The 19th Century

1801-1900

Great Lives from History

The 19th Century

1801-1900

Volume 3
Benjamin Henry Latrobe - Domingo Faustino Sarmiento

Editor
John Powell
Oklahoma Baptist University

Editor, First Edition
Frank N. Magill

SALEM PRESS
Pasadena, California   Hackensack, New Jersey

Editor in Chief: Dawn P. Dawson
Editorial Director: Christina J. Moose
Acquisitions Editor: Mark Rehn
Research Supervisor: Jeffry Jensen
Research Assistant: Rebecca Kuzins
Manuscript Editor: R. Kent Rasmussen

Indexer: Rowena Wildin Dehanke
Production Editor: Andrea E. Miller
Graphics and Design: James Hutson
Layout: Eddie Murillo
Photo Editor: Cynthia Breslin Beres
Editorial Assistant: Dana Garey

Cover photos: The Granger Collection, New York (Pictured left to right, top to bottom: Sitting Bull, Charles Darwin, Liliuokalani, Louisa May Alcott, Ludwig van Beethoven, Saʿīd ibn Sulṭān, Simón Bolívar, Cixi, Mark Twain)

Some of the essays in this work originally appeared in the following Salem Press sets: *Dictionary of World Biography* (© 1998-1999, edited by Frank N. Magill) and *Great Lives from History* (© 1987-1995, edited by Frank N. Magill). New material has been added.

Library of Congress Cataloging-in-Publication Data

Great lives from history. The 19th century, 1801-1900 / editor, John Powell.
    p. cm.
  "Editor, first edition, Frank N. Magill."
  Some of the essays in this work were originally published in Dictionary of world biography and the series of works collectively titled, Great lives from history, both edited by Frank N. Magill; with new material added.
  Includes bibliographical references and index.
  ISBN-13: 978-1-58765-292-9 (set : alk. paper)
  ISBN-10: 1-58765-292-7 (set : alk. paper)
  ISBN-13: 978-1-58765-295-0 (v. 3 : alk. paper)
  ISBN-10: 1-58765-295-1 (v. 3 : alk. paper)
  [etc.]
  1. Biography—19th century. I. Powell, John, 1954- II. Magill, Frank Northen, 1907-1997 III. Dictionary of world biography. IV. Great lives from history. V. Title: 19th century, 1801-1900. VI. Title: Nineteenth century, 1801-1900.
  CT119.G69 2006
  920.009′034—dc22

                                                                                    2006020187

First Printing

CONTENTS

CONTENTS

KEY TO PRONUNCIATION

Many of the names of personages covered in *Great Lives from History: The Nineteenth Century, 1801-1900* may be unfamiliar to students and general readers. For these unfamiliar names, guides to pronunciation have been provided upon first mention of the names in the text. These guidelines do not purport to achieve the subtleties of the languages in question but will offer readers a rough equivalent of how English speakers may approximate the proper pronunciation.

Vowel Sounds

Symbol	Spelled (Pronounced)
a	answer (AN-suhr), laugh (laf), sample (SAM-puhl), that (that)
ah	father (FAH-thur), hospital (HAHS-pih-tuhl)
aw	awful (AW-fuhl), caught (kawt)
ay	blaze (blayz), fade (fayd), waiter (WAYT-ur), weigh (way)
eh	bed (behd), head (hehd), said (sehd)
ee	believe (bee-LEEV), cedar (SEE-dur), leader (LEED-ur), liter (LEE-tur)
ew	boot (bewt), lose (lewz)
i	buy (bi), height (hit), lie (li), surprise (sur-PRIZ)
ih	bitter (BIH-tur), pill (pihl)
o	cotton (KO-tuhn), hot (hot)
oh	below (bee-LOH), coat (koht), note (noht), wholesome (HOHL-suhm)
oo	good (good), look (look)
ow	couch (kowch), how (how)
oy	boy (boy), coin (koyn)
uh	about (uh-BOWT), butter (BUH-tuhr), enough (ee-NUHF), other (UH-thur)

Consonant Sounds

Symbol	Spelled (Pronounced)
ch	beach (beech), chimp (chihmp)
g	beg (behg), disguise (dihs-GIZ), get (geht)
j	digit (DIH-juht), edge (ehj), jet (jeht)
k	cat (kat), kitten (KIH-tuhn), hex (hehks)
s	cellar (SEHL-ur), save (sayv), scent (sehnt)
sh	champagne (sham-PAYN), issue (IH-shew), shop (shop)
ur	birth (burth), disturb (dihs-TURB), earth (urth), letter (LEH-tur)
y	useful (YEWS-fuhl), young (yuhng)
z	business (BIHZ-nehs), zest (zehst)
zh	vision (VIH-zhuhn)

COMPLETE LIST OF CONTENTS

VOLUME I

VOLUME 2

VOLUME 3

VOLUME 4

COMPLETE LIST OF CONTENTS

List of Maps and Sidebars

Volume I

VOLUME 2

VOLUME 3

VOLUME 4

The World in 1801

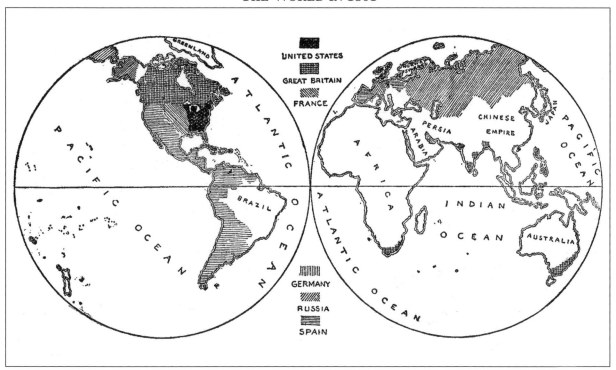

The World in 1900

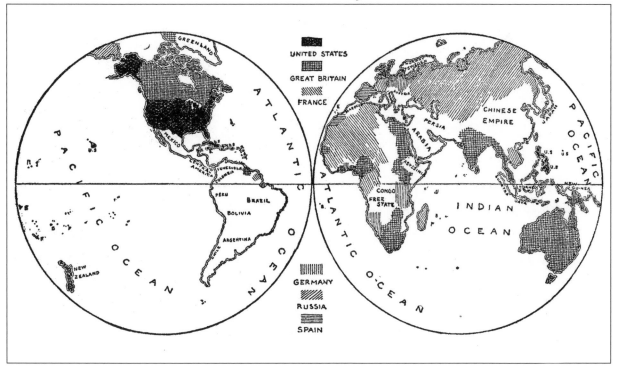

AFRICA AT THE END OF THE NINETEENTH CENTURY

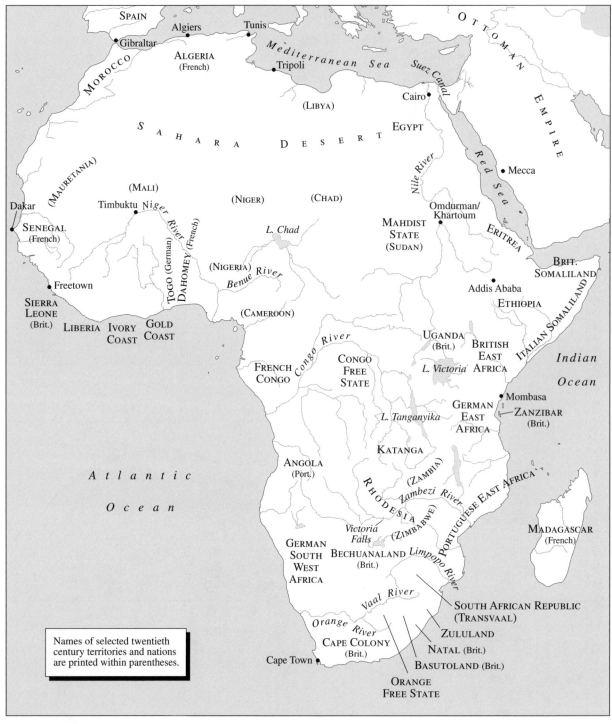

SPAIN

Gibraltar

Algiers

Tunis

MOROCCO

ALGERIA
(French)

Tripoli

Mediterranean Sea

Suez Canal

Cairo

(LIBYA)

EGYPT

S A H A R A   D E S E R T

OTTOMAN EMPIRE

Red Sea

Mecca

(MAURETANIA)

Dakar

SENEGAL
(French)

(MALI)

Timbuktu

Niger River

TOGO (German)

DAHOMEY (French)

(NIGER)

(CHAD)

L. Chad

(NIGERIA)

Benue River

Omdurman/
Khartoum

MAHDIST
STATE
(SUDAN)

ERITREA

BRIT.
SOMALILAND

Addis Ababa

ETHIOPIA

ITALIAN SOMALILAND

Freetown

SIERRA
LEONE
(Brit.)

LIBERIA   IVORY
COAST

GOLD
COAST

(CAMEROON)

FRENCH
CONGO

Congo River

CONGO
FREE
STATE

UGANDA
(Brit.)

L. Victoria

BRITISH
EAST
AFRICA

*Indian

Ocean*

Mombasa

GERMAN
EAST
AFRICA

ZANZIBAR
(Brit.)

L. Tanganyika

KATANGA

*Atlantic

Ocean*

ANGOLA
(Port.)

RHODESIA

(ZAMBIA)

Zambezi River

(ZIMBABWE)

PORTUGUESE EAST AFRICA

MADAGASCAR
(French)

Victoria
Falls

GERMAN
SOUTH
WEST
AFRICA

BECHUANALAND
(Brit.)

Limpopo River

Vaal River

SOUTH AFRICAN REPUBLIC
(TRANSVAAL)

ZULULAND

NATAL (Brit.)

Orange River

CAPE COLONY
(Brit.)

BASUTOLAND (Brit.)

Cape Town

ORANGE
FREE STATE

Names of selected twentieth
century territories and nations
are printed within parentheses.

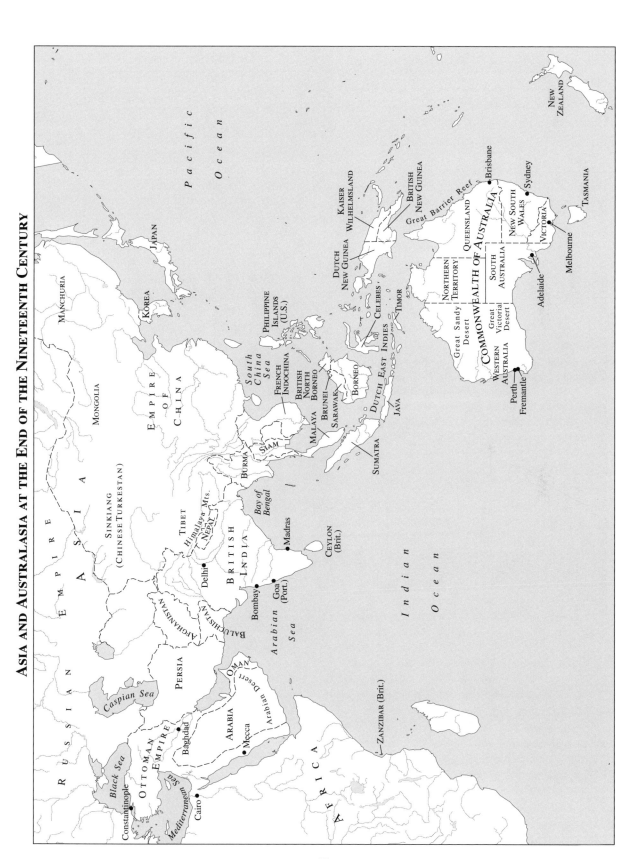

ASIA AND AUSTRALASIA AT THE END OF THE NINETEENTH CENTURY

RUSSIAN EMPIRE IN ASIA

MANCHURIA

MONGOLIA

SINKIANG (CHINESE TURKESTAN)

EMPIRE OF CHINA

KOREA

JAPAN

Pacific Ocean

TIBET

Himalaya Mts.

NEPAL

AFGHANISTAN

BALUCHISTAN

PERSIA

BRITISH INDIA

Delhi

Caspian Sea

Black Sea

Constantinople

OTTOMAN EMPIRE

Mediterranean Sea

Cairo

Baghdad

ARABIA

Mecca

OMAN

Arabian Desert

Arabian Sea

Bombay

Goa (Port.)

Madras

CEYLON (Brit.)

Bay of Bengal

BURMA

SIAM

FRENCH INDOCHINA

South China Sea

PHILIPPINE ISLANDS (U.S.)

BRITISH NORTH BORNEO

BRUNEI

SARAWAK

MALAYA

BORNEO

SUMATRA

Dutch East Indies

JAVA

CELEBES

TIMOR

DUTCH NEW GUINEA

KAISER WILHELMSLAND

BRITISH NEW GUINEA

Indian Ocean

ZANZIBAR (Brit.)

AFRICA

Great Barrier Reef

Brisbane

COMMONWEALTH OF AUSTRALIA

QUEENSLAND

NORTHERN TERRITORY

WESTERN AUSTRALIA

SOUTH AUSTRALIA

NEW SOUTH WALES

VICTORIA

Great Sandy Desert

Great Victoria Desert

Perth

Fremantle

Adelaide

Melbourne

Sydney

TASMANIA

NEW ZEALAND

EUROPE AT THE END OF THE NINETEENTH CENTURY

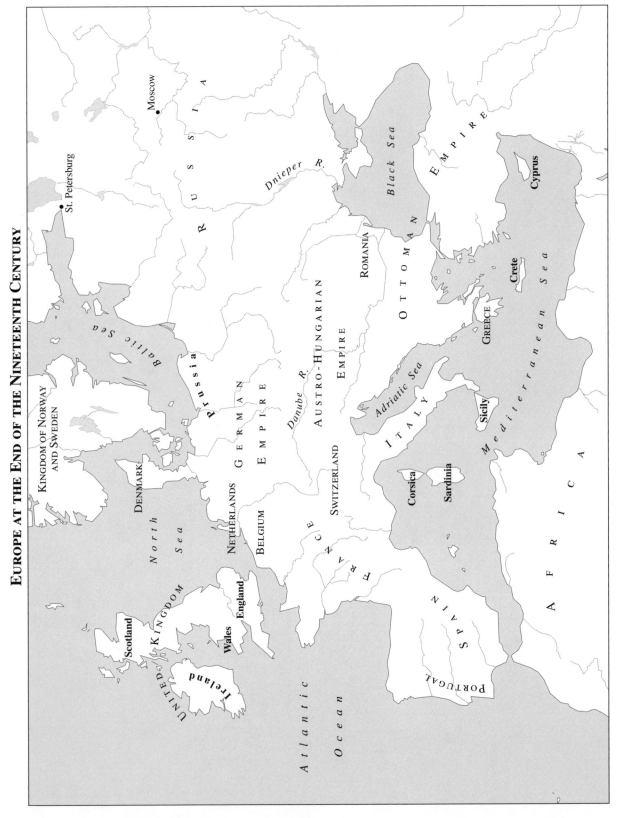

NORTH AMERICA AT THE END OF THE NINETEENTH CENTURY

Bering Sea

Bering Strait

Arctic Ocean

ALASKA

GREENLAND (Denmark)

Baffin Bay

KLONDIKE

DOMINION

Hudson Bay

OF CANADA

NEWFOUNDLAND

St. Lawrence River

Washington

Oregon

Montana

North Dakota

Minnesota

Great Lakes

Maine

Vermont

New Hampshire

Massachusetts

Idaho

Wisconsin

Michigan

New York

Rhode Island

Connecticut

Wyoming

South Dakota

Penn-sylvania

New Jersey

Nevada

Nebraska

Iowa

Indiana Ohio

Delaware

Utah

Colorado River

Colorado

Illinois

Ohio River

Maryland

California

Kansas

Missouri River

Kentucky

Virginia

West Virginia

Arizona (terr.)

Rio Grande

New Mexico (terr.)

Oklahoma (terr.)

Arkansas River

Tennessee

North Carolina

South Carolina

Mississippi River

Texas

Louisiana

Mississippi

Alabama

Georgia

MEXICO

Florida

Pacific Ocean

Gulf of Mexico

Atlantic Ocean

CUBA

HAITI

PUERTO RICO

JAMAICA

DOMINICAN REPUBLIC

CENTRAL AMERICA

Caribbean Sea

SOUTH AMERICA

SOUTH AMERICA AT THE END OF THE NINETEENTH CENTURY

Great Lives from History

The 19th Century

1801-1900

BENJAMIN HENRY LATROBE
American architect

The founder of the architectural profession in the United States, Latrobe had a genius that encompassed nearly every area of classical architecture but is noted most for his Greek revival influences.

BORN: May 1, 1764; Fulneck, near Leeds, Yorkshire, England

DIED: September 3, 1820; New Orleans, Louisiana

ALSO KNOWN AS: Benjamin Henry Boneval Latrobe (full name)

AREAS OF ACHIEVEMENT: Architecture, engineering

EARLY LIFE

Benjamin Henry Boneval Latrobe was born in England into a family of exiled French Protestants. Originally named de La Trobe, the family of Benjamin Henry Latrobe (as he usually signed himself) had been distinguished in religious, cultural, and business circles in Ireland, England, and Holland. Latrobe's father, Benjamin Latrobe, was educated at the University of Glasgow as well as in Europe. Converted from the Baptist faith to that of the Moravians (United Brethren), the senior Latrobe was an internationally recognized preacher and teacher, a Moravian leader whose headquarters at one time were in Fulneck. There, he married Anna Margaretta Antes. A Pennsylvanian with honored Revolutionary War ancestors and a wealthy, landowning father, she traveled to Fulneck at the age of fourteen to deepen her own Moravian learning. The sociability, cosmopolitanism, learned values, and interesting familial contacts surrounding young Benjamin were augmented by his parents' Moravian belief in directing education toward the broadening of children's individuality and tastes.

Thus, Latrobe's father, who returned to London to direct church interests better for the remainder of his life, placed Benjamin in Fulneck's Moravian school. Between the ages of four and fourteen, he acquired there a basic classical education: Latin, Greek, algebra, and geometry, as well as religious instruction. Then, following the example of an older brother and because of his father's dismay with the outbreak of the American Revolution in 1776, Benjamin was sent to Moravian schools in Niesky and Barby in German Silesia.

Little documentation exists of the seven years he spent in Europe. What is known is that, having established himself in London in 1783, Latrobe was fluent in French, German, and Italian and was proficient in Hebrew and Spanish as well. He also exhibited a knowledge and love of music. He had completed a translation of a popular German work on Frederick the Great, indicated an interest in military engineering, and manifested superior literary and artistic skills. Behind him, too, were invaluable friendships and acquaintances with European scholars and connoisseurs, which had led him deeply into philosophy, logic, ethics, a mastery of mathematics, sidereal navigation, and surveying.

At the age of twenty, Latrobe was a dark-haired, handsome, muscular young man, six feet, two inches in height. In addition to being privileged with an extraordinary background, he was ambitious, impetuous, childishly vivacious, and charming. He was also subject in young adulthood and throughout his life, however, to abnormal sensitivities, severe headaches, and sometimes debilitating depressions. Notwithstanding, he was remarkably accomplished and clearly gifted.

LIFE'S WORK

Technically, Latrobe was employed in the London Stamp Office from 1784 to 1794. However, the commencement of his lifetime career proceeded unhindered by a civil service post, for within two years he began working with John Smeaton. Smeaton, though trained as a lawyer, was in fact a renowned instrument maker and the designer and builder of, among other engineering feats, the famed Eddystone Lighthouse.

Latrobe was the first Englishman to designate himself as a "civil engineer"; as an acknowledged master, he founded Great Britain's first organization of civil engineers. Smeaton wrote extensively, was a friend of James Watt, and was a respected acquaintance of most upcoming architects and engineers; indeed, a whole generation of engineers sprang from association with him. Smeaton assigned Latrobe to work with his chief assistant, a master in his own right, William Jessop, chief inventor of the "edge rail," as well as the designer-builder of numerous canals, docks, and other harbor facilities. From 1786 into 1789, Latrobe served under Jessop on Rye Harbor's improvements and on construction of the Basingstoke Canal, both major engineering assignments.

Thanks to his achievements and his family and professional connections, Latrobe skipped the usual lengthy apprenticeships and joined the office of Samuel Pepys Cockerell, Cockerell being the founder of his own dynasty of great architects and officials. There, between 1789 and 1792, Latrobe variously helped design the Admiralty Building in Whitehall and took on private commissions, in the process making lifelong friends such as First Lord of the Admiralty Sir Charles Middleton.

Briefly, London was good to him. In 1792, he was able to establish his own architectural office. He became "surveyor" (designer) of London's police offices and conducted surveys for the Chelmer and Blackwater Navigation improvement. He also married Lydia Sellon and started his own family. Unhappily, Lydia died giving birth to their third child, and Latrobe suffered a nervous breakdown. That and a series of financial reverses shortly left him bankrupt and, in a sense, a professional failure. Only lands bequeathed to him by his mother in the United States allowed a way out of a sad situation. Further spurred on by a romantic, liberal attachment to American revolutionary principles and republican values, he abandoned England, landing in Norfolk, Virginia, in March, 1796.

Assisted by splendid references, Latrobe designed his first American house in Norfolk within months after landing and worked busily in Virginia until the end of 1798. He surveyed the upper Appomattox River for commercial navigational purposes, served as engineering consultant to the Dismal Swamp Land Company, and, receiving a gubernatorial appointment, designed and built the Virginia State Penitentiary in Richmond, which drew acclaim for the liberal philosophy of penology that it embodied. Finally, he designed a novel Richmond theater complex. During his Virginia years, Latrobe became a friend of Thomas Jefferson and Bushrod Washington and struck close acquaintances with George Washington and his family at Mount Vernon, with the Madisons and Randolphs—indeed, with most important social and political figures in Virginia. Moreover, keen observer that he had always been, he kept an exceptional journal and sketches of his journeys through the state.

Residing in Philadelphia until 1807 despite serious struggles and misfortunes, Latrobe reached new heights in his career. In 1800, he started his second family with his marriage to Mary Elizabeth Hazlehurst. With this stability and a genius for combining architecture and engineering skills possessed by no one else in the country, he designed many of his masterworks. By tapping the Schuylkill River and ingeniously utilizing steam power for pumping and distribution of purified water, he sanitized a basic service while masking his work behind beautiful buildings. With private and public commissions, he designed splendid private homes and completed designs for a national military academy, a monument to Washington, and the Chestnut Street Theater.

Latrobe was chosen both engineer and contractor of the Susquehanna River Survey, and he restored Nassau Hall at Princeton University. He designed Transylvania College for Henry Clay (and Clay's home) in Lexington, Kentucky, and the main buildings of Dickinson College, Carlisle, Pennsylvania, and he helped Jefferson with design of the University of Virginia. Three of his masterworks in Philadelphia were the Bank of Pennsylvania, the Bank of Philadelphia, and the University of Pennsylvania Medical School, while two others in nearby Baltimore were the first Roman Catholic cathedral in the United States and the Baltimore Exchange. He also surveyed, then served as chief engineer of, the great Chesapeake and Delaware Canal enterprise. Meanwhile, he designed a covered naval dry dock in Washington for Jefferson and accepted his appointment as the surveyor of the public buildings.

Because Latrobe enjoyed federal commissions or appointments during all but four of his twenty-four years in the United States, he was drawn to Washington in 1807. There, in addition to building the Washington Navy Yard and the Washington Canal, he designed, helped construct, and—after its destruction by the British— helped reconstruct the national Capitol, which was the subsequent standard for hundreds of American public buildings. He continued scores of other architectural interests: close association with Nicholas Roosevelt and Robert Fulton, among others, on the uses of steam power, development of public works, and contributions to learned societies. In 1819, he moved his family to New Orleans, drawn by son Henry's death (which occurred while he was working on a lighthouse of his father's design) and by the prospect of new commissions such as the Louisiana Bank, the Customs House, the unfinished lighthouse, and other private projects. Like his son, he died in New Orleans, on September 3, 1820, of yellow fever.

SIGNIFICANCE

Latrobe's genius encompassed nearly every area of classical architecture, though he is most noted for his Greek revival influences. Indeed, his work was marked by considerable originality and restrained and novel interpretations in the use of columns, domes, and masonry vaults and penditives. He founded and, through family and pupils, perpetuated professional architecture in the United States.

Throughout his career, Latrobe was plagued by personal and political hostilities and by chronic financial difficulties, in addition to the philosophy of impermanence and cheap construction that seemed an American style, yet his living was made almost entirely from his architectural and engineering works. Few aspects of civil engineering escaped his touch. He worked on surveys, canals, tunnels, waterworks, beach conservation, public buildings, universities, bridges, lighthouses, arsenals, and naval and port facilities. Before the professionalization of mechanical engineering, he joined with other pioneers in the design and use of steam power in manufactories, utilities, and land and water locomotion. His legacy also included journals, papers, drawings, and designs of the highest merit. Of great importance, his breadth of learning helped bridge the technological and artistic gap between the best British and European work and their adaptation to young republican America.

—*Clifton K. Yearley and Kerrie L. MacPherson*

Further Reading

Calhoun, Daniel H. *The American Civil Engineer, 1792-1843*. Cambridge, Mass.: MIT Press, 1960. Emphasizes the professionalization of civil engineering in the United States. Influences of West Point and state and federal sponsorship of public works are dealt with more extensively than the work of individuals such as Latrobe, who by mid-century would be eclipsed by task-oriented specialists. Excellent scholarly context for understanding the strengths and weaknesses of Latrobe's generation of architect-engineers with classical and continental educations.

Carter, Edward C., II, with Darwin H. Stapleton and Lee W. Formwalt. *Benjamin Henry Latrobe and Public Works: Professionalism, Private Interest, and Public Policy in the Age of Jefferson*. Washington, D.C.: Public Works Historical Society, 1976. Excellent, if brief, analysis of conflicting elements confronting early architect-engineers, by foremost experts on Latrobe's journals and papers.

Condit, Carl W. *American Building: Materials and Techniques from the First Colonial Settlements to the Present*. Chicago: University of Chicago Press, 1968. Chapter 5 is particularly pertinent to masonry and to Latrobe's and his contemporaries' employment of it.

_____. *American Building Art: The Nineteenth Century*. New York: Oxford University Press, 1960. Chapter 1 puts Latrobe's work in the context of previous American experience and later nineteenth century architectural and building directions.

Hamlin, Talbot. *Benjamin Henry Latrobe*. New York: Oxford University Press, 1955. The most thorough, scholarly, and personalized appreciation of Latrobe in all of his dimensions. Well written and an expert critical analysis of the great architect-engineer's trials, successes, and failures.

Latrobe, Benjamin Henry. *The Architectural Drawings of Benjamin Henry Latrobe*. Edited by Jeffrey A. Cohen and Charles E. Brownell. 2 vols. New Haven, Conn.: Published for the Maryland Historical Society and the American Philosophical Society by Yale University Press, 1994. The final two volumes in Latrobe's papers (see below), these drawings document his architectural career and the history of his buildings, including the U.S. Capitol, Bank of Pennsylvania, and Baltimore Cathedral.

_____. *The Correspondence and Miscellaneous Papers of Benjamin Henry Latrobe*. Edited by John C. Van Horne and Lee W. Formwalt. 3 vols. New Haven, Conn.: Yale University Press, 1988. The editors and Latrobe himself have made this an intriguing and readable volume of keen observations and literary merit.

Maynard, W. Barksdale. *Architecture in the United States, 1800-1850*. New Haven, Conn.: Yale University Press, 2002. Documents the development of American architecture from the age of Thomas Jefferson to the antebellum era. Good for placing Latrobe's work within the context of early nineteenth century American architecture.

Stapleton, Darwin H. "Benjamin Henry Latrobe and the Transfer of Technology." In *Technology in America: A History of Individuals and Ideas*, edited by Carroll W. Purcell, Jr. Cambridge, Mass.: MIT Press, 1981. Focuses upon an important aspect of Latrobe's contribution to American architecture and engineering as a result of his British and Continental training.

See also: Charles Bulfinch; Daniel Hudson Burnham; Henry Clay; Robert Fulton.

Related article in *Great Events from History: The Nineteenth Century, 1801-1900:* July 4, 1848: Ground Is Broken for the Washington Monument.

JOHN LAIRD MAIR LAWRENCE
British viceroy of India

One of the builders of British India, Lawrence made contributions that were crucial to the successful establishment of the administration of the Punjab and to the defeat of the great Indian mutiny of 1857.

BORN: March 4, 1811; Richmond, Yorkshire, England
DIED: June 27, 1879; London, England
ALSO KNOWN AS: First Baron Lawrence; Baron Lawrence of the Punjab and of Grately
AREA OF ACHIEVEMENT: Government and politics

EARLY LIFE

John Laird Mair Lawrence, the first Baron Lawrence, was the eighth of twelve children of Lieutenant Colonel Alexander Lawrence. A family friend was a director of the East India Company and, in 1827, he obtained an appointment in the company's civil service for John as he had earlier obtained military appointments for three of his brothers. At the time, instead of ruling India directly, the British government left its administration to the East India Company under a charter going back to the seventeenth century.

Lawrence spent two years in the company's training school at Maileybury, finishing in May, 1829. He sailed for India with his brother Henry, arriving in Calcutta in February, 1830. After studying Urdu and Persian at the College of Fort William, he was posted to Delhi. For the next fourteen years he served in civil posts in the area around Delhi as a magistrate and financial officer. He worked energetically and established himself as a competent administrator.

In 1839, a severe fever, which was almost fatal, interrupted his career and sent him home on invalid leave. Returning to England in 1840, he regained his health, traveled in Ireland and on the European continent, and, in August, 1841, was married to Harriet Catherine Hamilton, the daughter of a clergyman in Donegal. Though he was again sick with fever and was warned not to return to India, he disregarded the advice with characteristic stubbornness, resuming his career in the spring of 1843. His absence had not improved his position in the civil administration, where up to this time he had progressed only modestly.

LIFE'S WORK

In 1845, for the first time, Lawrence was able to bring his abilities to the attention of the governor-general and to make some professional progress in a substantial way.

The new governor general, Lord Hardinge, had just come out to India. The British had annexed the large province of Sind and were consequently at war with the neighboring Sikhs in the Punjab. Hardinge was eager to consolidate the rather shaky British position, and he called on Lawrence to supply the army with much-needed ammunition. Lawrence's determined energy won for him Hardinge's approval as he organized a great convoy of bullock-drawn carts and moved enough ammunition from Delhi to secure a victory that closed the First Sikh War decisively.

Lawrence's reward in 1846 was a post as administrator of one of the newly annexed provinces. His brother Henry, who had risen further than any of his brothers in the military service, was appointed the company's principal resident at Lahore. During his brother's absence from the post, Lawrence acted in his stead as the chief administrator of the entire area. In March, 1848, he held his province secure during the Second Sikh War, though he was attacked by sizable irregular forces. At the successful conclusion of the war, he urged that the entire Punjab be annexed quickly to prevent future trouble. This was done, and the highest level of administration was left to a board of three, to which Lawrence was appointed, his brother being named president.

The newly conquered Punjab, an area as large as France, had not even the rudiments of European-style administration, and all the structure of modern government, from roads to tax collection agencies, had to be created, a huge undertaking. To complicate the task, the military administrator, Sir Charles Napier, was critical of the civil administration, and the governing board could not agree within itself because Henry and John Lawrence, both men of strong views and fierce tempers, quarreled frequently. John was also attacked repeatedly by bouts of fever, which made the work no easier. At last, in 1853, the governor-general, Lord Dalhousie, while acknowledging their success, dissolved the board and made John Lawrence the chief administrator of the Punjab.

Although Lawrence cautioned the government against being drawn into the affairs of Afghanistan during the Crimean War, the government decided on a formal treaty with the emir and Lawrence was sent in March, 1855, to negotiate it. On the successful conclusion of the negotiation, he was rewarded with a knighthood. Having established a relationship with the emir, he was sent, early in 1857, to negotiate a second treaty.

Like many of the company's senior civil servants at the time, Lawrence saw no warning of the underlying discontents that produced the great mutiny of 1857; he applied for leave from his post only a few weeks before the subcontinent erupted in the most serious challenge British authority in India ever faced.

Lawrence's greatest moments came in the desperate danger of the weeks and months that followed. Mutineers besieged Delhi, and the Punjab was cut off. Lawrence was on his own, having to hold the province against the rebels and to mobilize its resources in suppressing the uprising elsewhere. With great coolness he collected all the reliable men he could find, striking swiftly at the mutineers and quieting much of the area. After a brief respite, he bent his efforts toward supplying the regular forces outside Delhi, seeing that that was the crucial situation. If Delhi fell, Lawrence would be unable to hold the territory, however vigorously he acted, for the whole province would rise against British rule. By August, the tide had turned and with the lifting of the siege of Delhi, the heart went out of the mutiny.

In the aftermath of the uprising, which had been crushed with great ferocity, bitterness lingered. Lawrence acted as a moderating figure, advising against further harsh reprisals, though during the fighting he had not hesitated to act with the greatest severity. Despite his own deeply evangelical temperament, he firmly opposed suggestions that the Indian administration be purged of all non-Christians, understanding that the only prudent course, if Great Britain were to continue to govern India, was to seek whatever accommodation could be made with the Indian people.

Lawrence's health had deteriorated seriously under the strain of the mutiny, and he returned to England, amid considerable popular acclaim for his heroism. When the furor was over, he settled down to work at the India Office in London as a member of the newly created Indian Council, although he did not find it satisfying employment, for it conferred no real power. He was offered the governorship of Bombay in 1860 but declined it. In November, 1863, on the death of the viceroy, Prime Minister Lord Palmerston offered Lawrence the position, and he accepted immediately. Only once before in the century had a civil servant been offered the highest position in the Indian government. For Lawrence it was the crowning moment of his long career.

Lawrence was viceroy for five years, from January, 1864, to January, 1869. Compared with the heroic years in the Punjab, they must have been frustrating. There were no great victories to be won, only the humdrum battles of successful administration. His predecessor had allowed government expenses to outrun revenues considerably, and Lawrence undertook to redress the balance by cutting back on expenditure. Though the deficit continued throughout his administration, he was harshly criticized by official India for the constraints imposed by his parsimony.

A terrible famine developed in Orissa that Lawrence was unable to alleviate, and a war in Bhutan that he could not avoid. His long experience governing the Punjab had taught him the wisdom of caution on the northwestern frontier. He resisted firmly pressures for expansion and meddling in the affairs of Afghanistan. Again, for this reluctance, he was criticized with some rancor. In an age in which many believed fervently in the desirability of expanding the empire, his was not a popular position, however sensible. In the long term, his judgment, that the natural limits of British power in that area had been reached, was sustained by history. Afghanistan proved indigestible and remained for another century the buffer zone between Russia and India.

In January, 1869, Lawrence left office and returned home to England, where he was finally awarded his peerage. He continued to play a significant part in politics during the 1870's as a member of the House of Lords. Though a reluctant speaker, he spoke often and to good effect, whenever the subject was India, and his judgment was respected, if not always heeded. His caution about imperial expansion meant that he often voted with the Liberals, though he was not a partisan. He was particularly active during the late 1870's in opposing the Conservative government's policy that led to the Afghan War of 1878-1879.

Though Lawrence kept active, serving on the boards of a number of charitable and public organizations, his health deteriorated markedly, and the onset of blindness limited what he could do. He continued to speak in the House of Lords to the end, dying only a week after his last speech, on June 27, 1879. He was buried in Westminster Abbey as a national hero.

SIGNIFICANCE

The first Baron Lawrence played a crucial part at one of the great turning points in the history of British rule in India. That history is, for the most part, the story of a small number of British soldiers and civil administrators governing a vast subcontinent of people whose languages, cultures, and values they neither shared nor fully understood.

The consolidation and expansion of British power seemed inevitable in an age of empire, but the explosion of 1857 showed how tenuous British control in India might be if the people of India chose to resist. Lawrence understood this fact clearly. The continuation of British rule depended on Great Britain's ability to understand the needs of India's people and to provide for them better than the traditional system and its rulers had been able to do. Although Lawrence showed that he could be as firm, and as ruthless, as any in putting down opposition, it was his own lifelong effort to understand India sympathetically that made it possible for him to rule successfully, both in the Punjab and then over the whole British Raj. In the end, it was as much his good sense as his heroic energy and courage that accounted for that success.

—*S. J. Stearns*

FURTHER READING

The Cambridge History of India. 6 vols. Cambridge, England: Cambridge University Press, 1922-1932. The standard work on Indian history. Despite its age, still provides a detailed overview, though the interpretation is naturally outdated.

Lee, Harold. *Brothers in the Raj: The Lives of John and Henry Lawrence.* New York: Oxford University Press, 2002. A joint biography of the two brothers, the first British administrators of the Punjab. Examines their lives, personal relationships, careers, and different approaches and disagreement over governing the Indian province.

Smith, Vincent A. *The Oxford History of India.* 3d ed. Oxford, England: Oxford University Press, 1958. A good general guide to Indian history and its literature.

Spear, Perceval. *India: A Modern History.* Ann Arbor: University of Michigan Press, 1961. An excellent, concise account of Indian history.

Steele, David. "John Laird Mair Lawrence." In *Oxford Dictionary of National Biography*, edited by H. C. G. Matthew and Brian Lee. New York: Oxford University Press, 2004. The standard biographical dictionary of British history features this brief overview of Lawrence's life and career.

Wolpert, Stanley. *A New History of India.* New York: Oxford University Press, 1977. Study providing a general review of Indian history and incorporating much new work.

Woodruff, Philip [Philip Mason]. *The Men Who Ruled India: The Founders.* London: Jonathan Cape, 1953. The first volume of a two-volume work by a member of the Indian Civil Service under British rule. The third section is relevant. The focus is on individuals, but they are put nicely in context. An appreciative and sympathetic commentary on British administration in India during the early nineteenth century.

_____. *The Men Who Ruled India: The Guardians.* New York: St. Martin's Press, 1954. Second and concluding volume of the preceding work. The first half of the book covers 1858-1909 and, like the first volume, focuses generally on individuals. Contains much of interest about Lawrence, his brother Henry, and the conditions under which the administrators struggled to work.

SEE ALSO: First Marquis of Dalhousie; Dadabhai Naoroji; Sir James Outram; Lord Palmerston.

RELATED ARTICLES in *Great Events from History: The Nineteenth Century, 1801-1900:* April 10, 1802: Lambton Begins Trigonometrical Survey of India; May 10, 1857-July 8, 1858: Sepoy Mutiny Against British Rule; 1885: Indian National Congress Is Founded.

EMMA LAZARUS
American poet

Lazarus began writing poems as a girl and published volumes of poetry, plays, translations, a novel, and many influential essays in Century *magazine and in the American Jewish press. She is best remembered for her sonnet "The New Colossus," which is engraved on the base of the Statue of Liberty.*

BORN: July 22, 1849; New York, New York
DIED: November 19, 1887; New York, New York
AREAS OF ACHIEVEMENT: Literature, social reform

EARLY LIFE
Emma Lazarus was born into an American Jewish family that had lived in New York for generations. One of her ancestors was a Sephardic Jew from Portugal who had fled the Spanish Inquisition and emigrated to the West Indies. Emma's father, Moses Lazarus, was a successful sugar merchant and one of New York's wealthiest men. He was a founder of the Knickerbocker Club and belonged to the influential Spanish-Portuguese Synagogue. Emma's mother, Esther Nathan Lazarus, belonged to a prominent New York family whose members were distinguished in the legal profession.

Emma, the fourth daughter born to the family, was named for one of the novelist Jane Austen's heroines. A boy and two more girls followed. The family enjoyed summers in fashionable Newport, Rhode Island. Emma and her older sisters were educated at home by private tutors; Emma in particular was considered too frail for schooling outside the house. She had a gift for languages and learned French, Italian, and German. She also immersed herself in children's stories and then in the volumes of her father's library. She was particularly taken with Sir Walter Scott, the Scottish novelist and poet, and with Greek and Roman mythology.

When the Civil War broke out, Emma was only eleven, but she was aware of the uncles and male cousins, dressed in Union blue, who arrived at her home at all hours to say tearful goodbyes to her parents. She wrote poems on war and on nature themes, and translated French and German poets. Her father retired in 1865 at the age of fifty-two and devoted himself to his children. When he saw Emma's notebooks, he was taken with her thirty original poems as well as with her translations of Heinrich Heine and Victor Hugo. He decided to have the manuscript printed for private circulation. *Poems and Translations by Emma Lazarus Written Between the Ages of Fourteen and Sixteen* appeared in 1866.

The book was received enthusiastically and, with the addition of ten new poems, was reprinted the following year for general circulation. To crown the events of Emma's eighteenth year, Moses Lazarus introduced her to Ralph Waldo Emerson, who was then in his sixties. Emerson, one of the most influential poets and writers of his time, asked the young poet to send a copy of her book to him in Concord, Massachusetts. He praised the book and offered constructive criticism, which led to a long and fruitful correspondence. He was to be an important influence on her work.

LIFE'S WORK
In the next few years, Emma Lazarus pursued nature, classical, and Jewish themes in her poetry. She wrote one of her best-known poems, "In the Jewish Synagogue at Newport," drawing on the historical resonance of the oldest synagogue in the United States and patterning it after Henry Wadsworth Longfellow's "The Jewish Cemetery at Newport." "Admetus," a long, romantic poem with scenes from Greek mythology, was accepted by *Lippincott's*, the leading literary magazine of the day, and became the title poem of her second collection. Emerson praised *Admetus, and Other Poems*, and Lazarus dedicated it to him over his objections. Published in 1871, the book was well received in the United States and earned rave reviews in England, where one critic compared Lazarus favorably to Robert Browning, one of the most erudite living English poets.

Lazarus's next project was a romantic novel titled *Alide*, based on a love incident in the life of Johann Wolfgang von Goethe, the great German writer whose work she had translated. When *Alide* was published in 1874, Lazarus sent a copy to Ivan Turgenev, a world-famous Russian novelist whom she revered. His response was reserved but positive; he praised her grasp of the German spirit and admired her depiction of character. Lazarus treasured his letter, and it may have offered her some comfort when *Parnassus*, a poetry anthology edited by her friend Emerson, appeared shortly afterward. It was an important anthology in which English and American poets were published together for the first time. When she found that she was omitted from *Parnassus* despite Emerson's years of praise for her work, Lazarus was deeply wounded. She wrote him a proud letter questioning his sincerity, but he did not answer.

Lazarus's mother died early in 1876, breaking up an

unusually close-knit family circle and prompting new poems on the theme of mother love. The following summer, after a year and a half of silence, Emerson and his wife invited Lazarus to visit them in Concord. It was a great adventure for the twenty-seven-year-old poet. She was immediately taken with Mrs. Emerson and developed a friendship with Emerson's daughter Ellen, who was ten years her senior. Among the people she met there was the poet and biographer William Ellery Channing, who took Lazarus to Henry David Thoreau's cottage at Walden Pond and presented her with the pocket compass that his old friend Thoreau had carried on his walks.

Lazarus returned to her literary life in New York, interspersed with summers in elegant Newport. Her poems continued to appear, and her name became widely known as her activities branched out into critical essays, book reviews, and profiles of prominent artists. Lazarus now began to recognize the limitations of her knowledge of the world and started to question the importance of her work. At about that time, Gustave Gottheil, a New York rabbi, asked her to translate some medieval Jewish hymns from German. These were the first of many that she was to translate from German, Spanish, and Hebrew sources and that were to appear over the years in the *Jewish Messenger.*

Emma Lazarus. (Library of Congress)

Lazarus next wrote a long, ambitious work titled *The Dance to Death.* This powerful verse-drama in five acts chronicles the martyrdom of the Jews of Nordhausen in 1349, when they were accused of causing the Black Plague and were sentenced to be burned to death. At the time, Lazarus neither showed it to anyone nor submitted it for publication. Her interest in her Jewish heritage found a new outlet in the life and work of the German Jewish poet Heinrich Heine. She translated many of his poems and wrote others based on Heine's notes that were found after his early death in 1856. A book grew from these endeavors, *Poems and Ballads of Heinrich Heine,* which included Lazarus's biographical study of the German poet.

The early years of the 1880's were marked by historical events that were to have a profound effect on Lazarus's work. A series of bloody riots against the Jewish population in Russia had caused hundreds of thousands of destitute Jews to flee to the United States. Lazarus visited the refugees at Ward's Island in the East River, where they were temporarily housed. The first task was to resettle the refugees, and she immediately started to raise funds for that purpose from her wide circle of acquaintances. In April of 1882, *Century* magazine carried an article by a Russian historian that justified the pogroms by vilifying Jews. Incensed, Lazarus wrote an answering essay that appeared in the May issue. She had found her cause, and with it, a new voice.

Lazarus wrote many new poems on Jewish themes and sent them to Philip Cowen, editor of the *American Hebrew.* She also sent him *The Dance to Death,* which he published in installments. In September of 1882, the verse-drama was published together with new poems in *Songs of a Semite.* Lazarus continued to visit the refugees on Ward's Island, occasions that stimulated new perspectives. In a burst of energy, Lazarus wrote "An Epistle to the Hebrews," which grew into fifteen articles that appeared in the *American Hebrew* between November, 1882, and February, 1883. The work was an appeal to American Jews to reflect upon their history and try to retain their special identities. "An Epistle" provoked great controversy, particularly in its support for the establishment of a Jewish state in Palestine.

Lazarus's reputation preceded her when she sailed to England in the spring of 1883 with her younger sister Annie. She was showered with invitations from the artistic elite of British society. She returned home in the autumn, and shortly after, she received an appeal from a fundraising committee for the gigantic new Statue of Liberty to be erected on Bedlow Island in New York Harbor. The

"THE NEW COLOSSUS"

Poet Emma Lazarus wrote this sonnet in 1883 in support of a fund organized to raise money to build the pedestal on which the Statue of Liberty was to be erected. The sonnet now appears on a bronze plaque at the statue's base. Its emotional appeal to the world's downtrodden peoples to come to the United States has remained a source of controversy into the twenty-first century.

> Not like the brazen giant of Greek fame,
> With conquering limbs astride from land to land;
> Here at our sea-washed, sunset gates shall stand
> A mighty woman with a torch, whose flame
> Is the imprisoned lightning, and her name
> Mother of Exiles. From her beacon-hand
> Glows world-wide welcome; her mild eyes command
> The air-bridged harbor that twin cities frame.
> "Keep, ancient lands, your storied pomp!" cries she
> With silent lips. "Give me your tired, your poor,
> Your huddled masses yearning to breathe free,
> The wretched refuse of your teeming shore.
> Send these, the homeless, tempest-tost to me,
> I lift my lamp beside the golden door!"

During Lazarus's lifetime, she was a strong and eloquent voice advancing provocative ideas on the history and future of the Jews. At a time when anti-Semitism was widespread, she wrote convincingly of the proud Jewish spirit. An ardently patriotic American, she had no difficulty reconciling this patriotism with her ethnic loyalty. She was one of the first Americans to take up the cause of a Jewish homeland, an idea that was not welcomed by the American Jews of her time.

Quiet, almost withdrawn, Emma Lazarus became an influential writer and intellectual who was admired by major contemporary figures. It cannot be known what Lazarus might have accomplished if she had lived, but in her thirty-eight years she became a widely known artist and important public advocate for causes whose time had not yet arrived.

—*Sheila Golburgh Johnson*

committee requested an original manuscript to sell at an auction along with manuscripts by Henry Wadsworth Longfellow, Walt Whitman, and Mark Twain. In reply, Lazarus wrote the sonnet "The New Colossus," a poem that was to ensure her immortality in a world of changing tastes and fashions.

The following year Lazarus fell ill, but she persevered in her work, writing a long poem that was intended to sum up her beliefs about the Jews. Influenced by Walt Whitman, she chose a new form: a cycle of lyrics made up of long, sprawling lines, which became "By the Waters of Babylon." Lazarus had apparently recovered from her illness when her father died in May of 1885. It was a numbing shock, and eight weeks later she departed for a tour of Europe with her sister Josephine. Lazarus spent two years abroad, although she was an invalid for much of that time. She finally returned to New York in 1887, where she died of cancer at the age of thirty-eight.

SIGNIFICANCE

Emma Lazarus's popular fame rests on her sonnet on the Statue of Liberty. Ironically, she herself never assigned any particular importance to that poem. Only through the efforts of a friend, Georgiana Schuyler, was "The New Colossus" inscribed on a plaque on the base of the Statue of Liberty in 1903, sixteen years after Lazarus's death.

FURTHER READING

Gordh, George. "Emma Lazarus: A Poet of Exile and Freedom." *The Christian Century* 103 (November 19, 1986): 1033-1036. In a careful reading of Lazarus's poetry, Gordh compares her early, romantic verse with the later work, which he finds imbued with a religious sensibility. "The New Colossus" is discussed at length.

Jacob, Heinrich E. *The World of Emma Lazarus*. New York: Schocken Books, 1949. Jacob uses a Freudian model to understand Lazarus, concluding that the major influence on her life was her father. This study is fanciful but interesting.

Lichtenstein, Diane. "Words and Worlds: Emma Lazarus's Conflicting Citizenships." *Tulsa Studies in Women's Literature* 6, no. 2 (Fall, 1987): 247-263. Lichtenstein demonstrates that Lazarus used her writing to achieve a resolution between her American and Jewish identities in the last decade of her life. The article also raises the issue of the poet's gender, another form of marginality that Lazarus forged into her unique identity.

Merriam, Eve. *Emma Lazarus: Woman with a Torch*. New York: Citadel Press, 1956. This biography studies Lazarus's life as it was reflected in her work. Merriam traces the poetry from the early focus on history and myth to its later engagement with events of her own time.

Omer-Sherman, Ranen. *Diaspora and Zionism in Jewish American Literature: Lazarus, Syrkin, Reznikoff, and Roth*. Hanover, N.H.: University Press of New England, 2002. Examines how Lazarus and three other Jewish American writers confronted the issues of Jewish nationalism and the fate of the diaspora.

Vogel, Dan. *Emma Lazarus*. Boston: Twayne, 1980. This work, one of a standardized series of monographs, offers the general reader a well-organized, concrete overview of the poet's life and work.

Young, Bette Roth. "Emma Lazarus and Her Jewish Problem." *American Jewish History* 84, no. 4 (December, 1996). Profile of Lazarus and her fight against anti-Semitism as evidenced in her work.

_____. *Emma Lazarus in Her World: Life and Letters*. Philadelphia: Jewish Publication Society, 1995. The author presents more than one hundred of Lazarus's letters that illuminate her life and personality and clarify her devotion to the cause of Jewish renewal.

SEE ALSO: Jane Austen; William Ellery Channing; Ralph Waldo Emerson; Heinrich Heine; Victor Hugo; Henry Wadsworth Longfellow; Sir Walter Scott; Charles Proteus Steinmetz; Henry David Thoreau; Ivan Turgenev; Mark Twain; Walt Whitman.

RELATED ARTICLE in *Great Events from History: The Nineteenth Century, 1801-1900:* October 28, 1886: Statue of Liberty Is Dedicated.

ROBERT E. LEE
American military leader

Perhaps the finest military tactician of his generation, Lee commanded the Army of Northern Virginia so brilliantly during the American Civil War that he helped to prolong the life of the Confederacy.

BORN: January 19, 1807; Stratford Hall, Westmoreland County, Virginia
DIED: October 12, 1870; Lexington, Virginia
ALSO KNOWN AS: Robert Edward Lee (full name)
AREA OF ACHIEVEMENT: Military

EARLY LIFE

One of the famous Lees of Virginia and fifth of seven children, Robert Edward Lee was born at the family estate of Stratford. His father, Colonel Henry "Light Horse" Harry Lee, had served with distinction as a cavalryman in the Revolutionary War and later as governor of Virginia, although he was financially insecure. His mother, Anne Hill Carter Lee, belonged to another aristocratic Virginia family. The family moved to Alexandria in Robert's fourth year, and he attended the local schools there. Because of the long absences and then the death of his father, Robert gradually took over the major care of his invalid mother. This intimate relationship shaped young Lee's character as one of quiet dignity, high moral integrity, and personal strength.

Desiring to emulate his father and to obtain a free education, Lee attended the United States Military Academy at West Point, where he performed as an outstanding cadet and was graduated second in a class of forty-six in 1829. Entering the engineer corps, he built and maintained coastal fortifications and river works. In June, 1831, he married his childhood friend Mary Anne Randolph Custis, the great-granddaughter of the wife of George Washington, at the opulent Custis estate at Arlington. Their marriage strengthened Lee's deep roots in his native state, though his devotion to his country enabled him to resist the temptation to settle down to the life of a country squire at Arlington, which he managed even while posted elsewhere, and where his seven children were reared. He ably performed the mundane tasks of a peacetime army engineer and held the rank of captain at the outbreak of the Mexican War in 1846.

LIFE'S WORK

Lee's genius as a field officer emerged during the Mexican War and placed him in the public eye. He received the brevet rank of major for his performance as a staff officer in the early campaigns, after which he transferred to the staff of General Winfield Scott for the major invasion of central Mexico. Lee contributed materially to the capture of Veracruz in April, 1847; through his ability and bravery in placing artillery and reconnoitering in several battles, he was promoted to brevet lieutenant colonel. After the attack on Chapultepec, in which he was wounded, he became brevet colonel.

Soon, however, Lee returned to routine duties, constructing fortifications near Baltimore and then, during 1852-1855, improving the course of study at West Point as superintendent. His reward was a transfer out of engineering to the Second Cavalry Regiment, with the rank of lieutenant colonel, policing the Indians in west Texas. In July, 1857, he assumed the colonelcy of the regiment. Home on leave during the fall of 1859, Lee was ordered to subdue John Brown's force, which had occupied the armory at Harpers Ferry (then part of Virginia) in Brown's stillborn attempt to incite a slave uprising in the South. After accomplishing the task, Lee returned to his regiment and, in 1860, assumed command of the Department of Texas.

A mild-mannered, even gentle officer with an excellent physique and devoted to the army and the flag, Lee dutifully obeyed his orders to return to Washington upon the secession of Texas from the Union in February, 1861. The next month, he was made colonel of the First Cavalry. By any measure the most able officer in the army, he was the logical choice to command the forces necessary to subdue the southern rebellion, a command offered him by the Lincoln administration upon the outbreak of the Civil War in mid-April, 1861. Following the secession of Virginia and considerable soul searching, however, Lee decided that his loyalty rested with his home state, whereupon he resigned his commission on April 23. He was given command of the Virginia militia and was soon appointed brigadier general in the new Confederate Army. Within months, his normal dark hair and mustache would be replaced by a full beard and hair completely grayed, the result no doubt of his awesome responsibilities.

Promoted to the full rank of general during the summer, one of five initially appointed, Lee first advised President Jefferson Davis in organizing the Confederate Army. He took command of the forces attempting to hold West Virginia in the Confederacy in August but was soundly defeated the next month at Cheat Mountain. Early in November, he assumed command of the coastal defenses of South Carolina, Georgia, and eastern Florida. Shortages of troops there led him to establish a strong defense against potential Union naval and amphibious penetrations. His strategy was faulty, however, because the Union had no intention of invading the interior in that quarter and instead attacked and successfully occupied key coastal positions merely for use as blockading stations for the navy.

Lee was recalled early in March, 1862, to help Davis organize the defenses of Richmond against the advance

Robert E. Lee. (Library of Congress)

of General George B. McClellan's army in the Peninsular Campaign. When the commander of the defending army, General Joseph E. Johnston, was wounded at Fair Oaks, Lee was given command on June 1, and he quickly reorganized his forces into the Army of Northern Virginia, a name he created. He masterfully countered McClellan's forces in the Seven Days' Battles, concluded on July 1, then swung north to defeat the army of General John Pope at the Second Battle of Bull Run in late August. Crossing the Potomac, Lee attempted to gain the support of Marylanders but was stopped by

McClellan in the Antietam campaign in September. He concluded the year by repulsing the bloody Union assaults on his well-placed army at Fredericksburg in December.

Lee's true genius in tactics lay in erecting field fortifications and in his remarkable ability to operate from the interior position—that is, to shift his forces between different points in his lines that were threatened by the larger numbers of the opposing Union armies. This tactic was best demonstrated in his stunning victory at Chancellorsville in May, 1863, when his army was half the size of that of the enemy. His greatest gamble occurred when he invaded Pennsylvania a month later. Frustrated from trying to turn the Union flanks at Gettysburg in July, he tried a frontal assault—"Pickett's charge"—that was virtually annihilated by the Army of the Potomac under General George G. Meade. As a result of this defeat, Lee was thereafter confined to the strategic defensive.

Lee fought a steadily losing battle against the vastly greater numbers and better-equipped troops of General Ulysses S. Grant's armies in the Wilderness Campaign during the spring of 1864. Lee's men, inspired largely by his towering leadership, stopped every bloody assault, but Lee was obliged to retreat each time, lest the larger Union forces turn his flank and cut him off from Richmond. As a result, Lee withdrew into the defenses of that city and adjacent Petersburg, to withstand what turned out to be a nine-month-long siege. Near its end, in February, 1865, he was finally made general in chief of all Confederate armies. It was, by this time, too late. He placed Johnston in command of the only other remaining major army, in the Carolinas; then, in April, he attempted to escape a fresh Union offensive at Petersburg to link up with Johnston. Grant cut him off at Appomattox Courthouse in Virginia, where Lee surrendered on April 9, effectively ending the Civil War. His three sons were with him, two of them major generals, one a captain.

Having lost his home at Arlington, which became the national cemetery, Lee assumed the presidency of Washington College at Lexington, Virginia, in October, 1865. For the next five years, in weakened health, he served effectively not only as a college administrator but also as a quiet symbol of reunion and restoration, burying the passions of the wartime bitterness and thereby setting an example for the defeated South. Following his death, the college was renamed Washington and Lee in his honor.

FROM UNION OFFICER TO CONFEDERATE GENERAL

In this letter of February 25, 1868, to Reverdy Johnson, Robert E. Lee attempts to counter unfounded rumors by explaining how and why he declined the opportunity to command the Union Army on the outbreak of the Civil War.

My Dear Sir: My attention has been called to the official report of the debate in the Senate of the United States, on the 19th instant, in which you did me the kindness to doubt the correctness of the statement made by the Honourable Simon Cameron, in regard to myself. I desire that you may feel certain of my conduct on the occasion referred to, so far as my individual statement can make you. I never intimated to any one that I desired the command of the United States Army; nor did I ever have a conversation with but one gentleman, Mr. Francis Preston Blair, on the subject, which was at his invitation, and, as I understood, at the instance of President Lincoln. After listening to his remarks, I declined the offer that he made me, to take command of the army that was to be brought into the field; stating, as candidly and courteously as I could, that, though opposed to secession and deprecating war, I could take no part in an invasion of the Southern States. I went directly from the interview with Mr. Blair to the office of General [Winfield] Scott; told him of the proposition that had been made to me, and my decision. Upon reflection after returning to my home, I concluded that I ought no longer to retain the commission I held in the United States Army, and on the second morning thereafter I forwarded my resignation to General Scott. At the time, I hoped that peace would have been preserved; that some way would have been found to save the country from the calamities of war; and I then had no other intention than to pass the remainder of my life as a private citizen. Two days afterward, upon the invitation of the Governor of Virginia, I repaired to Richmond; found that the Convention then in session had passed the ordinance withdrawing the State from the Union; and accepted the commission of commander of its forces, which was tendered me.

These are the ample facts of the case, and they show that Mr. Cameron has been misinformed.

I am with great respect,
Your obedient servant,
R. E. LEE.

Source: Robert E. Lee [Jr.], *Recollections and Letters of General Robert E. Lee* (New York: Doubleday, Page, 1904), chapter 2.

SIGNIFICANCE

Robert E. Lee became a legend in his own time, first to the embattled peoples of the South and, eventually, to the nation at large. He symbolized the plain fact that, rather than treason, the cause of the Confederacy had represented the playing out of the final contradiction of the American nation. North and South, geographically, economically, and socially distinct, could no longer coexist within the fabric of the Constitution. The southern plantation aristocracy, agrarian and founded upon slavery, had become an anachronism in the modern, industrialized Western world. Its ultimate survival could be obtained only by arms, in which contest Lee had been the supreme champion. His stately character, bearing, and professionalism represented the ideal of southern society. Though he had opposed slavery, secession, and even war as a final political solution, like so many of his generation, he had had to make the tragic, fateful decision to stand by his neighbors in defense of the only way of life they knew. In defeat, he accepted the course of history without rancor.

The contrast between Lee's conduct and that of his Union counterparts reflected the great shift in social values marked by the Civil War. He ordered his troops to abstain from plundering civilian property, failing to understand—unlike Grant, William T. Sherman, and Philip H. Sheridan—that the modern war that they were all waging was a harbinger of a new age of mass conflict, aimed at breaking civilian resistance with the use of modern industrialized machine weapons, thus destroying the socioeconomic institutions of an enemy. No better example of the adage that the Civil War was the last great war between gentlemen could be found than in the person of Robert E. Lee himself, the perfect gentleman of the long-past Age of Reason that had spawned his noble family.

Lee's achievements on the field of battle, however, established him as one of the greatest army commanders in history. Not merely an inspiring leader, he made correct, informed judgments about his enemy, then struck decisively. As a theater strategist defending his beloved Virginia, he became a master of the mobile feint, thanks largely to several able lieutenants. Stonewall Jackson's fast-moving so-called foot cavalry thrust into the Shenandoah Valley to draw away troops from McClellan during the Peninsular Campaign. J. E. B. Stuart's cavalry rode circles around the Union armies in every campaign. However, both these commanders were killed, in 1863 and 1864, respectively. Jubal A. Early's drive up the valley the latter year might have succeeded but for the deter-

mined riposte of Grant and Sheridan. In grand strategy, however, Lee was not adept, having misjudged Union intentions along the south Atlantic coast early in the war and never having the authority to mastermind Confederate fortunes until near the end of the struggle. He did not attempt to influence Davis beyond the Virginia theater.

Had Lee not been outnumbered most of the time, one can only conjecture what might have been the outcome of the war: As a tactician, he had no match in the Union army. The fatal flaw lay in the nature of the Confederacy itself, a politically loose grouping of rebelling states, devoid of effective central leadership. After Gettysburg, observed one of Lee's generals on the eve of Appomattox, the men had been fighting simply for him.

—Clark G. Reynolds

FURTHER READING

Blount, Roy, Jr. *Robert E. Lee: A Penguin Life*. New York: Lipper/Viking, 2003. Concise biography, written from the perspective of a southerner. Particularly strong in detailing Lee's life after the Civil War.

Connelly, Thomas L. *The Marble Man: Robert E. Lee and His Image in American Society*. New York: Alfred A. Knopf, 1977. An excellent interpretative analysis of Lee's reputation as a southern and national hero during and since the Civil War.

Dowdey, Clifford. *Lee*. Boston: Little, Brown, 1965. An excellent one-volume treatment of Lee's career, adding new materials and interpretations of Lee's performance at Gettysburg.

Fellman, Michael. *The Making of Robert E. Lee*. New York: Random House, 2000. Intellectual biography, focusing on Lee's psychology and ideas on race, slavery, and other issues. Describes how Lee struggled to reconcile his Christian virtue, humility, and sense of duty with his desire for success and fame.

Flood, Charles Bracelen. *Lee: The Last Years*. Boston: Houghton Mifflin, 1981. The best analysis of Lee's actions and achievements during the last five years of his life, including his reactions to the late war.

Freeman, Douglas Southall. *R. E. Lee*. 4 vols. New York: Charles Scribner's Sons, 1934-1935. The definitive biography, which dissects Lee's career with such detail and careful interpretation as to become the standard work for all students of Lee.

Johnson, Robert Underwood, and Clarence Clough Buel, eds. *Battles and Leaders of the Civil War*. 4 vols. New York: Century, 1887. The most comprehensive and reliable source of reminiscences of key Civil War leaders, including many of Lee's subordinates and opponents, with complete lists of the opposing armies and navies, down to the regimental and ship level. Excellent maps and illustrations.

Lee, Robert E. *Recollections and Letters of General Robert E. Lee by His Son Capt. Robert E. Lee.* 2d ed. Garden City, N.Y.: Doubleday, Page, 1924. An invaluable memoir, especially useful for insights into Lee's family relationships.

_____. *The Wartime Papers of R. E. Lee.* Edited by Clifford Dowdey and Louis Manarin. Boston: Little, Brown, 1961. Primary source material drawn from official records and private sources that offer insights into Lee's character and abilities as a commander.

Sanborn, Margaret. *Robert E. Lee.* 2 vols. Philadelphia: J. B. Lippincott, 1966-1967. A sound popular history based on the usual abundant primary and secondary sources.

Thomas, Emory M. *Robert E. Lee: A Biography.* New York: W. W. Norton, 1995. Comprehensive, analytical biography by a prominent Civil War historian. Thomas focuses on Lee as a person, portraying him as a man of many paradoxes.

SEE ALSO: John Brown; Jefferson Davis; Ulysses S. Grant; Stonewall Jackson; Abraham Lincoln; Winfield Scott.

RELATED ARTICLES in *Great Events from History: The Nineteenth Century, 1801-1900:* October 16-18, 1859: Brown's Raid on Harpers Ferry; July 21, 1861: First Battle of Bull Run; March 3, 1863: Union Enacts the First National Draft Law; July 1, 1863-November 25, 1863: Battles of Gettysburg, Vicksburg, and Chattanooga; November 15, 1864-April 18, 1865: Sherman Marches Through Georgia and the Carolinas; April 9 and 14, 1865: Surrender at Appomattox and Assassination of Lincoln; June 23, 1865: Watie Is Last Confederate General to Surrender.

ÉTIENNE LENOIR
French inventor

Lenoir invented a number of useful processes and devices, the most famous being an internal combustion engine. The significance of the later invention remains a matter of controversy, but there is little doubt that Lenoir's engine stimulated the efforts of the other pioneers of internal combustion engine design.

BORN: January 12, 1822; Mussy-la-Ville, Belgium
DIED: August 4, 1900; La Varenne-Saint-Hilaire, France
ALSO KNOWN AS: Jean-Joseph-Étienne Lenoir (full name)
AREA OF ACHIEVEMENT: Science and technology

EARLY LIFE
Although born in the French-speaking region of Belgium, Étienne Lenoir (ay-tyehn leh-nwahr) spent all of his productive life in France. He went to his adopted country at the age of sixteen in 1838 to begin work as a metal enameler. Within a few years, he had several inventions to his credit. In 1847, he patented an enameling process, in 1851 an electroforming process, in 1853 an electric-railway brake, and in 1865 an automatic telegraph that printed messages on a ribbon of paper. This telegraph was thus a forerunner of the ticker-tape machine. On January 24, 1860, he received a patent for his most famous invention—an internal combustion engine.

Interest in internal combustion engines was as old as the discovery of atmospheric pressure in the seventeenth century. Experiments and demonstrations that showed the power of atmospheric pressure working against or into a vacuum inspired a number of people to imagine an engine that could be powered by having atmospheric pressure drive a piston into a vacuum chamber. The difficulty in creating such an engine was in producing the vacuum—not once, but in rapid succession, because the piston must have continuous up-and-down motion. An obvious solution was to use gunpowder to burn the air in a chamber and to create a vacuum by allowing the resulting gas to cool. Christiaan Huygens actually constructed such engines, but they were impractical because of the incompleteness of the vacuum. The solution was the steam engine, as steam could drive the air from a chamber without an explosion and then be reduced to only one seventeen-hundredth of its original volume when converted to water.

There were suggestions for engines employing heated air rather than steam during the late eighteenth century, and some were in use by the end of the century. The real impetus for an internal combustion engine came, however, from the work of Sadi Carnot during the 1820's. Among the ideas about thermodynamics that Carnot established was the concept of a heat engine. He demonstrated that a steam engine was basically inefficient, because little of the heat produced to power it was actually used. He believed that an air engine would be much more efficient because more heat could be utilized.

By the time Lenoir appeared in Paris, the idea of an internal combustion engine was widespread and a number had been built, but none proved practical enough to be offered commercially. In addition to the familiarity of the idea, the stage was further set for Lenoir by the ready availability of natural gas for the gas lighting that was becoming common in Paris.

LIFE'S WORK

Lenoir's gas engine was the first internal combustion engine practical enough to be offered for sale in significant numbers. It ran on the natural gas piped into factories and businesses for lighting purposes or distillates of petroleum similar to modern gasoline. In 1897, Lenoir claimed in *France Automobile* that he used the engine to power a vehicle of some sort—probably a farm cart—for several trips between Joinville-le-Pont and Paris in 1863.

The Automobile Club of France conducted an investigation in 1900 and concluded that Lenoir had made the world's first automobile trip in May, 1862, between Paris and Vincennes. It has been observed that the discrepancy in dates is rather suspicious. These claims came at a time when there was controversy about who had invented the automobile, involving French and German inventors as well as their champions. Even if one assumes that Lenoir powered a vehicle with an internal combustion engine in 1862 or 1863, it was hardly more than a publicity stunt similar to the motorboat trips made on the Seine using his engine. He did nothing to develop a practical horseless carriage for his own use or for sale.

Although his engine was sold commercially and, in that sense, may be regarded as a success, there have been questions about the importance of his accomplishment. The most telling criticism of his work is that he did not understand the fundamental requirement for a truly successful internal combustion engine, namely that the gas must be compressed before firing. A further complaint is that he thought of his engine as nothing more than an advanced steam engine. In his patent application he stated:

> My engine cannot be classed among gas engines. Indeed, the functions of the gas I employ do not consist in

detonating or exploding it, thereby impelling the piston, as this has heretofore been done or suggested, but in the use of gas as a fuel that can be instantaneously and regularly ignited, and without producing any shock, for the purpose of heating the air that is mixed with it. The air thus dilated or expanded will act on the piston in the same manner as steam would in ordinary steam engines.

Despite his patent claims to have produced a gas engine unlike others, a company advertising brochure of 1864 pointed out that his engine was closely linked to those of previous inventors. It was stated that the Lenoir engine used Robert Street's piston with Philippe Lebon's double action, an ignition like that of Isaac de Rivas, and a cooling system similar to Samuel Brown's. Perhaps these claims and denials, as well as the similarity in appearance of the engine to stationary steam engines, were meant to reassure a buying public dubious about the idea of gas explosions.

Whether owing to the conservative buying habits of potential customers, design inadequacies, or both, the engine was not a commercial success. Lenoir had done engineering work for Gautier and Company of Paris and apparently convinced its proprietors of the merits of his design. This company backed him in forming the Société des Moteurs Lenoir in 1859. Some four thousand shares of stock were issued in the new company but no dividends appear ever to have been paid. The Parisian Gas Company took control of the engine in 1863 and paid Lenoir a pension in his old age.

Most of the engines were built under license from Lenoir's company. The Reading Iron Works in England built about one hundred. Two German companies built some, and the Lenoir Gas Engine Company of New York sold some at a cost of five hundred dollars for the half horsepower model and fifteen hundred dollars for the four horsepower version. The Marinoni and Lefebvre companies of Paris produced more than any of the foreign manufacturers, but, all told, fewer than five hundred were made.

The Lenoir engine resembled a stationary, double-acting, horizontal steam engine. With power being produced on each side of the piston, it was, in effect, the equivalent of a two-cylinder engine. Sliding valves connected to the crankshaft by rods that covered and uncovered ports to admit fuel and to exhaust spent fumes. The ignition system was electric. A battery provided power to an induction coil with a vibrating contact to provide a primary spark, and a sliding distributor alternated delivery of current between the two spark plugs. The electrical system was changed at least twice, as it never worked satisfactorily.

The final version used a rotary distributor with the rotor driven by the crankshaft. An unusual feature by comparison with later engines was that air and gas were admitted to the combustion chamber separately. This was the basis of Lenoir's claim that he had not produced an ordinary gas engine. He believed that the air should remain separate from the gas, at least in part, to provide a cushion between the explosion of gas and the piston head. However, the exhaust ports opened before the expansion was complete, and much of the heat produced was lost to the cooling water, in violation of Carnot's principles. The loss of heat also meant that there were problems with overheating and that a huge radiator was necessary. The company suggested a radiator capacity of one hundred gallons for the half horsepower model.

The engine was uneconomical for industrial applications. It consumed about one hundred cubic feet of gas per hour in the half horsepower model, and it had maintenance problems. Overheating caused the valves to stick, there was no self-contained means of recharging the batteries, and the spark plugs required frequent cleaning. Later versions of this type of engine, such as that of Pierre Hugon, provided for the injection of a spray of water into the cylinder to help in cooling, but the improvement was not enough to rescue the design. A steam engine of comparable size was as economical to operate and much less troublesome.

Carnot had observed that the most obvious way to produce a great change of temperature, as required in an efficient engine, was to compress the air used in the engine. Because compression was the key to success, Lenoir's noncompressing engine was out of production by the late 1860's, but he tried again during the 1880's with a four-cycle compression engine. It had poppet valves and other advances over his earlier model, including a 300 percent improvement in fuel consumption rates. This engine was produced for a while by the Mignon and Rouart Company.

Lenoir made no substantial profits from any of his inventions, but he did receive several honors. For his engine, he received a prize at the London Exposition of 1862 and several French prizes including that of the Marquis d'Argenteuil, which brought him twelve thousand francs, in 1886. His most prestigious award was the Legion of Honor, which he received in 1881 for the invention of the teletype machine in 1865. He died in relative obscurity and poverty in 1900.

SIGNIFICANCE

Even if Étienne Lenoir had not built an engine, his teletype machine and other inventions would have gained for him a respectable place in the story of modern technological development. It is, however, his production of the first commercial engine and, especially, his connection with the automobile that have brought him more attention than the other engine designers who were his contemporaries. He was not the first to build an internal combustion engine. In fact, by his own admission, his design depended almost entirely on the work of predecessors. Several hundred of his engines were built and sold, but, by all accounts, they were not suitable. It is on the automobile connection that his fame primarily rests.

Assessment of Lenoir's achievements is made difficult by the controversies surrounding the invention of the automobile. As indicated, national pride and the championing of personal favorites has made this a hotly debated subject. Moreover, the difficulty in defining exactly what constitutes the first automobile probably means that there will never be a clear ranking of its inventors.

The claims and counterclaims in France and Germany as to who invented the automobile brought some attention to Lenoir at the end of his life, but it was the Selden Patent Case that did the most to bring him to the attention of the English-speaking world. George Baldwin Selden obtained a United States patent on automobiles in 1895. Although he never built any automobiles, the Association of Licensed Automobile Manufacturers was formed to exploit the patent by selling the right to manufacture to other companies. Henry Ford challenged the patent, and in the subsequent trials, which lasted from 1903 to 1911, the Ford Company maintained that Selden's patent was invalid because practical automobiles predated the patent by a number of years.

A significant part of the Ford case was the claim that Lenoir had constructed an automobile in 1860. The Ford lawyers cited an article describing a self-propelled vehicle built by Lenoir that appeared in the June 16, 1860, edition of *Le Monde illustré*. There is no other evidence that this vehicle was ever built. Even Lenoir never claimed that he had built an automobile as early as 1860. The claims made for and by him during the late 1890's were also placed into evidence. When the Selden attorneys imported British experts to deny that an automobile could be powered by a noncompressing engine, the Ford Company actually built a copy of Lenoir's engine and used it to drive a Ford automobile. The attention drawn to Lenoir's name in this case has done much to establish him in the list of automobile pioneers.

Whatever one's opinion about Lenoir's importance as an inventor of the automobile, his engine stimulated the production of better engines and, ultimately, automobiles. All the pioneers of automobile design studied his engine. Those uninterested in automobiles were encouraged to build better stationary engines for industrial use, and Lenoir played a significant role in the transition from the age of steam to the age of oil.

—Philip Dwight Jones

FURTHER READING

Bishop, Charles W. *La France et l'automobile.* Paris: Librairies-Techniques, 1971. This French-language work gives considerable space to advocating Lenoir's importance and priority in developing engines and automobiles. The author carefully explains the invalidity of all complaints made against Lenoir or his engine. He is convinced that Lenoir invented the automobile and that others, such as Carl Benz and Gottlieb Daimler, were inspired by his inventions.

Cardwell, D. S. L. *From Watt to Clausius: The Rise of Thermodynamics in the Early Industrial Revolution.* Ithaca, N.Y.: Cornell University Press, 1971. Gives the early history of the effort to develop an efficient heat engine.

Cummins, C. Lyle, Jr. *Internal Fire: The Internal Combustion Engine.* Lake Oswego, Oreg.: Carnot Press, 1976. This is a history of the internal combustion engine. Although Lenoir's work is covered only in a portion of one chapter, it is one of the best accounts of his activities in English. Contains technical details, graphs, and illustrations of the engine.

Field, D. C. "Internal Combustion Engines." In *A History of Technology*, edited by Charles Singer et al. Vol. 5. New York: Oxford University Press, 1958. Details the general development of the internal combustion engine and dismisses the value of Lenoir's engine except for the observation that its limited commercial appeal encouraged others to attempt improvements.

Grayson, Stan. *Beautiful Engines: Treasures of the Internal Combustion Century.* Marblehead, Mass.: Devereux Books, 2001. The first chapter in this illustrated history of the internal combustion engine describes Lenoir's creation of "the seminal machine."

Mott-Smith, Morton. *The Concept of Energy Simply Explained.* Mineola, N.Y.: Dover, 1964. Presents the concepts of heat engines as well as major scientists who have dealt with the subject and their theories. Contains little mathematics, and the author does a good job of explaining theories simply without being simplistic.

Turner, A. J. *From Pleasure and Profit to Science and Security: Étienne Lenoir and the Transformation of Precision Instrument Making in France, 1760-1830.* Cambridge, England: Whipple Museum of the History of Science, 1989. Turner's monograph on Lenoir's life and his role in transforming the manufacture of scientific instruments accompanied the museum's exhibition, *La Citoyen Lenoir: Scientific Instrument Making in Revolutionary France.* Includes illustrations of compasses, telescopes, and other instruments displayed in the exhibit.

SEE ALSO: Carl Benz; Gottlieb Daimler; Rudolf Diesel; Nikolaus August Otto.

RELATED ARTICLES in *Great Events from History: The Nineteenth Century, 1801-1900:* 1860: Lenoir Patents the Internal Combustion Engine; February, 1892: Diesel Patents the Diesel Engine.

LEO XIII
Roman Catholic pope (1878-1903)

Considered one of the greatest leaders of the Roman Catholic Church during a period of crisis, Pope Leo XIII tried to maintain the strength and power of the Church in a world changing through industry, colonization, and governmental upheaval. He was not always successful, but he was a pioneer, aware of the needs of the modern Church.

BORN: March 2, 1810; Carpineto Romano, Papal States (now in Italy)
DIED: July 20, 1903; Rome, Italy
ALSO KNOWN AS: Vincenzo Gioacchino Pecci (birth name)
AREAS OF ACHIEVEMENT: Church government, religion and theology

EARLY LIFE

Pope Leo XIII was born Vincenzo Gioacchino Pecci in the hills south of Rome in central Italy. His parents, Colonel Ludovico Pecci and Anna Prosperi Buzi, were patrician, but neither wealthy nor of great nobility. The sixth in a family of seven children, Pecci began his education in Viterbo at the Jesuit college from 1818 to 1824. He was a brilliant student, with what became lifelong scholarly achievement in Latin. He continued his studies in Rome from 1824 to 1832 at the Roman College and in 1832 was admitted to the Academy of the Noble Ecclesiastics. He completed his religious studies at the University of the Sapienza between 1832 and 1837, concentrating in theology and civil and canon law. He was ordained in 1837.

In the same year, he was appointed a domestic prelate, and in 1838 he was named governor or apostolic delegate of Benevento by Pope Gregory XVI, who had praised Pecci's courageous service during the cholera epidemic of 1837. His success in this position, especially in reducing banditry and eliminating the inroads being made by liberals, led to his appointment in 1841 to the same position in Perugia. Although this area had similar problems to solve, Pecci went beyond his previous successes and improved the economy by building roads, establishing a farmers' savings bank, and gaining great popularity among the residents.

With these achievements, Pecci was sent to Belgium as nuncio, the pope's representative, in January, 1843, after having been consecrated titular archbishop of Damietta. Pecci spent three difficult years in Belgium, which finally ended when King Leopold requested of the pope that Pecci be recalled. The king and his prime minister, Nothomb, had been seeking to confer the right to name members of the university juries to the government. In this matter, crucial to the educational system of Belgium, Pecci sided with the bishops and Catholic politicians in opposition to the king. Even though the Catholic side won, the victory was empty for Pecci. Although this period appears to have been a failure, Pecci gained experience that helped form his future conservatism. During this time, his only extended observation of the more industrialized, liberal areas of Europe, he saw the behavior of a liberal political regime toward Catholics and learned to oppose it. As he fought against unionism, the compromise and agreement between Catholics and moderate liberals in Belgium, he came to be wary of liberal hands extended in compromise.

LIFE'S WORK

When Pecci left Belgium, he returned to Perugia, where he served as archbishop until 1878 and further solidified many of the ideologies that would serve him during his pontificate. Along with his brother Joseph, a Jesuit seminary professor, he worked to increase the numbers of clerics; modernize the curriculum at the seminaries; revive Thomism, the medieval Scholasticism based on the Aristotelianism of Thomas Aquinas; and establish the Academy of Saint Thomas in 1859. As a result of these activities, Pecci was named a cardinal in 1853.

During the period that he was archbishop in Perugia, Pecci was politically prudent and reserved. He protested the annexation of Perugia by the kingdom of Sardinia in 1860; on the other hand, he would not join Cardinal Giacomo Antonelli, the secretary of state to Pope Pius IX, in his methods of government and involvement in conflicts. Consequently, Antonelli considered Pecci an enemy and kept him from Rome. Following his moderate views as a Catholic, Pecci wrote his pastoral letters of 1874-1877, recommending that the Roman Catholic Church make conciliatory gestures toward contemporary society. Self-evident as it may seem, he recognized that the Church did not exist in a void, but rather in the quickly changing world of the late nineteenth century. These letters, in addition to his other achievements, gained for him the respect of Pius, and, when Antonelli died in 1877, Pecci was summoned to serve as camerlengo in the Roman curia, the chamberlain who oversees the Church when the pope dies.

When Pius died in 1878, Pecci was in a good position to be elected pope. Because this was the first conclave since the Holy See had lost its temporal power, Pecci's role as the leading moderate was important. He was indeed elected on the third ballot with forty-four of the sixty-one votes, after having received a plurality on the first ballot of nineteen votes, thirteen more than the second most favored candidate.

When he became Pope Leo XIII, Pecci was sixty-eight years old and in fragile health. These facts, combined with his delicate appearance, all indicated that his would be, at best, a brief transitional appointment. However, he was popular. Because the Italian government feared demonstrations in his support in St. Peter's Square and all over Rome, his crowning took place in private on March 3 in the Sistine Chapel so that he would not appear publicly on the loggia to bless the people as he wished to do.

Leo's acts on the evening of his coronation, however, foreshadowed the theme of his reign. He wrote letters to the German emperor, the Swiss president, and the Russian czar announcing his election and offering hope that the Church might come to better accord with their governments. Although doctrinally conservative, he sought

Leo XIII. (Library of Congress)

to maintain a strong role for the Church in the modern world.

In the course of his papacy, Leo wrote numerous encyclicals on subjects ranging from traditional piety to social issues. He wrote eleven encyclicals on the Blessed Virgin Mary and the Rosary, two each on the Eucharist and the redemptive work of Christ, and one on the renewal of the Franciscan Third Order. In the Jubilee Year of 1900, he consecrated the entire human race to the Sacred Heart of Jesus, an initiative begun by Pius, and in 1893 instituted a feast of the Holy Family. Becoming more conservative in the final few years or his life, he published new norms for censorship in 1897 and a new Index in 1900, and he set up a permanent Biblical Commission in 1902 after writing the encyclical on Bible study, *Providentissimus Deus* (1893; *On the Study of the Scriptures*, 1894).

Leo's ability to align such conservative piety to a new recognition of modern states is quite remarkable. It was accomplished, however, not with statements of accord with government, but rather with statements only of recognition. In 1878, the year of his coronation, Leo attacked socialism, communism, and nihilism in *Quod apostolici muneris* (*Concerning Modern Errors, Socialism, Communism, Nihilism*, 1895), and, in 1884, he wrote similarly on Freemasonry. He also acted to increase centralization within the Church, much to the disappointment of progressives.

At the same time, Leo wrote encyclicals on the relationship of the Church to sociopolitical order: *Diuturnum illud* (1881; *On Civil Government*, 1942) recognized the existence of democracy in God's world, *Immortale Dei* (1885; *On the Christian Constitution of States*, 1885) defined the spiritual and temporal spheres of power, and *Libertas praestantissimum* (1888; *Human Liberty*, 1895) viewed the Church as the true source of liberty. Most important was *Rerum novarum* (1891; *The Condition of Labor*, 1891), which advocated private property rights, fair wages, workers' rights, and trade unionism, while, predictably, condemning socialism and economic liberalism. Because of the positions presented in this encyclical, Leo came to be known as "the workers' pope."

In addition to these, Leo wrote encyclicals on social and intellectual issues. *Arcanum divinae sapientia* (1880; *On Christian Marriage*, 1880) is a highly conservative statement on marriage, identical in tone and thought to writings of his predecessors. On intellectual matters, however, he was more open to new ideas than the revival of old ones. Following his lifelong respect for and study of Thomism, he encouraged Catholics to incorporate fully Thomist metaphysics into Catholic philosophy in *Aeterni patris* (1879; *Scholastic Philosophy*, 1879). Leo also bridged the gap between Catholicism and the natural sciences by encouraging Catholics to study astronomy and the other natural sciences. He urged complete objectivity in all areas of scholarship done by Catholics; in an unprecedented ecumenical spirit, he opened the Vatican libraries to scholars of all faiths in 1883. This was begun in 1879, when he allowed the German historian Ludwig Pastor access to the secret archives of the Vatican.

In many ways, Leo was a far more political pope than was his successor, yet while he and his four secretaries of state had many diplomatic successes, he failed in matters closest to home, such as the achievement of accord with the Italian government. By 1887, Leo was willing to accept a compromise in which Italy would be entirely unified under the House of Savoy; the Papal States, a sixteen-thousand-square-mile area in central Italy, would be given to Italy; and an indemnification or compensation, offered under the Law of Guarantee, therefore would be received from Italy. The Italian government, however, wanted the abdication of the pope's sovereignty, which would lead inevitably to limited freedom for Leo himself and future popes. He made a counterrequest for a repeal of the anticlerical laws and restoration of papal rule for Rome, but it was denied. Thus, Leo was unable to achieve any resolution of conflict with the Italian government. None, indeed, was attained until the Lateran Treaty of 1929.

France also presented problems for the pope. With its republican government, France sought the separation of church and state, along with secular, social, and educational systems. Catholics within France were not enthusiastic in their support for the Church against their government. Soon, government recognition of all religious groups was required or the groups were to be disbanded. In 1880, the Jesuits were dissolved, followed in 1900 by the Congregation of the Assumptionists. Teaching orders went into exile, and the pope was unable to turn the tide, which became a crisis for his successor, Pius X.

Relations with England remained unchanged. At the beginning of his reign, Leo initiated a study seeking possible reconciliation with the Anglican Church. When such a unification proved impossible, he issued an apostolic letter in 1896, discouraging any move in this direction; yet he was responsible for the cardinalship of John Henry Newman in 1878.

Leo actively sought a reunion with the Oriental and Slavic Catholic churches, going so far as to praise the work of Saint Cyril and Saint Methodius in the encyclical *Grande munus* (1880) and to discuss rites and reunion in the apostolic letter of 1894. Again, he was unable to make concrete advances in this direction.

More satisfactory were Leo's efforts in Belgium, Germany, and Russia. He negotiated agreements with Belgium in 1884 and with Russia in 1894. In 1886-1887, he successfully achieved the repeal of the anticlerical laws in Germany (the Kulturkampf) and, in his sole diplomatic success, he mediated in Germany's dispute with Spain over the possession of the Caroline Islands in the Pacific Ocean in 1885. He was, however, unsuccessful in his attempt to keep Germany and Austria from joining Italy in the Triple Alliance in 1887. He was not invited to the Hague Peace Conference of 1899, because of the intransigence of the Italian government.

In other areas of the world Leo recognized the importance of colonialism to Christian evangelism, and he approved 248 sees, 48 vicarates or prefectures, and 2 patriarchates in Scotland, North Africa, India, Japan, and the United States. Although he criticized "Americanism," which would have attempted to modernize Catholicism, in a letter of 1899, he named the first apostolic delegate to the United States in 1892.

The twenty-five years of Leo's reign ended in 1903 with his death at the age of ninety-three. He far exceeded expectations in the longevity, the social concern, and the intellectual strength of his service to the Church.

SIGNIFICANCE

It was fortunate for the Roman Catholic Church that Leo XIII became the pope when the Western world was experiencing great turmoil. A brilliant man, he was able to steer the Church into a role in society that at once showed an awareness of the modern world but did not stray far from traditional church doctrine. The English writer Thomas Carlyle called him a great "reconciler of differences." Leo's was a strong voice against the growing popularity of socialism in Europe, yet he accepted democracy and advocated the rights of workers in the growing industrialized world.

Within his own church, Leo was able to create a clear role of spiritual leadership for the pope to replace the recently lost temporal powers of the Papacy. Although some scholars consider his learning antiquated, restricted, and perhaps obsessively concerned with Thomism, his intellectual breadth, strength of character, and devotion to service have brought him great praise. Even with his many failures, he is generally considered the greatest pope in three hundred years. Leo said of himself,

"I want to set the church so far forward that my successor will not be able to turn back." As a pioneer whose ideas shone even more brightly after his death, he clearly achieved this goal.

—Vicki Robinson

FURTHER READING

Bokenkotter, Thomas. "Social Catholicism and Christian Democracy." In *A Concise History of the Catholic Church*. Garden City, N.Y.: Doubleday, 1927. A scholarly and detailed narrative of the political world into which Leo was thrust at his ordination. Leo's charitable piety is shown as it affected the changing governments and economies of the entire Western world.

Burkle-Young, Francis A. *Papal Elections in the Age of Transition, 1878-1922.* Lanham, Md.: Lexington Books, 2000. Recounts how Leo XIII and his three successors rose to the papacy, providing previously unpublished details of church conclaves.

Gargan, Edward T., ed. *Leo XIII and the Modern World.* New York: Sheed & Ward, 1961. A series of nine essays by various scholars preceded by an introductory essay and followed by an extensive bibliography on Leo and his period in history. The essays stress Leo's theological contributions, especially as a Thomist, and his impact on the European and American political worlds of the late nineteenth century.

Holland, Joe. *Modern Catholic Social Teaching: The Popes Confront the Industrial Age, 1740-1958.* New York: Paulist Press, 2003. This examination of the Vatican's response to the Industrial Revolution includes a discussion of *Rerum novarum*, described as the first papal declaration of working people's rights.

Kretzer, David I. *Prisoner of the Vatican: The Popes' Secret Plot to Capture Rome from the New Italian State.* Boston: Houghton Mifflin, 2004. Using previously unopened Vatican archives, Kretzer recounts how Popes Pius IX, Leo XIII, and other members of the clergy sought to dismantle the new Italian state and regain control of Rome.

McCabe, Joseph. "Leo XIII." In *Crises in the History of the Papacy.* New York: G. P. Putnam's Sons, 1916. An objective appraisal of the life and accomplishments of Leo, which assesses him as the best pope in three hundred years but a failure in gaining influence upon the thoughts or actions of Western society.

Miller, J. Martin. *The Life of Pope Leo XIII.* Philadelphia: National Publishing, 1903. A five-hundred-page biography written in praise of Leo that was begun before his death, containing several drawings and photographs. The author writes conversationally and quaintly, quoting letters and relating anecdotes in dialogue. His purpose is the veneration of Leo, and nearly one-third of the book is devoted to a detailed description of Leo's final illness and death.

O'Reilly, Bernard. *Life of Leo XIII from an Authentic Memoir Furnished by His Order.* New York: Charles L. Webster, 1887. Authorized biography written by a Roman Catholic priest and issued by Mark Twain's own publishing firm.

Wallace, Lillian Parker. *Leo XIII and the Rise of Socialism.* Durham, N.C.: Duke University Press, 1966. A presentation of the juxtaposition of two major antagonistic ideologies of the nineteenth century, held on one side by Leo and his church and on the other by Karl Marx and his followers. This 464-page volume shows Leo's power as he stems the tide of Marxism in Europe with his intellectual and compassionate approach to the social problems of the industrial world.

SEE ALSO: Frances Xavier Cabrini; Thomas Carlyle; James Gibbons; Karl Marx; John Henry Newman; Pius IX; Mark Twain.

RELATED ARTICLES in *Great Events from History: The Nineteenth Century, 1801-1900:* May 20, 1882: Triple Alliance Is Formed; May 15, 1891: Papal Encyclical on Labor.

ANNA LEONOWENS
Indian-born English teacher and writer

Leonowens achieved posthumous fame as the teacher portrayed in the film Anna and the King of Siam *and the musical* The King and I, *both of which were inspired by her published memoirs. However, modern scholarship has shown that she falsified important details of her life and provided an inauthentic account of the royal court of Siam. Her most significant work came later, when she was a woman suffrage leader and promoted cultural, educational, and social improvements for the communities in which she lived.*

BORN: November 6, 1831; Ahmadnagar, India
DIED: January 19, 1915; Montreal, Canada
ALSO KNOWN AS: Anna Harriette Leonowens (full name); Mary Anne Harriette Emma Edwards (birth name)
AREAS OF ACHIEVEMENT: Education, literature

EARLY LIFE

The details of the early life of Anna Leonowens (LEE-on-OH-ihns) have long been obscured by her deliberate attempts to hide her Asian roots in order to protect her image as a proper Englishwoman. She claimed to have been born in 1834 in Wales, but records show that she was actually born in 1831 in India, where her father, Thomas Edwards, had gone for military service. He died there several months before she was born. Her widowed mother, Mary Anne Glasscott Edwards, gave her the name Mary Anne Harriette Emma Edwards. Her mother had also been born in India and appears to have some Asian ancestry—a fact that Leonowens later tried to hide. Within a year of her father's death, her mother remarried to achieve financial security.

Mary Anne's childhood home was unhappy. She loathed her stepfather and had to endure crowded military barracks, surrounded by soldiers and their families. Like other military children, she probably performed routine chores and attended the garrison's school, in which she would have read British and Indian history and literature. While exploring her local community, she learned Indian languages from her mother and became aware of Indian traditions and religions.

Historians believe that Mary Anne and her older sister, Elizabeth, briefly attended school in England, coming home in 1845, when Elizabeth was fifteen, an age at which children of British military personnel were expected to begin military service, work, or marry. Mary Anne was appalled when Elizabeth married an older

man, and she vowed that she would not wed merely for survival. Instead, she toured Egypt and the Middle East with the regiment's chaplain, the Reverend George Percy Badger.

Before Mary Anne departed on that trip, a military clerk named Thomas Leon Owens proposed marriage to her. After she returned to India, she married Leon Owens on December 25, 1849. They first settled at Bombay, then traveled to England and Australia. Mary Anne bore four children, two of whom survived infancy. She and her husband moved to Penang, in what is now Malaysia, where her husband died in May, 1859. The record of his death spelled his surname as one word, Leonowens—a form that Mary Anne used thereafter. At what point Mary Anne started calling herself "Anna" is uncertain. "Anna" may have been a family nickname, or it might have been a clue to her identity, as *anna* was also the name of a low-value Indian coin.

LIFE'S WORK

After her husband died, Anna Leonowens taught in Singapore to earn her living. Her pupils praised her storytelling. At that time, King Mongkut (Rama IV) of Siam (now Thailand) was interested in reforming and modernizing his autonomous kingdom and was seeking a tutor to teach him English and to educate his numerous royal children and wives about Western culture. The first European teachers whom he hired were all missionary wives who tried to convert his family to Christianity. As he was a former monk and devout Buddhist, he wanted a teacher who would not attempt to proselytize.

In February, 1862, Mongkut contacted Leonowens after the Siamese consul at Singapore recommended her as a teacher. Because of her part-Indian roots, Leonowens knew that racial prejudice within the British Empire might threaten her employment, so she saw working in Siam as an opportunity to re-create herself where no one knew her past to dispute facts. She severed contact with her sister, who she feared might expose her Asian background, and declared she was a respectable English widow working only to support her family. After sending her daughter to England, she traveled by steamer to Siam with her son. They arrived in Bangkok in March, 1862, and began their lives there living in the Grand Palace, a large walled compound adjacent to the Chao Phraya River.

Leonowens taught her royal pupils at a temple located within the Grand Palace's harem community. This area housed a population of several thousand women and children. Leonowens herself lived outside the Grand Palace's walls but had open access to the harem. Her worries about discrimination intensified when British expatriates living in Bangkok excluded her from social functions, despite her affiliation with the royal court. Missionaries, however, became her closest friends and accepted her.

Leonowens's royal students included Prince Chulalongkorn, the future King Rama V. Later, Leonowens implied that she had inspired and shaped that king's reform-oriented policies. She also later claimed to have helped King Mongkut write letters to Western recipients, suggesting words and phrasings that best communicated his intentions, while remaining compatible with Western diplomatic protocol.

In 1868, Leonowens left Siam, took her son to a school in England, and retrieved her daughter. After Mongkut died later that year, his heir did not ask Leonowens to return. Leonowens then moved to New Brighton, New York, where she started a school for teachers. James Fields, the editor of the *Atlantic Monthly*, expressed interest in Leonowens's years in Bangkok and persuaded her to write articles about her Siamese experiences for the magazine. Fields encouraged Leonowens to write more, and Leonowens published her first book, *The English Governess at the Siamese Court*, in 1870. She used that title, although she had never served as a royal governess. Her second book, initially titled *The Romance of the Harem* (1872), was reissued as *The Romance of Siamese Harem Life* (1873) in the United States and England.

Victorian reviewers praised Leonowens's books for denouncing slavery, but reviewers who were knowledgeable about Siam and its monarchy criticized the books' flaws and incorrect geographical names and historical dates and regarded Leonowens as a noncredible source. For example, her books contain detailed conversations with harem women, even though she was never fluent in the Siamese (Thai) language. She also wrote a sensational description of torture and a public execution that never occurred and claimed that prisoners were housed in underground dungeons that could not even exist in the riverside palace.

Leonowens also exaggerated her importance to the Siamese. In fact, court members often considered her a gossip and annoyance. Some critics charged that Leonowens plagiarized other writers' accounts of Siam to describe places where she had never been. Finally, Leonowens falsely stated her father had been a wealthy officer and provided different names for her family and sites associated with her childhood. However, contemporary critics did not question her family history, only misrepresentations of Siam. Siamese readers resented her depictions, suggesting she had written books solely to earn money.

Despite criticisms of her books, Leonowens enjoyed celebrity and was paid to lecture. In 1878, her daughter

---

KING MONGKUT INVITES LEONOWENS TO COME TO SIAM

After the Siamese consul at Singapore recommended to King Mongkut that he hire Anna Leonowens to teach in the royal household, the king sent the letter that follows directly to Leonowens. Of particular interest is the letter's specification that there is to be no Christian proselytizing.

ENGLISH ERA, 1862, 26TH FEBRUARY
GRAND ROYAL PALACE, BANGKOK
TO MRS. A. H. LEONOWENS:–
MADAM:

We are in good pleasure, and satisfaction in heart, that you are in willingness to undertake the education of our beloved royal children. And we hope that in doing your education on us and on our children (whom English, call inhabitants of benighted land) you will do your best endeavor for knowledge of English language, science, and literature, and not for conversion to Christianity; as the followers of Buddha are mostly aware of the powerfulness of truth and virtue, as well as the followers of Christ, and are desirous to have facility of English language and literature, more than new religions.

We beg to invite you to our royal palace to do your best endeavorment upon us and our children. We shall expect to see you here on return of Siamese steamer *Chow Phya*.

We have written to Mr. William Adamson, and to our consul at Singapore, to authorize to do best arrangement for you and ourselves.

Believe me
Your faithfully,
S. S. P. P. MAHA MONGKUT.

Source: Anna Harriette Leonowens, *The English Governess at the Siamese Court* (Boston: J. R. Osgood, 1870).

married a Nova Scotia banker, and Leonowens moved to Halifax to live with her daughter. She then often visited New York and Boston on writing and speaking business. After Czar Alexander II of Russia was assassinated in 1881, she traveled throughout Russia writing articles for the magazine *Youth's Companion*. That magazine offered her full-time editorial work, but she preferred to concentrate her attention on supplementing the educations of her five grandchildren. In 1884, she published *Life and Travels in India: Being Recollections of a Journey Before the Days of Railroads*.

In 1887, Leonowens acted as an art patron by planning an exhibition and speaking at fund-raising events to collect money for Halifax's Victoria School of Art (later known as the Nova Scotia College of Art and Design, which includes the Anna Leonowens Gallery). She edited *The Art Movement in America* in 1887 and published *Our Asiatic Cousins* in 1889. She also started community book clubs. She briefly lived in Germany, while her grandchildren were studying there, and returned to Halifax in 1893. A suffragist, she established the Halifax Local Council of Women, seeking civic improvements, and served as president of the Woman's Suffrage Association in 1895. Two years later, she attended the National Council of Women of Canada's conference at Halifax. While accompanying one of her granddaughters to Europe for musical training, she visited with King Chulalongkorn in London.

In 1901, Leonowens moved to Montreal, Quebec, where her son-in-law had transferred to another bank. A stroke later ruined her health, and she died in Montreal in January, 1915. Her obituary repeated the biographical errors she had created to preserve her carefully crafted image as a proper Englishwoman.

SIGNIFICANCE

Leonowen's memoirs, although tainted, provide valuable information about Siam that would otherwise be inaccessible to scholars. As an inside observer at the royal court, she was aware of routine life in the palace. By the 1940's, Leonowens's books had fallen out of print and her adventures were forgotten. All that changed in 1944, when Margaret Landon published a best-selling biography of her and popular culture appropriated her story. Landon perpetuated most of Leonowens's falsehoods about her life, believing that she was reporting facts. Those inaccuracies and misinformation remained when publishers reprinted editions of both Landon's and Leonowens's books.

Leonowens enjoyed her fame and profit but could not have envisioned that her life would one day inspire major motion pictures (*Anna and the King of Siam*, 1946; *Anna and the King*, 2000; *The King and I*, 1956); a Broadway musical, *The King and I* (1951); and even a television series, *Anna and the King* (1972) that would perpetuate her misinformation. Translations of her and Landon's books and films would spread her story worldwide, misleading readers and viewers who had no experience themselves with Siamese culture. Many Thais were outraged by the films that they considered disrespectful because no Westerner could influence and control Thai politics as Leonowens claimed to have done. Other Thais viewed the musical performances as comedies because they were so ludicrous. Mongkut's descendant emphasized Leonowens had not significantly affected royals. The Thai government later banned Leonowens's books, although some stores stocked them for tourists.

It was only in the late twentieth century that researchers began detecting inconsistencies in Leonowens's autobiographical information. They located documents to determine facts, yet missing records render Leonowens's true story incomplete.

—*Elizabeth D. Schafer*

FURTHER READING

Bristowe, William S. *Louis and the King of Siam*. London: Chatto and Windus, 1976. Biographer of Leonowens's son who discovered Leonowens's fabrications during his research and located vital and archival records to secure evidence countering the false autobiographical information Leonowens created.

Dow, Leslie Smith. *Anna Leonowens: A Life Beyond the "King and I."* Lawrencetown Beach, Nova Scotia: Pottersfield Press, 1991. Valuable for details concerning Leonowens's post-Siam life, especially her years in Canada. However, the book relies on her Siamese accounts and repeats many errors regarding her early life.

Landon, Margaret. *Anna and the King of Siam*. New York: John Day, 1944. Partially fictionalized and inaccurate portrayal of Leonowens's life in Siam based on her memoirs and family and contemporaries' recollections. This book is the source used for stage and screen adaptations.

Moffat, Abbot Low. *Mongkut: The King of Siam*. Ithaca, N.Y.: Cornell University Press, 1961. Describes the king's perspective of Leonowens. An appendix explores Leonowens's role as a historian of nineteenth century Siam.

Warren, William. *The Truth About Anna . . . and Other Stories.* Singapore: Archipelago Press, 2000. Discusses flaws in Leonowens's autobiographical and historical accounts and offers insights regarding Thai reactions to her memoirs.

Wyatt, David K. *Thailand: A Short History.* 2d ed. New Haven, Conn.: Yale University Press, 2003. Comprehensive account that provides context for Leonowens's interactions with Mongkut and Chula-longkorn and the significance of her educational employment.

SEE ALSO: Alexander II; Gia Long; Anna Jameson.
RELATED ARTICLES in *Great Events from History: The Nineteenth Century, 1801-1900:* August, 1858: France and Spain Invade Vietnam; April, 1882-1885: French Indochina War.

LEOPOLD II
King of Belgium (r. 1865-1909)

Leopold was the second constitutional monarch of the Belgian kingdom created during the 1830's. Frustrated by the constitutional restraints on his authority, he set up his own predatory private empire in Central Africa and earned a reputation as one of the most ruthless and unprincipled rulers in modern history.

BORN: April 9, 1835; Brussels, Belgium
DIED: December 17, 1909; Laeken, Belgium
ALSO KNOWN AS: Léopold-Louis-Philippe-Marie-Victor (full name); Leopold Lodewijk Filips Maria Victor
AREA OF ACHIEVEMENT: Government and politics

EARLY LIFE

Belgium's King Leopold II was born Louis-Philippe-Marie-Victor of Saxe-Coburg and Gotha. As the oldest son of Leopold I, king of the Belgians and his French queen, Louise-Marie Therese (Bourbon-Orleans), he was the heir to the throne to which his father had been elevated only five years earlier, and was, accordingly, named duke of Brabant at the age of eleven. His relationship to his parents was formal and distant, and he could often talk to his father only by appointment. During his adolescence, he was entered into the Belgian army and rose to the largely ceremonial rank of lieutenant general at the age of twenty.

On August 22, 1853, Leopold married the Austrian archduchess Marie-Henriette Anne von Hapsburg-Lothringen (1836-1902). With her, he had four children: one son, Leopold Ferdinand, and three daughters, Louise-Marie, Stephanie, and Clementine. However, his marriage was cold and devoid of affection, with little communication between husband and wife. Marie-Henriette Anne spent an inordinate amount of her time engaging in her passion for horses and horseback riding, and Leopold became increasingly obsessed with overseas trade, world geography, and imperial colonization schemes. Perhaps in part to offset what was lacking in his personal life, he traveled extensively. His globe-trotting took him to eastern Europe, Egypt, Spain, Burma, Ceylon (Sri Lanka), and the Dutch East Indies (Indonesia). On December 10, 1865, King Leopold I died and his son came to the crown as Leopold II, the second king of the Belgians.

LIFE'S WORK

Even prior to the beginning his reign, Leopold II evinced a restless energy and tendencies toward authoritarianism. Chafing under his constitutional role in the recently created kingdom of Belgium and the subordination of the monarchy to the Belgian parliament, he yearned to play a larger part in public affairs. He enthusiastically embraced the imperialist mentality that was sweeping across Europe during the mid-nineteenth century and was being championed by such articulate advocates as Great Britain's Benjamin Disraeli. Leopold fixed on the idea that Belgium must enter into the list of colonial powers and begin to carve out an overseas empire in Africa, Asia, and Oceania, as Britain and France were in the process of doing. To that end, he lobbied and campaigned with increasing intensity.

However, the political leadership, and indeed the climate of public opinion in Belgium, proved unfavorable to Leopold's ideas. Most Belgians believed that because their nation was small, it lacked the resources to acquire, maintain, and defend a far-flung empire. Leopold also met resistance to his ideas of increasing the size of the Belgian military establishment and felt further isolated from his own people when his legislative propos-

Leopold II. (Library of Congress)

als to expand spending on the army and navy were rejected.

Early in 1869, Leopold's only son, and heir, Leopold Ferdinand, the duke of Brabant, contracted pneumonia as a result of a fall into a frozen pond and died at the age of nine. After the child's death, Leopold seems to have become even more fanatical over the acquisition of colonies, drifting from one impractical scheme to another to secure a colonial possession through his own means and efforts, even if his nation would not do so. He considered such diverse areas as Argentina and Fiji before narrowing his interests to Central Africa during the early 1880's.

The explorations and reports of Henry Morton Stanley piqued Leopold's interest, and Leopold achieved a major public relations coup by recruiting Stanley—who

by then was taking on a heroic stature—as his spokesperson. He adroitly employed diplomacy, well-placed gifts, receptions, conferences, and connections to gain support for what he presented as a philanthropic program to eliminate Arab slave trading in the Congo River basin and to improve the living conditions of its peoples. To that end, he enlisted the support of U.S. president Chester A. Arthur, German chancellor Otto von Bismarck, and others.

Bismarck's support was especially important, as he personally convened the Berlin Conference of 1884-1885 in which most of Africa was partitioned among European nations. Leopold II was confirmed as the personal proprietor of a massive area of land south of the Congo and Ubangi Rivers. With Leopold himself—not Belgium—administering that vast area, the colony was dubbed the Congo Free State and an administrative center was set up in the town of Boma. The administrative apparatus set up under Leopold's ultimate control included his personal army and gendarmerie, the so-called Force Publique, and a corporative-governing structure, the International Association of the Congo.

Between 1885 and 1908, Leopold's Congo Free State degenerated into a regime of terror and exploitation. Although the Force Publique drove Arab slave traders from the region, a more vicious brand of slavery was established by Leopold's own minions. Leopold secured a monopoly on the increasingly lucrative world trade in ivory and rubber. Africans were forcibly conscripted for hard labor while their families and villages were held hostage, and severe penalties were inflicted when their productivity failed to meet designated quotas. As time went on the atrocities worsened into genocidal proportions: Villagers were burned alive, and the hands and feet of workers were cut off. Unconfirmed contemporary estimates of the numbers of people killed ran into the millions.

As revelations of the extent of the brutality leaked out, Leopold came under increased scrutiny. In response to pressure from international public opinion, he launched a propaganda campaign to gloss over the truth about his regime. In part, he sought to deflect attention by sponsoring a series of construction projects in Belgium, which were financed by proceeds from his Congo enterprise. However, evidence in published accounts, first by George Washington Williams in 1890, and later by E. D. Morel, Joseph Conrad, and William H. Sheppard, brought to light more gruesome details and led to the famous 1904 British parliamentary report on the Congo by Roger Casement.

On September 20, 1902, Queen Marie-Henriette Anne died. While returning from her subsequent funeral, Leopold survived an assassination attempt when an Italian anarchist fired into his coach. He was unscathed but af-terward became more open about his affair with the former Parisian prostitute Caroline (or Blanche) Delacroix, who had given him two sons. Disclosure of Leopold's affair, and his attempts to legitimize Caroline's children, made him even more unpopular with his subjects.

In March of 1904, Casement and Morel established the Congo Reform Association, and on May 10 of that same year, Stanley, Leopold's most powerful defender, died in London. Under mounting pressure, and in the face of further damning revelations, the Belgian parliament formally took the Congo away from Leopold on August 10, 1908, and placed it under national colonial governance. The colony was then known as the Belgian Congo until it became independent in 1960. Meanwhile, Leopold, who was discredited and still under fire, died on December 17, 1909. He was succeeded by his nephew, Albert I.

SIGNIFICANCE

Leopold's legacy was an ambivalent one for a long time after his death. The Congo atrocities for which he was responsible were to a great extent forgotten, or at least relegated to a historical footnote, and for many years Leopold was remembered in more benevolent terms as an empire-builder and sponsor of building projects. However, the troubles of the independent Congo after 1960 are traceable to the unprecedented level of exploitation, depopulation, and social disruption occurring during the Congo Free State years. It may also not be far from the truth that the rapid way in which the Congo atrocities, or "Rubber Terror," were lost to European memory may have instilled in the mind of German chancellor Adolf Hitler that when leaders of nations are involved in crimes, posterity is likely to look the other way, no matter how massive the crime.

—Raymond Pierre Hylton

"KING LEOPOLD'S SOLILOQUY"

At the request of the Congo Reform Association, Mark Twain wrote King Leopold's Soliloquy *as a polemic in which Leopold considers the charges made against him for his responsibility in the atrocities committed in the Congo Free State and responds with pious hypocrisies that ultimately condemn him. The soliloquy opens with Leoopold throwing down tracts that he has been reading, pounding a table with his fists, cursing, and kissing the crucifix hanging from his neck. He then begins his invective:*

— —!! — —!! If I had them by the throat! [*Hastily kisses the crucifix, and mumbles*] In these twenty years I have spent millions to keep the press of the two hemispheres quiet, and still these leaks keep on occurring. I have spent other millions on religion and art, and what do I get for it? Nothing. Not a compliment. These generosities are studiedly ignored, in print. In print I get nothing but slanders—and slanders again—and still slanders, and slanders on top of slanders! Grant them true, what of it? They are slanders all the same when uttered against a king.

Miscreants—they are telling *everything!* Oh, everything: how I went pilgriming among the Powers in tears, with my mouth full of Bible and my pelt oozing with piety at every pore, and implored them to place the vast and rich populous Congo Free state in trust in my hands as their agent, so that I might root out slavery and stop the slave raids, and lift up those twenty-five millions of gentle and harmless blacks out of darkness into light, the light of our blessed Redeemer, the light that streams from his holy Word, the light that makes glorious our noble civilization—lift them up and dry their tears and fill their bruised hearts with joy and gratitude—life them up and make them comprehend that they were no longer outcasts and forsaken, but our very brothers in Christ; how America and thirteen great European states wept in sympathy with me, and were persuaded; how their representatives met in convention in Berlin and made me Head Foreman and Superintendent of the Congo State, and drafted out my powers and limitations, carefully guarding the persons and liberties and properties of the natives against hurt and harm; forbidding whisky traffic and gun traffic; providing courts of justice; making commerce free and fetterless to the merchants and traders of all nations; and welcoming and safe-guarding all missionaries of all creeds and denominations. They have told how I planned and prepared my establishment and selected my horde of officials—"pals" and "pimps" of mine, "unspeakable Belgians" every one—and hoisted my flag, and "took in" a President of the United States, and got him to be the first to recognize it and salute it. Oh, well, let them blackguard me if they like; it is a deep satisfaction to me to remember that I was a shade too smart for that nation that thinks itself so smart. Yes, I certainly did bunco a Yankee—as those people phrase it. Pirate flag? Let them call it so—perhaps it is. All the same, *they were the first to salute it.* . . .

Source: Mark Twain, *King Leopold's Soliloquy: A Defense of His Congo Rule* (2d ed., Boston: P. R. Warren, 1905), pp. 5-7.

FURTHER READING

Gann, L. H., and Peter Duignan. *The Rulers of Belgian Africa, 1884-1914*. Princeton, N.J.: Princeton University Press, 1979. Describes the administration of the Congo Free State in terms of the day-today activities of the soldiers, police officers, and civil servants who carried out Leopold's directives.

Gondola, Charles Didier. *The History of the Congo*. Westport, Conn.: Greenwood Press, 2002. Sees Leopold as an arch-manipulator and public relations practitioner who was particularly adept at discovering the most effective ways of marshaling international support for his schemes.

Hochschild, Adam. *King Leopold's Ghost: A Story of Greed, Terror, and Heroism in Colonial Africa*. Boston: Houghton Mifflin, 1999. The most nearly definitive work on the subject of Leopold and the Congo Free State. The narrative is well constructed, and global reaction to the Congo genocide raises some particularly controversial points.

Kossman, E. H. *The Low Countries, 1780-1940*. Oxford, England: Clarendon Press, 1978. General history of the Low Countries that sees Leopold as less of a manipulator and more of an inept manager whose avarice allowed a bad situation to spiral out of control.

Morel, E. D. *Red Rubber: The Story of the Rubber Slave Trade Flourishing on the Congo in the Year of Grace 1906*. 1906. New York: Negro Universities Press, 1969. The book that was instrumental in exposing details of atrocities committed within the Congo Free State and launching an international investigation.

Nzongola-Ntalaja, Georges. *The Congo: From Leopold to Kabila—A People's History*. New York: Zed Books, 2002. Views Leopold's regime as having set the stage for the pattern of brutality, violence, and instability that have plagued the Congo to the present day.

Twain, Mark. *King Leopold's Soliloquy: A Defense of His Congo Rule*. Boston: P. R. Warren, 1905. Tract written by Mark Twain, who called Leopold a "bloody monster whose mate is not findable in human history." All proceeds from the tract's publication went to the Congo Reform Association. Its soliloquy is a polemic in which Leopold examines the charges made against him and replies with pious hypocrisies that ultimately condemn him. The booklet is illustrated with photographs of atrocities in the Congo; it has been reprinted several times, and some of the reprint editions contain the original illustrations.

SEE ALSO: Chester A. Arthur; Otto von Bismarck; Benjamin Disraeli; Charles George Gordon; Henry Morton Stanley; Tippu Tib; Mark Twain; George Washington Williams.

RELATED ARTICLES in *Great Events from History: The Nineteenth Century, 1801-1900:* 1873-1880: Exploration of Africa's Congo Basin; November 15, 1884-February 26, 1885: Berlin Conference Lays Groundwork for the Partition of Africa.

MIKHAIL LERMONTOV
Russian poet

As a poet during the Russian Romantic period, Lermontov left an impressive legacy of both lyric and narrative verse of lasting significance. He was also a dramatist and a novelist whose major work, A Hero of Our Time, *presaged the great realistic psychological novels of Leo Tolstoy and Fyodor Dostoevski.*

BORN: October 15, 1814; Moscow, Russia
DIED: July 27, 1841; Pyatigorsk, Russia
ALSO KNOWN AS: Mikhail Yurievich Lermontov (full name)
AREA OF ACHIEVEMENT: Literature

EARLY LIFE
The father of Mikhail Yuryevich Lermontov (lahr-muhn-tahf) was a poor Russian army officer, the descendant of a Scottish mercenary who had come to Russia during the early seventeenth century. He claimed relation to the twelfth century Scottish bard known as Thomas the Rhymer. A major success in his life was his marriage to seventeen-year-old Marya Arsenieva, the only daughter of the widowed Elizaveta Arsenieva, a member of the rich and powerful Stolypin family and the owner of a large estate, Tarkhany, in central Russia.

The death of Marya Lermontov in 1817, when the future poet was only three years of age, caused a one-sided power struggle for his custody between his grandmother and his father. Elizaveta Arsenieva desperately wanted to keep her young grandson in her household. She threatened to disinherit the child should he be removed from her and promised his disfavored father both money and the forgiveness of a previous debt if he would leave young Mikhail with her. Yury Lermontov therefore surrendered his son's custody and had only sporadic or indirect contact with him thereafter.

Lermontov's grandmother showered attention on the precocious boy. She hired foreign tutors, who taught him French and gave him the rudiments of Greek and Latin. He was given music lessons so that he was later able to compose tunes to accompany his own lyrics and was able to impress his contemporaries with his ability on the piano and on the violin. He was encouraged to draw and to paint, taking lessons from the artists A. S. Solonitsky and P. E. Zabolotsky, and his talent was so developed that his graphic oeuvre, consisting of more than four hundred oil paintings, aquarelles, sketches, and caricatures, is roundly praised by modern critics. It was Lermontov's early love of poetry, however, that was most thoroughly indulged. Having read Vasily Zhukovsky's translations of George Gordon, Lord Byron's verse, he desired to learn English so that he could read Byron's work in the original. Thus, when Lermontov was in his teens, a special tutor was engaged to impart this knowledge to him.

In addition to a remarkable home education, young Mikhail Lermontov received the benefit of three exciting journeys, made at ages three, five, and ten, to the Caucasus Mountains in the extreme south of Russia. The reasons for these journeys were both to avoid imminent visits at the Tarkhany estate by his father and to bolster his precarious health. Rheumatic fever and measles left him frail, and he developed a stoop-shouldered posture and sickly pallor, which later caused him considerable ridicule from his schoolmates, who nicknamed him "the frog."

The spectacular scenery and the unsubjugated tribes of the Caucasus Mountains made a lasting impression on Lermontov, an impression of adventure and romance in an exotic locale that found its way into many of his later works, both poetry and prose. He gained there an appreciation for freedom as an ideal apart from that of civilization, which he came to regard as corrupt.

In 1827, Arsenieva moved with Mikhail to Moscow. The next year, she enrolled him in an elite preparatory school attached to Moscow State University, the Nobles' Pensionate, which employed a number of prominent university professors as faculty. There, Lermontov read and discussed the works of such contemporary Russian poets as Zhukovsky, Konstantin Batyushkov, and especially Alexander Pushkin, whose work Lermontov zealously admired. During this period, Lermontov began his own literary activity, having one of his poems accepted for publication by the journal *Atheneum* in 1830. Thereafter, he wrote almost continually, entering into his notebooks epigrams, commentary, drafts of a drama, and a number of lyrics on nature, death, and love.

LIFE'S WORK

In 1830, Lermontov enrolled in Moscow University's department of ethics and politics, from which he soon transferred to the department of literature. His classmates in the university included a constellation of later luminaries of Russian social and political dissidence: Vissarion Belinsky, the social literary critic; Aleksandr Herzen, the seminal socialist thinker and editor of radical émigré publications; Nikolai Stankevich, the social philosopher and organizer of radical salons; and Ivan Goncharov, the prominent novelist.

Lermontov held himself aloof from these future stars, regarding himself as superior not only to them but to the faculty as well. He took part in one major scandal, in which an unpopular professor was driven out of the classroom, and he quarreled with one of his examination committees severely enough that, in 1832, he left the university, intending to move to the capital and to enroll at St. Petersburg University. The paperwork required by such a transfer was more than Lermontov's patience could endure, however, and he instead enlisted in the army—a move unpleasantly surprising to his grandmother, who used her influence to have him enrolled in the School of Ensigns of the Guards and Cavalry Cadets.

The literary production of Lermontov's university years is highlighted by the remarkable poem "Angel," which evokes the blissful prenatal memories of an earthbound soul. Prominent also is "Parus" ("The Sail"), in which Lermontov gives a symbolic portrait of a revolutionary. It is at this time too that Lermontov began his ten years of work on the romantic narrative poem "Demon," which remained unpublished in his lifetime as the result of censorship. A fallen angel's love for a mortal woman is related amid sparkling descriptions of Caucasian natural splendor. The university years also produced a cycle of poems connected with Lermontov's unreturned love for a young woman.

In the army, Lermontov tried to find acceptance among his fellow cadets by posturing as a daredevil and a womanizer. The highly affected social life of St. Petersburg increased his cynicism and his bitterness at his intellectual estrangement from his compatriots. He did pen some ribald songs and some bawdy verse but for the most part turned his attention to drama and prose. The best of his five plays, *Maskarad* (1842; *Masquerade*, 1973), reflects, through his moody villain Arbenin, his disillusionment with St. Petersburg society.

Influenced by the popular prose of Sir Walter Scott, Lermontov explored the genre of historical novel by beginning the unfinished *Vadim* (1832-1834; English translation, 1982), a contorted tale of unrequited love intertwined with the historical events of Russia's Pugachov Rebellion of 1773-1774. This work signaled the beginnings of Lermontov's work in prose, which continued through the unfinished society novel *Knyaginya Ligovskaya* (1836; *Princess Ligovskaya*, 1965) to the maturity of his masterpiece, *Geroy nashego vremeni* (1839; *A Hero of Our Time*, 1854).

Before Lermontov was commissioned an officer in Czar Nicholas I's Life Guard Hussars in 1834, he began a lifelong attachment to Varvara Lophukhina, the attractive daughter of family friends. Although Lermontov never married, his attachment to Lophukhina survived even her marriage to a man much her senior, of whom Lermontov disapproved. The relationship with her caused him considerable despair, which infused his verse thereafter with a note of brooding melancholy over the impossibility of love and happiness.

Lermontov's poetic response to the death by duel of Pushkin in 1837 earned for him instant fame. His poem "Smert poeta" ("The Death of a Poet") was circulated throughout the St. Petersburg literary salons. It blamed the capital society and its authorities for inciting Pushkin to the duel that caused his death. Largely as a result of this poem, Lermontov was arrested, tried, and sentenced to serve among the frontline troops fighting wild tribesmen in the Caucasus. The intercession of his grandmother and the publication of his patriotic poem about the victory over Napoleon I at Borodino softened the czar's attitude, however, and he was allowed to return to the capital.

The years 1838-1841 found Lermontov at the height of his popularity. His verse frequently appeared in the leading literary journals. It was during this time that his poems "Kazachia kolybelnaia pesnia" ("Cossack Lullaby") and "Vykhozhu odin ya na dorogu . . ." ("I Walk Out Alone onto the Road . . .") were published, providing the lyrics to well-known Russian songs. His Byronesque narrative poem "Mtsyri" ("The Novice") extolls the freedom experienced just before death by a native child pledged as a novice monk by his captors.

In 1840, *A Hero of Our Time* was published in book form. The protagonist, Pechorin, epitomizes the emotional isolation and intellectual frustration of his generation. Pechorin is the archetypical superfluous man later to be found in many Russian literary portrayals. His intellect tells him that he brings others only hardship and tragedy, but he lacks the moral certitude to change his ways. There is much autobiography in Lermontov's depiction of Pechorin, and it is a depiction in which every succeeding generation has found relevance.

A duel with the son of the French ambassador, in which only Lermontov was lightly wounded, caused him to he reassigned by the czar to frontline duty in the Caucasus. Lermontov so distinguished himself in battle that he was recommended for citation. He wrote a poem about the Battle of Valerik. On a self-granted furlough to the spa city of Pyatigorsk, he tormented a former cadet schoolmate, Nikolai Martynov, who challenged him to a duel. Outside the city, at the foot of Mount Mashuk, the duel took place. Martynov shot first, killing Lermontov outright. Thus, before the age of twenty-seven, Lermontov had inherited both Pushkin's literary fame and his personal fate.

SIGNIFICANCE

Western evaluations of Mikhail Lermontov's impact on world literature are often confined to discussing the influence of *A Hero of Our Time* on subsequent novels by Ivan Turgenev, Fyodor Dostoevski, and Leo Tolstoy, and on the stories of Anton Chekhov and Maxim Gorky, authors whose own influence is better established and more familiar. This discussion focuses on the addition of psychological examination, an inner dialogue of thought, to the realistic portrayal of the characters' actions. Questions of good and evil are left unresolved, at least in surface interpretations, much as Lermontov left unresolved in the minds of his readers the question of whether his main protagonist, Pechorin, is to be positively or negatively regarded; that is, is he seriously, or only ironically, to be considered a hero of our time? In literature of the previous Romantic period, good characters and evil characters were clearly delineated. In this, Lermontov's work is transitional and therefore important.

Russian evaluators of Lermontov's significance invariably foreground his contributions as a poet. His verse is well woven into the fabric of Russian society. Mothers sing his lullaby to their children. Children sing the words of his patriotic "Borodino" to Modest Mussorgsky's music in school. In a nation of poetry lovers, Lermontov's popularity is unmatched by any poet except Pushkin. Subsequent poets, such as Boris Pasternak, have dedicated works to Lermontov as if he were still alive. The permanence of his poetic legacy stems from the musicality of his verse—the sound of which so pleases the ear that memorization is effortless—and its direct appeal to primary emotions, feelings of love, freedom, and patriotism.

In sum, Lermontov was a person with severe problems relating to others. Early bereft of his parents, spoiled by his guardian, failed in academic credentials, restricted and hampered by authorities, he died before he was truly mature. However, his desire to find a soul mate, a confidant, became literary in method and, in the power and excellence of his still-developing talent, resulted in lasting achievement.

—Lee B. Croft

FURTHER READING

Bagby, Lewis, ed. *Lermontov's "A Hero of Our Time": A Critical Companion.* Evanston, Ill.: Northwestern University Press: American Association of Teachers of Slavic and East European Languages, 2002. Collection of essays offering various interpretations of and perspectives on the novel. Bagby's introduction includes a comprehensive biography of Lermontov and a discussion of his literary work.

Eikhenbaum, Boris M. *Lermontov.* Translated by Ray Parrot and Harry Weber. Ann Arbor, Mich.: Ardis, 1981. A seminal study by the renowned Soviet scholar on Lermontov's poetic method, focusing on the literary precedents of his figures of speech. Includes a multitude of citations of poetry from Lermontov's Russian predecessors and contemporaries. A last chapter is included that examines Lermontov's prose in the light of the development of Russian as a literary language.

Golstein, Vladimar. *Lermontov's Narratives of Heroism.* Evanston, Ill.: Northwestern University Press, 1998. Golstein examines the themes of heroism and individualism in three of Lermontov's poems, his play *The Masquerade,* and his novel *A Hero of Our Time.*

Kelly, Laurence. *Lermontov: Tragedy in the Caucasus.* New York: George Braziller, 1977. A biography of Lermontov that delves thoroughly into the influence on Lermontov's work of his time spent in the Caucasus Mountains. Both the childhood trips and the adult military sojourns are well treated. Appendixes include treatments of the relationship of Byron and Lermontov, an essay on Lermontov's poetry, and "The Official Report on the Death of Lieutenant Lermontov."

L'Ami, C. E., and Alexander Welikotny. *Michael Lermontov: Biography and Translation.* Winnipeg, Man.: University of Manitoba Press, 1967. An older-style biography, replete with the reminiscences of Lermontov's contemporaries about his character. A general outline of Russian history forms a significant part of this treatment. The second part of the book contains more than one hundred of Lermontov's poems in rhymed English translation as well as a small sample of prose.

Lavrin, Janko. *Lermontov.* London: Bowes and Bowes, 1959. The first widely available biographical treatment of Lermontov in English, introducing the reader not only to the personage of Lermontov but also to Russian history and Russian society of the early nineteenth century. Lermontov is seen as a key link in the historical development of Russian literature between the imitative eighteenth century and the world-leading literature of Russia's nineteenth century. Alexander Pushkin's influence is thoroughly treated.

Lermontov, Mikhail. *Major Poetical Works.* Translated with a biographical sketch, commentary, and an introduction by Anatoly Liberman. Minneapolis: University of Minnesota Press, 1983. A thorough detailing of Lermontov's life that takes good advantage of the previous works together with translations of more than one hundred of Lermontov's poems, not all of which had appeared in English previously. The translations have won much professional praise for their surprising poeticality that does not compromise accuracy. The text includes more than fifty illustrations and is wonderfully annotated and indexed.

Mersereau, John, Jr. *Mikhail Lermontov.* Carbondale: Southern Illinois University Press, 1962. A concise biography that manages to include much valuable detail. The focus is distinctly on Lermontov's development of a prose style, with more than half of the book devoted to an examination of *A Hero of Our Time.*

Powelstock, David. *Becoming Mikhail Lermontov: The Ironies of Romantic Individualism in Nicholas I's Russia.* Evanston, Ill.: Northwestern University Press, 2005. Comprehensive biography and analysis of Lermontov's writings. Powelstock maintains the seeming contradictions in Lermontov's life and work are actually evidence of a coherent worldview.

SEE ALSO: Lord Byron; Anton Chekhov; Fyodor Dostoevski; Aleksandr Herzen; Modest Mussorgsky; Napoleon I; Nicholas I; Alexander Pushkin; Sir Walter Scott; Leo Tolstoy; Ivan Turgenev.

RELATED ARTICLE in *Great Events from History: The Nineteenth Century, 1801-1900:* June 23-December 14, 1812: Napoleon Invades Russia.

FERDINAND DE LESSEPS
French diplomat and entrepreneur

Lesseps was a career diplomat, but though he never trained as an engineer, he is best known for his entrepreneurial abilities that led to the construction of the Suez Canal and the commencement of the transisthmian Panama Canal.

BORN: November 19, 1805; Versailles, France
DIED: December 7, 1894; La Chênaie, France
ALSO KNOWN AS: Vicomte de Lesseps; Ferdinand-Marie de Lesseps (full name)
AREAS OF ACHIEVEMENT: Diplomacy, business

EARLY LIFE

Ferdinand-Marie Vicomte de Lesseps (duh leh-sehps) was born into a family of diplomats, literally within a few meters of the great architectural expression of French monarchism, the palaces of Versailles. For several generations, the men of the family had been distinguished by their cultivation, vigor, belief in progress, extravagant lifestyles, and womanizing. Long before Ferdinand's birth, his granduncle, Dominique, had been ennobled for his public services, namely for his extraordinary around-the-world adventures that resulted in his presentation to Louis XVI as a national hero; Ferdinand's grandfather, Martin, had served as a diplomat at the Russian court of Catherine the Great; and his father, Mathieu, a friend of the great statesman Talleyrand, performed with distinction in Franco-Egyptian relations and, while posted to the United States, negotiated France's first commercial treaty with that country. Thus, there was a firm foundation for adventure, valor, and endurance in the family, all of which characterized Ferdinand's life and career.

Ferdinand's mother was the daughter of a prosperous French vintner who had settled in Spain, where she spent her life until her marriage, so that Ferdinand grew up speaking Spanish as well as French. He would later claim that his Spanish temperament led Panama to "seduce" him. Although his family reputedly was wealthy, in fact money was generally scarce. His mother's jewelry was often pawned, and his father died bankrupt. Ferdinand himself, while later to marry well and affect the high life, never enjoyed real wealth either.

Against this family background, Lesseps moved naturally into a diplomatic career, and while he had studied some law he was apprenticed, when he was nineteen, to an uncle then serving as France's ambassador to Portu-

gal. Subsequently, he refined his diplomatic apprenticeship, serving with his father until his father died in Tunis in 1832, after which the appointments he received were his own.

LIFE'S WORK

Lesseps's diplomatic career had come naturally, and he enjoyed it, as did his ravishing Parisian wife, Agnes, who not only bore him five sons (two lived to maturity) but also was a marvelous asset to the sociability expected of her diplomat husband. They were indeed a handsome couple, he well formed and dark eyed, with a memorable smile. The first seven years of his official work were spent in Egypt, then, variously, in Rotterdam, the Netherlands; in Malaga, Spain; and finally as France's minister to Spain in 1843.

Lesseps's interest in Suez was not born of interests in engineering; he enjoyed no training whatever along that line. Rather, it emerged from his partial adherence to the philosophy of the comte de Saint-Simon, who believed that private property and nationalism ought to be abolished and the world made over by scientists, engineers, industrialists, and artists.

Lesseps had met a coterie of French Saint-Simonian engineers during his duty in Egypt during the 1830's. This group, led by Prosper Enfantin, hoped to abolish war, end poverty, and generally reorder the world by great public improvements—railways, highways, and both a Suez and a Panamanian canal. For four years, perhaps with some financial assistance from Lesseps, Enfantin and his group labored to dig the canal but were ultimately defeated; indeed, their ranks were devastated by cholera. Although little had been accomplished, many Europeans continued to hope for a canal.

A career crisis diverted Lesseps once again from Suez. He was dispatched on a diplomatic mission to Italy. Lesseps was reprimanded for exceeding instructions and fired in 1848. By 1850, Napoleon III, by coup d'état, had made himself ruler of the Second Empire, had married one of Lesseps's distant cousins, and, surrounded by Saint-Simonians, had again urged great projects upon France. Meanwhile, political upheaval in Egypt had brought a new viceroy into power, Mohammed Said, whom Lesseps had befriended when Said was a boy. His diplomatic career finished and with Agnes dead the previous year, in 1854 Lesseps left his home at La Chênaie to join his old friend. Said, hopeful of launching his regime with some great enterprise, asked for Lesseps's advice: It was to dig a Suez Canal.

Tirelessly, meticulously watching details, and above all incessantly scurrying about the world raising or borrowing funds (half the money came from Frenchmen, the rest from Said and his successor), Lesseps justified a reputation as one of the nineteenth century's greatest entrepreneurs: patient, untiring, an imaginative propagandist, at times deceptive, and very much a shrewd actor-diplomat. On November 17, 1869, amid lavish fanfare, the 160-kilometer, sea-level canal opened. Although at most stages of its construction, Lesseps could have sold his rights and garnered great wealth, he was uninterested in money: He had the Suez dug for the good of humanity.

While being richly honored, lionized, and feted, Lesseps married the stunning young daughter of a wealthy friend and instantly started two great projects: founding what became a family of six sons and six daughters and planning a number of grandiose undertakings—a railway linking Paris, Moscow, Bombay, and Peking and the flooding of vast areas of the Sahara among them. Before the Parisian Geographical Society in 1875, he proposed elaboration of plans for an interoceanic isthmian canal.

Ferdinand de Lesseps. (Library of Congress)

To that end, he helped form the Société Civile Internationale du Canal Interocéanique de Darien, the so-called Türr Syndicate.

Both the syndicate and Lesseps's role in it would be, and remain, controversial. The intent of the Parisian Geographical Society was a binational effort composed of leading international scientists, ensuring an objective analysis of sites and possible problems; however, the Türr Syndicate agreed to handle everything. It did indeed make several expeditions; by 1882, it had contracted with the Colombian government in detail for a ninety-nine-year lease, financing, land concessions, rights of the syndicate to transfer its holdings to other individuals (or syndicates) but not to foreign countries, and distribution of profits.

Meanwhile, an international congress for the study of the isthmian canal convened in Paris in May, 1879. After much disappointing information, some disinformation, and intelligent conjecture, without consensus, Lesseps, who initially had seemed ineffectual, won his audience by declaring that for all insurmountable obstacles there existed men of genius to master them. Later in the day, another genius, a great engineer and the head of France's famed Corps de Ponts et Chaussées (bridges and highways), the only person present who had experience with construction in tropical America, warned of the deadly menaces of endemic, epidemic disease and of the impossibility of the sea-level canal (one without locks) upon which Lesseps was determined.

Lesseps ultimately carried the day. His victory in the congress would shortly cost tens of thousands of lives, the loss of millions by investors, ruin of the syndicate, scandals that historians have not yet entirely unraveled, judicial probes, and eventually the then-greatest real estate transaction in history when the United States bought the remnants of Lesseps's efforts under dubious circumstances.

Lesseps was magnificent in pursuit of his great objective: a Panamanian canal. He bought out the Türr Syndicate, created his own company, mesmerized general publics throughout Europe and the United States, and raised funds from a vast range of sources. He visited the Panama site; declared, with aplomb, that there were no insurmountable difficulties; hired a remarkable team of French engineers, whose general repute had been singular for nearly two centuries; mustered the great excavators necessary to gnaw their way through the terrain; provided the best housing and medical facilities then known for the protection of his aides, engineers, and workers; and launched the great dig in 1881.

Before disease and natural obstacles made obvious the impossibility of a sea-level canal, and before Americans undertook construction of a lock canal, Lesseps's crews had excavated nearly a third of the distance between Colón, on the Caribbean, and Panama City, on the Pacific: if not the most difficult portion, a sterling achievement nevertheless. However, by 1889, Lesseps's losses in life and money were too great. His grand enterprise was failed, bankrupt. Old and under financial pressures, he remained only vaguely aware of the press and judicial trials with which irate investors were crushing members of his family and colleagues, unaware that "Panama" had become a term of national opprobrium. Through his wife's protective care, the great adventurer sat at home in a seaman's peacoat, with his smoking cap and with his knees blanketed, wasting away, oblivious to the storms raging around his devastated enterprise. He died on December 7, 1894, at La Chênaie, and was quietly buried in Paris's Pére Lachaise Cemetery.

SIGNIFICANCE

Ferdinand de Lesseps was the complex scion of a distinguished family. A successful diplomat, he was shamelessly duped by the state he served, only to turn about and become the driving force behind two immensely important undertakings: the Suez and the Panama Canals. At the first he succeeded, at the second he failed. However, his success at Suez, certainly in global economic terms, far outweighed the financial disaster, and perhaps even the thousands of lives lost, in Panama.

For all Lesseps's deceptions, he was a heroic romantic, an inspired entrepreneur, suffused with the Saint-Simonian urge to remodel the world. In no technical or scientific sense did he qualify as an expert, and in an age in which the engineer and scientist became the forces with which to reckon, he relied upon his own fixations, rhetoric, and manipulations to launch his great enterprises. It had been the wisdom of Lesseps's father that he forget his great Panama scheme and settle for the undying fame earned at Suez. However, hubris and heroism are usually intertwined. It remains sufficient that his accomplishment, against great odds at Suez, matched his daring but partial failure at Panama—partial because it finally moved the United States to complete that singularly remarkable construction.

—Clifton K. Yearley

FURTHER READING

Allen, Frederick E. "Panama's Canal." *American Heritage* 51, no. 7 (November, 2000): 21. Describes Lesseps's role in the canal's construction.

Beatty, Charles. *Ferdinand de Lesseps: A Biographical Study*. New York: Harper & Brothers, 1956. An eminently readable, well-researched biography of genuine quality on one of the more vital personalities of the nineteenth century. Contains a fine bibliography, a chronology, and a useful double-columned index.

Cameron, Ian. *The Impossible Dream: The Building of the Panama Canal*. New York: William Morrow, 1972. A competent study that, while focused chiefly on the American effort, deals with Lesseps and the initial French enterprise, though it is less generous than other works on the real difficulties and progress made by the French. Contains a select bibliography and an adequate index.

Farnie, D. A. *East and West of Suez: The Suez Canal in History, 1854-1956*. Oxford, England: Clarendon Press, 1969. A large scholarly study that helps place the importance of Lesseps's work in perspective of the canal's subsequent history. Scholarly and well written, this work has several graphs; statistical tables; maps; a fine, extensive bibliography; and a superb index.

Fitzgerald, Percy. *The Great Canal at Suez*. Reprint. 2 vols. New York: AMS Press, 1978. Delightful reading, lending an ambience to the creation of the canal that is hard to find elsewhere. Although documentation is inserted in the text, there are no notes, bibliography, illustrations, or index.

Hicks, Bill. "The Great Divide." *Times Educational Supplement*, December 20, 2004, p. 8. A brief overview of Lesseps's career, focusing on the Panama Canal.

Karabell, Zachary. *Parting the Desert: The Creation of the Suez Canal*. New York: Alfred A. Knopf, 2003. A history of the canal, focusing on Lesseps and Egyptian ruler Muhammad Said. Karabell depicts Lesseps as a shrewd salesperson who viewed construction of the canal as a means of achieving his place in history.

McCullough, David. *The Path Between the Seas: The Creation of the Panama Canal, 1870-1914*. New York: Simon & Schuster, 1977. Although detailed treatment of Lesseps occupies only a portion of this marvelous work—winner of many prizes—it is easily the most readable and most thoroughly researched study of the wonder that is the canal. Contains great photographs, an extensive and first-rate bibliography of primary and secondary sources, and a useful index.

Schonfield, Hugh J. *The Suez Canal in Peace and War, 1869-1969.* Rev. ed. Coral Gables, Fla.: University of Miami Press, 1969. A readable, competent, and scholarly study, with the first six chapters covering Lesseps's planning and work. Contains seven useful appendixes. The index is full and useful.

SEE ALSO: James Buchanan Eads; Robert Fulton; Napoleon III; Talleyrand.
RELATED ARTICLES in *Great Events from History: The Nineteenth Century, 1801-1900:* October 26, 1825: Erie Canal Opens; November 17, 1869: Suez Canal Opens.

MERIWETHER LEWIS AND WILLIAM CLARK
American explorers

The Lewis and Clark expedition was the first organized exploratory expedition to cross the North American continent from the Atlantic to the Pacific coast within the geographical limits of the present United States. After serving as coleader of the expedition, Clark was for three decades one of the most important administrators of Indian affairs in the nation's history.

MERIWETHER LEWIS

BORN: August 18, 1774; Albemarle County, Virginia
DIED: October 11, 1809; Grinder's Stand, Tennessee

WILLIAM CLARK

BORN: August 1, 1770; Caroline County, Virginia
DIED: September 1, 1838; St. Louis, Missouri
AREA OF ACHIEVEMENT: Exploration

EARLY LIVES

Meriwether Lewis was born on a Virginia plantation. His father was William Lewis, who married Lucy Meriwether, after whom the future explorer was named. Meriwether had an older sister and a younger brother. The first Lewises in America, who were Welsh, migrated to Virginia during the mid-seventeenth century, where the family became planters. Meriwether's father was a lieutenant during the Revolutionary War, but he drowned while on leave in 1779. Six months later, Lucy married Captain John Marks. After the war, the Marks family moved to Georgia, but Meriwether soon went back to Virginia to live with his relatives. There he attended several small schools taught by parsons and received some tutoring, but his chief interest and delight was in rambling in the woods, hunting and observing nature. Although rather stiff and awkward as a child, Meriwether grew up to be a handsome young man.

When John Marks died in 1791, his widow returned to Virginia. She brought with her, besides Meriwether's brother and sister, a son and daughter she had borne her second husband.

A short time after his mother's return, Lewis became a soldier, as he was to remain most of his life. In 1794, he enlisted in the Virginia militia to help suppress the Whiskey Rebellion in western Pennsylvania. Liking this taste of military life, Lewis stayed in the militia until May, 1795, when he became an ensign in the United States Army. A few months thereafter, he was assigned to the "Chosen Rifle Company" that William Clark commanded, and during the short time that the two men were together, they became fast friends. Later that year, Lewis joined the First Infantry Regiment, and for the next four years he was engaged in a number of noncombatant duties, mainly on the Western frontier. In December, 1800, he was promoted to captain and became regimental paymaster.

It was while he was thus occupied that, in February, 1801, President-elect Thomas Jefferson wrote to invite Lewis to become his private secretary, probably with a view to naming him to command a transcontinental exploring expedition. Jefferson had thought about, and even planned for, such an undertaking since the United States had won its independence in 1783. In 1792, Lewis, then only eighteen years old, had volunteered for the assignment. Jefferson chose someone else, however, who failed to go.

Soon after coming to Washington, Lewis, under the president's direction, began to plan and prepare for the expedition. He obtained scientific and technical training from members of the faculty of the University of Pennsylvania; collected, with their advice, various kinds of equipment and supplies; and gathered information on his proposed route. Following congressional approval and funding of the mission and his formal designation as its commander, Lewis, early in 1803, with Jefferson's con-

Portraits of Meriwether Lewis (right) and William Clark (left).

currence, invited his friend William Clark, with whom he had maintained contact since they served together in the army, to be its coleader.

Clark was also born on his family's plantation in Virginia. He was the youngest of six sons and the ninth of ten children of John and Ann (Rogers) Clark. The Clarks had emigrated from England some time in the seventeenth century and, like the Lewises, had become planters. When the Revolution came, the Clarks were staunch patriots, and all of William's older brothers fought as officers in the War for Independence. The most famous was Brigadier General George Rogers Clark, who was the conqueror of the Illinois Country. William, who was too young to fight, stayed home. He received a little formal schooling and acquired the rudiments of learning, but mainly he developed the skills of a frontiersman: the ability to ride, hunt, and shoot.

When he was fourteen years old, Clark moved with his family to a new plantation near the falls of the Ohio at Louisville. As a young Kentucky frontiersman, Clark, a big, bluff redhead, served with the militia in several campaigns against the hostile Indian tribes living north of the Ohio River. In March, 1792, he was commissioned a lieutenant in the United States Army, and two years later he fought under General Anthony Wayne in the famous Battle of Fallen Timbers. In July, 1796, however, Clark

resigned his commission and returned home, where for the next seven years he managed his aged parents' plantation. It was there that, in July, 1803, he received Lewis's invitation to join him in leading a transcontinental exploring expedition and quickly accepted it.

LIVES' WORK
About the time Clark received his letter, Lewis, in the East, completed his preparations for the expedition and received final detailed directions from the president. The mission's purpose, as stated by Jefferson, was to explore the Missouri River up to its source in the Rocky Mountains and descend the nearest westward-flowing stream to the Pacific in order to extend the American fur trade to the tribes inhabiting that vast area and to increase geographical knowledge of the continent. With these instructions, Lewis left Washington for Pittsburgh. Descending the Ohio River by boat, he picked up Clark at Louisville, in late summer 1803. Together with a few recruits for the expedition, the two men proceeded to Wood River, Illinois, opposite the mouth of the Missouri, where they encamped early in December. During the next five months, Lewis and Clark recruited and trained their party and finished their preparations for the journey.

With everything in readiness, the expedition set out on May 14, 1804, for the Pacific. Lewis, still a captain in the First Infantry, was the expedition's official commander. Although commissioned only a second lieutenant of artillerists, on the expedition Clark was called "captain" and was treated in every way as Lewis's equal. During the journey, Lewis, a rather intense, moody introvert, spent much of his time alone, walking on shore, hunting, and examining the country. Because Lewis was better trained scientifically and the more literate of the two officers, he wrote most of the scientific information recorded in the expedition's journals. Clark, a friendly, gregarious individual, spent most of his time with the men in the boats. He was the expedition's principal waterman and mapmaker, and he was better able to negotiate with the Indians. Together, the two officers' dispositions, talents, and experience complemented each other superbly. Despite the differences in their personalities, they seem always to have enjoyed the best of personal relations.

In its first season's travel, the expedition advanced some sixteen hundred miles up the Missouri and went into winter quarters in a small fort, named Mandan for the nearest Indian tribe, situated in modern North Dakota. The following spring the expedition proceeded to the headwaters of the Missouri, made a portage of the Rocky Mountains, and descended the nearest westward-flowing tributaries of the Columbia as well as the Columbia itself. Lewis and Clark reached the Pacific by mid-November, 1805. After wintering a few miles from the ocean, in a post they called Fort Clatsop, for a nearby tribe, in March, 1806, the explorers set out for home and arrived in St. Louis in September, having long since been given up for lost by virtually everyone but Jefferson.

As rewards for their great achievement, the president appointed Lewis governor of Louisiana Territory and Clark its principal Indian agent and brigadier general of the territorial militia. Detained in the East by business related to the expedition and other matters, Lewis did not actually assume the governorship of the territory until March, 1808. He soon proved to be unsuited for the office by temperament and experience and quickly ran into trouble. He quarreled with Frederick Bates, the territorial secretary, and became unpopular with many of the people of the territory. He seldom reported to his superiors in Washington and failed to consult them on his policies and plans. As a result, he fell under their severe criticism, and he probably would not have been appointed to a second term of office had he survived the first.

In September, 1809, after only about a year and a half in office, Lewis left St. Louis for Washington, in order to try to straighten out his affairs with the government and to renew his efforts to get the expedition's journals published. On the way, while stopping at a tavern on the Natchez Trace, he was either murdered or committed suicide. Although the ev-

idence is inconclusive, there is reason to believe, as did Clark and Jefferson, that Lewis died by his own hand. Thus at the age of thirty-five ended the life of this great pathfinder.

Clark, in the meantime, was mainly concerned with improving relations and promoting trading activities with the Indian tribes of the territory and protecting the white settlers against the tribes of the Upper Mississippi who were allied with the British in Canada. Following

---

ARRIVAL ON THE PACIFIC COAST

This passage is extracted from William Clark's long journal entry for November 7, 1805—the day that he and Meriwether Lewis finally reached the Pacific coast. The eccentric spelling and capitalization are typical of the explorers' journal entries.

. . . after delaying at this village one hour and a half we Set out piloted by an Indian dressed in a Salors dress, to the main Chanel of the river, the tide being in we Should have found much dificuelty in passing into the main Chanel from behind those islands, without a pilot, a large marshey Island near the middle of the river near which Several Canoes Came allong Side with Skins, roots fish &c. to Sell, and had a temporey residence on this Island, here we See great numbers of water fowls about those marshey Islands; here the high mountanious Countrey approaches the river on the Lard Side, a high mountn. to the S W. about 20 miles, the high mountans. Countrey Continue on the Stard Side, about 14 miles below the last village and 18 miles of this day we landed at a village of the Same nation. This village is at the foot of the high hills on the Stard Side back OF 2 Small Islands it contains 7 indifferent houses built in the Same form of those above, here we purchased a Dog Some fish, wappato roots and I purchased 2 beaver Skins for the purpose of makeing me a roab, as the robe I have is rotten and good for nothing. opposit to this Village the high mountaneous Countrey leave the river on the Lard Side below which the river widens into a kind of Bay & is Crouded with low Islands Subject to be Covered by the tides we proceeded on about 12 miles below the Village under a high mountaneous Countrey on the Stard. Side. Shore boald and rockey and Encamped under a high hill on the Stard. Side opposit to a rock Situated half a mile from the Shore, about 50 feet high and 20 feet Diamieter, we with dificuelty found a place Clear of the tide and Sufficiently large to lie on and the only place we could get was on round Stones on which we lay our mats rain Continud. moderately all day & Two Indians accompanied us from the last village, they we detected in Stealing a knife and returned, our Small Canoe which got Seperated in the fog this morning joined us this evening from a large Island Situated nearest the Lard Side below the high hills on that Side, the river being too wide to See either the form Shape or Size of the Islands on the Lard Side.

Great joy in camp we are in View of the Ocian, this great Pacific Octean which we been So long anxious to See. and the roreing or noise made by the waves brakeing on the rockey Shores (as I Suppose) may be heard distictly . . .

Source: Meriwether Lewis, *History of the Expedition Under the Command of Captains Lewis and Clark to the Sources of the Missouri* (Philadelphia: Bradford and Inskeep, 1814).

Lewis's death, he was offered the governorship of Louisiana, but he declined it because he felt he lacked political experience. In June, 1813, however, the governorship of the Territory of Missouri, as the Louisiana Purchase was called after 1812, again became available, and this time Clark accepted it. During the War of 1812, which was then raging, Clark's chief responsibility was to defend the territory against the hostile Indians of the Upper Mississippi. After the war, Indian relations and the economic and political needs of the white settlers pouring into Missouri absorbed his time and interest.

Following Missouri's admission to the Union in 1821, Clark (an unsuccessful candidate to be the state's first governor) was appointed superintendent of Indian affairs at St. Louis and retained responsibility for the tribes of the Missouri and Upper Mississippi. Clark held this office until his death on September 1, 1838. As superintendent of Indian affairs, he played a major role in effecting the removal of Indians living east of the Mississippi and in Missouri to new lands in modern eastern Kansas.

Unlike Lewis, who never married, Clark was an affectionate family man. In 1808, he married Julia Hancock, with whom he had five children. Following Julia's death, in 1821 he married her cousin Harriet Kennerly Radford, a widow, who bore him two sons. Four of his sons lived to adulthood.

SIGNIFICANCE

Lewis and Clark's fame rests almost entirely on the success of their great expedition, one of the most extensive explorations undertaken in their time. They and their companions were the first American citizens to cross the continent and the first white men to traverse it within the area of the modern United States. During a journey that lasted a little more than twenty-eight months, the expedition traveled more than eight thousand miles. On the entire trip, only one man, Sergeant Charles Floyd, lost his life, and he died from a cause almost certainly unrelated to his exploring activities.

In their contacts with thousands of Indians, Lewis and Clark had only one minor violent encounter, which cost the lives of two Indians. The total expense of the undertaking was a little less than forty thousand dollars. Although Lewis and Clark did not find a commercially feasible route across the continent, as Jefferson hoped they would, they did make a significant contribution to the existing knowledge of the geography of a great part of North America. They also took a historic step toward opening the Trans-Mississippi West to American trade

and subsequently to American settlement, thus providing the basis for one of the strongest U.S. claims to the Oregon Country. Their great achievement stimulated the pride of the American people and served to make Americans aware of the vastness of the continent on which they lived.

Although Lewis's career after the expedition was short and hardly noteworthy, Clark's was long and eminently successful. In three decades of dealing with the tribes of the Upper Mississippi and the trans-Mississippi West, he carried out the policies of the federal government faithfully and effectively, helping to adjust relations peacefully between the Native Americans and the whites. In doing so, by the standards of his own time, he treated the American Indians fairly and sympathetically and, in return, had their respect and confidence.

—*John L. Loos*

FURTHER READING

Ambrose, Stephen E. *Undaunted Courage: Meriwether Lewis, Thomas Jefferson, and the Opening of the American West*. New York: Simon & Schuster, 1996. Best-selling account of the expedition by a prominent historian. Ambrose traveled along the expedition's route to the Pacific and painstakingly re-creates the activities and discoveries of the journey. The book also chronicles Lewis's tragic life in the years following the expedition.

Cutright, Paul Russell. *Lewis and Clark: Pioneering Naturalists*. Urbana: University of Illinois Press, 1969. This volume contains a wealth of detailed information on the scientific and technical aspects of the expedition, including fauna and flora discovered, topographic features discovered or named, and Native American tribes encountered.

Dillon, Richard. *Meriwether Lewis: A Biography*. New York: Coward-McCann, 1965. A noteworthy biography of Lewis, this somewhat sentimental and romantic work provides a relatively comprehensive treatment of the subject with emphasis on the expedition.

Jackson, Donald D., ed. *Letters of the Lewis and Clark Expedition, with Related Documents: 1783-1854*. Urbana: University of Illinois Press, 1962. A comprehensive collection of meticulously edited letters, memoranda, and other documents dealing with all aspects of the expedition, gathered from widely scattered sources.

Jones, Landon Y. *William Clark and the Shaping of the West*. New York: Hill & Wang, 2004. Focuses on

Clark's private life and public career in the thirty years following his expedition with Lewis. Includes discussions of Clark's duties in the Kentucky militia, his service as governor of the Missouri Territory, and his role as superintendent of Indian Affairs at St. Louis.

Lewis, Meriwether, and William Clark. *The Journals of Lewis and Clark.* Edited by Bernard De Voto. Boston: Houghton Mifflin, 1953. Based on the eight-volume Thwaites edition of *The Original Journals of the Lewis and Clark Expedition.* Edited by Rubengold Thwaites. 8 vols. New York: Dodd, Mead, 1904-1905. This single volume provides a good, readable narrative of that great enterprise that retains its flavor.

Ronda, James P. *Lewis and Clark Among the Indians.* Lincoln: University of Nebraska Press, 1984. An important, sophisticated, and engaging ethnohistorical study, this work chronicles the daily contact between the explorers and American Indians and shows that the expedition initiated important economic and diplomatic relations with them.

Slaughter, Thomas P. *Exploring Lewis and Clark: Reflections on Men and Wilderness.* New York: Random House, 2003. A revisionist view of the expedition, with Slaughter attempting to correct the myths and legends that he believes have surrounded it.

Steffen, James O. *William Clark: Jeffersonian Man on the Frontier.* Norman: University of Oklahoma Press, 1977. Steffen selectively and briefly sketches Clark's life, making an occasional reference to the intellectual framework that he believes explains it.

SEE ALSO: Albert Bierstadt; Alexander von Humboldt; Zebulon Pike; Sacagawea.

RELATED ARTICLES in *Great Events from History: The Nineteenth Century, 1801-1900:* May 14, 1804-September 23, 1806: Lewis and Clark Expedition; July 15, 1806-July 1, 1807: Pike Explores the American Southwest; May, 1842-1854: Frémont Explores the American West.

LI HONGZHANG
Chinese government administrator

Li Hongzhang played a leading role in China's Qing Dynasty, instituting reforms based on a moderate policy of Westernization known as self-strengthening, while in foreign affairs he adopted a firm but conciliatory attitude.

BORN: February 15, 1823; Hefei, Anhui, China
DIED: November 7, 1901; Tianjin, China
ALSO KNOWN AS: Li Hung-chang (Wade-Giles)
AREAS OF ACHIEVEMENT: Government and politics, diplomacy

EARLY LIFE

Li Hongzhang (lee hong-zhahng) came from a wealthy and successful literati family. His father, Li Wenan, was the holder of the highest imperial degree and had achieved that great status in 1838, along with Zeng Guofan. Li Wenan sent his son to Beijing to study with Zeng; in 1847, Li Hongzhang also acquired the highest degree. He began service in the Hanlin Academy and was being groomed as an important high official. Li's career underwent a dramatic shift in 1853, when he and his father returned home to raise a local militia to protect their region from the Taiping rebels. Through his connections

with Zeng, Li entered into the top ranks of the anti-Taiping forces in Anhui (Anhwei) Province. He served with great success in Anhui and Jiangxi (Kiangsi) Provinces until 1861. During this period, however, he had difficulties with his superiors, including Zeng, all of whom he believed were too cautious in taking the offensive.

Li was an unusually tall man for his time, more than six feet in height. As a young man, he was powerful and courageous; photographs taken in his sixties show a dignified, alert, and energetic man dressed self-assuredly in his official robes and with a small white beard. Li acquired enormous wealth in official service; at his death, his estate was estimated to be worth at least 500,000 Chinese ounces of silver, or several hundred million dollars. He used his wealth to sustain his political and family power; personally, he lived a plain and temperate life. Li had five brothers and six sons who profited from his prominence, both politically and financially, but none was as capable as he.

LIFE'S WORK

From 1860 to 1870, Li emerged from the ranks of Zeng's lieutenants to become a key regional official in the Lower Zhang Jiang River valley and commander of his own regional force, the Huai Army (so named after a region within Li's home province, Anhui, from which the army was raised). When Zeng assumed overall command of the anti-Taiping forces in 1860, he gave Li and the Huai Army a key role. Li joined in the campaign coordinated by Zeng that destroyed the Taipings in 1864. Three years later, still under Zeng's leadership, Li and his Huai Army implemented the offensive that destroyed the Nien rebellions in Shangdong (Shantung).

During the defense of Shanghai in 1862, Li incorporated into his forces the foreign-led and -armed "ever victorious army" and became an advocate of Western military technology. Cooperating with Zeng, Li played an important role in the establishment of small-arms factories in 1863-1864, the Kiangnan Shipyard in Shanghai in 1865, and the Nanjing Arsenal in 1867. These early self-strengthening projects were arms factories operated as official state enterprises and thus incorporated the nepotism and inefficiency typical of the Qing bureaucracy. All were headed by foreign technical experts, who were to train Chinese technicians while producing modern arms.

The production of these arsenals was available to Li's own regional forces, further increasing his power. Unlike Zeng, Li did not disband his provincial forces following the Taipings' defeat. He and a few others continued to command independent regional armies, a characteristic that gives a special feudal flavor to the late Qing Dynasty period (1860-1912), in which militarily strong officials such as Li are seen as the precursors of China's twentieth century warlords.

Li's early regional effort at military modernization is important because it was more effective than another program directed from Beijing by Prince Gong, a brother of the Xianfeng emperor. Gong understood the significance of Western military technology after the sacking of the Summer Palace at Beijing by an Anglo-French force in 1860, but his modernization efforts encountered delays and setbacks. Then Gong's power declined after the death of his brother, the emperor. The Empress Dowager Cixi consolidated her power behind the new child emperor Tongzhi, and she viewed Gong as a rival. By the 1870's, Gong was no longer a significant figure in Qing politics.

In 1870, when a crisis arose in Tianjin following a riot in which foreigners were killed, the dynasty turned to Zeng. Zeng's health was poor, so he recommended Li, who was then appointed governor general of Chihli (Hebei) and commissioner of the Northern Sea. Li quickly settled the Tianjin incident and proceeded during the next quarter century to wield enormous power from his posts at Tianjin, which combined control of military, trade, and diplomatic affairs for the whole of China north of Shanghai. Li also held several key positions in the central bureaucracy at Beijing, such as grand secretary (1872-1901), which further magnified his power.

Li maintained his positions through a combination of ability and political guile. He had relied upon Zeng until Zeng's death in 1872. Li cultivated Gong during the 1860's, when the prince's star was ascendant in Beijing. In 1875, he helped Cixi ensure the enthronement of her infant nephew as the Guangxu emperor, and he became an important supporter of her long domination of the dynasty's fortunes. Li's penchant for modernization put him at odds with more conservative officials, and his willingness to compromise in the face of foreign threats of force brought him into disrepute with hot-blooded young officials who hoped to best the foreigners in war. Thus, while enormously powerful, Li was both dependent upon a short-sighted and narrow empress dowager and open to challenge by other officials on a wide variety of grounds.

From 1870 to 1895, while based at Tianjin, Li followed a three-pronged foreign policy that combined moderate accommodation of foreign demands; construc-

Li Hongzhang. (Library of Congress)

tion of new Qing military power, especially a modern navy; and extension of Qing influence through the new diplomatic forms emerging in East Asia. Li assumed that the Qing Empire, like other ruling dynasties before, would continue to dominate all states in the region, including Russia and Japan, as well as the new trading powers such as Great Britain, France, Germany, and the United States. Although similar to European conceptions of a diplomacy based on a balance of power, Li's ideas derived from traditional Chinese notions of international politics, in which the foreigners' advantages are turned against themselves and China plays various foreign powers' ambitions against one another.

Li's diplomatic record from 1870 to 1895 is not distinguished by great successes. He was forced to accept extensions of Japanese power in the Ryukyu Islands and Taiwan, Russian power in the far western Ili valley, and the assertion of French power into Vietnam in the period from 1870 to 1885. Li was strongly criticized by more aggressive officials at the time for his role in these affairs as well as by later, nationalistic historians, who often cast Li as a venal traitor. Nevertheless, aside from the defeat in the Sino-French War in 1883-1885, a war Li knew the dynasty should have avoided, the Qing did not suffer any major defeats during this period.

The Sino-French War destroyed much of the Qing's military and naval modernization efforts south of Shanghai and had the effect of further increasing the weight of Li's Peiyang (Northern Sea) commissionership. Li undertook modernization programs in his region after 1870 that included the China Merchants' Steam Navigation Company, the Kaiping Coal Mines, textile factories, a telegraph system from Shanghai to Tianjin, new arsenals, a railroad at Tianjin, and a major naval base on the Liaodong Peninsula. Some of these mark a continuation of his pre-1870 pattern of military modernization; others included new forms of transportation and communication with commercial, diplomatic, and military advantages. Li also approved innovative forms of industrial operation involving less state control, a more active role for merchants, and greater opportunities for personal wealth for both the Chinese entrepreneurs involved and the Chinese officials, including himself.

During the late 1880's, Li undertook a diplomatic offensive in response to Japanese interest in extending their power into Korea. The complex machinations among the Koreans, the Qing Dynasty, and the Japanese unraveled in the fall of 1894 and produced the Sino-Japanese War (1894-1895). In this war, Li's Northern Sea fleet was destroyed, his armies were disgraced, and Japan won a

massive victory. Li's career never recovered from these defeats. Nevertheless, he was dispatched to Japan to negotiate a settlement and while there was wounded in an assassination attempt. Ashamed, the Japanese agreed to impose slightly less humiliating terms on the Qing.

As the distasteful peace with Japan was being concluded, Li became involved in a remarkable diplomatic maneuver known as the Triple Intervention. Seeking to offset Japanese power in Manchuria, Li concluded an agreement with Russia, Germany, and France to intervene and force Japan to give up the special privileges it had won from China in the First Sino-Japanese War. Japan grudgingly conceded to the international pressure but then was incredulous as the Qing Dynasty proceeded to bestow on Russia special privileges, including railway and naval-base rights, in Manchuria.

Li conducted negotiations on some of these matters in Europe and is believed to have accepted bribes from the Russian government for his favor to their interests in Manchuria. This charge of personal venality, combined with his compromise of Qing sovereignty in Manchuria, has sealed the unfavorable judgment of Li held by most historians of modern China. Li's late diplomacy in Manchuria began the rivalry between Japan and Russia over control of this region of China. That rivalry led to the Russo-Japanese War of 1905 and later produced the 1931 Japanese takeover of Manchuria, one of the critical steps on the way to World War II in the Pacific.

Li had no role in either the reform movement of 1898 or the Boxer Uprising of 1900. He appeared on the dynasty's behalf in 1901 to negotiate the settlement of the Boxer incident. He had little leverage because foreign armies occupied Beijing and the empress dowager and emperor were in self-imposed exile away from the court, while Li himself was known to be out of favor and devoid of real power. Li died before agreement was reached on the final terms.

SIGNIFICANCE

The failure of Li Hongzhang's efforts and the disgrace of his policies was much more than a great personal defeat. Li represented the best possibility that the Qing Dynasty had to accommodate itself to the rapidly changing world of the post-1850 era. He understood the need for China to adapt itself to an altered political and military situation in Asia and made some of the most enlightened efforts to encourage moderate modernization. These efforts were more successful than those of other Manchu and Chinese leaders but still fell far short of what was necessary.

Personally, Li was a decisive, innovative official who learned to act with restraint. His accommodation of Cixi can be interpreted either as a necessary compromise to the reality of court politics or as tragic misjudgment that doomed to failure all Li's carefully laid projects and plans. Whatever weaknesses that Li's stewardship contained, they remained largely unrecognized until the Sino-Japanese War, when all of his authority and glory were swiftly destroyed by the force of Japanese arms. Li's conception of what would happen to the dynasty and to China after this war remains a mystery, as does the full motivation behind his diplomatic maneuvers after 1895. The collapse of Li's own career by 1897 reflects the true decline of the Qing Dynasty's power and authority.

—David D. Buck

FURTHER READING

Bland, J. O. P. *Li Hung-chang*. London: Constable, 1917. Reprint. New York: Books for Libraries Press, 1971. A biography of Li. Bland was a reporter in China, and his account contains much of the foreign community's gossip about Li.

Chu, Samuel C., and Kwang-Ching Liu, eds. *Li Hung-Chang and China's Early Modernization*. Armonk, N.Y.: M. E. Sharpe, 1994. Collection of thirteen essays exploring Li as a modernizer, diplomat, and national official, and attempting to restore his name despite historical accusations of illegal financial activities and nepotism.

Folsom, Kenneth E. *Friends, Guests, and Colleagues: The Mu-fu System in the Late Ch'ing Period*. Berkeley: University of California Press, 1968. A rich and useful study of Li and his staff that contains many details about Li's life and career.

Hsu, Immanuel C. Y. *The Rise of Modern China*. 3d ed. New York: Oxford University Press, 1983. The author of this standard text is an authority on the self-strengthening period; the section entitled "Self-Strengthening in an Age of Accelerated Foreign Imperialism" puts Li's career into context.

Liu, K. C. "Li Hung-chang in Chihli: The Emergence of a Policy, 1870-1875." In *Approaches to Modern Chinese History*, edited by Albert Feuerwerker et al. Berkeley: University of California Press, 1967. Liu, who is a leading authority on Li, outlines Li's policies during his first years as governor-general and Northern Sea commissioner at Tianjan.

Spector, Stanley. *Li Hung-chang and the Huai Army*. Seattle: University of Washington Press, 1964. An important study that emphasizes Li's role in creating the system of regionally based military power in China after 1860.

SEE ALSO: Cixi; Zeng Guofan.

RELATED ARTICLES in *Great Events from History: The Nineteenth Century, 1801-1900:* 1860's: China's Self-Strengthening Movement Arises; May, 1900-September 7, 1901: Boxer Rebellion.

JUSTUS VON LIEBIG
German chemist

Liebig was one of the most important chemists of the nineteenth century. In addition to pioneering experimental research that transformed the basis of modern organic chemistry, his studies on agriculture led to the development of agricultural chemistry, and his systematic processes for training students became institutionalized within the German research university.

BORN: May 12, 1803; Darmstadt, Hesse-Darmstadt (now in Germany)
DIED: April 18, 1873; Munich, Germany
ALSO KNOWN AS: Justus Freiherr von Liebig; Justus Baron von Liebig
AREA OF ACHIEVEMENT: Chemistry

EARLY LIFE

Justus von Liebig (LEE-bihk) was the second of nine children of Johann Georg and Maria Karoline Moserin Liebig. His father was a dealer in pharmaceuticals and paint supplies, and Justus developed an interest in chemistry and experimentation at an early age. As a young boy, Liebig was especially fascinated with the explosive properties of silver fulminate, and his experiments with this material resulted in an explosion that prematurely ended his career as an apothecary apprentice.

After returning home for a short time, Liebig enrolled at the University of Bonn in 1820, where he studied under the chemist Wilhelm Gottlob Kastner. Later in life, Liebig was particularly critical of Kastner's inability to teach him chemical analysis and the lack of adequate laboratory equipment, but Liebig followed Kastner from Bonn to the University of Erlangen, where he received a doctorate in 1822. It was at Erlangen that Liebig became convinced of the need to study abroad, and he successfully persuaded the Grand Duke Louis I of Hesse to award him a grant to pursue his chemical education in Paris from 1822 to 1824.

In Paris, Liebig received the chemical training that proved to be decisive and pivotal in his professional career. He attended the lectures of Louis-Jacques Thénard, Pierre-Louis Dulong, and Joseph-Louis Gay-Lussac and also gained entrance into the latter's laboratory through the intervention of Alexander von Humboldt. Liebig would leave Paris thoroughly trained in critical thinking, in chemical analysis, and in the experimental methods necessary for making careful physical measurements, all hallmarks of the "new" chemistry first articulated by Antoine-Laurent Lavoisier at the close of the eighteenth century.

LIFE'S WORK

Liebig returned to Germany in 1824 as extraordinary professor of chemistry at the University of Giessen; his appointment was the result of Humboldt's successful efforts in convincing Louis I that the young chemist had exceptional promise. Although his laboratory initially consisted of only one room surrounded by benches along its walls with a coal stove at its center, Liebig would quickly rise from these humble beginnings to become Europe's most distinguished chemist, the consequence of his personal charisma, scientific skills, and technical ingenuity.

Until the time of Liebig, organic chemistry was for the most part an inexact descriptive science based upon a hodgepodge of conflicting observations and personal opinions. There existed no practical classificatory scheme for organic substances, and there was little consensus concerning the fundamental building block of these materials, the molecule. Further, it was generally

---

THE ADMIRABLE PROPERTIES OF GLASS AND CORK

In a collection of "letters" explaining basic concepts and applications of chemistry, Justus von Liebig discussed the contributions that such seemingly mundane materials as glass and cork had made to science.

And first, of Glass: every one is familiar with most of the properties of this curious substance; its transparency, hardness, destitution of colour, and stability under ordinary circumstances: to these obvious qualities we may add those which especially adapt it to the use of the chemist, namely, that it is unaffected by most acids or other fluids contained within it. At certain temperatures it becomes more ductile and plastic than wax, and may be made to assume in our hands, before the flame of a common lamp, the form of every vessel we need to contain our materials, and of every apparatus required to pursue our experiments.

Then, how admirable and valuable are the properties of Cork! How little do men reflect upon the inestimable worth of so common a substance! How few rightly esteem the importance of it to the progress of science, and the moral advancement of mankind!—There is no production of nature or art equally adapted to the purposes to which the chemist applies it. Cork consists of a soft, highly elastic substance, as a basis, having diffused throughout a matter with properties resembling wax, tallow, and resin, yet dissimilar to all of these, and termed suberin. This renders it perfectly impermeable to fluids, and, in a great measure, even to gases. It is thus the fittest material we possess for closing our bottles, and retaining their contents. By its means, and with the aid of Caoutchouc, we connect our vessels and tubes of glass, and construct the most complicated apparatus. We form joints and links of connexion, adapt large apertures to small, and thus dispense altogether with the aid of the brassfounder and the mechanist. Thus the implements of the chemist are cheaply and easily procured, immediately adapted to any purpose, and readily repaired or altered.

Source: Justus von Liebig, *Familiar Letters on Chemistry, and Its Relation to Commerce, Physiology, and Agriculture* (London: Taylor and Walton, 1844), letter 1.

---

thought that a vital force arising from life itself was necessary for the synthesis of an organic compound. These uncertainties and others related to organic chemistry were ultimately explained by Liebig and his students using data gained from chemical analyses derived from the use of his combustion apparatus. This simple glass triangle consisted of several bulbs filled with potash, and it enabled the chemist to determine the percentage of carbon in a compound with great accuracy, precision, and relative ease. The combustion apparatus proved to be at the heart of Liebig's success, revolutionizing both organic chemistry and nineteenth century chemical education.

The use of exact analysis did much to elucidate the nature of chemical compounds such as alcohols, aldehydes, ethers, and ketones during the late 1820's and 1830's. In the Giessen laboratory, where much of this compound characterization was done, large numbers of students, admitted on their talents and attracted by the low cost, flocked to the charismatic Liebig. Although their training encompassed both theoretical and practical chemistry, the combustion apparatus was an integral part of a systematic curriculum that enabled even the average worker to make valuable contributions.

Typically, the beginning student first sat in on Liebig's lectures on introductory chemistry and then was initiated in laboratory practices by doing qualitative analysis in which one characterizes a series of unknown compounds. Subsequently, a varied set of quantitative analyses was performed, followed by exercises in preparative chemistry in which certain substances were synthesized. After successfully completing these stages, the student was permitted to pursue independent research, often using the combustion apparatus to explore the reactions and compositions of organic substances. Because Liebig was editor of his own journal, *Annalen der Chemie und Pharmacie*, his students often had no problem in rapidly publishing their findings to a scientific community that by the 1840's recognized Giessen as the mecca of organic chemistry.

Without doubt, Liebig's scientific reputation resulted in the best and brightest students in chemistry coming to study with him at Giessen during the second quarter of the nineteenth century. Among his students were August Wilhelm von Hofmann, discoverer of aniline and the first director of the British Royal College of Chemistry; Friedrich August Kekule von Stradonitz, whose structural interpretation of benzene was crucial to development in structural organic chemistry; James Muspratt of England, who was a leader during the late nineteenth century in the British chemical industry; and Oliver Wolcott Gibbs, who was a key figure within the emerging chemical community of nineteenth century America. Indeed, Liebig's influence was truly international, as by the 1850's most important academic positions in Western Europe were filled by his former students.

Liebig's fame among his contemporaries and especially the public was perhaps not so much the result of his students and their work as the result of his opinions and writings on agricultural chemistry. In 1840, Liebig, weary after more than a decade of debate with the French chemist Jean-Baptiste André Dumas over the nature of organic molecules, gave a series of lectures on agricultural chemistry in Glasgow, Scotland, that subsequently would be the basis of *Die organische Chemie in ihrer Anivendung auf Agricultur und Physiologie* (1840; *Or-*

ganic Chemistry in Its Applications to Agriculture and Physiology, 1840). This work, which dealt with the uses of fertilizers, plant nutrition, and fermentation, was seriously flawed in its analysis but was so popular that by 1848 it appeared in seventeen editions and in nine languages, proving to be a powerful stimulus to the agricultural station movement in Europe and the United States.

In addition to his views on agriculture, Liebig also extended into the area of physiology and in 1842 expressed his views on nutrition and the chemical changes taking place within living organisms in *Die Thier-Chemie: Oder, Die organische Chemie in ihrer Anwendung auf Physiologie und Pathologie* (*Animal Chemistry: Or, Organic Chemistry in Its Applications to Physiology and Pathology*, 1842). Like his agricultural chemistry, Liebig's animal chemistry aroused criticism that ultimately was crucial to the late nineteenth century development of modern physiological chemistry.

In 1852, Liebig left Giessen for a modern, well-equipped laboratory in Munich, where he would continue to research and write on aspects of organic chemistry. Although the latter stages of his career were not as fruitful as those early years at Giessen, his legacy in terms of ideas and of followers was crucial to the shaping of modern civilization.

SIGNIFICANCE

Justus von Liebig perhaps did more than any other nineteenth century chemist in creating the modern synthetic world of the twentieth century. His reliance upon exact knowledge based upon chemical analysis resulted in the emergence of the discipline of organic chemistry, a field that has provided modern society with myriad synthetic products, including polymeric materials such as polyvinyl chloride, polypropylene, and synthetic rubber. However, Liebig did far more than influence the internal aspects of science, for his work on agricultural chemistry had enormous consequences in influencing what would become an ongoing agricultural revolution, and his speculations on physiology reoriented the course of medical research. Finally, his ideas on chemical education—ideas that continue to be practiced in universities today—mark perhaps his most lasting contribution, for most chemists trace their educational heritage to a small laboratory in Giessen and to its master, Justus von Liebig.

—John A. Heitmann

FURTHER READING

Beer, John J. *The Emergence of the German Dye Industry*. Urbana: University of Illinois Press, 1959. One important legacy of Liebig is in the creation of a modern synthetic world, the ultimate fruit of his many students working in industrial research laboratories during the last quarter of the nineteenth century. Beer's study carefully traces the emergence of the science-based dye industry and the role of Liebig's ideas in influencing its organizational development.

Brock, William H. *The Chemical Tree: A History of Chemistry*. New York: W. W. Norton, 2000. Includes information on Liebig's writings, his experiences at the University of Giessen, and his work on combustion analysis, farming and fertilizers, and other aspects of chemistry.

_____. *Justus von Liebig: The Chemical Gatekeeper*. Cambridge, England: Cambridge University Press, 1997. Reprint. 2002. Discusses Liebig's contributions to the field of organic chemistry, including his advocation of recycling sewage and replacing nutrients in the soil.

Ihde, Aaron J. *The Development of Modern Chemistry*. New York: Harper & Row, 1964. This survey work in the history of chemistry is excellent in characterizing the nature of organic chemistry during Liebig's lifetime. Discusses Liebig's contributions to organic, agricultural, and physiological chemistry as well as to the field of chemical education.

Levere, Trevor H. *Transforming Matter: A History of Chemistry from Alchemy to Buckyball*. Baltimore: Johns Hopkins University Press, 2001. This accessible history book includes information about Liebig's experiences at the University of Giessen in Chapter 10, "The Birth of the Teaching-Research Laboratory."

Lipmann, Timothy O. "Vitalism and Reductionism in Liebig's Physiological Thought." *Isis* 58 (1967): 167-185. A superb article that serves as a model for scholarship in the history of science. Lipmann demonstrates that while Liebig did not believe in the doctrine of vitalism as applied to organic compounds, he did adhere to the notion that a living force (*Lebenskraft*) was an essential part of physiological processes and necessary for the building up of organized structures in living bodies.

Morrell, J. B. "The Chemist Breeders: The Research Schools of Liebig and Thomas Thomson." *Ambix* 19 (1972): 1-47. A penetrating study that examines the pioneering contributions of Liebig in establishing the first modern scientific research school. Morrell analyzes Liebig's charismatic personality, the significance of the combustion apparatus, his ability to control the field of organic chemistry with *Annalen der Chemie und Pharmacie*, and his ability to secure financial and institutional resources.

Rossiter, Margaret W. *The Emergence of Agricultural Science: Justus Liebig and the Americans, 1840-1880*. New Haven, Conn.: Yale University Press, 1975. Traces the diffusion of Liebig's ideas on agriculture from Europe to the United States during the nineteenth century. By the conclusion of the Civil War, a powerful movement to establish agricultural experiment stations emerged, and Rossiter particularly focuses on the influence of Liebig on those scientists working at the Connecticut Station.

SEE ALSO: Joseph-Louis Gay-Lussac; Josiah Willard Gibbs; Sir William Robert Grove; Hermann von Helmholtz; Alexander von Humboldt; Dmitry Ivanovich Mendeleyev; Friedrich Wöhler.

RELATED ARTICLES in *Great Events from History: The Nineteenth Century, 1801-1900:* 1803-1808: Dalton Formulates the Atomic Theory of Matter; 1869-1871: Mendeleyev Develops the Periodic Table of Elements.

WILHELM LIEBKNECHT
German politician

Liebknecht was a founding member of the German Social Democratic Party and an extreme critic of authoritarian government in Germany. He was a delegate to the German Reichstag and editor of the Social Democratic Party newspaper Vorwärts. *His most important contribution was an effort to promote the ideals of democracy in the nineteenth century European socialist movement.*

BORN: March 29, 1826; Giessen, Hesse-Darmstadt (now in Germany)
DIED: August 7, 1900; Berlin, Germany
AREA OF ACHIEVEMENT: Government and politics

EARLY LIFE

Wilhelm Liebknecht (LEEP-k-nehkt) was the son of a government registrar, and his family was considered middle class by the standards of the early nineteenth century. One of three surviving children, Liebknecht benefited from his father's study of post-Napoleonic Enlightenment thought, and from an early age he was interested in social justice. By December, 1832, however, both of his parents were dead and the six-year-old orphan was reared by Karl Osswald, a theologian, who had been a close friend of the family.

By the time Liebknecht had reached his tenth birthday, what was left of his father's estate had disappeared. Although the sudden deaths of his parents and the descent into poverty must have made a lasting impression on him, Liebknecht seldom wrote of his childhood. His only lasting memories were of his uncle, the Reverend Friedrich Ludwig Weidig, a liberal democrat and author of fiery revolutionary tracts. Repeatedly jailed for his antimonarchist writings, in February, 1837, Weidig was apparently murdered in prison in Darmstadt. Although Liebknecht rarely referred to his uncle's death, evidence suggests that at this time he began to identify the authoritarian state as the source of his own bereavement and the problems of society.

Although reduced in circumstances, Liebknecht was still able to attend school, and it was education rather than hardship that pushed him in the direction of radical politics. In the autumn of 1845, Liebknecht left for Berlin to enroll at the university. Berlin was already an industrial city with a population approaching half a million, and the condition of the city's industrial workers, who were forced to live in appalling slums and to suffer brutal working conditions, made an instant impression on the young student.

Indeed, Liebknecht's course of study at the university perfectly complemented his introduction to working-class life. His major interests lay in philosophy and economics, and he read avidly in the works of the French socialist Claude Henri de Saint-Simon. As Liebknecht himself admitted, however, his real grounding in socialist thought began with his reading of Friedrich Engels's *Die Lage der arbeitenden Klasse in England* (1848; *The Condition of the Working Class in England in 1844*, 1887). This work persuaded Liebknecht to join the struggle against capitalism, and he cut his education short to join the liberal-democratic revolutions of 1848. The collapse of the revolutionary movement in 1849 forced Liebknecht to flee Germany.

LIFE'S WORK

Liebknecht's post-1848 travels took him to Switzerland and then to Great Britain. During his migration, he became acquainted with both Karl Marx and Engels. In 1850, he joined the Union of Communists and became a dedicated exponent of socialist political and economic theory. A proclamation of amnesty permitted Liebknecht to return to Berlin in 1862. He worked as a correspondent for various democratically oriented German and foreign newspapers and became a founding member, along with Ferdinand Lassalle, of the General German Workers' Association, an organization that favored workers' cooperatives financially supported by the state, universal suffrage, and a program of social legislation regulating wages and hours. In 1869, however, Liebknecht helped to create a new workers' party, the German Social Democratic Labor Party, a more radical organization that emphasized the class struggle and that demanded the abolition of class privileges in Prussia.

During the late 1860's, the two rival groups became parliamentary parties and sent representatives to the assembly of the North German Confederation, which had been created following the Prussian defeat of Austria in 1866. Liebknecht served as a Social Democratic delegate from 1867 to 1870 and vigorously attacked the reactionary policies of the Prussian Junker class and denounced Prussian militarism. Along with August Bebel, Liebknecht opposed the Franco-Prussian War of 1870-1871, fought against the annexationist plans of the Prussian government, and appealed for working-class solidarity with the Paris Commune of 1871. For his opposition to Germany's annexation of Alsace and Lorraine, Liebknecht was brought to trial in 1872 for treason against the state and sentenced to two years' imprisonment.

The Franco-Prussian War led to increased cooperation between the Social Democrats and Lassalle's Workers' Association. Many factional disputes disappeared with the unification of Germany and, by 1875, the two socialist parties resolved to join forces against capitalism and Prussian militarism. At the Socialist Congress at Gotha in May, 1875, a new German Social Democratic Labor Party was founded, and Liebknecht became one of the most influential party leaders, along with Lassalle and Bebel.

The Gotha Program reflected Liebknecht's democratic tendencies and was far from a radical socialist agenda. The party program called for such socialist measures as the abolition of "wage slavery" through the establishment of state-supported workers' cooperatives, but it also advocated many commonly held liberal-democratic policies, including universal suffrage, the secret ballot, guaranteed civil liberties, free public education, freedom of speech and assembly, and government-mandated social legislation. The republican nature of the Gotha Program engendered criticism from more doctrinaire socialists, including Marx. In 1875, Marx published his *Randglossen zum Gothaer Partei Program* (1875; *Critique of the Gotha Program*, 1938), a scathing ideological attack on the German Social Democrats. Nevertheless, Liebknecht repudiated Marx's denunciation, and the new party achieved impressive electoral gains in 1877. The party's moderate-democratic approach allowed it to increase its popular vote by 40 percent and helped it to capture twelve seats in the German Reichstag.

Following the Gotha meeting, however, German chancellor Otto von Bismarck took steps to prevent any further growth of socialism in Germany. As a result of Liebknecht's and other socialist leaders' opposition to Prussian policies during the Franco-Prussian War, Bismarck was inclined to regard all Social Democrats as enemies of the state. Therefore, in 1878, Bismarck persuaded the Reichstag to pass a series of antisocialist laws that suppressed all political and economic associations of the German socialists. Technically the German Social Democratic Party was not illegal, but party effectiveness was practically destroyed by curtailments in electoral funding and the harassment of party leaders. Liebknecht retained his democratic philosophy during this period and helped to retain party unity until the antisocialist legislation lapsed in 1890.

In 1890, Liebknecht became chief editor of *Vorwärts*, the central organ of the Social Democratic Party. During this period, and until his death in 1900, Liebknecht's socialist beliefs centered on the issue of the legitimacy of parliamentary activity in the context of the class struggle against capitalism and militarism. Liebknecht's position held that the workers' interests would be more effectively served by sending deputies to the Reichstag who would use the democratic system to achieve social, political, and economic reform. Liebknecht, Bebel, and other moderates helped mold the German Social Democratic movement into a responsible parliamentary party, defending workers' interests and political liberalism.

Liebknecht was especially responsible for formulating specific policies aimed at promoting social legislation, reducing the military budget, and eliminating economic protectionism. By the late 1890's, however, Liebknecht's position as party leader had diminished, largely as a result of his inexpert handling of intraparty strife. On the morning of August 7, 1900, Liebknecht suffered a fatal stroke while working at his office in Berlin. His leadership of the German Social Democrats fell to Bebel, Karl Kautsky, and Eduard Bernstein, but Liebknecht was eulogized as one who had helped to elevate a struggling socialist faction into the world's largest and most effective socialist party.

Significance

Wilhelm Liebknecht's achievement was to help to establish the world's first mass-based Marxist political party. He was a nineteenth century social democrat whose political philosophy was formed in the nexus of liberal democracy, Marxism, and nationalism. He was noted as being tolerant, humanitarian, and democratic. Although he did not excel as a statesman or political revolutionary, he was a master at political organization. His advocacy of revolutionary change was tempered with his abjuration of violence. He encouraged open discussion within his party, and he defended the right to hold dissenting viewpoints. In reaching decisions, he preferred persuasion and open voting to intimidation and deference to an elite party leadership.

Liebknecht rejected any form of conspiratorial action by a minority and based his socialism on the basic premise of mass participation. Liebknecht argued that the basic tool of working-class revolution remained education. Voluntary and enlightened mass participation in the revolutionary process was Liebknecht's aim. For him, the manipulative dictatorship of the proletariat always remained an incongruous part of Marxism. While most nineteenth century socialist movements indulged in sectarian debates and self-defeating intraparty rivalries, the German Social Democrats, largely as a result of Liebknecht's efforts, crystallized the socialist movement and forestalled party schism until 1917. Overall, Liebknecht's leadership molded the German socialists into a respected and effective workers' party and ultimately inspired the creation of modern European social democracy.

—William G. Ratliff

FURTHER READING

Braunthal, Julius. *History of the International*. Translated by Henry Collins and Kenneth Mitchell. 2 vols. New York: Praeger, 1976. This standard work on the Socialist International includes a discussion of Liebknecht's efforts in attracting German workers' attention to the First International. Places Liebknecht in the context of the early days of European socialism.

Dominick, Raymond H., III. *Wilhelm Liebknecht and the Founding of the German Social Democratic Party*. Chapel Hill: University of North Carolina Press, 1982. Dominick provides the standard biography of Liebknecht. His focus is on the philosophical struggle inherent in the founding of the German Social Democratic Party. He attributes to Liebknecht the party's emphasis on participatory democracy. Liebknecht is given credit for retaining party unity in the face of Prussian repression and ideological disputes within European socialism.

Hall, Alex. *Scandal, Sensation, and Social Democracy: The SPD Press and Wilhelmine Germany, 1890-1914*. Cambridge, England: Cambridge University Press, 1977. The author examines in detail the workings of such major Social Democratic organs as *Vorwärts* and provides a detailed discussion of Liebknecht's direction of the paper during the 1890's. Liebknecht is given credit for maintaining his democratic principles in the face of severe criticism from both the government and his own party's radical elements.

Lidtke, Vernon L. *The Outlawed Party: Social Democracy in Germany, 1878-1890*. Princeton, N.J.: Princeton University Press, 1966. This study is devoted largely to the struggle of the German Social Democratic Party during the period of Bismarck's antisocialist laws. Early chapters, however, deal in detail with Liebknecht's role in the founding of the party. The author emphasizes the impact of Liebknecht's liberalism in the formulation of party ideology.

Mukherjee, Subrata, and Sushila Ramaswamy, eds. *Wilhlem Liebknecht, His Thoughts and Works*. New Delhi: Deep & Deep, 1998. Contains Liebknecht's writings with some commentaries and a biographical sketch.

Pelz, William, ed. *Wilhelm Liebknecht and German Social Collections: A Documentary History*. Translated by Erich Hahn. Westport, Conn.: Greenwood Press, 1994. Presents Liebknecht through a sampling of his most renowned work. Whenever possible, the writings are included unedited, and each offering is preceded by an introduction placing the piece in context. Also included are essays by colleagues and those who knew Liebknecht personally.

Roth, Guenther. *The Social Democrats in Imperial Germany: A Study in Working-Class Isolation and National Integration*. Totowa, N.J.: Bedminster Press, 1963. This work is basically a sociological view of the integration of the German working class into German society. The author attacks party leaders, including Liebknecht, for denying strict Marxism in favor of watered-down liberalism. Credit is given, however, for Liebknecht's criticism of militarism and other evils of Prussian authoritarianism.

SEE ALSO: Otto von Bismarck; Friedrich Engels; Ferdinand Lassalle; Karl Marx.

RELATED ARTICLES in *Great Events from History: The Nineteenth Century, 1801-1900:* 1866-1867: North German Confederation Is Formed; 1867: Marx Publishes *Das Kapital*; 1871-1877: *Kulturkampf* Against the Catholic Church in Germany; January 18, 1871: German States Unite Within German Empire.

LILIUOKALANI
Queen of Hawaii (r. 1891-1892)

The last monarch of the Hawaiian kingdom, Liliuokalani struggled futilely to preserve her people's independence against the pressures of American annexation.

BORN: September 2, 1838; Honolulu, Hawaii
DIED: November 11, 1917; Honolulu, Hawaii
ALSO KNOWN AS: Mrs. John O. Dominis; Lydia Kamakaeha Paki; Lydia Kamakaeha (birth name)
AREA OF ACHIEVEMENT: Government and politics

EARLY LIFE

Born into Hawaii's royal family, Liliuokalani (leh-LEE-ew-o-kah-LAH-nee) was the daughter of a chief named Kapaakea and his wife, Keohokalole. Kapaakea was one of the fifteen counselors of the king, Kamehameha III. Immediately after her birth, she was adopted into another family. A woman named Konia was her foster mother, and her foster father was a chief named Paki. This practice of adoption was the custom among the leading families of Hawaii; it was a way to cement alliances among the chiefs, who were the nobility of Hawaii. All of Liliuokalani's ten brothers and sisters were also adopted into and reared by other families.

When Liliuokalani was four years old, she was enrolled in the Royal School, a boarding school run by American missionaries. The students of this school were all members of the royal extended family, which was made up of the families of the king and chiefs. In this school, Liliuokalani learned English and was taken to church every Sunday, but she said that she never got enough to eat. The school closed in 1848, when Liliuokalani was ten years old, and after that she attended a day school also run by American missionaries. Learning was important to Liliuokalani throughout her life.

After Paki's death in 1855, Liliuokalani continued to live in his home, along with her sister Bernice and Bernice's husband, Charles R. Bishop. The Bishops were to be a major influence on Liliuokalani's life.

Although at one time she was engaged to be married to Lunalilo (also known as Prince William), who would become king in 1873, she ultimately was married to the son of an Italian-born sea captain and a New England woman. The man was named John O. Dominis, and the marriage took place on September 16, 1862. The couple began their married life at Washington Place, the estate built by the groom's father for his family. This was to re-

main Liliuokalani's private residence throughout her life.

Much of Liliuokalani's adulthood before her accession as queen was spent on benevolent work for native Hawaiians. She was also a composer of music, and she wrote more than one hundred songs, including several Christian hymns, but is best known for the famous Hawaiian song "Aloha 'Oe." In 1887, she attended Queen Victoria of England's Jubilee celebration as an honored guest. She never had any children.

LIFE'S WORK

A year after Liliuokalani's marriage, King Kamehameha IV died, on November 30, 1863. Because the young king had recently lost his only son to illness, there was no direct heir to the throne. According to the Hawaiian Constitution of 1852, the king's brother was elected as the new monarch by the cabinet, the privy council, and the *kuhina nui* (the queen, who served as coruler with the Hawaiian king). He became known as Kamehameha V. By the time he died in 1872, a new constitution had been passed (in 1864) that gave the king the right to choose his own successor. The successor he had named, however, his sister Princess Victoria, had died in 1866, and he had named no one else.

Now it was up to the Hawaiian legislature to elect a new king from among the nobility. This was when Liliuokalani's former fiancé, Lunalilo, ascended the throne. He lived only a year longer, however, and also died without naming an heir. This time, Liliuokalani's brother Kalakaua was elected, and in 1877 she was chosen as heir to the throne. She served as regent from January to October of 1881 while the king was making a trip around the world, which gave her a taste of what it would later be like to be queen. She took this role again in 1890 and 1891 while the king was in California on a trip meant to restore his failing health. He died in January of 1891, however, leaving his sister Liliuokalani as queen.

Liliuokalani was proclaimed queen on January 29, 1891, at the age of fifty-two. She inherited a government that had been, throughout the nineteenth century, a mixture of Hawaiian tradition, British constitutional ideals, Victorian influence, and American interference brought by missionaries, adventurers, and politicians. Symbolic of this mixture were the combinations of names held by the Hawaiian nobility. (Liliuokalani was also known as Lydia Kamakaeha Paki and Mrs. John O. Dominis.) This mixture was strengthened by the frequency of intermarriage between Hawaiians and people of European American extraction, of which Liliuokalani's own marriage was an example.

Liliuokalani's brother, influenced by American businesspeople, had led Hawaii on a course toward ruin by trying to return to a more despotic form of government. This led to revolution in 1887 and to increased American influence, because in the new constitution of that year members of the nobility were to be elected by voters of large income and property, which in practice meant large numbers of Americans and others of foreign birth or ancestry. Hawaii was also under the grip of an economic depression as a result of the McKinley Tariff Act, which removed tariffs on other importers of sugar to the United States. Because sugar had become the center of Hawaii's economy, this act devastated the island nation.

Liliuokalani. (Hawaii State Archives)

This was the situation the new queen faced: political turmoil and economic difficulty. Her solution was to strengthen the monarchy. Liliuokalani was firmly opposed to the Constitution of 1887, which was far more democratic than previous constitutions had been. At the same time, the political strife and economic difficulties in the islands made the idea of annexation by the United States look rather appealing to some Hawaiians, and by 1892 there were secret organizations working toward that end.

After an attempt by the queen to promulgate a new constitution giving the monarchy more power, in January, 1892, a revolutionary committee took over the government and ended the monarchy, setting up a provisional government until a union with the United States could be worked out. The queen assented against her will, in order to avoid bloodshed, and retired to Washington Place. A treaty of annexation by the United States was drawn up and signed by the provisional government on February 14, 1893. It had not been acted upon, however, by the Senate of the United States by the time Grover Cleveland became president a few days later. A friend of Liliuokalani, Cleveland had received a letter from her about the coup d'état. After his inauguration, he withdrew the treaty from the Senate's consideration and launched a lengthy investigation into the matter. Meanwhile, the provisional government remained in power.

When it became clear that annexation was not imminent, a constitutional convention in 1894 set up what was to be the Republic of Hawaii. Liliuokalani protested to both the United States and Great Britain, but to no avail. An attempt to restore the monarchy was quickly squelched, leading to Liliuokalani's arrest and conviction on charges of treason. She was imprisoned in the Iolani Palace and forced to sign abdication papers. Hawaii was officially annexed to the United States on August 12, 1898, but the republic continued to govern the islands under the authority of the president of the United States.

Liliuokalani was pardoned in 1896, and in that year she traveled to the United States to visit her late husband's relatives, trying to forget her sorrows over recent events. She returned in August of 1898, her enthusiastic welcome home showing how much support she still retained among both native-born and foreign-born Hawaiians.

While in the United States, she wrote her autobiography, *Hawaii's Story by Hawaii's Queen* (1898), as well as translating an ancient Hawaiian poem. Liliuokalani died on November 11, 1917, in Honolulu, Hawaii.

"ALOHA 'OE" ("FAREWELL TO THEE")

According to tradition, Liliuokalani was inspired to compose "Aloha Oe" when she saw two lovers saying farewell to each other in the moonlight. The song also symbolized her own farewell to Hawaii's independence. The flowery Hawaiian language in which the song was primarily written is said not to translate well into English, which fails to convey the full depth of the sorrow that its Hawaiian phrases express. The song achieved new popularity during the early 1960's, when Elvis Presley sang it in the film Blue Hawaii *(1961).*

Ha'aheo ka ua i na pali,
Ke nihi a'e la i ka nahele,
E uhai ana paha i ka liko,
Pua ahihi lehua a o uka.

(Chorus)
Aloha 'oe, aloha 'oe,
E ke onaona noho i ka lipo,
One fond embrace a ho'i a'e au,
Until we meet again.

Proudly sweeps the rain clouded by the cliffs,
As onward it glides through the trees,
It seems to be following the liko,
The ahihi lehua of the vale.

(Chorus)
Farewell to thee, farewell to thee,
Thou charming one who dwells among the bowers.
One fond embrace before I now depart
Until we meet again.

Source: Mele Kalikimaka Web site, www.melekalikimaka.com/alohaoe .htm. Electronic text accessed on July 14, 2005.

ropean and American values and politics, could no longer remain independent. Although she resigned herself to Hawaii's annexation to the United States, she never agreed with the idea, always remaining convinced of the value of national autonomy for her islands.

Liliuokalani is something of a tragic figure. Trained and educated as a potential ruler, passionate about her country and her people, a woman of cosmopolitan learning and taste, she nevertheless came to power at a time when her method of rule came into conflict with the movement of history.

—*Eleanor B. Amico*

FURTHER READING

Kuykendall, Ralph S., and A. Grove Day. *Hawaii: A History, from Polynesian Kingdom to American State.* Englewood Cliffs, N.J.: Prentice-Hall, 1948. The parts of this book labeled books 3 and 4 (chapters 11 through 12) give a helpful chronicle of the events of the latter years of the Hawaiian kingdom. They help the reader understand the background to the situation that Liliuokalani inherited, as well as the outcome of her own reign.

Liliuokalani. *Hawaii's Story by Hawaii's Queen.* Rutland, Vt.: Tuttle, 1964. The queen's autobiography is the best source for learning about her early life. Although it is somewhat rambling, it is invaluable because it gives Liliuokalani's perspective on events in her own words. It ends with her return from the United States in 1898.

Loomis, Albertine. *For Whom Are the Stars?* Honolulu: University of Hawai'i Press, 1976. A highly readable and sympathetic account of the end of the Hawaiian monarchy, discussing the revolution and events leading up to it, the first failure to annex Hawaii to the United States, the founding of the republic, the rebellion of 1895, and the queen's arrest and trial.

"Native Hawaiians Seek Redress for U.S. Role in Ousting Queen." *The New York Times*, December 11, 1999, p. A20. A report about a group of Hawaiians seeking redress for the U.S. involvement in Liliuokalani's overthrow. Discusses then-president Bill Clinton's apology for the incident.

SIGNIFICANCE

Although her reign was Hawaii's last as an independent nation, Liliuokalani's impact on Hawaii's history cannot be denied. Because she was part of a tradition in which women played important roles, she never questioned her right to rule. Although she believed in a strong monarchy, Liliuokalani organized institutions for the improvement of the health, welfare, and education of her native Hawaiian compatriots. She was an educated woman who valued learning, and she was both an author and a composer. A native Hawaiian, she was also an enthusiastic participant in the Victorian-inspired society of her times. Her downfall was her accession to the throne at a time when her tiny kingdom, influenced as it was by both Eu-

Russ, William Adam, Jr. *The Hawaiian Republic, 1894-98, and Its Struggle to Win Annexation*. Selinsgrove, Pa.: Susquehanna University Press, 1961. This book follows up on Russ's earlier book (below). This volume analyzes the years of the Hawaiian Republic, between the time of Liliuokalani's abdication and Hawaii's annexation by the United States.

_____. *The Hawaiian Revolution, 1893-94*. Selinsgrove, Pa.: Susquehanna University Press, 1959. Analyzes in readable detail the events of the revolution that deposed Queen Liliuokalani. It also examines the involvement of the United States and American interests in the overthrow of Hawaiian autonomy.

Tate, Merze. *The United States and the Hawaiian Kingdom: A Political History*. New Haven, Conn.: Yale University Press, 1965. This book focuses on the period of Hawaiian history that included Liliuokalani's life and work: 1864 to 1898. Chapters 4 through 7 deal specifically with various events of her reign: her attempt to change the constitution, the revolution of 1893, and annexation by the United States.

Young, Lucien. *The Real Hawaii: Its History and Present Condition*. New York: Doubleday & McClure, 1899. An eyewitness account of the revolution of 1893 and the events that followed. The author was on a ship stationed at Honolulu at the time. Written to discount the reports of James H. Blount, the envoy of Liliuokalani to President Cleveland, the book gives an account of Hawaiian culture, history, and economy as well as of the revolution and its aftermath.

SEE ALSO: Grover Cleveland; Kamehameha I; William McKinley; Queen Victoria.

RELATED ARTICLE in *Great Events from History: The Nineteenth Century, 1801-1900:* January 24, 1895: Hawaii's Last Monarch Abdicates.

LIN ZEXU
Chinese scholar and government official

A respected scholar-official serving the Manchu Qing Dynasty, Lin led China's effort to eradicate the sale of opium by foreigners at Canton. The campaign succeeded but led to the first Opium War and the ignominious Treaty of Nanjing.

BORN: August 30, 1785; Houguuan, Fujian, China
DIED: November 22, 1850; Chaozhou, Guangdong, China
ALSO KNOWN AS: Lin Tse-hsü (Wade-Giles)
AREA OF ACHIEVEMENT: Government and politics

EARLY LIFE

Lin Zexu (lihn zay-chew) was the second child born to Lin Binri, a poor scholar. His father, hoping to emulate earlier family members by entering the government bureaucracy through the civil service exam system, could not rise beyond the initial *xiucai* (cultivated talent) degree and at the age of forty-one gave up his quest for the provincial level *juren* (recommended man) degree to run a private school to support his growing family (ultimately three sons and eight daughters). The young Lin Zexu grew up in a loving but impoverished family environment. His education began at home under his father's tutelage, and he entered school at the age of four. During his youth, he helped sell his mother's embroidery to make ends meet. A bright student, he entered the local academy at the age of nine and won the *xiucai* degree when fourteen. In an oral test to choose the best of the exam entrants, he bested a rival candidate many years his senior.

At the age of twenty, he passed the *juren* exams, which entitled him to go to Beijing to take the capital tests, but he could not afford to do so. Instead, he entered the local *yamen* (government office) as a clerk-scribe. When a New Year's greeting he wrote caught the attention of Zhang Shicheng, the Fujian (Fukien) provincial governor, Lin was summoned to neighboring Fuzhou (Foochow) to serve for three years on Zhang's staff.

Seven years after achieving *juren* status, Lin finally went to Beijing to take the highest-level exams. He attained *jinshi* (presented scholar) rank and entered the Hanlin Academy. His nine-year stay in Beijing gained for him considerable experience in handling the myriad governmental concerns brought to the attention of the six ministries at the top of the Qing bureaucracy. He also made valuable, lifelong contacts within the power structure, connections important for career advancement.

In 1819, Lin was sent to Yunnan in the southwest to be head examiner in the provincial exams. This was a stepping-stone to his first major appointment as intendant of the administrative circuit (*dao*) in the Hangzhou (Hangchow) area. In 1822, Lin went to Beijing and had an audience with the newly enthroned Daoguang emperor. The emperor praised Lin's work in the Hangzhou region and permitted Lin to return there. In succession, he was given posts in Jiangsu (intendant) and Zhejiang (salt monopoly controller) Provinces.

In 1823, Lin became surveillance commissioner of Jiangsu. By cleaning up a backlog of judicial cases with great impartiality and reforming the penal system, he earned the epithet "Lin as Clear as the Heavens." The following year, his mother died, requiring a return to his hometown for a custom-dictated three years of mourning. This period was interrupted twice, first to help in flood relief in Jiangsu along the Yellow River, and then to work in the salt monopoly administration. After a visit to Beijing in 1827, he was assigned to Xi'an (Sian) in Shanxi; there he became familiar with military affairs as a result of a nearby Muslim rebellion being quashed by the Qing military.

While Lin was serving as financial commissioner in Nanjing, his father died en route to joining him. This again necessitated a three-year absence from government service for official mourning in his native village. In 1830, Lin was back in the capital, awaiting a new assignment. During this stay, Lin renewed and made friendships with middle-echelon bureaucrats, men on the periphery of power yet close enough to the real problems to be concerned about the dynasty's ossifying rule. Lin was part of a coterie (often meeting socially as the Xuannan Poetry Society) of younger degree-holders, inspired by their study of "modern text" (*jinwen*) Confucian writings to seek practical solutions to problems of governing. When Lin received his next set of assignments, he left the capital, invigorated with ideas shared by a nascent group of intellectual-administrators devoted to practical statecraft.

In the next twenty months, Lin was given five different assignments: provincial administration commissioner, in turn, of Hubei (Hupei), Hunan, and Nanjing (Chiangning), followed by that of water conservancy director-general in Shangdong (Shantung) and Henan (Honan), and, in 1832, governor of Jiangxi (Kiangsu). He stayed in the latter post for five years. His tenure in Jiangxi under his friend Governor-General Taoshu added to his reputation. A new problem he encountered was the outflow of local silver used to pay for opium distributed into the hinterland from foreign sources at Canton (Guangzhou).

LIFE'S WORK

At the age of fifty-two, Lin was appointed governor-general of Hubei and Hunan. Increasingly, much of his time came to be concentrated on a matter that was by this time a major local and national concern—opium control. Trade between the Western powers and China, begun during the eighteenth century, originally was in China's favor, because European and American demand for tea leaves, raw silk, rhubarb, chinaware, and lacquer items far exceeded Chinese interest in Western woolens, tin, lead, furs, and linen. The anticommercial Manchu rulers only begrudgingly tolerated this trade, despite its profitability, and confined it to the southern port of Canton, where foreigners could not easily press on the dynasty their demands for diplomatic recognition.

The import of tea to England was lucrative to the Crown as a result of a 100 percent excise duty, but, because it could not be paid for only by the sale of Indian cotton to the Chinese, Britain had to bring in silver bullion from Mexico and Peru to pay its bills. A triangular trade among England, India, and China operated through the "Canton system" whereby foreign ships, stopping first at the Portuguese enclave Macao, would proceed with Chinese permission to Canton and sell their cargoes at a waterfront warehouse enclave through the *cohong* (*gonghong*) trade guild run by Chinese merchants supervised by the *hoppo* (customs official).

The British and the other foreigners tolerated this inconvenient system because it was lucrative. The trade imbalance in China's favor began to change with the export by the East India Company of opium from Bengal to Canton, starting during the 1770's. Opium was originally used for its reputed medicinal and aphrodisiac qualities, and, even though the Chinese repeatedly had outlawed its use, it became a popular drug, inhaled by pipe. The East India Company, to protect itself legally, consigned the opium transport and sale to private traders not bound by the intricacies of the formalistic Canton system. In 1834, the company's China trade monopoly was ended by the British parliament's response to domestic demands for free trade. The resulting free-for-all among opium dealers dramatically increased sales to the Chinese, and by the late 1830's anywhere from two to ten million Chinese had become addicted. In addition, the outflow of Chinese silver and the worsening exchange ratio between silver and Chinese copper coins (a problem Lin had confronted earlier) created economic havoc.

In China, a debate raged between those wanting to legalize the opium trade in order to control it and those favoring an end to it. The Daoguang emperor sided with the officials who opposed legalization, and Governor-General Deng Tingzhen cracked down on the Canton opium trade between 1836 and 1838. He was successful in dealing with the Chinese end of the problem but had difficulty with the foreign merchants. After the East India Company's monopoly ended, the Chinese, preferring to deal with a formal middleman rather than a host of competing foreign interests, asked the British to designate someone to be *taipan* (head merchant). The British, wanting official Chinese diplomatic recognition, sent, in 1833, Lord William John Napier, assisted militarily by Captain Charles Elliot.

In one stroke the British put a government official in a position formerly occupied by the East India Company, thus making trade, originally a private arrangement between the company and the cohong merchants, the official concern of the Crown. Increasingly, questions of commercial interests and national honor coalesced as the British, using commerce as a wedge, continued to attempt to persuade the Chinese to recognize their representative on a government-to-government basis.

Deng's antiopium campaign was successful. To preclude Deng from carrying out his threat to end all trade, the foreigners eventually reluctantly cooperated in the opium-suppression efforts. Smuggling by illegal profiteers, however, continued in the waters surrounding Canton. In Beijing pressure increased for the complete eradication of opium. Lin, successful in curbing opium use in his jurisdiction, was among the hard-liners. The emperor consulted with him personally and was impressed by his opium-elimination measures in Hubei and Hunan. On December 31, 1838, Lin was appointed imperial commissioner to eradicate the opium trade.

Lin arrived in Canton on March 10, 1839. The foreign community took his arrival calmly, viewing his subsequent crackdown on Chinese opium sellers and users as a continuation of the government's toughened policy. Lin's tack in dealing with the foreigners was to try to establish jurisdiction by getting them to accept Chinese legal rights and to convince them of the immorality of their actions. With imperial permission, he drafted two letters addressed to Queen Victoria, appealing to her moral propriety and common sense. Pointing out that opium smoking was a crime in England, he asked why her government promoted its use in his land and urged her to control her subjects' actions. These letters were widely circulated, for effect, among the foreign residents. A ship captain agreed to take a copy to England, but the foreign office refused to accept it.

On March 18, Lin ordered the surrender, through the *cohong* merchants, of all opium in the foreigners' possession and required all to sign a bond pledging, on penalty of death, no longer to engage in this trade. A token 1,036 chests were turned in. Dissatisfied, Lin attempted to coerce Lancelot Dent, a major opium supplier, to surrender himself to Chinese authority. Dent refused, and Elliot, fearing the worst, left Macao for Canton, arriving on the day before Lin enacted a total trade embargo and ordered all Chinese help out of the foreigners' compound, thus imposing a siege on the 350 foreigners trapped there. The standoff ended after six weeks on Elliot's promise to have the foreigners turn over all of their opium to Lin. This was readily done, because there no longer was a market and Elliot promised reimbursement. The forfeited 21,306 chests were emptied into a huge pit, and the opium was dissolved in seawater and lime, ending up in the ocean. Lin was victorious; however, by making his demands of Elliot, he now was dealing directly with a representative of the British government.

On May 24, all the British evacuated Canton for Macao. News of their confinement had infuriated the British public, and foreign secretary Lord Palmerston was bombarded with traders' petitions to be compensated for their losses. The British refugees thought they were secure in Portuguese Macao. The killing of a Chinese peasant on July 12 by some drunken British sailors at Kowloon, however, led to Lin's demand that the perpetrators be turned over to Chinese jurisdiction. This was refused. Lin had supplies to Macao cut off and ordered troops to surround it. The Portuguese evicted the British, who now sailed for Hong Kong. They were prevented from landing to replenish supplies. Elliot then ordered his ships to fire on some Chinese junks after being refused water and food.

By the fall of 1839 some British traders, aware that Americans were taking over their lucrative business in Canton, broke ranks with Elliot and decided to sign Lin's bond. On November 3, as some British traders were preparing to give in, a naval skirmish occurred at Xuanpi. Losing several ships, the Chinese retreated. On December 6, Lin ordered the end of all trade with the British. Unaware of this last event and responding to earlier provocations, the British parliament, after an acrimonious debate between Tories opposing a war to support opium smugglers and prowar politicians prodded by a strong China lobby with vested interests, voted by a narrow margin to retaliate.

A large British expeditionary force under Elliot's uncle arrived in Chinese waters in June, 1840. Anticipating this reaction, Lin fortified the Canton area. Coastal batteries at the Bogue were augmented with foreign-purchased guns, war-junks surrounded Canton waters, and chain blockades were put across the Pearl River. Peasant militia were mobilized in Guangdong (Kwangtung) Province. Martial arts fighters and Daoist magicians were also mustered. Lin wrote to the emperor that the large British warships were incapable of sailing up the Pearl River, adding that foreign soldiers, inept at fighting with swords and fists, could easily be routed.

Lin patiently waited for the British attack, but the fleet under Elliot's command, after blockading Canton, proceeded northward to deliver written ultimatums from Henry John Temple, Viscount Palmerston, directly to the court. After being refused at several ports, which were then blockaded, the British arrived in late August at the Peiho River near the Taku forts, protecting the approach to Beijing. The court was shocked that the local problem of Canton was now brought to its doorstep. Palmerston's letter of demands, putting most of the blame on Elliot's personal nemesis, Lin, was accepted. The emperor now saw Lin as a convenient scapegoat. On July 1, 1841, Lin was ordered into exile in remote Ili in Central Asia.

Lin's dismissal was merely an interlude in what became known as the Opium War. Diplomatic efforts to prevent further military action failed, and Elliot's military campaigns in the Canton delta eventually gave the British the upper hand. Sir Henry Pottinger, commanding a punitive naval force sent from India and England, followed up in 1841 with attacks on major Chinese ports. The Chinese reluctantly agreed on August 29, 1842, to the Treaty of Nanjing, requiring the payments of a war indemnity and reparations for seized opium, the opening of five coastal cities to trade and diplomatic residence, the abolishment of the cohong monopoly, and the ceding of Hong Kong.

Though in official disgrace, Lin was still a faithful servant to the dynasty. On his way to exile he was asked to fight a break in the Yellow River dykes at Kaifeng. While banished in Ili, he directed irrigation projects that reclaimed much land for farming. In 1845, he was recalled to service as acting governor-general of Shanxi (Shansi) and Gansu (Kansu), followed by posts in Shanxi and Yunnan. His final task was imperial commissioner to fight the Taiping rebels in the Guangxi (Kwangsi) region. He died on November 22, 1850, en route to this last assignment.

SIGNIFICANCE

Lin Zexu was a victim of two cultures; his Confucian upbringing and fidelity to the Qing required him to deal with the opium problem in an administrative and moralistic way that was outdated in the face of British might and the Western concept of foreign relations that denied China its self-assumed superiority. The Opium War, and Lin's role in it, marked a watershed in Chinese history. The "Middle Kingdom" would never recover from the burden of the "unequal treaties" begun at Nanjing, and the Western powers were not appeased by this first of many concessions to be extracted over the ensuing century. This happened despite Lin, not because of him.

Chinese Marxist historians use the Opium War as the beginning event in the history of modern China, the story of a collapsing feudal system ravished by foreign imperialism. Irrespective of ideology, Chinese everywhere respect Lin as a patriot who stood up to foreign aggression and the venal opium trade that symbolized it. His loyalty, though, was misplaced. It would take nationalism and revolution in the twentieth century to replace Lin's form of parochial dynastic allegiance before the Chinese would be able to reclaim their destiny for themselves.

—*William M. Zanella*

FURTHER READING

Chang, Hsin-pao. *Commissioner Lin and the Opium War.* Cambridge, Mass.: Harvard University Press, 1964. The most thorough study of the events leading to the Opium War are examined in the context of Lin's role in them. Uses Chinese and Western sources to give a well-rounded account, analyzing, from respective perspectives, the positions of the English and the Chinese. A portrait of Lin faces the title page. Includes copious notes, a glossary, and a bibliography.

Compilation Group for the "History of Modern China" Series. *The Opium War.* Beijing: Foreign Language Press, 1976. A booklet based on research by history professors at the University of Futan and Shanghai Teachers' University depicting Lin as one of "the capitulationists of the landlord class" who appeased Western imperialists in the Opium War; useful for understanding the Chinese Marxist historiographical approach.

Fairbank, John K., ed. *Late Ch'ing, 1800-1911, Part 1.* Vol. 10 in *The Cambridge History of China.* Cambridge, England: Cambridge University Press, 1978. Includes "The Canton Trade and the Opium War" by Frederic Wakeman, Jr., concisely narrating and analyzing the events before and after the war, including Lin's participation.

Liu, Lydia H. *The Clash of Empires: The Invention of China in Modern World Making.* Cambridge, Mass.:

Harvard University Press, 2004. A history of nineteenth century conflicts between the British Empire and the Qing Dynasty. Views the conflicts from the perspective of international law, modern warfare, and comparative grammar. The appendix features Lin's letters to Queen Victoria.

Mandancy, Joyce A. *The Troublesome Legacy of Commissioner Lin: The Opium Trade and Opium Suppression in Fujian Province, 1820's to 1920's*. Cambridge, Mass.: Harvard University Press, 2003. Describes Lin's efforts to end the opium trade and how he became a symbol of Chinese nationalism, elite activism, and opium reform during a 1908 opium suppression campaign.

Teng, Ssu-yü, and John K. Fairbank. *China's Response to the West: A Documentary Survey, 1839-1923*. Cambridge, Mass.: Harvard University Press, 1965. Lin's famous 1839 letter to Queen Victoria admonishing the British for their moral double standard in opium dealing and a short 1842 letter to a friend concerning the military superiority of the West are given in translation.

Waley, Arthur. *The Opium War Through Chinese Eyes*. New York: Macmillan, 1958. Uses Chinese documentary sources, Lin's diaries, and other writings to present the Opium War from a Chinese point of view.

SEE ALSO: Hong Xiuquan; Lord Palmerston; Queen Victoria.

RELATED ARTICLES in *Great Events from History: The Nineteenth Century, 1801-1900:* September, 1839-August 29, 1842: First Opium War; October 23, 1856-November 6, 1860: Second Opium War.

ABRAHAM LINCOLN
President of the United States (1861-1865)

A towering figure in American history, Lincoln played a leading role in the abolition of slavery and is generally credited with primary responsibility for preserving the Union through the unprecedented challenges of the Civil War.

BORN: February 12, 1809; near Hodgenville, Kentucky
DIED: April 15, 1865; Washington, D.C.
AREA OF ACHIEVEMENT: Government and politics

EARLY LIFE

Abraham Lincoln was born on the same date that the great British naturalist Charles Darwin was born. The place of his birth, Sinking Spring Place, was a farm three miles south of Hodgenville, Kentucky. Lincoln's mother was the former Nancy Hanks, and his father was Thomas Lincoln, both natives of Virginia whose parents had taken them into the Kentucky wilderness at an early age. Thomas Lincoln was a farmer and a carpenter. In the spring of 1811, they moved to the nearby Knob Creek Farm.

The future president had a brother, Thomas, who died in infancy. His sister, Sarah (called Sally), was two years older than he. Much has been made in literature of his log-cabin birth and the poverty and degradation of Lincoln's childhood, but his father—a skilled carpenter— was never abjectly poor. The boy, however, did not aspire to become either a farmer or a carpenter. A highly intelligent and inquisitive youth, he considered many vocations before he decided upon the practice of law.

In Kentucky during his first seven years, and in Indiana until he became an adult, Lincoln received only the rudiments of a formal education, about a year in total. Nevertheless, he was able to read, write, and speak effectively, largely through self-education and regular practice. He grew to be approximately six feet, four inches tall and 185 pounds in weight. He was angular and dark-complected, with features that became familiar to later generations.

Moving with his family to Spencer County, Indiana, in December, 1816, Lincoln learned to use the American long ax efficiently on the Pigeon Creek Farm, where his father constructed another simple log cabin. He grew strong physically, and, largely through books he was able to borrow from neighbors, he grew strong mentally as well. The death of his mother from "the milk sick" in the summer of 1818 left both the boy and his sister emotionally depressed until the arrival of their stepmother, Sarah Bush Johnston Lincoln, from Elizabethtown, Kentucky. This strong and resourceful widow brought love and direction back to Lincoln's life and introduced him to her lively children, Elizabeth, Matilda, and John D. Johnston, then aged twelve, eight, and five, respectively.

While in Indiana, Lincoln was employed in 1827 as a ferryman on Anderson Creek and on the Ohio River into which it flowed. Then, in cooperation with Allen Gentry and at the behest of Gentry's father, he took a flatboat full of goods down the Mississippi River to New Orleans in 1828. Another childhood companion of this time was Lincoln's cousin, Dennis Hanks, who, in his later years, would relate many colorful stories about the future president's boyhood.

In March, 1830, the family moved to central Illinois, where Thomas Lincoln had heard that the farming was superior. They situated their cabin on a stretch of prairie in Macon County, some ten miles west of Decatur. There Lincoln split many rails for fences, although not as many as would later be accredited to the Rail-Splitter. Another nickname he earned in Illinois that would serve him well in his later political career was Honest Abe. His honesty in business dealings became legendary.

Again, in the spring of 1831, Lincoln took a flatboat laden with supplies down the Mississippi River to New Orleans, this time commissioned by Denton Offutt and in the company of John Hanks and John D. Johnston. Hanks would later claim that the sight of a slave auction on this visit to the busy southern city stirred in Lincoln his famous opposition to slavery, but historians now discredit this legend. Upon his return, Lincoln, having reached maturity, struck out on his own for the village of New Salem, Illinois.

Abraham Lincoln. (Library of Congress)

LIFE'S WORK

Lincoln had been promised a store clerk's position in New Salem by Offutt and worked at this task for almost a year before the store "winked out." Then, in the spring of 1832, he served as a captain of volunteers in the Black Hawk War for thirty days. This service was followed by twenty days under Captain Elijah Iles and thirty days under Captain Jacob M. Early as a mounted private seeking to discover the whereabouts of the Indian leader for whom the war was named. While he saw no action, the war soon ended, and Lincoln returned home something less than a war hero.

Immediately upon returning to New Salem, Lincoln threw himself into an election for the lower house of the

Illinois state legislature but, having no reputation, failed to win the seat. He was a loyal supporter of Henry Clay for president and therefore a Whig, but Clay failed also. In desperation, Lincoln became a partner in a store with William Berry, but its failure left him with an eleven-hundred-dollar "national debt." In 1834, however, and in 1836, 1838, and 1840 as well, Lincoln won consecutive terms in the state house of representatives. He also served as postmaster of his village from 1833 to 1836 and as deputy county surveyor from 1833 to 1835. Effective in these roles and being groomed for a leadership position in the legislature by Whigs such as John Todd Stuart, Lincoln studied law and passed the state bar examination in 1836.

New Salem was too small a village to sustain a lawyer, and Lincoln moved to the new capital city of Springfield in April, 1837, to join the law firm of Stuart and Lincoln. This firm was successful, and Lincoln won more cases than he lost, but Stuart wanted to devote more time to his political career. In 1841, the partnership was dissolved, and Lincoln joined, again as junior partner, with the master lawyer Stephen T. Logan. Finally, in 1844, he formed his last partnership, taking on young William H. Herndon as his junior partner.

In 1839, Lincoln met his future wife, Mary Todd, at the home of her sister, Mrs. Ninian Edwards. Lincoln and Edwards were already Whig leaders and members of the influential Long Nine. Lincoln and Todd intended to marry in 1841, but on January of that year, he suffered a nervous breakdown, broke the engagement, and then cemented it again. Their marriage took place at the Edwards home on November 4, 1842. From this union would be born four children: Robert Todd (1843), Edward Baker (1846), William Wallace (1850), and Thomas, called Tad (1853). Lincoln was always a kind and caring husband and father. Their home, purchased in 1844, was located at Eighth and Jackson streets.

When Clay again ran for president in 1844, Lincoln campaigned energetically on his behalf, but Clay was defeated once again. Two years later, Lincoln canvassed the district on his own behalf and won his sole term in the U.S. House of Representatives over the Democrat Peter Cartwright. During this term, which ran from 1847 to 1849, the Mexican War was still in progress, and Lincoln followed the Whig leadership in opposing it. For this decision, he suffered among the voters at home and had to content himself with the single term. Before leaving Washington, however, he patented a device for lifting riverboats over the shoals.

During the early 1850's, Lincoln concentrated upon his legal practice, but perhaps his most famous legal case came much later, in 1858, when he defended Duff Armstrong successfully against a charge of murder. Lincoln was a friend of Duff's parents, Jack and Hannah, and took the case without charging a fee. His use of an almanac in this case to indicate the brightness of the moon on the night of the purported murder is justly celebrated in the annals of courtroom strategy.

The passage of the Kansas-Nebraska Act in 1854 and the Supreme Court decision in the *Dred Scott* case in 1856 aroused Lincoln's antislavery fervor and brought him back into active politics. In 1855, he campaigned as an Anti-Nebraska (later Republican) candidate for the U.S. Senate but was compelled to stand aside in favor of his friend Lyman Trumbull, the eventual victor. A year later, Lincoln campaigned on behalf of presidential candidate John C. Frémont. Then, in 1858, he contended with his archrival, Stephen A. Douglas, for another Senate seat.

Before engaging in the famous debates with Douglas, Lincoln gave his most famous speech to date at Springfield, in which he proclaimed, "A house divided against itself cannot stand . . . this government cannot endure permanently half slave and half free." This House Divided Speech set the tone for his antislavery attacks in the debates that followed. Lincoln was a Free-Soiler and was truly outraged by Douglas's amoral stance on slavery. Many observers thought that Lincoln had won the debates, but largely because of a pro-Democratic apportionment, Douglas won reelection. Nevertheless, the fame Lincoln achieved through these debates assured his consideration for a presidential nomination in 1860.

THE GETTYSBURG ADDRESS

One of the most famous speeches in American history, Abraham Lincoln's Gettysburg Address is noted for the brevity and poignancy of its language and for the fact that it paid tribute to the fallen of both the North and the South, while expressing faith in the ultimate preservation of the Union.

Fourscore and seven years ago our fathers brought forth on this continent a new nation, conceived in liberty and dedicated to the proposition that all men are created equal.

Now we are engaged in a great civil war, testing whether that nation or any nation so conceived and so dedicated can long endure. We are met on a great battle field of that war. We have come to dedicate a portion of that field, as a final resting place for those who here gave their lives that that nation might live. It is altogether fitting and proper that we should do this.

But, in a larger sense, we can not dedicate—we can not consecrate—we can not hallow—this ground. The brave men living and dead, who struggled here, have consecrated it, far above our poor power to add or detract. The world will little note, nor long remember, what we say here, but it will never forget what they did here. It is for this the living, rather, to be dedicated here to the unfinished work which they who fought here have thus far so nobly advanced. It is rather for us to be here dedicated to the great task remaining before us—that from these honored dead we take increased devotion to that cause for which they gave the last full measure of devotion—that we here highly resolve that these dead shall not have died in vain—that this nation, under God, shall have a new birth of freedom—and that government of the people, by the people, for the people, shall not perish from the earth.

The Republican Convention of that year was held in Chicago, where Lincoln was especially popular. Then, too, the original leading candidates, William Seward and Salmon Chase, detested each other; accordingly, their delegates turned to Lincoln as a "dark horse" when their favorites destroyed each other's chances. The Democrats then split their support with the dual nominations of Stephen A. Douglas and John C. Breckinridge. What was left of the old Whig Party split the South further by nominating as the Constitutional Union nominee John Bell of Tennessee.

Lincoln grew the dark beard associated with him during his campaign. He did not campaign actively but was elected over his divided opposition with 173 electoral votes, while Breckinridge amassed 72, Bell 39, and Douglas merely 12. Lincoln had the necessary majority of the electoral college but did not have a majority of the popular votes—no one did. The division in the country at large was made even more coldly clear when seven southern states seceded over his election.

Inaugurated March 4, 1861, Lincoln took a strong stand against secession; when newly armed Confederate troops fired upon and captured Fort Sumter on April 12-13, 1861, he announced the start of the Civil War by calling for seventy-five thousand volunteers and a naval blockade of the southern coast. Four more states then seceded, and the War Between the States began in earnest, lasting four years.

During the war, President Lincoln often visited the fighting front, intercepted telegraphic messages at the War Department, and advised his generals as to strategy. He was a remarkably able wartime leader, but he was deeply dissatisfied with his highest-ranking generals in the field until he "found his general" in Ulysses S. Grant.

In the midst of the struggle, Lincoln drafted his Emancipation Proclamation, calling for the freedom of the slaves. A few months later, in 1863, he wrote and delivered his most famous speech, the Gettysburg Address. This speech summed up the principles for which the federal government still fought to preserve the Union. Upon being reelected in 1864, over Democratic nominee General George B. McClellan, the president gave another stirring speech in his Second Inaugural Address. Final victory was achieved only after the defeat of Confederate general Robert E. Lee's Army of Northern Virginia at Appomattox Courthouse on April 9, 1865. Less than a week later, on April 14, Lincoln was assassinated by the southern partisan actor John Wilkes Booth at Ford's Theatre in Washington, expiring the following morning.

Secretary of War Edwin Stanton then was heard to say: "Now he belongs to the ages."

SIGNIFICANCE

More books have been written about Lincoln and more legends have been told about him than about any other individual in American history. This sixteenth president often is regarded as the greatest leader the United States has yet produced or is likely to produce, yet he came from humble stock, and little was given him that he had not earned.

Lincoln was the first Republican president, was twice elected, and had to fight a cruel war yet remained sensitive, humble, and magnanimous to the end. It was his intention, had he lived, to "bind up the nation's wounds" with a speedy and liberal method of reconstruction. His death assured the opposite, or Radical Reconstruction.

Lincoln's greatest achievements were the preservation of the federal Union and the liberation of the slaves. The former was achieved with the cessation of fighting in the South, which came only days after his death. The latter was brought about at last by the Thirteenth Amendment to the Constitution a few months later. However, the nobility and simple dignity that he brought to the nation's highest office are also a part of his legacy.

—*Joseph E. Suppiger*

FURTHER READING

Donald, David Herbert. *Lincoln*. New York: Simon & Schuster, 1995. A definitive, best-selling biography. Donald portrays Lincoln as ambitious, often defeated, and tormented by a difficult marriage, yet having a remarkable capacity for growth and the ability to hold the nation together during the Civil War.

Gienapp, William E. *Abraham Lincoln and Civil War America: A Biography*. New York: Oxford University Press, 2002. All but seventy pages of this biography deal with Lincoln's public and private life during his years in the White House. The book describes his handling of the Civil War, depicting him as a shrewd politician and an extraordinary military commander.

Guelzo, Allen C. *Lincoln's Emancipation Proclamation: The End of Slavery in America*. New York: Simon & Schuster, 2004. Examines how and why Lincoln persuaded himself to issue the proclamation, portraying him as a man with an inordinate understanding of his fellow citizens and the needs of the nation.

Herndon, William H. *Herndon's Lincoln: The True Story of a Great Life*. 3 vols. Chicago: Belford, Clarke,

1889. The color and dash of Lincoln's law partner almost make up for his lack of objectivity. Herndon is strongest when he speaks from experience, weakest when he deals with Lincoln's early years and personal relationships.

Kunhardt, Philip B., Jr. *New Birth of Freedom: Lincoln at Gettysburg*. Boston: Little, Brown, 1983. A concentrated examination of the background and circumstances of Lincoln's greatest speech, the Gettysburg Address. Vivid in the memory of a nation, this speech was considered a failure at the time by the president himself. Well written and beautifully illustrated, the book itself is one of the more important works dealing with a segment of Lincoln's life.

Lamon, Ward Hill. *The Life of Abraham Lincoln*. Boston: J. R. Osgood, 1872. Lincoln's longtime friend, fellow attorney, and marshal of the District of Columbia knew him well but was not particular about his sources. Certainly he relied too heavily upon Herndon's fulminations about the Ann Rutledge love affair (a myth) and Lincoln's stormy marriage to the former Mary Todd.

Nicolay, John G., and John Hay. *Abraham Lincoln: A History*. 10 vols. New York: Century, 1890. This major production is based upon Lincoln's personal papers but is rather laudatory. There is, perhaps, too much detail and too little insight in these volumes.

Oates, Stephen B. *With Malice Toward None*. New York: Harper & Row, 1977. An excellent scholarly biography, reflecting much new research. It is well written and well documented.

Sandburg, Carl. *Abraham Lincoln: The Prairie Years*. 2 vols. New York: Harcourt, Brace & World, 1926.

_____. *Abraham Lincoln: The War Years*. 4 vols. New York: Harcourt, Brace & World, 1939. These two sets are beautifully poetic but lacking in historical accuracy at times. Many readers have started with Sandburg, gained a sense for the subject, and gone on to develop a profound love of Lincolniana.

Thomas, Benjamin. *Abraham Lincoln*. New York: Alfred A. Knopf, 1952. One of the finest biographies of Lincoln available, combining a balanced scholarly-popular approach in one volume. It is a must for any shelf of Lincoln books.

Vidal, Gore. *Lincoln*. New York: Random House, 1984. The most celebrated novel yet written about Lincoln's presidential years. Well worth reading by those who would gain an understanding of his actions. Without psychoanalysis or unfettered pathos, Vidal has portrayed Lincoln and his wartime contemporaries with exceptional accuracy, taking only a few liberties with history.

SEE ALSO: Salmon P. Chase; Henry Clay; Stephen A. Douglas; John C. Frémont; Ulysses S. Grant; John Hay; Robert E. Lee; Mary Todd Lincoln; William H. Seward; Edwin M. Stanton.

RELATED ARTICLES in *Great Events from History: The Nineteenth Century, 1801-1900:* June 16-October 15, 1858: Lincoln-Douglas Debates; November 6, 1860: Lincoln Is Elected U.S. President; February 8, 1861: Establishment of the Confederate States of America; March 4, 1861: Lincoln Is Inaugurated President; January 1, 1863: Lincoln Issues the Emancipation Proclamation; March 3, 1863: Union Enacts the First National Draft Law; April 9 and 14, 1865: Surrender at Appomattox and Assassination of Lincoln.

MARY TODD LINCOLN
American First Lady

As the First Lady of the United States, Lincoln contributed to the survival of the Union cause during the Civil War. Her greatest strength was her political acumen in handling President Abraham Lincoln's political affairs.

BORN: December 13, 1818; Lexington, Kentucky
DIED: July 16, 1882; Springfield, Illinois
ALSO KNOWN AS: Mary Ann Todd (birth name)
AREA OF ACHIEVEMENT: Government and politics

EARLY LIFE

Mary Todd Lincoln was the fourth child of Robert S. Todd, a prominent Kentucky merchant, and Eliza Parker Todd. When Mary was six, her mother died from fever after childbirth. A year later, her father married Elizabeth Betsy Humphreys of Frankfort, Kentucky. Mary's new stepmother proved to be a very critical person, and Mary struggled in vain to win her approval, while her father busied himself with his store and was not around to provide encouragement. Feelings of abandonment would later become a reoccurring theme in Mary's life.

Mary's family belonged to the Lexington, Kentucky, aristocracy, and she received a good private education for a woman during the mid-nineteenth century. As she grew up, she became an excellent conversationalist and learned to speak French fluently. She stood only five feet, two inches in height when she reached maturity and had blue eyes, brown hair, and a fair complexion. She became active in southern social circles and was known for her vivacious personality, her love of fine things, her dancing, and her quick wit. At the age of twenty-one, she moved to Springfield, Illinois, to live with her older sister, Elizabeth, the wife of Ninian W. Edwards, the son of a former governor of the state.

In Springfield, Mary met Abraham Lincoln at a dance. Nine years her senior, Lincoln was an aspiring lawyer. After a lengthy courtship, marked by a broken engagement at one time during their relationship, they married on November 4, 1842. The couple proved to be opposites in temperament and physical appearance. The tall, gaunt Lincoln was introspective, socially awkward, and quiet, whereas Mary was extroverted, charming, and sometimes quite selfish. The marriage produced four sons: Robert Todd (born in 1843), Edward Baker (1846), William Wallace (1850), and Thomas "Tad" (1853). However, only Robert survived to adulthood. Mary her-

self faced several losses during this period. Her father died in 1849, and her son Edward died a year later from diphtheria.

LIFE'S WORK

Mary was ambitious. Realizing her husband's potential to climb the social ladder after he served in the Illinois legislature, she supported him in his endeavor to enter national politics, especially in his bid for one of Illinois's seats in the U.S. Senate, which he contested with Stephen A. Douglas in 1858. When Lincoln was elected president of the United States in 1860, Mary achieved her greatest goal in life. However, her life did not turn out as expected in the capital city, and heartache continued to follow her. As First Lady, she was publicly criticized for her lavish spending on parties and for redecorating the White House.

After Mary exceeded her allotted congressional budget for White House expenses, newspaper reporters dubbed her the "Republican Queen." On many occasions, she stated in her defense that the parties she staged were necessary to help relieve the emotional pressures caused by the Civil War, in which the nation was immersed throughout her husband's presidency. Although charges of disloyalty to the Union on her part were unfounded, her family connections to the South made some in the Washington elite suspect she was a Confederate sympathizer. Her sharp tongue and frequent temper tantrums also caused many people to turn against her over time. Her contemptuous manner alienated wives of other Washington officials as well.

Despite the public criticisms she received, Mary frequently visited military hospitals, comforting wounded soldiers with food and flowers and by reading to them. On one occasion, she raised one thousand dollars for a Christmas dinner in their honor. She also held fundraising events for the Contraband Relief Association to help former slaves after hearing about their plight from her good friend Elizabeth Keckley.

Mary's fragile mental and physical condition worsened after the death of her third son, twelve-year-old William, in 1862 and the loss of three stepbrothers during the war. As her mounting grief caused her to curtail social entertaining at the White House, her critics then charged that she was not fulfilling her social duties as First Lady. The assassination of her husband on April 14/ 15, 1865, caused her to have a complete mental and phys-

Mary Todd Lincoln. (Library of Congress)

ical collapse. She was with her husband at Ford's Theatre when he was shot by John Wilkes Booth.

After her husband's death, Mary spent several years obsessed with money. Convinced that she was becoming poverty stricken, she sold her wardrobe through New York dealers and then petitioned Congress for a larger widow's annuity. She spent three years living with her sons Robert and Tad. After Robert married, she and her youngest son moved to Europe. They returned to the United States in 1871, but Mary again became grief stricken when Tad died in July, at the age of eighteen, from a respiratory infection.

Over the next several years, Mary's mental health declined further, and she eventually fell into a deep depression. She continued to have illusions that her wealth was diminishing. Finally, Robert, her only surviving son, took her to court to have her declared legally insane in 1875. The jury agreed, and Robert had his mother placed in a private sanitarium called Bellevue in Batavia, Illinois. She was released four months later, and another jury found her sane the next year. Mary then went to live in Pau, a French town near the Pyrenees that was re-

nowned for its health spas, but she returned to the United States in 1880. Mary again went to live with her sister's family in Springfield, Illinois, where she died from a stroke on July 16, 1882, at the age of sixty-three. She was buried beside her husband in the Lincoln Tomb at Oak Ridge Cemetery in Springfield.

SIGNIFICANCE

Scholars often portray Mary Todd Lincoln as a tragic and much-maligned figure whose personal manner was constrained by nineteenth century mores. However, Mary's neuroses and selfishness contributed to her demise physically and mentally. Her intrusive nature as First Lady only served to upset key members of her husband's administration. She often believed that her personal tragedies outweighed those of other people who had experienced the same trials and tribulations.

Mary's most significant contribution was her unfailing support for her husband in his abilities and talents as a politician. She helped lift him to national political prominence by writing letters of endorsement, entertaining important figures, and offering cogent advice. Her help was especially important during his 1860 presidential election. She also proved to be a comforting influence for Abraham, and most important, helped ensure the stability of the Union.

—Gayla Koerting

FURTHER READING

Baker, Jean H. *Mary Todd Lincoln: A Biography*. New York: W. W. Norton, 1987. Biography that argues that Mary was a tragic figure, a victim of the nineteenth century social, political, and cultural constraints placed upon women.

_____. "Mary Todd Lincoln: Civil War First Lady." *White House Studies* 2, no. 1 (2002): 73-82. Brief overview of Mary's life, focusing on her actions as First Lady. Baker recounts her accomplishments and emotional problems that plagued Mary throughout her life.

Foster, Frances Smith, ed. *Behind the Scenes: Formerly a Slave, but More Recently Modiste, and a Friend to Mrs. Lincoln—Or, Thirty Years a Slave and Four Years in the White House*. Urbana: University of Illinois Press, 2001. This book is a reprint edition of an 1868 memoir by Elizabeth Keckley, a former slave who was a close personal friend of Mary Todd Lincoln. Keckley was the president of the Contraband Relief Association.

Neely, Mark E., and R. Gerald McMurtry. *The Insanity File: The Case of Mary Todd Lincoln*. Carbondale: Southern Illinois University Press, 1986. Case study of Mary's insanity trial from a social and legal history perspective that closely examines the Illinois sanity law.

Randall, Ruth Painter. *Mary Lincoln: Biography of a Marriage*. Boston: Little, Brown, 1953. Sympathetic biography of Mary that dispels many of the myths about her found in the memoir of William H. Herndon, a law partner of Abraham Lincoln who disliked Mary and published an unflattering account of her in 1889.

Schreiner, Samuel. *Trials of Mrs. Lincoln*. Lincoln: University of Nebraska Press, 2005. Schreiner describes how Lincoln was tried and judged insane by a jury. He describes his subject as a much-maligned woman whose eccentric behavior made her a burden to her husband and son.

Turner, Justin G., and Linda Levitt Turner. *Mary Todd Lincoln: Her Life and Letters*. New York: Alfred A. Knopf, 1972. Collection of 609 letters written by Mary to friends, creditors, and politicians.

Van der Heuvel, Gerry. *Crowns of Thorns and Glory: Mary Todd Lincoln and Varina Howell Davis: The Two First Ladies of the Civil War*. New York: E. P. Dutton, 1988. Examinaton of the lives of the wives of the presidents of the Union and the Confederacy during the Civil War. The author contends that Mary's volatile personality was her own worst enemy, overshadowing her wit and intelligence.

Winkler, H. Donald. *The Women in Lincoln's Life*. Nashville, Tenn.: Rutledge Hill Press, 2001. Study of the women who influenced Abraham Lincoln's life that concludes that his marriage to Mary was his "greatest tragedy."

SEE ALSO: Stephen A. Douglas; Abraham Lincoln; Dolley Madison.

RELATED ARTICLE in *Great Events from History: The Nineteenth Century, 1801-1900:* February 8, 1861: Establishment of the Confederate States of America.

JENNY LIND
Swedish singer

Through perseverance, hard work, and a uniquely charismatic personality, the "Swedish Nightingale," as Lind was known, became the most famous female singer of the nineteenth century, an internationally successful touring star, and a role model for her generation.

BORN: October 6, 1820; Stockholm, Sweden
DIED: November 2, 1887; Wynds Point, Herefordshire, England
ALSO KNOWN AS: Johanna Maria Lind (birth name)
AREA OF ACHIEVEMENT: Music

EARLY LIFE
Jenny Lind was born Johanna Maria Lind. Her parents, Anne-Marie Fellborg and Niclas Jonas Lind, lived together but did not choose to marry until their daughter was fifteen. For this reason, Jenny was placed in a foster home. Although considerate of her parents in later years, she was more devoted to her grandmother, who had instilled in her the spiritual values that would become a major part of her life.

After Lind's precocious singing ability was discovered by a member of the Swedish Royal Opera, she was

admitted to the court theater school at the age of nine. Her first major role was the part of Agathe in Carl Maria von Weber's opera *Der Freischütz* (1821; the marksman) at the Stockholm Opera on March 7, 1838. In 1840 Lind became a member of the Royal Swedish Academy of Music with the rank of court singer. Recognizing that her voice needed more extensive and better training, however, in 1841 she left to study in Paris, France, with vocal instructor Manuel García, Jr., brother of the famous early nineteenth century diva Maria García Malibran and son of the singer and impresario who had introduced Italian opera to the United States in 1825. After one year of intensive training with García, who was considered the world's greatest teacher of singing, Lind returned home and resumed her operatic career, which would last nineteen years.

LIFE'S WORK
In 1844 Lind began an extensive and successful European tour that included performances in Berlin, Hamburg, Cologne, Vienna, Copenhagen, and London. In addition to being a technically brilliant coloratura soprano with a range of two and three-quarters octaves and having perfect pitch, she impressed almost all of her contem-

poraries with her piety, simplicity, and instinctive dislike of celebrity. Her generous donations to charity wherever she performed also made her a unique symbol of virtue and goodness. The public had found a new heroine, and Lindomania soon swept Europe. Despite enthusiastic accounts by the press and large crowds wherever she appeared, Lind grew tired of theatrical life and chose to retire from the operatic stage in May, 1849, after more than six hundred performances in thirty operas. For the more than thirty years remaining in her professional life, she sang in oratorios and concerts.

Lind was not a beautiful woman; although she had typical Nordic blond hair and blue eyes, she had plain features with a broad mouth and wide nose. Some of her portraits were even enhanced to make her appear more romantically appealing. However, her remarkable charismatic stage presence transcended mere physical attractiveness. Dressed simply in blue or white and carrying flowers, this rather ordinary looking young woman seemed to many concertgoers to become an angelic being as soon as she began to sing. Along with a magnificent voice, she possessed a unique ability to make an emotional connection to her audiences.

In 1850 American impresario Phineas Taylor Barnum persuaded Lind to undertake a tour of the United States and Cuba. Despite his career as a showman of curiosities such as the midget Tom Thumb and overt frauds such as the Feejee Mermaid (a combination of a dead monkey and a fish), Barnum appreciated culture and genuinely admired Lind, and his offer was generous. For each concert, Lind would receive one thousand dollars plus all her expenses; she would choose the music to be performed and was allowed to give charity concerts when she wished. Barnum also agreed to manage her publicity, secure her lodgings and concert sites, and make other technical arrangements. Along with his potential profits, Barnum would gain respectability and even admiration as the man who brought Europe's greatest singer to the United States. The contract was signed in January, 1850, and on August 21, Lind and her entourage of eight, including a companion, her secretary, her pianist and musical director, servants, and her pet dog, left Liverpool, England, to begin a concert tour that lasted until May 27, 1852.

Enthralled by the sometimes fanciful accounts of her life in newspapers and literary magazines, a crowd of about thirty thousand people was waiting on the pier when Lind's party reached New York on September 1, 1850. She toured the city and gave concerts during most of September; the profits from two of these performances, a

sum of more than ten thousand dollars, were designated for charity. Lind then moved on to Boston and Philadelphia, where again she sang to capacity crowds.

At each stop, Barnum had arranged for the first few tickets to the opening performance to be auctioned to the highest bidders, a scheme that pitted individuals and even cities against each other; it was a publicity ploy that Lind disliked. The highest bidder in Philadelphia, for example, paid $625 for his ticket, although most seats could be purchased for three to seven dollars each. In Boston a young working girl purchased one of the cheaper tickets, declaring, "there goes half a month's earnings, but I am determined to hear Jenny Lind." On being told this, Lind asked her secretary to give her admirer a twenty-dollar gold piece. Similar acts of kindness in other cities and her well-publicized charity concerts illustrated not only Lind's generosity but also Barnum's media skills. He also approved of the marketing of a variety of items with her name, including Jenny Lind coats, hats, sewing machines, singing tea kettles, cigars, pianos, sofas, and bed frames.

Jenny Lind. (Library of Congress)

To appeal to large general audiences, Lind's concerts were a blend of several different types of music, a tradition that dated from at least the late eighteenth century. Along with overtures and arias from her popular operatic roles—including Vincenzo Bellini's *La sonnambula* (1831; the sleepwalker) and *Norma* (1831), Gaetano Donizetti's *Lucia di Lammermoor* (1835), Giacomo Meyerbeer's *Robert le Diable* (1831), Weber's *Der Freischütz*, and Wolfgang Amadeus Mozart's *Don Giovanni* (1787) and *Le nozze di Figaro* (1786; the marriage of Figaro)—were excerpts from sacred works, especially George Frideric Handel's *The Messiah* (1742) and Franz Joseph Haydn's *Die Schöpfung* (1798; the creation). Light popular songs such as "Home, Sweet Home" and "Echo Song," and settings of Robert Burns's "John Anderson, My Jo" and "Comin' Thro' the Rye" were always part of her programs. Lind knew instinctively that these simpler pieces would be more meaningful to many in her audience, however splendidly the classical works displayed the remarkable qualities of her voice.

In 1850 and 1851 Lind gave concerts in Baltimore; Washington; several southern cities, including Richmond, Charleston, and New Orleans; Havana, Cuba; and the Midwest, including St. Louis, Louisville, and Cincinnati. Her last (and ninety-fifth) performance before she terminated her contract with Barnum to develop her own touring schedule was held in Philadelphia's National Theater on June 9, 1851.

Now independent, Lind reorganized her troupe and revisited a number of cities in the North, the Midwest, and New England. In December, however, news of her mother's death temporarily halted the concert series. On February 5, 1852, she married her pianist and musical director Otto Goldschmidt, whom she had first met while touring in Europe. Though her concerts had brought her increased wealth, much of which she continued to give to charity, she was growing tired of traveling; after three final concerts in New York in May, 1852, the couple returned to Europe in early June.

With Lind's marriage, the adulation of the press became more subdued, but her international popularity remained. The Goldschmidts lived briefly in Dresden but in 1856 settled permanently in England. They had three children, one of whom wrote a biography of her mother (1926). Lind gave her last concert in 1880. Like many retired performers of the time, she became a teacher. Beginning in 1876, she devoted her energies to the Bach Choir founded and directed by her husband, and from 1883 to 1886, she was professor of singing at London's Royal College of Music. After a long illness, Lind died on November 2, 1887.

SIGNIFICANCE

Although Jenny Lind was the nineteenth century's most famous vocal star and was admired by millions of people, she was not above criticism. She was occasionally faulted for high ticket prices and her association with Barnum, and a few critics thought that her concert choices lacked originality or that she was excessively religious. Though shy and prone to stage fright, she was resolute where her performances were concerned; she won over a hostile audience who hissed her first Havana concert, and after a drunken crowd outside the performance hall spoiled her first visit to Pittsburgh, she returned for a successful second engagement.

No one disputed her commercial success. Barnum, with Lind's somewhat reluctant help, launched the first successful large-scale promotion of a performer. Music publishers profited handsomely from her fame, and several later singers began their careers as "new" Jenny Linds. Her programs of arias by composers she preferred, balanced by Scottish, British, and Swedish folk melodies, reinforced a long English and American tradition of shared popular culture that could be enjoyed by rich and poor alike. A hallmark of her success was that Lind was more than a splendid singer; she was a person with whom ordinary individuals could identify and whose lifestyle they could genuinely respect.

—*Dorothy T. Potter*

FURTHER READING

Barnum, Phineas Taylor. *Struggles and Triumphs: Or, Forty Years' Recollections of P. T. Barnum*. Buffalo, N.Y.: Warren, Johnson, 1871. Reprint. New York: Penguin Books, 1987. Ever the showman, Barnum tells a good story, and it is useful to read his version of his relationship with Lind because he was frequently accused of exploiting her for commercial purposes.

Dizikes, John. *Opera in America: A Cultural History*. New Haven, Conn.: Yale University Press, 1993. This comprehensive (612 pages) history of opera and its influence on American culture includes a chapter on Lind's American tour as well as references throughout the work. Dizikes's book is particularly helpful in placing the singer within the context of her time. It contains bibliographical notes and numerous illustrations.

Saxon, A. H. *P. T. Barnum: The Legend and the Man*. New York: Columbia University Press, 1989. In dealing specifically with Lind's career in relationship to

Barnum, this biography is more critical than most of the singer's personality, motivations, and failings, therefore providing a corrective to other more complimentary accounts. It contains valuable annotated notes and illustrations.

Schultz, Gladys Denny. *Jenny Lind, the Swedish Nightingale*. Philadelphia: Lippincott, 1962. This pleasantly written account deals not only with Lind's successes but also with the hardships in her early life and how she managed to overcome them. However, some aspects of the singer's life have been fictionalized, thus marring an otherwise interesting study.

Wagenknecht, Edward Charles. *Jenny Lind*. Boston: Houghton Mifflin, 1931. This brief (231 pages) biography considers Lind not only as a performer but also as a woman whose primary motivation was her spiritual life, for which she left the operatic stage to devote herself to concerts, oratorios, and eventually her marriage. It contains an extensive bibliography of articles and books about Lind.

_____. *Seven Daughters of the Theater*. Norman: University of Oklahoma Press, 1964. Lind's biography is the first in this series of famous women singers, actors, and dancers. Although Wagenknecht's account of Lind includes much material from his earlier full-length study, its juxtaposition with six related biographies provides a valuable study in contrasts.

Ware, W. Porter, and Thaddeus C. Lockard, Jr. *P. T. Barnum Presents Jenny Lind: The American Tour of the Swedish Nightingale*. Baton Rouge: Louisiana State University Press, 1980. This laudatory biography is one of the more recent studies of the singer. Focusing primarily on Lind's reception in America, it includes a number of useful reviews and descriptions of her and her concerts by contemporaries.

SEE ALSO: Hans Christian Andersen; P. T. Barnum; Gaetano Donizetti; Carl Maria von Weber.

RELATED ARTICLES in *Great Events from History: The Nineteenth Century, 1801-1900:* c. 1801-1850: Professional Theaters Spread Throughout America; April 10, 1871: Barnum Creates the First Modern American Circus.

JOSEPH LISTER
English physician

Combining skill as a laboratory scientist with great technical ability at surgery, Lister developed and helped to propagate antiseptic surgery, which fundamentally changed surgical procedures and saved uncounted lives.

BORN: April 5, 1827; Upton, Essex, England
DIED: February 10, 1912; Walmer, Kent, England
ALSO KNOWN AS: Baron Lister; Sir Joseph Lister
AREA OF ACHIEVEMENT: Medicine

EARLY LIFE

Joseph Lister was born in a town just east of London. His parents, Joseph Jackson and Isabella Lister, were Quakers, and the family—there were six children—was unusually close. Lister's father owned a prosperous wine business and was a scientist in his own right. His development of the achromatic lens made a significant improvement in the microscope, and he became a Fellow of the Royal Society. Paternal example helped Lister develop an interest in and skill at scientific investigation.

After his primary education in Quaker schools, Lister entered University College, London, the only option for non-Anglicans interested in medicine. Unlike most mid-nineteenth century medical students, Lister first studied for an arts degree. Then, following a brief bout with nervous problems, he began the study of medicine, taking his degree in 1852. He won a number of prizes for scholarship, served as house physician and surgeon at University Hospital, and became a fellow of the Royal College of Surgeons of England. Lister's decision to be a surgeon was an unlikely one, for with anesthesia being then only recently developed and the problems of infection still ill-understood, surgery was a brutal and little-respected specialty.

Two professors had significant influence on Lister. Wharton Jones, who did important work on blood circulation and inflammation, inspired an interest in the nature of inflammation that was important in the eventual understanding of infection. William Sharpey, one of the first modern physiologists, not only gave the young Lister a solid foundation in his field but also, when asked about the best way to get more experience, suggested visits to Edinburgh and the Continent. He also provided an introduction to James Syme, whose work at Edinburgh had made him the most distinguished surgeon in Great Britain and perhaps all of Europe.

Lister's visit to Edinburgh, planned for a month, lasted seven years, a period during which he completed his apprenticeship and began his career in earnest. His relationship with Syme was quickly one of friendship and mutual respect. He accepted a position as Syme's house surgeon, an unusually modest post for a man of his credentials. His willingness to serve as Syme's assistant seems to have reflected Lister's sincere desire to learn more, humility arising from his Quaker background, and perhaps some personal inclination. He not only found Syme extremely congenial but also married Syme's daughter, Agnes, in 1856. The match proved excellent. Agnes Syme Lister was better educated than most Victorian women, and she discussed and even helped her husband with his scientific work. The two, though sorry that they never had children, were devoted to each other until her death during an 1893 European tour.

In 1856, a year after Lister was made lecturer on surgery at the Edinburgh School of Medicine, he was appointed assistant surgeon at the Royal Infirmary. Scottish medicine had for years been at the intellectual forefront of the field, and so for Lister maturing in that country was, if not socially a plus, an excellent opportunity.

The mature Lister was taller than average, well built, and strong. As he aged, he tended to stoutness and wore "muttonchop" whiskers, shaving his chin and around his mouth. Contemporaries reported that he always gave an impression of health and vigor. In manner he was reserved and proper. Although he was unusually thoughtful of and kind to patients, his students gave him the nickname "the Chief" and did not find him particularly approachable. His manner appears to have been a mixture of his Quaker heritage—although he left the Society of Friends when he married outside it—and a natural shyness. His personality, combined with a strict forthrightness, did not help win supporters for his antiseptic theory.

LIFE'S WORK

Although identified with his later development of antiseptic surgery, Lister began serious scholarly work promptly after graduation—he published his first article in 1853—and continued research while working with Syme. In 1857, he made a presentation concerning inflammation to the Royal Society, though he had not yet begun to include infection as part of this work. Such experimentation was unusual for surgeons of the period.

In 1860, Lister, with eleven published research papers to his credit, was appointed surgeon at the Glasgow Royal Infirmary and elected a fellow of the Royal Society. His research expanded to the coagulation of blood, about which he gave a major address to the Royal Society in 1863. Over the next two years, the theory that was to dominate the rest of his life was developed. He became acquainted with the work of the French chemist Louis Pasteur concerning fermentation. This led to experiments testing whether putrefaction occurred in substances that air could not reach and the conclusion that hospital infections such as gangrene were caused by microbes in the air or on the hands and instruments of doctors and nurses. He decided that the cycle could be broken by the introduction of a proper antiseptic, and knowing that carbolic acid had been used to purify sewers at Carlisle, he decided to try a dilute mixture on the first appropriate case that came under his care.

Lister first used antiseptics on compound fractures. Such injuries were routinely treated by amputation because setting them almost inevitably resulted in blood poisoning and/or gangrene, and though the stump left after amputation almost always became infected, because the wound could drain, the patient sometimes survived. Using carbolic acid first directly in the wound and later increasingly as part of the dressing to exclude germs, Lister found that such fractures could be treated usually with no infection at all. Between March and July of 1867, *Lancet* carried in five installments the report of Lister's initial antiseptic treatments. Because of Lister's modest claims and the profession's conservatism about innovation, antiseptic surgery was initially taken as a method for the specific treatment of compound fractures rather than a general principle.

Over the next twenty years, Lister struggled to refine the antiseptic procedure and persuade his skeptical and sometimes self-serving colleagues to adopt it. His work ranged from such physiological studies as the importance of blood clots in healing to investigation of ligatures to replace the previously used silk and linen, which had to be pulled out of the wound once ulceration loosened them, often causing secondary hemorrhaging. He found that catgut treated with carbolic acid to prevent the passage of infection into the wound was absorbed by the body. In 1869, Lister returned to Edinburgh to replace Syme, who was ill and going into retirement, as Regius Professor of Clinical Surgery at the University of Edinburgh and Surgeon to the Royal Infirmary.

During the early 1870's, Lister began to use a spray made with carbolic acid to keep the air clean any time a wound was exposed and began to search for dressings that would be an effective barrier to infection. By the late 1880's, he had settled on gauze impregnated with cyanide of mercury and zinc. Although the spray was unpleasant and soon lost favor—Lister dropped it himself in 1887—its use coincided with increasing reduction of the use of carbolic acid in the wound itself, presaging the development of aseptic surgical techniques in the twentieth century.

Lister's wards were the healthiest in Edinburgh, as healthy as they had been in Glasgow, and he continued to expand his repertoire of operations. He was successfully applying surgical treatments to cases that would not have even been accepted into hospitals only a few years before. It is sad to note that his fame spread on the Continent—his wards were being visited by European surgeons by 1872—long before his British colleagues gave his techniques much more than scorn.

James Simpson, well known and respected for his introduction of anesthesia into the British Isles, had concluded that hospital infections could best be prevented by frequent replacement of facilities. He advocated quickly built wooden hospitals that could be abandoned when infections became rampant, and he acquired his considerable prestige not only in advancing his own ideas but also in deprecating those of Lister. Poorly conducted experiments with antiseptics, of course, failed, and the annoyed Lister resisted publication of much of his work lest it lead to more harm than good. Students and others who worked closely with Lister personally began slowly to spread the corrected antiseptic technique.

In 1877, Lister was invited to become Professor of Clinical Surgery at King's College in London. He was reluctant to leave Edinburgh, where he had become popular—his students organized a petition begging him to remain—and his fame was secure, but he felt duty-bound to go because London was the professional center of the country. Success in London would mean that his antiseptic techniques would gain a wide audience in short order, and thus he accepted the position, also becoming Surgeon to King's College Hospital.

Within a decade, Lister was a dominant figure in British medicine. Honors followed thick and fast. In 1883, he was created a baronet, and in 1897, he was raised to the peerage as Baron Lister. He retired from teaching in 1892 and private practice in 1896 but served as president of the Royal Society from 1895 to 1900. In 1896 and 1897, he helped reorganize the Jenner Institute of Pre-

ventive Medicine, which he had helped to found and that was later renamed the Lister Institute of Preventive Medicine. In 1902, Lister was selected as an original member of the Order of Merit, founded by King Edward VII, but in the following year he fell ill and was an invalid until his death on February 10, 1912.

SIGNIFICANCE

In many ways, Joseph Lister typified the Victorian era. Driven by the Nonconformist ethic calling for hard work and service, he also had the British genius for technology. Choosing to be a surgeon at a time when surgeons' most prized skill was speed at completing a procedure before the shock of the operation killed the unanesthetized patient and when infection killed many of those who survived surgery, he transformed the profession. Lister recognized the value of anesthesia and was among the first to slow his operations, preferring precision to speed. He then took advantage of scientific discoveries—his own but to a greater degree those of Pasteur—to develop antiseptic surgical techniques. The nineteenth century was a time when British manufacturers were preeminent in applying science to practice in the name of profit; Lister, in much the same way, applied it to the easing of human suffering.

—*Fred R. van Hartesveldt*

FURTHER READING

Cartwright, Frederick Fox. *Joseph Lister: The Man Who Made Surgery Safe*. London: Weidenfeld & Nicolson, 1963. Well written but based largely on secondary sources.

Cheyne, Sir William W. *Lister and His Achievement*. London: Longmans, Green, 1925. Written by a house surgeon and admirer of Lister. Includes a summary of Lister's life and a longer appendix appraising his work.

Dormandy, Thomas. *Moments of Truth: Four Creators of Modern Medicine*. Hoboken, N.J.: Wiley, 2003. Part 3 of this medical history book focuses on Lister and the development of antiseptic surgery.

Fisher, Richard B. *Joseph Lister*. New York: Stein & Day, 1977. A scholarly, well-researched biography, though a bit dry in style.

Gaw, Jerry L. *"A Time to Heal": The Diffusion of Listerism in Victorian Britain*. Philadelphia: American Philosophical Society, 1999. Examines several factors that helped spread Lister's antiseptic surgery techniques in mid-nineteenth century Britain. Those factors include medical administration, social interpretation, national competition, and experimental investigation. Aimed at readers with some technical knowledge of medicine.

Godlee, Sir Rickman John. *Lord Lister*. Oxford, England: Clarendon Press, 1924. A typical late-Victorian biography written by Lister's nephew. Includes much of Lister's correspondence.

Leeson, John R. *Lister as I Knew Him*. London: Balliere, Tindall and Cox, 1927. Reminiscences by a student and assistant of Lister. The style is chatty and personal, but the author did not know Lister intimately.

Turner, A. Logan, ed. *Joseph, Baron Lister: Centenary Volume, 1827-1927*. London: Oliver and Boyd, 1927. A collection of essays, including a biographical sketch, mostly by contemporaries, colleagues, and friends of Lister.

Waller, John. *Einstein's Luck: The Truth Behind Some of the Greatest Discoveries*. New York: Oxford University Press, 2002. An iconoclastic view of science. In Chapter 8, "Was Joseph Lister Mr. Clean?," Waller argues that Lister's antiseptic hospital wards were actually quite dirty.

Woodward, John. *To Do the Sick No Harm: A Study of the British Voluntary Hospital System in 1875*. Boston: Routledge & Kegan Paul, 1974. A useful and scholarly study. Excellent background for the study of Lister's work.

SEE ALSO: Emil von Behring; Louis Pasteur; Ignaz Philipp Semmelweis.

RELATED ARTICLES in *Great Events from History: The Nineteenth Century, 1801-1900:* October 16, 1846: Safe Surgical Anesthesia Is Demonstrated; May, 1847: Semmelweis Develops Antiseptic Procedures; 1867: Lister Publishes His Theory on Antiseptic Surgery.

FRANZ LISZT
Hungarian composer

Liszt revolutionized the art of piano playing and established the vogue of the recitalist. As a composer, he attempted to reconcile the trends of French and German Romanticism, created the musical genre of the symphonic poem, founded new innovations in harmony and form, and in his late works anticipated many devices of twentieth century music.

BORN: October 22, 1811; Raiding, Hungary
DIED: July 31, 1886; Bayreuth, Germany
ALSO KNOWN AS: Ferenc Liszt
AREA OF ACHIEVEMENT: Music

EARLY LIFE

Franz Liszt (lihst) was the son of Ádám Liszt, a clerk in the service of Prince Nikolaus Esterházy, the Hungarian noble family that had supported Joseph Haydn. An amateur cellist, the elder Liszt played in orchestras under Haydn and Ludwig van Beethoven and was his son's first teacher in piano.

Young Liszt showed phenomenal gifts for music as a child and began to study piano in his sixth year. His debut concerts in Sopron and Bratislava at the age of nine enabled him to acquire the support of several Hungarian nobles to finance his musical studies in Vienna under Karl Czerny and Antonio Salieri. Liszt soon acquired a reputation as a formidable sight reader. He published his first composition, a variation on a waltz by Anton Diabelli, in 1822, and in the following year made his debut in Vienna. The often-repeated story that Beethoven attended the concert and kissed the boy afterward cannot be proved, but it is certain that Liszt met Beethoven at his apartment and forever cherished the meeting.

Liszt continued his musical education in Paris. Denied admission to the Paris Conservatory because of his foreign citizenship, he studied privately with Anton Reicha and Ferdinando Paer. In 1824, he began his concert tours of England; until 1847, he was best known as a virtuoso pianist who revolutionized the art of playing that instrument and who was a pioneer in giving solo recitals performed from memory; he even invented the term "recital," to describe his solo programs in London in 1840.

The death of his father in 1826 and the rejection of his suit of Caroline de Saint-Cricq by her noble family brought about a period of depression when he contemplated entering the priesthood. During the early 1830's, he came under the influence of the Saint-Simonian movement and the liberal Catholicism of the Abbé Hughes-Félicité-Robert de Lamennais; both placed art in a central place in society. Liszt's first mature compositions, the *Apparitions* (1834), were written under La-mennais's influence, whereas his piano piece *Lyon* was influenced by a silk-weavers' strike there in 1834.

LIFE'S WORK

Liszt compensated for his lack of formal education by extensive reading and by seeking the company of writers. He was introduced to the Countess Marie d'Agoult, of German descent, who left her husband and children in 1835 to live with Liszt in Switzerland and Italy. The musical results of the sojourn were the first two volumes of the *Années de pèlerinage* (1835-1877; years of pilgrimage), featuring, in the first volume, nature scenes in Switzerland and, in the second, the art and literature of Italy. D'Agoult guided Liszt in his reading and interested him in the visual arts. They had three children. Blandine and Daniel died while in their twenties, but Cosima lived until 1930, to become the wife first of the pianist-conductor Hans von Bülow and then of the composer Richard Wagner.

Liszt's decision to return to concert playing in 1839 placed a strain on his relationship with d'Agoult, which ended in 1844 during a hectic period of concertizing all over Europe, performing as far afield as Portugal, Ireland, and Turkey, traveling under primitive conditions, and being subject to the kind of adulation given to modern rock stars. The main works of this period were his songs for voice and piano (highly expressive and unjustly neglected) and his opera paraphrases and transcriptions for the piano. The transcriptions are reproductions of the vocal music, but the paraphrases are virtual recompositions of the opera based on its main tunes; the most famous of these is the *Réminiscences de Don Juan* (1841), based on Wolfgang Amadeus Mozart's opera *Don Giovanni* (1787). During his tours of Hungary, he was able to hear authentic Gypsy music and re-created these sounds in his *Hungarian Rhapsodies* (1839-1847).

On his last concert tour in 1847, he met in Poland the Princess Carolyne de Sayn-Wittgenstein, with whom he began a lengthy relationship; because the czar of Russia would not grant her a divorce, she could not marry Liszt but was able to flee Russia with most of her money. Liszt, in turn, accepted an offer to become musical director of the court at Weimar and was able to abandon his career as a touring piano virtuoso in 1847 to devote himself to musical composition. He and Carolyne moved there during the following year.

During Liszt's thirteen years in Weimar, he revised most of his earlier compositions for publication and embarked on many ambitious musical projects that he had

Franz Liszt. (Library of Congress)

sketched earlier, such as his two piano concerti. During these years, Liszt invented the symphonic poem, an extended programmatic work for orchestra. His first two works in this genre, the so-called *Mountain Symphony* (begun 1848) and *Tasso* (begun 1849-1854), required assistance from others as Liszt was learning how to write for orchestra, but the next work, *Les Préludes* (1854), his best-known symphonic poem, shows his complete mastery of both form and instrumentation.

Among the best of Liszt's remaining nine works are *Orpheus* (1853-1854) and *Hamlet* (1858). The culmination of his orchestral works is his monumental *A Faust Symphony* (1854-1861), comprising three movements, character portrayals of the three main personages in Johann Wolfgang von Goethe's drama: Faust, Gretchen, and Mephistopheles. The less conventional *A Symphony to Dante's "Divina Commedia"* (1855-1856) was originally intended to accompany a stage performance with dioramas and does not follow normal symphonic form. A work of "absolute music" without an overt program is the Sonata in B Minor (1852-1853) for piano, the culmination of Liszt's experiments in harmony, form, and the construction of a large-scale work from a few ideas that are extensively developed and transformed.

While in Weimar, Liszt continued his altruistic gestures that got the music of his contemporaries performed. Earlier he had played the large piano works of Robert Schumann and Frédéric Chopin when their composers were physically unable to do so, and widened the audience for Beethoven's symphonies and Schubert's songs by arranging them for the piano. Now he devoted his energies to organizing and conducting performances of the operas of Richard Wagner, who was in exile in Switzerland after his participation in the abortive revolt in Dresden in 1849. Though Liszt had abandoned concertizing except for benefits and charities, he had a large number of piano students whom he taught without charge, and a coterie of ardent musical disciples. Disappointed at the lack of support he was receiving in Weimar from the new grand duke, who preferred the theater to music, Liszt resigned as musical director in 1858 and made it effective after a music festival in 1861, when he moved to Rome to join Carolyne.

The wedding of Liszt and Carolyne was to have taken place on Liszt's fiftieth birthday, but it was abruptly canceled; the reasons have yet to be revealed. Shortly thereafter, Liszt took the initial steps toward entering the priesthood; though he dressed in clerical clothes and was known as "Abbé Liszt," he did not complete the final stages of holy orders and thus could not say Mass or hear confessions. Not until 1865 was his entry into the religious life generally known. During this period, he wrote principally religious music, especially choral works such as the *Missa Choralis* (1865); two large oratorios, *Die Legende von der heiligen Elisabeth* (1857-1862) and *Christus* (1855-1866); the "Legends" for piano (1863); and the *Totentanz* (1849, revised 1853, 1859; dance of death) for piano and orchestra, a paraphrase of the *Dies Irae* (day of wrath) chant from the Requiem Mass.

In 1869, Liszt was reconciled with the Grand Duke of Weimar and began his *vie trifurquée* (three-pronged life) between Rome, Weimar, and Budapest. The third book of his *Années de pèlerinage* reflects his journeys, especially to Rome and Hungary. The best known of the works in this set is "The Fountains of the Villa d'Este" in Rome, where Liszt often stayed; this piece anticipates many of the impressionistic harmonic and coloristic effects of Claude Debussy and Maurice Ravel.

In Weimar and Budapest, Liszt held master classes in which he trained a new generation of pianists. His style of composition also changed to a spare, attenuated style, avoiding extensive developments or repetitions and using often unusual harmonic sonorities that he treated in unconventional ways. Many of these last pieces are extremely short, beginning and ending abruptly, without the extensive introductions or closes of his Weimar works. Publishers rejected these compositions, nearly all of which were published long after Liszt's death. Best known of these late works are the short piano pieces, such as "Unstern" (evil star) and "Nuages gris" (gray clouds) from the 1880's, and the *Via Crucis* (1879; the way of the cross) for chorus and organ.

Liszt's death in 1886 came, after an extensive tour of Belgium and England, in Bayreuth, Germany, where he had attended a festival of operas by his son-in-law Richard Wagner. The cause of death was pneumonia; he had earlier suffered from edema.

SIGNIFICANCE

Franz Liszt was a man of immense personal magnetism and charisma, as attested by the immense acclaim he received during his years as a virtuoso and reflected in later years during his charity concerts and appearances as a conductor. He attracted a devoted coterie of students, and though he failed to found a school of composition, he influenced virtually every composer of the second half of the nineteenth century and anticipated many of the devices and techniques of the twentieth.

A man of formidable energy, he composed about thirteen hundred works. He was one of the leading letter writers of the century, and, though he did not write the many books and essays attributed to him, he dictated their ideas, edited the text, and assumed responsibility for their final form. If one had to choose a single composer whose works sum up the nineteenth century's achievements, innovations, and also weaknesses, Liszt would be the most likely candidate.

—*Rey M. Longyear*

FURTHER READING

Arnold, Ben, ed. *The Liszt Companion*. Westport, Conn.: Greenwood Press, 2000. Collection of essays, including scholarly discussions of Liszt's life, writings and correspondence, reception, and analyses of the various types of music that he composed.

Fay, Amy. *Music-Study in Germany*. Chicago: Jansen, McClurg, 1881. Reprint. New York: Dover, 1965. This engagingly written firsthand account of Liszt's teaching in Weimar was written by one of his few

American pupils; her study also gives an incisive view of Germany shortly after unification.

László, Zsigmond, and Béla Mátéka. *Franz Liszt: A Biography in Pictures.* London: Barrie & Rockliff, 1968. This series of pictures and facsimiles of manuscripts and documents is arranged to provide a chronological account of Liszt's life, achievements, and circle of friends and students. An extensive commentary explains and connects the various illustrations.

Longyear, Rey M. "Ferenc (Franz) Liszt." In *Nineteenth-Century Romanticism in Music.* 3d ed. Englewood Cliffs, N.J.: Prentice-Hall, 1988. A brief survey of Liszt's musical style, emphasizing the Weimar and late works, which relates Liszt's music to that of the century as a whole. Liszt is also presented as a seminal composer for the twentieth century.

Merrick, Paul. *Revolution and Religion in the Music of Liszt.* Cambridge, England: Cambridge University Press, 1987. This interesting and controversial study emphasizes Liszt's music with religious import, particularly the choral works; the author tends to overstate his case in seeking hidden religious programs in some of the instrumental works.

Samson, Jim. *Virtuosity and the Musical Work: The Transcendental Studies of Liszt.* New York: Cambridge University Press, 2003. Focuses on three sets of etudes by Liszt, the first composed in 1826, with subsequent reworkings in 1837 and 1851. Samson describes how these compositions exemplify many of the characteristics of early Romantic era music, including the relationship of composer and performer, the concept of virtuosity, and the significance of recomposition.

Searle, Humphrey. *The Music of Liszt.* London: Williams & Norgate, 1954. A still-valuable survey of this prolific composer's works. Not too technically oriented for the person with limited musical background. Searle's book was a landmark in restoring Liszt's works to musical respectability after decades of neglect and disdain.

Searle, Humphrey, and Sharon Winklhofer. "Franz Liszt." In *The New Grove Early Romantic Masters I: Chopin, Schumann and Liszt*, edited by Nicholas Temperley. New York: W. W. Norton, 1985. A concise study, balanced between Liszt's life and his music, derived from Searle's article in *The New Grove* and revised by Sharon Winklhofer. The list of Liszt's approximately thirteen hundred compositions is particularly valuable.

Walker, Alan. *The Virtuoso Years, 1811-1847.* Vol. 1 in *Franz Liszt.* Rev. ed. Ithaca, N.Y.: Cornell University Press, 1987.

_____. *The Weimar Years, 1848-1861.* Vol. 2 in *Franz Liszt.* New York: Alfred A. Knopf, 1989. Walker's two-volume study is the most complete biography of Liszt. Though the focus is on his biography, some often insightful discussion is given to his music. Volume 2 provides the definitive account of his most productive years and shows Liszt not only as the musical director at Weimar but also as a composer, teacher, administrator, and writer on music.

Watson, Derek. *Liszt.* New York: Oxford University Press, 2000. Carefully researched biography, describing Liszt's life, work, and influence. Includes numerous musical examples, a detailed chronology, a list of compositions, and photographs.

SEE ALSO: Ludwig van Beethoven; Aleksandr Borodin; Johannes Brahms; Frédéric Chopin; César Franck; Edvard Grieg; Lola Montez; Modest Mussorgsky; Robert Schumann; Richard Wagner.

RELATED ARTICLE in *Great Events from History: The Nineteenth Century, 1801-1900:* April 7, 1805: Beethoven's *Eroica* Symphony Introduces the Romantic Age.

SECOND EARL OF LIVERPOOL
Prime minister of Great Britain (1812-1827)

As prime minister of Great Britain from 1812 to 1827, Liverpool led his nation to victory over Napoleonic France, rode out the domestic strife of the postwar years, and directed the economic recovery and liberal legislation of the 1820's.

BORN: June 7, 1770; London, England
DIED: December 4, 1828; London, England
ALSO KNOWN AS: Robert Banks Jenkinson (birth name); Baron Hawkesbury of Hawkesbury
AREA OF ACHIEVEMENT: Government and politics

EARLY LIFE

Robert Banks Jenkinson, who would become the second earl of Liverpool, was reared by his father, Charles Jenkinson, first Baron Hawkesbury and first earl of Liverpool. His mother, née Amelia Watts, the daughter of an ex-governor of Fort William in Bengal, died a month after he was born. His father was an adviser to George III, secretary at war under Lord North, and president of the Board of Trade under William Pitt the Younger.

Jenkinson was educated at Charterhouse and Christ Church, Oxford, emerging as an excellent classicist and historian, well versed in international affairs and political economy. While on the Grand Tour in 1789, he witnessed the storming of the Bastille, an experience that bred in him a lifelong distrust of mobs.

In 1790, Jenkinson was elected to Parliament at the age of twenty. However, he declined to sit as a minor and waited until 1792 to deliver his maiden speech, a well-received defense of Great Britain's handling of the Oczakov crisis. In 1793, his usefulness to the Tory government was demonstrated further by speeches answering Whig criticisms of the French war and demands for parliamentary reform, and Pitt rewarded him by appointment to the Indian Board of Control. For some years, he attended Parliament irregularly because of obligations in the Kentish militia, which he joined at the outbreak of war, and affairs of the heart. In 1795, he married the earl of Bristol's daughter, Louisa Theodosia Hervey, to whom he remained utterly devoted until her death. Despite his absences, Lord Hawkesbury (the courtesy title he assumed when his father received an earldom in 1796) was a valued supporter of the government. In 1799, he was made Master of the Mint, an appointment that gave membership of the Privy Council and a clear signal that Pitt had marked him out for further advancement.

Portraits of Hawkesbury reveal an ungainly figure with a long neck, awkward posture, and untidy appearance. He was a shy, sensitive man, respected in political circles for his modesty, integrity, and sound judgment. Although not a scintillating orator, his speeches were typically clear, well prepared, and effective, and it is understandable that Pitt, whose front bench was short of able speakers, should view him with favor. Nevertheless, appointment to the cabinet came unexpectedly early. After resigning over the Catholic question in 1801, Pitt persuaded Hawkesbury to support Henry Addington, who, desperate for the assistance of another minister in the Commons, gave him the Foreign Office at the age of thirty.

LIFE'S WORK

In the decade after joining the cabinet, Hawkesbury occupied all three secretaryships of state. As foreign secretary between 1801 and 1804, he negotiated the abortive Peace of Amiens (1802), a policy that was vehemently criticized by his predecessor, William Wyndham Grenville. In 1803, to help counter such attacks, he was raised to the House of Lords, where he led the Tories—initially as Baron Hawkesbury and, after his father's death in 1808, as earl of Liverpool—until retiring from politics. From 1804 to 1806, he was Pitt's home secretary and, after the latter's death, rejected a royal offer of the premiership because the cabinet had decided not to continue without its leader. Subsequently, he served as home secretary under the duke of Portland and secretary of war under Spencer Perceval, acquiring a reputation as a conciliator and a skilled administrator. By 1812, he was far more experienced than any of his ministerial colleagues, who elected him leader when Perceval was assassinated. The prince regent, after approaching a number of other politicians, endorsed this decision by making Liverpool prime minister on June 8, 1812.

At the time of its formation, there was little reason to expect Liverpool's administration to prove more resilient than any of its five predecessors in the previous eleven years. The most immediate threat was the issue of Catholic emancipation. Although personally opposed to the proposal that political rights be given to Catholics, Liverpool adopted a position of government neutrality on the question. This device maintained cabinet unity in 1812 and became a permanent feature of his policies. In the following three years, the government won immense popularity as a result of its contributions to Napoleon's defeat and the subsequent peace negotiations, and in 1814, Liverpool was made Knight of the Garter for his services to the country.

The period from 1815 to 1821 was the most difficult of Liverpool's career. During these years, he grappled with economic and social problems brought on by the end of the war; the government experienced continuous budgetary problems resulting from its reluctant abandonment of the wartime income tax. More obviously, the ministry's responsibility was the Corn Law of 1815, prohibiting importation until the domestic price reached eighty shillings a quarter. Viewed by Liverpool as a temporary measure to facilitate the agricultural sector's transition to peacetime conditions and reduce dependence upon foreign supply, the act provoked widespread outbursts against a self-interested landowning Parliament. Discontent was aggravated by economic distress, itself popularly attributed to the government's extravagance, and produced unprecedented calls for parliamentary reform, which culminated in the unfortunate "Peterloo Massacre" of 1819.

Lacking adequate information, Liverpool believed that there was an organized revolutionary movement and determined upon decisive action to maintain order. In 1817, habeas corpus was suspended, in 1819 the notorious Six Acts increased magistrates' powers against sedition, and a small number of suspects was jailed. These relatively mild measures silenced the radicals briefly but intensified their bitterness. After the accession of George IV in 1820, opposition rose to fever pitch around the figure of his adulterous wife, Caroline, whose return from the Continent obliged Liverpool to introduce a divorce bill and severely compromised him.

On one hand, Liverpool was vilified as the lackey of a licentious husband brutally attacking an innocent woman. On the other, his inability to carry the bill almost led to dismissal by the disgruntled monarch. By the time the affair was ended by Caroline's death in 1821, it appears to have taken a considerable personal toll of Liverpool, for afterward his characteristic good temper gave way increasingly to testiness and intolerance. His spirits were lowered further in 1821 by the death of Louisa, a devastating loss only partly cushioned by marriage to her close friend, Mary Chester, niece of Lord Bagot, in 1822.

Liverpool's public life took a favorable turn during the early 1820's as economic recovery dispelled social unrest and facilitated more constructive policies. In conjunction with able colleagues such as William Huskisson, Sir Robert Peel, and Frederick Robinson, he sought to eradi-

cate discontent by reducing economic instability and implementing moderate liberal reforms. In 1821, the Bank of England resumed cash payments, which had been suspended with inflationary consequences since 1797.

In 1826, the volatility of provincial credit was tackled by a statute prohibiting country bank notes under five pounds and permitting the erection of large joint-stock banks and Bank of England branches outside London. Similarly, to meet the population's need for steadier food supply and employment, the government attempted to regularize commerce by loosening trade restrictions and lowering duties on a broad range of imports. In addition, it passed a series of law reforms, including statutes that repealed the combination acts, halved the number of capital offenses, regulated judicial incomes, and improved provincial prisons. The government's liberalism was reflected also in its foreign policy, conducted until 1822 by Lord Castlereagh and afterward by George Canning. While pursuing the national interest, both vehemently opposed the efforts of the reactionary European powers to suppress revolutionary activity, and Canning in particular stirred patriotic spirit when he supported liberal and nationalist movements in Greece, Portugal, and South America.

By the mid-1820's, the government had regained its popularity but was seriously threatened by the perennial corn and Catholic questions. In 1826, in defiance of the agriculturalists, Liverpool prepared a corn bill replacing import prohibition below eighty shillings a quarter with a sliding scale of duties that would decline as the price rose. This was passed in a slightly altered form in 1828 and remained in force until 1846. The Catholic issue had become urgent because of Irish agitation and growing cabinet opposition to governmental neutrality. Liverpool believed that pro-Catholic aggression might destroy his ministry during the 1827 session. He suffered a cerebral hemorrhage on February 17 of that year, however, and played no further part in politics before his death on December 4, 1828. As he died without issue, he was succeeded as earl of Liverpool by his half brother, Charles Cecil Cope Jenkinson.

SIGNIFICANCE

As prime minister for fifteen years, a period exceeded only by Robert Walpole and William Pitt, the second earl of Liverpool exerted a profound influence on the development of British politics and public policy. Determined to enhance the authority of his office, he resisted both royal interference with the cabinet and the independent leanings of its members. After appointment by the premier, ministers were given considerable administrative scope, but general policy and major decisions were formulated in conjunction with him. Government was conducted in accordance with Liverpool's own moral code, a fact that helped to raise the public image of politicians and their expected standards of behavior. It also reflected his personal views, which represented, to a remarkable degree, the contradictory currents of early nineteenth century opinion and made him acceptable to both conservative and liberal wings of his party.

Liverpool's reverence for the traditional constitution was shared by the large, influential group of orthodox Tories. After he was replaced by the pro-Catholic Canning in 1827, their defection threw the party into chaos, and within five years the legislature had enacted Catholic emancipation and parliamentary reform. In contrast, Liverpool was progressive on other issues. Guided by the principles of political economy, he sought to promote industry and commerce, if necessary at the expense of the landed interest.

Liverpool's ministry's tariff policies inaugurated the Free Trade movement, which, after a hiatus under the Whigs during the 1830's, was resumed by Peel and came to be viewed as the basis of mid-Victorian prosperity. Similarly, the banking legislation laid the groundwork for Peel's later measures, and the law reforms paved the way for the radical work of Henry Brougham during the 1830's. In sum, although Liverpool is a little-known historical figure, his achievements were diverse and substantial. After leading Great Britain to victory over Napoleon and through the postwar troubles, he implemented constructive reforms that were to have important, long-term consequences.

—Ian Duffy

FURTHER READING

Brady, Alexander. *William Huskisson and Liberal Reform*. London: Oxford University Press, 1928. Dated but still useful essay on the nature and purposes of economic reforms. Particularly helpful on commercial legislation.

Brock, William Ranuf. *Lord Liverpool and Liberal Toryism, 1820 to 1827*. Cambridge, England: Cambridge University Press, 1941. 2d ed. Hamden, Conn.: Archon Books, 1967. Stimulating analysis of Liverpool's final years, especially valuable on his ideas and administrative methods. The second edition eliminates factual errors in the original.

Cookson, J. E. *Lord Liverpool's Administration: The Crucial Years, 1815-1822*. Hamden, Conn.: Archon Books, 1975. Excellent narrative of the government's reactions to events in the troubled years after Waterloo. Exposes the increasing influence of public opinion on policy and contains suggestive comments on Liverpool's administration as a whole.

Derry, John W. *Politics in the Age of Fox, Pitt, and Liverpool*. Rev. ed. New York: Palgrave, 2001. Describes how the British political system met the challenges of war, the French Revolution, and social and economic change during the late eighteenth and early nineteenth centuries.

Gash, Norman. *Lord Liverpool*. Cambridge, Mass.: Harvard University Press, 1984. A brilliant, superbly written portrait, good on all aspects of Liverpool's life, particularly his character and personal relations. Skillfully traces continuities between Liverpool's policies and those of Peel during the 1840's. Essential reading.

Hilton, Boyd. *Corn, Cash, Commerce: The Economic Policies of the Tory Governments, 1815-1830*. Oxford, England: Oxford University Press, 1977. Penetrating, controversial account of leading politicians' views on economic policy, based on parliamentary debates and private papers. Stresses the influence of pragmatic rather than doctrinal considerations.

Petrie, Sir Charles. *Lord Liverpool and His Times*. London: James Barrie, 1954. The only modern biography before that by Gash, this book provides an outline of Liverpool's career. Dwells excessively on background events and largely neglects economic matters.

Plowright, John. *Regency England: The Age of Lord Liverpool*. London: Routledge, 1996. Covers the period prior to the adoption of the Great Reform Act of 1832, describing the political issues of the time and how Liverpool's ministry responded to these issues.

Yonge, Charles Duke. *The Life and Administration of the Second Earl of Liverpool*. London: Macmillan, 1868. A three-volume biography with little analysis, but extensive quotations from Liverpool's papers reveal his reactions to specific events.

SEE ALSO: Henry Brougham; George Canning; George IV; Sir Robert Peel.

RELATED ARTICLES in *Great Events from History: The Nineteenth Century, 1801-1900:* November 20, 1815: Second Peace of Paris; December 11-30, 1819: British Parliament Passes the Six Acts; February 23, 1820: London's Cato Street Conspirators Plot Assassinations; October 20-30, 1822: Great Britain Withdraws from the Concert of Europe.

DAVID LIVINGSTONE
Scottish missionary and explorer

Although Livingstone is often remembered as a missionary, his real importance was as an explorer whose travels, together with moving appeals asking Britons to do something about the slave trade in the African interior, focused the eyes of the civilized world on previously unexplored regions of Africa and thereby helped to open that continent to the Western world.

BORN: March 19, 1813; Blantyre, Lanarkshire, Scotland
DIED: May 1, 1873; Chitambo's village near Lake Bangweulu, Central Africa (now in Zambia)
AREAS OF ACHIEVEMENT: Exploration, religion and theology

EARLY LIFE

The son of an impoverished tea vendor who was more interested in distributing religious tracts than in selling tea, David Livingstone was born near Glasgow, Scotland. Although he grew up in a large family under adverse economic circumstances, Livingstone managed, even though he began working in a cotton mill at the age of ten, to secure a solid education. He accomplished this by studying in every spare moment, and, while still in his teens, he determined to become a medical missionary.

Livingstone's preparations for such a career were successful, and when he completed his medical studies and became Dr. Livingstone in 1840, he was already unusual: It was simply unheard of for a factory boy from a poverty-stricken background to achieve such educational heights. Livingstone's original intention had been to serve in China, but the outbreak of the Opium War effectively ended this plan. Instead, he sought and won an assignment from the nondenominational London Missionary Society in South Africa. He reached Cape Town on March 14, 1841, and from there made his way into the interior to the mission station of Kuruman, Bechuanaland. This isolated outpost had been established by Robert Moffat, and a few years later, in 1845, Livingstone would marry Moffat's daughter, Mary.

LIFE'S WORK

For most of the first decade that he spent in Southern Africa, from 1841 to 1849, Livingstone devoted himself to the type of labors that were expected from missionaries. Livingstone founded three separate mission stations—Mabotsa, Chonuane, and Kolobeng—in the interior to the north of Kuruman. However, he quarreled incessantly with other missionaries and his superiors, and the sole convert he made, a chieftain named Sechele, soon lapsed. By 1849, frustrated with the routine of mission station life and increasingly attracted by the vast unexplored region to the north, he began traveling as a sort of itinerant missionary.

In truth, Livingstone's religious duties were increasingly subordinated to exploration, and it was in the field of discovery that Livingstone made his real mark. Between 1849 and 1852, he made three journeys, with the noted big-game hunter William Cotton Oswell as a companion, that altered the entire course of his career. The two men explored Lake Ngami and the upper reaches of the Zambezi River, and during these travels, Livingstone came to recognize the extent of Africa's internal slave trade.

Livingstone sent his wife and children, whom he regarded as impediments to his exploring ambitions, back to Great Britain in 1852, and following their departure, he continued his travels on the Zambezi. Between 1853 and 1856, he crossed the entire southern interior of Africa, traveling first to the Portuguese port of Luanda, Angola, on the west coast and then later following the course of the Zambezi to Quelimane, Mozambique, on the Indian Ocean. During the latter journey, which had commenced at Linyanti, he discovered the massive waterfalls on the Zambezi that he named Victoria Falls, in honor of the British monarch. After the completion of this journey, he returned to England for the first time since he had originally traveled to Africa.

Livingstone was already something of a geographical celebrity, thanks to contacts he had established with Sir Roderick Impey Murchison, the president of the Royal Geographical Society, and articles he had written for the society's journal. It was the appearance of his great book *Missionary Travels and Researches in South Africa* (1857), however, which brought Livingstone national fame. Livingstone completed the book shortly after returning home, and its appearance caused a sensation. He described his travels in detail and depicted the Southern African interior as a region that offered a fertile field for his countrymen to pursue the laudable and interconnected goals of commerce, Christianity, and civilization. So compelling was his book, together with a series of lectures that he made in England, that he secured government support for an exploratory mission on the Zambezi. Its primary purpose was to open the interior for parties of settlers who would bring British commerce and the benefits of their advanced society to the region.

After severing his formal ties with the London Missionary Society, in 1858 Livingstone returned to Africa as head of the Zambezi expedition. This undertaking was a fiasco from start to finish. Far from being the navigable river that Livingstone had imagined it to be, the Zambezi posed all sorts of obstacles as a potential highway to the interior. The Anglican missionaries who followed him suffered greatly from the climate, and Livingstone proved woefully inadequate as a leader in the conduct of the expedition. He quarreled with the other members of his party, death and disease took a heavy toll on the Universities' Mission that he had encouraged to come to the region, and his wife died while en route to join him. Ultimately, the British government, under growing protest, recalled him in 1863. Livingstone returned to England by way of India and arrived home on July 23, 1864.

Livingstone was no longer the conquering hero he had been in 1857, but his ill-fated Zambezi expedition had added appreciably to geographical knowledge of Africa.

David Livingstone. (Library of Congress)

By this juncture, he had become fascinated with the controversy surrounding attempts to discover the sources of the Nile, and thenceforth he abandoned all pretense of being a missionary. He rested in England in 1865 and wrote, in collaboration with his brother Charles, a book entitled *Narrative of an Expedition to the Zambezi and Its Tributaries* (1865). Shortly after it was published, he made his way back to Africa, and by early 1866, he was once more in the interior. Although his announced goals were to end the slave trade and advance Christianity, he had become virtually obsessed with the watershed of the Nile. The remaining seven years of his life would be spent in an unsuccessful search for the Nile's sources, and during most of this time, he would travel without European companions.

From 1866 to 1871, Livingstone traveled in the area of Lake Nyasa and the upper reaches of the Congo River. Among his discoveries were Lakes Mweru and Bangweulu, but these years cost him dearly in health. Indeed, when the journalist Henry Morton Stanley found him at Ujiji on Lake Tanganyika late in 1871, he was near death. With the medicines and supplies brought by Stanley, Livingstone quickly recovered. Together they explored portions of Lake Tanganyika and ascertained that that body of water was not a part of the Nile system.

The few weeks he spent with Livingstone influenced Stanley profoundly, and he did his best to persuade Livingstone to leave Africa. Livingstone refused, but he did open himself up to his traveling companion in a way that he had never done with any other person. He told Stanley of the horrible massacre of Africans by Arab slave traders that he had witnessed a few months earlier, and he shared his dreams of what he desired for the continent's future. Eventually, Stanley's anxiety to let the outside world know that he had "found" Livingstone led to his departure. The two separated at Unyanyembe (near the modern city of Tabora, Tanzania), with Livingstone determined to continue his explorations for the Nile's sources.

Livingstone's health, already seriously affected by recurrent bouts of malaria and years of unconcern for his physical state, degenerated rapidly. Livingstone's instruments had also been damaged in transit, and in his final days, he was for all practical purposes lost.

FIRST VISIT TO VICTORIA FALLS

David Livingstone is generally credited with discovering the great Victoria Falls on Central Africa's Zambezi River, but he was merely the first European to see the falls and report his observations to the world. When he made his first visit there in 1855, the falls were well known to Africans as Mosi-oa-Tunya (smoke that thunders), but he dubbed them "Victoria Falls," after the British queen, and the name stuck. His book Missionary Travels and Researches in South Africa *contains a long and detailed description of that visit, from which this passage is excerpted.*

After twenty minutes' sail from Kalai we came in sight, for the first time, of the columns of vapor appropriately called "smoke", rising at a distance of five or six miles, exactly as when large tracts of grass are burned in Africa. Five columns now arose, and, bending in the direction of the wind, they seemed placed against a low ridge covered with trees; the tops of the columns at this distance appeared to mingle with the clouds. They were white below, and higher up became dark, so as to simulate smoke very closely. The whole scene was extremely beautiful; the banks and islands dotted over the river are adorned with sylvan vegetation of great variety of color and form. At the period of our visit several trees were spangled over with blossoms. Trees have each their own physiognomy. There, towering over all, stands the great burly baobab, each of whose enormous arms would form the trunk of a large tree, beside groups of graceful palms, which, with their feathery-shaped leaves depicted on the sky, lend their beauty to the scene.... Some trees resemble the great spreading oak, others assume the character of our own elms and chestnuts; but no one can imagine the beauty of the view from any thing witnessed in England. It had never been seen before by European eyes; but scenes so lovely must have been gazed upon by angels in their flight. The only want felt is that of mountains in the background. The falls are bounded on three sides by ridges 300 or 400 feet in height, which are covered with forest, with the red soil appearing among the trees....

Source: David Livingstone, *Missionary Travels and Researches in South Africa* (London: J. Murray, 1857), chapter 26.

After days of being carried by the handful of retainers who continued to accompany him and being in a coma much of the time, Livingstone died in the predawn hours of May 1, 1873. Death came at a small village on the shores of Lake Bangweulu in what is now northeastern Zambia. His African companions eviscerated his body and embalmed it as well as they could before beginning the long journey back to the East African coast with it. After the party reached Zanzibar, Livingstone's remains were turned over to British authorities. Eventually, his body was taken to England and interred in London's Westminster Abbey on April 18, 1874.

SIGNIFICANCE

David Livingstone was a difficult and complex individual who was always surrounded by controversy. There can be little doubt that he was an abysmal failure as a missionary, husband, and father. He lacked the patience to pursue the daily drudgery required of missionaries to Africa in his era, and he was so lacking in sympathy and understanding for his wife that he drove her into alcoholism. Similarly, at least some of his children were disillusioned by Livingstone's total lack of parental concern. In contrast, his son-in-law, Robert Moffat, proved to be one of the most successful Protestant missionaries in nineteenth century Southern Africa, and he, too, would make important contributions to exploration. Against Livingstone's shortcomings stand his compassion for Africans and his almost superhuman determination as an explorer and exponent of Great Britain's civilizing mission on the African continent.

There is no disputing Livingstone's profound influence in directing British attention to what he called the "open, running sore" of the internal slave trade in eastern Africa. Similarly, his writings, his speeches, and the very nature of this controversial man captured the public imagination. In particular, his "last journey"—the final seven years he spent in Africa—fascinated the British public. There was something exceptionally poignant about the aging, ill man, struggling against all odds and frequently incommunicado as he sought to discover the sources of the Nile.

In the aftermath of his death, Livingstone came to be viewed almost as a saint. Modern observers realize that such adoration was misplaced. Nevertheless, Livingstone exerted a profound influence on the exploration and opening up of Africa to Western world. His death inspired Stanley to complete his unfinished geographical travels, and the attention he directed to Africa—both official and otherwise—loomed large in the "scramble" of the late 1870's and 1880's. Livingstone remains a frequently misunderstood figure who has attracted scores of biographers yet who still awaits a definitive biography. Thanks to the massive Livingstone Documentation Project launched in connection with the centenary celebrations of 1973, the wherewithal now exists at the National Library of Scotland for such a study.

—*James A. Casada*

FURTHER READING
Buxton, Meriel. *David Livingstone.* New York: Palgrave, 2001. Comprehensive biography based on recent scholarship, describing the complexities of Livingstone's personality.

Clendennen, Gary W., and I. C. Cunningham, comps. *David Livingstone: A Catalogue of Documents.* Edinburgh: Livingstone Documentation Project, 1979. A full listing of all known extant Livingstone documents, with a description and their location, which is invaluable for any serious study of the man. Cunningham prepared a supplement that was published in 1985.

Dugard, Martin. *Into Africa: The Epic Adventures of Stanley and Livingstone.* New York: Doubleday, 2003. Dual biography, focusing on both men's travels through Africa. Provides a detailed re-creation of their journeys; contrasts their personalities and thoughts about Africa.

Jeal, Tim. *Livingstone.* New York: G. P. Putnam's Sons, 1973. Although characterized by a certain overemphasis on debunking the Livingstone myth, Jeal's is perhaps the fullest, and certainly the most readable, of the many modern biographies of Livingstone.

Ransford, Oliver. *David Livingstone: The Dark Interior.* New York: St. Martin's Press, 1978. A detailed, carefully researched biography that is marred by the author's insistence that all Livingstone's life and actions can be explained by a disease that led to wide swings in mood ranging from deep depression to great elation.

Ross, Andrew C. *David Livingstone: Mission and Empire.* London: Hambledon and London, 2002. Scholarly account of Livingstone's life.

Seaver, George. *David Livingstone: His Life and Letters.* New York: Harper & Brothers, 1957. A solid life notable primarily for reprinting a number of interesting Livingstone letters.

SEE ALSO: Sir Richard Francis Burton; John Hanning Speke; Henry Morton Stanley; Tippu Tib.

RELATED ARTICLES in *Great Events from History: The Nineteenth Century, 1801-1900:* September, 1839-August 29, 1842: First Opium War; November 17, 1853: Livingstone Sees the Victoria Falls; 1873-1880: Exploration of Africa's Congo Basin; 1873-1897: Zanzibar Outlaws Slavery.

NIKOLAY IVANOVICH LOBACHEVSKY
Russian mathematician

Lobachevsky was the boldest and most consistent founder of a post-Euclidean theory of real space. His persistence in holding open his revolutionary line of inquiry into the reality of geometry helped to set the stage for the radical discoveries of twentieth century theoretical physics.

BORN: December 1, 1792; Nizhny Novgorod, Russia
DIED: February 24, 1856; Kazan, Russia
AREA OF ACHIEVEMENT: Mathematics

EARLY LIFE

Nikolay Ivanovich Lobachevsky (luh-buh-CHAYF-skuh-ih), whose parents were a minor government clerk and an energetic woman of apparently no education, was a member of what most nearly corresponded to a middle class in preemancipation Russia. As a government-supported student, he was recorded in school as a *raznochinets* (person of miscellaneous rank—not a noble, a peasant, or a merchant). Despite the early marriage of his mother, Praskovya, to the collegiate registrar Ivan Maksimovich Lobachevsky, the evidence strongly suggests that Nikolay and his two brothers were the illegitimate sons of an army officer and land surveyor, S. S. Shebarshin. Ivan Maksimovich Lobachevsky died when Nikolay, the middle son, was only five years old. The widowed Praskovya left Nizhny Novgorod and moved eastward along the Volga to the provincial center of Kazan. She enrolled all three boys in the local gymnasium (preparatory school). Nikolay attended the school between 1802 and 1807.

Lobachevsky's student years at Kazan University (1807 to 1811) were a time when Russia was eager to learn from the West and to give more than it had received. Lobachevsky was awarded Kazan's first master's degree for his thesis on elliptic movement of the heavenly bodies. He worked closely with Johann Martin Bartels, who had earlier discovered and taught Carl Friedrich Gauss, a great mathematician of the day.

Lobachevsky taught at Kazan University from 1811 until his mandated but most unwilling retirement in 1846. The tenure of Mikhail Magnitskii as curator from 1819 to 1826 was the school's most difficult period. A religious fanatic who attempted to give this particularly science-oriented university the atmosphere of a medieval monastery, Magnitskii was imprisoned in 1826 for his gross incompetence. He was particularly suspicious of the philosophy of Immanuel Kant. All the distinguished German professors left; for a time, the young Lobachevsky carried the burden of providing all the advanced lectures in mathematics, physics, and astronomy alone. His own development and integrity were only strengthened during this phase. It did Lobachevsky no harm that he too was anti-Kantian; he completely disagreed with Kant's view that Euclidean geometry was proof of the human mind's inborn sense of lines, planes, and space.

LIFE'S WORK

As a young professor in 1817, Lobachevsky was intrigued by the problem of Euclid's fifth postulate, which implies the possibility of infinitely parallel lines. More technically, one may draw a single line through a given point on a given plane that will never intersect another given line on the same plane. On one hand, this is not a simple axiom that has no need of proof. On the other, it cannot be proved. Two thousand years of general satisfaction with Euclidean geometry had seen many vain attempts to prove the fifth postulate and thereby give this geometry its final perfection. Such attempts became particularly frenzied in the eighteenth century. A rare few thinkers began to entertain the idea that the postulate was wrong, but they denied it even to themselves.

From 1817 to 1822, Lobachevsky made repeated attempts to prove the fifth postulate, already resorting to non-Euclidean concepts such as an axiom of directionality. Once he perceived the hidden tautology of even his best attempts, he concluded that the postulate must be wrong and that geometry must be put on a new foundation.

In addition to the resistance of intellectual tradition, Lobachevsky could expect little support in a country whose ruling house saw itself as the very embodiment of stability and conservatism. The unsettling implications of losing true parallelism and rocking the foundations of classical geometry were as unwelcome in czarist Russia as they could possibly have been anywhere in the world. This resistance makes Lobachevsky's boldness all the more impressive. Simultaneously and independently, two leading mathematicians of the day—Gauss in Germany and János Bolyai in Hungary—were facing the same conclusion as Lobachevsky. Despite their secure reputations, both refrained from pursuing the implications of negating the fifth postulate, correctly assessing that the world was not ready for it.

To exacerbate the radicalism of his approach in a highly religious country, Lobachevsky, though not an atheist, was a materialist in a most fundamental and original sense of the word. In his mathematical syllabus for 1822, he made the extraordinary statement:

> We apprehend in Nature only bodies alone; consequently, concepts of lines and planes are derived and not directly acquired concepts, and therefore should not be taken as the basis of mathematical science.

In 1823, Lobachevsky's full-length geometry textbook *Geometriya* was submitted to school district curator Magnitskii, who sent it to the St. Petersburg Academy of Sciences for review. The text was emphatically rejected, and Lobachevsky's difficulties with the academy began. A subsequent manuscript, "O nachalakh geometrii" (1829-1830; on the elements of geometry), was also submitted to the academy. Not only did the academy reject the manuscript but also an academician's flawed critique was fed to the popular press, which turned it into a lampoon of Lobachevsky.

The date February 7, 1826, marks the official debut of Lobachevskian geometry as an independent theory. On that day, Lobachevsky submitted to his department his paper entitled "Exposition succincte des principes de la géométrie avec une démonstration rigoureuse du théorème des parallèles." It was rejected for publication, as his colleagues ventured no opinion on it. Other major works continued to be largely ignored.

Nevertheless, the new school district curator who replaced Magnitskii, Count Mikhail Musin-Pushkin, was sufficiently impressed with Lobachevsky to make him rector of Kazan University in 1827. Thus began Lobachevsky's dual life as a brilliantly successful local administrator and a frustrated intellectual pioneer kept outside the pale of the St. Petersburg establishment. During his tenure as rector, Lobachevsky built Kazan University into an outstanding institution of high standards. He founded the scientific journal *Uchenye zapiski*, in which he published many of his works and that has flourished to the present day.

In 1846, Lobachevsky's life in the sphere of action fell apart, as he received a succession of blows: Musin-Pushkin was transferred to the St. Petersburg school district; the request to forestall Lobachevsky's mandatory retirement was denied; his eldest son, Aleksei, died of tuberculosis at the age of nineteen; his wife became seriously ill; his wife's half brother, dispatched to handle the sale of two distant estates, gambled away both the Lobachevskys' money and all of his own; and Lobachevsky's eyesight began to deteriorate. In the last year of his life, he was virtually blind, yet he dictated his best and strongest work, *Pangéométrie* (1855-1856). His views had evolved from rejection of Euclidean parallelism into a vision of reality that anticipated theories of the curvature of space and was validated by Albert Einstein's general theory of relativity.

SIGNIFICANCE

When Nikolay Ivanovich Lobachevsky's ideas first caught the imagination of a wide audience during the late nineteenth century, he was dubbed "the Copernicus of geometry," partly because of his Slavic origin (Nicolaus Copernicus was Polish), but far more because of the profound reorientation of thought that he set in motion. Lobachevsky forced the scale of earthly dimension as the measure of the universe off its pedestal, as Copernicus had earlier shattered the illusory status of Earth as the center of the solar system. This upheaval, which initially met with great resistance, forced the mind to focus on awesome phenomena that were not so much abstract as invisible to the human eye. Lobachevsky promoted bold and fruitful speculation about the nature of reality and space.

Pangéométrie, Lobachevsky's crowning work, opens: "Instead of beginning geometry with the line and plane, as is usually done, I have preferred to begin with the sphere and the circle." For this geometry, there are no straight lines or flat planes, and all lines and planes must curve, however infinitesimally. Yet, while pointing to modern concepts of the curvature of space, Lobachevsky does not abolish Euclidean geometry. In some areas, his geometry and Euclid's coincide. However, the latter is a limited case, whose relative certainties hold true on a merely earthly scale. In the conclusion to *Pangéométrie*, Lobachevsky correctly predicted that interstellar space would be the proving ground for his theory, which he saw not as an abstruse logical exercise but as the real geometry of the universe.

—*D. Gosselin Nakeeb*

FURTHER READING

Bell, E. T. *Men of Mathematics*. New York: Simon & Schuster, 1937. Reprint. 1986. Chapter 16, "The Copernicus of Geometry," focuses on Lobachevsky's life and mathematical discoveries.

Bonola, Roberto. *Non-Euclidean Geometry: A Critical and Historical Study of Its Development*. Translated by H. S. Carslaw. Mineola, N.Y.: Dover, 1955. Up-to-date for its time, and still relevant to the general reader. Focuses on a basic exposition of Lobachevsky's theories without the highly sophisticated applications thereof. Contains several relevant appendixes.

Greenberg, Marvin Jay. *Euclidean and Non-Euclidean Geometries: Development and History*. 3d ed. New York: W. H. Freeman, 1993. Includes information about Lobachevsky's discovery of the hyperbolic geometric.

Kagan, Veniamin Fedorovich. *N. Lobachevsky and His Contributions to Science*. Moscow: Foreign Language Press, 1957. A solid, basic account by one of the chief Russian experts on Lobachevsky. Omits most of the human-interest material to be found in Kagan's 1944 biography. Includes a bibliography, necessarily of primarily Russian materials.

Kulczycki, Stefan. *Non-Euclidean Geometry*. Translated by Stanisław Knapowski. Elmsford, N.Y.: Pergamon Press, 1961. Another introduction for the general reader, which updates but does not supplant Bonola.

Mlodinow, Leonard. *Euclid's Window: The Story of Geometry from Parallel Lines to Hyperspace*. New York: Free Press, 2001. Lobachevsky's contributions to geometry are briefly discussed in this book focusing on the work of five other mathematicians.

Shirokov, Pëtr Alekseevich. *A Sketch of the Fundamentals of Lobachevskian Geometry*. Edited by I. N. Bronshtein. Translated by Leo F. Boron and Ward D. Bouwsma. Groningen, Netherlands: P. Noordhoff, 1964. Written in Russian during the 1940's, it appears to have been aimed at the secondary-school mathematics student.

Smogorzhevsky, A. S. *Lobachevskian Geometry*. Translated by V. Kisin. Moscow: Mir, 1982. Partly accessible to the general reader but of particular interest to the serious student of mathematics. Emphasizes specific mathematical applications of Lobachevsky's theories.

Vucinich, Alexander. "Nikolay Ivanovich Lobachevsky: The Man Behind the First Non-Euclidean Geometry." *Isis* 53 (December, 1962). A substantial, well-written article, abundantly annotated to point the reader in the direction of all the basic sources, which are primarily in Russian. Highlights some avenues not mentioned elsewhere, such as Lobachevsky's role in the mathematization of science. Includes a balanced account of Lobachevsky's life.

SEE ALSO: Carl Friedrich Gauss; Henri Poincaré; Charlotte Angas Scott; Jakob Steiner.
RELATED ARTICLE in *Great Events from History: The Nineteenth Century, 1801-1900:* 1899: Hilbert Publishes *The Foundations of Geometry*.

LOBENGULA
King of the Ndebele (r. 1870-1894)

Lobengula was the second and last independent ruler of the Ndebele kingdom, which dominated what is now Zimbabwe before it was colonized. Tricked into signing a treaty he could not fully understand, he lost control of his kingdom to a chartered British company headed by Cecil Rhodes.

BORN: c. 1836; near Pretoria, Transvaal (now in South Africa)
DIED: January, 1894; near Bulawayo, Matabeleland (now in Zimbabwe)
ALSO KNOWN AS: Lobengula Khumalo (full name); Loben Gula; Ulobengula; Upengula
AREAS OF ACHIEVEMENT: Warfare and conquest, government and politics

EARLY LIFE

Little is known about the early life of Lobengula (loh-behn-GEW-lah) beyond the fact that he was born in the western part of the Transvaal around the time that the Ndebele kingdom was preparing to move north to relocate in the southwestern part of what is now Zimbabwe—a region that became known as Matabeleland. Lobengula was the son of the Ndebele founder-king Mzilikazi by a Swazi princess. As his mother was considered one of his father's lesser wives, he was not next in line for the kingship when his father died in September, 1868. However, the recognized heir, Nkulumane, had disappeared during the Ndebele migration into Matabeleland a generation earlier, and Lobengula was installed as king in 1870.

Lobengula was known for his intelligence and prodigious memory, both of which served him well in royal council meetings. Standing more than six feet tall and weighing a prodigious amount, Lobengula had a commanding presence. As a first act of his rule, he moved from his father's palace at Mhlahlandela and built a new chief village at Bulawayo. He then extended Ndebele domination over the Shona-speaking tribes to the north

and east and eventually came to rule much of the region of what is now Zimbabwe.

Lobengula was only the second ruler of the Ndebele kingdom. His father, Mzilikazi, created the kingdom after breaking away from service to the famous Zulu conqueror Shaka around 1822. He then established his own power base on the interior highlands of the Transvaal, using the Zulu fighting methods perfected by Shaka. In their new home in Matabeleland, the Ndebele (who were known to their Sotho- and Tswana-speaking neighbors as "Matabele") enjoyed much greater security than they had had in a series of settlements in the Transvaal during the 1820's and 1830's, when they had been repeatedly attacked by the Zulu, Afrikaners (Boers), and Griquas.

As Lobengula settled into power in Matabeleland during the 1870's, far to the south, the English immigrant Cecil Rhodes was making a fortune from his consolidation of the chaotic diamond mines at Kimberley. During the mid-1880's, he began making a second fortune in the new Witwatersrand gold mines of the Transvaal. Meanwhile, he and his associates were taking an increasing interest in the rumored mineral wealth of the Zimbabwe plateau, which had been known in earlier centuries for its gold mines.

LIFE'S WORK

Lobengula was a popular figure among the few European traders, hunters, and missionaries who entered his kingdom during the 1870's, and he gained a reputation for kindness to visitors. In 1875, he permitted the British missionary Charles Helm to establish the Hope Fountain Mission near Bulawayo. Over the years, he came to trust Helm. In 1879, Lobengula permitted three Jesuit missionaries to travel through Matabeleland, but he did not permit them to proselytize to his subjects.

In 1880, agents sent by Cecil Rhodes arrived at Bulawayo to negotiate concessions to prospect for gold in one limited part of the Matabeleland, in return for annual payments to Lobengula. The king signed the concession in September and renewed it the following year. In 1887, he signed two additional concessions. The holders of the mining concessions faithfully made the required payments to Lobengula in order to build a relationship of trust.

In early 1888, John Smith Moffat came to Bulawayo as an agent of the British government. His task was to convince Lobengula of the advantages he would receive by signing a treaty of friendship with the British. Moffat was a former missionary in Matabeleland and was also the son of the missionary Robert Moffat, who had been Mzilikazi's most trusted European friend and adviser. Moffat's past connections with the Ndebele kingdom placed him in a special position of trust with Lobengula, to whom he conveyed the idea that if he were to sign a treaty of friendship with the British government, he had everything to gain and nothing to lose. Such a treaty, Moffat promised, would protect Ndebele lands from the expansion of the Afrikaners, provide him with an annual income and arms, and develop Ndebele mineral wealth. After Lobengula signed the so-called Moffat Treaty on February 11, the path was cleared for Rhodes to send his own delegation later in the year.

In August, 1888, a three-man team led by Rhodes's business partner Charles Rudd arrived in Bulawayo to negotiate a new treaty that would give a syndicate headed by Rhodes a mineral rights concession. During negotiations that lasted two months, many members of Lobengula's royal council expressed their doubts about the wisdom of permitting European mining interests into their domain. However, the promise of a payment of one hundred pounds sterling per month and delivery of one thousand modern rifles with 100,000 rounds of ammunition in return for what appeared to be merely the right for a small number of British miners to explore for gold seemed too good an offer for Lobengula to turn down.

Before signing what became known as the Rudd Concession, Lobengula had his trusted friend Charles Helm translate the provisions of the treaty for him. This proved to be a costly mistake. Over the years, Helm had grown frustrated over the resistance of the Ndebele to Christian proselytizing and Lobengula's own lack of interest in changing traditional belief systems. Helm perceived that removal of Lobengula might open Ndebele society to Christianity. He therefore knowingly mistranslated a clause of the treaty that gave Rhodes's syndicate broad permission to take "whatever action they considered necessary" to exploit Ndebele mineral wealth. Without realizing it, Lobengula surrendered legal control of his country when he signed the concession on October 30, 1888.

With the Rudd Concession document in hand, Rhodes traveled to London to obtain permission to settle Central Africa under the auspices of the British government. In October, 1889, Queen Victoria signed a charter authorizing the newly created British South Africa Company (BSAC) to take control of territories north of the Limpopo River. As head of the chartered company, Rhodes was empowered to act as he wished without first obtaining government permission. He could make treaties, pass laws, and exercise police powers over the native population.

When Lobengula discovered that he had been deceived, he angrily protested to Queen Victoria and renounced the Rudd Concession. His protests, however, went unheeded. In 1890, the BSAC sent two hundred "pioneers" into Shonaland—over which the Ndebele had exercised control for four decades—accompanied by

---

LOBENGULA IN 1872

One of the most accomplished nineteenth century hunters in the region now known as Zimbabwe was Frederick Courteney Selous, who spent more than twenty years in the region. In this passage from a book he published in 1881, Selous describes his first meeting with the Ndebele king Lobengula nine years earlier.

The following morning Lobengula, king of the powerful tribe of the Matabele, came down to our waggons. He is man standing about 5 feet 10 or 11, strongly and stoutly built, and even at that date was growing very stout; he was then dressed in a greasy shirt and dirty pair of trousers, but I am happy to say that the during the last few years I have known him, he has discarded European clothing, and now always appears in his own native dress, in which he looks what he is—the chief of a savage and barbarous people. . . . He was attended by about fifty natives who had all been squatting in a semi-circle during the interview, but all of whom, immediately he rose to go, cried out, "How! How!" in a tone of intense surprise, as if some lovely apparition had burst upon their view; then, as he passed, they followed, crouching down and crying out, "Oh, thou prince of princes! thou black one! thou calf of the black cow! though black elephant!" etc. etc.

Source: Frederick Courteney Selous, *A Hunter's Wanderings in Africa* (London: Richard Bentley, 1881), p. 29.

two hundred heavily armed guards. This so-called Pioneer Column was led by Rhodes's close associate, Dr. Leander Starr Jameson. In September, the column established a township that they named Salisbury, after the serving British foreign minister. (That location is now the capital of Zimbabwe, Harare.) The members of the column and those who followed them were soon disappointed by the pitifully small amounts of gold that they found in the remains of mines that had been depleted centuries earlier. However, Rhodes had other plans to satisfy the pioneers and his company stockholders. Large tracks of fertile land, large cattle herds, and a mild climate made Lobengula's domain an appealing region for European settlement. The BSAC's offering of six-thousand-acre tracts attracted a flood of settlers to Mashonaland. By the turn of the twentieth century, more than 16 million acres would be settled by Europeans.

Meanwhile, Lobengula was becoming increasingly militant. When he sent a raiding party into a Shona village near the British base at Fort Victoria in July, 1893, the local settlers demanded that the company retaliate. It is unlikely that Lobengula—who never received rifles promised under the Rudd Concession—wanted war with the British. Nevertheless, in October, 1893, heavily armed forces under Jameson's command converged on Bulawayo. Lobengula's efforts to negotiate a peace were ignored. In several pitched battles, more than three thousand Ndebele warriors, armed mainly with spears and cowhide shields, died under the withering fire of Gatling guns and rifles, while Jameson's force suffered only one casualty. After having Bulawayo put to the torch, Lobengula fled north with his few remaining loyal warriors. He continued to send out emissaries to arrange for negotiations but failed to connect with the enemy commanders.

Lobengula's exact fate is unknown. He appears to have died from some disease in January, 1894. His remains were never found by the British. After Lobengula's death was reported, Jameson declared that all Ndebele land and cattle were the property of the BSAC. The company's defeat of Lobengula was more a symbolic victory than a complete conquest of the Ndebele, most of whom were little affected by their king's fall. However, major risings of both the Ndebele and the Shona peoples in 1896 were soundly crushed, and company control over most of present Zimbabwe was complete.

SIGNIFICANCE

Lobengula's life is significant for what it reveals about nineteenth century Africa. His father was caught in the tidal wave of Zulu expansion into South Africa, success-

fully breaking away to form his own kingdom. Both he and Lobengula expanded their rule to dominate the Shona people of Mashonaland. Lobengula's possible involvement in the elimination of Nkulumane, the rightful successor to the kingship, and his harsh exploitation of Shona communities indicate a ruthless side to his nature.

On the other hand, Lobengula's reign also illustrates the even more unscrupulous nature of European imperialism. Lobengula was duped into signing over control of his kingdom to a company created by England's most ambitious imperialist, Cecil Rhodes. Lobengula signed away not only mining concessions but also the farmland, cattle, and basic livelihoods of the Ndebele and Shona tribes. His domain later became the British crown colony of Southern Rhodesia, the vast majority of whose people became less than second-class citizens.

The great "scam" perpetrated on Lobengula forms a dismal chapter in the ethically bleak period after 1870, when European powers scrambled for control of Africa. The end result of Lobengula's downfall was the creation of a state in which a tiny European minority controlled the majority population. The descendants of the original European settlers in Rhodesia would pay a heavy price more than a century later, when the African government of independent Zimbabwe began seizing the rich lands of the country's remaining white farmers for redistribution to African citizens.

—*Irwin Halfond*

FURTHER READING

Bhebe, Ngwabi. *Lobengula of Zimbabwe*. London: Heinemann Educational Books, 1977. Brief illustrated account of Lobengula's life for African schools by an Ndebele historian.

Cloete, Stuart. *African Portraits: A Biography of Paul Kruger, Cecil Rhodes, and Lobengula, the Last King of the Matabele*. London: Simon, 2001. Originally published in 1969, this book contains clear biographical sketches of Lobengula and his nemesis, Cecil Rhodes.

Glass, Stafford. *The Matabele War*. London: Longmans, 1968. Fullest scholarly account of the war that ended Lobengula's reign.

Rubert, Steven C., and R. Kent Rasmussen. *Historical Dictionary of Zimbabwe*. 3d ed. Lanham, Md.: Scarecrow Press, 2001. Comprehensive reference work on Zimbabwe history that contains lengthy entries on the Ndebele, Lobengula, Jameson, Rhodes, and many other related subjects that are written by a specialist in Ndebele history.

Samkange, Stanlake. *On Trial for My Country*. London: Heinemann Education Books, 1967. Novel by an Ndebele historian in which Lobengula is called to account for the loss of his kingdom.

Watt, Duncan. *Legacy of Lobengula*. Singapore: Graham Brash, 1996. A study of the role played by Lobengula's fall in the development of Rhodesia.

SEE ALSO: Sir Robert Stephenson Smyth Baden-Powell; Cetshwayo; Cecil Rhodes; Samory Touré; Shaka; Tewodros II; Queen Victoria.

RELATED ARTICLE in *Great Events from History: The Nineteenth Century, 1801-1900:* October, 1893-October, 1897: British Subdue African Resistance in Rhodesia.

BELVA A. LOCKWOOD
American lawyer and social reformer

Lockwood obtained passage of federal legislation giving women equal pay for equal work in government service in the United States. She also was the first woman granted the right to plead cases before the U.S. Supreme Court and was a committed activist for women's rights.

BORN: October 24, 1830; Royalton, New York
DIED: May 19, 1917; Washington, D.C.
ALSO KNOWN AS: Belva Ann Bennett (birth name); Belva McNall
AREAS OF ACHIEVEMENT: Law, women's rights

EARLY LIFE

Belva Ann Bennett was the second of the five children of Lewis Bennett and Hannah Green Bennett. She attended country schools and completed her education by the age of fifteen. Her father's opposition to her educational ambitions, as well as a lack of funds, led her to begin a career in teaching. She taught school for four years before marrying Uriah McNall, a local farmer. The young couple moved to the country near Gasport, where Belva gave birth to a daughter, Lura. When her husband died in a sawmill accident in 1853, Belva returned to school to further her education in order to support herself and her child.

Belva McNall sold the farm and entered Gasport Academy. She also continued to teach school. As a teacher, she experienced at first hand inequities toward women when she was offered half the salary paid to male teachers. Angry and upset, she left her daughter with her parents and entered Genessee College, where she studied law, political economy, and the U.S. Constitution. On June 27, 1857, she received a bachelor of science degree from the college that was to become Syracuse University.

In 1857, Belva McNall became headmistress of Lockport Union School, where her daughter studied. For the next four years, she supervised the staff, taught courses, and, despite conservative disapproval, encouraged gymnastics, public speaking, nature walks, and skating for young women. She also taught at the Gainesville Female Seminary and later became proprietor of the Female Seminary in Oswego, New York. In 1866, while in her middle thirties, Belva McNall, with her daughter Lura, left for Washington, D.C. Her profession was still teaching, but she had political ambitions that would eventually take her far beyond the classroom.

In 1867, Belva McNall opened a school of her own. On March 11, 1868, she married Ezekiel Lockwood, a dentist and former Baptist minister. Their only child, Jessie, died in infancy. Ezekiel Lockwood assumed the administrative duties of his wife's school so that she could pursue a law degree. Denied admission to Columbia, Georgetown, and Harvard because she was not only a woman but also a married one, Lockwood was finally accepted at the National University Law School. She completed her studies in 1873 but was awarded her diploma only after she petitioned President Ulysses S. Grant, the school's ex officio president, to intervene on her behalf. Her husband, who had continued to supervise her school in Washington, was finally forced to close it because of his ill health. He died in 1877.

LIFE'S WORK

After judicial rules were changed and women were allowed to practice law in the District of Columbia, Belva Lockwood was admitted to the bar on September 24, 1873. She then embarked on a distinguished career in law. When one of her cases came before the Federal Court of Claims that winter, Lockwood was refused, because she was a woman, the right to plead a case. Her petition for admission to the Supreme Court of the United States (1876) was denied on the basis of custom, but Lockwood would not admit defeat. She petitioned Congress to pass a Declaratory Act or Joint Resolution "that no woman otherwise qualified, shall be debarred from practice before any United States Court on account of sex."

Reasoning that if women had the right to practice law they were entitled to pursue legal matters through the highest courts in the country, Lockwood pushed enabling legislation through Congress. By means of energetic lobbying, and with the support of such pro-suffrage senators as Aaron A. Sargent of California and George F. Hoar of Massachusetts, Lockwood secured the passage of the Lockwood Bill, which permitted women to practice before the Supreme Court. On March 3, 1879, she became the first woman to be admitted to the Bar of the U.S. Supreme Court. Three days later, she was admitted to the U.S. Court of Claims.

A year later, on February 2, 1880, in a striking demonstration of her commitment to racial equality, Lockwood appeared before the Supreme Court of the United States and made a motion that Samuel R. Lowery, an African American, be allowed to practice before the Supreme Court. Lowery, who was the principal of the Huntsville Industrial University in Alabama, became the first black southerner to practice law before the Supreme Court of the United States.

Lockwood became a familiar sight in Washington as she pedaled throughout the city on "Challenge No. 2," an English tricycle that she introduced to the nation's capital. She rode the vehicle to the Capitol, the courts—wherever her work led her. By 1890, Lockwood was well established in her law career, specializing in pension and claims cases against the U.S. government. It was this specialty that led her to one of the greatest legal triumphs of her career. The Cherokee Indian Nation secured Lockwood to represent it in claims against the U.S. government related to an 1891 treaty involving the sale and purchase of more than eight million acres of land known as the Cherokee Outlet. Lockwood was entrusted with defending nearly fifteen thousand Cherokee clients. After reviewing the numerous treaties and statutes that governed the history of the Cherokees, she filed a petition to uphold the claim of her Indian clients.

On March 20, 1905, the case of the Eastern and Emigrant Cherokees against the United States was decided before the Court of Claims. Following an impassioned argument by Lockwood, the chief justice agreed that the United States had broken and evaded the letter and spirit of its agreement with the Cherokees. Nevertheless, although he decreed that the Cherokees recover certain amounts due in the account rendered by the government, he could not bring himself to allow the full interest on those amounts. The case was appealed to the Supreme Court, where, on April 30, 1906, Lockwood again argued for the Indians and their rights. The court agreed and awarded the Cherokees five million dollars.

As a feminist, Lockwood did much to further women's rights. In 1867, she was one of the founders of Washington's first suffrage group, the Universal Franchise Association. During the 1870's and early 1880's, she was active in the Washington conventions of the National Woman Suffrage Association (NWSA). In January, 1871, Lockwood presented a memorial to the U.S. Senate on "The Right of Women to Vote."

Lockwood addressed congressional committees and drew up innumerable resolutions

Belva A. Lockwood. (Library of Congress)

and bills that would help bring equality to women in the United States. She circulated a petition at the meetings of the National and American Woman Suffrage Associations in New York that hastened the passage, in 1872, of legislation giving women government employees equal pay for equal work. In 1873, she represented a woman in a divorce case, charging the defendant with drunkenness, cruel treatment, desertion, and refusal to support. She won the case for her client, obtaining the decree of divorce and alimony with costs. Later, in 1896, as a member of a committee of the District Federation of Women's Clubs, she helped Ellen Spencer Mussey and others secure passage of a law liberalizing the property rights of married women and equal guardianship of their children in the District of Columbia. In 1903, she proposed the inclusion of woman suffrage clauses in the statehood bills for Oklahoma, Arizona, and New Mexico, which were then under consideration.

In 1872, Lockwood spoke at Cooper Union in New York on behalf of Victoria Woodhull's candidacy for president of the United States. Lockwood herself was nominated for president in 1884 by women representing the National Equal Rights Party. Her platform reflected her commitment to civil rights, temperance, and feminism. She encompassed equal rights for all, including African Americans, Indians, and immigrants. She advocated curtailment of the liquor traffic, reform in marriage and divorce laws, and universal peace. She flourished a banner inscribed on one side with the words "Women's Rights" and on the other with the word "Peace."

Although Lockwood's campaign alienated many members of the organized suffrage movement, including Susan B. Anthony, it generated much public interest. Astonishingly, she won the electoral vote of Indiana and half that of Oregon, nearly captured New Hampshire, and made a respectable showing in New York. A second campaign four years later was less successful. Her political aptitude was recognized by President Grover Cleveland, who sent her as the U.S. delegate to the Congress of Charities and Correction in Geneva, Switzerland.

Increasingly committed to the cause of world peace, Lockwood put much of her energy into peace organizations after the 1880's. One of the earliest members of the Universal Peace Union, Lockwood served at various times during the 1880's and 1890's on the union's executive committee and the editorial board of its paper, the *Peacemaker*, as a corresponding secretary and vice president, and as one of the union's chief lobbyists. She was the union's delegate to the International Peace Congress of 1889 and its successors; served as the American secre-

tary of the International Bureau of Peace, founded in Berne in 1891; and served on the nominating committee for the Nobel Peace Prize. In all these organizations, she agitated for the arbitration principle as a means of settling world problems.

Lockwood remained politically active into her later years. She continued lecturing well into her eighties and even campaigned for Woodrow Wilson. In 1909, she was awarded an honorary LL.D. degree by Syracuse University, and in 1913, she was presented with an oil portrait of herself by the women of Washington, D.C. The portrait now hangs in the Art Gallery of the National Museum.

Following the death of her daughter Lura in 1894, Lockwood's financial fortunes collapsed, and her last years were spent in ill health and relative poverty. She died at George Washington University Hospital in 1917 and was buried in the Congressional Cemetery in Washington. The funeral service held in the Wesley Chapel of the Methodist Episcopalian Church recalled the triumphs of her life, and the newspapers recorded her history. A scholarship was established in Lockwood's name, and a bust of Lockwood was unveiled by the Women's Bar Association of the District of Columbia to commemorate the seventy-fifth anniversary of her admission to the Supreme Court.

SIGNIFICANCE

Legally and socially, Belva A. Lockwood scored important victories for women. Marriage, she concluded, should be a civil contract in which property rights were equal. She rebelled against the law in the District of Columbia that could compel a man to support his illegitimate child but could not compel him to support his wife and his legitimate children. She worked for the reform of probate law and recognition of the rights of widows and orphans. Single-handedly, Lockwood moved the U.S. Congress to open the highest court to women lawyers. She fought for civil rights for all Americans. Up to the day she died, she worked for world peace.

Over the years of her practice, Lockwood gave aid, advice, and encouragement to women from all parts of the country who were attempting to become attorneys-at-law. Lockwood's hard-won battles, confidence, and fortitude are an inspiration to women throughout the world.

—*Diane C. Vecchio*

FURTHER READING

Curti, Merle. *Peace or War*. New York: Garland, 1972.

Curti discusses Lockwood's pacifism and her efforts

to advance peace on the national and international scenes.

Fox, Mary Virginia. *Lady for the Defense: A Biography of Belva Lockwood*. New York: Harcourt Brace Jovanovich, 1975. A useful, relatively recent treatment of Lockwood's life and work.

Klebanow, Diana, and Franklin L. Jonas. *People's Lawyers: Crusaders for Justice in American History*. Armonk, N.Y.: M. E. Sharpe, 2003. Contains short biographical chapters on ten civil rights attorneys, including Lockwood. Features a biography of her life and career, a chronology of key events in her life, a review of her major cases, and an annotated bibliography.

Norgren, Jill. "Lockwood in '84." *Wilson Quarterly* 26, no. 4 (Autumn, 2002): 12. Examines Lockwood's 1884 presidential campaign, describing her personal life and career and her opinions of woman suffrage.

Stanton, Elizabeth Cady, et al., eds. *History of Woman Suffrage*. New York: Arno Press, 1969. Contains informative accounts of the NWSA's Washington conventions, 1870 to 1874, in volumes 2 through 4 (1882-1902) and useful chapters on the District of Columbia in volumes 3 and 4.

Stern, Madeleine. *We the Women*. New York: Schulte, 1963. This work contains the most complete account available of Belva Lockwood's life. Stern discusses, at length, Lockwood's most celebrated court cases, including her own quest to practice before the Supreme Court. This is the best source to consult regarding Lockwood's commitment to women's rights, civil rights, and pacifism.

Whitman, Alden, ed. *American Reformers*. New York: H. W. Wilson, 1985. A brief but fairly thorough account of Lockwood's life, highlighting her women's rights and peace activism.

SEE ALSO: Susan B. Anthony; Grover Cleveland; Ulysses S. Grant; Victoria Woodhull.

RELATED ARTICLES in *Great Events from History: The Nineteenth Century, 1801-1900:* July 4, 1876: Declaration of the Rights of Women; February 17-18, 1890: Women's Rights Associations Unite.

SIR JOSEPH NORMAN LOCKYER
English astrophysicist

A pioneering, self-educated astrophysicist, Lockyer founded the world's premier general science periodical, the weekly journal Nature, *which he edited throughout its first fifty years.*

BORN: May 17, 1836; Rugby, Warwickshire, England
DIED: August 16, 1920; Salcombe Regis, Devonshire, England
AREAS OF ACHIEVEMENT: Astronomy, journalism

EARLY LIFE

Joseph Norman Lockyer was the son of Joseph Hooley Lockyer, a surgeon-apothecary in Rugby. His mother, who had been born Anne Norman, was the daughter of the squire of a Warwickshire village near Rugby. He had one sibling, a younger sister, and he was called Norman as he was growing up.

Lockyer's father had broad scientific interests and had been a founding member of the Rugby Literary and Scientific Institution. As a teenager, Lockyer's principal interest at school was not science but languages, especially Latin and Greek. In 1856, at the age of twenty, he went to the Continent for a year to study French and German. Upon his return to England, Lockyer obtained a temporary position at the War Office in May, 1857. In February of the following year he was appointed to a permanent clerkship in the War Office and appeared destined for a career in the civil service. In the same year he married Winifred James, whose father, William, had an important role in the early development of English railroads. Winifred possessed, as did her husband, an excellent knowledge of the French language, and after her marriage she became known as a translator of French scientific texts.

The Lockyers' first home was in the village of Wimbledon, an easy commute by train to London and the War Office. The Lockyers had nine children, seven boys and two girls, before Winifred died in 1879. Twenty-four years later, in 1903, Lockyer married Thomasine Mary Brodhurst, the fifty-year-old widow of a surgeon. She outlived Lockyer and after his death published a volume on Lockyer's life and work.

Lockyer was an energetic and forceful personality of medium height, somewhat thickset, who did not shrink from controversy. He was ambitious and an exceedingly hard worker, driving himself on several occasions to the point where he required a complete respite from work; nevertheless, he also enjoyed a variety of leisure activities, particularly golf, for which he coauthored *The Rules of Golf* (1896).

LIFE'S WORK

Lockyer's transformation from obscure War Office clerk to internationally known editor and scientist began in Wimbledon, where, influenced by new acquaintances, he took up astronomy as a hobby, purchasing a three-and-three-quarters-inch refracting telescope and becoming a fellow of the Royal Astronomical Society in 1861. On May 10, 1862, the *London Review* published his account of his observations of the transit of the shadow of Saturn's moon Titan across the planet's disc. The *London Review*'s editor subsequently invited Lockyer to submit an article each month under the title "Face of the Sky." Lockyer regarded this series as the beginning of his literary work.

Lockyer also became science editor and writer for the *Reader*, a new literary and scientific journal. When the *Reader* foundered after only a few years, Lockyer envisioned a weekly journal devoted exclusively to science. His idea appealed to the publisher Alexander Macmillan, and *Nature* was launched on November 4, 1869. *Nature* experienced financial difficulties in its early years, but thanks to Lockyer's enthusiasm and Macmillan's continued support it survived, showing a profit for the first time in 1899 and going on to become the world's most respected general scientific journal in the twentieth century and Lockyer's most lasting contribution. Lockyer was its editor throughout its first fifty years.

When the British government named a Royal Commission on Scientific Instruction and the Advancement of Science in 1870, Lockyer was delighted to be summoned from the War Office to be its secretary, a position he held until the commission issued its final report in 1875. The experience gave him a comprehensive knowledge of the strengths and weaknesses of science in Great Britain. Throughout his adult life he was an advocate of the state support of science. Upon the completion of the commission's work, Lockyer did not return to the War Office, being appointed instead to the government's Science and Art Department with responsibility for arranging an exhibition of significant laboratory and scientific teaching apparatus at London's South Kensington Museum.

Opened by Queen Victoria in 1876, the exhibition was a great success. In addition to arranging the exhibi-

tion, Lockyer was expected by the department to continue his by then significant astrophysical researches, and so he established a small government observatory, soon to be known as the Solar Physics Observatory. When in 1878 the government created a Solar Physics Committee, Lockyer sat on it as representative of the Science and Art Department. Nine years later, the committee became an advisory and supervisory board for the Solar Physics Laboratory still directed by Lockyer. Since 1881, Lockyer had taught astronomy at the Normal School of Science and the Royal School of Mines (renamed the Royal College of Science in 1890) in London. He was promoted to professor of astronomical physics in 1887.

While earning his livelihood in these various positions, Lockyer had from the 1860's pursued, frequently in his spare time, his research interests in the new field of astrophysics. In 1859, Robert Bunsen and Gustav Robert Kirchhoff, professors of chemistry and physics, respectively, at the University of Heidelberg in Germany had founded spectrum analysis on the principle that each element has its characteristic spectrum.

During the following year Kirchhoff had given an explanation of the dark, or Fraunhofer, lines in the solar spectrum, thereby revealing the chemical composition of the sun and at the same time initiating the science of astrophysics. Lockyer quickly became attracted to this new branch of astronomy—which utilized the new instrument the spectroscope, and also the camera, together with the traditional telescope—and just as quickly began to make his mark in it. During the early 1860's, a dispute had arisen concerning whether spots on the sun were hotter or cooler than the surrounding solar surface.

Lockyer devised a means of spectroscopically examining the light from individual sunspots, as opposed to the entire solar disc, and established that the spots are cooler than their surroundings. He then turned to a study of solar prominences, bright clouds of matter that were observed during solar eclipses to rise from the sun's surface into its corona, or atmosphere. Employing the method that he had devised for examining individual sunspots, Lockyer demonstrated in 1868 that prominences could be studied with the spectroscope at times other than solar eclipses, and, further, that, because of their bright line spectra, prominences were clouds of hot gas. Unknown to Lockyer, this conclusion had been independently reached by the French astrophysicist Pierre Jules César Janssen, using a similar method, a few weeks earlier. The French government honored Janssen's and Lockyer's simultaneous discovery by striking a medal with their portraits on it. On the strength of his original contributions to solar physics, Lockyer was elected a fellow of the Royal Society, Great Britain's most prestigious scientific society, in 1869.

Lockyer's further spectroscopic and astrophysical researches led him to formulate two bold hypotheses for which he became widely known. The first hypothesis concerned the dissociation of matter. At the time, during the 1870's, the concepts of atom and molecule (a combination of two or more atoms) were found to be useful in chemistry and certain branches of physics. For example, gaseous hydrogen was regarded as comprising hydrogen molecules, each consisting of two hydrogen atoms; the two spectra found in the laboratory to be characteristic of hydrogen, a band spectrum and a line spectrum, were attributed to the molecular and atomic forms of hydrogen, respectively.

It was believed that as the temperature of the hydrogen gas was increased, the molecules of hydrogen became dissociated into atoms, and so the band spectrum became replaced by the line spectrum. In the astrophysical realm, red stars, believed to be of relatively low temperature, exhibited band spectra; yellow stars, of higher temperature, such as the Sun, exhibited the line spectra of numerous elements, including the heaviest; and white stars, believed to be of yet higher temperature, displayed the line spectrum of the simplest element of all, hydrogen. From these and from other observations, Lockyer hypothesized in 1873 that with increasing stellar temperature heavier elements became dissociated into lighter ones and their common constituents.

In considering the constitutions of elemental atoms, Lockyer suggested an analogy with the composition of members of a hydrocarbon series that organic chemists had shown could be built up through successive additions of the radical CH_2. Earlier in the nineteenth century, a British physician, William Prout, had hypothesized that the hydrogen atom might be the building block of all other atoms.

At the annual meeting of the British Association for the Advancement of Science in 1879, Lockyer announced that he had been successful in partially decomposing several elements into hydrogen in the laboratory. Chemists were not convinced, however, and even though astrophysicists continued to support the dissociation hypothesis during the 1880's, by the end of the century they, too, had concluded that it was untenable. About that time a quite different view of atomic composition was beginning to take shape following Joseph John Thomson's discovery in 1897 of the astonishingly small parti-

cle, some two thousand times smaller than the hydrogen atom, soon to be known as the electron. In *The Chemistry of the Sun* (1887) Lockyer summarized his ideas on dissociation and answered criticisms of the dissociation hypothesis. He published a revised version of the hypothesis in *Inorganic Evolution as Studied by Spectrum Analysis* (1900).

In connection with the dissociation hypothesis, Lockyer had been unable to determine the constituents of atoms, but with the much grander meteoritic hypothesis he specified that meteors were the building blocks of the visible universe. As he claimed, "all self-luminous bodies in the celestial spaces are composed either of swarms of meteorites or of masses of meteoritic vapour produced by heat."

In 1866, two striking astronomical phenomena, a nova and the Leonid shower of meteors, greatly impressed Lockyer. He speculated that the phenomena might be related, that a nova might result from the collision of showers of meteors. Later, in 1874, in viewing Coggia's comet Lockyer adopted the idea, not original with him, that a comet consists of a shower of meteors whose frequent, mutual collisions cause the comet's luminosity. The spectroscopic study in the laboratory of available meteorites strengthened Lockyer's belief in the meteoritic nature of comets.

When the first nova to be examined systematically using the spectroscope developed a spectrum characteristic of a nebula in 1877, Lockyer argued that the observed spectroscopic changes could be interpreted as the result of a gradual cooling of meteors from the intense heat of their impact to the cooler state of a nebula. Hitherto, Lockyer had, like others, assumed nebulas to be the hottest bodies in the universe, which in cooling developed into stars that continued to fall in temperature over time. Now, on spectroscopic grounds, Lockyer argued that nebulas developed into *cool* stars that, on condensing, rose in temperature before becoming cool once more. He was aware that the teaching of the accepted view of stellar evolution, that stars are born hot and cool throughout their lives, ran against his argument.

Principally because of this disagreement with the prevailing view, the meteoritic hypothesis lost support among astrophysicists and perished. Lockyer published his views on stellar evolution in *The Meteoritic Hypothesis* (1890) and his further development of the meteoritic hypothesis in *The Sun's Place in Nature* (1897). *Inorganic Evolution as Studied by Spectrum Analysis* (1900) was the last of Lockyer's books to deal with both the meteoritic and the dissociation hypotheses.

During a visit to Greece and Turkey early in 1890, Lockyer became curious about the orientations of ancient temples. Later, in studying Egyptian temples, to which most of the available data referred, he argued that if their orientations had an astronomical basis, then determination of the orientations could lead to establishing the dates of construction of the temples. Lockyer determined that several temples at Karnak were oriented toward either the rising or the setting solstitial sun, while the pyramids and temples at Giza were oriented toward the equinoctial sun. He calculated that the temple of Amen-Ra at Karnak had been built about 3700 B.C.E.

Lockyer found that some temples were not oriented toward the sun, but instead toward bright stars, including Sirius. Lockyer went on to apply his ideas on orientation to Stonehenge and other ancient stone monuments in Great Britain. He concluded that they could be arranged in an evolutionary order: Avenues and cromlechs came first, and stone circles, representing a more advanced state of astronomical knowledge, came later. He believed that the sunrise orientations used in the earlier stage were related to the appearance of new vegetation in May, whereas those of the later stage were related to the summer solstice in June. In dealing with both Egyptian temples and British monuments, Lockyer made speculative, and controversial, excursions into mythology and folklore. His conclusions regarding the orientations of Egyptian temples were published in *The Dawn of Astronomy: A Study of the Temple Worship and Mythology of the Ancient Egyptians* (1894) and his views on British stone structures in *Stonehenge and Other British Monuments Astronomically Considered* (1906).

In 1901, Lockyer was obliged to retire from the Royal College of Science because of age regulations, but he continued as director of the Solar Physics Laboratory until 1911, when it was decided, to his profound disappointment and against his vigorous opposition, to transfer the observatory to Cambridge University. Lockyer's response to the transfer was to build an observatory at Sidmouth in Devonshire, which he directed until his death in 1920.

SIGNIFICANCE

Joseph Norman Lockyer was a self-educated and widely known man of broad interests, including scientific publishing, astrophysics, ancient astronomy, meteorology, education, the state support of science, and golf. During his busy life he played many roles, including those of civil servant, secretary to a royal commission on science, professor of astronomy, director of astronomical observatories, fellow of the Royal Society, president of the British Association for the Advancement of Science, and founder of the British Science Guild. Finally, he made substantial contributions: He was a leading astrophysicist, a sound experimentalist, and a bold theorizer, and he founded and edited *Nature*, which remains the world's foremost general scientific periodical. Lockyer's positive influence was felt by international scientists, British scientific institutions, the field of astrophysics, science in general, and even scholars and fields outside science. In recognition of his services to science in Great Britain, Lockyer was knighted in 1897.

—William McGucken

FURTHER READING

Chapman, Allan. *The Victorian Amateur Astronomer: Independent Astronomical Research in Britain, 1820-1920*. New York: John Wiley & Sons, 1998. Information about Lockyer's astronomical discoveries is included in this book about the work and significance of amateur astronomers in nineteenth century Britain.

Clerke, Agnes M. *A Popular History of Astronomy During the Nineteenth Century*. Edinburgh: A and C Black, 1885. Reprint. Decorah, La.: Sattre Press, 2003. The second part, "Recent Progress of Astronomy," provides useful accounts of various aspects of astrophysics during its first twenty-five years.

Lockyer, T. Mary, and Winifred L. Lockyer, with the assistance of Prof. H. Dingle. *Life and Work of Sir Norman Lockyer*. London: Macmillan, 1928. This volume consists of a chronology of Lockyer's life by Dingle based on materials gathered by Lockyer's second wife, Mary, and younger daughter, Winifred, and a series of useful essays on aspects of Lockyer's work, for example the dissociation hypothesis, not explained in the chronology.

McGucken, William. *Nineteenth-Century Spectroscopy: Development of the Understanding of Spectra, 1802-1897*. Baltimore: Johns Hopkins University Press, 1969. The second chapter, "Atoms and Molecules and the Further Extension of the Principle of Spectrum Analysis," includes a detailed discussion of Lockyer's dissociation hypothesis.

Meadows, A. J. *Early Solar Physics*. Oxford, England: Pergamon Press, 1970. Provides a good account of the development of solar physics during the second half of the nineteenth century. Reproduces original papers, including several by Lockyer, that contributed to that development.

_____. *Science and Controversy: A Biography of Sir Norman Lockyer*. Cambridge, Mass.: MIT Press, 1972.

This is the better of the two accounts of Lockyer's life and work. Although the author occasionally lapses into a chronological account, he enables the reader to see Lockyer within the context of his times. He also presents a fuller, more critical account of Lockyer the man.

SEE ALSO: Margaret Lindsay Huggins; Samuel Pierpont Langley; Daniel and Alexander Macmillan; Simon Newcomb; Queen Victoria.

RELATED ARTICLE in *Great Events from History: The Nineteenth Century, 1801-1900:* 1814: Fraunhofer Invents the Spectroscope.

HENRY WADSWORTH LONGFELLOW
American poet

Longfellow was the most popular of all living poets during his time, and he also worked to establish the study of modern languages and comparative literature in the United States.

BORN: February 27, 1807; Portland, Massachusetts (now in Maine)
DIED: March 24, 1882; Cambridge, Massachusetts
AREAS OF ACHIEVEMENT: Literature, education

EARLY LIFE
The second of Stephen and Zilpah Wadsworth Longfellow's eight children, Henry Wadsworth Longfellow was born in Portland, Maine, when Maine was still a part of the Commonwealth of Massachusetts. As a member of a loving, prosperous, and distinguished Unitarian family, the future poet seems to have had a happy childhood that included the scenes he would describe in "My Lost Youth." He was a gentle, precocious boy who started school when he was three. At the age of six, he enrolled in the Portland Academy, where he was still a student when, on November 17, 1820, "The Battle of Lovell's Pond," his first published poem, appeared in the *Portland Gazette* with merely "Henry" given as the author's name. His work did not receive unanimous acclaim: That evening, he heard a family friend disparage the poem.

In 1821 Longfellow passed the entrance examination for Bowdoin College; however, maybe because of his age, he remained at the Portland Academy another school year while working for college credit. It was not until the fall of 1822 that Longfellow, with his older brother, left home to study on the campus in Brunswick, Maine. While at Bowdoin, he studied hard, read avidly, joined a college literary club known as the Peucinian Society, had poems published in several off-campus periodicals, and, in 1825, graduated fourth in a class of thirty-eight.

As graduation approached, Longfellow feared that he would have to follow his practical-minded father's wish and study law instead of pursuing a literary career, but the Bowdoin trustees offered him the new professorship of modern languages, provided that he study in Europe at his own expense to prepare himself for the job. Having accepted the opportunity gladly, Longfellow sailed from New York on May 15, 1826, at the age of nineteen.

LIFE'S WORK
When his ship docked in France one month later, Longfellow began acquiring a knowledge of modern European languages and literature that would serve him well as a widely read author and translator. Although his intellect was hardly provincial before the voyage, his long, early visit to Europe made him a literary man of the world. His method of study was mainly one of informal immersion in the ordinary life of the countries he visited: France, Spain, Italy, Austria, Germany, the Netherlands, Belgium, and England.

Beginning his duties at Bowdoin in the fall of 1829, Longfellow became one of the first professors of modern languages in any U.S. college, because the traditional emphasis in languages had been on Latin and ancient Greek. As an innovative, enthusiastic teacher who could not find suitable materials, he had to translate or edit textbooks for his classes, trying to make modern European literature interesting for his students. During this period at Bowdoin, Longfellow put aside his ambition for fame as a creative writer and devoted himself more to scholarly articles than to poems and prose stories. His interest turned also to courtship, and on September 14, 1831, he married Mary Potter, an educated, intelligent, nineteen-year-old girl from his hometown.

Even before his wedding, Longfellow had grown dissatisfied with teaching at Bowdoin. By 1832 he was applying for other jobs, including ones outside the field of higher education. Then Longfellow, talented as he was, again had the sort of good luck that had let him avoid life as a lawyer: George Ticknor, who taught modern languages at Harvard, resigned his position and recommended Longfellow as his replacement. The Harvard administration accepted Ticknor's recommendation, with the inclusion of their own recommendation that Longfellow travel again to Europe, this time to enrich his knowledge of German. Having resigned from Bowdoin, Longfellow, with his wife and two of her friends, sailed across the Atlantic and docked in England on May 8, 1835.

After a stay in London, where Longfellow arranged for the British publication of *Outre-Mer: A Pilgrimage Beyond the Sea* (1833-1834), his new prose collection based on the journal he had kept during his first European tour, he and his party sailed for northern Germany, from which they traveled through Denmark to Sweden, where he studied the Swedish and Finnish languages. In the fall, they went to the Netherlands, where, in Amsterdam, Mary, who had been enduring a difficult pregnancy, suffered a miscarriage. After a while, when her health seemed better, they traveled to Rotterdam, forty miles away; there, on November 29, 1835, Mary died.

In his grief, Longfellow still believed he should continue his European studies and decided not to return to the United States with his wife's body but to study in Heidelberg, Germany. In the summer of 1836, while on a vacation in the Alps, Longfellow met Frances "Fanny" Appleton, who, still in her late teens, was a smart, pretty, and charming woman from a rich Boston family. A mutual attraction soon developed. However, the time that Longfellow had available for his second visit to Europe had almost expired, and in October he sailed for the United States.

Settling in Cambridge, Massachusetts, Longfellow began his official duties as Smith Professor of Modern Languages at Harvard, delivering his first lecture on May 23, 1837. In effect, he chaired a small academic department, besides teaching in the same attention-getting way he had taught at Bowdoin. He also wrote, but, unlike his writing during his stay at the smaller college, his writing at Harvard was more imaginative and autobiographical than scholarly. His loosely built novel *Hyperion*, published in the summer of 1839, tells in only slight disguise of his courtship of Appleton, who had rejected his marriage proposal in 1837. Still romantically interested in her, he sent her a copy of the book, apparently not realizing that she would object to having the courtship made so nearly public. It was not until 1843 that she encouraged Longfellow's attention, and on July 13 of that year they married, receiving as a gift from the bride's father Craigie House, the historic Cambridge mansion where Longfellow had been renting rooms.

Henry Wadsworth Longfellow. (Library of Congress)

Meanwhile, a few months after *Hyperion*, Longfellow's first volume of poetry, *Voices of the Night* (1839), was published; it contained "The Psalm of Life," which became one of his best-known poems, and marked the beginning of his immense popularity with critics and ordinary readers. In 1841 Longfellow published *Ballads and Other Poems*, which included "The Skeleton in Armor," "The Village Blacksmith," and "Excelsior."

The next year, while sailing home after a stay in Germany, Longfellow wrote eight short abolitionist poems published as *Poems on Slavery* (1842). After Longfellow married Frances in 1843, his literary productivity continued. Although he published one more novel, *Kavanagh* (1849), his big success came in poetry, not only in such short poems as "The Arsenal at Springfield" and "The Building of the Ship" but also in long narrative poems, especially *Evangeline* (1847), *The Song of Hiawatha* (1855), and *The Courtship of Miles Standish* (1858). In 1854, when Longfellow resigned his position at Harvard to give his full professional attention to writing, the president, accepting the resignation with regret, praised Longfellow for the fame he had brought the college.

"MY LOST YOUTH"

Often I think of the beautiful town
That is seated by the sea;
Often in thought go up and down
The pleasant streets of that dear old town,
And my youth comes back to me.
And a verse of a Lapland song
Is haunting my memory still:
"A boy's will is the wind's will,
And the thoughts of youth are long, long thoughts."

I can see the shadowy lines of its trees,
And catch, in sudden gleams,
The sheen of the far-surrounding seas,
And islands that were the Hesperides
Of all my boyish dreams.
And the burden of that old song,
It murmurs and whispers still:
"A boy's will is the wind's will,
And the thoughts of youth are long, long thoughts."

I remember the black wharves and the slips,
And the sea-tides tossing free;
And Spanish sailors with bearded lips,
And the beauty and mystery of the ships,
And the magic of the sea.
And the voice of that wayward song
Is singing and saying still:
"A boy's will is the wind's will,
And the thoughts of youth are long, long thoughts."

I remember the bulwarks by the shore,
And the fort upon the hill;
The sunrise gun, with its hollow roar,
The drum-beat repeated o'er and o'er,
And the bugle wild and shrill.
And the music of that old song
Throbs in my memory still:
"A boy's will is the wind's will,
And the thoughts of youth are long, long thoughts."

I remember the sea-fight far away,
How it thundered o'er the tide!
And the dead captains, as they lay
In their graves, o'erlooking the tranquil bay,
Where they in battle died.
And the sound of that mournful song
Goes through me with a thrill:
"A boy's will is the wind's will,
And the thoughts of youth are long, long thoughts."

I can see the breezy dome of groves,
The shadows of Deering's Woods;
And the friendships old and the early loves
Come back with a sabbath sound, as of doves
In quiet neighborhoods.
And the verse of that sweet old song,
It flutters and murmurs still:
"A boy's will is the wind's will,
And the thoughts of youth are long, long thoughts."

I remember the gleams and glooms that dart
Across the schoolboy's brain;
The song and the silence in the heart,
That in part are prophecies, and in part
Are longings wild and vain.
And the voice of that fitful song
Sings on, and is never still:
"A boy's will is the wind's will,
And the thoughts of youth are long, long thoughts."

There are things of which I may not speak;
There are dreams that cannot die;
There are thoughts that make the strong heart weak,
And bring a pallor into the cheek,
And a mist before the eye.
And the words of that fatal song
Come over me like a chill:
"A boy's will is the wind's will,
And the thoughts of youth are long, long thoughts."

Strange to me now are the forms I meet
When I visit the dear old town;
But the native air is pure and sweet,
And the trees that o'ershadow each well-known street,
As they balance up and down,
Are singing the beautiful song,
Are sighing and whispering still:
"A boy's will is the wind's will,
And the thoughts of youth are long, long thoughts."

And Deering's Woods are fresh and fair,
And with joy that is almost pain
My heart goes back to wander there,
And among the dreams of the days that were,
I find my lost youth again.
And the strange and beautiful song,
The groves are repeating it still:
"A boy's will is the wind's will,
And the thoughts of youth are long, long thoughts."

Source: Henry Wadsworth Longfellow, *The Complete Poetical Works of Henry Wadsworth Longfellow* (Boston: Houghton, Mifflin, 1902).

No famous writer has ever had a happier marriage. Tragedy, however, struck suddenly on July 9, 1861. While Frances was heating wax to seal locks of her daughters' hair, her dress caught fire. She raced to her husband in a nearby room, but he could not put out the flames in time, and she died the next day. Longfellow, badly burned on his hands and face, never fully recovered from her death. His sonnet "The Cross of Snow," written in 1879, suggests the emotional scar, and, with shaving difficult because of his facial scars, he grew the white beard that his admirers came to associate with him.

When Longfellow eventually resumed writing after his second wife's death, he produced the long collections of related poems *Tales of a Wayside Inn* (1863), which included "Paul Revere's Ride," and *Christus: A Mystery* (1872). He also wrote such separate long poems as *Aftermath* (1873), *The Hanging of the Crane* (1874), and *Morituri Salutamus* (1875). Furthermore, from 1867 to 1869, he added Dante's monumental fourteenth century Italian poem *La Divina Commedia* (1320; *The Divine Comedy*) to his impressive list of translations. Working almost until the end of his life, Longfellow added a last stanza to his own poem "The Bells of San Blas" on March 15, 1882. On March 24, having been sick only a short time, he died at Craigie House, twenty-five days after an admiring nation had celebrated his seventy-fifth birthday.

SIGNIFICANCE

As Longfellow's friend George Washington Greene said, no poet ever received such acclaim while he was living. In North America and in Europe, Longfellow triumphed both popularly and critically. In 1868, while he was on his last visit to England, Queen Victoria invited him to Windsor Castle. That in itself was a high honor, but even more indicative of Longfellow's fame was that some of the queen's servants, ordinarily nonchalant about seeing the powerful and the celebrated, hid in the halls to watch Longfellow as he walked by.

Amid all the praise, Longfellow lived as a gentleman, not merely in the sense that, with his second wife's fortune and the money from his books, he could keep an ample store of wine at Craigie House, but also in the sense that he gave himself graciously. Reserved though he normally was, his many friends loved him, and they included such well-known men as the English novelist Charles Dickens, the American novelist Nathaniel Hawthorne (who had been one of Longfellow's Bowdoin classmates), and the abolitionist senator of Massachu-

setts, Charles Sumner. Having become an institution, Longfellow found himself besieged at Craigie House by uninvited strangers and by unknown letter writers, yet he remained polite, even when the visitors and correspondents were boorish.

Almost inevitably, such a high reputation had to fall. Although some readers voiced objections to his poetry during his lifetime and shortly after his death, the outcry arose with the general anti-Victorianism that began during World War I. Among other features of his poems, critics targeted his notion of propriety in diction and subjects, his sentimentality, and his overt didacticism. However, a cry of protest against the harshest of the criticism eventually arose as well, and by the end of the twentieth century the mainstream critical opinion was that besides his contribution as an innovative professor in a new discipline, Longfellow enriched American literature. Although his rank among nineteenth century American poets is lower than that of Walt Whitman and Emily Dickinson and he belonged to what hostile sociological critics denounce as a privileged class, he remains important not only for what his contemporaries thought of him but also for what he wrote.

—*Victor Lindsey*

FURTHER READING

Arvin, Newton. *Longfellow: His Life and Work*. Boston: Atlantic-Little, Brown, 1963. Seeing Longfellow as a significant minor poet, Arvin is most helpful when he critically examines many of the works and explains why Longfellow's reputation fell.

Calhoun, Charles C. *Longfellow: A Rediscovered Life*. Boston: Beacon Press, 2004. Comprehensive biography. Calhoun seeks to rehabilitate Longfellow's fallen reputation by describing his importance as a nineteenth century culture maker who brought European culture to the United States, and as a proponent of multiculturalism and feminism.

Hirsh, Edward L. *Henry Wadsworth Longfellow*. University of Minnesota Pamphlets on American Writers 35. Minneapolis: University of Minnesota Press, 1964. This booklet contains ten pages of biography, thirty pages of well-balanced criticism of Longfellow's poetry and prose, one page about his reputation, and a three-page selected bibliography without annotation.

Longfellow, Samuel, ed. *Life of Henry Wadsworth Longfellow, with Extracts from His Journals and Correspondence*. 2 vols. Boston: Ticknor, 1886. This biography, prepared by a younger brother, withholds some information but has proved indispensable to all subsequent authors of full-scale biographies. For the most part, the author allows Henry Longfellow to speak for himself. Includes illustrations and an index.

_____. *Final Memorials of Henry Wadsworth Longfellow*. Boston: Ticknor, 1887. Printed in 1891 as the third volume of *Life of Henry Wadsworth Longfellow*, this book provides letters and journal entries to supplement the 1886 biography, especially for Longfellow's last fifteen years.

"Longfellow's Footprints." *Wilson Quarterly* 25, no. 3 (Summer, 2001): 99. Examines Longfellow's literary style, the criticisms of his approach to poetry, and his historical importance among poets.

McClatchy, J. D. "Return to Gitchee Gumee." *New York Times Book Review* 150, no. 51549 (October 22, 2000): 39. A profile of Longfellow, providing biographical information and describing readers' response to his poetry.

Wagenknecht, Edward. *Henry Wadsworth Longfellow: Portrait of an American Humanist*. New York: Oxford University Press, 1966. After a short narrative biography, Wagenknecht presents Longfellow topically as a Christian humanist, analyzing the man rather than his writings.

Williams, Cecil B. *Henry Wadsworth Longfellow*. Twayne's United States Authors Series 68. New York: Twayne, 1964. After a chronology and a chapter on Longfellow's "Image and Actuality," Williams devotes four chapters to biography, three to a sympathetic study of the works, and one to "Longfellow in Literary History and in Literature." The selected bibliography is annotated.

SEE ALSO: Charles Dickens; Emily Dickinson; Nathaniel Hawthorne; Julia Ward Howe; Emma Lazarus; Edgar Allan Poe; Charles Sumner; Queen Victoria; Walt Whitman.

RELATED ARTICLES in *Great Events from History: The Nineteenth Century, 1801-1900:* 1819-1820: Irving's *Sketch Book* Transforms American Literature; 1851: Melville Publishes *Moby Dick*; 1852: Stowe Publishes *Uncle Tom's Cabin*.

COUNTESS OF LOVELACE
English mathematician

During an age when women rarely were acknowledged for their scientific and technological pursuits, the countess of Lovelace wrote a paper describing the methodology for programming a forerunner of modern computers and is consequently credited as the first computer programmer.

BORN: December 10, 1815; Piccadilly Terrace, Middlesex (now in London), England
DIED: November 27, 1852; London, England
ALSO KNOWN AS: Augusta Ada Byron (birth name); Ada King; Lady Byron
AREA OF ACHIEVEMENT: Mathematics

EARLY LIFE

The countess of Lovelace was born Augusta Ada Byron. She was the only legitimate child of her father, the famed poet George Gordon, Lord Byron. Her mother was the former Anna Isabella (Annabella) Milbanke. A pair more mismatched than her parents would be difficult to imagine: Her mother was straitlaced and pious, and her father was profligate and unrestrained. Beset with scandal and gossip regarding Byron's unconventional lifestyle, the marriage was seemingly doomed to failure. Within a few months of Ada's birth, the couple formally separated, and Byron embarked on a self-imposed exile to the Continent, never to return to England. Ada was left in the care of her mother.

Annabella raised Ada with some assistance from her own parents, Sir Ralph and Lady Judith Milbanke Noel. She feared that her child might develop what she judged as the weaknesses of her departed husband—a free-ranging imagination, self-indulgent emotions, and uncurbed passions—and determined to rear the child in a manner designed to prevent the recurrence of such a disaster. Her corrective measures included hiring tutors whose instructions were to teach Ada only mathematics and sciences; they were never to mention her father or to provide any instruction in poetry. Ada was thus shielded from any information regarding her famous poet-father. Even her questions to her mother seeking information about her father were met with rebuke.

Ada grew up in virtual isolation until 1833, when she turned eighteen. In accordance with English aristocratic custom, she made her formal entrance into society through her presentation at the Royal Court of King William IV and Queen Adelaide in St. James's Palace. She also participated in a number of parties and balls that made up the "London season." These new developments constituted a life-changing experience for the long-sheltered Ada. She met many famous people, among them some who knew her father and others who were curious to know what the daughter of the famed poet was like. She also met many who were building reputations in new fields of science as the nineteenth century made the transition from romanticism with its emphasis on feeling and emotion to realism that celebrated rationality and embraced the new technological and scientific advances precipitated by the Industrial Revolution.

Ada's concentrated schooling in mathematics became her key to unlocking the doors of many intellectually gifted scientists then living in London. In the round of parties that she attended in 1833, she met Charles Babbage, who was gaining notice for his "difference engine," a theoretical machine for calculating number sequences. In 1834, she met Mary Somerville, a celebrated mathematician and scientist then visiting in London. In 1841, she met Charles Wheatstone, who was doing pioneering work with the electric telegraph.

LIFE'S WORK

Annabella's direction of Ada's education in mathematics had unanticipated, but fortuitous, results. Although her motive was to steer Ada away from the usual education for girls of the day and especially from the corrosive effects of the imagination, she did not plan to turn her daughter into a scientist, which would have been an unsuitable pursuit for a woman of rank. However, Annabella reveled in the attention Ada was receiving and her own chance to share the spotlight with her daughter. When Babbage invited Ada to see his work on the difference engine, Annabella quickly arranged for their visit. When they first attended one of Babbage's regular gatherings in the summer of 1833, Ada's response to a demonstration of what he termed his "mechanical universe" was dramatic. She determined to intensify her study of mathematics so that she could help Babbage in his work, and she wrote to him to pledge her support.

Meanwhile, Ada had the good fortune to develop a friendship with Mary Somerville, a frequent visitor at Babbage's socials and the wife of Dr. William Somerville, a physician at the Royal Hospital in Chelsea. Mary Somerville's fame rested in large part on her translating the work of the French mathematician and astronomer the Marquis de Laplace, as *The Mechanism of the Heavens* (1831). She also supplemented his text with diagrams and drawings to clarify the difficult concepts of the solar system. She had already attained the designation as London's "Queen of Science" and generously took on the role of mentor to the young Ada, welcoming her into her Chelsea home and into a rich family life that was unknown to Ada.

Somerville's son from an earlier marriage, Woronzow Grieg, also became Ada's valued friend and eventually her lawyer. During the spring of 1835, Ada met one of Grieg's former classmates from Trinity College at Cambridge, Lord William King. Following a brief courtship, she married him. A member of the landed aristocracy, King had large holdings in Somerset and Surrey on which he employed progressive ideas in farming and land use. In 1838, in recognition of his achievements, he was made the earl of Lovelace and Ada became the countess of Lovelace.

Ada afterward divided her time between the Lovelaces' palatial home in Somerset and their London home in St. James's Square. At that time, London offered numerous galleries and science exhibition sites that allowed the public to view the latest technological marvels. Ada routinely made the rounds of these exciting offerings, always with the unspoken hope that she would encounter something or someone to provide direction to the professional life for which she longed.

An opportunity for Ada to distinguish herself came quite by chance from her old friend Charles Babbage, who had moved beyond his difference engine to a more complex device that he called the analytical engine, a more advanced and powerful number cruncher than his earlier machine. Disappointed that the British government had offered little support for his project, Babbage accepted an invitation from a group of philosophers meeting in Turin, Italy, in October, 1842, to make a presentation on his analytical engine, an account of which Luigi Menebrea then published in French.

It happened that at that moment, Ada's friend Charles Wheatstone, whose electric telegraph machine Ada had admired, was engaged to recommend scientific articles in foreign journals for publishing in a new British journal, *Taylor's Scientific Memoirs*. He instantly thought of Ada to translate Menebrea's article, and thus Ada found her niche in the world of science. When she showed her translation to Babbage in the spring of 1843, he urged her to add explanatory notes because she understood the workings of his invention better than anyone else. Despite suffering from poor health and doubts about her adequacy for the task, Ada complied and produced detailed notes that turned out to be longer than the original article. Her efforts met with resounding success.

Just as Ada had achieved the possibility of a satisfying profession, however, her health failed. Always highly strung and sickly since childhood, she increasingly experienced debilitating attacks of a nervous disorder, which her physicians treated with sedatives and opiates that rendered her unable to function. Added to this condition, she developed uterine cancer, for which no remedy was then available. She died in London on November 27, 1852. At her request, her body was buried at Hucknall Torkard in Nottingham, in the vault next to her father.

SIGNIFICANCE

In an age when women were not encouraged to delve deeply into the sciences, Ada Byron Lovelace excelled in mathematics. Scholars disagree on the question of whether she should be considered the first computer programmer. However, the notes she provided for Babbage's analytical machine show that she herself provided the step-by-step instructions necessary to make his machine carry out its computations. In recognition of her contributions to computer science, the U.S. Department of Defense named one of its computer programming languages *Ada* in her honor during the 1980's.

—*Doris H. Meriwether*

FURTHER READING

Clayton, Jay. *Charles Dickens in Cyberspace: The Afterlife of the Nineteenth Century in Post-Modern Culture.* New York: Oxford University Press, 2003. A comprehensive overview of the place of science in nineteenth century society and a description of the interactions of the prominent figures.

Morrow, Charlene, and Teri Perl, eds. *Notable Women in Mathematics: A Biographical Dictionary.* Westport, Conn.: Greenwood Press, 1998. Concise, alphabetically arranged entries on the lives, works, and bibliographies of Lovelace, Somerville, and many other women scientists.

Shearer, Barbara S., and Benjamin Shearer. *Notable Women in the Physical Sciences.* Westport, Conn.: Greenwood Press, 1997. An overview of Lovelace's life and achievements that includes a useful bibliography.

Swade, Doron. *The Difference Engine: Charles Babbage and the Quest to Build the First Computer.* New York: Penguin Books, 2002. A readable account of the invention of the nineteenth century forerunner of the modern computer; includes a chapter on Ada Lovelace's contribution.

Toole, Betty Alexandra. *Ada, the Enchantress of Numbers: Prophet of the Computer Age.* Rev. ed. Mill Valley, Calif.: Strawberry Press, 1998. A useful study that provides a chronological collection of some of Ada's correspondence interspersed with biographical commentary.

Winston, Brian. *Media Technology and Society: A History from the Telegraph to the Internet.* London: Routledge, 1998. Offers a perspective on Charles Wheatstone's contribution to science.

Woolley, Benjamin. *The Bride of Science: Romance, Reason, and Byron's Daughter.* London: McGraw-Hill, 1999. A thorough discussion of Ada's role in the scientific revolution of her day and an overview of the achievements of science in her time.

SEE ALSO: Charles Babbage; Lord Byron; William Fothergill Cooke and Charles Wheatstone; Sophie Germain; Edvard Grieg; Charlotte Angas Scott; Mary Somerville; William IV.

RELATED ARTICLES in *Great Events from History: The Nineteenth Century, 1801-1900:* 1819-1833: Babbage Designs a Mechanical Calculator; May 24, 1844: Morse Sends First Telegraph Message.

SIR CHARLES LYELL
English geologist

One of the most important physical scientists of the nineteenth century, Lyell gave shape to the emerging science of geology with his theory of uniformitarianism, explaining past change from currently observable causes.

BORN: November 14, 1797; Kinnordy, Kirriemuir, Forfarshire, Scotland
DIED: February 22, 1875; London, England
ALSO KNOWN AS: First Baronet Lyell
AREA OF ACHIEVEMENT: Geology

EARLY LIFE

Sir Charles Lyell (LI-ehl) was born into a substantial London mercantile and naval family while his parents were staying on a Scottish estate, Kinnordy. The family spent the years of young Charles's boyhood in the south of England, where his father, also Charles, engaged in the gentlemanly pursuit of botanical collecting, especially of mosses. His father was a member of the Linnean Society and corresponded with many of the leading scientific men of the time.

Sickly as a boy, Lyell received a private grammar school education and matriculated at Exeter College, Oxford, in 1816. He acquired a standard classical education, receiving his B.A., with second-class honors, in 1819. In the same year, he moved to London to read law at Lincoln's Inn. He was called to the bar in 1822 and practiced law intermittently during the remainder of the 1820's. In London, he made a name for himself in broader intellectual circles as a regular contributor to the *Quarterly Review*. In 1826 alone, he provided examinations of the English university question, scientific institutions, and reviews of geology. Of medium height, with a large forehead and a slim build, he presented the gentlemanly exterior of proper dress and the demeanor of a young man of society, although his lifelong problem with weak eyes forced him to wear a squinting quizzical expression.

Lyell's geological reviews in the *Quarterly Review* reveal the increasingly central role that geology was playing in his life. His interest, aroused by William Buckland's mineralogy and geology lectures at Oxford in 1817 and 1818, had been supplemented by bits of geologizing with family friends, in Scotland, the south of England, and the Swiss Alps in 1818. Graduation from Oxford and his move to London brought him membership in the Geological Society of London and the Linnean Society in 1819.

Gradually, as Lyell's interest in geology changed from an avocation to a committed vocation, he became secretary of the Geological Society from 1823 to 1826 and in 1826 was elected a fellow of the Royal Society. Visits to France and geologizing in the Paris Basin with Constant Prévost in 1823, and Prévost's return visit in 1824, brought Lyell closer to the heart of specialized geology. It also led to his first Geological Society paper in 1824, in which he noted the equivalency of freshwater limestones in the Paris Basin to new limestones deposited in Scottish lakes. In his 1826 articles in the *Transactions of the Geological Society* in the *Quarterly Review*, he tentatively began theorizing about the nature of geological change.

During the 1820's, an amateur making original contributions to geology was not unusual. Geology was still in its Baconian, gentlemanly tradition of collecting and observing, with plenty of room for the gifted amateur. Although little theoretical framework for geology was accepted or recognized, a consensus existed that the Earth's geological past could be unraveled and ordered. This stratigraphic ordering was based on the agreement that superposition, the sequence or succession of rock strata appearing in the order in which they were deposited, the youngest at the top and the oldest at the bottom, indicated the relative age of each stratum.

This stratigraphic concept was combined with the ideas of William Smith and his map of 1816, showing that each stratum's different characteristic fossils also indicated relative age. The Geological Society of London had been founded in 1807 on the basis of this empirical, rather than theoretical, consensus, consciously shunning theorizing and stressing observation. Most geologists agreed that the science had been hindered by the extravagant assertions of systems-builders, such as Abraham Gottlob Werner in Germany and James Hutton of Scotland, who seemed to place theory above field experience.

By the late 1820's, Lyell was planning a popular "Conversations on Geology" to satisfy his geological and monetary needs. When he reviewed George Scrope's *Memoir on the Geology of Central France* (1827), however, the book focused his attention on the Auvergne in Central France, where a complex series of lava flows seemed to offer a unique key to geological forces and successions. In 1828, Lyell visited the Auvergne with Sir Roderick Impey Murchison, a retired army officer and amateur geologist who had taken up geology in part to satisfy his craving for outdoor activity and to supplement his passion for hunting.

Viewing the continually reexcavated river beds and successive lava flows suggested to Lyell analogies between past and present geological actions. From France, on what he called the best and longest geological tour he ever made—one that "made me what I am in theoretical geology"—he traveled to Italy with Murchison and then alone to southern Italy and Sicily. Struck by the number of fossil shells of living Mediterranean species, Lyell realized that one could order the Tertiary, or most recent, rocks according to the proportional relationship of living to extinct species. He also saw that past changes in land levels in the area of volcanic Mount Etna could be explained by analogy to present forces. The Italian trip forced him to change the scope of "Conversations on Geology" from a brief popular exposition to a major work.

LIFE'S WORK

By January, 1830, Lyell had clarified his ideas and published the first volume of *Principles of Geology*. This work presents a picture of the geological past as essentially uniform and explicable by analogy to currently operating forces. Lyell found no need for extravagantly violent alterations in forces and rejected the explanation adopted by the Catastrophists, who relied on irregular major convulsive change. Part of the basis of Catastrophism was the need to fit the biblical Flood, or deluge, into geological history (thus their alternative designation, Diluvialists). Lyell instead offered a picture of gradual, cumulative change in a uniform process; thus, his doctrine is called Uniformitarianism. He rejected any effort to explain the beginnings of the world, returning to the famous dictum of Hutton that no vestige of a beginning could be found.

To present a convincing argument, Lyell had to solve a number of problems, the first of which was climatic change. Most older fossils seemed to indicate a past tropical climate much warmer than the climate of Lyell's England. Most geologists explained the anomaly through the central heat theory, referring to an Earth formed out of fire and then cooling, such that the climate as a whole was slowly cooling over time. Lyell argued that climate was a local and variable phenomenon, dependent on relations of land and sea masses, showing that as the proportion of land and sea varied with uplifting and subsidence of land, climate varied around a stable norm, providing quite different climates and physical environments over time.

Sir Charles Lyell. (Library of Congress)

Volume 1 of *Principles of Geology* was an immediate popular success, with more than half the original edition sold by November, 1830. It met with less enthusiasm from the Catastrophists. Adam Sedgwick, in his 1831 presidential address to the Geological Society, pointed to the recent theory of Élie de Beaumont of France that mountain chains had been thrown up in parallel lines by great convulsions. Sedgwick then dismissed Lyell's theories and supported those of de Beaumont, because Lyell's work seemed to set out from deductive assumptions rather than empirical fieldwork.

In the second volume of *Principles of Geology*, which appeared in January, 1832, Lyell examined patterns left by living forms over geological time. If the stratigraphic record was to be intimately tied to the fossil record, then changes in life-forms over time had to be explained for fossils to be accurately used as indices. Because each successive formation displayed a gradually changing mix of different fossils, Lyell had to explain how the characteristic life-forms of each geological epoch had changed. He argued that species were discrete entities and rejected Lamarck's idea of continual transmutation and plasticity in favor of regular and periodic extinction of species. Then, as landforms and environments altered over time, some species would become extinct from the loss of suitable environment. Changing methods of rock deposition in marine or fresh waters and thus differing environments could explain gaps in the fossil record without reference to periodic catastrophes. The problem of the replacement of extinct species by new and different species remained an unsolved puzzle for Lyell.

The third volume of *Principles of Geology* appeared in 1833. While Lyell addressed some of his critics, the bulk of the volume was devoted to the direct application of the principles of the first two volumes to the rocks of the Tertiary. To divide the Tertiary, he introduced a new terminology, based on the proportional relationship of extinct to existing fossil forms. He also offered the names Eocene (dawn, recent), Miocene (less, recent), and newer and older Pliocene (more, larger, recent) to identify the succeeding epochs.

Principles of Geology propelled Lyell into the public and scientific eye. Revising it became the work of a lifetime. "Indeed," he once wrote, "I sometimes think I am in danger of becoming perpetual editor to myself." Over the next forty years, twelve editions appeared, each thoroughly revised and updated to reflect Lyell's own work and the work of his colleagues. In 1838, he published *Elements of Geology*, a work based on the theory of *Principles of Geology* but emphasizing the descriptive and practical. *Elements of Geology* became the first true geological textbook. With most of the purely descriptive material relegated to *Elements of Geology, Principles of Geology* remained his theoretical tour de force.

In 1832, in the forefront of his specialty, Lyell became professor of geology at King's College, London. He delivered only two series of lectures before resigning in 1834. The pressure of constant fieldwork and controversy prevented sufficient attention to the university. He made trips to the Pyrenees in 1830 to examine de Beaumont's theory of mountain building and to Sweden in 1834 to investigate the uplift of the lands of Scandinavia.

In 1832, Lyell married Mary Elizabeth Horner, daughter of Leonard Horner, a fellow of the Geological Society. A marriage tour of the Rhine, Switzerland, and France showed that he had married a woman with a fascination for and insight into geology. She became a skilled conchologist who helped him in his work, especially because of his weak eyes, often writing for him. Recognition and honors were heaped upon Lyell. In 1834, he received the Royal Medal of the Royal Society. From 1834 to 1836, and again in 1849, he served as president of the Geological Society. In 1848, Lyell was knighted by Queen Victoria, and through his friendship with Prince Albert he was named a commissioner of the Great Exhibition of 1851.

In 1841, Lyell stepped onto a new stage. He sailed for the first of four trips to North America. In the United States, he presented the Lowell Lectures in Boston, visited Benjamin Silliman at Yale, and toured New York State with James Hall of the New York Geological Survey. He was particularly struck by Niagara Falls and the possibility that the recession of the falls presented for explaining the passage of geological time.

Along the border of New York and Pennsylvania, Lyell was able to study the Devonian rocks, subject of a controversy then raging in England. After touring in the southern states, Lyell attended the spring, 1842, meeting of the American Association of Geologists and Naturalists in Boston. Finally, a tour of British North America took him through the St. Lawrence Valley and ended in the coal fields of Nova Scotia, where he met an enthusiastic young geologist, John William Dawson. Lyell's collaboration with and encouragement of Dawson would help him become one of the two greatest geologists of nineteenth century Canada. The trip was capped by the appearance of his two-volume work *Travels in North America with Geological Observations on the United States, Canada, and Nova Scotia* in 1845.

Lyell returned to North America in 1845, concentrating his attention on the Tertiary rocks of the South. His observations were published in *Second Visit to the United States of North America* in 1849. Lyell briefly visited a third time in 1852, when he worked in the South Joggins coal formations of Nova Scotia with Dawson. His final visit was in 1853, when he served as one of the British commissioners to the New York Industrial Exhibition, working closely again with Hall.

After an 1853-1854 visit to the island Madeira, Lyell concentrated on the species question. While studying the Madeira fossils, he was struck by the large number and variety of species, a discovery analogous to Charles Darwin's at the Galápagos Islands. Noting that every species must have come into existence near in time and place to closely allied species, Lyell began a series of seven note-books solely devoted to the subject.

This new focus brought him back into intimate contact with Darwin. In 1836, after Darwin had returned from his expedition on the *Beagle*, a working and personal friendship developed with Lyell. Initially, the relationship was one of Lyell as mentor and Darwin as student, for Darwin had used a copy of *Principles of Geology* on his expedition. Darwin's first published work after his return explicitly used and expanded Lyell's ideas. In his 1837 presentation to the Geological Society, Darwin argued for the elevation of South America through successive earthquake and volcanic action rather than a single convulsive upheaval. At the same time, Darwin presented a new theory of coral reefs, applying Lyellian principles, as the remnants of subsiding mountains, rather than Lyell's specific theory that they represented the tops of submerged volcanoes. This forced Lyell to alter his ideas, for as he wistfully recognized, "I must give up my volcanic crater theory for ever, though it costs me a pang at first, for it accounted for so much."

By 1856, Lyell consulted regularly with Darwin and urged him to publish his ideas promptly on the transmutation of species though natural selection, particularly after the revelation that Alfred Russel Wallace had come independently to the idea of natural selection and might forestall Darwin. Lyell and Joseph Hooker were instrumental in presenting both Darwin's and Wallace's ideas to the Linnean Society in July, 1858, and in impelling Darwin to publish his *On the Origin of Species by Means of Natural Selection* in 1859.

Although the Madeira species caused Lyell tentatively to accept Darwinian ideas of transmutation, he was unwilling to commit himself to the theory. Discovery of mammal remains in the supposedly reptile-dominated rocks of the Secondary epoch raised doubts about the change in species. Moreover, discovery of human-crafted implements in the later Pliocene deposits of France, shell mounds in Denmark, Lake Dwellings in Switzerland, and an apparently human skull at Neanderthal in Germany all focused Lyell's attention on the specific question of human origins.

Lyell's investigations culminated in 1863 with the publication of *The Geological Evidences of the Antiquity of Man*. In a tightly argued exposition, Lyell presented the evidence for a common parentage for human beings and the long period of time necessary for their development. He presented the evidence and then left his readers to reach their own conclusions; while the book offered a powerful argument in support of Darwin, Lyell did not

make his support for Darwin explicit. Darwin was disappointed in the lukewarm support, but as Lyell explained to him in an 1863 letter,

> I have spoken out to the utmost extent of my tether, so far as my reason goes, and farther than my imagination and sentiment can follow, which I suppose has caused occasional incongruities.

By 1864, however, Lyell expressed his full and unalloyed support for Darwin. The tenth edition of *Principles of Geology*, which appeared in 1868, was revised around a specifically Darwinian explanation for the transmutation of species.

SIGNIFICANCE

Sir Charles Lyell died on February 22, 1875, and was interred in Westminster Abbey, the final recognition for an illustrious career. The last years of his life had been marked by continuous honors. In 1864 he was made a baronet and elected president of the British Association for the Advancement of Science. Other honors included the Royal and Copley medals of the Royal Society and the Wollaston Medal of the Geological Society.

Lyell had provided the broad intellectual framework within which geology progressed in the nineteenth century. *Principles of Geology* is an enduring landmark in geology. In arguing for a geological past that changed through small, cumulative change, Lyell had defeated his Catastrophist opponents who supposed that nature changed primarily through violent and discontinuous means. His uniformitarian geology had provided a flexible model for research, as he demonstrated through his constant revision of *Principles of Geology*. He never abandoned the principles of uniformitarianism yet demonstrated a remarkable willingness to alter specific conclusions when presented with contradictory evidence.

Lyell always stood somewhat outside the geological establishment of Great Britain, with its central concern for the Baconian tradition. While Murchison and Sedgwick were crafting their Devonian, Silurian, and Cambrian systems in a practical, hands-on way within the stratigraphic consensus, Lyell was building his uniformitarian system.

Lyell also served as a link between British and North American geology, cross-fertilizing both. Lyell had brought the best of British geology directly to North America, which was then only beginning geological surveys and investigations. Through his books and papers for the Geological Society, he brought the new phenomena of North America back to Great Britain.

Fostering, aiding, and abetting Darwin, first as mentor and then as follower, Lyell contributed to a momentous scientific development in the nineteenth century. The personal scientific relationship was fruitful for both men, while Lyell's uniformitarian geological framework and analysis of fossil life changes were key to Darwin's hypothesis.

—William E. Eagan

FURTHER READING

Bolles, Edmund Blair. *The Ice Finders: How a Poet, a Professor, and a Politician Discovered the Ice Age.* Washington, D.C.: Counterpoint, 1999. Describes how interactions between Lyell, natural historian Louis Agassiz, and poet Elisha Kent Kane created public acceptance for the idea of an ice age.

Gillispie, Charles Coulston. *Genesis and Geology.* Cambridge, Mass.: Harvard University Press, 1951. Classic study of the "biblical" geology against which Lyell argued. May overstate the depth of biblical geology, but well worth studying for the interaction of science and religious views.

Gould, Stephen Jay. *Time's Arrow, Time's Cycle: Myth and Metaphor in Discovery of Geological Time.* Cambridge, Mass.: Harvard University Press, 1987. A revisionist account by the popular science writer, showing that Lyell's conception of geological time was essentially static, in contrast to the modern sense of "deep" time with its unimaginable immensity. Scholarly but accessible, and engagingly written. Illustrated.

Klaver, J. M. I. *Geology and Religious Sentiment: The Effect of Geological Discoveries on English Society and Literature Between 1829 and 1859.* New York: Brill, 1997. Explores Lyell's scientific and religious views about world antiquity and how these views were received by theologians, philosophers, poets, and novelists.

Lyell, Charles. *The Geological Evidences of the Antiquity of Man with Remarks on Theories of the Origin of Species by Variation.* London: John Murray, 1863. Four editions down to 1873. Clearly written and argued. Although it does not explicitly support Darwin, the evidence seems to do so.

_____. *Life, Letters, and Journals of Sir Charles Lyell.* Edited by K. M. Lyell. 2 vols. London: John Murray, 1881. A classic Victorian life-and-letters approach, filled with fascinating insights. Lyell's combative and epigrammatic style is allowed to come through.

_____. *Principles of Geology, Being an Attempt to Explain the Former Changes of the Earth's Surface by Reference to Causes Now in Operation.* 3 vols. London: John Murray, 1830-1833. Twelve editions down to 1875, in various formats and numbers of volumes. Widely available in many British and American editions, each of which is worth examining for his general theories. Remarkably easy to read, and written with an open and accessible style.

_____. *Travels in North America with Geological Observations on the United States, Canada, and Nova Scotia.* 2 vols. London: John Murray, 1845.

_____. *A Second Visit to the United States of North America.* 2 vols. London: John Murray, 1849. These two two-volume works are filled with fascinating comments on the American social and political scene, particularly on the slavery question, as well as geological observations. Interesting for the observations of an intelligent British tourist.

North, Frederick J. *Sir Charles Lyell: Interpreter of the Principles of Geology.* London: A. Baker, 1965. Popular, brief biography that deals with the essential facts and ideas clearly. A good introduction to the subject.

Rudwick, Martin, J. S. *The Great Devonian Controversy: The Shaping of Scientific Knowledge Among Gentlemanly Specialists.* Chicago: University of Chicago Press, 1985. Densely factual history of an important geological controversy that provides a context for the geological atmosphere in which Lyell was working. Worth plowing through.

Wilson, Leonard G. *Charles Lyell, the Years to 1841: The Revolution in Geology.* New Haven, Conn.: Yale University Press, 1972.

_____. *Lyell in America: Transatlantic Geology, 1841-1853.* Baltimore: Johns Hopkins University Press, 1998. The first two volumes of a projected three-volume definitive biography. Detailed and a gold mine of information.

SEE ALSO: Louis Agassiz; Georges Cuvier; Charles Darwin; Mary Somerville.

RELATED ARTICLES in *Great Events from History: The Nineteenth Century, 1801-1900:* July, 1830: Lyell Publishes *Principles of Geology*; 1854-1862: Wallace's Expeditions Give Rise to Biogeography; August, 1856: Neanderthal Skull Is Found in Germany; 1871: Darwin Publishes *The Descent of Man.*

MARY LYON
American educator

Combining a strong religious faith with a firm belief in the necessity of advanced training for women, Lyon served as the impetus for the creation of what is now Mount Holyoke College, the oldest continuing institution of higher learning for women in the United States.

BORN: February 28, 1797; Buckland, Massachusetts
DIED: March 5, 1849; South Hadley, Massachusetts
ALSO KNOWN AS: Mary Mason Lyon (full name)
AREAS OF ACHIEVEMENT: Education, women's rights

EARLY LIFE

The sixth of eight children, Mary Mason Lyon was the daughter of Aaron Lyon and Jemima Shephard Lyon, both of whom were descended from old New England stock. Mary Lyon's father, a veteran of the American Revolution and a struggling small farmer in western Massachusetts, died in 1802. Shortly after her husband's death, his widow made the decision to continue working the family farm with her children. While still a child, Lyon learned to perform many household chores; she also attended nearby one-room schools.

Upon her mother's remarriage in 1810, Lyon remained on the family farm in order to keep house for her brother, who paid her a salary of a dollar a week. This she saved for her education. In 1814, Lyon began to teach in summer schools for local children; she "boarded round," as was the custom. As she matured, Lyon turned into a sturdy, well-built woman who possessed blue eyes, auburn hair, and a fine complexion. Apparent from her youth was her warmth, great physical energy, and selfless concern for others.

In 1817, Mary Lyon drew upon her small inheritance and meager earnings and enrolled in Sanderson Academy, a new coeducational institution in Ashfield, Massachusetts. This school introduced her to such advanced subjects as astronomy and Latin. While at Sanderson, Lyon made the acquaintance of Thomas White, whose daughter Amanda became a close personal friend. Throughout Lyon's life, White acted as a confidant and supporter; he also carefully managed her money, serving eventually as executor of her estate.

In 1821, Lyon and Amanda White attended the Byfield (Massachusetts) Female Seminary. This school was headed by the Reverend Joseph Emerson, who firmly believed that permanent institutions of higher learning should be created for women. At Byfield, Lyon formed a lifelong friendship with Zilpah Grant, a teacher at the Academy. At that time, Lyon, who had been brought up in a religious household, became concerned about the state of her soul. In March, 1822, she was baptized and received into the Congregational Church. For the duration of her life, Lyon would remain a devout Christian.

By the mid-1820's, Mary Lyon could be found teaching and studying in a variety of institutions in Massachusetts and New Hampshire. It was not unusual for her to teach at one school during the fall and spring terms, and then to teach at another during the summer. In 1828, however, Lyon suffered from a severe case of typhoid fever. She decided that henceforth she would devote herself completely to one institution, the Ipswich (Massachusetts) Female Seminary. Her friend Zilpah Grant served as principal of the school.

Lyon's experiences at Ipswich proved instructive for her. The seminary had been founded with no endowment; she quickly realized that any successful educational institution had to be based on continuing funding that could ensure permanence. Also while she was at Ipswich, Lyon came to the conclusion that her goal in life was to be a teacher of teachers. This meant that, in the future, she would insist on minimum age requirements for her students, the study of sciences, and a curriculum that excluded such ornamental courses as conversational French or painting.

During the summer of 1833, in the midst of her Ipswich years, Lyon traveled through New York, Pennsylvania, and the Midwest. She visited numerous schools and colleges along her route. Urged to do so by generous local citizens, she seriously considered establishing a female seminary in Detroit, Michigan. After prayerful deliberation, Lyon decided against the Detroit plan. She returned to the East, where she became determined to create her own academy.

LIFE'S WORK

Although still teaching at the Ipswich Female Seminary, in 1834 Lyon began to meet with benevolent men such as Thomas White. These individuals supported her in her belief that what needed to be created was a new school for women that would be run by a disinterested board of trustees. Lyon hoped that in this proposed institution, teachers could be persuaded to accept low salaries and that students would do domestic work in a dormitory atmosphere. Such policies would help keep tuition low so that even girls of modest means could attend the school. The goal of the institution would be to educate women teachers.

During the next three years, Lyon worked unceasingly to make her dream a reality. Remaining humble and self-effacing, she exhibited a remarkable determination. For the most part, Lyon relied on wealthy male trustees to fund her institution. As these men raised the school's endowment, Lyon traveled throughout New England collecting money from women on farms and in small towns. It was her hope that the dormitory rooms of her students could be furnished from contributions made by such women.

After lengthy negotiations, Lyon's trustees made the decision to establish her school in South Hadley, which had made the best offer for it with a contribution of eight thousand dollars. The new institution would be named Mount Holyoke Female Seminary, after a nearby mountain. The Commonwealth of Massachusetts granted the school a charter in 1836. Soon thereafter, construction commenced. Lyon closely supervised this process.

On November 8, 1837, the barely completed seminary opened its doors to the eighty eager students who had been accepted for admission. According to Mary Lyon's original plans, all of her pupils were over seventeen, and everyone was required to engage in domestic work. The curriculum consisted of a three-year program that called for the concentrated teaching of courses over a short period of time. Science was emphasized, and guest lecturers such as Edward Hitchcock of Amherst College frequently came from nearby institutions. Public oral examinations proved to be a highlight of the end of each school year. Students also received religious training, a requirement upon which Lyon insisted. She hoped that all of her students would be "saved"; she frequently held religious meetings in her quarters to further this goal. The seminary directed much attention to foreign missions; it was not uncommon for students to enter this field of endeavor upon graduation. Lyon herself made a plea for increased missionary work when she published a short book, *A Missionary Offering*, in 1843.

Mount Holyoke Female Seminary quickly flourished. By the mid-1840's, enrollment had climbed to more than two hundred students. Because of the expanding size of the student body, new additions had to be made to the seminary's building. The curriculum also expanded in size; it became increasingly sophisticated with the introduction of such subjects as Latin and human anatomy. As the years passed, Lyon did less and less teaching. That job was performed by a handpicked group of recent graduates. Lyon herself acted as an administrator who oversaw all operations of Mount Holyoke. Increasingly, she seemed unable to delegate responsibility; the strain of many years of arduous effort were taking their toll. Hav-

ing long suffered from lung problems that weakened her resistance to other illnesses, Lyon died at Mount Holyoke of erysipelas in March, 1849. She was buried on the seminary's grounds.

Although Lyon's death dealt a severe blow to Mount Holyoke, it did not destroy it. For several years the institution foundered as its leadership remained uncertain. By the mid-1850's, however, this problem was solved and the school continued along on its path to permanence.

SIGNIFICANCE

Typical of many other early nineteenth century reformers, Lyon possessed a vision of how life could be improved for society as a whole. A woman of extraordinary enthusiasm, selfless determination, and loving compassion, she refused to be discouraged by adversity and she eagerly pursued her goal of providing a first-rate higher education for American women.

From her experiences in a variety of small New England institutions, Lyon learned that often a school's existence depended upon the health and good fortune of a single founder or teacher. To her, this was wrong. What she hoped to create with Mount Holyoke was an endowed and financially sound seminary whose control would be vested in a self-perpetuating board of trustees; these men would oversee the continuance of the institution through changes in leadership.

Furthermore, Lyon desired to prove that young women were as intellectually able as men, and that, like men, they were capable of doing advanced academic work. She dreamed that once Mount Holyoke achieved intellectual prominence, the American public would understand the advantages of educating women and go out and found other such institutions. To a great extent, this visionary plan came true, for by the late nineteenth century numerous "daughter" schools had been created that emulated Mount Holyoke's success. However, unlike its more secular counterparts, the seminary proved to be a deeply religious institution that was devoted to Christian piety and evangelism. In this respect, Lyon and Mount Holyoke were representative of the religiously motivated reform movements of the Second Great Awakening.

Whether consciously or unconsciously, Lyon also served to improve the quality of elementary and secondary education in the United States. As Mount Holyoke's fame spread, greater efforts were made by local teachers to prepare their students for the stiff entrance examinations that were required for entrance to the seminary. In addition, graduates of Mount Holyoke quickly came into demand as teachers in the United States and elsewhere in the world. Well-trained instructors inevitably improved the level of training in schools throughout the world.

What is amazing about Lyon's accomplishments is that they were carried out by a conservative individual who refused to challenge the prevailing social mores of her era. Unlike some of her more vocal contemporaries, Lyon avoided the limelight; she insisted upon achieving her goals through maintaining her ladylike composure and never stepping outside her prescribed sphere. This meant that, while she routinely relied on male benefactors for advice and financial support, she refused to appear before them at any meetings of her board of trustees. Thus, she never spoke publicly to mixed audiences, and most of her personal pleas for money were reserved for rural New England women.

The result of Lyon's efforts was the successful operation of Mount Holyoke Female Seminary, an institution that would achieve collegiate status in 1888. With a permanent endowment, secure leadership, low tuition, and a carefully structured living and learning environment, Mount Holyoke served as the model of women's higher education for generations to come.

—Marian E. Strobel

FURTHER READING

Cole, Arthur Charles. *A Hundred Years of Mount Holyoke College: The Evolution of an Educational Ideal.* New Haven, Conn.: Yale University Press, 1940. The best historical account of the first century of Mount Holyoke's existence. Approximately one-third of the volume is devoted to an explanation of the activities of Lyon.

Fiske, Fidelia. *Recollections of Mary Lyon with Selections from Her Instructions to the Pupils of Mt. Holyoke Female Seminary.* Boston: American Tract Society, 1866. Badly dated as a biography, this work is valuable for contemporary reminiscences of Lyon. Also included are selections from Lyon's lectures and Sabbath services.

Gilchrist, Beth Bradford. *The Life of Mary Lyon.* Boston: Houghton Mifflin, 1910. A traditional biography that is important for revealing early twentieth century attitudes toward Lyon.

Goodsell, Willystine. *Pioneers of Women's Education in the United States.* New York: McGraw-Hill, 1931. Placing Lyon in the company of Emma Willard and Catharine Beecher, Goodsell provides a brief biographical sketch and includes lengthy excerpts from Lyon's writings.

Green, Elizabeth Alden. *Mary Lyon and Mount Holyoke:* *Opening the Gates.* Hanover, N.H.: University Press of New England, 1979. The definitive biography of Lyon. Providing a clear, concise, and balanced narrative, the volume shows the results of impressive research in primary and secondary sources.

Hitchcock, Edward, comp. *The Power of Christian Benevolence Illustrated in the Life and Labors of Mary Lyon.* 2d ed. Northampton, Mass.: Hopkins, Bridgman, 1851. A complimentary account of Lyon's work as perceived by a close friend. The volume has historical importance as it is partially based on letters from Lyon that were later destroyed.

Levin, Miriam R. *Defining Women's Scientific Enterprise: Mount Holyoke Faculty and the Rise of American Science.* Hanover, N.H.: University Press of New England, 2005. Examines how Mount Holyoke's women science teachers established a niche for themselves and helped advance the institution from the time Lyon founded the college in 1837.

Lyon, Mary. *Mary Lyon Through Her Letters.* Edited by Marion Lansing. Boston: Books, Incoporated, 1937. An account of Lyon's life that was published to coincide with the one hundredth birthday of Mount Holyoke. Complimentary in tone, the book combines a narrative with excerpts from Lyon's letters.

Porterfield, Amanda. *Mary Lyon and the Mount Holyoke Missionaries.* New York: Oxford University Press, 1997. A study of Lyon and the Protestant missionary women she trained at Mount Holyoke. Porterfield views the college's missionary work as representative of American missionary thought before the Civil War.

Sklar, Kathryn Kish. "The Founding of Mount Holyoke College." In *Women of America: A History,* edited by Carol Ruth Berkin and Mary Beth Norton. Boston: Houghton Mifflin, 1979. An article-length account of Lyon's activities. Sklar emphasizes the role of evangelical religion in the founding of Mount Holyoke.

Woody, Thomas. *A History of Women's Education in the United States.* New York: Science Press, 1929. The classic work on its subject. Although dated in some of its interpretations, it is useful for placing Lyon's activities in their proper historical context.

SEE ALSO: Catharine Beecher; Alice Freeman Palmer; Emma Willard.

RELATED ARTICLES in *Great Events from History: The Nineteenth Century, 1801-1900:* May, 1823: Hartford Female Seminary Is Founded; November 8, 1837: Mount Holyoke Female Seminary Opens; September 26, 1865: Vassar College Opens.

JOHN MACARTHUR
Australian sheep breeder

MacArthur introduced to Australia merino sheep, which produce extremely high-quality wool. His initiative in importing fine stock from Spain and South Africa resulted in Australia's becoming one of the world's premier wool-producing countries and provided the basis for the continent's future economic development.

BORN: August 18, 1766; Stoke Damerel, Devonshire, England

DIED: April 11, 1834; Camden Park, New South Wales, Australia

ALSO KNOWN AS: John Macarthur; John "Merino" MacArthur

AREAS OF ACHIEVEMENT: Business, government and politics

EARLY LIFE

John MacArthur was the son of Alexander and Catherine MacArthur, who had returned to England after a period of residence in the West Indies and purchased a mercer and draper business in Plymouth, and settled down to raise their fourteen children. John was educated in a private school until he entered the army as an ensign in 1782. In October, 1788, at the age of twenty-two, he married eighteen-year-old Elizabeth Veal, the daughter of a lawyer who had been raised in the household of a cleric, the Reverend John Kingdon. Their first son, Edward, was born in 1789, shortly before John became a lieutenant in the New South Wales Corps.

Neither marriage to a woman raised in a religious household, fatherhood, or advancement in his profession had a beneficial effect on John MacArthur's character. Chronically discontented and short-tempered, he was recurrently embroiled in unpleasant social disputes. When his regiment was sent to Australia, he found sufficient fault with the captain of the ship that was to transport them there to provoke a duel before they had even left Plymouth. The actual voyage, which lasted seven months, was no happier than its inception, While they were at sea, Elizabeth gave birth to a premature daughter, who died and was buried at sea, while John engaged in a continuing quarrel with the captain, resulting in their being transferred to another vessel in the three-ship fleet in which they were sailing. They finally reached Port Jackson, the harbor of Sydney in what was then the convict colony of New South Wales, on June 28, 1790.

LIFE'S WORK

MacArthur's abrasive personality quickly led to a dispute with the colony's governor, Arthur Phillip, whose reprimand and displeasure barred the unpleasant young man from entrance into the upper levels of the colony's society. However, the arrival in February, 1792, of Major Francis Grose, newly assigned to the command of the New South Wales Corps, changed MacArthur's luck. Grose befriended the young man and appointed him regimental paymaster, a position that substantially increased his salary. A year later, when Grose was named acting governor of New South Wales, MacArthur was elevated to inspector of public works and was granted one hundred acres of excellent farmland along the Parramatta River, about fourteen miles from Sydney.

With the help of the cheap labor provided by convicts sent to New South Wales, MacArthur and his wife began clearing their land immediately. In November, 1793, they moved their family, which had grown by the addition of a daughter, Elizabeth, in 1792 and a son, James, earlier in 1793, to their new house on Elizabeth Farm. There MacArthur's family continued to grow. James died the following year, but John was born in 1794, Mary Isabella in 1796, a second James in 1798, William in 1800, and Emmeline Emily in 1808.

At Elizabeth Farm, MacArthur began experimenting with the cross-breeding of sheep. By importing stock from Ireland, Spain, and India, he hoped to be able to produce a breed that would adapt to the conditions of Australia and would produce marketable wool. His first attempts were not successful; the sheep that he bred produced only an inferior quality of wool. It was not until 1796, when he imported several merino sheep from South Africa, that he found a solution to his problem. The merinos, developed in Europe and world renowned for the exceptional quality of their wool, thrived under Australian conditions. Expanding his farm to three hundred acres, MacArthur developed a flock of merinos that showed immense economic promise.

Although MacArthur's sheep flock was improving, his position in Australian society was not. His friend, Governor Grove, was replaced by Governor John Hunter, who disapproved of MacArthur's ambition and litigious disposition. In September, 1796, MacArthur was forced to resign from his position as inspector of public works. In league with other disaffected officers of the New South Wales Corps, he worked at having Hunter replaced. Although his efforts were successful, Hunter's replacement, Philip Gidley King, proved to be no easier a governor with whom to deal.

Still in opposition to the government, MacArthur provoked and fought a duel with Lieutenant Governor Paterson. For wounding his superior, he was arrested and returned to England in November, 1801, to be court-martialed. Surprisingly, he was authorized to take with him his daughter Elizabeth and his son John to be educated in England, along with samples of his finest wool. During the long voyage to England, the document containing the indictment against him disappeared. After he arrived, the government consequently declined to court-martial him.

While MacArthur was in London, he discovered that the demand for wool far exceeded the available stocks. In 1803, he published a pamphlet, *Statement of the Improvement and Progress of the Breed of Fine Woolled Sheep in New South Wales*, that was designed to promote the sale of his Australian wool. This modest publication alerted the European wool market to the quality of Australian wool and launched the colonial wool industry that would make MacArthur both rich and famous.

In 1805, MacArthur returned to New South Wales, where Governor King had been replaced by William Bligh, a naval officer now famous for the mutiny of his crew aboard the HMS *Bounty* in 1789. Bligh was a resolute official, sent by the government to end the illegal rum trade that flourished among the officers and farmers of New South Wales. Not surprisingly, MacArthur opposed Bligh as he had earlier opposed King and Hunter.

With many of his fellow officers, MacArthur participated in the Rum Rebellion that deposed and imprisoned Bligh. MacArthur was tried in January, 1808, for his involvement in the rebellion but was acquitted. Afterward, he was tried for sedition and acquitted once again. He then took a lead role in the formation of a rebel government and was appointed colonial secretary.

In 1809, MacArthur sailed for England and spent the next eight years in London. He was under virtual, if not actual, arrest for his part in the Australian scandal. Finally, in 1817, he was cleared of all charges. Moreover, by then he had acquired the patronage of Lord Camden, who granted him five thousand acres of prime pastoral land in Camden, Australia, to develop his wool production, with the promise of five thousand additional acres if his enterprise succeeded.

After moving his family to the new estate in Camden, MacArthur built a finer house there and settled in to the process of expanding his flocks. Assisted by his son Wil-

liam in managing the estate, he spent his remaining years developing the region's agricultural capacities. With the wool industry well established, MacArthur and his son turned some of their attention to the production of wine as well. During his last years, his declining health led to severe mental difficulties that incapacitated him during the two years leading up to his death in 1834, at the age of seventy-eight.

SIGNIFICANCE

John MacArthur's political significance lies in his contentious career as a soldier and public official in Australia that culminated in the Rum Rebellion. However, he is not remembered primarily for that event. His more important legacy is his contribution to the economic development of Australia. He was not merely a contentious and unruly civil servant, he was also an ambitious and energetic farmer who actively sought out products and markets through which Australia could be transformed from a backwater convict colony into a thriving and important link in the structure of the world economy.

MacArthur's discovery of the ability of merino sheep to thrive in New South Wales, combined with his fortuitous opportunities to promote the sale of their wool in British and European markets, led to the development of one of Australia's most important industries. Moreover, his late experiments in viniculture pointed the way to another thriving Australian endeavor. Both of his original farms were still operating at the beginning of the twenty-first century, standing as monuments to his part in developing the economy that continues to support Australia today.

—Denyse Lemaire and David Kasserman

FURTHER READING

De Vries-Evans, Susanna. *Historic Sydney: The Founding of Australia*. Brisbane, Qld.: Pandanus Press, 1999. Readers will find this book particularly relevant to MacArthur because of the location of his estates in Parramatta and Camden, in the suburbs of Sydney.

Duffy, Michael. *Man of Honour: John Macarthur, Duellist, Rebel, Founding Father*. Sydney: Macmillan, 2003. Well-written and researched biography, tracing MacArthur's life and times until just after the 1808 Rum Rebellion.

Evatt, Herbert V. *Rum Rebellion: A Study of the Overthrow of Governor Bligh by John Macarthur and the New South Wales Corps*. Sydney: Angus & Robertson, 1938. The author examines the reasons for the Rum Rebellion and its consequences for New South Wales.

Hughes, Robert. *The Fatal Shore: The Epic of Australia's Founding*. New York: Alfred A. Knopf, 1986. This is an excellent description of the founding of Australia and the men and women who shaped the new country.

Woldendorp, Richard, Roger McDonald, and Amanda Burdon. *Wool: The Australian Story*. North Fremantle, W.A.: Fremantle Arts Center, 2003. This book is a good introduction to the development of Australia's wool industry, in which MacArthur played so important a role.

SEE ALSO: A. B. Paterson; Edward Gibbon Wakefield; W. C. Wentworth.

RELATED ARTICLES in *Great Events from History: The Nineteenth Century, 1801-1900:* December 6, 1801-August, 1803: Flinders Explores Australia; September 7, 1803: Great Britain Begins Colonizing Tasmania; August 16, 1835: Melbourne, Australia, Is Founded; 1851: Gold Is Discovered in New South Wales; 1868: Last Convicts Land in Western Australia.

THOMAS BABINGTON MACAULAY
English politician and historian

Macaulay was a prominent Whig politician and popular essayist, but his greatest achievement was The History of England from the Accession of James the Second, *a work of enduring popularity and influence.*

BORN: October 25, 1800; Rothley Temple, Leicestershire, England

DIED: December 28, 1859; Holly Lodge, Campden Hill, London, England

ALSO KNOWN AS: Baron Macaulay of Rothley; Lord Macaulay

AREAS OF ACHIEVEMENT: Government and politics, historiography

EARLY LIFE

Thomas Babington Macaulay (mah-KO-lih) was the first child of Zachary Macaulay, a descendant of Scottish highland chiefs, a merchant, a ship owner, a member of the Clapham Sect of Evangelical Anglicans, and a campaigner against the slave trade. Macaulay grew up in an atmosphere of stifling religious observance and self-examination that he rejected in later years, although still maintaining conventional Christian morality. He was a child prodigy who began to read voraciously at the age of three, thus beginning early to accumulate that vast array of facts with which he delighted his friends and belabored his enemies. He entered Trinity College, Cambridge, in 1818, and proceeded to win debating triumphs in the University Union and numerous academic prizes, including an award for his "Essay on the Life and Character of William III," who was to be the great hero of his historical masterpiece. After graduation, Macaulay studied law and was called to the bar in 1826, but he never put much effort into becoming a practicing lawyer.

In 1825, Macaulay began to contribute to the *Edinburgh Review*, the prestigious quarterly journal for intellectual Whigs. His second essay, discussing the poet John Milton and defending his radical politics during the English Civil War, made him an instant celebrity and star guest at Holland House, the very center of Whig society. Over the next twenty years, Macaulay wrote thirty-six articles for the *Edinburgh Review*, most of them ostensibly beginning as book reviews, but soon turning into long and independent essays. Macaulay at the age of twenty-five had mastered the style he was to wield for the rest of his life. The essays were vigorous and assertive, abounding in paradox and contrast, intimidating in their command of facts, confident in judgment, and exciting to read. His literary fame brought him some unexpected rewards. In 1828, Lord Lyndhurst made him a Commissioner of Bankruptcy, and in 1830, Lord Lansdowne used a pocket borough, Calne, which was under his control, to send the young Macaulay to Parliament.

Macaulay the public figure seemed assured and successful, but the private man was sometimes troubled and uncertain. He never married and concentrated his emotions completely on two younger sisters, Hannah and Margaret. By the 1820's, Macaulay's father, at one time very wealthy, had lost most of his money, and thereafter, Macaulay, though sometimes short of funds himself, felt obliged to help. He was, for a time, in much demand at fashionable dinner tables, and yet he often failed to impress at first sight. Many described him as a short, squat man with vulgar, though energetic, features, who talked interminably. He was also unusually clumsy and often had trouble tying his cravats properly or shaving without drawing blood.

LIFE'S WORK

Macaulay entered Parliament as a Whig, a member of the party of moderate reform, led by liberal aristocrats, proud of their descent from the families of the Glorious Revolution of 1688-1689, which had overthrown King James II, brought in William III, and asserted parliamentary supremacy. Macaulay was a man of the political center, or slightly left of center, but he asserted his moderate views with combative zeal. He delivered his maiden speech in April, 1830, in defense of a bill to remove civil disabilities from Jews. In March, 1831, he gave the first of a series of powerful orations supporting the Whig Reform Bill, which abolished many rotten or pocket boroughs (seats with few inhabitants, such as Calne, for which Macaulay sat), created new parliamentary districts, and gave the vote to most of the middle class, though not to the working class. It was a severely limited reform but was bitterly opposed by the Tories as threatening the social order.

The very reverse was true, argued Macaulay. The refusal to reform when reform was needed would create a justified discontent that would bring on revolution. "Reform," urged Macaulay, "that you may preserve." In June, 1832, the Reform Bill became law, and Macaulay returned to Parliament for one of the new constituencies, Leeds. He was acknowledged as a great orator and rising statesman. In December, 1833, he became the legal member of the newly created four-man Supreme Council of India at the amazing salary of ten thousand pounds a year. He planned to stay in India for five or six years, live splendidly on five thousand pounds a year (in fact he spent much less), and then return to England a rich man, able to follow his political and literary interests without financial concerns.

In February, 1834, Macaulay sailed for India accompanied by a small library of the Greek and Latin classics and by his adoring sister Hannah. His other favorite sister, Margaret, had, much to his distress, married the year before. Before the year was over, Hannah married Charles Trevelyan, a brilliant young official of the East India Company, and Macaulay received news that Margaret had died of scarlet fever.

Hannah was to remain Macaulay's closest friend and intimate, although she could not be as close as before. Macaulay felt lonely and devastated. He saved himself by rereading a good portion of Greek and Latin literature and by entering into hard and controversial work. He was fortunate in enjoying the backing of a reforming governor-general, but still had to fight harsh opposition in convincing the Supreme Council to abolish press censorship and to end certain privileges held by Englishmen appearing in Indian courts. He became president of the General Council of Public Instruction, which was bitterly split between the Orientalists, who wished to continue subsidizing native schools teaching traditional learning in Arabic, Persian, and Sanskrit, and the Anglicists, who wished to support only European learning taught in English. With his usual vigor and with even more than his usual intolerance of folly, Macaulay argued for English. In his famous "Minute on Indian Education" of February 2, 1835, he summed up Indian learning as:

> Astronomy, which would move laughter in girls at an English boarding school—History, abounding with Kings thirty feet high, and reigns thirty thousand years long—and Geography, made up of seas of treacle and seas of butter.

Macaulay despised Indian culture, but he did not despise Indians. He believed that Indian students could master the same curriculum as English students. His position became policy, and before the end of the century, several hundred thousand Indians were studying modern

Thomas Babington Macaulay. (Library of Congress)

THE HISTORY OF ENGLAND

The opening paragraph of Thomas Babington Macaulay's The History of England from the Accession of James II *lays out Macaulay's goals and distills his views on the subject.*

I purpose to write the history of England from the accession of King James the Second down to a time which is within the memory of men still living. I shall recount the errors which, in a few months, alienated a loyal gentry and priesthood from the House of Stuart. I shall trace the course of that revolution which terminated the long struggle between our sovereigns and their parliaments, and bound up together the rights of the people and the title of the reigning dynasty. I shall relate how the new settlement was, during many troubled years, successfully defended against foreign and domestic enemies; how, under that settlement, the authority of law and the security of property were found to be compatible with a liberty of discussion and of individual action never before known; how, from the auspicious union of order and freedom, sprang a prosperity of which the annals of human affairs had furnished no example; how our country, from a state of ignominious vassalage, rapidly rose to the place of umpire among European powers; how her opulence and her martial glory grew together; how, by wise and resolute good faith, was gradually established a public credit fruitful of marvels which to the statesmen of any former age would have seemed incredible; how a gigantic commerce gave birth to a maritime power, compared with which every other maritime power, ancient or modern, sinks into insignificance; how Scotland, after ages of enmity, was at length united to England, not merely by legal bonds, but by indissoluble ties of interest and affection; how, in America, the British colonies rapidly became far mightier and wealthier than the realms which Cortes and Pizarro had added to the dominions of Charles the Fifth; how in Asia, British adventurers founded an empire not less splendid and more durable than that of Alexander. Nor will it be less my duty faithfully to record disasters mingled with triumphs, and great national crimes and follies far more humiliating than any disaster. It will be seen that even what we justly account our chief blessings were not without alloy. It will be seen that the system which effectually secured our liberties against the encroachments of kingly power gave birth to a new class of abuses from which absolute monarchies are exempt. It will be seen that, in consequence partly of unwise interference, and partly of unwise neglect, the increase of wealth and the extension of trade produced, together with immense good, some evils from which poor and rude societies are free. It will be seen how, in two important dependencies of the crown, wrong was followed by just retribution; how imprudence and obstinacy broke the ties which bound the North American colonies to the parent state; how Ireland, cursed by the domination of race over race, and of religion over religion, remained indeed a member of the empire, but a withered and distorted member, adding no strength to the body politic, and reproachfully pointed at by all who feared or envied the greatness of England. Yet, unless I greatly deceive myself, the general effect of this chequered narrative will be to excite thankfulness in all religious minds, and hope in the breasts of all patriots. For the history of our country during the last hundred and sixty years is eminently the history of physical, of moral, and of intellectual improvement. Those who compare the age on which their lot has fallen with a golden age which exists only in their imagination may talk of degeneracy and decay: but no man who is correctly informed as to the past will be disposed to take a morose or desponding view of the present.

Source: Thomas Babington Macaulay, *The History of England from the Accession of James II* (Philadelphia: Porter & Coates, 1887?), vol. 1, chapter 1.

---

subjects in English. In May, 1835, Macaulay became head of the Law Commission that proceeded in two years to draw up a new, rational, and humane penal code, in large part composed by Macaulay, to replace the jumble of different systems in the various regions of India. The code was not put into operation until January of 1862, after the death of its creator, but it has remained the basis for Indian criminal law ever since. The rather inactive English barrister had become the lawgiver for India.

Macaulay returned to England in June, 1838. An uncle had left him a legacy of ten thousand pounds in 1836, which meant that Macaulay was able to accumulate the sum he was aiming at more quickly than he had expected.

While in India, he had written his longest and one of his most celebrated essays for the *Edinburgh Review*, a defense of Francis Bacon, whom Macaulay extolled as one of the fathers of inductive reasoning and experimental science. He also began to plan a large-scale history of England from 1688 to 1830.

Macaulay began to write the history in March, 1839, but returned to Parliament in September representing Edinburgh and entered Lord Melbourne's cabinet as secretary at war. The government fell in August, 1841, and Macaulay, while still in Parliament, now had more time to write. In 1842, he published *Lays of Ancient Rome*, vigorous ballads, written as if they were ancient Roman poems. Like all of his writings, they were an instant success. In 1843, he published *Critical and Historical Essays*, which brought together most of his articles from the *Edinburgh Review* and that sold several hundred thousand copies in England and in the United States in the next few decades. In 1846, the Whigs again formed a government, and Macaulay accepted the post of paymaster general because it would not take much time. In July, 1847, Macaulay lost his seat and decided to leave politics.

In 1849, Macaulay published the first two volumes of *The History of England from the Accession of James the Second* (1849-1855) to the acclaim of scholars and the appreciation of general readers. He had said earlier, "I shall not be satisfied unless I produce something which shall for a few days supersede the last fashionable novel on the tables of young ladies."

Tens of thousands of copies of Macaulay's book were sold within months and several hundred thousand before the end of the century. In 1852, Macaulay, with great reluctance, allowed the Whigs of Edinburgh to return him to Parliament, but he refused to take office again. He suffered a heart attack soon after, gave only a few speeches in the next few years, and resigned from Parliament in January, 1856. In December, 1855, volumes 3 and 4 of his historical study appeared. His publisher presented him with a check for twenty thousand pounds—a sum equivalent to more than one million dollars in modern U.S. currency.

Honors of all sorts showered upon Macaulay. In September, 1857, he became Baron Macaulay of Rothley, though he never spoke in the House of Lords. Macaulay did not live to complete his masterpiece. He died December 28, 1859, at Holly Lodge, Kensington, and was buried in Westminster Abbey. His sister, Hannah, now Lady Trevelyan, put together his final chapters to form volume 5, which appeared in 1861, and brought the story up to the death of King William III in 1702.

SIGNIFICANCE

Thomas Babington Macaulay was an important essayist, politician, and parliamentary orator. He achieved lasting importance, however, by providing India with an educational system and a law code, while he earned fame and recognition by writing *The History of England from the Accession of James the Second*. It is, first, an extraordinary work of literature. The characters, both heroes and villains, come alive as if in a novel. His battle scenes—Sedgemoor, Killiecrankie, Londonderry, the Boyne—are virtually refought as one reads them. The sympathetic reader, moreover, can almost believe that he is at

the deathbed of Charles II, in the court rooms of the ferocious Judge Jeffries, at the trial and execution of the noble Argyle, and in the crowd that welcomes William of Orange as he enters Exeter.

Macaulay did more than write extremely well. His research was on a far more thorough scale than that of English historians before him. He sought out new archives and walked over old battlefields. Macaulay's work also is an analysis of important political actions, their causes, and their consequences, written with the acute understanding of a man who had spent time in cabinet meetings as well as libraries. Macaulay did indeed see politics as central, but in the famous chapter 3, he devotes more than one hundred pages to the state of England in 1685, its towns, clergy, roads, stage coaches, highwaymen, inns, newsletters, wages of workers, female education, and much else. Much has been written on these topics since Macaulay, but no one before him had attempted anything as comprehensive. Macaulay, who has sometimes been criticized as too political in his interests, virtually invented social history.

Macaulay writes Whig history. It is sometimes Whig in a narrow and partisan sense as when Macaulay favors the Whigs, the liberal aristocrats who drove James II from the throne, and attacks the Tories who so often opposed them. It is also Whig history in the broader sense that traces, explains, and celebrates progress in human societies. It looks to the past for the origin of what men value in the present. Macaulay linked men and causes of the present with those of the past and brought new significance to both.

In his history, Macaulay only reached the year 1702, but he had planned to go to 1830, the eve of the battle over the Reform Bill in which the Whigs, this time with Macaulay among them, saved the nation once again, producing the right kind of fundamental constitutional change. Macaulay often refers in the multivolume study to later and even contemporary events. Thus, at the conclusion of the first two volumes that appeared in December, 1848, the end of the year in which revolutions had broken out in most of Europe, Macaulay states triumphantly,

> Now, if ever, we ought to be able to appreciate the whole importance of the stand which was made by our forefathers against the House of Stuart. All around us the world is convulsed by the agonies of great nations.

England, in contrast, has been at peace. "It is because we had a preserving revolution in the seventeenth century that we have not had a destroying revolution in the nineteenth."

Macaulay had critics in his day and afterward. He painted in primary colors. He was vigorous but not subtle and never appeared to doubt or even hesitate before pronouncing judgment on men and causes. At times, Macaulay was as partisan in writing history as when delivering parliamentary speeches. This lent passion to his work but sometimes produced bad judgments. He was clearly unfair to the Jacobite Viscount Dundee, the Quaker William Penn, and the great General Marlborough. Macaulay's critics have found flaws, but none that seriously diminishes the work. There are blemishes, but blemishes on a still great and imposing structure.

—Melvin Shefftz

FURTHER READING

Beatty, Richmond Croom. *Lord Macaulay: Victorian Liberal*. Reprint. Hamden, Conn.: Archon Books, 1971. A good middle-sized biography (almost four hundred pages); friendly, but critical.

Clive, John. *Macaulay: The Shaping of the Historian*. New York: Alfred A. Knopf, 1973. A magnificent full-scale biography covering Macaulay up to his return from India. It is both appreciative and critical. The definitive study for the early years.

Firth, Sir Charles. *A Commentary on Macaulay's History of England*. New York: Barnes & Noble Books, 1938. A full-length book, based on a series of university lectures, that evaluates and comments on Macaulay's history. Respectful, but critical.

Hamburger, Joseph. *Macaulay and the Whig Tradition*. Chicago: University of Chicago Press, 1976. An interesting though not always convincing study of Macaulay's political thought that asserts that he was too pessimistic to be a true Whig.

Levine, George. *The Boundaries of Fiction: Carlyle, Macaulay, Newman*. Princeton, N.J.: Princeton University Press, 1968. About a third of the book is a thoughtful analysis of Macaulay's history as imaginative literature.

Macaulay, Thomas Babington. *The History of England from the Accession of James the Second*. 4 vols. Reprint. London: J. M. Dent & Sons, 1972. A reprint of Macaulay's best known work.

Millgate, Jane. *Macaulay*. London: Routledge & Kegan Paul, 1973. An excellent short biography and analysis of the major writings.

Paget, John. *The New "Examen."* Reprint. Manchester, England: Haworth Press, 1934. This is an unusual book that was first published in 1861, though some parts appeared in the last two years of Macaulay's life. It is a vigorous and extended attack on Macaulay for misusing evidence in order to blacken William Penn, Viscount Dundee, and the duke of Marlborough, and to whitewash William III of responsibility for the Glencoe massacre. Paget goes too far, but he does score some valid points.

Thomas, William. *The Quarrel of Macaulay and Croker: Politics and History in the Age of Reform*. New York: Oxford University Press, 2000. Describes a longstanding literary feud between Macaulay and John Wilson Croker, the editor of Boswell's biography of Samuel Johnson. The feud began in the House of Commons in 1831, when Croker accused Macaulay of being ignorant about the French Revolution; eighteen years later, Croker wrote a scathing review of Macaulay's *History of England*. Thomas contrasts the two men's approach to history, and concludes that Macaulay was not the typical Whig historian of legend.

Trevelyan, George Otto. *The Life and Letters of Lord Macaulay*. 2 vols. London: Longmans, Green, 1876. An important and basic book, written by the son of Macaulay's beloved sister Hannah, who was himself a good historian. It is admiring and uncritical, limited naturally enough by familial piety.

Trevor-Roper, Hugh. Introduction to Macaulay's *Critical and Historical Essays*. London: Collins, 1965.

_____. Introduction to Macaulay's *History of England*. New York: Penguin Books, 1980. Two excellent introductory essays by a distinguished historian of the seventeenth century.

SEE ALSO: George Bancroft; William Edward Forster; Lord Jeffrey; James Mill.

RELATED ARTICLE in *Great Events from History: The Nineteenth Century, 1801-1900:* 1824: Ranke Develops Systematic History.

CYRUS HALL MCCORMICK
American inventor

McCormick revolutionized American agriculture through his invention of the reaper and his marketing innovations. He also helped to shape American theological development by his patronage of a northwestern seminary.

BORN: February 15, 1809; Rockbridge County, Virginia
DIED: May 13, 1884; Chicago, Illinois
AREAS OF ACHIEVEMENT: Agriculture, science and technology, philanthropy

EARLY LIFE

Cyrus Hall McCormick was born in his family home in the Virginia Valley. His father, Robert McCormick, and his mother, Mary Ann Hall, came from strong Scotch-Irish stock, and they represented two of the most influential families in the community. Cyrus was the eldest of eight children born to Robert and Mary Ann McCormick, two of whom died in their infancy.

McCormick's education was gained in a field school where he was taught the three R's, geography, and religion. At home he was daily instructed in the Shorter Catechism. Although Washington College (founded in 1782) was located at nearby Lexington, neither he nor any of his brothers received higher education. His constant instruction in the principles of the Bible and Calvinism molded his thought and faith throughout his life. He attended New Providence Church, eight miles from his home, and for several years led the congregation in singing. In 1834, he joined that church. Three years later he moved his membership to the Mount Carmel Presbyterian Meeting House at Steele's Tavern, it being closer to home.

Both of McCormick's parents were about five feet, eight inches in height. Cyrus was just under six feet tall. He was of powerful physique. This permitted him to work almost tirelessly in his later years, much to the dismay of associates who were obliged to follow him through the day. He once described himself thus: "My hair is a very dark brown,—eyes dark, though not black, complexion fresh and health good, 5 ft. 11 1/2 inc. high, weighing 200 lbs."

Much of McCormick's good health and strong physical condition he attributed to his refusal to drink alcohol and his disdain for smoking tobacco. Even as a youth he abstained from many of the debilitating habits of his peers. In 1857, at the age of forty-eight, he married Nancy Fowler. Before then, he had eschewed feminine companionship, but his new wife entered into his work, serving as a secretary who copied all his letters. Their marriage endured for twenty-six years and produced seven children.

LIFE'S WORK

McCormick's first reaper was demonstrated on the fields of Walnut Grove. It was a workable horsepowered reaper with a reciprocating cutting blade protected by metal fingers, a reel to bring the grain against the blade, a divider to separate the grain to be cut from the grain in the field, and a platform to catch the felled grain. In 1840, McCormick began to manufacture and sell his reapers locally. His first models exhausted the horses that pulled them, and they were constantly breaking down. So expensive were the repairs that hand reaping still remained the most economical way to harvest. In 1844, seeking increased sales, McCormick visited the Northwest. The large, flat fields of that region proved more conducive to his machinery than the small, rocky fields of Virginia. He moved his manufacturing operations to Chicago in 1847, and by 1850 he was producing McCormick reapers in his own factories.

Harvesting machinery thus became practicable through McCormick's inventions and those of Obed Hussey, a New Englander, who constructed a successful reaper in Cincinnati and obtained a patent in 1833, a year before McCormick received his; it is quite probable, however, that the latter's invention preceded Hussey's. The ensuing rivalry between the two inventors over patents and markets was long, bitter, and led to considerable controversy and numerous court battles.

McCormick's 1840 machine, in spite of its weaknesses, proved superior to Hussey's. As sales expanded, his reaper proved revolutionary. With only two men the McCormick machine could do ten times the work of two scythe or cradle harvesters. The reaper's entrance into the Midwest made extensive wheat growing possible, and it further encouraged frontier migration. William Seward once commented that McCormick pushed the line of civilization westward at least thirty miles per year.

McCormick entered the field of merchandising, and by 1856 more than four thousand McCormick reapers were being sold annually on the installment plan. On the eve of the Civil War, between eighty thousand and ninety thousand reapers were in use, primarily in midwestern farms. McCormick improved the method of harvesting hay. In 1856, he patented a two-wheeled mower with a flexible cutter bar. This permitted operation on rough, uneven ground. By 1860, a variety of types of mowing machines similar to modern mowers were on the market, for it was easy for inventors to make minor alterations to any of McCormick's machines—a practice that also involved him in numerous patent-infringement suits.

McCormick's inventions contributed indirectly to the ultimate Northern success in the Civil War, increasing the amount of grain and forage for human and animal consumption. His inventions permitted more men to leave the farm either to go into the army or to the city to work in factories that produced war materiel. The South, with its paucity of factories for civilian consumption, in addition to its hilly, rocky terrain, simply could not produce the necessary quantity of field-grown foodstuff.

McCormick entered the international trade scene with his reaper. He was awarded numerous prizes and medals for this invention, and in 1878, for the third time, he re-

Cyrus Hall McCormick. (Library of Congress)

ceived a grand prize at the French Exposition for his reaping and self-binding machine. The rank of officer in the Legion of Honor was also conferred upon him. At that time he was elected a corresponding member of the French Academy of Sciences, "as having done more for the cause of agriculture than any other living man." Reverdy Johnson remarked in 1859 that the McCormick reaper alone contributed an annual income of fifty-five million dollars to the whole country.

McCormick's religious training and discipline remained a part of his entire life. His Calvinistic philosophy was a source of comfort in the midst of his failures, and a beacon of direction through success. The greatest monument to his devotion to the church is the seminary that bears his name: McCormick Theological Seminary, located in Chicago. He stands in the company of men such as John D. Rockefeller, John Wanamaker, Jay Cooke, and W. H. Vanderbilt: successful businesspeople who contributed liberally to the institutions of their respective churches—institutions that now bear witness to their dedicated commitment.

McCormick represented that portion of the Presbyterian Church denominated the "Old School." His move to Chicago brought him into a strong New School community. His move to that city stirred within him religious pride to the point that he wanted more than merely an Old School congregation in which to worship, he desired a school of the prophets to train men to convert the Northwest to Old Schoolism.

A floundering seminary in New Albany, Indiana, attracted him, and it was primarily because of his beneficence that it was moved to Chicago in 1859. He ultimately endowed the seminary—the Presbyterian Seminary of the Northwest—with $100,000, a figure sufficient to underwrite four chairs. As the shadows of war began to creep across the Presbyterian horizon, none pleaded more than he that the church should not divide. When the war was over, he was in the front ranks of those who called for a reunion of the Old School wings, North and South, rather than a union of the Old School North with the New School, whose doctrinal soundness he questioned. He also contributed generously to several of the institutions of the southern Presbyterian Church in the days of reconstruction, helping them to get back on their feet.

At the Seminary of the Northwest—renamed the McCormick Seminary in 1886—McCormick fought to acquire and retain scholars from the Old School. For a time he appeared willing to tolerate a degree of liberalization within the seminary in order to increase financial support from other sources. When this additional financial support did not materialize, however, McCormick's financial contributions, and consequently his influence upon the seminary, increased. As a result, the seminary dominated the rapidly growing midwestern portion of the church, and exerted a large, if not decisive, influence on the Church's theological history at a critical point in the twentieth century. McCormick remained active in the Presbyterian Church until his death on May 13, 1884.

SIGNIFICANCE

The genius of Cyrus Hall McCormick lay in his unrelenting dedication to improving his inventions and his personal commitment to the Presbyterian Church; in him, vocation and faith were blended. He revolutionized agricultural economics. He initiated the installment plan, whereby ordinary farmers could afford to buy large machines. He made possible a more rapid expansion of the American drive to the West, and he presented his church with a valuable tool for the conversion of that portion of America. The Shorter Catechism, on which McCormick was nurtured as a youth, begins by asking: "What is the chief end of man?" McCormick's life was directed by the answer he learned by heart: "To glorify God and to enjoy Him forever."

—*Harold M. Parker, Jr.*

FURTHER READING

Brands, H. W. *Masters of Enterprise: Giants of American Business from John Jacob Astor and J. P. Morgan to Bill Gates and Oprah Winfrey.* New York: Free Press, 1999. A collection of profiles of 25 American entrepreneurs. Chapter 3, "Golden Grain," recounts how McCormick invented the reaper and established a harvesting machine company.

Hounshell, David A. "Public Relations or Public Understanding? The American Industries Series in *Scientific American.*" *Technology and Culture* 21 (1980): 589-593. Points out that the article regarding the McCormick Harvesting Machine Co. that appeared in a series of the *Scientific American* (May 14, 1881) was actually written and paid for as an advertisement.

Hutchinson, William T. *Cyrus Hall McCormick.* 2 vols. New York: Century, 1930. Reprint. New York: Da Capo Press, 1968. The definitive biography of McCormick. Thoroughly documented and based primarily on material in the McCormick Historical Association Library (Chicago).

Loetscher, Lefferts A. *The Broadening Church: A Study of Theological Issues in the Presbyterian Church Since 1869.* Philadelphia: University of Pennsylvania Press, 1957. Discusses the theological developments that emerged following the reunion of the Presbyterian Old School and New School in 1869. Presents McCormick's efforts to establish in Chicago a seminary grounded on Old Schoolism.

McClure, James G. K. *The Story of the Life and Work of the Presbyterian Theological Seminary Chicago Founded by Cyrus H. McCormick.* Chicago: Lakeside Press, R. R. Donnelley & Sons, 1929. Traces the history of the McCormick Theological Seminary, emphasizing the role of McCormick in establishing it in Chicago.

McCormick, Cyrus. *The Century of the Reaper: An Account of Cyrus Hall McCormick, the Inventor of the Reaper; of the McCormick Harvesting Machine Company, the Business He Created; and of the International Harvester Company, His Heir and Chief Memorial.* Boston: Houghton Mifflin, 1931. As the author admits in his foreword, "It must be obvious that I, his grandson, am not in a position to write a coldly impartial account of his contribution to history." Written on the occasion of the centennial celebration of McCormick's invention of the reaper. Weaves together the technological accomplishments with McCormick's religious propensities. Contains thirty-one illustrations.

Wendel, Charles H. *One Hundred Fifty Years of International Harvester.* Sarasota, Fla.: Crestline, 1981. A study of McCormick's business enterprises written to celebrate the sesquicentennial of McCormick's first reaper and to "show the evolution of the farm implement industry." Essentially a photographic essay, with a brief biography of McCormick. Contains short accounts of the numerous companies that joined to form the International Harvester Co.

SEE ALSO: Johnny Appleseed; Luther Burbank; Jay Cooke; J. P. Morgan; John D. Rockefeller.

RELATED ARTICLES in *Great Events from History: The Nineteenth Century, 1801-1900:* Summer, 1831: McCormick Invents the Reaper; October 14, 1834: Blair Patents His First Seed Planter.

SIR JOHN ALEXANDER MACDONALD
Prime minister of Canada (1867-1873, 1878-1891)

Macdonald not only had a major role in drawing up the British North America Act, which created the Dominion of Canada, but also, as Canada's first prime minister, brought about the new nation's territorial and political expansion from sea to sea. Within the British community, he paved the way for Canadians to determine their own foreign affairs and foreshadowed the principle behind the twentieth century's British Commonwealth of Nations.

BORN: January 11, 1815; Glasgow, Scotland
DIED: June 6, 1891; Ottawa, Ontario, Canada
AREA OF ACHIEVEMENT: Government and politics

EARLY LIFE

John Alexander Macdonald was the son of Helen Shaw, who was descended from a family of military professionals. After several generations of farmers on his father's side, his father, Hugh John Macdonald, was the first to earn a living from business. Ultimately, however, his business failed in Glasgow, and he, his wife, and children—John Alexander (then five years old), Margaret, Louisa, and James—traveled to Kingston, Upper Canada, to join Hugh John's in-laws, Lieutenant Colonel Donald Macpherson and his family, who had retired there. Macpherson helped the Macdonald family get settled, and the two families remained close.

After receiving the best education the local schools offered, at the age of fifteen years the young Macdonald was apprenticed to a Kingston lawyer, George Mackenzie. For a year or two, Macdonald worked as a messenger, a clerk, and a stenographer. At night he studied British law. Because Macdonald was advancing rapidly in his studies, Mackenzie put him in charge of a branch office. Macdonald then took over the law practice of his sick cousin, L. P. Macpherson. The latter recovered, and in 1835, with Mackenzie's death, Macdonald opened his own law office in Kingston. In the next year he was admitted to the bar.

Early in his legal career, Macdonald helped put down the 1837 insurrection. In the next year he participated in the capture of Americans who had invaded Canada. Even thought it might have damaged his career, Macdonald defended these men, as well as a man accused of raping a child. Macdonald provided them with the best legal advice, but he lost the cases. The men were hanged. Macdonald would continue in the practice of law, specializing in commercial law, first at Kingston and then at Toronto, with various partners, until his death in 1891. His clients were businesspeople and corporations.

Macdonald entered politics at the grassroots level, serving first as secretary for a local school board, then as alderman for Kingston. While serving in the latter office, he was elected to represent Kingston in the Canadian legislature. The British government had recently united Upper Canada and Lower Canada into Canada West (Ontario) and Canada East (Quebec) in the Act of Union of 1840. In one of his first addresses, Macdonald stated that the British Crown must be maintained in Canada. He never deviated from that stance, which remained his guiding principle.

Macdonald was nearly six feet tall, slender, and looked much like his English contemporary Benjamin Disraeli. He was not a good-looking man: His large nose dominated his face, and he became fair game for caricaturists. These "ugly" physical features were overcome by his natty dress, his keen sense of humor, his excellent memory for persons' faces and names, and his ease at making and keeping friends. Nevertheless, he was also noted for a caustic tongue and bad temper. He was never an orator, but rather a debater who made best use of the quick retort and the penetrating question. Though a clever tactician, Macdonald was a practical man who used practical means to achieve his goals. At times he was accused of being devious and unscrupulous.

In his early twenties, Macdonald often was ill. He became worse with the death of his father in 1841. To recuperate, he traveled to England and Scotland. In the latter country he met his cousin, Isabella Clark. After his return to Kingston, Isabella followed him. They were married soon afterward, in September of 1843. Within two years of the marriage, Isabella fell ill. She spent the rest of her life bedridden. Seeking a cure, Macdonald took her first to New York, then to Savannah, Georgia. He returned in six months; she stayed three years. In spite of her life-threatening illness, she gave birth to two sons, John Alexander (1847), who died at the age of thirteen months, and Hugh John (1850). Her illness, Macdonald's being deprived of her company, the huge medical bills, and later the additional pressures from the demands placed upon Macdonald by his constituency and his parliamentary obligations led Macdonald to become a heavy drinker. His alcoholism resulted in his having a number of short-term political reverses. He almost always turned those defeats into victories, however, through quick thinking and political machination.

LIFE'S WORK

During his wife's long years of illness (from 1845 until her death in December, 1857), Macdonald endured "the great struggle for power and place," as he defined it. In the Conservative government, he was receiver general from 1847 to 1848. The Conservatives and Macdonald were out of power from 1848 to 1854. In those years, "Responsible Government" was established by the Reformers (Liberals), with political power resting in the prime minister. It had been vested in the governor-general for Queen Victoria, Canada's monarch.

The Conservative Party almost destroyed itself in 1849. The empire's old economic organization was eroding with Great Britain's adoption of free trade. Poli-

tically, the government's Rebellion Losses Bill signified the end of the old imperial government. The result was that the Ultra-Conservatives went on a rampage in 1849, burning the Parliament building and demanding an end to the British connection and Canada's annexation to the United States. They came to their senses, but damage had been done. The parliamentarians moved the capital's site from Montreal, but because no permanent location could be decided on, it would alternate between Quebec and Toronto.

Macdonald disavowed himself of the Ultra-Conservatives. He helped form the British America League to work for confederation of all the provinces, for strengthening the British connection, and for adoption of a national commercial policy. Macdonald embraced Responsible Government. He worked within his party to destroy the Ultra-Conservatives—the Tory, Anglican, and Loyalist oligarchy (the family compact)—who had for so long dominated politics in Toronto, the capital of old Upper Canada.

Macdonald formed his own government by organizing a new political coalition once the Reformers (Liberals) left office in 1854. The Conservatives, along with the existing alliance of Upper Canadian Reformers, joined with the French majority political bloc. The coalition became a permanent political party, eventually the Progressive Conservative Party, known as the Liberal-Conservative Party, one of Canada's great political parties. Macdonald was the party's parliamentary leader. As attorney general, he established an elected legislative council, or upper house, in the provincial parliament. With the removal of the aged prime minister, Sir Allan McNabb, Macdonald became co-prime minister with Étienne P. Tache. Macdonald finally had power and place. Later George Étienne Cartier joined the cabinet, replacing Tache as co-prime minister. The partnership would end with Cartier's death in 1873.

Macdonald was an able, skillful, and clever politician. He proved it more than once. In 1858, he and Cartier had Queen Victoria select Canada's permanent capital; she chose Ottawa. The decision was presented to the legislature by Macdonald. The vote taken on the issue defeated the

Sir John Alexander Macdonald. (Library of Congress)

government. The Liberals under George Brown formed a new government. By law, all new cabinet appointees, including the prime minister, had to seek reelection. Macdonald refused to agree to a recess. While they were temporarily absent from Parliament, Macdonald, leader of the opposition, obtained a vote of no confidence in Brown's government. By ingenious political maneuvering, Macdonald secured his party's return to government, having been out of power for only two days.

During the mid-1850's, Brown introduced a new issue into the political scene. Representation in the legislature was shared equally by Canada West and Canada East, even though Canada West now had the greater population. Brown, from Canada West, demanded representation by population. In the Union, Canada West was stymied in matters of education, westward expansion, railway subsidies, and taxation. Macdonald stayed in power only with French Canadian bloc support. The latter was determined not to promote Canada West; the legislature as then constituted was a guarantee of their French Canadian identity. Regional and racial conflicts threatened destruction of the Canadian union.

The raging American Civil War exacerbated matters: During the war, serious disputes arose between Great Britain, British North America, and the United States. Because Great Britain was in charge of Canadian foreign affairs, any one of these disputes could have involved Great Britain and British North America (Canada) in war. For five long years, Macdonald believed that the Americans could (and would) invade his country and conquer it. Great Britain expected Canada to provide some contribution to defense. Macdonald and Cartier agreed. The Militia Bill's passage through the assembly failed. Conservative French Canadians refused to support their government. Macdonald, imbibing excessively, failed to provide the necessary leadership. His mother's death in October, 1862, had stripped him of any incentive he might have had.

Macdonald's government fell following an adverse vote in the legislature. He considered retiring from public life, but the Liberal government's ineptness changed his mind. When he knew the government was doomed, he got the assembly to vote no confidence in it. To save his government, the new prime minister, John Sandfield Macdonald, called a general election. The results returned the administration, but opposition and government were too evenly matched in the legislature—the Union of Canada was deadlocked.

To solve the constitutional dilemma, Macdonald accepted Brown's proposal for a new coalition to include Upper Canadian Reformers to bring about a federal union of all British North American provinces. Macdonald accepted leadership in drawing up a new constitution. In its drafting, he presided over meetings at Charlottestown, Quebec, and in London, England, where representatives of the Crown joined them. The British Parliament passed the resultant British North America Act in 1867, creating the Dominion of Canada to replace the Union of Canada.

In London, Macdonald married Susan Agnes Bernard, even though he barely knew her. Her brother was a member of the Office of the Attorney General, Canada West, and had once roomed with Macdonald. They had one daughter, Mary (1869-1933), who was confined from infancy to a wheelchair.

Before confederation was realized on July 1, 1867, Macdonald was disturbed by Fenian invasions from the United States, the American abrogation of the 1854 Reciprocity Treaty, and the Maritime Provinces' resistance in joining the Dominion. In 1867, however, Nova Scotia and New Brunswick came into the confederation. Macdonald followed through on a pledge given earlier to link the Maritime Provinces to Quebec by the building of the Intercolonial Railway.

The new federal parliament met in Ottawa in 1867, with Macdonald its first prime minister. A host of challenges faced the new government: the diverse claims of the French and English Canadians, the provinces' determination to maintain their rights, and the need for a continued British connection. In spite of these obstacles, Macdonald persevered, handling each problem as it arose. He was the Canadian representative among the British delegation that settled problems arising out of the American Civil War. From that time on, whenever Canadian interests were involved with a foreign country, Great Britain would include Canadians in any discussion or settlement.

Macdonald worked hard to enlarge the territorial boundaries of Canada from sea to sea. To forestall any American settlement of the western region, Macdonald arranged to purchase rights of the Hudson's Bay Company to the Northwest Territories, including the prairies. The Métis Red River rebellion under Louis Riel delayed its acquisition for several months. The rebellion, even though put down by military force, quickened Macdonald's decision to create the province of Manitoba (1870) and take it into the Dominion earlier than planned. He feared American intervention and the possibility of American annexation of the prairies.

Macdonald made possible the entry into the Dominion of British Columbia (1871) and Prince Edward Island

(1873). British Columbia demanded as her price the construction of a transcontinental railway across the empty plains and through the Canadian Rockies to the east. Macdonald's Quebec leader, Cartier, accepted, during the 1872 general election, campaign monies in return for a charter for the Pacific Railway Company. In the midst of the ensuing Pacific Scandal of 1873, Cartier died. Even though Macdonald proved that he had known nothing about the deal, he was forced to resign from the government. A new election was called, returning the Liberals to office, which they held from 1873 to 1878, a period of depression; they adopted free trade. In 1878, Macdonald returned to political power on the basis of the National Policy, a system of protection of Canadian manufacturers through imposition of high tariffs on foreign imports, especially American imports. The National Policy appealed to anti-Americans and Canadian nationalists and became a permanent part of Canadian economic and political life.

Macdonald's last years in office were politically difficult ones. He secured for a new Canadian Pacific Railway a charter in 1880. In spite of hardships encountered in its construction (Parliament had to appropriate funds far beyond original estimates), the line was in operation in the fall of 1885. As in 1870, the Indians and the Métis under Riel tried to stop western settlement. Canadian military forces—one of the soldiers was Macdonald's son, Hugh John—once again defeated them. Riel turned himself in. He was tried for treason, found guilty, and hanged, Macdonald refusing to pardon him. The French Canadians thought of Riel as a great hero; to the English Canadians he was a murderer. Several years before, he and Métis had executed an Ontario Orangeman, Thomas Scott. Riel's death intensified racial and religious tensions, severely hurt the Conservative Party in Quebec, and led to the French Canadian "nationalist" movement.

Macdonald wanted a strong national government. The federal power's right of disallowance over provincial legislation was challenged through the legal system. Great Britain's Privy Council often decided matters on appeal in favor of the provinces, resulting in a federal system much more decentralized than Macdonald wanted. In the face of provincial opposition, however, he had no choice. Macdonald's National Policy was successful during the first years of his return to power. With the return of depression, the opposition (Liberals) worked for its abandonment in favor of unrestricted reciprocity with the United States and their own return to political power.

To Macdonald, unrestricted reciprocity meant total surrender to the United States—loss of Canadian commercial autonomy, loss of fiscal freedom, and eventually the Dominion's annexation to the United States. The general election of 1891 was fought on this issue, and Macdonald and the Conservatives were victorious. Macdonald was pleased to see his son, Hugh John, a lawyer, elected to Parliament from Winnipeg, Manitoba. In the election, Macdonald overexerted himself. He died from heart failure in Ottawa, on June 6, 1891, and was buried in Kingston.

SIGNIFICANCE

For forty-seven years, Sir John Alexander Macdonald sat in a Canadian parliament. His cabinet experience encompassed forty-four years. In his lifetime he held seven cabinet posts, served as prime minister in the Union of Canada, and was singularly honored with his election as the first prime minister of the Dominion of Canada. He witnessed and, as prime minister, had a large role in the economic and political evolution of Canada, from its earliest years until it became an industrialized nation. More than any other single person, Macdonald "made" Canada and provided its character. As first prime minister of the Dominion of Canada, his greatest achievement was that he set forth the policy goals in domestic and external affairs for all future Canadian political leaders. If Macdonald was not Canada's greatest political leader, he certainly is numbered among her greatest.

—*Kathleen E. Dunlop*

FURTHER READING

Creighton, Donald Grant. *John A. Macdonald*. Vol. 1, *The Young Politician*. Boston: Houghton Mifflin, 1953. The first extended biography of Macdonald was written from contemporary sources by one of Canada's best historians. It portrays the life and times of Macdonald from his arrival in Kingston as a five-year-old boy from Scotland to the time he became the architect of the Dominion of Canada. Its one failing is that too much attention is given to provincial matters.

_____. *John A. Macdonald*. Vol. 2, *The Old Chieftain*. Boston: Houghton Mifflin, 1956. This book (also based on contemporary sources) is the definitive study of Macdonald and the history of the Dominion of Canada from its inception in 1867 to Macdonald's death in 1891.

"John A. Macdonald." *Maclean's* 114, no. 27 (July 1, 2001): 37. A profile of Macdonald, describing his career, role in the confederation of Canada, and involvement in Canadian politics.

Pope, Joseph. *Memoirs of the Rt. Honourable Sir John Alexander Macdonald, G.C.B., First Prime Minister* of the Dominion of Canada. 2 vols. Ottawa: J. Durie and Sons, 1894. Rev. ed. Toronto: Oxford University Press, 1930. This biography was the first to be based entirely on Macdonald's private papers and was the standard biography until Creighton's work (see above). Pope was Macdonald's private secretary for a number of years and became his literary executor; Pope's account is highly partial to Macdonald and the Conservatives.

Swainson, Donald. *The Rt Honourable Sir John A. Macdonald.* Toronto: Pagurian Press, 1968. Written in journalistic style, this work briefly narrates Macdonald's family background, his education, and his entrance into law, with the greater part dealing with his life's work in politics and his "creating" the Dominion of Canada. Macdonald's failings are not glossed over, but are considered in their proper context.

Waite, P. B. *The Life and Times of Confederation, 1864-1867: Politics, Newspapers, and the Union of British North America.* 3d ed. Toronto: Robin Brass Studio, 2001. Recounts the events leading to the 1867 confed-eration of the Canadian provinces, examining the role that politics and newspapers played in the process.

_____. *Macdonald: His Life and World.* Toronto: McGraw-Hill Ryerson, 1955. This work, as the title indicates, treats Macdonald's life and his world, with the emphasis on his world. Few works written about Macdonald address the places with which he was associated.

SEE ALSO: George Brown; Benjamin Disraeli; Alexander Mackenzie; Louis Riel; Queen Victoria.

RELATED ARTICLES in *Great Events from History: The Nineteenth Century, 1801-1900:* July 1, 1867: British North America Act; October 11, 1869-July 15, 1870: First Riel Rebellion; November 5, 1873-October 9, 1878: Canada's Mackenzie Era; 1875: Supreme Court of Canada Is Established; 1876: Canada's Indian Act; September, 1878: Macdonald Returns as Canada's Prime Minister; March 19, 1885: Second Riel Rebellion Begins.

WILLIAM HOLMES MCGUFFEY
American educator

A college president, professor, and Presbyterian clergyman in the Ohio Valley, McGuffey compiled the most famous series of school textbooks in American history. His six Eclectic Readers *sold more than 122 million copies between 1836 and 1920, and impressed upon young Americans the virtues of individual morality, thrift, hard work, and sobriety.*

BORN: September 23, 1800; Washington County, Pennsylvania
DIED: May 4, 1873; Charlottesville, Virginia
AREA OF ACHIEVEMENT: Education

EARLY LIFE
Born on his mother's family farm, William Holmes McGuffey was the second child and the eldest son of Alexander and Anna Holmes McGuffey. His mother had seven children before she died in 1829. His grandfather William McGuffey (1742-1836) and grandmother Ann McKittrick (1747-1826) had emigrated from Wigtown, Gallowayshire, Scotland, in 1774, sailing on the stormy Atlantic for thirteen weeks before landing in Philadelphia. His father was only seven years old when the family came to America, on the eve of the Revolutionary War. After a short stay in the city, the McGuffeys moved due west to carve out a farm in York County on the edge of the Appalachian mountains, which was their wartime home.

Like thousands of other Scottish immigrants, who traditionally disliked the British, the elder William McGuffey enlisted in the Pennsylvania regiments and served under General George Washington until the defeat of General Lord Cornwallis at Yorktown in 1781. In 1789, the family moved to the western edge of Pennsylvania, settling along Wheeling Creek in Washington County, south of Pittsburgh. Living among English and Scotch-Irish immigrants, the war veteran became known as "Scotch Billy." His son Alexander, nicknamed "Sandy," became a skilled frontiersman with his rifle, and with a friend, Duncan McArthur, became a scout and soldier in the Indian wars of the 1790's. They marched with General Anthony Wayne to drive the Indians out of the Ohio Territory.

After returning from the Miami Valley, Alexander married Anna Holmes in 1797, and they lived with her family in Pennsylvania, where three children were born:

Jane (in 1799); William Holmes (in 1800); and Henry (in 1802). When Ohio entered the Union in 1803, Alexander moved his family directly north from West Alexander and across the Pennsylvania state line into Trumbull (modern Mahoning) County, near Youngstown, Ohio, where he had erected a windowless log cabin. There, four more daughters and one son, Alexander, Jr., were born. As the oldest boy, William worked long hours on the Ohio farm to support the growing family. After he had left home, his mother died there at the age of fifty-three in 1829. Two years later, his father was remarried, to Mary Dickey, and in 1836, after the birth of three more daughters, he moved his family and father back to the Keystone state, where "Scotch Billy" died at the age of ninety-four.

McGuffey's early education began in the family's log cabin, where his mother taught her children the three R's. Local "subscription schools," generally taught by a young man or minister, provided further education. Like Abraham Lincoln in western Kentucky amid similar wilderness conditions, young McGuffey borrowed books from neighbors, memorized portions of the Bible and sermons, read before the fireplace, and taught his younger brothers and sisters. His father crafted an adjustable wooden candlestand that provided better light for his love of learning. Before his fourteenth birthday, "Master McGuffey" advertised opening his own school at West Union (modern Calcutta, Ohio), with a four-month term starting in September, 1814; forty-eight pupils paid two dollars each for his instruction.

McGuffey attended the Reverend William Wick's boarding school in Youngstown for a year or two, then took his high school level studies at the Old Stone Academy in Greersburg (modern Darlington), Pennsylvania, under the tutoring of Presbyterian minister and principal Thomas E. Hughs. From Greersburg he acquired sufficient command of classical languages for admission in 1820 to Washington College in Washington, Pennsylvania, near his birthplace. He found lodging with the head of the school and daily walked six miles to and from the college with President Andrew Wylie.

McGuffey majored in philosophy and languages, learning Latin, Greek, and Hebrew. During his senior year, with most of his classwork completed, McGuffey accepted a teaching position near Paris, Kentucky, for 1825-1826. On a visit to Lexington, the first president of Miami University, Robert Hamilton Bishop, happened to meet McGuffey and promptly offered him a professorship in languages at the Oxford, Ohio, land-grant college, at a salary of six hundred dollars per year. He ac-

William Holmes McGuffey. (Library of Congress)

cepted, and Washington College graduated him with honors at the end of the school year.

McGuffey began his ten-year career at Miami University at the age of twenty-six in the fall of 1826. The new professor impressed observers with his penetrating blue eyes, swarthy complexion, and dark hair. His rugged features were characteristically Scottish, and his height was average.

McGuffey's younger brother, Alexander Hamilton McGuffey (1816-1896), rode to Oxford with McGuffey and attended the village school before enrolling in William's language classes. At fifteen, Alexander entered Washington College, and he was graduated in 1836; that fall, he became a professor of languages at Woodward College in Cincinnati. He studied law at the Cincinnati Law School and was admitted to the Ohio bar as a lawyer in 1839.

During his first year on the faculty, William met Harriet Spining, a daughter of Judge Isaac Spining of Dayton, Ohio, when she was visiting her brother, Charles, a merchant in Oxford. They were married at her family home on April 3, 1827, and lived in a boardinghouse until McGuffey bought a four-acre corner lot with a frame house across the street from the college campus. By 1833, he had built a two-story, six-room red brick house onto the frame house to create the finest house in town. (It was sold to Miami University in 1958 and has been the McGuffey Museum since 1963.)

Four McGuffey children were born there: Mary Haines (in 1830), who married Dr. Walker Stewart of Dayton; Henrietta (in 1832), who married the Reverend Andrew D. Hepburn; William Holmes (in 1834), who lived only two weeks; and Charles Spining (in 1835). A fifth child, Edward Mansfield (born in 1838), was born in Cincinnati and died in Athens.

LIFE'S WORK

McGuffey's career encompassed teaching at four colleges, serving as president of two, preaching as an ordained Presbyterian minister, lecturing on educational topics, fighting for state common school systems in Ohio and Virginia, and compiling the first volumes of the famous McGuffey *Eclectic Readers* (1836-1837).

To meet the need for textbooks for the rising number of tax-supported public schools in the Mississippi Valley, the publishing house of Truman and Smith in Cincinnati began issuing common school books during the 1830's. In April, 1833, McGuffey entered into a contract with the firm to develop a series of texts—a primer, four readers, and a speller to rival Noah Webster's. Drawing on his knowledge of languages (he had mastered seven), and with the help of his wife and neighborhood children, he selected and graded reading materials by testing them with pupils gathered around a revolving octagonal table. The first and second readers were published in 1836, the third and fourth followed in 1837, and the McGuffey speller appeared in 1838. Dr. William E. Smith of Miami University wrote the most concise summary of the contents of the original editions and revisions:

> The *First Reader* introduced children to the code of ethics which ran through the four *Readers*—promptness, truthfulness, kindness, and honesty. . . . For the *Second Reader*, he chose stories about the heavens and the earth beneath, stories about table manners, fear of God, and behavior toward parents, teachers, and the poor. . . . The *Third Reader*, published in 1837, was much like other third readers of the time. Method and content were more formal than in the *Second Reader*. Rules were introduced for oral reading. Its fifty-seven lessons were made up of such stories as "The Moss-Covered Bucket," "The Dying Boy," and "George's Feast"—stories that readers

never forgot. . . . The objective of McGuffey's *Fourth Reader* (1837) was "reading aloud with sense, clearness, and appreciation." This *Reader*, introducing good prose and poetry, completed the *Eclectic Series*. McGuffey frequently used selections from the Bible and apologized for not using more.

> In 1838, the *Readers* were improved and enlarged. In 1844 the *Rhetorical Guide* by Alexander Hamilton McGuffey was placed on the market. It became the *Fifth Reader* in the *Eclectic Series*. . . . Later selections in the *Fourth* and *Fifth* were put in the *Sixth Reader*. . . . The late Dean Harvey C. Minnich and others have estimated that, on an average, each *Reader* was used by ten pupils before it was worn out or laid aside. Except the Bible, no other book or set of books has influenced the American mind so much.

McGuffey's contract for the original set allowed him a royalty of 10 percent on sales up to a limit of one thousand dollars. Beyond that the story is that the publisher annually sent him a barrel of smoked hams. Eventually, in the Civil War years, the publisher, then a millionaire, had the company grant McGuffey an annuity until his death.

In August, 1836, McGuffey resigned from Miami to accept the presidency of the revived Cincinnati College. His publisher was in Cincinnati, his brother Alexander had accepted a professorship at Woodward College, and Cincinnatians promised financial support. The panic of 1837, however, ruined the school, and in 1839 McGuffey accepted the presidency of Ohio University at fifteen hundred dollars a year. Friction with landowners and with students led to his resignation in 1843, and he returned from Athens to Cincinnati to teach at Woodward College. In 1845, elected to the chair of moral philosophy and political economy at the University of Virginia, McGuffey moved to Charlottesville, where he taught until his death in 1873. His wife, Harriet, died in 1850, and the next year he married Laura Howard; their child, Anna, died in Charlottesville at the age of five.

SIGNIFICANCE

The tremendous impact of McGuffey's readers upon American youth in more than 150 years, with more than 135 million copies in print, ranged even wider and deeper than numbers indicate. At least three generations of nineteenth century citizens were indoctrinated by the moral truths and personal values learned from literary selections of the *Eclectic Readers*. As a Presbyterian minister and as a professor, McGuffey perpetuated the Calvinistic virtues of hard work, thrift, and sobriety, commonly referred to as the Protestant ethic, through his extracts from English and American literature. His textbooks inculcated the character traits that upheld the ideal family, community, and nation. Honesty, industry, diligence, obedience, piety, and frugality were applauded; the evil consequences were clearly noted for those who ignored these lessons. Public schools soon shared in character-building along with the family and church.

McGuffey and his readers taught native and foreign-born Americans how to read and pronounce English words, how to read aloud and to speak effectively, and how to write and spell correctly. During the century of great immigration and an age when the written word predominated as the method of communication via newspapers, books, and magazines, the readers perpetuated the English language in the United States.

Admirers of McGuffey have long delighted in extolling the virtues of his textbooks as a Western product that brought enlightenment to rural and frontier folk; since 1960, scholars of history and sociology have declared that his lessons instilled the very virtues that industrial and urban societies needed among the working class in shops and factories of modern America. Critics of American common schools suggest that his textbooks served the rising middle classes but ignored the needs and traditions of the immigrants, the poor, and minorities in the pluralistic American culture.

—Paul F. Erwin

FURTHER READING

Crawford, Benjamin F. *William Holmes McGuffey: Schoolmaster of the Nation*. Delaware, Ohio: Carnegie Church Press, 1963. A short 105-page book that summarizes much of other authors' findings on McGuffey. Crawford's best contribution is his title for the book.

Gorn, Elliott J., ed. *The McGuffey Readers: Selections from the 1879 Edition*. Boston: Bedford/St. Martin's, 1998. An anthology of more than eighty selections from the six-volume 1879 edition. The selections are organized around twelve topics, including history, literature, virtues, vices, character, worth ethic, and citizenship. Includes an introduction by Gorn providing information about McGuffey's life, and his readers, lessons, and audience.

Lindberg, Stanley W. *The Annotated McGuffey: Selections from the McGuffey Eclectic Readers, 1836-1920*. New York: Van Nostrand Reinhold, 1976. A splendid sampling of the entire collection of materials in the readers with a brief but significant introduction describing the publisher's expertise, which the editor declares had much to do with the success of the series. Lindberg details how fortunate was the use of the word "eclectic" in the name of the series and how cleverly the publisher got the textbooks installed in the Confederate schools during the Civil War, where they captured the market thereafter.

Minnich, Harvey C. *William Holmes McGuffey and His Readers*. New York: American Book, 1936. Written by the dean of the School of Education of Miami University, this remains the best comprehensive McGuffey biography.

Ruggles, Alice McGuffey. *The Story of the McGuffeys*. New York: American Book, 1950. Written by the granddaughter of Alexander Hamilton McGuffey, who wished to relate the human side of the authors of the readers, this is a very readable, nonscholarly narrative of her distinguished relatives. Published by the same company that had printed the readers, this volume will be found in more libraries than any of the other biographies cited here.

Smith, William E. *About the McGuffeys: William Holmes McGuffey and Alexander H. McGuffey*. Oxford, Ohio: Cullen Printing, 1963. As historian and dean of the Graduate School of Miami and director of the McGuffey Museum Library, Smith worked with Harvey Minnich to honor McGuffey by founding the National Federation of McGuffey Societies. This twenty-eight-page booklet is the best introduction to the teamwork of the McGuffey brothers in the production of the readers. Smith also deftly describes the content of the various readers, the primer and speller, and the later revisions.

Sullivan, Dolores P. *William Holmes McGuffey: Schoolmaster to the Nation*. Rutherford, N.J.: Fairleigh Dickinson University Press, 1994. The first comprehensive biography of McGuffey since Minnich's (see above) book in 1963. Includes previously unpublished letters to McGuffey's family in Youngstown, Ohio.

Westerhoff, John. *McGuffey and His Readers: Piety, Morality and Education in Nineteenth Century America*. Nashville, Tenn.: Abingdon Press, 1978. Harvard Divinity School professor John Westerhoff provides a reassessment of the religious worldview undergirding the teaching McGuffey incorporated in his readers. A very readable volume that contains many other original writings of McGuffey that were not related to the textbooks.

SEE ALSO: Noah Webster.
RELATED ARTICLES in *Great Events from History: The Nineteenth Century, 1801-1900:* 1820's-1830's: Free Public School Movement; November, 1828: Webster

Publishes the First American Dictionary of English; March 2, 1867: U.S. Department of Education Is Created.

JOAQUIM MARIA MACHADO DE ASSIS
Brazilian writer

Because of his uniquely modern and boldly experimental contribution to narrative form and technique, as well as the universal appeal of his works, Machado is considered the greatest figure in nineteenth century Brazilian literature and a world master of the short story.

BORN: June 21, 1839; Rio de Janeiro, Brazil
DIED: September 29, 1908; Rio de Janeiro, Brazil
AREA OF ACHIEVEMENT: Literature

EARLY LIFE

The father of Joaquim Maria Machado de Assis (zhwah-KEEN mah-REE-ah mah-SHAH-doh deh ah-SEES), Francisco José de Assis, was a native of Rio de Janeiro, Brazil. He was the son of free mulattoes, and a housepainter by trade. Joaquim's mother, Maria Leopoldina Machado da Câmara, was a Portuguese woman from the Island of São Miguel in the Azores. His mother could read and write, and similarities observed between her handwriting and that of her son indicate that she may have taught her son how to read and write as well.

Machado had a younger sister, Maria, who died of measles in 1845; his mother died of tuberculosis in 1849, when he was ten years of age. His father remarried Maria Ignez da Silva on June 18, 1854, but he died ten years later, on April 22, 1864. Although the exact circumstances of the boy's early life as well as his relationship with his stepmother are matters of speculation among his biographers, it is believed that Machado did not get along with his stepmother or her family. Although one of his early poems is dedicated to a cousin, Henrique José Moreira, nothing else is known about this or any other relative.

It is believed that when he was ten years of age, Machado went to live with a priest who provided the boy with a primary education; Machado never attended secondary school. Largely self-taught, the young man was an avid reader, who educated himself by spending his free time at the Library of the Portuguese Cabinet of Reading. Nothing further is known of Machado until his fifteenth year, when one of his poems was published in the magazine *A Marmota.* Henceforth, his professional activities, at least, are well known. At the age of seventeen, he was a typesetter; at the age of nineteen, he was a proofreader; and at the age of twenty-one, he was on the editorial staff of the republican newspaper *Diário do Rio de Janeiro.*

By 1860, Machado had begun to gain recognition with theater criticism, articles, poems, and stories. At the age of twenty-five, he published a first volume of verse, *Crisálidas* (1864). The young man continued writing poems—more or less successfully—columns of clever and insightful commentary on current events, translations from French and English, and drama, but soon realized that fiction was the genre in which he was most proficient.

Machado was short and slight; his facial features were strong, although he was not considered handsome, and he was pronouncedly nearsighted. He was extremely conscious of his appearance and suffered from a lifelong inferiority complex because of his racial heritage. He was a victim of epilepsy; the illness was particularly pronounced during his early years and the last four years of his life—after the death of his wife.

Machado married Carolina Augusta Novaes (sister of the Portuguese poet Faustino Xavier de Novaes) on November 12, 1869, and in the same year became the assistant director of *Diário do Rio de Janeiro,* a post that he held until 1874. Machado and his wife remained devoted to each other throughout their marriage. During his lifetime, Machado never even ventured more than a few miles beyond the city limits of his native Rio. From 1873, his meager income as a writer was augmented by a position at the Ministry of Agriculture, where he served until his death in 1908. An exemplary civil servant, Machado never missed a day at the office.

During the period of Machado's novelistic production—his career as a novelist began in 1872 with the publication of *Resurreicão* (resurrection)—Romanticism was still flourishing, but the incursions of naturalism were soon apparent. In general, Brazilian Romanticism is characterized by lyric poetry, Indianism, poetry of the *mal du siècle*, and sociopolitical literature concerned with events such as abolition. The movement included the expansion of literary genres and was based on a veneration of nature and the observation and analysis of customs and characteristic types.

From the beginning of his novelistic career, Machado outlined an experimental literary form that contained some Romantic elements but was not strictly representative of the movement. Although his earlier novels utilize some Romantic devices, they also demonstrate many of the features to be found in his later works. In breaking with the movement, Machado freed himself not only from the school of Sir Walter Scott but also from all literary schools. With the publication of the novel *Yayá Garcia* (1878; *Iaia Garcia*, 1977), Machado ended the first phase of his literary career.

LIFE'S WORK

When he was already forty-two, Machado published his first great novel *Memórias póstumas de Bráz Cubas* (1881; *The Posthumous Memoirs of Brás Cubas*, 1951; better known as *Epitaph of a Small Winner*, 1952). The appearance of this work marks the beginning of the second, more powerful phase of Machado's career. In this period Machado violently attacked the naturalist movement, which he referred to as *realismo* (naturalism applied a scientific objectivity to the representation of reality). His advice to young writers in Portugal and Brazil was not to be lured into a movement that, despite its novelty, was already obsolete.

Machado took from the reigning schools, Romanticism and naturalism, only those elements that he chose to incorporate into his own aesthetic. In *Epitaph of a Small Winner*, he announced that he would make no concessions to popular literary fashion, despite the limited number of readers that the book would probably have. In that novel, Machado first introduced in his work archaic literary techniques of the eighteenth century. However, his archaism is surprisingly modern in, among other things, its formal fragmentation, use of ellipsis, and irony.

In one sense, Machado's fiction can be seen as a continuation of the work of the Brazilian writer José de Alencar. However, at a time when Alencar was still struggling to rid himself of Romantic attitudes and methods, Machado, quickly and with apparent ease, abandoned Romanticism, and Alencar, in the incredible maturity of *Epitaph of a Small Winner*. Whereas Alencar represented the clash and conflict of sharply delineated characters in concrete settings and in a series of well-staged confrontations, Machado developed the art of ambiguity and understatement. Instead of the social crit-

MACHADO DE ASSIS'S MAJOR WORKS

LONG FICTION

1872	*Resurreicão*
1874	*A mão e a luva* (*The Hand and the Glove*, 1970)
1876	*Helena*
1878	*Yayá Garcia* (English translation, 1977)
1881	*Memórias póstumas de Brás Cubas* (*The Posthumous Memoirs of Brás Cubas*, 1951; better known as *Epitaph of a Small Winner*, 1952)
1891	*Quincas Borba* (*Philosopher or Dog?*, 1954; also as *The Heritage of Quincas Borba*, 1954)
1899	*Dom Casmurro* (English translation, 1953)
1904	*Esaú e Jacob* (*Esau and Jacob*, 1965)
1908	*Memorial de Ayres* (*Counselor Ayres' Memorial*, 1972)

SHORT FICTION

1870	*Contos fluminenses*
1873	*Histórias da meia-noite*
1882	*Papéis avulsos*
1884	*Histórias sem data*
1896	*Várias histórias*
1937	*Histórias românticas*
1963	*The Psychiatrist, and Other Stories*
1963	*What Went on at the Baroness'*
1977	*The Devil's Church, and Other Stories*

DRAMA

Years in left column are earliest dates of production or publication.

1861	*Desencantos*
1864	*Quase ministro*
1866	*Os deuses de casaca*
1880	*Tu só, tu, puro amor*
1910	*Teatro*

POETRY

1864	*Crisálidas*
1870	*Falenas*
1875	*Americanas*
1901	*Poesias completas*

icism that in Alencar bordered on satire, he chose irony. Machado's characters are always plagued by their own demons: They are caught in a web of their own fears and dreams, and their vision of reality is entirely subjective.

Machado was deeply indebted to such British writers as Laurence Sterne. In the major works of both writers, the story is never presented directly to the reader but always through a first-person narration by the protagonist. The narrator, who is usually the main actor as well as the storyteller, becomes an unreliable witness. He is also so often compelled to discuss his own version of the facts that the novels become exercises in a new type of self-reflexive fiction. The text itself ultimately emerges as the protagonist.

In this second phase of Machado's writing, in addition to the short stories collected in *Histórias sem data* (1884; timeless stories) and *Várias histórias* (1896; stories), he wrote other novels. In the next twenty years he would complete a kind of trilogy with *Epitaph of a Small Winner, Quincas Borba* (1891; *Philosopher or Dog?*, 1954), and *Dom Casmurro* (1899; English translation, 1953). Before his death, he completed two extremely subtle novels, *Esaú e Jacob* (1904; *Esau and Jacob*, 1965) and *Memorial de Ayres* (1908; *Counselor Ayres' Memorial*, 1972).

Machado died in his native city of Rio in 1908. The Chamber of Deputies, in a special session, voted to hold a state funeral with civil and military honors. This was the first time in the history of Brazil that a literary man of humble origins was buried like a hero. The author was eulogized throughout Brazil, and in France a memorial service was held in his honor at the Sorbonne, with Anatole France presiding.

SIGNIFICANCE

A master of realistic and accurately detailed portrayal, Joaquim Maria Machado de Assis so subtly distorted the proud self-image of his generation that the brilliance of his critical eye was almost a century in being appreciated. In presenting the follies and foibles of his contemporaries, he was not only a faithful portraitist but also a judge. Yet, while Machado's writing reveals a bitter disillusionment with mankind, it exhibits the serenity of one who has learned to laugh at his own lost illusions and broken dreams.

Machado has achieved a unique place in Brazilian literature, above and beyond all artistic schools and cultural movements. Besides demonstrating insight, simplicity, and subtlety, his work reveals a spirit that ani-

mated the new generation of modernism. However, his novels about life in Rio are realistic psychological studies set in a middle-class milieu. No writer in Latin America has embraced as much and as varied a terrain as has this Brazilian author.

Many honors in recognition of his writing were bestowed on him, the first by the emperor in 1867. Finally, when the Brazilian Academy of Letters was founded in 1897, he was elected its first president and perpetually was reelected. Thus, although he was not widely known outside Brazil, his talents were appreciated and acknowledged during his lifetime. This acknowledgment has continued through the years.

—*Genevieve Slomski*

FURTHER READING

Bettencourt Machado, José. *Machado of Brazil: The Life and Times of Machado de Assis, Brazil's Greatest Novelist.* New York: C. Frank, 1962. This rather sentimental study focuses primarily on the life of Machado and secondarily on his work. Because little factual information exists on Machado's early life, and because Bettencourt does not reveal the sources of his information, his interpretation is interesting, although largely a matter of speculation. Includes a bibliography of primary and secondary works.

Caldwell, Helen. *Machado de Assis: The Brazilian Master and His Novels.* Berkeley: University of California Press, 1970. In this well-written and informative work of literary analysis, Caldwell discusses, after an introductory chapter, Machado's first four novels. Then follows a chapter on *Epitaph of a Small Winner*, one on *Philosopher or Dog?* and *Dom Casmurro*, and a concluding chapter on Machado's last two novels. Contains extensive footnotes and a brief biographical epilogue.

Graham, Richard, ed. *Machado de Assis: Reflections on a Brazilian Master Writer.* Austin: University of Texas Press, Institute of Latin American Studies, 1999. Collection of essays addressing the realistic elements in Machado's novels, particularly *Dom Casmurro*. The essayists debate if Machado was a late realist or a pioneering antirealist.

Maia Neto, José Raimundo. *Machado de Assis, the Brazilian Pyrrohonian.* West Lafayette, Ind.: Purdue University Press, 1994. Analyzes the quality of skepticism in Machado's work, tracing his skeptical philosophy to an ancient thinker, Pyrroho of Elis.

Nist, John. *The Modernist Movement in Brazil.* Austin: University of Texas Press, 1966. In this work, Nist attempts to describe and illustrate the modern spirit in Brazilian poetry and fiction. In the section devoted to Machado, Nist discusses Machado's antiromantic temperament and aesthetics in the context of the new social and political order in Brazil, assesses Machado's contribution to modernism, and praises the universality of his works. Nist's book contains a bibliography of general works on the Brazilian modernist movement.

Nunes, Maria Luisa. *The Craft of an Absolute Winner: Characterization and Narratology in the Novels of Machado de Assis.* Westport, Conn.: Greenwood Press, 1983. This brief but insightful work maintains that the most important element of Machado's art was his exploration of character. It is also the first study in English to apply systematically a philosophical and aesthetic critical apparatus to the texts of Machado, specifically that of narratology. Includes a bibliography of primary and secondary works.

Putnam, Samuel. *Marvelous Journey: A Survey of Four Centuries of Brazilian Writing.* New York: Alfred A. Knopf, 1948. In this survey, Putnam's purpose is to acquaint English-speaking readers with the main figures and currents in Brazilian literature of the past four centuries. In a rather lengthy chapter devoted to a discussion of Machado's work, "Machado de Assis and the End-of-the-Century Realists," Putnam places Machado's writing in the literary and social context of nineteenth century Brazil, and highlights the rebelliousness, originality, and universality of the author's work. Contains extensive footnotes, a bibliography, chronological tables, and reading lists.

SEE ALSO: Anton Chekhov; Anatole France; O. Henry; Clorinda Matto de Turner; Pedro II; Sir Walter Scott.

RELATED ARTICLE in *Great Events from History: The Nineteenth Century, 1801-1900:* September 7, 1822: Brazil Becomes Independent.

ALEXANDER MACKENZIE
Scottish-born prime minister of Canada (1873-1878)

After working as a building contractor and contributing to the construction of many of Canada's public works, Mackenzie moved into politics and became the new nation's second prime minister. In that capacity, he engineered greater political independence from Great Britain while encouraging an honest and democratic government at home.

BORN: January 28, 1822; Logierait, Perthshire, Scotland
DIED: April 17, 1892; Toronto, Canada
AREA OF ACHIEVEMENT: Government and politics

EARLY LIFE
Alexander Mackenzie was the son of Mary Stewart Fleming and Alexander Mackenzie, a Scottish carpenter who repeatedly relocated his family as he searched for work. After his father died in 1836, Alexander dropped out of school. At the age of sixteen, he was apprenticed to a stonemason. Four years later, he became a journeyman mason and moved to the town of Irvine, where he worked on the construction of a railway line and met fellow stonemason William Neil and his family.

Mackenzie became a close friend of the Neils and accompanied them when they emigrated to Canada aboard the sailing ship *Monarch* in 1842. He eventually settled with them in Kingston, a town that is now in Ontario. On March 28, 1845, he married Helen Neil, a daughter of William Neil. By that time, Mackenzie's brother Hope had left Scotland for Canada, and the remainder of the Mackenzie family followed in 1846.

Although his formal education ended when he was about thirteen, Mackenzie had continued to educate himself widely, if informally. Finding work in Canada as a mason proved more difficult than he had expected, so he became a building contractor in partnership with his brothers. With them, he worked on the Beauharnois and Welland canals, Fort Henry, and various churches, banks, courthouses, and jails in the region. He and his wife moved farther west to Sarnia (also now in Ontario) on the shores of Lake Huron in 1847. Five years later, Helen died. The following year, on June 17, 1853, Mackenzie married Jane Sym, the daughter of a neighbor.

LIFE'S WORK
Under the Act of Union, the British colonies of Upper Canada and Lower Canada had merged in 1841 to form the Province of Canada. The province was governed by a legislative assembly, and the city of Kingston, to which

Mackenzie and the Neils had emigrated in 1842, served as its capital from 1841 to 1844.

Mackenzie joined the liberal Reform Party (also known as the Clear Grits) soon after arriving in Canada and worked for the election of Reform candidate George Brown to the province's legislative assembly in 1851. The following year, he became the editor and publisher of a liberal newspaper, *The Lambton Shield*. Mackenzie's sense of duty also led to his involvement in local affairs as census taker, volunteer firefighter, school board trustee, and member of a temperance society—activities that along with his reputation for honesty helped him win election to the assembly himself in 1861. He would spend the rest of his life in politics.

The shape of British North America changed once again on July 1, 1867, when, under the British North America Act, several separate colonies were brought together to form the Dominion of Canada. The Province of Canada was again divided, with what had been Lower Canada becoming Quebec and Upper Canada becoming Ontario.

The Dominion's governor-general, Great Britain's representative in Canada, chose Conservative Party leader John A. Macdonald—another Scottish emigrant—to be the Dominion's first prime minister; Macdonald's position was confirmed by general elections in 1867. At the same time, Mackenzie was elected to the Dominion's new House of Commons; however, his old political ally George Brown, who had become leader of the Reform Party, was defeated, paving the way for Mackenzie to take his place as head of the party. From that new position of power, Mackenzie engineered the union of the Reform Party with several similar parties to form the loosely knit Liberal Party.

Mackenzie also served in the Ontario provincial assembly from 1871 to 1872, when dual representation—as such double legislative service was known—was abolished. The fact that Mackenzie had actually favored the bill abolishing such representation enhanced his reputation for selfless service to the nation.

Under Macdonald, the Conservative Party won a majority of seats in the 1872 elections. The following year, however, it was revealed that Macdonald's party had accepted a large contribution from a group subsequently chosen by the government to build a Pacific Railway into western British North America—a project that the Liberals had already attacked as too costly. In the wake of what became known as the "Pacific Scandal," Macdonald resigned. On November 7, 1873, Mackenzie was named prime minister by the governor-general. An elec-

tion held early during the following year gave the Liberals a majority in the House of Commons and confirmed Mackenzie in office.

As Canada's second prime minister, Mackenzie moved to strengthen the new Dominion's unity, although he was fiscally more careful than his predecessor. He himself directed the economically powerful Department of Public Works to assure its honesty. He also chose to build the Pacific Railway, which had been a condition for British Columbia's entry into the Dominion in 1871, in sections, linking the sections wherever possible with water routes and wagon roads.

Mackenzie also instituted a number of political reforms. Under his administration the right to vote was extended, election days were standardized, the secret-ballot system was introduced, and taverns were closed on election days. When Great Britain tried to intercede in negotiations between the Dominion and British Columbia governments, Mackenzie persuaded the British to allow the Canadians greater latitude in governing themselves. In addition, the creation of the Supreme Court of Canada in 1875 made it possible for the Dominion to review its own laws, thus decreasing the number of legal appeals to Britain.

Despite his achievements in the political sphere, Mackenzie proved unable to cope with the economic depression then affecting Canada and the rest of the world. An election in 1878 returned Alexander Macdonald and the Conservatives to power. Although poor health, including the loss of his voice, forced Mackenzie to resign leadership of the Liberal Party in 1880, he remained in parliament until his death in Toronto on April 17, 1892. He was buried in Sarnia.

SIGNIFICANCE

Alexander Mackenzie served as prime minister and member of Parliament during a crucial period in Canada's development. He worked successfully to extend democratic ideals within the Dominion, while at the same time limiting Britain's power to interfere in Canada's internal affairs. His policies thus paved the way for the even greater degrees of liberty and autonomy in Canada that were to follow.

Mackenzie's integrity and industriousness were acknowledged by all, but his inability to deal with Canada's economic problems has led critics to label him as having been too timid for his dynamic times—a verdict that was shared by a majority of Canada's voters when he was in politics. A man of working-class background and deep religious convictions, he was fiercely democratic in private as well as public life. Unlike preceding and succeeding prime ministers, he steadfastly refused a knighthood from the British crown.

—Margaret A. Dodson

FURTHER READING

Brown, R. Craig, ed. *The Illustrated History of Canada.* Toronto: Key Porter, 2002. An inviting and readable survey of Canadian history that places Mackenzie in the context of his times. Contains numerous black-and-white and color illustrations and bibliographical essays.

Buckingham, William, and George W. Ross. *The Hon. Alexander Mackenzie: His Life and Times.* Toronto: Rose, 1892. A pioneering if partisan biography of the politician written by two close friends that was published shortly after his death.

Riendeau, Roger. *A Brief History of Canada.* New York: Facts On File, 2000. A succinct history of Canada, supplemented with black-and-white illustrations,

maps, texts of key documents, and suggestions for further reading.

See, Scott W. *The History of Canada.* Westport, Conn.: Greenwood Press, 2001. A short survey, supplemented with appendixes and a bibliographic essay, that criticizes Mackenzie's leadership as ineffective.

Thomson, Dale C. *Alexander Mackenzie: Clear Grit.* Toronto: Macmillan, 1960. The standard modern biography, admiring but judicial, drawing extensively on papers made available since the early work of Buckingham and Ross.

SEE ALSO: George Brown; Sir John Alexander Macdonald; Sir Charles Tupper.

RELATED ARTICLES in *Great Events from History: The Nineteenth Century, 1801-1900:* July 1, 1867: British North America Act; November 5, 1873-October 9, 1878: Canada's Mackenzie Era; 1875: Supreme Court of Canada Is Established; September, 1878: Macdonald Returns as Canada's Prime Minister.

WILLIAM LYON MACKENZIE
Canadian journalist and politician

Working to establish for English Canada a political entity independent of British colonialism, Mackenzie devoted his life to a critique of English political authority in Canada and a demand for redress of grievances by English Canadians.

BORN: March 12, 1795; Springfield, Dundee, Forfarshire, Scotland
DIED: August 28, 1861; Toronto, Canada
AREAS OF ACHIEVEMENT: Government and politics, journalism

EARLY LIFE

William Lyon Mackenzie was the only child of Daniel and Elizabeth Mackenzie. His mother—who had been born Elizabeth Chalmers—an austere, demanding, and strong-willed adherent of the Presbyterian faith, was in her forties when she married. His father was in his mid-twenties, a weaver by trade with a reputation for carousing and pursuing life's pleasures. They were married on May 8, 1794, at Dundee, and three weeks after the birth of their only child, after having become blind, Daniel died, on April 9, 1795.

William Mackenzie's mother instilled in her son great pride in his family, tracing it back to the wars of the Scottish clans and participation with Charles Edward Stuart (the Young Pretender) in the critical battle at Culloden that culminated in English domination of Scotland. Both paternal and maternal grandfathers were named Colin Mackenzie, and William Lyon carried with him the belief that his family was specially endowed, but that its fortunes had been denied because of the English dominance following 1745. Throughout his life, he cultivated an attachment to the farmers and working classes while presuming a status equal to the wellborn and wealthy.

The untimely death of Mackenzie's father pushed his mother into poverty, compelling her to sell personal items from her dowry and the clothing of her late husband. Nevertheless, she sustained a fierce independence and faith in her religion, and strove for the education of her son. The youthful Mackenzie, always small in stature and reckless in nature, became a rowdy while at the same time he was a resolute student. He mimicked his teachers and haunted libraries and bookstalls. He pushed himself vigorously to gain attention throughout his life. From the age of five, when he entered school, until the day he died, Mackenzie found himself fighting the odds.

In his early teens, Mackenzie became a regular in the commercial reading room of the Dundee *Advertiser*, where he was the youngest member. He began to list by topic, number, and description all the works that he read. This reading continued until he arrived in Canada at the age of twenty. Divinity, geography, history and biography, poetry and drama, science and agriculture, and 352 novels, all were included in his 957-book reading list. Even his mother registered concern that his continual reading might disturb him. Nevertheless, Mackenzie persisted with his eclectic studies throughout his life, and his habit of filing away information and ideas was to sustain him in his newspaper work and in political debate.

At a scientific society, Mackenzie met and became friends with Edward Lesslie and his son James, both of whom were to become associated with him at various times and in various enterprises in Canada. With some help from friends, Mackenzie and his mother operated a store and lending library in the village of Alyth just north of Dundee, but the business failed and they returned to Dundee. Mackenzie also found time to travel to London and to France, where he did some work with newspapers, living a somewhat dissipated life of gambling and drinking and fathering an illegitimate son. The child, named James, was taken in by Mackenzie's mother, who brought him along when she later joined her son in the Americas. Mackenzie was later to marry a former schoolmate, Isabel Baxter, who would bear him thirteen children, only seven of whom survived childhood. The family, including his first son, was always central to Mackenzie's life and work.

In 1820, Mackenzie traveled to Canada with the prospect of setting up a business. Mackenzie had sworn off gambling and loose living and served notice to his creditors that he would make good his accounts, a promise that he kept. Arriving in Quebec, he immediately took a job as an accountant in Montreal, where he worked only for several weeks. He proceeded to set up a pharmacy and bookstore with a partner in the town of York and shortly thereafter opened a general store as a second enterprise in

William Lyon Mackenzie. (Library of Congress)

the town of Dundas, farther west. This second business also included a circulating library, and Mackenzie felt comfortable enough economically to marry. Given the dearth of women in frontier Canada, the choice of a bride was probably encouraged by his mother, who escorted Isabel to Canada.

Mackenzie's ambitions were still not realized, however, and he chose to end his business partnership and open a store of his own. His alert, agile mind did not seem suited to the mercantile life, for despite a fetish for efficiency and careful accounting, the mundane demands of a storekeeper's duty did not satisfy him. Mackenzie decided that his perceptions of society and government needed to reach an audience that could never be reached by a shop owner, despite the material comforts such a business guaranteed.

During the early nineteenth century, Canada was not a country that rewarded men of enterprise and ideas; in fact, British Canada was developing the same class structures as those found in Great Britain. Those who had fought in the Napoleonic Wars or the War of 1812 on the British side had been granted land and economic privileges in Canada that set them apart from immigrants such as Mackenzie. The town of York, which was to become the city of Toronto, was the capital of British Upper Canada, and, despite its small size, it was the center of English rule in North America.

The privileged families of Canada were a small and immensely powerful group perhaps best symbolized by the St. James Church and its powerful parishioners, which included the lieutenant governor of Upper Canada, Major General Sir Peregrine Maitland. Maitland's father-in-law was the duke of Richmond, governor in chief of all the colonies in North America. Presiding over the church was John Strachan, the first bishop of Toronto, who took seriously the obligation that the church was the center of Great Britain in Canada. Lands, schools, marriages, customs, and laws were subject to his administrative guidance. The leaders of both court and Parliament in Upper Canada were integral parts of the force of the church in the perpetuation of the Family Compact.

Dissenters from this conservative British contract of vested power did exist. Some, such as Dr. William Baldwin, stood in opposition politically while accepting Anglicanism as their faith. Men such as Mackenzie, a Presbyterian, however, were privy to neither the authority of that faith nor the economic, social, and political power. Had the dominant society of the day accepted him as one of its own, his rebellious career would never have developed. Given Mackenzie's background and the conditions he confronted in a developing colony that seemed to hold great promise for intelligent, aggressive, and ambitious settlers, his later actions can be understood.

At the top, British rule in Upper Canada, aside from the lieutenant governor, consisted of an appointed Executive Council of leading citizens who held acceptable ideas as to the direction the colony should take and whose advice generally guided their patron in Great Britain. This council was not responsible to the public or to any legislative body. Members were selected carefully and almost never asked to resign. As in Great Britain, British Canada had an upper house called the Legislative Council (modeled after the House of Lords), whose members were appointed by the lieutenant governor for life. Some members, such as Bishop Strachan, were members of both the Executive and the Legislative councils.

The House of Assembly, the lower house, was the forum for the common citizens and encouraged avenues for dissent. This dissent, however, was often negated by the power of the government to distribute funds to various troublesome areas. Though the sympathies of the majority of the people might lie with their elected delegates to the lower house, the conservatives still dominated Canada's policy. Expenditures were controlled by forces over which the lower house had no control. This condition allowed for the abuse of authority by the dominant Tory elements who were not accountable to any constituency and for the irresponsibility of critics and reformers who could eschew responsibility for promises that they had no power to fulfill. The paternal rule of the governing class became the focus of Mackenzie's new crusade.

The ending of Mackenzie's business partnership was not easy, and Mackenzie found it difficult to survive at first when he moved in 1823 to Queenston, in southern Ontario. He again started a store and attracted the help of Robert Randall, a member of the assembly. In Queenston, Mackenzie began the publication of his first and most outstanding newspaper, the *Colonial Advocate*, on May 18, 1824. The paper sought to influence elections to the assembly by comparing American political practices and institutions with those of Upper Canada.

Although Mackenzie did not challenge the British controls directly, agencies of the government, such as the post office, worked against him. Mackenzie immediately transferred his operations to York, and in November of 1824, he escalated his attacks against the Tory authority. His paper had some immediate success, but a competitive newspaper was begun, *Canadian Freeman*, which supported a more moderate approach to reform. Some historians believe that this paper was funded by conservative elements hoping to destroy Mackenzie's influence.

Undaunted, Mackenzie purchased new equipment and continued his forays against the establishment, which in turn escalated its pressure to remove Mackenzie. In the spring of 1826, he left Canada for Lewiston, New York, to avoid arrest for debt. During his absence, a gang of influential Tory citizens dressed as Indians destroyed his office and press in broad daylight. The magistrates did nothing to protect Mackenzie's property, and Mackenzie returned from New York to file suit and win compensation. With his settlement, he immediately paid off his creditors while capitalizing on his role as a martyr to free speech. The Tories, though chastened, resumed their harassment.

Mackenzie next took up the cause of American immigrants in Canada who sought the same rights as English settlers. Randall carried Mackenzie's petitions to London in 1827, an act that influenced the Colonial Office to order the upper legislature to guarantee full rights to

Americans living in Canada. In the same year, Mackenzie joined forces with a Methodist leader to protest attempts by Strachan to use funds from the sale of clergy lands to build his proposed King's College.

Mackenzie declared his candidacy for the assembly and engaged in direct correspondence with reform elements in both England and Lower Canada. Mackenzie used his newspaper effectively, publishing what he called a "black list" of his opponents. He won election on the Reform ticket that controlled the assembly but missed being elected Speaker. He now had a forum from which he could attack monopoly and vested interests. He argued against corporations dependent on public monies, against the practice of having an Anglican as chaplain of the assembly, and against the increasing indebtedness of the government.

In 1829, Mackenzie found time to go to the United States, where he observed at firsthand the enthusiasm surrounding the election of Andrew Jackson and the anticipation for an enlarged democracy. Mackenzie was struck by the economy of government in the United States and even admired the use of party patronage, which he hoped might be a means to revamp the Family Compact. He met Jackson personally and was intrigued by the twin ideas of hard money and antibanking monopolies. The success of a radical politician such as Jackson seemed to represent encouraged Mackenzie.

LIFE'S WORK

After Mackenzie visited the United States, his career took a new direction. Upon his return to Canada in 1830, he soon found that the legislature was dissolved because of the death of King William IV. A new governor of Upper Canada had replaced Maitland, and this new English leader, Sir John Colborne, worked to increase the numbers of English by financed immigration. He used the upper house to block legislation sought by the assembly that in turn weakened Mackenzie's reform group. During the 1830 elections, the Mackenzie forces lost their majority, gaining but twenty of the fifty-one seats.

Dismayed by what he regarded as tampering with the democratic process, Mackenzie gave up any pretense of association with conservative tradition. He challenged the church-state relationship while joining St. Andrews Presbyterian Church, which ironically had been established by Presbyterian Tories who also attended St. James, as was expected of members of the government. Mackenzie constantly attacked the government, which was in some disarray internally because of the governor's attempts to change the upper house without the

support of either the Executive Council or Strachan. Mackenzie was joined by other reformers in trying to gain control of certain revenues.

Attempts were made to remove Mackenzie while he traveled throughout Upper Canada with petitions listing grievances against the government, communicated again with reform elements in Lower Canada, which enraged Upper Canadian Tories, and encouraged the participation of new immigrants—especially the Americans and the Irish, who were enthusiastic about the attention he brought to them. His *Colonial Advocate* attacked conservative privilege; the Tories countered with petitions of their own and voted to expel him from the assembly. Hundreds of people stormed the assembly demanding that the governor dissolve Parliament. They were refused, but the people gained their revenge in a by-election that gave Mackenzie an overwhelming victory in January of 1832.

Five days later, the Tories expelled Mackenzie again, and the province was in civil disarray. Opposing groups clashed physically in the streets, meetings were disrupted, religious groups clashed openly, and in Hamilton a band of hoodlums was hired by a magistrate to attack Mackenzie. He decided to travel to Great Britain in the spring of 1832 to present his view of the situation to British authorities. While there, he wrote several articles for the London *Morning Chronicle* and drew up a document called *Sketches of Canada and the United States* (1833) for presentation to the people of Great Britain.

Mackenzie had once again been returned to the assembly, and while he was abroad, the Tories again expelled him for a third time. This time he was reelected by acclamation, much to the rage of his enemies. Their anger was heightened further when Lord Goderich, British colonial secretary, sent the governor a dispatch advising financial and political reform and an end to the Tory crusade against Mackenzie. The upper house refused to receive the dispatch, placing them in the difficult position of rejecting their superiors.

In the assembly, a close vote on the issue was approved, but Mackenzie was deprived of his vote and a call for a new election was refused. Learning of this, the colonial secretary dismissed both the attorney general and the solicitor general over Governor Colbourne's objections. The Mackenzie family now left London in triumph to tour Scotland, England, and France. It was a short-lived victory, however, for in April, 1833, a more conservative colonial secretary came into power and all that Mackenzie had accomplished was undone. Frustrated and in despair, he dropped the word "colonial" from his newspaper's title. He returned to Canada in late summer and in December he was again expelled from the assembly, only to be returned later in the same month.

Mackenzie now took advantage of the incorporation of York as the new city of Toronto by leading a slate of reformers to victory in the city elections. Elected as alderman and gaining a majority over the Tories, the redoubtable Mackenzie was chosen as the first mayor of Toronto. The Tory opposition sought to unseat him from that post and succeeded in early 1835, but meanwhile, in the fall of 1834, Mackenzie and the reformers again won a majority in the assembly, despite his publication of a letter that all but called for colonial independence.

In November, Mackenzie stopped publication of the *Advocate*, turning over its assets to a fellow reformer in the assembly. He then took on a committee assignment and in three months compiled a devastating record of grievances against past government administrations and a list of proposed remedies. A larger problem was a new lieutenant governor, Sir Francis Bond Head, whose conservatism was a throwback to the 1820's. He clashed openly with reformers in the assembly, dissolved the legislature, and openly campaigned on the issue of loyalty to the Crown. In July, 1836, Mackenzie met defeat at the polls.

Enraged at the injustice and corruption that he discovered following the election, Mackenzie immediately started another newspaper, called the *Constitution*. Given the circumstances, this paper was not overly radical, as it called only for specific constitutional change in Canada. This moderation was to change dramatically during the early months of 1837. Great Britain had begun to tighten its grip on Lower (French) Canada with new resolutions that took away all powers that the assembly in that region had over the executive authority of the governor. Mackenzie foresaw the same thing happening to Upper Canada and now began an outright protest. He moved about the province making speeches, raising funds, rallying people against the tyranny of the government, and proposing an alliance of the two Canadas in a common front. Some of his adherents began military training, while the Tories and the Orange Order to which many belonged harassed and physically attacked Mackenzie and his growing constituency.

Mackenzie counted on two things to work in favor of a successful revolution: the absence of the military, which had been sent to Lower Canada, and the belief that the mere threat of a massive assault on the government would avoid hostilities and bring capitulation. Lower Canada's rebellion was successfully under way, but Mackenzie had little communication with their movement.

Nevertheless, he suggested a common rebellion against Great Britain.

The date was set for the march on Toronto, and on November 15, Mackenzie published a constitution for the new government. He hired a former colonel, Anthony Van Egmond, to head the revolutionary army and wrote a declaration of independence to be distributed prior to the march. It was not lost on Mackenzie that Upper Canada was far more conservative, despite the general dissatisfaction with conservative rule, than Lower Canada. He planned to use large demonstrations of possible force to compel the government to capitulate. His plans began to unravel on the eve of the march because of a lack of communication with the various groups. Unanticipated resistance from conservative riflemen also threw the movement into disarray. In the end, the grand citizen rebellion dissipated into the countryside and many participants made their way to the United States.

After an abortive attack by the regrouped forces failed, despite some American help, Mackenzie was joined by his wife in Buffalo, where he was arrested for violating American neutrality. Seeing the futility of further hostilities, he brought the rest of his family to the United States and settled in New York. Old friends sent him what money they could, but poverty haunted his family at every turn. In 1839 he was found guilty on the neutrality violation and sentenced to a fine of ten dollars and a term of eighteen months in prison. He was still in the newspaper business, having founded *Mackenzie's Gazette*, and tried to run the paper from his Monroe County prison cell. The death of his mother while he was in prison was especially difficult. He believed that he had lost a guide and an anchor. He was pardoned in the spring of 1840 and gave up his paper.

Mackenzie's fierce independence demanded that any return to Canada be on his terms, and his old associates kept him informed of the changing conditions in the province. He took advantage of the new amnesty extended to the rebels of 1837 by the reform-minded government of Robert Baldwin in 1851. He wrote for his old friend James Lesslie's paper and also for the Niagara *Mail* while trying to make up his mind about returning permanently. Mackenzie took up residency, and in the spring of 1851 he was elected to the provincial parliament. He defeated one of the future powerbrokers in Canadian politics, George Brown. In office, Mackenzie was still effective in galvanizing attention against patronage, corruption, monopoly, sales of church lands, and use of public monies for church colleges. Ironically, his investigations forced the fall of the Baldwin government and he joined Lesslie in an attack on phony reformers. He alienated associates by exposing their culpability in passing legislation that increased debt. He even broke temporarily with Lesslie over attempts to edit a critical letter dealing with Crown Lands policy.

Mackenzie was still a figure to be reckoned with, and reformers sought him out to lead a true reform party. Mackenzie insisted on independence of thought and action, even turning down general editorship of his paper, the *Message*, with two others because stock ownership would be shared with investors who might compromise him. His work was an inspiration to his colleagues, who began to raise a Homestead Fund in his honor. Thomas D'Arcy McGee called him "the oldest living sentinel of public liberty in Canada." Mackenzie's newspaper began to take on a more conciliatory tone in his old age as he turned away from the idea of creating an independent constitutional state. He resigned his seat in the legislature, declined offers to run for the Legislative Council, and further refused to run for the mayor's office of Toronto. He began to renew friendships with old adversaries and shortly before his death, on August 28, 1861, entertained the notion of running again for the legislature.

SIGNIFICANCE

William Lyon Mackenzie stood as the conscience of a country that was not ready to realize the independence of people, place, and political institutions. The things Mackenzie sought for Canada would have reordered the status of Canada and perhaps accomplished an eventual unity of British and French regions. Mackenzie was a radical in every sense of the word. Within him there was a curious admixture that might be regarded as the birthright of the Scots—a durable distrust of the British, an intense devotion to Scotland, and a detached view of Europe.

It is not certain whether Mackenzie ever shared his countrymen's concern for the United States. Mackenzie trusted the spirit of democracy that he observed in the age of Andrew Jackson. Mackenzie's identification with the American politics of democracy was generally unacceptable, despite the real concerns for the corruption and the venality of the colonial administration and the Family Compact system. Mackenzie's words and actions struck at the heart of the issue of national identity. Being American to him meant more than mere geography. His life was consumed with the matter of what it meant to be a Canadian. Mackenzie was an important and even uncomfortable presence in Canada's struggle from colony to nation. He will endure as one of its true giants of democracy.

—Jack J. Cardoso

FURTHER READING

Craig, Gerald. *Upper Canada: The Formative Years*. Toronto: McClelland and Stewart, 1963. One of the first serious studies of the Family Compact and English colonial tradition. Critical of Mackenzie while praising conservative principles.

Dent, John Charles. *The Story of the Upper Canada Rebellion*. 2 vols. Toronto: C. B. Robinson, 1885. Particularly harsh on Mackenzie; a debunking of all that Mackenzie represented.

Flint, David. *William Lyon Mackenzie: Rebel Against Authority*. Toronto: Oxford University Press, 1971. Provides the broad chronology of Mackenzie's career but does not develop much of the politics or philosophy of the man. Has a useful bibliography.

Kilbourn, William. *The Firebrand: William Lyon Mackenzie and the Rebellion in Upper Canada*. Toronto: Clark Irwin, 1956. Perhaps the most readily available work on Mackenzie. Centers on interpreting the character of the protagonist rather than assessing all areas of controversy surrounding the man and his times.

Le Suer, William Dawson. *William Lyon Mackenzie: A Reinterpretation*. Toronto: Macmillan, 1979. Harshly critical of Mackenzie's career. Le Suer was a conservative in the Victorian tradition who opposed representative government as being nothing but partisan party-oriented and antithetical to the national concerns of Canada.

Lindsey, Charles. *The Life and Times of William Lyon Mackenzie*. Toronto: P. Randall, 1862. Defends Mackenzie, portraying him as a valiant reformer and promoter of an independent Canadian tradition.

Mackenzie, William Lyon. *1837: Revolution in the Canadas*. Edited by Greg Keilty. Toronto: N. C. Press, 1974. Both protagonist and editor join to establish that the Rebellion of 1837 was more than a passing phase in Canada's history. Views the rebellion as a joint struggle of Lower and Upper Canada against both the privileged entities of property and patronage and oppressive British colonial rule.

Sewell, John. *Mackenzie: A Political Biography of William Lyon Mackenzie*. Toronto: J. Lorimer, 2002. Generally sympathetic biography written by a former mayor of Toronto. Sewell argues that Mackenzie may be Canada's best model of a responsible politician.

SEE ALSO: Robert Baldwin; George Brown; William IV.

RELATED ARTICLE in *Great Events from History: The Nineteenth Century, 1801-1900:* October 23-December 16, 1837: Rebellions Rock British Canada.

WILLIAM MCKINLEY
President of the United States (1897-1901)

By strengthening the powers of the presidency, McKinley prepared the way for forceful executives of the twentieth century such as Woodrow Wilson, Theodore Roosevelt, and Franklin D. Roosevelt. His expansionist policies brought the overseas territories of Puerto Rico, the Philippines, Guam, and Hawaii into the American empire.

BORN: January 29, 1843; Niles, Ohio
DIED: September 14, 1901; Buffalo, New York
ALSO KNOWN AS: William McKinley, Jr. (full name)
AREA OF ACHIEVEMENT: Government and politics

EARLY LIFE

William McKinley, Jr.'s mother, née Nancy Allison, was descended from pious Scottish ancestors; his father, William McKinley, Sr., of Scotch-Irish and English Puritan descent, was an iron founder in Pennsylvania and Ohio. The elder McKinley's iron furnace brought only a meager living. The son grew up in a rural environment and attended the Methodist Church faithfully with his parents. When the family moved to the larger town of Poland, near Youngstown, Ohio, William was able to attend the academy there in preparation for college. He was able to complete only one term during 1860 at Allegheny College in Meadville, Pennsylvania; family financial reverses prevented resumption of his studies. Young McKinley had proved himself to be a good public speaker and a diligent, if not brilliant, student.

Because of his short stature—five feet, six inches tall—erect posture, and somber countenance, McKinley's physical appearance has often been compared to that of Napoleon Bonaparte. His gray, penetrating eyes gazed intently from a pale, serious face. McKinley did not have a sophisticated or cosmopolitan upbringing, yet he had a manner that was sedate and dignified. Those who knew him well were also aware of his good sense of humor and kindly disposition. He was abstemious, almost prudish in behavior. In early life, he disdained smoking, drinking, dancing, and gambling. In his middle years, however, he became addicted to the use of tobacco.

At the outset of the Civil War (1861), he enlisted as a private in the Twenty-third Ohio Volunteer Infantry. He participated in many of the major battles of the conflict, including the clash at Antietam. He rose rapidly through the ranks during his four years, attaining the rank of captain by 1864. He demonstrated impressive administrative abilities while serving on the staff of General Rutherford B. Hayes. His growing friendship with Hayes would serve him well in his later political career. He was mustered out of the service in 1865, with the brevet rank of major, a title that would often be used with his name.

After the war, McKinley studied law briefly at the Albany (New York) Law School and was admitted to the bar and set up his practice at Canton, Ohio, in 1867. This northeastern Ohio town became his home for the remainder of his life. In 1871, he married Ida Saxton, a young woman from a wealthy home. However, the couple enjoyed only two tranquil years of marriage before a severe nervous illness struck down Ida. Many of her later years were spent as a virtual invalid. William McKinley seemed to show infinite and unending compassion and devotion to his sick wife. He always found time during even his presidential years to minister to her needs.

LIFE'S WORK

William McKinley served twelve years as a Republican member of the U.S. House of Representatives, from 1877 to 1891, a period interrupted briefly by his loss of the 1882 election. The loss came from one of the periodic Democratic gerrymanders that plagued his career in Congress. He quickly became one of the leading proponents of protectionism in the House. His knowledge of the tariff issue and industrial questions helped him to secure a place on the Ways and Means Committee, a position that allowed him a major influence over revenue matters. He became chairman of the committee in 1889, after having lost in a battle for Speaker of the House to Thomas B. Reed.

McKinley's most important achievement in the Congress was the successful passage, in 1890, of a highly protectionist tariff that came to be known as the McKinley Act. The bill provided for a reciprocal lowering of the tariffs of two countries when a treaty to accomplish this could be negotiated. Several European states did enter into such arrangements with the United States. McKinley's tariff also reduced the excess revenue from the tariff that had been swelling the treasury. Sugar was placed on the free list, and American producers were compensated for this loss of protection by a subsidy of two cents a pound, paid to refiners. What had seemed to be McKinley's moment of triumph soon became abysmal defeat, however, when a storm of criticism from consumers brought about the defeat of many Republican congressmen in the 1890 elections, including McKinley himself.

The defeat in McKinley's district of Ohio in 1890 had been partly a result of another Democratic gerrymander rather than a wholesale repudiation of the candidate. His reputation still intact in Ohio, McKinley, with the backing of the wealthy Cleveland industrialist Marcus A. Hanna, won the governorship in 1891 and 1893. In 1892, Hanna tried to engineer the nomination of McKinley for president, but McKinley refused to encourage the movement because of his conviction that the Republican Party should stand by its incumbent president, Benjamin Harrison.

By 1896, when McKinley was ready to accept his party's nomination, a new issue had begun to overshadow the tariff question. Grover Cleveland's term (1893-1897) had been an era of severe depression and suffering, especially for the farmers. Many of those at the lower economic level began to see some hope in a new panacea. The monetization of silver would allow for inflation of the currency, bringing relief to debtors and a

William McKinley. (Library of Congress)

hoped for increase in agricultural prices. Such ideas were anathema to financiers and industrialists. The eastern aristocracy of wealth stood foursquare for the gold standard.

Although the "standpatters" had faith in McKinley as the apostle of protectionism, his record on the currency issue was less encouraging. He had in fact voted for overriding Hayes's veto of the Bland-Allison Act in 1878, a bill providing for the issuing of a moderate number of silver certificates. McKinley now took a position more reassuring to business. He favored a gold standard until such time as the other nations agreed to an international bimetallic (silver and gold) standard. It was not expected by most businesspeople that such an international agreement was likely.

In the election of 1896, McKinley ran against the prosilver candidate of the Democrats, William Jennings Bryan. In the campaign, McKinley stayed at his home in Canton, Ohio. He would appear on his front porch to make campaign speeches to supporters who were brought in by train for his rallies. The dignified campaign was in sharp contrast to the whirlwind tour of Bryan, who spoke from the rear of his train in numerous hamlets and towns along his path. To many, Bryan seemed a dangerous demagogue, while McKinley appeared to be an experienced and sane candidate who would restore prosperity and confidence. McKinley won by a comfortable margin.

One of McKinley's most important abilities as an administrator was a talent for choosing gifted men to work with him. However, he did choose a few men to serve in his first cabinet who proved unequal to the task. The elderly John Sherman was physically unable to carry on the duties of secretary of state at a time when international affairs were moving toward a critical stage. He served slightly more than a year. Later, McKinley chose such able men as John Hay, secretary of state; Philander Knox, attorney general; and Elihu Root, secretary of war.

During McKinley's first year as president, Congress passed a tariff that continued the high protectionist policies advocated by the president, the Dingley Act. The president sent emissaries to England to begin the process of sounding out other nations on the prospects for international bimetalism. The industrial nations had little interest in this proposal. The currency question would not be settled for McKinley until 1900, when the Congress passed the Gold Standard Act that declared that gold would be the only standard of value for the dollar. The debt-ridden farmers failed to receive the relief they sought. However, new discoveries of gold around the world did increase the supply of the precious metal slightly, and during McKinley's first term, the economy increased so markedly that most of the agrarian protest agitation died out.

The most significant theme of McKinley's presidency involved foreign affairs. Although McKinley came out of the Civil War with a strong aversion to war, events and pressures around him seemed to be carrying the nation toward war with Spain. In 1895, the Cuban people had begun a guerrilla war aimed at securing independence from Spain. The Spanish government appeared adamant in its determination to hold on to the last relics of empire in the New World. The United States found its interests inextricably involved in the fortunes of the rebels. The island's geographic proximity and its close economic ties made its destiny a major concern. The brutal treatment of Cubans in what were called "reconcentration" areas provoked sympathy and concern.

William Randolph Hearst's New York *Journal* and Joseph Pulitzer's New York *World* found the Cuban atrocities a ready-made source for the kind of sensational stories that could build up newspaper circulation. To the cry of the yellow journals were soon added the chorus of angry congressmen and senators. McKinley preferred the quiet path of diplomacy as a means of settling the issues between Spain and the United States, but an increase of pressure and tension in 1898 persuaded him to submit the issue to a Congress already determined upon war. In February, 1898, the destruction of the American battleship *Maine*, probably because of an internal explosion, incited further angry demands for war. The assumption that the Spanish had intentionally destroyed an American vessel was a highly unlikely one, but many Americans rashly made that assumption.

McKinley took a direct hand in guiding the conduct of the war that lasted only from April through August of 1898. Only the office of president was available to coordinate the activities of the war and navy departments. The war was primarily a naval affair fought in Manila Bay in the Philippines and near Santiago in Cuba. The navy demonstrated that it had finally achieved the modernity expected of a major power. It won decisive battles in both theaters. McKinley had entered the war for the avowed purpose of liberating Cuba from Spain, but during the course of the conflict, he made a decision to send troops to Manila to follow up the defeat of the Spanish fleet in the bay. The decision indicated a shift in direction, an apparent decision to use the conflict as a means of acquiring territory. McKinley directed the American

representatives at Paris to secure a peace treaty that included the acquisition from Spain of Puerto Rico, Guam, and the Philippine Islands.

The president easily defeated Bryan in the election of 1900. The slogan "a full dinner pail" reflected the reality that the agricultural crisis had eased and that workers were again finding employment. However, McKinley served only a half year of his second term before being succeeded by his vice president, Theodore Roosevelt. An anarchist, Leon Czolgosz, shot the president while he was attending the Pan-American Exposition at Buffalo. McKinley lived eight more days. Death came on September 14, 1901.

SIGNIFICANCE

As president, McKinley led the United States toward the creation of an overseas empire. Grover Cleveland had rejected an attempt to annex the Hawaiian Islands, but McKinley, fearing that Japan might gain a foothold, pressed for action. Congress annexed the islands by joint resolution in July, 1898. In 1899, McKinley acquired a settlement by treaty with Germany that recognized American control over a part of the Samoan Islands. The agreement granted Pago Pago to the United States, thus providing a strategically important South Pacific base for the navy. The Treaty of Paris of 1898, which ended the war with Spain, brought Puerto Rico, Guam, and the Philippines into the empire. Although Cuba was set free, it became a protectorate of the United States. McKinley's secretary of state, John Hay, began the process of removing barriers to the building of a canal by the United States. Negotiations to remove Britain's objections were begun but not finished before McKinley's death.

Although McKinley is usually not placed on most historians' list of the greatest American presidents, he did prepare the way for an increase in presidential influence and power in the twentieth century. He did not stand by idly while Congress conducted its business apart from the executive branch. He actively sought to influence legislation by suggesting the possibility of special sessions and by utilizing the veto threat. McKinley's direct guidance of the war effort also exemplifies his use of power in the fashion of a twentieth century president. Although he did not always explain his actions publicly, he seems to have been acting effectively and purposefully in his conduct of diplomacy. At the outset of his administration, he had to assert some control of foreign affairs because of the ineptness of the aged John Sherman. During McKinley's presidency, it became clear that the United States had reached great power. The power of the navy, demonstrated by the brief and spectacular victories of the Spanish-American War, dictated that the United States would have to be accepted as one of the major forces in international politics.

The strengthening of industry, trade, and the economy of the United States was McKinley's major domestic aim throughout his career. He tried to accomplish this aim primarily through the tariff and by avoiding policies that would be injurious to the business community. Later economic experience seems to show that the nation might have profited from freer trade and a slight inflation of the currency. Just before his death, McKinley seems to have been intimating that he was reconsidering the tariff issue himself.

—Richard L. Niswonger

FURTHER READING

Armstrong, William H. *Major McKinley: William McKinley and the Civil War*. Kent, Ohio: Kent State University Press, 2000. Recounts McKinley's experiences in the Ohio Infantry during the Civil War, and how these experiences defined him for the rest of his life. Also describes McKinley's life after the war, including his legal work defending freed slaves and his efforts to restore unity to the country by reaching out to former Confederate soldiers.

Glad, Paul W. *McKinley, Bryan, and the People*. Philadelphia: J. B. Lippincott, 1964. A brief study of the election of 1896 and its two main antagonists. The book provides a summary of the issues that led to the dramatic contest between Bryan and McKinley. It offers an analysis and contrast of the two men.

Gould, Lewis L. *The Presidency of William McKinley*. Lawrence: University Press of Kansas, 1981. Gould argues effectively that McKinley was the first modern president. Many historians have seen McKinley as Hanna's puppet and as being too weak to resist the pressures for war. This book is especially useful in that it offers a carefully reasoned alternative to the traditional view. Gould believes that McKinley was an effective administrator who increased the powers of the presidency and thus prepared the way for the imperial presidency of the twentieth century.

Leech, Margaret. *In the Days of McKinley*. New York: Harper & Brothers, 1959. This book combines scholarship and an entertaining writing style; it is carefully researched and provides details of McKinley's personal life. Leech is generally sympathetic to her subject and has authored one of the best full-length biographies of McKinley available.

Morgan, Howard Wayne. *America's Road to Empire: The War with Spain and Overseas Expansion*. New York: John Wiley & Sons, 1965. This is a brief work but a useful one for insights on McKinley's diplomacy, leading up to the Spanish-American War. It suggests that McKinley did not rush impetuously into war as pressures built up in the nation. There had been a patient and sincere diplomatic offensive aimed at preventing conflict, but this effort had been beset by Spanish temporizing.

_____. *William McKinley and His America*. Syracuse, N.Y.: Syracuse University Press, 1963. This book, along with Leech's work, is one of the two most important full-length biographies of McKinley. Morgan's chief contribution is his deep understanding of the political background of the Gilded Age. Morgan is known as a revisionist on the era. He disagrees with those who view the period as little more than a generation of political, social, and economic degeneracy.

Phillips, Kevin. *William McKinley*. New York: Times Books/Henry Holt, 2003. In his analysis of McKinley's presidency, Phillips concludes McKinley was a "near great" president, whose place in history has been diminished because he was unable to complete his second term. Phillips describes how McKinley began transforming the United States into a global military power, and how many of McKinley's goals were later accomplished by President Theodore Roosevelt.

SEE ALSO: Grover Cleveland; Marcus A. Hanna; Benjamin Harrison; John Hay; Rutherford B. Hayes; Joseph Pulitzer.

RELATED ARTICLES in *Great Events from History: The Nineteenth Century, 1801-1900:* March 13, 1887: American Protective Association Is Formed; 1895-1898: Hearst-Pulitzer Circulation War; January 24, 1895: Hawaii's Last Monarch Abdicates; November 3, 1896: McKinley Is Elected President; April 24-December 10, 1898: Spanish-American War; February 4, 1899-July 4, 1902: Philippine Insurrection; September 6, 1899-July 3, 1900: Hay Articulates "Open Door" Policy Toward China.

DANIEL AND ALEXANDER MACMILLAN
English book publishers

The Macmillans started as booksellers and eventually founded Macmillan and Company, which would eventually become a major world publishing enterprise that endured into the twenty-first century.

DANIEL MACMILLAN

BORN: September 13, 1813; Island of Arran, Buteshire, Scotland
DIED: June 27, 1857; Cambridge, England

ALEXANDER MACMILLAN

BORN: October 3, 1818; Irvine, Ayrshire, Scotland
DIED: January 26, 1896; London, England
AREA OF ACHIEVEMENT: Business

EARLY LIVES

The Macmillan brothers were of Scottish stock, sons of Duncan and Katherine Crawford Macmillan, who had a dozen children. Born in 1766, Duncan Macmillan lived on the Island of Arran. He succeeded his father-in-law in running a small farm. On this farm Daniel Macmillan was born in 1813. By 1816, the family had moved to Irvine in Ayrshire, where Alexander was born in October of 1818.

Duncan's death in 1823 left the family hard-pressed. The eldest son, Malcolm, a schoolmaster who later became a Baptist clergyman, at the age of twenty-five became head of the family and did what he could to help keep it solvent. Nevertheless, financial exigencies forced Daniel, only three months past his tenth birthday, to become self-supporting. He was apprenticed to Maxwell Dick, a local bookseller, for seven years and was paid a small wage.

Young Daniel was so dependable that when Dick went to London on business in 1828, he was able to leave his teenage apprentice in charge. Daniel learned from Dick how to buy, sell, and bind books. Dick also taught Daniel how to handle and groom horses. The apprenticeship was largely a positive experience for Daniel, a frail child, of normal height, perilously thin, whose lungs were weak.

Alexander, the younger brother, attended Irvine Academy, where he enjoyed the more vigorous games his classmates played. He and Daniel both were accustomed to seeing their mother, a woman of intellect, read voraciously, and they both early developed a similar love of books.

When Daniel's apprenticeship ended, the seventeen-year-old was in bad health. After working for booksellers in Stirling and in Glasgow, in 1833, Daniel sailed for London, a sixty-three-hour journey, to seek his fortune. He sought work there as a bookseller but found a more compatible job in a Cambridge bookstore, where he went at half the salary that Simpkin's in London had offered him. He remained for three years in Mr. Johnson's Cambridge bookshop.

In 1836, a year after his mother had died, Daniel returned to Scotland. Alexander by this time had an ill-paying job as usher in a school and was destitute. When Daniel was offered a job in London at Seeley's in Fleet Street, he took it, and three years later, in 1839, he had arranged for Alexander to work in the same bookstore. Daniel, who shared lodgings with Alexander, assiduously promoted the younger man's education.

By late 1842, the two brothers could think of opening their own bookstore, which they did in Aldersgate Street early the following year. Because of the shop's out-of-the way location, it did not show a profit, although it attracted some of London's most prestigious intellectuals. By June, 1843, the brothers had the chance to buy Mr. Newby's shop in Cambridge and did so. Alexander kept his job at Seeley's for a while to assure them of a secure income. Daniel left Seeley's to devote full time to running the bookstore. Alexander was as active in the new venture as his job at Seeley's permitted.

Before long, the brothers began a small publishing operation in connection with the new bookshop. By November 10, 1843, the first book bearing the Macmillan imprint was in the British Museum Library. By this time, both brothers were deeply in debt. Daniel had lung problems against which he constantly struggled. Then, early in 1844, he had a life-threatening hemorrhage, brought on by the long hours his new enterprise required.

LIVES' WORK

Before Daniel moved to Cambridge, he had become friends with Archdeacon Julius Charles Hare, to whom he had written about one of Hare's religious books. Through Hare, Daniel came to meet some of the notable writers of his day, among them F. D. Maurice, whose religious books had gained considerable celebrity. Religious books were best sellers in that era, so it was commercially prudent for publishers to have as many of them as possible on their lists of offerings.

The archdeacon and his brother helped finance the Macmillans when they bought Newby's bookshop in Cambridge, lending them five hundred pounds at 4 percent interest. Despite Daniel's continued ill health, the shop prospered. The most notable intellectuals from Cambridge University flocked to it, as did Cambridge students, who looked upon it as a second university.

Daniel was aware early of the need for re-editions of books by some notable writers, including Jeremy Taylor, John Donne, Henry Moore, and John Milton. He was too much in debt to do much about publishing these new editions, although in 1844 he published an edition of William Law's 1723 answer to Bernard de Mandeville's *Fable of the Bees* (1714, 1723), with a preface by Maurice.

At about this time, the Macmillans had the opportunity to buy for six thousand pounds a bookselling business, run by Thomas Stevenson, that had flourished in Cambridge for almost a century. The challenge of expanding in this way was great, and the only way the brothers could meet it was to take on a partner, a wholesale drug merchant.

In 1845, the brothers moved their enterprise to 1 Trinity Street, and it is there that William Wordsworth, William Makepeace Thackeray, and Charles Kingsley were their guests. The Macmillans were becoming a force in British publishing. Both brothers were charming and patient. They made writers believe that the Macmillans had their best interests at heart and understood what they wanted to accomplish in their writing. An aura of trust and mutual understanding surrounded the brothers' dealings with writers.

Alexander, a man of impeccable intellect and firm ideas, could respect people at odds with his thinking if their reasoning was sound. He had strong persuasive gifts and avoided intellectual confrontation; he took the arts seriously, and creative artists immediately sensed the depth of his devotion to the arts; and he stood ready to defend his authors. These qualities served him admirably as a publisher. When Cambridge University took Maurice's professorship from him in 1853, Alexander lent Maurice his support and kept his controversial books in print.

Through Maurice, the Macmillans published the work of Charles Kingsley, the first author to bring them considerable financial success. Within a decade of their first venture in publishing, the Macmillans had published scores of books, many of them translations from the classics, for which a ready market existed. One of their enduring successes was the publication in 1852 of John Llewellyn Davies and David James Vaughan's translation of Plato's *Republic*, a book that went into countless editions and still sold well a century after it first appeared. Kingsley's *Phaethon* and Isaac Todhuner's *Differential Calculus* appeared in 1852 and were dependable sellers for years to come. In 1855, Macmillan press issued a reprint of Maurice's 1853 book, *Prophets and Kings of the Old Testament*, which sold briskly.

On September 4, 1850, Daniel had married Frances Orridge. A desperately ill man, Daniel continued to live for only a little more than six years. During his brief marriage, he fathered four children. By 1852, however, it was necessary for him to be away from Cambridge frequently to breathe the sea air that gave him some relief from his illness. He and Alexander carried on a voluminous business correspondence during Daniel's absences. Despite his illness and absence from the Macmillan Publishing Company, Daniel continued to be intimately involved in forming its policies, in soliciting manuscripts, and in directing the course those manuscripts took.

During the early 1850's, Great Britain's uncertain economic climate placed the Macmillans under financial pressure. Nevertheless, they had faith in their basic business policies, knowing that their company could survive periods of economic instability. Daniel, although ill, had worked from 1854 with Kingsley as Kingsley wrote *Westward Ho!* (1855), which proved to be one of Macmillan's continuing windfalls, its earnings proliferating markedly after 1889, when the sixpenny edition of the work appeared.

When Daniel died, on June 27, 1857, Kingsley's current novel, *Two Years Ago*, was breaking sales records, and the Macmillans, while not yet wealthy, were in a financially promising position. Upon Daniel's death, Alexander, who had run the day-to-day operations of the company, became its head.

Shortly after Daniel's death, Alexander opened a branch of the company in London. His nephew, Robert Bowes, who had worked for the company since 1846, ran this operation. Alexander routinely went to London on Thursdays and stayed overnight. During these visits, London's literati flocked to the Henrietta Street offices in Covent Garden, where Alexander was at home to all comers. It was during these bristling sessions that the idea of *Macmillan's Magazine* (1859-1907) was incubated. Alexander launched the magazine, and it became a force in establishing the course of both British and American writing during the nearly fifty years of its existence.

By 1863, Alexander was appointed publisher to the University of Oxford. He had moved his prosperous publishing company from Cambridge to London. Some of the most notable authors of the nineteenth century wrote for Macmillan, which by then had published Thackeray, Walter Pater, Alfred, Lord Tennyson, Mrs. (Margaret) Oliphant, Thomas Hardy, Thomas Hughes, Christina Rossetti, and Cardinal John Henry Newman.

In 1867, Alexander made his first trip to the United States and was well received. Although he had not gone abroad to establish an American Macmillan, the idea now seemed feasible to him. Daniel's sons and his own were of an age that they would soon be entering the business, and an American branch provided just the sort of testing ground they needed. By November, 1869, the company had an American branch. Macmillan books printed after 1870 listed both London and New York on their imprint.

SIGNIFICANCE

Daniel and Alexander Macmillan established one of the most influential and diverse publishing companies in the world. They were good businesspeople, well seasoned in their trade. Their chief skill, however, was their ability to identify and nurture talent. They had endless patience in their dealings with authors. They were willing to take risks by publishing works that might not sell, but by doing so, they achieved some of their most remarkable successes.

These two men, rising from humble origins and working against substantial economic and personal handicaps, helped establish the intellectual tone of the age in which they lived by making available to readers the most exciting and controversial ideas of their day. Their company, now in its second century, still affects the intellectual direction of the English-speaking world.

—*R. Baird Shuman*

FURTHER READING

Foster, James. *A Bibliographical Catalogue of Macmillan and Company's Publications from 1843 to 1880*. London: Macmillan, 1891. This comprehensive list shows the broad range of books that issued from Macmillan and Company during the days when Daniel and Alexander had their most direct influence upon it.

Graves, Charles L. *The Life and Letters of Alexander Macmillan*. London: Macmillan, 1910. Although not comprehensive, Graves's edition of the letters has an interesting interspersion of biographical data. The letters are well chosen and illuminate the early history of Macmillan and Company.

James, Elizabeth, ed. *Macmillan: A Publishing Tradition*. New York: Palgrave, 2002. Collection of essays recounting the history of the company since its founding in 1843, based on recent research in the archives of the British Library. The essays explore Macmillan and Company's nineteenth century business strategy, the company's expansion into India and the United States, relations with Thomas Hardy, W. B. Yeats, Alfred, Lord Tennyson and other authors, children's publishing, and *Macmillan's Magazine*.

Macmillan, Alexander. *The Letters of Alexander Macmillan*. Edited by George Macmillan. Glasgow, Scotland: University Press, 1908. These letters reflect both the range of authors with whom Alexander Macmillan dealt and the careful attention he lavished on them.

Morgan, Charles. *The House of Macmillan: 1843-1943*. London: Macmillan, 1944. This book remains the comprehensive history of the founding of the Macmillan company and provides a detailed biographical background of both of its founders as well as valuable information about other members of the Macmillan family.

Packer, Lona Mosk, ed. *The Rossetti-Macmillan Letters*. Berkeley: University of California Press, 1963. This collection of 133 letters written to Alexander Macmillan and other officials of Macmillan and Company by Dante Gabriel, William Michael, and Christina Rossetti, between 1861 and 1889, reveals Alexander's gentle and understanding handling of one of his notable authors and demonstrates the cordiality of the Rossettis' relationship with their publisher.

Seiler, Robert, ed. *The Book Beautiful: Walter Pater and the House of Macmillan*. New Brunswick, N.J.: Athlone Press, 1999. Contains Pater's letters to his publisher, written between 1872 and 1917. The letters, which have been annotated by Seiler, describe Pater's literary career and activities at Macmillan and Company.

SEE ALSO: Thomas Hardy; Sir Joseph Norman Lockyer; John Henry Newman; Walter Pater; William Makepeace Thackeray; William Wordsworth.

RELATED ARTICLE in *Great Events from History: The Nineteenth Century, 1801-1900:* 19th century: Development of Working-Class Libraries.

WILLIAM CHARLES MACREADY
English actor and dramatist

The mid-nineteenth century's most influential actor-manager, Macready laid the foundations for reforms that helped to forge the modern theater, restored uncorrupted Shakespeare texts to the stage, and gave solid encouragement to the contemporary "new drama."

BORN: March 3, 1793; London, England
DIED: April 27, 1873; Cheltenham, England
AREA OF ACHIEVEMENT: Theater

EARLY LIFE

The mother of William Charles Macready was an actor and the daughter of a respectable surgeon. His father was an improvident, womanizing actor-manager and son of a Dublin upholsterer, whose personal and theatrical tastes and notorious example were to influence his son profoundly: The seeds were sown early of Macready's lifelong professional caution and private propriety.

The delusions of genteel grandeur of the elder Macready led to his son's entering Rugby school in 1803. There Macready gained both a liking of his own for polite society and a taste for the classics. By 1808, stimulated by the intellectual rigor of his studies, he had formed hopes of going to Oxford and preparing for the bar, but these were forever and bitterly dashed when his father's near-bankruptcy forced the sixteen-year-old Macready to undertake the comanagement of his company. This baptism of fire in theatrical business was supplemented by a visit to London in 1809 to learn fencing and study the reigning stars of his profession.

On June 7, 1810, Macready made his first stage appearance, playing Romeo in white silk stockings and dancing pumps, a costume not calculated to flatter an actor of only medium height and rather heavy on his feet, who possessed (in addition to a noble brow) not only the large blue eyes but also the flat face and irregular features of the Irish. Nevertheless, his success was considerable, and continued so for six prosperous provincial years.

LIFE'S WORK

On September 16, 1816, Macready finally stepped onto the stage of a London theater. His Covent Garden debut, delayed by his caution, occasioned many favorable and some perceptive reviews:

Mr. Macready strikes us as having a better conception of his Author's meaning [than Kean]. He trusts more to plain delivery and proper emphasis—and consequently has less occasion for starting—pointing—and slapping his forehead.

The instant comparison to Edmund Kean, the great and well-established romantic actor of the age, anticipated the jealous rivalry that swiftly developed. Also of interest is the immediate critical recognition of the more natural style of acting that Macready brought to the stage. There are indications, too, of why the more intellectual Macready would become the preeminent actor-collaborator of the 1830's and 1840's, working directly and with success with authors.

For three years after this auspicious beginning, however, to his own disgust, Macready was relegated to playing a selection of gothic and melodramatic "heavies." His luck turned in 1819, when his Richard III caught the public's fancy. Then, in 1820, a poverty-stricken and eccentric first-time playwright named Sheridan Knowles sent Macready a manuscript. He decided at once to stage it. *Virginius*, with its combination of sensibility with a plea for the rights of man, caught the spirit of its age, and eminently suited the talents of its star. Macready's success as the noble centurion raised him to the top of his profession.

In a few short years, however, his relationship with the Covent Garden management had soured sufficiently for his contract to be canceled. Thus, on October 13, 1823, he made his first appearance at Drury Lane, where he was to stay for thirteen years that did little to enhance his reputation, and during which Kean refused to act with him. His unhappiness was somewhat mitigated in 1823 by his marriage (prudently later in life), in 1826 by the first of several trips to the United States.

In 1835 occurred a famous incident. Macready's sense of angry frustration at the low status of tragedy in the theater (reduced to a mere part of a miscellaneous entertainment) boiled over. On April 29, focusing this anger on the figure of the Drury Lane manager, money-minded Alfred Bunn, he called him a "damned scoundrel" and knocked him down. It says much for the nature of the audiences of the period that Macready's popularity increased after this outrageous assault.

The later 1830's saw Macready premiering several of Edward Bulwer-Lytton's highly acclaimed historical

William Charles Macready. (Library of Congress)

dramas, Sir Thomas Noon Talfourd's *Ion* (1836), another influential major play of the "new drama," and Robert Browning's *Strafford* (1837), written for Macready at his own request. As often in Macready's career, this last was a critical rather than a popular success, and yet another factor in the cementing of his friendships with these eminent literary figures, as well as John Forster and Charles Dickens (who dedicated to Macready his *Nicholas Nickleby*, 1838-1839).

On September 20, 1837, Macready opened the Covent Garden season (1837-1838) for the first time as manager, himself playing Leontes in a restored text of *The Winter's Tale*. He gathered about him a powerful company, together with a troupe of pantomimists—crucial in the recouping of the three thousand pounds he was said to have lost by Christmas. In February, he had a remunerative hit with Bulwer-Lytton's *The Lady of Lyons: Or, Love and Pride* (1838). In his second season as manager (1838-1839), the most notable performances were of William Shakespeare's *The Tempest* (originally produced in 1611; an elaborate revival); of Bulwer-

Lytton's *Richelieu: Or, The Conspiracy* (1839), which took the town by storm; and of Shakespeare's *Henry V* (pr. c. 1598-1599; with staging supervised by Bulwer-Lytton, Dickens, Forster, W. J. Fox, and the artists Daniel Maclise and Clarkson Stanfield)—another resounding success.

The next highlight in Macready's career was his second period of management, again for two seasons, this time at Drury Lane. The hit of the 1841-1842 season was *Acis and Galatea* (1842), a pantomime by W. H. Oxberry, with Stanfield's scenery and George Frideric Handel's music. Macready himself scored a great personal success in the title role in another restored "problem" Shakespeare play, *King John* (pr. c. 1596-1597), on October 24, 1842. On June 14, 1843, he appeared for the last time as manager, in his "keynote" role of Macbeth. After this high point, remunerative and well-received trips to the United States and Paris aside, he played mostly in the provinces, returning to London on November 22 to play his last new part, Philip Van Artevelde, in his own somewhat botched adaptation of Henry Taylor's play, regarded by contemporaries as a species of nineteenth century *Hamlet* (pr. c. 1600-1601).

At the end of 1848, however, came the low point of his career, in one sense, when his last trip to the United States ended in tragedy. Poor reception of the highly popular American actor Edwin Forrest in England, and American discontent with recent unflattering portraits of the country by Mrs. Frances Trollope and Dickens, erupted into a full-scale riot at the Astor Place Opera House in New York during a Macready performance as Macbeth on May 10, 1849. Troops were called in, and twenty-two people were left dead. Macready himself, whose characteristic lack of tact had not helped the situation, was ignominiously smuggled away and sent back to England.

Macready's farewell to the stage came in 1851, shortly after the death of a daughter, the first of many domestic tragedies: Only three of his twelve children outlived him. He left the stage, by choice, while he was still near the height of his powers and resisted the temptation of a comeback. On February 28, he played Macbeth for the last time, at Drury Lane. On March 1, a public dinner for six hundred, hosted by Bulwer-Lytton, with speeches by Dickens and William Makepeace Thackeray, paid him the tribute his age believed was his due. He withdrew to the gentleman's residence he had purchased in Dorset, and later to Cheltenham (with a second wife, married 1860), where he died at the age of eighty-one, on Sunday, April 27, 1873.

SIGNIFICANCE

In his farewell address, William Charles Macready asked his last theater audience to give him credit for two things: his efforts "to establish a theatre, in regard to decorum and taste, worthy of our country, and to have in it the plays of our divine Shakespeare fitly illustrated." He succeeded. In the words of the sonnet Alfred, Lord Tennyson wrote for his farewell dinner: "Thine is it that our drama did not die,/ Nor flicker down to brainless pantomime."

Macready by no means banished money-spinning pantomime from the theater (although he did draw the line at trained lions and prostitutes); what he did was disentangle it from serious drama. Other aspects of his management similarly combined practicality with principle: Preeminent among his reforms, crucial to the development of modern theater, was his insistence on regular full rehearsals. Also influential was his concept of the play as a coherent artistic whole.

Macready's other great achievement lies in the support he gave the legitimate theater of his time. Bulwer-Lytton declared of him: "He has identified himself with the living drama of his period, and by so doing he has half created it." The playwrights wrote for him, visualizing Macready as their Virginius, Ion, Richelieu, or Strafford: What Tennyson called his "moral, grave, sublime" stage persona was the heroic type of the period.

Indeed, even in his limitations, the essence of Macready's era was distilled. His popularity is evidence of a public preference for the domestic over the sublime. He was a self-made businessperson with social ambitions, an "eminent Victorian" before his time. For William Hazlitt, even his Macbeth was "a mere modern, agitated by common means and intelligible motives." For Leigh Hunt, Macready was proto-Victorian respectability itself: "Violent or criminal pains he makes simply violent and criminal. Nothing remains to him, if his self-respect, in the ordinary sense of the word, is lost."

Macready's limitations are insignificant compared with his personal failings. Had he not been humorless and prone to ungovernable and childish rages and sulks, less egocentric, and better able to attract the loyalty and

best efforts of his companies, there is no doubt that his periods of management would have been longer, more successful, and more influential in reviving a degraded theater. As it was, company members were treated with a snobbish and haughty contempt that can be traced to Macready's fundamental dislike of what he saw, in quintessentially Victorian terms, as his dirty trade, as such diary entries as this, for April 26, 1843, testify:

> [My] darling children acted *Comus* in the drawing room after dinner, interesting and amusing me very much; they recited the poetry very well indeed, and only gave me a fear lest they should imbibe a liking for the wretched art which I have been wasting my life upon. God forbid!

—*Joss Marsh*

FURTHER READING

Agate, James Evershed, ed. *These Were Actors: Extracts from a Newspaper Cutting Book, 1811-1833*. London: Hutchison, 1943. Reprint. New York: Benjamin Blom, 1969. This absorbing collection of contemporary reviews gives pride of place to Macready's great rival, Kean, and bitingly witty short shrift to the "eminent tragedian" himself. Well worth reading for context, balance, and sheer enjoyment.

Archer, William. *William Charles Macready*. London: K. Paul, Trench, Trübner, 1890. Reprint. New York: Benjamin Blom, 1971. Still brilliantly readable and reliable. Focuses on the four crucial seasons of management.

Baker, Kevin. "The Riot that Remade a City." *American Heritage* 50, no. 7 (November, 1999): 20. Describes the aftermath of the Astor Place riot, which resulted in social reform activities and the construction of Central Park. Also describes the rivalry between Macready and actor Edwin Forrest and the social conditions in New York City that sparked the riot.

Donohue, Joseph, ed. *1660 to 1895*. Vol. 2 in *The Cambridge History of British Theatre*. New York: Cambridge University Press, 2004. Includes information about Macready's roles and repertoire, his Shakespearean productions, and his establishment of a "respectable" theater.

Downer, Alan S. *The Eminent Tragedian: William Charles Macready*. Cambridge, Mass.: Harvard University Press, 1966. Lively and well documented. Locates Macready in his theatrical context; analyzes the "Macready style" and contribution to the stage. Final chapter is an "ideal" reconstruction of Macready's famed *Macbeth* in performance, drawing on his heavily annotated prompt books, reminiscences, and reviews.

Macready, William Charles. *Macready's Reminiscences, and Selections from His Diaries and Letters.* Edited by Sir Frederick Pollock. New York: Macmillan, 1875. Macready's autobiographical account of his life until 1826, followed by a slightly circumspect but nevertheless fascinating selection from the actor's diaries. Alternately frankly self-lacerating and pompously self-centered.

Rowell, George. *The Victorian Theatre: A Survey.* London: Oxford University Press, 1956. The standard work on the theater from 1792 to 1914, with solid but never stolid coverage of the "new drama" of the 1830's and 1840's. Invaluable thirty-page bibliography.

Shattuck, Charles H., ed. *Bulwer and Macready: A Chronicle of the Early Victorian Theatre.* Urbana: University of Illinois Press, 1958. Correspondence covering the years of collaboration between the actor-manager and the lionized author. Excellent sixteen-page introduction.

Southern, Richard. *The Victorian Theatre: A Pictorial Survey.* Newton Abbot, England: David and Charles, 1970. Concise information on theatrical scenery, staging and architecture, Victorian audiences, and Victorian "stars" and shows; supplements a wealth of photographs, drawings, paintings, and diagrams.

Trewin, J. C. *Mr. Macready: A Nineteenth Century Tragedian and His Theatre.* London: George G. Harrap, 1955. A more personal, psychological account; thorough, with illustrations and a helpful bibliography.

_____, ed. *The Pomping Folk in the Nineteenth Century Theatre.* London: J. M. Dent & Sons, 1968. A survey in the words of actors Macready, Helen Faucit, and Fanny Kemble; dramatist Bulwer-Lytton and authors Thackeray and Dickens; managers Edward Stirling and Alfred Bunn (from *The Stage: Both Before and Behind the Curtain,* 1840); drama critics Clement Scott and Henry Morley (from *The Journal of a London Playgoer*); and others.

SEE ALSO: Charles Dickens; Edwin Forrest; Henry Irving; Edmund Kean; Fanny Kemble; William Makepeace Thackeray; Frances Trollope.

RELATED ARTICLES in *Great Events from History: The Nineteenth Century, 1801-1900:* c. 1801-1850: Professional Theaters Spread Throughout America; 1850's-1880's: Rise of Burlesque and Vaudeville.

DOLLEY MADISON
American First Lady

First Lady Dolley Madison's popularity and social acumen made her a political asset to President James Madison. The leading social figure in the capital city for years, she was arguably the most beloved and important American woman of her times, and she served as a role model for future First Ladies.

BORN: May 20, 1768; Guilford County, North Carolina
DIED: July 12, 1849; Washington, D.C.
AREA OF ACHIEVEMENT: Government and politics

EARLY LIFE

Dolley Madison was the daughter of John and Mary Coles Payne, who moved to Piedmont, North Carolina, from Virginia. It was there that Dolley was born in 1768. The following year, the Payne family moved back to their native Virginia. In 1783, after freeing his slaves, John again moved his family, this time to Philadelphia, Pennsylvania, where the Paynes raised their eight children in the strict disciplinary tradition of the Quaker Society of Friends. Dolley was also raised modestly, as her father had failed in business.

In 1790 Dolley married John Todd, Jr., a successful lawyer and Quaker. Dolley and John had two sons: John Payne in 1790 and William Temple in 1792. Tragedy struck when the yellow fever epidemic hit Philadelphia in 1793 and claimed the lives of Dolley's husband, both of his parents, and Dolley's son William, leaving her a young widow with an infant child. The strong-willed Dolley was determined to persevere and make something of herself. Among her many courters at this time was the "Father of the Constitution" and author of the Bill of Rights, Representative James Madison of Virginia. They seemed to make an unlikely couple, as the longtime bachelor James was seventeen years Dolley's senior. He was also unlike most of the dashing gentlemen of his time, because he had not been a soldier, did not dance, and did not ride horses. However, Dolley eventually fell for the intelligent but dour James. They were married on September 15, 1794, and enjoyed a happy but childless marriage. After abandoning her Quaker roots for James's Episcopalianism, she was disowned by the Quakers.

LIFE'S WORK

Dolley appears to have completely shed her conservative Quaker upbringing after her second marriage and developed a love of music, gardens, and socializing. She also acquired a taste for fashion that could not have been further from the social standards of the day that included bright colors, scandalously low-cut dresses, and a bold hairstyle of large curls. Incredibly, for much of the early nineteenth century she was at the center of social life in Washington, D.C. During this time, Dolley was quite possibly the most widely known and beloved woman in the country. A highly capable woman, Dolley managed the Madison family plantation when James was away in Washington, D.C. Admired for her outgoing, pleasant personality, her legacy belongs to her famous social events. Even among present-day First Ladies, Dolley is widely considered to have been the most talented social hostess in the history of the White House. In this endeavor she was aided by what appears to have been a deep, selfless, and genuine love of people and a knack for remembering everyone's name.

In 1801, newly elected President Thomas Jefferson appointed James as his secretary of state. As a widower, Jefferson asked James's wife Dolley to help serve as the White House's social hostess. For eight years she presided over the social affairs of the Jefferson White House. This was followed by another eight years during which her husband was president of the United States from 1809 to 1817. It was Dolley who presided over the nation's first inaugural ball in 1809.

Among the Washington social crowd and much of the nation, Dolley was hailed as "Queen Dolley," "Lady Presidentress," or the "Queen of Washington City." Her socials were the events of the social season, and all of Washington awaited an invitation. Breaking with tradition, she served American dishes for dinner (even contacting people all over the country for recipes), rearranged rooms to better accommodate her guests, and defied convention by sitting at the head of the table at dinners.

Dolley Madison. (Library of Congress)

Dolley set a precedent for future First Ladies when she renovated and redecorated the White House. Strategically, she invited members of Congress to the White House so they could see the poor condition of the building; after securing congressional funding for the renovation project, she even worked with the supervising architect. She successfully blended European flair with American homespun simplicity in her entertaining and invited a wide array of guests to the White House. Although the historical record is far from complete, she seems to have made a positive impression on almost every visitor to the White House. She also emerged as a fashion trendsetter as the nation took a keen interest in her taste for European attire, jewels, bird plumes, and even what became known as "the Dolley Madison turban." Details of her social events and attire were reported in newspapers.

Along with her successful social role, she was the perfect political partner for James. In comparison with his subdued seriousness, she was funny, talkative, and engaging. As was the norm for women of the eighteenth and nineteenth centuries, Dolley had little formal education and was not as well read or intellectual as her predecessor, Abigail Adams. She had been tutored at her childhood plantation home in Virginia and had received some education at a Quaker school in Pennsylvania. Yet, in an era during which women rarely spoke publicly and took no interest in politics, Dolley functioned as an adviser to her husband on both social and political matters. She traveled with him, campaigned with him, and appeared in public with him. James was proud of his wife's accomplishments. He appears to have recognized her social abilities and his limited interpersonal skills. He often sought and took her advice, appreciating her political astuteness, warm personal touch, and legendary tact.

Even though James had been the secretary of state, it was Dolley who was the diplomat. She took no formal or public role in politics and claimed to not be interested in political affairs. However, her actions revealed her many political contributions to James's presidency. Many historical accounts exist of Dolley disarming her husband's political opponents, charming his potential supporters, and captivating statesmen, dignitaries, and other White House guests. Dolley made sure she invited every member of Congress to dinner at least once during legislative sessions. In doing so, she was a century ahead of her time as the first presidential spouse to blend White House social events with political agendas. She also held socials in honor of U.S. accomplishments, including the capture of British ships during the War of 1812.

When the British sacked the capital city and set the White House ablaze during the War of 1812, Dolley was among the last Americans to leave. The president and cabinet had already evacuated the city. Refusing pleas to abandon the capital city, Dolley watched the approach of the British through a spy glass. Unconcerned about her own safety, she thought to load as many White House archives as possible (including official papers, china, and silver, as well as such artifacts as the famous Gilbert Stuart portrait of George Washington) onto a wagon while the British army literally marched into the city. With a wagon full of priceless items, she fled to Virginia at the last possible moment. Her courageous act inspired a nation stung by the defeat and the August 24, 1814, burning of the White House. After the war an unfazed but heroic Dolley continued entertaining in her temporary quarters in a private home on Penn Avenue in Washington, D.C. She proclaimed to a cheering city, "We shall rebuild Washington!"

SIGNIFICANCE

After James's second term as president ended in 1817, he and Dolley returned to Montpelier, their plantation home

in Virginia, where they enjoyed a comfortable retirement highlighted by the many visitors and guests who attended Dolley's parties. Dolley continued to support her husband's political work by taking dictation for him through his failing health during the last years of his life. James Madison died in 1836 and, in the autumn of 1837, Dolley returned to the capital city to live. She moved into a small home that James had built some years earlier. Back in Washington, Dolley returned to the social and political life, enjoying an honorary seat on the Senate floor, attending social events, and receiving lifetime franking privileges from Congress. She wisely sold James's official papers to the government for $30,000 to both assure their preservation and provide for herself financially. She remained a central figure until her death in 1849.

Dolley Madison loved living in the White House and was perhaps the first presidential spouse as well as one of the few women prior to the twentieth century to develop an identity of her own beyond that of her husband. She fashioned the social side of the office of First Lady and consequently became a role model for many future First Ladies. On her death, President Zachary Taylor aptly described her as "Our First Lady for a half-century."

—Robert P. Watson

FURTHER READING

Anthony, Carl Sferrazza. *First Ladies: The Saga of the Presidents' Wives and Their Power, 1789-1961.* New York: William Morrow, 1990. Contains a chapter on each First Lady, including Dolley. Anthony provides both personal and political details of Dolley's life.

Arnett, Ethel Stephens. *Mrs. James Madison: The Incomparable Dolley.* Greensboro, N.C.: Piedmont Press, 1972. A source for Dolley's life before meeting James Madison and later in the White House. Examines her personality and character.

Cote, Richard N. *Strength and Honor: The Life of Dolley Madison.* Mount Pleasant, S.C.: Corinthian Books, 2004. A well-researched, comprehensive biography of the woman Cote describes as the "best loved first lady of the nineteenth century."

Gould, Lewis L., ed. *American First Ladies: Their Lives and Their Legacy.* New York: Garland, 1996. Contains a chapter on each First Lady that includes an examination of their contributions to the presidency. Includes a helpful bibliography.

Hunt-Jones, Conover. *Dolley and the "Great Little Madison."* Washington, D.C.: American Institute of Architects Foundation, 1977. Hunt-Jones explores the

Madisons' marriage, their long life together, and Dolley's influence on her "Great Little Madison."

Ketcham, Ralph. *James Madison: A Biography*. Charlottesville: University Press of Virginia, 1990. Insights on the life and presidency of the fourth president. Dolley is discussed periodically, but it also benefits one studying Dolley to know James Madison, his times, and life in the Madison White House.

Madison, Dolley. *The Selected Letters of Dolley Payne Madison*. Edited by David B. Mattern and Holly C. Shulman. Charlottesville: University Press of Virginia, 2003. Contains a carefully edited selection of letters to and from Madison. Also features short, factual essays placing Madison's letters within the con-

text of her life and times, and biographies of the people mentioned in the letters.

Truman, Margaret. *First Ladies: An Intimate Group Portrait of White House Wives*. New York: Random House, 1995. Contains numerous discussions of Dolley's sense of style, famous social events, renovation of the White House, and heroism during the War of 1812. The book is written in a conversational, nonacademic style and is very readable.

SEE ALSO: Mary Todd Lincoln; Zachary Taylor.

RELATED ARTICLE in *Great Events from History: The Nineteenth Century, 1801-1900:* June 18, 1812-December 24, 1814: War of 1812.

THE MAHDI
Sudanese Islamic revolutionary

The Mahdi led an Islamic reform movement that swept away the Sudan's Turkish-Egyptian colonial administration and created a new Islamic fervor in northern Sudan. His movement also provided an ideology for later jihad movements throughout the Muslim world.

BORN: August 12, 1844; Dirar Island off Dongola, Sudan

DIED: June 22, 1885; Omdurman, Sudan

ALSO KNOWN AS: Muḥammad Aḥmad ibn as-Sayyid ʿAbd-Allāh (full name); Al-Mahdī

AREAS OF ACHIEVEMENT: Religion and theology, warfare and conquest, government and politics

EARLY LIFE

The Mahdi was born Muḥammad Aḥmad ibn as-Sayyid in the western part of what is now Sudan. He was a member of an Arabized Nubian family. His parents relocated to Karari, some twelve miles north of Khartoum, where his brothers together with their father, Abdallah, entered into a boat-building business. However, Muḥammad himself pursued religious studies, as his great-grandfather, a respected Islamic scholar, had done. He studied in Khartoum and in Karari. He became a pupil of prominent religious teachers in the Gezira and Berber regions of central Sudan, such as Sheikh al-Amin al-Suwaylih and Sheikh Muḥammad al-Dikayr ʿAbdallah Khujali.

Muḥammad admired the ascetic life and mystic experiences of the Sufis and joined the Sufi order (*Tarīqah*) of

the Sammānīya in 1861. After studying Sufism for seven years, he was certified as a Sammānīya sheikh and married a daughter of his grand uncle, Aḥmad Sharfi. In 1870, he and his brothers established a base on Aba Island on the Nile above (south) Khartoum—a place attractive to his boat-building brothers because of its reserves of wood. There Muḥammad built a mosque and started teaching the Qurʾān. He soon endeared himself to the tribes of the island.

Over the next ten years, particularly after 1879, Muḥammad traveled widely: to Dongola, Sennar, and Kordofan, among other places in Sudan. During his travels, he observed widespread dissatisfaction of the Sudanese peoples against Turkish rule (*Turkiyā*). Widespread discontent and unrest had generated an apocalyptical expectation among many people, especially in northern Sudan, that the degenerate world would be dissolved and an authentic Islamic state would arise under the rule of a new messenger of God known as the Mahdi.

Muḥammad Aḥmad was an eloquent and elegant preacher who had a charismatic personality and an impressive physical charm. He was brawny and tall, with a bald forehead and an aquiline nose. He was praised for his "infallibility" and was considered by many to be the "perfect man." His distinctive attributes, together with his claims of being descended from the Prophet Muḥammad, through al-Ḥasan, the son of the Prophet's daughter Fāṭima and her husband ʿAlī ibn Abī Ṭālib, added to the growing perception that he himself was the awaited Mahdi.

One of the notable people who recognized Muḥammad as the Mahdi was ʿAbdullahi ibn Muḥammad, a nomadic Baqqara Arab from southern Darfur, who fell in a swoon after seeing him at al-Massalamiya on the Blue Nile during March, 1881. This incident resulted in a conversion experience that convinced Muḥammad that he had indeed been elected by God (Allah) as a messenger. ʿAbdullahi then became Muḥammad's close associate, or *khalifa*.

LIFE'S WORK

After joining with ʿAbdullahi, Muḥammad went to Kordofan to present himself as the Mahdi and urged that region's people to eschew the present world for the world to come. His message echoed the familiar teachings of the Sufis in the Sudan, and the people of Kordofan quickly flocked under his banner, taking an oath of allegiance (*baylʾa*). His followers came to be known as the *ansars*—which translates literally as "madmen."

Muḥammad then made a triumphant return to Aba Island, where on June 29, 1881, he publicly proclaimed his new identity as the Mahdi and urged important leaders of the region to abolish the agrarian tax and join him in a holy war, or jihad. The Egyptian governor-general of Kordofan, Muḥammad Rʾuf Pasha, dispatched a military expedition to Aba Island with the intention of arresting the troublemaker in August, 1881. However, on August 12, the government's army was routed by Muḥammad's followers, who established a base at Jabal Qadir (renamed Jabal Massa) in the Nuba Mountains on August 31.

The governor (*mudir*) of Fashoda, Rashid Bey Ayman, decided to launch a surprise attack on Muḥammad's headquarters at Jabal Qadir in early December but did not first obtain official permission from the governor-general of Kordofan. Acting on information about Rashid's plan obtained from a Kinana woman, Muḥammad ambushed the attackers on December 9, and Rashid Bey was killed in action. On May 30, 1882, Muḥammad's followers overwhelmed a seven-thousand-man Egyptian force led by Yusuf Pasha Hasan al-Shallali near al-Ubayyiḍ and seized its weapons and ammunition. Muḥammad followed up this victory by laying siege to El-Obeid, which was defended by Muḥammad Said Pasha. The town fell to the Mahdi's followers on January 19, 1883.

On November 5, the Mahdi scored another major victory over government forces at Sheikan that were commanded by the British colonel William Hicks. On December 23, the Turkish-Egyptian administration in the western Sudan collapsed following a victory of the Mahdi's followers at Darfur, where Rudolf Slatin Bey

was in charge. On April 12, 1884, Baḥr al-Ghazāl surrendered to a Mahdi force commanded by Karamallah Muḥammad Kurqusawi. The Mahdi had converted the Baqqārah tribes of the western Sudan and the riverain peoples, and the Bīja tribes of the east went over to the Mahdist commander, ʿUthmān ibn Abī Bakr Diqna.

The Mahdist forces then targeted Khartoum, the center and symbol of Turkish-Egyptian rule in the Sudan. Between 1873 and 1879, Khartoum had been administered by Governor-General Charles George Gordon, a British officer employed by the Turkish-Egyptian authorities. Gordon was trying to implement a modernization program—including an effort to abolish the slave trade—that was seen by the Sudanese people as an attempt to Christianize the region. After Gordon had left in 1879, Raʾuf Pasha became governor-general.

The politics of the Sudan were further complicated in 1882 by the fact that Great Britain began occupying Egypt in September of that year, and it thereby assumed responsibility for Egypt's share of the administration of the Sudan. Because of the deteriorating situation of the Sudanese government, the British decided to withdraw their forces from the Sudan and planned the withdrawal in consultation with the Turkish khedive, who oversaw the administration of Egypt. They sent Gordon to the Sudan to organize the withdrawal. Gordon reached Khartoum on February 18, 1884. By April, he managed to evacuate some 2,500 foreigners. However, he had also decided as early as February 26 to suppress the Mahdi's jihad.

Meanwhile, the Mahdi's forces encircled Khartoum, spreading their jihad in the adjacent Berber region. By May, they had cut off Khartoum from the outside world. In September, the vanguard of the Madhi's followers, commanded by ʿAbd al-Raḥmān al-Nūjumī, reinforced the Mahdist army already operating in Khartoum under the command of MuḥammadʿUthmān Abu Qarja. Shortly thereafter, the main Mahdist force reached the city. On January 5, 1885, the Fort of Omdurman—across the Nile River from Khartoum—surrendered to the Mahdi, who captured Khartoum on the night of January 25. Gordon was killed while defending his palace against the insurgents.

After establishing a new capital north of Omdurman, Muḥammad Aḥmad transformed his spiritual leadership into a theocratic rule. However, on June 16, 1885, he became ill from a fever. He may have been poisoned—as was rumored—or, perhaps more plausibly, was infected with typhus virus. In any case, he died in Omdurman on June 22. His *khalifa*, ʿAbdullahi ibn Muḥammad, succeeded him as the ruler of the Sudan.

SIGNIFICANCE

Muḥammad Aḥmad's religious revolt, or Mahdiya, was one in a series of Islamic revivalist and fundamentalist movements during the nineteenth century. Others included those of Wahhābīya in Arabia, the jihad of Shehu ʿUthman dan Fodio in Nigeria, and the Sanūsīya in Cyrenaica in North Africa.

Muḥammad Aḥmad's brief regime as the Mahdi played a significant role in the era of "new imperialism" of the late nineteenth century. By overthrowing the Turkish-Egyptian rule, it contributed substantially to the formation of the nation state of the Sudan that would arise during the mid-twentieth century. The political and spiritual role played by the family of Muḥammad continued to influence the history of post-independent Sudan.

—*Narasingha P. Sil*

FURTHER READING

Bermann, Richard A. *The Mahdi of Allah: The Story of the Dervish Mohammed Ahmed.* New York: Macmillan, 1932. A much acclaimed popular, rather than scholarly, biography.

Collins, Robert O. *The Southern Sudan, 1883-1898: A Struggle for Control.* New Haven, Conn.: Yale University Press, 1962. Well-written and authoritative, though brief, account of the Mahdist jihad era in the Sudan.

Holt, Peter M. "The Mahdia in the Sudan, 1881-1898." *History Today* (March, 1958): 187-195. A succinct summary of Holt's monograph on the subject (see below). A must for a preliminary understanding of Mahdism.

_____. *The Mahdist State in the Sudan, 1881-1898: A Study of its Origins, Development, and Overthrow.* 2d ed. Oxford, England: Clarendon Press, 1970. Well-researched and written, a magisterial account of the Sudanese Mahdiya.

Shaked, Haim. *The Life of the Sudanese Mahdi: A Historical Study of Kitab Sa'adat al-Mustahdi bi-Sirat al-Imam al-Mahdi . . . by Ismail b. ʿAbd al-Qadir.* New Brunswick: Transaction Books, 1978. Ismail's sacred biography provides intimate details of the divine calling of Muḥammad Aḥmad and his "miraculous" victories in numerous battles in connection with his jihad.

Wingate, Francis R. *Mahdism and the Egyptian Sudan.* 1891. 2d ed. London: Frank Cass, 1968. A work by an officer of the Turkish-Egyptian government that is based on military and government documents, as well as some limited Mahdist sources. In spite of its occasional anti-Mahdi bias, this is a valuable account of the Mahdi's campaigns by a distinguished contemporary.

SEE ALSO: Muḥammad ʿAbduh; The Bāb; Muḥammad Bello; Charles George Gordon; Jamāl al-Dīn al-Afghānī; Menelik II; ʿUthman dan Fodio.

THOMAS ROBERT MALTHUS
English political economist

The original professor of political economy, Malthus will be forever linked to discussions of the population problem. Terms such as "Malthusian economics" and "neo-Malthusianism" have achieved a permanent place in the English language and reflect the controversy that his work engendered.

BORN: February 13, 1766; the Rookery, near Dorking, Surrey, England
DIED: December 23, 1834; St. Catherine, near Bath, Somerset, England
AREA OF ACHIEVEMENT: Economics

EARLY LIFE

Thomas Robert Malthus was born on his father's estate. Some biographies incorrectly list February 14, the day of his baptism, as his birthdate. His father, Daniel Malthus,

was an Oxford-educated lawyer and a gentleman of some means, as well as an intellectual of the Enlightenment and a devotee of the French thinker Jean-Jacques Rousseau.

Malthus grew up in a genteel, intellectually invigorating environment provided by his father, who was caught up in the exciting ideas of the Age of Reason and the French Revolution. Indeed, Malthus's great work was initially a reaction to many of those ideas, especially the notion that through the use of reason, humankind could achieve perfection. Privately educated under a series of tutors, Malthus entered Jesus College of Cambridge in 1784 when he was eighteen. There he won prizes in Latin and English grammar, but his chief study was, as his father had suggested, mathematics. In that area, he was graduated as Ninth Wrangler (high honors) and was awarded a fellowship.

Upon graduation, Malthus took religious orders in 1788 and became a pastor in the Church of England, taking charge of the rectory in the village of Surrey in 1793. In 1804, he gave up his fellowship and married Harriet Eckersall, his cousin and eleven years his junior. A devoted family man, his home life appears to have been quite stable, and his wife was reputed to have been a charming hostess. He sired three children—two sons and a daughter who died when she was seventeen, the one note of tragedy in his personal life.

Malthus was a handsome man, with an aristocratic nose, sharp eyes, and a high forehead. He dressed as a gentleman of the day and wore his curly hair short with sideburns. Contemporary sources generally indicate that his personality, despite the heated controversy that ensnared him, was genuinely amiable and pleasant. Even his worst enemies frequently noted his sincerity and fairness. He was, by all reports and in spite of the terrible things that have been said about him, a gentle man.

Thomas Robert Malthus. (Library of Congress)

LIFE'S WORK

In 1805, Malthus received an appointment as professor of history and political economy at the newly founded East India College, the purpose of which was to train civil servants for work in India. This was the first such professorship established, and Malthus retained it until his death. He was a dedicated teacher, called "Pop" by his students.

By the time he left religious work for education, Malthus had already written the book that resulted in his historical significance: *An Essay on the Principle of Population, as It Affects the Future Improvement of Society, with Remarks on the Speculations of Mr. Godwin, M. Condorcet, and Other Writers* (1798). Despite his other contributions, it was this work that marked him as a man of controversy. The original work was fairly short and published anonymously, but it became widely read, quickly sold out, and generated considerable discussion, not all of it positive. From 1799 to 1802, Malthus traveled widely throughout Europe, going as far as Russia, collecting additional data on his theory that the growth of population will always outstrip the production of food. The second edition, of 1803, was greatly expanded, and while critics still quote from the first edition, it is the 1803 version that represents the fuller accounting of Malthusian principles. During his lifetime, *An Essay on the Principle of Population* went through six editions, and extracts and complete renditions remain in print.

Malthus was both attacked and admired in his day. In 1819, he was elected a Fellow of the Royal Society, and in 1821 he became a charter member of the Political Economy Club, along with David Ricardo, his close friend, and James Mill. In 1824, he received admission as a royal associate into the Royal Academy of Literature. Also a member of the French Institute and the Royal Academy in Berlin, in 1834 he became a Charter Fellow of the Statistical Society. During the Christmas vacation of 1834, he and his family visited his father-in-law at Claverton, Bath. There, on December 23, Malthus died of a heart attack. He is buried in Bath Abbey. His wife survived him by thirty years.

Students of Malthus and Malthusian economics can easily become confused by the controversy surrounding Malthus and particu-

---

ESSAY ON THE PRINCIPLE OF POPULATION

In the preface to his famous work on population, Thomas Malthus explains what led him to take up the subject and what he hopes that his essay will achieve.

The following Essay owes its origin to a conversation with a friend, on the subject of Mr [William] Godwin's essay on avarice and profusion, in his *Enquirer*. The discussion started the general question of the future improvement of society, and the Author at first sat down with an intention of merely stating his thoughts to his friend, upon paper, in a clearer manner than he thought he could do in conversation. But as the subject opened upon him, some ideas occurred, which he did not recollect to have met with before; and as he conceived that every least light, on a topic so generally interesting, might be received with candour, he determined to put his thoughts in a form for publication.

The Essay might, undoubtedly, have been rendered much more complete by a collection of a greater number of facts in elucidation of the general argument. But a long and almost total interruption from very particular business, joined to a desire (perhaps imprudent) of not delaying the publication much beyond the time that he originally proposed, prevented the Author from giving to the subject an undivided attention. He presumes, however, that the facts which he has adduced will be found to form no inconsiderable evidence for the truth of his opinion respecting the future improvement of mankind. As the Author contemplates this opinion at present, little more appears to him to be necessary than a plain statement, in addition to the most cursory view of society, to establish it.

It is an obvious truth, which has been taken notice of by many writers, that population must always be kept down to the level of the means of subsistence; but no writer that the Author recollects has inquired particularly into the means by which this level is effected: and it is a view of these means which forms, to his mind, the strongest obstacle in the way to any very great future improvement of society. He hopes it will appear that, in the discussion of this interesting subject, he is actuated solely by a love of truth, and not by any prejudices against any particular set of men, or of opinions. He professes to have read some of the speculations on the future improvement of society in a temper very different from a wish to find them visionary, but he has not acquired that command over his understanding which would enable him to believe what he wishes, without evidence, or to refuse his assent to what might be unpleasing, when accompanied with evidence.

The view which he has given of human life has a melancholy hue, but he feels conscious that he has drawn these dark tints from a conviction that they are really in the picture, and not from a jaundiced eye or an inherent spleen of disposition. The theory of mind which he has sketched in the two last chapters accounts to his own understanding in a satisfactory manner for the existence of most of the evils of life, but whether it will have the same effect upon others must be left to the judgement of his readers.

If he should succeed in drawing the attention of more able men to what he conceives to be the principal difficulty in the way to the improvement of society and should, in consequence, see this difficulty removed, even in theory, he will gladly retract his present opinions and rejoice in a conviction of his error.

Source: Thomas Robert Malthus, "Preface," in *An Essay on the Principle of Population* (London: J. Johnson, 1798).

---

larly by arguments advanced in his name that actually bear no relation to the man or his ideas. It is best to begin by asking how did Malthus come to write *An Essay on the Principle of Population* and what did he say in it? As the subtitle suggests, Malthus wrote in response to certain ideas put forth by the reforming Englishman William Godwin and the equally perfectionistic Frenchman, the Marquis de Condorcet. Simply stated, Godwin and Condorcet believed that with the use of reason and education there could be no end to human progress. They both foresaw continued physical, intellectual, and moral advancement until a perfect society resulted. In discussing these ideas with his father, Malthus entered certain objections to such a happy view, and his father suggested

that he put them in writing. Thus came about the first *An Essay on the Principle of Population*.

Like so many of his contemporaries, Malthus admired science and mathematics, and he believed in a natural law that would inevitably prevent human perfection. The secret lay in the mathematical ratios that he understood to govern the growth of population and the production of food. Population, he said, increased geometrically, while food or agriculture could be increased only arithmetically. Thus, human population would increase by the following ratio: 1, 2, 4, 8, 16, 32, 64, 128, and so forth. Food, however, would increase thus: 1, 2, 3, 4, 5, 6, 7, 8. To many in this early age of science, and an age so eager to discover natural laws, the simple proof that Malthus offered seemed inescapable: There would never be enough food to feed the world's population.

To the question of what could be done about this situation, Malthus had little in the way of encouraging answers. In his day, there were no dependable methods of birth control (which was at any rate regarded as immoral), and abortion was illegal. The only natural limits to population growth appeared to lie in war, disease, and poverty. This depressing situation gave rise to attacks on Malthus and to his being called the Dismal Parson and to political economy becoming known as the Dismal Science. There were simply no checks on population that Malthus could find that did not come under the heading of either vice or misery. In the second edition in 1803, Malthus introduced the notion that a possible curb on population growth might rest in what he called "moral restraint," by which he meant the social responsibility to bear no more children than parents could properly maintain. Although the addition of moral restraint is the greatest change that Malthus made in his theory, the inherent weakness of this restriction, because it depends on individual control, is and was obvious.

Viciously attacked during his lifetime, Malthus and his ideas actually became even less popular in the second half of the nineteenth century. Marxists were particularly bitter in finding that Malthusian economics was merely a tool of the capitalist society to keep the poor oppressed. Humanitarians found the theory hard-hearted and mean-spirited and rejected it vigorously. More important, the mathematical analysis employed by Malthus simply did not withstand rigorous scrutiny. Food, critics observed, was organic, and thus it also increased geometrically. Additionally, technological advances made in agriculture seemed almost to eliminate hunger. By 1900, Malthus was generally dismissed as a pseudoscientist who had leaped to a gross generalization. The only school of thought that continued to embrace Malthus was that of some social Darwinists (and, indeed, Charles Darwin had been influenced by Malthus) who found the population theory acceptable in the light of their emphasis on the struggle for survival.

In the twentieth century, however, Malthus emerged as an important symbol in a concept known as neo-Malthusianism. Ironically, this movement advocated birth control, which Malthus opposed as immoral. Nevertheless, after World War II it became apparent that in many areas of the world, particularly in underdeveloped countries, population was growing at an alarming rate. As the prospect, and often the reality, of famine loomed in Africa and Asia, calls for government-sponsored birth control programs mounted. Some attempts were made in India and China. The problem, however, continues, as does the image of Malthus in this monumentally important issue.

SIGNIFICANCE

Whatever the flaws of his analysis, Thomas Robert Malthus must be regarded as the founder of demographic studies. In addition, he was an important and influential figure in the development of early nineteenth century economic thought. His influence on Darwin was certainly of enormous importance, as was his work on the diminishing returns of agricultural production. The Malthusian legacy is most evident in the continued use and misuse of his name, which has become synonymous with population studies and the population problem.

—*Roy Talbert, Jr.*

FURTHER READING

Avery, John. *Progress, Poverty, and Population: Rereading Condorcet, Godwin and Malthus.* London: Frank Cass, 1997. Traces the history of the debate during the late eighteenth and early nineteenth centuries between utopian optimists, such as Condorcet and Godwin, and pessimists, such as Malthus, about the effects of population growth upon society.

Dupaquier, Jacques, et al., eds. *Malthus Past and Present.* New York: Academic Press, 1983. A selection of papers presented in 1980 at the International Conference on Historical Demography. Contains useful information on the influences on Malthus, the conditions of his time, and the neo-Malthusian movement.

Elwell, Frank W. *A Commentary on Malthus's 1798 Essay on Population as Social Theory.* Lewiston, N.Y.: Edwin Mellen Press, 2001. An analysis of the essay that seeks to eliminate some of the dogma and misinterpretation surrounding Malthus's theories and present his ideas with more subtlety and complexity. Includes a reprint of the original essay.

James, Patricia. *Population Malthus: His Life and Times.* London: Routledge & Kegan Paul, 1979. An excellent biography.

Meek, Ronald L., ed. *Marx and Engles on Malthus: Selections from the Writings of Marx and Engles Dealing with the Theories of Thomas Robert Malthus.* London: Lawrence and Wishart, 1953. The Marxist condemnation of Malthus in the nineteenth century.

Petersen, William. *Malthus*. Cambridge, Mass.: Harvard University Press, 1979. Reprint. New Brunswick, N.J.: Transaction, 1999. An intellectual biography that properly sets the work of Malthus into the context of early nineteenth century thought.

Turner, Michael, ed. *Malthus and His Time*. London: Macmillan, 1986. Further selections, somewhat more technical, from the 1980 international conference on historical demography.

Wood, John Cunningham, ed. *Thomas Robert Malthus*. 4 vols. London: Croom Helm, 1986. A detailed and quite helpful overview of the work and importance of Malthus, including selections from contemporary sources to the 1980's.

SEE ALSO: Charles Darwin; James Mill; Francis Place; David Ricardo.

RELATED ARTICLES in *Great Events from History: The Nineteenth Century, 1801-1900:* 1854-1862: Wallace's Expeditions Give Rise to Biogeography; November 24, 1859: Darwin Publishes *On the Origin of Species*; 1882: First Birth Control Clinic Opens in Amsterdam; 1883: Galton Defines "Eugenics."

ÉDOUARD MANET
French painter

In a relatively short career, Manet challenged the conventions of European art by creating a body of paintings, drawings, and etchings manifesting novel approaches both to form and to content. His works and his career were the focal points of the struggle for artistic independence waged by a generation of French artists and writers during the mid-nineteenth century.

BORN: January 23, 1832; Paris, France
DIED: April 30, 1883; Paris, France
AREA OF ACHIEVEMENT: Art

EARLY LIFE
Édouard Manet (mah-nay) was born in Paris at 5 rue de Grands Augustins, a street bordering the Seine, not far from the Cathedral of Nôtre Dame. His father, Auguste Manet, was a high official in the Ministry of Justice. At the time of Édouard's birth, his mother, Eugénie-Désirée Manet, was twenty years old, fourteen years her husband's junior. The family was prosperous from the beginning, and in keeping with its social status Eugénie Manet held twice-weekly receptions for the influential associates of her husband; Auguste, nevertheless, preferred the company of scholars and ecclesiastics to that of his colleagues.

From the ages of six to eight, Manet attended the Institut Poiloup in Vaugirard; in his twelfth year, he began studies at a boarding school, the Collège Rollin, where he befriended Antonin Proust, who later wrote about his childhood friend. During these school years, Manet and Proust frequently visited the Louvre, accompanied by the former's maternal uncle, Captain Édouard Fournier, who encouraged his nephew's interest in art by paying for drawing lessons.

Though Édouard excelled at drawing and soon expressed his wish to follow an artistic career, Auguste Manet's ambition for his eldest son was that he become a lawyer (Édouard's brothers, Eugène and Gustave, born in 1833 and 1835, were to become civil servants). Because his teachers at the Collège Rollin had found him "distracted" and "slightly frivolous," in July, 1848, Auguste Manet proposed a compromise in which Édouard would apply to the École Navale, or naval school. Failing the entrance examination, he embarked on a training ship instead, sailing on December 8 for Rio de Janeiro, Brazil. He is reported to have found the cruise boring; after his return to France in June, 1849, having again failed the entrance examination, he was finally allowed to study for an artistic career. By January of 1850, he had registered as an art student to copy paintings in the Louvre, and in September he and Antonin Proust joined the studio of Thomas Couture, a noted painter of innovative, though not revolutionary, sympathies.

Soon after his return from the sea voyage, Édouard and his brother Eugène began to take piano lessons from a young Dutch woman, Suzanne Leenhoff. It seems clear that his association with Suzanne quickly blossomed into love, and when she became pregnant in the spring of 1851, Manet, who was still required to obtain his father's permission to go out at night, succeeded in keeping his liaison a secret from him. The child born to Suzanne Leenhoff was registered as the son of a probably fictitious Koëlla but was presented socially as Suzanne's younger brother, Léon. It was not until 1863, more than a year after the death of Auguste Manet, that Suzanne Leenhoff and Manet were married.

Living in his parents' home, and with their financial support for his study of art, Manet continued working at the studio of Couture during the early 1850's. His relationship with his teacher was frequently stormy, and Manet acquired a reputation as a rebellious pupil, but Couture was in many ways a good choice of teacher. He represented a middle ground between the academic side of French art, with its often-rigid adherence to tradition, and the experimental, individualistic tendencies of artists such as Honoré Daumier and Gustave Courbet. Manet was, by nature, a somewhat conservative personality—he was always well dressed, even fashionable, and he enjoyed the civil pleasures of bourgeois life—but as an artist he challenged from the outset many of the conventions of painting, even as he learned from the masters of the past.

LIFE'S WORK

After leaving Couture's studio in 1856, Manet occasionally brought his works to the master for criticism, a circumstance that must have been more than a polite gesture. Manet's interest in tradition was profound, but his studies of the past were undertaken to achieve a personal understanding of the old masters rather than to emulate their styles. Like many young Parisian artists, Manet often copied paintings in the Louvre and elsewhere. He was particularly attracted to Spanish masters such as Diego Velázquez but also copied works by Peter Paul Rubens and Eugène Delacroix, from whom he personally requested permission to copy *The Barque of Dante*.

Equally important for Manet's future as an artist, however, was his devotion to recording the life of the Paris boulevards, where he daily observed the activities of all levels of society. Despite his comfortable family background, Manet had an instinctive appreciation for the urban poor, and in 1859 he submitted his painting *The Absinthe Drinker* to the Salon, a biennial exhibition of art that was judged by the established painters of the day. *The Absinthe Drinker* is based in part upon Manet's observation of a ragpicker named Collardet, part of a legion of characters who were increasingly visible as a result of the redevelopment of Paris begun in 1853 under the direction of Baron Eugène Hausmann. Although such a subject was considered appropriate for the popular press, it was thought too vulgar for the Salon, and Manet's painting was rejected. In 1861, however, two of his works were accepted into the exhibition; one

Édouard Manet.

of them, *The Spanish Singer*, received an honorable mention.

At this time in his career, Manet's art had been noticed appreciatively by a few knowledgeable critics, but his audience was comparatively small. An event in 1863 changed not only Manet's relationship to the public but also that of a generation of French artists. This was the Salon des Refusés, an exhibition held by order of Emperor Napoleon III, which was to include all of the work rejected by the jury from the regular Salon of 1863. The emperor's decree invited the public to be the final judge of the quality of the art rejected, and the public responded with tumultuous curiosity and derision.

Manet's principal submission, *Déjeuner sur l'herbe* (luncheon on the grass), while appreciated by a discerning few, was taken by many visitors to the exhibition to be the flagship of artistic revolt. The work shows a nude woman with two fashionably dressed men in a modern parklike setting, and although the painting is based upon various historical prototypes, its broad, painterly technique and contemporary setting seem intended to challenge the public's artistic taste and its moral standards. *Déjeuner sur l'herbe* marks the beginning of a widespread but often-hostile interest in the dissident claims of modern art; the polarization of the art world into "academics" and the "avant-garde" had begun.

In Manet's paintings of the early 1860's, one sees the influence of his friend the poet Charles Baudelaire. In an essay written years earlier, Baudelaire had called for an art based upon "the heroism of modern life" that would show "how great and how poetic we are with our neckties and our varnished boots." Manet's emphasis on clothes, costume, fashion, and other aspects of everyday life, rather than giving a trivial view of society, shows urban life as a complex network of signs that require a skilled interpreter. The emergence of the city as the fulcrum of modern culture is one of the implicit themes of Manet's art, though this is seen more often in his graphic works than in his paintings.

Manet caused another public outcry at the Salon of 1865 with his *Olympia*, which depicts a nude courtesan, attended by a black servant and a cat, looking impudently toward the viewer. One critic advised that "women on the point of giving birth and proper young girls would be well-advised to flee this spectacle," and two guards were stationed by the painting, which had already been removed to an obscure and dishonorable location within the immense exhibition. The audacity of *Olympia* far outdistanced that of *Déjeuner sur l'herbe*, and in addition to suffering criticism on account of the theme, Manet came under attack for the structure and technique of the painting. Courbet said that it looked flat, like a playing card, and a newspaper critic accused Manet of "an almost childish ignorance of the fundamentals of drawing."

It is clear that Manet, though not systematically courting the disfavor of the public, was willing to suffer incomprehension both of his treatment of subjects and of his style. He was fully capable of painting appealing subjects in a more traditional manner, but for complex reasons he ruled out forms of compromise that might have gained for him a higher level of public esteem. He subsequently painted popular pictures, such as *The Good Glass of Beer* (1873), and though he wished for broad acceptance of his art he was never inclined to pursue it.

In many of his works of the 1870's Manet sought an increasing naturalism by emphasizing lighter colors and more varied surfaces. In paintings made in 1874 at Argenteuil, a few miles northwest of Paris, Manet drew close to the group that became known that year as the Impressionists. He borrowed the light and color of his younger friends Claude Monet and Pierre-Auguste Renoir, but his canvases are more deliberately composed and are much less extraverted than theirs of the same period. Some critics who had been sympathetic to Manet's work, including the novelist Émile Zola, considered Manet's technical gifts unequal to his ambition of painting in the open air; others recognized that these works were, in part, the result of exacting formal experimentation. In a famous remark made in 1890, the painter Maurice Denis asserted that

> a painting—before it is a battle horse, a nude woman, or some anecdote—is essentially a flat surface covered with colors assembled in a certain order.

To a significant extent, Manet's work of the 1870's is a precocious fulfillment of this concept, particularly in a work such as *The Rue Mosnier with Pavers* (1878), which brings the spontaneous brushwork, subtle coloration, light, and movement of the Argenteuil paintings back to the streets of Paris. Manet had by this time developed fully a means of drawing with strokes of paint that both represents objects in space and unifies the painting as an assemblage of shapes and colors.

In late 1878, Manet began to have trouble with his leg, and by September of the following year he was seeking treatment for it. The precise nature of his ailment has never been specified, but it seems likely that he was suffering from the advanced stages of a syphilitic infection contracted in his youth. During his last three years, he was in pain, and small drawings and oil paintings began to take the place of larger works, reflecting his diminished mobility.

There are a number of fine portraits and still lifes dating from 1880 through 1882, and there is also one major subject painting, *A Bar at the Folies-Bergère*. This work, which is about three feet high by four feet wide, is widely considered to be one of Manet's finest works. It shows a barmaid at the celebrated Paris "café-concert," standing behind a marble counter on which have been placed bottles of ale and champagne, a compote with mandarin oranges, and a glass holding two pale roses. Behind the melancholy and distracted young woman, a mirror reflects a brightly lit crowd that seems unaware of a trapeze artist whose green-slippered feet are whimsically shown in the upper left-hand corner of the painting. There are many subtle, calculated ambiguities concerning things viewed either directly or in reflection.

Manet seems to have decided, at the end of an artistic career often criticized for a lack of psychological insight, to address the human element in one final, haunting but luminous canvas. In early April, 1883, as Manet's health precipitously declined, he briefly considered taking lessons in miniature painting from a friend, but by April 20 his condition required that his left leg be amputated, and on April 30 he died.

SIGNIFICANCE

Édouard Manet has been celebrated as a rebellious artist who was rejected by his own time; however, such a stereotyping of his career ignores not only the complexities of his personality and artistic production but also the varieties of response that his work elicited from his contemporaries and from the generation that followed. For years, many critics and art historians fostered the notion of a noble, progressive lineage of art that was engaged in perpetual conflict with a defensive, static "establishment" art supported by reactionary social forces; Manet, quite understandably, was installed as the great progenitor of the progressive trend. As the discipline of art history established a broader foundation of fact and methodology during the first half of the twentieth century and the issues of mid- and late-nineteenth century art became both clearer and more intricate, the assessment of Manet's achievement in particular came to be seen more as a problem in defining the changing relationship of artists and audiences than of arriving at objectively valid, stabilized conclusions about his paintings.

Manet was somewhat conservative by temperament, but he was also creatively independent. Though many of his images involved adaptations of ideas and images borrowed from the past, and thus appealed to aspects of public taste, other elements of his work were vibrantly novel and challenged both the visual imagination and social consciousness of his contemporaries. These contrasting elements in Manet dictated that he could not rely on conventional taste to provide him with a constituency; his success was one that might be earned only by tremendous labor and courage. Finally, it was a largely posthumous success.

In his later career, Manet frequently despaired at the inconsistency with which his work was received, believing, perhaps somewhat naïvely, that it should suffice for an artist to present sincere work. Like many of his contemporaries, he hoped that the public would be able to recognize and value sincerity and commitment and would reward it at least as strongly as virtuosity and predictability. In hoping for this kind of relationship with an ever-expanding mass audience, Manet presents to history a modernity of outlook in keeping with the adventurousness of his finest paintings.

—C. S. McConnell

FURTHER READING

Adler, Kathleen. *Manet*. Oxford, England: Phaidon Press, 1986. An excellent source of collateral illustrations concerning Manet's life and times, as well as his art and its sources. The text emphasizes the eclectic nature of the artist's work and provides an integrated view of modern scholarship concerned with Manet's place in nineteenth century art.

Bataille, Georges. *Manet*. New York: Rizzoli, 1983. Françoise Cachin, in her introduction to this reprinting of Bataille's 1955 essay, shows how the author's view of Manet was colored by his close association with the artistic trends of his own time. Nevertheless, she concedes, Bataille's essay has "unusual penetration and appeal."

Blunden, Maria, and Godrey Blunden. *Impressionists and Impressionism*. New York: Rizzoli, 1977. Manet is accorded only his share of attention in this survey volume, but contemporary photographs and documents, many of which are seldom reproduced, vividly reveal Manet and his contemporaries. Text and images are presented in a loosely integrated but nevertheless effective manner.

Cachin, Françoise, et al. *Manet: 1832-1883*. New York: Metropolitan Museum of Art, 1983. This large, indispensable volume was issued in connection with a major international exhibition organized to commemorate the one hundredth anniversary of the painter's death. There are several fine essays, and the book is illustrated with hundreds of exemplary color and black-and-white plates, most of which are discussed in some detail by accompanying text.

Fried, Michael. *Manet's Modernism: Or, The Face of Painting in the 1860's*. Chicago: University of Chicago Press, 1996. Fried seeks to provide a more accurate idea of Manet's place in art history by describing how Manet's art was received by his contemporaries.

Mauner, George. *Manet, Peintre-Philosophe: A Study of the Painter's Themes*. University Park: Pennsylvania State University Press, 1975. The author is one of many who have sought to provide a corrective to a once-prevalent view of Manet as a painter obsessed with structural matters and indifferent to meaning; his scholarly arguments are involved but clearly stated. The lack of color plates does not diminish the book's interest.

Rewald, John. *The History of Impressionism*. New York: Museum of Modern Art, 1946. Rev. ed. 1973. This masterly chronological study of the Impressionists does full justice to nine artists in addition to Manet, but Manet's art is unquestionably the author's touchstone. There is an excellent annotated calendar covering the years 1855-1886, as well as an extensive bibliography and an index.

Schneider, Pierre. *The World of Manet, 1832-1883*. New York: Time-Life Books, 1968. The popular format of this book should not be allowed to obscure the fact that it contains a wealth of information. The quality and variety of its reproductions are matched by an intelligent, readable text.

Sloane, Joseph C. "Manet." In *French Painting Between the Past and the Present: Artists, Critics, and Traditions from 1848 to 1870*. Princeton, N.J.: Princeton University Press, 1973. The author's emphasis is upon the reaction of critics and the public to Manet's paintings of the 1860's, and he shows why the artist's innovations were met with resistance. The text as well as an excellent bibliography is unrevised from the original 1951 edition.

Tucker, Paul Hayes, ed. *Manet's "Le Déjeuner Sur L'Herbe."* New York: Cambridge University Press, 1998. Essays offering various interpretations of one of Manet's best-known paintings.

Wadley, Nicholas. *Manet*. London: Paul Hamlyn, 1967. This survey of the artist's paintings is valuable principally for its good color plates, which are briefly annotated. A modest essay is complemented by a chronology and extensive quotations from Manet and his contemporaries.

SEE ALSO: Charles Baudelaire; Mary Cassatt; Paul Cézanne; Gustave Courbet; Edgar Degas; Eugène Delacroix; Napoleon III; Pierre-Auguste Renoir; Émile Zola.

RELATED ARTICLES in *Great Events from History: The Nineteenth Century, 1801-1900:* March, 1814: Goya Paints *Third of May 1808: Execution of the Citizens of Madrid*; May 15, 1863: Paris's Salon des Refusés Opens; April 15, 1874: First Impressionist Exhibition.

MERI TE TAI MANGAKAHIA
New Zealand suffragist

Though details of her life are little known, Mangakahia is an iconoic figure in women's rights in New Zealand, where she voiced the demands of Maori women to vote and run for office. Her political involvement and writings expressed Maori women's interest in land and government reforms to improve conditions for Maoris in New Zealand.

BORN: May 22, 1868; Whakarapa, New Zealand
DIED: October 10, 1920; Panguru, New Zealand
AREAS OF ACHIEVEMENT: Women's rights, government and politics

EARLY LIFE
Meri Te Tai Mangakahia (MEH-dih Teh Tie MAH-nuh-KUH-Hih-Uh) was born near Hokianga Harbour on New Zealand's North Island. Maori kinsmen respected her father, Re Te Tai, who later served as tribal chief of Te Rarawa in the Hokianga district. Mangakahia's mother, Hana Tera, had been previously married. Mangakahia was her first child with Re Te Tai.

Few records exist to document Mangakahia's childhood. However, her experiences were probably typical of those of most nineteenth century Maori children. In the primarily rural society in which she lived, Maori elders would have expected her to perform chores to help members of her immediate and extended families and her community. Maoris honored the connections among the descendants of the first Polynesians who settled New Zealand. They identified their tribes (*iwi*) by their immigrant ancestors' names. Maori tribes sometimes fought one another, but they also resolved differences in social gatherings and made alliances in legal matters. Most male Maoris revered women, including them in community decisions and respecting their authority.

As a child, Mangakahia probably was aware of her people's history and the land conflicts between Maoris and British settlers. When Europeans, whom the Maori called Pâkehâ, began settling New Zealand during the early nineteenth century, they wanted to buy Maori lands. In 1840, Maoris, including women, and Pâkehâ signed the Treaty of Waitangi. The treaty made them British subjects, recognized their independence, and assured them that their lands were secure. However, imprecise translations of the treaty later caused misinterpretations.

The 1852 New Zealand Constitution Act allowed male property owners of all ethnicities to vote for members of the colonial legislature. The expanding Pâkehâ population provoked conflicts when settlers seized Maori land. Maori men and women fought in Land Wars. The 1865 Native Land Act provided a forum, the Native Land Court, for Maoris, including women, to make legal claims to confiscated lands. The court oversaw land sales and leases. Maoris petitioned the British government to honor the 1840 treaty and improve land legislation by allowing them to serve in the colonial legislature. The 1867 Maori Representation Act created four Maori parliamentary positions for men only.

The Maori population dropped from more than 100,000 people in 1840 to approximately 43,000 people during the 1890's. European settlers, who numbered 625,500 in 1890, encouraged assimilation. Many Maoris accepted some European practices, especially educational opportunities. Assured free schooling, Maori students learned about government protocol, which helped tribal land petitions. Mangakahia, who was growing up through this period, attended school at Auckland's St. Mary's Convent.

LIFE'S WORK
During the early 1890's, Mangakahia married a widower named Hamiora Mangakahia, who had already been married twice. She then lived with her husband on a property that he owned at Whangapoua on the North Island's Coromandel Peninsula. Mangakahia tended her husband's children and gave birth to four more of her own.

Mangakahia's marriage gave her entry in Maori political forums. Her husband had served as an assessor in the Native Land Court and was active in politics, dedicating his career to protecting Maori lands. Frustrated by unchanging and restrictive British land policies and inadequate representation in parliament, Maori tribal representatives, including Mangakahia's husband, established a separate Maori parliament in 1892 to achieve self-determination and demand promised treaty rights. They named their autonomous government Te Kotahitanga (union). Representatives selected Mangakahia's husband as the parliament's first premier. British law required the transfer of married women's land to their husbands, but Mangakahia and most Maori women wanted to regain control of property rights and have a voice in political decisions. They supported Te Kotahitanga in addition to woman suffrage efforts and the Woman's Christian Temperance Union.

Mangakahia traveled to Waipatu on Hawke's Bay with her husband for the 1893 meeting of Te Kotahi-

tanga. Probably because of the official status of Mangakahia's husband, other women attending the meeting asked her to represent them. On May 18, 1893, she gave the women's petition to the speaker of Te Kotahitanga's lower house, asking him to request representatives to consider allowing women to vote for future assembly members. Mangakahia then became the first woman to speak before the Maori parliament when she was asked to elaborate on the contents of the petition.

During her speech, Mangakahia boldly demanded that Maori women be given both voting rights for and the right to become members of parliament. Her demands went beyond those of other contemporary suffragists in New Zealand and internationally. Mangakahia asserted that Maori women deserved to have those rights because they owned, inherited, and managed property according to long-established Maori customs, and they also paid land taxes. She argued that many women were more capable land managers than men. She also recommended that if women were to appeal Maori land issues to Great Britain's Queen Victoria, the queen—as a woman— might be more receptive to the appeal than she would be to male chiefs.

Representatives at the meeting liked Mangakahia's speech, but Akenehi Tomoana, whose husband, Henare Tomoana, was a political rival, pressured the group to delay action. Mangakahia argued that the group's first priority should be to secure parliamentary recognition of Te Kotahitanga and not women's rights. The male representatives postponed discussion at that conference, despite promises to consider Mangahakia's proposals, which were recorded in the proceedings of the Maori parliament. Individual Maori tribes selected women to address the parliament at later sessions.

While women were becoming increasingly involved in the Maori parliament, New Zealand's official parliament still forbade women even to speak in its sessions. That situation suddenly changed in September, 1893, when the governor granted all New Zealand women voting rights. Maori women became able to vote on either Maori rolls or European rolls, if they owned property worth specified amounts. Maori women then began establishing committees to discuss such social and political issues as alcoholism, marital abuse, and the preservation of Maori women's skills and traditions. Te Kotahitanga finally approved Mangakahia's ideas in 1897.

Details about Mangakahia's life after she addressed Te Kotahitanga in 1893 are vague. She probably accompanied her husband as he pursued political activities and belonged to women's committees to discuss Maori and national politics and raise money for parliamentary expenses. Mangakahia edited the women's column in the newspaper *Te Tiupiri* (the jubilee) with Niniwa i te Rangi, the Maori parliament's record keeper. They encouraged women representing all the Maori tribes to interact and communicate ideas about individual and community concerns. Mangakahia discussed women's issues and sought tolerance and equality for both Maoris and women generally. Voting records for the 1919 election include her name, but she probably voted prior to that.

Mangakahia supported her husband when he endured the false accusations of political foes that he mishandled parliamentary funds. He continued to attend meetings despite those conflicts and the fact that his poor health confined him to a wheelchair. On June 4, 1918, he died at Whangapoua. As his estate executor and trustee, Mangakahia was permitted to reside on the Whangapoua property that her children inherited. Instead, she moved to live with relatives on family property at Panguru near her birthplace. After suffering from severe influenza, she died there on October 10, 1920.

SIGNIFICANCE

Mangakahia spoke on behalf of most Maori women when she demanded the right to vote and choose political representation. Her efforts mobilized women to seek control of their lives and form groups to achieve social improvement. She rallied Maoris to persevere despite intimidation and discouragement and inspired and unified women in her generation and its successors.

In 1919, New Zealand's parliament passed the Women's Parliamentary Rights Act, which made all New Zealand women eligible for election to the national parliament. Finally, in 1935, a Maori woman named Rehutai Maihi campaigned to represent the Northern Maori district; however, she lost because Maori elders were unsupportive of women politicians. In 1949, Iriaka Ratana won the Western Maori position and served in parliament for twenty years. Increasing numbers of Maori women obtained employment in parliamentary and governmental positions, and political activists have studied Mangakahia's ideas and tactics to resolve modern issues.

Mangakahia's leadership secured respect from both Maori and white suffragists. During the 1993 New Zealand woman suffrage centennial, Mangakahia was included with other suffrage pioneers in the bronze Kate Sheppard National Memorial to woman suffrage dedicated at Christchurch. At the 2003 Suffrage Day, speakers praised Mangakahia, stressing how she had influenced the success of 1893 suffrage legislation for all New Zealand women.

—Elizabeth D. Schafer

FURTHER READING

Ballara, Angela. "*Wahine Rangatira:* Maori Women of Rank and Their Role in the Women's *Kotahitanga* Movement of the 1890's." *New Zealand Journal of History* 27, no. 2 (October, 1993): 127-139. Discusses differences between the motivations of Maori and European suffragists—their motivations, methods, and political aspirations.

Brooking, Tom. *The History of New Zealand.* Westport, Conn.: Greenwood Press, 2004. Useful history that balances information about Maoris and Europeans, examining land and suffrage topics.

Grimshaw, Patricia. *Women's Suffrage in New Zealand.* 2d ed. Auckland, New Zealand: Auckland University Press, 1987. Comprehensive account that describes the contributions of Maori women to achieve voting rights for both Maoris and all women in New Zealand.

Macdonald, Carolyn, Merimeri Penfold, and Bridget Williams, eds. *The Book of New Zealand Women.* Wellington, New Zealand: Bridget Williams Books, 1991. Profiles Mangakahia and other notable Maori women and suffragists. Includes a reproducton of the page from the parliamentary proceedings of her speech in Maori.

Rei, Tania. *Māori Women and the Vote.* Wellington, New Zealand: Huia Publishers, 1993. Excellent overview of Maori women's political activity published for the suffrage centennial. Features Mangakahia's portrait on the cover.

Walker, Ranginui. *Struggle Without End (Ka whawhai tonu matou).* Rev. ed. Auckland, New Zealand: Penguin, 2004. A Maori history of New Zealand, stressing the Maoris' ongoing efforts to maintain secure political rights and protect their distinct cultural identity.

Williams, John A. *Politics of the New Zealand Maori: Protest and Cooperation, 1891-1909.* Seattle: University of Washington Press, 1969. Examines the political leadership of Mangkahari's husband, especially his efforts to protect Maori lands.

SEE ALSO: Sir George Grey; Richard John Seddon; Queen Victoria; Sir Julius Vogel.

RELATED ARTICLE in *Great Events from History: The Nineteenth Century, 1801-1900:* September 19, 1893: New Zealand Women Win Voting Rights.

HORACE MANN
American educator

As a legislator and educator, Mann initiated the first state mental hospital and the first comprehensive system of public education in the United States.

BORN: May 4, 1796; Franklin, Massachusetts
DIED: August 2, 1859; Yellow Springs, Ohio
AREAS OF ACHIEVEMENT: Education, government and politics

EARLY LIFE

Horace Mann was the fourth of five children of Thomas Mann, a farmer in Franklin, Massachusetts, and the former Rebecca Stanley of nearby Attleboro. Mann traced his American roots, on his father's side, back to William Man, who came to Massachusetts Bay Colony in 1635. None of his ancestors achieved any distinction before him. When he later looked back on his youth, he could not remember a time when he and the family did not work together planting, cultivating, and harvesting. As Franklin became a center of bonnet-making, Mann braided straw for women's bonnets. He would later believe strongly in the value of work and would work hard all his life. However, he would also come to believe that he had been made to work too hard in childhood.

At twelve years of age, Mann rejected the Calvinism of his town's ministers and began to construct for himself a more benevolent interpretation of Christianity by which to live. He was also critical of the teachers in Franklin's one-room schools, although up to the age of fifteen, he never attended school for more than eight or ten weeks out of the year. As the town library held few books, none suitable for children, opportunities for self-education were also severely limited.

Aspiring to a college education, Mann received tutoring from a minister who happened to be a Brown University graduate. Like a number of other boys from his area, Mann enrolled in Brown, where he excelled in composition and oratory and was graduated in 1819 at the head of his class. Thereupon he studied law in Litchfield, Connecticut, and after an apprenticeship in Dedham, Massachusetts, he was admitted to practice there in 1825. Thus, at the age of twenty-nine, this industrious young man had yet to establish himself in his profession.

LIFE'S WORK

Prophetically, the event that brought Mann into prominence locally was a speech that marked a patriotic occasion involving three famous political figures. When Presidents John Adams and Thomas Jefferson both died on the fiftieth anniversary of the signing of the Declaration of Independence, Dedham chose Mann to speak at a memorial service, and among his listeners was President John Quincy Adams. Then as later, the eloquence of this tall, intense lawyer commanded the attention of all who valued the art of public speaking.

Mann's law practice blossomed after this 1826 speech, and in 1827 his district sent him to the Massachusetts House of Representatives, where he worked vigorously for the establishment of railroads and the industrialization of his region. His penchant for reform emerged in his efforts in behalf of the temperance movement, but seeing the issue as a social rather than specifically religious one, he rejected the sectarian bias of those who dominated the movement. Nevertheless, his bill to restrict the licensing of liquor vendors became law in 1831.

Mann's interest in institutional reform dated from his inspection of the Dedham House of Correction in 1828, where he found appalling conditions, especially among mentally disturbed inmates. He began immediately to collect information on the insane confined in county jails throughout Massachusetts and proposed the establishment of a state facility to care humanely for these forgotten people, many of whom he correctly surmised would be able to return to society. He struggled personally with the difficult problem of an architectural design adequate to solve the problems of noise, sanitation, and security. The result was the State Lunatic Hospital at Worcester, which opened early in 1833.

These projects coincided with his courtship of Charlotte Messer, their marriage in 1830, and her death less than two years later. Crushed by this personal tragedy, Mann withdrew from politics and reform activities for a time, but in 1834, encouraged by friends, including Elizabeth and Mary Peabody, he campaigned successfully for a seat in the Massachusetts senate. In his second one-year term, he was elected its president and used his power to promote various reforms. This gray-haired and gaunt but energetic legislator found his cause of causes in the plight of the Massachusetts common schools, poorly funded and, in many communities, nonexistent. After Governor Edward Everett and the legislature cooperated to establish a state board of education in 1837, a governor's committee, realizing the importance of forceful leadership at the outset, chose Mann as its first secretary.

Knowing little about education, Mann pored over the relatively few books available on the subject. Convinced that "in a republic ignorance is a crime," Mann found too few resources available to dispel it in 1837, a year of nationwide financial panic. Available town reports informed him that schools were regularly small, shabby, and crowded, teachers unprepared and underpaid, and parents skeptical of the utility of public education. Many young teachers—Henry David Thoreau in Concord and Herman Melville in Pittsfield among them—soon quit in disgust.

Although he might have retained his senate seat, Mann judged his new task a full-time one and declined candidacy in the fall of 1837. He consulted with friends such as Samuel Gridley Howe, first director of the school eventually to be known as the Perkins Institute for the Blind, and William Ellery Channing, Unitarian minister and friend of reformers; he visited schools, gathering, organizing, and interpreting data from around the state; and on January 1, 1838, delivered the first of his twelve famous *Annual Reports* (1838-1849) to the Board of Education.

Over the next twelve years, Mann promoted the establishment of normal schools for the training of teachers, organized teachers' conventions at which he and other educators lectured, established the *Common School Journal*, urged more systematic curricula, largely overcame public apathy and suspicion, and began the task of extending educational opportunity to agrarian families and to the children of poor laborers in the mushrooming manufacturing towns. Throughout his stewardship, controversy swirled around Secretary Mann. Independent New Englanders balked at the idea of imposing an educational system too closely resembling the highly systematic Prussian model that attracted Mann and his supporters, who considered some degree of centralization of educational authority and standardization of school curricula, methods, and administrative procedures essential to progress. Not the least controversial of Mann's proposals was mandatory full-time schooling for all children up to the age of sixteen—not necessarily in common schools but to the state's satisfaction.

In the midst of these duties, Mann married Mary Peabody, a quiet but strong-willed woman who had long loved the now middle-aged reformer. She bore him three sons and shared his enthusiasms. After the death of John Quincy Adams in February of 1848, the Whigs nominated Mann for the former president's seat in the U.S. House of Representatives. Elected in April of that year, Mann quickly established himself as an uncompromising foe of slavery. Thus, when Daniel Webster supported

Henry Clay's Compromise of 1850, Mann broke with Webster, and the latter's forces retaliated by blocking Mann's renomination later that year. Despite this setback, Mann was returned to Congress as the nominee of the Free-Soil Party.

Two years later, the founders of a new college in Yellow Springs, Ohio, sought Mann as its first president even as the Massachusetts Free-Soilers were nominating him for governor. When Mann's hoped-for coalition of antislavery Whigs, Democrats, and Free-Soilers fell short of victory, Mann accepted the presidency of the new Antioch College. Established by a Protestant sect called "the Christian Connexion," which Mann judged sufficiently liberal in its tenets, Antioch also pleased him with its then rare commitment to coeducation. However, the college was soon reeling under the sort of sectarian wrangling that its new chief officer had always tried to avoid. In addition, Mann sent out confusing signals with his strict disciplinary code and aversion to the conservative theology so often associated with it. His lack of financial experience also hampered him. Contemporaneously with Antioch's first graduation in 1857—another panic year—the trustees were forced to declare bankruptcy.

Mann was now in his early sixties, tall and dignified, with an abundant shock of gray hair, his eyes deep-set under bushy brows, his wide mouth set in the determined way he had always displayed in a crisis. Two years later, a group of Mann's friends purchased the college and restored it to solvency. The years in Yellow Springs had taken a terrible toll on Mann physically, however, and he had little vitality left. The ill president retained his oratorical gift to the last; his last speech, at the 1859 baccalaureate services, proved to be one of his best, ending with the admonition to the graduates: "Be ashamed to die until you have won some victory for humanity." He died only a little more than a month later, on August 2, 1859.

SIGNIFICANCE

Had Horace Mann never turned his considerable talents to education at all, he would still rank as a notable American. His work on behalf of the mentally ill alone represents a victory for humanity, as the institutions all over the United States now usually designated "state hospitals" make clear. At a time when only occasional private philanthropy stood between the mentally disturbed and a life of unbroken degradation and captivity, Mann made their cause public business and a matter of public conscience.

Among the few in his age to understand the importance of conducting social reform on a nonsectarian basis, Mann often risked the opposition of fellow reformers by refusing to allow religious denominations to capture and dominate the causes they shared. His uncompromising attitude was both a strength and a weakness. When he managed to sweep aside obstacles to reform, as in the areas of public education and mental health, he effected great changes in a short time. On other occasions, by alienating possible supporters and rousing the active hostility of opponents, he did his causes little good.

A measure of Mann's educational influence is the extent to which his controversial ideas have become conventional wisdom. Mann, more than any other single person, is responsible for bringing Massachusetts, and in turn the nation, to acknowledge the importance of providing public education for all mentally competent citizens. Also considered radical when he proposed it was the concomitant idea that the state might require schooling for youths up to the age of sixteen. His measures to improve the profession of teaching—the normal schools, conferences, the *Common School Journal*, and many others—enormously increased the status and effectiveness of teachers.

Mann moved adroitly between legislative and professional educational positions. Resigning a post of political sway for a thankless job as secretary of a new state board with little support among the powerful, he succeeded by the unlikely method of writing a series of annual reports to his superiors. Again, late in his career, he gave up politics to devote himself to a troubled fledgling college, and although his health broke under the strain, he brought Antioch to the point where it could survive and take its place among the more respected American colleges.

Trained in the oratorical mode considered vital to political success during the early decades of the republic, Mann used his eloquence not to extend his personal prestige but to bring about humanitarian reforms. He renounced the career of political leadership for which he was so obviously qualified to foster the education of people both rich and poor, male and female, black and white, at levels from elementary school to college. He could afford to yield power because of a gift he manifested most strikingly when, as in his years as a school board secretary, his power was most circumscribed: a capacity for moral leadership that he invariably exercised to increase the well-being of his fellow citizens.

—*Robert P. Ellis*

FURTHER READING

Downs, Robert B. *Horace Mann: Champion of Public Schools*. Boston: Twayne, 1974. A biography empha-

sizing Mann's educational ideas and their influence. This short work is essentially uncritical and relies chiefly upon secondary sources.

Gibbon, Peter H. "A Hero of Education." *Education Week* 21, no. 38 (May 29, 2002): 33. A profile of Mann, containing information about his life and career, his opinions of education, character, and citizenship, and his campaign to improve public schools.

Gutek, Gerald L. *Historical and Philosophical Foundations of Education: A Biographical Introduction*. Upper Saddle River, N.J.: Merrill, 1997. This historical overview of education includes a biography of Mann, examining his philosophy and impact upon education.

Hinsdale, Burke Aaron. *Horace Mann and the Common School Revival in the United States*. New York: Charles Scribner's Sons, 1898, 1937. This relatively detailed study gives a turn-of-the-century perspective on Mann.

Hubbell, George Allen. *Horace Mann, Educator, Patriot, and Reformer: A Study in Leadership*. Philadelphia: William F. Fell, 1910. Hubbell was an Antioch College professor who wrote many articles on Mann. As its title suggests, the book is more appreciative than critical, but Hubbell knew his subject better than all but two or three of Mann's biographers.

Mann, Mary Tyler Peabody. *Life of Horace Mann*. Boston: Walker, Fuller, 1865. Reprint. Miami: Mnemosyne, 1969. Mann's widow occasionally depicts scenes, such as that of his death, which go beyond the scope of any other Mann biographer, but this work (which is perhaps the second most valuable of the books on Mann) deserves particular notice for its generous selections from his letters and journals.

Messerli, Jonathan. *Horace Mann: A Biography*. New York: Alfred A. Knopf, 1972. An educator himself, Messerli is most interested in his subject's educational reforms, but this book is the longest, most thorough, and most painstakingly documented work on Mann. As such, it must be regarded as the standard biography, although it does have some drawbacks. Its full index is idiosyncratically organized (especially the ten pages of "Mann, Horace" entries) and difficult to use. Messerli seldom attempts to generalize, to fuse his welter of detail into an interpretive whole. His style, however, is clear and entirely serviceable.

Morgan, Joy Elmer. *Horace Mann at Antioch*. Washington, D.C.: National Education Association, 1938. A lengthy labor of love by a Mann enthusiast, this work is only partly biographical, the rest being Morgan's compilation of tributes, Mann's Antioch speeches, and some other material of interest only to devotees of the college.

Tharp, Louise Hall. *Until Victory: Horace Mann and Mary Peabody*. Boston: Little, Brown, 1953. Readers seeking an intimate view of two kindred spirits will enjoy this book. Although Tharp does not convey a sense of the basis of Mann's greatness, this book is professionally researched and accurate as well as eminently readable.

Williams, Edward I. F. *Horace Mann, Educational Statesman*. New York: Macmillan, 1937. In many respects this book is superseded by that of Messerli, yet it remains a useful middle-length biography.

SEE ALSO: John Quincy Adams; William Ellery Channing; Henry Clay; Samuel Gridley Howe; Herman Melville; Elizabeth Palmer Peabody; Henry David Thoreau; Daniel Webster.

RELATED ARTICLES in *Great Events from History: The Nineteenth Century, 1801-1900:* 1820's-1830's: Free Public School Movement; 1820's-1850's: Social Reform Movement.

HENRY EDWARD MANNING
English Protestant cleric

Manning combined a deep Christian faith with an active Christian conscience. As an Anglican cleric he was an avid reformer and the leader of the Oxford Movement. After he converted to the Roman Catholic faith, he continued his careers as theologian, reformer, and philanthropist and contributed greatly to the rebirth of Catholicism in England.

BORN: July 15, 1808; Copped Hall, Totteridge, Hertfordshire, England
DIED: January 14, 1892; London, England
AREAS OF ACHIEVEMENT: Religion and theology, social reform, philanthropy

EARLY LIFE

Henry Edward Manning was the third and youngest son of William Manning, a West Indian merchant and parliamentarian, and his second wife, Mary, the daughter of Henry Leroy Hunter. The Hunter family claimed Italian extraction, "Hunter" being the English equivalent of the Italian name "Venature." As a youngster, Manning was educated at Harrow, and on April 2, 1827, he matriculated at Balliol College, Oxford.

While Manning was at Balliol, his father suffered severe financial problems that eliminated any possibility of his son's pursuing a career in Parliament. Instead, the younger Manning applied himself to his studies and received a first-class degree in 1830. He then obtained a post in the colonial office. At the suggestion of Favell Lee Bevar, an evangelical Anglican, he considered a career in the Church and then returned to Oxford at Merton College to study for the priesthood in the Church of England. On December 23, 1832, he was ordained and at once took a curateship at Wollavington-cum-Graffham, Sussex. In 1833, he received his master's degree and was installed as rector, and in the same year he married Caroline Sargeant, the late Rector John Sargeant's third daughter.

As a parish priest, Manning was deeply loved by his parishioners and devoted to their care. He successfully rebuilt the churches in his parish. Manning participated in the Ecclesiastical Commission of 1835 and was active on the diocesan boards of the National Society for Promoting the Education of the Poor.

In 1837, Manning was appointed to the rural deanery of Midhurst. It was there that Mrs. Manning died of tuberculosis on July 24, 1837. Manning was deeply sorrowed by his wife's death. His marriage, although childless, had been extremely happy. Manning's affection for his wife can be seen in the fact that he observed the anniversary of her death until he died.

In 1840, Manning was advanced to the Archdeaconry of Chichester. Manning's appointment was hailed as a "blessing for the church" by *The Christian Remembrance*. Advancement to a bishopric or an even higher post seemed assured. At this point, as an important figure in the Church of England, Manning showed no sympathy toward the Church of Rome. Indeed, he preached against papal power. However, Manning not only believed in one holy, catholic, and apostolic Church but also espoused baptismal regeneration, apostolic succession, and Richard Hooker's theory of the Eucharist. He also hated the idea of the Erastian state and deplored the decline of the church parliament of convocation. Nevertheless, Manning was not active in the Tractarian, or Oxford, Movement until the secession to Rome of Newman and W. G. Ward. At that point, Manning became one of the leaders of the movement. He was liked and trusted by most of his colleagues in the Church.

LIFE'S WORK

The year 1847 was a momentous one for Manning, marking a decisive turning point in his life. A tour of the Continent impressed him with the vitality of the Roman Catholic Church and the difficulty of explaining the Anglican position to foreigners. Upon his return to England, Manning resumed his activities. The year 1850, however, brought Manning to a decision. In that year, George Gorham, a Calvinist theologian, was refused appointment to a living because of his holding that divine grace was not imparted at baptism. The bishop's refusal was reversed on an appeal to the Judicial Committee of the Privy Council, an action that invited controversy.

A protest was circulated that stated that to regard an article of faith as a debatable question meant that the Anglican Church could not assure its members the grace of the sacraments and the remission of sins. Manning signed the protest but, significantly, his good friend William Ewart Gladstone did not. At this point, Manning was asked to consider the founding of an Anglo-Catholic "free church" but declined on the grounds that "three hundred years ago we [England] had left a good ship for a boat. I am not going to leave a boat for a tub."

On top of this decision, the bull reestablishing a Roman Catholic hierarchy in England caused 1850 to be dubbed the year of papal aggression. Thousands of meetings were held protesting papal authority, including one in Chichester Cathedral on November 22, 1850. This was Manning's last official act in the Anglican Church. He renounced his archdeaconry and withdrew to London, where he was a communicant at St. Paul's, Knightsbridge.

On April 6, 1851, Passion Sunday, Manning was received into the Church of Rome at the Jesuits Church, Mayfair, London. He was confirmed by Cardinal Nicholas Wiseman on April 11, tonsured on April 29, admitted to four minor orders on April 30, admitted to the subdiaconate on May 25 and to the diaconate on June 8, and ordained to the priesthood on June 15.

The fall of 1851 saw Manning at the Academie di Nobili Ecclesiastici in Rome. He spent the next three years studying at the college and summering in England and Ireland. Pope Pius IX took great interest in Manning and from the beginning saw him frequently on a private

basis. On January 24, 1854, he was given the degree of doctor of divinity by the pope and made provost of the chapter at Westminster. On May 31, 1857, he was installed as superior of the Congregation of the Oblates of St. Charles at St. Mary's Church, Bays Water, which he had founded.

For the next eight years, Manning devoted his time to preaching, to teaching in the slums of Westminster, and to the defense of the temporal power of the pope. In 1860, he received the title of monsignor.

Upon the death of Cardinal Wiseman on February 23, 1865, Manning preached the funeral sermon. On April 30, 1865, the pope appointed Manning to the vacant see of Wiseman over three other candidates. He was consecrated archbishop on June 8, 1865, in the largest Catholic assembly seen since the Reformation. On September 29, 1865, Pius IX conferred the pallium on Manning.

As archbishop, Manning made full use of his powers, and he continued to do so after he became a cardinal ten years later. For the rest of his life, he devoted his time not only to theological writings but also to humanitarian causes. He was not interested in building a Catholic cathedral in London, although in 1903 the Catholic Westminster Cathedral was opened on ground Manning had acquired.

Manning was active in improving and expanding the Catholic school system. He established a diocesan seminary of St. Thomas at Hammersmith. From 1880 to 1887, he served on the Royal Commission of Education and was responsible for much of the work in the Education Act of 1891 that dealt with voluntary schools. He also advocated temperance and abstained from alcohol for the last twenty years of his life. He campaigned for restrictive legislation on the alcohol traffic and founded the temperance society known as the League of the Cross.

Manning was active also in the Irish nationalist movement, favoring home rule, reform of the land laws, and disestablishment of the Irish church. On the labor front, Manning sat on the royal commission of 1884-1885 for improving working-class housing. He was interested in workers' rights, child-labor laws, better housing, better education, and relief for the starving poor. In the famous London Dockers' Strike of August, 1889, it was Manning's exceptional powers as a diplomat and advocate of labor rights that ended the strike peacefully on September 16—hence the name for the strike's resolution, "the Cardinal's peace."

In his theological writing, Manning was an Ultramontane for his support of the supremacy of papal power and the doctrine of infallibility. He wrote in defense of communion in one kind, the doctrine of the Sacred Heart, and on the Holy Spirit. Despite his deep devotion to papal power, Manning remained devoted to England and the growth of ecumenism. He worked with the Nonconformists on education bills. Again and again, Manning held the position that England had never deliberately rejected the Roman Catholic faith but rather had been robbed of it by its rulers. He believed that Protestanism would eventually become extinct because of its accommodations to modern rationalism, and he hoped for England's return to the Roman fold. He did not live to see it, for he died on January 14, 1892, from bronchitis. Manning was buried in St. Mary's Cemetery, Kensal Green. His net worth was less than three thousand pounds because of his devotion to charity.

SIGNIFICANCE

Henry Edward Manning's early career reflected the spiritual complexities of the Oxford Movement. His search for spiritual peace and his growing disillusionment with the true significance of state control were feelings with which many Anglicans could identify. Moreover, although Manning had regarded his submission to Rome as the end of his career as a cleric, this did not prove so. Manning, unlike Newman, retained the affection of most Anglicans while being deeply appreciated by members of the Roman Catholic Church. Under Manning's leadership, the Roman Catholic Church in England grew in numbers and influence. At the same time, Manning continued his devotion to all the humanitarian causes for which he had worked throughout his clerical career. He was a hero to the poor and the working class regardless of their religious affiliation.

Manning was not, however, simply an ecclesiastical statesman. He was a prolific theological writer, although much of his work was polemical in regard to papal power. He believed that Roman Catholicism was most concerned with the predicament of the worker in the modern state. In this, he presaged modern Catholic views of the world and the Church as being one sphere.

Manning's influence lies in his deep contribution to the revival of Roman Catholicism within England during the nineteenth century. Less obvious is the impact of his commitment to the welfare of the common man. In his humanitarian efforts, Manning served England well as both an Anglican and a Catholic.

—*Rose Ethel Althaus Meza*

FURTHER READING

Fitzsimons, John. *Manning: Anglican and Catholic*. Westport, Conn.: Greenwood Press, 1951. An excel-

lent account of Manning's conversion to Roman Catholicism. Emphasizes Manning's belief that the Church of England was the closest approximation to a perfect church but that only Rome could sustain his intellectual, sentimental, and emotional nature.

Gray, Robert. *Cardinal Manning: A Biography*. New York: St. Martin's Press, 1985. Gives a detailed description of Manning's High Church background and belief in good works. Shows that the estrangement between Gladstone and Manning after his conversion was a result of Gladstone's fear of papal political power. A valuable study of Manning's dedication to humanitarian causes, which stemmed from his belief that the Church must stand in contrast with the uncaring modern state system.

Leslie, Sir Shane. *Cardinal Manning: His Life and Labours*. London: Burns, Oates and Washbourne, 1921. Reprint. New York: P. J. Kenedy, 1954. The thesis of this biography is that Manning was a theologian who, although born into Anglicanism, was by nature destined for Rome. An interesting undercurrent of this book is its examination of how prominent Victorians were disillusioned by the Church of England's apathy toward the social problems of the day. Valuable for its insights into Manning's contemporaries as well as its account of his life and thought.

McClelland, Vincent Alan. *Cardinal Manning: His Public Life and Influence, 1865-1892*. London: Oxford University Press, 1961. A detailed study of Manning's career as the head of the Roman Catholic Church in England. Stresses Manning's contributions to the lives of workers in England. Provides a clear picture of Manning's working habits, his differences with Newman, and his contributions to the social history of nineteenth century England.

Newsome, David. *The Convert Cardinals: John Henry Newman and Henry Edward Manning*. London: John Murray, 1993. Examines the lives of both men, describing how they gave up secure careers in the Anglican Church for more dubious futures as converted Catholics. Newsome devotes a chapter to Manning's literary and philosophical genius, restoring Manning's reputation against criticism by Strachey and others.

_____. *The Wilberforces and Henry Manning: The Parting of Friends*. Cambridge, Mass.: Harvard University Press, 1966. A detailed, scholarly examination of Manning's relationship with his cousin William Wilberforce and the other Wilberforces. Stresses that the estrangement between them was a result of the

Wilberforces' unwillingness and/or inability to understand why he left the Church of England. Newsome contends that the basis of this difference concerned the role of the Church—Anglican or Roman Catholic—in modern society.

Pereiro, James. *Cardinal Manning: An Intellectual Biography.* New York: Oxford University Press, 1998. Examines Manning's life and thought during both his Anglican and Catholic periods, tracing his intellectual development and describing the personal crisis he experienced.

Reynolds, E. E. *Three Cardinals: Newman, Manning, and Wiseman.* London: Burns, Oates, 1958. This book, although only partly concerned with Manning, is important for the insight it gives on the development of his spiritual thought. Reynolds contends that Manning was most influenced by the thought of St. Thomas Aquinas and Richard Hooker, and that Man-

ning became a Roman Catholic not by conversion but because of what he believed as an Anglican.

Strachey, Lytton. *Eminent Victorians.* London: Chatto & Windus, 1918. Reprint. New York: Capricorn Books, 1963. A dated and acerbic minibiography of Manning and other prominent Victorians; exaggerates Manning's egotism and minor weaknesses. Strachey's biting if not vindictive style reveals, however, how deep a loss the Church of England believed Manning to be.

SEE ALSO: William Ewart Gladstone; John Henry Newman; Pius IX; E. B. Pusey.

RELATED ARTICLES in *Great Events from History: The Nineteenth Century, 1801-1900:* July 14, 1833: Oxford Movement Begins; October 9, 1845: Newman Becomes a Roman Catholic; December 8, 1869-October 20, 1870: Vatican I Decrees Papal Infallibility Dogma.

DANIEL MANNIX
Irish-born cleric and Australian politician

Mannix became the hero of working-class Roman Catholics for his articulate and outspoken views in favor of Ireland and against British and Protestant influences in Australia that he believed threatened their rights to equality and justice.

BORN: March 4, 1864; Charleville, County Cork, Ireland
DIED: November 6, 1963; Melbourne, Victoria, Australia
AREAS OF ACHIEVEMENT: Government and politics, religion and theology

EARLY LIFE
Daniel Mannix was the son of the former Ellen Cagney and Timothy Mannix, a prosperous tenant farmer in Ireland's County Cork. He was the first of eight children, of whom three died in infancy and another died as a young man in New York. Educated at first at the parish school and then by the Christian Brothers, he enrolled at a classical school, a preliminary to entering the priesthood, at the age of twelve. He was a studious lad; while later boarding at St. Colman's College, Fermoy, he won a scholarship to Maynooth Seminary, where from 1882 his academic achievements set a standard by which all other students came to be measured.

Resembling his tall, slim mother in appearance, Mannix was ordained on June 8, 1890, and, after a year's postgraduate study, taught logic, metaphysics, and ethics at Maynooth. Qualifying for a doctorate of divinity in 1895 and receiving rapid promotion, first to the chair of higher philosophy and then, at the age of thirty-one, to the chair of moral theology, he also became a contributing editor to the *Irish Ecclesiastical Record.* By 1903, Mannix was college president.

During this time, Mannix acquired a reputation as a cold, abstemious, but competent administrator, a disciplinarian who held himself apart from the Gaelic revival then in progress. His main achievement was to gain affiliation for Maynooth to the Irish National University (established in 1908) and a seat on the senate for himself.

LIFE'S WORK
Mannix was forty-eight and president of Maynooth. The future looked very promising. Some imagined that he would succeed Archbishop William Walsh of Dublin. The Vatican, however, agreed to the request of Archbishop Thomas Carr of Melbourne that Mannix be appointed his coadjutor and his successor. A former vice president of Maynooth, a recognized scholar, and a firm believer in the value of a Catholic-run school system, Carr had held the archbishopric since 1886. He never

consulted Mannix about his coming to Melbourne, and Mannix never questioned his appointment.

On his arrival in Melbourne on March 23, 1913, Mannix was incensed to find a policy of compulsory, free, and secular education in operation. In 1870, state aid to church schools had been abolished and continuing attempts, especially by Catholics and Anglicans, to have it restored were unsuccessful. Convinced that secular education was a "great stain upon the statute books of this free and progressive land," Mannix made its removal a paramount objective. Though state aid was not reinstated in his lifetime, he never ceased to confront politicians with the issue.

In the 1911 census only 3 percent of the Australian population were recorded as Irish born but more than 22 percent were Roman Catholics, most of Irish descent. Surprisingly few approved of the Irish rebellion (the Easter Rising) in 1916; their sympathy was aroused, however, at Great Britain's tough response. Although official church policy was to stay on the sidelines, Mannix opposed Labour prime minister William Morris Hughes's proposal to introduce conscription for overseas service when recruiting numbers started to fall during World War I. Mannix argued, among other things, that by removing troops from Ireland, Great Britain would have enough men to continue the fight against Germany without drawing on more Australians.

Although in favor of supporting Great Britain in the war, Australians narrowly rejected conscription for overseas service in a referendum held on October 28, 1916. Expelled from the Labour Party for contravening the spirit of its platform, which was opposed to compulsion, Hughes led a "Win the War" party to victory at elections held the following May. Yet, despite a bitter campaign in December, a second referendum was lost by an increased margin. Once in favor, this time Victoria was opposed.

It is difficult to know how important Mannix's role was. Hundreds of thousands attended mass rallies to hear him exercise his renowned sarcastic wit, and yet a majority in the more populous state of New South Wales voted no in both referenda without Mannix to lead them. Hughes was not quite the ogre Mannix painted him. He had privately intervened on Irish demands for independence with British prime minister David Lloyd George, and he had quickly given assurances that Australia would not follow New Zealand's lead by requiring priests to argue for exemption before a magistrate. There is no doubt, Professor Patrick O'Farrell writes, that Catholic influence was much stronger in the Labour Party after the expulsion of Hughes and his followers: Only three out of

twenty-four federal members of Parliament who left the party were Catholics. This did not result, however, in the more Catholic-minded party that Mannix desired.

Despite Vatican displeasure, Mannix continued his attack on Great Britain's Irish policy. In mid-1920, he was feted in the United States for his views, appearing at Madison Square Garden in New York City with the Irish Republican leader, Eamon de Valera. Mannix's planned visit to Ireland, however, was aborted by the British government. In a dramatic move, he was taken from the passenger steamer en route and landed by destroyer in England. Thus thwarted, he went on to Rome, where he persuaded Pope Benedict XV to censure British conduct in Ireland. Mannix never faltered in his support of de Valera and the republican cause. By 1925, when he was able to enter Ireland freely, he was said to be the only episcopal supporter of de Valera in all of Ireland and Australia.

During World War II, Mannix defended Irish neutrality, but by that time communism, not the British, absorbed most of his attention. Again he went on the attack. In line with Vatican policy, in 1937 the Australian National Secretariat of Catholic Action had been established. A decision was taken in September, 1945, by Australian bishops to expand its political wing, the Catholic Social Studies Movement, which became known simply as the Movement. One of its founders was his protégé, Bartholomew Augustine Santamaria, who proposed that the Movement copy its enemy's organizational methods by creating cells with which to infiltrate the labor movement and counter communist elements. Once its existence became public during the mid-1950's, the activities of the Movement caused a rift among Catholics and a split in the Labour Party far more damaging than that of 1916-1917.

SIGNIFICANCE

Daniel Mannix was not a humble man. During his presidency at Maynooth he got into a dispute with Father Michael O'Hickey, professor of Irish language studies since 1896, who wanted Irish to be made compulsory for university entrance. Postgraduate students supporting Hickey became so rebellious that Mannix closed the center and expelled five students, all ordained priests. Dismissed from his post, Hickey appealed to the Rota in Rome. By the time the tribunal concurred with Mannix that the matter was one only of seminary discipline, he had departed for Melbourne.

The rector of the Irish College in Rome, who was not consulted about Mannix's appointment, believed in

1912 that Australia should direct its own destiny. The Vatican unwittingly, however, sent a man who came to believe that being Irish was almost synonymous with being Catholic.

From 1820, successive colonial governments had allowed the gradual establishment of a Roman Catholic Church hierarchy in Australia. Its early members were actually paid from the public purse. A shortage of English priests meant that the majority of priests were recruited in Ireland, and so by the 1890's, powerful English Benedictine forces in Sydney had been silenced. From 1914, however, priests trained at St. Patrick's College in Manly, Sydney, were outspokenly in favor of Rome's policy of a native-born, locally trained clergy, and from 1930, Manly-trained priests were made bishops.

While allowing Catholic laity a greater say in church affairs, Mannix favored Irish-trained, preferably Maynooth, clergy. He was rude to the apostolic delegate Archbishop John Panico, whose arrival in March, 1936, was seen as a further attempt by the Vatican to limit Irish influence in the Australian church. In February, 1937, a Manly product, Justin Simonds, became the first Australian-born archbishop on his appointment to Hobart, Tasmania; in 1943, this was followed by the elevation of Sydney-born Norman T. Gilroy to the archbishopric of Sydney. Mannix remained, however, an unrepentant Irishman, a self-confessed supporter of the Sinn Féin.

Coming to Australia apparently crystallized Mannix's Irishness. Whereas at Maynooth he was prepared to receive royalty, in Melbourne during the visit of Queen Elizabeth II in 1954 he would not relax his rule of declining invitations to Government House. He widened the rift between Catholics and Protestants by refusing to allow Catholic participation in any ceremonies including a religious segment. Partly because of his determination, the religious component was dropped from the trooping of the colors ceremony at military colleges and the traditional Anzac Day (April 25) service at Melbourne's Shrine of Remembrance. Even on the death of his old antagonist, Dr. Frederick W. Head, the Anglican archbishop, he would not enter St. Paul's Cathedral, waiting outside to join his funeral procession.

Mannix seemed to completely disregard the effect of his much-publicized anticonscription activities on the welfare of the ordinary Catholic worker, whom he claimed to represent. Discrimination by employers and landlords against those with German connections gradually embraced Catholics, who came to be regarded by some as disloyal, partly understandably at least in Victo-

ria, where their archbishop made practically no concessions to the fact that he lived in a country where most were still happy with the British connection, nearly 80 percent were non-Catholic, and (even among Catholics) republican sentiments were minute. He accused others of sectarianism but constantly indulged in its practice himself. He did mellow in some ways: In 1937 he made conciliatory gestures to Hughes that resulted in the regular exchange of birthday greetings. He never gave way, however, on the big issues.

Despite his time at Maynooth and his acknowledged intellectual abilities, Mannix wrote (or at least published) no great works, not even any polemics on his strongly held beliefs. On the contrary, he destroyed almost all of his private papers that may have helped one to understand the man. It is interesting to contrast Mannix with his contemporary in Brisbane, Archbishop James Duhig. Duhig was also Irish-born; he became archbishop the same year as Mannix. He came to Australia at the age of thirteen, however, after his family first moved to Yorkshire, England, and then to Queensland. Perhaps that is why the more moderate position Duhig adopted was in many ways more attuned to the Australian way of thinking.

Unlike Mannix, Duhig took part in community activities and fostered good relations with other religious groups. Like Mannix, he never received a cardinal's cap. Both experienced disappointment when in 1946 the cardinalship went to Archbishop Gilroy. Admirers believed it a tremendous insult to Mannix, but their efforts to achieve this honor for him were unsuccessful. With his death, the great Irish influence on the Catholic Church declined.

—Annette Potts

FURTHER READING

Garden, Don. *Victoria: A History*. Melbourne, Vic.: Nelson, 1984. A good general history of Victoria, helpful for putting Mannix and his activities into the Victorian setting.

Gilchrist, Michael. *Daniel Mannix: Priest and Patriot*. Melbourne, Vic.: Dove Communications, 1982. Gilchrist uses sectarian and state aid controversies to highlight Mannix's role as priest and uses the issues of conscription, Ireland, and communism to show him as a patriot.

McKernan, Michael. "Catholics, Conscription, and Archbishop Mannix." *Historical Studies* 17 (April, 1977): 299-314. McKernan shows the division among Catholic attitudes toward Mannix's conscription stand.

O'Farrell, Patrick. *The Catholic Church and Community in Australia: A History*. Melbourne, Vic.: Nelson, 1977. Written by a well-regarded Catholic historian, this general history includes a substantial and diverse bibliography.

_____. *The Irish in Australia*. Sydney: New South Wales University Press, 1987. This study complements O'Farrell's history of the Roman Catholic Church in Australia (see above).

Santamaria, B. A. *Daniel Mannix: The Quality of Leadership*. Melbourne, Vic.: Melbourne University Press, 1984. By a leading Melbourne Catholic conservative who from the 1930's worked closely with Mannix and led the Catholic Social Studies Movement in its campaign against communism.

SEE ALSO: William Morris; Daniel O'Connell; Charles Stewart Parnell.

RELATED ARTICLES in *Great Events from History: The Nineteenth Century, 1801-1900:* May 9, 1828-April 13, 1829: Roman Catholic Emancipation; June, 1886-September 9, 1893: Irish Home Rule Debate Dominates British Politics.

ALESSANDRO MANZONI
Italian novelist

Among his writings in various genres, Manzoni authored the great Romantic historical novel The Betrothed, *an acknowledged world masterpiece and much-beloved expression of Italian culture that contributed to the unification of Italy and to the Italian language.*

BORN: March 7, 1785; Milan, Lombardy, Austria (now in Italy)
DIED: May 22, 1873; Milan, Italy
ALSO KNOWN AS: Alessandro Francesco Tommaso Antonio Manzoni (full name)
AREA OF ACHIEVEMENT: Literature

EARLY LIFE

Alessandro Manzoni (mahn-DZOH-nee) was born into the aristocratic liberal circles of late eighteenth century Milan, which, influenced by the Enlightenment, was the leading political and intellectual center of preunification Italy. His maternal grandfather was Cesare Beccaria, an economist and jurist whose lectures anticipated the theories of Adam Smith and Thomas Robert Malthus and whose influential work *Dei delitti e delle pene* (1764; *An Essay on Crimes and Punishments*, 1767) reformed thinking on penology. Beccaria introduced the modern view that punishments should be for the purpose of protecting society, not for taking vengeance on criminals. Among Beccaria's close friends were such writers as Giuseppe Parini and the brothers Pietro and Alessandro Verri. The young Manzoni idolized his grandfather and his grandfather's friends, who provided him with role models and a liberal outlook.

Young Manzoni seriously needed such role models, because his parents took little interest in his upbringing. His mother, Giulia Beccaria Manzoni, resembled her own mother, Teresa de' Blasco Beccaria, a lovely but scandalous lady who caused discord between Cesare Beccaria and his family and friends and who finally died of venereal disease. Young Giulia became involved in an affair with Giovanni Verri, the pleasure-seeking younger brother of Pietro and Alessandro Verri. In an attempt to end the affair, Pietro Verri arranged her marriage to Pietro Manzoni, a stolid middle-aged member of the Lecco landed gentry. The marriage was a disaster from the beginning, but then young Manzoni was born (no one is sure whether Pietro Manzoni or Giovanni Verri was his actual father). With no talent or taste for motherhood, Giulia farmed him out to a wet nurse, a peasant woman who cared for him in her home. Eventually, Giulia and Pietro Manzoni separated, and Giulia fled to London and then Paris with a rich Milanese banker, Carlo Imbonati.

Manzoni spent his childhood and youth in a series of boarding schools. From 1791 to 1798, he attended schools in Merate and Lugano run by the Somaschi friars, and from 1798 to 1801 he was at schools in Magenta and Milan run by the Barnabite fathers. A sensitive child, he longed for his mother (he and Pietro Manzoni never cared for each other), endured the bullying of headmasters and other students, and led a miserable existence. Besides reducing him to a shy, withdrawn individual prone to assorted lifelong paranoias, one notable result of his religious schooling was to turn him into a youthful atheist. When he was sixteen, Manzoni's formal education ended, and he moved into a Milan townhouse with an aunt (a former nun), who introduced him to a life of dissipation, which included gambling and women. At the age of sixteen, Manzoni also wrote his first surviving verse, including the unpublished four-quarto poem "Il trionfo della Libertà" ("The Triumph of Liberty").

In 1805, his mother and Carlo Imbonati invited him to join them in Paris, but before Manzoni arrived, Imbonati died, leaving Manzoni's mother a fortune. While Manzoni consoled her, she introduced him to the literary salons of Paris. There Manzoni absorbed the brilliant conversations of writers, philosophers, and politicians that, combined with his avid reading of French literature, made him extremely fluent in French. He became friends with a number of French intellectuals, particularly the literary and historical scholar Claude-Charles Fauriel, who remained a lifetime friend and correspondent. Gradually, however, events began to occur that would draw Manzoni away from Paris. In 1807, Pietro Manzoni died, leaving Manzoni the family estate in Lecco. Then in 1808 Manzoni married Henriette Blondel (who changed her name to Enrichetta), a sixteen-year-old Swiss Calvinist, and in 1810 Enrichetta, Manzoni, and his mother all converted to Catholicism and returned to Italy.

Alessandro Manzoni. (Library of Congress)

LIFE'S WORK

Most commentators cite Manzoni's conversion as the turning point in his life, but a more propitious event might have been his marriage to Blondel, who probably influenced his conversion. Gentle, loving, and strong, she provided Manzoni with the family life and stability that he had never had before. With Manzoni's mother, they settled near Milan on the Brusuglio estate that his mother had inherited from Carlo Imbonati (in 1813 Manzoni also purchased a home in Milan and in 1818 sold the Lecco estate). They proceeded to have a houseful of children while Manzoni practiced agronomy and wrote.

Among the first fruits of his conversion were the *Inni sacri* (1812-1815; *The Sacred Hymns*, 1904), followed by an essay defending Catholicism, *Osservazioni sulla morale cattolica* (1819; *A Vindication of Catholic Morality*, 1836). Then, however, Manzoni turned to history for inspiration in writing two verse tragedies, *Il conte di Carmagnola* (1820; the count of Carmagnola) and *Adelchi* (1822), which, like most Romantic dramas, are hardly suited for the stage, although *Adelchi* was performed. He also wrote an ode on the death of Napoleon, "Il cinque maggio" (1821; "The Napoleonic Ode," 1904), and *Lettre à M. *** sur l'unité de temps et de lieu dans la tragédie* (1823) defending Romantic drama. His next work was the first version of his masterpiece, the long historical novel *I promessi sposi* (1827, 1840-1842; *The Betrothed*, 1828, 1951). Manzoni then spent the next fifteen years rewriting, revising, and polishing *The Betrothed*.

Aside from his literary publication, Manzoni led a retiring and tranquil life on his farm among his family. He needed such a placid life, because he still suffered from phobias (for example, he reputedly weighed his clothes several times a day) and nervous disorders that occasionally left him incapacitated. The various portraits of Manzoni suggest his nervous disposition through his slimness and his long, thin nose that seemed to grow sharper with age. Otherwise, the portraits show a man with regular, almost handsome features whose dark hair and sideburns gradually turned white over the years.

Manzoni's tranquillity was disturbed only by a series of deaths in his family. One child died in 1811, another in 1823, and in 1833 the most shattering blow of all occurred, his beloved wife died. Before Manzoni could recover from her death, their eldest child, Giulia, died in 1834. Needing the supportive companionship of a wife, Manzoni in 1837 married a widow, Teresa Borri Stampa, who brought along stepchildren. The intermittent deaths of his many children continued, and Manzoni outlived all except two. These somber events may help account for Manzoni's turning away from poetry and fiction in his later life to take up the study of history, literary theory, and language. Manzoni published an account of the seventeenth century Milan plague, *Storia della colonna infame* (1842; *The Column of Infamy*, 1845), appended to the final version of *The Betrothed*. Later writings included *Del romanzo storico* (1845), which theorized about historical novels; *Dell'invenzione* (1850), a theoretical work concerning creativity; and *Dell'unità della lingua e dei mezzi di diffonderla* (1868), a report on the Italian language commissioned by the government.

As this last work indicates, Manzoni received much official recognition during his later years. In 1860, the newly unified Italy granted him a pension and made him a senator; he was visited by foreign government dignitaries and by other writers. Most satisfying, however, was the unofficial veneration heaped upon him by the Italian people. Few writers have lived to see such adoration. His death on May 22, 1873, was considered a national tragedy. Giuseppe Verdi's *Messa da requiem* (*Requiem Mass*) was composed and performed in Manzoni's honor the following year.

SIGNIFICANCE

The writing of *The Betrothed* presented Alessandro Manzoni with a unique problem that most modern writers face only in translation. That is, at the time Manzoni wrote, not only was Italy divided into different states ruled by various rulers, but also Italians spoke provincial dialects. There was no unified or standard Italian language. Like other Italian writers at the time, Manzoni briefly considered writing his novel in French, but patriotic sentiments prevailed: How could the great Italian novel be written other than in Italian? Manzoni wrote the first version of *The Betrothed* in his native Lombardy dialect, sometimes called Milanese, but he was dissatisfied with the first version as soon as it appeared.

Manzoni decided to rewrite the whole novel in the Tuscan dialect, which Dante had used for his *La divina commedia* (c. 1320; *The Divine Comedy*), and that Manzoni considered the purest and most graceful Italian dialect. For purposes of learning the Tuscan dialect, Manzoni made several visits to Florence and grilled any Florentine visitors. Experts in the Italian language still find Lombardisms in *The Betrothed*, but the novel gained such immense popularity that, together with Dante's *The Divine Comedy*, it is credited with establishing the Tuscan dialect as standard Italian.

The unification of the Italian language only begins to account for Manzoni's achievements in *The Betrothed*. By balancing the good-hearted but shrewd Italian peasant against the disorder and tyranny of Spanish rule in seventeenth century Lombardy, *The Betrothed* fueled the nineteenth century Risorgimento movement that was still trying to throw off foreign rule and unify Italy. It is no wonder that when unification came about Manzoni was hailed as both poet and patriot.

Religious readers also found cause for praise in Manzoni's theme of divine Providence working through history. Finally, a reader looking for a good story was bound to be enthralled by the novel's long, suspenseful plot, its memorable characters, and its climax during the Milan plague. When Manzoni gratefully acknowledged the influence of Sir Walter Scott on *The Betrothed*, Scott generously replied that it was by far the best novel Manzoni had ever written.

—Harold Branam

FURTHER READING

Barricelli, Gian Piero. *Alessandro Manzoni*. Boston: Twayne, 1976. A competent and useful source containing a brief biography followed by a critical survey of Manzoni's writings, concentrating on *The Betrothed*. Includes an annotated bibliography.

Caserta, Ernesto G. *Manzoni's Christian Realism*. Florence, Italy: Leo S. Olschki, 1977. Focuses on Manzoni as a Christian writer. Begins with an examination of his aesthetic theory, then traces his development as a Christian writer from the *Inni sacri* through *The Betrothed*.

Chandler, S. B. *Alessandro Manzoni: The Story of a Spiritual Quest*. Edinburgh: Edinburgh University Press, 1974. Another competent critical survey of Manzoni's writings, concentrating on *The Betrothed*. Includes a fairly extensive bibliography.

Colquhoun, Archibald. *Manzoni and His Times*. New York: E. P. Dutton, 1954. The best biography of Manzoni in English, written by the translator of the definitive English version of *The Betrothed*. Provides a context of extensive social and family background and includes sixteen pages of photographs.

De Simone, Joseph Francis. *Alessandro Manzoni: Esthetics and Literary Criticism*. New York: S. F. Vanni, 1946. A dull but informative source, originally a Columbia University Ph.D. thesis. The first part traces Manzoni's aesthetics through three phases—classicism, Romanticism, and "negation of his poetic work"—while the second part surveys Manzoni's critical opinions of other writers, primarily French and Italian.

Ginzburg, Natalia. *The Manzoni Family*. Translated by Marie Evans. New York: Seaver Books, 1987. A translation of *La famiglia Manzoni* (1983). Using letters and other old documents, the author constructs a loose account of Manzoni's family from 1762 to 1907, concentrating on his mother, his two wives, his friend Claude Fauriel, and his children.

Matteo, Sante, and Larry H. Peer, eds. *The Reasonable Romantic: Essays on Alessandro Manzoni*. New York: Peter Lang, 1986. An anthology of seventeen original essays (a few using deconstruction techniques) written by new and established Manzoni scholars to introduce Manzoni. The first section is a general introduction, followed by sections on Manzoni and Romanticism, language, history, and religion.

Reynolds, Barbara. *The Linguistic Writings of Alessandro Manzoni: A Textual and Chronological Re-construction*. Cambridge, England: Heffer, 1950. Originally a University of London Ph.D. thesis. A bit of scholarly detective work that uses Manzoni's published and unpublished writings to reconstruct his changing theories on language, particularly on how to achieve a standard Italian language.

Wall, Bernard. *Alessandro Manzoni*. New Haven, Conn.: Yale University Press, 1954. A short introduction to Manzoni's life and works, marred by its brevity and stereotypical thinking, but still useful.

SEE ALSO: Vincenzo Gioberti; Thomas Robert Malthus; Sir Walter Scott; Giuseppe Verdi.

RELATED ARTICLES in *Great Events from History: The Nineteenth Century, 1801-1900:* 1814: Scott Publishes *Waverley*; December, 1816: Rise of the Cockney School; October 1-December 15, 1856: Flaubert Publishes *Madame Bovary*.

JOHN MARSHALL
American jurist

During his long tenure as chief justice of the United States, Marshall used his considerable intelligence, personal charm, and political skills to make the Court the chief arbiter of constitutional doctrine, firmly establishing what had been the weakest branch of the national government as an equal with Congress and the executive.

BORN: September 24, 1755; Germantown (now Midland), Virginia
DIED: July 6, 1835; Philadelphia, Pennsylvania
AREA OF ACHIEVEMENT: Law

EARLY LIFE

John Marshall was the eldest of fifteen children. His father was a planter of moderate means who in time became a wealthy leading citizen of Virginia and later of Kentucky, serving in numerous official capacities in both states. Through Mary, the Marshall family was connected to most of the important families of Virginia. Growing to manhood among the landed gentry molded John Marshall's character, yet his too casual and occasionally sloppy appearance was at odds with his background. John Marshall's education was a typical blend, for the sons of southern colonial gentry, of intermittent and limited formal instruction by tutors in the classics and informal instruction by his parents in reading, writing, and elementary mathematics. The few books in the family library included several on law and served as Marshall's introduction to the subject; from his family's participation in state and local government, he learned about politics.

Only nineteen years old in 1774, when the chain of events beginning with the Boston Tea Party led to the American War of Independence, John Marshall followed his father's example and enthusiastically took the patriots' side in the quarrel with England. He was a popular first lieutenant in the local militia when the fighting started but followed his father into the Continental army as soon as it was formed. He served with distinction until independence was nearly won, rising to the rank of captain and becoming something of a hero. He fought in several battles, was wounded, and was with George Washington at Valley Forge.

During a lull, while stationed in Virginia, Marshall studied law and other subjects for three months at the College of William and Mary in Williamsburg. His law teacher was George Wythe, one of the most respected colonial lawyers, with whom Thomas Jefferson, Marshall's cousin, had also studied. Although short, Marshall's legal education was better than most, because there were no law schools in America. The College of William and Mary was one of the few to offer any law classes as part of the undergraduate curriculum. Most lawyers learned only by self-study while working as a clerk in a practicing attorney's office. During these months of study, he also met and began courting Mary Willis Ambler, known all of her life as Polly.

Marshall had passed the bar examination and received his license to practice from Governor Thomas Jefferson in August of 1780. He returned to Oak Hill in Fauquier County, the family estate, to begin his career. In April of 1782, Marshall was elected to represent his county in the House of Delegates. In the state capital, Richmond, Marshall was introduced to a world beyond that of the country lawyer and landed gentry, and his ambition to be part of it was fired. Marshall renewed his courtship of Polly Ambler, whose family now lived in Richmond, and they were married on January 3, 1783, when he was twenty-seven and she was nearly seventeen. Marshall decided to move to Richmond to practice and became a leading member of the bar within three years.

LIFE'S WORK
The man who had joined the mainstream of Virginia's affairs was a commanding, lean figure, six feet in height, black-haired, with a nearly round face and strong, penetrating black eyes, complimented by a smile that seemed to disarm everyone. Honest, capable of sustained hard work, and possessed of a probing intellect, Marshall was also a gregarious man who loved games and athletic activity and who radiated a captivating friendliness. By nature, he was a gracious person, although he did not have a polished manner. As happened with so many patriots who actively participated in the military and political events of the War of Independence, Marshall had acquired a deep sense of nationalism from his travels through the former colonies and the comradeship of men from all parts of the emerging nation. The fact that this new nation should survive and prosper became a concern of Marshall for the remainder of his life.

Marshall worked hard to build his Richmond practice. He held various official positions with the state and local governments but refused any that would seriously interfere with his private law work. A major reason was Polly's poor health after 1786. Their second child died shortly after birth, and then Polly miscarried a few months later. The shock of these two tragedies brought on a nervous breakdown from which Polly never totally recovered. For the remainder of their long married life

John Marshall. (Library of Congress)

and through the eight children yet to come, Polly could not abide crowds or noise. It was necessary to have servants to perform the routine household duties, and Marshall personally did the family marketing.

The condition of the nation worried Marshall throughout the 1780's. He thought the national government was too weak to protect the new nation from foreign threats or to restrain state governments from abuses of power. For this reason, he wholeheartedly supported the work of the Constitutional Convention of 1787 to create a "more perfect union." Elected as delegate to Virginia's special convention to decide whether to adopt the new national constitution, he spoke strongly for it. Once the issue was favorably resolved, however, and the new national government instituted under the leadership of his idol, George Washington, Marshall's attention returned to the practice of law.

Marshall refused all offers of appointment to national office, including the cabinet, until 1797, when he accepted what he thought would be a short-term diplomatic appointment from President John Adams. When Marshall returned to the United States in July of 1798, he was feted as a national hero for his part in what had become known as the XYZ affair. George Washington persuaded him to capitalize on his public recognition and run for a seat in the House of Representatives. Washington had persuaded him to agree to leave his lucrative private practice by convincing him that the republic was in danger from the development of political factionalism.

In the conventional wisdom of his day, Marshall believed that political factions were a threat to the smooth and stable operation of a republican government. Factionalism stirred up the masses to interfere in the affairs of government, best left to the better educated and propertied gentry, who alone could be expected to function from motives of civic virtue and on the basis of practical common sense. Although willing to fight for fundamental principle, Marshall was a man who otherwise believed in moderation and compromise on matters of policy; he saw that political polarization, if unchecked, would eventually destroy the nation. In Congress, he became the leading House spokesperson for President Adams's moderate Federalist administration. In recognition of his service he was promoted to secretary of state in 1800, and, when the Federalists lost the election that year, to chief justice of the United States in 1801. Marshall would remain chief justice until 1835, the year he died.

The Supreme Court in 1801 had serious problems with low public esteem, low pay, poor morale, and rapid turnover of justices. The Court had developed no corporate sense of identity. Marshall's first innovation was to persuade the justices not to give their written opinions *seriatim*—that is, each justice writing his own. Instead, in most cases Marshall persuaded the justices to confer until they reached a consensus so that a single opinion could be issued for the majority. Marshall correctly reasoned that the Court's decisions would be much more authoritative if the majority spoke with one voice. The institution of this practice was the single most important reason for the rise of the Supreme Court to equality with the other branches of government. To facilitate the development of collegiality, he also encouraged the justices to lodge at the same Washington, D.C., inn during the one- to two-month yearly sessions.

A distinctive feature of the American system of government is the power of its courts to declare actions by other parts of the government unconstitutional. This power, called judicial review, had not yet been exercised except by some state courts (with mixed results) when Marshall became chief justice. The first instance of the power's use arose out of the fury of President Jefferson and his party over the famous Midnight Appointments of President Adams in 1801, in the case of *Marbury v. Madison* (1803). The case involved a request that the Supreme Court issue a writ of *mandamus* (a court order) to Secretary of State James Madison. The Court's decision, written by Marshall, first lectured Jefferson and his party on their failing in the practice of principles of good government and then announced that the writ of *mandamus* requested in this case could not be issued because section 13 of the Judiciary Act of 1789, which gave the Court the power to issue the writ, was unconstitutional.

This self-denial by the Court was a shrewd political maneuver. In its first big constitutional case under Marshall, the Court had exercised judicial review and declared an act of Congress unconstitutional, and there was nothing anyone could do about it. It was also a brave act in the face of the enormous antijudiciary bias of the Jeffersonians. Although the Court did not declare another act of Congress or the president unconstitutional during Marshall's tenure, it did so for state laws on a number of occasions. Thus, the practice as well as the principle of judicial review was established.

After 1805, the political pressure on the Court decreased, partly because the government's attention was increasingly focused on foreign affairs and partly because, under Marshall, the Court had acquired greater respect and, therefore, greater independence. The work of the Court now centered more on two objectives: the supremacy of the national government and the preservation and protection of rights. The two were directly related in Marshall's view.

The point in establishing the supremacy of the federal Constitution, statutes, and treaties over the states was to counter the threat to inalienable rights from abuses of power by the states. Marshall perceived this as the most serious threat of all. For example, the Constitution prohibited the states from interfering with the obligations of the parties to a contract, yet many states were doing just that in numerous ways. In a long line of cases interpreting the "contract clause," Marshall's court fashioned from it a powerful defense of the private citizens' right to whatever property they had come by honestly. In the famous trial of Aaron Burr for treason, Marshall interpreted the Constitution to prevent the charge of treason from becoming an instrument to punish political enemies.

In *Gibbons v. Ogden* (1824), Marshall's court struck down a law creating a steamboat monopoly, not only because it infringed on federal power to regulate interstate commerce, but also because the Constitution's framers had given the commerce power to Congress in order to establish the whole of the United States as a free trade area and the steamboat monopoly violated freedom of commerce. The issue of slavery presented a serious problem for Marshall; on one hand, the slave owner's property right had to be protected, like any other property right, but on the other hand, Marshall thought that black slaves had the same rights as white people. It seemed to him that the only solution to this dilemma was the American Colonization Society. This organization hoped to remove all black slaves from the United States to Liberia, Africa.

The Jackson years disheartened Marshall. He hated the viciously partisan character assassinations of the Jackson campaign, and he feared that universal manhood suffrage, a major Jacksonian goal, could only result in politicians pandering to the prejudices of the common people. He also believed the states' rights orientation of the Jackson appointees to the Court threatened all of his work to establish the supremacy of the Constitution, guarantees of rights, and the restraint of state uses of power.

As Marshall increasingly saw himself as a relic of the past, he found it necessary to compromise on some issues to save at least something of his work. When Polly died in 1831, he was desolate and felt very much alone. There were, however, some positive moments. When Jackson stood up for the supremacy of the national government in 1832 against South Carolina's attempt to nullify a national tariff, Marshall relented somewhat in his dislike of the old general. Although unable to stop Georgia from brutally removing the Cherokee Indians from the state and humiliated at seeing the state of Georgia flout the Supreme Court's decision forbidding the removal—the Court had no means of enforcing it and the president would not—a remedy was provided. President Jackson's Force Bill, passed by Congress in connection with the Nullification Crisis, provided the Court with its own officials to enforce future decisions.

In 1835, Marshall was seventy-nine when he suffered a spinal injury in a stagecoach accident from which he never fully recovered. He also suffered from serious liver trouble. When told that his time was short, he put his affairs in order and, on July 6, 1835, he died.

SIGNIFICANCE

Marshall built better than he knew. He was mistaken in his beliefs about political parties and the superior governing abilities of the gentry, but practices he established

for the Court and many of his judicial doctrines are still important. Supreme Court majorities continued after Marshall generally to speak with one voice. His example of collegial leadership remains the standard for chief justices. The defense of property rights based on the contract clause and his interpretation of the commerce clause contributed significantly to the legal environment necessary for the free enterprise economic system to flourish. Treason remains only a crime and not a weapon against the enemies of whatever politicians are in power.

In raising the visibility and authority of the Supreme Court to a position of equality with the other branches, Marshall created a potent force for political stability within the American system of government. This was his most important achievement. The government's ability to correct its mistakes through the Supreme Court's exercise of the power of judicial review inspires confidence and trust in all levels of the system. The Supreme Court became the guardian and final arbiter of the Constitution, establishing the primacy of the constitutional principles of the nation's founders. In 1801, when John Marshall became chief justice, none of this was certain to evolve, but the fundamentals were all in place when he left, thirty-four years later. During that time, he wrote 519 of the Court's 1,106 opinions, including 36 of the 62 involving major constitutional questions. John Marshall had a major hand in creating the most balanced and equable judicial system in the world.

—Richard L. Hillard

FURTHER READING

Baker, Leonard. *John Marshall: A Life in Law.* New York: Macmillan, 1974. A good biography of Marshall's professional life; includes some private matters as well. Explains many details about how Marshall and the legal system in his time worked. Also explains his reasoning in his Supreme Court decisions.

Baxter, Maurice G. *Daniel Webster and the Supreme Court.* Amherst: University of Massachusetts Press, 1966. A superb and scholarly examination of the relationship between Daniel Webster, one of the leading constitutional lawyers of his day and a Marshall supporter, and the development of judicial doctrine by the Supreme Court during much of Marshall's tenure as chief justice.

Beveridge, Albert J. *The Life of John Marshall.* 4 vols. Boston: Houghton Mifflin, 1916-1919. Detailed and wonderfully told story, yet sadly lacking in balance, making Marshall seem a heroic savior of his nation against arch-villains. Even so, these four volumes are still the starting point for Marshall scholarship.

Faulkner, Robert K. *The Jurisprudence of John Marshall*. Princeton, N.J.: Princeton University Press, 1968. Definitive examination of the political philosophy of Marshall. Traces the origins to a mix of the theories of John Locke, American nationalism, and the respect for landed gentry typical of the classical Romans, especially Cicero.

Horwitz, Morton J. *The Transformation of American Law: 1780-1860*. Cambridge, Mass.: Harvard University Press, 1977. Mentions Marshall only briefly. Probably the best one-volume legal history of the era to date. Emphasis is on the transformation of English law in the colonies into a modern national legal system and how this transformation aided economic development.

Newmyer, R. Kent. *John Marshall and the Heroic Age of the Supreme Court*. Baton Rouge: Louisiana State University Press, 2001. Focuses on Marshall's legal philosophies, analyzing some of his Supreme Court decisions and placing his beliefs in historical context. Describes how Marshall's experiences as a soldier in the Revolutionary War, his legal career, and his childhood in Virginia influenced his constitutional thinking.

_____. *The Supreme Court Under Marshall and Taney*. New York: Thomas Y. Crowell, 1968. A succinct but thorough and perceptive study of the Marshall Court in the context of the people and events of the times. The Marshall chapters concentrate on Marshall as chief justice, and little of his personal life is included.

Robarge, David. *A Chief Justice's Progress: John Marshall from Revolutionary Virginia to the Supreme Court*. Westport, Conn.: Greenwood Press, 2000. Focuses on the formative influences in Marshall's life before he joined the U.S. Supreme Court, including his upbringing in Virginia, military service, legal career, and experiences as a federalist and diplomat.

Simon, James F. *What Kind of Nation: Thomas Jefferson, John Marshall, and the Epic Struggle to Create a United States*. New York: Simon & Schuster, 2002. Describes how Marshall, a proponent of federalism, and Jefferson, an advocate of states rights, engaged in a lengthy competition to determine the direction of the newly created United States.

Stites, Francis N. *John Marshall: Defender of the Constitution*. Boston: Little, Brown, 1981. This is an excellent short biography of Marshall. Well researched and carefully written, it brings together in a reasonable synthesis the voluminous scholarship available on Marshall.

SEE ALSO: Aaron Burr; Joseph Story; Daniel Webster.

RELATED ARTICLES in *Great Events from History: The Nineteenth Century, 1801-1900:* February 24, 1803: *Marbury v. Madison*; March, 1805-September 1, 1807: Burr's Conspiracy; March 16, 1810: *Fletcher v. Peck*; March 6, 1819: *McCulloch v. Maryland*; March 2, 1824: *Gibbons v. Ogden*; May 28, 1830: Congress Passes Indian Removal Act; March 18, 1831, and March 3, 1832: Cherokee Cases.

JOSÉ MARTÍ
Cuban poet, journalist, and nationalist leader

A gifted writer and political leader, Martí dedicated his life to the struggle for Cuba's independence from Spain, and his poetry ranks him among the finest Latin American writers. Although he died as the final war for Cuban independence began, he remains a powerful patriotic symbol for all Cubans.

BORN: January 28, 1853; Havana, Cuba
DIED: May 19, 1895; Dos Ríos, Cuba
ALSO KNOWN AS: José Julían Martí y Pérez (full name); Pépé
AREAS OF ACHIEVEMENT: Government and politics, literature

EARLY LIFE

José Martí (mahr-TEE) was born in Cuba, the son of Spanish parents Leonor Pérez and Mariano Martí y Navarro. His father was a soldier in a Spanish army that was sent to Cuba to discourage independence movements. By the time José was born, several uprisings had been suppressed, and offers by the United States to buy the island from Spain had been rejected.

In 1865, the twelve-year-old José became a student in Havana, where his teacher, Rafael Maria Mendives, fostered Martí's literary and political interests. At an early age, José showed writing talent and a passion for Cuban independence. He began writing patriotic plays, poems, and essays, and in 1869 printed his own newspaper, *Patria Libre* (free homeland).

In 1868, while Martí was still a student, a new war for independence began under the leadership of Carlos Manuel Cespedes; it would continue for ten years. During that war, Spanish authorities used increasingly harsh methods to suppress dissent, and executions—often for nonviolent offenses—and imprisonments increased. On the strength of a letter found in the home of a friend, Martí himself was arrested and imprisoned in 1869. The following year, he was sent to work in a rock quarry until he was deported to Spain.

After arriving in Spain in 1871, Martí began his university education but also continued writing in support of Cuban independence. In 1871, he wrote an essay on political prisons in Cuba that eloquently described the plight of sick old men and frightened young boys who were sent to work in Cuban quarries, where they were whipped and afflicted with smallpox and cholera. Written in a dramatic, emotional style, Martí's essay reveals a thorough training in classical rhetoric that was to benefit him later as a speaker.

After graduating from the University of Zaragoza in 1874, Martí traveled throughout Europe, where he made the acquaintance of the French writer Victor Hugo. He also visited New York. In 1875, he settled in Mexico, where he worked as a journalist, teacher, and dramatist.

LIFE'S WORK

During the two years that Martí spent in Mexico, he made regular contributions to newspapers and magazines, often on political topics. During that period he became familiar with Mexican history and doubtless became more aware of the 1846-1848 war between the United States and Mexico that ended with the United States taking possession of a large portion of northern Mexico that included California, Arizona, and New Mexico. Martí's dramatic work soon attracted a following.

Martí became acquainted with officials in the Mexican government, but these relationships put him at risk after the ruling administration was overthrown by the militarist Porfirio Díaz. In 1876, Martí left Mexico and settled in Guatemala, where he became a friend of Rubén Darío, one of the leading modernist poets in Latin American literature. Martí spent one and one-half years in Guatemala as a professor and a journalist.

While Martí was in Guatemala, he may have engaged in a love affair similar to the one described in his poem "La Niña de Guatemala" (the girl of Guatemala). In 1877, he returned briefly to Mexico, where he married Carmen Zayas Bazan and then returned with his bride to Guatemala. Political troubles intervened once again when the president of Guatemala removed a friend of Martí's from his position. Martí then took his wife back to Cuba, where his only son was born. He again engaged in revolutionary activities and was again deported to Spain. From there, he went to New York in 1880, spent a brief period teaching and writing in Venezuela, and then settled down in New York in 1881.

Martí's approximately fifteen years in New York were marked by his intense activity on behalf of Cuban independence, social activism, teaching, and writing. He soon became the leader of both New York's Cuban exile community and the Cuban Revolutionary Party. In Cuba, the ten-year independence struggle had concluded unsatisfactorily during the late 1870's. However, the so-called "little war" of 1880 was a sign of continued nationalist

José Martí. (Library of Congress)

where there were large numbers of Cuban emigrants working in cigar factories. Martí's group planned the war of independence and raised enough money to outfit three steamers to transport weapons to Cuba; however, the ships were seized by the United States.

In 1895, Martí landed in Cuba and wrote daily letters from the battlefield. However, he died in his first hostile engagement with Spanish troops, while leading a charge at Dos Rios in 1895. The war continued until 1898, by which time the independence forces were in control of much of the devastated and burned-over countryside. By then, the United States—which feared a truly independent Cuba, as Martí had predicted—intervened on the pretext of a Spanish attack on the USS *Maine*. American forces took control of the entire island and occupied it until 1902 and on several later occasions. The United States continued to dominate Cuba's government until Fidel Castro's revolution in 1959.

SIGNIFICANCE

In the twenty-first century, José Martí remains an icon to Cubans of conservative and radical political beliefs. Standing in Havana's Plaza of the Revolution is an enormous statue of Martí. Several editions of his *Complete Works* have been sponsored by both conservative and Marxist governments in Havana, and the Castro government has used Martí's writings for both children's school texts and adult literacy programs.

Martí's observations of the United States during the late nineteenth century provide unique insights into American social history. He praised American leaders such as Abraham Lincoln and Grover Cleveland but also vividly described the lynching of a black man in the South and the deplorable conditions under which Native Americans lived. He observed and wrote in detail about political conventions, social customs, and even sports.

Martí's writings promoted democracy in Latin America, and he envisioned a Spanish America—which he called "Our America"—as a community of nations that would not be overwhelmed by their powerful English-speaking neighbor to the north. Although he admired American enterprise, he expressed in his writings his concerns that the need of American industry for foreign markets could eventually consume and marginalize Latin America.

In the field of Latin American poetry, Martí is considered an important modernist, ranked alongside Rubén Darío. He led a break with the Romanticism of the past and initiated an almost surrealistic poetry, sometimes of dream images, that foreshadowed the work of others. His

unrest, and Martí became close to the rebel Cuban generals Maximo Gomez and Antonio Maceo.

As Martí wrote for papers in Argentina, Venezuela, and Mexico and edited *La America* in New York, he refined his ideas about the Cuban revolution. Fearing the danger of a Cuban military dictatorship, he broke with Maceo and Gomez, and he also feared the possibility of American intervention. Against the backdrop of the American war with Mexico, Martí was suspicious of American imperialistic designs. He was also aware of the oppression of African Americans and Native Americans within the United States. He described a lynching in striking detail and sent it to papers in Latin America.

Martí's literary activity during that period was also intense. He wrote the poetry for *Versos libres* (free verses) and *Versos sencillos* (simple verses), and *Ismaello*. He started a magazine for children, *La Edad de Oro*. He stressed the importance of education and taught a class for black Hispanics.

Meanwhile, Martí traveled extensively around the United States and the Caribbean and spoke before members of Cuban exile groups about his plans for the Cuban revolution—especially in Tampa and Key West, Florida,

poetry is still popular in Cuba, whose highly literate population have an exceptional appreciation of literature.

—*Timothy C. Frazer*

FURTHER READING

Kirk, John M. *José Martí: Mentor of the Cuban Nation.* Tampa: University Presses of Florida, 1983. After a review of differing interpretations of Martí's work, Kirk analyzes the growth of Martí's political thought through a detailed examination of the writings. Particularly insightful is Kirk's discussion of how Martí's prison experience influenced his ideas about the independence struggle. Includes an extensive bibliography and a detailed chronology.

Martí, José. *Selected Writings.* Translated and edited by Esther Allen. New York: Penguin Books, 2002. The introduction by Roberto González Echevarría includes an overview of Martí's life and a critical review of his political and literary writings, followed by a year-by-year chronological outline of Martí's life and a two-page list of suggested readings. The volume contains more than four hundred pages of Martí's writings in English translation, including samples of his poetry, his personal letters, his dispatches to newspapers, and his notebook and diary excerpts.

Perez, Louis J., ed. *José Martí in the United States: The Florida Experience.* Tempe: Arizona State University Center for Latin American Studies, 1995. Focuses on Martí's work with the exile Cuban populations in Florida, especially Tampa and Key West.

Shonookal, Deborah, and Mirta Muñez, eds. *José Martí Reader: Writings on the Americas.* New York: Ocean Press, 1999. A collection of translated writings, less extensive than Allen's, but with a thirteen-page introduction by Ivan A. Schulman, one of the leading American students of Martí and his poetry, that offers a thorough overview of Martí's poetical works and scholarship about them.

SEE ALSO: Grover Cleveland; Rubén Darío; Porfirio Díaz; Victor Hugo; Abraham Lincoln; Clorinda Matto de Turner.

RELATED ARTICLES in *Great Events from History: The Nineteenth Century, 1801-1900:* October 10, 1868-February 10, 1878: Cuba's Ten Years' War; April 24-December 10, 1898: Spanish-American War.

HARRIET MARTINEAU
English writer and social commentator

Sometimes called the first woman sociologist, Martineau wrote numerous books, pamphlets, and articles on social and economic issues that helped shape political life in both England and North America. Her writings on slavery, laissez-faire economics, and women's education were particularly influential.

BORN: June 12, 1802; Norwich, Norfolk, England
DIED: June 27, 1876; Ambleside, Westmorland, England
AREAS OF ACHIEVEMENT: Sociology, literature, women's rights

EARLY LIFE

Harriet Martineau (mahr-tih-noh) was the sixth of eight children of Thomas Martineau, an English cloth manufacturer whose family was of French Huguenot descent. The family's active involvement in the freethinking Norwich Unitarian community helped form attitudes of skepticism, rationalism, and reliance on systematic inquiry. Harriet owed a better education to Unitarianism than was standard among middle-class English girls of her day. She first attended a boys' day-school that admitted a few girls and later went to a boarding school run by an aunt in Bristol. At the latter, she studied with the Reverend Lant Carpenter, a distinguished scholar. Harriet was sickly as a child, and when she was around the age of twelve was increasingly plagued by deafness. That disability helped steer her to focus her attention on writing by preventing her from becoming a governess or teacher.

In later life Harriet remembered her mother as having been harsh and distant—a woman who belittled her appearance, reinforcing intellectual pursuits at the expense of feminine social development. Harriet's impression of a nonnurturing mother is corroborated by her younger brother, James, to whom she was particularly close. He later became a Unitarian minister, scholar, and church administrator of some distinction. When he entered the university in 1822, he encouraged Harriet to begin writing as a way of correcting the disparity in opportunities available to men and women.

Harriet began her writing career by publishing two articles in the *Monthly Repository*, a Unitarian journal. She continued to live at home, contributing occasional anonymous articles to the periodical press and augmenting the household economy with fancy needlework. In 1826, she became engaged to Hugh Worthington, a friend of James, but he died before a marriage could take place.

Meanwhile, the Martineau family manufacturing business, which had been declining for some time, failed in 1829. Faced with the necessity of supporting herself, Harriet attempted, unsuccessfully, to set up a correspondence school, and approached William Fox, the editor of the *Monthly Repository*, about payment for her contributions. He offered her fifteen pounds per year. From 1829 through 1832, Harriet was the journal's chief and only paid contributor. She also accepted other writing assignments, and by 1832 was beginning to establish a reputation as a perceptive social commentator.

LIFE'S WORK

In her autobiography, Martineau expressed gratitude for the financial difficulties that forced her to become a full-time writer. "I had henceforth liberty to do my own work in my own way," she wrote, "for we had lost our gentility." Following a suggestion of James, she planned a series of stories that would illustrate social and economic themes and persuaded Charles Fox, William Fox's brother, to underwrite the series. The resulting *Illustrations of Political Economy*, which appeared in twenty-five monthly installments during 1832-1834, was a solid success. The principles that Martineau illustrated covered much of the same territory as John Stuart Mill's later *Principles of Political Economy* (1848) and reached a much wider readership. Each of Harriet Martineau's stories contained an appendix explaining its important points. Martineau continued the series with *Illustrations of Taxation* (1834), decrying, among other things, the national debt, and *Poor Laws and Paupers* (1834), which was instrumental in passage of Great Britain's 1834 Poor Law Act.

In September of 1834 Martineau embarked on a journey to the United States, intending to write a book on American society and to test her methods of sociological observation. She spent nearly two years in this arduous

Harriet Martineau. (Library of Congress)

venture, the most notable episode of which was a meeting of the Ladies' Anti-Slavery Society on Boston in August, 1835. Convinced of the evil of slavery on philosophical and economic grounds, and now having witnessed the ugly practice at firsthand in the United States, she publicly announced her support for abolition at the Boston meeting.

Upon Martineau's return to England in 1836, she produced three books: *Society in America* (1837), which is among the most thorough sociological studies of a society in the nineteenth century, *Retrospect of Western Travel* (1838), an engaging picture of America, and *How to Observe Morals and Manners* (1838), a handbook for sociological investigation. *Society in America* decries slavery and also dwells on how the subordinate position of women was incompatible with the democratic ideals of the nation. During this period of her life, Martineau also wrote *Deerbrook* (1843), her only full-length novel, which is noteworthy for the sympathetic portrayal of an unmarried, marginalized governess.

In 1839, Martineau was stricken with a prolapsed uterus and ovarian tumor that left her debilitated and in constant pain. Over the next five years, she lived in seclusion in Tynemouth, near Newcastle, under the care of her physician brother-in-law, Thomas Greenhow, who diagnosed her problem as "excessive anxiety of the mind." From her sickbed Martineau wrote a novel about Haiti, a series of popular children's stories, and *Life in the Sickroom* (1848), a handbook offering advice for invalids.

After five years, Martineau decided to consult the mesmerist Spencer Hall. Several hypnosis sessions with Hall made her felt well enough to leave her house. Within four months, she was pronounced cured. Now a firm convert to mesmerism, she quarreled with Greenhow, who published a pamphlet detailing her case, claiming that he had nearly effected a cure before Hall appeared. Exactly what happened is uncertain, except that Hall got Martineau off the opiate addiction to which she had succumbed under Greenhow's care.

After Martineau was restored to health, her first action was to purchase property in Ambleside in the Lake District, and have a modest house built on it. There she lived for the remainder of her life, conducting a healthy rural lifestyle and enjoying the company of literary neighbors, who included the aging poet William Wordsworth and poet Matthew Arnold.

Among the works that Martineau produced over the next ten years were *Household Education* (1849), *History of England During the Thirty Years Peace* (1849-1850), and a translation of Auguste Comte's *Course in Positive Philosophy*. In 1846, she toured Egypt and the Middle East; her observations on that tour formed the basis for *Eastern Life: Past and Present* (1848). *Eastern Life* is more than a travelogue or a collection of sociological observations, as it attempts to trace the development of religious thought from its polytheistic origins in ancient Egypt through increasing abstraction to what Martineau saw as its logical endpoint: rationalism, positivism, the perfectibility of humans through intellect and industry, and a deity that, if it existed at all, had become irrelevant. Martineau herself had similarly evolved from a freethinking Unitarian to a decided agnostic.

In 1854, after enjoying a decade of robust good health, Martineau fell ill again. Convinced that her heart was about to fail, she returned to Tynemouth and began writing her autobiography, a frank, analytical assessment that leaves unanswered few questions about her private life, philosophy, and motivations. Martineau was actually undergoing a recurrence of the old ovarian tumor. Although she never completely regained her health, she lived for another twenty-two years and spent most of them in Ambleside. During this period, she became a regular correspondent for the *Daily News*, to which she contributed commentaries on the Crimean War of 1853-1856, the Indian Mutiny of 1857, and the U.S. Civil War of 1861-1865. By addressing the concerns of the textile manufacturing interests while maintaining an uncompromising proabolition stance, she was able to help sway British public opinion against intervening on the side of the Confederacy in the American Civil War.

Martineau's last cause involved women's rights. She used her pen to campaign vigorously against the Contagious Diseases Acts of 1864 and 1869 because they provided for detaining and examining suspected prostitutes without permitting them due process of law. By 1866, she had become too ill to write. After suffering from severe bronchitis, she died at Ambleside on June 27, 1876.

SIGNIFICANCE

Harriet Martineau would have scorned the label of "feminist." In contrast to some of her contemporaries, she valued objectivity above all else and sought to distance her sex from her principles. Among those principles was equality of opportunity, which led naturally to advocacy of woman suffrage and access to higher education for women. As an abolitionist, Martineau helped shape British foreign policy. In the area of economic justice, her acceptance of Thomas Malthus's views on population and Adam Smith's views on free trade led her to oppose factory safety legislation and laws regulating wages and hours and to support the draconian New Poor Law of 1834.

Martineau was popular in her own day because she had a gift for transforming abstract social thought to concrete narratives that caught the popular imagination and was able to reduced masses of observations and anecdotes to coherent moral tales. A generation after she died, she was all but forgotten, as the problems she had helped solve faded into obscurity. However, the late twentieth century revival of interest in women's issues has helped rescue her from obscurity, placing her in perspective as a perceptive, influential mid-Victorian thinker who brought a distinctive woman's voice into the male-dominated field of sociology.

—Martha A. Sherwood

FURTHER READING

Easley, Alexis. *First Person Anonymous: Women Writers and Victorian Print Media*. Aldershot, England: Ashgate, 2004. Provides both a specific and a general picture of the publishing climate in which Harriet Martineau worked.

_____. "Gendered Observations: Harriet Martineau and the Woman Question." In *Victorian Women Writers and the Woman Question*, edited by Nicola Diane Thompson. Cambridge, England: Cambridge University Press, 1999. Contrasts Martineau's objectivity and distancing herself from gender identity with contemporary feminists.

Hoecker-Drysdale, Susan. *Harriet Martineau: The First Woman Sociologist*. Providence, R.I.: Berg Publications, 1992. Showcases the American trip and provides contemporary context for mid-nineteenth century sociology.

Pichanik, Valerie Kossev. *Harriet Martineau: The Woman and Her Work, 1802-1876*. Ann Arbor: University of Michigan Press, 1980. A comprehensive

biography that emphasizes the development of Martineau's outlook in the context of contemporary rationalist philosophy.

Thomas, Gillian. *Harriet Martineau*. Boston: Twayne, 1985. Part of a series of books on individual authors, this volume focuses on Martineau's major works and provides summaries of them.

SEE ALSO: Matthew Arnold; Annie Besant; Barbara Leigh Smith Bodichon; Josephine Butler; Auguste Comte; Octavia Hill; Anna Jameson; John Stuart Mill; Lucretia Mott; William Wordsworth.

RELATED ARTICLES in *Great Events from History: The Nineteenth Century, 1801-1900:* August 28, 1857: British Parliament Passes the Matrimonial Causes Act; August, 1867: British Parliament Passes the Reform Act of 1867.

KARL MARX
German political philosopher

Marx may be the most influential political philosopher in world history; his ideas concerning modes of economic distribution, social class, and the developmental patterns of history have profoundly influenced theories in philosophical and economic thought and have helped shape the political structure of the modern world.

BORN: May 5, 1818; Trier, Prussia (now in Germany)
DIED: March 14, 1883; London, England
ALSO KNOWN AS: Karl Heinrich Marx (full name)
AREAS OF ACHIEVEMENT: Economics, philosophy

EARLY LIFE
Karl Marx was born into a Jewish family in Prussia's southern Rhineland area. After the Napoleonic Wars, when the Rhineland was rejoined to Protestant Prussia, Marx's father, a public lawyer, had converted to Christianity. In 1830, the young Marx entered the Trier secondary school and pursued the traditional humanities curriculum. In the fall of 1835, he entered the University of Bonn as a law student but left the following year to enroll at the University of Berlin. His studies were concentrated on law, history, and the works of the then-leading philosophers Johann Gottlieb Fichte and Georg Wilhelm Friedrich Hegel.

Marx was graduated in 1841, after writing his doctoral dissertation, and returned to Bonn, where he became involved with his friend Bruno Bauer in left-wing politics and in the study of the materialist philosophy of Ludwig Feuerbach. In April, 1842, he began writing radical articles for the *Rheinische Zeitung* (Rhenish gazette), and he assumed its editorship in Cologne that October. He married in June, 1843, and moved to Paris that October.

In August, 1844, Marx met Friedrich Engels in Paris, and the two began a productive collaboration. Marx's articles had angered the Prussian government, and in February, 1845, he moved to Brussels. In 1848, the year of revolutions in many European countries, Marx was ordered to leave Brussels; he returned to Paris and then to Cologne. He was again compelled to leave in 1849 and went to London, where he would remain for the rest of his life.

LIFE'S WORK
Marx's lifelong critique of capitalist economy began in part as an analysis of the then-dominant Hegelian system of philosophical Idealism. Influenced to a degree by Feuerbach's materialism, Marx rejected Hegel's metaphysical vision of a *Weltgeist*, or Absolute Spirit. It was not metaphysical Spirit that governed history but rather material existence that determined consciousness. The

ways in which an individual was compelled to seek physical necessities such as food, shelter, and clothing within a society profoundly influenced the manner in which a person viewed himself and others. As Hegel (and others) suggested, the course of history was indeed a dialectical process of conflict and resolution, but for Marx this development was determined to a great extent by economic realities.

Whereas Hegel saw dialectical process (thesis/antithesis/synthesis) as one of ideas, for Marx it was one of class struggle. Hence Marx's position is called dialectical materialism. He stood in staunch opposition to the prior philosophical tradition of German Idealism and thinkers such as Immanuel Kant, Fichte, and Hegel. German philosophy, he believed, was mired in insubstantial theoretical speculation when concrete and practical thought about the relationship between reality—especially economic and political realities—and consciousness was needed. In general, Marx was a synthetic thinker, and his views represent a mixture of German materialist philosophy such as that of Feuerbach; the French social doctrines of Charles Fourier, Comte de Saint-Simon, and Pierre-Joseph Proudhon; and British theories of political economy such as those of Adam Smith and David Ricardo.

Marx's philosophical position of a dialectical materialism suggests a comprehensive view of social organization—which is, broadly speaking, a dimension of human consciousness—in all its manifestations. The determinant of all societal forms is its economic base (*Basis*), that is, the means of production and the distribution of its produced wealth. All aspects of human social interaction, what Marx called the superstructure (*Überbau*), are influenced and shaped by the economic base and its consequent relationships of power among social classes.

The superstructure ultimately involves a society's educational, legal, artistic, political, philosophical, and scientific systems. The nature of the economic base—above all the power relationships of the classes—tends to be reproduced in an overt or covert fashion in the various dimensions of the societal superstructure. The pedagogical curriculum of the school system, for example, might reproduce or reinforce in some unconscious manner the inequality of the social classes upon which the mode of production is based. Various aspects of the artistic or cultural dimensions of a society (a novel, for example) might also incorporate in symbolic expression the nature of the economic base. Thus Marx's economic theories provide an account for a wide variety of phenomena.

Karl Marx. (Library of Congress)

In capitalist political economy, the individual must sell his physical or intellectual labor, must sell himself as a commodity, in order to survive. Thus, Marx's early writings, such as *Ökonomische und philosophische Manuskripte* (1844; *Economic and Philosophic Manuscripts of 1844*, 1947), deal with the pivotal concept of alienation (*Entfremdung*) as a central aspect of the worker's experience in capitalism. Because the worker is reduced to an exploited commodity or object, this is above all a condition of dehumanization (*Entmenschlichung*). The individual is alienated or divorced from his full potential as a human being. Committed to long hours of labor in a factory, the worker—and this means man, woman, and child—has no time to develop other facets of the personality. In a capitalist society, individuals are estranged not only from aspects of their own selves but also from others in that the labor market is a competitive one, and workers must outdo one another in order to survive. In its crudest form, capitalist economy, Marx would assert, is a kind of Darwinian "survival of the fittest," in which the weak—those who cannot work—must perish.

In his *Die deutsche Ideologie* (1845-1846; *The German Ideology*, 1938), Marx discusses earlier forms of social organization, such as tribal or communal groups, in which the estrangement of the individual in industrialist society was not yet a crucial problem. His vision of an ideal socialist state would be one in which the individual might, for example, manufacture shoes in the morning, teach history in the afternoon, and play music in an orchestra in the evening. In other words, a person would be free to utilize or realize all dimensions of the self. This idealized notion of social organization in the writings of the young Marx indicates the utopian influence of Romantic thought upon his initial critique of capitalist society.

In 1848, after the Paris revolts of that same year, Marx and Engels published *Manifest der Kommunistischen Partei* (*The Communist Manifesto*, 1850), a booklet that has become the best-known and most influential statement of Marxist ideology. It presents a brief historical sketch of bourgeois society and suggests that capitalism will eventually collapse because of its inherent pattern of cyclical economic crises and because of the worsening situation of the worker class, or the proletariat, in all capitalist nations. The proletariat has become, they argue, more conscious of its situation, and a worker revolution

---

THE COMMUNIST MANIFESTO

The history of all hitherto existing societies is the history of class struggles.

Freeman and slave, patrician and plebeian, lord and serf, guild-master and journeyman, in a word, oppressor and oppressed, stood in constant opposition to one another, carried on an uninterrupted, now hidden, now open fight, a fight that each time ended, either in a revolutionary re-constitution of society at large, or in the common ruin of the contending classes.

In the earlier epochs of history, we find almost everywhere a complicated arrangement of society into various orders, a manifold gradation of social rank. In ancient Rome we have patricians, knights, plebeians, slaves; in the Middle Ages, feudal lords, vassals, guild-masters, journeymen, apprentices, serfs; in almost all of these classes, again, subordinate gradations.

The modern bourgeois society that has sprouted from the ruins of feudal society has not done away with class antagonisms. It has but established new classes, new conditions of oppression, new forms of struggle in place of the old ones. Our epoch, the epoch of the bourgeoisie, possesses, however, this distinctive feature: it has simplified the class antagonisms. Society as a whole is more and more splitting up into two great hostile camps, into two great classes, directly facing each other: Bourgeoisie and Proletariat.

From the serfs of the Middle Ages sprang the chartered burghers of the earliest towns. From these burgesses the first elements of the bourgeoisie were developed.

The discovery of America, the rounding of the Cape, opened up fresh ground for the rising bourgeoisie. The East-Indian and Chinese markets, the colonisation of America, trade with the colonies, the increase in the means of exchange and in commodities generally, gave to commerce, to navigation, to industry, an impulse never before known, and thereby, to the revolutionary element in the tottering feudal society, a rapid development.

The feudal system of industry, under which industrial production was monopolised by closed guilds, now no longer sufficed for the growing wants of the new markets. The manufacturing system took its place. The guild-masters were pushed on one side by the manufacturing middle class; division of labour between the different corporate guilds vanished in the face of division of labour in each single workshop.

Meantime the markets kept ever growing, the demand ever rising. Even manufacture no longer sufficed. Thereupon, steam and machinery revolutionised industrial production. The place of manufacture was taken by the giant, Modern Industry, the place of the industrial middle class, by industrial millionaires, the leaders of whole industrial armies, the modern bourgeois.

Modern industry has established the world-market, for which the discovery of America paved the way. This market has given an immense development to commerce, to navigation, to communication by land. This development has, in its time, reacted on the extension of industry; and in proportion as industry, commerce, navigation, railways extended, in the same proportion the bourgeoisie developed, increased its capital, and pushed into the background every class handed down from the Middle Ages.

We see, therefore, how the modern bourgeoisie is itself the product of a long course of development, of a series of revolutions in the modes of production and of exchange.

Each step in the development of the bourgeoisie was accompanied by a corresponding political advance of that class. . . .

Source: Karl Marx, "Bourgeois and Proletarians," in *The Communist Manifesto*, edited by Friedrich Engels (Chicago: C. Kerr, 1888).

is inevitable. The international communist party presents a revolutionary platform in which the workers are the ruling class in charge of all capital production. Marx and Engels call for a worker revolt to overthrow the "chains" that bind them.

Marx wrote and published *Zur Kritik der politischen Ökonomie* (1859; *A Contribution to a Critique of Political Economy*, 1904), which became a preliminary study for the first volume of his and Engels's planned multivolume analysis of capitalist political economy, *Das Kapital* (1867, 1885, 1894; *Capital: A Critique of Political Economy*, 1886, 1907, 1909, better known as *Das Kapital*). Marx actually completed only the first volume; the second and third were edited from his notes by Engels, who was helped on the third by Karl Kautsky. This work is a more technical economic analysis of the capitalist mode of production with the intention of revealing "the economic law of motion" that underlies modern (industrial) society.

It would be beyond the scope of this study to provide a detailed summary of this complex work, but a few words of general explanation may be given. Marx discusses economic issues such as the labor theory of value and commodities, surplus value, capital production and accumulation, and the social relations and class struggles involved in capital production. Capital accumulation, the central goal and justification of the system, is beset by certain internal contradictions, such as periodic episodes of moderate to extreme market inflation and depression and a tendency toward monopoly. These inherent conditions usually have their most deleterious effects upon the wage laborer. Such cycles will eventually lead to economic collapse or revolutionary overthrow by the proletariat. In general, Marx's analyses were flawed—especially the labor theory of value upon which much of this work is based—and could not account for adaptive changes in the capitalist system.

In December, 1881, Marx's wife, Jenny, died, and his daughter died the following year. Marx himself, after a life of overwork and neglect of his health, died in 1883.

SIGNIFICANCE

Karl Marx was a critical social and economic philosopher whose materialist analyses of bourgeois capitalist society initiated a revolution that has had profound effects on the development of human civilization. Despite some of the later ideological, and at times quasi-religious and fanatical, adaptations of his thought, the basic philosophical assumptions of Marx's approach remain hu-

manistic and optimistic; they are based upon fundamental notions of the European Enlightenment, that is, that human reason can successfully alleviate the problems of life. Alienation is, for example, in Marx's view (as opposed to modern existential thought) a historical and societal phenomenon that can be overcome through a change in the social-economic order. Marxism has remained a vital intellectual position and therefore possesses much relevance to the modern world.

Subsequent developments of Marxist thought have resulted in Communist Party revolutions in a number of countries, such as that led by the ideologue Vladimir Ilich Lenin within czarist Russia in 1917 or that of the popular leader Mao Zedong in the People's Republic of China in 1949. These revolutions have involved pogroms and mass executions of certain segments of the population, usually elements of the landed bourgeoisie. This was the case under the rule of Joseph Stalin in Soviet Russia. These socialist governments became reified, for the most part, at the intermediate stage of a party dictatorship rather than the essentially free state of the people that Marx had ideally envisioned.

Marx's philosophy has led to fruitful thought in areas other than social and economic thought. The notion that the power relationships of the economic base effect in various ways the manifestations of the societal superstructure has produced an analytical mode called ideological criticism, in which the hidden dimensions of class ideology are revealed in their social expressions. This has been especially productive in the field of literature and the arts. Marxist analyses of literary texts have yielded new insights into the nature of literary production and its relationship to society at large. The Hungarian critic Georg Lukács, for example, wrote many excellent books and essays on the history of European literature, establishing a new model of Marxist interpretation and criticism.

—Thomas F. Barry

FURTHER READING

Bottomore, Tom, ed. *Karl Marx*. Englewood Cliffs, N.J.: Prentice-Hall, 1973. An excellent collection of essays by prominent scholars on various aspects of Marx's thought. Contains a selected bibliography.

Henry, Michel. *Marx: A Philosophy of Human Reality*. Translated by Kathleen McLaughlin. Bloomington: Indiana University Press, 1983. An important critical work by a French scholar who gives close readings and interpretations of Marx's key texts.

Lee, Wendy Lynn. *On Marx*. Belmont, Calif.: Wadsworth/Thomson Learning, 2002. A brief overview of Marx's philosophy designed to introduce students to his ideas. Discusses his thoughts on several subjects, including human nature, labor and alienation, and dialectics.

McLellan, David. *Karl Marx: His Life and Thought.* New York: Harper & Row, 1973. An excellent critical biography of Marx by a prominent Marxist scholar. Contains a good bibliography.

_____. *Marx Before Marxism.* New York: Harper & Row, 1970. An excellent study of Marx's important early years as a student and the development of his initial ideas. Contains a selected bibliography.

Rockmore, Tom. *Marx After Marxism: The Philosophy of Karl Marx.* Malden, Mass.: Blackwell, 2002. Seeks to interpret Marx's philosophy from an apolitical perspective, without the ideology that dominated many previous analyses. Focuses on Marx's relationship with Hegel.

Singer, Peter. *Marx.* New York: Oxford University Press, 1980. A brief but informative introduction to Marx's life and major ideas. Contains suggestions for further reading.

Suchting, W. A. *Marx: An Introduction.* New York: New York University Press, 1983. A good critical biography of Marx presented chronologically and by topic. Contains helpful guide for further reading.

Wood, Allen W. *Karl Marx.* 2d ed. New York: Routledge, 2004. Provides an explanation of Marx's ideas from a philosophical perspective.

SEE ALSO: Mikhail Bakunin; Friedrich Engels; Charles Fourier; Georg Wilhelm Friedrich Hegel; Ferdinand Lassalle; Wilhelm Liebknecht; Pierre-Joseph Proudhon; David Ricardo.

RELATED ARTICLES in *Great Events from History: The Nineteenth Century, 1801-1900:* February 17, 1815: Treaty of Ghent Takes Effect; 1839: Blanc Publishes *The Organization of Labour*; February, 1848: Marx and Engels Publish *The Communist Manifesto*; September 28, 1864: First International Is Founded; 1867: Marx Publishes *Das Kapital*.

CLORINDA MATTO DE TURNER
Peruvian writer

In a long career of publishing and writing, Matto de Turner crusaded for the modernization of Latin America, particularly her native Peru, by opening society to the indigenous populations and women. She helped found the literary genre known as indigenismo, *or Indianism, and worked tirelessly for the education of women and their participation in all areas of public life.*

BORN: November 11, 1852; Cuzco, Peru
DIED: October 25, 1909; Buenos Aires, Argentina
ALSO KNOWN AS: Grimanesa Martina Mato (birth name)
AREAS OF ACHIEVEMENT: Literature, social reform, women's rights

EARLY LIFE

Clorinda Matto de Turner was born Grimanesa Martina Mato, the daughter of Ramón Mato Torres and Grimanesa Concepción Usandivaras, in the former capital of Peru's precolonial Inca Empire. She grew up on her father's hacienda in the village of Paullo north of Cuzco. She was a tomboy as a child and was nicknamed "Clorinda," after the Italian poet Torquato Tasso's name for a woman disguised as a Persian warrior in his 1575 epic poem *Gerusalemme liberta* (Jerusalem delivered). She grew up with Quechua-speaking Indians on the family hacienda and in nearby villages and learned the language, beliefs, and customs of the descendants of the Incas. In 1862, she entered a boarding school in Cuzco, where she completed her studies in 1868. On July 27, 1872, at the age of seventeen, she married Joseph Turner, an English physician and businessperson, with whom she lived in Tinta, southeast of Cuzco.

With the encouragement of her husband, Clorinda began writing short stories, poems, essays, legends, and historical vignettes. Many of her early writings highlighted the virtual enslavement of the Indians and the need for an opening of society to women, beginning with their education. Using several pseudonyms, she submitted her work to local newspapers. Eventually she returned to her childhood nickname, Clorinda, and added a *t* to her Galician surname, Mato, making it "Matto"—a Quechua word for coca leaf harvest.

In 1876, Matto began publishing a weekly in Cuzco with the support of her husband and her father. This weekly included many of her own *tradiciones*, short historical fictions similar to those written by Ricardo Palma. These pieces attracted the attention of literary salons in Lima, and during the following year, the novelist Juana Manuela Gorriti awarded Clorinda a golden pen as Peru's outstanding young writer.

LIFE'S WORK

Shortly after Matto received her first recognition as a writer, Peru suffered a disastrous defeat at the hands of Chile in the 1879-1884 War of the Pacific. The war plunged the Peruvian economy into chaos, and when Matto's husband died in 1881, his estate was deeply in debt. Matto and Turner had no children. Matto never remarried and tried for two years to manage her husband's businesses but could not repay their debts.

In 1883, Matto moved to the southern Peruvian town of Arequipa, where she took up the position of editor of *La Bolsa* (the exchange). The first woman in the Americas to serve as editor of an important daily newspaper, she championed women's causes and blossomed as a writer and a publisher. She also published two volumes of her *tradiciones* in 1880 and the first of two volumes of *Perú: Tradiciones cuzceñas* (Peru: tales of old Cuzco) and the first of many textbooks for female students in 1884. During that same year her play *Hima-Súmac* about a young Indian heroine was performed before an appreciative audience. Meanwhile, Matto argued repeatedly in her essays and editorials for society to recognize that women were as intelligent as men but had deeper faith and more tender hearts.

At the end of 1885, after finally paying off all her husband's debts, Matto moved to Lima. There she continued publishing her biographies and sketches and was welcomed in the literary circles of Peru's capital city. By the end of 1887, she had formed her own salon. Along with Manuel González Prada and other elite Peruvians who felt humiliated by their nation's defeat in the war with Chile, Matto was convinced that Peru needed to modernize by reforming its European institutions. However, rather than encourage more European immigration, these reformers sought to reinvigorate Peru by uniting the nation's existing European and indigenous populations through education and social and cultural improvements. Peruvians, Matto argued, needed to open more schools and factories and build a better future with the labor of all Peruvians, learning and working side by side.

In 1889, Matto became the editor of *El Perú Ilustrado*, the most prestigious weekly magazine in the nation. The following year, however, the archbishop of Lima declared that an article by a Brazilian that was published in *El Perú Ilustrado* contained heretical ideas. The ensuing controversy led to Matto's excommunication from the Roman Catholic Church and her resignation as editor of the magazine.

In 1889, Matto published the first book in a trilogy of novels that broke new literary ground. *Aves sin nido* (birds without a nest), *Índole* (character) in 1891, and *Herencia* (heredity) in 1895 deplored the sufferings of the indigenous population at the hands of indifferent and abusive landowners, greedy government officials, and lecherous priests. Matto's novels realistically described the wretched living conditions in the Andes, depicted the white elites as villains, and cast the exploited native Peruvians as heroes. Immediate commercial successes in Peru and some other countries, the books provoked powerful reactions from the elites and the institutions they controlled. Speakers in the Peruvian congress condemned Matto. The archbishop of Lima forbade the faithful to purchase, read, or discuss her writings, and mobs burned her literature and effigies.

In 1892, Matto established a feminist print shop, hired a female staff, and published a new weekly magazine, *Los Andes*, which she dedicated to women's issues and the success of Peru's Constitutional Party. In the Revolution of 1895, the Conservative Party leader Nicolás Piérola seized power. During fighting in Lima, mobs looted Matto's home, destroyed her publishing company, and burned unpublished manuscripts of her articles and novels. Piérola deported Matto, who relocated in Buenos Aires, Argentina.

The literary world of Argentina welcomed Matto immediately. In December, 1895, the male-only salon Atheneum broke its custom and invited Matto to address its members. Matto chose the topic women workers in South America. The subject of women's conditions and the need for improvement remained the focus of her energies through the rest of her life. She supported herself by teaching, lecturing extensively, writing textbooks and articles, and establishing and operating the family magazine *El Búcaro Americano*. She also translated the gospels and the Acts of the Apostles into Quechua for the American Bible Society.

Women's education, acceptance in the professions, and equal treatment in the workplace were constant subjects of Matto's interest during her last years. On October 25, 1909, she died in Buenos Aires, at the age of fifty-five, of pulmonary congestion. Fifteen years later, on November 30, 1924, her long exile ended when her body was reburied in the Cementario General in Lima.

SIGNIFICANCE

Clorinda Matto de Turner left a large volume of writing in several genres. She pioneered in the school of realism and virtually founded the school of *indigenismo*. She wrote hundreds of essays on Peruvian folkways and more than two hundred biographies exalting the lives of influential women. In her articles, speeches, and editorials, she championed the elevation of women's conditions in the private and public spheres of society. Her textbooks improved the curriculum for school girls.

The few writings of Matto that are still being read during the twenty-first century are read mostly by academics and their captive audiences. The real significance of Matto's life is the course of her life itself. With the death of her husband, she rose from personal depression and bankruptcy to become a self-made person, transforming herself from Grimanesa Martina Mato de Turner into Clorinda Matto de Turner.

Matto was born and was reared as a dependent among the landed elite but became a self-supporting entrepreneur. She also became a writer, a publisher, a business owner, a teacher, and a public speaker. The streets, schools, and public buildings that now bear Matto's name throughout Latin American nations testify to the recognition of the importance of her life and the possibilities that life holds for others. Like Torquato Tasso's warrior Clorinda, Clorinda Matto de Turner struggled against great odds to be herself. Unlike the imaginary Clorinda who died a tragic and untimely death, Matto overcame the barriers placed in her path and lived a full life.

—*Paul E. Kuhl*

FURTHER READING

Berg, Mary G. "The Essays of Clorinda Matto de-Turner." In *Reinterpreting the Spanish American Essay: Women Writers of the Nineteenth and Twentieth Centuries*, edited by Doris Meyer. Austin: University of Texas Press, 1995. Berg points out that while Matto's novels brought her fame, her essays constituted the bulk of her writings. Berg's analysis emphasizes the feminist character of Matto's writings, particularly during her exile in Argentina.

Matto de Turner, Clorinda. *Birds Without a Nest: A Story of Indian Life and Priestly Oppression in Peru*. Edited and emended by Naomi Lindstrom. Translated by J. G. H[udson]. Austin: University of Texas Press, 1996. Lindstrom has reprinted the 1904 English translation of *Aves sin nido*, restored passages excised by the squeamish J. G. H., and placed sections in their original order. She introduces the work with a fine discussion of Matto de Turner and the literary milieu of Peru at the end of the nineteenth century.

_____. *Torn from the Nest*. Edited by Antonio Cornejo Polar. Translated by John H. R. Polt. New York: Oxford University Press, 1998. This modern translation of *Aves sin nido* follows an extensive discussion of Matto de Turner and Peruvian literature.

Meyer, Doris, ed. *Rereading the Spanish American Essay: Translations of Nineteenth and Twentieth Century Women's Essays*. Austin: University of Texas Press, 1995. Contains two samples of Matto's essays. The first is a short biographical essay of Francisca Zubiaga de Gamarra, who was a soldier like Tasso's Clorinda. The second is a lecture to Argentina's National Council of Women.

SEE ALSO: Fanny Calderón de la Barca; José Martí; Domingo Faustino Sarmiento; Flora Tristan.

RELATED ARTICLE in *Great Events from History: The Nineteenth Century, 1801-1900:* c. 1820-1860: *Costumbrismo* Movement.

GUY DE MAUPASSANT
French writer

Maupassant was one of the major literary figures at the end of the nineteenth century to help move short fiction away from the primitive folktale form to the short story of psychological realism. His most significant contributions to the form may be found in such affecting realistic stories as "Boule de Suif" and such powerful tales of psychological obsession as "The Horla."

BORN: August 5, 1850; Château de Miromesnil, near Dieppe, France

DIED: July 6, 1893; Passy, Paris, France

ALSO KNOWN AS: Henri-René-Albert-Guy de Maupassant (full name)

AREA OF ACHIEVEMENT: Literature

EARLY LIFE

Henri-René-Albert-Guy de Maupassant (moh-pah-sahn) was the first son of Laure Le Poittevin and Gustave de Maupassant, both from prosperous bourgeois families. When he was eleven and his brother Hervé was five, his mother, an independent-minded woman, risked social disgrace to obtain a legal separation from her husband. With the father's absence, Maupassant's mother became the most influential figure in the young boy's life.

At the age of thirteen, he was sent to a small seminary near Rouen for classical studies, but he found the place unbearably dreary and yearned for home, finally getting himself expelled in his next-to-last year. He returned home to the influence of his mother, as well as her brilliant brother Alfred and his student and friend Gustave Flaubert. At the age of eighteen, Maupassant was enrolled at the Lycée de Rouen, and he began law studies soon afterward in Paris, only to have these studies interrupted by the Franco-Prussian War, for which he enlisted. After the war, he gained a position in the Naval Ministry, but under the tutelage of Flaubert he began to publish poetry and stories in various small journals. He also became part of a group of literary figures, including Alphonse Daudet, Émile Zola, and Ivan Turgenev, who met regularly at the home of Flaubert.

LIFE'S WORK

Maupassant's first published story, "La Main d'écorché" (1875; "The Skinned Hand," 1909), which was reworked in 1883 as simply "La Main" or "The Hand," belongs to a tradition of supernatural short fiction that is as old as legend itself; in reworking the story, however, Maupassant grounded it in the revenge-tale tradition popularized by his countryman Prosper Mérimée and at the same time managed to make the story an ironic comment on supernatural fictions.

With the publication of "Boule de Suif" (1880; English translation, 1903), a tale that Flaubert praised extravagantly, Maupassant ceased working for the government and devoted himself to a career as a writer, excelling especially in the genre of the *conte*, or short story, which was quite popular at the time in periodical magazines and newspapers. Before achieving this initial success, however, Maupassant contracted syphilis, which was to take his life after a relatively brief writing career of ten years.

After the success of "Boule de Suif," the touching story of the prostitute who reluctantly goes to bed with a Prussian officer in order to procure the release of her traveling companions, only to be scorned by them, Maupassant began to write anecdotal articles for two newspapers, the practice of which served as preparation for writing the short stories that were to make him famous.

Maupassant's first full volume of short fiction appeared in 1881 under the title of his second important story, "La Maison Tellier" (1881; "Madame Tellier's Establishment," 1903), a comic piece about a group of prostitutes who attend a First Communion. After the success of this book, Maupassant published numerous stories in newspapers and periodicals. These stories were reprinted in volumes containing other Maupassant stories. Many of his stories created much controversy among the French critics of the time because he dared to focus on the experiences of so-called lowlife characters.

In addition to the realistic stories of the lower classes, Maupassant experimented with mystery tales, many of which are reminiscent of the stories of Edgar Allan Poe. Instead of depending on the supernatural, these stories focus on some mysterious dimension of reality that is justified rationally by the central character. As a result, the reader is never quite sure whether this realm exists in actuality or whether it is a product of the narrator's obsessions.

After having published as many as sixty of Maupassant's stories, the newspaper *Gil-Blas* began the serialization of his first novel, *Une Vie* (*A Woman's Life*, 1888), in February, 1883, which was published in book form two months later. The year 1884 also saw the publication of Maupassant's most famous short story and his most widely read novel. The story, "La Parure" (1884; "The Necklace," 1903), has become one of the most famous short stories in any language. Indeed, it has become so famous that it is the story that most commonly comes to mind when Maupassant's name is mentioned, despite the fact that most critics agree that Maupassant's creation of tone and character in such stories as "Boule de Suif" and "La Maison Tellier" is much more representative of his genius than this ironically plotted story about a woman who wasted her entire life working to pay back a lost necklace, only to discover that it was fake.

"Le Horla" (1887; "The Horla," 1890), a story almost as famous as "The Necklace," is often referred to as the first sign of the syphilis-caused madness that eventually led to Maupassant's death. As a story of psychological horror, however, it is actually the pinnacle of several stories of madness with which Maupassant had previously experimented. The story focuses on the central charac-

ter's intuition of a reality that surrounds human life but remains imperceptible to the senses. Told by means of diary entries, the story charts the protagonist's growing awareness of his own madness as well as his lucid understanding of the process whereby the external world is displaced by psychic projections.

What makes "The Horla" distinctive is the increasing need of the narrator to account for his madness as the result of something external to himself. Such a desire is Maupassant's way of universalizing the story, for he well knew that human beings have always tried to embody their most basic desires and fears in some external but invisible presence. "The Horla" is a masterpiece of hallucinatory horror because it focuses so powerfully on that process of mistaking inner reality for outer reality—a process that is the very basis of hallucination. The story is too strongly controlled to be the work of a madman.

Moreover, those who argue that with the writing of "The Horla" Maupassant was already going mad cannot explain the fact that the following year he published the short novel *Pierre et Jean* (1888; *Pierre and Jean*, 1890), which is one of his best-conceived and best-executed works. This work was his last major contribution, however, for after its publication his intensive production of stories slowed almost to a halt, and he began to complain of migraine headaches, which made it impossible for him to write. His eyesight began to fail, his memory faded, and he began to suffer from delusions.

Just after the first of the year in 1892, Maupassant had to be taken to a sanatorium in a straitjacket after having slashed his own throat in a fit of what he himself called "an absolute case of madness." In the sanatorium, he disintegrated rapidly until he died on July 6, 1893.

SIGNIFICANCE

Guy de Maupassant is one of those writers whose contribution to literature is often overshadowed by the tragic facts of his life and whose unique experimentation is often ignored in favor of his more popular innovations. Too often it is his promiscuity and profligate Parisian lifestyle that receive the most attention from the casual reader. As if to provide evidence for the payment Maupassant had to make for such a lifestyle, these readers then point to the supposed madness-inspired story "The Horla" as a fit ending for one who not only wrote about prostitutes but also paid for their dangerous favors with his life. However, Maupassant's real place as a writer belongs with such innovators of the short-story form as Anton Chekhov, Ivan Turgenev, Ambrose Bierce, and O. Henry.

Guy de Maupassant. (Library of Congress)

Too often, whereas such writers as Turgenev and Chekhov are admired for their so-called lyricism and realistic vignettes, such writers as Bierce and O. Henry are scorned for their so-called cheap narrative tricks. Maupassant falls somewhere in between. On one hand, he mastered the ability to create the tight, ironic story that depends, as all short stories do, on the impact of the ending. On the other hand, he had the ability, like Chekhov, to focus keenly on a limited number of characters in a luminous situation. The Soviet short-story writer Isaac Babel has perhaps paid the ultimate tribute to Maupassant in one of his stories by noting that Maupassant knew the power of a period placed in just the right place.

Maupassant had as much to do with the development of the short-story genre during the late nineteenth century as did Chekhov, although in somewhat different ways. Yet, because such stories as "The Necklace" seem so deceptively simple and trivial, his experiment with the form has often been ignored.

—Charles E. May

FURTHER READING

Bloom, Harold, ed. *Guy de Maupassant*. Philadelphia: Chelsea House, 2004. One in a series of books aimed at introducing students to the works of prominent authors. Includes an introduction by Bloom, a brief biography, and plot summaries and critical analysis of "Boule de Suif," "Madame Tellier's Establishment," and "The Necklace."

Fusco, Richard. *Maupassant and the American Short Story: The Influence of Form at the Turn of the Century*. University Park: Pennsylvania State University Press, 1994. Provides a detailed analysis of the structure of Maupassant's short stories and measures his influence on the short stories of Ambrose Bierce, O. Henry, Kate Chopin, and Henry James.

Ignotus, Paul. *The Paradox of Maupassant*. London: University of London Press, 1966. A biographical and critical study that focuses much more on the unsavory aspects of Maupassant's life than it does on the excellence of his fiction. Ignotus insists, with little evidence to support his arguments, that Maupassant was primarily driven by his sexual appetites, perversions, and immoralities.

Lerner, Michael G. *Maupassant*. New York: George Braziller, 1975. Primarily a biographical study, although discussion of the publication of Maupassant's work is often accompanied by some brief discussion of how his novels and stories are influenced by and in turn reflect his own social milieu.

Steegmuller, Francis. *A Lion in the Path*. New York: Random House, 1949. Not only the best biographical study of Maupassant but also one of the most perceptive critical estimates of Maupassant's works; it is the one indispensable book on Maupassant by an excellent biographer and critic who clearly understands the important role that Maupassant plays in the history of French literature.

Sullivan, Edward D. *Maupassant: The Short Stories*. Great Neck, N.Y.: Barron's, 1962. Although little more than a pamphlet-length introduction to some of Maupassant's basic themes and story types, this valuable study can serve to orient the reader to Maupassant's contribution to the short-story form. Particularly helpful is Sullivan's attempt to place Maupassant's short stories within their proper generic tradition.

_____. *Maupassant the Novelist*. Princeton, N.J.: Princeton University Press, 1954. A study of the basic themes and technique of Maupassant's novels, as well as an attempt to synthesize his aesthetic and critical ideas from his essays and newspaper articles. Sullivan admits that Maupassant was a "natural" short-story writer but argues that a study of his novels provides an opportunity to study Maupassant's creative process.

Wallace, A. H. *Guy de Maupassant*. New York: Twayne, 1973. A conventional biographical and critical study that adds little to Steegmuller's earlier work. Wallace focuses on Maupassant's use of fictional themes and obsessions taken from his own life, primarily the cuckoldry of his father, the women in his life, and his madness.

SEE ALSO: Ambrose Bierce; Anton Chekhov; Kate Chopin; Gustave Flaubert; O. Henry; Henry James; Edgar Allan Poe; Ivan Turgenev; Émile Zola.

RELATED ARTICLE in *Great Events from History: The Nineteenth Century, 1801-1900:* c. 1865: Naturalist Movement Begins.

FREDERICK DENISON MAURICE
English theologian

Maurice was one of the most respected theologians in an age when religious crisis was a part of almost every person's life. His efforts to support educational and social reforms, specifically his involvement with the movement known as Christian Socialism, had a significant beneficial impact on the working classes.

BORN: April 29, 1805; Normanton, England
DIED: April 1, 1872; London, England
ALSO KNOWN AS: John Frederick Denison Maurice (full name)
AREAS OF ACHIEVEMENT: Education, religion and theology

EARLY LIFE

Born on the English coast during the year in which Admiral Horatio Nelson defeated the French in the Battle of Trafalgar, John Frederick Denison Maurice (he dropped his first name early in his adult life) was the only surviving son of Unitarian minister Michael Maurice and his wife, Priscilla. Frederick and his five sisters, along with two cousins who moved in with the family while Frederick was quite young, grew up in a deeply religious household whose history was, by any standards, most unusual. Originally, the family adhered to the father's strict Unitarian beliefs. In a hectic period beginning in 1814, however, the family members began to fall away from that creed. Maurice's older sisters, and then his mother, adopted a Trinitarian stance influenced strongly by Calvinism and Evangelicalism. Although the younger children were reared Unitarian, the tense atmosphere that existed in the household was certainly in part responsible for Frederick's eventual decision to accept the notion of the divinity of Christ and to move closer toward Anglicanism, a faith he ultimately embraced in 1831.

Maurice was educated by his father to prepare for admission to Cambridge, where he matriculated in 1823. There, though he was not ready to subscribe to the Thirty-nine Articles (a condition required for receiving a degree), he pursued studies that would eventually prepare him for a career in law. He studied under Julius Hare, a compassionate and learned tutor who helped him explore various academic and theological questions. From Hare, he learned of the idea of Absolute Truth, and he was taught that it was each person's responsibility to search for it. While at Cambridge, Maurice took the lead in forming a club for undergraduates who met periodically to discuss important political, philosophical, and literary subjects: the Apostles Club, perhaps the most famous of such societies, which eventually numbered among its members John Sterling, Arthur Henry Hallam, and Alfred, Lord Tennyson.

In 1826, Maurice left Cambridge without taking a degree and went to London to continue his study in law. There, he actually spent considerable time in literary activities, including service as editor for two separate periodicals. Maurice also worked on a novel, *Eustace Conway*, which was eventually published in 1834. Religious questions continued to plague him, however, and to "discipline" himself, as he put it, in his studies he decided to renew his formal education; this time, however, he enrolled in the more conservative Oxford University, where he associated with such men as the young William Ewart Gladstone. He received a bachelor of arts degree from Oxford in 1831.

The years 1831-1834 were crucial in Maurice's spiritual development and hence in determining his future. In 1831, after years of contemplation and study, he converted to Anglicanism. Three years later, he took orders, embarking on a career that would bring him to prominence within a short time.

LIFE'S WORK

Maurice began his ministry firmly convinced that the traditional view of religion based on the notion of the Fall was wrongheaded, for people had spent too much time wrangling over the problems of sin and damnation and had given too little attention to the fact that the essence of Christian theology was the presence (or potential presence) of Christ in every person. Maurice had been heavily influenced by theologians Edward Irving and Thomas Erskine, as well as by the religious writings of Samuel Taylor Coleridge. His studies and his reading of the Bible led him to believe that faith must be based on God's revelation of himself to people; people must, he thought, come to know God intimately, as a friend. That view he preached in his first curacy at Bubbenhall and for years while serving as chaplain at Guy's Hospital, a post he assumed in the fall of 1835.

By 1835, Maurice had come to recognize that the Thirty-nine Articles were no inhibition to humankind's personal search for God; certainly the requirement that young men subscribe to them was no cause for anyone to stay away from the universities. To support his position, Maurice published *Subscription No Bondage* (1835), in which he argued that the Articles simply provided a framework within which theological inquiry could proceed; they were not, he claimed, a set of rules that limited one's exploration for the truth. This position seemed to place him in alignment with members of the Oxford Movement, but Maurice was not ready to go as far as the most extreme thinkers of that group. He broke with them openly over the question of the nature of baptism, which he saw as a sign of the continuing relationship God has with every person.

Growing increasingly dissatisfied with such tenets as the Oxford Movement proposed and with other issues with which he found himself continually at odds, Maurice decided to outline his own theological beliefs in a series of "Letters to a Quaker." These sermons he published in 1838 as *The Kingdom of Christ*, a volume he revised in 1842 in order to clarify his basic beliefs. In that work, Maurice displayed his dissatisfaction with the Tractarians of Oxford and affirmed his notion that human beings are saved through personal relationships with Christ. For Maurice, the Kingdom of Heaven already exists—in every person who has established this relationship.

During the 1830's, Maurice's friendship with Sterling led to marriage for the theologian. Though shy and unassuming by nature, Maurice was not without passion, and during 1837 he found a woman who stirred feelings of love within him: Anna Barton, Sterling's sister-in-law. The two were married on October 7, 1837, and were soon blessed with two sons. Anna Maurice did not live to see her children grow up or her husband bring to fruition many of the projects and publications for which he is most remembered; she died of illness in March, 1845.

Maurice was selected to serve as professor of English literature and modern history at King's College, London, in 1840. Not a strong lecturer, he nevertheless captivated audiences with the sincerity of his presentations and remained popular and influential in the various professorships he held throughout his career.

When, in 1846, King's College established a program of religious studies, Maurice was given an additional appointment as professor of theology, a position that permitted him to influence young men who were themselves training for the clergy. The same year, he was appointed chaplain at Lincoln's Inn, where his weekly sermons were well received by the young men studying for the bar. During the same period, he was asked to deliver several lecture series. As the Boyle Lecturer, he pioneered the study of comparative religions; as the Warburton Lecturer, he spoke eloquently on St. Paul's Epistle to the Hebrews.

During the 1840's, Maurice began to attract a following, both through his teaching and especially through his writings. In 1844, influenced by his reading of *The Kingdom of Christ*, author and social worker Charles Kingsley began a lifelong friendship with Maurice. They were joined by J. M. Ludlow, a more radical socialist, in an effort to help improve the living conditions and the education of the London poor; their movement became known as Christian Socialism. Ludlow pressed for more radical solutions to current ills, but Maurice held out to effect such reforms within existing social and political structures.

The trio engaged in several schemes, including publication of several journals, to assist the working poor and to raise the conscience of their countrymen to the plight of the less fortunate. In 1848, Maurice and his followers were first encouraged and then dismayed by the rise and subsequent collapse of the Chartist movement.

Frederick Denison Maurice. (Library of Congress)

By the end of the 1840's, Maurice's personal life took a new turn. He had always been close to his old tutor, Julius Hare, who had married Maurice's sister Esther in 1844. In 1848 and 1849, Maurice was finding another reason to visit the Hare family: Julius's sister Georgiana. They became engaged early in 1849 and were married July 4 of that year.

Because his appointment at King's College, Maurice had devoted much of his life to education. That commitment went beyond his lecturing; for example, in 1848 he was instrumental in establishing Queen's College to educate young women. As early as 1850, Maurice was working to promote education for working men as a means of bettering their lot. His first efforts were directed at assisting various Working Men's associations to conduct independent programs, but it was not long before he found himself at the center of a movement to establish the Working Men's College. Perhaps he would not have been as heavily involved as he eventually became had it not been for a change in his fortunes at King's College.

Maurice was freed of his commitment to King's College in 1853—but not because he had sought release. On the contrary, he was dismissed from his professorships, largely through the efforts of the principal of the college, Dr. Jelf, and conservative members of the Board of Trustees, who objected to his position on eternal punishment, published in his *Theological Essays* (1853). Though his prose was never crystal-clear to even the most discerning reader, Maurice seemed to suggest in *Theological Essays* that he could not accept the notion of eternal punishment. To theologians educated in a system that stressed the significance of the Fall and the ever-present threat of eternal damnation, such an idea appeared heretical. Despite objections from some board members, including Gladstone, the trustees voted to oust Maurice from the college.

That dismissal proved fortunate in some ways, because it permitted Maurice to become principal of the Working Men's College, which opened in 1854. Men who labored by day in London's factories and trade shops attended classes in the evenings. The college offered instruction in a number of subjects and attracted a faculty of noteworthy educators and intellectuals, including John Ruskin, who taught drawing.

Though he was no longer a professor of theology after 1853, Maurice continued to be an important voice on theological issues for the next decade and to cause consternation among those who opposed what they considered to be Maurice's unorthodox views. His appointment to St. Peter Vere Chapel in 1860, made by the Crown

through the Board of Public Works, caused quite a stir; the editors of the *Record*, a paper long opposed to Maurice, lobbied to have the appointment canceled. Maurice continued to publish his own theology in volumes and pamphlets, the most important of which were *What Is Revelation?* (1859), *The Claims of the Bible and of Science* (1863), and *Moral and Metaphysical Philosophy* (1850-1862). These works, and his criticisms of the works of others, showed the essentially conservative bias of his thinking, despite his liberal notions about Hell. He objected strongly to the controversial collection of radical religious writings *Essays and Reviews* (1860), which argued that the Bible should be criticized in the same fashion as other books. Similarly, he took issue with Bishop John Colenso over the publication of the bishop's study *The Pentateuch and Book of Joshua Critically Examined* (1862-1879), because Colenso argued that some of the writings were forgeries.

In 1866, Maurice finally regained a position within the traditional academic community when Cambridge University appointed him Knightsbridge Professor of Casuistry, Moral Theology and Moral Philosophy. He held the appointment until his death. Failing health caused him to reduce his work as the decade turned; he finally succumbed on April 1, 1872, and was buried in the family plot at Highgate.

SIGNIFICANCE

No theologian in the nineteenth century was more committed to the idea that the Church should be one than was Frederick Denison Maurice. His constant attempts to show that sectarian division was artificial and against the will of God influenced many in his lifetime and became an important source of inspiration for later theologians and clergy. Even more significant was Maurice's insistence on the personal relationship that exists between God and humankind, a commitment that led him to pronounce that the Kingdom of God exists in every person who comes to know his or her maker personally. Not only in theology, though, has Maurice's impact been felt in England: The Christian Socialist movement was important in the steady progress that liberalism made during the century to improve the lot of the poor and the working classes and to promote the dignity of the individual. Modern British democracy owes a debt to Maurice for his work in this area.

—Laurence W. Mazzeno

FURTHER READING

Brose, Olive J. *Frederick Denison Maurice: Rebellious Conformist*. Athens: Ohio University Press, 1971. A scholarly study of Maurice, focusing on the influence he exerted on Victorian theological issues. Especially detailed analysis of Maurice's conversion to Anglicanism and its impact on his life and opinions.

Courtney, Janet E. *Freethinkers of the Nineteenth Century*. Reprint. Freeport, N.Y.: Books for Libraries Press, 1967. Reprinted from the original 1920 edition, this book includes a brief biographical sketch of Maurice as well as similar sketches of other important intellectuals in nineteenth century England.

Davies, W. Merlin. *An Introduction to F. D. Maurice's Theology*. London: S.P.C.K., 1964. Largely based on Maurice's important work, *The Kingdom of Christ*, this study presents a summary of his theology, making a strong case for the primacy of Maurice's belief in Christ and his personal relationship with God as an underpinning of his work as a social and educational reformer.

Higham, Florence. *Frederick Denison Maurice*. London: S.C.M. Press, 1947. A brief, conversationally written biography that highlights Maurice's movement toward acceptance of Christian Socialism as a necessary consequence of his theological inquiry. Contains a good discussion of his association with Working Men's College and with such figures as Richard Trench, John Sterling, Charles Kingsley, J. M. Ludlow, and F. J. Furnivall.

Maurice, Frederick. *The Life of Frederick Denison Maurice*. 2 vols. London: Macmillan, 1884. Lengthy biography compiled by Maurice's son from letters, family papers, and reminiscences provided by friends. Contains hundreds of important excerpts from Maurice's letters. A primary source of information for scholars and for others interested in Maurice's life and opinions.

Rogerson, J. W. *The Bible and Criticism in Victorian Britain: Profiles of F. D. Maurice and William Robertson Smith*. Sheffield, England: Sheffield Academic Press, 1995. Examines the Old Testament interpretations of Maurice and Smith.

Schroeder, Steven. *The Metaphysics of Cooperation: A Case Study of F. D. Maurice*. Amsterdam: Rodopi, 1999. An analysis of Maurice's theological views, placed within the context of Victorian Britain and the ideas of Samuel Taylor Coleridge.

Vidler, Alec R. *Witness to the Light: F. D. Maurice's Message for To-day*. New York: Charles Scribner's Sons, 1948. An extensive analysis of Maurice's theological views, relying heavily on excerpts from Maurice's own writings. Contains a chapter on Maurice's views of Christian Socialism, including his assessment of the relationship between individual nations and established religions.

Wood, H. G. *Frederick Denison Maurice*. Cambridge, England: Cambridge University Press, 1950. A series of lectures outlining Maurice's theological position, examining his critique of Newman's writings and statements, and commenting on Maurice's study of comparative religion.

Young, David. *F. D. Maurice and Unitarianism*. New York: Oxford University Press, 1992. Analyzes the influence of Unitarianism on Maurice's life and teaching.

SEE ALSO: Samuel Taylor Coleridge; William Ewart Gladstone; John Ruskin.

RELATED ARTICLE in *Great Events from History: The Nineteenth Century, 1801-1900:* August, 1867: British Parliament Passes the Reform Act of 1867.

MATTHEW FONTAINE MAURY
American scientist

A universal scientist, Maury did not limit his endeavors to one field; instead, he researched the land, sea, and air and showed how they are inextricably linked to one another. He brought the study of physical geography and oceanography into the modern age.

BORN: January 14, 1806; Spotsylvania County, Virginia

DIED: February 1, 1873; Lexington, Virginia

AREAS OF ACHIEVEMENT: Geography, science and technology

EARLY LIFE

A descendant of French Huguenots, Matthew Fontaine Maury (mo-ree) was the fourth son in a family of five sons and four daughters. His father, Richard Maury, was an unsuccessful tobacco farmer who was forced, before Matthew reached the age of five, to move his family to Tennessee in search of better land. Matthew's mother, née Diana Minor, was from a prominent Virginia family of Dutch descent.

Young Matthew grew up in a strict household. His father was a disciplinarian who believed that children must never question an order from a parent and should never speak unless spoken to. The elder Maury wanted his son to become a farmer and could not understand Matthew's passionate love for books and learning. In 1818, at the age of twelve, the young boy was enrolled in Harpeth Academy for a formal education and studied there until 1825. He proved to be an excellent student in all subjects and showed a particular aptitude for languages. Disappointed by the lack of books at school and at home, Matthew spent much time at his uncle Abram's nearby house, where books were plentiful. There, Matthew met John Bell, a future United States senator, and Sam Houston, a future governor of Tennessee and military hero. These contacts were to help young Maury later in his naval career.

In 1823, Matthew's eldest brother, John, contracted yellow fever and died at sea. The twenty-eight-year-old naval lieutenant had served as a role model for Matthew. John's death caused the grief-stricken father to forbid Matthew to enter West Point, as the young man had desired. Instead, in 1825, Maury contacted then Congressman Houston and requested help in obtaining a naval commission. Richard Maury was so angered that he refused to communicate with his son for many years.

LIFE'S WORK

Matthew was assigned as a midshipman on the frigate *Brandywine*, bound for France. He had hoped to improve his education aboard the vessel but soon found that he would have to teach himself navigation, because the teacher aboard became impatient with the midshipmen's lack of interest. During the voyage, Maury realized how inadequate and outdated the navy's navigational materials were.

In August, 1826, the *Brandywine* departed New York for a three-year tour around South America. In Chile, Maury was transferred to the *Vincennes*, which patrolled the western coast of South America in response to the political unrest created in several countries by the wars for independence being waged against Spain. In July, 1828, the *Vincennes* received orders to circumnavigate the globe, the first American naval vessel to accomplish that two-year mission.

Although Maury loved the life of a sailor, he longed to marry and rear a family. Years before, Maury had fallen in love with Ann Herndon, a distant cousin. They were engaged in the summer of 1831, but the wedding was postponed until 1834, because Matthew received orders to leave on another three-year voyage. (He and his wife had seven children, three boys and four girls.) It was on this passage that he wrote the first of many articles, "On the Navigation of Cape Horn," published in the *American Journal of Science and Arts* in July, 1834. He also started writing a new navigation textbook that explained the mathematical principles behind the formulas used to derive longitude. This concept was a departure from the rote method then used to learn navigation. In April, 1836, his book *A New Theoretical and Practical Treatise on Navigation* was published. It soon became the official textbook for instructing midshipmen in navigation techniques. Partly as a result of the acclaim that this publication received, Maury was promoted to the rank of lieutenant in June, 1836.

Maury was anxious to return to sea duty, but at that time, there were too many officers and not enough ships in the navy. Finally, in 1838, the young sailor was assigned to a vessel surveying harbors on the North Carolina and Georgia coasts. When the survey was completed, Maury was given leave to visit his aging parents. On October 17, 1839, returning to active duty, Maury received a severe fracture of his leg when the stagecoach in which he was riding overturned.

The injury ended Maury's sailing duties, because it permanently crippled him. During a long period of recovery, he turned to writing articles for the highly respected *Southern Literary Messenger*, exposing what he considered to be the deteriorating condition in the United States Navy. The articles written in 1840 and 1841, under the pen name "Harry Bluff," called for a revision in the promotion ranks, a four-year naval academy stressing a curriculum that included languages, the sciences, international law, and mathematics in order to educate properly future naval officers. He also stressed greater efficiency in ship construction. In 1845, the United States Naval Academy was established, a result, in part, of Maury's articles. The true identity of Harry Bluff became known, and Maury received praise as well as criticism for the publicity he had brought to the navy.

Photographs of Maury show him as a stocky individual, five feet, six inches tall. He was described as having a soft voice with a southern accent, and as a meticulous dresser who walked with a slight limp.

In 1842, Maury was appointed as superintendent of the Depot of Charts and Instruments in Washington, D.C. He was responsible for maintaining the accuracy of the navigational instruments and charts issued to departing navy ships. He soon discovered that most of the navigation charts used by the navy had been compiled by foreigners and were outdated. He therefore began the monumental task of examining old ship logs and calculating prevailing winds, currents, and water temperature conditions for various sailing routes. By 1847, he was able to publish the *Wind and Current Chart of the North Atlantic*.

This work provided such accurate navigational information and so reduced the sailing times on commercial sea routes that other nations began requesting copies of Maury's charts. To keep his charts current, Maury obtained abstract logs from American navy and merchant captains, which contained the latest meteorological observations. Later, he compiled a chart that provided information on the migration patterns and habits of sperm and right whales.

In 1844, Maury was appointed as the first superintendent of the new Naval Observatory in Washington, D.C. The observatory studied and recorded astronomical, hydrographical, and meteorological data and phenomena. Maury's reputation as a scientist had grown greatly, and even though he had not received a college education, the University of North Carolina bestowed an honorary master of arts degree upon him in May, 1847, to honor his contributions to scholarship. In July of 1853, Maury received an honorary law degree from Columbian College (modern George Washington University).

The year 1853 marked the start of the successful Brussels Conference. This meeting was called by the United States to seek the cooperation of the major seafaring nations in a project to exchange marine meteorological data, which Maury used to make new charts of the world's oceans. In 1854, Cyrus Field consulted Maury regarding the feasibility of laying a transatlantic telegraph cable. Maury had conducted deep-sea soundings and told Field that the project would be possible. After two failures, a short-lived cable did link Europe and the United States, but it was not until 1866 that a final link across the Atlantic was achieved.

By 1854, Maury's publisher suggested that he should consider writing a popular treatment of his studies of the oceans in order to take advantage of commercial possibilities. In 1855, the first edition appeared under the title *Physical Geography of the Sea*. It appealed to the general reader and included material on the winds and currents of the sea, temperature data, theories on the circulation of ocean waters, and descriptions of the flora and fauna of the oceans.

For all of Maury's scientific achievements and fame, both at home and abroad, there was to occur an event that was to spell an end to his scientific research and association with the United States Navy. His home state, Virginia, passed an ordinance of secession on April 17, 1861, five days after forces of the Confederate States of America fired upon Fort Sumter. Maury resigned from the navy on April 20, 1861, offered his services to the governor of Virginia, and was immediately appointed to the Governor's Executive Council.

Maury started working on plans for the construction of electric and mechanical "torpedoes" (mines) that could be used to break the Union naval blockade of Virginia ports. By July, 1861, Maury had experimented with powder charges and fuse devices that could be used in the construction of mines. On the night of July 7, Maury led a small raiding party in an attack upon the Union blockading fleet in Hampton Roads. The effort did not succeed in sinking any Union ships, because the fuse device would not detonate the two-hundred-pound powder charge in the mine. In June, 1862, however, Maury mined the James River below Richmond with electrically detonated torpedoes, discouraging Union gunboat movement below that city.

In August, 1862, Maury was sent on a successful secret mission to Europe in order to secure ships and munitions for the Confederacy. He also attempted to influence

European public opinion to favor the Southern cause. While abroad, Maury continued his investigations of electrical torpedoes.

In May, 1865, Maury was ordered back to the South with torpedoes to be used in the defense of Galveston, Texas. Before he reached Confederate soil, he was informed that the war was over. Maury decided to sail to Mexico and offer his services to Maximilian, the French-supported emperor, because he could not be assured of receiving an amnesty from the United States. He planned to establish a colony for displaced Confederates in Mexico, but the scheme did not succeed.

In March, 1866, Maury traveled to England for a reunion with his wife and decided not to return to Mexico. While in England, he received a doctor of laws degree from Cambridge University. He was offered academic positions at universities in Tennessee and Virginia. (During the war, he had refused offers from Russia and France.)

In 1868, Maury finally accepted a position at the Virginia Military Institute as professor of physics and superintendent of the Physical Survey of Virginia, a project designed to investigate the natural resources of that state and utilize them to improve Virginia's depressed economic condition. On several occasions after he took the position, other universities attempted to hire Maury away from Virginia, but he remained loyal to his home state, even in peacetime.

By January, 1873, Maury's health had seriously deteriorated. He attempted to continue a speaking tour, calling for the establishment of a national weather bureau and crop reporting system to aid farmers, but his strong will alone was not enough to sustain his failing body. He died peacefully on February 1, 1873, at his home in Lexington, Virginia.

SIGNIFICANCE

During his lifetime, Maury embodied the spirit of nineteenth century America. A zeal for inquiry, discovery, and improvement may be said to have characterized Maury's America. Nevertheless, he was, perhaps, a man with even stronger commitments and goals than the average person. His inquiring mind spoke of his commitment to discovery. His desire to share his discoveries with ordinary citizens spoke of his commitment to the dissemination of knowledge. His loyalty to Virginia in war and strife spoke of his commitment to a principle, an ideal. Maury's concern for education was mirrored in the publication of his school geographies and wall maps, designed for elementary school use, and in his attempt to establish an agricultural college at the Virginia Military Institute.

Maury was a self-made man in an era of self-made men. He had no college education in the sciences and was criticized by some university-trained scientists for his lack of formal schooling. (Foreign governments and kings showered Maury with honors and memberships in many learned societies for his efforts in charting the oceans.) However, he possessed the gift of observation and an experimentation-oriented intellect that allowed his successes to surpass those of many of his more formally educated critics.

Maury was not afraid to dream. Goals that some would have thought impossible or too difficult to achieve, Maury readily accomplished. He was a nineteenth century American possessing those attributes that made this country unique among the nations. By showing that determination, patience, and hard work, even in the face of adversity, could bring achievement, his example for Americans of any century should not be ignored.

—Charles A. Dranguet, Jr.

FURTHER READING

Bullock, James D. *The Secret Service of the Confederate States in Europe: Or, How the Confederate Cruisers Were Equipped*. 2 vols. New York: Thomas Yoseloff, 1959. Maury is only mentioned briefly in connection with his secret service mission to Europe during the Civil War. However, the book still provides a first-hand account by the Confederate States' naval representative in England of efforts to buy and arm ships for the Confederate navy.

Corbin, Diana Fontaine Maury. *A Life of Matthew Fontaine Maury, U.S.N. and C.S.N.* London: Sampson Low, Marston, Searle, and Rivington, 1888. This laudatory book by one of Maury's daughters contains much personal history of Maury and his family. Includes letters to and from Maury. However, there are many factual errors throughout the work.

Hawthorne, Hildegarde. *Matthew Fontaine Maury: Trail Maker of the Seas*. New York: Longmans, Green, 1943. Written more in the style of a historical novel, this very readable work is a good introduction to Maury's life. It suffers, though, from a lack of documentation and does not have the benefit of new archival material drawn upon by later works.

Hearn, Chester G. *Tracks in the Sea: Matthew Fontaine Maury and the Mapping of the Oceans*. Camden, Maine: International Maritime/McGraw-Hill, 2002.

Comprehensive biography, describing how Maury's career paralleled the U.S. rise as a maritime power. Focuses on Maury's experiences as the first superintendent of the U.S. Naval Observatory, when he charted the oceans' surface currents and wind systems.

Jahns, Patricia. *Matthew Fontaine Maury and Joseph Henry: Scientists of the Civil War*. New York: Hastings House, 1961. This work presents a not-too-flattering and possibly overly critical treatment of Maury. It does, however, point out some of his faults and personality clashes with other scientists of the era that earlier biographers glossed over.

Lewis, Charles Lee. *Matthew Fontaine Maury: The Pathfinder of the Seas*. Annapolis, Md.: United States Naval Institute, 1927. General overview of Maury's life. Not much about his personal life but contains a good chapter on how his family and friends viewed him before the Civil War. The best early biography, but lacks documentation or bibliography.

Wayland, John Walter. *The Pathfinder of the Seas: The Life of Matthew Fontaine Maury*. Richmond, Va.: Garrett and Massie, 1930. This highly readable book is particularly good on Maury's Tennessee years; it has been superseded by later biographies but still provides an enjoyable introduction to its subject.

Williams, Francis Leigh. *Matthew Fontaine Maury: Scientist of the Sea*. New Brunswick, N.J.: Rutgers University Press, 1963. The best and most accurate biography, based on primary sources in the Library of Congress, National Archives, and the Maury Collection at the University of Virginia. Contains an excellent bibliography and a valuable list of Maury's published works.

SEE ALSO: Joseph Henry; Sam Houston; Maximilian.

RELATED ARTICLES in *Great Events from History: The Nineteenth Century, 1801-1900:* c. 1845: Clipper Ship Era Begins; July 27, 1866: First Transatlantic Cable Is Completed.

MAXIMILIAN
Austrian emperor of Mexico (r. 1864-1867)

A liberal, romantic idealist, the young Austrian archduke Maximilian was placed on the French-created throne of Mexico as emperor and attempted sweeping reforms, only to be rejected by the majority of Mexican people, deserted by his French supporters, and executed.

BORN: July 6, 1832; Vienna, Austria
DIED: June 19, 1867; Querétaro, Mexico
ALSO KNOWN AS: Archduke Ferdinand Maximilian Joseph van Habsburg (full name); Maximilian of Habsburg
AREA OF ACHIEVEMENT: Government and politics

EARLY LIFE

Mexico's Emperor Maximilian was born an Austrian archduke, Ferdinand Maximilian van Habsburg. Some historians have speculated that his father was Napoleon Francis Charles, the duke of Reichstadt and son of the French emperor Napoleon I. Reichstadt is known to have been a close friend of his mother, Archduchess Sophia (née Wittelsbach), a Bavarian princess who was the wife of the archduke Charles Francis, the son of Austrian emperor Francis II (r. 1792-1835). What-

ever the truth of that rumor, however, Ferdinand Maximilian was officially considered the second son of Charles Francis.

Favored by his mother when he was young, Maximilian—as his family called him—was noted for his vibrant personality and inquisitive intelligence. In his personality, he differed markedly from his two brothers. At the age of thirteen he determined upon pursuing a career in the navy.

In 1848, when Maximilian was sixteen, revolutions swept through Europe and rocked the Austrian monarchy to its foundations. Archduchess Sophia worked hard to preserve the throne for her oldest son, Francis Joseph (Franz Josef). On December 2, 1848, she succeeded, when the incompetent Emperor Ferdinand abdicated, and her equally weak-minded husband renounced his claim to the throne. Eighteen-year-old Francis Joseph was then crowned emperor.

As the next in line to his brother, Maximilian was now a conspicuous figure at court. He became the center of controversy because of his outspoken liberal opinions, which were at odds with those of Francis Joseph and most of his court, and his criticisms of government policy on Hungary. In 1850, he was sent far from Vienna to join the navy in Trieste, then part of the Austrian province of Venetia-Lombardy.

LIFE'S WORK

Maximilian spent the next few years cruising on the Mediterranean in naval vessels and being dispatched on occasional diplomatic missions. In September of 1854, he was promoted to rear admiral and proved to be an exceptionally able administrator. He launched a program of reform and modernization that contributed to the naval victories the Austrians were to achieve during the Seven Weeks' War of 1866. In 1857, he was promoted to the rank of vice admiral.

On July 28 of 1857, Archduke Maximilian married Princess Charlotte, daughter of King Leopold I of Belgium. At the time of her wedding, Charlotte changed the form of her name to the Germanic Carlota. The couple would have no children. Meanwhile, Maximilian was appointed imperial viceroy to the province of Venetia-Lombardy on September 6, 1857. His liberal leanings and conciliatory policies even toward Italian nationalists aroused the opposition of Count Gyulai, the military commander of that province, who eventually turned Maximilian's brother Francis Joseph against him. Maximilian was relieved of his office of viceroy in 1859, shortly before the Franco-Austrian War wrested control of Lombardy away from Austria and gave it to the kingdom of Sardinia-Piedmont.

Around that same time, a civil war arose in Mexico that became known as the Reform War; it lasted from 1858 to 1860 and divided the country between liberals and conservatives. The war ended in victory for the liberals and their leader, President Benito Juárez. Thousands of exiled Mexican conservative leaders then went into exile in Europe. Among these exiles were José Hidalgo and José Maria Gutierrez d'Estrada, who gained the favor of Empress Eugenie, the wife of French emperor Napoleon III. The empress, the Mexican exiles, and Napoleon's half brother, the duke de Morny, convinced Napoleon that intervening in Mexico on behalf of the conservative faction was a project worth undertaking.

In 1861, Napoleon saw his chance when the impoverished Mexican government defaulted on loans from France, Spain, and Great Britain. The three nations accordingly dispatched expeditionary forces to Veracruz, Mexico, in January of 1862. The Spanish and British troops withdrew several weeks later, but the French remained and attempted to take control of the country for the conservatives. Juárez and his partisans began a war of resistance that continued even after the French drove the Juaristas out of Mexico City in June of 1863.

With French troops in control of Mexico's capital, Napoleon and the Mexican conservatives campaigned to persuade Maximilian to accept the crown of emperor of Mexico, which had once been briefly held during the early 1820's by Agustín de Iturbide, who styled himself Emperor Agustín I. At first reluctant, Maximilian agreed to do so only under pressure from his wife and after receiving assurances that the military situation was under control and that the majority of the Mexican people wanted him. A plebiscite of Mexican voters arranged by French occupation forces seemed to confirm this.

After a bitter confrontation with his brother, Francis Joseph, who insisted that Maximilian renounce his rights as an Austrian archduke, Maximilian resentfully signed the Act of Renunciation and left for Mexico. There he was proclaimed emperor on April 10, 1864, and was crowned on June 10. However, he soon discovered that he had been deceived. The plebiscite had been rigged, and there was deep opposition to his regime, which was merely propped up by French arms. Nonetheless, he committed himself to the task of governing his new country.

It was not long before Maximilian alienated both the conservatives who had expected him to carry out their political agenda and the Roman Catholic Church, which had expected to have its properties and privileges restored. Maximilian rejected the conservative program and proceeded to confirm the liberal and anticlerical provisions of Juárez's administration.

Just as Maximilian was losing what little support he had in Mexico, Napoleon III was under pressure from the international community to withdraw from Mexico. Tensions arose among France, Prussia, and the United States. Up to that time, the United States had been enmeshed in its own civil war. The United States made it known that it considered the French intervention in Mexico to be a violation of the Monroe Doctrine, which explicitly forbade European meddling in Western Hemisphere affairs. After the U.S. government threatened to send troops into Mexico in 1866, Napoleon began withdrawing French troops from Mexico.

Disregarding warnings that his regime was doomed, Maximilian refused to desert what he had come to believe was his sacred duty to the Mexican people. Carlota left for Europe in an attempt to persuade Emperor Napoleon and Pope Pius IX to preserve her husband's throne. Carlota not only failed, but she also suffered a mental breakdown and lapsed into insanity. In the meantime,

Maximilian, with his support rapidly eroding, evacuated Mexico City and made a last stand at Querétaro, where he was captured by Juaristas on May 15, 1867. Despite numerous entreaties for clemency, Juárez considered Maximilian to pose an unacceptable threat to Mexico's security and ordered his execution. On June 19, 1867, Maximilian and two of his generals, Tómas Mejia and Miguel Miramon, were shot by firing squads.

SIGNIFICANCE

Though sometimes derided as a lackey of Napoleon III, Maximilian was in most respects an innocent whose grip on reality was tenuous at best and who died sincerely believing in the righteousness of his cause. His death and the collapse of the French intervention sullied the reputation of Napoleon III in the eyes of the international community and may have contributed to the Second French Empire's downfall in 1870. In Mexico, Napoleon's own downfall confirmed Juárez's triumph but only intensified the already-poisoned political atmosphere there. The major victor in the entire affair was the United States, which was on its way to assuming the status of a great power and whose firm stance against the French intervention was perceived as having made the French back down.

—Raymond Pierre Hylton

FURTHER READING

Blasio, José Luis. *Maximilian: Emperor of Mexico: Memoirs of His Private Secretary*. New Haven, Conn.: Yale University Press, 1934. A firsthand but biased account by a person who was close to Maximilian but who did not himself play an important role in major events.

Harris, Alfred Jackson, and Kathryn Abbey. *Napoleon III and Mexico: American Triumph over Monarchy*. Chapel Hill: University of North Carolina Press, 1971. A slanted account that takes the view that the downfall of Maximilian's regime was in effect a victory for United States ideals and policy over the reactionary forces of Europe.

Haslip, Joan. *The Crown of Mexico: Maximilian and Empress Carlotta*. New York: Holt, Rinehart and Winston, 1972. A sympathetic but factually sound portrayal of the emperor that depicts him as talented and well-intentioned victim of the cynical *realpolitik* of his times.

Shorris, Earl. *The Life and Times of Mexico*. New York: W. W. Norton, 2004. The author stresses the theme of Maximilian as the idealistic dreamer caught up in forces that he was never able to comprehend.

Sinkin, Richard N. *The Mexican Reform, 1855-1876: A Study in Liberal Nation-Building*. Austin: Institute of Latin American Studies, University of Texas at Austin, 1979. A broad study of Mexican politics during the Juárez era.

Smith, Gene. *Maximilian and Carlota: A Tale of Romance and Tragedy*. New York: William Morrow, 1973. Although this narrative rambles at times, it nonetheless makes controversial points, particularly about Maximilian's parentage, and provides interesting reading.

Wasserman, Mark. *Everyday Life and Politics in Nineteenth Century Mexico: Men, Women and War*. Albuquerque: University of New Mexico Press, 2000. An informative account that provides some insights into the background of the events of the 1860's. Includes an excellent time line.

SEE ALSO: Francis Joseph I; Benito Juárez; Matthew Fontaine Maury; Napoleon I; Napoleon III; Pius IX; George Washington Williams.

RELATED ARTICLES in *Great Events from History: The Nineteenth Century, 1801-1900:* March, 1805-September 1, 1807: Burr's Conspiracy; December 2, 1823: President Monroe Articulates the Monroe Doctrine; October 31, 1861-June 19, 1867: France Occupies Mexico.

JAMES CLERK MAXWELL
Scottish physicist

Both a theoretical and an experimental physicist as well as a notable mathematician, Maxwell founded modern field theory and statistical mechanics, mathematically describing interactions of electrical and magnetic fields that produce radiant energy, thus confirming the existence of electromagnetic waves that move at light speed. He also elaborated theories of the mechanics and kinetics of gases and a theory of Saturn's rings.

BORN: June 13, 1831; Edinburgh, Scotland
DIED: November 5, 1879; Cambridge, England
AREA OF ACHIEVEMENT: Physics

EARLY LIFE

An only child, James Clerk Maxwell was reared by devout Episcopalian parents who, in a generally impoverished Scotland, enjoyed the comforts of Middlebie, a modest landed estate, and other small properties. Though rarely practiced, his father's profession was law. Between his parents and grandparents, James was a descendant of middle-level government officials, landed developers of small mines and manufactories, and acquaintances of such famous Scotsmen as Sir Walter Scott and the great geologist John Hutton, although none of Maxwell's immediate kin displayed unusual drive or distinction.

Maxwell's boyhood was that of a happy, unusually observant, and well-loved child to whom were imparted clear religious and moral precepts that prevailed throughout his life. His health was sometimes delicate, and between his fourteenth and sixteenth years he learned that he was nearsighted and afflicted with a persistent ear infection. Regardless of whether these infirmities were contributory, he manifested a shyness and reserve, a superficial impression of dullness, though not unfriendliness, that remained permanent characteristics.

In his earliest years, Maxwell had no formal education. Clearly, despite his affection for the outdoors, his mother introduced him to John Milton's works, as well as other classics, and he became a catholic, voracious reader prior to his entrance into the prestigious Edinburgh Academy in 1841. There, for six years, if at first unenthusiastically, he pursued a classical curriculum. Equally important, Maxwell's father introduced him into the meetings of the Edinburgh Society of Arts and the Royal Society, where he met D. R. Hay, a decorative painter interested in explaining beauty in form and color according to mathematical principles.

Stimulated by his own prior interest in conic forms, Maxwell was encouraged to pursue such inquiries seriously, one result being his receiving of the academy's Mathematical Medal (he also took first prize in English verse) in 1846. A second consequence stemmed from his introduction to Dr. James D. Forbes, of Edinburgh University, subsequently a lifelong friend, for Forbes sent the young Maxwell's ". . . Description of Oval Curves, and Those Having a Plurality of Foci" to be included in the *Proceedings of the Edinburgh Royal Society* the same year. At the age of fifteen, Maxwell, in sum, was already recognized by Forbes and other mentors as an original, proficient, and penetrating mind, confirmation of this coming with publication by the Royal Society of two additional papers in 1849 and 1850, one dealing with the theory of rolling curves, the other with the equilibrium of elastic solids. These achievements came while Maxwell attended the University of Edinburgh, steeping himself in natural philosophy (a Scottish intellectual specialty of great logical rigor), mathematics, chemistry, and mental philosophy.

LIFE'S WORK

Precocious, already credited with natural genius, Maxwell entered Cambridge University (first Peterhouse but soon Trinity College) in 1850. There, he swiftly came under the direction of William Thomson, popularly known for helping lay the Atlantic cable but academically to gain fame as Lord Kelvin, expert on the viscosity of gases and collaborator with James Joule in experiments on properties of air, heat, and electricity and in thermodynamics. Maxwell's superb tutor, William Hopkins, simultaneously brought discipline and order to Maxwell's incredible range of knowledge. Graduated in 1854, Maxwell shortly was made a Fellow of Trinity College and was authorized to lecture. By 1856, however, he accepted a professorship in natural philosophy at Marischal College, whose reorganization as the University of Aberdeen in 1860 caused him to move to King's College, London, still professing natural philosophy. He took with him to London the daughter of Marischal's principal, Katherine Dewar, whom he had married in 1858. They were to have no children.

Maxwell remained at King's until 1865. From students' perspectives, he was a poor instructor; his voice, mirroring his shyness, was husky and monotonal; his explanations were pitched beyond their grasp, particularly

James Clerk Maxwell. (The Granger Collection, New York)

geometry; mechanics; Saturn's rings; and electromagnetism and electricity, which began with Michael Faraday's lines of force and eventuated in Maxwell's theory of the electromagnetic field, in the electromagnetic theory of light, and, among other electrical investigations, in establishing standards for the measurement of resistance for the British Association.

Maxwell published in each of these seven areas, but he is undoubtedly best known for his works on electricity and magnetism. His papers "Faraday's Lines of Force" and "Physical Lines of Force," presented between 1855 and 1861, were seminal studies. Originally confessing little direct knowledge of the field in which Michael Faraday worked, Maxwell nevertheless sought to demonstrate mathematically that electric and magnetic behavior was not intrinsic to magnetic bodies or to conductors, that rather, this behavior was a result of vaster changes in the distribution of energy throughout the ether, albeit by unknown means.

In a 1864 paper titled "On a Dynamical Theory of the Electromagnetic Field," Maxwell further demonstrated that electromagnetic forces moved in waves and that the velocity of these waves in any medium was the same as the velocity of light, thus paving the way for an electromagnetic theory of light. In connection with his many published papers, Maxwell also wrote a textbook, *Theory of Heat* (1871), a study in dynamics, *Matter and Motion* (1876), and gathered and edited the *Electrical Researches of Henry Cavendish* (1879). His own *An Elemental Treatise on Electricity* was published posthumously, in 1881.

While Maxwell recovered from his erysipelas and remained in good health until 1877, though in his prime, he fell ill again with painful dyspepsia. For nearly two years, Maxwell treated himself and kept silent on his illness. By 1879, when he acknowledged it to physicians, his disease was diagnosed as terminal, and he died at Cambridge on November 5, 1879.

SIGNIFICANCE

James Clerk Maxwell is probably the only nineteenth century physicist whose reputation became greater in the twentieth century than it had been in his own century. Rarely have such capacities for inventiveness, exposition, experiment, and mathematical descriptiveness been brought to bear by one man in the physical sciences. He gave new direction and substantiation to Faraday's work and effected a bridge to the investigations of Heinrich Hertz, who did in fact measure the velocity of electromagnetic waves, confirm that these waves indeed be-

when he was lecturing workingmen. In addition, both his wife's health and his own seemed precarious. Upon arrival at King's, he had been infected with smallpox, and in 1865 a riding accident resulted in erysipelas, which seriously drained him. Perhaps persuaded by these circumstances, he retired to the family farm at Glenair until 1871, when Cambridge University offered him a new chair in experimental physics. Because the university's chancellor had presented funds to it for a modern physical laboratory, subsequently the world-famous Cavendish Laboratory, Maxwell devoted himself to designing and equipping it, alternating between spending academic terms there and summers at Glenair. He completed this task in June, 1874.

Contrary to superficial appearances, Maxwell's theoretical and experimental work proceeded steadily from his entrance into Trinity College until his death. Before completion of the Cavendish, he had converted his London home into an extensive laboratory, and the results of his investigations were both continuous and impressive. They basically fell into seven seemingly disparate but actually related areas: experiments in color vision and optics, which later had important consequences in photography; studies in elastic solids; explorations in pure

THE COLOR SPECTRUM

A major part of James Clerk Maxwell's research was into color vision and optics. Here he discusses a basic truth about the nature of the color spectrum.

When we mix together blue and yellow paint, we obtain green paint. This fact is well known to all who have handled colours; and it is universally admitted that blue and yellow make green. Red, yellow, and blue, being the primary colours among painters, green is regarded as a secondary colour, arising from the mixture of blue and yellow. [Isaac] Newton, however, found that the green of the spectrum was not the same thing as the mixture of two colours of the spectrum, for such a mixture could be separated by the prism, while the green of the spectrum resisted further decomposition. But still it was believed that yellow and blue would make a green, though not that of the spectrum. As far as I am aware, the first experiment on the subject is that of M. Plateau, who, before 1819, made a disc with alternate sectors of prussian blue and gamboge, and observed that, when spinning, the resultant tint was not green, but a neutral gray, inclining sometimes to yellow or blue, but never to green. Prof. J. D. Forbes of Edinburgh made similar experiments in 1849, with the same result. Prof. [Hermann von] Helmholtz of Konigsberg, to whom we owe the most complete investigation on visible colour, has given the true explanation of this phenomenon. The result of mixing two coloured powders is not by any means the same as mixing the beams of light which flow from each separately. In the latter case we receive all the light which comes either from the one powder or the other. In the former, much of the light coming from one powder falls on particles of the other, and we receive only that portion which has escaped absorption by one or other. Thus the light coming from a mixture of blue and yellow powder, consists partly of light coming directly from blue particles or yellow particles, and partly of light acted on by both blue and yellow particles. This latter light is green, since the blue stops the red, yellow, and orange, and the yellow stops the blue and violet.

Source: James Clerk Maxwell, "On the Theory of Compound Colours with Reference to Mixtures of Blue and Yellow Light," *Report of the British Association* (1856).

of X rays and ultraviolet light. Even in metallurgy, he was credited with the invention of an automatic control system. In short, his inquiries ranged from the macrocosm to the microcosm and were ultimately knit together and described mathematically in the tradition of Newton.

—*Clifton K. Yearley*

FURTHER READING

Campbell, Lewis, and William Garnett. *The Life of James Clerk Maxwell*. London: Macmillan, 1882. 2d ed. New York: Johnson Reprint Corp., 1969. This remains the most detailed and accurate nineteenth century view of Maxwell. Maxwell's letters were added in the second edition of 1884. Lifelong friends and associates, the authors supply a full account of his personal life and a detailed review of his scientific contributions as they were understood during the 1880's. Though in need of intelligent editing, this is an extremely informative study. Readily available in major libraries.

Domb, Cyril, ed. *Clerk Maxwell and Modern Science*. London: Athlone Press, 1963. Six commemorative essays by scientists who place Maxwell's contributions in twentieth century perspective. Excellent for general readers; reflective and instructive. Readily available in major science libraries.

Garber, Elizabeth. "James Clerk Maxwell and Thermodynamics." *American Journal of Physics* 27 (February, 1969): 146-155. Excellent, readable scholarly analysis of Maxwell's anticipation and subsequent stimulation of Willard Gibbs's work in thermodynamics. Readily available in most science libraries.

Harmon, P. M. *The Natural Philosophy of James Clerk Maxwell*. New York: Cambridge University Press, 1998. An introduction to Maxwell's physics and his world view, based upon the author's lecture series.

Larsen, Egon. *The Cavendish Laboratory*. London: Edmund Ward, 1962. Places Maxwell's preparation and subsequent work at this remarkable research lab-

haved precisely like light, and showed therefore that light and electromagnetic waves were one and the same. Practical evidence of the importance of this work is manifest in modern electronics, in radio, television, and radar.

Maxwell was the effective founder of field theory and of statistical mechanics, with enormous implications for theoretical and tabletop physics, not only for questions that he clarified but also for those that he raised. Similarly, his curiosity about the rings of Saturn led him productively into study of the kinetic theory of gases, adding to the work of John Herapath, Rudolf Clausius, and Joule by treating the velocities of molecules statistically. His conclusions about the nature of light made physical optics a branch of electricity, providing a basis for the study

oratory in perspective. Readable. Availability limited to major libraries.

Mahon, Basil. *The Man Who Changed Everything: The Life of James Clerk Maxwell.* Chichester, England: Wiley, 2003. Sympathetic biography written by a longtime admirer of Maxwell's work. Describes all of Maxwell's work in the physical sciences.

Maxwell, James Clerk. *The Scientific Letters and Papers of James Clerk Maxwell.* 3 vols. Edited by P. M. Harmon. New York: Cambridge University Press, 1990-2002. Contains almost all of Maxwell's correspondence and manuscripts written between 1846 and 1879, including his reference reports to the Royal Society, documents regarding the Cavendish Laboratory, and his letters to other scientists that document his wide involvement in the scientific community.

SEE ALSO: Michael Faraday; Josiah Willard Gibbs; Hermann von Helmholtz; Baron Kelvin; Wilhelm Conrad Röntgen; Mary Somerville.

RELATED ARTICLES in *Great Events from History: The Nineteenth Century, 1801-1900:* October, 1831: Faraday Converts Magnetic Force into Electricity; June, 1896: Marconi Patents the Wireless Telegraph.

GIUSEPPE MAZZINI
Italian nationalist leader

Mazzini was the most influential leader of the Risorgimento—the Italian national unification movement. His political activities and philosophy were carried beyond Italy and inspired fledgling nationalist and democratic reform movements throughout the world.

BORN: June 22, 1805; Genoa, Ligurian Republic (now in Italy)

DIED: March 10, 1872; Pisa, Italy

AREAS OF ACHIEVEMENT: Government and politics, philosophy

EARLY LIFE

The son of a well-to-do Genoese family, Giuseppe Mazzini (maht-TSEE-nee) was a sickly but precocious child, who could scarcely walk until the age of six. His mother, Maria Drago, practiced the morally rigorous Catholic doctrine of Jansenism and provided the young Mazzini with Jansenist tutors. His political education began at home under the influence of his father, Giacomo—a renowned physician and a professor at the University of Genoa. Mazzini's father, like many educated Italians, had embraced the nationalist and democratic ideas of the French Revolution. These ideas endured even after the Napoleonic Wars, when authoritarian rule had been restored to the various Italian states. Giacomo and other Italian patriots nurtured hopes for democratic reform, independence from foreign rule, and ultimately a united Italy.

As a young man, Mazzini was deeply moved by the suffering of others and was recklessly generous in his charity. He tended to be melancholy, always dressed in black—as if in mourning—and enjoyed long, solitary walks. At the University of Genoa, he studied law, but his real interest was in history and literature. He organized a student group to study censored books and wrote provocative essays for several literary journals. The Italian universities during the 1820's were a conduit for subversive political organizations. During his student years, Mazzini became involved with a secret revolutionary society—the Carbonaria. The July Revolution of 1830 in France inspired the group's members, known as the Carbonari, to plot insurrections in Piedmont and other Italian states. Government officials uncovered the conspiracy and arrested hundreds of suspects, including Mazzini. He defended himself successfully in court, but the Piedmontese authorities forced him into exile. At the age of twenty-six, he left Genoa for France.

LIFE'S WORK

The failure of the Carbonari insurrections during 1830-1831 led Mazzini to organize his own secret society, Young Italy. Through this group, he hoped to bring a youthful energy and idealism to the movement for Italian independence and unification. His sincerity and the quiet strength of his convictions won for him a devout following. His agents distributed the newspaper *Young Italy* and established affiliated societies throughout the Italian peninsula. In 1833, Mazzini joined with nationalists from other countries to found Young Europe. This organization embodied the aspirations of many European nationalities seeking to break free of the Austrian and Russian empires and to establish their own independent states with democratic institutions. Mazzini's European network of secret societies made him a notorious figure. The Austrian government considered him an international terrorist, a threat to the entire European order. However, to the peoples of Europe who chafed under authoritarian rule, he appeared as a symbol of liberty.

The insurrections organized during the 1830's by Mazzini and his followers failed to ignite a popular uprising in Italy. For his subversive activity, he received the death sentence in absentia from a Piedmontese court in 1833. His life in exile took him from France to Switzerland to Great Britain. He traveled like a fugitive—under the constant threat of arrest and imprisonment. To survive these difficult years in exile, he relied on the loyalty of his followers and the generous financial support from his mother. Once in London, he devoted his time to writing for popular journals and to publishing his own newspaper. His most notable work during his years in exile was *Doveri dell'uomo* (1860; *The Duties of Man*, 1862). Through his many editorials, essays, commentaries, and correspondence, he shaped and refined his political philosophy. He became a celebrated figure among intellectuals and reformers in Great Britain and the United States. At the same time, he generated international sympathy for the Italian cause.

Mazzini based his philosophy on a profound belief in God, in human progress, and in the fundamental unity and cooperation of humankind. The banner of Young Italy best summarized his thought: "Liberty, Equality, Humanity, Unity." These words had universal application. For Mazzini, liberty meant the elimination of all despotism, from tyranny in Italy to slavery in the American South. His belief in equality extended to women as well as men, and for this he won the admiration and devotion of many women's rights advocates in Europe and the United States. His faith in humanity was expressed in the Latin epithet *Vox populi, vox Dei* (the voice of the people is the voice of God). He believed that the Italian unity would be forged through a spontaneous, general uprising of the Italian people. Mazzini's call for unity transcended national boundaries. He envisioned no less than a brotherhood of nations, beginning with a new federation of European states—a United States of Europe—with the new Italy in the vanguard.

Mazzini's religious faith bordered on mysticism. However, despite his religious convictions and his Catholic education, he had no room for the authority of the pope, either as civil ruler of the Papal States or as the spiritual leader of the Christian world. Although sympathetic to the plight of the working class, he rejected the materialist, atheistic character of socialist philosophy and avoided emphasizing class conflict as the Marxists would later do. Instead, he advocated worker-aid associations and a spirit of cooperation between labor and capital. He sought to extend the Christian ethic from the home to the workplace to the halls of government and spoke more of duties and responsibilities than of rights and privileges.

The popular revolts in Europe during 1848-1849 gave Mazzini the opportunity to return to Italian soil. He arrived in Milan in April, 1848, shortly after the city's heroic five-day uprising against Austrian rule. Despite the generous welcome extended to the exiled patriot, Mazzini represented only one of several political factions vying for leadership. He left Milan after a failed attempt to organize the city's defenses against the returning Austrian army.

Mazzini's second opportunity to create a new Italy came in November, 1848, when the populace of Rome revolted, drove Pope Pius IX from the city, and established a republican government in the Papal States. Maz-

Giuseppe Mazzini. (Library of Congress)

zini entered Rome as an elected leader and immediately implemented his reform program. Church lands were confiscated and redistributed to the peasants, church offices became shelters for the homeless, and public works provided labor for the unemployed. The new republic lasted only a few months. In response to the pope's plea for intervention, the French government dispatched an army to central Italy. The French occupied the Papal States and won control of Rome, despite a tenacious, monthlong defense of the city led by Giuseppe Garibaldi. Mazzini, devastated by the turn of events, left Rome and once again went into exile.

Mazzini's direct influence on Italian politics waned after the failed revolutions of 1848. The work of Italian unification passed to the hands of the Piedmontese prime minister Count Cavour, who preferred international diplomacy to popular uprisings to achieve his goals. Mazzini maintained contacts with republican groups who attempted several unsuccessful, sometimes tragic, insurrections during the 1850's. These failures provoked public criticism even from his supporters. He made several secret trips to Italy and in one instance was arrested and imprisoned briefly near Naples.

Mazzini held stubbornly to his republican principles. Elected to the Italian parliament in 1865, he refused his seat because of the required oath of allegiance to the monarch. He also rejected the general amnesty offered to him by the king in 1871. He spent his last years in Pisa and lived to see Italy unified with Rome as its capital. His political legacy was continued by his followers, many of whom championed further democratic reforms in the parliamentary politics of postunification Italy.

SIGNIFICANCE

Giuseppe Mazzini was the international spokesperson for Italian unification and the Italian people. Ironically, he knew little of his own country. He spent much of his life in exile and, before 1848, had never traveled in central or southern Italy. Much of his knowledge of Italy came from history texts and secondhand reports from visitors, and he did not have many contacts with working-class Italians. His concept of "the people" was a middle-class intellectual's romanticized notion, far removed from the brutish existence of the Italian peasant.

Mazzini was not a profound philosopher; many of his writings are characterized by vagaries, inconsistencies, and temperamental ramblings. Despite these shortcomings, his life had a mythical, heroic quality, and his political philosophy had universal appeal. He personified the idealism, optimism, and faith in humanity that motivated many nineteenth century reformers in Europe and the United States. Even Indian and Chinese nationalists invoked Mazzini's name in their efforts to create new democratic nations. They all found inspiration in his life and in his thoughts on political freedom, social equality, economic cooperation, and the brotherhood of nations.

Many of Mazzini's ideas seemed unrealistic in his own time, but some had a prophetic ring, and others have become even more relevant in the twentieth century. His hopes for an Italian republic were finally realized in 1946. His proposals for worker associations and a reconciliation between labor and capital proved far more constructive than did Karl Marx's vision of unmitigated class conflict, and his dream of a United States of Europe anticipated the post-World War II movement toward a unified European community.

—Michael F. Hembree

FURTHER READING

Griffith, Gwilym O. *Mazzini: Prophet of Modern Europe*. London: Hodder & Stoughton, 1932. The best written of the English biographies, this work offers an uncritical study with emphasis on Mazzini's theology.

Hales, Edward E. Y. *Mazzini and the Secret Societies*. New York: P. J. Kenedy & Sons, 1956. A critical study of Mazzini's early years. Hales highlights the climate of conspiracy to which the young Mazzini was drawn and describes the making of the Mazzini "myth." Contains a helpful annotated bibliography.

Hinkley, Edyth. *Mazzini: The Story of a Great Italian*. Reprint. Port Washington, N.Y.: Kennikat Press, 1970. First published in 1924, this sympathetic biography emphasizes Mazzini's profound religious convictions and the universal character of his philosophy.

King, Bolton. *Mazzini*. London: J. M. Dent & Sons, 1902. The first serious English study of Mazzini. King offers a generous portrayal of Mazzini as a historical agent of political and moral progress. Includes an appendix containing several of Mazzini's letters and a bibliography listing many of Mazzini's writings published in English during the nineteenth century.

Lovett, Clara M. *The Democratic Movement in Italy, 1830-1876*. Cambridge, Mass.: Harvard University Press, 1982. Places Mazzini in the broader context of a complex and diverse democratic political movement.

Mack Smith, Dennis. *Mazzini*. New Haven, Conn.: Yale University Press, 1994. Biography examining Mazzini's ideological influence and his place within the political and intellectual climate of the mid-nineteenth century. Mack Smith portrays Mazzini as an astute but largely unrecognized prophet of the idea of European community.

Mazzini, Giuseppe. *Life and Writings of Joseph Mazzini.* 6 vols. London: Smith, Elder, 1890-1891. A comprehensive collection of Mazzini's writings available in English.

Salvemini, Gaetano. *Mazzini.* Translated by I. M. Rawson. Stanford, Calif.: Stanford University Press, 1956. An English translation of Salvemini's study, originally published in 1905 and revised in 1925. His commentary provides a good, critical introduction to Mazzini's thought and writings but contains little biographical information.

Sarti, Roland. *Mazzini: A Life for the Religion of Politics.* Westport, Conn.: Praeger, 1997. Biography exploring the relationship between Mazzini's life and his ideas.

SEE ALSO: Count Cavour; Giuseppe Garibaldi; Vincenzo Gioberti; Karl Marx; Pius IX.

RELATED ARTICLES in *Great Events from History: The Nineteenth Century, 1801-1900:* 1831: Mazzini Founds Young Italy; January 12, 1837: Mazzini Begins London Exile; January 12, 1848-August 28, 1849: Italian Revolution of 1848; May-July, 1860: Garibaldi's Redshirts Land in Sicily; March 17, 1861: Italy Is Proclaimed a Kingdom.

SECOND VISCOUNT MELBOURNE
Prime minister of Great Britain (1834, 1835-1841)

A man of wit, urbanity, and cynicism, Melbourne was an archetypal aristocratic Whig politician. As prime minister during the early nineteenth century, he helped set a pattern for future governmental reforms. He also was a crucial influence on the young Queen Victoria.

BORN: March 15, 1779; Melbourne House, London, England

DIED: November 24, 1848; Brocket Hall, Hertfordshire, England

ALSO KNOWN AS: William Lamb (birth name); Baron of Kilmore; Baron Melbourne of Melbourne

AREA OF ACHIEVEMENT: Government and politics

EARLY LIFE

William Lamb, the second Viscount Melbourne, was born in his family home, Brocket Hall in Hertfordshire. His father, Peniston Lamb, squandered the family fortune but secured a title of nobility by means of his loyalty to the ministry of Lord North and his friendship with the Prince of Wales (later George IV). His mother, née Elizabeth Milbanke, brought a fortune to the marriage and took a deep interest in her son's education. After tutoring at home, Melbourne studied at Eton, at Trinity College, Cambridge, at Lincoln's Inn (where he qualified as a lawyer), and as a private student of history, economics, and political science in Glasgow. An intelligent and well-read man, he had only begun his career in law when, at the death of his elder brother in 1805, he became heir to the family title. He gave up the law for politics, as was the duty of a man in his position.

Melbourne sat in the House of Commons from 1806 to 1812 and again from 1816 to 1829; he entered the House of Lords upon his father's death in 1829. At first an advanced Whig who opposed the war against France, Melbourne moderated his opinions as he moved into the orbit of George Canning, the leader of the moderate Conservatives. Although Melbourne rarely spoke in debates, Canning and the Prince Regent liked him; when Canning became prime minister in 1827, Melbourne was appointed Irish secretary. At that time, the Conservative domination of British politics was beginning to break up under the pressures of the movements to abolish slavery, to give Roman Catholics political rights, and to reform the electoral system. Melbourne followed the liberal followers of Canning into opposition, and when Earl Grey formed a Whig ministry in 1830, Melbourne was named home secretary.

As home secretary (1830-1834), Melbourne was responsible for maintaining public order in England and Ireland. This was no small task, for the kingdom seemed on the verge of revolution. Daniel O'Connell's Catholic Association held mass rallies to demand home rule for Ireland; factory workers marched to demand a ten-hour working day; agricultural laborers burned hayricks and tried to organize a union. Middle-class Nonconformists wanted to crush the power of the Church of England and the landed gentry. Philosophical Radicals advanced Prussian or French centralization as the model for Great Britain to follow in reforms. As home secretary, Melbourne sought to find a middle ground among these competing voices, mediating differences between factory owners and workers, members of the Church of England and Nonconformists, Whigs and Radicals.

As a minister of state, Melbourne was a reasonably efficient man of business who paid attention to the actions of his civil servants and was evenhanded within the limits of his political views. (Although he is remembered by left-wing historians as the man responsible for exiling to Australia the Tolpuddle Martyrs, who had tried to organize a farm workers' union, Melbourne opposed both legislation to repress the free exercise of dissent and the use of police spies to infiltrate working-class movements.) Whiggish in his toleration for religious dissent, he exhibited a healthy skepticism for reformers who did not have to bear the responsibility for the practical consequences of their theoretical radicalism. His politics were as moderate as his demeanor was affable.

A handsome and sophisticated man, Melbourne was known for his cynical flippancy and religious skepticism. He was reputed to be lazy, both personally and politically, but that was a pose. He liked attractive women and was cited as a correspondent in several divorce actions, most notably that of Mrs. Caroline Norton. Melbourne's marriage to Lady Caroline Lamb (née Ponsonby) was an unhappy one. Lady Caroline had many affairs, and her liaison with the poet Lord Byron was an open scandal. The couple separated in 1825; the fact that their only child, a son, was mentally impaired only added to Melbourne's domestic unhappiness. Thus Melbourne's cynicism, flippancy, and skepticism concealed inner pain.

LIFE'S WORK

Melbourne was prime minister from July to November of 1834, and again from April, 1835, to August, 1841. (In the interval, the Conservative Sir Robert Peel held office.) Melbourne faced two great problems during his premiership: the pressure for reforms of institutions in church and state, and the accession to the throne of the eighteen-year-old Queen Victoria.

The coming to power of the Whigs in 1830 and the reform of Parliament in 1832 had opened the floodgates for reform. All sorts of political, economic, social, and religious groups, representing important divisions within British society, expected the reformed Parliament to be attentive to their desires. Taken together, their desires, had they been gained, would have resulted in a radical restructuring of British institutions. Religious Nonconformists objected to the Anglican established church's right to collect local taxes (tithes) and its monopoly on higher education; some wanted to separate church and state. Industrialists and merchants wanted an end to protective tariffs and the abolition of all government restrictions on the way that they did business. Workers wanted the state to protect them from their powerful employers by limiting the length of the working day and by inspecting factories to uncover hazardous working conditions. Humanitarians wanted the state to help the West Indian slaves, the children, and the poor. The middle classes wanted to increase their political power at the expense of the landed gentry.

The Whigs, especially Lord Melbourne, were moderate liberals. On the one hand, they believed in religious freedom, in the classical economics of Adam Smith and David Ricardo, and in the paternalistic duty of those better able to help others. On the other hand, the Whigs also believed that democracy led to social disorder and tyranny, either of a dictator (as revolutionary France showed) or of a fickle and ignorant majority (as the republican United States showed). Moreover, they were practical politicians who wanted to gain power and, once having gained power, remain in power. The Whigs understood that they had to balance all competing demands, giving something to each, but not enough to all, if government was to proceed. They charted a careful and moderate path in such matters as the New Poor Law, the Municipal Corporations Act, state aid to education, the tithe question, Irish grievances, and the civil registration of births, marriages, and deaths.

As prime minister, Melbourne presided over a cabinet of Whig grandees, some of whom were able, and all of whom thought highly of themselves. Melbourne was able to keep the peace by acting as mediator and by restraining some of the more activist ministers, although in a genial way. When necessary, however, he could be firm, as in the case of Lord Brougham, the brilliant but erratic Lord Chancellor. Melbourne excluded Brougham from his second ministry, but did it in a way that minimized Brougham's anger.

In his relationship with Queen Victoria, Melbourne did three important things. First, he taught her the ins and outs of politics, of the great questions of the day, and of the personalities of public figures. This tutoring was invaluable for a young, inexperienced monarch. Second, he helped Albert of Saxe-Coburg-Gotha adjust to his role as prince consort and Victoria's husband. This task was extremely delicate, for Albert as husband broke up the close personal relationship between queen and prime minister. Nevertheless, Melbourne not only made room for Albert, but also introduced him to the art of British politics. Third, Melbourne helped the queen understand the role of the monarch in a constitutional system. The queen tried to maintain contact with him after he went into opposition in 1841, but he resisted this unconstitutional relationship and helped Peel, the new prime minister, establish a good working relationship with the monarch.

Melbourne led the Whig opposition until he suffered a stroke in 1842. Thereafter he withdrew gradually from active politics and spent more and more time at Brocket Hall, his country estate in Hertfordshire, where he died on November 24, 1848.

SIGNIFICANCE

A skeptic, rationalist, and epicure, very much in the mold of the eighteenth century, the second Viscount Melbourne served in and later presided over the Whig ministries of the 1830's, a time that historians call "the decade of reform." A believer in moderation, consensus, and reasonable reform, he charted for the Whigs a middle course, between the pressures of Nonconformists and middle-class philosophical radicals on the left and the reaction of Anglicans and Conservatives on the right. The moderate nature of his party's programs allowed the liberal Conservatives, led by Peel, to pursue a policy rather more reformist than their right wing would otherwise have accepted. This circumstance promoted stability and evolutionary tendencies in British politics.

In his relationship with Queen Victoria, Melbourne contributed greatly to the Hanoverian monarchy's adjustment to the more parliamentary and responsible constitutional system of the nineteenth century, a system in which the monarch was expected to support, or at least not to oppose actively, that politician whose party commanded a parliamentary majority gained through honest elections. Melbourne, then, contributed to the stability of the British monarchy and to its ability to survive into the twentieth century.

—*D. G. Paz*

FURTHER READING

Arnstein, Walter L. *Britain Yesterday and Today: 1830 to the Present.* Vol. 4 in *A History of England.* 4th ed. Lexington, Mass.: D. C. Heath, 1983. A very readable survey of English history; useful for background.

Cecil, David. *Melbourne.* Indianapolis: Bobbs-Merrill, 1954. A beautifully written study by one of the masters of the art of biography.

Douglass, Paul. *Lady Caroline Lamb: A Biography.* New York: Palgrave Macmillan, 2004. This biography of Lamb's mentally unstable wife provides details of their marriage and Lamb's life before his political ascent.

Finlayson, Geoffrey B. A. M. *England in the Eighteen Thirties: Decade of Reform.* London: Edward Arnold, 1969. A brief but thoughtful, clear, and succinct analysis of the reform tendencies of the day.

Gash, Norman. *Politics in the Age of Peel: A Study in the Technique of Parliamentary Representation, 1830-1850.* London: Longmans, 1953. This and the following study are essential reading for anyone concerned with the politics of the 1830's and 1840's.

_____. *Reaction and Reconstruction in English Politics, 1832-1852.* Oxford, England: Clarendon Press, 1965. An overview of the forces that determined how politics functioned, written by the dean of the political historians who study the 1830's and 1840's.

Melbourne, W. L. *Lord Melbourne's Papers.* Edited by Lloyd C. Sanders. London: Longmans, Green, 1889. Reprint. New York: Kraus Reprint, 1971. A reasonably accurate edition of Melbourne's political correspondence, the originals of which are at the Royal Archives at Windsor Castle.

Mitchell, Austin. *The Whigs in Opposition, 1815-1830.* Oxford, England: Clarendon Press, 1967. A scholarly study of how the Whigs conducted themselves in opposition and prepared for taking office in 1830.

Mitchell, L. G. *Lord Melbourne, 1779-1848.* New York: Oxford University Press, 1997. Biography recounting the personal and public lives of Melbourne. Describes his relationship with Queen Victoria, both as her advisor and her spurned lover.

Southgate, Donald. *The Passing of the Whigs, 1832-1886.* New York: St. Martin's Press, 1962. Seeks to show how the Whigs emerged from the late eighteenth century with a coherent party program, but ultimately failed to attract the mass electorate of the late nineteenth century.

Ziegler, Philip. *Melbourne: A Biography of William Lamb, Second Viscount Melbourne.* New York: Alfred A. Knopf, 1976. An excellent biography, well grounded in documentary sources, that convincingly links Melbourne's personal life and political style.

SEE ALSO: Lord Byron; George Canning; First Earl of Durham; George IV; Daniel O'Connell; Sir Robert Peel; David Ricardo; Queen Victoria; William IV.

RELATED ARTICLES in *Great Events from History: The Nineteenth Century, 1801-1900:* September 9, 1835: British Parliament Passes Municipal Corporations Act; June 28, 1838: Queen Victoria's Coronation.

HERMAN MELVILLE
American writer

The author of Moby Dick, *Melville was one of the towering figures of nineteenth century American literature. With great power and insight into humankind's ambiguous nature, he helped prove that American literature could equal that of England.*

BORN: August 1, 1819; New York, New York
DIED: September 28, 1891; New York, New York
AREA OF ACHIEVEMENT: Literature

EARLY LIFE

Herman Melville was the second son of Allan and Maria Gansevoort Melvill. (The final *e* was added to the family name after Allan's death in 1832, perhaps to indicate the family's connection with the aristocratic Melville clan of Scotland.) He grew up in the shadow of his older brother, Gansevoort, for whom the family had high expectations. In contrast, his mother found seven-year-old Herman "very backward in speech and somewhat slow in comprehension." The Melvills wanted all of their children to excel because of the family's prominence.

Maria's father was considered the richest man in Albany, New York, a Revolutionary War hero after whom a New York City street was named, and Allan's father participated in the Boston Tea Party. Allan Melvill did his best to keep up the appearance of prosperous respectability, moving several times to larger and more comfortable houses in better Manhattan neighborhoods, yet this surface prosperity belied his problems with his business, importing fine French dry goods. In 1830, he closed his shop and moved the family to Albany, leaving unpaid bills behind.

Allan's worries about his new Albany business drove him mad just before he died in January, 1832, and his two oldest sons had to go to work. (Maria was left with four sons and four daughters.) While sixteen-year-old Gansevoort took over his father's fur store and factory, Herman became a bank clerk. He wanted more than a career in commerce, however, and quit the bank in 1835 to work in the family store while attending the Albany Classical School. In 1837, he qualified to be a teacher and was in charge of a one-room school near Pittsfield, Massachusetts, for one term.

After his family moved to Lansingburgh, New York, in 1838, Melville studied engineering and surveying at the Lansingburgh Academy. After failing to obtain a job on the Erie Canal, he, like many restless young men from families with financial problems, went to sea, sailing on the *St. Lawrence* with a cargo of cotton to Liverpool in June, 1839. Despite presenting this trip as a miserable experience in *Redburn: His First Voyage* (1849), Melville thrived on the freedom from family responsibilities. The only negative aspect of the journey was his horror at the poverty of the Liverpool slums. He returned home that fall to teach at the Greenbush Academy near Lansingburgh and contributed a gothic horror sketch to the local newspaper. He made another important trip in the summer of 1840 along the Great Lakes and the Mississippi and Ohio Rivers.

Unable to secure a profitable or interesting position on land, Melville sailed for the Pacific on the whaler *Acushnet* in January, 1841. Life on this ship was unpleasant, so Melville and a shipmate ran away in the Marquesas and spent twenty-six days in the valley of the Typees, who were alleged to be cannibals. He then signed on the *Lucy Ann*, an Australian whaler, in August, 1842. This time, conditions were even worse than those on the *Acushnet*, and Melville was put ashore in Tahiti and briefly held as a mutineer. He joined another whaler, the *Charles and Henry*, that November. Discharged in Hawaii, he worked as a clerk and bookkeeper at a Honolulu general store.

Throughout these travels, Melville was appalled at the way supposed civilization was being imposed upon the islanders primarily by missionaries. Having seen enough of the exotic and of the depravities of his fellow white men, he enlisted in the navy in August, 1843, so that he could sail to Boston on the *United States*. His cynicism about civilized behavior was further hardened on this voyage as he saw 163 seamen and apprentices flogged.

LIFE'S WORK

Back home, because travel literature, especially that about the South Seas, was in vogue, Melville began writing a book. Realizing that he could not rely completely upon his memory and untested descriptive skills, he read numerous books about voyages to the Pacific. Such researches into factual material to support his stories continued throughout his career.

The result of Melville's labors was *Typee: A Peep at Polynesian Life* (1846). He combined his experiences and his reading with his imagination to produce a romantic adventure that was rejected by the first publisher to whom it was submitted because it could not possibly be

Herman Melville. (Library of Congress)

true. Gansevoort, in London as secretary to the American legation, showed his brother's manuscript to John Murray, who agreed to publish it, and an American publisher was also soon found. Gansevoort became ill and died a few months later, creating an additional pressure on Melville to succeed.

Typee received praise from both American and British critics, including, in unsigned reviews, Margaret Fuller, Nathaniel Hawthorne, and a then-unknown Walt Whitman. The American edition sold an impressive 5,753 copies in its first year. Melville based his second book, *Omoo: A Narrative of Adventures in the South Seas* (1847), on his *Lucy Ann* and Tahiti experiences, again borrowing material from other sources. *Omoo* sold as well as *Typee*, but both were attacked in religious journals for their unflattering view of missionaries.

During this time, Melville had met and fallen in love with a Boston friend of his sister Helen. Elizabeth Shaw was the daughter of Lemuel Shaw, chief justice of Massachusetts and a boyhood friend of Melville's father. Elizabeth may have been attracted to Melville, who stood five feet, nine and a half inches, had a stocky build, oversized ears, small blue eyes—and later a big black beard—because his experiences and prospects as an artist seemed romantic to someone who had led a relatively tame existence. They were married August 4, 1847, and began sharing a Manhattan house with his mother, sisters, and brother Allan and his new wife.

Melville started his third novel intending simply to repeat his formula of blending his seagoing experiences and his research, but his reading of German romances and the poetry of George Gordon, Lord Byron, John Keats, and Percy Bysshe Shelley, together with his affection for his young wife, turned *Mardi and a Voyage Thither* (1849) into a whimsical Polynesian romance. He injected philosophy and political commentary in *Mardi* as well, presenting a theory of history in which American freedoms are not the products of the country's institutions but are made possible by the geographical fact of a constantly diminishing frontier. Melville also wanted the United States to refrain from meddling in European affairs and from imperialism in its own hemisphere. Throughout his career, he criticized the ways in which American society fell short of the ideals it professed.

Melville had hoped *Mardi* would be a popular success, but reviewers were unfriendly, one calling it "a transcendental *Gulliver,* or *Robinson Crusoe* run mad." Because his first child, Malcolm, had just been born, he felt compelled to delay the more ambitious work he wanted to do. Because something commercial was called for, he planned "a plain, straightforward, amusing narrative of personal experience—the son of a gentleman on his first voyage to sea as a sailor—no metaphysics, no conic-sections, nothing but cakes and ale."

Melville wrote *Redburn* to this prescription, quickly followed by a similar novel, *White-Jacket: Or, The World in a Man-of-War* (1850), based on his duty on the *United States* (*White-Jacket* is said to have contributed to ending flogging in the United States Navy). His expectations for the novels were rewarded when both were well received by critics and the public.

Melville believed that these five books had exhausted the interesting incidents in his life, so he went to Europe in the autumn of 1849 hoping to collect material he could use in new books. Returning to America, he planned to write about an American exile in Europe, but Richard Henry Dana, Jr., suggested that he do for the whaling industry what he had done for the navy in *White-Jacket* and what Dana had done for the merchant marine in *Two Years Before the Mast* (1840). Melville agreed and promised Dana "a strange sort of book," though not as strange as *Mardi.*

Feeling cramped living with his relatives in New York, Melville moved his wife and son in 1850 to a 145-acre farm near Pittsfield, where he met Hawthorne at a gathering of leading literary figures. Melville spoke to his fellow writers of the potential greatness of American literature, and in reading Hawthorne's *Mosses from an Old Manse* (1846) soon afterward, he found confirmation of American genius. Melville interrupted his work on *Moby Dick: Or, The Whale* (1851) to write "Hawthorne and His Mosses," in which he argued that the literature of the United States could rival that of England, that an American writer with the intellectual capacity of Hawthorne could create art on Shakespearean levels. Melville deliberately tried for this kind of greatness in *Moby Dick*, his ambition matching Captain Ahab's obsession with the white whale.

Although some reviewers perceived the originality and power of *Moby Dick*, many misunderstood and attacked it. *United States Magazine and Democratic Review* found it full of "bad rhetoric, involved syntax, stilted sentiment and incoherent English." *Southern Quarterly Review* considered the parts not dealing with the white whale "sad stuff, dull and dreary, or ridiculous." Even Melville's close friend and staunchest supporter, Evert Duyckinck, a prominent editor and critic, disliked the novel.

Acknowledging that the reading public was predominantly female, Melville decided to direct his next book toward feminine tastes. He was further motivated by having received an average of only twelve hundred dollars for his books and by being in debt to Harper's, his American publisher. In attempting to create a gothic romance in the manner of Hawthorne's *The House of the Seven Gables* (1851), however, Melville became recklessly carried away as he had with *Mardi*, ignoring his commercial judgment in his effort to "find out the heart of a man."

MELVILLE'S NOVELS

1846	*Typee: A Peep at Polynesian Life*
1847	*Omoo: A Narrative of Adventures in the South Seas*
1849	*Mardi, and a Voyage Thither*
1849	*Redburn: His First Voyage*
1850	*White-Jacket: Or, The World in a Man-of-War*
1851	*Moby Dick: Or, The Whale*
1852	*Pierre: Or, The Ambiguities*
1855	*Israel Potter: His Fifty Years of Exile*
1857	*The Confidence Man: His Masquerade*
1924	*Billy Budd, Foretopman*

Pierre: Or, The Ambiguities (1852), a story of love, murder, and suicide, with overtones of incest, was rejected by Melville's English publisher and almost unanimously vilified by reviewers for its "impurity." When only 283 copies were sold during the first eight months after publication, Melville finally began to be discouraged by his prospects as a writer. His family thought there was a danger of his work affecting his mental health and set out to find for him a more profitable and less demanding occupation, such as a foreign consulship. Melville was hardly ready to abandon his writing and turned much of his attention to well-paying magazine stories, the best of which are "Bartleby the Scrivener" (1853) and "Benito Cereno" (1855). He was encouraged enough by this success to write his long-planned American-exile novel, *Israel Potter: His Fifty Years of Exile* (1855), keeping what he had learned about the interests of magazine readers constantly in mind. This satirical look at the Revolutionary War and its aftermath sold well and brought Melville, who had four children by then, closer to financial security than he had ever been.

Melville's next book, however, *The Piazza Tales* (1856), a collection of stories, was unsuccessful, and his family believed that the writing of *The Confidence Man: His Masquerade* (1857) was ruining his health. They decided that he needed a vacation, and Judge Shaw paid for him to go to Europe and the Holy Land. Melville hoped to have some sort of simple religious faith restored on this trip but found the Holy Land more unattractive and uncomfortable than inspiring.

Melville returned home to find *The Confidence Man*, a satirical allegory based upon his Mississippi River trip years before, a critical and commercial failure. His brother-in-law, Lemuel Shaw, Jr., felt it belonged to "that horribly uninteresting class of nonsensical books he is given to writing," the view of most of his relatives of most of his work. Melville chose not to write any further, because doing so would upset his family.

Instead of writing, Melville took to the lecture circuit, speaking on statuary in Rome and the South Seas throughout the Northeast and Midwest in 1857-1859, but these lectures were only moderately successful. He next turned to poetry, but he had no illusions about popular success, creating his art simply to satisfy himself, especially because no publishers were interested in his poems.

After failing to obtain a consulship, Melville traded his farm for the Manhattan house of his brother Allan. He also began writing Civil War poems based upon newspaper accounts and one visit to the front lines. He paid for the publication of *Battle-Pieces and Aspects of the War* (1866) and lost four hundred dollars on the venture.

In 1867, he submitted to his family's wishes and became a deputy customs inspector in New York for four dollars a day, later reduced to $3.60. He continued writing poetry, and Peter Gansevoort, his uncle, gave him twelve hundred dollars to publish *Clarel: A Poem and Pilgrimage in the Holy Land* (1876), his most significant poetry. After its publication, he settled into a daily routine of work, family obligations, and the frequent illnesses associated with age.

Contrary to legend, Melville's novels were not completely forgotten. They sold about one hundred copies yearly during 1876-1880 and twice that many in 1881-1884, and W. Clark Russell, the popular English writer of sea stories, praised him as "the greatest genius" the United States had produced. At the age of sixty-five, Melville found himself without financial worries for the first time, primarily because of money his wife inherited from her parents, and he retired from the customhouse in December, 1885.

Melville privately published two collections of poems during this time of leisure: *John Marr and Other Sailors* (1888) and *Timoleon* (1891). In 1888, after neglecting fiction for thirty years, he started a long-planned project based upon a famous case in which a sailor was perhaps unjustifiably hanged at sea. (A cousin of Melville presided over the court-martial.) He may also have been exploring his feelings about the apparent suicide of his son Malcolm in 1867 and the death in 1886 of his other son, the unhappy, wandering Stanwix. He completed *Billy Budd, Foretopman* before dying of enlargement of the heart of September 28, 1891. This short novel was not published until 1924 after biographer Raymond M. Weaver discovered it in 1919, concealed in a tin breadbox.

SIGNIFICANCE

New editions of *Typee, Omoo, White-Jacket,* and *Moby Dick* were published in 1892 and, surprisingly, found a market, going through forty-four editions in the United States and Great Britain by 1919, when Melville's work began to be widely rediscovered and reassessed. The Melville revival exploded during the 1920's with several books and articles, led by Weaver's 1921 biography. By this time, readers were more accustomed to symbolism and psychological fiction and recognized the originality and power of Melville's writing, with many proclaiming *Moby Dick* the Great American Novel for its insight into the contradictory motives underlying so much of American experience. Equally important is what D. H. Lawrence describes as "the peculiar, lurid, glamorous style that is natural to the great Americans" and that stems "from the violence native to the American Continent, where force is more powerful than consciousness." *Moby Dick* is, in Alfred Kazin's words, "a hymn to the unequalled thrust that lifted America to the first rank."

Melville's famous skepticism and cynicism resulted from a very American restlessness of the intellect and the spirit. As Hawthorne wrote of his friend, "He can neither believe, nor be comfortable in his unbelief; and he is too honest and courageous not to try to do one or the other." Melville was more bitter about not making money as a writer than about not receiving the recognition he deserved. He would have been content, as he was in his last years, simply to write for himself. He even described himself as "a happy failure."

Melville had integrity as an artist, an inherent inability to be satisfied with giving superficial readers what they wanted. *Moby Dick* is a masterpiece because its author dared to attempt so much. As he wrote Evert Duyckinck in 1849, "I love all men who *dive*. Any fish can swim near the surface, but it takes a great whale to go down stairs five miles or more." More than anything, Melville stands for the courage to risk failure.

—Michael Adams

FURTHER READING

Anderson, Charles R. *Melville in the South Seas.* New York: Columbia University Press, 1939. Lengthy, detailed account of the most important period of Melville's life, with analysis of how he used these experiences in his art. Attempts to separate fact from fiction.

Gilman, William H. *Melville's Early Life and "Redburn."* New York: New York University Press, 1951. Most detailed account of Melville's life from 1819 to 1841, with the emphasis on his voyage to Liverpool.

Hardwick, Elizabeth. *Herman Melville.* New York: Viking Press, 2000. A brief but insightful overview of Melville's life and work, written by a prominent literary critic and novelist.

Kazin, Alfred. *An American Procession.* New York: Alfred A. Knopf, 1984. Study of American literature from 1830 to 1932 places Melville's work in the context of a literary tradition and offers a good, brief sketch of Melville as writer and man.

Leyda, Jay. *The Melville Log: A Documentary Life of Herman Melville, 1819-1891.* 2 vols. New York: Harcourt, Brace & World, 1951. Amazingly complete document based on letters to, from, and about Melville, journals, publishers' files, newspaper articles, Melville's marginalia in the books he read, and similar sources. Arranged in a day-by-day chronology. Supplemented in 1969.

Miller, Edwin Haviland. *Melville*. New York: George Braziller, 1975. Psychoanalytical biography offers the most complete view of the Melville-Hawthorne friendship.

Mumford, Lewis. *Herman Melville*. New York: Harcourt, Brace & World, 1929. Interpretation of Melville's life based on his writings, including letters and notebooks. Concerned more with the writer's view of his world than with the details of his life.

Parker, Hershel. *Herman Melville: A Biography*. 2 vols. Baltimore: Johns Hopkins University Press, 1996-2002. An exhaustive two-volume biography written by a lifelong Melville scholar.

Robertson-Lorant, Laurie. *Melville: A Biography*. New York: Clarkson Potter, 1996. Comprehensive biography based on newly discovered Melville family letters. Provides new insight into Melville's life and an analysis of his literature.

Sealts, Merton M., Jr., comp. *The Early Lives of Melville: Nineteenth-Century Biographical Sketches and Their Authors*. Madison: University of Wisconsin Press, 1974. Compiles biographical material by those who knew Melville, including his wife and granddaughters. Reveals how he was perceived in his time.

Weaver, Raymond M. *Herman Melville, Mariner and Mystic*. New York: George H. Doran, 1921. First book-length biography of Melville by the scholar who virtually discovered him. Weakened by treating Melville's fiction as fact and by saying little about the last thirty years of his life.

SEE ALSO: Lord Byron; James Fenimore Cooper; Margaret Fuller; Sarah Josepha Hale; Nathaniel Hawthorne; Washington Irving; John Keats; Percy Bysshe Shelley; Walt Whitman.

RELATED ARTICLE in *Great Events from History: The Nineteenth Century, 1801-1900:* 1851: Melville Publishes *Moby Dick*.

GREGOR MENDEL
Austrian geneticist

Mendel's work was almost unknown during his lifetime, and he died without receiving any significant recognition. However, he demonstrated the rules governing genetic inheritance with a novel statistical approach to experiments in plant hybridization, and after his work was recognized, his ideas transformed the field of genetics.

BORN: July 22, 1822; Heinzendorf, Austria (now Hyncice, Czech Republic)
DIED: January 6, 1884; Brünn, Austro-Hungarian Empire (now Brno, Czech Republic)
ALSO KNOWN AS: Gregor Johann Mendel (full name)
AREAS OF ACHIEVEMENT: Biology, science and technology

EARLY LIFE

Gregor Johann Mendel (MEHN-dehl) was the only son of Anton Mendel, a peasant, and his mother was the daughter of a village gardener. He had four sisters, two of whom died early, but Veronica, born in 1820, and Theresia, born in 1829, survived. The Mendel lineage included other professional gardeners. Fortunately for his future career, Mendel went to a village school where the teacher taught the children about natural science. Mendel was exposed early to the cultivation of fruit trees, at the school as well as at home, where he helped his father with the family orchard. Mendel attended secondary school in the year 1833 and then spent six years in the gymnasium in Troppau, where he did well overall.

Mendel's nervous physical reaction to stress, which partially determined Mendel's choices and possibilities in later life, became evident when he was a student. Initially, when Mendel's father, unable to work because of serious injuries, had to give his son-in-law control of the farm in 1838, Mendel gave private lessons to make money. The stress affected him to such a degree that he had to miss several months of his fifth year at the gymnasium in order to recover.

Mendel started a philosophy course at the Philosophical Institute at Olmütz in 1840 but was unable to find tutoring jobs. He fell ill again and spent a year with his parents. His sister Theresia offered to support him out of her dowry so he could continue his studies. With her aid,

Mendel completed the two-year course in philosophy, physics, and mathematics, which would have led to higher studies. He did well enough that one of his professors, who had lived in an Augustinian monastery for nearly twenty years, recommended Mendel to the same monastery.

LIFE'S WORK

Mendel entered the Augustinian monastery, taking the name Gregor, on October 9, 1843, out of sheer financial necessity. It proved, however, to be a fruitful decision. Though he felt no great vocation to be a monk, he found himself in the environment most conducive to his studies; it was at the monastery that Mendel was able to concentrate on those studies in meteorology and, more significant, plant reproduction that made him a pioneer in genetics.

The abbot of the monastery was actively involved in encouraging agricultural studies, so Mendel was surrounded by other scholars and researchers. The nervous disposition that had affected him as a student continued to plague him, for he would become ill when he visited invalids. Useless as a pastor, he was assigned instead to the gymnasium in Znaim as a substitute teacher. In this capacity, Mendel was successful and was encouraged to become a teacher permanently, if he could pass the required examinations for a license.

Ironically, this careful researcher never made much headway in official academic circles, though his education was crucial to shaping the course of his experiments. He failed to pass all the examinations to become a permanent teacher and was sent to the University of Vienna to study natural science more thoroughly. From October, 1851, to August, 1853, Mendel was in the intellectually stimulating company of men such as Franz Unger, a professor of plant physiology, who asserted that the plant world was not fixed but had evolved gradually—a view that caused much controversy.

From Christian Doppler and Andreas von Ettingshausen, both physicists, Mendel most likely acquired the technique of approaching physical problems with mathematical analysis. He served as a demonstrator at the Physical Institute in Vienna and became adept at the physicist's approach to a problem. In 1855, Mendel took the teachers' examination again but fared even worse; he became sick after writing the first answer and was apparently so ill subsequently that his father and uncle came a long way to visit him. Because he never tried the examinations again, Mendel remained a substitute teacher for sixteen years, kind, conscientious, and well liked.

In 1856, he began his experiments with garden peas. It was known at the time that the first generation reproduced from hybrids tended to be uniform but that the second generation reverted to the characteristics of the two original plants that had been crossbred. Such facts were observable, but the explanations remained unsatisfactory. In *An Introduction to Genetic Analysis* (1976, 1981) the authors note that before Mendel, the concept of blending inheritance predominated; that is, it was assumed that offspring were typically similar to the parents because the essences of the parents were contained in the spermatozoon and the egg, and these were blended at conception to form the new offspring. Mendel's work with pea plants suggested another theory, that of particulate inheritance; this theory postulated that a gene passes from one generation to the next as a unit, without any blending.

As several historians of science have noted, Mendel approached this problem of heredity in hybrids as a physicist would, and this may account for some of the suspicion surrounding the success of Mendel's famous experiments with garden peas. Instead of making many

Gregor Mendel. (Library of Congress)

observations of natural life and then looking for the general pattern, as was the conventional approach of biologists, Mendel determined the problem first, devised a solution to the problem, then undertook experiments to test the solution. Mendel prepared the groundwork for his experiments by testing thirty-four varieties of peas to find the most suitable varieties for research. From these, he picked twenty-two to examine for two different traits, color and texture. He was then able to trace the appearance of green and yellow seeds, as well as round and wrinkled ones, in several generations of offspring. By literally counting the results of his hybridization, he found the ratio of dominant genes to recessive ones: 3 to 1. In effect, he demonstrated that there was a rule governing inheritance.

When he finished his experiments with peas in 1863, Mendel was well aware that his conclusions were not what the scientific knowledge of the time would have predicted. To confirm his findings, he experimented with the French bean and the bush bean, crossed the bush bean with the scarlet runner, and got the same 3:1 ratio, though in the last case, he could not obtain the same ratio for the white and red colors. He spoke about his work at two meetings of the Naturforschenden Verein (natural science society) and was asked to publish his lecture in 1866. Only a few of the forty copies made have been recovered: One of the most important recipients was Carl von Nägeli, a leading botanical researcher who had written about the work of preceding experimenters. Nägeli found it impossible to accept Mendel's explanation but did engage in discussion with him; the two corresponded from 1866 to 1873. Nägeli's influence was not altogether salutary, for he set Mendel on a futile track experimenting with *Hieracium*, which, as was established later, breeds slightly differently.

In 1868, Mendel was promoted to abbot of the monastery. He became involved in a controversy about taxes on the monastery and eventually, in 1871, abandoned his studies of hybrids. A heavy smoker toward the end of his life, Mendel developed kidney problems, which led to a painful illness. Theresia, the sister who had helped him pay for his education with her dowry, was also there for his last days, taking care of him until he died in January of 1884.

SIGNIFICANCE

Gregor Johann Mendel's work was not rediscovered for thirty years, by which time three other researchers— Hugo de Vries, Carl Erich Correns, and Erich Tschermak von Seysenegg—had, working independently, drawn some of the same conclusions. Thus, Mendel's work in itself did not directly influence the history of science, for it was not well known. Even his original explanations of meteorologic phenomena, particularly of a tornado that struck his birthplace, Brno, in 1870, was ignored. He died without achieving the full recognition he deserved.

The explanation for his contemporaries' lack of appreciation for his work can only be speculative. For example, Mendel's successor destroyed his private papers; furthermore, scientists at the time considered Mendel's experiments to be a hobby and his theories the "maunderings of a charming putterer." In part, Mendel's use of numerical analysis, so different from the conventional working procedures of biologists up to that time, may have been suspect. Mendel's personal qualities, which enabled him to reduce a puzzling problem to its bare essentials, may also have been a contributing factor to his obscurity. Though widely read in scientific literature and an active participant in the affairs of his community, he was a modest and reticent man, who compressed twenty years of scientific work into four short papers.

This lack of fanfare concerning his discoveries was not rectified until a young priest discovered Mendel's official documents, preserved in monastery archives, in the first decade of the twentieth century. Only then were Mendel's conscientious, careful, painstaking work and the results that he achieved fully appreciated. As L. C. Dunn notes, there had been several experiments with hybridization before Mendel. Among his predecessors, Josef Gottlieb Kölreuter was an important figure, for it was he who produced the first plant hybrid with a planned experiment in 1760.

What Mendel did that no one else thought to do was to apply statistical analysis to an area of study that had not habitually conceptualized problems numerically. By so doing, he was able to discover specific and regular ratios. With this apparently simple technique, Mendel was able to formulate the rules of inheritance and thus give birth to the science of genetics.

—Shakuntala Jayaswal

FURTHER READING

Dunn, L. C. *A Short History of Genetics: The Development of Some of the Main Lines of Thought, 1864-1939*. New York: McGraw-Hill, 1965. As indicated in the subtitle, this is a study of the development of the main lines of thought in genetic studies from 1864 to 1939. Contains chapters on Mendel and on the aftermath of Mendelism. Includes photographs, a glossary, a bibliography, and an index.

Henig, Robin Marantz. *The Monk in the Garden: The Lost and Found Genius of Gregor Mendel, the Father of Genetics*. Boston: Houghton Mifflin, 2000. Biography of Mendel, recounting his life, experiments, and the importance of his genetic discoveries. Includes bibliography, notes, and index.

Iltis, Hugo. *Life of Mendel*. Translated by Eden Paul and Cedar Paul. London: Allen & Unwin, 1932. Researched and written by the man who helped to rediscover Mendel and preserve his remaining papers. One of the best biographies of Mendel. Includes illustrations, color plates, and an index.

Mendel, Gregor. *Experiments in Plant-Hybridisation*. Foreword by Paul C. Mangelsdorf. Cambridge, Mass.: Harvard University Press, 1965. Reprinted to celebrate the centennial of Mendel's lectures on his groundbreaking experiments. The foreword contains a concise explanation of the experiments and their significance.

Olby, Robert C. *Origins of Mendelism*. New York: Schocken Books, 1966. Places Mendel's work in the context of those who came before him. Starts with Kölreuter and his hybridization experiments, includes a discussion of Charles Darwin's genetics, and concludes with the work of the three who replicated Mendel's work independently. Contains an appendix, an index, plates, and suggested readings at the end of each chapter.

Orel, Vítězslav. *Gregor Mendel: The First Geneticist*. Translated by Stephen Finn. New York: Oxford University Press, 1996. An account of Mendel's life and activities as a scientist and a monk. Describes how his genetic ideas were received by his contemporaries and in the years following his discoveries.

Sturtevant, Alfred H. *A History of Genetics*. New York: Harper & Row, 1965. Provides a historical background of genetics from before Mendel through the genetics of mankind. Lively discussion of the controversy over Mendel's near-perfect results. Includes a chronology of genetics history, a bibliography, and an index.

Suzuki, David T., Anthony J. F. Griffiths, and Richard C. Lewontin. *An Introduction to Genetic Analysis*. 2d ed. San Francisco: W. H. Freeman, 1981. A chapter on Mendelism provides a clear explanation of Mendel's experiments, using contemporary terminology. Includes problems, with answers, a glossary, a bibliography, and an index.

SEE ALSO: Charles Darwin; Francis Galton; Sir Edwin Ray Lankester.

RELATED ARTICLES in *Great Events from History: The Nineteenth Century, 1801-1900:* 1865: Mendel Proposes Laws of Heredity; 1899-1900: Rediscovery of Mendel's Hereditary Theory.

DMITRY IVANOVICH MENDELEYEV
Russian chemist

Although he did important theoretical work on the physical properties of fluids and practical work on the development of coal and oil resources, Mendeleyev is best known for his discovery of the periodic law, which states that the properties of the chemical elements vary with their atomic weights in a systematic way. His periodic table of the elements enabled him accurately to predict the properties of three unknown elements, whose later discovery confirmed the value of his system.

BORN: February 8, 1834; Tobolsk (now Tyumen Oblast), Siberia, Russia
DIED: February 2, 1907; St. Petersburg, Russia
ALSO KNOWN AS: Dimitri Mendeleev
AREA OF ACHIEVEMENT: Chemistry

EARLY LIFE

Dmitry Ivanovich Mendeleyev (myehn-dyih-LYAY-yehf) was born in an administrative center in western Siberia. He later recalled that he was the seventeenth child, but a sister claimed that he was actually the sixteenth child, and many scholars state that he was the fourteenth. His mother, Marya Dmitrievna Kornileva, came from an old merchant family with Mongolian blood. She became deeply attached to her youngest son and played an influential role in shaping his passionate temperament and directing his education. His father, Ivan Pavlovich Mendeleyev, was a principal and teacher at the Tobolsk high school, but shortly after his son's birth he became totally blind. The modest disability pension he received did not allow him to support his large family, and so Marya, a remarkably able and determined woman, reopened a glass factory that her family still owned in a village near Tobolsk. She ran it so successfully that she was able to provide for her family and complete her younger children's education.

In the Tobolsk schools, young Dmitry, an attractive curly-haired, blue-eyed boy, excelled in mathematics, physics, geography, and history, but he did poorly in the compulsory classical languages, Latin in particular. Tobolsk was a place for political exiles, and one of Dmitry's sisters wedded an exiled Decembrist, one of those who tried unsuccessfully in December, 1825, to overthrow Czar Nicholas I. He took an active interest in Dmitry, taught him science, and helped form his political liberalism.

Toward the end of Mendeleyev's high school education, a double tragedy occurred: His father died of tuberculosis and his family's glassworks burned to the ground. By this time, the older children had left home, leaving only Dmitry and a sister with their mother, who decided to seek the help of her brother in Moscow. After Dmitry's graduation from high school in 1849, Marya, then fifty-seven years old, secured horses and bravely embarked with her two dependent children on the long journey from Siberia. In Moscow, her brother, after first welcoming them, refused to help his nephew obtain an education on the grounds that he himself had not had one. Marya angrily left Moscow for St. Petersburg, where she again encountered difficulty in getting her son either into the university or into the medical school.

Finally, through a friend of her dead husband, Mendeleyev's mother secured a place for him in the faculty of physics and mathematics of the Main Pedagogical Institute, the school his father had attended. Three months later, Marya died, and not long afterward her daughter succumbed to tuberculosis. Mendeleyev, who also suffered from tuberculosis, later wrote that his mother instructed him by example, corrected him with love, and, in order to consecrate him to science, left Siberia and spent her last energies and resources to put him on his way.

Mendeleyev received a good education at the Pedagogical Institute. One of his teachers had been a pupil of Justus von Liebig, one of the greatest chemists of the time. In 1855, Mendeleyev, now qualified as a teacher, was graduated from the Pedagogical Institute, winning a gold medal for his academic achievements.

Worn out by his labors, he went to a physician, who told him that he had only a short time to live. In an attempt to regain his health, he was sent, at his own request, to the Crimea, in southern Russia. He initially taught science at Simferopol, but when the Crimean War broke out, he left for Odessa, where he taught in a local lyceum during the 1855-1856 school year and where, aided by the warm climate, his health improved. In the autumn of 1856, he returned to St. Petersburg to defend his master's thesis. He succeeded and obtained the status of privatdocent, which gave him the license to teach theoretical and organic chemistry at the University of St. Petersburg.

LIFE'S WORK

In his teaching, Mendeleyev used the atomic weights of the elements to explain chemistry to his students. This did not mean that he believed that chemistry could be completely explained by physics, but his work on isomorphism and specific volumes convinced him that atomic weights could be useful in elucidating chemical properties. To improve his understanding of chemistry, he received in 1859 a stipend for two years' study abroad.

In Paris, Mendeleyev worked in the laboratory of Henry Regnault, famous for his studies on chlorine compounds, and at the University of Heidelberg, where he had the opportunity to meet Robert Bunsen, Gustav Kirchhoff, and other notable scientists. Because his weak lungs were bothered by the noxious fumes of sulfur compounds in Bunsen's laboratory, Mendeleyev set up a private laboratory to work on his doctoral thesis on the combination of alcohol and water. In the course of his research at Heidelberg, he discovered that for every liquid there existed a temperature above which it could no longer be condensed from the gas to the liquid form. He called this temperature the absolute boiling point (this phenomenon was rediscovered a decade later by the Irish scientist Thomas Andrews, who called it the "critical temperature," its modern descriptor). In September, 1860, Mendeleyev attended the Chemical Congress at Karlsruhe, Germany, and met the Italian chemist Stanislao Cannizzaro, whose insistence on the distinction between atomic and molecular weights and whose system of corrected atomic weights had a great influence on him.

Upon his return to St. Petersburg, Mendeleyev resumed his lectures on organic chemistry. Because he lacked a permanent academic position, he decided to write a textbook on organic chemistry, which became a popular as well as a critical success. In 1863, he began to act as a consultant for a small oil refinery in Baku. In this same year he was married to Fezova Nikitichna Leshcheva, largely because one of his sisters insisted that he needed a wife. The couple had two children, a boy,

Vladimir, and a girl, Olga. The marriage was not happy, however, and quarrels were frequent. Eventually, Mendeleyev and his wife separated. He continued to live in their St. Petersburg quarters, while his wife and children lived at their country estate of Boblovo. In 1864, Mendeleyev agreed to serve as professor of chemistry at the St. Petersburg Technical Institute while continuing to teach at the university. A year later, he defended his doctoral thesis on alcohol and water, arguing that solutions are chemical compounds indistinguishable from other types of chemical combination.

A turning point in Mendeleyev's career occurred in October, 1865, when he was appointed to the chair of chemistry at the University of St. Petersburg. While teaching an inorganic-chemistry course there, he felt the need to bring to this subject the same degree of order that had characterized his earlier teaching of organic chemistry. Because he could find no suitable textbook, he decided to write his own. The composing of this book, eventually published as *Osnovy khimii* (1868-1871; *The Principles of Chemistry*, 1891), led him to formulate the periodic law. It was also one of the most unusual textbooks ever written. Unlike most textbooks, it was not a recycling of traditional material. It had instead a novel organization and an abundance of original ideas. It was also a curious blend of objective information and personal comment in which footnotes often took up more space than the text.

In organizing his ideas for the book, Mendeleyev prepared individual cards for all sixty-three elements then known, listing their atomic weights and properties, which showed great dissimilarities. For example, oxygen and chlorine were gases, whereas mercury and bromine were liquids. Platinum was very hard, whereas sodium was very soft. Some elements combined with one atom, others with two, and still others with three or four. In a search for order, Mendeleyev arranged the elements in a sequence of increasing atomic weights. By moving the cards around, he found that he could group certain elements together in already familiar families. For example, in the first table that he developed in March of 1869, lithium, sodium, potassium, and the other so-called alkali metals formed a horizontal row. In some groups he left empty spaces so that the next element would be in its proper family.

Mendeleyev's analysis of his first arrangement convinced him that there must be a functional relationship between the individual properties of the elements and their atomic weights. One of the many interesting relationships he noticed concerned valence, the ability of an element to combine in specific proportions with other elements. He observed a periodic rise and fall of valence—1, 2, 3, 4, 3, 2, 1—in several parts of his arrangement. Because valence and other properties of the elements exhibited periodic repetitions, he called his arrangement in 1869 the periodic table. At the same time he formulated the periodic law: Elements organized according to their atomic weights manifest a clear periodicity of properties. He had been thinking about information relevant to the periodic law for fifteen years, but he formulated it in a single day. Mendeleyev would spend the next three years perfecting it, and in important ways he would be concerned with its finer points until his death.

When Mendeleyev's paper was read by a friend at the Russian Chemical Society meeting in 1869, the periodic table did not evoke unusual interest. Its publication in German met with a cool reception. Mendeleyev's opponents, who were especially censorious in England and Germany, were suspicious of highly imaginative theoretical schemes of the elements; many scientists before Mendeleyev had proposed such systems, which resulted in little of practical benefit for chemists.

Mendeleyev believed that if he could convince scientists of the usefulness of his system, it would attract followers. Therefore, he tried to show how his table and periodic law could be used to correct erroneously determined atomic weights. More significant, he proposed in an 1871 paper that gaps in his table could be used to discover new elements. In particular, he predicted in great detail the physical and chemical properties of three elements, which he called eka-aluminum, eka-boron, and eka-silicon, after the Sanskrit word for "one" and the name of the element above the gap in the table.

Mendeleyev's predictions were met with great skepticism, but when, in 1875, Paul Lecoq de Boisbaudran discovered eka-aluminum in a zinc ore from the Pyrenees, skepticism declined, especially after chemists learned that the element's characteristics had been accurately foretold by Mendeleyev. When, in 1879, Lars Nilson isolated eka-boron from the ore euxenite, even fewer skeptics were to be found. Finally, in 1879, when Clemens Winkler in Germany found an element in the ore argyrodite that precisely matched Mendeleyev's predictions for eka-silicon, skepticism vanished. In fact, Winkler used Mendeleyev's predictions of a gray element with an atomic weight of about 72 and a density of 5.5 in his search (he found a grayish-white substance with an atomic weight of 72.3 and a density of 5.5). These new elements were given the names gallium (1875), scandium (1879), and germanium (1886), and their discovery led to the universal acceptance of Mendeleyev's periodic law.

In addition to campaigning for his periodic system, Mendeleyev during the 1870's spent time on his technological interests. He was a patriot who wanted to see such Russian resources as coal, oil, salt, and metals developed properly. With this in mind, he visited the United States in 1876 to study the Pennsylvania oil fields. He was critical of the American developers' concentration on the expansion of production while ignoring the scientific improvement of industrial efficiency and product quality. Upon his return to Russia, he was sent to study his country's oil fields, and he became critical of the way they were exploited by foreign companies. He urged Russian officials to develop native oil for the country's own benefit. From his experience in the oil fields, Mendeleyev developed a theory of the inorganic origin of petroleum and a belief in protective tariffs for natural resources.

In the year of his American trip, Mendeleyev underwent a domestic crisis. At a sister's home he had met Anna Ivanovna Popov, a seventeen-year-old art student, and fallen desperately in love with her. Anna's family opposed the relationship and made several attempts to separate the pair, resorting finally to sending her to Rome to continue her art studies. Mendeleyev soon followed her, leaving behind a message that if he could not wed her, he would commit suicide. She was mesmerized by this passionate man who, with his deep-set eyes and patriarchal beard, looked like a biblical prophet. She agreed to return to Russia and wed him, but the couple discovered that, according to the laws of the Russian Orthodox Church, Mendeleyev could not be remarried until seven years after his divorce.

Mendeleyev eventually found a priest who was willing to ignore the rule, but two days after the marriage the priest was dismissed and Mendeleyev was officially proclaimed a bigamist. Despite the religious crisis, nothing happened to Mendeleyev or his young wife. As the czar told a nobleman who complained about the situation: "Mendeleyev has two wives, yes, but I have only one Mendeleyev." The second marriage proved to be a happy one, and the couple had two sons and two daughters. Anna Ivanovna introduced her husband to art, and he became an accomplished critic and an astute collector of paintings.

During the 1880's and 1890's, Mendeleyev became increasingly involved in academic politics. Ultimately, conflict with the minister of education prompted him to resign from the University of St. Petersburg. At his last lecture at the university, where he had taught for more than thirty years, the students gave him an enthusiastic ovation. His teaching career at an end, Mendeleyev turned to public service, where he was active in many areas.

When the Russo-Japanese War broke out in February, 1904, Mendeleyev became a strong supporter of his country's efforts, and Russia's defeat disheartened him. By this time, Mendeleyev was not only the grand man of Russian chemistry but also, because of the triumph of the periodic law, a world figure. In 1906, he was considered for a Nobel Prize, but the chemistry committee's recommendation was defeated by a single vote, mainly because his discovery of the periodic law was more than thirty-five years old. Though he missed winning the Nobel Prize, he was showered with many awards in Russia and in many foreign countries. His end came early in 1907, when he caught a cold that developed into pneumonia. His chief consolation during his final illness was the reading of *A Journey to the North Pole* (*Les Anglais au pôle nord*, 1864; English translation, 1874) by Jules Verne, his favorite author.

SIGNIFICANCE

Dmitry Ivanovich Mendeleyev's name has become inextricably linked with the periodic table, but he was not the first to attempt to develop a systematic classification of the chemical elements. Earlier in the century, Johann Döbereiner, a German chemist, had arranged several elements into triads—for example, calcium, strontium, and barium—in which such properties as atomic weight, color, and reactivity seemed to form a predictable gradation. John Newlands, an English chemist, arranged the elements in the order of atomic weights in 1864 and found that properties seemed to repeat themselves after an interval of seven elements.

In 1866, Mendeleyev announced his "law of octaves," in which he saw an analogy between the grouping of elements and the musical octave. Several other attempts at a systematic arrangement of the elements were made before Mendeleyev, some of which were known to him. Many scholars credit the German chemist Lothar Meyer as an independent discoverer of the periodic law, since in 1864 he published a table of elements arranged horizontally so that analogous elements appeared under one another.

Other scholars contend that Mendeleyev's table was more firmly based on chemical properties than Meyer's and it could be generalized more easily. Furthermore, Mendeleyev was a much bolder theoretician than Meyer. For example, he proposed that some atomic weights must be incorrect because their measured weight caused them to be placed in the wrong group of the table (Meyer was reluctant to take this step). In most instances Mendeleyev's proposals proved to be correct (although the troublesome case of iodine and tellurium was not resolved until the discovery of isotopes). Finally and most notably, Mendeleyev was so impressed with the periodicity of the elements that he took the risk of predicting the chemical and physical properties of the unknown elements in the blank places of his table. Although his table had imperfections, it did bring similar elements together and help make chemistry a rational science and the periodic law an essential part of chemistry.

The periodic table grew out of the theoretical side of Mendeleyev's scientific personality, but he also had a practical side. He made important contributions to the Russian oil, coal, and sodium-carbonate industries. He served the czarist regime in several official positions. Nevertheless, he did not hesitate to speak out against the government's oppression of students, and his sympathy for the common people led him to travel third-class on trains. Though he held decidedly liberal views, it is wrong to see him as a political radical. Perhaps he is best described as a progressive, because he hoped that the czarist government would correct itself and evolve into a more compassionate regime.

Had Mendeleyev lived a few more years, he would have witnessed the complete and final development of his periodic table by Henry Moseley, whose discovery of atomic number by interacting X rays with various elements led to the use of the positive charge of the nucleus as the true measure of an element's place in the periodic table. Throughout the twentieth century, the periodic table, which owed so much to Mendeleyev, continued to be enlarged by the discovery of new elements. It was therefore appropriate that a new element (atomic number 101), discovered in 1955, was named mendelevium, in belated recognition of the importance of his periodic law.

—*Robert J. Paradowski*

FURTHER READING

Farber, Eduard, ed. *Great Chemists*. New York: John Wiley & Sons, 1961. This collection of more than one hundred biographies of chemists contains an excellent short biography of Mendeleyev. Nontechnical and contains ample references to both primary and secondary literature.

Gordin, Michael D. *A Well-ordered Thing: Dmitri Mendeleev and the Shadow of the Periodic Table.* New York: Basic Books, 2004. Biography focusing on Mendeleyev's professional years. Gordin recounts how Mendeleyev used his periodic table as a means of garnering attention for himself and as a platform for social change in imperial Russia.

Ihde, Aaron J. *The Development of Modern Chemistry.* New York: Harper & Row, 1964. Ihde traces the development of chemistry largely through its disciplines, for example, inorganic chemistry, organic chemistry, physical chemistry, and the like. Discusses Mendeleyev's life and work in a chapter on the classification of elements. Contains an excellent and extensive annotated bibliography.

Jaffe, Bernard. *Crucibles: The Lives and Achievements of the Great Chemists*. New York: Simon & Schuster, 1930. This book tells the story of chemistry through the lives of some of its greatest practitioners. The approach is popular, uncritical, and accessible to young readers and those with little knowledge of chemistry. The chapter on Mendeleyev contains a good basic treatment of his life and his discovery of the periodic law.

Strathern, Paul. *Mendeleyev's Dream: The Quest for the Elements*. London: Hamish Hamilton, 2000. A popular, accessible history of chemistry, describing the work of scientists from ancient Greece through the nineteenth century. As the title suggests, the book describes how Mendeleyev conceived of the periodic table in a dream, and details his contributions to the development of chemistry.

Van Spronsen, Johannes W. *The Periodic System of Chemical Elements: A History of the First Hundred Years*. Amsterdam: Elsevier, 1969. Several books have been written about the periodic system of chemical elements and its history, but this one, written to commemorate the hundredth anniversary of the periodic system, is the best. Van Spronsen analyzes Mendeleyev's achievement in great detail. Based on original sources, the book requires some knowledge of chemistry for a full understanding of the analysis. Generously illustrated with diagrams, photographs, and graphs.

Weeks, Mary Elvira. *Discovery of the Elements*. Edited by Henry Leicester. 7th ed. Easton, Pa.: Journal of Chemical Education, 1968. This book, which has served chemists as a rich source of information about the elements—chemical, technical, historical, and biographical—has been made even more valuable by this new edition prepared by Leicester. The material on Russian chemists, including Mendeleyev, has been expanded. Extensively illustrated and thoroughly understandable to readers with a modicum of chemical knowledge.

SEE ALSO: Aleksandr Borodin; Justus von Liebig; Nicholas I; Aleksandr Stepanovich Popov; Wilhelm Conrad Röntgen; Jules Verne.

RELATED ARTICLES in *Great Events from History: The Nineteenth Century, 1801-1900:* 1803-1808: Dalton Formulates the Atomic Theory of Matter; 1869-1871: Mendeleyev Develops the Periodic Table of Elements.

FELIX MENDELSSOHN
German composer

Mendelssohn was one of the great composers of the Romantic period. His music is noted for its exceptionally melodic qualities and its ability to capture a mood. It has been continually performed and studied from his time into the twenty-first century.

BORN: February 3, 1809; Hamburg (now in Germany)
DIED: November 4, 1847; Leipzig (now in Germany)
ALSO KNOWN AS: Jacob Ludwig Felix Mendelssohn-Bartholdy (full name)
AREA OF ACHIEVEMENT: Music

EARLY LIFE

Felix Mendelssohn (MEHN-dehls-zohn) was an unusually gifted and precocious child musically and was the most prominent member of an exceptionally talented family. He worked long and diligently, absorbed in his music, aware of his subtle talent and discernment in music. He loved taking walks in the woods and often wrote down the notes he heard the birds singing. His first musical influence was his mother, Leah, an expert pianist and vocalist. When Felix was only four years old, she gave him five-minute piano lessons, soon extended as the music capivated Felix's imagination. At the age of eight, Felix began music lessons with Karl Friedrich Zelter, the director of Berlin's Singakademie. Before long, the young musical genius was composing fugues, songs, operettas, violin and piano concerti, and piano quartets. He performed Sunday concerts in his home and even conducted a small orchestra.

Abraham Mendelssohn, Felix's father, was a prominent German banker, and his fashionable home was one of the intellectual and musical centers of Berlin. The excitement of learning reigned in Felix's "childhood castle," a home bustling with activity, servants, and tutors. Rebecka sang, Paul played the violoncello, and the eldest child, Fanny, played the piano almost as well as Felix. The children wrote their own newspaper, called at first

"The Garden Paper" and, later, "The Tea and Snow Times." They made paper lanterns to decorate the trees in the garden for dances. Felix particularly loved the park, where he rode his horse. He played billiards and chess and practiced the piano, organ, and violin. He learned landscape drawing and calligraphy.

Felix, a gentle, cheerful, kindly person, was handsome, self-confident, and even-tempered. His hair was dark black and his eyes, dark brown. He dressed elegantly, was very sociable, and loved good meals and stimulating companionship. He was sharply critical of his own work, revising five or six times pieces that had already been performed successfully.

LIFE'S WORK

In a sense, Mendelssohn began his life's work before he was ten years old, inasmuch as he was already busily composing music by that age. It was, however, the composition of his early masterpiece, *A Midsummer Night's Dream* (1826), at the age of seventeen that launched him into a serious career as a composer.

An early extended trip throughout Germany and Switzerland gave Mendelssohn a love of travel. He visited most of the beautiful, historical, cultural, and scenic places of Europe, carrying his sketchbook with him. His first visit to England and Scotland in 1829, at the age of twenty, began his lifelong attraction to English culture. The English were similarly enchanted with both Mendelssohn and his music. Even on this first visit he conducted the London Philharmonic.

Also in 1829, Mendelssohn helped to revive the singing of Johann Sebastian Bach's *Saint Matthew Passion*, which he had studied for years. Beginning in 1827, Mendelssohn and his friends assembled a small, dependable choir that met one evening a week for practice of rarely heard works. They secured permission to present the work at the Berlin Singakademie. Mendelssohn shortened the work drastically. He omitted many of the arias and used only the introductory symphonies of others. He edited passages for greater brevity. The performance was a historic success. The chorus numbered 158 and the orchestra included many from the Royal Orchestra. The king was in the royal loge with members of his court. Twenty-year-old Mendelssohn conducted without a score, as he knew the music and lyrics from memory. The historical effect was a Bach revival in Europe.

Despite his many musical activities, Mendelssohn had a very active social life and was often invited by families with girls of marriageable age. He was wealthy, cultured, courteous, handsome, of good moral character, and had a promising future. Mendelssohn chose for his wife Cécile Jeanrenaud, the daughter of a leading Huguenot minister in Frankfurt, who had died in 1819. Mendelssohn became acquainted with Cécile on one of his extended musical engagements in Frankfurt and finally realized that he was in love with this beautiful, charming girl, nine years his junior. Cécile and Mendelssohn were married on March 28, 1837, in the Reformed French Church in Frankfurt. The ceremony was performed in French. A friend wrote special music for the

Felix Mendelssohn. (Library of Congress)

wedding; Mendelssohn's "Wedding March" from *A Midsummer Night's Dream* had yet to come into fashion.

The couple spent their honeymoon in the upper Rhine valley and in the Black Forest. It was a wondrous and creative time: Mendelssohn sketched the outlines of half a dozen works. Mendelssohn was a devoted and content husband and Cécile an ideal wife. She loved her domestic life and was an excellent and charming hostess and a cheerful companion to her husband. She was a pious and orthodox Protestant, as was Mendelssohn. The couple had five children, one of whom died at the age of nine.

In 1833, Mendelssohn wrote the *Italian* Symphony and his oratorio on the life of the Apostle Paul. In 1835, he became conductor of the Leipzig Gewandhaus Orchestra and continued in that post for the rest of his life. Mendelssohn loved the Psalms and set many of them to music. In 1840, he finished *Hymn of Praise* (Second Symphony), with its delicate melodic contrasts so characteristic of Mendelssohn. The choral movement is mostly from Scripture, "Let everything that hath life and breath praise the Lord!" Mendelssohn also wrote the melody for "Hark, the Herald Angels Sing," and his *Reformation* Symphony (Fifth Symphony) expands on Martin Luther's "A Mighty Fortress Is Our God." In 1846, Mendelssohn completed and directed his oratorio *Elijah* to enthusiastic response. He soon began the opera *Lorelei* and his oratorio on the life of Christ, *Christus*, but he was unable to complete either. In May of 1847, his sister Fanny suddenly died. Mendelssohn lived only six months longer and died of a cerebral hemorrhage on November 4, 1847, at the age of thirty-eight.

SIGNIFICANCE

Felix Mendelssohn excelled in Romantic musical scene painting. His two most important symphonies are geographically identified: the *Italian* and the *Scottish*, which was dedicated to Queen Victoria, whom he met during his concert tours of England. The *Italian* pictures the spirited and sunny, vibrant south, and the *Scottish* has its own peculiar northern beauty. His works *The Hebrides* (1830-1832) and *Meeresstille und glückliche Fahrt* (1828-1832; calm sea and prosperous voyage) continue to influence musical seascapes. The listener can almost hear the sounds of the sea. Mendelssohn in fact listened to the waves and the gulls and ships and the water rushing into Fingal's Cave and recorded the sounds he heard in musical transcription, just as he had recorded the songs of birds in the gardens of his boyhood home.

It was no doubt an advantage to Mendelssohn to be born into a family of wealth so that he could concentrate unreservedly on his art. He worked exceptionally hard, however, and was motivated by a sense of duty and a desire to excel. He was Jewish by birth but had been baptized into the Christian faith. His philosophy of life, morals, and music all reflected a sincere orthodox faith. Mendelssohn agreed with Bach's philosophy of sacred music, that music should "form an integral part of our service instead of becoming a mere concert which more or less evokes a devotional mood."

How is music different from verbal communication? When someone asked Mendelssohn the meanings of some of his songs in "Songs Without Words," he responded:

> genuine music . . . fills the soul with a thousand things better than words. . . . Only the song can say the same thing, can arouse the same feelings in one person as in another, a feeling which is not expressed . . . by the same words.

Mendelssohn's music continues to evoke strong feelings.

—*William H. Burnside*

FURTHER READING

Blunt, Wilfrid. *On Wings of Song: A Biography of Felix Mendelssohn.* New York: Charles Scribner's Sons, 1974. A particularly interesting biography because of the many illustrations, anecdotes, and quotations from primary sources. An excellent introduction for the general reader. Includes cultural and scenic descriptions by Mendelssohn himself during his early nineteenth century travels in Switzerland, Germany, and Scotland.

Brown, Clive. *A Portrait of Mendelssohn.* New Haven, Conn.: Yale University Press, 2003. An account of Mendelssohn's life and work, featuring previously unpublished sketches by the composer. Brown argues that Mendelssohn was not a musical lightweight, but an innovative, cerebral composer who influenced twentieth century music.

David, Hans T., and Arthur Mendel, eds. *The Bach Reader: A Life of Johann Sebastian Bach in Letters and Documents.* New York: W. W. Norton, 1945. Valuable for a study of Mendelssohn because of the chapter on Mendelssohn's revival of the *Saint Matthew Passion.* Part of the eleven-page account is Edward Devrient's first-person account of the revival.

Kupferberg, Herbert. *The Mendelssohns: Three Generations of Genius.* New York: Charles Scribner's Sons, 1972. Places Mendelssohn in historical context by giving a one-hundred-page biographical sketch of his father, Abraham Mendelssohn, and his grandfather Moses Mendelssohn. Kupferberg also gives brief sketches of the lives of many others in the Mendelssohn family and shows them to be, men and women, a remarkable clan. The last chapter follows the Mendelssohns into the twentieth century. Includes a genealogical chart.

Marek, George R. *Gentle Genius: The Story of Felix Mendelssohn.* New York: Funk & Wagnalls, 1971. A very interesting biography. The lengthy quotations from the Mendelssohn correspondence and the many pictures enhance the book's value. Some of Mendelssohn's charming landscape drawings are also reproduced. "A Mendelssohn Calendar" is included.

Mendelssohn, Felix. *Letters.* Edited by G. Sheldon-Goth. New York: Pantheon Books, 1945. A fascinating collection of personal letters. Indispensable in giving insights into the personality, character, and thinking of Mendelssohn.

Mercer-Taylor, Peter, ed. *The Cambridge Companion to Mendelssohn.* New York: Cambridge University Press, 2004. Collection of essays analyzing Mendelssohn's life and music. Includes discussions of Mendelssohn and German art music; Mendelssohn and Judaism; Mendelssohn's symphonies, chamber music, keyboard works, and other compositions; and the reception for Mendelssohn's music.

Nichols, Roger. *Mendelssohn Remembered.* London: Faber & Faber, 1997. Popular biography, containing excerpts from Mendelssohn's letters and journals, contemporary reviews, and recorded conversations with family, friends, and acquaintances.

Todd, R. Larry. *Mendelssohn: A Life in Music.* New York: Oxford University Press, 2003. Comprehensive biography. Todd analyzes Mendelssohn's compositions and rejects the common view that he only composed sentimental pieces.

Werner, Eric. *Mendelssohn: A New Image of the Composer and His Age.* Translated by Dika Newlin. London: Free Press of Glencoe, 1963. A long and complete biography of Mendelssohn. Includes detailed technical and artistic discussions of all Mendelssohn's major works, including musical scores as examples.

SEE ALSO: W. S. Gilbert and Arthur Sullivan; Charles Gounod; Robert Schumann; Queen Victoria.

RELATED ARTICLE in *Great Events from History: The Nineteenth Century, 1801-1900:* April 7, 1805: Beethoven's *Eroica* Symphony Introduces the Romantic Age.

MENELIK II
Emperor of Ethiopia (r. 1889-1913)

Menelik unified Ethiopia after it had experienced centuries of political fragmentation, consolidated the ancient Christian heritage against growing Muslim influence, and saved Ethiopia from European colonialism. He laid the foundations for Ethiopia's transformation from a medieval, feudal empire to a modern state.

BORN: August 17, 1844; Ankober, Shoa (now in Ethiopia)
DIED: December 12, 1913; Addis Ababa, Ethiopia
ALSO KNOWN AS: Sahle Mariam; Menilek II
AREAS OF ACHIEVEMENT: Government and politics, warfare and conquest

EARLY LIFE

Emperor Menelik II (MEHN-eh-lihk) was born Sahle Mariam in the court of his father, Haile Malakot, a leading prince of the Ethiopian province of Shoa. Chronicles and oral tradition reflect some uncertainty as to the details of the birth: Sahle Mariam may have been born out of wedlock, possibly the result of Haile Malakot's infatuation with a concubine. However, the traditional sources, while almost ignoring Sahle Mariam's father—whose reign appears to have been less than illustrious—often make much of the piety and reputation of the child's mother.

In Ethiopia, where the nobility put much importance on genealogy, these were matters of enormous concern for Sahle Mariam's career. These concerns caused Haile Malakot's father, the mighty Sahle Selassie who had led the resurgence of the Christian, Amharic-speaking nobles in Shoa earlier in the nineteenth century, to intercede. Sahle Selassie and his influential queen, Bezzabbesh, saw that the parents of Sahle Mariam were married in a civil ceremony shortly after the child's birth. In order to erase any further question of Sahle Mariam's pedigree, Sahle Selassie rechristened the child Menelik II. He prophesied that Menelik would restore the empire of Ethiopia to the ancient greatness wrought by Menelik I, the offspring of a legendary union between Solomon, the king of ancient Israel, and Sheba, Queen of south Arabia.

In Menelik's youth, however, there were others with similar aspirations. Ethiopia was just emerging from the *Zamana Masafent* (age of the princes), a long period of disunity and internal chaos. The most notable of the early unifiers was Theodore, ruler of the province of Gonder. In 1856, Theodore's forces defeated the Shoan levies and

incorporated the province. Menelik's father died of malaria during the final campaign against Theodore. Menelik himself, now the designated heir to the throne of Shoa, became a ward of Theodore at his fortress capital of Magdela. There, Menelik received the favored treatment and education due a noble. He completed religious training and developed excellent military skills. Above all, Menelik obtained the practical experience necessary for success as a ruler and statesman in his own right. He also formed lasting alliances with other noble children from far-flung parts of Ethiopia.

Theodore's enterprise began with great promise. He envisioned an Ethiopia of law and order and of conciliation between Muslims and Christians. As his reign progressed, however, he resorted increasingly to force, infuriated by the resistance of Muslim principalities and deeply suspicious of intrigue. Theodore may well have been demented in his final years. After 1864, he executed members of the court on a whim and imprisoned members of the British diplomatic mission. The latter indiscretion brought a British military expedition; Theodore committed suicide as it was about to storm Magdela in 1868.

LIFE'S WORK

The disintegration of Theodore's authority set the stage for Menelik's emergence. In 1865, the Shoan nobles revolted and beseeched Menelik to return. He escaped Magdela under cover of darkness to return to Ankober. By 1866, Menelik was firmly in command in Shoa. From the moment of his return, Menelik dreamed of succeeding where Theodore had failed, in ruling a united Ethiopian empire.

In 1872, after four years of intrigue and dynastic struggles, Yohannes IV was crowned emperor of Ethiopia at the ancient capital of Aksum in the north. Yohannes managed to hold together the tenuous unity imposed by Theodore. Only Menelik's homeland of Shoa remained outside the empire.

Menelik's ambitions—indeed his durability as an independent ruler—required outside support. Theodore's notoriety, and the British punitive expedition of 1868, had shattered Ethiopia's isolation and exposed the country to outside pressures. The opening of the Suez Canal in 1869 greatly increased European interest in the countries along the Red Sea. Egypt, ruled by the ambitious modernizer Ismāʿīl Pasha, pushed its authority deep into the

Sudan, west of Ethiopia, and in 1865 occupied the old Turkish port of Mesewa on the Ethiopian coast. Menelik cultivated an alliance with the Egyptians in the hope of forcing Yohannes IV to divide his attention between two opponents rather than concentrate on Shoa. The Egyptians, however, were devastated by Yohannes's forces when they attempted to move inland in 1875. Yohannes's predominantly Greek advisers urged him to articulate a pan-Christian front in the Middle East against both Egyptian and Turkish ambitions. Yohannes also had reached an understanding with the British, who were alarmed at the pace of Egyptian expansion in northeast Africa.

In 1883, tribes in the Sudan rose in rebellion against Egyptian rule. Under the leadership of a Muslim cleric who styled himself as Mahdi (savior), tens of thousands of Sudanese Muslims invaded western Ethiopia in 1887 and sacked Gonder, massacring its inhabitants. Yohan-

Menelik II. (Library of Congress)

nes retaliated the following year by butchering sixty thousand Mahdist troops, but he was wounded in the battle and died shortly thereafter.

The throne now went to Menelik II, and his reign proved among the greatest in Ethiopian history. Menelik immediately set about pushing Ethiopia's frontiers west toward the Nile and south toward Lake Victoria. He incorporated vast quantities of trade into the empire, thus filling his usually extended exchequer. Menelik departed from the crusading ways of his predecessors by restoring religious liberty and ending the persecution of Muslims and pagans. His method of establishing a dominant culture in Ethiopia was economic and diplomatic rather than military. When new regions were added to the empire, he sowed them with strategically placed settlements of lesser Amhara nobles and Christian clergy, whose increasing control of commerce provided an incentive for the Christianization of many areas. Even tribes who remained Muslim adopted the trappings of Christian, Amhara noble etiquette and fashion.

One of Menelik's most lasting contributions to modern Ethiopia was the establishment of a new capital at Addis Ababa (new flower) in a relatively sheltered location on the central plain. The region around Addis Ababa contained many of the oldest and most venerated Christian monasteries in the country. Founding the capital there not only reiterated Menelik's commitment to the Christian tradition of Ethiopia but also brought to an end the practice of changing capitals each time a new dynastic line or regional nobility assumed power. Eucalyptus trees, imported by Menelik to provide shade for government buildings in Addis Ababa, soon spread throughout Ethiopia and helped reforest some of the barren and denuded hillsides of the country. Telegraph communication, and later the beginnings of a telephone system, tied together the outlying regions of the huge, mountainous country. In 1897, a French firm completed a direct railway link between Addis Ababa and the Red Sea coast at Djibouti.

Menelik is best known for transforming Ethiopia's role in international affairs from that of potential prey of European colonialism to that of a factor in the regional balance of power. He did so by successfully confronting Italy's bid to incorporate Ethiopia into its colonial domain. In 1882, the Italians purchased the port of Aseb from a private trading company and began to expand along the Red Sea coast. Italian ambitions triggered British occupation of northern Somalia and a French landing at Djibouti in 1885. At first, Menelik deferred to the Italians. Under the Treaty of Uccialli of May, 1889, Menelik recognized Italian sovereignty on the coast and agreed to link his foreign policy with that of Italy. Four years later, however, with Italian columns steadily pushing inland and nearby provincial governors calling for assistance, Menelik prepared for war. After several inconclusive skirmishes, the decisive battle came at Adwa on March 1, 1896, where the Ethiopian army crushed an Italian force.

The news of Adwa electrified the world; it was a stunning reverse of the forces of colonialism hitherto judged irresistible. Within months, a new treaty finalized the Italian colonial frontier with Ethiopia. Emboldened, Menelik pushed his borders westward, joining with France in 1898 in an effort to control the Upper Nile by planting his flag alongside the French at Fashoda (modern Kodok). Ethiopia thus became a factor in a major Anglo-French diplomatic crisis. In 1902, Menelik agreed to the Treaty of Addis Ababa, in which Great Britain and Ethiopia, negotiating on equal terms, reached agreement on placement of the western frontier.

Menelik grew frail in his final years. In 1909, he relinquished the government to a regency in the name of his grandson, Lij Yasu, whose Muslim leanings led to renewed strife and political intrigue. Menelik's new imperial administration and cultural latticework of Christian-Amhara tradition survived the crisis, however, and continued to support Ethiopia as a nation.

SIGNIFICANCE

Menelik II ruled Ethiopia at a crucial time in its history, when the country was emerging from its own dark age and opening itself up to the world. He accomplished the rarest of feats in assimilating the military and technological advances of Europe while turning religion, tradition, and an antiquated class structure toward productive ends. In doing so, he saved Ethiopia from the fate of the rest of Africa, which fell under European rule. For nearly a century, the culture, economy, and political system of Ethiopia bore his stamp.

—*Ronald W. Davis*

FURTHER READING

Abir, Mordechai. *Ethiopia: The Era of the Princes, the Challenge of Islam, and the Reunification of the Christian Empire, 1769-1855*. New York: Praeger, 1968. Analyzes the crucial period of disunity from the mid-eighteenth to the mid-nineteenth century, when the power of the traditional Christian nobility was in decline and Ethiopia faced the challenge of a revitalized Islam. Excellent on the importance of trade expansion and fiscal control.

Berkeley, George Fitz-Hardinge. *The Campaign of Adowa and the Rise of Menelik*. Reprint. New York: Negro Universities Press, 1969. A reprint of a 1902 edition that examines the enormous impact of the Ethiopian victory at Adwa, and the consequent rise of the country's international prestige on the intellectual and political environment of African American society.

Caulk, Richard A. "Minilik II and the Diplomacy of Commerce." *Journal of Ethiopian Studies* 17 (1984): 63-76. Discusses the emperor's commercial and diplomatic aplomb in gaining control of the productive means of his country and in balancing the opportunities and dangers of increased trade with Europeans.

Darkwah, R. H. Kofi. *Shewa, Menilek, and the Ethiopian Empire, 1813-1889*. London: Heinemann, 1975. Monographic coverage of the period with emphasis on the later portion. Extensive coverage of agriculture and other economic issues, suppression of the slave trade, and military organization. Contains a useful bibliography.

Horvath, R. J. "The Wandering Capitals of Ethiopia." *Journal of African History* 10 (1969): 205-219. Discusses the locations of the capital in various periods; also useful as a brief synopsis of Ethiopian politics and society prior to the nineteenth century.

Marcus, Harold G. *A History of Ethiopia*. 1994. Updated edition. Berkeley: University of California Press, 2002. An overview of Ethiopian history from prehistoric times through 1991. All but the first eighty of the book's 394 pages deal with Ethiopia since the country's reunification under Menelik II in 1889.

_____. *The Life and Times of Menelik II of Ethiopia: 1844-1913*. Oxford, England: Clarendon Press, 1975. Reprint. Lawrenceville, N.J.: Red Sea Press, 1995. The primary focus is on Menelik's relations with Ethiopian noble dynasties and European powers. Extensive political narrative. Excellent bibliography.

Rosenfeld, Chris Prouty. *A Chronology of Menilek II of Ethiopia, 1844-1913*. East Lansing, Mich.: African Studies Center, 1976. A diary of the life and reign of Menelik gleaned from many different sources. Major foreign developments correlated with those in Ethiopia. A must for research on the period.

SEE ALSO: Tewodros II.

RELATED ARTICLE in *Great Events from History: The Nineteenth Century, 1801-1900:* April, 1868: British Expedition to Ethiopia.

ADAH ISAACS MENKEN
American actor and poet

Menken won notoriety throughout the United States and Europe for her scandalous performances in Mazeppa, *in which she appeared on stage apparently nude, strapped to the back of a wild horse—an image that shocked nineteenth century audiences and contributed to the creation of burlesque theater and the liberation of nineteenth century women.*

BORN: June 15, 1835; either Memphis, Tennessee, or Chartrain (now Milneburg), near New Orleans, Louisiana

DIED: August 10, 1868; Paris, France

ALSO KNOWN AS: Ada McCord; Adelaide McCord; Ada Bertha Theodore; Adel Theodora; Dolores Adios Fuertes; Great Unadorned

AREAS OF ACHIEVEMENT: Theater, literature

EARLY LIFE

Little is known about the early life of Adah Isaacs Menken, largely because she later deliberately created misleading legends about herself. Not even her birthplace is known for certain, and there is some suggestion that her father may have been a prosperous freed slave who worked in New Orleans. Her early years certainly introduced her to a varied background, for she spoke German, French, Spanish, Hebrew, and Latin. It is also known that during her early years she danced with the New Orleans French Opera and appeared in circus equestrian acts. Menken herself also claimed to have attended college in Nacogdoches, Texas.

In 1856, Adah married Alexander Isaac Menken, a well-known Jewish theatrical musician. She later claimed to have published during that same year a book of poems titled *Memories*, under the pseudonym Indigina. In 1857, she made her stage debut in Shreveport, Louisiana, as Pauline in Edward Bulwer-Lytton's play *The Lady of Lyons* (1838). Over the next two years, she earned her living as a dancer and circus performer in Shreveport, Nashville, and New Orleans. A woman who was always ready to defy convention, she took to smoking cigarettes in public. When she refused to stop, her husband left her.

LIFE'S WORK

The crucial year in Menken's career was 1859, when she moved to Cincinnati, Ohio, where she embraced Judaism. She also published a series of poems in *The Cincinnati Israelite* and in *The New York Sunday Mer-*

cury. Before the year was out, she moved to New York, where she made her stage debut in *The Soldier's Daughter* in March. To maintain herself she worked frequently in variety shows as a black-faced minstrel and even once impersonated the distinguished actor Edwin Booth in a satire on his production of William Shakespeare's *Hamlet* (pr. c. 1600-1601).

During that period, Menken met and fell in love with the famous Irish prize fighter John Carmel Heenan. To marry Heenan, she secured a rabbinical diploma dissolving her marriage to Alexander Menken but retained Menken as her stage name throughout the rest of her life. However, her marriage to Heenan actually constituted bigamy because she failed to obtain a legal divorce through New York State courts. To make matters worse, Heenan took to beating her at night and eventually left her with a son who died in infancy. Their divorce was ultimately made legal in 1862. During Menken's brief marriage to Heenan, she apparently learned to box from her husband, and in later years she claimed that she had boxed professionally.

In 1861, Menken came to the stage role that would make her fame and fortune throughout the remainder of her life: the title role in *Mazeppa: Or, The Wild Horse of Tartary*, a melodrama about the tribulations of a young boy adapted in 1830 by Henry M. Milner from Lord Byron's 1819 poem "Mazeppa." What made Menken's performance noteworthy and, indeed, notorious, was not only her playing the role of a young boy but also her appearance in the play's climatic scene, in which she was strapped to the back of a wild horse that leapt and bucked across the stage. That sensational image alone would have been spectacular; however, Mazeppa was also supposed to be nude. That scene had originally employed a dummy strapped to the horse. However, Menken insisted on playing the scene herself and created a realistic impression of nudity by wearing a skin-tight outfit that matched her coloring, with only a small skirt around her waist. In an age in which women were clothed from neck to toe and when the mere sight of a woman's bare ankle was considered provocative, Menken's choice of costume was audacious and scandalous. However, the daring costume also brought her fame and fortune, and soon she became the highest-paid female actor in the United States. A photograph of Menken on horseback in her famous role was widely distributed during her lifetime and is still reproduced in many books on the history of theater.

From New York, Menken took the production of *Mazeppa* to San Francisco where it opened to a sold-out audience at Maguire's Opera House, with Junius Brutus Booth, Edwin's Booth's brother, as Menken's costar. Menken became the toast of San Francisco and was even made an honorary member of that city's Hook and Ladder Fire Company. Soon, she was traveling throughout the United States presenting *Mazeppa* to large and shocked, but obviously appreciative, audiences. The question of scandal aside, Menken was apparently very good in her role. She had spent several years acquiring her skills as an actor, and the many years she had spent

performing equestrian acts in circuses aided her in handling the climatic moment in the play.

In addition to *Mazeppa*, she starred in several other plays, including *Dick Turpin, The French Spy, Three Fast Women*, and *The Child of the Sun*, in each of which she received good reviews. However, *Mazeppa* was always her main vehicle. When she performed in the play in San Francisco, Mark Twain wrote a review and later sought her out as a friend when she appeared in Virginia City, Nevada. Other notable literary figures, including Bret Harte, were also her friends, and they encouraged her to write more poetry, especially in the new free verse

MARK TWAIN REVIEWS *MAZEPPA*

THE MENKEN—WRITTEN ESPECIALLY FOR GENTLEMEN

When I arrived in San Francisco, I found there was no one in town—at least there was no body in town but "the Menken"—or rather, that no one was being talked about except that manly young female. I went to see her play "Mazeppa," of course. They said she was dressed from head to foot in flesh-colored "tights," but I had no opera-glass, and I couldn't see it, to use the language of the inelegant rabble. She appeared to me to have but one garment on—a thin tight white linen one, of unimportant dimensions; I forget the name of the article, but it is indispensable to infants of tender age—I suppose any young mother can tell you what it is, if you have the moral courage to ask the question. With the exception of this superfluous rag, the Menken dresses like the Greek Slave; but some of her postures are not so modest as the suggestive attitude of the latter. She is a finely formed woman down to her knees; if she could be herself that far, and Mrs. H. A. Perry the rest of the way, she would pass for an unexceptionable Venus. Here every tongue sings the praises of her matchless grace, her supple gestures, her charming attitudes. Well, possibly, these tongues are right.

In the first act, she rushes on the stage, and goes cavorting around after "Olinska"; she bends herself back like a bow; she pitches headforemost at the atmosphere like a battering ram; she works her arms, and her legs, and her whole body like a dancing-jack: her every movement is as quick as thought; in a word, without any apparent reason for it, she carries on like a lunatic from the beginning of the act to the end of it. At other times she "whallops" herself down on the stage, and rolls over as does the sportive pack-mule after his burden is removed. If this be grace then the Menken is eminently graceful. After a while they proceed to strip her, and the high chief Pole calls for the "fiery untamed steed"; a subordinate Pole brings in the fierce brute, stirring him up occasionally to make him run away, and then hanging to him like death to keep him from doing it; the monster looks round pensively upon the brilliant audience in the theatre, and seems very willing to stand still—but a lot of those Poles grab him and hold on to him, so as to be prepared for him in case he changes his mind. They are posted as to his fiery untamed nature, you know, and they give him no chance to get loose and eat up the orchestra. They strap Mazeppa on his back, fore and aft, and face upper most, and the horse goes cantering up-stairs over the painted mountains, through tinted clouds of theatrical mist, in a brisk exciting way, with the wretched victim he bears unconsciously digging her heels into his hams, in the agony of her sufferings, to make him go faster. Then a tempest of applause bursts forth, and the curtain falls.

The fierce old circus horse carries his prisoner around through the back part of the theatre, behind the scenery, and although assailed at every step by the savage wolves of the desert, he makes his way at last to his dear old home in Tartary down by the foot lights, and beholds once more, O, gods! the familiar faces of the fiddlers in the orchestra. The noble old steed is happy, then, but poor Mazeppa is insensible—"ginned out" by his trip, as it were. Before the act closes, however, he is restored to consciousness and his doting old father, the king of Tartary; and the next day, without taking time to dress—without even borrowing a shirt, or stealing a fresh horse—he starts off on the fiery untamed, at the head of the Tartar nation, to exterminate the Poles, and carry off his own sweet Olinska from the Polish court. He succeeds, and the curtain falls upon a bloody combat, in which the Tartars are victorious. . . .

Source: "Letter from Mark Twain, San Francisco, September 13, 1863," *Virginia City Territorial Enterprise*, September 17, 1863.

form. Menken married and divorced one of these literary acquaintances, the Civil War satirist Robert Newell, better known as Orpheus C. Kerr ("office seeker"). She also married and divorced James Barkley, a southerner about whom little is known. Through the turmoil of her private life she continued to star in *Mazeppa* and crossed the Atlantic Ocean in 1864 to take the production to Europe, where it was a great success.

In London, where Menken appeared at Sadler's Wells Theater, Menken attracted the friendship of such important literary figures as Henry Wadsworth Longfellow, Algernon Swinburne, and Dante Gabriel Rosetti. In France she met and carried on a romantic relationship with the famous French novelist Alexandre Dumas, *père*. Meanwhile, in addition to making frequent stage performances, she continued to write poetry and dedicated a new volume of poems to her friends Charles Dickens and George Sand. After Menken gave birth to her second son in November, 1866, Sand honored her by serving as the short-lived boy's godmother.

In August, 1868, Menken was rehearsing for a show in Paris when she suddenly collapsed on stage. Over the following week, her condition did not markedly improve, but she returned to rehearsals, only to collapse again. On August 10, she died, at the age of only thirty-three years. Physicians were unable to agree on a diagnosis; some attributed her condition to tuberculosis, others thought she had cancer, and still others thought she might have had a ruptured appendix. There was no post-mortem examination. Menken's final book of poetry, *Infelicia*, appeared one week after her death.

SIGNIFICANCE

In an age when respectable women were expected to be quiet and genteel in their public life and to demur to their husbands and other men in all matters, Adah Isaacs Menken was a startling phenomenon. Her first husband abandoned her because she refused to stop smoking cigarettes in public. That did not stop her from marrying and divorcing three other husbands during an age when divorce was not common.

However, Menken's artistic adventures were more significant than her complex private life. Known as an accomplished actor, she flew in the face of convention by appearing on stage seemingly in the nude, both shocking and delighting polite society. Her innovation in the theater of the times would be the first step toward the creation of American burlesque. Not only was she an actor of accomplishment and some infamy, but she was also a poet and the friend, and even lover, of some of the most significant literary figures of the day. She may well be considered one of the first of modern public celebrities. She accomplished all this in a lifetime that spanned only thirty-three years.

—*August W. Staub*

FURTHER READING

Banham, Martin, ed. *The Cambridge Guide to the Theatre*. Cambridge, England: Cambridge University Press, 1995. A good general guide to the theater with an informative entry on Menken.

Eiselein, Gregory, ed. *"Infelicia" and Other Writings by Adah Isaacs Menken*. Alberta, Canada: Broadview Press, 2002. An edition of her book of poetry and of other works by Adah Isaacs Menken.

Gascoigne, Bamber. *World Theatre: An Illustrated History*. Boston: Little, Brown, 1968. The emphasis in this book is on the visual theater, and it contains an excellent description of how the "wild horse" scene in *Mazeppa* was staged.

Mankowitz, Wolf. *Mazeppa: The Lives, Loves, and Legends of Adah Isaacs Menken*. New York: Stein & Day, 1982. Fascinating and thorough biography of Menken, with many illustrations.

Sentilles, Renee. *Performing Menken: Adah Isaacs Menken and the Birth of American Celebrity*. Cambridge, England: Cambridge University Press, 2003. A study of how Menken was the first woman of the theater to create herself as a celebrity and how that phenomenon has continued in American history.

SEE ALSO: Sarah Bernhardt; Edwin Booth; Lord Byron; Charles Dickens; Alexandre Dumas, *père*; Fanny Kemble; Lillie Langtry; Henry Wadsworth Longfellow; George Sand; Ellen Terry; Mark Twain.

RELATED ARTICLE in *Great Events from History: The Nineteenth Century, 1801-1900:* 1878-1899: Irving Manages London's Lyceum Theatre.

OTTMAR MERGENTHALER
German-born American inventor

Mergenthaler invented Linotype, the most widely used automatic typesetting system before the advent of computerized photocomposition, thus revolutionizing the production of printed matter.

BORN: May 11, 1854; Hachtel, Württemberg (now in Germany)
DIED: October 28, 1899; Baltimore, Maryland
AREAS OF ACHIEVEMENT: Science and technology, business

EARLY LIFE

The third of five children born to Johann George and Rosine (Ackermann) Mergenthaler (MERH-gehn-tah-lehr), Ottmar Mergenthaler grew up in a family of schoolteachers. After an unexceptional grade school education in Ensingen, to which his family had moved, his father attempted to enroll him in a seminary in preparation for a career as a teacher. His early interest in engineering, however, and his skill at repairing all kinds of mechanisms, including the village clock, overcame his father's desire. Mergenthaler rejected the seminary, opting instead for an apprenticeship with a maker of watches and clocks.

Mergenthaler was fourteen when he began his apprenticeship with Louis Hahl in Bietigheim. He completed his apprenticeship in 1872, having shown himself to be a talented and ambitious mechanic. These were difficult times in Mergenthaler's homeland. Soldiers returning from the Franco-Prussian War were flooding the labor market. Economic reforms were disrupting established patterns of everyday life. To avoid military service himself and to further his career, he arranged to emigrate to the United States to work for Hahl's son, August, who was already an established instrument maker in Washington, D.C.

Although Washington was more of a governmental center than a manufacturing city, its skilled mechanics benefited from their proximity to scientific agencies and the patent office. August Hahl's shop concentrated on making electrical and meteorological apparatus, and Mergenthaler distinguished himself as an ingenious and dexterous mechanic. Curious and sensitive to a fault, he was also anxious to prove his competence and to make a success of himself in his adopted homeland. Bearded, with a high forehead, wavy dark hair, and deep-set eyes, he conveyed an intense, almost brooding presence.

The United States into which Mergenthaler arrived was different in several respects from the Germany he left. Mergenthaler grew up in a society in which precision and pride in craft were highly valued. In the United States, economic gain and productivity were more evident priorities. Germany had a more rigid class system and was developing a strong tradition of centralized state interference in the economy. In the United States, careers tended to be more open to the talented, and there was relatively greater opportunity for individual entrepreneurship. Mergenthaler seemed to be in his element.

LIFE'S WORK

Mergenthaler's introduction to the printing trade came in 1876, after Hahl's shop had been moved to Baltimore because it was more of an industrial center than Washington. Ironically, it was a Washington court reporter, James O. Clephane, who envisioned a means of transferring a printed page by means of a new kind of typewriter. He took his idea to an inventor, Charles Moore, who had developed a prototype. Moore brought his device to Hahl's shop for refinement. Mergenthaler was entrusted with the job of perfecting this machine and determining if it would serve its purposes. After three years of work, he decided that neither this idea nor a subsequent papier-mâché process would ever succeed. He also became obsessed with the idea that he could develop a successful machine to compose type automatically.

Mergenthaler became Hahl's partner in 1878 and continued there until 1883, when he established his own instrument-making and machine shop in Baltimore. From 1876 until his death in 1899, wherever Mergenthaler worked, it was the perfection of mechanical type composing that held his attention. Clephane continued to encourage him and found financial backing for his early endeavors.

In 1883, Mergenthaler produced a machine that used relief figures on long bands to make a papier-mâché mold of a line of type from which a metal line could be cast. In 1884, he developed a second so-called band machine, which aligned recessed dies on the bands from which a metal type line could be directly cast. Mergenthaler recognized that using individual brass molds for each character would improve the quality of the cast line and the machine's ability to redistribute molds for reuse. Despite the opposition of his financial backers, organized into the National Typographic Company, Mergenthaler worked on developing this new machine rather than producing the band model.

In 1885, Mergenthaler tested his new machine, and in the summer of 1886 the first one was installed at the *New York Tribune*. Whitelaw Reid, the *New York Tribune* editor and a financial backer of the machine, is reputed to have given the machine its name by exclaiming his amazement at the "line o' type" produced.

Several newspaper publishers formed a syndicate to support Mergenthaler's device, and they immediately sought to encourage its production for use on their papers. Mergenthaler opposed their efforts to move rapidly into manufacturing because he felt that significant improvements were needed. Nevertheless, the machine went into production, with Mergenthaler making improvements along the way. By 1888, disputes between Mergenthaler and his business partners reached a crisis and he resigned from the company, reorganized in 1885 as the Mergenthaler Printing Company.

Mergenthaler set up his own company to build parts and assemble machines for the syndicate that controlled the rights to the invention. He continued to make dozens of patented improvements on the Linotype. In 1890, he developed a new model Linotype that was more efficient and more reliable. In 1891, he was induced to rejoin the syndicate, renamed this time the Mergenthaler Linotype Company. He resigned in anger again in 1895 after the company president unsuccessfully requested that Mergenthaler's name be removed from the title.

Struck by tuberculosis in 1894, Mergenthaler spent the last years of his life perfecting his invention, battling for recognition and financial reward, and struggling to regain his health. He moved with his wife and three surviving children to New Mexico in 1897 but soon returned to Baltimore, where he died on October 28, 1899.

As completed, the Linotype combined the processes of composing text, casting type, and redistributing the molds. Type molds, called matrices, were held in a magazine. By working on a keyboard, the operator assembled in sequence individual matrices for letters, numbers, or marks. The line of assembled matrices was automatically spaced to the desired length by expanding wedges. Then it was held in front of a casting mechanism as molten type metal was forced into the molds. The completed line of type, called a slug, was then dropped into a galley, ready to be joined by the next line. Finally, after casting, the matrices were automatically carried back to the magazine and distributed to their original places to be reused. When the galley was full, the slugs were taken away to be prepared and arranged for printing.

The machine provided several advantages over handset type. First, it was about four to five times as fast as hand composition. Second, it allowed each publication to be printed from what was, in essence, new, unworn type. Third, composed matter could be stored for later printing without tying up expensive foundry type and depriving compositors of type to use on other jobs.

The Linotype faced a number of competitors, a few of which had been in limited use for years while others were introduced almost simultaneously with Mergenthaler's invention. In 1891, the American Newspaper Publishers Association invited the makers of fourteen machines to compete in a typesetting machine contest. Only four machines were eventually tested and, although not considered the best, the Linotype performed well enough to encourage several newspaper publishers to place orders.

Not surprisingly, the Linotype caused concern among skilled printing workers. During the 1890's, no fewer than twelve thousand journeymen printers, most often older men or those without a permanent job, lost their positions. Their union, the International Typographical Union, developed a set of policies to bring the machine predominantly under the control of the union rather than attempting to oppose its introduction. It thus set a precedent followed by many other American trade unions in response to technological innovations.

The Linotype's influence spread beyond the printing office itself. Newspaper publishers began to insist that reporters and editors use typewriters so that Linotype operators would not be slowed by unreadable manuscript. American type founders quickly learned that the Linotype was cutting into orders for new type. A group of them responded in 1892 by forming a new corporation, the American Type Founders Company, to benefit from economies of scale, reduced competition, and promotional activities.

The Linotype rapidly overwhelmed its competition in machine typesetting. About two hundred of the initial model, the Blower, were manufactured by 1890; between 1890 and 1892, more than 350 of the improved model were made; and more than seven thousand of the perfected Model 1 were in use by 1901. More than ninety thousand of the machines had been produced in the United States by 1971, when domestic production ended, and another forty thousand had been produced in foreign factories. Nearly all American daily and even weekly newspapers were produced on Linotypes during the early 1960's, when the shift to computer-based technologies began in earnest.

SIGNIFICANCE

Ottmar Mergenthaler's single contribution to American, indeed world, culture came in the form of a perfected machine for automatically composing printing type. This invention transformed the printing trade and contributed to increasing the amount and speed with which printed material reached the public. It reduced the labor costs of employing printers and increased their ability to produce large quantities of text in a short time. This was particularly important in the newspaper trade, where time was of the essence. Although initially more appropriate for producing text than advertisements, the Linotype increased the total size of papers and encouraged more advertising. Although it imposed some limits on typefaces and page design, it was sufficiently flexible to meet the aesthetic needs of most publishers.

In some ways, Mergenthaler epitomized the ironies of American industrial history. An immigrant who saw the United States as a land of opportunity, Mergenthaler achieved a significant level of success and acclaim, having contributed materially to his adopted homeland, yet he was unwilling to compromise his craftsperson's principles in the face of economic pressures and was unable to create a practical balance between technical and business affairs.

—William S. Pretzer

FURTHER READING

Barnett, George E. *Chapters on Machinery and Labor.* Cambridge, Mass.: Harvard University Press, 1926. Includes Barnett's seminal essay on the economic and labor aspects of the Linotype's introduction. Provides the best conceptual discussion of the pace of introduction and its impact.

Chappel, Warren. *A Short History of the Printed Word.* New York: Alfred A. Knopf, 1970. An accessible, generally reliable history of printing in world context. Covers intellectual, aesthetic, and technical aspects of printing. Places the mechanization of typesetting into the context of other nineteenth century changes in the book trades.

Huss, Richard E. *The Development of Printers' Mechanical Typesetting Methods: 1822-1925.* Charlottesville: University Press of Virginia, 1973. A chronological survey of typesetting devices, particularly strong on technical descriptions of their mechanisms. Includes 294 individual items with illustrations of most.

Jennett, Sean. *Pioneers in Printing.* London: Routledge & Kegan Paul, 1958. A series of biographies of influential individuals in the book trades. Places Mergenthaler's work in the context of others working on mechanical typesetting. Gives a good, brief introduction to the complex business arrangements surrounding the Linotype.

Kahan, Basil. *Ottmar Mergenthaler: The Man and His Machine: A Biographical Appreciation of the Inventor on His Centennial.* New Castle, Del.: Oak Knoll Press, 2000. Recounts Mergenthaler's efforts to find appreciation for his Linotype, and his battles with typographical unions and financiers.

Kelber, Harry, and Carl Schlesinger. *Union Printers and Controlled Automation.* New York: Free Press, 1967. A thorough discussion of the impact of the Linotype and subsequent technological changes on printing labor. Contains a complete analysis of the development of attitudes toward technology by the International Typographical Union.

Mengel, Willi. *Ottmar Mergenthaler and the Printing Revolution.* Brooklyn, N.Y.: Mergenthaler Linotype, 1954. Produced for the centenary anniversary of Mergenthaler's birth, this volume relies heavily upon Mergenthaler's autobiography for its discussion of the Linotype. Also includes helpful material on earlier efforts to mechanize typesetting.

Mergenthaler, Ottmar. *Biography of Ottmar Mergenthaler and History of the Linotype.* Baltimore: Author, 1898. Written in the third person, this publication was pulled together by Mergenthaler just before his death after an original manuscript and notes were destroyed in a fire. The biography is an indispensable source, full of information and insights unavailable elsewhere. It is marred, however, by an understandably one-sided and frequently bitter perspective.

Thompson, John S. *The Mechanism of the Linotype; History of Composing Machines.* 2 vols. Chicago: Inland Printer, 1902-1904. Reprint. New York: Garland, 1980. Originally published as serials in a trade journal, these two works constitute a basic source written by a former Mergenthaler employee. Contains a complete technical description of the Linotype and its operation and maintenance, as well as comparisons with other typesetting devices.

SEE ALSO: Thomas Alva Edison; Mark Twain; John Walter II.

RELATED ARTICLE in *Great Events from History: The Nineteenth Century, 1801-1900:* 1819-1833: Babbage Designs a Mechanical Calculator.

METTERNICH
Austrian politician and diplomat

As Europe's preeminent champion of post-French Revolution conservatism, Metternich was the chief architect in the reconstruction of the European map after the fall of Napoleon I. As minister of foreign affairs, and, later, as Austria's state chancellor, he presided for more than three decades over the political and diplomatic workings of the continent he had restored until the revolutions of 1848 swept him from power and ushered in a new generation of leaders.

BORN: May 15, 1773; Coblenz, Archbishopric of Trier (now in Germany)

DIED: June 11, 1859; Vienna, Austro-Hungarian Empire (now in Austria)

ALSO KNOWN AS: Clemens Wenzel Nepomuk Lothar Von Metternich (full name); Prince von Metternich

AREAS OF ACHIEVEMENT: Diplomacy, government and politics

EARLY LIFE

Clemens Wenzel Nepomuk Lothar von Metternich (MEHT-ehr-nihk) was born, not within the vast hegemonous region that made up the Austro-Hungarian Empire, but in the small German state of Trier, ruled by prince-bishops, one of whom, during the early seventeenth century, had been a Metternich. His father, Count Franz Georg Karl von Metternich, had represented the elector of Trier at the Imperial Court of Vienna, and, at the time of his son's birth, had reversed that role and was representing the Austrian emperor in his homeland. As a result, young Clemens was reared in the Rhineland, and he remained fond of this region all of his life. His mother, Countess Beatrix Kagenegg, was a woman of considerable culture, intelligence, and charm, whose sophistication and elegance were more French than Germanic. These qualities she passed on to her son, who was always more at home with the language and Old World manners of the country of his greatest adversary, Napoleon I, then he was with his own.

In 1788, at the age of fifteen, he was sent to study diplomacy at the University of Strasbourg. There, he studied under a celebrated professor, Christoph Wilhelm Koch, who was an ardent proponent of creating a conservative counterbalance that would oppose the growing nationalist sentiment in Europe. The following year saw the outbreak of the French Revolution, which spread to Strasbourg in 1790. Abhorring the destructive violence of the Revolution, Metternich left Strasbourg for Mainz, where he enrolled in the university. He abandoned that city before the arrival of the French revolutionary troops to join his father in Brussels, where the count was prime minister of the Austrian Netherlands. From there, young Metternich was sent on a minor diplomatic mission to England in 1794, the first of his career. Upon his return later that year, he rejoined his family in Vienna, where they had fled after the ever-growing fury of the French Revolution had deprived them of their position in Brussels and their home in Coblenz.

In September, 1795, Metternich married Eleonore von Kaunitz, but it was not a love match. While a student at Mainz, Metternich had been initiated into the erotic privileges of a young nobleman, and he was to show a lifelong predilection for the company of a great variety of attractive women that his steadily increasing political status made available to him, even using some of these amorous liaisons to great diplomatic advantage. His was not merely a marriage of convenience but of opportunity as well, for his bride was the granddaughter of the powerful Wenzel von Kaunitz, state chancellor to the late Empress Maria Theresa. By marrying into this family of tremendous political and social prestige, Metternich at last had entrée into the exclusive imperial inner circle of influence from which he could make his bid for high office.

LIFE'S WORK

During his first ten years of service as an ambassador for the Austrian emperor, Metternich witnessed the final dissolution of the ancient Holy Roman Empire, whose (by this time) symbolic and powerless crown had traditionally rested on the head of the reigning Habsburg monarch in Vienna. After serving as Austrian minister to the Saxon court in Dresden and the Prussian court in Berlin, where his anti-French efforts were thwarted, Emperor Francis I placed his young ambassador in the front ranks of the battle, and in 1806 Metternich presented his credentials to France's newly self-declared emperor, Napoleon, at Saint Cloud.

In Paris, he became well informed as to the internal workings of the French Empire through his many important connections and his vast network of spies, which became legendary. For all of these advantages, his initial diplomatic efforts with the brilliant French tyrant proved to be a costly failure to his own country. Overestimating the effect of the 1808 Iberian uprising against the Bonapartes, he precipitated Austria into a war against France that ended disastrously for the Austrians in the Battle of Wagram (1809). Recalled to Vienna by the emperor, Metternich was appointed minister of foreign affairs, in which capacity he bought time for an exhausted Austria by giving Napoleon one of Francis's daughters as a bride. The match with the Archduchess Marie Louise (ironically a grandniece of Louis XVI's tragic queen, Marie Antoinette) was a calculated psychological maneuver to flatter Napoleon, whose character Metternich had closely studied during his tenure in Paris. Austria could now remain independent from the seemingly invincible French Empire, preserving the autonomy it needed to recoup its losses.

While Napoleon turned his attention and his Grande Armée from Austria to Russia, Austria quietly rearmed and Metternich tried to preserve the shaky balance of power in Europe, striving to keep the momentary status quo he had bought at so high a price. Austria now needed France to remain strong. Fearing the creation of a Prussian empire after French assault had awakened a dormant sense of German nationalism, and mindful of the threat of a Russian invasion of Europe if France collapsed, Metternich needed to counterbalance these threats with French power until Austria was again fit to face its dangerous adversary.

Metternich. (Library of Congress)

Metternich found his moment with France's catastrophic and surprising defeat in Russia in 1812. Confident of Austria's rejuvenation, he concluded a treaty with Russia and Prussia in June, 1813. Metternich negotiated with France for a separate peace treaty, but Napoleon hesitated, and in August of that year Austria declared war on France. During the following October, Francis bestowed on his most illustrious subject the hereditary title of prince. Holding close the South German states as allies to block any Russo-Prussian aggrandizement during this final conflict with France, Metternich arrived in Paris in May, 1814, after Napoleon's defeat at Waterloo and subsequent abdication, with the upper hand to sign the Treaty of Paris and open the way to the Congress of Vienna (September, 1814, to June, 1815).

Employing his own great charm and worldliness along with the music for which Vienna is legendary,

Metternich attracted Europe's most powerful and glamorous figures to the Austrian capital for the "Congress that Danced," giving that city for the first and only time in its history the distinction of being the center of European politics. It was a splendid social occasion with an unending round of balls and festivities. It was also the most important political congress in a generation, and Europe's future hinged on the negotiations that took place there during those nine months.

Conservative by temperament, upbringing, and education, Metternich was further persuaded by the horror of two decades of pan-European war to restore the Continent to its pre-Napoleonic form. Additionally, he sought to replace the Habsburgs' traditional but meaningless role as the preeminent monarchs of Europe by establishing for them a real leadership over loose confederations of German and Italian states. To this end he proposed the creation of an imperial German title to be borne by the Austrian emperor. Furthermore, he wanted to restore France to its pre-Revolutionary War status with the old royal house of Bourbon, giving it equal footing with its conquerors to counter the threat of Russian dominance.

Metternich failed in Germany and in Italy, primarily through the archconservatism of his own emperor. Francis embraced the idea of power in Italy, where Austria was initially welcomed with enthusiasm, but he mishandled it and only succeeded in agitating the feeling of national unity that his foreign minister had thereby tried to avoid; he refused the title of German emperor, leaving Austrian influence in the German states on an equal footing with Prussia. With France, Metternich was successful. France's Talleyrand and England's Castlereagh concluded an alliance with Metternich to keep in check the Russo-Prussian pact that had taken place.

That was the essential balance of power when the Congress broke up, and it established a European order that lasted well into the middle of the century. During most of that time Metternich was custodian of that order, making him the virtual prime minister of Europe. With patience, insight, and an uncanny ability to see through the heated rhetoric and quickly shifting currents of the time, Metternich triumphed over the more imposing figures of his generation, yet he was unable to defeat the new ideas that they had helped unleash. With England withdrawn from continental politics, republican restlessness in France, and nationalistic fervor in the German and Italian states, Metternich, by now Austrian state chancellor, could not prevent in 1848 the eruption of revolutions that swept through the great European capitals. Hated by now as a reactionary and the leading figure of repressive government, Metternich was forced to resign on March 13, 1848. He went into exile in England for three years but returned to Vienna, where he died in 1859 in his eighty-sixth year.

SIGNIFICANCE

A cursory investigation of Metternich's many and varied achievements could give the impression that the subject was a genius. This, however, would do him an injustice because, though he may have possessed a kind of genius, the genius of his day was Napoleon and Metternich was his enemy. Although Metternich and his ilk eventually triumphed over Napoleon, it was the more prosaic qualities of patience, industry, and levelheadedness that won for him the war after losing most of the battles.

Metternich was not a visionary, but a practical man. Imagination, great style, and charm he did possess; in-deed, he often depended on these qualities. Beyond this, however, Metternich was built to last long after the dust had settled and there was work still to be done. He saw his age through to its end and beyond, living long enough to see himself vilified by the very generation whose future he had striven to preserve. The conservatism he reimposed on Europe lasted nearly forty years until it was swept away forever by men such as Napoleon III, Giuseppe Garibaldi, and Otto von Bismarck, who were, if not his political heirs, certainly his successors. Seen from a modern, liberal perspective, it is easy to label those four decades as reactionary and oppressive. They were also four decades of a desperately needed peace, perhaps the longest such period that Europe has ever known.

—Pavlin Lange

FURTHER READING

Bertier de Sauvigny, G. de. *Metternich and His Times.* Translated by Peter Ryde. London: Darton, Longman & Todd, 1962. Written one hundred years after its subject's death, this biography is a good introduction to Metternich and his world. Most of this work is devoted to the comments of Metternich and his contemporaries, while the author serves as a guide to the Austrian minister's life.

Cecil, Algernon. *Metternich, 1773-1859: A Study of His Period and Personality.* London: Eyre & Spottiswoode, 1933. A thorough and engaging biography of Metternich and his times. The great statesman's life is recounted with an imagination that counterbalances its frequently difficult scholarly approach. Inaccessible to the lay reader, this book of moderate length is a penetrating account of Metternich's professional life.

Haas, Arthur G. *Metternich, Reorganization, and Nationality, 1813-1815: A Story of Foresight and Frustration in the Rebuilding of the Austrian Empire.* Wiesbaden, Germany: Franz Steiner Verlag, 1963. For those interested in a detailed, documented, blow-by-blow account of the crucial negotiations and renegotiations that followed the resettlement of Europe after Napoleon's fall, this book is thorough and easy to understand.

Kissinger, Henry A. *A World Restored: Metternich, Castlereagh, and the Problems of Peace, 1812-22.* Boston: Houghton Mifflin, 1957. A biography of a celebrated nineteenth century statesman by a celebrated twentieth century statesman before the latter was well known. This is a good, if somewhat dry, introduction to Europe after Napoleon.

Metternich, Prince Clemens von. *Memoirs of Prince Metternich, 1773-1835.* 5 vols. Edited by Prince Richard Metternich. Translated by Mrs. Alexander Napier and Gerard W. Smith. New York: Charles Scribner's Sons, 1880-1884. Completed in 1844 by Metternich himself and brought to publication twenty years after his death by his son, Prince Richard, here is an account of his life from his birth to the Congress of Vienna. Recounted with the clarity and arrogance for which he was well known. Contains important documents and correspondence.

Schroeder, Paul W. *Metternich's Diplomacy at Its Zenith, 1820-1823.* Austin: University of Texas Press, 1962. An account of Metternich's years of diplomatic supremacy following the Congress of Vienna. Using maps to help illustrate this history, Schroeder describes the first years of Metternich's chancellory when his plan for Europe was most successful.

Seward, Desmond. *Metternich: The First European.* New York: Viking Press, 1991. Seward portrays Metternich as the consummate statesman of his time, and describes how he sought to sustain a framework for Eu-

ropean nations to live in relative harmony. The author argues that Metternich's concepts of unity anticipated the more recent creation of the European community.

SEE ALSO: Friedrich von Beust; Otto von Bismarck; Viscount Castlereagh; Francis Joseph I; Giuseppe Garibaldi; Karl von Hardenberg; Napoleon I; Napoleon III; The Rothschild Family; Carl Schurz; Talleyrand.

RELATED ARTICLES in *Great Events from History: The Nineteenth Century, 1801-1900:* April 11, 1814-July 29, 1830: France's Bourbon Dynasty Is Restored; September 15, 1814-June 11, 1815: Congress of Vienna; June 8-9, 1815: Organization of the German Confederation; November 20, 1815: Second Peace of Paris; July 2, 1820-March, 1821: Neapolitan Revolution; October 20-30, 1822: Great Britain Withdraws from the Concert of Europe; December 2, 1823: President Monroe Articulates the Monroe Doctrine; 1824: Ranke Develops Systematic History; January 12, 1848-August 28, 1849: Italian Revolution of 1848; September 12, 1848: Swiss Confederation Is Formed.

JULES MICHELET
French historian

France's greatest national historian, Michelet was one of the guiding forces of modern historical writing. His contributions included coining the concept of the "Renaissance" and calling attention to the role of geography in human history.

BORN: August 21, 1789; Paris, France
DIED: February 9, 1874; Hyères, France
AREAS OF ACHIEVEMENT: Historiography, philosophy

EARLY LIFE

Jules Michelet (meesh-leh) was the only child of a poor Parisian printer. His early life was one of material privation but deep familial love. Forced to work in his father's establishment from an early age, the youth lived a solitary life and experienced few of the common joys of childhood. His only pleasure came from his long walks after hours in the famous cemetery, Père Lachaise, and his occasional visits to Lenoir's Museum. It was from the latter that he first experienced a vivid realization of history and a fascination with the past.

Michelet's antagonism toward the Church and toward monarchy, which would loom so large in his later writings, stemmed, in part, from his youth. The family of the future historian, already in dire poverty, was reduced to absolute destitution during the Reign of Terror as Robespierre's henchmen combed the streets of Paris, jailing and executing men whose manuscripts his father had published. Fearing for his life, the elder Michelet first curtailed his printing projects and was finally forced to terminate his business by the government. Unemployment led to debts for which his father was arrested in 1808 and incarcerated for nearly a year. The collapse of his father's occupation and his ensuing imprisonment engendered in Jules a hatred of Napoleon I, clerics, and the empire that endured to his death. In his last work, *Histoire du XIXe siècle* (1872-1875; history of the nineteenth century), he continued to spew forth the vitriolic opinions inculcated during his childhood.

Although financial problems led to marital strife, both parents agreed on one thing; Jules should be formally educated whatever the cost. After being tutored in Latin by a family friend, Michelet entered Lycée Charlemagne in 1812, which proved to be socially disastrous. His life of solitude had not prepared him for the competitive academic world, and the small, sensitive, shy lad became the object of endless verbal and physical abuse. The owl in daylight, as one source described him, endured the abuse and, capitalizing on his native intelligence, innate writing skills, and untiring work habits, became the top student in his class.

Michelet's brilliant academic career won for him a teaching position at the Collège Sainte-Barbe in 1822. In 1827, he published a translation of Giambattista Vico's *Principi di scienza nuova d'intorno alla comune natura delle nazione* (1744; *The New Science*, 1948) that brought him both public acclaim and an appointment to teach history and philosophy at the École Normale Supérieure, a position he held until 1838, when he accepted a chair at the Collège de France. In addition to his academic positions, he served as head of the history section of the National Archives from 1830 to 1852.

LIFE'S WORK

The philosophical foundation for Michelet's seventeen-volume *Histoire de France* (1833-1867; partial translation as *The History of France*, 1844-1846) and the seven-volume *Histoire de la révolution française* (1847-1853; *History of the French Revolution*, 1972), his life's work, slowly evolved in 1827 as he came under the influence of German Romanticism. Vico, the little-known Neapolitan philosopher, taught Michelet that all history was universal, constantly in motion, and that humanity was the common element unifying all ages. Men die, but humanity, the receptacle for human wisdom, lives on.

A still-embryonic scholar, Michelet first expressed his historical philosophy in *Introduction à l'histoire universelle* (1831; introduction to universal history), maintaining that history was nothing more than the story of liberty: humankind's ongoing struggle to free itself from nature and fatality. As history was constantly in motion, he likened it to the movement of the sun. It rose in the east, in India, moved westward to Persia, Greece, Rome, and culminated in France. In his typically unabashed, chauvinistic manner, Michelet explained that France was superior to the rest of Europe in culture and civilization and, being such, was the new apostle of liberty. Along this line of reasoning, France became synonymous with humanity, and France alone would control the destiny of humankind. Thus, in Vico, Michelet found both a philosophy of history and a mission. His life's

work would be to show how the French people fostered and nourished the spirit of liberty.

The History of France filled seventeen volumes, took thirty-four years to write, and was a labor of love. Of the seventeen volumes, only the first six merit serious consideration. These six, written between 1833 and 1844, are based on primary sources, contain no obvious bias, and reflect a unique historical method. Michelet's objective was to treat the "whole of the parts"—the land, its people, events, institutions, and beliefs—but it was the people who were the important element. The remaining eleven volumes (written between 1854 and 1867), covering the end of the Middle Ages to the Revolution, are inferior, as Michelet was forced to write them without full benefit of manuscripts and documentation. Michelet, having been relieved of his professorship and archival position for refusing to swear an oath of allegiance to Napoleon III, voices in volumes seven through thirteen his hostility toward the monarchy and toward Christianity.

In the interval that divided his work on *The History of France*, Michelet turned his attention to the French Revolution. Using the turmoil of 1789 as a backdrop, he painted a gloomy picture of the state of affairs in France; he maintained that the Church, supported by the monarchy, was threatening education, which had been an essential reform of the Revolution. In both *History of the French Revolution* and *Le Peuple* (1846; *The People*, 1846), he maintained that France was once again suffering under the tyranny of Christian monarchy and it was time for the people to sally forth and rekindle the light for justice and liberty. In *History of the French Revolution*, the voice is that of a revolutionary as Michelet becomes one of the common people who won the triumph for law and justice in 1789. His objective was to stir the masses. So effective was his effort that he has been credited with being instrumental in instigating the revolutions of 1848, which, in addition to his refusal to swear allegiance to Napoleon, cost him his academic post at the Collège de France as well as his archival position.

Deprived of rank and income, Michelet was forced to move to the countryside with only the company of his young wife, Athenais, to comfort him. As his own suffering paralleled his father's at the hands of the government, it is not surprising that when he resumed work on *The History of France* an obvious bias against the government ran through the remaining volumes. In January, 1874, the great historian fell ill, and a month later, on February 9, 1874, he died of a heart attack. Although initially interred at Hyères, France, in May, 1875, his body was later exhumed, and, before thousands of public offi-cials, students, and friends, he was buried a second time at Père Lachaise, where he had spent his happiest mo-ments as a child.

SIGNIFICANCE

Jules Michelet was a product of the Romantic move-ment, the world of color, passion, and poetry, but his love for France became excessive. So intense were his emo-tions that he could not see life as it was. As his patriotism turned into idolatry and as he deified the French people and the Revolution, it became impossible for him to ex-plain the terror of the age. Although his work must be ad-mired for its novelty and beauty, it must also be scorned for its mysticism.

Despite Michelet's flaws, his labors were not without merit. He was the first to use the term "Renaissance" to refer to a specific period in history. He was the first to in-sist that geography was a determining factor in shaping a state. He was the first to make widespread use of artifacts in interpreting the past. He was the first to assign a major role to common persons as the molder of their own desti-nies. If his excessive love for France distorted his analy-sis, his historical method was destined to play a major role in inspiring future historians to view the past in its totality.

—*Wayne M. Bledsoe*

FURTHER READING

Geyl, Pieter. *Debates with Historians.* Rev. ed. Cleve-land: World, 1958. Provides good balance to Gooch's work (see below), as Geyl is critical of Michelet. Although attention is given to both *The History of France* and *History of the French Revolution*, the lat-ter is emphasized. The major criticism is Michelet's attempt to use emotionalism and sentimentality to make wrong appear right.

Gooch, G. P. *History and Historians in the Nineteenth Century.* 2d ed. New York: Barnes & Noble Books, 1952. The best work on nineteenth century historiog-raphy in English. Gives one of the more favorable views of Michelet. Gooch notes the historian's bias toward the monarchy, his anticlerical position, and his excessive adoration of France.

Kippur, Stephen A. *Jules Michelet: A Study of Mind and Sensibility.* Albany: State University of New York Press, 1980. This biography considers Michelet's childhood, social status, and intellectual development as they contributed to his work as a historian and pro-fessor. Kippur examines Michelet's ideas on France, religion, and "the people." Gives a good analysis of Michelet's major works and is a balanced account.

Mitzman, Arthur. *Michelet, Historian: Rebirth and Romanticism in Nineteenth Century France.* New Haven, Conn.: Yale University Press, 1990. Places Michelet's work within the context of nineteenth cen-tury Romanticism.

Orr, Linda. *Jules Michelet: Nature, History, and Lan-guage.* Ithaca, N.Y.: Cornell University Press, 1976. Orr provides excellent coverage of Michelet's non-historical writings. Gives particular attention to his writings on natural science. Traces Michelet's search for patterns of coherence in nature, which influenced his historical works. Draws upon Michelet's journal to provide fascinating insight into the personal as-pects of his private life.

Rigney, Ann. *Imperfect Histories: The Elusive Past and the Legacy of Romantic Historicism.* Ithaca, N.Y.: Cornell University Press, 2001. Rigney analyzes the work of Michelet and other historians of the late eigh-teenth and early nineteenth centuries to describe how they strove to provide an alternative account of every-day experience.

Thompson, J. W. *A History of Historical Writing.* Vol. 2. Magnolia, Mass.: Peter Smith, 1967. This good source gives a chronological account of the major aspects of Michelet's life. Particularly good on the problems leading to Michelet's anticlerical stance in his history of the Revolution. Advocates dividing Michelet's works into two categories for analysis.

SEE ALSO: Lord Acton; Jacob Burckhardt; Aleksandr Herzen; Napoleon I; Napoleon III; Leopold von Ranke.

RELATED ARTICLES in *Great Events from History: The Nineteenth Century, 1801-1900:* 1824: Ranke De-velops Systematic History; 1843: Carlyle Publishes *Past and Present.*

ALBERT A. MICHELSON
German-born American physicist

Michelson was the first American to win a Nobel Prize in Physics, which he received for determining the length of the standard meter in terms of wavelengths of light. His significant contributions to physics and optics include measurement of the velocity of light, of the ether drift, of the rigidity of the earth, and of the diameter of stars, as well as development of the interferometer.

BORN: December 19, 1852; Strelno, Prussia (now Strzelno, Poland)
DIED: May 9, 1931; Pasadena, California
ALSO KNOWN AS: Albert Abraham Michelson (full name)
AREA OF ACHIEVEMENT: Physics

EARLY LIFE

Strelno (modern Strzelno), the town in which Albert Abraham Michelson was born, was predominantly Polish in population and tradition but was located in German territory at time of Michelson's birth. Michelson's mother, Rosalie Przlubska, was the daughter of a businessperson, and the effect of her early teachings made Albert resist the lure of easy money all of his life. At the time of Albert's birth, his father, Samuel Michelson, was the proprietor of a dry-goods shop. Political upheavals in Europe in 1848 accelerated anti-Semitism there, and late in 1855, the Michelsons decided to emigrate to California. They traveled by steamer to Panama; made the laborious trip across the Isthmus by muleback, canoe, and train; and boarded another boat to San Francisco, where Samuel's sister and brother-in-law, Belle and Oscar Meyer, were living.

After arriving in Northern California, the Michelsons settled in Murphys, a mining town in the heart of the gold country, where Samuel opened a store. Young Albert took violin lessons from a local prospector who was a fine musician. Albert's parents realized that their son was bright and decided that he needed a better education than was available in the mining town. They boarded him with his cousins in San Francisco to finish the last two years of grammar school, and he matriculated to San Francisco Boys High School. The principal, Theodore Bradley, recognized the boy's exceptional mechanical abilities and took him into his own home.

While Michelson was in high school, his father moved the family to Virginia City, Nevada, and opened a business there. After graduation at the age of sixteen,

Michelson went to Nevada's famous mining town and took the competitive examination for the U.S. Naval Academy at Annapolis at the Storey County Court House. He lost the appointment to the son of a man who had been injured in the Civil War. Undaunted, the young man solicited letters of recommendation and made the long train trip alone across the country, determined to petition the president for an appointment.

After arriving in Washington, Michelson learned that President Ulysses S. Grant walked his dogs at a regular hour. He then waited on the White House steps and approached the president with his petition. The president advised him that the appointments-at-large had been filled, but Michelson implored the president to consider another appointment. Impressed with the young man who would not take no for an answer, the president suggested that Albert visit Annapolis. Three days later, President Grant named him the eleventh appointee-at-large. This characteristic of attempting the impossible became a pattern in Michelson's life.

When Michelson entered Annapolis in June, 1869, he made a striking figure clad in his naval uniform with his chiseled features, jet-black hair, and deep-set hazel eyes. He appeared taller than his five feet seven or eight inches because of an elegant and dignified bearing. While at the academy, he excelled in optics, acoustics, and drawing but always had time for fencing, boxing, music, and painting. His spirited independence and youthful exuberance were not evident in gunnery class, and a superior officer scolded that he might eventually be of some use to his country if he paid more attention to his gunnery than to science. No one knew at that time that this ensign would become one of the greatest American scientists.

Upon graduation, Michelson served for two years at sea and then returned to the academy as an instructor in the department of physics and chemistry headed by Admiral William T. Sampson. He met the admiral's niece, Margaret Heminway, and they married in 1877 and had two sons and a daughter.

LIFE'S WORK

The speed of light had interested scientists for centuries, including Galileo Galilei, Armand-Hippolyte-Louis Fizeau, and Jean-Bernard-Léon Foucault. This was to become the all-consuming question of Michelson's life. Eager to use demonstrations in his physics class, he gathered crude pieces of apparatus lying about the laboratory, spent ten dollars of his own money, and modified Foucault's earlier experiment. The young ensign was able to make a more accurate measurement of the speed of light than had ever before been achieved. The superintendent of the United States Navy's nautical almanac office, Simon Newcomb, appointed Michelson to a position in a government-sponsored project to determine the velocity of light. Michelson quickly surpassed his peers and even his seniors, as he had an uncanny ability to devise experimentation techniques.

In 1880, Michelson secured a leave of absence from the Navy and spent two years in Europe studying under Hermann von Helmholtz at the University of Berlin, Georg Hermann Quincke at Heidelberg University, and Marie Alfred Cornu at the Collège de France and the École Polytechnique in Paris. Scientists of the nineteenth century believed that light was propagated through a luminiferous ether that filled all space around the earth. The inquisitive Michelson wondered whether the existence of this luminiferous ether could be proved or disproved. This was a big idea, but big ideas appealed to him. He began studying light interference patterns and reasoned that an instrument was needed for measuring distances that would be far beyond the range of the most powerful microscope invented. In 1881, he developed this delicate instrument, which became known as the Michelson interferometer, and performed his first ether-drift experiment in Europe. He calculated a negative result on the motion of the ether relative to the earth, but scientists at that time hesitated to accept this challenge to their belief.

Michelson decided to devote his life to science, reasoning that staying in the Navy would thwart this career. He resigned to become professor of physics at Case School of Applied Science in Cleveland, Ohio. He was appointed corresponding member of the British Association for the Advancement of Science in 1884, named associate fellow of the American Academy of Arts and Sciences in 1885, and received his first honorary doctoral degree from Western Reserve University the following year.

In 1885, Michelson met Professor Edward Williams Morley, a well-estab-

lished chemist. Michelson must have learned much from this versatile scientist, and Morley's influence on Michelson's work has not been adequately acknowledged. They collaborated on light experiments, and Michelson worked day and night, neglecting food and rest. He reached the point of nervous exhaustion and had to take time away from the experiments. When he returned, Michelson and Morley submitted a joint paper to the *American Journal of Science* reporting negative results from the ether-drift experiment. In 1887, they conducted an experiment to see if light traveled in the same velocity in any direction and discovered no observable difference.

Scientists of the nineteenth century had reasoned that because the earth moves around the sun at approximately eighteen miles per second, the speed of a light beam traveling with the earth's orbital motion should be greater than that of a beam traveling in the opposite direction. The negative result of the Michelson-Morley experiment provided the raw material that stimulated the theory of relativity. It proved that there were not different velocities of light. This discovery was catastrophic to the mechanical theory of science, which had received support

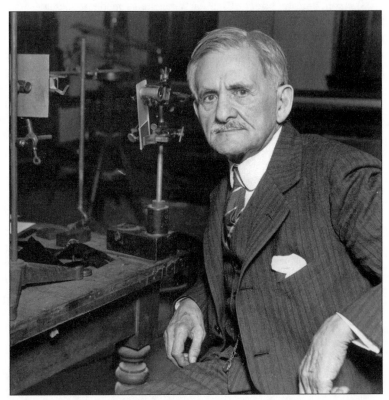

Albert A. Michelson. (Library of Congress)

since the time of Sir Isaac Newton. The two scientists worked together until 1889.

Michelson left Case Institute to teach at Clark University between 1889 and 1892. His first sojourn into astronomy began at this time when he took his equipment to Lick Observatory in California and actually measured Jupiter's satellites. In 1892, he moved to the University of Chicago and assumed the position as head of the department of physics but continued working on experiments in astronomy, spectroscopy, geophysics, and optics. He also lectured to graduate students.

By the end of the nineteenth century, Michelson was considered to be one of the twelve greatest scientists in the world, yet he remained modest. When he was teaching, he gave credit to all the scientists for their contributions, but the students noticed that when he started describing current experiments and results that were clearly more significant than the preceding ones, he neglected to cite the author. The puzzled students questioned another instructor about this strange behavior. The instructor laughingly resolved the problem. The mysterious experiments had been those of Albert Abraham Michelson, and the renowned scientist had not wanted to call undue attention to his own work.

Michelson was more interested in his scientific work than in a social life, and his first marriage ended in divorce in 1897. Some sources present an austere, forbidding, overwrought picture of him at that time, but in December, 1899, he married Edna Stanton, a former student, and life with his second wife and their three daughters seemed to be happier.

Michelson continued to be productive during this period of time and developed an echelon spectroscope with high enough resolution to indicate optical evidence of molecular motion associated with temperature. By 1905, he had completed a ruling engine that had 110,000 lines on a six-inch square of glass, which he referred to as the "she-devil." This instrument was later used by astronomers to discover the innermost secrets of the atom.

In 1907, Michelson received the Nobel Prize in Physics for establishing the length of the meter in terms of cadmium light. A few years earlier, the International Conference on Weights and Measures had made the metric system the scientific standard and deposited a platinum-iridium bar in a well-guarded vault at Severes. The Franco-Prussian War brought to the forefront the idea that the bar, which established the length of the meter, would be lost. Scientists suggested that measurement of a length of light wave would be more permanent.

Michelson attempted this experiment, as he was able to measure the wavelengths of various gases with his versatile interferometer. After experimenting with sodium and mercury, he settled for the bright red line of cadmium light. He announced that 1,553,163.5 wavelengths of the red line of the metal cadmium were equal to the length of the platinum-iridium standard. The Nobel Prize was awarded to him for accomplishment in precision measurements.

Michelson was also interested in zoology. He related the phenomenon of the iridescent colors of hummingbirds, butterflies, and beetles to interference and reflection of light. In his book *Studies in Optics* (1927), he noted that the diamond beetle had diffraction grating ruled on its wings as fine as two thousand to the inch. Meanwhile, Michelson remained active in naval affairs throughout his life. He commanded the Illinois Naval Militia for years. During World War I, he served as a lieutenant commander in the Navy and patented five optical range-finders for naval vessels.

Ever reaching for new planes, Michelson used his interferometer to indicate the substance of the earth's interior, and, in 1920, he was the first to measure the angular diameter of a distant star. The Royal Astronomical Society of England recognized this achievement by presenting its gold medal to him, but this was only one of numerous medals and prizes from scientific societies that he was awarded. Michelson received six honorary doctoral degrees during his lifetime. Although he disliked publicity, he did realize the value of promotion in obtaining money for his projects, and was always gracious in his dealings with people.

In his later years, Michelson still held himself erect, maintaining the quiet demeanor of his youth. His hair was white, and he wore a close-cropped gray mustache. He enjoyed tennis, bridge, chess, and billiards. He would discuss these subjects socially, but he preferred to keep his science and art, which were so dear to his heart, in the laboratory and the studio.

Michelson always believed that his greatest experimental work was still ahead of him. He considered it great fun to do the arduous work involved in setting up experiments and overseeing the technical difficulties. When he was in his seventies, he once again determined to measure the velocity of light. He worked with George Ellery Hale at Mount Wilson Observatory on five sets of light measurements between 1924 and 1927. He was dissatisfied with these tests because of the obstruction of valley haze and smoke and constructed an experiment in a vacuum tube where light could travel in empty space. He was directing this work when he became ill, but the dedicated man, then in his late seventies, carried on the work from his sickbed. He dictated the introduction of a scientific paper to astronomer Francis Pease, and when the report was published posthumously, the title was "On a Method of Measuring the Velocity of Light," the same title of his first paper when he was an ensign in the Navy. He died on May 9, 1931, of a cerebral hemorrhage.

SIGNIFICANCE

Albert Abraham Michelson obtained world attention for American science at a time when European scientists were inclined to characterize Americans as lacking in scientific capabilities. It is evident that his contributions helped forward the theory of relativity, though it would be an overstatement that Albert Einstein's theory was a generalization of the Michelson-Morley experiment or that the theory of relativity could not have been arrived at without this experiment. Michelson has often been called "the man who measured the stars," but he was more than this. His major contributions include precision optical measurements of the velocity of light, of the ether drift, of the length of the standard meter, of the angular diameters of stars, and of the rigidity of the earth; developmental experimentation in the young field of spectroscopy; and invention of the harmonic analyzer, in addition to the Michelson interferometer. His efforts extended to the precision of measurement represent an extraordinary contribution to scientific knowledge.

Michelson always had the greatest respect for the Navy, where he received his start. The Navy did not forget him and, in 1948, honored his memory with the construction of a laboratory for basic and applied research at the U.S. Naval Ordnance Test Station at China Lake in California's Mojave Desert. In 1969, Michelson Hall, housing the science department, was dedicated at Annapolis in honor of its graduate of the class of 1873. The building stands over the area of the old seawall where Michelson made his earliest measurements of the speed of light. His papers, accumulated over a period of thirty years by Ted McAllister, curator of Michelson Museum at the Naval Weapons Center at China Lake, have been transferred to this facility.

Few Americans are chosen for the Hall of Fame. Michelson was selected to receive this honor; the tribute ceremony and unveiling of the bust took place on October 21, 1973, at the Hall of Fame for Great Americans at New York University. His own words were chosen as the inscription on the bronze tablet that accompanies the sculpture:

> It seems to me that scientific research should be regarded as the painter regards his art, as the poet his poems, and the composer his music.

Michelson was a splendid scientist, a fine naval officer, a talented artist, and an honored educator. He will be long remembered for his significant contributions to physics and optics.

—Evelyne L. Pickett

FURTHER READING

Ball, Philip. "Quantum Gravity: Back to the Future." *Nature* 472, no. 6974 (February 5, 2004): 492. Describes how Michelson and Morley's experiments with light waves influenced Einstein's theory of relativity.

Bennett, Jean M., D. Theodore McAllister, and Georgia M. Cabe. "Albert A. Michelson, Dean of American Optics: Life, Contributions to Science, and Influence on Modern Day Physics." *Journal of Applied Optics* 12 (October, 1973): 2253. Excellent article that not only summarizes Michelson's life but also details his scientific experiments in a readable fashion. Compiled by the curator of the Michelson Museum, who spent thirty years compiling the Michelson papers. One of the most concise sources available. Well documented. Thorough bibliography.

Holton, Gerald. *Thematic Origins of Scientific Thought.* Cambridge, Mass.: Harvard University Press, 1973. Systematically attacks any relationship between Einstein, Michelson, and the "crucial" experiment. Persuasive that the Michelson-Morley experiment had no effect on Einstein's theory of relativity.

Jaffe, Bernard. *Men of Science in America.* New York: Arno Press, 1980. Jaffe has done a considerable service for students of the history of science in this assortment of materials dealing with scientists in the United States. Sound and scholarly, the book presents Michelson's participation as a catalyst in the revolution of modern physics.

_____. *Michelson and the Speed of Light.* Garden City, N.Y.: Doubleday, 1960. A well-balanced biography of Michelson. Includes descriptions of his experiments. Designed for popular reading but contains relatively few errors. Excellent bibliography. Thematic approach correlated chronologically.

Livingston, Dorothy Michelson. *The Master of Light: A Biography of Albert A. Michelson.* New York:

Charles Scribner's Sons, 1973. An admirable book that falls short of being a scientific biography as it lacks the critical analysis of scientific and technical matters essential in such a work. Written by Michelson's daughter, it gives a picture of the man rather than the scientist.

Ronan, Colin A. *Science: Its History and Development Among the World Cultures*. New York: Hamlyn, 1982. Mentions Michelson in passing but provides a detailed account of the events, in chronological order, in the fields of science during Michelson's life. Relates to the Michelson-Morley experiment.

Swenson, Loyd S., Jr. *Genesis of Relativity: Einstein in Context*. New York: Burt Franklin, 1979. Good detail of the Michelson-Morley experiment and its contribution to the theory of relativity. Readable and within reach of the average student. A valuable study.

Tyson, Neil deGrasse. "Speed Limit." *Natural History* 114, no. 1 (February, 2005): 18. Discusses the various studies that determined the speed of light, including the experiments of Michelson and Morley.

SEE ALSO: The Becquerel Family; Josiah Willard Gibbs; Ulysses S. Grant; Hermann von Helmholtz; Simon Newcomb; Alfred Nobel; Wilhelm Conrad Röntgen.

RELATED ARTICLES in *Great Events from History: The Nineteenth Century, 1801-1900:* November 9, 1895: Röntgen Discovers X Rays; December 14, 1900: Articulation of Quantum Theory.

JAMES MILL
English philosopher

A utilitarian propagandist and theorist, Mill shattered neat boundaries of modern special scholarship with his intellectual and practical interests. He believed in the perfectibility of humankind and regarded morality as more important than religion.

BORN: April 6, 1773; Northwater Bridge, Logie Pert, Forfarshire, Scotland
DIED: June 23, 1836; London, England
AREAS OF ACHIEVEMENT: Historiography, philosophy, economics

EARLY LIFE

James Mill was the son of a poor Scottish shoemaker of the same name. His mother, Isabel Fenton, was the daughter of a formerly wealthy farmer. Both parents were stern Puritans, but James's mother was ambitious and tried to bring up her son to be a gentleman and a minister. He was educated at Montrose Academy, after which he met Sir James and Lady Jane Stuart, who made it possible for him to attend Edinburgh University. Mill entered there in 1790 and stayed for seven years, living with the Stuarts and tutoring their only child, Wilhelmina.

At Edinburgh, Mill became interested in Greek thought, particularly Plato and the Socratic method he would later use on his own son John. Dugald Steward, a professor of moral philosophy, gave James a taste for studies and a moral consciousness that were to stay with him for life. Here he also met Henry Peter Brougham and Francis Jeffrey—later literary associates—and Thomas Thomson, a fine scientist who became Mill's lifelong friend.

Mill was licensed to preach in 1798, but his sermons were unsuccessful and he received no parish call. In 1802, he accompanied Sir John Stuart to London and the Parliament, where he observed the House of Commons and developed his interest in politics. Probably because of later opposition to religion and the aristocracy, Mill chose to forget his early days, and even though he later became an advocate of the free press, he maintained one's young life was not for public knowledge.

During the early nineteenth century, Mill began to write for journals, the *Anti-Jacobin Review*, the *Literary Journal*, which he helped establish with his Scottish friends, and the *St. James Chronicle*. In this new setting, he wrote two essays that signaled his future thought, one on the corn trade (1804), in which he defended landholders who profited from the export of grain, and the other a translation of Charles François Dominique de Villers's *Essai sur l'esprit et l'influence de la reformation de Luther* (1804; *Essay on the Spirit and Influence of the Reformation*, 1805) wherein, with the help of Thomson, he championed the progress of the human mind following an age of religious faith.

In 1805, Mill married Harriet Burrow and settled in Pentonville. Contrary to the thinking of Thomas Malthus, whom Mill would eventually support, he fathered nine children, educating the oldest, John Stuart, in his own philosophy to eventually became the spokesman of utilitarianism. After his literary jobs failed, Mill struggled to survive economically, adding to his own debts those of his bankrupt father. Hoping to free himself financially, Mill began work on his *History of British India*, but that was to take twelve years until it was published in 1817. In the meantime, in 1808, he met Jeremy Bentham, a man who was to determine the tone and character of the rest of his life.

LIFE'S WORK

Almost immediately, Mill became the devoted disciple of Bentham, whose philosophy of utilitarianism—promoting the greatest good for the greatest number—needed practical application. Bentham wanted Mill close at hand, so he provided housing at Queen's Square and supported him financially. Unlike the fanciful Bentham, Mill was stern and rigid, but the two conversed almost daily and, with the exception of a major quarrel in 1814, agreed that they needed each other if their thinking was to have a lasting effect.

Able from his family training and schooling to speak and write clearly and forcefully, Mill began to use the press and the public forum to further Bentham's goals. By 1810, he had dropped his theology and became an open critic of the established church. He began to write for the *Edinburgh Review*, and though Brougham's and Jeffrey's editing concealed Mill's connections to Bentham, Mill still was able to externalize utilitarian views in many areas—emancipation, foreign affairs, economics, and penal reform. In his article "Commerce Defended" he reversed his earlier defense of wealthy landowners to become an overt opponent of the aristocracy.

Mill was also interested in education. John Stuart Mill in his *Autobiography* (1873) speaks of how his father brought him up to be a rigorous rationalist at the expense of both feeling and sentiment. During the 1810's, Mill championed the Lancasterian theory of education (teaching the poor to read and write, and having students help each other learn), as opposed to the church schools, which dwelt on the study of the catechism. He later espoused Bentham's chrestomathic method (adult education in utilitarian tendencies), but generally his efforts to promote a lasting method failed.

Mill was more fortunate in the area of governmental reform. Supporting the Radicals, he was instrumental in increasing their representation in Parliament and promoted the consequent changes in government policy. Mill was able to work with men of vastly different

persuasions—William Allen, a Quaker, and the Evangelical Zachary Macaulay—to accomplish such things as prison reform and legislation abolishing the slave trade. He continued to write, publishing articles on freedom of the press and governmental reform in the supplement to the *Encyclopædia Britannica* from 1815 to 1824. His thinking on democratic government was rooted not in human rights but on the utilitarian principle that it best served the interests of all classes.

Between 1806 and 1817, Mill worked on his *History of British India*, which was to become the definitive work on that country. In his history, he focused on the importance of democratic government run as in England, not by the native peoples. Mill knew little of the class system in India, but he used that factor as an argument for objectivity. This work not only established Mill as an authority on India but also brought him employment with the East India House, thus securing his financial future for life; it also gave him the freedom to pursue the goals of utilitarianism and the Radical Party.

By the middle of the 1820's the Radicals had become a major power in England, and there were many good men who supported the cause because of Mill—men such as David Ricardo, Francis Place, and George Grote. It was at that time that Mill's brilliant son assumed the leadership of the group, leaving the older Mill with the opportunity to write and pull strings in the background. When the Radical magazine *Westminster Review* began publication in 1824, Mill for the first time was free to write without the restraints placed upon him by other publications.

In 1832, the Reform Bill passed the English Parliament, enabling the country to accomplish democratic reform without the violence of the French Revolution. Though the Whigs claimed victory and the Tories were thankful that bloodshed had been averted, it was the Radicals who provided a solid theoretical and practical basis for the historic bill. Mill had advocated middle-class governance rather than aristocratic control, progress through political reform rather than violent takeover, and education through the press rather than religious indoctrination, and these were the factors that prevailed. Having suffered from lung disease for several months, Mill died of bronchitis on June 23, 1836. He was buried in Kensington Church.

SIGNIFICANCE

James Mill was at the height of his intellectual powers when England was undergoing a most significant time of unrest and change. Basically, he was a propagandist and a reformer, with philosophical underpinnings in the British empiricists. Unlike Thomas Hobbes, however, he was not an egoistic hedonist but believed in the perfectibility of humankind quite apart from divine grace. For him, morality was more important than religion, though he based his morality on utilitarian principles rather than on any inherent right or the goodness of humankind.

In Bentham, Mill found a mentor and a rational basis for cultural change. These two met in the context of Bentham's interest in legal reform, but their mutual concerns spread to many fields—economics, government, psychology, ethics, and education. For the Utilitarians, the Church of England was spiritually dead and the aristocracy inherently selfish. Hence the importance of democratic (by which Mill meant middle-class) control to best satisfy the greatest number of people.

Sometimes called the last great eighteenth century man, Mill, mostly because of his Scottish past, was well-educated and highly disciplined. It was in England, however, that he became convinced that the intellect was humankind's greatest asset. Mill rejected Romantics, such as Samuel Taylor Coleridge, for he was unimaginative himself, and thoroughly distrustful of feelings. Moreover, he was disinclined to socialism, as were William Cobbett and Robert Owen, who believed that government, rather than any class, should be responsible for the just treatment of the people.

Perhaps Mill's greatest gift, apart from his skillful pen and ability to articulate precise positions, was his propensity in work for common goals with people of widely differing points of view and to persuade others to go along with utilitarian ends. Harriet Grote (wife of the future historian) said of Mill:

> Before many months ascendancy of James Mill's powerful mind over his younger companion made itself apparent. George Grote began by admiring his wisdom, the acuteness, the depth of Mill's character. Presently he found himself enthralled in the circle of Mill's speculations, and after a year or two of intimate commerce there existed but little difference in point of opinion between master and pupil.

Even Thomas Macaulay, the champion of Whig politics and industrial progress, who had attacked the *Encyclopædia Britannica*'s "Essay on Government," came to admire Mill in the end.

Mill was not an original thinker, but he held his intellectual convictions with vigor. By the mid-1820's,

when his son began to lead the Radicals, it became evident that Mill was a success. John Stuart Mill would eventually go beyond his father, incorporating the importance of feeling and imagination into his vision of the world, but he saw in James Mill, if not a good husband and father, certainly a disciplined teacher who gave him an intellectual advantage few parents pass on to their children.

The Reform Bill was perhaps the single most significant event of the first half of the nineteenth century in England, and James Mill had a giant's part in its conception and passage. Though few agree with him now, he championed a philosophy that had an enormous impact in the shaping of Western civilization and perhaps still remains a subconscious, if not conscious, part of us all.

—*Thomas Matchie*

Further Reading

Bain, Alexander. *James Mill: A Biography*. London: Longmans, Green, 1882. Reprint. New York: Augustus M. Kelley, 1966. Dated, but still the most thorough account of Mill's life.

Bonner, John. *Economic Efficiency and Social Justice: The Development of Utilitarian Ideas in Economics from Bentham to Edgeworth*. Brookfield, Vt.: E. Elgar, 1995. Examines the economic theories of Mill, Bentham, and other utilitarians.

Halevy, Elie. *The Growth of Philosophical Radicalism*. Translated by Mary Morris. 3 vols. London: Farber and Gwyer, 1928. Reprint. New York: Augustus M. Kelley, 1955. Traces the evolution of utilitarianism from its philosophical roots in John Locke and David Hume, details the changes in Mill and Bentham as they worked together, and captures the essence of Mill's debates leading up to the Reform Bill. A good reference book from a Continental perspective.

Hamburger, Joseph. *James Mill and the Art of Revolution*. New Haven, Conn.: Yale University Press, 1963. A book about radical strategy: how Mill employed extraparliamentary means—the press, petitions, public meetings—to change the English constitution. A scholarly work that gives a larger picture for understanding Mill's time.

Mill, James. *James Mill: Selected Economic Writings*. Edited by Donald Winch. Chicago: University of Chicago Press, 1966. Best biographical sketch; relates Mill's life to his economic and political contributions. Includes a bibliography of Mill's works, some of which are reprinted with interesting introductions that trace the development of his thought.

Mill, John Stuart. *Autobiography and Literary Essays.* Edited by John M. Robson and Jack Stillinger. London: Routledge & Kegan Paul, 1981. Mill recounts the place of Bentham in his father's life and the rationalistic education he got during the time James was closest to Bentham. Short and moving in parts. The essay "Utilitarianism" in this volume is more wordy but represents John's defense of his father's philosophy of life.

Plamenatz, John. *The English Utilitarians.* London: Basil Blackwell and Mott, 1949. A succinct and thoughtful study of how Hume, Bentham, and James and John Stuart Mill each contributed to utilitarianism. Chapter 6 is a pithy analysis of James Mill and his accomplishments.

Schultz, Bart, and Georgios Varouxakis, eds. *Utilitarianism and Empire.* Lanham, Md.: Lexington Books, 2005. Collection of essays examining how Mill and other English utilitarians conceived of race and the role race played in their political and ethical programs. Includes an analysis of Mills's *History of British India* and his views on the "Negro question."

Stephen, Leslie. *The English Utilitarians.* 3 vols. London: Duckworth, 1900. Reprint. New York: Augustus M. Kelley, 1968. Scholarly but readable study of a complex time. Volume 2 is a thematic analysis of Mill's involvement in politics, economics, legal changes, and church reform. Other chapters explain his relationship to movements (Whiggism and socialism) as well as key personalities (Thomas Robert Malthus and David Ricardo). A good source book.

SEE ALSO: William Cobbett; Samuel Taylor Coleridge; Thomas Robert Malthus; John Stuart Mill; Robert Owen; Francis Place; David Ricardo.

RELATED ARTICLES in *Great Events from History: The Nineteenth Century, 1801-1900:* 1817: Ricardo Identifies Seven Key Economic Principles; June 4, 1832: British Parliament Passes the Reform Act of 1832.

JOHN STUART MILL
English philosopher

Desiring the greatest possible happiness for individual men and women and an England of the greatest possible justice and freedom, Mill questioned all assumptions about knowledge and truth and made what was observed the starting point of his discussions.

BORN: May 20, 1806; London, England
DIED: May 7, 1873; Avignon, France
AREAS OF ACHIEVEMENT: Philosophy, economics

EARLY LIFE

John Stuart Mill was the eldest of nine children born to James Mill and Harriet Burrow. His father, the son of a shoemaker, was helped by a patron, Sir John Stuart, to attend the University of Edinburgh, where he studied philosophy and divinity. He qualified for a license to be a preacher but soon lost his belief in God. In 1802, in the company of Sir John Stuart, who was then a member of Parliament, James Mill went to London to earn his living as a journalist.

Two years after the birth of his son, John Stuart Mill, James Mill began his association with Jeremy Bentham, twenty-five years older and the founder of utilitarianism.

James Mill became Bentham's disciple and the principal disseminator of utilitarianism; along with free trade, representative government, and the greatest happiness of the greatest number, another major belief of utilitarianism is that through education the possibilities for improving humankind are vast. The association between James Mill and Bentham, therefore, was to have a profound effect on the childhood, and indeed on the entire life, of John Stuart Mill, for he became the human guinea pig upon whom Bentham's ideas on education were acted out. Under the direction of his father, John Stuart Mill was made into a Benthamite—in John's own words, "a mere reasoning machine."

James Mill began John's education at the age of three, with the study of Greek, and it was not long before the boy was reading Aesop's Fables. By the time he was eight and began the study of Latin, he had read a substantial body of Greek literature, including the whole of the historian Herodotus and much of Plato. In the opening chapter of the *Autobiography* (begun in 1856 but published posthumously in 1873), Mill gives a detailed account of his prodigious feats of reading. Much of his studying was done at the same table at which his father did his writing.

On the morning walks on which he accompanied his father, Mill recited the stories about which he had read the day before. In the *Autobiography*, he states: "Mine was not an education of cram. My father never permitted anything which I learnt to degenerate into a mere exercise of memory." The purpose of the education was to develop the greatest possible skills in reasoning and argumentation. Those skills then were to be used for the improvement of humanity.

In the year of John's birth, James Mill began to write a work that would be eleven years in the making, his *History of British India* (1817). In the *Autobiography*, John tells of his part in the making of that formidable work, reading the manuscript aloud while his father corrected the proof sheets. He goes on to say that the book was a great influence on his thinking. The publication of the *History of British India* led directly to James Mill's appointment to an important position in the East India Company, through which he was able to have a considerable impact upon the behavior of the English in India.

The final episode in James Mill's education of his son was the work they did with David Ricardo's treatise *On the Principles of Political Economy and Taxation* (1817). On their daily walks, the father gave lectures to the son drawn from Ricardo's work. On the following day, the son produced a written account of the lecture, aimed at clarity, precision, and completeness. From these written accounts, James Mill then produced a popularized version of Ricardo, *Elements of Political Economy* (1821); this exercise in the thinking of Ricardo also formed the basis of one of John Stuart Mill's great works, the *Principles of Political Economy* (1848). When he and his father finished with Ricardo, John was fourteen and was allowed to be graduated from James Mill's "academy."

John then spent a year living in France with Samuel Bentham, brother of Jeremy. When he returned to England, he began the study of law with John Austin, a lawyer who was a friend of his father and Bentham. It was during this period that Mill had one of the greatest intellectual experiences of his life, the reading of one of Bentham's great works, which, edited and translated into French by Bentham's Swiss disciple Étienne Dumont, has come to be known as the *Traité de législation civile et pénale* (1802). Mill was exhilarated by Bentham's exposure of various expressions, such as "law of nature" and "right reason," which convey no real meaning but serve to disguise dogmatisms.

Mill also was greatly impressed by the scientific statement in this work of the principle of utility. Reading Bentham's statement of the principle "gave unity to my conceptions of things." Mill says in the *Autobiography* that at this time all of his ideas came together: "I now had opinions; a creed, a doctrine, a philosophy." He had been transformed: "When I laid down the last volume of the *Traité*, I had become a different being."

In 1823, James Mill obtained for his son a position in the same department as the one in which he worked at the East India Company. For the next thirty-five years of his life, John Stuart Mill worked in the office of the Examiner of India Correspondence. This was for Mill his "professional occupation and status." He found the work wholly congenial and could think of no better way to earn a steady income and still be able to devote a part of every day to private intellectual pursuits.

LIFE'S WORK

It was in the *London and Westminster Review*, founded by Bentham, that Mill's first writings of significance appeared in 1824 and 1825. Among others were essays on the mistaken notions of the conservative *Edinburgh Review* and on the necessity of absolute freedom of discussion. In 1826, however, at the age of twenty, Mill became seriously depressed and experienced what has come to be known as his "mental crisis," a period in his life discussed in detail in the *Autobiography*. Mill explains that at the age of twenty he suddenly found himself listless and despairing and that he no longer cared about the purpose for which he had been educated. He had to confess to himself that if all the changes in society and in people's attitudes were accomplished for which he, his father, and Bentham were working, he would feel no particular happiness. He had been taught that such accomplishments would bring him great happiness, but he realized that on a personal level he would not care. Thus, he says, "I seemed to have nothing to live for."

The *Autobiography* tells of his dramatic recovery. He read of a boy who, through the death of his father, suddenly had the responsibility for the well-being of his family thrust upon him. Feeling confident that he was capable of doing all that was expected of him, the boy inspired a similar confidence in those who were dependent on him. Mill claimed that this story moved him to tears: "From this moment my burden grew lighter. The oppression of the thought that all feeling was dead within me, was gone. I was no longer hopeless: I was not a stock or a stone."

Mill added that he learned two important things from his mental crisis. First, asking whether you are happy will cause you to be happy no longer. Second, stressing

---

MORAL INFLUENCES IN MILL'S YOUTH

I was brought up from the first without any religious belief, in the ordinary acceptation of the term. My father [James Mill], educated in the creed of Scotch Presbyterianism, had by his own studies and reflections been early led to reject not only the belief in Revelation, but the foundations of what is commonly called Natural Religion. I have heard him say, that the turning point of his mind on the subject was reading [Joseph] Butler's *Analogy*. That work, of which he always continued to speak with respect, kept him, as he said, for some considerable time, a believer in the divine authority of Christianity; by proving to him that whatever are the difficulties in believing that the Old and New Testaments proceed from, or record the acts of, a perfectly wise and good being, the same and still greater difficulties stand in the way of the belief, that a being of such a character can have been the Maker of the universe. He considered Butler's argument as conclusive against the only opponents for whom it was intended. Those who admit an omnipotent as well as perfectly just and benevolent maker and ruler of such a world as this, can say little against Christianity but what can, with at least equal force, be retorted against themselves. Finding, therefore, no halting place in Deism, he remained in a state of perplexity, until, doubtless after many struggles, he yielded to the conviction, that concerning the origin of things nothing whatever can be known. . . .

It would have been wholly inconsistent with my father's ideas of duty, to allow me to acquire impressions contrary to his convictions and feelings respecting religion: and he impressed upon me from the first, that the manner in which the world came into existence was a subject on which nothing was known: that the question, "Who made me?" cannot be answered, because we have no experience or authentic information from which to answer it. . . .

I am thus one of the very few examples, in this country, of one who has not thrown off religious belief, but never had it: I grew up in a negative state with regard to it. I looked upon the modern exactly as I did upon the ancient religion, as something which in no way concerned me. . . .

Source: John Stuart Mill, *Autobiography* (London: Longmans, Green, Reader, and Dyer, 1873), chapter 2.

---

right thinking and good behavior is not enough; one must also feel the full range of emotions.

It is thought that the intensity of his relationship with his father was the main cause of Mill's crisis. He adored and worshiped James Mill, and thus found it impossible to disagree with him. In recognizing the value of feeling, however, the son was rejecting his father's exclusion of feelings in determining what is desirable. As John came out of his depression, he let himself take an interest in poetry and art; William Wordsworth's poetry was a medicine to him, bringing him joy, much "sympathetic and imaginative pleasure." He was further helped in his emotional development with the beginning, in 1830, of his platonic love affair with Harriet Taylor and, in 1836, by the death of his father.

In 1830, Mill began to commit to paper the ideas that were to go into his first major work, *A System of Logic* (1843). Mill had come to believe that sound action had to be founded on sound theory, and sound theory was the result of sound logic. He was aware of too much argumentation that was not based on clear thinking; in particular, what were no more than habitual beliefs were frequently represented as truths. The subtitle of *A System of Logic* helps to explain Mill's intention: "Being a Connected View of the Principles of Evidence and the Methods of Scientific Investigation."

Although Mill and the utilitarians regarded experience or observation as the exclusive determinant of truth, of considerable influence in both Great Britain and on the Continent were those who believed that truth could be known through intuition. Those who started with intuition, Mill believed, started with nothing more than prejudices, and these prejudices then provided justification for untrue doctrines and harmful institutions. In *A System of Logic*, Mill attempted to combat what he considered prejudices with philosophy by establishing a general theory of proof. Insisting that "facts" were facts only if they could be verified by observation, Mill argued the necessity of ascertaining the origins of individual ideas and belief systems.

The publication of *A System of Logic* established Mill as the leader of his school of thought, now known as Philosophical Radicalism. *A System of Logic* became the most attacked book of its time, and Mill responded by revising to take account of the attacks; over the remaining thirty years of his life, Mill took the book through eight editions. His response to the criticisms of *Principles of Political Economy* was similar; he saw that treatise through seven editions.

As *A System of Logic* was an attempt to overthrow the dominance of the intuitionists, *Principles of Political Economy* was an attempt to liberate economic thinking from his own utilitarian predecessors, especially his father and David Ricardo. In the preliminary remarks, Mill says:

> It often happens that the universal belief of one age of mankind—a belief from which no one *was*, nor without an extraordinary effort of genius and courage, *could* at that time be free—becomes to a subsequent age so palpable an absurdity, that the only difficulty then is to imagine how such a thing can ever have appeared credible.

By 1848, the descriptions of economic activity by his predecessors had gained the status of natural law among the newly dominant middle class; to behave otherwise than to sell as dearly as possible and to buy as cheaply as possible, including human services, was to violate natural law. Mill thought it necessary to consider the effects of economic behavior on individuals and on society. He refused to accept the idea that there must be no interference with the playing out of economic forces.

Unlike his predecessors, Mill saw feasible alternatives to the system of laissez-faire and private property. He refused to accept the idea that there was nothing to be done about the suffering and injustices wrought by the system. He could not passively accept a system in which remuneration dwindles "as the work grows harder and more disagreeable, until the most fatiguing and exhausting bodily labour cannot count with certainty on being able to earn even the necessaries of life." He would consider communism as an alternative if there were no possibility of improving the system then at work. He insists, though, that a comparison with communism must be made "with the regime of individual property, not as it is, but as it might be made." Thus, Mill comes to advocate that the "Non-Interference Principle," sacred to his predecessors, must not be regarded as inviolable.

One of the markets in which interference by government is justified is education, which, as governed by the free market, was to Mill "never good except by some rare accident, and generally so bad as to be little more than nominal." However, education is the key to elevating the quality of life, for well-educated persons would not only understand that true self-interest depends upon the advancement of the public interest; they also would be thoroughly impressed with the importance of the population problem. Mill was a whole-hearted Malthusian and believed that there could be no permanent improvement of society unless population be under "the deliberate guidance of judicious foresight."

Another of the many high points of *Principles of Political Economy* is the chapter on the stationary state, in which Mill rejects the desirability of indefinitely pursuing higher rates of economic development. Mill was "not charmed with the ideal of life held out by those who think that the normal state of human beings is that of struggling to get on, that the trampling, crushing, elbowing, and treading on each other's heels are the most desirable lot of human kind." The ideal economic state of society for Mill is that in which "no one is poor, no one desires to be richer, nor has any reason to fear being thrust back, by the efforts of others to push themselves forward."

On Liberty (1859) is one of the most influential works in all of Western literature. It is a justification of the value of individuality, to the individual and to the individual's society. Written during a period of rigid, although informal, social control, *On Liberty* is an encouragement for the individual to do and say whatever he or she wishes to do or say. The work consists of five chapters, the first of which is a history of the contention between liberty and authority. The objective of this introductory chapter is to show that whereas limiting political tyranny used to be a foremost goal, in his own time and country it is the tyranny of public opinion that must be withstood and limited. The tyranny of the majority is an evil against which society must guard, for the tendency of the majority is to coerce others to conform to its notions of proper behavior and right thinking. Mill asserts that the "engines of moral repression" are growing and that a "strong barrier of moral conviction" must be raised against them.

In the chapter "Of the Liberty of Thought and Discussion," Mill argues the necessity of providing freedom for the expression of any and all opinions. Preventing an opinion from being expressed is an evil act against all humanity; even if the opinion happens to be false, the truth could be strengthened by its collision with the false opinion. If, however, the silenced opinion happens to be true, an opportunity to move toward truth has been lost. Only when it is possible to hear one's own opinions contradicted and disproved can one feel confidence in their truth. Throughout history, the most eminent of persons have believed in the truth of what turned out to be foolish notions or have engaged in conduct that later appeared to have been irrational. However, progress has been made; fewer people are prone to holding foolish opinions and behaving irrationally. That has happened because errors are correctable. People learn from experience, but they also learn from discussion, especially discussion on how experience is to be interpreted. "Wrong opinions and practices gradually yield to fact and argument: but fact and argument, to produce any effect on the mind, must be brought before it."

"Of Individuality, As One of the Elements of Well-Being" is perhaps *On Liberty*'s most potent chapter. In it, Mill argues that both the highest development of the individual and the good of society require that the individual human being be free to express his or her individuality. Mill regards individuality as a "necessary part and condition" of civilization, instruction, education, and culture. Different modes of living need to be visible in a society; where there is no individuality, there is no impetus for either other individuals or the society as a whole to improve. The visible individuality of some forces others to make choices, and it is only in making choices that various human faculties are developed—"perception, judgment, discriminative feeling, mental activity, and even moral preference."

Where there are no opportunities to choose, the feelings and character are rendered "inert and torpid, instead of active and energetic." Human beings must be free to develop themselves in whatever directions they feel the impulse, and the stronger the impulses the better. Should eccentricity be the result, then it should be remembered that "the amount of eccentricity in a society has generally been proportional to the amount of genius, mental vigor, and moral courage which it contained." The chief danger of the time is that so few dare to be eccentric. "Every one lives as under the eye of a hostile and dreaded censorship." This suppression of individuality can make a society stagnant.

Soon after the appearance of *On Liberty*, Mill began work on *Utilitarianism* (1863). About half the length of the former, it is, despite its title, a great humanistic work. Mill stretches Bentham's very limited concept of human motivation from the absolutely egotistic or selfish to include the altruistic. Bentham believed that experiences fell into one of two categories, pleasurable or painful, and that within each category there were quantifiable differences in such qualities as intensity and duration; Mill believed that in regard to pleasure there are two different kinds, higher and lower. The higher pleasures, which include knowledge, the experience of beautiful objects, and human companionship, Mill asserts, are more valuable than the lower, animal pleasures. Mill felt it necessary to make this distinction because whenever he came across the term "utilitarianism" the term seemed to sanction the lower pleasures and excluded the higher. Mill wished to rescue the term from the "utter degradation" into which it had fallen.

Rather than encouraging degradation, utilitarianism encourages the development of nobility. Truly noble persons always have the effect of making other people happy. Utilitarianism, therefore, could only attain its end—the greatest happiness of the greatest number—through the general cultivation of nobleness of character, not selfishness. Indeed, Mill insists,

> In the golden rule of Jesus of Nazareth we read the complete spirit of the ethics of utility. To do as you would be done by, and to love your neighbor as yourself, constitute the ideal perfection of utilitarian morality.

Doing as one would be done to is at the heart of Mill's discussion of relations between the sexes in *The Subjection of Women* (1869). Centuries-old customs and laws have subordinated women to men, but the test of true virtue is the ability of a man and woman to live together as equals. One reason why they often do not is that the law favors men. That is seen particularly when the law returns women to the custody of the very husbands who have physically abused them. Another reason they do not usually live together as equals lies in what women are taught is proper behavior toward men. Women are taught to be submissive and to make themselves attractive, but men are not taught to behave similarly toward women.

Such an imbalance in the way men and women relate to each other is doomed: "this relic of the past is discordant with the future and must necessarily disappear." Throughout his life, Mill sought equality and justice for women, not only because he believed strongly in the abstractions "equality" and "justice" but also because he believed that equality and justice in their relationships would improve and make happier both men and women. Mill's last years were devoted to public service. A few months before his death he was involved in beginning the Land Tenure Reform Association, for which he wrote in *The Examiner* and spoke publicly. Mill died at Avignon on May 7, 1873.

SIGNIFICANCE

In the nineteenth century, John Stuart Mill was England's most thoughtful and most wide-ranging writer on the subjects of how truth could be determined, what was good for the individual human being, and what was good for society as a whole. As a result of his consideration of these questions, he is known as a great champion of fundamental civil liberties and an opponent of all forms of oppression. He is one of the two great defenders in English, along with John Milton, of the necessity of the freedoms of thought, expression, and discussion.

For the most part, Mill's discussions in print are dispassionate and disinterested; he sincerely sought knowledge and truth, regardless of the sources from which ideas came. Without preconceptions of how it must have been, he sought to understand the past. Without contempt, he listened to and read his philosophical opponents in order to find and make use of whatever germs of truth there might be in their positions. He was always open to modifying and correcting what he had said previously. Aware of the brutality in humankind's past, he was never cynical about human nature nor pessimistic about humanity's long-term future.

Mill was optimistic about the desire and capacity of men and women to make themselves better persons, not all people certainly, but enough to have the net effect of improving society. He respected the complexity of human nature and human behavior. Never quick to rush to judgment, he saw that even an immoral action might have a sympathetic side or have qualities of beauty to it. John Stuart Mill was a very wise man, the nineteenth century's Socrates. Generations of students have been nourished on his works, and rightly so.

—Paul Marx

FURTHER READING

Capaldi, Nicholas. *John Stuart Mill: A Biography*. New York: Cambridge University Press, 2004. Biography focusing on Mills's intellectual development. Traces the influences in Mills's life that contributed to his philosophy.

Ellery, John B. *John Stuart Mill*. New York: Twayne, 1964. A book of one hundred pages that efficiently highlights and connects "the rare spirit of the man," the ideas of the man, and the spirit and ideas of the age in which he lived.

Glassman, Peter. *J. S. Mill: The Evolution of a Genius*. Gainesville: University of Florida Press, 1985. A fascinating analysis of Mill's life and writings from a psychoanalytic point of view. Glassman argues that long into adulthood Mill was struggling to repair the damage done to his emotional life and imagination by his father's domination.

Levin, Michael. *J. S. Mill on Civilization and Barbarism*. London: Routledge, 2004. Examines Mills's ideas of the stages leading from barbarism to civilization, his belief in imperialism as part of the civilizing process,

and his thoughts on the blessings and dangers of modernization.

Mazlish, Bruce. *James and John Stuart Mill: Father and Son in the Nineteenth Century*. New York: Basic Books, 1975. A very thorough discussion of the entangled personalities and ideas of the two Mills.

Mill, John Stuart. *Essays on Politics and Culture*. Edited by Gertrude Himmelfarb. Garden City, N.Y.: Doubleday, 1962. Contains eleven lesser-known essays, including the two seminal works "Bentham" and "Coleridge." In a twenty-page introduction, Himmelfarb discusses Mill's "peculiar brand of conservatism."

_____. *John Stuart Mill: A Selection of His Works*. Edited by John M. Robson. New York: Odyssey Press, 1966. Contains all of *On Liberty* and *Utilitarianism*; selections from the *Autobiography, A System of Logic*, and *The Subjection of Women*; and passages from eighteen other essays. Robson's twenty-page introduction is excellent.

Packe, Michael St. John. *The Life of John Stuart Mill*. London: Seckar and Warburg, 1970. Especially good on Mill's relationship with Harriet Taylor, the woman with whom Mill had a platonic love affair for twenty years while she was married and whom he married in 1851, two years after her husband's death.

Robson, John M. *The Improvement of Mankind*. Toronto: University of Toronto Press, 1968. A comprehensive examination of Mill's social and political thought by a sympathetic critic who writes excellent prose.

Ryan, Alan. *J. S. Mill*. London: Routledge & Kegan Paul, 1974. Focuses on seven of Mill's major works; summarizes them and relates them to the issues of the time that gave Mill the impetus to write.

West, Henry R. *An Introduction to Mill's Utilitarian Ethics*. New York: Cambridge University Press, 2004. An interpretation of Mills's essay on Utilitarianism.

SEE ALSO: Thomas Carlyle; James Mill; David Ricardo; Henry Sidgwick; Alfred, Lord Tennyson; William Wordsworth.

RELATED ARTICLES in *Great Events from History: The Nineteenth Century, 1801-1900:* 1817: Ricardo Identifies Seven Key Economic Principles; January 12, 1837: Mazzini Begins London Exile; September 2, 1843: Wilson Launches *The Economist*; 1859: Mill Publishes *On Liberty*.

MARIA MITCHELL
American astronomer

The first woman in the United States to become a professional astronomer, Mitchell discovered a comet in 1847 and became the most famous American female scientist of her time, as well as a leading voice for educating women in the sciences.

BORN: August 1, 1818; Nantucket, Massachusetts
DIED: June 28, 1889; Lynn, Massachusetts
AREA OF ACHIEVEMENT: Astronomy

EARLY LIFE

Maria Mitchell was born into a Quaker seafaring community that encouraged women to become self-reliant and well educated. Her mother and grandmother were both teachers. Her father, William Mitchell, was also a teacher who had a part-time position with the U.S. Coast Survey, for which he observed stars to check the accuracy of the chronometers that were used to tell time and chart longitude on whaling ships. From the age of twelve, Maria counted seconds for her father. She attended the academy of Cyrus Peirce, served as her father's teaching assistant at the age of sixteen, and opened her own school at the age of seventeen.

In 1836, Maria closed her school to accept the job of librarian for the Nantucket Athenaeum, which had just been founded. She taught herself mathematics, astronomy, German, and Latin by reading the books from the collection. These included textbooks by Charles Hutton and Nathaniel Bowditch and treatises by Joseph-Louis Lagrange, Pierre-Simon Laplace, and Karl Friedrich Gauss. At night, she and her father continued to study the sky, making observations with a circle and transit lent by West Point and a four-inch equatorial telescope from the Coast Survey. William Mitchell was by that time a clerk for Pacific Bank; his employers provided living quarters in which he built an observatory.

LIFE'S WORK

During a dinner party on October 1, 1847, Maria Mitchell slipped away to use the family telescope and noticed a previously unknown comet at a position five degrees above the North Star. She and her father monitored the comet for several days, computed its orbit, and shared the discovery with William Bond, the director of the Harvard Observatory. Bond then communicated the Mitchells' observations and calculations to the European scientific community. Their findings were published in England's *Monthly Notices of the Royal Astronomical*

Society, and King Frederick VII of Denmark awarded to Maria the gold medal that he had offered to the first person to discover a comet with a telescope. In 1848, Maria Mitchell was elected the first female honorary member of the American Academy of Arts and Sciences, and the Seneca Falls Woman's Rights Convention cited her achievement.

Mitchell's discovery made her one of the most famous astronomers in the United States, and she was invited to join the Coast Survey in 1849. She computed the position of Venus for the *American Ephemeris and Nautical Almanac* and assisted with a survey of the Maine coast in 1852. Meanwhile, she was elected to the American Association for the Advancement of Science in 1850, and she wrote scientific articles and began to travel outside Nantucket more frequently. She continued to work at the Athenaeum even as her fame grew but finally quit in 1856 to chaperon a wealthy girl on tours of the American South and Europe. After the girl returned home to the United States, Mitchell remained in Europe to meet other astronomers. During that trip, she became the first woman admitted to the Vatican Observatory; however, she was allowed to enter the observatory only during the daytime.

When Mitchell returned to the United States, a group that called itself "Women of America" presented her with a five-inch equatorial telescope, built by Alvan Clark, that permitted her to make more precise observations. She continued to work as a computer and field researcher for the *Nautical Almanac*. After her mother died, she moved to Lynn, Massachusetts, with her father and established a small observatory. By this time, she had become a nominal Unitarian in her religious beliefs, but she maintained Quaker values of simplicity and abolitionism. Because of her opposition to slavery, she boycotted southern cotton and always wore silk clothing.

As the U.S. Civil War came to an end in 1865, Mitchell accepted an invitation to become professor of astronomy and director of the observatory a new women's college that was being founded by Matthew Vassar. The twelve-inch telescope at Vassar College was the third-largest in the United States. Mitchell never married, so her father again accompanied her to the college campus at Poughkeepsie, New York.

At Vassar, Mitchell became known as a demanding but respected instructor who treated her students as intellectual equals and involved them directly in scientific work. For example, she and her students recorded the passage of four thousand meteors during a meteor shower in 1868. Mitchell also wrote papers on double stars, the daily photography of sunspots, an 1878 solar eclipse, and the satellites of Jupiter and Saturn that originated in part from her teaching practices. She also successfully challenged the college on the level of her salary, which was half that of younger and less-accomplished male professors. In 1869, she was elected to the American Philosophical Society.

In 1873, when Mitchell visited Europe a second time, she met with proponents of higher education for women and was ready to campaign nationally for women's rights. Afterward, she became a founder and the president (1875-1877) of the American Association for the Advancement of Women (AAW). She encouraged women to join AAW and to present scientific papers at its annual meetings. She believed both that women benefited from scientific education and that science needed women's special skills in detailed observations and teaching. From 1876 to 1888, Mitchell chaired the AAW's science committee, which prepared yearly reports on women in science. She also conducted open-ended surveys to determine where opportunities in science for women actually existed in 1876 and 1880. On June 28,

Maria Mitchell. (Library of Congress)

1889, she died in Lynn, Massachusetts, toward the end of her seventy-first year.

SIGNIFICANCE

As an astronomer and educator, Maria Mitchell played a seminal role for women in the history of science. She repeatedly proved by example that women could contribute new knowledge and observations. She was the most famous American female scientist of the nineteenth century. She received honorary degrees from Indiana University (1853), Rutgers Female College (1870), and Columbia University (1887). Mitchell always sought to bring other women along with her. For example, her students included the academic and scientific leaders Mary Whitney, Christine Ladd-Franklin, and Ellen Swallow Richards. She promoted collaborative approaches to science in her teaching and involved her students in important research. She spoke out publicly for women and helped create a place for them in which to raise their voices through the AAW.

Despite the honors she accumulated, Mitchell always saw herself as a data collector rather than as some kind of genius. Although she hoped women would hold academic positions as professionals, she expected that most of her students would remain amateurs. She was careful never to challenge men directly in her speeches. Meanwhile, the importance of the AAW as an advocate for scientific education for women ran its course during the 1880's, as other, specialized women's organizations emerged. The AAW then shifted its emphasis to philanthropy and eventually became the General Federation of Women's Clubs.

Mitchell's significance was symbolic as well as concrete. She herself was well aware that because few women were in the scientific community, those who wished to succeed were expected to demonstrate exceptional abilities. Her willingness to talk about that double standard inspired later generations of women, who founded the Maria Mitchell Association in 1902 to preserve Mitchell's Nantucket home. In 1908, an observatory was built at her home where student research is still carried out under the auspices of Harvard astronomers.

—Amy Ackerberg-Hastings

FURTHER READING

Albers, Henry, ed. *Maria Mitchell: A Life in Journals and Letters.* Clinton Corners, N.Y.: College Avenue Press, 2001. A well-documented account by an emeritus Vassar professor that is especially strong at conveying Mitchell's daily routine and intellectual energy.

Kendall, Phebe Mitchell. *Maria Mitchell: Life, Letters, and Journals.* Boston: Lee and Shepard, 1896. A mostly accurate account by Mitchell's sister, who destroyed several of Mitchell's papers.

Kidwell, Peggy. "Three Women of American Astronomy." *American Scientist* 78 (1990): 244-251. Describes the scientific contributions of Mitchell, Annie Jump Cannon, and Cecilia Payne-Gaposchkin and discusses what each of these women said about the role of women in astronomy.

Kohlstedt, Sally. "Maria Mitchell and the Advancement of Women in Science." In *Uneasy Careers and Intimate Lives: Women in Science*, edited by Prina G. Abir-Am and Dorinda Outram. New Brunswick, N.J.: Rutgers University Press, 1987. Emphasizes Mitchell's teaching techniques and advocacy for women's education. Concludes that Mitchell employed deliberate strategies for a changing but cautious world.

Oles, Carole. *Night Watchers: Inventions on the Life of Maria Mitchell.* Cambridge, Mass.: Alice James Books, 1985. Poems inspired by and drawn from Oles's study of Mitchell's manuscripts. Provides a literary perspective on Mitchell's significance and personal idiosyncracies.

Wright, Helen. *Sweeper in the Sky: The Life of Maria Mitchell.* Reprint. Clinton Corners, N.Y.: Attic Studio Press, 1997. A popular biography by a Vassar alumna and astronomer that carefully reconstructs Mitchell's childhood.

SEE ALSO: Friedrich Wilhelm Bessel; Williamina Paton Stevens Fleming; Margaret Lindsay Huggins; Pierre-Simon Laplace; Sir Joseph Norman Lockyer; Ellen Swallow Richards.

RELATED ARTICLE in *Great Events from History: The Nineteenth Century, 1801-1900:* January 1, 1801: First Asteroid Is Discovered.

THEODOR MOMMSEN
German historian

Mommsen transformed the study of Roman history by correcting and supplementing the literary tradition of the ancient historians with the evidence of Latin inscriptions. Going beyond the usual focus on the generals and emperors, Mommsen championed study in all aspects of ancient societies.

BORN: November 30, 1817; Garding, Schleswig (now in Germany)
DIED: November 1, 1903; Charlottenburg, Germany
ALSO KNOWN AS: Christian Matthias Theodor Mommsen (full name)
AREA OF ACHIEVEMENT: Historiography

EARLY LIFE

Now considered a German historian, Theodor Mommsen (MOM-zehn) was born a Danish subject in a town that later became part of Germany. The eldest son of a poor Protestant minister, he was reared in Oldesloe, where he was educated by his father until 1834, when he attended school in Altona, outside Hamburg. In 1838, he entered the University of Kiel to study jurisprudence, which at the time involved a thorough grounding in Roman law. Under the influence of Friedrich Karl von Savigny's writings on the interrelationship of law and history, Mommsen's interest shifted to Roman history by the time he completed his doctorate in 1843. Equally influential were Otto Jahn's lectures on epigraphy, the study of inscriptions, which convinced Mommsen of the need for a complete collection of Latin inscriptions.

With a grant from the Danish government, Mommsen traveled through Italy from 1844 to 1847, collecting inscriptions and studying ancient Italian dialects. At the suggestion of the Italian scholar Bartolomeo Borghesi, he concentrated on Naples, and his subsequent monograph, *Inscriptions regni Neapolitani Latinae* (1852; inscriptions of the Latin Neopolitan kingdom), impressed scholars with its philological method and organization.

When Mommsen returned to take a post in Roman law at the University of Leipzig in 1848, Schleswig was agitating for union with Prussia. An ardent German patriot, Mommsen was caught up in the revolutionary nationalism, and his academic career was momentarily interrupted. Slightly injured in a street riot, Mommsen stayed behind when his brothers took up arms against the Danish crown, and instead he furthered the cause as editor and writer for the *Schleswig-Holsteinische Zeitung*.

In the reaction after the failed uprising, Mommsen was eventually dismissed from his teaching post in 1851. After a period of what he termed exile in Zürich, he returned to Germany in 1854 to teach at the University of Breslau, before settling permanently in Berlin, first with the Berlin Academy of Sciences and then with the University of Berlin.

LIFE'S WORK

Nineteenth century scholars, Germans in particular, applied scientific methods to the humanities in the belief that just as Charles Darwin had demonstrated the laws of natural selection, they could discover the laws of historical and social evolution. Some scholars were led by the evolutionary analogy, with its emphasis on the survival of the fittest, to dismiss questions of morality in their desire to establish the inevitability of historical development. This was especially true in Germany, where the nationalistic yearning for political unification had been building ever since Napoleon I's power over the German states had been broken. Consequently, German scholars often found it easy to let supposedly objective science serve political ends.

Theodor Mommsen. (Library of Congress)

Mommsen never overtly subverted scholarship to nationalism; however, the tendency was manifest in his most famous work, *Römische Geschichte* (1854-1856; *The History of Rome*, 1862-1866), which covers Roman history up to the end of the republic. Never intending to write for a general audience, Mommsen was approached in 1851 by his future father-in-law, the publisher Carl Reimer, who persuaded him to undertake the project.

Immediately famous, even notorious, *The History of Rome* was not only the first comprehensive survey of Roman history but also a passionate narrative of the rise and fall of the republic, brought to life by Mommsen's vivid and partisan portraits of historical personalities. With a dynamic, journalism-influenced style, Mommsen drew on familiar political and historical incidents and presented even abstract ideas in concrete imagery to make Roman history accessible to a wide audience.

The History of Rome impressed the scholarly community with its rigorous questioning of the ancient historians, but it was faulted for not citing sources or acknowledging any possible differences in interpretation. Moreover, many believed that he went so far in his demythologizing that he falsely recast Roman history in terms of his biased perspective of German politics.

These critics feared that *The History of Rome*'s adulatory depiction of Julius Caesar as the savior of Rome dangerously glorified power and buttressed Prussian militarism. Despite a belief in the generally progressive and civilizing effect of the emergence of powers such as Rome or Germany, Mommsen was not authoritarian so much as elitist, believing that the best government was that of an intellectual aristocracy in support of an enlightened leader such as Caesar. Because the closest example in German history was Prussian leadership in the tradition of Frederick the Great, Mommsen initially supported Prussia's central role in German unification.

However, when other Germans surrendered to, even welcomed, outright domination, masterfully managed by the German chancellor Otto von Bismarck, Mommsen felt betrayed. He opposed the extralegal and self-interested ambitions of Bismarck in Germany and of Napoleon III in France, though *The History of Rome* was often used to justify their actions. Mommsen served in both the Prussian and German legislatures, where he resisted Germany's colonial and economic policies. When he denounced protectionism as a swindle, Mommsen was brought into court by Bismarck on a charge of libel.

Though acquitted, Mommsen largely withdrew from politics after 1884.

It was in the calmer arena of the university that Mommsen made his more important though less famous contributions to scholarship. Mommsen's collection of Neapolitan inscriptions had made it obvious that he was the man to undertake a more comprehensive cataloging of all Latin inscriptions, a project already begun by the Berlin Academy. He was appointed editor in 1858 and worked on the project the rest of his life, demonstrating the highest standards of scholarly and organizational brilliance. To eliminate any possibility of forgery or error, he insisted on the examination of the actual inscriptions instead of secondhand reports. With the first volume of the monumental *Corpus inscriptionum Latinarum* (1863-1902; collection of Latin inscriptions), Mommsen transformed Roman historiography by providing it with an extensive factual basis. At the time of Mommsen's death, *Corpus inscriptionum Latinarum* contained 130,000 inscriptions in fifteen volumes, six of which he edited himself.

Though this would have been the life's work of other men, Mommsen also reconstructed Roman law in *Römisches Staatsrecht* (1871-1888; Roman constitutional law) and *Römisches Strafrecht* (1899; Roman criminal law). In the tradition of Savigny, Mommsen examined Roman law not as an abstract system but as a cultural and historical development determined by power struggles in the Roman Republic and Empire.

Despite reiterated plans to continue *The History of Rome*, Mommsen did almost no work on a narrative history of the empire. Instead, he published *Das Weltreich der Caesaren* (1885; *The Provinces of the Roman Empire from Caesar to Diocletian*, 1886), which, though termed a continuation of his *The History of Rome* and accessible to the nonscholar, is quite different from the earlier work. Nonnarrative and nonpartisan, *The Provinces of the Roman Empire* is a study based on the Latin inscriptions gathered from the areas that were once under Roman domination, revealing the empire to have been far more stable than the traditional focus on dynastic struggles suggested.

Over the years, Mommsen became a well-known character in Berlin. Active up to his death at the age of eighty-five, he worked late each night but arrived at the university each morning at eight, even using the tram ride to read. Although he was neither a graceful man nor, with his shrill voice, a particularly good lecturer, he commanded absolute respect. Mesmerized by his piercing blue eyes and intellectual authority, his students sat in to-

tal silence as Mommsen raced through prepared lectures. Rigorous in his criticism, he was equally generous in his assistance to his former students and left a lasting legacy with the generation of scholars he trained to his own exacting standards of research. At a time when solitary labor was still normal for scholars, Mommsen contributed to many cooperative efforts, started several international journals, and helped found the International Association of Academies in 1901.

Said by some to be intolerant of equals, Mommsen was no recluse, surrounding himself with students, friends, and a large family. Marie Reimer, to whom Mommsen was married in 1854, bore him sixteen children and for nearly fifty years provided her husband with a comfortable and supportive domestic life.

SIGNIFICANCE

Theodor Mommsen is universally acknowledged as one of the nineteenth century's most important historians. In his own lifetime, Mommsen's eminence was recognized when he was awarded the Nobel Prize in 1902. Because so much of his work dealt with matters of interest only to scholars, however, his fame is overshadowed by that of the great narrative historians, such as Leopold von Ranke.

With his amazing capacity for work, Mommsen put his name to more than a thousand published articles in his nearly sixty-year career. Highly regarded for an imaginative handling of voluminous statistics and detail as well as memorable epigrams and pithy summations, most of Mommsen's writing is still of interest mainly to specialists. Except for his *The History of Rome*, he wrote little narrative history, focusing instead on gathering and interpreting the inscriptions on stone and coins left by the Romans and correcting the less reliable written tradition. The *Corpus inscriptionum Latinarum*, which continues to grow, is indispensable for Roman studies, as are his studies of Roman law; yet much of his other work was superseded even in his own lifetime as others built on his pioneering work and methodology.

Throughout his career, Mommsen represented the best in humanistic scholarship. Dedicated to putting all studies on the most rigorous scientific footing, Mommsen never lost sight of the human element, which transcends national and racial considerations. Despite the controversy still surrounding *The History of Rome*, Mommsen's positive estimation of Caesar is shared by most scholars today, and his animated style exerted a beneficial influence on later German writing. His emphasis on the nonliterary sources encouraged scholars to shift their attention away from dynastic history to many areas of ancient societies. Welcoming innovative ideas and methods regardless of their political or personal consequences, Mommsen was always more interested in forwarding scholarship than in preserving his preeminence.

—Philip McDermott

FURTHER READING

Broughton, T. Robert S. Introduction to *The Provinces of the Roman Empire*, by Theodor Mommsen. Chicago: University of Chicago Press, 1968. Provides biography with an overview of Mommsen's major works and a discussion of reasons for his not finishing *The History of Rome*. Examines Mommsen's innovative scholarship and traces his influence on historiography into the mid-twentieth century. Contains a bibliography.

Gooch, George Peabody. "Mommsen and Roman Studies." In *History and Historians in the Nineteenth Century*. London: Longmans, Green, 1913. Chronological overview of Mommsen's life and his major work, detailing his many interests and activities along with contributions to the work of others. Conceding Mommsen's historical biases and tendency to esteem the victorious too highly, Gooch ranks Mommsen along with Ranke for demythologizing Roman history and encouraging new trends in scholarship. Contains valuable bibliographical footnotes.

Haverfield, F. "Theodor Mommsen." *The English Historical Review* 19 (January, 1904): 80-89. An obituary assessing Mommsen's character and contribution. In a review of Mommsen's main works, Haverfield analyzes the historian's remarkable combination of imagination, hard work, and organizational brilliance. Stresses Mommsen's pioneering use of inscriptions and cooperative projects in scholarship.

Kelsey, Francis W. "Theodore Mommsen." *Classical Journal* 14 (January, 1919): 224-236. A comprehensive biographical and character sketch with attention to the influences of Mommsen's teachers and colleagues. Argues that Mommsen was not so much an innovator as a brilliant and diligent realizer of the innovations of others. Details Mommsen's helpfulness as a teacher and includes a portrait of his happy domestic life.

Thompson, James Westfall, and Bernard J. Holm. *A History of Historical Writing*. Vol. 2. New York: Macmillan, 1942. Contends that through mastery of scholarship and a scientific approach to evidence, Mommsen revolutionized the study of Roman history. Examines Mommsen's elitist views and adulation of Caesar, dismissing their connection to German militarism and anti-Semitism. Includes a biographical sketch, a physical description, and a good bibliography.

SEE ALSO: Otto von Bismarck; Charles Darwin; Napoleon I; Napoleon III; Barthold Georg Niebuhr; Leopold von Ranke; Friedrich Karl von Savigny.

RELATED ARTICLE in *Great Events from History: The Nineteenth Century, 1801-1900:* 1824: Ranke Develops Systematic History.

JAMES MONROE
President of the United States (1817-1825)

As president of the United States and author of the Monroe Doctrine, Monroe set forth a basic principle of American foreign policy that has endured into modern times.

BORN: April 28, 1758; Westmoreland County, Virginia
DIED: July 4, 1831; New York, New York
AREA OF ACHIEVEMENT: Government and politics

EARLY LIFE

James Monroe came from a good but not distinguished family of Scottish origin. His father was Spence Monroe, and his mother was Elizabeth Jones Monroe, sister of Judge Joseph Jones, a prominent Virginia politician. James was the eldest of four children. His formal education began at the age of eleven, at a private school operated by the Reverend Mr. Archibald Campbell, which was considered the best school in the colony. At the age of sixteen, after the death of his father, Monroe entered the College of William and Mary upon the advice of his uncle, Judge Jones, who was to have a formative influence upon Monroe's life.

At the College of William and Mary, the Revolutionary War intruded, and Monroe, with his education unfinished, enlisted, in the spring of 1776, as a lieutenant in a Virginia regiment of the Continental Line. Slightly more than six feet tall, with a large, broad-shouldered frame, the eighteen-year-old was an impressive figure. He had a plain face, a rather large nose, a broad forehead, and wide-set, blue-gray eyes. His face was generally unexpressive, and his manners were simple and unaffected. He fought in the battles at Harlem and White Plains, and he was wounded at Trenton. During 1777 and 1778, he served as an aide, with the rank of major, on the staff of William Alexander, Lord Stirling. As an aide, Monroe mingled with the aides of other commanders and other staff officers, among them Alexander Hamilton, Charles Lee, Aaron Burr, and the Marquis de Lafayette. This interlude broadened his outlook and view of the ideals of the Revolution, which he carried with almost missionary zeal the remainder of his life.

After participating in the battles of Brandywine, Germantown, and Monmouth, Monroe resigned from Stirling's staff in December, 1778, and returned to Virginia to apply for a rank in the state line. Unable to secure a position, Monroe, upon the advice of Judge Jones, cultivated the friendship of Governor Thomas Jefferson, and

he formed a connection as a student of law with Jefferson that continued until 1783. This was the beginning of a long and valuable relationship, especially for Monroe. In 1782, Monroe was elected to the Virginia legislature, thus beginning a political career that lasted for more than forty years and brought him eventually to the highest office in the land.

LIFE'S WORK

In 1783, Monroe was elected to the Congress of the Articles of Confederation. He was an active and useful member, and he gained invaluable experience. He cultivated a friendship with James Madison, who was introduced to him by Jefferson. Monroe was identified with the nationalists, but his strong localist and sectional views made him cautious. He was particularly opposed to John Jay's negotiations with Don Diego de Gardoqui, the first Spanish minister to the United States, which threatened the western navigation of the Mississippi River. Monroe helped to defeat the negotiations, thereby gaining great popularity in the Western country, which lasted all of his political life.

Monroe's congressional service expired in 1786. He returned to Virginia intending to become a lawyer. By this time, he had married Elizabeth Kortright, the daughter of a New York merchant, on February 16, 1786. She was attractive but formal and reserved. Years later, she proved to be a marked contrast to her predecessor as hostess of the White House, Dolley Madison.

Monroe set up a law practice at Fredericksburg, Virginia, but he was not long out of politics. He was again elected to the Virginia legislature. He was also a delegate at the Annapolis Conference, but he was not chosen for the federal convention. In 1788, Monroe was elected to the Virginia convention for ratification of the Constitution. Here he joined with the opponents of the Constitution, fearing that the government would be too strong and would threaten Western development.

Monroe soon joined the new government, however, after losing a race for the House of Representatives against James Madison. He was elected to the U.S. Senate in 1790 and served there until May, 1794. He took an antiadministration stand, opposing virtually all of Secretary of the Treasury Alexander Hamilton's measures. It was a surprise, therefore, when he was selected as the new United States minister to France in June, 1794. Relations between the United States and France were at a low ebb. President George Washington apparently believed that Monroe, whose pro-French attitude was well known, would improve relations as well as appease the Republican Party at home.

Moved by his sympathies and a desire to satisfy the French, Monroe addressed the French National Convention in a manner that brought a rebuke from Secretary of State Edmund Randolph. Monroe was unable to defend Jay's treaty to the French, and he was considered too pro-French in the United States. In 1796, he was recalled by the new secretary of state, Timothy Pickering. When he returned, Monroe responded to innuendoes about his conduct with a nearly five-hundred-page pamphlet entitled *A View of the Conduct of the Executive, in the Foreign Affairs of the United States* (1797), revealing his belief that he had been betrayed by the administration. Although attacked by Federalists, among Westerners and his friends, his reputation was enhanced.

Monroe's diplomatic career was not finished. After an interlude as governor of Virginia (1799-1802), Monroe was chosen to return to France to assist Robert R. Livingston in negotiations to purchase New Orleans. Monroe always believed that his arrival in France was the decisive factor in convincing Napoleon Bonaparte to shift his position and offer the entire Louisiana Territory to the United States. Livingston had, however, already opened the negotiations and, with Monroe's assistance, closed the deal.

In 1804, Monroe went to Spain to "perfect" the American claim that the Louisiana Purchase included West Florida. The Spanish would not budge, and Monroe returned to England in 1805. In London, Jefferson matched Monroe with William Pinkney to negotiate with the British to end the practice of impressments and other disputes that had arisen between the two countries. The Monroe-Pinkney Treaty of December, 1806, gained few concessions but apparently satisfied the two American ministers. President Jefferson and Secretary of State Madison, however, rejected the treaty, and Jefferson did not submit it to the Senate.

Monroe returned to the United States in December, 1807, in an angry mood. He allowed his friends to present him as a presidential contender against Madison. Although Monroe's ticket was swamped in Virginia, ending his effort, he still had support in Virginia, for he was elected to the Virginia legislature in 1810, and the next year, to the state's governorship.

In 1811, Monroe and Madison were reconciled. Monroe accepted the offer of secretary of state. Relations between the United States and Great Britain had so deterio-

rated that Monroe concluded, as had Madison, that war must result. Monroe sustained the president's policy and the declaration of war on June 18. As secretary of state, Monroe supported Madison's decision to enter negotiations with the British and helped him select an outstanding negotiating team. Thereafter, Monroe had little influence upon the negotiations that resulted in the Treaty of Ghent, which ended the War of 1812.

Monroe emerged from the war with his reputation generally unscathed, and he was a leading contender for the presidency. The congressional caucus in 1816, however, partially influenced by a prejudice against the Virginia dynasty, accorded him only an eleven-vote margin to win the nomination. The discredited Federalists offered only token opposition, and Monroe won easily. His years in the presidency (1817-1825) are often referred to as the Era of Good Feelings. The Federalist Party gradually disappeared and offered no opposition. Monroe was reelected in 1820, only one vote short of a unanimous vote. He sought to govern as a president above parties. He took two grand tours, one to the North and the other to the South, and was well received wherever he went. Monroe also appointed some Federalists to office.

The outward placidity of these years, however, was belied by ferment below the surface. The question of slavery was raised to dangerous levels in the debate over restrictions upon the admission of Missouri to statehood. Monroe did not interfere in the debate, and he readily signed the compromise measure. Other issues during his presidency revealed the dissension within his party—for example, the debate over Jackson's invasion of Florida, army reduction, and internal improvements.

Diplomatic successes included neutralizing the Great Lakes, arbitrating the fisheries question, establishing the northern boundary of the Louisiana Purchase as the forty-ninth parallel, and joint occupation of Oregon with Great Britain. Much of the success of these negotiations was a result of Monroe's able secretary of state, John Quincy Adams. After Jackson's foray into Florida, Adams got Spain to transfer Florida to the United States and to settle the border extending to the Pacific Ocean.

The Monroe Doctrine, issued in 1823, capped off these diplomatic successes. It arose out of American fears that European nations would intervene to subdue the newly independent countries in South America. Invited by the British to join in a statement warning against intervention, Monroe, at the urging of Adams, issued a unilateral statement warning Europe not to interfere in the affairs of the Western Hemisphere.

THE MONROE DOCTRINE

In his December, 1823, state of the union address to the U.S. Congress, President James Monroe laid out a policy regarding European interference in the affairs of Western Hemisphere nations that has since become known as the Monroe Doctrine.

At the proposal of the Russian Imperial Government, made through the minister of the Emperor residing here, a full power and instructions have been transmitted to the minister of the United States at St. Petersburg to arrange by amicable negotiation the respective rights and interests of the two nations on the northwest coast of this continent. A similar proposal has been made by His Imperial Majesty to the Government of Great Britain, which has likewise been acceded to. The Government of the United States has been desirous by this friendly proceeding of manifesting the great value which they have invariably attached to the friendship of the Emperor and their solicitude to cultivate the best understanding with his Government. In the discussions to which this interest has given rise and in the arrangements by which they may terminate the occasion has been judged proper for asserting, as a principle in which the rights and interests of the United States are involved, that the American continents, by the free and independent condition which they have assumed and maintain, are henceforth not to be considered as subjects for future colonization by any European powers. . . . It was stated at the commencement of the last session that a great effort was then making in Spain and Portugal to improve the condition of the people of those countries, and that it appeared to be conducted with extraordinary moderation. It need scarcely be remarked that the results have been so far very different from what was then anticipated. Of events in that quarter of the globe, with which we have so much intercourse and from which we derive our origin, we have always been anxious and interested spectators. The citizens of the United States cherish sentiments the most friendly in favor of the liberty and happiness of their fellow-men on that side of the Atlantic. In the wars of the European powers in matters relating to themselves we have never taken any part, nor does it comport with our policy to do so. It is only when our rights are invaded or seriously menaced that we resent injuries or make preparation for our defense. With the movements in this hemisphere we are of necessity more immediately connected, and by causes which must be obvious to all enlightened and impartial observers. The political system of the allied powers is essentially different in this respect from that of America. This difference proceeds from that which exists in their respective Governments; and to the defense of our own, which has been achieved by the loss of so much blood and treasure, and matured by the wisdom of their most enlightened citizens, and under which we have enjoyed unexampled felicity, this whole nation is devoted. We owe it, therefore, to candor and to the amicable relations existing between the United States and those powers to declare that we should consider any attempt on their part to extend their system to any portion of this hemisphere as dangerous to our peace and safety. With the existing colonies or dependencies of any European power we have not interfered and shall not interfere. But with the Governments who have declared their independence and maintain it, and whose independence we have, on great consideration and on just principles, acknowledged, we could not view any interposition for the purpose of oppressing them, or controlling in any other manner their destiny, by any European power in any other light than as the manifestation of an unfriendly disposition toward the United States. In the war between those new Governments and Spain we declared our neutrality at the time of their recognition, and to this we have adhered, and shall continue to adhere, provided no change shall occur which, in the judgement of the competent authorities of this Government, shall make a corresponding change on the part of the United States indispensable to their security.

The late events in Spain and Portugal shew that Europe is still unsettled. Of this important fact no stronger proof can be adduced than that the allied powers should have thought it proper, on any principle satisfactory to themselves, to have interposed by force in the internal concerns of Spain. To what extent such interposition may be carried, on the same principle, is a question in which all independent powers whose governments differ from theirs are interested, even those most remote, and surely none of them more so than the United States. Our policy in regard to Europe, which was adopted at an early stage of the wars which have so long agitated that quarter of the globe, nevertheless remains the same, which is, not to interfere in the internal concerns of any of its powers; to consider the government de facto as the legitimate government for us; to cultivate friendly relations with it, and to preserve those relations by a frank, firm, and manly policy, meeting in all instances the just claims of every power, submitting to injuries from none. But in regard to those continents circumstances are eminently and conspicuously different.

It is impossible that the allied powers should extend their political system to any portion of either continent without endangering our peace and happiness; nor can anyone believe that our southern brethren, if left to themselves, would adopt it of their own accord. It is equally impossible, therefore, that we should behold such interposition in any form with indifference. If we look to the comparative strength and resources of Spain and those new Governments, and their distance from each other, it must be obvious that she can never subdue them. It is still the true policy of the United States to leave the parties to themselves, in hope that other powers will pursue the same course. . . .

Source: James Monroe, "State of the Union Address," December 2, 1823.

In 1824, the unity of the party was shattered by a contest between several strong rivals for the presidency. William H. Crawford, Monroe's secretary of the treasury, secured the caucus nomination from a rump group of congressmen, but other contenders, including Adams, Jackson, and Henry Clay, threw the vote into the House of Representatives. Clay threw his support to Adams, who won the presidency. In the aftermath, new coalitions were formed and eventually another two-party system emerged.

Monroe did not exert any political leadership during this period. It was not his temperament to operate in the new style of politics emerging as the Age of the Common Man. In many ways, he was obsolete when he left the presidency. His last years were spent making claims upon the government for past service. He received $29,513 in 1826, and he got an additional $30,000 in 1831, but this did not stave off advancing bankruptcy. In 1830, upon the death of his wife, he moved to New York City to live with a daughter and her husband. He died there on July 4, 1831.

SIGNIFICANCE

Monroe, the third of the Virginia triumvirate, has generally been ranked below his two predecessors in intellectual ability, although he has been ranked higher than either for his administrative skills. Monroe was more narrowly partisan and sectional, but he tried to be a president of all the people. The question has been raised, however, as to what extent he understood the role of the president as a party leader. It is to be noted that the party disintegrated under his presidency, but that may be a result, in part, of the decline of the Federalist Party as an effective opposition.

During his last years, Monroe was much concerned about his reputation. His concern reflects the essentially political cast of his mind. His letters throughout his life concerned almost exclusively political matters. An experienced and even a sensitive politician, he was an anachronism by the end of his presidency. Monroe was the last representative of the generation of the Founders. His idea of government by consensus was out of place in the new democratic politics of the Age of the Common Man.

Monroe's legacy was his Americanism. If he was at times narrow and sectional, he was always an American. His Monroe Doctrine aptly expressed the feelings of his fellow Americans that the Western Hemisphere was where the principles of freedom would be worked out and show the way to Europe and the rest of the world. His

career was long and successful, and his public service, if not brilliant, was useful to his country.

—C. Edward Skeen

FURTHER READING

Ammon, Harry. *James Monroe: The Quest for National Identity*. New York: McGraw-Hill, 1971. The most comprehensive biography. This book is well researched and well written. The interpretations are favorable to Monroe.

Cresson, William P. *James Monroe*. Chapel Hill: University of North Carolina Press, 1946. Until Ammon's book, this was the standard biography. Engagingly written, it lacks rigorous analysis. The point of view of the author is also favorable to Monroe.

Cunningham, Noble E., Jr. *Jefferson and Monroe: Constant Friendship and Respect*. Chapel Hill: University of North Carolina Press, 2003. This 80-page book describes the relationship of the two men that began when Monroe was a military aide to Jefferson during the Revolutionary War.

_____. *The Presidency of James Monroe*. Lawrence: University Press of Kansas, 1996. Cunningham outlines the major domestic and foreign policy issues that confronted Monroe during his two terms in office, including the first Seminole War, the Missouri Compromise, and the Monroe Doctrine. He portrays Monroe as a cautious president, lacking the education or intellect of Jefferson or Madison, but still an effective leader.

Dangerfield, George. *The Era of Good Feelings*. New York: Harcourt, Brace & World, 1952. Brilliantly written, this work, though superficial in many places, is still an excellent account of Monroe's presidency.

Hart, Gary. *James Monroe*. New York: Times Books, 2005. An analysis of Monroe's presidency by Hart, a former U.S. Senator from Colorado. In Hart's view, Monroe, a former military man, was concerned about homeland security in the United States, and initiated a series of treaties, annexations, and military actions aimed at securing the United States from foreign attack.

Monroe, James. *The Autobiography of James Monroe*. Edited by Gerry Stuart Brown. Syracuse, N.Y.: Syracuse University Press, 1959. Monroe's own view of his early career (the narrative extends only to 1805). Partly written to advance his claims upon the government, and partly to leave his own record of his career, Monroe's narrative does not always achieve objectivity.

Perkins, Dexter. *Hands Off: A History of the Monroe Doctrine.* Rev. ed. Boston: Little, Brown, 1955. In part a summary of a three-volume study by the same author and the considered judgment of the authority on the Monroe Doctrine.

Styron, Arthur. *The Last of the Cocked Hats: James Monroe and the Virginia Dynasty.* Norman: University of Oklahoma Press, 1945. Less a biography than a collection of the author's favorable opinions of Monroe. Written in a spritely manner, but there is more style than substance.

SEE ALSO: John Quincy Adams; Aaron Burr; Henry Clay; DeWitt Clinton; Dolley Madison.

RELATED ARTICLES in *Great Events from History: The Nineteenth Century, 1801-1900:* May 9, 1803: Louisiana Purchase; 1811-1840: Construction of the National Road; February 17, 1815: Treaty of Ghent Takes Effect; February 22, 1819: Adams-Onís Treaty Gives the United States Florida; December 2, 1823: President Monroe Articulates the Monroe Doctrine; December 1, 1824-February 9, 1825: U.S. Election of 1824.

LOLA MONTEZ
Irish-born dancer and actor

Montez was a dancer and actor who inspired the work of poets, playwrights, musicians, painters, kings, and politicians. She traveled extensively as a performer and was romantically linked to the king of Bavaria and famous writers and composers. Toward the end of her career, she turned away from scandalous stage antics to lecture on "female beauty," recommending temperance, exercise, and cleanliness over cosmetics as safeguards of beauty.

BORN: February 17, 1821; Grange, County Sligo, Ireland
DIED: January 17, 1861; New York, New York
ALSO KNOWN AS: Elizabeth Rosana Gilbert (birth name); Marie Dolores Eliza Rosanna Gilbert; Lola Montes
AREAS OF ACHIEVEMENT: Music, theater

EARLY LIFE

Lola Montez (MAHN-tehz) was born Elizabeth Rosana Gilbert. Her mother, Eliza Oliver, claimed to be a descendant of a Spanish family of high pedigree. She married Edward Gilbert, a British army officer of the Imperial Regiment in 1820. Most accounts paint a lonely picture of Elizabeth's childhood, part of which she spent in India, where her father died in September, 1823. A year later, her mother married a man named Patrick Craigie.

In late 1826, when Elizabeth was not quite six years old, she was sent back to England, where she arrived the following year. She later wrote in her memoirs that she did not see her mother again until 1837, when her mother apparently tried to marry her off to an aging man. The

sixteen-year-old Elizabeth instead eloped with an army officer named Thomas James. The couple later married legally on July 23, 1837, in Ireland. However, James's commission to India in 1839 was the death knell for what was apparently a doomed union. Two years later, Elizabeth returned to London alone. By most accounts, she was by this time a particularly striking young woman. She had vivid blue eyes, ivory skin, ebony hair, and a curvaceous figure.

LIFE'S WORK

The erratic stage career of Lola Montez began in 1842, after the fact that Elizabeth had had an adulterous affair with a man named George Lennox was discovered, and her husband petitioned for a legal separation. Elizabeth then reportedly studied under the gifted actor Fanny Kelly before taking up dance instruction in Spain. Her return to London as a "Spaniard" must have appeared authentic because she was engaged by the director of Her Majesty's Theatre, Benjamin Lumley. Elizabeth danced the Spanish cachucha dance *El Olano* (also spelled *El Oleano*) for her debut on June 3, 1843, before the king of Hanover, Queen Adelaide, and the duchess of Kent. It was probably around this time that Elizabeth began calling herself Lola Montez, as Lumley billed her as "Donna Lola Montez of the Teatro Real, Seville."

Lola's specialty at that time was so-called "Andelusian" dances. The fact that she performed in both *El Olano* and *La Sevillana* at Covent Garden in July, 1843, suggests that her dancing skills were impressive, otherwise, she would not have gotten such engagements. European performances followed: the *El Olano* in Dresden, Germany, in early August, 1843; *Le Bal de Don Juan* at the Paris Opera on in March, 1844; and *Der Verwunschene Prinz* in Munich, Germany, in October, 1846. During this period, her rumored lovers included the Polish composer Franz Liszt; Alexandre Dujarier, a Parisian journalist; the French novelist Alexandre Dumas, *père*; and King Ludwig I of Bavaria.

Between late October, 1846, and early 1848, Lola's acting career stalled as she played mistress to King Ludwig in Bavaria. Meanwhile J. S. Coyne's farce *Lola Montez: Or, Countess for an Hour* was licensed by the Lord Chamberlain in London and debuted at the Haymarket Theatre on April 26, 1848. Curiously, Lola's earlier, anonymously written piece, *Lola Montez: Ou, La Countess d'une heure*, was not licensed on the grounds that it pertained to a living monarch—King Ludwig. Coyne's adaptation of her play was later reprised as *Pas de Fascination; Or, The Catching of a Governor* at the Haymarket Theatre on May 22, 1848.

In 1851, Lola returned to the stage after she reportedly married George Trafford Heald—who was apparently an officer in the Life Guards—on July 19, 1849. However, several weeks later, she was charged with bigamy. She jumped bail, fled London, and roamed through continental Europe before taking dance instruction from the noted Parisian ballet instructor Jardin Mabille. She returned to dancing in September.

Lola made her American debut at New York City's Broadway Theatre in an original ballet called *Betly the Tyrolean* on December 29, 1851. After four performances there, she danced a *pas d'Andalusia* in the grand Spanish ballet *Un Jour de carneval à Seville* (carnival day in Seville) on January 5, 1852. Her career was boosted by numerous, well-publicized benefit nights, in which performers received most of the box-office proceeds, and a widely reported incident in which Lola evidently pummeled a man backstage in Boston in April.

Lola performed in C. P. T. Ware's drama *Lola Montez in Bavaria* when it premiered in New York on May 25, 1852, and toured St. Louis and New Orleans afterward. Meanwhile, her publicity was supplemented by occasional stories about her physically assaulting men. For example, she boxed her dancing master George Smith about the ears in June, 1852, and assaulted the prompter of the Varieties Theatre New Orleans in April, 1853. Lola's public sensations were coupled with her performances such as the spider dance, a saucier version of *La tarentule*, an Italian folk dance. The popular American actress Caroline Chapman later achieved an even greater success by performing her own version of the spider dance in San Francisco in June, 1853.

Lola Montez. (Library of Congress)

Lola began a tour of California goldfields after she met and married the editor of the *San Francisco Whig* Patrick Hurdy Hull on July 2, 1853. Rumors that she was seeking a divorce from Hull began to surface as early as October. In June, 1855, she sailed to Australia in the company of yet another lover, Noel Folland (sometimes spelled Follin). In August, she opened *Lola Montez in Bavaria* at Sydney's Victoria Theatre. Her other staple pieces included *The Follies of a Night* by James Robinson Planche, *Maidens Beware*, *Anthony and Cleopatra*, and the comedy *Morning Call*. Into addition to her spider dance, which she presented in Australia in September, she performed the *Neapolitan Sattirella*, the *El Olle*, and a nautical hornpipe.

After separating from her theatrical company, Lola went to Melbourne. As in America, her feisty temper became a hallmark of her Australian tour. She publicly horsewhipped the editor of the *Ballarat Times* in February, 1856, and later accused him of slander. Soon afterward, she herself was so viciously attacked by the wife of her manager that she was unable to perform. When she sailed back to San Francisco in June, 1856, Folland mysteriously disappeared overboard.

After reaching the United States, Lola performed in

San Francisco and New York but by August, 1857, her attentions were shifting from dancing to lecturing. In lecture tours through the United States and Canada, her topics included "Beautiful Women," "Heroines and Strong-Minded Women of History," "Gallantry," "Comic Aspects of Fashion," and "Slavery." Her abrupt change of careers later inspired the Reverend Francis Lister Hawks's tract *Is Not This a Brand Plucked Out of the Fire? The Story of the Penitent: Lola Montez* (1867).

Some researchers have suggested that syphilis, which Lola may have contracted from Alexandre Dumas, *père*, was the cause of her death in New York on January 17, 1861. She was appears to have been survived by a daughter named Elise who had been fathered by the French journalist Dujarier, with whom she had had an affair during the 1840's.

SIGNIFICANCE

The many enduring cross-cultural narratives that Lola Montez inspired lie at the heart of her significance. King Ludwig's infamous decision to make her the "Countess of Lansfeld" in 1847 remains as compelling a part of her legacy as the nuggets of gold that prospectors are said to have thrown onto her stages during her Australian tour in 1855.

Just as Montez influenced others, she had her own influences. For example, her authentic costuming and use of iconic props were influenced by prima ballerinas such as Fanny Elssler and Maria Taglioni. Lola's garter and *mantilla* became trademarks of her blatant sexuality, and the Spanish flavor of Elssler's *La tarentule* was certainly the source for Lola's spider dance. Lola's advocacy of female emancipation in her lectures was probably encouraged by women such as the French writer George Sand and soprano Madame Rosina Stoltz.

More significant, perhaps, was Lola's extraordinarily aggressive role in the construction of her own public persona. Years before the great French actor Sarah Bernhardt gained notoriety on and off the stage, Lola made herself famous with her stage antics and inflammable temper. The name "Lola Montez" became synonymous with the male "breeches" that she sometimes wore, the pungent cigars she smoked, and her involvement in controversial political issues, such as women's rights.

Interestingly, Lola's Australian tour coincided with a tour of the American lecturer Caroline H. Dexter, who spoke on the hazards of contemporary women's attire

and advocated wearing "bloomers." Lola met Dexter during her voyage to Australia. Afterward, Dexter's attention must have been drawn to Lola's often critical press. In September, 1855, Dexter wrote to *Bell's Life in Sydney and Sporting Review* to denounce the "unwholesome prejudice against the foully stigmatized and deeply injured Lola Montez." The letters that both Dexter and Lola wrote to Australian newspapers are significant. They remain as rare examples of mid-nineteenth century women who succeeded in having their "political" views published under their own names. Because of this, both Dexter and Montez rank as remarkable figures in early Australian media history.

—Nicole Anae

FURTHER READING

D'Auvergne, Edmund B. *Lola Montez: An Adventuress of the Forties*. London: T. W. Laurie, 1909. Despite its age, still a seminal source on Montez's life.

Goldberg, Isaac. *Queen of Hearts: The Passionate Pilgrimage of Lola Montez*. New York: John Day, 1936. This book retains its merit as an important reference.

Hall, Humphrey, and Alfred John Cripps. *The Romance of the Sydney Stage by Osric*. Sydney: Currency Press, 1996. Includes information regarding Lola's early life and gives details of her Australian tour.

Holdredge, Helen. *Lola Montez*. London: Alvin Redman, 1957. A meticulously researched source on Montez's entire life.

Lola Montes: The Tragic Story of a Liberated Woman. Melbourne, Vic.: Heritage Publications, 1973. This anonymously published text extensively acknowledges the work of Goldberg, Holdredge, and D'Auvergne and pays particular attention to Montez's tour of the Australian goldfields.

Seymour, Bruce. *Lola Montez: A Life*. New Haven, Conn.: Yale University Press, 1996. Thorough and nearly definitive biography. Should be read in conjunction with John W. Frick's review in *Victorian Studies* 40, no. 4 (Summer, 1997): 688-689.

SEE ALSO: Sarah Bernhardt; Alexandre Dumas, *père*; Fanny Elssler; Franz Liszt; Adah Isaacs Menken; George Sand; Ellen Terry.

RELATED ARTICLE in *Great Events from History: The Nineteenth Century, 1801-1900:* March 12, 1832: *La Sylphide* Inaugurates Romantic Ballet's Golden Age.

SUSANNA MOODIE
English writer and pioneer in Canada

A modestly sophisticated pre-Victorian Englishwoman who was roughly tested by immigrant life in Upper Canada, Moodie recorded strong emotional responses to her experiences in autobiographical writings that make her a central figure in nineteenth century Canadian literature.

BORN: December 6, 1803; Bungay, Suffolk, England
DIED: April 8, 1885; Toronto, Ontario, Canada
ALSO KNOWN AS: Susanna Strickland (birth name); Susanna Strickland Moodie
AREA OF ACHIEVEMENT: Literature

EARLY LIFE

Susanna Moodie was born Susanna Strickland, the youngest of six daughters and the sixth of eight children born to Thomas and Elizabeth (Homer) Strickland of Suffolk, England. An eccentric and precocious child with red hair and wide gray eyes, she experience wide swings between high spirits and depression that were taken as signs of her romantic temperament. Her father, who had been a manager of Greenland Dock at Rotherhithe on the River Thames, moved his family to the rural quiet of the Norfolk-Suffolk border-country, renting a manor farm called Stowe House that was beloved by his children, who gathered every morning in the parlor for lessons. The older children enacted scenes from Shakespearean plays or studied Greek and Latin under their father's supervision, while the younger children were taught to read by their mother. Afternoons were spent in the garden, on the farmland, or other local places.

In 1808, Susanna's family moved into Reydon Hall, a huge, drafty Elizabethan manor house in much disrepair, and Susanna and her siblings were schooled principally in mathematics, geography, sewing, handicrafts, theology, and literature. However, when Susanna's father died in May, 1818, the family was in precarious financial straits. Lacking money for dowries, the daughters could not make many trips to London, where social and literary opportunities flourished. Nevertheless, the oldest daughter, Elizabeth (born in 1794) did find a publishing and editing career in London. The two sons, Samuel (born in 1805) and Thomas (born in 1807), left England for ventures overseas. The remaining daughters remained in Reydon Hall, with Agnes (born in 1796), Catharine (born in 1802), and Susanna launching literary careers.

Competition broke out among the literary sisters, with domineering Agnes—the first of the sisters to see her work in print—eventually settling on history as her subject. Sweet-tempered and placid Catharine preferred nature, while impulsive, defiant Susanna turned to verse and first-person narratives. Susanna renounced the Church of England in favor of Congregationalism. She also changed her politics and became involved in the abolitionist movement.

In 1831, Susanna's life changed more dramatically after she married thirty-four-year-old Lieutenant John Dunbar Moodie, a cheerful Scot who had served in South Africa. Moodie played the flute, composed poetry, and wrote beautiful love letters but disliked his genteel poverty. In 1832—after the birth of their first child, Catharine—Susanna and her family boarded the *Anne*, a relatively small sailing ship crammed with seventy-two cheap-fare passengers, and sailed for Upper Canada.

LIFE'S WORK

After arriving in Canada, the Moodies settled first in Hamilton Township, near Port Hope. While living in three different residences over eighteen months, they suffered continual antagonism from "Yankee" neighbors. Nevertheless, Susanna began to publish in North America, placing poems in New York's *The Albion* and *The Emigrant* and in *The Canadian Literary Magazine*, *The North American Quarterly Magazine*, and various provincial newspapers.

In 1834, the Moodies acquired an uncleared lot near present-day Lakefield in Douro Township, where another daughter (Agnes) and three sons (John Alexander, Donald, and John Strickland) were born. John Moodie served in the Peterborough militia during the Mackenzie Rebellion. After he was appointed sheriff of Hastings County in 1839, the family moved to Belleville, a comparatively cosmopolitan town that was the most important settlement between Kingston and Toronto. Its Loyalist founders could trace their roots in Upper Canada back three generations. However, Belleville's thriving economy did not camouflage its contentious politics, which pitted Tories against Reformers, Methodists against Anglicans, Irish against Scots, and Roman Catholics against Protestants.

As sheriff, John Moodie tried to remain neutral in local politics, but his enemies tried to ruin him by ensnaring him in nuisance lawsuits. Family tragedies—the death of a newborn son (George) in 1840, a fire in the family's rented cottage during the same year, and the

CANADA'S FUTURE PROSPECTS

In this extract from the final chapter of Roughing It in the Bush, *Moodie expresses some of her feelings about her life in Canada and predicts a prosperous future for the new land.*

The preceding sketches of Canadian life, as the reader may well suppose, are necessarily tinctured with somewhat somber hues, imparted by the difficulties and privations with which, for so many years the writer had to struggle; but we should be sorry should these truthful pictures of scenes and characters, observed fifteen or twenty years ago, have the effect of conveying erroneous impressions of the present state of a country, which is manifestly destined, at no remote period, to be one of the most prosperous in the world. Had we merely desired to please the imagination of our readers, it would have been easy to have painted the country and the people rather as we could have wished them to be, than as they actually were, at the period to which our description refers; and, probably, what is thus lost in truthfulness, it would have gained in popularity with that class of readers who peruse books more for amusement than instruction.

When I say that Canada is destined to be one of the most prosperous countries in the world, let it not be supposed that I am influenced by any unreasonable partiality for the land of my adoption. Canada may not possess mines of gold or silver, but she possesses all those advantages of climate, geological structure, and position, which are essential to greatness and prosperity. Her long and severe winter, so disheartening to her first settlers, lays up, amidst the forests of the West, inexhaustible supplies of fertilising moisture for the summer, while it affords the farmer the very best of natural roads to enable him to carry his wheat and other produce to market. It is a remarkable fact, that hardly a lot of land containing two hundred acres, in British America, can be found without an abundant supply of water at all seasons of the year; and a very small proportion of the land itself is naturally unfit for cultivation. To crown the whole, where can a country be pointed out which possesses such an extent of internal navigation? A chain of river navigation and navigable inland seas, which, with the canals recently constructed, gives to the countries bordering on them all the advantages of an extended sea-coast, with a greatly diminished risk of loss from shipwreck!

Little did the modern discoverers of America dream, when they called this country "Canada," from the exclamation of one of the exploring party, "Aca nada,"—"there is nothing here," as the story goes, that Canada would far outstrip those lands of gold and silver, in which their imaginations revelled, in that real wealth of which gold and silver are but the portable representatives. The interminable forests—that most gloomy and forbidding feature in its scenery to the European stranger, should have been regarded as the most certain proof of its fertility. . . .

Source: Susanna Moodie, *Roughing It in the Bush* (3d ed., London: R. Bentley, 1854), chapter 28.

drowning of their son John Strickland in 1844—weighed heavily on the Moodies. Nonetheless, the family managed to survive and make important friends, including Robert Baldwin, later known as the founder of Canada's responsible government; John Lovell, the most famous Canadian printer-publisher of his era; and Joseph Wilson, a bookstore owner, publisher, and distributor.

While living as a pioneer woman, Susanna continued to write. She smoked a clay pipe as she worked in her vegetable garden and fed the poultry in her backyard, but she also produced controversial stories and articles that did not endear her to some notable figures in Belleville. Because her formative world was English, pre-Victorian, and conservative, she always thought of herself as an Englishwoman who was compelled to reveal the problems of Canadian society and life. After she befriended John Lovell, the editor of the Montreal magazine *The Literary Garland*, she received regular remuneration for her writing, and from 1839 to 1851, she was the magazine's

most prolific and versatile contributor. During that period, she and her husband coedited *The Literary Garland* and *The Victoria Magazine*. The latter publication was also becoming an outlet for the other Strickland sisters. Many of the poems, sketches, and serial fiction that she published in those journals were later reworked into book form for the English publisher Richard Bentley.

Though her literary output was large, Susanna Moodie's fame as a writer rests primarily on two books: *Roughing It in the Bush: Or, Life in Canada* (1852) and *Life in the Clearings Versus the Bush* (1853). In both books, she forsook her fondness for the kind of romance that she found in the novels of Sir Walter Scott, one of her major literary influences. Both books are hard to classify because they contain elements of poetry, fiction, travel writing, autobiography, and social analysis. Some critics believed them to be loose in structure; others argued that their unity rests on Moodie's sense of self as revealed by her personal voice, sense of humor, and middle-class values. This sense of self gives *Roughing It in the Bush* its force and vividness, as Moodie continually struggles with the loss of the Old World or with New World potentiality. What ultimately emerges from the text is its author's adaptation to her experiences.

Structured as an account of a trip from Belleville to Niagara Falls, *Life in the Clearings* is a more good-humored book, although its description of social life in Canada—of which Belleville serves as a microcosm—is slowly displaced by extraneous material. Moodie reveals herself to be puritan and progressive, a genteel English traditionalist and an eager proponent of democracy. Her book's anomalies may indicate a "Canadianness" in their balancing of extremes. Moodie is firmly optimistic as her book concludes with an affirmation of a new Canadian identity.

In 1863, when Susanna was approaching sixty years of age, she and her husband retired to a small cottage on the outskirts of Belleville. There Susanna divided her time between nursing her ailing husband and writing a long novel, *The World Before Them* (1868). In the fall of 1869, her beloved husband died, and she plunged into chronic gloom, loneliness, and ill health. As her body declined, she was forced to live with her children in Belleville, Seaforth, and Toronto, and with her sister Catharine in Lakefield. She lived long enough to oversee the publication of the first Canadian edition of *Roughing It in the Bush* before she died in Toronto on April 8, 1885.

SIGNIFICANCE

Although initially unpopular among Canadian readers because of its sentimentality about the Old World and the sometimes snobbish distance that Susanna Moodie puts between herself and others, *Roughing It in the Bush* has achieved the status of a Canadian literary classic as social history, autobiography, personal essay, and miscellany. Moodie's humor, enthusiasm, frustration, and depression inform the text, and the book is full of suspense and color.

Moodie's characters are a cross section of bush society, and the book offers lessons about early immigrant experience in a new, often rugged and hostile land. As Moodie puts aside some of her early social and cultural prejudices so she can come to terms with her new world, her writing reduces its reliance on conventional phrases and sentiments about civilization and the wilderness. In this way, both Moodie and her sister Catharine Parr Traill—another noted writer in Canada—helped lay the foundation of a literary tradition that still endures in the country.

It is unlikely that Moodie ever felt in control of her destiny in Canada, but as she took note of the transformation of the rough colony of 1832 into a vigorous, prosperous nation, she helped to shape the culture of her adopted country. While her sister Catharine was important for descriptions of landscape and natural history, Moodie was important for her evocations of colonial society, even though her personal relationship with the country was ambivalent. The most important books of both sisters are still in print and are studied in universities across the land.

—Keith Garebian

FURTHER READING

Fowler, Marian. *The Embroidered Tent: Five Gentle-women in Early Canada*. Toronto: Anansi, 1994. A mixture of scholarship and journalism, with notable wit, this book offers a fast-moving narrative about Elizabeth Simcoe, Catharine Parr Traill, Susanna Moodie, Anna Jameson, and Lady Dufferin.

Gray, Charlotte. *Sisters in the Wilderness: The Lives of Susanna Moodie and Catharine Parr Traill*. Toronto: Viking Press, 1999. A brilliantly clear picture of two sisters from England who became Canadian literary icons. Shows character of backwoods and clearings of Upper Canada and uses the sisters' correspondence, personal papers, and published works. Meticulously researched, beautifully told and illustrated.

Peterman, Michael. *Susanna Moodie: A Life*. Downsview, Ont.: ECW Press, 1999. This first critical biography of Susanna Moodie takes readers into her precocious English childhood, then follows her development as an independent-minded young gentlewoman with a social conscience and love for writing, a devoted farm wife, mother, and true pioneer.

Thurston, John. *The Work of Words: The Writing of Susanna Strickland Moodie*. Montreal: McGill-Queen's University Press, 1996. A comprehensive examination of the entire range of Moodie's writing that aims to dispel some of the myths about her life and work.

SEE ALSO: Robert Baldwin; Anna Jameson; William Lyon Mackenzie; Sir Walter Scott; Thomas Talbot; Catharine Parr Traill.

RELATED ARTICLES in *Great Events from History: The Nineteenth Century, 1801-1900:* October 23-December 16, 1837: Rebellions Rock British Canada; February 10, 1841: Upper and Lower Canada Unite.

DWIGHT L. MOODY
American cleric

In mass evangelistic campaigns, Moody preached a message of salvation and brought spiritual revival to the United States and England. One of the most influential religious leaders of the Gilded Age, he instituted new strategies and techniques in mass evangelism that were copied by countless later evangelists.

BORN: February 5, 1837; Northfield, Massachusetts
DIED: December 22, 1899; Northfield, Massachusetts
ALSO KNOWN AS: Dwight Lyman Moody (full name)
AREA OF ACHIEVEMENT: Religion and theology

EARLY LIFE

Dwight Lyman Moody was the sixth of nine children. His father, Edwin Moody, died when he was four, leaving the family with no provision for their future. With determination, hard work, and assistance from others, Dwight's mother, Betsey Holton Moody, kept the family together and reared them in a strict, loving, devout home. Because he was impatient with school and needed to work, Moody had little formal schooling. Always conscious of this lack, he was for many years hesitant to speak in public and only gradually attained the ability to preach.

At the age of seventeen, Moody left Northfield and obtained work as a shoe salesperson in the store of his uncle, Samuel Holton. Ambition, boundless energy, natural wit, and unorthodox selling methods made him an unusually successful salesperson.

As a condition of employment, Moody had to attend Holton's church, the Mount Vernon Orthodox Congregationalist Church. Reared as a Unitarian, Moody had never heard the message that was preached at Mount Vernon: that Jesus Christ had died for all men, risen from the dead, and lived to be the Savior and friend of all who trusted Him. Moody resisted this idea for some time, but when his Sunday-school teacher asked him privately for a response, Moody gave himself and his life to Christ. From that date forward, April 21, 1855, Moody had a new purpose in life.

In 1856, Moody moved to Chicago and within two years was earning more than five thousand dollars a year. His ambition was to succeed in business and accumulate the wealth to support his philanthropic work.

Needing an outlet for his energy and Christian zeal, Moody started a mission Sunday school in 1858. In two years, the regular attendance grew to 450 children. By 1864, the school had outgrown two buildings, and members wanted to form a church. The Illinois Street Church was founded that year, later becoming Moody Memorial Church.

In 1860, Moody resigned his business position to devote himself full time to Christian work. He joined the fledgling Young Men's Christian Association (YMCA) and, in 1865, became its president. Through the years, he was one of the foremost fund-raisers for YMCA buildings and activities. During the Civil War, the YMCA held evangelistic services for the soldiers, and though still unpolished, Moody became an effective and practiced preacher. He also visited personally with the soldiers.

In 1862, Moody married Emma Revell, a beautiful and well-educated girl of nineteen. They differed sharply in personality traits. Although Emma Moody was poised, retiring, and conservative, her husband loved publicity and practical jokes and was impulsive, quick-tempered, and outspoken. Though she suffered from poor health, he was robust and was always active. Practical and orderly, she handled most of her husband's correspondence and the family's finances. He depended on her good judgment and learned self-discipline from her. With all of his brusqueness, he was warm, tenderhearted, and sensitive to others. Humble and peace-loving, he was quick to apologize when he had wronged another. Under his wife's influence, Moody mellowed and improved in manners and speech.

During the 1860's, the YMCA expanded its work among the poor of Chicago. The association set up a distribution system for food and clothing using Moody's mission staff as workers. Moody organized literacy and Americanization classes. Also, the YMCA sponsored evangelism of the poor and, under Moody's leadership, citywide distribution of religious tracts.

As president of the YMCA, Moody became responsible for traveling to national conventions. At the same time, he participated in Sunday-school conventions and interdenominational "Christian conventions." Because he played a prominent role in YMCA work and the Sunday-school movement, Moody was well known as a colorful and effective speaker. At a convention Moody heard Ira Sankey sing and persuaded Sankey to leave his home and business and to join him as an associate. This partnership led Moody in a new direction.

LIFE'S WORK

After much prayer and soul-searching, Moody concluded that God was calling him to full-time evangelism. In June, 1873, Moody and Sankey sailed for England. After an inauspicious beginning, the two met with minor success in Newcastle and then preached to huge crowds in Edinburgh and Glasgow.

Throughout 1874, Moody moved slowly through Scotland and Ireland, then reached England in 1875. Moody would select a local person to coordinate plans for the campaign, and he insisted on cooperation among the local churches. He encouraged people to hold prayer meetings to pray for his work.

Attendance at the revivals required a huge building and, at times, a special temporary structure was built. Meetings were publicized in circulars and through home visitation.

As the evangelists approached London, the question was whether London would accept this uneducated preacher with his simple and direct messages. Short and heavyset, he wore a full beard on his round, ruddy face. Good-humored with a rich, full laugh, he walked quickly and spoke loudly. Although Moody received criticism from the press, his popularity seemed assured from the beginning of his London meetings. It was estimated dur-

Dwight L. Moody. (Library of Congress)

ing the four-month campaign that Moody spoke to more than two million people.

Moody returned to the United States as an international figure, receiving numerous requests for speaking engagements. After a short time at Northfield, Moody and Sankey held campaigns in Brooklyn, Philadelphia, and New York. After these campaigns, a visit to the South and a tour of the Midwest brought the two evangelists back to Chicago. In the fall of 1876, they began a revival in Chicago that lasted until mid-January, 1877. Following this revival, they held campaigns in Boston, Baltimore, St. Louis, Cleveland, and San Francisco.

Moody proved to be a sought-after speaker for the remainder of his life, and he traveled in North America and Britain with his message of revival. Recognizing a need for trained laymen to work in the churches, he established schools to instruct new converts. The Northfield School for Girls opened in 1879, followed by the Mount Hermon School for Boys in 1881. Their purpose was to provide a preparatory school education that would encourage the development of Christian character and prepare the students for Christian service. Moody did not consider himself an educator; rather, he obtained funds, facilities, and personnel for his schools.

In 1880, Moody held the first summer Bible conference at Northfield, with his friends and himself as speakers. The goal was to give lay readers increased understanding of the Bible and to foster spiritual renewal. These readers would then return to work in their churches with greater power. In 1886, the conference was expanded to include college students.

Chicago was the setting for another of Moody's ventures into education. Friends had long hoped for a permanent school there, and Miss Emma Dryer, with Moody's encouragement, had founded a small training school. Under Moody's direction, the Chicago Bible Institute officially opened on September 26, 1889. The school's purpose was to train Christian workers and equip them to serve in city missions. After Moody's death, the name was officially changed to Moody Bible Institute.

In 1894, Moody became convinced that masses of people could be reached if Christian books were available in inexpensive editions. A colportage department was begun at the Chicago Bible Institute, with students often distributing the books. In his later years, Moody developed a concern for prisoners, and books from the institute's colportage line were provided to prison libraries.

Moody had continued his revival preaching from 1878 to 1899, and he was speaking at Kansas City when his fatal illness struck. He hastened home to Northfield, and there he died on December 22, 1899.

SIGNIFICANCE

A man of incredible energy and authority, Moody was an evangelist to the masses and brought spiritual renewal to urban centers, both in the United States and abroad. The most significant religious leader of the Gilded Age, he instituted new strategies and techniques in mass evangelism that have been used by later evangelists. These included his methods of planning, organization, and publicity. By enlisting cooperation among the churches, he proved that evangelism could be above denominationalism.

Living in the midst of a change from traditional conservatism to a liberal outlook in theology, Moody nevertheless maintained a deep belief in a literal interpretation of the Bible and its fundamental creeds. His message typified the thought of the evangelical Protestant movement. Out of the millions who heard him speak, many became converted and carried on his message.

In Moody's era, Christian elementary and secondary schools had not come into existence. The schools he established at Northfield were innovative in their approach as Christian education. The Chicago Bible Institute was the second significant Bible school started up in the United States and became the impetus for others. His use of lay people in his work—Moody himself was never ordained—and his Christian schools ushered in the age of the lay worker in the Church.

Moody's influence was felt in evangelical circles long after his death. Probably more than his theology, his personality and fierce concern for humankind have inspired others to continue his work. His compassion, humility, and earnest message of salvation remain an example for other evangelists.

—*Elaine Mathiasen*

FURTHER READING

Dorsett, Lyle W. *A Passion for Souls: the Life of D. L. Moody*. Chicago: Moody Press, 1997. This biography provides an admiring yet balanced depiction of Moody by describing his virtues, faults, struggles, and triumphs.

Evensen, Bruce J. *God's Man for the Gilded Age: D. L. Moody and the Rise of Modern Mass Evangelism*. New York: Oxford University Press, 2003. Uses contemporary newspaper accounts to examine the influence of the popular press on Moody's rise to fame between 1873 and 1877. Evensen concludes that the press and Moody had a mutually beneficial relationship: The press used Moody to attract readers, and Moody used the press for free advertising.

Findlay, James F., Jr. *Dwight L. Moody: American Evangelist, 1837-1899*. Chicago: University of Chicago Press, 1969. The single best scholarly biography. Includes an analysis, though inadequate, of Moody's personality, theology, and techniques of evangelism. Examines critical shifts in the social and religious thought of the nineteenth century, placing Moody in historical perspective. A review of Moody's home life and later accomplishments is included.

George, Timothy, ed. *Mr. Moody and the Evangelical Tradition*. London: T&T Clark, 2004. Collection of ten essays examining Moody's doctrine, preaching methods, and his role in nineteenth century revivalism.

Getz, Gene A. *MBI: The Story of Moody Bible Institute*. Chicago: Moody Press, 1969. A comprehensive account of the growth and expanion of Moody Bible Institute and its varied ministries. Getz describes Moody's role in the institute's founding and early years.

Gundry, Stanley N. *Love Them In*. Chicago: Moody Press, 1976. Balanced, comprehensive evaluation of Moody's theology and how it related to his evangelistic campaigns. Within the historical context, Gundry considers Moody's doctrine in matters such as Calvinism, perfectionism, speaking in tongues, and the life of the believer. He stresses how Moody viewed the Gospel and its message of salvation.

Hopkins, C. Howard. *History of the Y.M.C.A. in North America*. New York: Association Press, 1951. A valuable resource as it examines the interplay of influences between Moody and the YMCA. Details the work Moody did for the YMCA in organization, fundraising, and evangelism.

McLoughlin, William G., Jr. *Modern Revivalism: Charles Grandison Finney to Billy Graham*. New York: Ronald Press, 1959. Attempting to explain the significance of revivalism in the social, intellectual, and religious life of America, McLoughlin examines the lives of major revivalists, including Moody. He analyzes their social environment and their effect on American life. Includes a description of the work of Moody's associate, Ira Sankey.

Moody, William R. *Dwight L. Moody*. Rev. ed. New York: Macmillan, 1930. Just before his death, Moody commissioned his son to write this official biography. Though eulogistic, it is complete and invaluable in any study of Moody's life.

Pollock, John. *Moody*. Chicago: Moody Press, 1983. A readable, inspirational biography. Although it is not a theological analysis, Moody's personality is illuminated, and the detailed story gives information not found in other biographies.

Sankey, Ira D. *My Life and the Story of the Gospel Hymns*. Chicago: Bible Institute Colportage Association, 1907. Because Ira Sankey was Moody's associate in his evangelistic campaigns, his autobiography gives insight into the way Moody conducted services. Also included are anecdotes that further aid in the understanding of Moody's personality.

SEE ALSO: Alexander Campbell; Frances Willard.
RELATED ARTICLES in *Great Events from History: The Nineteenth Century, 1801-1900:* May, 1819: Unitarian Church Is Founded; 1835: Finney Lectures on "Revivals of Religion."

J. P. MORGAN
American financier and philanthropist

As an extraordinarily successful investment banker and a conspicuous philanthropist, and one of the most prominent art collectors of his day, Morgan symbolized an era of aggressive capitalism.

BORN: April 17, 1837; Hartford, Connecticut
DIED: March 31, 1913; Rome, Italy
ALSO KNOWN AS: John Pierpont Morgan (full name); J. Pierpont Morgan
AREAS OF ACHIEVEMENT: Business, patronage of the arts

EARLY LIFE

John Pierpont Morgan had remarkable parents. His father, Junius Spencer Morgan (1813-1890), owned part of a large mercantile house in Hartford, advanced to a larger one in Boston, and finally became partner, then successor to the wealthy George Peabody, an American who made his career banking in London. Junius settled there in 1854 and lived in England for the remainder of his life. Morgan's mother, Sarah Pierpont, came from the family of a brilliant preacher in Boston, much given to abolitionism and other reforms.

Young Morgan received his formal education in Hartford, in Boston, in Vevey, Switzerland, and at the University of Göttingen. Seriously ill as a teenager, he had a long and successful convalescence in the Azores. At the age of twenty, he began his career as a clerk in Duncan, Sherman, and Company in New York. Two years later, while traveling in the Caribbean to study the sugar and cotton markets, he bought, without authorization, a cargo of unwanted coffee with a draft on his employers. They complained but accepted the profit of several thousand he earned by wholesaling the coffee in New Orleans.

In 1860, Morgan set up his own company. He had plenty of business from his father in London and also took advantage of many opportunities to buy and sell in the booming commercial city of New York. In 1861, he married Amelia Sturges, after courting her for several years. She was clearly in the advanced stages of tuberculosis, but Morgan, daring in love as well as in business, gave up all commercial activities and took his stricken bride to Algiers and then to Nice, hoping to cure her. He failed, returning to the United States as a widower in 1862. He formed a partnership with his cousin, Jim Goodwin, and called the firm J. P. Morgan and Company, Bankers.

Writers hostile to Morgan claim that he selfishly pursued profit during the Civil War years, trading in gold against the government's fluctuating greenbacks, buying a substitute for three hundred dollars under the Conscription Act, and on one occasion buying obsolete arms from the federal government in the East and then selling them to General John C. Frémont in the West at an enormous profit.

Morgan never apologized for his own actions, but writers friendly to him have argued that recurrent fainting spells, from which he suffered as a young man, made him unfit for military duty; that he served the Union cause well as an agent for Junius Morgan, who was staunchly pro-Union and placed United States bonds in England; and, finally, that two other men arranged and carried out the affair of the arms. Morgan was involved only as their banker, extending a short-term loan. Furthermore, the weapons were improved by rifling the barrels, and the young entrepreneurs, whatever their motives, did what the disorganized Department of the Army could not manage: They delivered arms at a reasonable price to the desperately needy Western army.

On one point, however, there is no dispute: Morgan spent that part of the war that followed his disastrous first marriage in making money as rapidly as he could. In September, 1864, he took in new partners and reorganized as Dabney, Morgan and Company. At twenty-seven, he was a leader in the financial life of the largest U.S. city. However, he was already launched in his career of philanthropy, helping to raise money for the wounded and widowed and working effectively to establish and enlarge the Young Men's Christian Association (YMCA). In 1865, he married Frances Tracy, one of the six daughters of attorney Charles Tracy. The Tracys were fellow communicants at St. George's Episcopal Church in the Bowery, which Morgan had joined in 1861 and attended for the remainder of his life.

Largely free, at this point, of the illnesses and spells that had marred his youth, Morgan stood well over six feet, with powerful shoulders, penetrating eyes, and the air of one born to command. In later life, he would grow portly and suffer painfully from acne rosacea, an inflammation of the skin which settled especially in his nose. He doted on his and Frances's four children, Louisa, Jack (John Pierpont Morgan, Jr.), Juliet, and Anne. In the summer of 1869, Morgan and his wife, accompanied by two relatives, rode the new transcontinental railroad to Utah and to California, where they toured extensively by stagecoach and horseback. Returning East, the Morgans occupied a comfortable new home at Six West Fortieth Street. In 1871, troubled by nervous disorders, Morgan briefly considered retiring. Instead, he accepted a new partnership with the powerful Drexels of Philadelphia. He would be a full partner and would head their New York office under the title of Drexel, Morgan, and Company.

J. P. Morgan. (Library of Congress)

LIFE'S WORK

To understand the later fame of Morgan, the investment banker, one must first understand how and why he became involved with the railroads of the United States. From their earliest beginnings around 1830 to the Civil War, American railroads were generally small affairs, connecting neighboring cities or connecting cities with important rivers or seaports. Most companies supposed that they could not manage more than five hundred miles of track. The two systems that thoroughly refuted this thinking, the New York Central and the Pennsylvania, were quite exceptional until Congress, offering large land grants, encouraged the building of transcontinental railroads.

Some firms can begin business with little capital investment and grow on earnings; others, including railroads and electric power systems, are expensive to build and cannot be put into operation or earn money until everything is in place, including the employees. Thus, the quantities of federal land given to the Western railroads were not the source of huge profits that they have been claimed to be. The railroads had to be built and operating, and the land had to be well along toward settlement, before any of those lands were salable. Railroads, the most important and transforming feature of the American economy in the nineteenth century, relied entirely on borrowed capital for their construction and initial operation. Furthermore, they had to be public corporations, their stock for sale in markets throughout the world; otherwise, the enormous sums required would not be forthcoming. This feature led almost inevitably to the separation of management from stockholders, too numerous and too scattered to exercise a coherent will on railroad affairs.

Stockholders all had one thing in common: They wished to protect their investments. It was therefore logical that investment bankers, whose income derived largely from marketing stocks and bonds, would wish to protect their own business positions by assuring the quality of the stocks and bonds being sold. Morgan was thus drawn into railroad affairs by a desire, born of necessity, to see that railroads were properly and efficiently managed, so that the stockholders and bondholders would be properly rewarded for their investments. Furthermore, he clearly saw what Cornelius Vanderbilt, Thomas A. Scott, and Jay Gould had seen earlier: The future of American railroading lay in building large, integrated systems, in which a single corporation controlled not only trunk lines but also feeders and operated without competition.

Morgan's first adventure was a colorful skirmish with the most notorious railroad pirates of the age, Gould and Diamond Jim Fisk, in a battle for the control of the Albany and Susquehanna. There is a legend that Morgan kept control of a crucial stockholders meeting by hurling the burly Fisk down a flight of stairs, scattering his henchmen as though they were tenpins. If true, this was the only time Morgan gained control of a railroad by hand-to-hand combat. In 1879, he performed a more sedate but much more lucrative feat in marketing William Vanderbilt's 250,000 shares (87 percent of those in existence) of New York Central Stock without suffering any depreciation or exciting any move to displace the railroad's management.

The year 1880 brought another enormous challenge, converted into enormous profits, not because Drexel, Morgan, and Company charged high brokerage fees but because it was handling so much money. In this case, it was a question of marketing forty million dollars in bonds for the improvement of the Northern Pacific, a transcontinental that had suffered bankruptcy and reorganization in the Panic of 1873. Great though his resources were, Morgan could not finance such enormous sales of stocks and bonds entirely through his own and his father's partnerships. He brought in other major banking houses, in the United States and abroad, discreetly organized in syndicates. To help protect the in-

vestments so arranged, Morgan, or one of his trusted partners or friends, became director of the refinanced railroad. Morgan later helped to finance and manage dozens of railroads.

Morgan was involved in the finances of the federal government on four major occasions. With other leading bankers, he helped refinance the federal debt under President Ulysses S. Grant. In the summer of 1877, Morgan committed another of his unexpected and extraordinary moves: He lent the army money with which to pay its troops, largely engaged in the Western Indian wars, after a distracted Congress had adjourned without renewing their appropriation. Because the army was not authorized to borrow, Morgan had paid out more than two million dollars at his own risk; Congress, however, appropriated funds to repay the banker. Much more effort was required to save the United States Treasury's gold reserve in the depression of 1893.

A combination of laws, more popular than wise, had forced the Treasury to sell gold until it was on the brink of bankruptcy; the Panic of 1893 had further started a general flight of gold back to Europe. To save the situation, Morgan had to form a syndicate of American and European bankers both to loan gold to the government at acceptable rates and to check the flow of gold from the Treasury out of the country. Furthermore, Grover Cleveland, whose party was rapidly coming under the control of Populists and Bryanites, was extremely reluctant to accept help from the only people who could give it, the "monied interests of Wall Street."

Morgan's greatest triumphs and defeats came toward the end of his life. In 1901, he formed a combination to buy out Andrew Carnegie and merge his steel colossus with several other companies. The resulting United States Steel Corporation, the first "billion dollar corporation," renewed charges of monopoly and chicanery. Morgan then turned to a merger of the Northern Pacific with its regional rival, the Great Northern, by means of a holding company, the Northern Securities Company. Theodore Roosevelt, the Progressive president, ordered a prosecution that the government won in 1904, and the merger fell apart.

Ever the patriot, Morgan returned in 1907 to lead yet another syndicate of bankers to prevent a financial panic. One of the New York banks saved on that occasion had chiefly working people for its depositors. Morgan ordered his company to save them even if he lost money; in fact, he did. In the last year of his life, Morgan was summoned before the Pujo Committee, which charged him with destroying competition by controlling all the large banks, railroads, and steel companies of the United States through interlocking directorships and stock proxies. Morgan stoutly denied the charge, claiming that his methods guaranteed the proper management of business by men of high character.

At St. George's Church, Morgan led the vestry in hiring W. S. Rainsford, an Emerson-inspired Progressive who introduced a community center, a house for deaconesses (Episcopal women doing social work, in this case), an industrial school, a summer camp, and a seaside resort for working-class women and children, all of which Morgan helped plan and most of which he financed. He also helped maintain the church near his summer home, served on the committee that planned the cathedral, and attended every national triennial convention of his church until his death.

Always something of a collector, Morgan began buying rare and old works of art on a stupendous scale after the death of his father. As a collector, Morgan displayed the decisiveness and flair that had characterized his business career. A trustee of the Metropolitan Museum from its fledgling days, he became its most active member in the last fifteen years of his life and left it priceless collections of paintings, ceramics, armor, and other objets d'art. For his collection of rare manuscripts and books, he built his own library next to the home at 219 Madison Avenue that he had built in 1881. It would later be administered as a public reference library. Collecting art went nicely with Morgan's lifelong habit of traveling abroad. He spent almost every summer in England, France, Italy, and, on several occasions, Egypt, where he often visited archaeological digs. He died during one of his periods of travel in Rome, Italy, on March 31, 1913.

SIGNIFICANCE

J. P. Morgan's power grew because of the unusual combination of boldness and good sense, ruthlessness and responsibility, that made up his complex personality. The failure of the American people, between 1836 and 1913, to have any sort of central bank created rare opportunities for investment bankers with strong connections to foreign centers of capital. Hating waste, inefficiency, and conflict, Morgan used his growing financial power to impose order on the railroad and steel industries, reducing competition and calling into question the Adam Smith economics that most educated people took seriously. Democrats also feared the growing power of rich men who appeared responsible to no one but themselves. Morgan, thus, stirred up controversy and antagonism; yet, on his death in 1913, he left a legacy of responsibility

in business and civic affairs and a priceless collection of art for the enjoyment of, literally, millions.

—*Robert McColley*

FURTHER READING

Allen, Frederick Lewis. *The Great Pierpont Morgan.* New York: Harper and Brothers, 1949. A readable biography that does justice to Morgan while stating the full case against him.

Canfield, Cass. *The Incredible Pierpont Morgan: Financier and Art Collector.* New York: Harper and Row, 1974. Richly illustrated and with superb color plates, this is a delightful book on Morgan.

Chandler, Alfred D., Jr. *The Visible Hand: The Managerial Revolution in American Business.* Cambridge, Mass.: Belknap Press of Harvard University Press, 1977. A comprehensive business history, placing Morgan exactly in context.

Chernow, Ron. *The House of Morgan: An American Banking Dynasty and the Rise of Modern Finance.* New York: Simon & Schuster, 1991. A meticulously detailed and well-written chronicle of four generations of Morgans, tracing the family's banking empire from its beginning in Victorian London to the stock market crash of 1987. Also describes the influence that the Morgan banks have exerted on the Western economy for the past two centuries. Winner of the National Book Award.

Gras, N. S. B., and Henrietta Larson. "J. P. Morgan: 1837-1913." In *The Coming of Managerial Capitalism: A Casebook on the History of American Economic Institutions*, edited by A. D. Chandler and R. S. Tedlow. Homewood, Ill.: Richard D. Irwin, 1985. An outstanding short treatment of Morgan's business affairs and their significance.

Hughes, Jonathan. *The Vital Few: American Economic Progress and Its Protagonists.* Boston: Houghton Mifflin, 1966. A splendid interpretive history with a graceful chapter on Morgan.

Rainsford, W. S. *The Story of a Varied Life: An Autobiography.* Garden City, N.Y.: Doubleday, Page, 1922. Rainsford was rector of Morgan's church for twenty-two years and, for all of his spiritual condescension, the only informed witness to Morgan's strenuous service.

Satterlee, Herbert L. *J. Pierpont Morgan: An Intimate Portrait.* New York: Macmillan, 1939. A narrative chronicle by Morgan's son-in-law, in whose eyes the financier was a great and good man. Dull, but full of family information not available elsewhere.

Sinclair, Andrew. *Corsair: The Life of J. Pierpont Morgan*. Boston: Little, Brown, 1981. A stylishly written book in the muckraking tradition, slightly marred by the repetition of the unlikely theory that Morgan resented his rich and powerful father right up to the old gentleman's death in 1890.

Strouse, Jean. *Morgan: American Financier*. New York: Random House, 1999. A balanced, detailed account of Morgan's life, describing his business dealings, social life, personality, and interests, such as his art collection. Strouse explains complex financial material in an easily understandable style.

Tomkins, Calvin. *Merchants and Masterpieces: The Story of the Metropolitan Museum of Art*. New York: E. P. Dutton, 1970. Richly illustrated, this work places Morgan's collecting and ambitions for the museum in proper context.

SEE ALSO: Andrew Carnegie; Grover Cleveland; Ralph Waldo Emerson; John C. Frémont; Ulysses S. Grant; James Jerome Hill; Nikola Tesla; Cornelius Vanderbilt.

RELATED ARTICLES in *Great Events from History: The Nineteenth Century, 1801-1900:* October 21, 1879: Edison Demonstrates the Incandescent Lamp; December 8, 1886: American Federation of Labor Is Founded.

LEWIS HENRY MORGAN
American anthropologist

Extending kinship studies, first among the Iroquois, then to cultures around the world, Morgan devised a theory of social and cultural evolution that provided both a theoretical model for late nineteenth century anthropology and a theory of early family evolution that Karl Marx would use in his interpretation of history.

BORN: November 21, 1818; Aurora, New York
DIED: December 17, 1881; Rochester, New York
AREA OF ACHIEVEMENT: Scholarship

EARLY LIFE

Lewis Henry Morgan was the son of Harriet Steele and Jedediah Morgan. His father, a wealthy landholder, died when he was eight, and the farm's operation was placed in the hands of young Morgan's older brothers. After receiving an education at the Cayuga Academy in Aurora and being graduated from Union College in 1840, Morgan decided to pursue a career in law. In Aurora, while reading for his bar exams, Morgan joined a secret men's organization called the Grand Order of the Iroquois. Morgan's participation and leadership in this organization proved to be the beginning of his ethnological career. In order to model the order after the political organization of the six Indian nations of New York, known as the Iroquois Confederacy, Morgan and other members of the club made trips to several Iroquois reservations to study their history and culture.

Later, Morgan took an active role in protesting the loss of Iroquois land, specifically reservations of the Seneca—one of the six Iroquois nations—to a land company, and he even traveled to Washington to present a petition to the president and the Senate on behalf of the Seneca. For his support of the Seneca Indians in this matter and his continuing interest in their culture, the Seneca adopted Morgan as a member of the Hawk clan.

In 1844, Morgan moved to Rochester, New York, and opened a law office. This career move did not deflect Morgan from his preoccupation with Indian studies. Not only did he supply Indian artifacts to the Regents of the University of New York, for what would later become a collection of the New York State Museum, but he also wrote a series of articles that appeared under the title "Letters on the Iroquois Addressed to Albert Gallatin," published in the *American Whig Review* (1847-1848).

Morgan later revised and expanded these letters into *League of the Ho-dé-no-sau-nee, or Iroquois* (1851), now considered the first full ethnography of an American Indian group. Morgan dedicated the book to Ely S. Parker, a Seneca Indian whom Morgan met in an Albany bookstore and who was instrumental in helping Morgan collect Seneca data. If Morgan never lived among the Indians, as some writers have claimed, neither was he an armchair ethnologist. He read what books he could find on the Iroquois and then complemented this reading with extensive fieldwork. Indeed, Morgan proved to be one of the first ethnologists to rely heavily on data collected in the field for the construction of ethnological theories.

The publication of Morgan's work on Iroquois history and culture drew the attention of others in the new science of ethnology, including the Indian agent, historian, and ethnographer Henry Rowe Schoolcraft and archaeologist Ephraim George Squier. After the publication of his book on the Iroquois, Morgan hoped to put aside his study of Indians and devote himself to his career in law. His marriage to his cousin Mary Elisabeth Steele, in 1851, strengthened his desire to succeed in his law career.

LIFE'S WORK

Morgan's early law career in Rochester proved unspectacular. Unknown and without influential friends, Morgan supported himself on local collection cases and occasional criminal cases. In time, he became known more for his public lectures at the Mechanic's Institute and at the Rochester Athenaeum than as a trial lawyer. These lectures, as well as his book on the Iroquois, eventually introduced Morgan to the elite society of Rochester. Through these contacts, he invested in railroad and mining companies in the Upper Peninsula of Michigan. By the late 1850's, through wise investments, he had acquired a modest fortune that allowed him to retire from legal practice during the early 1860's. Except for brief stints in the New York assembly in 1861 and the New York senate from 1868 to 1869, Morgan devoted the remainder of his life to ethnology.

Morgan's return to anthropological studies really began in 1857. In 1856, Morgan attended the meetings of the American Association for the Advancement of Science. Impressed with the papers he heard, Morgan decided to return the following year and deliver a paper on Iroquois kinship. This paper grew out of Morgan's earlier research and his discovery that the Iroquois determined kinship differently from the way of Anglo-Americans. Morgan suspected that other Indian tribes exhibited similar kinship patterns, but he had no opportunity to test this theory until the summer of 1858, while traveling in Upper Michigan.

In Upper Michigan, Morgan met some Ojibwe Indians and was excited to discover that their system of kinship was essentially the same as that of the Iroquois. It occurred to Morgan that kinship systems might be linked to a people's economy. Morgan noted that North American Indian kinship systems, which he termed classificatory, seemed to be associated with a hunting-gathering horticultural economy. Assuming that kinship systems changed slowly and then only when a people's economy changed, Morgan believed such systems to be quite old. If they were ancient and if similar systems could be found in other parts of the world, Morgan believed that

this would constitute proof of the migration of American Indians from the Old World.

Because the origin of the American Indian remained an important question throughout the first half of the nineteenth century, Morgan believed that discovering an Old World connection would be a major contribution to the young science of ethnology. Seeking an answer to these questions, Morgan made four trips, between 1859 and 1862, to Indian tribes west of the Mississippi River to collect kinship information.

On these trips, Morgan interviewed missionaries, schoolteachers, merchants, government agents, Indian traders, and steamboat captains, checking and rechecking the data he received from his talks with Indians from various reservations. He also sent questionnaires to missionaries and government agents around the world to learn how other non-European cultures determined kinship. Out of these travels and research came his *Systems of Consanguinity and Affinity of the Human Family* (1871). Discovering that the method of designating kinship that he first found among the Iroquois Indians also existed in Asia, Morgan became convinced of the Old World origin of the American Indians.

Morgan's trips to the West and his examination of conditions in various Indian communities made him sharply critical of the federal government's handling of Indian affairs. His shock and frustration over educational and health facilities available to Indians poured out in a series of articles triggered by the public outcry at the deaths of General George A. Custer and his troops at Little Bighorn. In "Factory Systems for Indian Reservations," "The Hue and Cry Against the Indians," and "The Indian Question," all published in the *Nation*, Morgan castigated the government for its treatment of Indians and blamed Custer's death on the government's longstanding mismanagement and indifference to reservation administration. Morgan claimed that Indians could not be civilized quickly and that teaching them farming might not be the best approach to changing their behavior. Change would take time, and American society would have to be patient in their expectations for the Indian.

Along with many others, Morgan sharply criticized government Indian policy. His reputation, however, rests not on these attacks but on his study of Indian kinship, which led him to theorize about the history and nature of the family. His evidence convinced him that the family had evolved through gradual stages from promiscuity to monogamy. This idea contributed to the development of Morgan's theory of human social and cultural evolution through stages of savagery, barbarism, and civilization. He developed these ideas in his next and best-known work, *Ancient Society: Or, Researches in the Lines of Human Progress from Savagery Through Barbarism to Civilization* (1877). After the publication of *Ancient Society*, Morgan published little. A section on the evolution of house architecture and home life originally intended for *Ancient Society* and deleted by the publishers because of its length was published separately as *Houses and House-Life of the American Aborigines* in 1881.

Although Morgan's primary contribution to American scholarship came through his work in anthropology, he also made contributions to natural history. Intrigued by the question of whether animals operated through instinct or reason, Morgan set out to investigate this question through an extensive study of the American beaver. Through his thorough examination of beaver behavior, Morgan concluded that beavers, in particular, and animals, in general, did indeed use reason. With the publication of *The American Beaver and His Works* (1868), Morgan became the foremost authority on the beaver. The study impressed both famed Harvard zoologist Louis Agassiz and English evolutionist Charles Darwin.

SIGNIFICANCE

Morgan began writing at a time when American ethnology still stressed collection and classification, with little emphasis on the interpretation of these accumulating data. His evolutionary theory moved American ethnology beyond mere classification to a larger consideration of humankind and their place in space and time. By placing American Indian ethnology into the larger context of human social evolution or human history, Morgan proved a pioneer in the development of the science of anthropology.

Morgan's legacy to anthropology is considerable. His studies of kinship and theories of social evolution became the model for anthropological study in the second half of the nineteenth century and influenced, in both Europe and the United States, the development of social anthropology into the twentieth century. His accomplishments were recognized by Charles Darwin, Henry Adams, Francis Parkman, and Karl Marx. Morgan's election to membership in the American Academy of Arts and Sciences, the National Academy of Science, and the American Association for the Advancement of Science, in which he served as president, indicates the esteem in which he and his ideas were held by the scientific community.

The work of Lewis Henry Morgan embodied much of the optimistic spirit that prevailed in nineteenth century America, a spirit that enthusiastically emphasized laws of progress for both the individual and society. Morgan's theory of social evolution—the evolution of society through levels of savagery and barbarism to civilization—well expressed this fundamental belief in progress.

—*Robert E. Bieder*

FURTHER READING

Bieder, Robert E. *Science Encounters the Indian, 1820-1880: The Early Years of American Ethnology.* Norman: University of Oklahoma Press, 1986. Contains a chapter on Morgan discussing his views on Indians and considering his influence on American anthropology.

Eggan, Fred. *The American Indian: Perspectives for the Study of Culture Change.* Chicago: Aldine, 1966. A series of lectures given by Eggan at the University of Rochester's Morgan Lectures, which focused on Morgan's contributions to the study of American Indian social organization.

Fortes, Meyer. *Kinship and the Social Order: The Legacy of Lewis Henry Morgan.* Chicago: Aldine, 1970. Also lectures in the University of Rochester's Morgan Lecture series. Fortes explores the larger scope of Morgan's ideas on kinship and social order in contemporary anthropology.

Morgan, Lewis Henry. *Lewis Henry Morgan: The Indian Journals, 1859-1862.* Edited by Leslie A. White. Ann Arbor: University of Michigan Press, 1959. Reprint. New York: Dover, 1993. Morgan's journals of his four trips, relating experiences among the Western Indians.

_____. *Pioneers in American Anthropology: The Bandelier-Morgan Letters, 1873-1883.* Edited by Leslie A. White. Albuquerque: University of New Mexico Press, 1940. A collection of letters between Morgan and his foremost American disciple.

Resek, Carl. *Lewis Henry Morgan: American Scholar.* Chicago: University of Chicago Press, 1960. A brief but well-written biography of Morgan.

Stern, Bernhard Joseph. *Lewis Henry Morgan: Social Evolutionist.* Chicago: University of Chicago Press, 1931. A dated but still useful biography of Morgan, written by a sociologist and social theorist.

Stocking, George W. *Race, Culture, and Evolution: Essays in the History of Anthropology.* New York: Free Press, 1968. Contains a chapter in which Morgan's anthropological theories are considered, along with those of his English contemporaries E. B. Tylor and Herbert Spencer.

Tooker, Elisabeth. *Lewis H. Morgan on Iroquois Material Culture.* Tucson: University of Arizona Press, 1994. As part of his study of Iroquois culture, Morgan collected five hundred objects, almost all of which were destroyed in a 1911 fire. The book contains illustrations of the objects; it also reprints Morgan's field note descriptions of the objects and his reports to the New York State officials who sponsored his research.

Also includes a brief overview of Morgan's life and career.

SEE ALSO: Henry Adams; Louis Agassiz; George A. Custer; Charles Darwin; Albert Gallatin; Karl Marx; Francis Parkman.

RELATED ARTICLES in *Great Events from History: The Nineteenth Century, 1801-1900:* 1871: Darwin Publishes *The Descent of Man*; February 8, 1887: General Allotment Act Erodes Indian Tribal Unity.

WILLIAM MORRIS
English writer and designer

Morris's influence on book design has been almost as profound as his impact on the decorative arts and the course of modern design; his key contribution to the growth of modern British socialism was practical, financial, and philosophical; he was also a powerful force in the revival of narrative poetry and the rediscovery of Norse literature, and an influential romantic and utopian writer.

BORN: March 24, 1834; Walthamstow, near London, England
DIED: October 3, 1896; Hammersmith, near London, England
AREA OF ACHIEVEMENT: Art

EARLY LIFE
The future socialist William Morris was born into upper-middle-class comfort. The son of a nondescript Evangelical mother and a businessperson father, he was brought up in a series of semirural residences near Epping Forest, where he acquired a love of natural form that would later manifest itself in his designs. At Marlborough public school, from January, 1848, until December, 1851, he benefited not from studying (because the school, then newly founded, was rather lax and rough) but from having free access to beautiful countryside and the wealth of historic buildings in the area. This resulted in his coming to know, as he later said, "most of what was to be known about English Gothic."

In 1853, Morris entered Exeter College, Oxford. In 1854, he made the first of several summer trips abroad that expanded his conception of art and architecture. During this period, the writings of essayist and reformer

John Ruskin proved to be a revelation to Morris, clarifying his unconventional beliefs. Also critical to his development was Thomas Carlyle's upholding of the virtues of the medieval past over the vices of the present.

At Exeter, Morris made two friendships that would last his lifetime and inform his work. Most important, the idealistic enthusiasm for things medieval of future painter Edward Burne-Jones confirmed Morris's own. The two gathered about them a group of friends, the "Brotherhood," dedicated to a "Crusade and Holy Warfare against the age"; for the twelve months of 1856, they published the *Oxford and Cambridge Magazine* (largely funded by Morris, who in 1855 came into an income of nine hundred pounds a year). At the same time, after taking his degree, in January, 1856, Morris articled himself to George Edmund Street, one of the most prominent architects of the revived English Gothic. In his Oxford office, he met and became friends with young architect Philip Webb.

Another major influence of the Oxford years was the Pre-Raphelite painter-poet Dante Gabriel Rossetti, who swayed Morris toward painting and away from architecture: Crucially, Rossetti's painting was medieval in inspiration and tended to emphasize the decorative. The influence is apparent in one of Morris's few extant paintings, a mural executed at the new Oxford Union Debating Hall in 1857. His model was seventeen-year-old Jane Burden, daughter of an Oxford groom: In 1859, in the teeth of Victorian convention, Morris married her. In a poem in his first volume, *The Defence of Guenevere* (1858), he pays tribute to the beautiful and enigmatic Jane; it points, too, at the loneliness he would later suffer in this marriage. Her great "mournful" eyes "[are] most times looking out afar,/ Waiting for something, not for me/ *Beata mea Domina!*"

LIFE'S WORK

Anticipating the birth of two daughters in 1861 and 1862, in 1860 Morris joined with Webb to build himself a house. At this moment, Morris's path started to unroll before him. "Red House," so called for the color of its brick, left uncovered in defiance of architectural convention, has been said to have initiated plain, unostentatious modern domestic design. The problem of what to do about aesthetically satisfying interior decoration and furniture led directly to the formation of Morris and Company.

The aim of "the Firm," which involved painters Rossetti and Ford Madox Brown as well as Webb and Burne-Jones, was to reinstate decoration as one of the fine arts. As its prospectus stated, it was concerned with everything from paintings "down to . . . the smallest work susceptible of . . . beauty." It was so successful that by 1866, only four years after the first Morris wallpaper, "Daisy," the Firm was decorating rooms at St. James's Palace. Gradually, as he mastered each craft, Morris expanded its scope to include, besides painted windows and mural decoration, furniture, metal and glassware, cloth and paper wall-hangings, embroideries, jewelry, dyed and printed silks and cottons, and carpets and tapestries. He created more than six hundred designs for the Firm, basing his designs on natural forms, primarily flowers, but always retaining a structural pattern. His designs are characterized by his firm calligraphic line (anticipating the style of art nouveau) and suggestions of movement, growth, and fullness.

At the height of these activities, in 1869, Morris was visited by Henry James, who remembered the bearded and still somewhat bohemian designer as "short, burly and corpulent, very careless and unfinished in his dress. . . . He has a very loud voice and a nervous restless manner and a perfectly unaffected and business-like address." As a younger man, Morris had been rather poetically beautiful, though not when in the throes of his occasional childish rages, during which he would bang his head on the walls.

There had been a lull in poetic production between *The Defence of Guenevere* and publication of Morris's next major works, *The Life and Death of Jason* in 1867 and *The Earthly Paradise*, a series of intricately interweaved narrative poems, in 1868-1870. These brought Morris instant success and popularity. Meanwhile his first translations of Icelandic sagas were published in 1869; their influence is apparent in much of his writing after the lonely and escapist *The Earthly Paradise*, most powerfully in his acclaimed epic *Sigurd the Volsung* (1876), the immediate cause of his being considered for the prestigious post of professor of poetry at Oxford: He declined to be considered (as later he would decline to be nominated for the post of poet laureate upon the death of Alfred, Lord Tennyson, in 1892).

By 1881, when the Firm moved to larger premises, there was essentially little difference between Morris the businessperson and any other Victorian capitalist. Contrary to eulogizing tradition, he did not entirely spurn machines (spurning instead "the great intangible machine of commercial tyranny"). Although he provided rather better pay and conditions, work in the Firm was boring: Certainly, it did not reach Morris's Ruskinian, medieval-Gothic ideal of delight and self-expression in work. After he had become a committed socialist, Morris was even more aware of the ironies of his position, as well as its benefits, such as his ability to fund socialist activities and the socialist press. However, he operated the way his society dictated he must in order to operate at all.

William Morris. (Library of Congress)

What Morris called his "conversion" to radical political activism came about gradually from 1876, in protest against the "dull squalor" of his civilization. By the early 1880's, he had openly committed himself to socialism, and despite some problems within the Socialist League, which he helped to found in 1884, he remained faithful to this cause until he died, not only writing political poetry (*Chants for Socialists*, 1883-1886; *The Pilgrims of Hope*, 1885), pamphlets, and tales, but also editing the League's journal *Commonweal*, from 1885 to 1890, selling it on the streets, speaking at workingmen's clubs and on street corners throughout the country, and braving arrest during the "free-speech" disturbances of 1886.

Philosophically, socialism gave Morris an analysis that provided firmer foundations for his belief that art has its roots in the social and political body, and will wither if that body is not in good health. High Victorian capitalist society, as his reading of the works of Karl Marx impressed upon him, was sick; nothing less than revolution was needed, and accordingly he would work for it. From the late 1870's, Morris went on to express these beliefs in the many lectures and publications, often spin-offs from his design work, on which rests his reputation as a pivotal figure in the development of the modern conception of culture. His analysis was deepest and most eloquently expressed in *A Dream of John Ball* in 1886 (a mix of romance and the philosophy of history) and in the utopian socialist vision *News from Nowhere* in 1890. Between 1889 and his death in 1896, Morris also published eight prose romances, set in a semimythological past, which prefigure the fantasies of C. S. Lewis and J. R. R. Tolkien.

The third of these tales, *The Story of the Glittering Plain*, was the first book to be published, in 1890, by the Kelmscott Press. It was Morris's great "typographical adventure" that revitalized English printing, then at a low ebb, stimulating experimentation and a proliferation of private presses. His insistence that the best books are "always beautiful by force of the mere typography" led to his designing two alphabets and producing more than six hundred designs for initials, borders, and ornaments. Between 1891 and 1898, when his executors wound up the Press, fifty-two books were produced; his 1896 Kelmscott edition of the works of Geoffrey Chaucer has been pronounced the finest book ever produced. Morris lived long enough to see it finished, but the punishing round of his many activities took its toll at last, and he died at the age of sixty-two.

SIGNIFICANCE

The greatest pattern designer of the nineteenth century,

William Morris has had a lasting effect upon the look and thought of the modern world because of his attempt to uphold in practice his Ruskinian belief in truth to nature, his respect for his materials, his fight for quality workmanship in a world already engulfed by shoddy mass production, and the protofunctionalism he came to advocate, expressed in his famous dictum: "Have nothing in your house that you do not know to be useful or believe to be beautiful."

Beyond even this, Morris was one of the most searching, and certainly the best-rounded, critics of English society and culture in the nineteenth century. He made in action, in his own life, the kind of links between poetry, politics, art, and society that are usually left to academics. His work was unified and therefore made more influential by a core of essentially simple ideas: to make life more worth living, less complicated, and more beautiful for more people. As he wrote in an 1894 article, "How I Became a Socialist": "Apart from the desire to produce beautiful things, the leading passion of my life has been and is hatred of modern civilization." He refused to believe, he added, that all the beauty of the world was destined to end "in a counting-house on the top of a cinder heap."

—*Joss Marsh*

FURTHER READING

McCarthy, Fiona. *William Morris: A Life of Our Time*. New York: Knopf, 1995. Scholarly, comprehensive biography that describes the full range of Morris's endeavors and interests. Places Morris's life and career within the context of Victorian architecture, politics, and literature.

Mackail, J. W. *The Life of William Morris*. London: Longmans, 1899. Reprint. Benjamin Blom, 1968. The standard, authorized biography, written at the request of Burne-Jones, with unhampered access to papers of the family and the Firm. A skillful patchwork of extracts from Morris's own writings, diaries, and letters, as well as Mackail's quietly elegant and highly readable narrative.

Morris, May, ed. *William Morris: Artist, Writer, Socialist*. London: B. Blackwell, 1936. Reprint. 2 vols. New York: Russell and Russell, 1966. The invaluable insights of Morris's beloved and politically sympathetic daughter, also the editor of the twenty-four volumes of *The Collected Works of William Morris* (1910-1915).

Morris, William. *The Collected Letters of William Morris*. Edited by Norman Kelvin. 2 vols. Princeton, N.J.: Princeton University Press, 1984. Excellent edition, with a solid introduction, chronology, more than thirty illustrations per volume (including reproductions of letters, plus designs, places, and people), indexes of subjects and correspondents, and unobtrusive footnoting.

_____. *Selected Writings and Designs*. Edited by Asa Briggs. Harmondsworth, England: Penguin Books, 1962. Includes two short autobiographical pieces. Helpfully organized under the headings of "Romance" (including his best poetry), "Commitment," "Socialism," and "Utopia" (the first half of *News from Nowhere* is printed in full). Excellent but short introduction by Briggs and good interleaved central section on Morris as designer by Graeme Shankland.

Naylor, Gillian. *The Arts and Crafts Movement: A Study of Its Sources, Ideals, and Influence on Design Theory*. Cambridge: Massachusetts Institute of Technology Press, 1972. More than one hundred illustrations, nine in color, of designs, fabrics, furniture, and household objects. Morris takes his place in a well-organized survey leading from Augustus Pugin through to Frank Lloyd Wright and the modern "efficiency" style.

Pevsner, Nikolaus. *Pioneers of Modern Design: From William Morris to Walter Gropius*. 3d ed. Harmondsworth, England: Penguin Books, 1970. First published in 1936. A compelling case for the crucial influence of Morris, despite his medievalism, for the modern movement. Makes clear the connections between interior and pattern design, architecture (including the work of Webb), and painting. Heavily illustrated.

Stansky, Peter. *William Morris*. New York: Oxford University Press, 1983. This excellent brief study in the Past Masters series is less a collection of the essential facts than a reflective essay upon the essential Morris. Thoroughly readable and frequently witty.

Thompson, E. P. *William Morris: Romantic to Revolutionary*. Rev. ed. London: Merlin Press, 1977. A monumental, primarily political study by the author of the classic work *The Making of the English Working Classes* (1963). Traces how Morris's intense romanticism came to unite with his political idealism.

Vallance, Aymer. *William Morris: His Art, His Writing, and His Public Life, a Record*. Kennebunkport, Maine: Milford House, 1971. Reprint of second edition of 1898. Draws extensively on contemporary reviews, criticism, and opinions. Heavily and attractively illustrated.

Waggoner, Diane, ed. *"The Beauty of Life": William Morris and the Art of Design*. New York: Thames & Hudson, 2003. Published to accompany an exhibition presented at the Huntington Library and the Yale Center for British Art. Contains essays about Morris's stained glass, interior decoration, and bookmaking, the activities of Morris & Company, and Morris's influence on British design and the American Arts and Crafts movement.

SEE ALSO: Aubrey Beardsley; Thomas Carlyle; Henry James; Karl Marx; John Ruskin; George Edmund Street.

RELATED ARTICLES in *Great Events from History: The Nineteenth Century, 1801-1900:* July 14, 1833: Oxford Movement Begins; Fall, 1848: Pre-Raphaelite Brotherhood Begins; 1861: Morris Founds Design Firm; 1884: New Guilds Promote the Arts and Crafts Movement.

SAMUEL F. B. MORSE
American inventor

As one of the primary inventors of the telegraph, Morse developed and implemented a system of electric communication that revolutionized the availability of information and forever changed the sense of world distances.

BORN: April 27, 1791; Charlestown, Massachusetts
DIED: April 2, 1872; New York, New York
ALSO KNOWN AS: Samuel Finley Breese Morse (full name)
AREAS OF ACHIEVEMENT: Engineering, science and technology

EARLY LIFE

Samuel Finley Breese Morse was born in the shadow of Boston, a center for politics and communication—pursuits that his own life and work would eventually revolutionize. The first son of the young Calvinist minister Jedidiah Morse and his New Jersey wife Elizabeth Breese, he was called Finley as he was growing up. Three years after he was born, a brother, Sidney Edwards, was born, and the next year, Richard Cary followed.

The Morses had great expectations of their sons, who were born into a family with a strong history of education: Their mother's grandfather had been president of Princeton College, and their father, Pastor Morse, earned a degree from Yale and wrote the first geography text in America. When the boys started school, however, they showed distinctly different aptitudes for study. Their father characterized Finley as the hare, quick to lose interest and change paths; Sidney, he said, was the tortoise of the family, stubborn and steadfast; Richard, the youngest Morse to survive birth, was more like Sidney than he was like Finley. Though the younger siblings were of different temperaments, they would often later come to the aid of their older brother: easing his financial woes, caring for his children after his first wife's death, and offering an editorial forum for discourses on the telegraph.

Morse's parents believed that the discipline of education would benefit their firstborn. They sent him off to Phillips Academy in Andover, Massachusetts, at the tender age of seven. His aptitude in the classroom was not legendary, though his aptitude for drawing proved somewhat greater and was encouraged by the family. By the time he studied at Yale, Morse was able to sponsor his affinity for cigars and wine with miniature portraits on ivory. Further encouragement from a meeting with the artist Washington Allston, whom Morse would later

credit as his mentor, prompted him to set some goals. Young Morse yearned to go abroad to study painting with Allston and Benjamin West. With some persuasion, his parents agreed to send him to England. There, at the Royal Academy of London, he learned to work in other media: charcoal, marble, and oils. West lent his work a critical eye and often turned the callow artist back to finish works he had thought completed. Soon, England recognized his talent and diligence with a gold medal from the Adelphi Society of Arts for his sculpture of the dying Hercules.

Morse returned to the United States (via a nearly two-month voyage), convinced of the historical genre's preeminence as "the intellectual branch of art." Commissions of such works were not readily available, however, and he had to resort to portrait work for subsistence. His pursuit of commissions took him up and down the eastern seaboard. In Concord, Massachusetts, he met his bride-to-be, Lucretia Pickering Walker. The wedding was postponed until he could save enough money to set up winter housekeeping in Charleston, South Carolina, where he had been awarded a commission for a portrait of President James Monroe.

Charleston, however, was only a temporary residence, and eventually Morse was forced by impecunity to leave his wife in New Haven, where his entire family seemed to be toiling without benefit of regular salary. He traveled continually to paint and dreamed of the means to live in the same house as his wife and children. That dream was never realized while Lucretia lived. In fact, he learned of Lucretia's death days after the event, while he was in Washington to paint the Marquis de Lafayette.

The Lafayette portrait, which hangs in New York's city hall, is not without critical acclaim. At least one art historian deems it worthy of nomination to the Golden Age of American portrait painting. Portrait painting, especially for civic commission, offered a regular income, but the two large-scale historical works Morse hoped to exhibit for profit did not. Morse conceived of these historical pieces in a grand manner. One, *Congress Hall*, otherwise known as *The Old House of Representatives*, shows the National Hall during a session of Congress and includes likenesses of the congressmen, achieved from individual sittings, as well as Jedidiah Morse, Benjamin Silliman, and a Pawnee chief.

The other, *The Louvre*, shows a room at the museum, the Salon Carré, complete with more than forty great paintings. When he thought of these works initially (nearly ten years apart), Morse wanted to create something that would appeal to the common person, though the historical genre was to his mind the most elevated of art forms. With *Congress Hall*, Morse thought each man would at least recognize his representative and have an interest in seeing him at work. *The Louvre*, he thought, would open the treasures of the Old World to Americans, who were rarely privileged to see these masterpieces.

Morse dreamed of an additional historical commission to decorate panels at the new Capitol, but the commission went to someone else; in this case, perhaps, art's loss directly contributed to science's gain.

LIFE'S WORK

When there is a question of who was the first to invent a machine or a process, research often shows more than one person working with similar ideas, though the one has no knowledge of the others' works. Such was the case with the invention of the telegraph. In 1832, while Morse was returning from Europe aboard the packet ship *Sully*, isolated from libraries, laboratories, and scientific journals, he formulated his first hypotheses regarding the possibility of transmitting information by electric impulses.

Morse's only formal education in matters of electricity had been lectures during his junior year at Yale when Silliman and Jeremiah Day gave demonstrations there. Morse himself experimented with electricity in the basements of Yale, apparently for reasons of native curiosity. Outside the classroom, Silliman, who was Morse's neighbor, and James Dwight Dana, an acquaintance with more than passing knowledge of electromagnetism, rounded out Morse's knowledge of electricity.

Long out of Yale by 1832, Morse had not read current scientific journals and was not aware that, at the same time, there were men experimenting in England with semaphore telegraphs—that is, those that worked with visual signals. On board the *Sully*, he was inspired in a conversation on electromagnetism with Dr. Charles T. Jackson to note that information could be sent electrically. With that grain of thought he began investigating possibilities for transforming the potential into a reality.

Morse's shipboard sketch pad shows his early ideas for a code based on dots and dashes and for devices to send and record messages. Upon his arrival at his brother's house in New York City, he began work on a prototype. With an old canvas stretcher and sawtooth type that he had forged at his sister-in-law's hearth, he produced a rudimentary model of a machine that would make electricity useful to humankind. The forces that had confronted Morse as artist, however, now played upon Morse the inventor: The initial stroke of genius demanded systematic revisions and fresh income if it were to be developed fully. Nevertheless, Morse was too active to be incapacitated by despair over lack of remuneration for his art or invention. He was busy running the National Academy of Design (he was among its founders), running for mayor of New York, and accepting the first art professorship at New York University (NYU).

To further his telegraphic work, Morse contracted several partners. These partners agreed that any new discoveries made regarding the telegraph would become public under Morse's name. The original partners, Leonard Dunnell Gale, Alfred Vail, and that cantankerous man, most often cast as a villain in stories of the telegraph, F. O. J. "Fog" Smith, contributed money and ideas to development of the telegraph.

Two crucial contributions by scientists made Morse's telegraph work. A professor, Joseph Henry, had discovered a principle that, though made public in 1831, did not come to Morse's attention until after he had made preliminary investigations. Henry discovered that increasing the number of turns in a coil increased the power of the current. Morse's partner Gale, who brought Henry's law to Morse's attention, was responsible for persuading Morse to change his primitive battery, designed for quantity, into one of intensity. This factor, with Morse's concept of an electric relay, enabled the telegraph to be effective over great distances.

Morse continued wrapping wires around and around his NYU studio, testing and demonstrating his remarkable new device. In 1837, he applied for his first telegraph patent in the form of a caveat to protect his preliminary inventions. They included a code of dots and dashes (to become, eventually, the "Morse code"), a mechanism for sending information and another for receiving, a method of laying wire, and a code dictionary. During that same year, Morse began petitioning Congress to accept and implement his system on a national basis.

Congress let the initial telegraph offer pass it by as Morse set sail for Europe to secure foreign patent rights. Europe, though enthusiastic about the abilities of the electromagnetic telegraph, would not bless it with the official sanction of patent.

This European excursion, however, was not completely futile. Morse learned the newly discovered photographic process of Jacques Daguerre and resorted to it as a means to gain additional funds for his research concerning the telegraph. His trained artistic eye and his direct knowledge of the process from study with Daguerre in France made him an ideal teacher. In time, the success of Morse's students, who literally kept him from the brink of starvation, earned for him the epithet "Father of Photography."

Physically, Morse showed the effects of years of struggle. He looked haggard, and his clothes were shabby with wear. In this condition Morse returned to Washington, D.C., wooing Congress with demonstrations. At last, Congress awarded him money to build a line between Baltimore and Washington in 1843. This line reported to the Capitol the results of the national presidential conventions held in Baltimore and broadcast the first formal message, "What hath God wrought?"

After financial remuneration was forthcoming with the spread of lines across the country, Morse became the subject of suit and countersuit as others tried to claim rights of invention and expansion in this new and as yet unregulated field. Morse energetically fought off these attacks. His mind was active with thoughts of a transatlantic cable, a new wife, and a home in the country that he could share with his children. After the trials and disappointments of his earlier years, Morse lived to enjoy universal approbation and financial success. At the time of his death, on April 2, 1872, his invention was in use throughout the world.

SIGNIFICANCE

Morse lived at the vanguard of a communications revolution. Trained as a painter, he combined knowledge of composition that would convey a message without words with the technology of Daguerre's picture-taking method to train the men who would record the Civil War through the eye of the camera. The photographic images, along with the news of the war transmitted instantly by telegraph, reported the immediate and shocking news of the war to the folks at home. This ability to unite and make useful abstract theories is a trademark of the American inventor.

As a communicator, Morse was always ready to serve—through his portraits and historical genre paintings, through working on the public relations of trying to fund experimentation, and in having the foresight and magnanimity to encourage Congress to establish this new machine under the auspices of the postal system. Even when pressed with other responsibilities, he ran for mayor of New York City, appeared at the statue erection in Central Park, and helped found the National Academy of Design. In each case, his motivation was the desire to contribute to society rather than to promote himself.

Though Morse was a nativist, he worked to make the telegraph a force for international communication, and his success in making the world much smaller was clearly demonstrated in the memorial services held upon his death: Telegrams arrived at the nation's capital from as far as Egypt and from all over the United States as well.

—Ellen Clark

FURTHER READING

Boorstin, Daniel J. *The Americans: The Democratic Experience.* New York: Vintage Books, 1974. Includes an examination of the spirit and character peculiar to the American innovator-entrepreneur.

Coe, Lewis. *The Telegraph: A History of Morse's Invention and Its Predecessors in the United States.* Jefferson, N.C.: McFarland, 1993. Coe, a former Morse telegrapher, traces the genesis of the telegraph from 1832. Recounts the creation of the first transcontinental telegraph line and analyzes the telegraph's impact on the Civil War.

Harlow, Alvin F. *Old Wires and New Waves.* New York: D. Appleton-Century, 1936. A comprehensive look at long-distance communication via signal, from Trojan War signal fires to the American telephone.

Larkin, Oliver W. *Art and Life in America.* New York: Holt, Rinehart and Winston, 1960. Though not as specific as the author's *Samuel Morse and American Democratic Art,* published in 1954 in Boston by Little, Brown, this text seems more readily available. Explores Morse's standing among other artists of the period. Very good on the contrasts between pursuit of the arts in the New World and the Old.

Mabee, Carleton. *The American Leonardo: A Life of Samuel F. B. Morse.* New York: Alfred A. Knopf, 1944. The standard Morse biography. Mabee writes a unified account of a man whose varied interests are a delight and challenge to follow.

_____. *Memorial of Samuel Finley Breese Morse, Including Appropriate Ceremonies of Respect at the National Capitol and Elsewhere.* Washington, D.C.: Government Printing Office, 1875. One measure of a man's life is the mourning of his passing. The ceremonies described here were particularly modern, uniting electronically virtually the entire world in a common bond of gratitude and sorrow.

Morse, Samuel F. B. *Samuel F. B. Morse: His Letters and Journals.* 2 vols. Edited by Edward Lind Morse. New

York: Houghton Mifflin, 1914. Begins with Morse's first thoughts of telegraphic communication while aboard the packet ship *Sully*.

Silverman, Kenneth. *Lightning Man: The Accursed Life of Samuel F. B. Morse.* New York: Alfred A. Knopf, 2003. Meticulously researched biography portraying Morse as a restless, naïve dreamer, who, despite the success of his invention, believed he was a failure.

Vail, Alfred. *The American Electro Magnetic Telegraph.* Philadelphia: Lee and Blanchard, 1845. Reprint. *Eyewitness to Early American Telegraphy.* New York:

Arno Press, 1974. Explains the workings of the telegraph, illustrated with fully labeled diagrams.

SEE ALSO: Mathew B. Brady; Samuel Colt; Carolina Coronado; Joseph Henry; James Monroe.

RELATED ARTICLES in *Great Events from History: The Nineteenth Century, 1801-1900:* May 24, 1844: Morse Sends First Telegraph Message; October 24, 1861: Transcontinental Telegraph Is Completed; July 27, 1866: First Transatlantic Cable Is Completed; June, 1896: Marconi Patents the Wireless Telegraph.

WILLIAM THOMAS GREEN MORTON
American dentist and medical pioneer

In his discovery and development of the anesthetic uses of ether inhalation, Morton made one of the most important contributions to medicine of the nineteenth century. However, rival claims to the discovery produced one of the most acrimonious debates in the history of medicine.

BORN: August 9, 1819; Charlton, Massachusetts
DIED: July 15, 1868; New York, New York
AREA OF ACHIEVEMENT: Medicine

EARLY LIFE

William Thomas Green Morton was born to James Morton, a farmer of Scottish descent, and his wife, Rebecca Needham, a native of Charlton, Massachusetts. A sternly religious upbringing, a wholesome and plain family life, and a boyhood filled with farm tasks formed Morton's character. His father insisted on a proper education, enrolling him in several country academies from the age of twelve. The boy wanted to become a physician, but his hopes vanished when a business venture undertaken by his father failed.

In 1836, Morton moved to Boston, making a living as a clerk and salesperson for several firms. He hated the drudgery and crassness of business life, choosing a career in dentistry with the opening of the first American dental school, the Baltimore College of Dental Surgery, in 1840. One year later, he apprenticed himself to Horace Wells, a young dentist from Hartford, before establishing his own practice in Farmington, Connecticut. In 1842, he met Elizabeth Whitman, daughter of a prominent Farmington family. The Whitmans were disturbed by their daughter's interest in him, the owner of no prop-

erty and a dentist, dentists then being regarded as ignorant "tooth-pullers." Determined to marry, Morton convinced them that dentistry was a temporary occupation; he intended to become a physician. The marriage took place in May of 1844; the first of the Mortons' children, William James Morton, became an important neurologist and a pioneer in the use of X rays.

Morton was a tall, dark-haired, handsome man, neat and methodical, mild and agreeable in manner. He maintained his dignity and composure through the long years of the bitter ether controversy, never attempting to retaliate against his enemies despite the relentless attacks on his character.

LIFE'S WORK

Prior to his marriage, Morton had formed a partnership in Boston with Wells in order to exploit the development of a noncorrosive dental solder for attaching false teeth to plates. Artificial teeth were hinged monstrosities set over the roots of old teeth, leaving the face swollen, the solder coloring and corroding the teeth. The two young dentists devised enameled teeth that they attached with their new solder to a hingeless plate. To fit the plate snugly in the mouth, however, required the removal of the roots of the old teeth. No one would accept their innovations unless they found a means to overcome the extremely painful extractions.

By the end of 1843, the partnership failed for lack of patients. Wells returned to Hartford and Morton remained in Boston, both intent on succeeding in dentistry. During their development of the solder, they sought the advice of an expert chemist, Charles T. Jackson, a European-trained physician, chemist, and geologist. In 1844,

Morton became Jackson's private student, boarding in his house, first alone and then with his wife, hoping to prepare himself for entrance into Harvard Medical School.

During 1844-1845, his dental practice flourished, and his income enabled him to buy a farm in West Needham (modern Wellesley) near Boston. Morton became a specialist in prosthetic dentistry and prospered by his thoroughness and his skill in excavating and filling cavities.

During the summer of 1844, Morton discussed with Jackson the need to control pain. He had tried many pain remedies, but none was satisfactory. Jackson gave him a bottle of ether and urged him to try his "toothache drops" as a local painkiller for filling teeth. He also learned from Jackson that physicians used ether as an inhalant in treating respiratory ills, believing it to be a possible cure for tuberculosis and other lung diseases.

Morton used the ether drops, finding that he could remove tooth decay and fill cavities painlessly. He noticed that often the region near the tooth became numb and wondered whether ether had wider possibilities. Morton wanted to experiment with ether. What happens upon inhaling it? Was it dangerous? Might it be an effective painkiller for all aspects of dentistry, including the extraction of the stumps and roots of old teeth? He experimented with ether inhalation into 1846, using animals of all kinds, including his pet spaniel.

In August of 1846, Morton purchased a new supply of ether in Boston. His two apprentices submitted to ether inhalation but became excited rather than quieted. He sought Jackson's advice on September 30, careful not to tell him about his inhalation experiments but only about the problems he was having with different samples of ether. Jackson informed him that ether varied considerably in quality and that he must use only pure, highly rectified ether.

Events happened swiftly on September 30; obtaining the best-quality ether, Morton induced unconsciousness in himself for about seven minutes, recovering with no ill effects. On that same day, a patient, Eben Frost, came to him with a painful toothache. Morton persuaded him to have his tooth extracted under ether.

During the next two weeks, he successfully etherized about one hundred patients, developing an inhaler in the form of a glass globe that had two necks to allow both ether and air to be inhaled. Suddenly, his horizons widened beyond dentistry. A young surgeon, Henry Jacob Bigelow, appeared at his office, having become aware of his ether experiments and wanting to observe some painless tooth extractions. Through Bigelow, Morton

arranged a public demonstration at Massachusetts General Hospital on October 16, 1846. John Collins Warren, the preeminent surgeon in Boston and founder of Massachusetts General and of the *New England Journal of Medicine*, agreed to perform surgery on an etherized patient.

Warren removed a three-inch tumor from the neck of a young man, Gilbert Abbott, with Morton administering the inhalant. Before a large audience, the hitherto exceedingly painful operation proceeded smoothly, with no cry or struggle from Abbott, the first public demonstration that ether could prevent the pain of surgery. Anesthesia quickly became routine at Massachusetts General. (The Boston physician Oliver Wendell Holmes introduced the name "anesthesia" in November.) The very newness of the procedure caused concern, however, and the case records of etherized patients at the hospital never mentioned anesthesia; only after its general acceptance were the records altered to record that it had been used.

Prior to the surgical demonstration, Morton visited Richard M. Eddy, patent commissioner in Boston, to inquire whether his painless tooth extraction method could be patented. The visit reveals his determination to secure a monopoly; he planned to sell licenses for the use of ether and gain a royalty on the price of all inhalers. On October 21, Eddy informed him that the process was patentable but that Jackson should be included, because he had provided essential information. Jackson knew Eddy and convinced him that he had been essential to the discovery. Although Morton did not share their opinions, he agreed to an arrangement whereby Jackson received 10 percent of the profits, while turning over the responsibility of the patent to Morton. He received the patent on November 12.

Morton failed to appreciate the professional opposition to his scheme of licenses and royalties. Bigelow, in a hectic meeting, told him that he should give his discovery to the world for the relief of human suffering. Morton, however, believed that he had to control his procedure to prevent its misuse, granting licenses only to qualified people, and candidly admitted that he wanted to make a living from his discovery. He did convince Bigelow of his good intentions and expressed his willingness to surrender the patent if the government would take it over and reward him for the discovery.

Problems began immediately. Morton had just received a bill for one thousand inhalers when he learned that they were inferior to a simple bell-shaped sponge saturated with ether. The Massachusetts Medical Society protested the procedure because it was for private profit and a secret remedy. (Morton had disguised the nature of the agent by adding a red dye and calling it "Letheon.") He soon saw his hopes of controlling anesthesia and gaining a financial reward dashed. As physicians realized that the readily available ether was the active agent, there was no need to buy a patented preparation.

Morton may have been disappointed by the turn of events, but surgeons were not. Surgical anesthesia spread with unprecedented speed, far more rapidly than earlier innovations such as vaccination or later ones such as antisepsis. Bigelow was once again the key figure in alerting physicians to the discovery. His detailed report in the *Boston Medical and Surgical Journal* was the first in a professional journal, copies of which spread the news throughout the United States and Europe. Etherization was in use in American, English, and French hospitals by the year's end. By 1848, anesthetics were in use in dentistry, obstetrics, and therapeutics, as well as in surgery.

The ugliest aspect of the ether controversy was the dispute between Morton and Jackson. In mid-November of 1846, Jackson was claiming full credit for the discovery of anesthesia. He asserted that he had been experimenting with ether since 1841, had discovered its anesthetic properties, and had instructed Morton in how to use it in his dental practice and in how to seek a surgical demonstration. Jackson used his prestige and influence to press his case in both the popular press and professional journals and before such bodies as the American Academy of Arts and Sciences and the French Academy of Sciences.

For the remainder of his life, Morton had to face attacks on his character and ability, Jackson using Morton's faulty education and the fact that he was a mere dentist to make him out to be an unscrupulous profit-seeker and fraud. His life became exceedingly troubled. He lost his dental practice, and creditors demanded payments on loans; he was ruined financially. Supporters petitioned Congress to give adequate compensation for his discovery of anesthesia. During the 1850's, Congress introduced two bills appropriating $100,000, but active supporters of Jackson, Wells (who successfully used nitrous oxide for tooth extractions), and several other claimants prevented any appropriation. A direct appeal by Morton to President Franklin Pierce led to a promise of a reward, but the presidential promise proved worthless. With the coming of the Civil War, the cause was lost. During that war, Morton served with distinction as an anesthetist in field hospitals.

In 1868, Morton went to New York in an agitated state over a pro-Jackson article in the *Atlantic Monthly*, determined to defend himself with a reply. While there, he suffered a fatal stroke. Following his interment, Boston citizens donated a monument bearing a moving tribute to him as the inventor of anesthetic inhalation. In 1873, Jackson visited the site; still obsessed with Morton, he began to scream and flail wildly. He had to be restrained, and he remained confined to a mental institution until his death in 1880.

SIGNIFICANCE

Anesthesia is the greatest contribution of American science to nineteenth century medicine. Until 1846, all surgical operations were done without anesthesia: Patients were strapped or held down, struggling in agony over the cutting, speed being the prime requisite of surgeons. Anesthesia freed patients of pain, while giving surgeons the gift of time.

The ether controversy reflected the medical profession's disarray during the 1840's: full of disputes over causes and cures with no central authority to confer legitimacy to an innovation. In addition, Morton violated four norms of the medical profession. He patented his "Letheon," patented pain cures being synonymous with quackery. He indulged in promotional advertising. He was a dentist, dentists being regarded with mistrust as mere empirics. Last, he engaged in a bitter, unprofessional quarrel over priority that tarnished both the image of anesthesia among physicians and whatever reputation the disputants possessed.

Despite the violation of these taboos, Morton's discovery spread with remarkable speed, because the benefits of ether were so evident. It did prevent pain. Leading surgeons saw ether as primarily benevolent and humane; it relieved human suffering, hence its rapid, general acceptance.

—*Albert B. Costa*

FURTHER READING

Davis, Audrey B. "The Development of Anesthesia." *American Scientist* 70 (September/October, 1982): 522-528. A superb essay by a historian of science, relating the development of anesthesia to the context of nineteenth century surgery and dentistry.

Fülöp-Miller, René. *Triumph over Pain*. Translated by Eden Paul and Cedar Paul. New York: Literary Guild of America, 1938. A comprehensive study of the search for pain relief, focusing on the American discovery of anesthesia. Not a scholarly work, but absorbing reading.

Ludovici, L. J. *The Discovery of Anesthesia*. New York: Thomas Y. Crowell, 1962. A fine biography of Morton. More concerned with the personalities of the characters and why they behaved as they did than other works.

MacQuitty, Betty. *Victory over Pain: Morton's Discovery of Anaesthesia*. New York: Taplinger, 1971. A clear, dramatic story of Morton and his career set against life in pre-Civil War America. Well written, with an emphasis on Morton's struggle to secure recognition.

Pernick, Martin S. *A Calculus of Suffering: Pain, Professionalism, and Anesthesia in Nineteenth-Century America*. New York: Columbia University Press, 1985. A brilliant book. Pernick goes beyond a history of surgical anesthesia to consider how the medical profession confronted the discovery and the implications of anesthesia for society. Social history at its finest.

Wolfe, Richard J. *Tarnished Idol: William Thomas Green Morton and the Introduction of Surgical Anesthesia: A Chronicle of the Ether Controversy*. San Anselmo, Calif.: Norman, 2001. Meticulously researched revisionist biography of Morton. Wolfe acknowledges that Morton conducted the first successful public demonstration of anesthesia in 1946 but credits him with little else regarding the discovery of anesthesia. In Wolfe's opinion, Morton created a "sanitized and idealized" image of himself, when he was actually a man of "limited talent" and "many faults."

Woodward, Grace Steele. *The Man Who Conquered Pain: A Biography of William Thomas Green Morton*. Boston: Beacon Press, 1962. A vivid, elegantly written biography of Morton. Woodward's study was based on hitherto unavailable letters and other unpublished material of the Morton family. Very good at describing the medical atmosphere of early nineteenth century Boston.

SEE ALSO: Sir Humphry Davy; Oliver Wendell Holmes; William James; Joseph Lister; Franklin Pierce.

RELATED ARTICLES in *Great Events from History: The Nineteenth Century, 1801-1900:* October 16, 1846: Safe Surgical Anesthesia Is Demonstrated; November 4, 1854: Nightingale Takes Charge of Nursing in the Crimea.

LUCRETIA MOTT
American social reformer

An eloquent advocate of the abolition of slavery and of equality for women, Mott devoted her life to working toward those goals and made a fundamental contribution to the eventual winning of woman suffrage.

BORN: January 3, 1793; Nantucket, Massachusetts
DIED: November 11, 1880; near Philadelphia, Pennsylvania
ALSO KNOWN AS: Lucretia Coffin (birth name)
AREAS OF ACHIEVEMENT: Social reform, women's rights

EARLY LIFE

Lucretia Coffin was the daughter of the master of a whaling vessel. Her parents, Thomas and Anna Folger Coffin, were hardworking Quakers. Although public education was not available, Lucretia learned to read and write as a young child, probably attending Quaker schools. In 1804, Thomas Coffin, who had lost his ship, moved the family to Boston, where he became a successful merchant. Here the children could be educated, and when Lucretia showed particular talent, she was sent to Nine Partners Boarding School, a Quaker academy in southeastern New York. She became an academic success, met James Mott—her future husband—and got a lesson in discrimination when she discovered that James was paid five times as much as a woman with the same title at the school.

In 1809, the Coffin family moved to Philadelphia, and James Mott followed, taking a job in the family business. In 1811, James and Lucretia were married. They experienced several years of hard times because of the depression that followed the War of 1812, but eventually they settled in Philadelphia, where James established a successful business. Lucretia, despite having two small children, took a job teaching. Four more children followed, but Mott's son Thomas died in 1817. As the children began to spend time at school and her husband prospered, Mott had time to read many books, including Mary Wollstonecraft's *Vindication of the Rights of Women* (1792), which had a strong influence on her. Mott began to speak in Quaker meetings and during the early 1820's was approved as a Quaker minister.

LIFE'S WORK

For Lucretia Mott, faith was always important, and it led her to desire justice for all, including slaves and women. Although she always wanted to avoid controversy, when issues she cared about arose, she was often outspoken. During the early 1830's, she befriended William Lloyd Garrison, a leading abolitionist who founded the New England Anti-Slavery Society. When women's groups were called for, Mott helped found the Philadelphia Female Anti-Slavery Society and held some office for virtually every year of its existence. Mott was soon a leader in the Anti-Slavery Convention of American Women, and when its 1838 meeting was met by riots and arson in its meeting hall, it was the Mott home at which convention leaders reconvened.

Mott soon found equality an issue within the abolitionist movement. In 1838, the Massachusetts branch of the Anti-Slavery Society gave women the right to vote. A decision on the issue was blocked at a regional meeting, and a debate began at the 1839 national convention. After the five sessions adjourned without a decision, Garrison managed to get agreement that the organization's roll would include all persons, but a number of leading abolitionists were opposed, maintaining that the organization was being diverted from the issue of slavery.

In 1840, the British and Foreign Anti-Slavery Society issued invitations for a world convention, and Mott was elected as one of the American delegates. The British group had indicated that women were not wanted, and Mott arrived to find that the credentials of female delegates were not being honored. Despite an angry debate, the decision stood, and Mott had to sit in the visitors' gallery, where she was joined by Garrison and the other American delegates. Mott did not speak at the convention, preferring to defer to proper authority even when it was mistaken.

After the convention Mott traveled in Britain—it was her one trip abroad—and visited such luminaries as Harriet Martineau. In Scotland, it was suggested that she address the Glasgow Emancipation Society, but the directors demurred. The city's Unitarian Church, however, welcomed her, and she gave her address there. During this trip, she also began a friendship with Elizabeth Cady Stanton, with whom she would fight discrimination against women. The two were close until Mott's death in 1880.

Lucretia Mott. (Library of Congress)

Mott's attitude about slavery was quite clear: It was unmitigated evil and should be ended forthwith. She rejected any idea of compensation for slave owners as adding to the immorality, and she urged abolitionist groups to stop debating the ethical and philosophical implications of the institution—for her, these were settled anyway—and stick to the practical question of ending it. She argued for "free produce"—that is, refusing to conduct any trade in goods produced by slaves—but northern economic interests in southern goods and commerce were too large for such a boycott to win many friends even among abolitionists. In theory, she rejected colonization and even flight as solutions to slavery because the numbers who escaped did not even equal the natural increase of the enslaved population. In practice, however, she supported the Underground Railroad, freely opening her home to fugitives. She was an active supporter of many escapees, including Henry "Box" Brown, who had himself nailed into a packing box and shipped to her friend Miller McKim.

During the early years of the 1840's, Mott was often ill. Her husband, however, had become prosperous enough to give up his business so that the family could pursue other interests. The Mott home was known for its hospitality to its many guests, including Garrison, Theodore Parker, Frederick Douglass, and Sojourner Truth. As her health allowed, Mott continued her preaching, mostly at Quaker and Unitarian meetings. Having rejected orthodox Quaker theology in 1827, she faced charges of heresy as well as denunciations for daring, as a woman, to speak in church. Never ruffled, she spoke to hostile audiences—including slave owners—forthrightly and firmly.

Although she never gave up her work toward abolition, during the late 1840's Mott became more and more involved in the crusade for women's rights. In 1845, she made her first public call for woman suffrage in a speech to the Yearly Meeting of Ohio Quakers. Three years later, in an address to the American Anti-Slavery Society titled "The Law of Progress," she lamented the lack of improvement in the condition of women. It was after this speech that Mott fell in with a suggestion by Elizabeth Cady Stanton that there should be a women's rights convention.

The future stars of the women's movement, Stanton and Susan B. Anthony, were virtually unknown, so the much better known Mott emerged as the person in the public eye at the first Woman's Rights Convention, which met at Seneca Falls, New York, July 19 and 20, 1848. Mott and others drew up a Declaration of Sentiments modeled on the Declaration of Independence, but the women were so unsure of themselves that they asked James Mott to preside at their meeting. The convention then debated the declaration paragraph by paragraph, ultimately passing them all unanimously.

Mott had been somewhat reluctant to press the issue of suffrage, but, urged on by Stanton and Frederick Douglass, she agreed to it. In the end, she was the most frequent speaker at Seneca Falls. At a follow-up meeting two weeks later in Rochester, New York, she responded to critics who asserted that the women were ignoring St. Paul's injunction that they be subservient to their husbands by noting that most of the complainers had ignored the saint's advice not to marry. The 1853 convention met in Philadelphia only to be so disrupted by hostile demonstrations that Mott, the presiding officer, was forced to adjourn it. An invitation to move to Cleveland was accepted, and despite some tension, the meeting was completed without interruption.

Although she was beginning to experience some physical decline during the 1850's, Mott made many efforts on behalf of the abolitionist and women's rights

crusades. In 1849, she agreed to make a speech to counter the traditional misogynist position taken by Richard Henry Dana during a lecture series in Philadelphia. Her "Discourse on Women," tracing the history of women's achievements and reiterating her position that female inferiority was a function of systematic repression and denial of opportunity, was printed.

A second edition appeared in 1869 in response to requests from feminists in England. During the early 1850's, Mott confronted Horace Mann and the new National Education Association on the issue of equal pay for women teachers, though without much immediate success. She also continued to speak for the abolitionist cause, traveling as far south as Maysville, Kentucky, where, despite some significant hostility, she presented her case for freedom. Although she took no public position on John Brown's raid on Harpers Ferry—Quaker principles of pacifism overrode even the urgency of freeing slaves—she did shelter Mrs. Brown while she was trying to visit her husband in the weeks before his execution.

In 1857, the Mott family moved to Roadside, a comfortable estate between New York and Philadelphia. The move was intended in part to get Lucretia away from the stress of her numerous commitments. Although her health was somewhat restored by rest, she was sixty-four years old and beginning increasingly to feel her age. A pacifist, she was torn by the Civil War, but after the conflict she tried to preserve the antislavery society to support the freedmen. She was also active in the Free Religious Association, which had been formed in 1867 to encourage an end to sectarian strife. She also continued her activities with the Equal Rights Convention.

When that organization began to split during the 1870's, Mott tried vainly to heal the breach. The feminists divided into the National Woman Suffrage Association, led by Elizabeth Cady Stanton and Susan B. Anthony, and the American Woman Suffrage Association, headed by Lucy Stone and Julia Ward Howe. Mott remained with her longtime friends Stanton and Anthony but deeply regretted the split. Mott's activities decreased steadily throughout the late 1860's and 1870's. She died on November 11, 1880, at Roadside.

SIGNIFICANCE

Lucretia Mott was an unusual woman. In an age when most people objected to women ministers, she was an eloquent advocate for her faith. Not only did she speak effectively within Quaker meetings, but she also had the confidence to challenge the leadership on points of theology. Her preaching and erudition won the respect of many, although no woman in the first half of the nineteenth century could have achieved full acceptance in the pulpit. Believing that she was in the right, she was unruffled by criticism and continued to speak as she deemed appropriate.

Mott was less unusual in the ranks of the abolitionists, which included many women, white and black. Nevertheless, her dignified mien and public speaking ability gave her a leadership role. The strength of her conviction led her to take risks, speaking out during the 1830's when the antislavery position was far from popular and going into hostile areas—even the South. She fought diligently for her view that the antislavery forces should insist on total abolition immediately and should use the economic weapon of refusing to trade in products produced by slave labor. Although she was unsuccessful in winning support for the latter position, she provided the abolitionist movement with one of its best examples of idealism and principle.

Faced with serious sexual discrimination within the ranks of the abolitionists, Mott emerged as a champion of women's rights. At a time when most of the eventual champions of the feminist movement were young and unknown, Mott was a respected and respectable leader. If Elizabeth Cady Stanton and Susan B. Anthony, in 1848, could be dismissed as part of a radical fringe, Lucretia Mott could not. As a minister whose knowledge and conviction were well established and as a mainstay of the abolitionist movement, she gave the fledgling women's movement a credibility that would have taken much time and effort to gain without her leadership. She did not live to see the triumph of equal rights for women, but she did much to give the movement the impetus necessary to obtain them.

—*Fred R. van Hartesveldt*

FURTHER READING

Burnett, Constance. *Five for Freedom: Lucretia Mott, Elizabeth Cady Stanton, Lucy Stone, Susan B. Anthony, Carrie Chapman Catt.* Reprint. New York: Greenwood Press, 1968. Originally published in 1953, this is an effective and well-written biography that gives a thorough account of Mott's life and career.

Cromwell, Otelia. *Lucretia Mott.* Cambridge, Mass.: Harvard University Press, 1958. A scholarly, well-researched biography that sets Mott's life and activities in the context of nineteenth century America, this work is somewhat lacking in critical analysis of the subject.

Hallowell, Anna. *James and Lucretia Mott: Life and Letters.* 5th ed. Boston: Houghton Mifflin, 1896. An early biography made particularly valuable by the inclusion of correspondence. Overly supportive of the Motts.

Mott, Lucretia. *Lucretia Mott: Her Complete Speeches and Sermons.* Edited by Dana Greene. New York: Edwin Mellen Press, 1980. A convenient source of much of Mott's writing that provides an excellent means of gaining an understanding of her philosophy and ideas.

_____. *Selected Letters of Lucretia Coffin Mott.* Edited by Beverly Wilson Palmer, Holly Byers Ochoa, and Carol Faulkner. Urbana: University of Illinois Press, 2002. Contains a selection of Mott's letters written between 1813 and 1879, providing an understanding of her public and private lives. The letters are annotated, and a guide to the correspondence is published as an appendix.

Stewart, James B. *Holy Warriors: The Abolitionists and American Slavery.* New York: Hill & Wang, 1976. A useful survey of abolitionism that is extremely valuable in setting Mott's work and views in the context of the movement as a whole.

SEE ALSO: Susan B. Anthony; Amelia Bloomer; John Brown; Frederick Douglass; Lydia Folger Fowler; William Lloyd Garrison; Julia Ward Howe; Horace Mann; Harriet Martineau; Theodore Parker; Elizabeth Cady Stanton; Lucy Stone; Sojourner Truth.

RELATED ARTICLES in *Great Events from History: The Nineteenth Century, 1801-1900:* 1820's-1850's: Social Reform Movement; July 19-20, 1848: Seneca Falls Convention; May 28-29, 1851: Akron Woman's Rights Convention; May 10, 1866: Suffragists Protest the Fourteenth Amendment; December, 1869: Wyoming Gives Women the Vote; July 4, 1876: Declaration of the Rights of Women; February 17-18, 1890: Women's Rights Associations Unite.

MUḤAMMAD ʿALĪ PASHA
Governor of Egypt (1805-1848)

By applying strong-arm techniques so as to ensure central-government control, Muḥammad ʿAlī transformed Egypt from an ungovernable and unproductive province of the Ottoman Empire into a largely autonomous state supported by an impressive military apparatus. That was done by combining Ottoman "new order" reform priorities with European technical contributions, especially in the areas of military and agricultural modernization.

BORN: 1769; Kavala, Macedonia, Ottoman Empire (now in Greece)
DIED: August 2, 1849; Alexandria, Egypt
ALSO KNOWN AS: Mehmet Ali
AREA OF ACHIEVEMENT: Government and politics

EARLY LIFE

Although Muḥammad ʿAlī Pasha was born into a family that originated in Albania, it was in the Ottoman Turkish province of Macedonia (in modern Greece) that the first biographical information concerning him was recorded. His father's position as a ranking Ottoman bureaucrat serving the sultanate of Selim III (who ruled between 1789 and 1808) was significant for the future career of Muḥammad. One of Selim's main goals was to use loyal servants of the state to create, in the place of the by then severely inefficient Janissary corps and imperial administrative system, an army and government of "the new order" (*nizam-ul Cedid*). Without actually being members of the new order elite military unit that Selim had consciously copied from contemporary European models, both his father and the young Muḥammad were heavily influenced by the visible efficiency of new order Ottoman institutions.

When the sultan needed a capable lieutenant to accompany a force of irregular Albanian troops sent to reoccupy the Ottoman province of Egypt (after the retreat of Napoleon I's famous 1798-1802 expeditionary force on the Nile), he chose Muḥammad. The future governor of Egypt entered history in early adulthood, not as an Albanian and certainly not as an Egyptian, but as a loyal Ottoman military officer.

LIFE'S WORK

Muḥammad's rise to power as an Ottoman governor and then a virtually independent ruler of Egypt between 1805 and 1848 was tied to his ability to centralize (in typical Ottoman new order fashion) governmental control over military, bureaucratic, and economic functions. He began this process in Egypt by befriending rival local groups and playing each against the others. Then he gradually and systematically reduced each of his temporary allies to dependence on his sole will. In stages, for example, the army under the new governor's command ceased to be Albanian and was replaced by trainees under new order officer candidates selected by Muḥammad.

Some of those selected to take the place of Albanian irregulars and residual (pre-1798) *mamlūk* (foreign slave elite) military grandees were already Ottoman professionals. Others were retrained *mamlūks*. Any elements likely to resist Muḥammad's restructuring of the province's military forces were eliminated either by being reassigned (the case of Albanians sent to combat Wahhabi tribes in Arabia after 1811) or by being mercilessly killed (the fate of many *mamlūk* beys in 1811).

After he was in firm political and military control over Cairo's governorate, Muḥammad proceeded to introduce a series of major internal reforms that would help strengthen his position. First, Egypt's old *mamlūk*-dominated tax farm system (*iltizamat*) was replaced by a single tax (*ferda*) collected by direct salaried agents of the governor. Proceeds from taxes were used not only to expand and train the new military establishment (by bringing more professionals, including, after 1815, retired Napoleonic officers) but also to invest in publicly sponsored agricultural innovations. These included new irrigation canals engineered to increase productivity during the low Nile season and the introduction of new internationally marketable crops. The latter, especially silk and cotton, were brought under cultivation according to strictly controlled governmental terms.

By the early 1820's, the effectiveness of Muḥammad's authority as governor of Egypt was so obvious that his sultanic sovereign, Mahmud II, called on him (in 1826-1827) to send troops to help subdue Greek insurrectionists. Had this expedition been successful, Muḥammad might well have been named to the high imperial post of Ottoman grand vizier. Instead, the Concert of Europe powers, worried about Ottoman repression of the Greek independence movement but also seriously concerned about Muḥammad's dominant, monopolistic control over the conditions of cash-crop trade (especially cotton) in Egyptian ports, intervened militarily at Navarino in 1827 and forcibly removed him from the Ottoman theater. Sultan Mahmud was thus robbed of the possibility of having a grand vizier and military commander capable of reversing Istanbul's obvious decline.

The result was that Muḥammad redoubled his determination to make Egypt strong. State monopolistic controls over agricultural production methods and marketing were increased (in a specifically agricultural-labor code, or *ganun al filahah*, in 1829), and the army was expanded to include, for the first time, large numbers of Egyptian peasant recruits. In 1831, this army, under the command of Muḥammad's son Ibrahim, seized control of Mahmud's Syrian province, including the key Levant trade subzones of Lebanon and Palestine. Egypt's governor then extended to Syria the same iron-handed controls over taxes, agricultural production, and trade that applied in Egypt, creating a sort of mini-empire, this time at Mahmud's expense.

For eight years, Muḥammad and Ibrahim reigned supreme over this expanded Arab state of Egypt, Greater Syria, and the Red Sea coast province of Arabia. By 1839, it was clear that the European powers that had intervened at Navarino in 1827 were determined that an

Muḥammad ʿAlī Pasha. (Library of Congress)

even greater show of force against Muḥammad might be necessary. When the Battle of Nezib occurred in June, 1839, the Ottomans were so soundly defeated that Mahmud's successor Abulmecid might well have been removed by Muḥammad. Such a development would have made it possible to put the revolutionary reform methods of the latter in place throughout the Ottoman Empire. To avoid this, the London Convention of 1840 produced an international ultimatum to Muḥammad: either withdraw to a hereditarily guaranteed Egyptian governorate and abandon commercial monopolies over the Levant zone as a whole or confront a joint European force.

Muḥammad's decision to save his Egyptian governorate (which eventually became the hereditary possession of his family, a situation that ended only with the overthrow of King Faruk in 1952) saved him from a nearly certain military disaster in 1840. The terms that the Ottoman sultan imposed on Cairo during the last eight years of his rule, however, made it clear that the new order principles that had built Muḥammad's power would not survive long. Egypt's cotton monopoly was dismantled and its army cut back to a mere eighteen thousand men. By the time of his death in 1849, Muḥammad had begun to rely on practices of ruling patronage (private land grants for privileged political supporters and members of the ruling family, decentralization of taxation with benefits for privileged elements, and the like) that would characterize Egypt's decline and eventual chaotic drift toward foreign colonial domination in the third quarter of the nineteenth century.

SIGNIFICANCE

Muḥammad ʿAlī Pasha's governorate in Egypt represented a successful application of Ottoman imperial new order reform priorities to a single regional province. After the old forms of inefficient military and fiscal organization were removed and restored state authority became unchallenged, the productive potential of Egypt became very promising. Because of what proved to be possible in Egypt under the right conditions, future prospects for the eastern Mediterranean basin as a whole took on new importance. From a position of relative unimportance until 1798, Egypt emerged in the brief span of twenty years, between

1820 and 1840, to occupy a key position of international strategic importance that it would hold throughout the nineteenth and into the twentieth century.

Muḥammad's strongly autocratic reforms may have been necessary to ensure the maintenance of order and expanded productivity in the local context of the Egyptian province. When they were expanded beyond this local context, however, it became apparent that parties who were accustomed to the Ottoman status quo prior to 1798, especially where open trade in Levantine agricultural and transit trade products were concerned, were not keen to see other areas of the empire fall under Muḥammad's control.

The effects of Muḥammad's expanded governorate over Syria and Lebanon proved to be controversial, both for the interests of internal social and economic subgroups (especially the Maronite Christians) and, ultimately, for the foreign powers who drafted the 1840 London Convention on the "Egyptian crisis." After the latter decided to intervene to reverse Muḥammad's gains, a pattern was set for the future intermingling of foreign imperial priorities and vested (if not to say reactionary) local interest groups leery of centrally imposed government reform priorities.

—*Byron D. Cannon*

FURTHER READING

Abdel-Rahim Mustafa, Ahmed. "The Breakdown of the Monopoly System in Egypt After 1840." In *Political and Social Change in Modern Egypt*, edited by Peter M. Holt. New York: Oxford University Press, 1968. Deals specifically with the internal and international consequences of the Concert of Europe's decision, in 1840, to force free market conditions on Muḥammad's governorate. Particularly useful for its discussion of the terms of the Anglo-Ottoman Commercial Treaty of 1838, which became after 1840 the basis for European dealings, not only in cotton but also in other agricultural products that Muḥammad's monopoly system had defined as the basis of a nationalistic (or protectionist) economy for the Egyptian province as early as the 1820's.

Baer, Gabriel. *A History of Landownership in Modern Egypt, 1800-1950*. New York: Oxford University Press, 1962. Baer's study contains perhaps the best-documented examination of the Muḥammad decentralized tax farm (*iltizam*) system and its linkages with land ownership and patterns of cultivation. The chapter on Muḥammad's reforms examines his success not only in boosting administrative efficiency by replacing the *iltizams* but also in the effect such changes had on agricultural productivity.

Daly, M. W., ed. *Modern Egypt from 1517 to the End of the Twentieth Century*. Vol. 2 in *The Cambridge History of Egypt*. New York: Cambridge University Press, 1998. Chapter 6, written by Khaled Fahmy (see below), chronicles the events and significance of Muḥammad's governorate.

Dobrowolska, Agnieszka, and Khaled Fahmy. *Muḥammad ʿAlī Pasha and His Sabil*. Cairo: American University in Cairo Press, 2005. After his son, Tusun, died in 1816, Muḥammad commemorated his son by constructing a *sabil* (public cistern and water dispenser) in Cairo. This book describes how the *sabil* was built, used, changed, and restored over time, and provides information about Muḥammad's life and personality.

Fahmy, Khaled. *All the Pasha's Men: Mehmed Ali, His Army, and the Making of Modern Egypt*. New York: Cambridge University Press, 1997. Examines Muḥammad's military reforms and recruitment policies. Fahmy counters historians who maintain Muḥammad's military and economic reforms sought to create an independent Egyptian state; he argues Muḥammad wanted to establish hereditary rule of an Egyptian province within the Ottoman Empire.

Holt, Peter M. *Egypt and the Fertile Crescent, 1516-1922*. Ithaca, N.Y.: Cornell University Press, 1966. Deals with the general history of Egypt and its relations with surrounding Ottoman provinces. Contains a chapter on Muḥammad's governorate in part 3: "The Last Phase of Ottoman Rule." Because both Syria and Lebanon are part of Holt's general history, this book makes it possible to place the phenomenon of the Egyptian occupation of 1831-1841 in a comparative historical context.

Hunter, F. Robert. *Egypt Under the Khedives, 1805-1879*. Pittsburgh: University of Pittsburgh Press, 1984. Part 1 of this book is devoted to a concentrated analysis of Muḥammad's reign, which the author characterizes as "the emergence of the new power state." In addition to its concise synopsis of Muḥammad's governorate, this work contains the most comprehensive coverage, in one book, of the reigns of his immediate successors, Abbās the Great, Saʿīd Pasha, and Ismāʿīl Pasha. The study of these successors is needed to gauge the long-term effects, both positive and negative, of what Muḥammad had accomplished, both in the area of political institutions and in their supporting social and economic structures.

Sayyid-Marsot, Afaf Lutfi. *Egypt in the Reign of Mu-hammad Ali*. New York: Cambridge University Press, 1984. Deals not only with the close circles of elites, both Egyptian and foreign, who had a hand in the construction of Muḥammad's state system but also with the measurable effects of the changes that he introduced. Very valuable, for example, for its investigation of the industrial and commercial sectors of

Egypt's economy under Muḥammad, which complemented developmental efforts in agriculture.

SEE ALSO: Muḥammad ʿAbduh; Napoleon I.
RELATED ARTICLES in *Great Events from History: The Nineteenth Century, 1801-1900:* 19th century: Arabic Literary Renaissance; September 13, 1882: Battle of Tel el Kebir.

JOHN MUIR
Scottish-born American naturalist

Combining his skills as a scientist, explorer, and writer, Muir played a significant role in the conservation movement and in the development of the United States National Park system and left a legacy that has kept his name honored in the twenty-first century.

BORN: April 21, 1838; Dunbar, Scotland
DIED: December 24, 1914; Los Angeles, California
AREAS OF ACHIEVEMENT: Exploration, geography

EARLY LIFE
John Muir (mewr) was the eldest of three sons and the third of eight children of Ann Gilrye Muir and Daniel Muir. His father grew up under the harshest poverty imaginable but eventually gained stature as a middle-class grain merchant and became a Presbyterian of severe Fundamentalist religious beliefs. He worshiped a God of wrath who found evil in almost every childish activity. Typically, John and his playmates would leave the yard, and his tyrannical father would fly into a rage and punish the innocent lad. When his father did not have the total devotion of his entire family, he would punish them with the greatest severity.

In 1849, at the age of eleven, John and his family immigrated to the United States in search of greater economic opportunity. The Muirs moved to Portage, Wisconsin, an area that had a fine reputation for wheat growing, where they purchased farmland. John marveled at the beauty of the countryside. He kept busy with farm chores and read at night when he was thought to be asleep. He also developed an early love of machinery and began the practice of waking at one in the morning to go to his cellar workshop to build things out of scraps of wood and iron. His father considered his inventions a waste of time, but John built a sawmill, weather instru-

ments, waterwheels, and clocks. In 1860, at the age of twenty-two, he displayed his inventions at the state fair in Madison. His gadgets were well received, but his dour father only lectured him on the sin of vanity.

At this juncture in his life, John decided to leave home to make his own way. First, he moved to nearby Madison and attended the University of Wisconsin. He followed no particular course of study; he took classes that interested him. He seemed more concerned with learning than with earning a degree. Muir excelled in the sciences and also enjoyed the outdoor laboratory of nature. A tall, disheveled, bearded man with penetrating, glacial-blue eyes, Muir eventually grew tired of the regimentation of college. He liked books, but he loved experience more. Some men from the university were leaving to fight in the Civil War. Muir was twenty-five years old and in his junior year of school, but he decided to leave also.

From Madison, he journeyed into Canada to take odd jobs and to study the botany of the area. Later, he turned up in Indianapolis, Indiana, working in a carriage shop. With his inventive mind, he proved a success in the factory environment until one day he suffered an eye injury while working on a machine. The puncture wound affected both eyes, and soon he lost his eyesight. After a month of convalescence in a darkened room, his vision slowly returned. With a new lease on life and his eyesight fully restored, Muir decided to abandon the factory world and enjoy nature.

LIFE'S WORK
In September of 1867, Muir began a walking tour that would take him from Louisville, Kentucky, to the Gulf Coast of Florida. He found the wildlife and plants of the South fascinating. His travels took him through Kentucky, Tennessee, Georgia, and Florida, until he reached

the Gulf at Cedar Key. He had no particular route planned, other than to head south. He was not disappointed in what he found on his four-month trek and decided to continue his journey. He had often read the exciting travel accounts of Alexander von Humboldt, who had explored widely in South America. Such exploration was Muir's dream also, but it was interrupted by a three-month bout with malaria. When he was almost recovered, he set off for Cuba, but, upon reaching that tropical island and after waiting for a southbound ship for a month, he settled on a new destination.

Muir believed that California offered the best climate for his malarial disorder and also afforded an environment of substantial botanical interest. He made the long journey to the West and settled in beautiful Yosemite Valley, which was snuggled in the Sierra Nevada. At times, he worked as a sheepherder and at a lumber mill, but he spent most of the time exploring the beautiful countryside, taking notes of his findings, and looking for one more glorious site of the wondrous Sierra. In 1869, Muir and a friend built a one-room cabin of pine logs near Yosemite Falls, and this became his home. He had famous visitors such as Asa Gray, the Harvard botanist, the novelist Therese Yelverton, and the renowned Transcen-

John Muir. (Library of Congress)

dentalist Ralph Waldo Emerson. With all, he shared the exhilarating scenes of the high country.

After four years in Yosemite Valley, Muir moved to San Francisco and dreamed of other trips. He traveled up the coast to Oregon and Washington and climbed Mount Shasta and Mount Rainier. He also made six excursions to Alaska, where he climbed mountains and studied glaciers. His favorite area was Glacier Bay in southern Alaska, but he loved any place where he could find a mountain to climb. During his stay in Alaska, he also studied the customs of the Tlingit Indians.

Muir also found time for romance. A friend introduced him to Louisa Strentzel, daughter of horticulturalist Dr. John Strentzel and owner of a large fruit ranch east of San Francisco, near the town of Martinez. Louisa and John were married on April 14, 1880. At the same time, he became the overseer of the Strentzel ranch and introduced changes that brought production to peak efficiency. Muir grafted one hundred varieties of pears and grapes onto the best strains. His effective management of the ranch provided him with economic security. For the next ten years, he neglected his writing and mountain climbing, but he and his wife grew reasonably prosperous and reared their two daughters, Wanda and Helen.

Nine years after his marriage, Muir took an important trip back to Yosemite. With him was Robert Underwood Johnson, an old friend and editor of the influential *The Century*. The two were dumbfounded by the changes that had taken place in the Sierra during such a short time. Sheep and lumberjacks had created great devastation in the valley and high country. Forest land was bare, and grass root structures were severely damaged by the sharp hoofs of the sheep. Johnson was moved to action. He promised to lobby influential congressmen, and he encouraged Muir to convince the American public of their conservationist cause and the need to take action before it was too late. Muir accepted the challenge and, in two well-argued articles published in *The Century*, he convinced many readers of the desperate need to preserve some of the natural wonders of the California highlands.

In 1890, the federal government rewarded the efforts of Muir, Johnson, and other conservationists by creating Yosemite National Park. Other victories followed when Congress established Mount Rainier, the Grand Canyon, the Petrified Forest, and parts of the Sierra as national preserves. The following year, Muir worked for the passage of legislation that eventually allowed President Benjamin Harrison to set aside thirteen million acres of forest land and President Grover Cleveland, twenty-one mil-

HETCH HETCHY VALLEY

It is generally recognized that California's Yosemite Valley is one of the most scenically beautiful places in the world. Less well known is the fact that a nearby second valley, Hetch Hetchy, rivaled Yosemite in natural beauty and geological splendors until its river was dammed and the valley was flooded during the early twentieth century. Here, John Muir describes the wonders of Hetch Hetchy before it was destroyed.

Yosemite is so wonderful that we are apt to regard it as an exceptional creation, the only valley of its kind in the world; but Nature is not so poor as to have only one of anything. Several other yosemites have been discovered in the Sierra that occupy the same relative positions on the Range and were formed by the same forces in the same kind of granite. One of these, the Hetch Hetchy Valley, is in the Yosemite National Park about twenty miles from Yosemite and is easily accessible to all sorts of travelers by a road and trail that leaves the Big Oak Flat road at Bronson Meadows a few miles below Crane Flat, and to mountaineers by way of Yosemite Creek basin and the head of the middle fork of the Tuolumne.

It is said to have been discovered by Joseph Screech, a hunter, in 1850, a year before the discovery of the great Yosemite. After my first visit to it in the autumn of 1871, I have always called it the "Tuolumne Yosemite," for it is a wonderfully exact counterpart of the Merced Yosemite, not only in its sublime rocks and waterfalls but in the gardens, groves and meadows of its flowery park-like floor. The floor of Yosemite is about 4000 feet above the sea; the Hetch Hetchy floor about 3700 feet. And as the Merced River flows through Yosemite, so does the Tuolumne through Hetch Hetchy. The walls of both are of gray granite, rise abruptly from the floor, are sculptured in the same style and in both every rock is a glacier monument.

Standing boldly out from the south wall is a strikingly picturesque rock called by the Indians, Kolana, the outermost of a group 2300 feet high, corresponding with the Cathedral Rocks of Yosemite both in relative position and form. On the opposite side of the Valley, facing Kolana, there is a counterpart of the El Capitan that rises sheer and plain to a height of 1800 feet, and over its massive brow flows a stream which makes the most graceful fall I have ever seen. . . .

So fine a fall might well seem sufficient to glorify any valley; but here, as in Yosemite, Nature seems in nowise moderate, for a short distance to the eastward of Tueeulala booms and thunders the great Hetch Hetchy Fall, Wapama, so near that you have both of them in full view from the same standpoint.

Source: John Muir, *The Yosemite* (New York: Century, 1912), chapter 16.

(1911), *The Yosemite* (1912), and *The Story of My Boyhood and Youth* (1913). In these works, he richly illustrated the growth of a conservationist mind and presented forceful arguments for preservation and ecological protection.

In his last years, Muir traveled to Europe, South America, and Africa, always learning and experiencing what he could. Seventy-six years of life and accomplishment came to an end in December of 1914, when Muir died in Los Angeles on Christmas Eve.

SIGNIFICANCE

For John Muir, it had been a full life. Forced to make a decision at an early age between machines and inventions on one hand and nature and conservation on the other, he chose the path of mountains, flowers, and preservation. In nature, he found his cathedral, and there he preached the gospel of conservation, preservation, and ecology. He walked the wilderness paths with Ralph Waldo Emerson and Theodore Roosevelt; in the end, he convinced many of his contemporaries of the rightness of his ideas.

Muir lived at a time when the United States was becoming a great industrial leader in the world. Nevertheless, he was able to point to the wisdom of preserving many natural wonders of the American West. Although an earlier generation had plundered the East, his efforts and those of others helped to save significant portions of the West, to create

lion acres more. Muir continued the conservationist cause by helping to create the Sierra Club in 1892. He became the club's first president, and the members vowed to preserve the natural features of the California mountains.

With the total support of his wife, Muir decided to abandon the ranch work and concentrate on furthering his writing career. In 1894, he published *The Mountains of California* and followed it with *Our National Parks* (1901), *Stickeen* (1909), *My First Summer in the Sierra* large national parks and forest preserves, and to protect the ecological systems so necessary for the survival of nature.

—*John W. Bailey*

FURTHER READING

Badè, William Frederic. *The Life and Letters of John Muir*. 2 vols. New York: Houghton Mifflin, 1924. The best collection of Muir's letters.

Ehrlich, Gretel. *John Muir: Nature's Visionary*. Washington, D.C.: National Geographic Society, 2000. Insightful biography, containing many quotations from Muir's unpublished journals and his other writings. Well illustrated with landscape photographs.

Fox, Stephen R. *John Muir and His Legacy: The American Conservation Movement*. Boston: Little, Brown, 1981. This is a biography of Muir, a chronological history of the conservation movement from 1890 to 1975, and an analysis of what conservation means in historical terms.

Melham, Tom. *John Muir's Wild America*. Washington, D.C.: National Geographic Society, 1976. A good place to begin the study of Muir. Beautiful illustrations and sound background history.

Nash, Roderick. *Wilderness and the American Mind*. New Haven, Conn.: Yale University Press, 1967. This work traces the idea of wilderness from an early view as a moral and physical wasteland to its present acceptance as a place to preserve. John Muir emerges as one of many significant figures in this intellectual transformation.

Smith, Herbert F. *John Muir*. New York: Twayne, 1964. Approaches Muir through his writings as literary works and places him in the context of Transcendentalist literature.

Turner, Frederick. *Rediscovering America: John Muir in His Time and Ours*. New York: Viking Press, 1985. A good, sound coverage of Muir's life in the context of his times and the development of the United States.

Williams, Dennis C. *God's Wilds: John Muir's Vision of Nature*. College Station: Texas A&M University Press, 2002. Examines Muir's views of nature, morality, and conservation, locating their source in his nineteenth century Calvinist upbringing.

Wolfe, Linnie Marsh. *Son of the Wilderness: The Life of John Muir*. New York: Alfred A. Knopf, 1945. Reprint. Madison: University of Wisconsin Press, 2003. A well-written biography based on solid research that shows the many-faceted dimensions of Muir's personality.

SEE ALSO: Grover Cleveland; Ralph Waldo Emerson; Asa Gray; Benjamin Harrison; Ferdinand Vandeveer Hayden; Alexander von Humboldt.

RELATED ARTICLE in *Great Events from History: The Nineteenth Century, 1801-1900:* March 1, 1872: Yellowstone Becomes the First U.S. National Park.

MODEST MUSSORGSKY
Russian composer

A major figure in the Russian national school, Mussorgsky was the most original composer among the so-called Mighty Five. He excelled in creating dramatic works and songs in which natural speech inflections determined the vocal line, thus creating a striking realism, or naturalism.

BORN: March 21, 1839; Karevo, Pskov, Russia
DIED: March 28, 1881; St. Petersburg, Russia
ALSO KNOWN AS: Modest Petrovich Mussorgsky (full name)
AREA OF ACHIEVEMENT: Music

EARLY LIFE

Modest Petrovitch Mussorgsky (mew-SORG-skee) was descended from wealthy landowners. His father, Peter, and his mother, Julia Chirikova, had four sons. The first two died in infancy; the third, Filaret, survived the youngest, Modest, by some twenty years. Much of what is known about the composer's early years is drawn from some drafts (one in Russian, two in poor French) that he wrote himself and from the scattered recollections of his brother. Mussorgsky's familiarity with Russian folklore is attributed to the family nurse, while his skill at the piano is credited to the lessons he took from his mother and, during the period 1849-1854, from Anton Herke in St. Petersburg. Mussorgsky, according to his own account, was able to play some small pieces by Franz Liszt by age seven and a concerto by John Field at the age of eleven.

In August, 1849, Modest and Filaret were taken by their father to St. Petersburg. There, Modest entered a preparatory school while studying with Herke; in 1852, he followed Filaret to the School for Cadets of the Guard. In this environment, the embryonic military man was exposed to a life of drinking, gambling, dancing, and debauchery. Although serious study was not a highly prized virtue at the institution, Mussorgsky seems to have taken an interest in history and German philosophy. His musical inclinations resulted in the dedication of a piano piece, *Porte-Enseigne Polka*, to his fellow students; it was published at the expense of his proud father, who died in 1853. Mussorgsky participated in the school choir and made a cursory study of old Russian church music, including some of the works of Dmitri Bortnyanski, though he did little composition.

In 1857, however, a year after leaving the cadet school, he met Aleksandr Dargomyzhski and César Cui; through them, he became acquainted with Stasov and Mily Alekseyevich Balakirev. At musical gatherings of these men and other artists, Mussorgsky was exposed to the music of such luminaries as Hector Berlioz, Franz Liszt, Robert Schumann, and Mikhail Ivanovich Glinka, much of it performed on the piano. He then sought Balakirev as a teacher of composition. Shortly thereafter, he resigned his commission. Under Balakirev's guidance, the youthful creator produced various early pieces, some of which were later lost.

Nervous disorders, at least in part attributed to excessive drinking, appeared as early as 1858. A visit to the estate of family friends near Moscow in 1859 for a rest resulted in a turn from a cosmopolitan outlook to a Russian orientation. On January 23, 1860, Anton Rubinstein conducted the orchestral version of Scherzo in B-flat major, thus marking Mussorgsky's public debut as a composer. Another nervous crisis ensued, but after spending the summer at the estate of friends, the composer pronounced himself cured of the "mysticism" with which he had been afflicted.

LIFE'S WORK

In 1861, an imperial decree declared the emancipation of the serfs, and Mussorgsky was immediately enmeshed in family difficulties associated with the change in the social order. Over the next two years, he was obliged to spend considerable time aiding his brother in managing the family estate. Mussorgsky, however, was not musically inactive during this period. The *Intermezzo in modo classico* (1860-1861) for piano and such songs as "Tsar Saul" (1863) manifest a musical maturity. The opera *Judith* by composer-critic Aleksandr Serov, performed on May 28, 1863, and a reading of Gustave Flaubert's *Salammbô* (1862) that autumn, impelled the composer to to write a libretto based on *Salammbô*. Mussorgsky's mélange of verse, with liberal borrowings from Russian poets and from Heinrich Heine, took its stage directions from Flaubert's work. The accompanying music, which occupied his attention until 1866, contains borrowings from his earlier piece *Oedipus in Athens*, and some portions of *Boris Godunov* are prefigured.

In December of 1863, as a consequence of a major downturn in his financial status, Mussorgsky took a position as collegiate secretary in the engineering department of the Ministry of Communications, and, on February 1, 1864, he was elevated to the post of assistant head clerk in the barracks section of the same department. In December, 1866, Mussorgsky was made titular councilor, but, on May 10, 1867, he was fired. In late 1863, the composer joined a commune with five other young men, lived together with them in a flat, and engaged in discussions on life and art.

The group was strongly influenced by the novel *Chto delat'?* (1863; *What Is to Be Done?*, c. 1863), by Nikolay Chernyshevsky, written during the author's imprisonment in the fortress of St. Petersburg. The burning issue with which Mussorgsky wrestled from this point onward was the subordination of art to life, as proposed by Chernyshevsky. Musical works that exemplify this turn in his creative thinking are the two-piece *From Memories of Childhood* and *Rêverie* (both compositions dating from 1865). That year was, indeed, a pivotal one. Following his mother's death, Mussorgsky's alcoholism became so serious that a case of delirium tremens caused the severing of his ties with communal life. His recovery at his brother's flat allowed him to resume work, but the seeds of destruction were sown.

Salammbô was abandoned, probably because Mussorgsky had come to grips with his technical deficiencies and his lack of empathy, at the time, for the Eastern coloration the work demanded; however, in January, 1867, *The Destruction of Sennacherib* for chorus and orchestra was completed, and, late in 1866, such songs as "Darling Savishna," "You Drunken Sot," and "The Seminarist" flowed from his pen. Naturalism and irony were by then mainstays of the composer's vision, and, as he provided his own texts to each of these three efforts, there is a distinctly personal level embodied therein. A modest degree of recognition was bestowed on the beleaguered artist when, with the earlier "Tell Me Why" (1858), "Darling Savishna" and "Hopak" were published in 1867, Mussorgsky's first creative efforts to appear in print since the youthful *Porte-Enseigne Polka*.

In 1866, Mussorgsky, who had for some years been interested in Nikolai Gogol's tale "St. John's Eve" even to the point of considering it for an opera, wrote a piece based on the tale as a tone poem for orchestra. This work became *Night on Bare Mountain* (popularized in the film classic *Fantasia*, 1940). The unusual tonalities, intentionally "foul and barbarous," disturbed the sensibilities of his more conventional contemporaries, and the work was never performed in Mussorgsky's lifetime. During this same period, an orchestral setting of the *Intermezzo in modo classico* (with an added trio) and an unfinished tone poem inspired by the Pan-Slav Congress, *King Poděbrad of Bohemia*, give witness to the several directions in which Mussorgsky was moving.

After a hiatus of several years, Mussorgsky returned to the Dargomyzhski circle at a time when "Dargo" was working on *The Stone Guest*, based on Aleksander Pushkin's play. By this time, he was officially a member of what Vladimir Stasov called "The Mighty Handful," known familiarly as "The Five." He also rejoined the ranks of the employed by accepting an appointment as assistant head clerk in the forestry department in the Ministry of Imperial Domains. Early in 1868, he busied himself with song composition, composing "The Orphan" and "Eremushka's Lullaby." In June of 1868, he set the first act of Gogol's comedy *The Marriage*, and a few months later he commenced composition on *Boris Godunov*, based in part on a play by Pushkin, and with a libretto fashioned by the composer.

Unlike the usual fits and starts that accompanied many of his large-scale works, Mussorgsky's energy and intensity were such that *Boris Godunov* was completed by December 15, 1869. Although Dargomyzhski died on January 5 of that year, his influence is notable. The Imperial Theatre rejected *Boris Godunov* for its "extraordinary modernism": The piece departed from custom and operatic tradition; for example, it lacked a major female character. Undeterred, Mussorgsky set about to revise by excising politically objectionable material and by adding two "Polish Scenes" that included a female character, Marina, and a closing "Revolutionary Scene." Individual portions, such as the "Coronation Scene" and the "Polonaise," received favorable receptions, but the Committee of the Theater remained implacable in their shortsightedness.

On February 17, 1873, Eduard Nápravník directed the "Inn Scene" and the "Polish Act" at the Marinsky Theatre. Cui reported that the ovations were unprecedented. A full production was finally mounted on February 8, 1874, with Nápravník again on the podium. Although the public was enthusiastic (Mussorgsky took some thirty curtain calls), the critics were, for the most part, unmoved. The composer could take solace in that the public had at last recognized his immense talent. The realism and the intensity of the drama struck a nerve in the audience of the time that set into motion a new way of thinking about opera.

While *Boris Godunov*'s travails occupied several years of his lifetime, Mussorgsky, nevertheless, busied himself with other grand projects. During much of 1873 and 1875-1876, he devoted his attention to *Khovanshchina*, another historical opera; sustained periods of heavy drinking prevented uninterrupted work, however, and his last efforts on this work date from 1880. Nikolay Rimsky-Korsakov completed the work in 1886.

During the summer of 1873, Mussorgsky began to share living quarters with a distant relative, the amateur poet Count Arseny Golenishchev-Kutuzov. The latter provided the texts to two song cycles, *Sunless* (1874) and *Songs and Dances of Death* (1875-1877). The six *Sunless* songs, reflecting a morbid text, contain much of Mussorgsky's characteristic melodic recitative, but with increased attention to subtle shadings in harmony reflective of changes in mood. The piano is used in a most original manner to evoke or to suggest the appropriate atmosphere.

In the *Songs and Dances of Death*, there emerges a series of vividly painted dramas in cameo. The vocal declamation, now at a level of perfection, is blended with a melodic line that grips and sustains the listener's attention. Golenishchev-Kutuzov provided the texts for two more individual songs, "Forgotten" (1874) and "The Vision" (1877). Mussorgsky wrote the texts to his remaining songs, "Epitaph" (1874), "The Nettle Mountain" (1874), and "Sphinx" (1875); only the latter was actually completed.

Stasov, who was growing increasingly alarmed at Mussorgsky's dementia, encouraged the latter to visit Liszt, who had made known his admiration for *The Nursery*, a song cycle published in 1872. Mussorgsky declined; instead, he devoted his energy both to composition and to his civil service position. In June of 1874, he created the piano suite *Pictures from an Exhibition*, inspired by the architectural drawings and paintings of his friend Victor Hartmann, who had died only the year before. The musical depiction of such drawings as *The Gnome, The Old Castle, The Hut of Baba-Yaga*, and the concluding *Great Gate at Kiev*, unified by a recurring "Promenade" theme, include bold and unconventional harmonies that unsympathetic critics referred to as "crude" and "barbaric."

Mussorgsky and Glinka's sister were involved in the jubilee celebrations for Osip Petrov, the bass whose role of Varlaam in *Boris Godunov* set the standard for others to follow; during this general time frame (spring, 1876), the composer returned to a projected comic opera based on Gogol's "Sorochintsy Fair," which he had begun two years earlier. By 1878, he had abandoned the work once again. Another regression in his battle with the bottle caused Stasov to intercede with the state controller for the purpose of transferring Mussorgsky to his own control department. As the state controller was a devotee of folk songs and an admirer of "The Five," he complied willingly with the entreaty; furthermore, he gave Mussorgsky permission to take a three-month leave in order to accompany the contralto Darya Leonova on a concert tour through central Russia and the Crimea. Delighting in the scenery, Mussorgsky composed some pleasant but inconsequential piano pieces and the popular "Song of the Flea."

In November, 1879, Rimsky-Korsakov conducted excerpts from *Khovanshchina* in St. Petersburg. As the new year began, however, Mussorgsky was relieved of his duties in the Control Department. Friends came to his rescue by providing funds, with the stipulation that he complete *Khovanshchina* and *Sorochintsy Fair*. Neither composition was completed. Leonova provided him with employment as her accompanist and as a teacher of theory and arranger of duos, trios, and quartets for use by students in her singing school. At her summer residence at Oranienbaum, Mussorgsky conceived a plan for a suite for orchestra with harp and piano based on motives from folk tunes he had collected on his tours.

On February 15, 1881, Mussorgsky received the applause of the audience at a performance of *The Destruction of Sennacherib* given by Rimsky-Korsakov at the Free School of Music. Only eight days later, he suffered an apparent stroke on a visit to Leonova, and, on the following day, he was taken unconscious to the Nikolaevsky Military Hospital. Periods of lucidity enabled the noted portrait painter, Ilya Repin, to produce, in four sittings, the most frequently reproduced painting of the unruly genius; in it, he appears haggard and disheveled. According to Repin, a misguided attendant gave Mussorgsky a bottle of brandy to help celebrate his impending birthday. Craving the alcohol, Mussorgsky disobeyed doctor's orders and, at five in the morning on March 28, 1881, he died.

SIGNIFICANCE

In his last year of life, Mussorgsky provided a statement of his artistic principles: "Art is a means of communicating with people, not an aim in itself." Only artist-reformers, he stated, such as Giovanni Palestrina, Johann Sebastian Bach, Christoph Gluck, Ludwig van Beethoven, Berlioz, and Liszt, create art's laws, but these laws are not immutable. Art for its own sake was anathema to

Mussorgsky; he believed that art should reflect life and communicate the common experiences of the human condition. Mussorgsky had particular empathy for the peasant class, despite his privileged early years; this earthiness, in fact, becomes a distinguishing feature of some of his most profound musical utterances.

During Mussorgsky's formative years, the many and varied influences of Glinka, Balakirev, Schumann, and Liszt, among others, are readily identifiable, as are the technical deficiencies that created a host of detractors and that caused Rimsky-Korsakov and others to rework some of Mussorgsky's pieces. Later, Mussorgsky aimed at the musical representation of human speech, but, from time to time, elements of Russian folk song are discernible, and they establish the lyrical quality that gives his work its unique blend of antipodal musical forces. His gift for satire is most observable in the songs, revealing Mussorgsky as a keen observer of all aspects and stations of life. His extraordinary talent for penetrating the inner recesses of the soul is nowhere better demonstrated than in *Boris Godunov*; because of this ability, the harmony, which would otherwise appear to be amateurish, seems perfectly suited to the requirements of dramatic expression.

Starting with the best intentions, "the fixers," such as Rimsky-Korsakov, were determined to complete, to reorchestrate, and to revise much of Mussorgsky's corpus. It has been argued that these refurbishings made the compositions accessible to audiences at large and contributed to their publication; however, the prettification of such masterworks as *Boris Godunov* and *Night on Bare Mountain* have stripped them of their raw, rough-hewn strength. Now that the original versions are available, there is no justification for automatically opting for the well-known revisions.

—*David Z. Kushner*

FURTHER READING

Brown, David. *Musorgsky: His Life and Works*. New York: Oxford University Press, 2002. A scholarly account of Mussorgsky's life and compositions. Devotes several chapters to analyses of the composition and music of Mussorgsky's operas, particularly *Boris Godunov*.

Brown, Malcolm Hamrick, ed. *Musorgsky: In Memoriam, 1881-1981*. Ann Arbor, Mich.: UMI Research Press, 1982. A collection of essays dealing with various aspects of Mussorgsky's life and music. Among the most informative and revelatory are "Musorgsky and the Populist Age," by Richard Hoops; "Musorgsky's Interest in Judaica," by Boris Schwarz; "Musorgsky's Choral Style," by Vladimir Morosan; "Editions of *Boris Godunov*," by Robert William Oldani; and "Musorgsky and Shostakovitch," by Laurel E. Fay.

Calvocoressi, Michael D. *Modest Mussorgsky, His Life and Works*. London: Rockliff, 1956. A major biographical study, this work contains musical illustrations, portraits of "The Five," and a catalog of Mussorgsky's compositions. A chronological account of the composer's life and works is followed by two excellent chapters devoted to "Technique and Style."

_____. *Mussorgsky*. London: J. M. Dent & Sons, 1946. This book, part of Dent's Master Musicians series, presents the salient facts about Mussorgsky and his music. There are fine musical illustrations to highlight the descriptive analyses of important compositions. The appendixes are of practical value, including a calendar of Mussorgsky's life with an adjoining column relating to contemporary musicians.

Emerson, Caryl. *The Life of Musorgsky*. New York: Cambridge University Press, 1999. Compact biography that seeks to alter some of the misconceptions about Mussorgsky's life.

Leyda, Jay, and Sergei Bertensson, eds. *The Musorgsky Reader: A Life of Modest Petrovich Musorgsky in Letters and Documents*. New York: W. W. Norton, 1947. This valuable source is essentially a life of Mussorgsky in letters and documents. They are presented in chronological order and appear in their entirety in English translations. The footnotes provide excellent explanatory data.

Montagu-Nathan, M. *Mussorgsky*. Reprint. New York: AMS Press, 1976. This book, part of the Masters of Russian Music series, is divided into four parts: career, Mussorgsky as operatic composer, choral and instrumental works, and songs. Emphasis is placed on what the author perceives as the high points in the composer's career. A brief commentary is provided on all the major works.

Orlova, Alexandra. *Musorgsky's Days and Works*. Edited and translated by Roy J. Guenther. Ann Arbor, Mich.: UMI Research Press, 1983. This work contains an exhaustive day-by-day account of Mussorgsky's life; it is, in effect, a biography in documents. Material is drawn from letters, diaries, newspaper and journal articles, and reviews. Sheds much new light on Mussorgsky's travels with Darya Leonova.

Riesemann, Oskar von. *Mussorgsky*. Reprint. Translated by Paul England. New York: AMS Press, 1970. This popular biography encompasses all aspects and phases of the composer's life. Despite occasional errors in small details, the book has much to admire, and the material is presented in a logical and orderly manner.

SEE ALSO: Ludwig van Beethoven; Hector Berlioz; Aleksandr Borodin; Gustave Flaubert; Nikolai Gogol; Heinrich Heine; Franz Liszt; Nikolay Rimsky-Korsakov; Robert Schumann; Peter Ilich Tchaikovsky.

RELATED ARTICLES in *Great Events from History: The Nineteenth Century, 1801-1900:* March 3, 1875: Bizet's *Carmen* Premieres in Paris; August 13-17, 1876: First Performance of Wagner's Ring Cycle; December 22, 1894: Debussy's *Prelude to the Afternoon of a Faun* Premieres; January 14, 1900: Puccini's *Tosca* Premieres in Rome.

MUTSUHITO
Emperor of Japan (r. 1867-1912)

As the first Japanese emperor in two and one-half centuries to exercise real power, Mutsuhito oversaw his nation's rapid modernization and expanding contacts with the outside world after renewed contact with Western nations brought the collapse of the isolationist shogunate.

BORN: November 3, 1852; Kyōto, Japan
DIED: July 30, 1912; Tokyo, Japan
ALSO KNOWN AS: Mutsuhito Shinnō (full name); Meiji; Meiji Tennō; Sachi no Miya
AREA OF ACHIEVEMENT: Government and politics

EARLY LIFE

Mutsuhito (mewt-sew-hee-toh) was the son of one of the many concubines of his father, Emperor Kōmei. At the time of Mutsuhito's birth, the emperor was the titular ruler of Japan, but in reality all power was in the hands of an official known as the shogun, who theoretically governed in the emperor's name. The Tokugawas—from whom all shoguns were selected—had been the de facto rulers of Japan since they had unified the island nation 250 years earlier, after a century of civil war.

Mutsuhito was the only one of Kōmei's six children to survive to adulthood. By most accounts he was a somewhat spoiled, protected, and delicate child who was often prone to temper tantrums. He had a lively curiosity, however, and took great interest in things exotic and foreign. Unlike his father, he was attracted to the increasing number of Westerners who were entering Japan during the 1850's and 1860's. Until the mid-1850's the Tokugawa shogunate had successfully kept most Westerners out of Japan since they had come to power. Japan's isolation from the Western world lasted until an American flotilla under Commodore Matthew Perry forced open the country in 1854.

In early 1867, Emperor Kōmei died of smallpox at the young age of thirty-six, and Mutsuhito inherited his throne at the even younger age of fourteen, At that time, both the imperial court and the Tokugawa shogunate were growing panicky about growing Western influence in Japan, and the government was consequently in political confusion. The long period of seclusion and peace had greatly weakened the Tokugawa government, and its vulnerability became readily apparent when the ruling shogun was unwilling or unable to turn the Westerners away. Local and middle-level politicians—who saw what had happened to China and other Asian nations after concessions had been extracted by the West—feared for Japan's survival. Young leaders of four southern domains set aside their differences with one another and revolted against the shogunate. In 1868, they called for the restoration of imperial power and abolition of the shogunate and seized the imperial palace in Kyōto. After the coup was completed, Mutsuhito authorized its actions, and his reign became known as the Meiji era, which means era of enlightened rule.

The new government, consisting of a coalition of revolutionaries from the rebellious domains and their sympathizers in the imperial court, gradually extended imperial control over the whole nation. In a symbolic twenty-two-day trek, the young emperor was carried on a palanquin to the new capital, Tokyo; the procession comprised three thousand soldiers and servants. Six months later, Mutsuhito returned to Kyōto to marry Princess Haruko, a woman two years older than him.

LIFE'S WORK

The new Meiji government believed that only by emulating Western nations could it make Japan strong enough to stand up to the West. The government enacted a series of radical and draconian laws that almost instantaneously transformed all aspects of Japanese life. The rigid feudal class system was abolished, and the samurai gave up their swords to a conscripted European-style military. Compulsory education was established, and Western experts were recruited to teach in the new universities. Within only a few decades, Japan was transformed from an decentralized agrarian economy to a major industrialized power. A constitution was written and adopted, and an elected parliamentary legislative body, the Diet, was established for the first time.

Historians still debate the role that the Meiji emperor played in these dramatic changes. Some of his harshest critics have claimed that he personally did little more than drink sake, dally with his concubines, and watch sumo wrestling. However, they have underestimated his influence. Even if he did nothing else, his release of several important edicts set the moral tone of the Meiji state. His very progressive Charter Oath of April, 1868, established how the new government was to treat its citizens. It pledged equality for all people and promised that all "evil customs" of the past would be eliminated.

The Imperial Rescript to Soldiers and Sailors—prepared at the emperor's direction in January, 1882—

Mutsuhito. (The Granger Collection, New York)

was designed to offer guidance to the military. As a code of ethics for the new armed forces, it demanded of commoner recruits loyalty to the emperor and the new Meiji state, rather than to local warlords or provinces. The emperor did several things to reinforce the symbolic connection between the military and his throne: He presented his edict directly to the army minister in an unprecedented ceremony at the imperial palace. He also often wore a military uniform himself and frequently attended military exercises, watched maneuvers, and presided over graduations at the military academies.

The emperor's Imperial Rescript on Education of October 30, 1890, was one of the most far-reaching statements of policy of the Meiji state. It was read at school functions and ceremonial occasions, and students were required to memorize it. It was an unabashedly Confucian document, extolling the virtues of filial piety, unquestioned obedience to authority, and reverence for the imperial system. It claimed that the Japanese were a unique people, united and tied to the land by bonds of blood, common history, and the emperor. Nationalistic in outlook and intent, it served as a tool for political indoctrination in the schools until the end of World War II.

SIGNIFICANCE

Probably no emperor in Japan's fifteen hundred years of recorded history was more important than Meiji, and none experienced such sweeping change. Today the name Meiji is synonymous with progress and modernization, and he became the symbol around which the new state was both constructed and interpreted. If he was, as some have claimed, a figurehead of actors and politicians with their own agendas for a modern Japan, he played his role well. Both he and Empress Haruko were public figures, meeting heads of state, giving garden parties for foreign dignitaries, and even sometimes mingling with commoners. Both often wore Western dress, and Haruko was visibly active with social causes and charities, such as the Red Cross and education for girls. By their own actions, the emperor and empress were ambassadors for a new, Westernizing, Japan.

The Meiji emperor was also the nominal commander in chief of Japan's armed forces, and he led them to victory in two major conflicts, the Sino-Japanese War of 1894-1895 and the Russo-Japanese War of 1904-1905. These victories established Japan as a new force to be reckoned with in the eyes of the international community. The territories that he won gave the Japanese an overseas empire, an expansion that would not end until World War II. Moreover, as the head priest of the Shinto religion, the emperor gave spiritual legitimacy to the parochial nationalism of the new state.

Though Mutsuhito assumed the throne as an inexperienced youth, barely into his teens, he grew in stature during his reign, as did his nation in the world. The death of the Meiji emperor in 1912 symbolically represented the completion of Japan's transformation from an isolated Asian agrarian society to one of the world's most important economic and military powers at the start of the twentieth century.

—*James Stanlaw*

FURTHER READING

Gluck, Carol. *Japan's Modern Myths: Ideology in the Late Meiji Period.* Princeton, N.J.: Princeton University Press, 1985. A provocative study of the symbols and discourse of Meiji Japan. The chapter on the development of the modern emperor's new roles is especially enlightening here.

Irokawa, Daikichi. *The Culture of the Meiji Period.* Translated by Marius Jansen. Princeton, N.J.: Princeton University Press, 1985. A classic account of the people and culture of Mutsuhito's Japan by one of the country's foremost historians.

Jansen, Marius. *The Making of Modern Japan*. Cambridge, Mass.: Harvard University Press, 2000. One of the best single-volume histories of modern Japan by one of its best Western historians. Jansen gives a wonderful explanation of how the imperial restoration occurred, and about one-third of the book is devoted to Meiji life and culture.

Keene, Donald. *Emperor of Japan: Meiji and His World*. New York: Columbia University Press, 2002. This nine-hundred-page biography—drawing on the official Japanese record of the emperor's life—is the definitive study of Mutsuhito in any language, written by America's preeminent specialist on Japanese literature.

Lebra, Takie Sugiyama. *Above the Clouds: Status Culture of the Modern Japanese Nobility*. Berkeley: University of California Press, 1993. While focusing more on Mutsuhito's successors, this ethnography and history of the imperial line by a noted Japanese anthropologist gives much insight into the daily life and manners of Japan's extended royal family, many of whose structures came into formal existence during Mutsuhito's reign.

Seagrave, Sterling, and Peggy Seagrave. *The Yamato Dynasty: The Secret History of Japan's Imperial Family*. New York: Broadway Books, 1999. A controversial and scandal-focused history of Japan's imperial family by two investigative reporters. The two chapters on Mutsuhito contain some colorful anecdotes not found in the usual references.

SEE ALSO: Ii Naosuke; Itō Hirobumi; Saigō Takamori.
RELATED ARTICLES in *Great Events from History: The Nineteenth Century, 1801-1900:* March 31, 1854: Perry Opens Japan to Western Trade; January 3, 1868: Japan's Meiji Restoration; January-September 24, 1877: Former Samurai Rise in Satsuma Rebellion; August 1, 1894-April 17, 1895: Sino-Japanese War.

DADABHAI NAOROJI
Indian nationalist leader

A liberal political leader who became the second president of the Indian National Congress in Calcutta and the first Indian elected to the British parliament, Naoroji was a moderate spokesperson for India and is considered by many to have been a primary founder of the Indian nationalist movement.

BORN: September 4, 1825; Bombay, India
DIED: June 30, 1917; Bombay, India
ALSO KNOWN AS: Grand Old Man of India; Mr. Narrow Majority
AREA OF ACHIEVEMENT: Government and politics

EARLY LIFE

Although born in India, Dadabhai Naoroji (dah-dah-bay now-ROH-jee) was a Parsi—a descendant of Persian followers of Zoroaster who fled to India to avoid religious persecution. In 1831, when he six years of age, his father died. His mother was not a well-educated person, but she realized the importance of education, and as she raised him, she ensured that he focused on his studies. He did so and received academic prizes at school and college. He was eventually sent to Elphinstone College in Bombay and was part of its first graduating class.

On August 26, 1852, when the first political party in Bombay, the Bombay Association, was established, Naoroji became a member. Two years later he became the first Indian professor at Elphinstone College, which made him an assistant professor of mathematics and natural philosophy. The following year, however, he resigned and was one of a group of three Indians who traveled to London to start the Parsi trading business Cama & Company. In London, he dedicated himself to business and to serving as a spokesperson for India in England, but he left the company in 1858. He then spent two periods in India but by April, 1865, was back in England almost permanently after founding his own trading company.

LIFE'S WORK

During the first dozen years of Naoroji's residence in England, he dedicated his life to business and to being an informal representative of India, explaining the Indian viewpoint to British people who were interested in India or who were responsible for Indian policies, both in and outside Parliament. He traveled regularly between England and India and acted as a bridge between British interested in India and Indians active in politics in India. He believed that if British policy was to be reformed then British people needed to be informed about the Indian situation and the Indian perspective.

Naoroji was a moderate who worked for the improvement of British rule in India, not for its elimination. He argued that more government positions held by British employees should be given to Indians and that the amount of money spent on the military in India should be reduced. In 1866, he formalized his lobbying activities in England by founding the East India Association. One of the issues for which he fought was holding Indian civil service examinations in England and in India simultaneously so that Indian candidates not have the disadvantage of having to travel to England to sit for the examinations. He was successful, and in 1870 examinations began to be held both in London and in India.

In 1871, the East India Association was transformed into the India Lobby, and branches were set up in Calcutta, Madras, and Bombay. In 1871 and 1872, Naoroji testified before a parliamentary committee in the House of Commons on Indian objections to the drain on Indian resources. He was now a recognized spokesperson for India in both India and England.

In 1873, Naoroji returned to India to become the *dewan*, or prime minister, of the princely state of Baroda, a post he held for just over one year. He reformed the government of the state in order to demonstrate that an Indian administration could bring benefits to the people. During the 1880's, he was a member of the Bombay Municipal Corporation. Maintaining the Parsi tradition of philanthropic activities, he endowed a number of schools that catered to girls and the poor and also formed literary societies, for which he became an honored figure in Bombay. In 1883, he established a newspaper, *Voice of India*, to express his views and to give greater publicity to the positions of the India Lobby. In 1885, he was nominated for a seat in the Bombay Legislative Council by the British.

In 1886, Naoroji failed in his attempt to be elected a member of Parliament for a district in London, but in 1892 he achieved the greatest extent of his fame when he won election in the London constituency of Finsbury. After winning by only three votes, he was given a nickname that, when spoken with an Indian accent, became a pun on his name: "Mr. Narrow Majority." His election inspired many young Indians at this time, including the future nationalist leader and creator of Pakistan, Mohammad Ali Jinnah (1876-1948), who was then living in

England. Naoroji's criticism of the financial plight of India impelled the British to set up a royal commission of investigation, on which Naoroji served as the only Indian member.

A voluminous correspondent, Naoroji was also the author of numerous papers and books on Indian affairs. He wrote a paper, "Poverty in India," which he first presented to the East India Association in 1870 and later expanded and published as a book, *Poverty and Un-British Rule in India*, in 1901. In a comparative analysis of fifteen countries, he looked at national and per capita incomes, agricultural and nonagricultural output, taxation, and a number of other indices and concluded that Great Britain drained wealth from India that benefited a small number of people in Britain and India, while increasing poverty for the majority of Indians. This, he argued, brought great dishonor to Britain because it was not only a material drain on India but also a moral drain on Britain. Naoroji's "drain of wealth" thesis, while neither new nor Naoroji's own invention, was used by all Indian politicians until independence in 1947 to argue that British rule impoverished India and therefore India should become free.

In 1907, a split occurred in the Indian National Congress between the moderates, led by Gopal Krishna Gokhale (1866-1915), and the extremists, led by Bal Gangadhar Tilak (1856-1920), over whether the party should fight for reform or independence. Naoroji was asked to be president of the party for the third time, to maintain party unity, even though he was considered by some to be too moderate and too Anglicized to have a faith in the British sense of justice that had been overtaken by history. At the end of Dadabhai Naoroji's life, in 1917, he was affectionately known as the "Grand Old Man" of the Indian nationalist movement, and that term has remained his moniker in India today.

SIGNIFICANCE

Naoroji was a close associate and intimate friend of Gopal Krishna Gokhale, and he influenced Mohandas K. Gandhi, who regarded both Gokhale and Naoroji as his gurus, or mentors. Naoroji's "drain of wealth" theory was adopted by many Indians and gave them the intellectual arguments to oppose colonial rule. As a member of the British parliament, his criticism of British rule in India helped to create a political climate that British rule should end. It put the British on the defensive. As a result, he is today regarded as a primary founder of the Indian nationalist movement.

—*Roger D. Long*

FURTHER READING

Grover, Verinder, ed. *Dadabhai Naoroji*. Vol. 12 in *Political Thinkers of Modern India*. New Delhi: Deep and Deep, 1990. Part 1 of this volume contains twenty-four of Naoroji's writings and speeches on a large number of topics, especially on economic and financial matters. The second part includes eight short appreciations of Naoroji, his relationships, and his influence.

Jones, Kenneth W. *Socio-Religious Movements in British India*. Cambridge, England: Cambridge University Press, 1989. One in the series "The New Cambridge History of India," it places Naoroji's thought in comparative perspective with the numerous other reform movements from the eighteenth to the twentieth century.

Nanda, B. R. *The Moderate Era in Indian Politics: Dadabhai Naoroji Memorial Prize Fund Lecture*. Delhi: Oxford University Press, 1983. This short lecture places Naoroji's career in historical perspective when moderates dominated Indian politics between the 1880's and 1920. With the ascendency of Gandhi and his technique of *satyagraha* and his noncooperation movement, Indian nationalist politics became strident.

Naoroji, Dadabhai. *Poverty and Un-British Rule in India*. Delhi: Ministry of Information and Broadcasting, Government of India, 1962. This is a reprint of Dadabhai's seminal work of 1901 that was influential among a generation of nationalists.

Zaidi, A. M., ed. *The Grand Little Man of India: Dadabhai Naoroji—Speeches and Writings*. Vols. 1-2. New Delhi: Indian Institute of Applied Political Research, 1984-1988. Thirty-three speeches in volume 1 are divided into Naoroji's "Congress Speeches," "Speeches in the House of Commons," and "Miscellaneous Speeches and Addresses." Volume 2 contains ten of his statements, speeches, and papers plus a four-page autobiographical extract, in which Naoroji offers an account of his early life and a character sketch of his mother.

SEE ALSO: Sir Sayyid Ahmad Khan; Mahadev Govind Ranade; Rammohan Ray; Iswar Chandra Vidyasagar; Vivekananda.

RELATED ARTICLE in *Great Events from History: The Nineteenth Century, 1801-1900:* 1885: Indian National Congress Is Founded.

NAPOLEON I

First consul (1799-1804) and emperor (r. 1804-1814/1815) of France

Napoleon was one of the greatest military generals in history, and he also made lasting contributions to the laws and civil administration of France and other lands. However, he also left a darker legacy—that of dictatorial rule that was the precursor to modern fascism.

BORN: August 15, 1769; Ajaccio, Corsica
DIED: May 5, 1821; Saint Helena Island
ALSO KNOWN AS: Napoleon Bonaparte (birth name); Bonaparte; Little Corporal; Little Corsican
AREAS OF ACHIEVEMENT: Government and politics, military

EARLY LIFE

Although he was a native of the island of Corsica, Napoleon Bonaparte was sent to French military schools in Brienne and Paris, where he became known as "the little corporal" because of his small stature. Commissioned to the artillery in 1785, he later took part in fighting on behalf of the French Revolution. In 1793, he was promoted to brigadier general, but he was imprisoned the next year when the forces in power changed from the radical Jacobins to Thermidorean reactionaries intent on stopping the reign of terror that had made the revolution turn on its own members. He was soon released, however, and back in favor in October, 1795, when he dispersed a Parisian mob threatening the government.

A politically helpful marriage and victories in the field, especially in northern Italy, increased Napoleon's prestige. Other spectacular victories in Egypt, coupled with a weak government at home that was overthrown in 1799, led to his elevation as first consul in the new government. A plebiscite was held confirming his enormous popularity, and by 1801 (the year in which he made peace with the Roman Catholic Church, one of the revolution's greatest enemies) he was the supreme dictator of France.

Napoleon's remarkable early success was in part a matter of good fortune and in part the product of an unconquerable will and energy that took the maximum advantage of every political and military opportunity. Given the chaos of the revolutionary years, it is not surprising that a military man with political prowess should do so well. With France under siege and surrounded by hostile powers, Napoleon's victories could be viewed (rather romantically) as having saved the revolution from destruction. At the same time, his own steadiness of purpose prevented warring factions from destroying the revolution from within.

LIFE'S WORK

Napoleon I was to keep France in the paramount position to which he had brought it in only a few years. If France was to be secure, it had to dominate the European continent. Thus Napoleon intervened successfully in Austria, Italy, and Germany—all enemies of the revolution. England, with its control of the sea, was a major target, but Napoleon repeatedly failed in attempts to destroy British military power in Egypt and on the European continent.

By 1804, Napoleon had himself proclaimed emperor. What had once been a man of humble origins, whose energies and talents had been released by revolutionary actions, now increasingly became an individual identifying his personal successes with the glory of the state. England, Austria, Russia, and Sweden formed an alliance against him, but on December 26, 1805, he overwhelmingly defeated their armies at Austerlitz. By 1808, he was master of the Continent, with only the sea power of England to thwart his imperial plans.

Although Napoleon had made significant legal reforms in France, he relied increasingly on the force of his own personality to rule. Rather than developing some kind of governmental structure that might perpetuate his rule or forming a strong general staff that could carry through with his military plans, he relied almost exclusively on his own genius. As a tireless worker and supremely organized person, he counted on being able to switch rapidly from one issue to another or from one field of battle to another. He had a detailed grasp of both civil and military matters that was awesome, and he refused to delegate the authority that accrued from his command of the components of power.

Napoleon thought, mistakenly, that he could use members of his own family as extensions of his will. Thus he conferred the thrones of Holland and Westphalia on his brothers Louis and Jerome. He made his stepson, Eugène, a viceroy of Italy and his third brother, Joseph, king of Naples and later of Spain. Few of these familial appointments were successful, either because his relatives were incompetent or because they acted independently of his wishes. However, he continued to act as though he could invent a royal line for himself, having his marriage to Joséphine (who was unable to bear his child) annulled in 1809 so that he could marry the daughter of the Austrian emperor Francis II, Marie-Louise, who bore him a son.

Between 1808 and 1814, Napoleon continued to triumph in war, but at great cost to his country. A defeat he suffered in May, 1809, in a battle with the Archduke Charles at Aspern, demonstrated his vulnerability. Nevertheless, he drove his forces on, invading Russia in June, 1812, with an army of 500,000 men, the largest collection of troops ever mobilized in Europe. Although he made it to Moscow, the Russians had devastated their own country along the route of his advance, depriving him of the sustenance of the land and exacerbating his problems with supply lines that became overextended. With winter overtaking him, the Russians struck back, reducing his huge army to one-fifth of its original size, so that he had to hasten back to Paris to prepare a defense against an invasion. When Paris fell on March 31, 1814, Napoleon abdicated and was exiled to Elba.

A much lesser man might have accepted the verdict of history. It was a measure of the esteem Napoleon could still compel that he was able to escape and rally France once more. In his effort to reconstruct his em-

Napoleon I. (Library of Congress)

pire, he liberalized certain features of the French constitution, but, before he could truly mobilize public opinion, he was forced into battle at Waterloo (June 12-18, 1815), the decisive defeat of his career. In exile on Saint Helena Island, Napoleon assiduously built up the myth of himself as the revolution's man, the conqueror who had meant to liberate Europe from reactionary elements.

SIGNIFICANCE

Napoleon I's impact on his time and on subsequent events has been extraordinary. First, there was his conceit that Europe could be unified under the rule of one man. Napoleon established a cult of personality, a disturbing phenomenon that would be repeated in the bloody rules of Joseph Stalin and Adolf Hitler in the twentieth century. Hitler, in particular, suffered from delusions of grandeur that had their precedent in Napoleon. Both leaders, in fact, were bold military strategists who imagined that if only they took over the details of command the world could be shaped according to their desires. Napoleon established the modern model for the world-historical individual who believes in the triumph of his will.

The great Marxist critic Georg Lukács has argued that Napoleon's movement of masses of men across a continent resulted in the development of a historical consciousness in which millions of men suddenly saw their fate linked to the fate of millions of others. Even when Lukács's Marxist bias is discounted, his evocation of Napoleon's ability to motivate millions of people takes on an inspiring and frightening aspect. Napoleon took the ideas of democracy, of popular rule, and of government by the majority and turned them into another tool of the dictator. At the height of his own popularity, at crucial periods in his career, Napoleon used plebiscites to legitimate his military and imperial ambitions.

Historians of various biases continue to argue over Napoleon's significance, for they recognize in his example a powerful lesson on personality and politics. At the beginning of his career, Napoleon was seen as the outcome of a revolutionary movement and as the very type of man whom the forces of history had shaped to rule. However, by the end of his career, large parts of Europe regarded him only as a dictator who camouflaged his tyranny in the rhetoric of the revolution.

The comparison with Hitler is, again, apposite. There is virtually nothing in Hitler's record that can be salvaged, no vision of a united Europe worth contemplating. The difference between him and Napoleon can be gauged by imagining what would have happened if each man had been able to conquer all of Europe. Hitler's ideology was founded on excluding and exterminating various groups of people. Napoleon's ideology was based on the principle of inclusion. Armies were defeated in the field, and, though civilian populations also suffered in the Napoleonic Wars, the emperor had no final solution, no master plan, to rid Europe of undesirable elements. If Napoleon did betray much of the revolution, he also left a code of law and an enviable legacy of civil administration. He is not the monster Hitler was precisely because he evolved from the context of a revolution, which in practice he may have subverted but which he also supported in a way that still influences scholars of this period.

—Carl Rollyson

FURTHER READING

Cronin, Vincent. *Napoleon: An Intimate Biography*. London: Collins, 1971. As the title suggests, this biography aims to give a close-up view of the man. Written in a clear, conversational style, this is by no means one of the classic works on Napoleon, but it is an accessible way of studying a figure who has been layered with so many different interpretations. The notes and the index sections are helpful guides to further research.

Geyl, Pieter. *Napoleon, For and Against*. London: Jonathan Cape, 1949. This study by a great Dutch historian is essential reading. With great clarity and impartiality he relates the various reactions to Napoleon that still govern writing on him today. Geyl is an acute student of nationalism and shows how nationalistic reactions to Napoleon color much of the writing that has been done on him.

Hobsbawm, E. J. *The Age of Revolution: Europe, 1789-1848*. London: Weidenfeld & Nicolson, 1962. Napoleon cannot really be understood apart from his age. This classic history by one of the most important British historians of the century brilliantly evokes a sense of the historical period and of social and political change.

Johnson, Paul. *Napoleon*. New York: Viking Press, 2002. Concise biography, providing an overview of Napoleon's life and career. Johnson portrays Napoleon as an opportunist whose militarism and style of governance planted the seeds for warfare and totalitarianism in the twentieth century.

Jones, R. Ben. *Napoleon: Man and Myth*. London: Hodder & Stoughton, 1977. Should be read after consulting one of the standard biographies of Napoleon. Divided into chapters on historical background, Napoleon's civil and military career, and the impact of his myth, this is a useful study that includes maps, bibliographies, and chronologies of important periods and events.

Kircheisen, F. M. *Napoleon*. New York: Harcourt, Brace, 1932. One of the standard biographies of Napoleon, condensed in this edition from nine volumes and more than five thousand pages of text. Based on extensive archival research and reading in sources in many languages, but still a readable and informative study. Well indexed with maps and illustrations.

Lefebvre, Georges. *Napoleon: From 18 Brumaire to Tilsit, 1799-1807*. New York: Columbia University Press, 1969.

_____. *Napoleon: From Tilsit to Waterloo, 1807-1815*. New York: Columbia University Press, 1969. These volumes are a translation of what is generally considered to be the greatest biography of Napoleon. Although it focuses on the man, the biography opens with a first chapter that helpfully situates him in the context of his revolutionary times.

Palmer, R. R. *The Age of Democratic Revolution: A Political History of Europe and America, 1760-1800*. 2 vols. Princeton, N.J.: Princeton University Press, 1959-1964. This is a particularly lucid overview of the Napoleonic period. Palmer's balanced prose and helpful bibliography are essential and should be read in conjunction with Hobsbawm's classic study.

Schom, Alan. *Napoleon Bonaparte*. New York: HarperCollins, 1997. Scholarly, detailed biography covering all facets of Napoleon's life and career. Schom is unusually candid about his subject's character flaws and failures.

Thompson, J. M. *Napoleon Bonaparte: His Rise and Fall*. New York: Oxford University Press, 1952. A standard biography relying extensively on Napoleon's correspondence. It is somewhat unusual for being structured in chapters strictly devoted to the many countries on which Napoleon had an impact. Contains notes and an index.

SEE ALSO: Alexander I; Viscount Castlereagh; Charles XIV John; Joséphine; Napoleon III; Michel Ney; Duke of Wellington.

RELATED ARTICLES in *Great Events from History: The Nineteenth Century, 1801-1900:* May 9, 1803: Louisiana Purchase; September 25, 1804: Twelfth Amendment Is Ratified; December 2, 1805: Battle of Auster-litz; May 2, 1808: Dos de Mayo Insurrection in Spain; May 2, 1808-November, 1813: Peninsular War in Spain; June 23-December 14, 1812: Napoleon Invades Russia; July 22, 1812: Battle of Salamanca;

September 7, 1812: Battle of Borodino; October 16-19, 1813: Battle of Leipzig; April 11, 1814-July 29, 1830: France's Bourbon Dynasty Is Restored; June 18, 1815: Battle of Waterloo; November 20, 1815: Second Peace of Paris.

NAPOLEON III
President (1848-1852) and emperor (r. 1852-1870) of France

The nephew of Emperor Napoleon I, Napoleon III, was president of the Second French Republic and emperor of the Second Empire. He was one of the key figures, sometimes unwittingly, in the political unification of both Italy and Germany, and was also greatly responsible for the rebuilding of Paris.

BORN: April 20, 1808; Paris, France
DIED: January 9, 1873; Chislehurst, Kent, England
ALSO KNOWN AS: Charles Louis Napoleon Bonaparte (birth name); Louis Napoleon
AREA OF ACHIEVEMENT: Government and politics

EARLY LIFE

Louis Napoleon Bonaparte was born in Paris in 1808. His father, also Louis Napoleon, was a younger brother of the French emperor Napoleon I. His mother, Hortense, was the daughter of the emperor's first wife, Joséphine, from an earlier marriage. The marriage of Louis Napoleon and Hortense was not a success, and rumors persisted regarding their child's paternity. After Napoleon I's final defeat at Waterloo and exile to St. Helena, all the Bonapartes were forced out of France. Hortense, having separated from her husband, settled in Switzerland, where Louis Napoleon was educated to the dual heritage of the French Revolution and the imperialism of Napoleon I. Both traditions formed his character.

As a young man, Louis Napoleon was a romantic figure. Of average height for the day, about five feet, five inches, he had a pale complexion and dark, curly hair. Women were greatly attracted to him, perhaps because of his name. It is impossible to ascertain when his own political ambitions first matured, though it is probable that he saw himself as a man of destiny at an early age. Louis Napoleon's older brother died in 1831, and Napoleon I's son by his second wife, the so-called duke of Reichstadt, died in 1832, leaving Louis Napoleon as the political head of the Bonaparte family. In 1836, he attempted his first coup d'état against the French government of King Louis-Philippe. It failed ignominiously,

and after his arrest he was exiled, first to the United States and then, after his mother's death, to London.

In 1840, the British government consented to the return of Napoleon I's body to France from St. Helena, where he had died in 1821. Hoping to take advantage of the Bonaparte legend, Louis Napoleon again attempted a coup against Louis-Philippe. It, too, utterly failed, and he was sentenced to imprisonment for life. During the next few years, Louis Napoleon wrote and studied. He authored various works, identifying himself with the heritage of Napoleon I. In 1844, he published "Extinction du paupérisme" (the extinction of poverty), which, contrary to the laissez-faire ideology of the times, advocated government intervention in the economy. In 1846, he escaped from prison and within a few hours was back in England, but no closer to power.

LIFE'S WORK

The year 1848 was a revolutionary year in Europe and in France. In February, Louis-Philippe was overthrown. Initially, Louis Napoleon was unable to profit by the change, but after a working-class uprising in May and June, which alarmed the middle and upper classes, his opportunity came. Abandoning the monarchy, the French established the Second Republic, and Louis Napoleon was elected president, receiving almost 75 percent of the vote. His uncle's reputation, his own activities against the former regime, his economic program, the divisions among his opponents, and perhaps merely the times made Louis Napoleon president of France.

The government of the Second Republic was modeled after the American presidential system rather than the parliamentary form of England. Louis Napoleon lacked a political party of his own, and the newly elected French assembly owed him little loyalty. In addition, the presidential term was for four years with no immediate reelection allowed. Finally, there were Louis Napoleon's own ambitions and his heritage. Those factors guaranteed still another revolution, this time, ironically, by Louis Napoleon against his own government. "Operation Rubicon"

Napoleon III. (Library of Congress)

itself was a standoff, but the emperor reaped credit for his diplomacy that led to peace.

During the nineteenth century, national unification was perceived by many to be both logical and necessary. Napoleon was sympathetic toward Italian unity. Nevertheless, it was easier for Napoleon to become involved in Italian affairs than to get out of them. In 1849, he had alienated both Italian nationalists and Catholics when he intervened in Roman affairs. Expecting to be welcomed, instead the French were opposed both by liberals on the Left, who had recently established a republic in Rome, and by conservative Catholics on the Right.

In spite of Napoleon's support of Italian national aspirations, for some Italian patriots he moved too slowly, and in 1858 there was an attempt to assassinate him. Napoleon supported Sardinia's aim of eliminating Austria from Italy, but he envisioned not a strong united Italy but a federated state that would look to France and himself for guidance. His decision to wage war against Austria was risky, lacking as it did the support of most European governments, and after initial victories, Napoleon agreed to peace. Sardinia was not pleased, but France obtained Savoy and Nice as a result of the newest Napoleon's imperialism. Italian unification remained for the future, and Napoleon's intervention had failed to satisfy any of the participants.

Perhaps the major accomplishment of the Second Empire was the rebuilding of Paris. Here, too, Louis Napoleon was inspired by his uncle's accomplishments. Even as late as 1848, Paris was in many ways a medieval city, but, with the assistance of Georges Haussmann, Napoleon made Paris into one of the first modern and planned cities in Western civilization. The Seine River was no longer a public sewer, the city streets were widened, trees planted, parks provided, and gaslights added, making Paris the famous City of Lights. Undoubtedly, the emperor wished to create a monument to his rule—he saw himself as a second Caesar Augustus building a new Rome—but there were economic and strategic considerations. Jobs would be created, and the wider, straighter streets would make it more difficult for the Parisians to rebel against his regime.

As emperor, Napoleon faced the responsibility of providing an heir. After canvassing several European princesses, the imperial eye fell upon Eugenie de Montijo,

was successful, in December, 1851, but at the cost of many arrests, 370 lives lost, and twenty thousand exiled, damaging the legitimacy of his rule. However, in a carefully worded plebiscite, the voters approved the coup d'état, and a year later, in another plebiscite, they overwhelmingly voted to abolish the Second Republic and replace it with the Second Empire, with Louis Napoleon as Emperor Napoleon III.

The creation of the Second Empire caused considerable fear among other European governments as possibly portending the revival of the military imperialism of Napoleon I. Napoleon III, however, publicly stated that his empire would be an empire of peace; as president, he had proposed to the British and Prussian governments that naval and land armaments be reduced, although nothing came of it. Early in his reign, Russian pressure on the Turkish Ottoman Empire ignited the fears of both France and England about Russia's territorial ambitions and its perennial quest for warm-water ports. The result was war in the Crimea in 1854. For Napoleon, the determining factor was his desire for an alliance with England, the old enemy, more than fear of Russia. The war

daughter of a Spanish nobleman and his part-Scottish wife. For Napoleon, it was a love match, unpopular with many of his advisers; yet Eugenie, for all of her beauty and charm, was ultimately not a suitable consort. She gave birth to a son, the prince imperial, in 1856, but she and the emperor were not close and Eugenie often pursued policies independent of those of Napoleon. In particular, she was a strong supporter of the Papacy during the era of Italian unification, and she was the energetic sponsor of French adventure in Mexico whereby the Austrian Archduke Maximilian was placed on the throne of that unwilling country. In time, Maximilian's position became untenable, and the Austrian was executed by his Mexican subjects.

The 1860's saw a change in policy as the emperor slowly began moving toward the creation of a more liberal empire. The earlier high tariff policies, which had benefited French industrialists, were modified and freer trade with Great Britain instituted. The assembly was given additional powers, and in elections republican and Royalist opponents of the imperial regime, although still in the minority, improved their numbers.

Napoleon III had claimed to be a socialist, and during the 1860's he allowed the development of labor unions, but his policies and approaches were more paternalistic than democratic. By the end of the decade, the empire was more liberal than at its beginning but in reality still more despotic than democratic. If given sufficient time, Napoleon's empire might have evolved into something approximating the constitutional monarchy of Victorian England, but it faced many obstacles. Its violent birth in 1851 and its opposition from both the Left and the Right—from republicans and from Royalists—created problems that were difficult to surmount. Napoleon's advisers were often marginal political figures who lacked prominence and political stature. Napoleon's health was poor, and his own personality was more suited to the seeking of power than to the wielding of it. He remained more the conspirator than the statesman.

It was Napoleon's ultimate misfortune to face one of the most astute statesman of modern European history. Otto von Bismarck of Prussia desired a united Germany, a Germany created by blood and iron. In 1866, Prussia defeated the Austro-Hungarian Empire in only six weeks, which led the northern German states into a federation.

In 1870, Bismarck turned his talents against Napoleon. The vacant Spanish throne was offered to a Catholic prince of the Protestant ruling house of Prussia. The French feared that they would find themselves encircled by Germans. Napoleon's government demanded that the Prussian king apologize for the affair, but Bismarck made the diplomatic conversations appear that the Prussian rejection of the French demand was harsher and more dismissive than it was in reality. The French public, including Eugenie, demanded war with Prussia, and against his own inclinations Napoleon weakly succumbed. War was declared in 1870. It was an unmitigated disaster. Napoleon III was captured by the Prussians and soon abdicated. The Second Empire was over.

SIGNIFICANCE

Napoleon III chose exile in England. In France, the war against Prussia continued briefly, but ultimately Germany prevailed and the French were forced to surrender the provinces of Alsace and Lorraine. The Second Empire was replaced by the Third Republic. Napoleon III died in his English exile in 1873. His son and heir, the prince imperial, the hope of the Bonaparte dynasty, joined the British army in South Africa. He was killed in action against the Zulu in 1879. Eugenie survived until 1920; she lived long enough to see Alsace and Lorraine restored to republican France after World War I.

Although Napoleon's diplomatic accomplishments were sometimes significant and his economic policies showed vision, the ease with which he was swept away in the events of 1870 suggests that his hold upon France was extremely superficial. He ruled for more than twenty years—longer than his famous uncle—but other than on Paris, his ultimate impact was slight. He remained the political adventurer and the dreamer to the end.

—*Eugene S. Larson*

FURTHER READING

Bresler, Fenton. *Napoleon III: A Life*. London: Harper-Collins, 1999. Popular, accessible biography providing a wealth of detail and a thorough analysis of Napoleon's personal life and public career.

Bury, J. P. T. *Napoléon III and the Second Empire*. London: English Universities Press, 1964. Bury, also a biographer of Leon Gambetta, a leading republican opponent of Napoleon III, has here written one of the best introductions to the Second Empire.

Corley, T. A. B. *Democratic Despot: A Life of Napoleon III*. New York: Clarkson N. Potter, 1961. This study notes two of the elements found in Napoleon, the popular and the autocratic, and the emperor's attempt to reconcile them. The author takes Napoleon's intellectual attempts seriously, arguing that he was the first modern politician but failed as a statesman.

Gooch, Brison D., ed. *Napoleon III, Man of Destiny:*

Englightened Statesman or Proto-Fascist? New York: Holt, Rinehart and Winston, 1963. This volume is a compendium of excerpts by various historians of Napoleon, allowing the reader to sample differing interpretations of the emperor and his regime. The subtitle captures its scope.

Pinkney, David H. *Napoleon III and the Rebuilding of Paris.* Princeton, N.J.: Princeton University Press, 1958. The author concentrates upon the creation of modern Paris under the leadership of the emperor and Georges Haussmann. The City of Lights is perhaps the major monument to the Second Empire, showing both its strengths and its weaknesses.

Price, Roger. *The French Second Empire: An Anatomy of Political Power.* New York: Cambridge University Press, 2001. Chronicles Napoleon's political career, examining how he was elected president, devised a coup to establish the Second Empire, and used the empire's power to initiate liberal reforms and wage a disastrous war against Prussia.

Thompson, J. M. *Louis Napoleon and the Second Empire.* New York: Noonday Press, 1955. This analysis of Napoleon ultimately finds the emperor lacking the necessary qualities to succeed in the inheritance left to him by Napoleon I. Suggesting the author's interpretation, each chapter begins with a quotation from *Hamlet.*

SEE ALSO: Otto von Bismarck; Joséphine; Maximilian; Napoleon I.

RELATED ARTICLES in *Great Events from History: The Nineteenth Century, 1801-1900:* February 22-June, 1848: Paris Revolution of 1848; December 2, 1852: Louis Napoleon Bonaparte Becomes Emperor of France; July 6, 1854: Birth of the Republican Party; August, 1858: France and Spain Invade Vietnam; July 11, 1859: Napoleon III and Francis Joseph I Meet at Villafranca; March 17, 1861: Italy Is Proclaimed a Kingdom; October 31, 1861-June 19, 1867: France Occupies Mexico; May 15, 1863: Paris's Salon des Refusés Opens; June 15-August 23, 1866: Austria and Prussia's Seven Weeks' War; July 19, 1870-January 28, 1871: Franco-Prussian War; September 1, 1870: Battle of Sedan; January 18, 1871: German States Unite Within German Empire.

JOHN NASH
English architect

The most outstanding architect of the Regency period in English history, Nash left a legacy of villas and refurbished estates throughout the British Isles. He designed Regent's Park and Regent Street in London and extensively redesigned and added to the Royal Pavilion at Brighton and to Buckingham Palace.

BORN: September 1752; London, England, or Neath Glamorgan, Wales
DIED: May 13, 1835; East Cowes Castle, Isle of Wight, England
AREA OF ACHIEVEMENT: Architecture

EARLY LIFE
Few details of John Nash's early life exist. He was apparently born in London to Welsh parents. His father, probably named Robert Nash, was a millwright from Lambeth, Wales. No facts remain of his mother's background, other than that she was also Welsh. Robert Nash died young, sometime before his son reached the age of seven.

His mother apprenticed the boy to work at about age fourteen to an architect, Robert Taylor (who appears to have had his office near their home). As was customary for indentured boys, Nash worked in Taylor's office for a period of seven years. He performed menial tasks at first and then rose, with age and experience, to more skilled labor. In his later years, Nash believed that he had had a rather wild personality as a boy; others described him as outgoing and ambitious, even in his youth—traits that characterized him throughout his life.

Shortly after finishing his apprenticeship, Nash married Jane Elizabeth Kerr on April 28, 1775, just outside London. Theirs was not a happy union; Jane spent money much more quickly than her husband could earn it. In the first years of their marriage, Nash was struggling to find a place in London as a builder. At the age of twenty-five, he was contracted by John Rushout to refurbish eight old houses on the northwest corner of Bloomsbury Square, London. Nash, however, had problems finding renters for these houses (part of his contractual duties). He had sent Jane to live temporarily in South Wales in June of 1778, in order to prevent her from incurring more debts in London, but by 1782, he owed a considerable amount of money to both Rushout and his wife's creditors.

Also in 1782, Nash began divorce proceedings against her, but the process during that period was extremely complex and lengthy, so he had no great hope of resolving his financial and marital problems soon. On September 30, 1783, court records show that Nash had declared himself bankrupt; his London property was sold to pay off his bills.

LIFE'S WORK

The next report of Nash finds him residing in Carmarthen, Wales, in early 1784. There he temporarily worked with a young architect, Samuel Simon Saxon. The two men reroofed a local church, St. Peter's, in 1785. Nash, now slightly known as an architect in Carmarthen, became an adviser for the planning of a new jail. In late 1792, he was the architect chosen to build this jail in Carmarthen; it was his first public building. Nash at this time became affiliated with the Whig Party, whose candidate, John Vaughan, was elected to sit in Parliament from 1779 to 1784.

Probably through Vaughan's influence, Nash received his next jobs; he planned and built the jail at Cardigan in 1793 and another in Hereford, England, finished in 1796. By the time this last jail was completed, Nash was again living in London. During the early 1790's, Nash's other public-works projects included at least three bridges, two of stone and an innovative one of iron. Iron was a medium in which Nash was a pioneer builder; almost no one had used iron in public construction prior to his work with it.

Nash also gained his early reputation as a builder of villas, or country houses. They were a departure from the farmhouse-type residences built in the previous centuries in the English countryside. Nash completed twelve houses of this kind in England and Wales early in his career (prior to 1800). Through Thomas Johnes in Cardiganshire, one of his clients, Nash met two men who would greatly influence his future tastes in architecture, Uvedale Price and Richard Payne Knight.

Both Price and Knight were leading advocates of a concept of artistic, landscape, and house design known as the picturesque. This aesthetic theory affirmed that buildings should be designed and constructed so as to fit comfortably and beautifully with their natural surroundings. When Nash designed a small triangular house for Price in 1797 at Aberystwyth, the architect clearly saw how advantageous picturesque planning could be. This house, called Castle House, had three distinct views from each of its three windows: One faced the ocean, another faced a range of cliffs, and the third faced a ruined castle.

On December 17, 1798, his first wife having died, Nash married Mary Anne Bradley, the daughter of a coal merchant. This marriage seems to have been more felicitous for Nash. He and Mary Anne socialized easily and frequently entertained his professional friends at home. The couple would have no children, but a wide circle of friends and relatives would remain devoted to them throughout their lives. At the time of this marriage, Nash also purchased land at East Cowes on the Isle of Wight; there he would build for himself a small but comfortable Gothic-style country home near the sea. In addition, he and his wife maintained a London home during his active years as an architect.

When Paul Cobb Methuen in Wiltshire wished to enlarge his Elizabethan era house, he hired Nash, along with Humphry Repton, to do the landscaping. Repton, a reputable landscaper in the picturesque tradition, was to work on several houses with Nash in the next five years. One of their greatest successes together was completed in 1799—Luscombe Castle, Devon. The varied elements Nash designed for this house combined picturesque traits with a Gothic influence. An outstanding feature of this house was its octagonal tower; another, which was also a typical feature of Nash's houses, was a plain interior. Nash seemed least interested in the interior decoration of his buildings; he is also regarded as a much better designer than a builder. He could be hasty and careless in the actual construction of buildings, while meticulously careful with their initial designs. Designing was clearly where his enthusiasm was centered.

As the nineteenth century opened, Nash was beginning to enjoy a rather solid reputation as an architect, particularly of country houses for the wealthy classes. His success may in part be attributed to his social affability; he got along well with his clients.

Nash did not cut a prepossessing figure; he was a short man with a stocky shape. He also had a round head with a bulbous nose and small eyes. He was, however, a charming and generous man, who made a good impression on the people he met. He was not afraid to take large financial risks in order to finance some of his more speculative building projects. His enthusiasm for his projects also encouraged investors to back these costly architectural works.

One of the projects about which Nash was most excited at this point in his career was the construction of Blaise Hamlet, a picturesque grouping of nine old-fashioned thatched-roof cottages for the retired servants of John S. Harford of Blaise Castle, Bristol. Each cottage had a unique design, and each was carefully executed for beauty and comfort. These innovative cottages were constructed between 1809 and 1811. They mark an end in Nash's career, for he soon turned from private residences to public building and planning in London.

Marylebone Park in London, the property of the monarchy, was to be redesigned as an integral unit. Several wealthy investors had hoped to buy sections of the park for their own use, and the English government wished to stifle such speculation. As requested by the government agencies involved, Nash submitted his designs for the development of Marylebone Park, as well as for a new street that would connect it to Charing Cross. Nash's report of 1811 is a convincing document; it shows that he had thoroughly studied the area to be developed, had a great command of design, and was compelling when he promised the future success of his ideas for the area. In August of 1811, Prime Minister Spencer Perceval somewhat modified Nash's plan by suggesting that fewer country villas be built on the park land and more open space be left. Nash incorporated Perceval's ideas into his designs, and he limited the number of villas to fifty.

In June of 1812, the plan for the new park and its connecting street were made public. It was clear that the new street would create a large highway through northwest London. Many present dwellings would have to be demolished to make room for the new road; shrewdly, Nash had designed this highway so that of the 741 houses to be bought and removed, 386 already belonged to the Crown.

Parliament and its agencies fully supported Nash and his visions for the new park and street. Two builders, Samuel Butler and James Burton, also came forward to help Nash develop his grand designs into actual buildings. Burton especially invested his time and services heavily in building seventy-four houses, or about one-quarter of all the houses on the new street. As work progressed on the new highway, it was officially named Regent Street in January of 1819. On this immense project Nash himself fulfilled many functions: He worked as a surveyor, an engineer, and a financial manager, in addition to his duties as architect.

During the construction of Regent Street, Nash was officially in the employ of the prince regent (later to become King George IV). The prince liked Nash and admired his hard work. After the death of the prince's personal architect, Henry Holland, in 1806, Nash gradually assumed his duties.

Holland had designed the royal residence at Brighton, which became known as the Royal Pavilion. In 1818 and 1819, Nash added to the exterior of this as yet incomplete building. By 1823, when all of his exterior designs were in place, the result was an exotic palace that combined elements of Indian, Chinese, and Gothic styles of architecture. It was a versatile piece of work on Nash's part with a splendid picturesque effect.

At about this same time, Nash and his investors were completing the first villas inside the new London park, named Regent's Park. In 1818, Burton constructed his own house and moved in the next year. Other homes in and around the park were built in attached rows called terraces, usually having one unifying facade designed by Nash. From 1822 to 1823, J. M. Aitkens built Hanover Terrace. In 1824, Cambridge Terrace was begun by Richard Mott and Chester Terrace by Burton. In 1826, William Nurse built Cumberland Terrace, followed by William Smith's Kent Terrace, completed in 1827. Despite all these houses, Regent's Park retained a rural atmosphere with beautiful landscaping and sufficient open spaces to make it a comfortable place of residence. Between 1819 and 1823, Nash constructed his own home on the lower section of Regent Street.

After Nash's outstanding success on the ambitious Regent's Park and Regent Street project, he was still to redesign and rebuild another major London monument. In June of 1825, at the age of seventy-two, Nash began to reconstruct Buckingham Palace for King George IV. It was a laborious assignment, and Nash had to work hastily because the aging king wished to move into his new residence. Architectural critics often assert that Buckingham Palace was a case in which Nash's designs were clearly not well executed when built.

The beautiful concepts that Nash put on paper did not translate well to the palace itself. By 1829, Parliament was upset by the large costs Nash had accumulated in redesigning the palace; Nash, at the behest of the king, had spent considerably more money than the government had officially appropriated for his work. The allotted price of improvements to Buckingham Palace was set by law at £252,690 in 1826. By 1830, the money spent had risen to £613,269, and more work remained to be done. Nash was greatly disheartened by the death of the king on June 26, 1830. Nash now had no royal patron, and a parliamentary committee was investigating his work on the palace. The committee found him to be innocent of any wrongdoing, but he was hurt by the adverse publicity.

Also in 1830, Nash suffered a minor stroke that left him afflicted by headaches and giddiness for the remainder of his life. He retired to his Gothic-style castle at East Cowes, where he entertained his friends and family in his declining years. He died at his home on May 13, 1835.

Significance

John Nash was the premier architect of the Regency period in English history. He left a legacy of villas and refurbished estates in several areas throughout England, Ireland, and Wales. Among his most celebrated and photographed houses is Cronkhill near Shrewsbury in Shropshire, which Nash designed and built in 1802. It is considered to be the first Italianate villa erected on English soil. The design cleverly and neatly combines one round tower, one square tower, and a colonnade into a charming, integral whole.

Other of Nash's significant buildings influenced architects and city planners long after his own era. In 1816, he produced in England the first covered shopping arcade, the Royal Opera Arcade in Pall Mall; in this he may have been inspired by similar structures in Paris. Also in London is Nash's United Service Club Building of 1826, a stately piece of work that initiated the concept of one unit to house a major club in the city; many other architects would follow Nash's example in the decades to come.

John Nash was an innovative English architect whose imagination and skill in building design and city planning will long be appreciated. Above all, his versatility in combining several architectural styles in his work will be remembered.

—*Patricia E. Sweeney*

Further Reading

Betjeman, John. *A Pictorial History of English Architecture.* New York: Macmillan, 1972. The twelve essays in this source first appeared in a series in a London newspaper. The section on the Regency period contains detailed information on Nash. Readable and engaging. The many color photographs are beautiful.

Evans, Tony, and Candida L. Green. *English Cottages.* New York: Viking Press, 1982. Nash's work on cottages is found here in the section on picturesque cottages. The authors consider him a pioneer in that field of building, and they focus attention on his Blaise Hamlet. The illustrations are striking, and captions are ample and informative.

Mansbridge, Michael. *John Nash: A Complete Cata-*

logue. Oxford, England: Phaidon, 1991. A chronological inventory of the buildings, bridges, and monuments designed and built by Nash in Great Britain and Ireland. Mansbridge summarizes the details of each project and its architectural significance. Also includes an introduction by John E. Summerson, a noted Nash authority.

Muthesius, Stefan. *The English Terraced House.* New Haven, Conn.: Yale University Press, 1982. Discusses Nash's terraced houses of the early and mid-1820's. The variety of the terraces on Regent Street is highlighted and explained in detail. Readable and well researched. Nearly 250 illustrations are included.

Pilcher, Donald E. *Regency Style, 1800-1830.* London: B. T. Batsford, 1947. Another well-illustrated book, which includes some of Nash's finest buildings in London. Pilcher's scholarship is impeccable, and his style is entertaining. A valuable book.

Richards, J. M. *The National Trust Book of English Architecture.* New York: W. W. Norton, 1981. Richards describes and praises Nash's brilliant planning of Regent Street and its varied architecture. Some details are provided on Nash's private life. Richards also discusses Nash's other London landmarks as well as his country houses. An accessible study, intended for the general reader.

Summerson, John E. *Architecture in Britain, 1530 to 1830.* New York: Penguin Books, 1977. Summerson devotes much space to an analysis of Nash's career as an architect. He also places Nash in perspective among other famous English architects. The two hundred illustrations include both photographs and building plans. A helpful bibliography accompanies each chapter.

_____. *The Life and Work of John Nash, Architect.* Cambridge, Mass.: MIT Press, 1980. Summerson is the preeminent authority on Nash, and his book devotes ample space to Nash's private life as well as to his professional career. Detailed, scholarly—an invaluable source, although there are relatively few illustrations.

See also: Sir Charles Barry; Samuel Butler; George IV; Francis Greenway; Sir George Gilbert Scott; George Edmund Street.

Related article in *Great Events from History: The Nineteenth Century, 1801-1900:* 1884: New Guilds Promote the Arts and Crafts Movement.

JAMES NASMYTH
Scottish inventor

Nasmyth developed and successfully marketed a pioneering class of industrial metalworking machines, principally the steam hammer, contributing to Great Britain's role as the center of the Industrial Revolution.

BORN: August 19, 1808; Edinburgh, Scotland
DIED: May 7, 1890; London, England
ALSO KNOWN AS: James Hall Nasmyth (full name)
AREAS OF ACHIEVEMENT: Engineering, science and technology

EARLY LIFE

James Hall Nasmyth (NAY-smihth) was born in Edinburgh, into a family of Scottish artists. He was the youngest of nine children of Alexander Nasmyth, a prominent Edinburgh painter, and Barbara Foulis, a member of the Scottish aristocracy. As a child, James assisted in his father's studio, mixing paints and working wood and metal on the family's foot-powered lathe. Together with five of his brothers and sisters, James developed skills as a graphic artist that were to remain with him throughout his working life.

In 1821, Nasmyth entered the Edinburgh School of Arts while receiving more intensive technical training from his father. The fine arts and the applied arts of metallurgy, draftsmanship, and mathematics worked together in Nasmyth's upbringing. In frequent visits to the forges, foundries, and factories of industrial Edinburgh, Nasmyth sharpened a keen interest in the methods of machine manufacture, building his own stationary steam engine by the age of seventeen.

With his father's assistance, Nasmyth secured a position in 1829 as personal assistant to Henry Maudslay, one of England's most noteworthy mechanical engineers. In his London shops, Maudslay built steam engines and many pioneering machines for the working of wood and metal. Several of the country's most prominent machine-tool builders received their initial exposure to engineering practice in Maudslay's shops, including Joseph Clement, William Muir, Joseph Whitworth, and Richard Roberts. After three years with Maudslay, Nasmyth returned to Edinburgh to manufacture the machines that he would need to set up practice as an independent manufacturer of metalworking machines. By 1834, he had accumulated sufficient goods and capital to establish himself in Manchester, at the heart of the Lancashire manufacturing industry.

Nasmyth's shop stood on the first floor of a former cotton mill, where his success in building heavy tools and steam engines for the surrounding mills quickly taxed the limited quarters. In late 1835, Nasmyth undertook a search for a new site to satisfy his growing needs for proper space, for access to better transport, and for greater prominence among Lancashire factory owners in need of new machinery.

LIFE'S WORK

At Patricroft, a short distance west of Manchester, Nasmyth found a site offering all the advantages he sought: a large plot of land at the intersection of the Bridgewater Canal and the main road and railway connecting Manchester with Liverpool. With the financial backing of a Manchester investment firm and various other sources of capital, Nasmyth set about the construction of the Bridgewater Foundry. Unlike his Manchester shop, this new enterprise was to include the entire range of workshops necessary to execute all classes of heavy work from their inception to delivery.

By 1838, Nasmyth was overseeing the operation of a complete machinery-design department, iron and brass foundries, machine and erecting shops, forge shop, pattern shop, and various other lesser shops, the whole connected by a network of rail transport. Aided by the business skills of his brother, George, and his partner Holbrook Gaskell, Nasmyth began a rapid climb to the upper reaches of British industrial enterprise. Between 1838 and his retirement from the firm in 1856, the Bridgewater Foundry produced the full range of heavy machine tools then in use: lathes, planers, shapers, slotters, boring mills, and drilling machines. Many of Nasmyth's own machinery designs were incorporated into the output. Also produced at Bridgewater were steam locomotives, hydraulic presses, stationary and marine steam engines, and pumps. Although the considerable business success of the Bridgewater Foundry was the key element in Nasmyth's own prosperity, it was the production of the steam hammer that created his reputation as one of the preeminent British engineers of the Victorian age.

The steam hammer appeared at a time when the hammering or forging of iron had reached the limits of existing technology. By the 1830's, blacksmiths could not effectively produce such large iron forgings as engine shafts or ships' anchors without considerable labor and time spent at water-powered trip hammers, frequently re-heating the piece and gradually working the iron up into its rough form.

Although the first practical use of the steam hammer occurred in France in 1841, at the Schneider works in Le Creusot, in 1838 Nasmyth had conceived the general form such a machine would take and the needs it could fill. With the addition of controls designed by his works manager, Robert Wilson, the steam hammers that Nasmyth began producing in 1843 became symbolic as well as immensely practical giants of the industrial age, towering structures with ponderous steam-driven hammer-heads that would crash down on red-hot iron masses to rough out enormous piston rods, crankshafts, anchors, and cannon. The great force exerted by each blow of the hammer both reduced the forging time dramatically and produced a metallurgically superior product. Nasmyth's tight control over the patented features of his hammers, along with Bridgewater's production capacities, ensured a steady demand for steam hammers produced there until well after his departure in 1856.

By the end of the century, steam hammers would give way to hydraulic presses in producing large forgings of greater strength and integrity. Nevertheless, Nasmyth hammers remained in use in factories throughout the world, their quick action and powerful blows rendering them invaluable to the production of many industrial goods.

Largely on the strength of his steam hammer sales, Nasmyth had amassed a considerable fortune by the age of forty-eight, when he chose to leave the firm and devote himself to private scientific pursuits. Astronomical studies became one of his chief interests, and he coauthored an account of his observations of the Moon in 1874. As with many other men of his age who left behind a life of busy industrial pursuits, Nasmyth began to seek answers to some of the ancient riddles of the day: the origin of the pyramids, early alphabets, and various astrological speculations. He also traveled widely, took up photography, and resumed his interest in painting.

A portion of Nasmyth's retirement was spent defending his claim to the invention of the steam hammer, a campaign that had developed into a nationalistic debate between advocates of French and British engineering practice. Although most popular accounts of the hammer's appearance still credit Nasmyth as its originator, contemporary records do indicate that French engineers independently conceived, built, and used a steam hammer prior to its construction by Nasmyth. The autobiography that Nasmyth completed in 1883 established his reputation among his countrymen, a reputation he rightly deserves as the steam hammer's chief advocate and one of Great Britain's most successful machine-tool innovators.

SIGNIFICANCE

Mirroring the careers of many self-taught British engineers before the professionalization of the field, James Nasmyth had early been trained in the handicrafts that were an essential foundation of all engineering. His skills as a machinist and his knowledge of machine design and steam engineering are well documented. Of his forty-three mechanical innovations, he patented nineteen, including a safety foundry ladle, cotton press, rolling mill, pile driver, and iron-making process.

As the head of a major industrial works, Nasmyth sought to retain shop-floor control of his workforce of several hundred men, to resist union demands, and to introduce machinery that would limit the degree of skill needed to operate it. A principal feature of the machine tools Nasmyth developed and used at the Bridgewater Foundry was the automatic motion, or feed, of their cutting tools, reducing the need for experienced machinists. Less knowledgeable machine tenders, often young boys, could operate such machines with ease.

Nasmyth's opposition to organized labor, including its system of apprenticeship, resulted in several labor actions against his firm and may have played a role in his early retirement. His view of skill as a marketable product subject to agreement solely between employer and employee did not fare well in the early period of the industrial workers' rights movement but did allow Nasmyth to compile a highly successful record as a builder of revolutionary industrial machinery.

—*David Shayt*

FURTHER READING

Briggs, Asa. *Iron Bridge to Crystal Palace: Impact and Images of the Industrial Revolution*. London: Thames and Hudson, 1979. A richly illustrated treatment of the sweeping influences of industrialization in Great Britain from 1779 to 1851, this thin volume depends less on authoritative research than it does on more than two hundred visual impressions of industry selected from popular literature, technical publications, and art galleries.

Cantrell, John A. *James Nasmyth and the Bridgewater Foundry*. Manchester, England: Manchester University Press, 1985. This thorough study of the economic and technical history of Nasmyth's Bridgewater years dispels many of the excessively heroic notions associated with the man and his principal product, the steam hammer. The author uses business records and correspondence to unravel the actual roles played by Nasmyth and his contemporaries in the success of the business.

Clayre, Alasdair, ed. *Nature and Industrialization.* Oxford, England: Oxford University Press, 1977. In his later years, Nasmyth was saddened by the damaged landscapes wrought by industry. This anthology of British prose and poetry confronts many of industry's social side effects—good and evil. The words of Charles Dickens, William Wordsworth, Alfred, Lord Tennyson, and Thomas Carlyle are used extensively.

Landes, David S. *The Unbound Prometheus: Technical Change and Industrial Development in Western Europe from 1750 to the Present.* 2d ed. Cambridge, England: Cambridge University Press, 2003. The broad sweep of European industrialization from 1750 to the late twentieth century is examined in this textbook study. Landes attempts to explain why Europe was industrialized first by studying the processes of industrial growth in Great Britain, France, and Germany.

Mayr, Otto, and Robert C. Post, eds. *Yankee Enterprise: The Rise of the American System of Manufactures.* Washington, D.C.: Smithsonian Institution Press, 1981. The proceedings of a symposium held at the Smithsonian, this collection of essays from distinguished historians of technology examines the reasons that industrialization emerged so rapidly and successfully in the United States, specifically in the manufacture of interchangeable parts.

Nasmyth, James Hall. *James Nasmyth, Engineer: An Autobiography.* London: John Murray. Reprint. Edited by Samuel Smiles. Baton Rouge, La.: B of A Communications, 1985. Written in part to refute allegations that there was French precedent to Nasmyth's invention of the steam hammer, this self-appraisal edited by Samuel Smiles glorifies Nasmyth's personal attributes in explaining his engineering and business success. Many statements are clarified by Cantrell, above.

Rolt, Lionel Thomas Caswell. *Tools for the Job.* London: B. T. Batsford, 1965. Reprint. London: Her Majesty's Stationery Office, 1986. A technical history of the five major machine-tool groups (turning, drilling, planing, milling, and grinding), this study places Nasmyth's metal-cutting innovations in their British and American contexts.

Smiles, Samuel. *Industrial Biography: Iron Workers and Tool Makers.* London: John Murray, 1863. Reprint. New York: Augustus M. Kelley, 1967. Smiles uses the biographies of several commercially successful British engineers, including Nasmyth, to highlight the benefits of self-reliance and hard work in improving one's economic welfare. His romantic accounts of engineering enterprise found large audiences in Victorian England and helped establish the popular image of Nasmyth as the sole inventor of the steam hammer.

SEE ALSO: Marc Isambard Brunel; Richard Trevithick; George Westinghouse.

RELATED ARTICLES in *Great Events from History: The Nineteenth Century, 1801-1900:* March 11, 1811-1816: Luddites Destroy Industrial Machines; 1855: Bessemer Patents Improved Steel-Processing Method.

THOMAS NAST
German-born American cartoonist

One of the greatest American editorial cartoonists, Nast created lasting works of art that expressed his personal and political convictions while reflecting the hopes and dreams of a generation, and his work influenced political events of his time.

BORN: September 27, 1840; Landau, Bavaria (now in Germany)
DIED: December 7, 1902; Guayaquil, Ecuador
AREA OF ACHIEVEMENT: Art

EARLY LIFE

Thomas Nast was born in army barracks in Landau, Germany, where his father, also called Thomas Nast, was a musician in the Ninth Regiment Bavarian Band. The elder Nast and his wife, Apollonia Apres, had three children before Thomas was born. Two boys died at an early age, so that Nast's only playmate was an older sister. In 1846, the Nast family decided to move to the United States, because of the father's political affiliations and the threat of revolution in Germany. While the elder Nast served in the French and American navies, his family moved to New York. He joined them four years later.

Young Thomas Nast had by this time developed considerable artistic talent. His crayon drawings thrilled fellow students and teachers, but Nast did not enjoy school. Finally, his parents allowed him to take art classes instead, first with Theodore Kaufmann and later, Alfred Fredericks. Nast's formal education soon ended, when he showed some of his work to Frank Leslie, publisher of *Frank Leslie's Illustrated Newspaper*. Leslie was impressed with the boldness, if not talent, of this short, round-faced, pudgy, fifteen-year-old German with dark hair and olive skin. After Nast's successful completion of a difficult assignment, Leslie hired him at four dollars a week.

Nast worked diligently for *Frank Leslie's Illustrated Newspaper* over the next four years, receiving much technical training from Sol Eytinge, a coworker and good friend. Nast's drawings during this early period frequently reflected his humorous personality in their subject matter and his study of the English illustrators John Leech, Sir John Gilbert, and Sir John Tenniel, in methodology. Perhaps most significant for the future, however, was Nast's first battle with corruption. Frank Leslie discovered that while dairy owners sold "swill milk" from diseased cows, New York city officials were looking the

other way. With Nast's vivid depictions of the squalid conditions in these dairies, *Frank Leslie's Illustrated Newspaper* brought the issue to the forefront of the news and created a public outcry, which quickly defeated the promoters of the contaminated milk. In this first campaign against corruption, Nast learned that his art could have tremendous political power—a lesson he would not forget.

When Nast left *Frank Leslie's Illustrated Newspaper* in 1859, to work for the *New York Illustrated News*, he covered events such as the funeral of John Brown and the John Heenan-Tom Sayers fight in England. Then, hearing of Giuseppe Garibaldi's invasion of Italy, Nast left England to join the great liberator. While witnessing and recording only a few skirmishes, Nast found upon his return home in February, 1861, that his reputation had grown considerably. Later that year, on the day before his twenty-first birthday, a dignified looking Nast with a recently grown mustache (which became his trademark) married the refined and lovely Sarah Edwards. She would become not only the mother of his five children but also the author of many of the captions for his artwork. Their Niagara Falls honeymoon was a pleasant escape from the realities of a country torn by the Civil War.

LIFE'S WORK

At the outbreak of the Civil War, Nast determined to do what he could for the sacred Union. A more devoted patriot could not be found, especially one with his battlefield experience. Consequently, *Harper's Weekly*, a pictorial newspaper begun in 1857, hired Nast to illustrate the events of the war. This association with *Harper's Weekly* would provide Nast the perfect forum for the expression of his ideas and the development of his art.

Nast soon began to create imaginative works that aroused the patriotism and commitment of his northern audience, pictures that made the Confederate soldier the embodiment of evil and the Union soldier the defender of justice. Nast's fervent support of the Union was recognized by President Abraham Lincoln, who called Nast his best recruiting sergeant.

After the Civil War, Nast used his art to support the Republican Party, which to him represented freedom and equality for the slaves and punishment of the treasonous South. Thus, when President Andrew Johnson adopted a lenient Reconstruction policy for the South, Nast retaliated with his first use of caricature, the comic distortion of identifiable men. In 1868, Nast used this art form in the campaign to elect Ulysses S. Grant, the hero of the war, to the presidency. With his satiric caricatures of the Democratic presidential candidate from New York, Governor Horatio Seymour, Nast not only helped Grant but also established a national reputation for himself.

The following year marked the beginning of Nast's most widely acclaimed political battle. In his crusade against the corrupt Tweed Ring of New York City, Nast's work matured in technique, composition, and power. Nast's enemies were the Tammany Hall Democrats who controlled the New York state legislature, the immigrants, the courts, the police, and, to some extent, organized crime. Nast made the four Tweed Ring leaders—city boss William Marcy Tweed, Peter Barr Sweeny, Richard B. Connolly, and A. Oakey Hall—famous with his caricatures. A cartoon entitled "Shadows of Forthcoming Events" (June 4, 1870) revealed the areas of corruption—schools, elections, street cleaners, the fire department, the board of health, saloons—and the men who were responsible for these conditions.

Thomas Nast. (Library of Congress)

For two years, Nast bombarded the enemy with artistic accusations. His most viciously direct cartoon indicting ring members was "Who Stole the People's Money?" (April 19, 1871), in which corrupt officials stood in a circle, pointing to one another and proclaiming, "Twas Him." Ring members became so frightened over this cartoon that Tweed tried to stop Nast's attacks by threats and then bribery. Nast, true to his principles, vowed not only to continue his fight but also to put the Ring leaders behind bars. With increased public awareness and an honest tabulation of the ballots, the Tweed Ring was defeated in the 1871 election. Although Nast did not win a single-handed victory over the Tweed Ring, one of his caricatures of Tweed did help officials in Spain identify and capture the American fugitive, who died in jail in 1878.

During the early 1870's, Nast continued to support the Republican Party and its candidates, especially Grant, his hero. Nast even created the symbol for the Republican Party, the Republican elephant, and popularized the Democratic donkey in his cartoons. For his assistance in the 1876 campaign of Rutherford B. Hayes, the Republican Party offered Nast ten thousand dollars, but he refused to accept money for expressing his convictions.

Nast became disillusioned with the Republican Party, however, when President Hayes restored home rule to the South in the Compromise of 1877. By 1884, Nast's political dilemma had reached its climax. He could not back James G. Blaine, Republican presidential candidate, because Blaine sponsored Chinese exclusion, a policy contrary to Nast's belief in equality. Nast therefore abandoned the Republicans for the Democratic candidate, Grover Cleveland, whose fiscal policy and personal and political philosophies were more acceptable. However, even though Cleveland won the election, Nast's political influence would never be the same. In 1886, the forty-six-year-old Nast ended his fruitful career with *Harper's Weekly.*

Though Nast continued freelance work and even tried to establish his own paper with the motto *Principles, not Men,* he soon realized that only one area of his work remained popular—his Christmas sketches. For more than twenty-five years, the Christmas issue of *Harper's Weekly* had contained Nast's drawings of Santa Claus, the jolly, fat, fur-clad, white-bearded legend whom Americans still recall at the holiday season. Nast's inspiration for the character came from his childhood memories of Pelze-Nicol—the local name for the German Saint Nicholas who awarded good children with toys and bad ones with switches. Appropriately, Nast's last publication was a Christmas drawing for *Leslie's Weekly* in 1901.

SIGNIFICANCE

Thomas Nast more completely represents life in late nineteenth century United States than most prominent men of his day, for he not only lived it, but he also captured its essence in his artistic creations. His career began at a time when intense nationalism was of primary importance to his country; his Uncle Sam became the symbol of patriotic feeling. After the Civil War, an era of political Reconstruction caused heated debates among American politicians. Nast became a pictorial contributor to these debates as a Radical Republican. Wherever he saw a threat to American democracy, he pounced on it—whether it took the form of the Ku Klux Klan in the South or the Tweed Ring in New York.

Nast's caricatures and cartoon symbols were given life by the intensity of his principles. The popularity of his Tammany tiger, empty dinner pail, and rag baby of inflation reveals more about society in this period than any political speech or statistical study. For twenty-five years, Nast was a molder of public opinion, intuitively sensing the public mood and responding with drawings that stirred the public mind to thought or action. However, by the 1890's, things had changed. The public had grown tired of moral and political crusades. Nast's popularity decreased rapidly, his finances dwindled, and, in 1902, he was forced to accept a gift from his beloved country—a consulship in Ecuador, where he died from yellow fever.

Nast's death indicated the end of an era, but he left a powerful legacy of images: the Republican elephant, the Democratic donkey, Uncle Sam, and the jovial figure who spreads happiness to all humankind, Santa Claus. Moreover, he left the story of a dedicated American whose pursuit of a perfect society with liberty and justice for all could never end.

—*Alice Taylor*

FURTHER READING

Harper's Weekly, 1859-1886. The original publications of Nast's drawings are an essential source of information in tracing his development and analyzing his contribution.

Hess, Stephen, and Sandy Northrop. *Drawn and Quartered: The History of American Political Cartoons*. Montgomery, Ala.: Elliott & Clark, 1996. This illus-trated history features Nast's cartoons mocking Boss Tweed and Tammany Hall.

Keller, Morton. *The Art and Politics of Thomas Nast*. New York: Oxford University Press, 1968. Shows how Nast's work reflected the post-Civil War belief that society can be reformed. Weak regarding Nast's artistic techniques.

Lordan, Edward J. *Politics, Ink: How America's Cartoonists Skewer Politicians from King George III to George Dubya*. Lanham, Md.: Rowman & Littlefield, 2005. Chapter 3 of this cartoon history features information on Nast and other political cartoonists whose work was published between 1860 and 1900.

Nast, Thomas. *Thomas Nast's Christmas Drawings*. Introduction by Thomas Nast St. Hill. New York: Dover, 1978. A reprint of the work published by Harper and Brothers in 1890, which compiled Nast's Christmas drawings of almost thirty years. Three illustrations and the introduction by Nast's grandson have been added.

Paine, Albert Bigelow. *Th. Nast: His Period and His Pictures*. New York: Macmillan, 1904. Nast selected Paine to write this comprehensive biography. Provides sympathetic insight into Nast's personal life while presenting the history of an era. Used by all subsequent biographers. Several facsimile reprints were published during the 1970's.

Smith, Kristen M., and Jennifer L. Gross, eds. *The Lines Are Drawn: Political Cartoons of the Civil War*. Athens, Ga.: Hill Street Press, 1999. Nast's work is included in this collection of 138 comics, cartoons, and caricatures about the Civil War that were originally published by the popular press and printing houses.

Vinson, J. Chal. *Thomas Nast: Political Cartoonist*. Athens: University of Georgia Press, 1967. A scholarly work that condenses the Paine biography, concentrating on those aspects of Nast's career that made him a powerful influence on the politics of his day.

SEE ALSO: James G. Blaine; John Brown; Grover Cleveland; Giuseppe Garibaldi; Ulysses S. Grant; Rutherford B. Hayes; Andrew Johnson; Abraham Lincoln; Carl Schurz; William Marcy Tweed.

RELATED ARTICLES in *Great Events from History: The Nineteenth Century, 1801-1900:* September 3, 1833: Birth of the Penny Press; September 24, 1869-1877: Scandals Rock the Grant Administration.

CARRY NATION
American social reformer

An activist in the temperance and women's rights movements, Nation gained international notoriety by smashing saloons and is remembered as the most outstanding nineteenth century icon of the temperance movement. She also demonstrated the strength and place of women in temperance reform.

BORN: November 25, 1846; Garrard County, Kentucky
DIED: June 9, 1911; Leavenworth, Kansas
ALSO KNOWN AS: Carry Amelia Moore (birth name)
AREAS OF ACHIEVEMENT: Social reform, women's rights

EARLY LIFE

The daughter of George Moore and Mary Campbell Moore, Carry Nation was born Carry Amelia Moore. (The name "Carry" was written in her illiterate father's hand in the family Bible with that spelling.) She grew up amid the slave culture of Kentucky. Her father was a prosperous planter and stock trader; her mother suffered from a delusionary mental illness and assumed she was Queen Victoria, demanding the appropriate degree of respect from those around her.

At the age of ten, Carry was converted at a Campbellite revival, an event that had a profound effect on her spiritual development. Her early secular education was limited because her family moved at least a dozen times between Kentucky, Missouri, and Texas before she was sixteen. She did manage, however, to attend a teacher's college in Missouri, where she earned a teaching certificate.

Carry's father lost his slaves and land as a result of the Civil War, and took his family back to Missouri, settling in Belton. Carry met and fell in love there with a young army physician, Charles Gloyd. They were married on November 21, 1867; however, because of Gloyd's alcoholism and fierce devotion to the Masonic Lodge, the marriage deteriorated soon after the nuptials. Despite her love for Charles, she never persuaded him to stop drinking, which he did in the company of his fellow Masons, and within two years of their marriage he was dead, leaving Carry with an infant daughter, Charlien, who may have grown up insane, an elderly mother-in-law, and an intense dislike for both alcohol and secret societies.

For several years, Carry supported herself, her daughter, and her mother-in-law by teaching in a primary school in Holden, Missouri. In 1877, she married David Nation, an attorney, minister, and editor who was nineteen years her senior. They had little in common, and for Carry it proved to be an unhappy match. They lived for several years in Texas, where Carry supported the family by running a hotel. In 1890, they moved to Medicine Lodge, Kansas, where David became a minister and then left the pulpit to practice law. His practice grew large enough to free Carry from the necessity of supporting the family, and as a result, she became active in the temperance movement as well as in religious and civic reform. Because of her interest in charitable activities, the residents of Medicine Lodge called her Mother Nation. Her second marriage also deteriorated, however, and in 1901 Carry's husband divorced her.

LIFE'S WORK

Before David and Carry Nation moved to Kansas, a constitutional amendment adopted in 1880 had made it a dry state. This occurred nearly half a century before the passage of the Eighteenth Amendment and fifty years after the beginning of the temperance movement in the United States. In Kansas, a legal technicality allowed liquor in its original container to be served. Carry, believing that she had a divine mission to stop the drinking of alcoholic beverages, organized a chapter of the Women's Christian Temperance Union (WCTU) with the intention of driving out the "wets" (those who drank).

Carry's first major confrontation took place in 1899, when, in the company of several other WCTU members, she managed through nonviolent means to shut down seven liquor distributors. During the following year, she changed her tactics when she traveled twenty miles by buggy to smash three "joints," or saloons, using rocks and brickbats, in Kiowa, Kansas. Carry rationalized that because those establishments were illegal, they had no protection under the law; therefore, she had the right to destroy them. From Kiowa she went to Wichita, where she used a hatchet to destroy the bar in the Hotel Carey. This venture resulted in several thousand dollars of property damage for the saloon owner and seven weeks in jail for Nation. From there it was on to Enterprise and then the state capital, Topeka, for several days of bar chopping. Each incident earned for her more time in the local jail, usually for disturbing the peace.

Prior to her appearance in Topeka, Nation's activities had been of the hit-and-run variety. She would typically break up a few saloons and then either leave town or go to

Carry Nation. (Library of Congress)

jail. Realizing that she could not single-handedly close down all the offending liquor establishments in Kansas, she intended to use Topeka as a focal point for an organization that, she hoped, would achieve her goal.

After holding an unsuccessful meeting with the governor of Kansas, Carry Nation set about to organize her mostly feminine supporters into an army of Home Defenders. Led by General Nation, who was ably supported by assistant generals, the force numbered several hundred. Nation accepted numerous speaking engagements to spread her message that the only way to close the joints was to increase the agitation against them. In keeping with her message, she took her Home Defenders on the offensive, smashing the ritzy Senate Saloon. In the melee, Nation, who was often in physical danger, received a nasty cut on the head. Despite the destruction, the bar reopened within hours, selling beer, whiskey, and souvenirs from the wreckage.

Carry Nation's actions exacerbated the split in the temperance movement: on one hand, between the sexes, and on the other hand, between those who supported such violence as necessary and those who took a more passive and traditional approach to the liquor control is-

sue. Nation helped to focus the issue of prohibition in Kansas. Generally, the Prohibitionists, who represented the more radical fringe, supported her tactics, while the Women's Christian Temperance Union leadership, made up mostly of Republicans or Populists, opposed them. Those who opposed Nation disliked her taking the law into her own hands, and they rejected her argument that the joint owners, being lawbreakers themselves, deserved to be put out of business violently.

Nation supported herself and paid her fines by means of lecturing, stage appearances, and the sale of souvenir miniature silver hatchets. For a time, she earned as much as $300 a week. To help with her finances, she employed a management firm, and she later hired her own manager, Harry C. Turner. However, Nation had little business sense, giving away most of her money to the poor and to temperance groups, not all of which were legitimate.

Nation also took on a few publishing ventures to spread the word. At varying times, *The Smasher's Mail*, *The Hatchet*, and *The Home Defender* appeared. While in Topeka, she wrote her autobiography, *The Use and Need of the Life of Carry A. Nation* (1905).

Although she spent the majority of her time in the temperance crusade in Kansas, she did venture to the East Coast, where she visited both Yale and Harvard. However, on both occasions she allowed herself to be portrayed as a buffoon, thus adding to the negative image surrounding her. She later toured England, where again her welcome was less than expansive.

Physically, Carry Nation was a large woman. Nearly six feet tall, she weighed approximately 175 pounds and was extremely strong. When she and her minions broke up the Senate Saloon, she lifted the heavy cash register, raised it above her head, and smashed it to the ground.

After less than a decade in the public spotlight, however, her health failed, and she retired to a farm in the Ozark Mountains of Arkansas. She spent the last several months of her life in a Leavenworth, Kansas, hospital and died there on June 9, 1911. After her death, friends erected a monument at her gravesite with the inscription "She hath done what she could."

SIGNIFICANCE

Carry Nation's impact is both real and symbolic. She did show the nation that direct action can help to focus attention on a moral issue. When, in 1901, Nation went to speak to the Kansas legislature, she told them that since she was denied the vote, she would have to use a stone, and use the stone (or hatchet, to be more specific) she did. The joints she smashed were not significant in terms of her impact on temperance and prohibition. In fact, at least a few of them reopened within hours or days of her visit. Her impact had to do with her ability to rally support to her cause. She focused attention on the issue of alcohol consumption. Representing the views of a majority of Kansans, she showed them that one individual could make a difference.

Nation also had a significant impact on women's rights. She certainly broke with the traditional roles of woman as wife and mother, although she did fulfill both roles. At a time when few women engaged in public protest, Nation was at the cutting edge of that activity. She opened a home in Kansas City for women who had suffered at the hands of male alcoholics. She determined that her activity had been made necessary by a male-dominated world—as a woman, she did not have access to political power. As time went on, however, Nation appeared to be moving toward nonviolent direct action and away from saloon smashing. The masthead of her newspaper *The Hatchet* (1905) encouraged women to seek the vote instead of resorting to the hatchet.

Carry Nation has been badly treated by most of her biographers. In part, she was responsible for her own bad reputation. In her autobiography, she perhaps revealed too much of her personal and religious life, thus exposing herself to criticism. She played into the hands of her critics when she made outrageous statements or visited college campuses where she should have expected to be placed in a bad light. Her methods appeared unfeminine in a decade when feminine virtue was extolled. She also became the victim of the eastern press, which delighted in poking fun at the crude ways of westerners by mocking Nation as a social misfit and a religious freak.

Carry Nation died almost a decade before the passage of the Eigh-

teenth Amendment, which outlawed the manufacture, distribution, sale, and consumption of alcoholic beverages. Whether people remembered her in 1919 is not of great importance; the amendment passed in part at least because she focused the attention of many Americans on

---

AN UNFRIENDLY MOB IN KANSAS

Carry Nation's work of smashing saloons naturally made her some enemies. In her autobiography she recalls a particularly unpleasant experience that she had in Kansas.

While in Enterprise I got a telegram from Holt, signed by the "Temperance Committee," it read: "Come here and help us break up dives." This little town was only twelve miles from Enterprise. In going to the train that night there seemed to have been some one hiding on every corner throwing eggs. My dress was covered with them. I got to Holt at midnight. When I got off the train, I then knew it was a plot to injure me for no one was there to meet me, and I saw some suspicious men keeping in the dark. I got in a hack and went to a hotel. I asked for the women but all had retired. I went up to my room, which was very small. It had one window which was raised an inch with a lath under it, and I thought it strange at the time that the landlord should have let the window down, but I was very tired and dropped asleep almost as soon as I touched the bed. About two o'clock I was awakened with a smothered feeling, struggling for breath. I jumped for the window, which I threw up, for the room was full of the most poisonous odor, as of cigarettes, and other smells. I knew that there were persons at the door puffing the poison in. I sat at the window and listened and in about fifteen minutes I heard some one whistling and saw through the transom that a light was coming. A man stopped at my door and knocked.

"What do you want?"

"I want to speak to you," he replied.

"What is it?"

"I want to speak to you."

God showed me in a vision two men crouched on each side of the door ready to either catch or slug me, if the door was opened.

"I see you sluggers on each side of the door. You villain, you have tried to murder me by throwing poison in my room and now you are trying something else."

"There is a mob here after you."

"You are a liar," I answered.

"There is a committee wants to speak to you."

"You are telling lies in order to have me open my door."

He left and went down below, and for ten minutes there was a great tramping of feet and I could hear the landlord making out as if he was dispersing a crowd. I watched from my window and saw two men walking away. I certainly was thankful for a lock on my door. Next morning when ready to leave my room, I looked up and down the passages well; then I hurried and did not feel safe, until I got on the outside. I asked a little boy if there were any Christians in Holt.

"No, but there are some in the country."

Source: Carry Nation, *The Use and Need of the Life of Carry A. Nation* (rev. ed. Topeka, Kans.: F. M. Steves & Sons, 1905), chapter 9.

---

the issue of prohibition. Whether one was for or against temperance, it would have been difficult in the first decade of the twentieth century to ignore the issue, especially when Carry Nation went storming into bars with hatchet in hand. She also died a decade before the passage of the Nineteenth Amendment, which granted women the right to vote. Her statements to the Kansas legislature, as well as her newspaper's masthead, indicate that Carry Nation well knew the power of the ballot and the importance of working for the right of women to vote.

—Duncan R. Jamieson

FURTHER READING

Asbury, Herbert. *Carry Nation*. New York: Alfred A. Knopf, 1929. This older biography paints Nation as a social misfit.

Bader, Robert Smith. *Prohibition in Kansas*. Lawrence: University Press of Kansas, 1986. This general history of prohibition in Kansas contains a positive chapter on Carry Nation and her contribution to the temperance movement.

Flexner, Eleanor. *Century of Struggle: The Woman's Rights Movement in the United States*. Rev. ed. Cambridge, Mass.: Belknap Press of Harvard University Press, 1975. Provides an excellent starting point for anyone interested in the women's rights movement.

Grace, Fran. *Carry A. Nation: Retelling the Life*. Bloomington: Indiana University Press, 2001. Grace contradicts earlier biographers who portrayed Nation as crazy, fanatical, and either over- or undersexed. She presents a more complicated portrait of Nation, tracing the roots of her religious piety and social activism, and describing how contemporaries admired Nation's riveting speeches and political courage.

Gusfield, Joseph. *Symbolic Crusade: Status Politics and the American Temperance Movement*. Urbana: University of Illinois Press, 1963. An interesting and useful history of the temperance movement from its nineteenth century roots to the passage of the Eighteenth Amendment.

Lewis, Robert Taylor. *Vessel of Wrath: The Life and Times of Carry Nation*. New York: New American Library, 1966. A relatively recent biography written in negative terms.

Mattingly, Carol. *Well-Tempered Women: Nineteenth Century Temperance Rhetoric*. Carbondale: Southern Illinois University Press, 1998. Recounts the techniques and rhetoric women used to create the Women's Christian Temperance Union and campaign for prohibition.

Nation, Carry. *The Use and Need of the Life of Carry A. Nation, Written by Herself*. Topeka, Kans.: F. M. Steves & Sons, 1905. Nation's autobiography sets the negative tone for her biographers.

Schwarz, Frederic D. "1900." *American Heritage* 51, no. 3 (May/June, 2000): 107. Describes Nation's campaign to close bars in Kiowa, Kansas, that served liquor to customers in 1900.

SEE ALSO: Amelia Bloomer; Anna Howard Shaw; Queen Victoria; Frances Willard.

RELATED ARTICLES in *Great Events from History: The Nineteenth Century, 1801-1900:* 1820's-1850's: Social Reform Movement; February 17-18, 1890: Women's Rights Associations Unite.

LORD NELSON
English naval leader

Nelson is perhaps the most venerated figure in British naval history. His innovative tactics in battle and his determination to achieve total victory over the enemy made him one of the most successful admirals in naval history and helped to establish the tradition of British perseverance until final victory could be won.

BORN: September 29, 1758; Burnham Thorpe, Norfolk, England
DIED: October 21, 1805; off Cape Trafalgar, Spain
ALSO KNOWN AS: Horatio Nelson (birth name); Viscount Nelson; Sir Horatio Nelson; Viscount Nelson of the Nile and Burnham Thorpe
AREA OF ACHIEVEMENT: Military

EARLY LIFE

Horatio Nelson was born in an Anglican parsonage in the English county of Norfolk. He was the sixth of eleven children of Edmund and Catherine Nelson. His father, a devout, educated man, was a minister in the Church of England and was following his own father's occupation, although without much financial reward. Catherine Nelson came from a family that owned much land and occupied a respected position on the social ladder; her father was the prebendary of Westminster, and her maternal grandmother was the sister of Sir Robert Walpole, the first prime minister in English history. The Walpoles resided nearby, at Houghton, and the second Lord Walpole of Wolterton acted as godfather to young Nelson when he was christened.

As a young boy, Nelson was sent by his father to three separate schools in Norfolk, but some of his major personal beliefs he developed at home. Although his mother died when he was only nine years old, Nelson remembered that it was from her that he became aware that France was England's ancient enemy. From his father, he learned about piety and obedience to God, and throughout his naval career he often expressed his pleasure at being able to serve God as well as his country.

Young Nelson was always sensitive to criticism, and he displayed his emotions publicly. In future years, as an officer in the fleet, he continued to display these same feelings, even though it was a tradition for naval officers to keep their feelings well hidden from their men. This practice, however, coupled with an unusually large measure of common sense, a genuine interest in the welfare of his men, and a willingness to lead his crew personally into battle, helped to produce the feelings of awe, re-

spect, and loyalty that his men always held for him. Nelson received many serious injuries in the line of duty, and members of his crew, who were the most likely to be injured or killed in close combat with the enemy, trusted him as an officer who would actually lead them into battle and not simply watch their actions from a safe distance.

In the meantime, after the death of Catherine Nelson it was increasingly difficult for Edmund Nelson to provide proper care for all of his children, and they gradually left home to obtain independent positions. For Horatio, an interest in the sea had been slowly developing. From his hometown, he could easily catch sight of the North Sea and the ships that sailed its waters almost constantly, and on occasion he would sail some of his paper boats down one of the streets of Burnham Thorpe. His desire to go to sea, however, seemed to represent a most unlikely choice for a boy of his physical build: His rather thin face was highlighted by a large, protruding nose and piercing blue eyes, and he possessed a frail body that would attain a height of less than five feet, six inches by adulthood. Throughout his life, he would be plagued by a constant cough, and he often had difficulty sleeping at night. Fits of depression troubled him from time to time, and occasionally he was unable to keep his food down. Later in life, he would be afflicted with seasickness if forced to remain for long on a small vessel.

These problems notwithstanding, Nelson, at the age of twelve, sought to go to sea. His father registered no objections, and his uncle, Maurice Suckling, who held the position of post-captain in the navy at the time, agreed to obtain a position for his young nephew on his own ship, the *Raisonnable*, in spite of his personal doubts about Nelson's physical qualifications.

Suckling's ship was to sail to the Falkland Islands to defend Great Britain's position in a dispute with Spain over the ownership of those islands. This voyage, which was Nelson's first at sea, ended peacefully, and subsequently the young man was placed with John Rathbone, an officer who had served under Suckling during the Seven Years' War and who was now commanding a ship for the trading firm of Hibbert, Purrier, and Horton. Under Rathbone's guidance, the young Nelson sailed on a voyage to the West Indies, and it was this voyage that convinced him that he wanted to spend the rest of his life in the Royal Navy.

LIFE'S WORK

Nelson's naval career began in 1773, when he served as a coxswain on a scientific expedition to the Arctic. He subsequently was assigned as a midshipman in the waters off India, and by the age of nineteen, he was commissioned with the rank of lieutenant. Throughout his career as an officer, Nelson worked hard to keep morale high on his ships. He regularly invited other officers to fine dinners in his quarters and tactfully inquired as to the welfare of the members of their families. Although he expected absolute obedience, he never forgot the basic needs of his men; their living quarters were equipped with stoves to prevent dampness, and in the evenings, they were allowed to play music and to dance.

At the time Nelson was commissioned, the American Revolution was in progress, and he spent much of the war on duty in the West Indies. After the war ended, Nelson, now a post-captain, remained in the islands until 1787. It was on this peacetime tour that he met Frances Nesbit, the widowed niece of John Herbert, the president of the island of Nevis. On March 11, 1787, Nelson married the woman he said would keep him happy for the rest of his life.

During his courtship, however, Nelson aroused the ire of the local planters and merchants by refusing to allow

Lord Nelson. (Library of Congress)

them to trade with ships from the United States. Although the Board of Trade defended Nelson's actions, he became so unpopular that he returned to England two months after his marriage in 1787. From 1787 to 1793, Nelson lived quietly with his family in Burnham Thorpe, a virtual social outcast because of the many complaints from the wealthy residents of the West Indies. When war with France appeared imminent in 1793, however, his unpopularity faded and he was assigned to the Mediterranean fleet under Admiral Samuel Hood.

On this tour of duty, Nelson saw military action around Corsica. As was his custom, he took little precaution for safety and was standing right up at the batteries outside Calvi on July 12, 1794, when he was hit in the right eye by sand and rocks from a French shell. As a result of this injury, he permanently lost the use of his eye, although it was never removed.

After a brief period of recuperation, Nelson was eventually assigned to the command of Admiral John Jervis, who commanded a fleet of fifteen ships of the line and was known for his strict discipline. On February 14, 1797, off Cape St. Vincent, Jervis attacked a Spanish fleet of twenty-seven ships of the line by moving his ships in a line between the leading and the trailing Spanish columns. Nelson, however, realized that the enemy segments would be able to join before the British move could be completed, and without orders he pulled his own ship out of the line and blocked the advance of the Spanish flagship. In the fierce fighting that followed, Nelson personally boarded and captured two Spanish ships. When the battle ended, the Spanish had lost four ships of the line, while the British had lost none. For Nelson, who had risked a court-martial by breaking naval tradition, Jervis had only words of praise. Both men were subsequently rewarded; Jervis became the earl of St. Vincent, and Nelson was promoted to the rank of rear-admiral and became a Knight of the Bath.

St. Vincent, convinced by now of Nelson's abilities, next sent him to capture a Spanish treasure ship in the harbor of Santa Cruz, on the island of Teneriffe, in the Canary Islands. On July 24, 1797, Nelson, in typical fashion, led the attack himself, but a musket ball shattered his right arm. Within hours, surgeons amputated the arm just above the elbow, and Nelson's tour of duty had come to an end.

After a brief recuperation in England, Nelson was sent to watch the French fleet at Toulon. When this fleet sailed for Egypt in May, 1798, he gave chase and finally came upon it in late July in Aboukir Bay, just east of Al-

A LETTER TO EMMA HAMILTON

Lord Nelson's amorous relationship with Lady Hamilton nearly ruined his naval career, but he maintained that relationship until the end of his life. This letter to Hamilton, written on July 31, 1801, deals mainly with mundane subjects and mentions Horatia, Hamilton's daughter by Nelson. Nelson signs his name "Nelson & Bronte," using the ducal title conferred on him by the king of Sicily.

MY DEAREST EMMA,

Did not you get my letter from Sheerness on Thursday morning, telling you I was just setting off for Deal; as I have no letter from you of yesterday, only those of Wednesday, which went to Sheerness? It has been my damned blunder, and not your's; for which I am deservedly punished, by missing one of your dear letters. They are my comfort, joy, and delight.

My time is, truly, fully taken up, and my hand aches before night comes.

I got to bed, last night, at half past nine; but the hour was so unusual, that I heard the clock strike one. To say that I thought of you, would be nonsense; for, you are never out of my thoughts.

At this moment, I see no prospect of my getting to London; but, very soon, the business of my command will become so simple, that a child may direct it.

What rascals your post-chaise people must be! They have been paid every thing. Captain Parker has one receipt for seven pounds odd, and I am sure that every thing is paid; therefore, do not pay a farthing. The cart-chaise I paid at Dartford.

You need not fear all the women in this world; for all others, except yourself, are pests to me. I know but one; for, who can be like my Emma? I am confident, you will do nothing which can hurt my feelings; and I will die by torture, sooner than do any thing which could offend you.

Give ten thousand kisses to my dear Horatia. . . .

Ever, for ever, your's, only your,

NELSON & BRONTE.

Best regards to Mrs. Nelson, the Duke, and Lord William.

I have totally failed for poor Madame Brueys.

Bonaparte's wife is one of Martinique, and some plan is supposed to be carried on.

Source: Horatio Nelson, *The Letters of Lord Nelson to Lady Hamilton* (London: T. Lovewell, 1814), vol. 1, letter 13.

exandria. Admiral Francis Brueys, the French commander, had placed his thirteen ships of the line close to the shoals offshore, so that only the seaward side of his ships could be attacked by Nelson. Because of his strong position, Brueys did not bother to clear his guns on the landward side of his ships, and he was caught completely by surprise on August 1, 1798, when Nelson sent five of his thirteen ships of the line between the French fleet and the shoals offshore. Panic broke out among the French as they were fired on from two sides at once, and although Nelson himself was wounded in the forehead, his victory in the Battle of the Nile was assured

when Brueys's flagship, *L'Orient*, exploded. By dawn of the next day, only two of the French ships had escaped; Nelson had not lost a single ship, and for his efforts he was made Baron of the Nile.

From Egypt, Nelson sailed to Naples, where his famous affair with Lady Emma Hamilton led to the birth of a daughter, Horatia. This affair, however, severely damaged Nelson's reputation; when he returned to England in 1799, he found himself rejected by both society and his wife. In January, 1801, Horatio and Frances Nelson permanently separated.

The Admiralty, however, still needed Nelson's services, and he was assigned as second in command to Sir Hyde Parker on an expedition to detach Denmark from the League of Armed Neutrality. Parker, who fought by the book, cautiously agreed to Nelson's plan to attack the harbor of Copenhagen at its least defended point by sailing through a narrow, shallow waterway that was considered impassable for ships of the line. Nelson attacked on April 2, 1801, but when the Danes put up unexpected resistance Parker ordered him to withdraw. In response, Nelson placed his telescope to his blind eye, reported that he could see no such order, and scored a major victory within the hour. Once again, Nelson had disobeyed the orders of a superior officer, but he was praised by Sir Thomas Masterman Hardy, Nelson's flag captain, and was made a viscount for his victory.

Lord Nelson subsequently remained in England until 1803, when war with France was renewed. Now a vice-admiral, he was named commander in chief for the Mediterranean Fleet and began to cover the fleet of Admiral Pierre de Villeneuve at Toulon. Villeneuve made various efforts to join up with other ships of the French fleet, but Nelson pursued him closely and eventually engaged him in battle off Cape Trafalgar on October 21, 1805. In this action, Nelson's twenty-seven ships broke the enemy line of thirty-three in two places, in the rear and in the center. Typically, Nelson led the attack on the center himself, but about one hour and twenty minutes after the battle had begun, a musketeer in the rigging of the French ship *Redoutable* fatally wounded Nelson, who fell with a bullet through his spine. Before he died, however, he learned that eighteen of the enemy ships had been destroyed or captured and that not one of his own vessels had been lost. With his last words, he thanked God that he had been able to do his duty.

Nelson's body was returned to England, where on January 9, 1806, it received one of the most impressive funerals in all British history. According to his wishes, Nelson was buried in St. Paul's Cathedral.

SIGNIFICANCE

Even before his death, Lord Nelson was regarded as a legend, and the circumstances surrounding his funeral merely added to that mystique. Captain Benjamin Hallowell of the *Swiftsure* had given his commander, as a victory souvenir, a beautiful wooden coffin fashioned out of part of the main mast of *L'Orient* after the Battle of the Nile, and it was in this coffin that the famous admiral was buried.

Memories of the funeral faded, but people never forgot that Nelson was the first British commander to seek not merely victory but also total destruction of the enemy fleet. The victory at Trafalgar ended Napoleon I's hopes for an invasion of Great Britain and became a symbol of British inspiration in the dark days when Adolf Hitler was putting forth every effort to conquer the island kingdom.

Nelson's legacy is well represented by preservation of his last ship, the *Victory*, a ship of the line of one hundred guns that became a national monument. Nelson himself is also remembered in London's Trafalgar Square, where his statue stands as a constant reminder of the man who saved Great Britain from one of the greatest threats in its long history.

—*David W. Krueger*

FURTHER READING

Bowen, Marjorie. *Patriotic Lady*. New York: D. Appleton-Century, 1936. A useful work that presents much detailed information about the personalities of Nelson and Hamilton. The coverage of Hamilton's first meeting with Frances Nelson is particularly interesting. Well researched, the work includes a good index and a helpful bibliography.

Coleman, Terry. *The Nelson Touch: The Life and Legend of Horatio Nelson*. New York: Oxford University Press, 2002. Well-researched, balanced biography of Nelson, whom the author describes as "a paramount naval genius and a natural born predator."

Hattersley, Roy. *Nelson*. New York: Saturday Review Press, 1974. The style is easy to follow, and many drawings and portraits are included. Although he covers Nelson's major victories, Hattersley also takes time to bring out the personality behind those victories. The index is most helpful for the general reader.

Howarth, David. *Trafalgar: The Nelson Touch*. New York: Atheneum, 1969. One of the most readable of all books about Nelson, this work concentrates upon the admiral's last campaign. Howarth provides specific details; he also covers Nelson's close relations with the men who served under him. An excellent index and many maps and drawings enhance the scholarly nature of this work.

Mahan, Alfred T. *The Influence of Sea Power upon History, 1660-1783*. Boston: Little, Brown, 1890. A standard work in the field, Mahan's book helps the reader to understand why control of the sea is so important during wartime. Nelson's tactics at Aboukir Bay and Trafalgar are analyzed, and his general manner in battle is also discussed.

_____. *The Influence of Sea Power upon the French Revolution and Empire, 1793-1812*. 2 vols. Boston: Little, Brown, 1892. A famous work in the field, featuring maps, drawings, explanatory footnotes, and an extremely complete index. Contains helpful coverage of Nelson's campaigns in detail, with emphasis upon the tactics that he introduced.

Marcus, Geoffrey J. *The Age of Nelson: The Royal Navy, 1793-1815*. New York: Viking Press, 1971. An excellent, well-researched work complete with maps, many illustrations, footnotes, and a thorough list of sources for additional reading. Quite helpful in its discussion of Nelson's relations with Jervis.

Pope, Dudley. *The Great Gamble*. New York: Simon & Schuster, 1972. A complete account of the Copenhagen campaign, Pope's work provides footnotes, maps, and a full bibliography. Discussion of the contrast in the personalities of Nelson and Parker is especially helpful. Virtually any fact that the reader desires to know about the Copenhagen campaign may be found in this book.

Sugden, John. *Nelson: A Dream of Glory, 1758-1797*. New York: Henry Holt, 2004. The first of a projected two-volume definitive biography. Sugden makes excellent use of primary sources to present Nelson's life and career in all of their complexity and to place them within the context of eighteenth century naval service.

Vincent, Edgar. *Nelson: Love and Fame.* New Haven, Conn.: Yale University Press, 2003. A perceptive, empathetic look at Nelson's professional and emotional lives, describing the causes and effects of his insatiable desire for admiration and attention.

Warner, Oliver. *Nelson's Battles.* New York: Macmillan, 1965. Warner provides detailed information about Nelson's major engagements; an appendix lists all the ships and captains who served with Nelson at Aboukir Bay, Copenhagen, and Trafalgar. Excellent maps, many portraits, and frequent quotations from Nelson and his contemporaries.

_____. *Victory: The Life of Lord Nelson.* Boston: Little, Brown, 1958. A well-written, detailed life of Nelson in which considerable emphasis is placed upon personalities as well as major campaigns. Includes an extensive bibliography and a most complete index.

SEE ALSO: Napoleon I; Duke of Wellington.

RELATED ARTICLES in *Great Events from History: The Nineteenth Century, 1801-1900:* October 21, 1805: Battle of Trafalgar; 1889: Great Britain Strengthens Its Royal Navy.

SIMON NEWCOMB
Canadian-born American astronomer

As superintendent of The American Ephemeris and Nautical Almanac and later as director of the U.S. Naval Observatory, Newcomb undertook a complete revision of the data used for calculating the positions of the planets, and his work led to the adoption of a new set of international standards for astronomical calculations.

BORN: March 12, 1835; Wallace, Nova Scotia, Canada
DIED: July 11, 1909; Washington, D.C.
AREAS OF ACHIEVEMENT: Astronomy, mathematics

EARLY LIFE

Simon Newcomb was taught by his father, an itinerant Nova Scotia schoolmaster, but otherwise had no formal education as a child. Nevertheless, he developed an intense interest in learning and felt keenly deprived by the intellectual poverty of the primitive rural area in which he grew up. He later described his childhood as "one of sadness," likened its primitive conditions to growing up at the time of the American Revolution, and titled the chapter of his autobiography on his childhood "The World of Cold and Darkness."

At the age of sixteen, Newcomb entered into apprenticeship with an herbalist but soon became disenchanted with the man's unscientific practices and left Canada. In Maine, he signed aboard a ship that sailed for Salem, Massachusetts, where he rejoined his father, who had moved there previously. The two then moved to Maryland, where Simon taught in rural schools for two years. In 1856, he became a private tutor near Washington, D.C., and took advantage of the location by frequently visiting libraries in the capital city. In that setting, Newcomb finally began to experience the intellectual stimulation that he had craved. During his spare time, he studied such subjects as religion, economics, and astronomy.

In 1857, Newcomb took a job at *The American Ephemeris and Nautical Almanac*, which was then located in Cambridge, Massachusetts, and also began studying mathematics and conducting research at Harvard University. One of his first noteworthy achievements was a study of the orbits of the asteroids. His findings showed that it was unlikely that the asteroids had formed from the breakup of a planet, as was then widely supposed. In 1860, he participated in one of the most ill-fated eclipse expeditions in history. The journey required travel by rail, stagecoach, and canoe into remote central Canada and was repeatedly delayed by storms and flooded rivers. Members of the expedition finally reached a site for viewing the eclipse after twenty-four hours of non-stop canoe travel, only to have the eclipse itself hidden from their view by clouds.

LIFE'S WORK

When the U.S. Civil War broke out in 1861, a number of officers at the U.S. Naval Observatory resigned in order to join fighting units, and Newcomb was appointed to fill one of the vacancies. In 1864, he and other observatory staff members were called to active duty for a short time when Confederate forces briefly threatened to attack Washington, D.C.

As Newcomb gained experience in astronomical calculations, it became apparent to him that the best available tables for predicting the positions of the moon were yielding unacceptably large errors. In 1870, he took advantage of an eclipse expedition to Gibraltar to visit most of the major observatories of Europe and to make an extended visit to Paris.

Newcomb's visit to Paris in May, 1871, came at a remarkably unfortunate time. The Franco-Prussian War had only recently ended, and Paris was under siege and occupied by a revolutionary government, the Commune, which would be violently suppressed not long after Newcomb's departure. Although Newcomb described Paris in a letter as a "slumbering volcano," he was nevertheless able to spend six weeks at the Paris Observatory without mishap. During that time, he was delighted to discover many good records of the moon's position dating back to 1675—three-quarters of a century earlier than previously known historical data. He termed this discovery the greatest find he ever made.

Precise predictions of the motions of the sun, moon, and planets are necessary for accurate navigation and timekeeping. When Newcomb assumed the post of superintendent of *The American Ephemeris and Nautical Almanac* in 1877, the almanacs then being issued by various nations differed significantly in the fundamental quantities they used in calculating planetary predictions. To improve the accuracy of the predictions, Newcomb and his assistants had to recalculate the positions of the stars and planets from original observations. They also had to detect, assess, and correct errors in existing almanacs. Of this work, Newcomb said:

One might almost say it involved repeating, in a space of ten or fifteen years, an important part of the world's work in astronomy for more than a century past.

The work of Newcomb and his collaborators set such a high standard that an international conference in 1896 agreed to use their data compiled as the basis for all astronomical calculations. Despite this recognition of his work, Newcomb once wrote that he had never been able to confine his attention to astronomy "with that exclusiveness which is commonly considered necessary to the highest success in any profession." This was a remarkable admission from a scientist who achieved the highest success in his profession.

Another of Newcomb's interests quite separate from astronomy was economics. He first became recognized

---

THE POSSIBILITY OF LIFE ON THE MOON

The moon being much the nearest to us of all the heavenly bodies, we can pronounce more definitely in its case than in any other. We know that neither air nor water exists on the moon in quantities sufficient to be perceived by the most delicate tests at our command. It is certain that the moon's atmosphere, if any exists, is less than the thousandth part of the density of that around us. The vacuum is greater than any ordinary air-pump is capable of producing. We can hardly suppose that so small a quantity of air could be of any benefit whatever in sustaining life; an animal that could get along on so little could get along on none at all.

But the proof of the absence of life is yet stronger when we consider the results of actual telescopic observation. An object such as an ordinary city block could be detected on the moon. If anything like vegetation were present on its surface, we should see the changes which it would undergo in the course of a month, during one portion of which it would be exposed to the rays of the unclouded sun, and during another to the intense cold of space. If men built cities, or even separate buildings the size of the larger ones on our earth, we might see some signs of them.

In recent times we not only observe the moon with the telescope, but get still more definite information by photography. The whole visible surface has been repeatedly photographed under the best conditions. But no change has been established beyond question, nor does the photograph show the slightest difference of structure or shade which could be attributed to cities or other works of man. To all appearances the whole surface of our satellite is as completely devoid of life as the lava newly thrown from Vesuvius. We next pass to the planets. Mercury, the nearest to the sun, is in a position very unfavorable for observation from the earth, because when nearest to us it is between us and the sun, so that its dark hemisphere is presented to us. Nothing satisfactory has yet been made out as to its condition. We cannot say with certainty whether it has an atmosphere or not. What seems very probable is that the temperature on its surface is higher than any of our earthly animals could sustain. But this proves nothing.

Source: Simon Newcomb, *Side-Lights on Astronomy and Kindred Fields of Popular Science: Essays and Addresses* (New York: Harper & Brothers, 1906).

as an economist with a short book warning of the dangers of debased currency during the Civil War. In 1886, he published *Principles of Political Economy*, a 550-page book in which he approached economics in a way that might be expected from an astronomer: by stating simple, fundamental laws and then developing the consequences of those laws in greater and greater detail. However, Newcomb was quite aware of the limitations of economics as a science and its weaknesses in deciding policy.

One of Newcomb's less successful scientific efforts was his analysis of the possibility of powered heavier-than-air flight. He reasoned that the ability of a craft to fly depended on the area of its wings and therefore on the square of its dimensions, but concluded, incorrectly, that the aircraft's weight would increase as the cube of its dimensions, and therefore any machine large enough to support a human being would be impossibly heavy. What Newcomb failed to anticipate was that future construction methods would employ materials that maintained the necessary strength but reduce weight. More important, he failed to take into account the importance of wing cross-section in generating lift. Newcomb published an analysis of the problem in a news magazine, *The Independent*, in October, 1903. Less than two months later, two bicycle builders, Wilbur and Orville Wright, successfully flew a heavier-than-air craft at Kitty Hawk, North Carolina, after making careful studies of lift and wing design.

In 1908, Newcomb was diagnosed with cancer of the bladder. He died on July 11, 1909, in Washington, D.C.

SIGNIFICANCE

The awe that Newcomb felt as a young man when he finally came into contact with a world of learning never entirely left him. His autobiography suggests a man interested in almost everything he encountered. He wrote about historically obscure assistants with the same personal attention that he applied to the most illustrious scientists of his day. He spent far more effort describing the events around him and the people he met than he did on the technical details of his own work.

Precise projections of the motions of astronomical bodies are necessary for accurate navigation. After Newcomb assumed the post of superintendent of *The American Ephemeris and Nautical Almanac*, he developed measurements that served as the international standard for accuracy until 1984. His measurements were superseded only after the development of radar-ranging of planets and spacecraft, electronic computers, and improved mathematical techniques made it possible to

achieve even greater accuracy. Nevertheless, in the twenty-first century, numerous astronomical computer programs were still using simplified versions of Newcomb's original methods.

Newcomb received a large number of scientific honors during his lifetime. In addition, Cape Newcomb, Greenland, was named after him, as was the World War II naval surveying ship the USS *Simon Newcomb*. Craters on the Moon and Mars bear his name, as does an asteroid named Newcombia. In 1978, the Royal Astronomical Society of Canada founded the Simon Newcomb Award to honor achievements in astronomical writing. When the the Astronomical Society of the Pacific awarded him a medal, it stated that Newcomb "has done more than any other American since [Benjamin] Franklin to make American science respected and honoured throughout the entire world."

—*Steven I. Dutch*

FURTHER READING

Carter, Bill, and Merri Sue Carter. *Latitude: How American Astronomers Solved the Mystery of Variation*. Annapolis, Md.: Naval Institute Press, 2002. Careful measurements of the positions of stars show that the earth does not rotate smoothly on its axis but wobbles slightly. Newcomb's precise determination of star positions were central to the discovery and understanding of this phenomenon.

Dick, Steven J. *Sky and Ocean Joined: The U.S. Naval Observatory, 1830-2000*. Cambridge, England: Cambridge University Press, 2003. Newcomb's directorship of the U.S. Naval Observatory propelled the institution into the front ranks of world astronomical centers and occupies a prominent place in this history of the observatory.

Moyer, Albert E. *A Scientist's Voice in American Culture: Simon Newcomb and the Rhetoric of Scientific Method*. Berkeley: University of California Press, 1992. Biography, focusing on Newcomb's advocacy of the scientific method, and how his position spurred support for science and raised numerous social, culture, and intellectual issues.

Newcomb, Simon. *Principles of Political Economy*. New York: Augustus M. Kelley, 1966. A reprint of Newcomb's book of 1886. Newcomb the economist was strikingly like Newcomb the astronomer, viewing the world as the rational product of predictable forces. However, Newcomb was not a blind believer in economic forces, and he also stressed the limitations of economics in making societal decisions.

_____. *The Reminiscences of an Astronomer.* Boston: Houghton Mifflin, 1903. Newcomb's rambling autobiography is written in somewhat stuffy Victorian prose but beneath the formality, Newcomb's interest in people and events both great and small shows through.

SEE ALSO: Williamina Paton Stevens Fleming; Margaret Lindsay Huggins; Samuel Pierpont Langley; Albert A. Michelson; Maria Mitchell.

RELATED ARTICLES in *Great Events from History: The Nineteenth Century, 1801-1900:* January 1, 1801: First Asteroid Is Discovered; 1814: Fraunhofer Invents the Spectroscope.

JOHN HENRY NEWMAN
English religious leader

Newman was a leading figure in the Oxford Movement, which brought religious issues to the forefront of the Victorian consciousness. After his conversion to Roman Catholicism, he became the leading Catholic figure in Great Britain, writing eloquently about religion and education and influencing the course of theological and administrative practices within the Catholic Church in Great Britain and throughout the world.

BORN: February 21, 1801; London, England
DIED: August 11, 1890; Birmingham, England
AREA OF ACHIEVEMENT: Religion and theology

EARLY LIFE

The eldest of six children, John Henry Newman grew up in a close-knit family and was educated at Dr. Nicolas's school at Ealing, near London. At the age of fifteen, shortly before he matriculated at Oxford, Newman underwent a period of extreme mental crisis, which he later described as his conversion, and became deeply religious, convinced that God had destined him for a high calling. His reading during this period led him to appreciate the early church fathers and to fear the Roman Catholic Church's influence in the modern world.

In the fall of 1816, Newman's father took his son to Oxford and enrolled him at Trinity College. Newman did not actually move to the university until the following summer, when he began a period of intense study in the classics and mathematics. His performance during his first year earned for him a prestigious scholarship, but he was bitterly disappointed in 1820 when he failed to gain a coveted first in either classics or mathematics.

Believing that his performance at Trinity did not truly represent his abilities, Newman applied for a fellowship at Oriel College. The examiners found him clearly the best applicant, and in April, 1822, he joined the college, where he was to achieve fame and then notoriety. At Oriel, he became acquainted first with Edward Pusey, Edward Copleston, Richard Whately, and Edward Hawkins, and later with Richard Hurrell Froude and John Keble. In 1825, Newman was ordained an Anglican priest. For the next several years he combined duties as an educator at the college and at Alban Hall, with priestly functions as vicar of St. Mary's Church, Oxford.

An extended trip through Sicily led to a serious illness, which forced Newman into a lengthy period of convalescence on the Continent. He returned to Oxford in time for his friend John Keble's famous sermon on national apostasy, which initiated what came to be known as the Oxford Movement.

LIFE'S WORK

Newman and his Oxford colleagues took advantage of the outcry generated by Keble's sermon to bring before the public their thoughts on the proper role of the Church. In September, 1833, Newman published his thoughts on Apostolic Succession in a small pamphlet, or tract, which he had delivered all over Great Britain. This first pamphlet was followed by dozens of others during the next eight years, written by various Tractarians, as Newman's group was called. Intended to establish the right of the Anglican Church to the title of "catholic," *Tracts for the Times* eventually led many to believe that the Church of Rome, not that of Canterbury, was the only body to preserve the true spirit of early Christianity.

Newman's polemical *Tract Ninety*, in which he argued that even Roman Catholics could subscribe to the Thirty-nine Articles, caused such a stir that the tracts were terminated. Newman himself had grown to believe that the Anglican Church was not a "via media," as he had once argued so eloquently. In 1841, he left Oxford to reside at the parish house in nearby Littlemore, where he spent four years agonizing over his own religious future.

John Henry Newman. (Library of Congress)

Finally, he broke openly with the Church of England: On October 9, 1845, he was baptized into the Roman Catholic Church.

The Anglican Church hierarchy was shaken by this move; the Roman Catholic community was elated. Within two years, Newman completed his studies in Rome and was ordained a priest, receiving from the pope a commission to establish in Great Britain an Oratory like those of Saint Philip Neri. Newman established his community in 1848, in Birmingham, bringing into it several men who had converted at or about the same time.

The move into the bosom of Rome had ironic consequences. In the Anglican Church, Newman had been one of the chief spokespersons for conservative values; as a Roman Catholic, he found himself immediately cast as the champion of liberalism. Newman's belief in individual intellectual inquiry and in participation by the laity in the government of the Church set him at odds with numerous bishops and priests who viewed centralization of all authority as essential to the health of the "one true Church."

These differences of opinion caused Newman considerable difficulty for almost two decades. Even within his own community at Birmingham he faced controversy. Several of the Oratorians, recent converts to Roman Catholicism, had found great solace in practicing the extreme forms of worship common in Italian churches. These men were disillusioned with Newman's moderate tone toward non-Catholics. Eventually, the community split, with a group establishing a separate Oratory in London under Frederick William Faber, one of Newman's most trusted friends and followers.

Newman was not eager to challenge openly the Church of England; rather, he wanted to lead British Catholics to the Church of Rome through conciliatory measures. That plan was made especially difficult almost from the outset when, in 1850, the pope decided to reestablish bishops in residence in Great Britain; since the sixteenth century, the country had been a "mission" for the Roman Catholic Church, without a designated diocesan headquarters. To make matters worse, Nicholas Wiseman, first archbishop of Westminster, inflamed public opinion by suggesting that the Catholic Church was "reclaiming" England. Protestants rallied against this "papal aggression," and Newman found himself explaining to both Catholics and Protestants that the Church had no temporal aims.

During the early 1850's, the Irish bishops, wanting to establish an independent university to provide Catholics with an education not influenced by the Protestant institutions of higher learning, sought out Newman to found a Catholic university in Dublin. Initial efforts were promising. In 1852, Newman delivered a series of lectures in Ireland, outlining his plans for the school, which were later collected under the title *The Idea of a University Defined and Illustrated* (1852). Newman wanted to build a university on the model of Oxford, where classical and scientific learning were the cornerstones of education. The bishops wanted little of such independent thinking; instead, they had hoped that the new colleges would indoctrinate students in Catholicism. Newman tried for several years to compromise and bring the school into existence; the effort eventually failed, and in 1858 he resigned.

During this period, Newman found himself embroiled in a lawsuit, brought against him by a former priest, Giacinto Achilli. Having fled to Great Britain, Achilli entertained Protestants by railing against the Church of Rome; in response, Newman, knowing Achilli to be a philanderer, castigated him in print. When Achilli sued, Newman was unable to obtain from Rome or from Archbishop Wiseman the documents he needed for a defense. Though a friend went to Rome and brought back witnesses against Achilli, Newman was still found guilty and ordered to pay a fine. Public outcry against what appeared to be Protestant injustice brought Newman considerable support, financial as well as moral; with the excess funds that were sent to him by well-wishers Newman was able to build a church for the university in Dublin.

Almost immediately after he resigned from his position at the University in Dublin, Newman found himself at the center of another controversy over the *Rambler*, a monthly Catholic lay magazine that often questioned church authorities. To quell growing dissatisfaction, Newman agreed to become the editor, but his own practices were not acceptable to the bishops, who had originally objected. Newman was forced to resign almost immediately after he had assumed the editorship, but not before he published an influential article, "On Consulting the Faithful in Matters of Doctrine." His liberal ideas on the role of the laity—ideas based on his study of the Church and its early history—caused him to be accused of heresy and left him under a cloud with those in Rome.

Vindication for Newman came slowly and began not within the church he had adopted but rather within his country. The publication of an article by Charles Kingsley in 1864, in which Kingsley accused Newman of condoning lies as a means of promoting the Catholic faith, forced Newman to clear his reputation by explaining his conversion. The series of letters Newman published in the spring of 1864 were collected into a volume that became the most important religious autobiography of the century: *Apologia Pro Vita Sua*. The work was praised by both Protestants and Catholics for its sincere presentation of a man's search for truth. After its publication, Newman became reconciled with several of the friends whom he had abandoned when he converted two decades earlier. *Apologia Pro Vita Sua* was followed in 1870 by *An Essay in Aid of a Grammar of Assent*, which explains how one can find assurances in faith that go beyond the merely intellectual.

In 1870, Newman was invited to the First Vatican Council to help determine an important and controversial issue: papal infallibility. He declined. He believed in the doctrine but feared that the council would declare the pope infallible in all of his pronouncements. He need not have been concerned. The council adopted a more circumscribed definition, that the pope spoke infallibly only on matters of faith and morals.

In 1878, Oxford honored Newman when officials of Trinity College elected him as the first Honorary Fellow. Not until Leo XIII became pope, however, did Newman gain the ecclesiastical recognition he deserved. One of the new pope's first acts was to make Newman a cardinal. After some initial concern, and an attempt by Henry, Cardinal Manning, of Westminster to thwart the appointment, Newman eventually accepted the honor, and he was elevated to the cardinalate in May, 1879. The pope allowed Newman to retain his residence at the Oratory in Birmingham, where he died on August 11, 1890.

SIGNIFICANCE

John Henry Newman's influence on the Catholic Church in England during the nineteenth century cannot be overestimated. His own conversion was the catalyst that led dozens of others to adopt the Roman rule. Within the Church, he served as a constant voice for liberalism, stressing the dignity of individuals and the importance of the laity. Many of his ideas about the role of the laity formed the basis for later decisions of the Second Vatican Council in 1965, seven decades after his death.

Similarly, Catholic education has accepted a number of Newman's ideas. His influence on Catholic colleges and universities both in Great Britain and in America has been significant. As Newman had urged, while most Catholic institutions of higher learning offer a liberal education that includes the study of theology, they also teach secular subjects and allow students to confront the evils of the world directly, offering guidance rather than trying to isolate students from life's challenges.

Though Newman was a poet of some merit, his major contributions to British letters are his volumes of prose, especially his spiritual autobiography, his analysis of the nature of belief, and his writings on education. In an eloquent yet accessible style, he explored his subjects with great erudition and sincerity. His works continue to be read as examples of the essay at its best.

—*Laurence W. Mazzeno*

FURTHER READING

Blehl, Vincent Ferrer. *Pilgrim Journey: John Henry Newman, 1801-1845*. New York: Paulist Press, 2001. A study of Newman's religious development, focusing on the Oxford Movement.

Bouyer, Louis. *Newman: His Life and Spirituality*. Translated by J. L. May. New York: Meridian Books, 1965. Detailed biography illuminating the complex psychology of its subject. Excellent analysis of Newman's motives for his conversion, his belief in the importance of the laity, and his insistence on the need for intellectual inquiry for all Catholics. Makes extensive use of Newman's diaries and letters.

Culler, A. Dwight. *The Imperial Intellect: A Study of Newman's Educational Ideal*. New Haven, Conn.: Yale University Press, 1955. Well-researched study of Newman's life, focusing primarily on his thinking, writing, and action concerning education. Excellent discussions of *The Idea of a University*, and of Newman's efforts to found such an institution.

Dessain, Charles Stephen. *John Henry Newman*. 2d ed. Stanford, Calif.: Stanford University Press, 1971. Brief biography by the editor of Newman's letters. Concentrates on Newman's religious life and the controversies surrounding his conversion and his dealings with the hierarchy in Rome. Excellent analysis of Newman's lifelong quest to understand and propagate the notion of revealed religion.

Hollis, Christopher. *Newman and the Modern World*. Garden City, N.Y.: Doubleday, 1968. Biographical sketch that examines Newman's ideas and contributions to religion as they affected his contemporaries and the subsequent actions and pronouncements of the Roman Catholic Church. Good source of information about both the major events of Newman's life and the impact his writings have had on the changes brought about by the Second Vatican Council.

Martin, Brian. *John Henry Newman: His Life and Work*. New York: Oxford University Press, 1982. Brief, highly readable biographical sketch, profusely illustrated. Provides short analyses of Newman's major works, including his novels. Stresses the difficulties Newman had in dealing with the conservative party within the Catholic Church.

Trevor, Meriol. *Newman*. Vol. 1, *The Pillar of the Cloud*; Vol. 2, *Light in Winter*. Garden City, N.Y.: Doubleday, 1962. The standard biography. Provides well-documented sources, illustrations, and an extensive index.

Turner, Frank M. *John Henry Newman: The Challenge to Evangelical Religion*. New Haven, Conn.: Yale University Press, 2002. Examines Newman's early years at Oxford and in the Church of England to trace his religious development and eventual conversion to Roman Catholicism.

Ward, Wilfrid. *The Life of John Henry Cardinal Newman*. 2 vols. London: Longmans, Green, 1912. First major biography of Newman; makes extensive use of personal correspondence and private papers, as well as anecdotes from those who knew him. Despite the title, deals almost exclusively with the years Newman spent as a member of the Roman Catholic Church.

Yearley, Lee H. *The Ideas of Newman: Christianity and Human Religiosity*. University Park: Pennsylvania State University Press, 1978. Scholarly study that analyzes Newman's attitudes toward humankind's innate need for religion. Contains a good bibliography.

SEE ALSO: Matthew Arnold; Thomas Arnold; Thomas Hill Green; Leo XIII; E. B. Pusey.

RELATED ARTICLES in *Great Events from History: The Nineteenth Century, 1801-1900:* July 14, 1833: Oxford Movement Begins; October 9, 1845: Newman Becomes a Roman Catholic.

MICHEL NEY
French military leader

Ney was arguably the most celebrated of the twenty-six marshals who served the French Empire throughout the Napoleonic Wars. He is primarily remembered for his leadership during the retreat from Moscow and at Waterloo.

BORN: January 10, 1769; Saarlouis, France
DIED: December 7, 1815; Paris, France
ALSO KNOWN AS: Prince de la Moskowa; Duke d'Elchingen; Bravest of the Brave
AREA OF ACHIEVEMENT: Military

EARLY LIFE

Michel Ney (nay) was born twenty years before the outbreak of the French Revolution. The second son of Pierre Ney, a cooper, and Marguerite Grevelinger, he was trained as a notary public and as an overseer of mines but discovered that his inclinations lay in martial pursuits. In 1788, one year before the revolution, he joined the light cavalry and from 1789 fought in the French republican armies.

Ney underwent his baptism of fire from 1792 to 1794, when he rose to the ranks of sergeant major and subsequently of captain. The tall, sturdily built, blue-eyed Ney was already a superb horseman and swordsman and was skilled in drill and maneuver. He had also acquired the reputation for reckless courage and a hot temper, which, combined with his flaming red hair, earned for him the nickname of "Le Rougeaud," or "the red-headed one."

From 1794 to 1799, Ney advanced steadily to the rank of general of division. His military talent was complemented by an immense personal charisma. He led his men from the front rank, an exposure to danger that endeared him to the soldiery of France. Already, he had been wounded three times and had been temporarily captured. In 1800, Ney contributed to the French victory at Hohenlinden. Thereafter, the future emperor of France, Napoleon, took an interest in him. In 1802, Ney was further connected to Napoleon through marriage to Aglaé Louise Auguié, a friend of Napoleon's wife. When Napoleon was crowned in 1804, he elevated Ney to the distinguished position of marshal.

LIFE'S WORK

From 1804 to 1815, the French Empire under Napoleon fought successive wars against seven coalitions of enemies. The foundation of Napoleon's rule was the military, and at the top of the military was his personally created body of twenty-six marshals. Ney was France's most celebrated marshal and the one most remembered by posterity, even if he was not its most consistently talented member. During the 1805-1807 campaigns in Central Europe, Ney demonstrated both his talents and his weaknesses. One of his greatest victories was the Battle of Elchingen, during which he surrounded an Austrian army at Ulm. Ney then subdued the Austrian Tyrol.

Against the Prussians at Jena, however, he attacked too precipitously, nearly cutting off his VI Army Corps. The impetuous Ney then provoked a foraging incident in eastern Prussia in January, 1807, which developed into the Battle of Eylau. Eylau was the first real check to Napoleon's Imperial Grand Army, but Ney partially redeemed himself by staving in the Russian right flank and causing their withdrawal. Ney's redemption was completed after the Battle of Friedland, wherein his advance led to a decisive defeat of the Russian army and directly to the Treaty of Tilsit. Out of gratitude, Napoleon created Ney duke of Elchingen in June, 1808.

Ney's years in Spain, from August, 1808, to March, 1811, were less happy. Spain, the scene of a bloody guerrilla war, damaged many French officers' reputations, and Ney's was no exception. Initially, Ney led his VI Army Corps to minor victories, and in 1810 he participated in the invasion of Portugal under Marshal André Masséna. Ney captured the fortress of Ciudad Rodrigo and fought, indecisively, at Bussaco. The French highwater mark was reached at Torres Vedras, and, thereafter, the British, Spanish, and Portuguese armies slowly rolled back the French. Ney's gallantry and inspiration held the exposed rear guards together, but another side to his personality was revealed: a general lack of cooperation with his fellow marshals and with his superior. That situation resulted in his being dismissed by Masséna in 1811.

Napoleon, however, was seldom disturbed when his marshals drew daggers against one another, and he lost no time in appointing Ney head of the military camp of Boulogne, a post he held from August, 1811, to February, 1812. In April, 1812, Ney was put in charge of the III Army Corps in the greatest French army yet assembled, which was preparing to invade Russia and bring Czar Alexander I back into an economic line more favorable to Napoleon's continental system. Instead, it was the French who were brought to heel in the beginning of the end for the French Empire.

Conversely, however, Ney's reputation prospered. On August 17, Ney was the first to go into Smolensk, where he was again wounded; at Borodino, on September 7, he pushed back Prince Pyotr Ivanovich Bagration's troops. The French occupied Moscow a week later. However, the Russian field army had not been decisively beaten, and the czar would not come to terms. Moreover, a mysterious fire in Moscow robbed the French of their winter quarters. The cataclysmic French retreat began on October 19. As in Spain, Ney was placed in command of the dangerous rear guard. There, amid snows, harassed by Cossacks, and low on supplies, Ney led by such heroic personal example and élan that Napoleon respectfully named him "the bravest of the brave." Ney was reportedly the last Frenchman to have left Russian soil. Next to Napoleon, Ney had emerged the most renowned soldier of France. In recognition, Napoleon created Ney Prince de la Moskowa, in March, 1813.

After the disaster in Russia, much of Europe rallied against the French, and Ney fought a series of battles in German states in 1813. After receiving yet another wound and achieving an indecisive victory at Lützen, Ney blundered at Bautzen, where he had been in command of several corps. Briefly recovering at Dresden, Ney was defeated at Dennewitz and failed to take Berlin. His critics would note that his effective span of control was one corps and that he was not usually successful with a larger body. Defeated at last in 1813, Napoleon and Ney fell back on France, engaging in some of their most classic if smaller battles in an effort to keep their country from being overrun. Sensing the end, Ney was one of the first marshals to call for Napoleon's abdication. That fact set the stage for Ney's increasing political involvement, which went so much against his temperament and natural ability.

When Napoleon was exiled to Elba, the returned Royalist government under Louis XVIII eagerly employed such a preeminent marshal as Ney on its own behalf. Complicating events, Napoleon escaped in February, 1815, and began raising a new army with which to conquer France and, ultimately, Europe. That situation put Ney in a terrible quandary, for he owed Napoleon his career and owed nothing to the aristocrats, who looked upon him as a mere upstart. Although Napoleon's chances seemed dim, Ney could see that the army rank and file largely longed for a return to the former days of glory. Ney deserted to Napoleon, an act for which he would later pay with his life.

During the Waterloo Campaign in June, 1815, Ney commanded the left wing in the Battle of Quatre-Bras.

Uncharacteristically, Ney's actions on June 16 were dilatory. He incorrectly assessed the situation and failed to take the strategic crossroads. Napoleon's own choice of ground at the Battle of Waterloo on June 18 was unfortunate, and his method of frontal attack was equally so. Further, even though Ney's capabilities in the grander scale had already been tested and found not to be his strongest feature, Napoleon chose to entrust to him the conduct of the main assault at Waterloo.

Repeatedly and courageously, Ney charged against the well-prepared British defenses, exhausting the French cavalry. Unable to break through to Brussels, the French were themselves struck in the right flank by the Prussians. As a word, "Waterloo" has become synonymous with defeat. Napoleon was exiled to the remote island of St. Helena, and Ney was tried and executed by the Bourbon Royalists on December 7, 1815. Out of respect for France's hero, "the bravest of the brave" was allowed to conduct his own firing squad beside the wall of the tranquil Luxembourg Gardens in Paris.

SIGNIFICANCE

Michel Ney's life may be considered a failure if one only reflects that the cause he served failed. If, above all, the age symbolized the drift away from monarchy, the seeds

Michel Ney. (Library of Congress)

had at least been planted. From a personal view, Ney's career was spectacular. Few have risen from completely obscure origins to become a marshal and a prince. Ney was a successful man before Napoleon chose him as one of the elect, but Ney largely owes his historical reputation to his service in Napoleon's French Empire while under the banner of the Imperial Grand Army. Had there been no Napoleon, Ney might well have been marked by posterity as no more than one of the many newly promoted republican generals.

Ney's career as a marshal of France was made more because of his outstanding bravery than from any qualified skill as a military strategist. That judgment is not to belittle Ney's overall martial talent. Ney's personal example, energy, charismatic inspiration, and willingness to share risks made him an exceptional leader of men and France's greatest period soldier second only to Napoleon.

From 1815 to 1848, France struggled between its traditions of monarchy and its increasingly republican leanings. The Bourbons understandably forbade the erection of a statue to Ney's memory, until their own downfall in 1848. In 1852, however, the nephew of Napoleon secured by plebiscite the mantle of hereditary emperorship, and the following year a statue of Ney was commissioned. The statue stands in the Carrefour de l'Observatoire in Paris as an eternal tribute to a national military hero of France.

—David L. Bullock

FURTHER READING

Chandler, David G. *The Campaigns of Napoleon.* New York: Macmillan, 1966. This work is the best single-volume work on the period. Ney appears in the index, and his name covers an entire column of entries. Invaluable for understanding Ney's position in the Imperial Grand Army. Excellent maps indicate where Ney fought. Although it is appreciative of Ney's role throughout, the chapters concerning Russia and Waterloo are especially rewarding.

_____. *Dictionary of the Napoleonic Wars.* New York: Macmillan, 1979. The entry on Ney fills approximately two pages and includes a picture. The subject is covered chronologically. Key events are set off by asterisks, which permit cross-referencing and therefore a more complete explanation.

_____, ed. *Napoleon's Marshals.* New York: Macmillan, 1987. This is the best account of the twenty-six marshals so far published. Each marshal is presented in a separate section authored by a separate period scholar and includes a picture of the subject. Ney is covered by Peter Young. A map and analysis of the Battle of Elchingen help to explain Ney as a commander. His talents may be easily compared and contrasted to those of his fellow marshals.

Delderfield, R. F. *The March of the Twenty-Six: The Story of Napoleon's Marshals.* London: Hodder & Stoughton, 1962. The book is illuminating because it deals with the interactions of the marshals in a chronological sequence. Thus, it is complementary to works that adopt a sectional subject approach. Ney is indexed throughout the text.

Esposito, Vincent J., and John Robert Elting. *A Military History and Atlas of the Napoleonic Wars.* New York: Frederick A. Praeger, 1964. The atlas is without doubt the best military atlas on the Napoleonic period and, because of the rising cost of publication, may stand indefinitely as the definitive work. The maps offer a complete understanding of Ney's positions during the campaigns. Coverage is comprehensive, and each map is supported by an oversize page of linking narrative.

Horricks, Raymond. *Military Politics from Bonaparte to the Bourbons: The Life and Death of Michel Ney, 1769-1815.* New Brunswick, N.J.: Transaction, 1995. Comprehensive biography, describing Ney's life and military career within the context of French politics during and after the reign of Napoleon I.

Marshall-Cornwall, Sir James. *Napoleon as Military Commander.* London: B. T. Batsford, 1967. This book offers a literate exposition that is well illustrated with detailed maps and a chronological table. Presents a balanced account of Napoleon's career. Ney is frequently referenced in the index and may be briefly related against the larger background of his leader.

Morton, John Bingham. *Marshal Ney.* London: Arthur Barker, 1958. Only two chapters cover the 1812-1815 period. Three chapters review the politics of the second restoration or the events surrounding Ney's trial. The work adequately portrays the ineptitude of Ney in the climate of shifting politics.

Young, Peter. *Napoleon's Marshals.* New York: Hippocrene Books, 1973. The section on Ney is not as comprehensive or informative as Young's section in Chandler's edited *Napoleon's Marshals.* Four pictures of Ney and a color plate of the marshal in uniform provide the finest single, illustrative coverage, but the Chandler book is to be preferred in most respects.

SEE ALSO: Alexander I; Gebhard Leberecht von Blü-
cher; Napoleon I.
RELATED ARTICLES in *Great Events from History: The
Nineteenth Century, 1801-1900:* June 23-December 14, 1812: Napoleon Invades Russia; June 18, 1815:
Battle of Waterloo; November 20, 1815: Second
Peace of Paris.

NICHOLAS I
Emperor of Russia (1825-1855)

*As ruler of the Russian Empire, Czar Nicholas I
partially succeeded in restoring the historic power and
position of the autocracy in Russian life and European
affairs. His reign marks the high point of Russian
conservative reaction to the French Revolution,
Napoleonic Europe, and the Decembrist Revolt.*

BORN: July 6, 1796; Tsarskoye Selo (now Pushkin),
Russia
DIED: March 2, 1855; St. Petersburg, Russia
ALSO KNOWN AS: Nickolay Pavlovich (birth name)
AREA OF ACHIEVEMENT: Government and politics

EARLY LIFE

Czar Nicholas I was born Nikolay Pavlovich. He was
the third surviving son of Russia's Emperor Paul I and
Empress Maria Fyodorovna, a former princess of Württemberg. Being the third son, Nicholas was not expected
to rule in his own right but rather to serve one of his elder
brothers, the future czar Alexander I or the Grand Duke
Constantine Pavlovich. Consequently, Nicholas was not
initially prepared to rule but rather was given a traditional, conservative, military education. What liberal
training Nicholas did receive probably came from one of
his tutors, the German economist Heinrich Storch. Nicholas proved to have no mind for abstraction; he was interested in science and technology and was especially talented in mathematics. Like his father before him, he took
a strong interest in military affairs.

Nicholas's natural conservatism was profoundly
deepened during the last years of Alexander's reign, after
1812-1814, and as a result of the Decembrist Revolt in
1825. After he returned from the Congress of Vienna, Alexander—and Russia through him—came under the
sway of conservative German mystical Romanticism
from the West. Opposition arose from young reform-
minded noble military officers and civil servants, who
staged demonstrations in St. Petersburg to influence
the new czar, Constantine, upon the somewhat sudden
death of the childless Alexander in 1825. Unbeknown
to the Decembrists, however, Constantine secretly had

renounced his right to succeed in 1822, in favor of Nicholas, when he had married a Roman Catholic Polish aristocrat. When they realized that Nicholas was the new
emperor, the Decembrists went into rebellion in St. Petersburg and Kiev. The Decembrist Revolt was thoroughly crushed, and Nicholas I saw it as a manifestation of the liberal treason of much of the nobility, an
attitude that set the tone for his entire reign at home and
abroad.

LIFE'S WORK

Not only did the Decembrist Revolt strengthen Nicholas's conservative resolve, but also it forced him to rebuild the historic power of the Russian autocracy and
concentrate on internal affairs over foreign relations
throughout most of his reign. To do this he surrounded
himself with reasonably talented conservative and reactionary advisers in key positions, many of whom
came from military backgrounds. Together they created and enforced the state ideology of official nationalism, with its four-pronged attack: autocracy, orthodoxy, nationality, and legitimacy. Autocracy meant the
historic direct, divine-right absolutism of the czar; orthodoxy reaffirmed Russian Orthodoxy as the one true
faith and condoned the persecution of all dissenters,
especially Roman Catholics, Muslims, and Jews; nationality called for the protection of the unique Russian
character from the decadence of the West; and legitimacy was a guide for foreign policy, allowing for intervention abroad to preserve the antirevolutionary status
quo.

To create a degree of bureaucratic efficiency, Nicholas did not reform the bureaucracy as such; rather, he
added yet another layer, His Majesty's Own Imperial
Chancery, which was more directly responsible to him.
It contained six sections: Sections 1 and 6 dealt with
charity and welfare, respectively. Section 2, under Count
Michael Speransky, successfully carried out the codification and some modernization of Russian law from
1833 to 1835, a prelude to the judicial reforms to come

under the reign of Alexander II in 1864. Section 4 managed the conquest of the Caucasus Mountains region, which began under Nicholas and continued in the reigns that followed.

Part of Armenia was secured in a war with Persia in 1826-1828 and the eastern shore of the Caspian Sea in a war with Turkey in 1828-1829. Section 5, under General Paul Kiselyov, considered the reform of serfdom. Nicholas wanted to do something about this pressing problem, which had kept Russia economically and socially backward, had in large part precipitated the Decembrist Revolt, and had constantly fueled debate and dissent in the Russian Empire. As with so many important matters, however, he never committed himself to doing anything about it.

The most infamous of these sections, though, was the third, the secret police, under General Alexander Benckendorff. Based on French Revolutionary and Napoleonic models, it was a modern, professional police establishment through which Nicholas controlled dissent, monitored public opinion, propagandized his people, and otherwise enforced his will. Through the third section, censorship was maintained, and famous troublesome intellectuals such as Peter Chaadayev, Alexander Pushkin, Nikolai Gogol, Vissarion Belinsky, and Aleksandr Herzen were hounded and controlled. Nevertheless, under Nicholas, dissent (especially that dissent inspired by the West) continued to grow.

Nicholas did not see art as propaganda but believed that it was able to portray attitudes; he was therefore determined that the attitudes portrayed be the correct ones. He fancied himself as an artist and an architect, and he played a personal role in the rebuilding of the Winter Palace and the completion of St. Isaac's Cathedral in St. Petersburg.

Section 3 acted and reacted efficiently and helped Russia to suppress the Polish uprisings of 1830-1831 and move against Russian dissidents to prevent trouble in 1848; Russia and Great Britain were the only two major European countries not to experience upheavals in 1848. Nicholas's Russia even sent troops abroad to quell a rebellion in Hungary in 1848. With section 3, Nicholas laid the basis for the modern Russian and Soviet police states. In this regard, Nicholas eventually came to be known as the "gendarme of Europe."

Nicholas I. (The Granger Collection, New York)

Nicholas reenergized the pattern of "defensive modernization" for the Russian Empire first set by Czar Alexei Mikhailov and his son Peter the Great during the late seventeenth and early eighteenth centuries. Russia did not have an original industrial revolution, and Nicholas believed it necessary for Russia to modernize cautiously to protect itself from the aggressive tendencies of the West and to avoid coming under the sway of Western decadence. Western expertise and capital therefore were allowed to come into Russia only slowly and selectively. For example, under Nicholas the first railroad in Russia was completed in 1838, not primarily to foster internal economic development but to move troops more efficiently between Moscow, St. Petersburg, and Kiev to control possible social disorder.

Meanwhile, intellectuals of opposing Slavophile and Westernizer groupings debated the past, present, and future of Russia and sought to influence the czar and his policies. Slavophiles such as Sergei Khomyakov and the Aksakovs usually were supportive, while Westernizers such as Belinsky were much more critical. Through its control of government spending, it was really the Ministry of Finance under the reactionary Count Yegor Kankrin that was in charge of modernization and reform during much of Nicholas's reign.

A haphazard commitment to improve education also was made. A heavy emphasis was placed on science and technology. New schools and curricula were established and the older ones expanded by Minister of Public Instruction Sergei Uvarov in the years 1833-1848, marking the end of the period of reaction to the Decembrist Revolt. Soon, however, the educational system, especially as manifested by the universities, was seen as responsible for stimulating the development of a radical intelligentsia. The universities came to be distrusted, greater centralized control was instigated, and the period of post-1848 reaction ensued.

Despite the efforts at reform and modernization, the Russian defeat in the Russian-provoked Crimean War (1854-1856) at the end of Nicholas's reign showed how far the Russian Empire had declined from great power status and how backward it was. The defeat spurred Nicholas's son and successor, Alexander II, to initiate a major era of reform, beginning with the emancipation of the serfs in 1861.

SIGNIFICANCE

Nicholas I was the last Russian czar to embody the historical definition of the autocrat. Through the strength of his conservative character and the power of his will, he reconstructed the autocracy of Ivan the Great, Ivan the Terrible, and Peter the Great in his own image. However, in the process of this atavistic quest he retarded and often hurt Russia and its people. His stifling of progressive development, furthering of bureaucratic absolutism, expensive militarism and foreign adventurism, and general lack of progressive accomplishment left those who followed in his footsteps with a growing number of aggravated problems with which to cope.

However, while Nicholas did not stop Russia's slide from greatness, he did prepare the way for some of the accomplishments of his successors. The addressing of the problems of serfdom and the codification of law facilitated the later reforms of Alexander II. He furthered the march of the Russian Empire across Eurasia and into China. Defensive modernization helped bring on the Russian Revolution, and modernization continued through the Soviet period of Russian history to the present. Nicholas was a strong ruler but not a positive one, and his antireform reactionary conservatism was out of step with the needs of his country, the times in which it

existed, and the modern world. In trying to strengthen the Russian Empire, Nicholas actually weakened it severely.

—Dennis Reinhartz

FURTHER READING

Blackwell, William L. *The Beginnings of Russian Industrialization, 1800-1860*. Princeton, N.J.: Princeton University Press, 1968. Largely a study of the important period under Nicholas in the history of Russian industrialization prior to the actual Russian industrial revolution. Very good on the role of the state in stimulating Russian industrialization and modernization.

Golovin, Ivan. *Russia Under the Autocrat Nicholas the First*. London: H. Colburn, 1846. A critical account of the first two decades of Nicholas's reign written by a member of one of Russia's more important aristocratic families. A valuable primary source on the life and times of Nicholas and his Russia.

Grunwald, Constantin de. *Tsar Nicholas I*. Translated by Brigid Patmore. New York: Macmillan, 1955. Somewhat romanticized and very traditional, but for years the standard biography of Nicholas. Stresses foreign affairs.

Ingle, Harold N. *Nesselrode and the Russia Rapprochement with Britain, 1836-1844*. Berkeley: University of California Press, 1976. Centering on the activity of Nicholas's principal foreign minister, Count Karl Nesselrode, this work addresses the cold war relationship that developed between Russian and Great Britain in the nineteenth century. A good study of Nicholas's unsuccessful attempt to transfer his conservative values to European affairs.

Kagan, Frederick W. *The Military Reforms of Nicholas I: The Origins of the Modern Russian Army*. New York: St. Martin's Press, 1999. Thorough, scholarly study of Nicholas's reign and reorganization of the Russian army during the 1830's, written by a professor at the U.S. Military Academy. Aimed at scholars and serious students of Russian history.

Kohn, Hans, ed. *The Mind of Modern Russia: Historical and Political Thought in Russia's Great Age*. New York: Harper & Row, 1955. Commentary and documents on Russian intellectual history in the nineteenth century. The first seven chapters deal with the reign of Nicholas. A classic text.

Lincoln, W. Bruce. *Nicholas I: Emperor and Autocrat of All the Russias*. Bloomington: Indiana University Press, 1978. Largely synthetic, but very good and readable. A definitive and up-to-date standard biography of Nicholas.

Monas, Sidney. *The Third Section: Police and Society Under Nicholas I*. Cambridge, Mass.: Harvard University Press, 1961. Excellent on the third section and its various activities and on the early modern Russian police state of Nicholas. An unmatched standard.

Pinter, Walter McKenzie. *Russian Economic Policy Under Nicholas I*. Ithaca, N.Y.: Cornell University Press, 1967. A study of Russian "defensive modernization" under Nicholas I. Especially good on the philosophy and activities of Nicholas's minister of finance, Count Kankrin.

Riasanovsky, Nicholas V. *Nicholas I and Official Nationality in Russia, 1825-1855*. Berkeley: University of California Press, 1959. An excellent study that concentrates on the construction of the conservative Rus-sian state ideology of official nationality by Nicholas and his advisers. Reveals in part the complex personality of Nicholas I.

SEE ALSO: Alexander I; Alexander II; Francis Joseph I; Nikolai Gogol; Aleksandr Herzen; Mikhail Lermontov; Alexander Pushkin.

RELATED ARTICLES in *Great Events from History: The Nineteenth Century, 1801-1900:* December 26, 1825: Decembrist Revolt; September 24, 1829: Treaty of Adrianople; November 29, 1830-August 15, 1831: First Polish Rebellion; October 4, 1853-March 30, 1856: Crimean War; March 3, 1861: Emancipation of Russian Serfs.

BARTHOLD GEORG NIEBUHR
German historian

Niebuhr was an extraordinarily able historian who, through meticulously researched as well as voluminous books and published lectures, founded the modern German school of critical historical scholarship, one objective of which was regeneration of the Prussian state.

BORN: August 27, 1776; Copenhagen, Denmark
DIED: January 2, 1831; Bonn, Prussia (now in Germany)
AREA OF ACHIEVEMENT: Historiography

EARLY LIFE

Barthold Georg Niebuhr (NEE-bur) was the son of the noted German philologist and Arabian traveler Karsten Niebuhr. Although the Niebuhrs lived in Denmark and appeared to be Danish, they regarded themselves as German by virtue of having lived in Denmark's Dithmarschen district, where for centuries Germans maintained separate, nearly independent rights, within the disputed duchies of Schleswig-Holstein.

By his own description, Barthold's childhood was that of a physically weak, almost chronically ill, and dreamy boy who lived in worlds of his own imaginative creation, which throughout life he regarded as dangerous to thought, justice, and morality. Indeed, from child to adult, he remained short, thin, and constitutionally nervous and excitable. Not surprisingly, having seldom passed beyond his house and garden, and being the only son of a then-famous father, he was precociously studious by disposition almost from infancy. He evinced predilections for ancient and modern languages, mathematics, geography, history, and political economy. Nevertheless, until he was an adolescent ready for university he received his education at home.

Already formidably equipped intellectually, Barthold entered the University of Kiel eager to avoid narrow specialization and to master everything available in Kiel's curriculum, from philosophy to mathematics, physics, chemistry, natural history, additional languages, Roman law, European constitutions, and antiquities. The purpose of this ambitiously catholic intellectual immersion was preparation for public service: Niebuhr wanted to become, on his father's advice, not an academician but a man of practical affairs.

LIFE'S WORK

Impatient to get on, Niebuhr thus abandoned the university in January, 1796, to serve as secretary to the Danish minister of finance, a post for which he seemed well adapted, considering his early and continuing interest in Danish-German land tenures (hence finance), curiosities that bent increasingly toward Europe's classical origins. After two years' service at the ministry, Niebuhr left to spend 1798-1799 between London and Edinburgh. These were years that generated interesting, if superficially critical, observations on British life and institutions to his father and the Moltke family. Although

Niebuhr later developed immense admiration for most things British, particularly their practicality and liberties, his encounters at the time left him feeling that the quality of German conversation and thought was far superior.

Consequently Niebuhr returned to Denmark, married in 1801, and resumed various high-status official positions: assessor in the East Indies Company's commerce department and director of the Copenhagen Royal Bank as well as of the Commercial Company of the East Indies. The great Prussian statesman-reformer Freiherr vom Stein soon drew him into Prussian service, initially to negotiate Dutch and English loans (essential during Prussian participation in the Napoleonic Wars), then as Frederick William III's privy councillor during the Saxony campaign of 1813, and finally, from 1816 to 1822, as Prussian ambassador to Rome.

Although Niebuhr's responsibilities in Prussia's wartime officialdom were complex and onerous, his relations with Stein and State Chancellor Karl von Hardenberg became strained. Stein had misread Niebuhr both as a practical man of affairs and as a politician; accidentally, Stein had recruited a pedant. "Niebuhr," Stein remarked, "is no use save as a dictionary whose leaves one turns over." Niebuhr, a staunch Protestant, regarded Hardenberg as immoral and complained repeatedly that he detested the public duties that he executed for Stein. Essentially what he preferred all along was an exclusive devotion to historical scholarship.

Time and fortune favored him. Selecting faculty for the newly founded University of Berlin in 1810, Prussia's distinguished philologist, educational reformer, and, at the time, Minister of Education Wilhelm von Humboldt appointed Niebuhr professor of ancient history, a position with singular requirements for philological genius. Although dedicated to free research, the university's faculty was also dedicated to Prussia's internal reformation and enhancement of the state's power against the powerful menace posed by France under Napoleon I. Niebuhr was second to none in his advocacy of these objectives. Prussia's great field marshal Helmuth von Moltke described young Niebuhr as a true representative of the Prussian mind.

Popular as a lecturer with students, savants, and colleagues alike, Niebuhr, drawing upon years of previous research, converted these lectures into the first two volumes of the *Römische Geschichte* (1811-1812; *The Roman History*, 1827). Combined, the brilliance of his lectures and the fresh contributions of his first major publications solidly established his professional

reputation. In these works, Niebuhr was the first scholar to attack the arcane problems of ancient Italian ethnology.

Niebuhr sought to illuminate the lasting importance of the legends of ancient kings passed down to the Roman historian Livy, not as historically evidential but, through his novel philological, legal, and religious evidence, as persisting social beliefs among subsequent generations of Rome's plebeian populace. He also sought to concentrate upon the social consequences of economic and political questions such as the Roman state's agrarian problems: that is, to unravel the complexities of Rome's agrarian laws, thereby differentiating public from private ownership uses and rights. Perhaps equally important were his efforts, born of intense empathy with his materials, to perceive interrelationships between ancient institutions and to develop a pragmatic sense for their everyday operations.

Outstanding as a historian, Niebuhr nevertheless returned to public life in 1813, reassuming a role in financial negotiations with the Dutch, witnessing Prussia's humiliation at the passage of Napoleon's troops through Berlin and defeat at the Battle of Bautzen, and suffering exhaustion as well as the burden of his wife's serious illness.

Prompted in 1815 by the deaths of his wife and father and the nearly simultaneous settlement of Napoleon's fate at Waterloo, Niebuhr quickly remarried and, through appointment as Prussian ambassador to the Vatican, left Berlin for Italy which, though central to his scholarship, he had never visited. Though loathing Italians generally, much as he did the French, he vastly enriched his scholarship during his seven-year "exile" in Italy. At Verona Cathedral, he unearthed the manuscript find of a lifetime: the corpus of the legal textbook by second century Roman legist Gaius, from which subsequent knowledge of early Roman law derives.

Despite the chaos of the Vatican Library, Niebuhr found and published fragments of Cicero's speeches. With such professional triumphs and a growing, happy family life, he cheerfully abandoned Italy in 1823 for a resumption of professorial duties in Bonn, where, despite occasional commands from Berlin for consultations, he established residence. There he revised and republished two volumes of his Roman history, plus, in three volumes, his *Vorträge über die römische Geschichte* (1828-1830; *Lectures on Roman History*, 1850), and delivered what became his three-volume *Vorträge über altbekannt Geschichte* (1829-1830; *Lectures on Ancient History*, 1852). Drawn into the December cold of 1830 to seek late news on the French revolt—and deposition—of Charles X, Niebuhr, who had lived in fear of Napoleon's revolutionary France, contracted pneumonia and died in Bonn on January 2, 1831.

SIGNIFICANCE

Notwithstanding his precocious erudition as applied to the attempts of Stein and Hardenberg to strengthen Prussia in confrontations with the aggressive expansions of Napoleon's revolutionary France and not discounting his successful and complex financial, consultative, and diplomatic services to Prussia, Barthold Georg Niebuhr was too passionate, excitable, physically vulnerable, and moral to earn renown in the political arena. A supporter of liberal reformers in the Prussian sense, Niebuhr, like those whom he served, mistrusted the general public's capacities either to strengthen the state or to contribute directly to German unification under the aegis of Prussia. Rather, unlike the popular origins of revolutions in France, which Niebuhr and most liberal Germans abhorred, he believed that a strong, unified Prussian state would have to extend liberalism from above.

In this context, the focus of his historical work on classical societies, on Rome particularly, was not entirely fortuitous. Rome and its institutions had been a great unifying force in Western civilization; thus, to dissect and explore Rome's evolution, strengths, and weaknesses was to instruct—or remind—intelligent Germans how better they might proceed with their own nation-building. In that didactic sense, his work would be followed by many of his colleagues, disciples, and immediate successors.

Unquestionably, Niebuhr's critical historical methodology and his penchant for solid documentation and detailed philological scrutiny of the ancient institutions upon which his work was focused distinguished him from his predecessors. Justifiably, he deserves foremost rank as a founder of modern historical methodology and as the first historian to illuminate the institutional, legal, religious, and popular recesses of ancient and classical Roman history particularly. However, his writings are so densely detailed and he so lacked the gift of broad conceptualization that he was sharply criticized by Theodor Mommsen, Leopold von Ranke, and others of his more famous, if indebted, successors. Seldom read or cited by twentieth century historians in his field, he nevertheless was recognized as a major historian during the nineteenth century for his influence on the development of scientific history.

—Clifton K. Yearley

FURTHER READING

Barnes, Harry Elmer. *A History of Historical Writing*. Norman: University of Oklahoma Press, 1938. Written for nonspecialists, this is a clear general exposition of the evolution of modern historical craftsmanship. Niebuhr is appropriately cited in context but is not a principal subject. His influences, however, are well noted. Contains a brief index.

Croce, Benedetto. *History: Its Theory and Practice*. New York: Harcourt, Brace, 1921. Croce, a great Italian philosopher, presents a sophisticated synthesis of historical craftsmanship over the past two centuries, differentiating modern approaches from older, less evidential narrative, often fictional, styles. Niebuhr is briefly placed in context. Contains a brief index.

Fowler, W. Warde. *Roman Essays and Interpretations*. Oxford, England: Clarendon Press, 1920. An able, if sympathetic, scholarly narration of Niebuhr's career. This is a useful and sound account. Clearly written for nonspecialists. Contains a few notes.

Gooch, G. P. *History and Historians in the Nineteenth Century*. New York: Longmans, Green, 1913. A clear and authoritative account, which in chapter 1 deals effectively with Niebuhr's minor predecessors and amply with Niebuhr's own critical contributions. Niebuhr is cited only in reference to other nineteenth century historians throughout Gooch's study. Contains footnotes.

Guilland, Antoine. *Modern Germany and Her Historians*. Reprint. Westport, Conn.: Greenwood Press, 1970. Although there are minor errors, this work does an especially able job in chapter 1, "The Forerunners: Niebuhr." Contains footnotes and a useful, double-columned index.

Thompson, James Westfall. *The Eighteenth and Nineteenth Centuries*. Vol 2 in *A History of Historical Writing*. New York: Macmillan, 1942. Written brilliantly for both specialists and nonspecialists by a distinguished historian and historiographer, this extensive study is the best recent assessment of the subject. Footnotes are extensive and informative, and substitute for the lack of an overall bibliography. Contains a superb twenty-six-page double-columned index.

Ziolkowski, Theodore. *Clio the Romantic Muse: Historicizing the Faculties in Germany*. Ithaca, N.Y.: Cornell University Press, 2004. Examines how a sense of history permeated German thought from 1790 to 1810, influencing the disciplines of philosophy, theology, law, and medicine. Includes biographical information on German scholars whose work exemplified this Romantic historicism, including chapters on the University of Berlin and Niebuhr's lectures on Roman history.

SEE ALSO: Karl von Hardenberg; Theodor Mommsen; Napoleon I; Leopold von Ranke; Freiherr vom Stein.
RELATED ARTICLE in *Great Events from History: The Nineteenth Century, 1801-1900:* 1824: Ranke Develops Systematic History.

NICÉPHORE NIÉPCE
French inventor

Niépce was a tenacious researcher who, despite rural isolation, succeeded in creating first a method of photomechanical reproduction and subsequently the earliest method of permanently recording the image of the camera obscura.

BORN: March 7, 1765; Chalon-sur-Saône, France
DIED: July 5, 1833; Chalon-sur-Saône, France
ALSO KNOWN AS: Joseph-Nicéphore Niépce (full name)
AREA OF ACHIEVEMENT: Science and technology

EARLY LIFE

Nicéphore Niépce (nee-say-fohr nyehps) was born into a prosperous bourgeois family with several estates in the Burgundy region of France. His father, Claude, was a lawyer who, suspected of sympathy for the king during the upheavals of the French Revolution, had to flee his home for a time. Four children were born to Claude and his wife. Their firstborn was a daughter and the second was a son, also named Claude, who was born in 1763. Though Claude was a lifelong friend and collaborator of his younger brother Nicéphore, a third brother, Bernhard, born in 1773, appears to have had no part in their photographic research.

Nicéphore and Claude were educated at a Catholic seminary in their hometown. Nicéphore is thought to have been intended by his father for the priesthood, and he taught briefly at the seminary following his studies there until the revolution caused the religious order to be dispersed. In 1792, not long after the death of his father, Nicéphore joined an infantry regiment of Napoleon I's army, an act that may have been conceived partly as a way of allaying suspicions about his own political sympathies; in any case, military service was mandatory for a man of his age. Achieving the rank of lieutenant in May, 1793, he traveled to Italy and participated in the campaign there in the following year but soon fell victim to typhoid fever. Resigning his commission, he

returned to France, living in the Mediterranean city of Nice, where he was employed by the district administration.

Nicéphore married in Nice in 1795, and two years later, while he pursued family business affairs in Cagliari, the capital of the island of Sardinia, a son, Isidore, was born to the young couple. Claude had accompanied his brother on this trip, and it appears that they had conducted some unsuccessful experiments in an attempt to capture the image created in the camera obscura, an optical device consisting of a lens and a box, or chamber, within which an image could be viewed. The camera obscura had been used for centuries both as a technical aid for draftsmen and as a popular entertainment, but the Niépce brothers' experiment was perhaps the first such use of the apparatus. Only a few years later, Thomas Wedgwood and Sir Humphry Davy were to attempt a similar experiment in England, also without success.

Both brothers returned to their home in Chalon-sur-Saône in 1801. The family's remaining wealth allowed them to continue pursuing a variety of research. From their childhood, Claude and Nicéphore had shown a penchant for experimentation, making working-scale model machines together. Over the next few years, they worked on an ambitious invention that they called the "Pyréolophore," an ancestor of the internal combustion engine.

Pyréolophore is a coinage based on Greek words that translates roughly as "producer of wind and fire." Air was mixed in a piston cylinder with lycopodium, a highly flammable plant spore, producing a controlled explosion powerful enough to propel a boat up the Saône River at twice the speed of the current. This invention, remarkable for its time, was patented by decree of Napoleon on July 20, 1807, from Dresden, Germany. The Niépce brothers continued to refine the Pyréolophore over the next twenty years with the hope of exploiting it commercially, but documentation does not suggest the importance of this endeavor relative to the work in photography, which occupied their attention during many of the same years.

It is known that the Niépce brothers conducted work in the cultivation of textile plants and the extraction of indigo dye but without creating successful business ventures based upon their efforts. Much of the work of Nicéphore and Claude seems to have been motivated more by curiosity than hope of financial gain. Nicéphore has been referred to by modern commentators as "a modest provincial amateur scientist" and as "a dilettante inventor (in the best sense of the word)," and it is certain that the prestige given to science and technology by the European Enlightenment exerted an influence upon him.

Even the few existing published images of Nicéphore bear witness to his ties to the rational outlook of the eighteenth century, though they date from a much later period: His portrait is rendered in the neoclassical style, the reserved, formal kind of art typical of the latter half of the century, instead of in the more expressive and emotional Romantic style of the years of his maturity. These portraits, consisting of a sketch by his son, Isidore, a sculpture from 1853 by Jean August Barre based upon it, and a drawing from 1795 by C. Laguiche, depict Niépce as having a long but well-proportioned face and aquiline nose, and also possessing unmistakably gentle eyes that evoke a kindly personality.

LIFE'S WORK

Niépce conducted various researches at his country estate, Le Gras, in the village of Saint-Loup-de-Varennes, just south of Chalon-sur-Saône. Claude moved to Paris in 1816 to be better able to promote the Pyréolophore, but by then the brothers had begun to experiment in earnest with light-sensitive materials. The path to resuming the project that they had begun in 1797-1798 began with Nicéphore's interest in lithography, a new method of reproduction of drawings that had been introduced by Aloys Senefelder in 1798 in Munich, Germany. In 1812, a French nobleman had attempted to make the method better known in France, and by 1813, a craze for it had swept the nation.

Nicéphore had begun by etching the stones drawn upon by his son, Isidore, but because the stones were of indifferent quality, he tried using pewter plates instead. Soon after father and son began this project, Isidore joined the army. Nicéphore, having little aptitude for drawing, turned from reproducing drawings to a search for a method of copying engravings onto his lithographic plates. The technique that he tried involved first oiling

or waxing an engraving in order to make it transparent, then placing it atop a plate that had been coated with a light-sensitive material. These early experiments do not seem to have been successful, but in 1822, employing a form of asphaltum called bitumen of Judea as the light-sensitive coating, his efforts resulted in an effective method he named "heliography," derived from the Greek roots meaning "sun" and "drawing."

In the early instances, these copies were made upon glass plates. The emulsion-coated plate was then exposed through the oiled engraving to the light of the sun for two or three hours. The areas of the asphaltum emulsion that had received ample exposure through the transparent paper alone were hardened by the action of light, but the areas of the emulsion lying under the dark areas of the print remained unhardened and were readily washed away by a solvent of lavender oil and turpentine.

Niépce's first attempts to record the image of a camera obscura began in April of 1816. A sheet of paper sensitized with silver chloride was exposed in one of three small cameras for an hour or more, resulting in a faint negative image. These negatives were treated in nitric acid in an attempt to fix them, but Niépce knew that the acid was bound to attack the image. A second problem with this method was the reversal of the values of the original scene, which he tried to solve by making a print using the camera negative in much the same way that he had used an engraving in his first attempts at photolithography. Some of these prints seem to have survived in a faded condition into the 1860's.

Two other approaches to recording the camera image were the use of substances that bleach in the presence of light and the attempt to capture an image on metal and lithographic stone in order to use it for printing plates, but neither of these was successful. In the next several years, Nicéphore experimented with other light-sensitive emulsions, communicating his research in guarded letters to Claude, who had moved to London in August of 1817. Little of Nicéphore's side of the correspondence survives, apparently because Claude destroyed the letters in order to forestall discovery of their line of inquiry.

As Nicéphore's method of heliography became more refined, the possibility of using it to record the camera obscura image presented itself. The first partial success in this endeavor dates from 1824 and is reported in an optimistic letter to Claude dated September 16, 1824, which mentions images captured on stone and glass. Nicéphore's attempt to etch the stones ended in failure, however, because the image was too faint. The following year, Nicéphore experimented with zinc and copper plates and in 1826 tried pewter.

Aided by improved optics and by accumulated expertise in the preparation and handling of plates, in 1827—probably in June or July—Niépce produced the image that is today regarded as the first photograph, in the accepted sense of "a permanent image of a natural scene made with a camera." It is a view taken from an upper-story window at Le Gras, showing a courtyard of the estate with a wing of the main building on the left, some trees and a low building described as a bake house in the center, and a tower on the right.

Judging from the somewhat contradictory lighting of the objects in the picture, the exposure probably lasted about eight hours. This 6½-by-8-inch plate, which lay undiscovered in England until 1852, is part of the Gernsheim collection at the University of Texas, a legacy of the indefatigable historian who tracked it down. There is no conclusive proof that it is the first photograph, but since most of Nicéphore's trials were made from the same upper-story window of the house, it can be little different from other results achieved at this time that may have been lost; presumably, it is one of the best examples of his work, because it is one that he took to England with him in 1827 on a visit to see his ailing brother, Claude.

In early 1826, Niépce had ordered a camera obscura from the noted Paris opticians Charles and Vincent Chevalier, and he asked a cousin, who was to visit there, to buy the instrument for him. In conversation with Charles Chevalier, the cousin described the intended use of the specially equipped camera and even showed him an example of heliography. This unauthorized revelation soon reached another customer of the Chevaliers, the painter and scenic designer Jacques Daguerre, an ambitious man who was known principally as the proprietor of the diorama, a popular entertainment that simulated famous places and events by means of the manipulation of illusionistically painted scrims, lighting, auditory effects, and other theatrical devices.

Daguerre had been conducting experiments toward fixing the image of the camera obscura—though without documented results—and upon hearing of the work of Niépce, wrote to him to gain information about his processes. Daguerre's first inquiries were all but rebuffed; Niépce was perhaps justifiably suspicious of a stranger whose motives he could not assess. After more than a year of correspondence, however, Daguerre won a response from Niépce by sending him a drawing. Niépce replied with a heliographic printing plate showing the Holy Family and a proof from it. The two men met for the first time in Paris in September, 1827, while Niépce was en route to London to visit his brother, and they met again in early 1828 on the return journey.

During 1829, Daguerre slowly won Niépce's confidence, and when Niépce decided to write a handbook explaining his research, it was Daguerre's advice that Niépce should attempt to find a way of getting a large profit out of the invention before publication, apart from the honor it would gain for him. Niépce then invited Daguerre to become a partner in perfecting heliography, and in December, 1929, they signed a ten-year contract to perfect and exploit the process.

The partnership was, in many ways, an unequal one, with Niépce supplying a far greater portion of the combined technical experience. Daguerre's potential contribution, however, was far from negligible; he was a man of great energy, a skilled entrepreneur who was perhaps perfectly suited to direct the commercial exploitation of a successful photographic process (although in this episode of photographic history, as in many later ones, the financial value of the technology was surprisingly elusive).

Niépce had attempted to launch heliography in late 1827, during his visit to London. While staying at Kew, near the Royal Botanical Gardens, Niépce had become acquainted with Francis Bauer, a well-known botanical draftsman. Bauer, recognizing the importance of Niépce's experiments, suggested that Niépce address a meeting of the Royal Society on the topic of heliography. A notice on heliography, accompanied by several examples, was prepared but was never presented, ostensibly because Niépce was unwilling to disclose the entirety of his work and was himself disqualified by the society's rules from making a presentation.

Niépce returned to France in early 1828, disappointed by the lack of interest in his work and saddened by the death of his brother, who seems in his last months to have suffered from delusions, including one in which he regarded the Pyréolophore as a kind of perpetual-motion machine. These personal setbacks may well have helped pave the way for Niépce's partnership with Daguerre, to whom the burden of experimentation began to pass during the early 1830's. Little physical evidence remains of the work of either Niépce or Daguerre from these years. A glass plate picturing a still life of a table set for a meal, known only from a mediocre halftone reproduction of 1891, was smashed in 1909 by a demented professor who was supposed to conduct scientific tests on it. This object may have been the work of Niépce, of Daguerre, or even of Niépce's cousin Abel Niépce de Saint-Victor, who took up the heliographic process again in 1853.

By 1829, Niépce felt ready to write a book about his discoveries. Several drafts of an outline exist, and they are quite logical, showing that Niépce was putting his photographic experiences into useful form, perhaps with some thought of his posthumous reputation. Although his partnership with Daguerre remained valid, his productive contribution to it clearly appears to have diminished in the period immediately following its inception. On July 5, 1833, Niépce died of a stroke; he was sixty-eight years old.

SIGNIFICANCE

Nicéphore Niépce was neither an artist nor a scientist but made a contribution to each field at a time when art and science were more naturally related than they became during the Industrial Revolution. His research was less systematic than that of the scientists of his day, and he appears not to have had productive contacts with specialists who could aid his experiments. However, as a generalist, he succeeded where better-qualified people had failed. One reason for this may have been his determination; another is surely that he had the leisure and the resources, over a long period of time, to let his accumulated experiences coalesce into practical steps toward his goals.

It is interesting to speculate on how events might have developed if particular circumstances had differed. In the case of Niépce's inability to publish his notes in England during his sojourn there, there is strong justification for the view that, had he been successful in publicizing heliography in 1827, a series of communications between various noted individuals would almost certainly have resulted in the development, before 1830, of a photographic method based upon paper negatives. Not only would Daguerre's partnership with Niépce have been forestalled, along with the daguerreotype process that was its legacy, but also the great intellectual gifts of the Englishman William Henry Fox Talbot might not have been directed into photography. Whether this course of events would have had any truly lasting effect upon the art or technology of photography is, however, debatable, especially since both Niépce and Daguerre were cognizant of the possible advantages of emulsions coated upon glass plates, the method that was soon to triumph over both Daguerre's and Talbot's processes.

Though there is scant evidence of artistic intention in Niépce's research, his photograph from the window at Le Gras has assumed a monumental significance within the art of photography; as an item of photographic incu-

nabula, it has taken on an aura that is more than sentimental. Technically primitive, it nevertheless announces the beginning of a new era in communication and a new dimension of artistic sensibility.

—C. S. McConnell

FURTHER READING

Batchen, Geoffrey. *Burning with Desire: The Conception of Photography*. Cambridge, Mass.: MIT Press, 1997. A revisionist history of photography, tracing how the desire to photograph emerged from eighteenth and early nineteenth century ideas about landscape and nature. Batchen argues that early photographers, such as Niépce and Daguerre, were not interested in capturing reality, but wanted to "deconstruct" reality.

Braive, Michel F. *The Era of the Photograph: A Social History*. London: Thames & Hudson, 1966. In addition to a brief memoir of Niépce by his descendant, photographer Janine Niépce, this book offers several illustrations of Niépce memorabilia not found elsewhere.

Daval, Jean-Luc. *Photography: History of an Art*. New York: Rizzoli, 1982. This book treats Niépce only in passing, but it offers a rare reproduction of one of his heliographs that represents his experiments more accurately, perhaps, than the enhanced and even retouched illustrations available in other sources.

Fouque, Victor. *The Truth Concerning the Invention of Photography: Nicéphore Niépce, His Life and Works*. Translated by Edward Epstean. New York: Tennant and Ward, 1935. This difficult-to-find translation of a work originally published in 1867 contains the correspondence between Claude and Nicéphore Niépce, but the material is adequately available in the standard modern sources.

Gernsheim, Helmut. "The 150th Anniversary of Photography." *History of Photography: An International Quarterly* 1 (January, 1977): 3-8. An indication of Gernsheim's eminence in the study of the history of photography is given by the fact that this personal memoir is the lead item in the inaugural issue of this journal. The article is an account of his discovery in 1952, by scholarly instinct and luck, of the image now recognized as the first photograph.

Gernsheim, Helmut, and Alison Gernsheim. *The History of Photography from the Camera Obscura to the Beginning of the Modern Era*. New York: Oxford University Press, 1955. Rev. ed. London: Thames & Hudson, 1969. For years this was the standard detailed survey of the history of photography. This book displays both the authors' thoroughness and their affection for the subject. There are hundreds of excellent illustrations as well as notes, an index, and a bibliography meeting high scholarly standards.

_____. *The Origins of Photography*. New York: Thames & Hudson, 1982. Essentially an adaptation of material from the Gernsheims' 1969 history of photography, this volume covers the photographic medium only until the end of the era of the calotype and daguerreotype. This book is better designed than its predecessor but contains fewer illustrations pertaining to Niépce.

Gorman, Jessica. "Photography at a Crossroads." *Science News* 162, no. 21 (November 23, 2002): 331. Examines the future of historical photos in the digital age. Includes information about Niépce's creation of the first heliograph and Gernsheim's attempt to locate it.

Newhall, Beaumont. *Latent Image: The Discovery of Photography*. Garden City, N.Y.: Doubleday, 1967. This is the best survey of the technical research pursued by Niépce, Daguerre, Talbot, and others. Written in an entertaining narrative style, this book by a leading historian of photography tells the human side of the story as well.

_____, ed. *Photography: Essays and Images, Illustrated Readings in the History of Photography*. New York: Museum of Modern Art, 1980. The rather dry documentation of material that survives from Niépce's experiments was understandably omitted from this collection, but the book vividly shows the cultural context of the search for a photographic technology. Indispensable to students of the early history of photography is the reprinting of the entire text of an 1857 article by Lady Elizabeth Eastlake, who affectionately calls Niépce the "philosopher of Chalon."

Scharf, Aaron. "The Mirror with a Memory." In *Pioneers of Photography: An Album of Pictures and Words*. London: British Broadcasting Corporation, 1975. This chapter contains generous excerpts from Niépce's diaries and correspondence as well as a highly amusing chart showing his linguistically oriented attempt in 1832 to derive a name for "photography" from Greek roots.

SEE ALSO: Jacques Daguerre; Sir Humphry Davy; Napoleon I.

RELATED ARTICLES in *Great Events from History: The Nineteenth Century, 1801-1900:* January, 1839: Invention of Daguerreotype Photography Is Announced; 1878: Muybridge Photographs a Galloping Horse.

FRIEDRICH NIETZSCHE
German philosopher

Though Nietzsche's writings were mostly ignored during his lifetime, they became a bellwether in the twentieth century for radical philosophical, psychological, linguistic, and literary critiques of Western culture. Through a series of remarkable works of German prose, Nietzsche sought to smash the idol of Christian morality and liberate a few who might follow after him into a triumphant and tragic this-worldly life.

BORN: October 15, 1844; Röcken, Saxony, Prussia (now in Germany)
DIED: August 25, 1900; Weimar, Germany
ALSO KNOWN AS: Friedrich Wilhelm Nietzsche (full name)
AREA OF ACHIEVEMENT: Philosophy

EARLY LIFE
Born in a German parsonage, Friedrich Wilhelm Nietzsche (NEE-cheh) was named for the reigning king of Prussia, Friedrich Wilhelm IV, who had the same October 15 birth date. His father, Karl Ludwig Nietzsche, was a Lutheran pastor; his mother, Franziska Nietzsche (née Oehler), was the daughter of a Lutheran pastor. (The union produced two other children, Elisabeth in 1846 and Joseph in 1848, who died shortly before his second birthday.)

With the death of his father in 1849, Friedrich would spend most of his early life surrounded by women: his mother, his sister, his paternal grandmother, and two maiden aunts. The family moved in 1850 to Naumburg, in Thuringia, where the young Nietzsche attended elementary school and a private preparatory school. In 1858, he entered Germany's most renowned Protestant boarding school, the Schulpforta, on a scholarship. There he met Paul Deussen, also a student, who became one of his few lifelong friends; Deussen found Nietzsche to be deeply serious, "inclined to corpulence and head congestions," and extremely myopic.

Nietzsche was graduated from the school at Pforta in 1864 with a classical education; that same year, he entered the University of Bonn to study theology and philology, the latter under Friedrich Wilhelm Ritschl. Unable to fit into the rowdiness of student life at Bonn— despite his entertaining students on the piano—Nietzsche abandoned any pretense of theological studies and transferred in 1865 to the University of Leipzig, where his friend Ritschl had gone. Writing to his sister Elisabeth about his abandonment of the Christian faith, Nietzsche told her that he had become a disciple of the truth, wherever it led; he could not be content with a religious happiness. During that same year, the serious Nietzsche told Deussen that a recently published "life of Christ" by David Strauss was disingenuous in its removal of the miraculous Christ from the Gospels while holding on to his precepts. "That can have serious consequences," said Nietzsche; "if you give up Christ you will have to give up God as well."

The year 1865 was remarkable for two other reasons. As Deussen later wrote, Nietzsche had told him that a street porter, asked to take him to a restaurant in Cologne, instead had delivered him to a brothel. Speechless, Nietzsche soon left. Deussen speculated that his friend remained a lifelong virgin. There is much scholarly debate on the subject, but it seems likely that Deussen was wrong. Because there is no indication in Nietzsche's correspondence that he ever had sexual relations with a woman of his own class, it is probable that in 1865 or later Nietzsche acquired syphilis at a brothel. Early in 1889, he would collapse into insanity.

It was in 1865 that Nietzsche encountered the works of the pessimistic philosopher Arthur Schopenhauer, and though Nietzsche was later to renounce his allegiance to Schopenhauer's perspective, and his anti-Semitism, by late in 1865 he had announced that he had become a follower. The Leipzig years, from 1865 to 1869, saw Nietzsche taken under Ritschl's wing as his protégé, the development of his friendship with Erwin Rohde, and the entrance of composer Richard Wagner into his life. After hearing Wagner's music in 1868, Nietzsche became a convert; meeting with the composer that same year, Nietzsche found that Wagner, too, loved Schopenhauer. However, as he would do with Schopenhauer, Nietzsche would one day reject Wagner.

Nietzsche entered into the cavalry company of an artillery regiment in October of 1867, but in March of the next year he suffered a serious chest injury while trying to mount a horse. On extended health leave from the military, Nietzsche resumed his studies in Leipzig; in 1869,

Friedrich Nietzsche. (Library of Congress)

the university (on Ritschl's recommendation) conferred a doctorate on Nietzsche on the strength of his published philological writings and without the customary examination and dissertation required for a German degree. During that same year, Basel appointed Nietzsche to the chair of classical philology; he was twenty-four, no longer a citizen of Prussia, now a resident of Switzerland.

LIFE'S WORK

In the two decades of sanity that remained to Nietzsche, he would battle often against long periods of ill health, especially after 1870, when he fell victim to dysentery and diphtheria while serving as a medical orderly with the Prussian army in the Franco-Prussian War (1870-1871). On his return to Basel to resume his teaching chores in philology (he was an unsuccessful applicant to the chair of philosophy), Nietzsche was plagued with frequent bouts of nausea and exhaustion.

For a time, his one surcease was his friendship with Wagner. From 1869 until Wagner moved to Bayreuth in 1872, Nietzsche visited the composer and his wife, Cosima, some twenty-three times at the Wagner residence at Tribschen, near Lucerne. The composer welcomed a disciple; yet his increasing use of Christian images, especially in his last opera, *Parsifal*, sickened Nietzsche, as did Wagner's anti-Semitism. By 1878, their friendship had been sundered.

Nietzsche's first book broke with tradition. *Die Geburt der Tragödie aus dem Geiste der Musik* (1872; *The Birth of Tragedy out of the Spirit of Music*, 1909) was far from being a classical philological study burdened by arcane footnotes. Instead, Nietzsche had written a speculative treatment of what he found to be two competing forces in ancient Greek life—the Dionysian, representing potentially destructive passion, and the Apollonian, representing reason and restraint. Greek tragedy had fused the two, but, with the triumph of Socrates, the Apollonian was in the ascendant. (Much later Nietzsche would redefine the Dionysian impulse as a sublimated or perfected "will to power" and would ally himself with Dionysus.)

Nietzsche was granted a leave of absence from Basel in 1876 because of ill health, but his continued headaches, vomiting, and deteriorating eyesight led to his resignation in May, 1879, with a pension of three thousand Swiss francs a year for six years. From that time onward, Nietzsche increasingly became an enigma to his friends. His publication of the aphoristic *Menschliches, Allzumenschliches: Ein Buch für freie Geister* (1878; *Human, All Too Human*, 1910, 1911) was characterized by Wagner as the beginning of Nietzsche's slide into madness. Nietzsche cut his intellectual mooring to Schopenhauer as well, writing a friend that he no longer believed what the philosopher had said.

In the decade beginning in 1879, Nietzsche, moving from boardinghouse to boardinghouse, always seeking new curatives, lived in the French Riviera, Italy, and Switzerland, a virtual recluse. His letter writing was a substitute for most human contact. Suffering almost ceaseless pain, Nietzsche turned within—as if the pain itself were a spur to creativity, or as if, through his project of revaluing traditional Christian values, his literary genius would master his physiology.

There was much emotional pain as well. His friendship with philosopher Paul Rée (who was investigating the psychological basis of religious belief), which had begun in 1873, was marred when in 1882 both men met Lou Salomé (later the wife of Orientalist F. C. Andreas, friend of Sigmund Freud, and mistress of the poet Rainer Maria Rilke) and both proposed—Nietzsche apparently

through Rée. Declining both requests, Salomé counterproposed a platonic ménage à trois; Nietzsche's sister Elisabeth learned of the plan, took him to task for his immorality, and informed their mother of Nietzsche's behavior. The three continued in one another's company, but by November, with Salomé and Rée having departed, Nietzsche realized that he had been abandoned.

In January, 1883, in only ten days, Nietzsche penned the first part of what was to become his literary masterpiece, *Also sprach Zarathustra: Ein Buch für Alle und Keinen* (1883-1885; *Thus Spake Zarathustra*, 1896). His only work of fiction, the book (completed in 1885, the fourth and final part privately printed from Nietzsche's own funds) brings a biblical narrative style to parody the Socratic and Christian wisdom teachings, and to bring to "everyone and no one" (the subtitle) the teachings of the *Übermensch* (variously translated "superman" or "overman"). A more explicit elucidation of Nietzsche's philosophical orientation came in 1886 with *Jenseits von Gut und Böse: Vorspiel einer Philosophie der Zukunft* (*Beyond Good and Evil*, 1907), and, in 1887, *Zur Genealogie der Moral* (*On the Genealogy of Morals*, 1896). Books streamed from Nietzsche's pen. In the last year of his sanity, 1888, he wrote five of them, including *Der Antichrist* (1895; *The Antichrist*, 1896) and *Ecce Homo* (1908; English translation, 1911), the last a semiautobiographical overview of Nietzsche's published works.

Several months of euphoria preceded Nietzsche's descent into madness, but following his collapse in the Piazza Carlo Alberto, in Turin, Italy, on January 3, 1889—he had seen a cab driver beating his horse and had flung himself around the horse's neck—the darkness was complete. For the next eleven years, Nietzsche was variously cared for in a Basel asylum, by his mother in Naumburg (until she died in 1897), and by his sister in Weimar.

Elisabeth, married in 1885 to anti-Semite Bernhard Förster (who committed suicide in 1889), managed to gain control of Nietzsche's literary estate and began zealously to refashion her brother's image into that of a proto-Nazi. She withheld *Ecce Homo* from publication for twenty years after Nietzsche had written it, established a Nietzsche archive, and compiled and published a series of notes Nietzsche himself had never intended for publication. She edited it and titled it *Der Wille zur Macht* (1901; *The Will to Power*, 1910).

Only in the last year of his sanity did Nietzsche begin to receive important public notice, a result primarily of the philosophy lectures given by Georg Brandes at Copenhagen. It seems ironic that the first commercial successes of the man who wanted to be understood came at the hands of his sister, who carefully crafted a mythical Nietzsche. Poignantly, it was the ever-prescient Nietzsche who had written in *Ecce Homo*, "I have a terrible fear I shall one day be pronounced holy. . . ." Nietzsche died in Weimar on August 25, 1900, not yet fifty-six, his mane of hair and his shaggy mustache still dark brown.

SIGNIFICANCE

There is much scholarly dispute over the nature of Friedrich Wilhelm Nietzsche's philosophy, and even over whether he intended to have one. In his mature works, from *Thus Spake Zarathustra* on, many themes seem important to Nietzsche, from the concept of the overman, the idea of eternal recurrence, of a man being in love with his own fate and thus triumphant in it, to the psychological origins of traditional morality, the nature of the will to power in human affairs, and the death of God, the last announced by a madman in section 125 of *Die fröhliche Wissenschaft* (1882, 1887; *The Joyful Wisdom*, 1910). However, in Nietzsche's modified aphoristic style, his themes receive no systematic exploration; scholarly interpretations are legion.

Nietzsche's analysis of the psychology of the priest, and of Christian morality, anticipated Freud. Traditional morality has quenched the instinct for life, and has pronounced sexuality, nobility of self, and intellect to be evil; the afterlife is promised only to those who submit to the priest, to the slave morality, the *ressentiment* of those who are weak. Nietzsche's message was that the sickness, the life-denying morality of the Church, must be replaced by the message of the overman; though perhaps an unachievable ideal, the overman is able to fall in love with every aspect of his fate and, without self-deception, to will the eternal repetition of every part of his life. God is dead—the new learning killed him—but the late nineteenth century slumbered on in its nihilism, unaware of the consequences. Nietzsche's message of triumph and tragedy fell on deaf ears during his lifetime.

Nietzsche's insights, often not fully developed, have been mined by twentieth century existentialists such as Albert Camus, deconstructionists such as Jacques Derrida and Michel Foucault, phenomenologists such as Martin Heidegger, religious thinkers such as Paul Tillich and Martin Buber, novelists such as Thomas Mann and Hermann Hesse, and playwright George Bernard Shaw; Sigmund Freud and Carl Jung also felt Nietzsche's influence. As a man "born posthumously," Nietzsche is a key to understanding the twentieth century's most influential and most deeply perplexing currents of thought.

—Dan Barnett

FURTHER READING

Gilman, Sander L., ed. *Conversations with Nietzsche: A Life in the Words of His Contemporaries*. Translated by David J. Parent. New York: Oxford University Press, 1987. Fully aware of Elisabeth Förster-Nietzsche's tendencies to mythologize her brother, this anthology draws carefully on her letters, and those from dozens of other correspondents and writers, to paint a picture of Nietzsche as others knew him. Accessible to the general reader, who will be struck by the varying impressions Nietzsche made on those around him.

Hayman, Ronald. *Nietzsche: A Critical Life*. New York: Oxford University Press, 1980. A chronological account of Nietzsche's life and work. Includes a helpful timeline and a section of photographs. Hayman draws extensively upon Nietzsche's letters, especially in detailing Nietzsche's many illnesses. Attempts to integrate the man with his philosophy but is sometimes murky and cryptic.

Higgins, Kathleen. *Nietzsche's Zarathustra*. Philadelphia: Temple University Press, 1987. A cleanly written and accessible exploration of the book Nietzsche considered his best. Higgins finds thematic and structural unities when the book is considered from the literary standpoint. The first chapter draws on Nietzsche's life and letters during the time of the composition of *Thus Spake Zarathustra* to reveal Nietzsche's serious concerns behind the sometimes-mocking prophet. The twelve-page bibliography is useful.

Hollingdale, R. J. *Nietzsche: The Man and His Philosophy*. Baton Rouge: Louisiana State University Press, 1965. A sympathetic chronological and interpretive narrative, contending that, in the end, one is left with Nietzsche the man and not with some movement or philosophical system. A standard work by one of Nietzsche's English-language translators.

Kaufmann, Walter. *Nietzsche: Philosopher, Psychologist, Antichrist*. 4th ed. Princeton, N.J.: Princeton University Press, 1974. A standard and important account of Nietzsche's life and thought by one of his modern English-language translators. The extensive thirty-page annotated bibliography of primary and secondary sources is invaluable. Included are samples of Nietzsche's handwriting. Kaufmann attempts to smooth Nietzsche's rough edges even as he removes the onus of Elisabeth's manufactured image of her brother. Somewhat dated, as it takes issue with many works on Nietzsche published early in the twentieth century.

Small, Robin. *Nietzsche and Rée: A Star Friendship*. New York: Oxford University Press, 2005. Explores the two men's friendship, common ideas, and novel approach to philosophy. Describes how their collaboration played a crucial role in the development of Nietzsche's philosophy.

Solomon, Robert C., and Kathleen M. Higgins, eds. *Reading Nietzsche*. New York: Oxford University Press, 1988. Based on papers presented at a 1985 seminar on Nietzsche at the University of Texas at Austin. Twelve Nietzsche scholars in the Anglo-American tradition provide insightful interpretations of most of the Nietzsche canon. A ten-page bibliography of primary and secondary sources, including works on specific texts, is extremely valuable in directing first-time readers of Nietzsche into the mountain of Nietzsche studies. Works in the continental tradition are also cited in the bibliography.

Welshon, Rex. *The Philosophy of Nietzsche*. Montreal: McGill-Queen's University Press, 2004. An introductory overview of Nietzsche's thought, organized by subject, including chapters on morality, religion, nihilism, metaphysics, truth, logic, and the will to power.

SEE ALSO: Georg Wilhelm Friedrich Hegel; Friedrich Wilhelm Joseph von Schelling; Arthur Schopenhauer; Richard Wagner.

RELATED ARTICLE in *Great Events from History: The Nineteenth Century, 1801-1900:* April, 1807: Hegel Publishes *The Phenomenology of Spirit*.

FLORENCE NIGHTINGALE
English nurse and social reformer

Following a deeply rooted passion to serve God and combining it with a strong will and intellect, Nightingale revolutionized the nursing profession and the design and conditions of medical care and hospital facilities.

BORN: May 12, 1820; Florence (now in Italy)
DIED: August 13, 1910; London, England
ALSO KNOWN AS: Lady of the Lamp
AREA OF ACHIEVEMENT: Medicine

EARLY LIFE

Florence Nightingale was named after the romantic Italian city of Florence, Italy, in which she was born. Her mother, Frances (Fanny) Nightingale, thirty-two, was a socially ambitious and strong-willed woman. Her father, William Edward Nightingale, twenty-five, was a scholarly and liberal Cambridge man. Florence had one older sister, Parthe, and when the family returned to England, the sisters' education was first handled by governesses but soon taken over by their father. Thus, both girls received a broader and more liberal education than many women of their day. This early introduction to a competitive and intellectual world rather than a purely social and domestic one would be a great influence on Nightingale.

As a teenager, Nightingale was surrounded by relatives and friends, family visits and excursions to foreign countries, and the usual round of social events and gossip. Although she engaged in all the domestic and social obligations and was quite popular, she felt, as early as seventeen, a desire to do something more productive and useful with her life. She was expected to marry well and rear a family; still, Nightingale wanted more. In between social engagements, therefore, she would retreat into a private world of dreaming and writing what she later called her "private notes." Then, in 1837, she wrote in one of her diaries that God had called her to his service, but for what she was not sure. For the next sixteen years she would be tormented by this uncertainty. During these years, she unhappily continued to lead the social life that her mother prescribed, but she managed to find the time for isolated hours of self-reflection as well as visiting and nursing sick relatives.

In 1839, both Nightingale sisters were presented at court, and there Florence met Henry Nicholson, who wooed her for six years before she finally refused his marriage proposal. She could give no concrete reason other than her desire to do God's will, whatever that was. Again, she was overwhelmed by uncertainty about what her life's work should be, and her spells of quiet frustration and spiritual agony worried her mother. After all, Nightingale was attractive, if not beautiful, with dark reddish hair, gray eyes, a gay smile, and a sense of humor tempered with a sharp intellect and curiosity.

In 1842, another suitor presented himself: Richard Monckton Milnes, a member of Parliament, a linguist, and a social reformer of sorts; in short, he seemed the perfect mate for Nightingale. Her feelings were nevertheless divided, for in that year she learned of the work being done at the Institute of Deaconesses at Kaiserwerth, Germany, regarding the training of nurses in hospital work. For two years, she kept this knowledge to herself; then one day she tentatively voiced a desire to devote her life to nursing. Her family, especially her mother, rejected the idea completely, and for the next six years Florence suffered from the denial both spiritually and physically. She believed that God had called her again, yet since she was unable to follow his calling, she thought she must be somehow unworthy. The best she could do was nurse sick relatives, friends, and villagers. By 1847, she had worked herself into a state of ill health, marked by migraines, chronic coughing, and a near breakdown.

Nightingale went to Rome in 1848 to regain her spirits and health. There, she met Sidney Herbert and his wife, Liz; her friendship with Sidney marked a turning point in her life. After this meeting, she soon rejected her long-waiting suitor Richard Milnes, again disappointing her family. Now alone and desperate for an answer to God's calling, she made her way (with the help of friends) to Kaiserwerth, Germany, but her family flatly refused to allow her to enter the school.

By that time, Nightingale was ill and suicidal; thus, she defied her family and in 1851, at the age of thirty-one, entered the questionable profession of nursing. Her rebellion did little good, however, for when she returned to England she found herself facing her mother's anger. Again, she was plunged into the social life and for the next two years suffered as she followed her mother's will, and, periodically, nursed the sick under the guidance of the Sisters of Charity in Paris. Then, in 1853, Liz Herbert made a decision on Florence's behalf; she recommended her as the new superintendent at the Institution for the Care of Sick Gentlewomen in London. Florence's nursing career then began in earnest.

LIFE'S WORK

As superintendent of the institution for the next fourteen months, Nightingale surprised the committee that appointed her in two respects. First, the "ministering angel" they had thought that they recruited proved to be a tough-minded and practical administrator who completely reorganized the hospital, from food and beds to medical supplies and sanitary conditions. Second, Nightingale insisted that any poor and ill woman should be admitted, not only those who were members of the Church of England.

With a fight, Nightingale got most of what she wanted. She also wanted trained nurses, however, and this request was not easy to fulfill. Nightingale therefore began to formulate plans to establish a training school for nurses along the lines of Kaiserwerth. Her plans were interrupted, however, when England and France declared war on Russia in March, 1854. War reports in *The Times* stated that while England and France were victorious in battle, the casualty rate was alarmingly high. In October, Nightingale left England for the shores of the Black Sea with a handful of poorly trained nurses. As a result, she made her way into the annals of the Crimean War.

Once again, the Herberts, this time Sidney, opened the way for Nightingale by appointing her superintendent of the Female Nursing Establishment of the English General Hospitals in Turkey, a position never before held by a woman. It was a revolutionary step, and she took it gladly. However, her initial enthusiasm was soon

Florence Nightingale. (Library of Congress)

replaced by dogged determination, for what she found in the hospitals at Scutari was appalling. Despite assurances by the cabinet ministers in the War Office that everything was in order, Florence found the hospital and medical conditions deplorable. Besides a lack of basic medical supplies (bandages, splints, stretchers), nourishing food, adequate clothing, and clean water, the hospital was overrun with filth, vermin, and backed-up cesspools. In addition, the wounded, the diseased, and the dead were all crowded together in rooms with little or no ventilation. Foresight, luckily, had prompted Nightingale to bring supplies, equipment, and food with her, and while it was not nearly enough, it did help.

Lack of supplies, however, was not Nightingale's only obstacle. Even though her position was an official one, she met with stubborn resistance from the military doctors and staff in Scutari. War and women, even if they were nurses, did not mix. Slowly and steadily, however, Nightingale began her nurses on a cleanup campaign. The job was difficult, yet in time, the men were cleaned, clothed, and fed, and the hospital was scrubbed and emptied (as much as possible) of the overflowing dirt. Her next task was to request the rebuilding of the Barrack Hospital; again she met with opposition, but using her own money and influence, she managed to get the men better quarters.

Nightingale's final triumph came when the doctors (or at least most of them) relented and finally allowed her and her nurses actually to care for the patients and assist the doctors. Thus the "bird," as she was called, became more than merely a "ministering angel," the "lady of the lamp"; she used her official position and her passion to serve God and got things done, thus earning her title as administrative chief.

The struggle was long and slow, for Nightingale was battling men who were set in their ways; they not only objected to a woman coming that close to military matters but also stubbornly refused to admit that there was any sort of problem with the medical system. However, Nightingale demanded change, and she had

some powerful people on her side: Sidney Herbert, Dr. Sutherland, the Home government, *The Times*, public opinion, and the queen herself. Therefore, using whatever and whomever she could, Nightingale was able to reform the hospitals at Scutari, as well as some of the army's medical policies. Within a year after her arrival in the Crimea, the rate of mortality among wounded soldiers dropped dramatically.

Nightingale not only was bent on improving the physical conditions of the men but also wanted to do something for their emotional state as well, for morale was extremely low. She set up, to the surprise and outrage of her opposition, reading and recreational rooms for the soldiers, assisted them in managing and saving some money from their salaries, and held classes and lectures for them; in short, she treated them like human beings. In the middle of all this change, she was still battling military and government officials and religious leaders who were upset by the lack of religious segregation among both the nurses and the patients. Nightingale refused, however, to

---

"OBSERVATION OF THE SICK"

Florence Nightingale's Notes on Nursing *was one of the earliest books to offer nurses practical and realistic advice on how to care for patients. Its chapter titled "Observation of the Sick" addresses the simple question of how to determine when a patient is getting well.*

There is no more silly or universal question scarcely asked than this, "Is he better?" Ask it of the medical attendant, if you please. But of whom else, if you wish for a real answer to your question, would you ask? Certainly not of the casual visitor; certainly not of the nurse, while the nurse's observation is so little exercised as it is now. What you want are facts, not opinions—for who can have any opinion of any value as to whether the patient is better or worse, excepting the constant medical attendant, or the really observing nurse?

The most important practical lesson that can be given to nurses is to teach them what to observe—how to observe—what symptoms indicate improvement—what the reverse—which are of importance—which are of none—which are the evidence of neglect—and of what kind of neglect.

All this is what ought to make part, and an essential part, of the training of every nurse. At present how few there are, either professional or unprofessional, who really know at all whether any sick person they may be with is better or worse.

The vagueness and looseness of the information one receives in answer to that much abused question, "Is he better?" would be ludicrous, if it were not painful. The only sensible answer (in the present state of knowledge about sickness) would be "How can I know? I cannot tell how he was when I was not with him."

Source: Florence Nightingale, *Notes on Nursing: What It Is, and What It Is Not* (New York: D. Appleton, 1872), chapter 13.

let narrow-minded sectarian differences get in her way, and by July, 1856, a few months after the declaration of peace, Nightingale considered her work in the Crimea complete. As she returned to England, news of her accomplishments preceded her, and the queen invited her to the court for the purpose of awarding her a brooch that bore a St. George's cross and the royal cipher encircled in diamonds surrounded by the words "Blessed are the merciful."

After her struggles and successes at Scutari, Nightingale's work was far from finished: For the next fifty years, she kept fighting for hospital reform. Doctors diagnosed a nervous condition and heart trouble, telling her that if she did not take an extended rest she could die. Nightingale refused flatly and continued her work, which had become both a passion and a mission. When she was ill and tired, she read and wrote letters or reports from her bed. When she felt well enough, she visited influential people and hospitals trying to implement her reforms.

The army hospital at Scutari had been only the beginning; now Nightingale went after the Army Medical Department itself. Her supporters remained loyal and hardworking; in fact, they were joined by her Aunt Mai and Sir Harry Varney. However, she also gained two formidable enemies—Lord Panmure, secretary of state for war, and Dr. Andrew Smith, head of the Army Medical Department. Together, they either denied the need for reforms or managed to undermine her work. Nightingale had met resistance before, however, and their opposition did not stop her.

As in the Crimea, so too in England Nightingale used her friends, her influence, and her social position to initiate change in medical procedures, sanitary conditions, hospital design, and patient care (both physical and emotional). She wrote an eight-hundred-page report, *Notes on Matters Affecting the Health, Efficiency, and Hospital Administration of the British Army* (1858), and *A Contribution to the Sanitary History of the British Army During the Late War with Russia* (1859), which was submitted to the Royal Commission. Members of the commission received the report favorably, and as a result, drastic changes were initiated according to Nightingale's recommendations between the years 1859 and 1861.

Nightingale was then contacted by the Sanitary Commission (an organization set up at her suggestion) and asked to investigate army medical conditions in India. By then, she had become quite a medical authority, and her reputation was spreading with the help of a published book entitled *Notes on Hospitals* (1859), which

completely revolutionized hospital construction and administrative practices. Then, in 1860, the Nightingale Training School for Nurses at St. Thomas's Hospital opened, and in the same year, Nightingale published *Notes on Nursing: What It Is, and What It Is Not*. Nightingale's establishment of a nursing hospital earned for her her reputation as the founder of modern nursing. Just when it seemed Nightingale was succeeding in all of her reforms, however, disaster struck. Sidney Herbert, her most powerful ally, became ill and soon died, and with his death her open door to the world of men and politics shut slightly. Nevertheless, over the next ten years, 1862-1872, she managed to initiate and enact many changes despite the hostility of the War Office.

By this time, however, Nightingale's health was again causing her problems, and she settled in a house on South Street, where she remained for the rest of her life, practically bedridden. Invalid she might be, but inactive and unproductive she was not. She had a constant stream of visitors (from friends to public officials both domestic and foreign) who came seeking her advice and expertise on hospital matters. Thus, from her bed, she dictated letters, reports, and policies regarding the construction of hospitals and the training of nurses; still she wanted to do more. Having devoted her life to the physical comfort of humankind, she now turned inward to her own metaphysical condition, reading everything that she could. As in her early adult years when she wrestled with religious questions and callings, she returned to a state of spiritual and intellectual turmoil.

Nightingale's last ten years, which she should have spent reveling in her accomplishments, were spent, instead, trying to satisfy unanswerable longings and questions. She became increasingly sentimental and senile. The once-thin, strong-minded woman had become a rather fat, simpleminded patient. The world had all but forgotten her. In 1907, sick and confused, she received the Royal Order of Merit; she was the first woman ever to be awarded this honor. It was presented to her in her bedroom, and her only reply was, "Too kind, too kind." Three years later, nearly blind, she died in her sleep on August 13, 1910.

SIGNIFICANCE

Florence Nightingale has been pictured as a quiet, meek, self-sacrificing angel of mercy moving softly among dimly lit hospital corridors and beds filled with wounded soldiers. In short, she has been envisioned as the "lady of the lamp." Although she did spend many hours comforting the sick in this manner, this is only a partial and romanticized portrait of her. What is often not realized or remembered is that Nightingale was more than a nurse; she was a hospital reformer and administrator. Thus, although her role as nurse was a difficult task, both physically and emotionally, she also faced a more difficult task: She was a woman trying to do a man's job in a society that, generally speaking, opposed her.

Luckily for Nightingale, she was also living in a time of great change. She was not alone in her passion and determination to change the health conditions of Great Britain; others, many of them women, were also fighting for changes in laws and customs, as well as social standards and attitudes. While she crusaded for more humane medical treatment and modern facilities, others were crusading for woman suffrage, the need for welfare for the poor and sick, and a general change in attitude toward education and status.

Although not outwardly concerned with these other changes, Nightingale must have been influenced by this growing climate, which challenged the Victorian status quo. Although Nightingale's name may remain synonymous with nursing, her impact on hospital design, construction, and administration has remained strong even into the late twentieth century.

—Deborah Charlie

FURTHER READING

Cook, Sir Edward. *The Life of Florence Nightingale*. 2 vols. London: Macmillan, 1913. An exhaustive biography based on a comprehensive study of Nightingale's diaries and letters, in addition to material written about her in both government and medical reports, including those from the Crimean War. The study also describes how friends and family viewed Nightingale, based on their letters and memoirs. As a research tool, this is a valuable work.

Gill, Gillian. *Nightingales: The Extraordinary Upbringing and Curious Life of Miss Florence Nightingale*. London: Hodder & Stoughton, 2004. Biography of Nightingale, placing her life within the context of her family and her relationships with family members.

Huxley, Elspeth. *Florence Nightingale*. New York: G. P. Putnam's Sons, 1975. A well-written and readable biography exploring in great detail both Nightingale's personal history and her public life. It also includes a good overview of the historical and social world in which she moved. The book is well documented by excerpts from Nightingale's diaries and letters, as well as government publications. Huxley's approach is both thematic and novelistic.

Longford, Elizabeth. *Eminent Victorian Women*. New York: Alfred A. Knopf, 1981. Longford's chapter on Nightingale is a clear and well-written chronology of her life and accomplishments. There is some editorializing regarding Nightingale's other biographers and her romanticized or exaggerated image. Longford's account is marred by her cryptic references to Nightingale's relationship with other women and her growing concern for matters intellectual and mystical.

Nightingale, Florence. *Florence Nightingale: An Introduction to Her Life and Family*. Vol. 1 in *The Collected Works of Florence Nightingale*, edited by Lynn McDonald. 16 vols. Waterloo, Ont.: Wilfrid Laurier University Press, 2001- . The first volume of this sixteen-volume collection contains essays examining Nightgale's life and the themes found in her work, as well as selected correspondence and some of Nightingale's writings. Subsequent volumes contain Nightingale's correspondence, journals, diaries, and other writings about a wide range of subjects, including theology, mysticism, public health care, hospital reform, and the Crimean War.

Schnittkind, Henry Thomas, and Dana Lee Thomas. *Living Biographies of Famous Women*. New York: Doubleday, 1959. A brief and straightforward account of Nightingale's work during and after the Crimean War. The chapter mentions, in passing, her early and later years but concentrates primarily on the highlights of her career between the years 1856 and 1862. Contains little specific information or analysis.

Strachey, Lytton. *Eminent Victorians*. New York: Modern Library, 1918. Strachey devotes five chapters to Nightingale in this study of famous Victorians (she is the only woman he includes). These well-written and well-documented chapters concentrate not only on Nightingale's personal life and career but also on the social and political milieu in which she lived. The author's point of view is so close to the actual time in which Florence worked that Strachey's work has a tone and sense of familiarity with both his subject and the times.

SEE ALSO: Clara Barton; Elizabeth Blackwell; Elizabeth Fry.

RELATED ARTICLES in *Great Events from History: The Nineteenth Century, 1801-1900:* November 4, 1854: Nightingale Takes Charge of Nursing in the Crimea; May 12, 1857: New York Infirmary for Indigent Women and Children Opens.

ALFRED NOBEL
Swedish inventor and philanthropist

Nobel invented dynamite and blasting caps and held patents for more than 350 inventions, but he is remembered mostly for the provision he made in his last will for the distribution of the income from the bulk of his estate to provide annual prizes to those who confer upon humankind the greatest benefits in the fields of physics, chemistry, physiology or medicine, literature, and peace.

BORN: October 21, 1833; Stockholm, Sweden
DIED: December 10, 1896; San Remo, Italy
ALSO KNOWN AS: Alfred Bernhard Nobel (full name)
AREA OF ACHIEVEMENT: Science and technology

EARLY LIFE

Alfred Bernhard Nobel spent his life in one sort of pursuit yet is enshrined in history for something quite different. He was the fourth son of Immanuel and Andriette Nobel. His father was a visionary, an inventor whose fortunes swung from one extreme to another. When the family's fortunes were reduced, his mother operated a food shop to supplement their income. Shortly before Alfred's birth, Immanuel's business in Sweden foundered. In 1837, Immanuel made an attempt to reestablish himself in Finland but failed. By 1842, however, he was a modestly successful manufacturer of mechanical devices in St. Petersburg, Russia. He flourished there until 1858, when the Russian government canceled its contracts, creating for him a new round of financial difficulties.

During his time in Russia, Immanuel had become fascinated with the explosive qualities of nitroglycerin, realizing that if the substance could be controlled it would have tremendous potential as military weaponry as well as for use in heavy industry and mining. Alfred, frail, colorless, and thin, was a sickly child with a spinal defect, who early shared this interest in nitroglycerin with his father. Often he was too ill to attend school, and, in Russia, he was taught exclusively by tutors. He showed a natural gift for languages, acquiring them as he traveled. He had lived in Finland and Russia, and he spoke Swedish at home. Between the ages of seventeen and nineteen, Nobel traveled in Germany, France, and the United States, learning languages as he went. Nobel, always dedicated to work, was a perfectionist, always demanding more of himself than more healthy people do.

Nobel and his brothers Ludvig and Robert worked in their father's plant in St. Petersburg. When it faced an impending financial disaster in 1858, Nobel, because of his fluency in English, was sent to England to try to negotiate financing for the business. He failed in this attempt, however, and his defeated father returned to Sweden. Nobel and his brothers remained in Russia, but in 1863, Nobel returned to Sweden to work with his father. Granted his first patent in 1857, Nobel was now on the way to discovering how to control nitroglycerin for commercial use. His invention of the blasting cap changed forever the way mining, massive construction, and war would be conducted.

LIFE'S WORK

Liquid nitroglycerin is among the world's most volatile substances. Nobel's device for igniting it, the blasting cap, consisted of a charge of gunpowder that could be ignited by a fuse and was attached to liquid nitroglycerin. This blasting cap gave workers who set the device time to seek shelter from the ensuing explosion. So revolutionary was this invention that Nobel gained fame in a matter of months, but his life was not free from sorrow, difficulty, and loneliness.

Just a year after the blasting cap was invented, Nobel's younger brother, Emil, a twenty-one-year-old student who worked in his brother's laboratory making detonators, was in the laboratory when it caught fire and exploded, killing five people who were working there, including Emil. The loss of this young son was so devastating to Immanuel that he soon suffered a paralytic stroke, from which he never recovered. Nothing, however—not even Emil's death—could shake Nobel's belief in what he was doing, and he proceeded to open explosives factories across Europe and in the United States.

So great was his confidence that Nobel yielded his patent rights when he opened foreign factories, agreeing that instead of receiving royalty payments he would receive a substantial share of the proceeds from each factory. It is this arrangement that caused him to be numbered among the world's wealthiest people by the time he died.

Nitroglycerin is a dangerous substance because it decomposes quickly; this decomposition inevitably leads to explosions. Few people realized during the 1860's and 1870's just how dangerous nitroglycerin was to work with. Two years after Nobel's laboratory exploded in 1864, a ship carrying nitroglycerin exploded and capsized near Panama, killing seventy-four people. Within

Alfred Nobel. (The Nobel Foundation)

months of that explosion, a San Francisco warehouse, in which liquid nitroglycerin was stored, exploded, killing another fourteen people. Nobel's factory near Hamburg, Germany, was completely destroyed by an explosion less than a year after it opened.

Continuing disasters impelled Nobel to find a safe way to store and ship nitroglycerin. Ever the inventor and thinker, Nobel knew that he had to find a way to turn nitroglycerin into a solid substance. He realized that he had to combine the liquid with something that could absorb it, and he finally settled on a siliconlike substance, kieselguhr, which was porous and would not add anything chemically to the substance with which it was mixed. After nitroglycerin was mixed with kieselguhr, it could be formed into shapes, wrapped in paper, then transported or stored. The result was dynamite, so named by Nobel from the Greek word for power, *dunamis.*

With this advance in the latter part of the 1860's, Nobel was able to establish factories all over the world to mass-produce one of the world's most destructive substances. The production of his plants increased from a mere 11 tons in 1867 to more than 3,000 tons in 1874,

and to almost 67,000 tons produced by ninety-three factories—in all of which he had a financial interest—by the year of his death. Everyone connected with the production of dynamite was becoming rich; Nobel, however, because he shared in the profits of every dynamite factory in the world, was quickly gaining a financial position unheard of in Europe since the days of the Medicis.

Nobel's interest in invention never waned. After he invented dynamite, he invented an explosive gelatin more powerful than nitroglycerin, virtually impervious to shock and unaffected by moisture, which predated the sophisticated plastic explosives now available. Before Orville and Wilbur Wright flew their airplane at Kitty Hawk, North Carolina, in 1903, Nobel was experimenting with aerial photography as an expedient and accurate means of cartography, mounting his cameras on rockets. He was involved with experiments to find ways of synthesizing silk, rubber, and leather far in advance of the synthetic production of nylon, synthetic rubber, and vinyl a half century after his death. His smokeless gunpowder, *balliste,* first patented in 1887, was in great demand by armies throughout the world and added considerably to Nobel's coffers.

Through all this time, Nobel wandered from one place to another, buying houses in Paris, where he spent a considerable amount of time; at San Remo, Italy, where he bought the villa in which he eventually died; and in Sweden at Bofors, where he spent the last summer of his life. Nobel never married and his romantic involvements were never notably fulfilling, although he had a long, quite distant relationship with an Austrian, Sofie Hess, much his junior, to whom he wrote nearly daily and whom he supported during the later years of his life even though she had been married to someone else.

SIGNIFICANCE

In his final years, Alfred Nobel speculated that he would die alone, unattended by anyone who loved him; his prediction was accurate. He spent the summer of 1896 at his home, Björkborn in Bofors, after which he went to his home in Paris, and then to San Remo. His health was failing, but he continued to work, write to his friends, and plan. On December 10, 1896, Nobel collapsed in his laboratory, and that evening, with only his servants present, Nobel died of heart failure.

On November 27, 1895, Nobel had drafted a holograph will, replacing one that left his vast fortune essentially to relatives, servants, and friends. The new will, for which Nobel will be forever remembered, substantially reduced his personal bequests. It directed that his residual estate be invested conservatively and that the income from these investments be used to establish annual prizes to be awarded with no reservations regarding nationality to those people whose activities are deemed to be of the greatest benefit to humankind in the fields of physics, chemistry, physiology or medicine, literature, and peace.

Nobel's will was contested and was in litigation for more than three years. Afterward, however, a system was established for the distribution of the income in the form of Nobel Prizes, the first set of which were awarded in 1901. As the income from the Nobel trust has increased, the size of each award has grown to the point that in 2005 the typical prize was worth over $1.3 million, more than thirty times what the same award had been worth fifty years earlier.

The list of Nobel laureates, which has now been expanded to include a sixth field, economics, contains the names of international giants in their fields: scientists of the stature of Albert Einstein, Marie Curie, and Linus Pauling; writers such as William Faulkner and T. S. Eliot; physicians and physiologists such as Ivan Pavlov and Sir Alexander Fleming; and advocates of world peace such as Woodrow Wilson and Albert Schweitzer. The Nobel legacy is great because of the endowment he established to recognize those who contribute most to the benefit of humankind.

—R. Baird Shuman

FURTHER READING

Bergengren, Erik. *Alfred Nobel: The Man and His Work.* New York: Thomas Nelson and Sons, 1962. This brief overview of Nobel's life is supplemented by a list of Nobel institutions and of the awards that have been granted. It is particularly valuable for its discussion of Nobel's inventions and for its detail about the growing use and sales of dynamite. The research is extremely careful.

Evlanoff, Michael, and Marjorie Fluor. *Alfred Nobel: The Loneliest Millionaire.* New York: Ward Ritchie Press, 1969. This book is a study of Nobel's personal isolation and of his attempts to escape from his loneliness. It relates his establishing the Nobel Prizes to his guilt about the destructive effects of dynamite. Nobel is portrayed as a sensitive man with few roots, one whose intellect was a chief and isolating concern.

Contains a list of all Nobel laureates from 1901 to 1968.

Fant, Kenne. *Alfred Nobel: A Biography.* Translated from the Swedish by Marianne Ruuth. New York: Little, Brown, 1993. Portrays Nobel as an isolated and melancholy misanthrope, convinced of life's absurdities.

Jackson, Donald Dale. "The Nobility of Alfred Nobel." *Smithsonian* 19 (November, 1988): 201-224. This substantial article, both meticulously researched and extremely well written, focuses on Nobel's pessimism and loneliness and on their causes, relating these conditions to his establishing the Nobel Prizes. Jackson has intriguing notions concerning Hess, the young woman in Nobel's life.

Nobelstiftelsen. *Nobel: The Man and His Prizes.* Rev. ed. New York: Elsevier, 1962. This authorized biography has chapters by eminent representatives from the five fields in which the awards were originally granted as well as a biographical chapter by Henrick Schück and a chapter on Nobel and the Nobel Foundation by Ragnar Sohlman. This book is a good starting point for those wishing to know more about Alfred Nobel.

Sohlman, Ragnar. *The Legacy of Alfred Nobel: The Story Behind the Nobel Prizes.* Translated by Elspeth Harley Schubert. London: Bodley Head, 1983. This book was published originally in Swedish under the title *Ett Testamente* in 1950. Sohlman was Nobel's assistant in the last three years of his life and served as one of the executors of his will, giving him a significant role in establishing the Nobel award mechanism. Sohlman knew intimately the details of Nobel's business and life, and he presents these details clearly and directly in this excellent book, which also contains a copy of Nobel's will.

SEE ALSO: Bertha von Suttner.

RELATED ARTICLES in *Great Events from History: The Nineteenth Century, 1801-1900:* October, 1867: Nobel Patents Dynamite; 1888-1906: Ramón y Cajal Shows How Neurons Work in the Nervous System; December 11, 1890: Behring Discovers the Diphtheria Antitoxin; November 9, 1895: Röntgen Discovers X Rays; November 27, 1895: Nobel Bequeathes Funds for the Nobel Prizes.

ANNIE OAKLEY
American sharpshooter

An expert markswoman and consummate performer, Oakley traveled throughout the United States and Europe demonstrating her shooting skills during an era when shooting was almost exclusively a man's sport.

BORN: August 13, 1860; Darke County, Ohio
DIED: November 3, 1926; Greenville, Ohio
ALSO KNOWN AS: Phoebe Anne Moses (birth name)
AREA OF ACHIEVEMENT: Sports

EARLY LIFE

Phoebe Anne Moses—who was nicknamed Annie—was the fourth daughter born to the Quakers Jacob and Susan Moses of rural Darke County, Ohio. When Annie was still a young child, Jacob taught her to hunt and to trap. After Jacob's death from exposure in 1866, Susan and her eight children were left destitute. Young Annie was sent to the county poor farm, but she was soon chosen by a young farmer to be a companion for his wife and infant daughter. Although it was common for poor children to be farmed out, the ten-year-old Annie's fate was unusually cruel; she was overworked and physically abused by the farmer. For two years she was virtually a slave. In 1872, Annie fled, returning to the poorhouse, where she lived with the new superintendent and his wife as a member of their family. Under their care she attended school.

When Annie was fifteen, she returned to her mother. The enterprising young woman capitalized on her adroitness with firearms, entering into a business arrangement with a local merchant in which she supplied him with small game that was shipped to Cincinnati hotels. From that time forward, Annie earned her living with her shooting, proudly paying her mother's mortgage and boasting throughout her life that she had never had money other than what she personally had earned. From her early years of depredation Annie learned frugality. Throughout her life, she shrewdly managed and invested her earnings, thereby enabling herself and her husband to live their retirement years in comfort.

LIFE'S WORK

Annie Moses—in 1882 she adopted the stage name Oakley—was twenty-one when she met her future husband, sharpshooter Frank Butler. Exhibition shooting was at its peak in popularity when Butler, who was traveling in Ohio with a variety show, competed in a contest

against Annie Moses. Although women sharpshooters were relatively common, Butler was surprised by the youthful, petite Annie Moses, who appeared to him to be a little girl. Moses outshot Butler that day, which marked the beginning of their courtship. The two married one year later.

During their early married years, Oakley and Butler toured variety theaters and skating rinks. It was at one such show that Oakley met the Lakota (Sioux) chief Sitting Bull, who became fond of her, naming her *Watanya Cicilla*, or "Little Sure Shot." The two would meet again when they both worked for Buffalo Bill Cody's Wild West Show. Butler soon realized he was outdistanced by Oakley's prowess and her showmanship; he retired from exhibition shooting to become Oakley's manager.

In 1884, after a short stint with the Sells Brothers Circus, the still relatively unknown Oakley applied to Buffalo Bill Cody for a sharpshooting position in his Wild West Show. Although he initially refused her, after the sudden departure of his star marksman, Captain Adam Bogardus, Cody gave Oakley a three-day trial. He was delighted with "Missie"—as he called her—and with only a brief interruption, Oakley remained with Cody's outfit until 1902.

Bursting into the arena sporting her trademark loose, dark, curly hair and her meticulously hand-sewn costumes of short skirts and leggings, Oakley was in constant motion during her ten-minute act. She leaped over a table to grasp her gun after a clay target had already been released, shot upside down, backward while looking in a hand mirror, and occasionally from horseback and from a bicycle. She clowned with audiences by feigning horror over missed shots, which she did intentionally so that she would not be accused of cheating. She shot cigarettes from her husband's mouth and potatoes from her dogs' heads, and she split a playing card turned sideways. Athletic and quick, Oakley was one of the finest shots, and clearly the most engaging exhibition shooter, of her era.

At the height of its popularity during the 1880's, Buffalo Bill and his Wild West Show presented a spectacle of heroic cowboys and villainous horse-riding Plains Indians. Its massive cast of Indians, including for a year the famous Sitting Bull, and fancy-riding cowboys recreated shootouts, stagecoach attacks, and mock battles, thrilling audiences and generating an idealized image of the West in the minds of Americans and Europeans alike.

Cody's outfit was the first and best of the numerous Wild West shows that became the inspiration for film Westerns of a later era. The youthful athlete Oakley became an audience favorite, attaining international superstar fame. Her life, along with Cody's, was mythologized.

After drawing record crowds at Staten Island and Madison Square Garden in 1886, the Wild West Show traveled in 1887 to London, where Oakley was universally praised by audiences and reporters. In England, the once-poor country girl charmed royalty and traveled in upper-class social circles. Remarkably, Oakley was accepted at elite British gun clubs, where, despite being a woman, she was admired for her expert shooting. In London, she began teaching women to shoot, a tradition she continued for the rest of her life. Women were as capable of shooting as men, she believed, and she advocated the carrying of personal arms as a means of self-defense.

Oakley left Cody's show in 1887 for reasons that are obscured because neither Cody nor Oakley discussed the matter. During that year, she engaged in numerous

Annie Oakley. (Courtesy, Nutley Historical Society Collection, Nutley, New Jersey)

exhibitions and matches, in which she had also participated when touring with the Wild West Show in order to earn prize money and gain publicity. In 1885, for example, she attempted to shoot, after loading the guns herself, 5,000 glass balls in one day, scoring 4,722 and breaking a record for the last 1,000, of which she missed only 16. She set several other records, including one for American doubles scoring—two traps released simultaneously. During 1888, Oakley also traveled on the variety circuit performing trick shooting on stage, spent a short time with Pawnee Bill's Wild West Show, and starred in her first theatrical play, *Deadwood Dick: Or, The Sunbeam of the Sierras*. Although the critics despised the play, they wrote favorable reviews of Oakley. By early 1889, Oakley returned to Cody's show, where she remained as a star performer until she retired in 1902.

By 1892, Oakley's legend was firmly established; she had charmed London society, had become the darling of the newspapers, had achieved recognition at shooting clubs in England and the United States, and had even had clubs named for her. In 1889, she had extended her reputation to continental Europe when she traveled with Cody's Wild West Show to France, Italy, and Germany. In 1893, even the United States Army admitted her expertise by sending representatives to learn from her while she performed at the Chicago World's Fair.

Oakley's apparent youthfulness generated much of her stage appeal. Only five feet tall and weighing approximately 110 pounds, the petite Oakley astounded audiences with feats of endurance with heavy guns. In 1902, when her hair suddenly turned white, and she could no longer project the image of a young girl, Oakley and Butler retired from the Wild West Show. She again tried acting, with a play called *The Western Girl*, written expressly for her and showcasing her marksmanship. This time, the play was successful with both critics and the public.

In 1903, Oakley's relationship with the press was abruptly shattered when newspapers throughout the country printed a story originating in Chicago with William Randolph Hearst's news service. Reportedly, Annie Oakley had been arrested stealing a man's pants to support her cocaine habit. She was represented as a destitute drug addict. A woman claiming to be Annie Oakley had indeed been arrested, but the newspapers had failed to confirm her identity, and she was, in fact, merely a burlesque impersonator of Oakley. In one of the largest libel suits ever initiated, Oakley sued and won settlements from newspapers throughout the country. Her battle to clear her reputation lasted for nearly five years and absorbed much of her energy. During that time, she performed some of her best trapshooting, establishing her reputation among the elite of the sport.

Oakley officially retired from show business in 1913, after having spent a brief time with the Young Buffalo Wild West Show. Butler and Oakley moved to an idyllic spot on the Eastern Shore of Maryland, but after a lifetime spent on the road, they could not easily reconcile themselves to a sedentary lifestyle. They soon resumed traveling. During World War I, Oakley toured army camps demonstrating her shooting. She also campaigned for the Red Cross. Amid plans to reenter show business in 1922, Oakley was partially paralyzed in a car accident, which ended her career. She died on November 3, 1926, and was followed eighteen days later by her husband, Frank Butler.

SIGNIFICANCE

In an era when shooting was considered a men's sport, Annie Oakley advocated that all women be taught to shoot. She viewed guns as providing a form of independence for women, who, when armed and trained, would no longer be forced to rely on men for their protection. During her lifetime, Oakley estimated that she had trained more than fifteen thousand women and considered that women were as capable as men. She advocated providing shooting instructors and rifle ranges in schools for both boys and girls.

In other ways, Oakley was patently less iconoclastic. She jealously guarded her social reputation among upper-class Britons and Americans, bridling at challenges to her femininity, and when she was not performing, she functioned in what she deemed to be ladylike fashion: dressing conservatively, refraining from alcohol, and sharing a close monogamous relationship with her husband. During the suffragist movement, she condemned bloomers, which she considered unladylike, and "bloomer women." She did not advocate women's voting rights. She claimed that women should not "go in for sport so that they neglect their homes." After retiring to the Eastern Shore of Maryland, however, Oakley found herself to be a failure at homemaking. "I went all to pieces under the care of a home," she reported.

Interestingly, during the Spanish-American War in 1898, Oakley had written President William McKinley, requesting to be sent to the Cuban front. During World War I, she likewise wrote to the secretary of war, proposing the establishment of an armed women's regiment for home defense. Although her suggestions were never seriously entertained, her intent was genuine. Annie Oakley, according to her own definition of femininity, achieved fame and success in a predominantly male field that required strength, stamina, and great skill.

—*Mary E. Virginia*

FURTHER READING

Blackstone, Sarah J. *Buckskins, Bullets, and Business: A History of Buffalo Bill's Wild West*. Westport, Conn.: Greenwood Press, 1986. A concise, detailed account of Cody's Wild West, describing the variety of acts and the logistics of moving the massive show from one engagement to another. Blackstone provides the best analysis of the impact of Cody's show on the development of the myth of the American West.

Kasper, Shirl. *Annie Oakley*. Norman: University of Oklahoma Press, 1992. Extensively utilizing newspapers and Annie Oakley's own scrapbooks, journalist Kasper has written an interesting and detailed biography of Oakley in which she has attempted to separate myths from documentable facts about Annie Oakley's life. Easily supplants earlier works as a definitive biography. Contains photographs, an index, and a bibliography.

McMurtry, Larry. *The Colonel and Little Missie: Buffalo Bill, Annie Oakley, and the Beginnings of Superstardom in America*. New York: Simon & Schuster, 2005. A dual biography of Oakley and Buffalo Bill. Oakley is portrayed as a quiet, reserved, and frugal woman, with a talent for showmanship and self-promotion.

Riley, Glenda. *The Life and Legacy of Annie Oakley*. Norman: University of Oklahoma Press, 1994. Scholarly biography, providing an evaluation of Oakley's legend and influence. Riley describes how Oakley sought to reconcile her public image as an athletic western woman with her private perception of herself as a genteel model Victorian wife.

Rosa, Joseph G., and Robin May. *Buffalo Bill and His Wild West: A Pictorial Biography*. Lawrence: University Press of Kansas, 1989. As its title indicates, this book is liberally illustrated. It contains a section summarizing Annie Oakley's career with, and apart from, Cody's Wild West Show. Contains a bibliography and an index.

Russell, Don. *The Lives and Legends of Buffalo Bill*. Norman: University of Oklahoma Press, 1960. Russell's nearly five-hundred-page book on Buffalo Bill places Oakley's life in the context of Cody's Wild West Show. Russell provides the most detailed history available of Cody's outfit.

SEE ALSO: Calamity Jane; William Cody; William Mc-
Kinley; Sitting Bull.
RELATED ARTICLES in *Great Events from History: The
Nineteenth Century, 1801-1900:* 1850's-1880's: Rise of Burlesque and Vaudeville; c. 1871-1883: Great
American Buffalo Slaughter; April 10, 1871: Barnum
Creates the First Modern American Circus.

DANIEL O'CONNELL
Irish social reformer

*Once the leader of the struggle for Roman Catholic
emancipation in the British Empire, O'Connell is
identified with the principles of religious freedom and
separation of church and state, nonviolent reform
movements, early democratic organizations, and the
upholding of the rule of law.*

BORN: August 6, 1775; near Carhen, Cahirciveen,
County Kerry, Ireland
DIED: May 15, 1847; Genoa, kingdom of Sardinia
(now in Italy)
ALSO KNOWN AS: The Liberator
AREA OF ACHIEVEMENT: Social reform

EARLY LIFE
Daniel O'Connell was born in a town on the southwest
coast of Ireland that was situated at the western end of
Iveragh, a mountainous peninsula running forty miles
out into the Atlantic from the Lakes of Killarney. Its
mountains and sea inlets afford beautiful scenery, and
nowhere more so than at Derrynane, where O'Connell's
family lived from the beginning of the eighteenth century
(Derrynane is now preserved as a national monument).
Iveragh had retained much of the Gaelic culture so that
O'Connell was born into a society in which perhaps a
majority of the people knew no English.

Roman Catholic landlords, the O'Connells were the
principal family in Iveragh for some centuries before
O'Connell was born in 1775. Fostered out at birth to a
tenant of his father, in accordance with Gaelic custom, he
returned to his parents' house at the age of four, knowing
no English. He was the eldest son in a family of ten children. His father ran a general store in Cahirciveen and invested his profits in the purchase of land. His mother was
a daughter of John O'Mullane, a Catholic small landlord
of old family in County Cork.

When he was still a boy, O'Connell was adopted as
heir by his rich but childless uncle at Derrynane. Receiving his first schooling at Derrynane, he then proceeded to a boarding school near the city of Cork. In

1791, he was sent to France, first to the college of St.
Omer and then to the English college at Douai. In January, 1793, Douai was closed by the French revolutionary
government, and O'Connell left for England as virtually
a refugee, a day or two after the execution of Louis XVI.
He spent the next three years as a law student in London
and then obtained his uncle's permission to complete his
legal studies in Dublin, where he was called to the bar in
1798.

Moderately tall and broadly built, O'Connell looked
impressive and distinguished rather than handsome,
though his expressive blue eyes were commented upon.
Having a powerful voice, he was one of the famous orators
of his day, being able to appeal to more educated audiences as well as to great crowds. Although actively engaged in politics, he built up one of the largest practices of
his day at the Irish bar. Because of his skill in defending
great numbers of poor Catholics against charges they considered unjust, he early won widespread popular fame.

In 1802, O'Connell married his distant cousin, Mary
O'Connell, one of the eleven penniless children of a
County Kerry physician. For this impecunious marriage,
he was disinherited by his uncle. Three years later, however, uncle and nephew were reconciled, and eventually
O'Connell was bequeathed Derrynane and a third of his
uncle's estate. The marriage was a happy one, the only
cause of distress being his extravagance, which left him
always in debt. The charge that he was a womanizer is
not supported by historical evidence. The fact that the
charge has been made can be explained by the fact that
he was the last of the Gaelic folk heroes, and all these
heroes from prehistory onward had a reputation for sexual energy—it was seen as part of their greatness—and
O'Connell was no exception.

O'Connell entered politics in 1800, when he organized a meeting of Dublin Catholics to oppose the enact-
ment of the Union between Great Britain and Ireland
(whereby the Irish Parliament was abolished, and Ireland
for the future elected representatives to the British Parliament). He seems to have been the only member of the

Catholic propertied classes to oppose the Union. By 1805, he was an energetic member of the Catholic Committee, a body of landlords, businesspeople, and lawyers who sought full freedom and equality for Catholics so that they could enter Parliament and government service and not remain a subject people.

LIFE'S WORK

Politics in Great Britain and Ireland was at that time a matter for landlords and members of the upper-middle classes, for aristocratic dinner parties, and, to a lesser extent, for committees and small public meetings. O'Connell was to alter this pattern when he founded the Catholic Association in 1823, which proved to be the first great popular democratic organization. In February, 1824, he introduced the penny-a-month plan, whereby tens of thousands of the poorer classes were enrolled and politically instructed. By the end of 1824, the whole country was roused, and for the next four years the Catholic Association exerted strong pressure on the British government. In 1828, there occurred a by-election for County Clare, and O'Connell was induced to contest it, the first Catholic to stand for Parliament since the seventeenth century.

It was realized from the start that the Clare election would be decisive. The contest was bitter, and O'Connell, who could be scurrilous, left nothing unsaid or undone to ensure victory. Special contingents of army and police stood by to deal with popular violence, but there was none. Instead, as great numbers gathered in and around the county town of Ennis, where the polling took place, the officials of the Catholic Association with the assistance of the clergy imposed strict discipline, even to the extent of banning the consumption of liquor. On the fifth day of the polling, when the count was two-to-one in O'Connell's favor, the Tory candidate conceded victory. Organized, disciplined, and instructed, the masses had shown their power. In the weeks that followed, the two chief members of the Tory cabinet, the duke of Wellington as prime minister and Sir Robert Peel as home secretary (the minister in charge of Ireland), decided that Catholic emancipation must be enacted. Accordingly, in the spring of 1829, Peel introduced the bill that was passed by both houses without difficulty and received the royal assent in April.

The reasons for which the anti-Catholic Tory government conceded emancipation have frequently been misunderstood. The threat of civil war in Ireland is usually given as the reason, but that factor would not have been sufficient if the British body politic were united in de-

Daniel O'Connell. (Library of Congress)

fense of the Protestant establishment in Ireland. There was no such unity. The Whigs and their Radical supporters, who together made up half of the House of Commons, were sick of the long agitation for emancipation. Though not necessarily committed to any principle of religious freedom, they did respond to the Whig tradition of government by consent.

Also, some of the more liberal of the Tories were prepared to concede. Should the Tory administration, by rejecting emancipation, provoke a civil war in Ireland, they might find themselves voted out of office and replaced by a Whig government willing to enact the measure. There was the additional consideration that twenty or thirty Catholics might be returned for Irish constituencies at the next general election, and the Mother of Parliaments could look ridiculous if she refused them admission. In demanding emancipation for Catholics, O'Connell was careful to ask for it only on the general principle of freedom and equality for men of all religions. As early as 1807, he rested his case "on the new score of justice—of that justice which will emancipate the Protestant in Spain and Portugal, the Christian in Constantinople."

After being elected to Parliament, O'Connell applied his energies to a large number of causes. These included the extension of the parliamentary and local government suffrages; the Tolpuddle Martyrs; Poles persecuted by czarist Russia; Jewish emancipation; separation of church and state in Catholic as well as in Protestant countries, and even in the Papal States; free trade and especially the repeal of the Corn Laws; and the abolition of black slavery. In pursuing these aims, he was the leading Radical in the British Parliament during the 1830's.

With the passing of the emancipation bill, O'Connell hoped for great things for Irish Catholics, but his hopes were only partly realized. The Tories and the more conservative of the Whigs were determined to maintain Protestant dominance in Ireland and not to admit Catholics to office. In the general election of 1834, however, the Whigs lost their overall majority and were forced to come to terms with O'Connell if they wished to maintain a stable government. They negotiated an arrangement whereby O'Connell's party of some twenty-five members of Parliament would support the Whigs and keep them in power provided they admitted Catholics to the Irish administration and sponsored certain reforms. As a consequence, the Protestant monopoly of power was broken, and Catholics were appointed to the civil service, the judiciary, and high posts in a modernized and expanded police force. The legislative reforms demanded by O'Connell were passed by the Commons but amended in an anti-Catholic direction by the House of Lords. Nevertheless, gains were made.

When the Tories returned to power in 1841 with a large majority in the House of Commons, O'Connell believed that he could look for no further reforms. When his year as lord mayor of Dublin ended in October, 1842, he threw himself into the struggle for Repeal, that is, the repeal of the Act of Union. British political opinion was determined to uphold the Union, seeing Repeal as involving sooner or later the breaking away of Ireland from the empire. It was also considered that control of Ireland was essential to British military security.

The question the historian must ask is: How could a perceptive politician such as O'Connell, with a long experience of British politics, believe that he could win Repeal? The only answer that makes sense is that he knew he could not; he was using the carrot of Repeal to rouse the Catholic masses so that, as in the case of Catholic emancipation, he could intimidate a British government into granting not Repeal but major reforms. Whatever his purpose, he had the Repeal Association hold great public gatherings known as monster meetings throughout the country, at which he made menacing speeches. Peel's

nerve held, however, and in October of 1843, he called O'Connell's bluff by proclaiming that he would speak at the monster meeting announced for Clontarf outside Dublin. O'Connell called off the meeting.

Peel, however, was not the proverbial Bourbon. He realized that the Repeal movement was a response to real grievances, and in the years left to him as prime minister he enacted several reforms pleasing to the Catholic clergy and middle-class Catholics in general, and he planned to enact a measure giving tenant farmers a degree of legal security. Unfortunately for Irish Catholics, Peel was driven from office in 1846 by the Whigs (aided by O'Connell) and a majority of his own Tory Party, as soon as he had enacted the repeal of the Corn Laws.

The Repeal movement brought to the fore a group of idealistic young men who soon came to be known as the Young Irelanders. On the declared policy of Repeal, they were ostensibly at one with O'Connell, but there were fissures under the surface. Where he drew his political principles from the *philosophes* (excluding Jean-Jacques Rousseau) and the English Rationalists, such as Thomas Paine, William Godwin, and Jeremy Bentham (who though a zealous Catholic in his maturity had been a Deist as a young man), the Young Irelanders subscribed to Romantic Nationalism, the ideology then sweeping through Europe. O'Connell saw the nation as a collective unit, as the sum of all of its parts, whereas the young men of the movement realized that a nation is first and foremost a tradition; from that reality, they drew conclusions that bore little practical relevance to their own day but which would inspire later generations.

Unrealistic in the context of contemporary politics, the Young Irelanders demanded that the small Repeal Party should act independently of the Whig and Tory parties in the British Parliament and that O'Connell must not renew his "alliance" with the Whigs; they rightly suspected that, contrary to his declared policies, he intended to do just that. Though he tolerated much public criticism from the Young Irelanders, he often acted as if the Repeal Association were his private property and as if he were not bound by its decisions.

The break between old and young came in July, 1846, on the question of violence. O'Connell insisted that all members of the Repeal Association must adhere to the principles of nonviolence and constitutionalism, on which the association had been founded and to which the members had pledged their allegiance repeatedly since then. The Young Irelanders insisted that these alleged principles were merely policies. They were constitutionalists by preference, but they considered that the use of violence might be necessary at some time in the future should constitutional methods fail. The two positions were mutually exclusive. The majority of the population sided with O'Connell, regardless of whether they understood the points at issue, but it was his last victory. Within months, the famine was ravaging the country, and by February, 1847, O'Connell knew himself to be dying. On the advice of his doctors, he set out on a pilgrimage to Rome but died on the way at Genoa on May 15, 1847.

SIGNIFICANCE

Daniel O'Connell deserved the title "the Liberator," which was bestowed on him by his followers after Catholic emancipation. Though he had able Catholic lieutenants and received valuable cooperation from a number of Irish Protestants, he was the central figure in politically instructing and organizing a subject people. Catholic emancipation was the first political victory they knew after two centuries of discouragement and failure, and it was irreversible.

The Catholic Association was the first popular democratic organization of the modern world. O'Connell was the first Catholic political leader and perhaps the first politician in any major Christian denomination in Europe to espouse the dual principles of religious freedom and separation of church and state. In the years from Catholic emancipation until his death, he was the outstanding European opponent of black slavery. As a practitioner of nonviolent reform, he ranks with Mahatma Gandhi and Martin Luther King, Jr. He embraced and expanded the British Whig tradition of government by consent that owed much to another Irishman, Edmund Burke. Future generations may well recognize him as the greatest upholder of the rule of law—not merely of law as made by one's own people but also of law as made by others—that Western civilization has produced.

—*Maurice R. O'Connell*

FURTHER READING

Hinde, Wendy. *Catholic Emancipation: A Shake to Men's Minds*. Oxford, England: Blackwell, 1992. Focuses on Irish history in the period from January, 1828, through April, 1829, highlighting the events and personalities that brought the question of Catholic emancipation to a crisis, culminating in O'Connell's election.

McCartney, Donal, ed. *The World of Daniel O'Connell*. Dublin: Mercier Press, 1980. Fourteen articles, mostly of high quality, describing O'Connell's image abroad, his role in the British Parliament, his attitude to black slavery, and his influence on the Liberal Catholic movement in Western Europe.

Moley, Raymond. *Daniel O'Connell: Nationalism Without Violence*. New York: Fordham University Press, 1974. A popular biography by a distinguished American political commentator.

Nowlan, Kevin B., and Maurice O'Connell, eds. *Daniel O'Connell: Portrait of a Radical*. New York: Fordham University Press, 1985. Eight articles on various aspects of O'Connell, notably his association with Gaelic Ireland, his social and economic ideas, and his role in British politics.

O'Connell, Daniel. *The Correspondence of Daniel O'Connell*. Edited by Maurice R. O'Connell. Dublin: Irish University Press, 1972-1980. Thirty-five hundred private letters to and from O'Connell.

O'Faoláin, Seán. *King of the Beggars: A Life of Daniel O'Connell, the Irish Liberator, in a Study of the Rise of the Modern Irish Democracy*. London: Nelson, 1938. Entertaining biographical study of O'Connell's personality. Intuitive rather than scholarly, it is the only work on O'Connell before 1960 that merits consideration.

O'Ferrall, Fergus. *Catholic Emancipation: Daniel O'Connell and the Rise of Irish Democracy, 1820-30*. Atlantic Highlands, N.J.: Humanities Press, 1985. Comprehensive study of the Catholic Association as the modern world's first democratic mass movement. Both grassroots organization and its effect on high politics are described.

Taylor, William Cooke. *Reminiscences of Daniel O'Connell: During the Agitations of the Veto Emancipation and Repeal*. Edited by Patrick Maume. Dublin: University College Dublin Press, 2005. This biography, originally published shortly after O'Connell's death, is based on eyewitness accounts and O'Connell's memoirs and articles. Although Taylor sympathized with O'Connell's struggle for Catholic liberation, he argues that O'Connell's abusive oratory hindered emancipation.

Trench, Charles Chenevix. *The Great Dan: A Biography of Daniel O'Connell*. London: Jonathan Cape, 1984. Historically sound and entertaining, this biography is written with wit and insight.

Williams, Leslie. *Daniel O'Connell, the British Press, and the Irish Famine: Killing Remarks*. Edited by H. A. Williams. Burlington, Vt.: Ashgate, 2003. Examines anti-O'Connell reports in nineteenth century

English metropolitan newspapers and illustrated journals to determine how this coverage affected British response to the Irish famine.

SEE ALSO: Fourteenth Earl of Derby; Sir Robert Peel; Duke of Wellington.

RELATED ARTICLES in *Great Events from History: The Nineteenth Century, 1801-1900:* January, 1802: Cobbett Founds the *Political Register*; May 9, 1828-April 13, 1829: Roman Catholic Emancipation; June 4, 1832: British Parliament Passes the Reform Act of 1832; 1845-1854: Great Irish Famine.

JACQUES OFFENBACH
French composer

Offenbach composed one hundred operettas and a major opera that virtually defined this form of musical theater through his characteristic mixture of gaiety, spontaneity, and infectious melody and thus became the first great influence in the process of internationalizing the operetta.

BORN: June 20, 1819; Cologne, Prussia (now in Germany)
DIED: October 5, 1880; Paris, France
ALSO KNOWN AS: Jacob Eberst (birth name)
AREA OF ACHIEVEMENT: Music

EARLY LIFE

One of the greatest figures in the history of operetta, Jacques Offenbach (O-fehn-bahk) was born Jacob Eberst, the second son of a peripatetic Jewish cantor and music teacher. His father, Isaac Eberst, was a poor man who, when not singing in the synagogue of his hometown, Offenbach-am-Main, Germany, supplemented his income as a music teacher by playing the fiddle in local cafés. Called "the Offenbacher" on his travels, Isaac thus adopted "Offenbach" as his legal surname.

Jacob clearly inherited more than his father's name, for the boy, along with his brother Julius, early showed a marked talent for music. Offenbach himself noted that he had learned to play the violin by the time he was seven, but by age ten he discovered the cello and it was with this instrument that the young man became a professional musician. Frail and thin throughout his life, Offenbach belied his appearance by playing the cello with the same high-spirited vivacity that was to characterize his music.

Offenbach's talent was in need of greater nourishment than that which could be obtained in Cologne, so in October, 1833, Isaac arranged for his son to go to Paris to enroll in the conservatoire, the pinnacle of musical opportunity. The story goes that Offenbach was at first denied admission on the grounds that he was not French,

upon which he took up his cello and began playing a piece at first sight. The admissions committee did not let him finish but took his hand and welcomed him as a pupil. Offenbach began to study the violin, but within a year the young man left the conservatoire, probably from the need to earn a living. At fifteen, Jacob, now Jacques, Offenbach secured a job as cellist in the orchestra of the Opéra-Comique.

The business of music in Paris of the late 1830's was primarily a theatrical enterprise. Composers often conducted their own works and promoted them as well, and it was not uncommon for a composer of waltzes and social music to lead a sixty-piece orchestra in cafés along the boulevards. The young Offenbach submitted several of his waltzes to the leading composer-impresarios of the day, and one of his first, "Fleurs d'hiver" ("Winter Flowers"), was a popular success. By January, 1839, Offenbach, at the age of nineteen, gave his first public concert. Soon thereafter, he was asked to write the music for a vaudeville, *Pascal et Chambord*. Produced in March, 1839, the piece was a failure.

Undaunted, Offenbach continued to perform as virtuoso cellist and to teach. Over the next few years, he composed a number of cello works and performed in Germany and before the queen of England. Thus, the salon and the drawing room—not the theater—dictated both the setting and the style for the compositions of Offenbach during the 1840's. His music was light, simple, generously diverting, and, above all, well crafted. The ballads and songs of this period are interesting in at least two respects. First, they often contain the melodic germs of his later work, for Offenbach had a lifelong practice of recasting earlier material. For another, they often contain elements of humor—such as the cello simulating a kazoo—that were to make his great operettas so distinctive.

It was, indeed, just this element of humor bordering on impertinence that—more than even the local musical politics—probably kept Offenbach from serious notice.

Jacques Offenbach. (Library of Congress)

Though he was known throughout the 1840's as a cellist and minor composer of songs and other salon pieces, his own ambition to write a musical work for the Opéra-Comique was spurned by the management of that theater. Meanwhile, Offenbach converted to Catholicism and married Herminie d'Alcain in 1844.

LIFE'S WORK
The revolutions of 1848 that made France, nominally at least, a republic precipitated Offenbach's departure to Germany. The father of a young girl, he was as poor as a freelance composer of dance music could be, but he continued to pursue his ambition of writing for the musical stage and had his first work of this kind produced in Cologne. The work went virtually unnoticed. Now approaching thirty, Offenbach returned to Paris to see Louis Napoleon, nephew of Napoleon I, installed as emperor of France. The so-called Second Empire had begun and with it the rising fortunes of Offenbach.

During his career as cellist and salon composer, he had met the director of the Théâtre-Française, the serious theater for all state-approved tragedies and comedies. In

1851, the director appointed Offenbach conductor of the house, hoping that the young cellist's musical abilities and vivacious personality would bring back the audiences lost to administrative and artistic chaos. As conductor, Offenbach presented not only the music of other composers but also, more pertinent to his own career, his own compositions. Before long, his own incidental music to plays and his entr'actes (music played during the intermissions) began to gain attention.

Now in a position to write the kind of light, witty theater music that he perceived as lacking on the French stage, he dedicated himself unceasingly to the task. From this period of the early 1850's, Offenbach began to compose an astonishing number of "little operas." In 1855 alone, he produced no less than twelve one-act operettas. This was the year in which he left his official post at the Théâtre-Français and opened his own theater, the Bouffes-Parisiens. Restricted now only by his own cleverness, Offenbach flourished. By his own admission, his major vice now and throughout the rest of his life was work. He wrote incessantly, steadily, and quickly. In 1856, eight operettas came from his fecund pen, and in 1857 seven more. These early operettas, such as *Ba-ta-clan* (1855), *La Bonne d'enfants* (1856), and *Les Deux Pêcheurs* (1857), possess a lyrical charm and freshness that characterize much of the composer's best music, but they fall victim to clumsy and dated librettos and are thus seldom heard or performed.

After producing almost thirty operettas in five years, Offenbach composed what was to be his first, and perhaps best-known, major work. Unlike his previous compositions, *Orphée aux enfers* (1858) is more ambitious in scope (two acts), more serious in the variety of musical types, and, above all, more witty in its parody of some of French society's most cherished traditions. Offenbach's chief librettist for the work was Ludovic Halévy, who, along with Henri Meilhac, was to write the book for Georges Bizet's *Carmen* (1875). Together, they provided Offenbach with the librettos for his finest operettas.

Offenbach's love of satire and parody infused the music of *Orphée aux enfers* with the sparkling wit and innocent naughtiness that became the composer's hallmark and a distinctive element of French operetta for the remainder of the century. Taking the Greek myth of Orpheus and Eurydice as its source, the operetta pokes fun at the pantheon of gods who talked not like Greek divinities but Second Empire boulevardiers, ladies and gentlemen of mid-nineteenth century French society. Along the way, there are musical parodies of Christoph Gluck, composer of the 1762 serious version of the Orpheus and

Eurydice story, and of scenes from Italian opera. The finale consists of the famous cancan, during which the gods and goddesses cavort in a frenzied bacchanal.

Orphée aux enfers made Offenbach famous and rich, though money was never his constant companion. His generosity, love of luxury, and overall beneficent prodigality always kept the composer within view of his creditors. However, his prodigality of money was at least equaled by his prodigality of genius as one after another operetta reached the stage. Between *Orphée aux enfers* in 1858 and his next great operetta, *La Belle Hélène* of 1864, Offenbach composed another twenty-eight works, including a ballet, *Le Papillon* (1860), and a three-act parody of medieval France, *Geneviève de Brabant* (1859). The latter contained a famous section that was later adapted by the United States Marine Corps for its well-known hymn.

When in 1860 the Opéra-Comique at last commissioned a work from him, Offenbach offered *Barkouf*. A ridiculous libretto about a dog that becomes head of state was coupled with music that the public, for once, did not understand. The work drew the disdain of music critics and composers such as Hector Berlioz, who attacked Offenbach's use of strange and awkward harmonies. *Barkouf* represents one of the few times Offenbach overextended himself and clearly illustrates the fatality of musical stage works in thralldom to a bad libretto. Offenbach was not to make the same mistake again. *La Belle Hélène* is regarded by many as his most brilliant operetta. For his source, the composer once again returned to Greek mythology, this time to the legend of Helen of Troy. Although conservative critics condemned the work for its blasphemy of Homer, the public knew better. With *La Belle Hélène*, Offenbach reached the zenith of his career. His orchestration now bore a richer chromatic harmony, evidence of Richard Wagner's influence, and the music sparkled with a brilliant libretto.

La Belle Hélène was followed by a series of witty and gently mocking operettas. Offenbach had become the darling of the Second Empire, even as he gaily laughed at it. With the Franco-Prussian War of 1870, however, the Second Empire tottered, and when it fell Offenbach's own success and the quality of his work soon also declined. He continued to write operettas, but he began imitating himself, revising earlier productions and depending increasingly on the spectacular and the impressive rather than on spontaneity.

Always pressed for money because of lavish spending, Offenbach accepted an offer to conduct concerts in the United States as part of the centennial celebration of 1876. During a three-month tour, he played excerpts from his work in New York, Philadelphia, and Chicago. Despite some critical reserve at the naughtiness of some of his operettas, Offenbach impressed many by his personality, and the tour was an ultimate success. His impressions of his American experience were published in Paris the following year.

By the late 1870's, however, two conditions had altered Offenbach's life, one physical, the other artistic. Afflicted by gout for a number of years, Offenbach was enduring more continuous pain as his ailment wracked his already frail body. Additionally, his dream of being taken seriously as a composer now manifested itself in his determination to write a masterwork of opera. He had been making sketches for a work based on stories by the German Romantic writer E. T. A. Hoffmann since 1875, but he wrote with uncharacteristic deliberation, signifying a more serious commitment rather than a decline in creative powers.

By 1880, Offenbach completed the score of his masterpiece, *Les Contes d'Hoffmann*. By October of that year, however, the disease precipitated heart failure, and Offenbach died on October 5, 1880. The orchestration of his great opera was completed by a family friend, Ernest Guiraud. Offenbach's masterpiece was thus performed in 1881, after his death, at the Opéra-Comique, the very theater in which he first dreamed of being recognized.

SIGNIFICANCE

Though Jacques Offenbach did not actually invent the operetta, he did infuse the form with those elements of gaiety and good-natured fun that became the model for subsequent works of the kind. His influence on later masters such as W. S. Gilbert and Sir Arthur Sullivan and the Viennese composer Johann Strauss—whom Offenbach first urged to write operettas—is indelible; Offenbach must thus be regarded as a seminal figure in making operetta an international art form.

Gioacchino Rossini, himself an operatic master, referred to Offenbach as "the Mozart of the boulevards." The similitude is apt not only because Wolfgang Amadeus Mozart was Offenbach's idol—Offenbach kept a book of Mozart's music always by his bedside—but also because, like Mozart, Offenbach had a unique gift for melody and for lucidity of style. Like Mozart's, Offenbach's music is almost always perfectly suited to the context in which it is placed and which it thus defines. His melodies are among the most infectious ever written.

The connection with Rossini, who lived in Paris during Offenbach's greatest triumphs, is also pertinent in an artistic sense. Like Rossini, Offenbach understood the dramatic excitement generated at the end of a scene by the use of a galloping rhythm combined with a crescendo. His use of brass instruments particularly heightened the vitality of the melodic line. Finally, Offenbach's music epitomizes the saucy, high-spirited, and supremely confident atmosphere of Paris during the middle years of the nineteenth century.

—Edward Fiorelli

FURTHER READING

Bordman, Gerald. *American Operetta: From "H.M.S. Pinafore" to "Sweeney Todd."* New York: Oxford University Press, 1981. Contains a brief history of the popularity of Offenbach in the United States, particularly citing his *La Grande-Duchesse de Gérolstein* (1867) as an influence on later American operetta formats.

Faris, Alexander. *Jacques Offenbach.* New York: Charles Scribner's Sons, 1980. This is probably the best biography in English. Himself a conductor, Faris presents a well-balanced, though often too minutely detailed, study. Includes liberal examples of musical notation and technique. Contains an excellent bibliography, including a complete chart of all Offenbach's work, published and unpublished.

Hadlock, Heather. *Mad Loves: Women and Music in Offenbach's "Les Contes d'Hoffman."* Princeton, N.J.: Princeton University Press, 2000. An analysis of Offenbach's last operetta, describing how the work was created and comparing it to Offenbach's previous compositions. Hadlock maintains *Les Contes d'Hoffman* was the culmination of Offenbach's career and a century of Romantic culture.

Kracauer, Siegfried. *Offenbach and the Paris of His Time.* London: Constable, 1937. Reprint. Cambridge, Mass.: MIT Press, 2002. A sociological study of the theatrical and artistic traditions within which Offenbach lived and worked. Though accurate, the study tends to emphasize the political and revolutionary aspects of Offenbach's works.

Lamb, Andrew. *One-Hundred-and-Fifty Years of Popular Musical Theatre.* New Haven, Conn.: Yale University Press, 2000. Lamb begins his history of musical theater with a discussion of Offenbach's operettas. Although chapter 1 focuses on "Paris and the Rise of Offenbach," there are other references to the composer throughout the text.

Mordden, Ethan. *The Splendid Art of Opera: A Concise History.* New York: Methuen, 1980. Contains an excellent chapter on musical comedy that credits Offenbach with internationalizing operetta and examines the "remarkably innovative" *Les Contes d'Hoffmann.*

Offenbach, Jacques. *Orpheus in America: Offenbach's Diary of His Journey to the New World.* Translated by Lander MacLintock. Bloomington: Indiana University Press, 1957. Offenbach's memoir of his American concert tour. His breezy prose serves as a revealing correlative to his musical style. Contains an excellent brief biographical introduction by the translator.

SEE ALSO: Hector Berlioz; Georges Bizet; Léo Delibes; W. S. Gilbert and Arthur Sullivan; Napoleon I; Gioacchino Rossini; Johann Strauss; Richard Wagner.

RELATED ARTICLE in *Great Events from History: The Nineteenth Century, 1801-1900:* October 10, 1881: London's Savoy Theatre Opens.

BERNARDO O'HIGGINS
Supreme director of Chile (1817-1823)

O'Higgins is widely regarded by Latin Americans as the George Washington of Chile. Inspired by both the American and the French Revolutions, he followed the lead of the great Argentine general José de San Martín and helped Martín liberate Chile from Spanish colonial rule. Although he was not a political administrator, O'Higgins was able to inspire both the troops under his command and the Chilean civilian population to overthrow a long-detested regime.

BORN: August 20?, 1778; Chillán, viceroyalty of Peru (now in Chile)
DIED: October, 24, 1842; Lima, Peru
ALSO KNOWN AS: Bernardo Riquelme
AREAS OF ACHIEVEMENT: Government and politics, military

EARLY LIFE

Born in what is now Chile when it was still under Spanish rule, Bernardo O'Higgins was the illegitimate son of an Irishman, Ambrosio O'Higgins, who distinguished himself in the Spanish government's Chilean bureaucracy and as viceroy of Peru. His mother was a Chilean woman of impoverished background. O'Higgins went to primary school in Lima, Peru, and London, England. The latter school was especially important. A bright and energetic student, O'Higgins met Latin American anti-Spanish revolutionaries in London whose liberation ideas stayed with him, greatly influencing his later military career.

When his father died, O'Higgins went back to Chile to oversee lands that his father had willed him. From all appearances, he was but one of many wealthy, ambitious young Chileans who, benefiting greatly from the hacienda system of landholding, would spend the rest of his life overseeing a large estate. However, perhaps as a result of the revolutionary contacts he had made in England, O'Higgins grew increasingly bitter about the ongoing Spanish occupation of Chile, resolving to help free the country from these bonds in a future struggle for independence.

Together with other patriotic, anti-Spanish aristocrats of liberal tendencies, O'Higgins in 1810 joined a group of delegates to Chile's congress, which was attempting to decide the country's political future. Unfortunately for all concerned, the congress was violently divided over which kind of governmental system Chile required. Some wanted a return to old ways of doing things, instituted centuries earlier by the conquering Spanish; others

favored a republican form of government; still others hoped for a complete transformation of society that would do away with the past. Those who were not interested in the radical approach decided that working with others in the Santiago congress who failed to share their utopian vision of Chile was futile; thus, they left the congress, an act that allowed their political foes, calling themselves the Executive Power, to claim control of the Chilean government.

The rebels were ruthlessly defeated by José Carrera, who had fought against Napoleon I's army in Spain. Carrera, in a manner confusing to friend and enemy alike, supported constitutional reform while continuing allegiance to Spain's King Ferdinand, the latter action having been to camouflage true anti-Spanish intent.

The new constitution created a ruling triad, which included O'Higgins, who zealously believed in the reform of both society and government and in the creation of a benevolent state encouraging the betterment of the human condition. O'Higgins's first efforts were quashed by Peru's viceroy when the combined forces of O'Higgins's and Carrera's armies were routed in 1814, a rout that allowed the capture of Santiago, Chile, by Spanish forces and a setback to the budding revolution that resulted.

O'Higgins narrowly avoided being executed by the vengeful government forces; he took his army—what remained of it—over the Andes Mountains to Argentina, in itself a heroic feat. Discouraged by this untimely defeat, O'Higgins appeared to have become merely one more victim of the Spanish occupation, which was victoriously reasserting itself in the New World. In this defeat, Chile was joined by other countries elsewhere in Spanish America—Guatemala, Mexico, and Peru—that unsuccessfully battled oppression.

LIFE'S WORK

O'Higgins is often referred to as the liberator of Chile as well as a kind of George Washington figure. Like Washington, O'Higgins suffered early defeats, only to pull together his beaten forces and win the war. After the loss in 1814 to Spanish and loyalist troops, O'Higgins, like Washington, had the good fortune to have help from outside his nation. Argentina's José de San Martín, governor of Cuyo Province, was able to give O'Higgins the right sort of assistance when he most needed it. Actually, without San Martín's expertise in military matters as well as his experienced army, the liberation of Chile would most likely have remained a dream unfulfilled. This tall, handsome man was clearly a classic leader who, like O'Higgins, had the respect of his troops. San Martín became O'Higgins's mentor and friend.

The campaign for the independence of Chile began in 1817 at Mendoza, Argentina, where San Martín gathered together great amounts of ammunition and guns for the coming war. Buenos Aires was in the mood to supply what O'Higgins needed—another bit of good fortune.

In O'Higgins, San Martín recognized a strong, purposeful young leader, with whom he could share military leadership. However, what faced them both was the daunting prospect of moving an army across Andean passes much more than three thousand meters in elevation. Nevertheless, supplies, including equipment designed for traversing gullies and ravines, were readied, though O'Higgins was not certain that they would take them where no army had gone.

Using the Los Patos and Uspollata passes in the Andes, the troops united under San Martín and O'Higgins met the Spanish and Chilean loyalists near Santiago at the town of Chacabuco. It was O'Higgins, however, who achieved the greatest triumph in that battle: He rose from relative obscurity that day to be numbered among Latin America's most illustrious liberators. San Martín also added to his already impressive reputation as a military genius.

Bravely, with little thought to his personal safety, O'Higgins led two sweeping cavalry charges into the Spanish ranks, causing the latter considerable losses and creating confusion in the ranks. These great attacks set the stage for San Martín's being offered the supreme directorship of Chile, as the new title was known. San Martín, however, graciously declined the position. The title was given to O'Higgins, an honor he happily accepted.

The independence of Chile was proclaimed by O'Higgins on February 12, 1818. Because of Spanish and loyalist entrenchment in the southern part of the country, however, the war was not over. It took San Martín's brilliant defense of Santiago and the repulse of counterforces at Maipu, near the capital on April 5 of that year, before O'Higgins could truly announce that Chile was free of its long Spanish occupation.

Deeply indebted to San Martín, who took over the Maipu battle after O'Higgins himself had fallen ill, O'Higgins returned the favor by assisting his friend in the battle to liberate Peru, the astute O'Higgins realizing that if the fledgling Chilean government were to survive, it would require that Peru and other neighboring states be free from Spanish enslavement. To this end, he joined San Martín once more, this time in acquiring a flotilla of

ships, which were presented to a Scottish sailor, Thomas Cochrane, who created a Chilean fleet that was superior to anything operating in the Southern Pacific region. On August 20, 1820, the fleet left Valparaiso, and it included at least eight well-armed men-of-war and various other vessels. In September of 1820, the army under San Martín's command invaded southern Peru while Cochrane blockaded the Peruvian coastline, attacking several Spanish ships in the process.

For O'Higgins, however, the main arena was no longer battle, but warfare of the political sort, wherein he would have to take charge of a newly free nation without any Latin American precedents to follow that would suit Chile's unique situation. To O'Higgins, the only workable way to govern a turbulent, newly freed country such as Chile was for him to declare himself a virtual dictator, which he did.

It was O'Higgins's and Chile's misfortune—since O'Higgins was a man of tremendous ability—that he could not be as successful a leader as he had been a soldier. It may have been that he lacked the skills that were needed to govern effectively, and it may have been the case that he simply was not interested in politics. Whatever the cause, history records that after trying to force various liberal social reforms on unwilling Chileans, O'Higgins was forced to resign as supreme director. In 1823, O'Higgins was deposed peacefully and sent into exile in Peru, where he stayed until he died.

O'Higgins was a true reformer by nature, his most pressing interest being in educational reform, for he believed that Chileans deserved to have widespread—even universal—public education. Thus, he re-created the once-defunct Instituto Nacional in Santiago and opened a number of schools for the people under the auspices of the English educator James Thompson.

O'Higgins also ordered that aristocratic titles and coats of arms be abolished and asked that estate entailment, the backbone of the hacienda system, be destroyed, measures that infuriated the rich landlords of Chile, who became convinced that O'Higgins was a threat to their pleasant, tradition-bound lifestyle. Other high-minded ideas of O'Higgins outraged more than the elite members of Chilean society, for he wanted to do away with cockfighting and bullfighting, both highly popular pursuits among the poor. The enslavement of black people, another popular institution, was also declared immoral by O'Higgins, much to the general consternation of the populace. To add to his problems, it was not only the rich who were angry but also the liberals and moderates from whose ranks O'Higgins himself had risen. Moreover, powerful military men found the director's ideas intolerable, and this turned out to be O'Higgins's undoing, for the military, under the leadership of Ramón Freire, led the revolt that ousted him in 1823 and sent him into Peruvian exile.

It was Chile's misfortune to lose one as capable as O'Higgins in its national infancy, when it needed a strong leader. After his departure, more than ten different directors came to and left office, each of them trying in his own way to keep Chile from disintegrating completely. Although stability did eventually come to Chilean government, it was a long time in coming.

SIGNIFICANCE

Whatever ill might be said of Bernardo O'Higgins's last years in Chile, he remains that nation's greatest hero and its political benefactor supreme. Without him, Chile might have languished under Spanish rule for several more decades than it did. O'Higgins knew that the time had come for Latin American nations in general to rise up against their colonizers.

Along with Simón Bolívar, San Martín, and, most recently, Fidel Castro, O'Higgins is one of the Latin American men of destiny who profited from a political and social climate in which revolutionary thought and action could flourish. The lessons drawn from France's bloody revolution and from the inspirational American experience in its war with England taught people of intellect and patriotism living after those revolutions had triumphed that it was possible to fight against and eventually conquer the most powerful of tyrannies. Notions also drawn from the French and American conflicts that became current in Latin America's revolutionary period—freedom, liberty, and self-direction—helped O'Higgins fight against Spanish oppressors, for older notions about being subservient to foreign masters seemed stale and lifeless.

Although it was not transformed immediately from a distant province of New Spain into a modern nation after O'Higgins and San Martín won the war of independence, Chile would eventually become known as one of Latin America's most reliably democratic nations. O'Higgins was shrewd enough and sufficiently visionary to realize that an opportunity had finally presented itself. He alone was able to take appropriate actions that would lead to the destruction of Spanish power in his part of the world. If he was not a dynamic politician or even a well-loved one, he created the new Chile almost single-handedly, and for that Chileans owe him much.

—*John D. Raymer*

FURTHER READING

Collier, Simon. "The Story or Part of It at Least." In *From Cortes to Castro: An Introduction to the History of Latin America, 1492-1973*. New York: Macmillan, 1974. An insightful reevaluation of the political, social, religious, and economic currents shaping Latin American history over several centuries. A valuable account of the liberation movement led by O'Higgins and San Martín.

Collier, Simon, and William F. Sater. *A History of Chile, 1808-2002*. 2d ed. New York: Cambridge University Press, 2004. A chronicle of political, social, economic, and cultural developments in Chile from independence until the early twenty-first century. Includes information on O'Higgins.

Eyzaguirre, Jaime. *O'Higgins*. 3d ed. Santiago, Chile: Editorial Zig Zag, 1950. An excellent biography that is likely the finest one about O'Higgins. The author has at times an overinflated opinion of O'Higgins's attributes, yet the book does full justice to his seminal role in Chile's struggle for independence.

Harvey, Robert. *Liberators: Latin America's Struggle for Independence, 1810-1830*. Woodstock, N.Y.: Overlook Press, 2000. A history of Latin America's struggle to overthrow Spanish rule, focusing on O'Higgins and six other liberation leaders.

Kinsbruner, Jay. *Bernardo O'Higgins*. New York: Twayne, 1968. An invaluable contribution to O'Higgins scholarship that goes into considerable depth about O'Higgins's revolution and how he achieved all that he did in such a short time. Includes a selective bibliography.

Mehegan, John J. *O'Higgins of Chile: A Brief Sketch of His Life and Times*. London: J & J Bennett, 1913. One of the better general introductions to the life and times of O'Higgins.

Worcester, Donald E., and Wendell G. Schaeffer. "The Wars of Independence in the South." In *The Growth and Culture of Latin America*. 2 vols. New York: Oxford University Press, 1970-1971. Discusses how Chilean society evolved during and after the revolution O'Higgins helped lead. Also good for placing O'Higgins in a historical context.

SEE ALSO: Simón Bolívar; Napoleon I; José de San Martín; Antonio José de Sucre.
RELATED ARTICLES in *Great Events from History: The Nineteenth Century, 1801-1900:* March, 1813-December 9, 1824: Bolívar's Military Campaigns; September 7, 1822: Brazil Becomes Independent.

FREDERICK LAW OLMSTED
American landscape architect and critic

Olmsted traveled extensively in the antebellum South and wrote some of the best critical descriptions of American slavery on the eve of the Civil War. Considered the founder of the profession of landscape architecture in the United States, he also designed Central Park in New York City and other urban parks across the country.

BORN: April 26, 1822; Hartford, Connecticut
DIED: August 28, 1903; Waverly, Massachusetts
AREA OF ACHIEVEMENT: Architecture

EARLY LIFE

Frederick Law Olmsted (OHM-stehd) was the son of a prosperous dry-goods merchant. His family's material wealth and deep roots in the community gave Olmsted both the economic freedom and the personal confidence to pursue a leisurely course toward his major life works. On the other hand, he was physically frail and suffered from an eye problem that hampered his efforts at formal education. Olmsted was attracted to strenuous outdoor physical activity as compensation for his physical weakness and developed a keen appreciation of nature and the outdoors. During his early years, Olmsted acquired a taste for travel, and by the time he was in his mid-teens he had made several lengthy trips through various regions of the northeastern United States and Canada.

Olmsted matriculated at Yale, where he studied engineering, but his eye problem prevented regular study, and after practical training in surveying he worked briefly and unhappily for a dry-goods firm in New York City. This was followed by an extremely unpleasant year's experience as a sailor on a voyage to China. Returning to Yale, he studied agricultural science and engineering and then undertook practical training as a farmer on 130 Staten Island acres purchased by his father. As he became absorbed with scientific agriculture, Olmsted began to publish articles on rural subjects and drifted toward a career as a writer.

LIFE'S WORK

During the 1850's, Olmsted embarked upon his first noteworthy career as he traveled extensively and published accounts of his journeys. His first book, *Walks and Talks of an American Farmer in England* (1852), was well received and demonstrated his aptitude for keen social observation. It is also significant that Olmsted was quite favorably taken with the landscape and rural life of the country, reflecting his continuing interest in the scenic. With sectional tension between North and South escalating, he was commissioned by *The New York Times* to travel through Dixie and report on the region's social and economic conditions.

Olmsted was chosen because of his connections among rationalist intellectual circles, his moderate antislavery views, and his established literary reputation. Although the publisher of *The New York Times* was himself a moderate Free-Soiler, Olmsted was not chosen primarily because of his views on slavery but because of his reputation as a perceptive observer who could produce an objective report on the "peculiar institution."

In December of 1852, Olmsted began a fourteen-month tour that took him through much of the South and as far as Texas and across the Rio Grande. He sent back lengthy letters over the signature "Yeoman," which were published on the first page of the newspaper, beginning in February, 1853. These were followed by several volumes under various titles, which were finally distilled into his classic two-volume work, *The Cotton Kingdom* (1861).

Olmsted's works were immediately hailed by contemporaries as the most important sources of objective information about the life and customs of the slaveholding states and became significant references as Europeans discussed the relative merits of the Northern and Southern causes in the American Civil War. Olmsted's works remain essential sources for modern historians, who regard them as classic contemporary portrayals and analyses of the plantation slavery system of the antebellum South. If Olmsted had done nothing else, his descriptions of slavery would have established his lasting reputation, but, remarkably, even as he was producing these works, he was embarking upon a second career for which he would become even better known.

In 1857, because of his continuing interest in landscape, Olmsted accepted the position of superintendent of the preparatory work on Central Park in New York City. Soon after, with his partner Calvert Vaux, Olmsted won the competition to provide a new design for the park. He signed his plans with the title "Landscape Architect" under his name, supposedly becoming the first to use this title formally. In 1858, he became the park's chief architect and began to implement his and Vaux's plan to make the park both materially and artistically successful. His work was interrupted by service during the Civil War as general secretary of the United States Sanitary Commission, the forerunner of the American Red Cross, but by this time his philosophy of landscape design was well established.

Olmsted started from the premise that it is essential for human beings to maintain a balance between civilization and nature in their lives and that for city dwellers, particularly, it is imperative that places should be provided as retreats from the pressures of overcrowded, overly civilized urban existence. Although he had an appreciation for nature in the raw, "wilderness," Olmsted's real preference was for the pastoral, a natural environment that was ordered, designed, structured, but which provided the illusion of nature's own handiwork. Thus, the construction of Central Park would involve the movement of tons of dirt, the creation of lakes, sunken roads, bridges, and other features to manufacture the illusion of nature for the city dweller. Ironically, considering the fact that much of his later career was spent in the service of the wealthy and influential, Olmsted's interest in urban parks was shaped in part by a strong democratic impulse to provide facilities where all classes could find refuge and recreation.

In 1863, Olmsted left Washington to become superintendent of John C. Frémont's Mariposa mining estates in California, and while there he became a leading figure in the movement to set aside the Yosemite and Mariposa "big tree" reservations that culminated in the establishment of Yosemite Park. Yosemite eventually became part of the national park system. Olmsted was a consistent promoter of preserving scenic regions and often manufactured "wilderness" areas as part of his design scheme for urban parks.

After the Civil War was concluded, Olmsted returned to New York City and carried Central Park nearly to completion. When the project was begun, the site was an area containing pig farms and squatters' shacks that had no distinguishing physical features; twenty years and the labor of more than thirty-eight hundred workers were required to construct the hills, lakes, and paths that became so important to New Yorkers. Central Park established Olmsted's reputation and became the prototype for urban parks across the United States.

Olmsted's services were now much in demand, and he moved on to design additional parks for New York City and other cities across the nation, the Capitol grounds in Washington, D.C., a preservation plan for the Niagara Falls area, and numerous college campuses. Some consider his design for the system of lagoons, wooded islands, and plantings in Chicago's Jackson Park for the Columbian Exposition in 1893 his crowning achievement. He also became a fervent advocate of suburban living, balancing the features and values of both city and country in new planned communities on the borders of older urban centers. Olmsted and Vaux designed suburbs for several cities, the most famous being Chicago's Riverside, which opened in 1869.

Olmsted's design of the U.S. Capitol grounds. (Library of Congress)

1707

Frederick Law Olmsted. (Library of Congress)

Emotionally exhausted by the constant political maneuvering and compromise required for work in the public sector, in his later years Olmsted retreated to the service of precisely those wealthy plutocrats whose stranglehold on scenic outdoor areas his urban parks had helped to break. His clients included Andrew Carnegie, Leland Stanford, and George Vanderbilt, for whom he helped design the famous Biltmore estate in North Carolina. Olmsted suffered a mental collapse in 1893 and disappeared from public view until his death in 1903.

SIGNIFICANCE

Frederick Law Olmsted was one of those amazingly talented individuals who was able to achieve striking success in several areas. He was a gifted social observer and writer who left some of the best contemporary American descriptions and analyses of the life and economy of the antebellum South. Shaped by an aesthetic appreciation for wilderness and the pastoral and by a strong democratic impulse, Olmsted became a passionate advocate of

the need for balance between urban and natural experiences if one were to maintain a healthy existence. He thus became the first great proponent and designer of large urban parks that would be open to all people and allow city dwellers to maintain that necessary balance in their lives. His Central Park in New York City was the progenitor of the urban parks movement in the United States, and Olmsted fathered the profession of landscape architecture.

—James E. Fickle

FURTHER READING

Beveridge, Charles E., and Paul Rocheleau. *Frederick Law Olmsted: Designing the American Landscape.* Edited and designed by David Larkin. Rev. ed. New York: Universe, 1998. A survey of Olmsted's landscape projects, with textual descriptions and color photographs. The text also discusses Olmsted's work as an administrator and social reformer.

Fein, Albert. *Frederick Law Olmsted and the American Environmental Tradition.* New York: George Braziller, 1972. Evaluates Olmsted's significance in the broad development of environmentalism.

Huth, Hans. *Nature and the American: Three Centuries of Changing Attitudes.* Berkeley: University of California Press, 1957. Discusses Olmsted's work as a landscape architect, as well as his efforts in the campaigns to preserve Yosemite and the area around Niagara Falls.

Mitchell, John G. "Frederick Law Olmsted's Passion for Parks." *National Geographic* 207, no. 3 (March, 2005): 32. An overview of Olmsted's life, philosophy, and landscape projects, richly illustrated with color photographs.

Newton, Norman T. *Design on the Land: The Development of Landscape Architecture.* Cambridge, Mass.: Belknap Press of Harvard University Press, 1971. Includes an assessment of Olmsted's role in the development of the profession.

Olmsted, Frederick Law. *The Slave States Before the Civil War.* Edited by Harvey Wish. New York: G. P. Putnam's Sons, 1959. Wish has written an excellent introduction discussing Olmsted's life and publications.

Robczynski, Witold. *A Clearing in the Distance: Frederick Law Olmsted and America in the Nineteenth Century.* New York: Scribner, 1999. Comprehensive biography, describing Olmsted's occupations and interests and his vision for the American landscape. Olmsted is portrayed as a humanist who saw city parks as a civilizing force for a growing urban population.

Roper, Laura Wood. *FLO: A Biography of Frederick Law Olmsted*. Baltimore: Johns Hopkins University Press, 1973. The definitive biography, combining social history with a nuanced portrait of its subject. Makes generous use of Olmsted's letters. Massively documented, though lacking a bibliography.

Runte, Alfred. *National Parks: The American Experience*. Lincoln: University of Nebraska Press, 1979. Although the focus is upon cultural and economic influences in the creation of the American national park system, this work also discusses the contributions of

Olmsted to park design, wilderness appreciation, and the Yosemite and Niagara Falls campaigns.

Tobey, George B. *A History of Landscape Architecture: The Relationship of People to Environment*. New York: American Elsevier, 1973. Includes considerable material dealing with Olmsted.

SEE ALSO: Daniel Hudson Burnham; Andrew Carnegie; John C. Frémont; Leland Stanford.

RELATED ARTICLES in *Great Events from History: The Nineteenth Century, 1801-1900:* August-December, 1857: Texas's Cart War; May 1-October 30, 1893: Chicago World's Fair.

OSCEOLA
Native American leader

Allegedly a participant in the First Seminole War, Osceola became a leader of the Seminoles who refused to be moved west of the Mississippi; he initiated the Second Seminole War.

BORN: c. 1804; Tallassee on the Tallapoosa River near present-day Tuskegee, Alabama

DIED: January 30, 1838; Fort Moultrie, Charleston, South Carolina

AREA OF ACHIEVEMENT: Warfare and conquest

EARLY LIFE

Osceola later insisted, and some historians maintain, that both his father (whose name is now longer known) and mother (Polly Copinger) were Creeks and that his mother later married an Englishman, William Powell. However, a study by Patricia R. Wickman provides impressive evidence that Powell was indeed Osceola's father, that Copinger's grandfather (James McQueen) and father were white, and that the boy also had black ancestors, as did many children who were born in the Upper Creek town of Tallassee. Nevertheless, Osceola was considered to be an Upper Creek, like his mother.

Osceola's mother's uncle, Peter McQueen, was chief of the village where Osceola was born and became a leader of the Red Sticks during the Creek War of 1813-1814. As that conflict escalated, many Creeks fled from Alabama into Florida. Among the refugees were Osceola and his mother, who followed McQueen and became separated from Powell during the migration. The young Osceola was captured by Andrew Jackson's troops dur-

ing his 1818 campaign in Florida, but he was released because of his age. Allegedly he fought against Jackson in the First Seminole War.

LIFE'S WORK

Osceola settled in central Florida after Jackson's campaign and, like many dislocated Creeks, became known as a Seminole. He was never a hereditary chief, nor was he apparently ever elected to such a post; however, in the controversy surrounding the signing of the treaties of Payne's Landing in 1832 and of Fort Gibson in 1833, both of which provided for the relocation of the Seminoles to the West, he emerged as a leader of those who opposed removal.

A heated clash with Wiley Thompson, the federal Indian agent for central Florida, made Osceola an outlaw. Abolitionists later wrote that Thompson aided two slave catchers to capture one of Osceola's wives, who was a mulatto, but there is no evidence for this tale. Instead, the conflict apparently originated when Thompson called a council at Fort King to confirm the earlier treaties. Most of the Seminoles who were present silently refused to sign the documents placed before them, but Osceola allegedly plunged a knife through the agreement. Again, no contemporary account supports this story.

Other confrontations in the summer of 1835 led Thompson to have Osceola imprisoned in shackles, but Osceola was released when he agreed to support removal. Rather than abide by his agreement with Thompson, Osceola organized Seminole resistance and killed Charley Emathla, a chief who had supported emigration.

Osceola and his followers then attacked a baggage train during December, 1835. Later that same month, he killed Thompson, while allies ambushed a force of more than one hundred regulars and killed all but three of them. On New Year's Eve, 1835, a large party led by Osceola attacked another detachment of regulars and punished them severely in the First Battle of the Withlacoochee, where Osceola was wounded slightly in the hand or arm but escaped capture.

This began the Second Seminole War, which would last until 1842. Until his capture in 1837, Osceola was the primary target of army operations because the U.S. military recognized his importance as a leader in the resistance. Participants in the campaigns against him noted that many of his followers were black. They would have supported him instead of the hereditary chiefs, and his desire to protect them may have been part of his motivation for continuing to fight long after his health began to fail. His evasion of army columns and bold attacks made him something of a folk hero in the United States, but it also earned him the hatred of military leaders, especially

Osceola. (Library of Congress)

after he liberated more than seven hundred Indians held in a detention camp in June, 1837.

In October, 1837, General Thomas S. Jesup, frustrated by Osceola, treacherously accepted his request for a parley under a flag of truce. The Seminole leader, who was then suffering from malaria, and more than eighty of his followers were captured at their camp near Fort Peyton in a flagrant violation of the truce. Despite the public outcry, he was taken to Fort Mellon at St. Augustine, where two of his wives and two children, as well as his half sister and others, joined him. These two wives may have been the two sisters he had married in accordance with Creek custom, though there appear to have been others.

After several other Seminoles escaped, Osceola and his group were transferred on New Year's Eve, 1837, to Fort Moultrie at Charleston, South Carolina. There his health declined rapidly, and he died on January 30, 1838. Allegations vary as to the cause of his death, but most agree that his depression contributed to his rapid demise. Wickman says that quinsy, or tonsillitis complicated by an abscess, was the immediate cause of Osceola's death, and both malaria and recurring fevers were contributing factors in his declining health.

SIGNIFICANCE

Osceola was buried outside Fort Moultrie on Sullivan Island with military honors, but before interment his head was removed by Frederick Weedon, the physician who had attended him during his fatal illness. It was displayed in a medical museum maintained by Valentine Mott of the Medical College of New York until the building was allegedly destroyed by fire in 1866.

The betrayal of Osceola destroyed any realistic hope of unity among the Seminoles. The war continued sporadically until 1842, when most of the surviving Seminoles moved West, as his family had after his death. Only a few remained in the swamps. The circumstances of Osceola's fight, capture, and death, which were often misrepresented, made him a folk hero to many. No fewer than twenty towns in the United States now bear his name, as do three counties, two townships, one borough, two lakes, two mountains, a state park, and a national forest.

—*Richard B. McCaslin*

FURTHER READING

Boyd, Mark F. "Asi-Yaholo, or Osceola." *Florida Historical Quarterly* 23 (January-April, 1955): 249-305. This is an overview of Osceola and the events of his life.

Covington, James W. *The Seminoles of Florida*. Gainesville: University Presses of Florida, 1993. Covington covers the history of the Seminole Indians, their relations with the U.S. government, and the social conditions under which they lived during various periods.

Hartley, William, and Ellen Hartley. *Osceola: The Unconquered Indian*. New York: Hawthorn Books, 1973. This illustrated biography of Osceola includes bibliographic references.

Mahon, John K. *History of the Second Seminole War, 1835-1842*. Gainesville: University Presses of Florida, 1967. Mahon's detailed study of the Second Seminole War includes illustrations, maps, and a bibliography.

Missall, John, and Mary Lou Missall. *The Seminole Wars: America's Longest Indian Conflict*. Gainesville: University Press of Florida, 2004. A history of the three Seminole wars, examining their causes and significance in American history.

Wickman, Patricia R. *Osceola's Legacy*. Tuscaloosa: University of Alabama Press, 1991. Wickman interweaves a biography of Osceola with the history of the Seminoles and considers the implications of the events of his lifetime for later interactions between Native Americans and the U.S. government. The book contains a bibliography and an index.

SEE ALSO: Andrew Jackson; Winfield Scott; Zachary Taylor.

RELATED ARTICLES in *Great Events from History: The Nineteenth Century, 1801-1900:* November 21, 1817-March 27, 1858: Seminole Wars; 1830-1842: Trail of Tears.

SIR WILLIAM OSLER
Canadian physician

Osler published the original Principles and Practice of Medicine, *a classic text for many years, and transformed medical education by extending it beyond the classroom to the patient's bedside.*

BORN: July 12, 1849; Bond Head, Canada West (now Ontario), Canada
DIED: December 29, 1919; Oxford, England
AREA OF ACHIEVEMENT: Medicine

EARLY LIFE
Any reading of the life of Sir William Osler (OHS-ler) quickly reveals an individual of widely varied interests and great vitality. He cared deeply for people and was loved in return by young and old alike. He had a special fondness for the young. Born in Ontario, near Lake Simcoe, he was the youngest of nine children of an Anglican clergyman. Life on the frontier of Canada during the mid-nineteenth century was far from easy, and the earnings of a clergyman not great, yet what was lacking in material comfort was made up in the closeness and love of the family. A nurturing of intellect and an abundance of books instilled in the children the desire for education, and somehow from the meager funds available, Featherstone and Ellen Osler saw several sons through university and into professions.

Endowed with a fine mind as well as a small but wiry and healthy body, Osler excelled at both scholarship and sports. A sprightly sense of humor embroiled him in high jinks, a characteristic that would mark him throughout life. While at Weston School, one such prank ended with Osler, along with his fellows, in the Toronto jail. The Matron of Weston failed to appreciate their humor, of which she was the butt, and charged them with assault and battery.

Nevertheless, Osler pursued his studies with diligence. In this, he had the rare good fortune to cross the paths of not one, but two gentlemen who became his mentors and friends. They were friends to one another as well, and the available correspondence is indicative of the warm affection that the three shared. The first of these was the Reverend W. A. Johnson, who had opened Weston, the boarding school to which Osler was sent in preparation for university study. There, he came under Johnson's influence, and this good man became affectionately known as "Father" Johnson, not so much for his priestly calling as for his genuine caring for the students, especially Osler.

Father Johnson had a passion for botany, and young Osler became his companion and collaborator in this pursuit, an activity that helped to prepare him for the course he was to follow. The sharing of specimens and information went on for years, along with microscopic examination of specimens gathered on numerous forays into the woods and waters of the area.

The second individual to have significant impact upon the course of Osler's life was the physician Dr. William

Bovell, in whose home Osler lived when he attended Toronto University. As a young man, Osler began preparation for the ministry, following his father's steps. Shortly, however, exposed to Bovell's remarkable mind as well as his vast library, Osler became interested in medicine. (Ironically, Bovell began theological studies and eventually took a charge in the West Indies, but the friendship continued.)

Transferring to McGill College, Osler completed his clinical study there in 1872. The faculty, upon his graduation, conferred a special award, remarking on the "originality and research" of his thesis that was illustrated with "33 microscopic and other preparations of morbid structure."

LIFE'S WORK

It was the custom of the time for young medical graduates to make a tour of medical facilities and schools in Europe. As his parents were not in a position to support such a venture financially, an older brother, himself bound for Scotland and pleased to have the company of his lively young brother, paid the cost of transportation. Osler continued his study in Vienna, in Berlin, and in London, allowing himself to expand his knowledge and experience.

Osler continued his microscopic studies, and a notation in his laboratory notebook records that on the fourteenth of June, 1873, he began studies of his own and others' blood as well as that of various animals, and there appear drawings of what he observed. Here was the beginning of his study of the circulatory system and the identification of platelets as a component of the blood. So passed two frugal but rewarding years. Then, in 1874, a request came for Osler to return to McGill as a lecturer in the medical school. Acceptance of this offer inaugurated Osler's long and distinguished career as professor, clinician, scholar, and humanitarian.

Osler is said to have humanized the whole of medical practice. He was unusual not only for the respect he

---

THE ORIGINS OF MEDICINE

In 1913, Sir William Osler delivered a series of lectures on the evolution of modern medicine at Yale University. In his first lecture, he offered a speculation on the relationship between medical and magical beliefs.

Modern anthropologists claim that both religion and medicine took origin in magic, "that spiritual protoplasm," as Miss Jane Harrison calls it. To primitive man, magic was the setting in motion of a spiritual power to help or to hurt the individual, and early forms may still be studied in the native races. This power, or "mana," as it is called, while possessed in a certain degree by all, may be increased by practice. Certain individuals come to possess it very strongly: among native Australians today it is still deliberately cultivated. Magic in healing seeks to control the demons, or forces, causing disease; and in a way it may be thus regarded as a "lineal ancestor of modern science," which, too, seeks to control certain forces, no longer, however, regarded as supernatural.

Primitive man recognized many of these superhuman agencies relating to disease, such as the spirits of the dead, either human or animal, independent disease demons, or individuals who might act by controlling the spirits or agencies of disease. We see this today among the negroes of the Southern States. A Hoodoo put upon a negro may, if he knows of it, work upon him so powerfully through the imagination that he becomes very ill indeed, and only through a more powerful magic exercised by someone else can the Hoodoo be taken off.

To primitive man life seemed "full of sacred presences" connected with objects in nature, or with incidents and epochs in life, which he began early to deify, so that, until a quite recent period, his story is largely associated with a pantheon of greater and lesser gods, which he has manufactured wholesale. Xenophanes was the earliest philosopher to recognize man's practice of making gods in his own image and endowing them with human faculties and attributes; the Thracians, he said, made their gods blue-eyed and red-haired, the Ethiopians, snub-nosed and black, while, if oxen and lions and horses had hands and could draw, they would represent their gods as oxen and lions and horses. In relation to nature and to disease, all through early history we find a pantheon full to repletion, bearing testimony no less to the fertility of man's imagination than to the hopes and fears which led him, in his exodus from barbarism, to regard his gods as "pillars of fire by night, and pillars of cloud by day."

Source: William Osler, *The Evolution of Modern Medicine* (New Haven, Conn.: Yale University Press, 1921), chapter 1.

---

showed his students but also for the new collegial relationship that he established among physicians. More important still, the patient-physician relationship was revolutionized. Medical education was extended beyond the confines of the classroom and into the hospital, where patients rather than disease became the focus. If the situation appears to have changed during the late twentieth century, it may be that Osler's wisdom has been forgotten. "Don't ask the doctor; ask the patient" is a Yiddish proverb, but it could stand well as the motto of Osler's life and practice.

Another particular concern of Osler was his insistence that learning must be an ongoing process. Addressing young graduates in 1875, he exhorted them to "be students always" and to keep up their reading (as he himself never failed to do). In 1913, a few short years before his death, he greeted students at Yale as "fellow students." On another occasion, he urged the student body at McGill to seek as much truth as possible, stating:

> No human being is constituted to know . . . the whole truth. . . . The truth is the best you can get with your best endeavor [and] an earnest desire for an ever larger portion.

Looking at another facet of this exceptional human being, it appears that Osler never met a stranger. Harvey Cushing, in his superlative biography of the man, records one especially poignant yet characteristic event that illustrates this. In the autumn of 1875, Osler chanced to meet an English businessperson in Montreal. The young man contracted smallpox and died. While attending the patient, Osler learned the address of his parents, and so he wrote to them, describing the illness and death of their son and conveying his sympathy. Many years later, he provided to the man's sister a photograph of the grave.

Osler's flair for jest, which belies his sober, even severe, countenance in surviving photographs, caused him to assume the pseudonym of "Egerton Y. Davis, M.D." for purposes of satire and humor, addressing numerous issues in essays and letters. (Years later, he occasionally and affectionately referred to his son as "Egerton, Jr.") The byline surfaced from time to time over a number of years, gaining considerable attention.

In 1884, while in Leipzig, Osler was offered the Chair of Clinical Medicine at the University of Pennsylvania, which he is said to have accepted based on the flip of a coin. McGill's loss became Pennsylvania's gain. While in Philadelphia, Osler made significant contributions: He revived a faltering professional organization and founded and supported a student club, both of which he valued as a means of professional sharing and mutual support.

Johns Hopkins University was developing a medical school, and in 1891, officials at the university invited Osler to Baltimore. While awaiting the opening of the school, he prepared his *Principles and Practice of Medicine* (1892), which became a standard text for many years. By 1930, in its eleventh edition, the book had been translated into at least four other languages. Later revisions, edited by others, never quite captured the style and flow of the original. Osler became, too, a part of the brilliant medical staff at Johns Hopkins, which was known as the "Big Four."

Osler returned to Philadelphia briefly in 1892 to marry Grace Revere Gross, the widow of a colleague and great-granddaughter of Paul Revere. Years later, in Oxford, their home was familiarly referred to as the "Open Arms." One of their children died in infancy, and their son, Revere, grew to adulthood only to die in the trenches of France in 1917. It was a grief that Osler took to his own grave.

A request to accept the chair as Regius Professor of Medicine at Oxford took the Oslers to England in 1904. There William Osler was to spend his remaining years, serving with great distinction. On the occasion of the coronation of King George V in 1911, a baronetcy was bestowed, and Osler became Sir William—"much to the embarrassment of my democratic simplicity," he reported to a friend in a letter.

For some years Osler had been subject to episodes of bronchitis, and, in October of 1919, a severe cold developed into bronchitis and bronchopneumonia. Osler was unable to fend off this final illness, and he died on December 29, 1919.

SIGNIFICANCE

When Sir William Osler died, he was widely known and admired in his profession and beyond. He brought freshness and humanity to the practice of medicine and humor to those around him. His example remains today and is acclaimed in his profession as unique. This fact was made apparent when, in 1951, a committee of his fellows republished those speeches and essays deemed to be his best in order to give medical students "a taste of Osler." These works show that his wide interests were not separate from medicine.

Osler believed profoundly, and proclaimed repeatedly to his students, that history, the classics, and an understanding of human behavior were essential to the holistic practice of medicine. An individual in need of medical care, he was convinced, seeks the attention and comfort of a fellow human being before drugs and treatment. Such wisdom is timeless, as fresh in the twenty-first century as in Osler's own time.

—*Mary Wilson Sage*

FURTHER READING

Bliss, Michael. *William Osler: A Life in Medicine.* New York: Oxford University Press, 1999. The first definitive biography since Cushing's book (see below). Bliss portrays Osler as a brilliant, compassionate, and influential physician and teacher.

Bryan, Charles S. *Osler: Inspirations from a Great Physician*. New York: Oxford University Press, 1997. A collection of Osler's writings providing advice on everyday living.

Cushing, Harvey. *The Life of Sir William Osler*. 2 vols. Oxford, England: Clarendon Press, 1925. This is the exhaustive biography from which the bulk of the information for this essay was drawn. It was written by one who knew medicine and surgery at first hand and who himself taught surgery at Johns Hopkins University, where Osler had served on the first faculty. This work won the Pulitzer Prize.

Foucault, Michel. *The Birth of the Clinic*. Translated by A. M. Sheridan Smith. New York: Vintage Books, 1973. Foucault describes this as "an archeology of medical perception." It examines the development of medical knowledge and practice, confirming that the modern entity of the teaching hospital was brought into being only in the nineteenth century. It was this forum that Osler introduced to the United States and in which he practiced as professor of medicine at Oxford.

Journal of the American Medical Association 210, no. 12 (1969). The entire issue is devoted to Osler. Published fifty years after his death.

Osler, William. *The Principles and Practice of Medicine*. New York: D. Appleton, 1892. 18th ed. Edited by Abner McGehee Harvey. New York: Appleton-Century-Crofts, 1972. This is a later edition of the textbook originally compiled by William Osler. It continues to be revised and updated by the faculty of Johns Hopkins University for use as a text in the medical school.

_____. *Science and Immortality*. Boston: Houghton Mifflin, 1904. Publication of the lectures Osler delivered at Harvard University in 1904.

_____. *Selected Writings of Sir William Osler*. New York: Dover, 1951. Collection of Osler's essays and addresses spanning the adult years of his life. These writings demonstrate the breadth of his knowledge and interests as well as his fluency with the English language.

SEE ALSO: Samuel Hahnemann; Joseph Lister.

RELATED ARTICLE in *Great Events from History: The Nineteenth Century, 1801-1900:* October 5, 1823: Wakley Introduces *The Lancet*.

NIKOLAUS AUGUST OTTO
German inventor

Otto invented the first internal combustion, four-stroke engine that was the forerunner of the modern gasoline automobile engines that transformed world transportation during the twentieth century.

BORN: June 10, 1832; Holzhausen, Nassau (now in Germany)
DIED: January 26, 1891; Cologne, Germany
AREA OF ACHIEVEMENT: Science and technology

EARLY LIFE

Nikolaus August Otto was born in a small German village on the banks of the Rhine River. His father, postmaster and innkeeper in the village, died shortly after his birth. As a child, he was bright and did well in school, and his mother wanted, at first, to enter her son in higher education. The unrest of 1848 changed her mind, however, and she decided that the business world would provide a better future for him. Accordingly, he gave up high

school (where he had been a star student) and went to work.

Otto's first job was as a clerk in a small-town grocery store. From there he moved to a job as a clerk in Frankfurt, and eventually became a traveling salesperson for a wholesale grocer, working out of Cologne. In 1860, still a traveling salesperson, Otto read a newspaper account of a gas engine built by a Frenchman, Étienne Lenoir. The Lenoir engine was well known at this time, and Otto studied it carefully. As the piston of the Lenoir engine moved down the cylinder, it drew in a mixture of gas and air. An electric spark ignited the air/gas mixture halfway through the stroke, creating the power necessary to push the piston to the bottom of the cylinder. Each piston was doubled-sided, so the piston returned to its original position when the same steps were repeated on the opposite side. It is important to note that this engine did not compress the air/gas mixture and that it relied on illuminating gas (used in homes and street lamps) for its fuel.

Lenoir had trouble getting it to run smoothly under a load.

LIFE'S WORK

With strong links to rural regions both in his boyhood and in his job, Otto was bothered by the fact that the Lenoir engine relied on a fuel that was available only through a system of pipelines found in the cities. He saw that the internal combustion engine had the potential to become an important source of power in a wide variety of applications, and he determined to make an engine that could be used in city and village alike. He devised a carburetor for the Lenoir engine that enabled the engine to receive fuel from a tank rather than a pipeline. Although his patent application for the carburetor was rejected, he continued to work on the internal combustion engine.

In 1861, Otto commissioned Michael Zons, an instrument maker and machine-shop owner in Cologne, to build a Lenoir engine. Otto studied this engine carefully in an attempt to make it run smoothly under a load. The main problem with the engine was the shock of detonation on the piston. While he was experimenting with this engine, Otto stumbled across a phenomenon that would later pay him great dividends. He drew in the air/gas charge and then, instead of allowing the piston to continue down the cylinder, he moved it back up toward the cylinder head, compressing the charge. Otto was surprised to find that the detonation was so violent as to turn the engine through several revolutions. This was the principle upon which he would later base the four-stroke cycle. After continued experimentation with the Lenoir engine, Otto decided that the difficulties were too great and turned to a new type of engine: the atmospheric engine.

The atmospheric engine resembled an upward-pointing cannon with gears and levers attached. As the motion of the flywheel pulled the piston up, air and gas were drawn in beneath the piston. At the same time, the piston pushed the air above it out of the cylinder and into a tank, where it was stored at above-atmospheric pressure. The combustion of the air/gas mixture pushed the piston up at high velocity to the top of the cylinder, creating a vacuum in the cylinder below the piston. The piston's own weight and the pressure difference between the air in the holding tank and the vacuum in the cylinder then returned the piston to the bottom of the cylinder.

Zons built a one-half horsepower model of the atmospheric engine for Otto in 1863. In order to develop the engine, Otto obtained financial backing from Eugen Langen, son of a wealthy industrialist, and they entered

Nikolaus August Otto. (The Granger Collection, New York)

into a formal business agreement in March of 1864. With Langen's help, Otto refined the atmospheric engine. After three years of work, the Otto and Langen engine was shown at the 1867 Paris Exposition, winning the grand prize. Having built a successful engine, Otto and Langen now needed to manufacture and sell their product. They found more capital, created the Gasmotorenfabrik Deutz corporation in 1872, and shortly thereafter were selling their engines around the world.

The Otto and Langen engine proved to be popular; five thousand were eventually built. The engine's reliance on atmospheric pressure (the final version did not have the holding tank for air) posed a serious limitation, however, by limiting its output to a maximum of three horsepower. Furthermore, it was extremely noisy and vibrated strongly when in operation. In response to these shortcomings, Otto began to think about a new type of engine (possibly reviewing his earliest experiments with the Lenoir engine) in which the air/gas mixture was compressed in the cylinder before ignition. The engine then used one stroke each for the intake, compression, ignition (and expansion), and exhaust functions. In such an engine there was only one power stroke for every four piston strokes, hence the name "four-stroke cycle." This was a bold step, considering that the double-acting steam engine—the dominant power technology of the time—used each stroke as a power stroke.

Otto was concerned that detonation of the compressed air/gas mixture would produce a violent explosion capable of damaging the engine. To lessen the shock of detonation, he devised a concept known as the "stratified charge," in which the richest mixture would be farthest from the piston, with successive layers of air and exhaust gases filling the remainder of the cylinder. Otto believed that this would create a gradual burning instead of a violent explosion. The stratified charge was so important to Otto that it constituted the main claim in his patent, rather than the four-stroke cycle or the compressed charge.

Otto built the first of these engines in 1876 at the Gasmotorenfabrik Deutz works. Even the rough prototype demonstrated the many advantages of the four-stroke engine to Otto and his partners. Compared to the atmospheric engine (and others of the time) the four-stroke engine produced, for the same displacement and engine weight, far more horsepower. In addition to erasing the three-horsepower ceiling of the atmospheric engine, the new engine operated with much less noise and vibration, earning the nickname "Silent Otto." Gasmotorenfabrik Deutz refined the prototype and eventually marketed the engine with great success. By the turn of the century, Otto's firm had built twenty-four thousand engines.

In 1882, the first of several claims against Otto's patent rights arose. He was to spend the rest of his life defending himself against these claims. The most damaging came from a competitor who wanted to void Otto's patent on the four-stroke cycle on the basis of an obscure pamphlet written in 1862 by the French engineer Alphonse-Eugène Beau de Rochas. Rochas had clearly stated the principles of the four-stroke cycle in his pamphlet, but apparently he never realized its significance and never built an engine operating on those principles. Nevertheless, in 1886 Otto lost his German patents on the four-stroke cycle. He considered the patent suits an attack upon his honor, and the defeat in 1886 left him an embittered man. The legal battle continued until 1890, when the last appeal ended. On January 26, 1891, Nikolaus Otto died of heart failure in Cologne.

SIGNIFICANCE

Automobiles using Nikolaus August Otto's engine appeared on the roads of Europe only ten years after he built the prototype, and less than two decades later the Wright

brothers' aircraft was propelled by a four-stroke engine. The predominant type of automobile engine in the twenty-first century is a direct descendant of Otto's 1876 engine. One asset of Otto's engine is its flexibility, thanks to its small size, low weight, and the multitude of possible configurations (vertical, horizontal, single or multiple cylinders, ability to run on many kinds of fuels, and the like). Although Otto placed more faith in the stratified-charge concept than was probably warranted, he did, nevertheless, build the first successful engine to operate on the four-stroke cycle. For his persistence in solving the problems he encountered and for seeing them through to their respective solutions, he deserves the credit as that engine's inventor.

—*Brian J. Nichelson*

FURTHER READING

Bryant, Lynwood. "The Origin of the Automobile Engine." *Scientific American* 216 (March, 1967): 102-112. This article concentrates on the intellectual process by which Otto arrived at the 1876 engine. Bryant notes that Otto believed in the stratified charge to the end, although most other experts believed that the charge should be as homogeneous as possible. The many illustrations and photographs are a great help in understanding the technical details of Otto's engines. No documentation.

_____. "The Origin of the Four-Stroke Cycle." *Technology and Culture* 8 (April, 1967): 178-198. Examines Otto's claim to inventing the four-stroke cycle. In a carefully documented and reasoned argument, Bryant shows that while others had the idea of a four-stroke cycle, credit for invention should go to Otto. The section on Rochas, the cause of much grief to Otto, is of special interest.

_____. "The Silent Otto." *Technology and Culture* 7 (Spring, 1966): 184-200. Asks why Otto was successful after so many others had been trying to assemble an internal combustion engine for seventy-five years. Traces his thought through fifteen years of development; points out that only in 1876, having gained much practical experience, was Otto ready to accept the four-stroke cycle he had discovered accidentally in 1862. In addition to the usual sources, Bryant has assembled evidence directly from the patent records.

Csere, Csaba. "Nikolaus Otto and His Remarkable Compression Stroke." *Car and Driver* 39, no. 8 (February, 1994): 7. Describes some of Otto's designs for the four-stroke cycle engine; explains his partnership with Eugen Langen.

Cummins, C. Lyle, Jr. *Internal Fire*. Lake Oswego, Oreg.: Carnot Press, 1976. Written by the son of the founder of the Cummins Engine Company, this book is an absorbing account of the internal combustion engine from the seventeenth century to the present. Chapters 8 and 9 deal specifically with Otto. Cummins is not afraid to differ with other historians and generally provides good support for his arguments.

Goldbeck, Gustav. "Nikolaus August Otto, Creator of the Internal-Combustion Engine." In *From Engines to Autos: Five Pioneers in Engine Development and Their Contributions to the Automotive Industry*, by Eugen Diesel, Gustav Goldbeck, and Friedrich Schilderberger. Chicago: H. Regnery, 1960. Goldbeck recounts the highlights of Otto's life and his accomplishments in the development of his engine. Lacks documentation but appears reasonably accurate. Is less sterile than many sources in that Goldbeck tries to reveal a more human side to the successes and failures Otto experienced.

Grayson, Stan. *Beautiful Engines: Treasures of the Internal Combustion Century*. Marblehead, Mass.: Devereux Books, 2001. Chapter 2 in this illustrated history of the internal combustion engine describes Otto's engine.

Karwatka, Dennis. "Technology's Past." *Tech Directions* 61, no. 8 (March, 2002): 10. Describes how Otto created his four-stroke cycle engine.

SEE ALSO: Carl Benz; Gottlieb Daimler; Étienne Lenoir.

RELATED ARTICLES in *Great Events from History: The Nineteenth Century, 1801-1900:* May, 1876: Otto Invents a Practical Internal Combustion Engine; January 29, 1886: Benz Patents the First Practical Automobile.

SIR JAMES OUTRAM
British imperialist

Using a mixture of military force and sound administrative techniques, Outram helped to complete the construction of the British imperial system in India during the evolution from rule by the East India Company to direct imperial domination.

BORN: January 29, 1803; Butterley Hall, Derbyshire, England
DIED: March 11, 1863; Pau, France
AREA OF ACHIEVEMENT: Government and politics

EARLY LIFE

James Outram was the son of Benjamin Outram, a civil engineer who introduced iron rails to mining traffic. His mother, Margaret Anderson, was a Scottish agricultural writer's daughter. His father died in June, 1805, leaving heavy debts from his building of an iron foundry. Margaret Outram returned with her children to her native Aberdeen, Scotland, where James was educated at the Marischal College. Outram was an indifferent-looking man with swarthy complexion and curly hair; Lady Canning, wife of one of India's governor-generals, said that he "was a very common looking little dark Jewish man, with a desponding slow hesitating manner."

Although of puny build, Outram was athletic and adventurous; he enlisted as a cadet in the Indian army at the age of sixteen and arrived in Bombay in August, 1819, where he was posted for several years to various regiments, learning the military trade. Outram's generous nature was demonstrated early, when he stipulated that part of his pay be reserved for his mother. Outram also became a first-class outdoorsman: He was credited with more than half of the "first spears" thrown at tigers on hunting trips that he accompanied from 1822 to 1824, and he kept a lifelong interest in the hunt.

LIFE'S WORK

Outram's career as soldier and administrator assumed its shape in the middle and late 1820's. In April, 1825, he was made agent for the East India Company for much of Khandesh, a province north of Bombay that had recently devolved to the British. In that capacity, he pacified the Bhils—a race of nomads resisting British authority—and, gaining their admiration through his hunting prowess, succeeded in turning most of them into loyal subjects. This process, completed by 1835, rested on Outram's technique of converting the village *patels* (leaders) into officers of the government. After a Bombay interlude during which Outram married his cousin, Margaret Anderson, he carried out the same process of annexation by force and then pacification of

Gujarat, a native state to the west of Khandesh (1835-1838).

In 1838, Outram became involved in the expanding British effort to bring order to the Sind, a region lying west of the Indus River. He was appointed aide-de-camp to Sir John Keane, the general in charge of trans-Indus operations. In August, 1839, Outram commanded an expedition across Afghanistan in pursuit of Dost Mohammed, whom the British had rejected as ruler of that country. Posing as an Afghan, Outram made an eight-day ride in November, 1839, through enemy territory to advise the Bombay government of Kalat's siege, an exploit that made him famous all over India. Despite Outram's audaciously successful raids against various Afghan and Baluchi tribesmen, the British were not victorious in the First Afghan War and eventually withdrew from the country, considerably humiliated.

Perhaps to compensate for recent disasters, the Indian government then determined to annex the Sind. Outram—who had been appointed political agent of Lower Sind in 1839 and of Upper Sind in 1841—was a non-interventionist, preferring to work with the local emirs to maintain the security of India's frontiers, but he could not stem the desire of the governor-general, Lord Ellenborough, for a cheap victory. General Sir Charles Napier was sent in June, 1842, to pacify the Sind, virtually superseding Outram in authority.

Seeing that Outram could not protect them against Napier, the Sind leaders rebelled; Outram defended the British residency at Hyderabad, the Sind's capital, against eight thousand Baluchi tribesmen (February, 1843). Napier used this as an excuse to annex the Sind, cynically referring to his action as "a very advantageous, useful, humane piece of rascality." Although he liked Napier, Outram bitterly condemned the Sind annexation during a visit to England in May, 1843, as a breach of faith with the emirs and as "tyrannical—positive robbery." Such outspokenness angered many in the Indian government, even though Outram was made a brevet lieutenant colonel in July, 1843, in recognition of his past service in Afghanistan and the Sind.

Upon his return to India at the close of 1843, Outram was charged with conducting military operations against the Maratha rebels, south of Bombay toward Portuguese Goa. These having been successfully concluded, he was made resident of Satara in May, 1845, and then of Baroda in May, 1847—the highest civilian position possible within the Bombay administration. Baroda's government was corrupt, and with characteristic forthrightness, Outram criticized both Baroda's native ruler and local company officials in a report of October, 1851. The incensed Bombay administration removed Outram from his position in March, 1852; the company director in London upheld the removal while praising Outram's energy and honesty.

After another sojourn in England, Outram returned to India, where Lord Dalhousie (governor-general, 1848-1856) reappointed him resident at Baroda. Shortly afterward, Outram was transferred in April, 1854, to Aden, at the mouth of the Red Sea, as political agent and commandant of the garrison. The intense heat there weakened his health, and Outram was sent back to India and named resident at Oudh in December, 1854.

Oudh—last of the Muslim-ruled native kingdoms besides Hyderabad—lay strategically situated on the Ganges, between Delhi and Calcutta. Thus, it was a prime target of the East India Company's "doctrine of lapse," which called for annexation if native rule was considered incompetent. Oudh's rulers were undeniably bad; they had been previously warned that their maladministration would end in a British takeover. In March, 1855, Outram reported from Lucknow, the capital of Oudh, that conditions there were deplorable. The British could either run Oudh's affairs while leaving the king his title, or annex the state. Outram recommended the latter course, Dalhousie the former; the London authorities decided in Outram's favor. As the Oudhian ruler would not sign a treaty ending his sovereignty, Dalhousie proclaimed annexation on February 13, 1856, simultaneously naming Outram the chief commissioner.

Oudh's absorption helped bring on the Indian Mutiny of 1857, because many of the sepoys (soldiers employed by the East India Company) lived there. Already disaffected by the prohibition of wife-burning, by the use of bullets greased with taboo animals' fat, and by rumors of British intent to Christianize India, the sepoys decided to rebel, after the much-respected Outram left India in mid-1856 as a result of ill health. Lord Charles Canning, Dalhousie's successor as governor-general, wanted Outram back in Oudh, but Prime Minister Henry Palmerston sent the popular general to Persia instead, in early 1857, to lead a brief and successful war with that power. By the time Outram returned to Bombay, the Sepoy Mutiny had begun.

The stage was set for the central event of Outram's career—the relief of Lucknow, where the British garrison, some loyal sepoys, and several hundred dependents lay besieged in the British residency. Lord Canning intended him to raise the siege, but Outram waived his powers to Major General Sir Henry Havelock, an older officer whom he admired; unwisely, Outram continued to give "advice" freely, thus undercutting Havelock's authority. Nevertheless, with about 3,100 troops, both Havelock and Outram fought their way into Lucknow from Cawnpore fifty miles away on the Ganges, in only a week—September 19-25, 1857. However, their force was too small to evacuate the residency, and they were besieged there in turn. Sir Colin Campbell, the British commander in India, finally relieved Outram on March 19, 1858, with an additional force of five thousand men. The garrison and dependents were then evacuated, although Havelock soon died of dysentery. Outram was left temporarily in charge of the Alambagh—a palace near Lucknow—to guard the city, while Campbell dealt with the rebellion in nearby Cawnpore.

As India passed under direct British rule following the mutiny's collapse, Outram became the toast of the country. He was appointed military member of the Governor-General's Council, received Parliament's thanks and a baronetcy, was made a lieutenant general in the Indian army, and received a large annual pension. Suffering from chronic asthma and bronchitis, Outram left India forever in July, 1860, returning to London to write his memoirs. He died while wintering at Pau, in southern France, on March 11, 1863, and was honored with burial in Westminster Abbey.

SIGNIFICANCE

Sir James Outram was one of the most honorable and sensitive British officials in India during the years of evolution from rule by the East India Company to direct imperial domination. As a military man, he was always well liked by his officers and soldiers. Despite some of his questionable military decisions—notably his waiving of command to Havelock at Lucknow—no one ever questioned his integrity and bravery; Napier's characterization of Outram in November, 1842, as "the Bayard of India, without fear and reproach," was richly deserved.

As a civil administrator, Outram was well respected, even loved, by the Indians and was known to be sympathetic toward them (for example, as the mutiny collapsed, he argued successfully with Canning to show clemency to sepoys who surrendered quickly). Rare among British officials of his time, Outram sensed the growth of Indian nationalism, saying of the Sepoy Mutiny, "It is absurd to call this a military rebellion." Although Outram's fame faded after his death, he should

be remembered as a statesman who tried to soften the frequently oppressive process of British imperialism in India.

—*Thomas John Thomson*

FURTHER READING

Edwardes, Michael. *Battles of the Indian Mutiny*. London: B. T. Batsford, 1963. A detailed military history of the Sepoy Mutiny. Outram's activities during the Lucknow campaign are exhaustively outlined, and criticized, in chapters 8-15. One of Batsford's British Battle series.

Gardiner, Brian. *The East India Company*. New York: McCall, 1972. Outram's career is covered in the context of the institution that, at the end of its rule in 1858, controlled one-fifth of the world's population. The author stresses the strangeness of an entity that was neither company nor government.

Goldsmid, F. J. *James Outram: A Biography*. 2 vols. London: Smith, Elder, 1880. One of two full-length biographies of Outram. Heavily dependent on Outram's letters and other documents. There is no attempt to be evenhanded; the work is well written but overly adulatory.

Hibbert, Christopher. *The Great Mutiny: India, 1857*. New York: Viking Press, 1978. A narrative history of the Sepoy Mutiny by a prolific historian and biographer. Hibbert draws on the memoirs of Outram and of practically every other major figure in the uprising. Good personal characterization of Outram.

Holmes, Thomas Rice Edward. *A History of the Indian Mutiny, and of the Disturbances Which Accompanied It Among the Civil Population*. London: W. H. Allen, 1883. Rev. ed. London: Macmillan, 1913. A good, but dated, treatment of the mutiny. Outram is prominently mentioned, and his personality and actions praised as knightly and chivalric. See especially chapter 9.

Kinsley, D. A. *They Fight Like Devils: Stories from Lucknow During the Great Indian Mutiny, 1857-1858*. New York: Sarpedon, 2001. A military history of the Lucknow campaign that includes excerpts of personal accounts by European participants. Contains information about Outram's role in the campaign.

Trotter, Lionel J. *The Bayard of India: A Life of General Sir James Outram*. London: J. M. Dent & Sons, 1909. A shorter biography than Goldsmid's, and highly partial to Outram.

Woodruff, Philip. *The Men Who Ruled India: The Founders*. New York: Schocken Books, 1964. A study of the impact of the British on India. Although admitting the faults of their rule, the author hoped that they would be remembered for their positive contributions. Outram is mentioned in passing, although positively.

SEE ALSO: First Marquis of Dalhousie; John Laird Mair Lawrence; Dadabhai Naoroji.
RELATED ARTICLES in *Great Events from History: The Nineteenth Century, 1801-1900:* April 10, 1802: Lambton Begins Trigonometrical Survey of India; 1885: Indian National Congress Is Founded.

ROBERT OWEN
Welsh social reformer

Best known for his utopian community of New Harmony in Indiana, Owen was both one of the leaders of the early Industrial Revolution and one also of its greatest critics. He developed the cotton-spinning factory while demonstrating the efficiency and productivity that resulted from the benevolent treatment of workers. He pioneered in educational reform and became the chief spokesman for the cooperative movement.

BORN: May 14, 1771; Newtown, Montgomeryshire, Wales
DIED: November 17, 1858; Newtown, Montgomeryshire, Wales
AREA OF ACHIEVEMENT: Social reform

EARLY LIFE

Born into a Welsh family of modest means, Robert Owen attended a small local school only until the age of nine. His education was considerably advanced through his own determined reading. By his account, he read, during his youth, a book each day. At the age of ten, he left home to seek his fortune, working as a shop-boy in textile stores, eventually making his way to Manchester in 1786 just as the Industrial Revolution, centered on the textile industry in cities such as Manchester, was beginning.

Owen was fifteen when he arrived in Manchester, and his success came early. He worked for three years as a shop assistant, but by early 1791 he had become a partner in a small cotton mill, and by the age of twenty he was the manager of a large, industrialized cotton-spinning factory. In this mill, Owen introduced the first use of American sea-island cotton, thus beginning the demand for that crop produced in the southern portion of the United States. The thread produced in Owen's spinning factory was generally recognized to be of superior quality, and he was regarded, at this early age, as the master of this new industry. By 1795, he was manager and co-owner of the large Chorlton Twist Company and was on his way to amassing an enormous fortune.

Through business connections, Owen met Miss Anne Caroline Dale, the daughter of David Dale, a wealthy textile industrialist in New Lanark, Scotland. Owen not only fell in love with Miss Dale, but also determined to buy her father's factories. With the financial backing of his partners, the deal was made, and the New Lanark Twist Company formed, with Owen as sole manager and part owner. On September 30, 1799, he and Caroline were married, making their home in New Lanark. Given his later radical views on marriage, it would be impossible to term theirs a happy union.

As the new century opened, Owen approached his twenty-ninth birthday. He was a good-looking young man, whose sensitive mouth and eyes were checked by a furrowed brow and prominent nose. In his youth, he affected the hairstyle and dress of the romantic, and he looked almost poetic. As he grew older, however, and his utopian ideas caused heated attacks against him, Owen appeared more somber, dressing in black broadcloth that accented his rugged looks. Financial success came early in Owen's life, and with the new century he looked forward to addressing a wide array of social problems, and with his enormous creditability as an industrialist he was confident he could change the world for the better.

LIFE'S WORK

As a cotton-mill owner and manager, Owen first achieved national, and even international, recognition as a result of the reforms he instituted for his workers. In those early days of the Industrial Revolution, working conditions were worse than poor; they were deplorable. Along with the long hours of dehumanizing drudgery in the dreary factories, the poor sanitation, the terrible overcrowding, and the absence of schools were the associated problems of drunkenness, theft, and other vices. Most notorious of all was child labor. Owen found that among his two thousand employees were some five hundred pauper children as young as the age of six.

Owen determined to improve these conditions and the lives of his workers. As early as 1806, when his factory and others closed as a result of the American embargo, Owen persuaded his partners to take the extraordinary step of continuing to pay wages while his mills sat idle. With such an attitude, he won the loyalty and admiration of his employees, who surpassed all others in their productivity. He greatly improved housing, sanitation, and the physical plant in general. He provided free medical care, opened a company store where prices were low, controlled the sale of whiskey, and docked the pay of public drunkards. This benevolence was not without the price of authoritarianism, and Owen ran New Lanark with a firm hand, even levying fines for sexual promiscuity. Nevertheless, these measures were remarkably successful in improving not only the lives of his employees but also the output of his mills. In the latter regard, Owen proved a superb manager in reorganizing the factory system and in evaluating individual production.

These reforms were expensive, and Owen was always at odds with his partners over the cost of his social experiments. In 1813, he formed a new company, this time with partners of a more kindred spirit, one of whom was Jeremy Bentham, the leader of the Utilitarians. This new arrangement allowed Owen to proceed with the enterprise that was closest to his heart: education. He believed, as he often said, that man's character was not made by him but for him; that is, environment played a greater role than heredity. Education was the answer to creating a proper environment and building good character. In 1814 at New Lanark, he began building an "institution for the formation of character," which included facilities for education, public meetings, and a nursery school, an idea new in Great Britain at the time.

Owen expressed virtually all of his philosophy in a pamphlet that appeared in 1813: *A New View of Society: Or, Essays on the Principle of the Formation of the Human Character*. This essay, coupled with the great success of his factory system, brought him international attention, and he was in contact with many of the great leaders of his world. Visitors flocked to see New Lanark, including the Grand Duke Nicholas, the future czar of Russia. Owen was much admired, and his philanthropy

was widely praised. He worked hard for legislation that would improve working conditions, and he was largely responsible for the Factory Act of 1819, although he was disappointed with its limitations.

Owen's early success went to his head, and he came to believe that he could solve all of society's problems. Within a few years, he declined from being a highly regarded industrialist to being dismissed as an eccentric crank. The first hint of his radical ideas came on January 1, 1816, when he gave the main address at the opening of his institute. On that occasion, he dismissed all existing institutions as false and based on erroneous principles.

Owen claimed to have discovered new foundations that would allow the creation of a perfect society, and he asserted that his ideas were supported by world leaders, philosophers, and educators. The following year, he proposed that the problem of the poor could be solved by having them live in small communal villages based on agriculture. Owen summarized this plan and its call for so-called Villages of Cooperation in the *Report to the County of Lanark, of a Plan for Relieving Public Distress*

Robert Owen. (Library of Congress)

and *Removing Discontent, by Giving Permanent, Productive Employment to the Poor and Working Classes, Under Arrangements which Will Essentially Improve Their Character, and Ameliorate Their Condition, Diminish the Expenses of Production and Consumption, and Create Markets Co-extensive with Production* (1820).

What really damaged Owen's reputation, however, was his deliberate and public assault on organized religion, a surprise attack that he delivered in a London address on August 21, 1817, and an attitude that doomed his other reform schemes by their association with atheism. Afterward, his continued baiting of the clergy compounded his notoriety. However, Owen remained firmly unshaken in his purpose. Next he proposed that a community be founded where his principles could be tested. At his own expense, he created such a model at New Harmony in Indiana in 1825. The experiment lasted for three years and attracted a broad range of weird reformers and misfits as well as sincere adherents to Owen's principles of cooperation and association. The end was foreordained: New Harmony, after using up most of Owen's fortune, failed, and Owen returned to Great Britain in 1829.

In 1828, Owen had sold his share of the New Lanark Company. In 1831, his wife died, and all of his surviving children lived in the United States. Alone and no longer a wealthy industrialist, Owen became the chief spokesperson for a movement that was later termed utopian socialism (to distinguish it from Marxist socialism). Indeed, the actual term "socialism" seems to have become popular in meetings of the Association of All Classes of All Nations, which Owen founded in 1835. He worked tirelessly on behalf of his form of socialism, for cooperation, and against religion. He also openly opposed the institution of marriage and in his later life expressed a deep interest in spiritualism.

By the mid-1830's, Owen was actively involved in the trade union movement, establishing the Grand National Consolidated Trades Union, which for a time had a membership of more than half a million. His several organizations went through numerous name changes, and all were ultimately unsuccessful. In 1858, he became seriously ill and requested that he be taken back to his native village of Newtown. There, on November 17, 1858, he died. By his wish, he was buried in a churchyard next to the graves of his parents. His three sons did well in the United States. Robert became a member of Congress and a diplomat, David was a geologist, and Richard was a college professor.

SIGNIFICANCE

Despite the controversy and failures that accompanied his life, Robert Owen left a remarkable set of legacies. In industry, he proved that high wages and good employee relations improve productivity. In education, his nursery school idea and the importance of environmental influences became standard concepts. His theories on cooperation gave birth to the cooperative movement, which demonstrated remarkable endurance. His attempt to build a model community was repeated numerous times in the nineteenth and twentieth centuries. The impetus he gave to the trade union movement was of particular historical significance. Despite the unfortunate personality traits that made him combative and difficult to deal with, he played a leading role in the attempt to resolve the social consequences of the early Industrial Revolution.

—*Roy Talbert, Jr.*

FURTHER READING

Cole, Margaret. *Robert Owen of New Lanark*. New York: Augustus M. Kelley, 1953. A brief and general but useful introduction.

Donnachie, Ian. *Robert Owen: Owen of New Lanark and New Harmony*. East Linton, Scotland: Tuckwell, 2000. Reprint. Edinburgh: Birlinn, 2005. Comprehensive biography of Owen, describing his work as a factory owner and social reformer.

Harvey, Rowland Hill. *Robert Owen, Social Idealist*. Berkeley: University of California Press, 1949. A scholarly, yet highly readable, biography.

Holloway, Mark. *Heavens on Earth: Utopian Communities in America, 1680-1880*. New York: Library Publishers, 1951. 2d ed. New York: Dover, 1966. Properly includes Owen's New Harmony experiment and Owen's influence in America.

Jones, Lloyd. *The Life, Times, and Labours of Robert Owen*. 2 vols. London: Sawn, Sonnenschein, 1890. Reprint. New York: AMS Press, 1971. This early biography is useful because the author, born in 1811, was an adult during Owen's later years.

Noyes, John Humphrey. *History of American Socialisms*. Philadelphia: J. B. Lippincott, 1870. Reprint. New York: Dover, 1966. This work, by one of the most famous American utopians, includes contemporary accounts of New Harmony and other Owenite communities.

Owen, Robert. *A New View of Society and Other Writings*. London: Everyman's Library, 1966. One of the most important and the most generally available works by Owen.

Podmore, Frank. *Robert Owen: A Biography*. 2 vols. London: Hutchinson, 1906. Reprint. New York: Haskell House, 1971. First published in 1906, this remains the standard biography of Owen.

Royle, Edward. *Robert Owen and the Commencement of the Millennium: A Study of the Harmony Community*. New York: St. Martin's Press, 1998. Chronicles life at Harmony in Hampshire, England, one of the two utopian communities personally established by Owen.

Thompson, Brian. *Devastating Eden: The Search for Utopia in America*. London: HarperCollins, 2004. A history of two experimental communities at Harmony, Indiana. George Rapp initially founded a Christian community there in 1815; ten years later, he sold the town to Owen, who renamed it New Harmony and established a socialist society. Thompson describes life in both communities, chronicling their successes and failures.

SEE ALSO: Alexander Campbell; William Edward Forster; James Mill; David Ricardo; Frances Wright.

RELATED ARTICLES in *Great Events from History: The Nineteenth Century, 1801-1900:* Spring, 1814-1830: Communitarian Experiments at New Harmony; February 23, 1820: London's Cato Street Conspirators Plot Assassinations; May 8, 1838-April 10, 1848: Chartist Movement; 1839: Blanc Publishes *The Organization of Labour*.

NICCOLÒ PAGANINI
Italian composer

From his own time to the twenty-first century, Paganini has been considered one of the greatest violinists the world has ever known. He was the founder of the freelance virtuosi. His astonishing feats of skill on the violin, his uncanny dramatic flair, and the compelling rumors and legends spawned by his colorful lifestyle all combined to captivate the imagination of audiences throughout early nineteenth century Europe and distinguish him as one of the most intriguing figures in music history.

BORN: October 27, 1782; Genoa, Republic of Genoa (now in Italy)
DIED: May 27, 1840; Nice, Kingdom of Sardinia (now in France)
AREA OF ACHIEVEMENT: Music

EARLY LIFE

The northern Italian culture into which Niccolò Paganini (PAH-gah-nee-nee) was born venerated musicians as much as any other great musical culture in history. Considering the great deal of money available to musical talent at that time, it was quite natural that a family as poor as the Paganini's would raise a gifted child such as Niccolò to no other end than the complete development of his talents. Paganini's mother, Teresa, was a pious woman who claimed that while he was being born, an angel came to her and told her that the child would be the greatest violinist the world had ever known. The young Niccolò grew up under his mother's gentle yet constant prompting to fulfill this divine commission. His father, Antonio, had a more direct and demanding influence on the development of his talents. Antonio worked at the Genoa harbor but was a gifted amateur musician. Although he spent most of his time drinking, gambling, and scheming of ways to get rich, he found time to teach Niccolò the mandolin at the age of five and the violin at the age of seven.

Paganini claimed that within a few months of learning the violin he could play anything on sight. Antonio, recognizing his son's talents and willing to exploit any financial prospect, forced Paganini to practice from morning until night. When he could teach Paganini no more, he arranged for his son to take lessons with Giacomo Costa, the foremost violinist in Genoa. Paganini played in church three times per week to help pay for his tuition, and Antonio set up concerts throughout Genoa, where Paganini played his own compositions and varia-

tions on standard pieces to great applause. At the age of thirteen, Paganini went with his father to Parma, where he studied composition for one year and then made an extensive and successful concert tour throughout northern Italy. Paganini constantly chafed against Antonio's severity, and although he did make a few concert tours between the ages of fifteen and eighteen, he spent most of this time in his room practicing and composing, as much to avoid contact with his father as to attain perfection in his art.

LIFE'S WORK

In September of 1801, at the age of eighteen, Paganini finally extracted himself from his father's control and set out on a path that was to make him the talk of Europe. He pleaded to be allowed to go to a festival in Lucca, Italy, where he would be able to demonstrate his talents to travelers from all over southern Europe. His father reluctantly consented on the condition that he take his older brother. The two set out for the festival, and Paganini met with great success.

When the festival ended in December, Niccolò, having tasted the sweet nectar of freedom, sent his brother home alone and decided to remain in Lucca. For three years he lived the life of a freelance artist and indulged the passions of youth that had been long suppressed under his father's strict rule. His performances earned him a great deal of money, which he gambled away and then earned back at his next concert. Several times he had to pawn his violin to pay a debt of honor. While his violin was in hock he was in desperate need of an instrument with which to perform a concert. A wealthy businessperson lent him a Guarneri violin and was so moved by the performance that he insisted Paganini keep it. Although he would later give up gambling altogether, it was a major feature of his stay in Lucca and would prove to be the source of a great financial failure near the end of his life.

Paganini's amorous adventures during this period in Lucca and throughout his life were legendary. He was not an attractive man, but his genius and magnetic personality gave him an appeal that captured the hearts of women wherever he went. The most important aspect of this period in Lucca, however, was his development as a performer of the first order. His early teachers had been closely associated with opera and the theater, which surely contributed to his sense of the dramatic and, combined with a financial opportunism he inherited from his father, gave him a keen sense of how to work an audience. His physical appearance also contributed to his popular appeal. His cadaverous presence was so alarming that it led to endless rumors of his associations with the devil, which he initially exploited for publicity but later regretted.

Paganini's programs were filled with music of his own composition—the works of other violinists and composers not being difficult enough for him—which emphasized his technical prowess and his ability to perform amazing tricks such as imitating the sound of farm animals and playing entire pieces on a single string that anyone else would find difficult playing on all four strings. This thrilled his audiences and earned him a great deal of money, but his propensity to pander to low tastes led critics to label him a charlatan.

Although this criticism is deserved to some extent, those who were most vocal in this regard had not heard him play, basing their judgments on reports of his performances and in reaction to the startling phenomenon of

Paganini that swept all of Europe. The most incredulous of critics had only personally to experience a performance to be disabused of the worst of this notion. Even while acknowledging dismay for his antics, the greatest composers and musicians of his day, including Franz Schubert, Franz Liszt, Gioacchino Rossini, Hector Berlioz, and Giacomo Meyerbeer, paid him homage as a master. He cut himself an enigmatic figure from those early days in Lucca and remained such throughout his life.

In 1805, Napoleon Bonaparte named his own sister, Elise, regent of Lucca. She appointed Paganini court conductor and solo violinist. Besides performing several times per week, his duties also included giving violin lessons to Elise's husband. After serving four years in this capacity, Paganini resumed his career as a freelance artist, delighting audiences all over the Lombardy region of Italy. In 1813, he gave a triumphant concert in Milan. He had considered following this performance with an international tour but was retained for thirty-six more concerts in Milan and then proceeded with an extensive tour of Italy. He would not leave his native land for another fifteen years.

By the time Paganini set out for Vienna in 1828, he was known throughout Europe, his fame having spread by travelers who returned home from Italy with reports of his amazing skills as well as fantastic rumors of his notorious lifestyle. After five months in Vienna, Paganini set out on a two and one-half year tour of Germany, Bohemia, and Poland. In 1831 he visited Paris, France, for the first time and later that year made the first of two tours of England. Everywhere he went, his concerts sold out even though he charged twice as much for tickets as any other performer. His performances invariably exceeded his reputation.

In 1834, Paganini returned to Italy and purchased an estate near Parma. For a brief time he took a post with Napoleon's second wife, Marie Louise, who was then the duchess of Parma. Paganini spent the remaining years of his life giving concerts and dabbling in the violin trade, buying and selling fine instruments as a hobby during his extensive travels. In 1836, he became enmeshed in a failed scheme to open a casino in Paris that was to bear the name Casino Paganini. An easy target because of his wealth and fame, Paganini was

Niccolò Paganini. (Library of Congress)

ruined by the lawsuits that followed this debacle. He left Paris in 1838 hoping to return to Genoa, but he was not to live much longer. He did not have a strong physical constitution, and his life had been filled with extended periods of illness. In 1840, still embroiled in litigation over the casino venture, his frail health, compounded by years of living on the road and the pressures of his recent financial setbacks, failed him. He died in Nice, unable to complete his journey home.

SIGNIFICANCE

Public subscription concerts had been common for nearly one hundred years prior to Paganini's life, but only as a supplement to the support a musician received from wealthy patrons. With the rise of republican sentiment in Europe during the early nineteenth century, a new class of citizen emerged with new aesthetic demands that made public concerts a practical option for the musician who understood these demands. Paganini was the first to take advantage of these changing conditions. He defined the role of the freelance musician for generations to come, and his influence extended from the likes of Liszt to the modern rock band.

The legendary aspects of Paganini's colorful life and showmanship are fascinating, but it is his achievements as a composer and an artist that preserve his place in history. Although many of his compositions are flashy pieces of technical wizardry lacking musical substance, there are a few pieces that are premier works for the violin. His greatest compositions are his twenty-four caprices, a collection of violin studies exercising all the technical elements necessary to master the instrument. The ability to play this work remains a primary criterion for consideration as a master violinist. These caprices have also been the subject of transcriptions as well as theme and variations by numerous composers. His six violin concertos are highly regarded and are still a part of the standard concert repertoire.

—Richard L. Mallery

FURTHER READING

Courcy, G. I. C. *Paganini: The Genoese*. Norman: University of Oklahoma Press, 1957. Reprint. New York: Da Capo Press, 1977. This book is one of two classic biographies on Paganini in English. The appendixes include a genealogy of the Paganini family, two autobiographical sketches by Paganini himself, a list of compositions, a list of instruments owned by Paganini, and an extensive bibliography of pre-1950 works on Paganini.

Pulver, Jeffrey. *Paganini: The Romantic Virtuoso*. Herbert Joseph, 1936. Reprint. New York: Da Capo Press, 1970. This book is a classic work on Paganini and includes an extensive bibliography compiled by Frederick Freedman.

Roth, Henry. *Violin Virtuosos: From Paganini to the Twenty-first Century*. Los Angeles: California Classics Books, 1997. Roth traces the phenomenon of the violin virtuoso from Paganini to contemporary performers. Includes chapters on women violinists, American and Russian violinists, and the nature of the violin as art.

Sheppard, Leslie, and Herbert R. Axelrod. *Paganini*. Neptune City, N.J.: Paganiniana, 1979. A complete compendium of material related to the life and works of Paganini. This collaboration includes an engaging biography; hundreds of drawings and pictures of Paganini, his contemporaries, and modern performers of his compositions; reproductions of Paganini-related ephemera; stylistic samples and analysis of Paganini's music; a Paganini discography; and a facsimile of the twenty-four caprices.

Stratton, Steven S. *Niccolò Paganini: His Life and Work*. Westport, Conn.: Greenwood Press, 1971. The first half of this short book is a biography of Paganini, while the second half provides a detailed analysis of his life, his artistic merit, and his significance as a composer.

Sugden, John. *Paganini*. London: Omnibus Press, 1986. This book was originally published in 1980 as *Paganini: Supreme Violinist or Devil's Fiddler?* by Midas Books. It is a brief biography with many pictures and drawings. Appendixes include a select bibliography, a discography, and a list of derivatives of Paganini's life and works in popular and serious culture.

SEE ALSO: Hector Berlioz; Franz Liszt; Gioacchino Rossini; Franz Schubert; Clara Schumann; Theodore Thomas.

RELATED ARTICLE in *Great Events from History: The Nineteenth Century, 1801-1900:* December 22, 1894: Debussy's *Prelude to the Afternoon of a Faun* Premieres.

ALICE FREEMAN PALMER
American educator and social reformer

The second president of Wellesley College, Palmer championed the cause of educational reform for women, greatly influencing attitudes of educators and society at large concerning the need for high-quality education for women at every level.

BORN: February 21, 1855; Colesville, New York
DIED: December 6, 1902; Paris, France
ALSO KNOWN AS: Alice Elvira Freeman (birth name)
AREAS OF ACHIEVEMENT: Education, women's rights

EARLY LIFE

Alice Freeman Palmer was born Alice Elvira Freeman. She was the oldest of four children of James Warren Freeman and Elizabeth Josephine Higley Freeman. When she was nine years old, her father decided to pursue his interest in medicine in the hope of improving the family economic situation. Elizabeth Freeman assumed full support of the children for two years and her husband received his degree from the Albany Medical College in 1864. Alice's early education came mostly from her parents. Her mother and grandmother had experience as schoolteachers, and her father was adventurous and inquisitive. The family was deeply religious and active in promoting moral and social causes. Alice was given household responsibilities that often included the care of younger siblings. She gained much practical knowledge and developed a deep love of nature that she carried into adulthood. At three years of age, Alice had taught herself to read; by the next year, she began to attend the village school. In the one-room school, however, educational stimulation was limited.

In 1865, Dr. Freeman moved his family to the nearby village of Windsor, New York, to begin his medical practice. Alice was enrolled at Windsor Academy, a coeducational preparatory school where she came into contact with formal, rigorous education for the first time. The academy's teachers came from prestigious institutions such as Harvard and Andover, and Alice excelled in her work. At the age of fourteen, she became engaged to a theology professor. She soon realized, however, that her own goals in life depended on her receiving adequate education. She viewed marriage as an equal partnership that would be impossible without an education equal to that of her mate. Six months after the young professor left for seminary at Yale, Alice broke the engagement.

The Freeman family lived in relative poverty to which the members responded with a certain resourcefulness and creativity. Although the parents valued education, for financial reasons it was decided that the funds available must go to Alice's brother, who would one day likely be in a position of supporting a family of his own. Alice had been preparing diligently at Windsor to enter college and was willing to sacrifice whatever was necessary to attend. She bargained with her parents that if they would even partially finance her higher education, she would take on no family responsibilities of her own until each of her three siblings had received the education they desired, and her father gave his consent.

Alice had thought of entering newly founded Vassar College, but was not satisfied that the college would offer women as rigorous an education as men received at the finest schools. Instead, she chose to travel far from home and take entrance examinations at the University of Michigan, one of the few universities in the country offering a coeducational program. However, she failed the examinations. During her interview, however, she attracted the attention of the university president, who interceded on Alice's behalf.

Alice was allowed six months to prove her suitability as a student. This she did admirably and, after years of financial hardship and sometimes ill health, graduated in 1876, with a bachelor of arts degree. Family finances had deemed it necessary for Alice to interrupt her studies in 1875 and take a temporary position as preceptress at a struggling high school in Ottawa, Illinois. From the outset, her skill as an administrator was evident. She negotiated smoothly with faculty and students and designed quality courses of study. Nevertheless, finishing her own education was her priority, and she returned as soon as possible to the university despite pleas from the community to remain.

LIFE'S WORK

After graduation from the University of Michigan, Alice Freeman embarked on a succession of difficult years as she fulfilled her resolution to help her family and educate her siblings. Jobs were low paying and not always of her choice; however, her record of achievements was no less than excellent in each situation. She taught in a girls' seminary in Lake Geneva from 1876 to 1877 and from 1877 to 1879 at the high school of Saginaw, Michigan. In 1877, she received her first invitation to teach at

Alice Freeman Palmer. (Library of Congress)

Wellesley College as an instructor of mathematics, but refused for personal reasons. In 1878, Henry Fowle Durant, the founder of Wellesley, contacted her again with the offer of a position in the Greek department. Her sister Stella, to whom she was devoted, was ill and needed her care. Again, she declined. Stella died in 1879, and, although it was a time of deep sorrow for Alice, she was freed to go about her work with a more independent spirit. When Durant called for the third time, she accepted the chairmanship of the history department in 1879, and went to Wellesley.

The college had been founded by Durant and his wife in an effort to promote the same kind of education for women that was offered to men in the United States. The ideals were in close kinship with those that Freeman upheld, and she worked tirelessly with the young women whom she taught. The college was experimental and liberal in its program of studies, and Durant was insistent that research and laboratory work were more important than simply learning from a textbook. This placed a large demand on the faculty not only to lecture but also to prepare detailed reading lists from which the students worked. Shortly after Durant's death in 1881, Ada L. Howard, the president of Wellesley, resigned. Alice Freeman, whose work had shown dedication and con-

summate skill, was chosen at the age of twenty-six to be vice president of the college and acting president. In 1882, she became the second president of Wellesley, where her talent as an administrator and organizer of human resources found an ideal outlet.

During her six years as president, much of Freeman's time was spent stabilizing the academic and administrative structure while implementing goals Durant had set for the college. She organized the Academic Council made up of heads of the academic departments to which she turned often for advice and consultation in academic matters. Standing faculty committees were formed and a building program was begun that included a gymnasium and dormitories. Networks were created with feeder high schools in the country, and the preparatory school was discontinued. Freeman's full energy then went into improving the collegiate program by raising academic standards and simplifying and standardizing the courses of study that were offered. Although tuition was increased, Freeman also endeavored to make more scholarships available to students. Her contacts in the field and keen sense of people's abilities also culminated in successful efforts to build the faculty.

Alice Freeman's professional life was not restricted to the Wellesley campus, but extended to matters of general education. She was instrumental in establishing the Association of Collegiate Alumnae in 1882 (forerunner of the American Association of University Women), which brought together educated women nationwide who were interested in raising standards of education for women. She served two terms as president in 1885-1886 and 1889-1890. In 1884, she was one of three American delegates elected to attend the International Conference on Education in London.

In 1887, Alice Freeman's life took a new turn. A friendship with Harvard philosopher George Herbert Palmer developed into a romance, and the two were married on December 23. Having decided that her work at Wellesley was finished and the college was ready for a time of quiet growth and the watchful care of someone new, she resigned her position shortly before her marriage, much to the despair of the college and of her public, especially those who felt she had compromised her profession for marriage. Instead, she envisioned her future as an opportunity to continue to pursue her goals within the comfort of a lifestyle that for the first time included leisure.

Alice was constantly available for public addresses and gave unselfishly of her time to any organization that supported the ideals of excellence in education, particularly that of women. She remained on the executive committee of the Board of Trustees at Wellesley until her death and was active as well in the founding of Radcliffe College as separate from, but affiliated with, Harvard. Her work was separate from that of her husband, but each received ample support and respect from the other. The couple spent several sabbaticals in Europe, where they traveled many miles on bicycle enjoying the countryside. Alice and her husband also spent many summers at the Palmer family farm in Boxford, Massachusetts, twenty-five miles north of Boston, where they enjoyed tranquillity not possible in the city.

In 1891, Alice Palmer was one of five delegates from Massachusetts chosen to attend the World Columbian Exhibition in Chicago, an event that highlighted the work of international women in many professions, including education. In 1892, she received a doctoral degree from the University of Michigan. In the same year,

she was invited by the new University of Chicago to serve as their dean of women. Although Alice and her husband were both offered positions, they decided not to leave Boston. The university's president, William Rainey Harper, was determined to entice the most capable woman he knew in the field and persisted in modifying the conditions until she agreed to serve. She was required to spend only twelve weeks' residence in Chicago, allowed to elect her own sub-dean, and released from any teaching responsibilities. She stayed until 1895, having established policies on which others could build.

Palmer's professional activity continued and included work with the Woman's Home Missionary Society of the Presbyterian Church and the Women's Educational Association, an organization founded in Boston in 1891 and of which she was president for nine years. The Massachusetts Board of Education appointed her to its membership in 1889, and she helped to raise levels of high school education in the state and ensure free high school education for every citizen. In 1902, while on sabbatical with her husband, Alice Palmer died in Paris of a heart attack at the age of forty-seven.

SIGNIFICANCE

Alice Freeman Palmer was a true pioneer in the field of education for women. Her life was spent in preparation for her work and in professional endeavors that helped to drastically change the quality of academic opportunity offered to women in the United States. Her accomplishments were numerous, and, fortunately for society, came early in her brief life. She had a gift for working among people that called for the best from them and herself. Recognition included honorary degrees from Columbia University in 1887 and Union University in 1896.

In 1920, Palmer became the second youngest person to be named to the Hall of Fame at New York University, which recognizes professionals from a variety of fields. She left no writing for posterity other than a few articles and a book of romantic poems called *A Marriage Cycle*

WHY GO TO COLLEGE?

After retiring from the presidency of Wellesley College in 1887, Alice Freeman Palmer frequently spoke before public groups. On one occasion, she lectured on the subject of why women should go to college. This concluding excerpt from her lecture sums up her thoughts on that subject.

Such are some of the larger influences to be had from college life. It is true all the good gifts I have named may be secured without the aid of the college. We all know young men and women who have had no college training, who are as cultivated, rational, resourceful, and happy as any people we know, who excel in every one of these particulars, as have the college graduates about them. I believe they often bitterly regret the lack of a college education. And we see young men and women going through college deaf and blind to their great chances there, and afterwards curiously careless and wasteful of the best things in life. While all this is true, it is true too that to the open-minded and ambitious boy or girl of moderate health, ability, self-control, and studiousness, a college course offers the most attractive, easy, and probable way of securing happiness and health, good friends and high ideals, permanent interests of a noble kind, and large capacity for usefulness in the world. It has been well said that the ability to see great things large and little things small is the final test of education. The foes of life, especially of women's lives, are caprice, wearisome incapacity and petty judgments. From these oppressive foes we long to escape to the rule of right reason, where all things are possible, and life becomes a glory instead of a grind. No college, with the best teachers and collections in the world, can by its own power impart all this to any woman. But if one has set her face in that direction, where else can she find so many hands reached out to help, so many encouraging voices in the air, so many favoring influences filling the days and nights?

Source: Alice Freeman Palmer, *Why Go to College?* (New York: T. Y. Crowell, 1897).

(1915). Her lasting mark was made, however, through her interaction with students and faculty and her willingness to involve herself fully with important causes in cooperation with others, thus bringing many worthwhile ideas to fruition. Her efforts made a difference for all women who have followed her as she opened the doors to educational and professional challenges never before possible.

—*Sandra C. McClain*

FURTHER READING

Bordin, Ruth B. *Alice Freeman Palmer: The Evolution of a New Woman*. Ann Arbor: University of Michigan Press, 1993. The most recent biography of Palmer, Bordin's work gives an excellent account of Palmer's achievements, impact, and interaction with other prominent figures in the struggle for equal education for women.

Kenschaft, Lori J. *Reinventing Marriage: The Love and Work of Alice Freeman Palmer and George Herbert Palmer*. Urbana: University of Illinois Press, 2005. Examines the couple's attempt to create a new type of marriage that would allow both partners to pursue satisfying careers. Kenschaft uses the couple's correspondence and other sources to trace the Palmers' changing relationship.

Palmer, George Herbert. *The Life of Alice Freeman Palmer*. Boston: Houghton Mifflin, 1924. Written by her husband, this biography offers an intimate look at Alice Palmer's life and work. Some correspondence and poetry are included.

Palmieri, Patricia A. "Here Was Fellowship: A Social Portrait of Academic Women at Wellesley College, 1895-1920." *History of Education Quarterly* 23 (Summer, 1983): 195-214. A scholarly article that discusses the lives of various figures encountered by Palmer during her tenure as professor and then as president of the college.

Storr, Richard J. *Harper's University: The Beginnings*. Chicago: University of Chicago Press, 1966. This history of the University of Chicago gives insight into Palmer's tenure as the first dean of women.

Weimann, Jeanne Madeline. *The Fair Women*. Chicago: Academy Chicago, 1981. This account of the Women's Building at the World's Columbian Exposition discusses Palmer's involvement with the education exhibition.

Wein, Roberta. "Women's Colleges and Domesticity: 1875-1918." *History of Education Quarterly* 14 (Spring, 1974): 31-47. The article explores activity at Wellesley and Bryn Mawr at a time when decisions made had a major effect on whether female education would continue to perpetuate feminine passivity or foster independence.

SEE ALSO: Elizabeth Cabot Agassiz; Catharine Beecher; Olympia Brown; William Rainey Harper; Charlotte Angas Scott; Emma Willard.

RELATED ARTICLES in *Great Events from History: The Nineteenth Century, 1801-1900:* May, 1823: Hartford Female Seminary Is Founded; September 26, 1865: Vassar College Opens.

LORD PALMERSTON
Prime minister of Great Britain (1855-1858, 1859-1865)

Palmerston made aggressive use of military and naval power to ensure security for British commerce, while attempting to work closely with France to avoid war.

BORN: October 20, 1784; Westminster, London, England

DIED: October 18, 1865; Brocket Hall, Hertfordshire, England

ALSO KNOWN AS: Henry John Temple (birth name); Third Viscount Palmerston; Baron Temple of Mount Temple; Pam

AREAS OF ACHIEVEMENT: Government and politics, diplomacy

EARLY LIFE

Born Henry John Temple, the future Lord Palmerston sprang from a long line of Anglican Irish aristocrats. His education at Harrow, Edinburgh University, and finally at St. John's College, Cambridge, earned for him a nobleman's degree, without examinations. He had no need, however, for such academic favors. His intelligence and talents would have ensured success even if he had been forced to compete for the prizes that the accident of noble birth thrust upon him.

Since the seventeenth century, the Temples had been Whigs. The reign of George III, however, had seen the emergence of the "king's party." Although under George I and George II (1714-1760) Toryism had been equated with treason, it enjoyed renewed respectability under George III (1760-1820). The road to any kind of patronage lay through personal loyalty to the king. He was determined to assert royal prerogative, as far as he could, without forgetting that since the Glorious Revolution of 1688-1689, British sovereigns had owed their crowns to Parliament rather than to divine right.

It is thus not a matter of an abandonment of Whig ideals, but a simple, pragmatic need to wear the king's colors that made the second Viscount Palmerston identify with what came to be called the "New Tory" Party, for forty years. At the death of the second Viscount on April 17, 1802, Henry John Temple succeeded to his father's title and estates as the third Viscount Palmerston. At the age of eighteen, he still had his university studies ahead of him. Appropriately, this scion of a Whig family was most profoundly influenced at Edinburgh by Professor Dugald Stewart, the leading Whig philosopher of the day.

It is, however, understandable that this bright, personable, and independently wealthy Irish peer chose to wear the Tory label when he first entered political life, in 1807. Whether as a Tory at the beginning of his career or as a Whig and a Liberal at the end, he was fundamentally an heir of the Glorious Revolution, mistrustful of royal power and devoted to a Parliament whose destinies were guided by educated and propertied aristocrats.

As an Irish peer, Lord Palmerston was eligible to seek election in the British House of Commons. At the age of twenty-two, he began his fifty-nine-year career in Parliament as the representative of a pocket borough whose voters had been bought by wealthy patrons on his behalf. It must be understood that no element of scandal attached to buying and selling votes in underpopulated boroughs. The rationale of the borough mongers asserted that only thus could able young politicians be recognized and helped to an early start in their careers.

Although almost immediately offered cabinet rank, Lord Palmerston contented himself with the noncabinet post of Secretary-at-War for twenty years, until 1828. He was apparently happy doing an efficient job at the War Office, showing no signs of ambition as he made his way through London society. He earned a name as a fashion setter, a womanizer, and a dilettante writer for political journals. He could have been dismissed as a brilliant young man who was wasting his talents and was destined to remain a second-rater. Although he made a few parliamentary addresses on foreign affairs, he took no real interest in diplomacy. It was to be the last thirty-five years of his long career that would earn for him the sobriquet "Most English Minister" and to identify him as the embodiment of John Bull.

Lord Palmerston delayed matrimony until 1839, when he was married to the widow of Lord Cowper, Emily, née Lamb, sister of Prime Minister Lord Melbourne. The newlyweds had long been intimate during the lifetime of Lord Cowper, and gossip ascribed the paternity of Lady Cowper's younger children to Lord Palmerston. In any event, those children became his heirs.

LIFE'S WORK

Lord Palmerston owed his first attainment of cabinet rank to the prime ministership of that arch Tory, the duke of Wellington. He resigned in 1828, in loyalty to his friend William Huskisson, who had been forced out of the cabinet after a major split with the Iron Duke. Thrown into opposition, Palmerston interested himself in diplomatic matters, for the first time. At last, the talented dabbler had found his forte. In June, 1829, he delivered one of the great parliamentary speeches of his career, establishing his reputation as a man who understood foreign affairs. Immediately, Lord Grey, the Whig leader, formed an alliance with the disaffected Tory. In September, 1830, Wellington invited Palmerston to return to the cabinet. The offer was refused, unless Wellington would include Lord Grey in a sort of Cabinet of National Unity. Wellington, quite predictably, declined the proposal. From that hour, most of Palmerston's biographers count him as having returned to his ancestral Whig origins.

When in 1830 Lord Grey attained the prime ministership after forming his own coalition of Whigs and disaffected Tories, Palmerston attained the office of Foreign Secretary at last. He held it until 1841 and again in 1846-1852.

Lord Grey's greatest achievement was the parliamentary Reform Bill of 1832. In Palmerston's domain at the Foreign Office, his accomplishments assumed a gigantic stature of their own. In France, the senior line of the House of Bourbon was overthrown and replaced by its cadet branch, the House of Orleans, personified by Louis-Philippe, who reigned as king of France until overthrown in turn by the revolutions of 1848. Italian and Polish nationalists also made 1830 a revolutionary year, with suicidal results. Closer to Great Britain, however, a Belgian revolt against the king of the Netherlands required forceful British action, and it was the Belgian crisis that established Palmerston's reputation for brilliance in statecraft.

There was the gravest danger that Austria, Russia, and Prussia might intervene with armed force to assist the king of the Netherlands to regain Belgium. After all, the union of all the Low Countries under the Dutch sovereign had been one of the achievements of the Congress of Vienna, designed to prevent either French or Prussian aggression across that natural military highway formed by the flat Netherlands. Seen in that way, Lords Grey and Palmerston would have preferred to see the unity of the Netherlands preserved. As a realist, however, Palmerston perceived that there was no way of forcing French-speaking Walloons and Flemish Belgians, almost entirely Roman Catholic, to accept the sovereignty of the Calvinist Protestant Dutch House of Orange, which had unwisely treated the Belgian provinces as subordinate appendages rather than as fully participating states in a United Kingdom of the Netherlands.

Palmerston and Grey were ready to settle for an independent Belgium, provided that Louis-Philippe did not regard it as a means to French aggrandizement. It took all

Palmerston's skill, and a neat balance of conciliatory gentleness and bullying firmness, to get an adventuresome French army withdrawn from Belgium and to persuade Louis-Philippe not to press the claims of one of his sons to be king of Belgium. At the same time, he had to restrain the Dutch from using force to repress the Belgian revolt, a repression that would have made it more difficult to control the French.

Fortunately for Great Britain, France, and the Belgians, the Polish and Italian revolts of 1830 kept Austria, Prussia, and Russia so preoccupied that Palmerston was able to create an independent Belgium. As a crowning touch, the London Conference of 1831 obtained the consent of all the major powers to the erection of an independent Belgium. The king selected for the new state was Prince Leopold of Saxe-Coburg-Saalfeld, the widowed former son-in-law of Great Britain's King George IV. It was an incidental but significant bonus that Leopold was the uncle both of the future Queen Victoria and her consort, Prince Albert. The queen selected for him, and imposed as an act of statecraft, was a daughter of Louis-Philippe, king of France. Thus, everyone obtained something, the appearance of Anglo-French entente was maintained, the Belgians were freed, yet British security in the Low Countries seemed assured. Only the king of the Netherlands might complain of unrequited loss.

Palmerston took an aggressive role in settling disputed claims to the Spanish and Portuguese thrones, and in finding husbands for Donna Maria of Portugal and Isabella of Spain who would pose no threat to British interests. Although sympathetic to the Greek struggle for independence from Turkey, he devoted the last thirty years of his life to building and protecting a strong Ottoman Turkish barrier against Russian and French expansion.

Palmerston interested himself in active support for Protestant missionaries in the Levant and briefly toyed with the idea of a Jewish commonwealth in Palestine. Even after he had abandoned that idea, he continued to offer the most aggressive protection to the Jews of that area. Palmerston saw no contradiction between his drive to protect minorities on Turkish soil, whether Jews, Protestants, Druze, Samaritans, or Armenians, and his determination to save the Turkish Empire. After all, France used its role as protector of Roman Catholicism, and Russia used its protectorate of Orthodox Christianity to build power bases in the East. Palmerston merely concluded that a strong British presence in the Levant was the best possible protection for Turkey against Russian or French ambitions.

When, from 1839 to 1841, Mehmet Ali, the viceroy of Egypt, threatened to rip Syria out of Turkish hands, in close alliance with Louis-Philippe's France, Palmerston landed troops at Beirut and Acre, threatened to cut off the Egyptians, who were advancing against Turkey, and forced Egyptian retreat beyond the Sinai Desert. In the London Conference of 1841, he restored the sultan's authority in Syria, Palestine, and the Sinai, repulsed the French, and closed the Bosphorus and Dardanelles to warships in peacetime. As usual, however, he allowed a small prize even to the losers, awarding the title of hereditary viceroys of Egypt to Mehmet Ali and his heirs.

Making what can only be described as high-handed use of British power, Palmerston did not hesitate to bombard the Greek port of Piraeus in 1850 and to rip Hong Kong from China, all in the name of the right of British merchants and seamen to pursue trade without danger to their persons or property, even if the trade was in opium. Even imperial Great Britain threatened him with censure for going too far with gunboat diplomacy, but Palmerston always managed to rescue himself with an appeal to British pride, comparing anyone who carried a British passport to St. Paul, who could say, *Civis Romanus sum*, or "I am a British subject," and be sure that he could travel where he willed.

Palmerston, like his longtime rival and ultimate partner Lord John Russell, did not hesitate to ignore Queen Victoria's clear constitutional right to be informed of all the details of foreign policy. Whether fearing that she would refuse her assent, or out of simple impetuosity, the great Liberal duet had no hesitation about showing the queen only as much as she might be expected to approve, and writing secret instructions to British envoys abroad on private stationery, bearing no indication of the writer's cabinet office. The fact that Queen Victoria referred to Lords Palmerston and Russell as "those terrible old men" is scarcely surprising.

Most of Palmerston's biographers bemoan the fact that he was not foreign secretary during the disaster known as the Crimean War. At the end of the war, when all that was left was to repair the damage as well as possible, he became prime minister at the age of seventy-one. He held that office for the first time in 1855-1858. His constant preoccupation for the rest of his life was to remain Napoleon III's confidant and collaborator to avert any possibility that Bonapartist adventurism might start anew the wars he remembered clearly from his youth.

Palmerston was an enthusiastic supporter of Italian unification. He was one of the original authors of the intervention in Mexico and was also the first to abandon any military role in that country in 1862, though he did recognize Emperor Maximilian during his short-lived empire.

Palmerston proclaimed his neutrality during the American Civil War, but his every gesture offered moral and material support to the Confederacy. To ardent Northerners such as the historian George Bancroft, Palmerston came to personify British hostility toward the United States.

Palmerston's second and final tenure of the prime ministership, 1859-1865, witnessed British ineffectiveness during the Polish Revolt of 1863 as well as the German-Danish war of 1864. To the end, however, Palmerston was in control of policy; on his deathbed he was engaged in checking, line by line, the text of a new Belgian treaty. He died, two days before his eighty-first birthday, on October 18, 1865.

SIGNIFICANCE

Lord Palmerston remained a man of the eighteenth century whose unconcern for the rigid conventions of Victorian Great Britain never alienated the public. Perhaps, in a perverse sort of way, he charmed a generation of Englishmen who could not imagine behaving privately as he behaved so nonchalantly in public. He was the delight of cartoonists, always the bully prizefighter with his shirt off, ready to knock the crowns off the heads of kings. He was adept at manipulating the press. Throughout his later career, his financial interests in newspapers that carried his "leaked news" and "authentic" copies of state papers was a matter of debate. Above all else, this aristocrat, so hostile to democracy, understood the role of the printing press in exploiting public opinion.

It was his good fortune to live during Great Britain's era of Splendid Isolation, when, safe behind her ocean wall and guarded by the greatest navy in the world, London needed neither allies nor long-term treaties to feel secure. In the springtime of free trade, British goods could undersell competitors, and no foreign products threatened British prosperity. Lord Palmerston dwelt in an age of optimism, fearless of the future.

—Arnold Blumberg

FURTHER READING

Bell, Herbert C. F. *Lord Palmerston*. Hamden, Conn.: Archon Books, 1966. A solid two-volume study, giving a splendid overview of the life of the third Viscount Palmerston.

Blumberg, Arnold. *The Diplomacy of the Mexican Empire, 1863-1867*. Malabar, Fla.: Krieger, 1987. Makes use of British diplomatic correspondence that reveals

Palmerston's original authorship of the London Convention of 1861, authorizing British, French, and Spanish military intervention in Mexico. It traces the British withdrawal of 1862 and the subsequent British diplomatic attitude toward Maximilian's empire.

Brown, David. *Palmerston and the Politics of Foreign Policy, 1846-1855*. New York: Palgrave, 2002. An analysis of the conditions in Great Britain which influenced Palmerston's foreign policy. Describes the impact of Palmerston's foreign policy upon the development of the Liberal Party and how he mobilized public opinion in support of his foreign policy goals.

Case, Lynn M., and Warren F. Spencer. *The United States and France: Civil War Diplomacy*. Philadelphia: University of Pennsylvania Press, 1974. Reveals the close Anglo-French entente maintained by Lords Palmerston and Russell concerning the policy pursued toward the Union and the Confederacy.

Chambers, James. *Palmerston, "The People's Darling."* London: John Murray, 2004. Comprehensive biography tracing Palmerston's life and career, describing the personal and professional characteristics that made him one of the most influential statesmen in British history.

Ingle, Harold N. *Nesselrode and the Russian Rapprochement with Britain, 1836-1844*. Berkeley: University of California Press, 1976. Describes the brief period when Russia made a sincere effort to come to an amicable understanding with Great Britain for a division of the Near Eastern pie.

Southgate, Donald. *"The Most English Minister": The Policies and Politics of Palmerston*. New York: St. Martin's Press, 1966. This readable study brings Palmerston to life and describes the impact of the man on British policy.

Thomas, Daniel H. *The Guarantee of Belgian Independence and Neutrality in European Diplomacy, 1830's-1930's*. Kingston, R.I.: D. H. Thomas, 1983. Palmerston's greatest accomplishment and his lifelong preoccupation were tied in with Belgian independence and neutrality. This massive volume is the best study of the subject.

Victoria, Queen of Great Britain. *Regina v Palmerston: The Correspondence Between Queen Victoria and Her Foreign and Prime Minister, 1837-1865*. Edited by Brian Connell. London: Evans Brothers, 1962. Uses the letters exchanged to trace the gradual deterioration of their personal relationship. Connell allows the correspondents to speak for themselves but intersperses his own comment, making the entire series understandable and entertaining for the amateur historian.

Webster, Sir Charles. *The Foreign Policy of Palmerston, 1830-1841: Britain, the Liberal Movement, and the Eastern Question*. 2 vols. New York: Humanities Press, 1969. This two-volume work deals only with Palmerston's first term as Foreign Secretary. It is, nevertheless, the key to understanding his philosophy on international relations, applicable to his entire career. Making extensive use of unpublished primary sources, including Palmerston's papers, this ambitious study is definitive.

Ziegler, Paul R. *Palmerston*. New York: Palgrave Macmillan, 2003. Biography describing how Palmerston, though an aristocrat, identified with the people of Great Britain and helped usher them into the modern age.

SEE ALSO: George Bancroft; Henry Brougham; Richard Cobden; Fourteenth Earl of Derby; Benjamin Disraeli; George IV; Lin Zexu; Maximilian; Napoleon III; Baron John Russell; Queen Victoria; Duke of Wellington.

RELATED ARTICLES in *Great Events from History: The Nineteenth Century, 1801-1900*: July 29, 1830: July Revolution Deposes Charles X; September, 1839-August 29, 1842: First Opium War; September 12, 1848: Swiss Confederation Is Formed; August 28, 1857: British Parliament Passes the Matrimonial Causes Act; July 26, 1858: Rothschild Is First Jewish Member of British Parliament; August, 1867: British Parliament Passes the Reform Act of 1867; November 17, 1869: Suez Canal Opens.

THEODORE PARKER
American cleric and social reformer

A scholar with a strong social conscience, Parker was an influential Transcendentalist who helped shape American Unitarianism and was a leader in the abolitionist cause during the years leading up to the U.S. Civil War.

BORN: April 24, 1810; Lexington, Massachusetts
DIED: May 10, 1860; Florence, Italy
AREAS OF ACHIEVEMENT: Philosophy, social reform

EARLY LIFE

Theodore Parker was born into a Massachusetts family with a history of patriotic activity, including service at Lexington and Bunker Hill during the American Revolution. Parker grew up on stories about this heritage and often referred to it when he was crusading for the liberty of black Americans. His parents John and Hannah (Segur Stearns) Parker inspired many aspects of his life. The youngest of eleven children, Parker was a bit spoiled by his mother, who often read the Bible to him and who encouraged the development of his strong conscience.

Books were readily available in Parker's home as his father frequently purchased them and had access to a lending library. At school, although he could not attend full-time, Parker quickly showed his scholarly potential but was terrified by the theology of divine retribution found in the primers of that day; it was an interpretation he later rejected totally. The loss of his mother when Parker was thirteen years old left him with more and more work to do at home, and his formal secondary education ended three years later. Parker spent the next seven years teaching school and trying to accumulate enough money in order to attend the Harvard Divinity School.

In 1832, with the help of an uncle, Parker was able to open his own school at Watertown, Massachusetts. The school was quickly successful, so that, while he was still aiding his elderly father, Parker's financial situation improved. At his boardinghouse, he met Lydia Cabot, his future wife. She was the sort of woman he preferred: loving, cooperative, and supportive. Although he was often to work with strong-minded, intellectual women, Parker was never comfortable with them. Parker became friends with the Reverend Convers Francis, who provided books and scholarly guidance. Francis introduced the young Parker to the antislavery movement and to the idealistic philosophy of scholars such as Immanuel Kant and G. W. F. Hegel, which strongly influenced his thought.

He also began to explore modern biblical criticism. In 1834, Francis found a scholarship for him, and Parker sadly left Watertown for the Harvard Divinity School. Over the next two years he earned a degree and a reputation for frugal living, hard study, lightheartedness, and theological radicalism.

LIFE'S WORK

It took Parker a year to get a pulpit after he was graduated. Perhaps he was tainted with Transcendentalism or, as Unitarian ministers often were, perceived as too intellectual. Perhaps his awkward bearing, prematurely balding head, square frame, and large hands hardened by farm work resulted in a poor impression. Whatever the cause, Parker used the time to fill temporarily empty pulpits, to marry Lydia, and to begin his translation of and commentary on W. M. L. De Wette's *Beiträge zur Einleitung in das Alte Testament* (1806; *A Critical and Historical Introduction to the Canonical Scriptures of the Old Testament,* 1843). It was on this book that his scholarly reputation was grounded. Parker was among the first Americans to study and apply the higher biblical criticism that was being developed by German scholars.

In May, 1837, Parker accepted a call from a church in West Roxbury, Massachusetts. Over the next decade, Parker worked on developing his philosophical and theological ideas. He was already in the Transcendentalist school with Ralph Waldo Emerson and Henry David Thoreau, for he was convinced that sensory data confirmed only limited phenomena. The great moral truths, he believed, being self-evidently true, transcended such confirmation. These were known to the human conscience and depended on no outside authority. In May, 1841, he preached a sermon entitled "The Transient and Permanent in Christianity," arguing that all the supernatural trappings of the religion and even Jesus himself might be proven false or nonexistent without weakening the essential truth of Christianity. Each person must find the Kingdom of Heaven within himself, he argued.

Unitarianism, which was still largely a branch of Congregationalism, supposedly rejected creeds, but these ideas that Parker elaborated in subsequent years outraged many. After his 1841 sermon, Parker could find few ministers who were willing to exchange pulpits with him, and the friends who did, including those who did not agree with him, faced congregational protests and even withdrawals. Undaunted, Parker criticized his colleagues freely, and eventually he was asked to resign from the Boston Association of Congregational ministers, a demand that he refused.

Convinced of God's enduring love—eternal damnation was, he believed, impossible, for it would make eternal life a curse—he renounced the religion of guilt and retribution that had tormented his childhood. A good man, a kind man, a just man, a loving man was a Christian regardless of whether he believed the traditional theology of that sect. Reason was a God-given tool, but in religion, as in Transcendentalist philosophy, intuition carried man to greater truths. With this emphasis on the individual's discovery of truth within himself, it should have been impossible for Parker to argue that anyone's beliefs were wrong. However, he often did.

Although becoming controversial among Boston's ministers, Parker was also becoming known as a Transcendentalist philosopher. His articles and reviews appeared in many journals and were a staple of the Transcendentalist organ *The Dial*, which first appeared in 1840. In this same period, Parker's friend George Ripley founded the utopian community Brook Farm. Like Ralph Waldo Emerson, Parker chose not to join. Many who did also joined his West Roxbury congregation, and Parker often visited the farm. This exposure to intellectuals stimulated Parker's thought, which appeared as seven lectures that constituted the book *A Discourse on Matters Pertaining to Religion*, published in 1842. Writing—he had finished the two volumes on De Wette and another volume of collected articles—lecturing, preaching, parish duties, and disputes took their toll, and in September, 1843, he and Lydia left for a year in Europe. He spent this vacation visiting scholars and philosophers whom he admired.

Upon his return from Europe, Parker, more convinced than ever that Transcendentalism was the only feasible form of religion, intended to prove his point. The demands of his congregation and calls for lectures that had to be written quickly always prevented him from doing the scholarly work he wanted. The old controversies were quickly renewed when, in December, 1844, he suggested the possibility that God might send humanity greater Christs in the future. His piety and respect for Jesus were undeniable, yet he was willing neither to limit God's love and power nor to assume that the revelation of one age was adequate for another.

More and more, Parker was heard with respect, and early the next year a Boston group created a church for him. Although sad to leave friends in West Roxbury, Parker was eager to be part of the intellectual ferment of

the city, and the new Twenty-eighth Congregational Society, under his leadership, became the largest parish in Boston and possibly in the United States. Parker made many new friends, including such luminaries as William Lloyd Garrison, Charles Sumner, Julia Ward Howe, and Horace Mann, and became mentor of a few young Unitarian ministers such as Starr King.

In Boston, the childless Parker family was enlarged by the adoption of a young, distant cousin of Lydia. Parker also worked on his beloved library, which was becoming one of the largest private collections in New England, though increasingly during the 1850's lecture fees that had bought books were diverted to support the needs of fugitive slaves. From 1847 to 1850, Parker wrote for and helped edit *The Massachusetts Quarterly Review*, a new Transcendentalist journal. Although never the intellectual force that its founders intended it to be, the *Review* did give Transcendentalists, including Parker, an outlet for their ideas.

During the 1840's, Parker moved into the general social reform movement of the mid-nineteenth century. The cozy, self-satisfied, formulistic rut that even Unitarians had fallen into was not for him. He spoke of the virtues (though against the state imposition) of temperance, the importance of equality for women, the evils and un-

Theodore Parker. (Library of Congress)

christian nature of the Mexican War, and the need for penal reform as well as many other reforms.

Increasingly, however, justice for black Americans came to dominate not only his reform impulse but virtually all of his efforts. In 1845, Parker joined Emerson and Charles Sumner in refusing to speak at the New Bedford Lyceum because black people had been refused membership. He was driven by the memory of his forebears' fight to win liberty from Great Britain to make liberty a reality for all. Although he did not know the peculiar institution at first hand, he recognized its transcendent evil quality just as he recognized the transcendent virtues of Christianity. He amassed a powerful statistical argument that slavery was not economical, but his true power as an abolitionist came from his fervor in invoking the higher law of morality in opposing slavery. Did the Bible accept slavery? he asked, and if the answer was affirmative, he insisted, then the Bible was wrong. On the issue of slavery, as on theological issues, the intuitive truth was not to be denied. Parker would do as he believed Jesus had done: reject statute in favor of what he knew to be right.

Galvanized to greater effort by the Fugitive Slave Law of 1850, Parker became a leader of the Boston Vigilance Committee organized to prevent return of escaped slaves to the South. He called for resistance in the same spirit that the Stamp Act had once been resisted. Men who came for William and Ellen Craft, runaway slaves who were parishioners of Parker, were driven from Boston by abuse and threats. When he married the Crafts, Parker, with an eye for the dramatic gesture, presented to William a Bible for the care of their souls and a sword for the care of his wife's freedom. It would be a sin to hate those who would reenslave them, he told the Crafts, but not to kill in order to preserve their freedom if no other means were available.

Parker's radicalism grew. When Thomas Sims was being taken back to Georgia in 1852, Parker eloquently denounced the "kidnaping" in public and urged the Vigilance Committee to attack the ship on which Sims was confined. The passage of the Kansas-Nebraska Act in 1854 only made matters worse, and Parker, in May of that year, helped organize an abortive raid on the courthouse where the recently arrested fugitive Anthony Burns was held. After Burns was taken away, Parker was indicted along with several others who had supported the raid. Parker was delighted with the idea of presenting his own defense and prepared quite a speech for that purpose. When the indictment was quashed on technical grounds, he had to be satisfied with publishing the defense.

Although he refused to attend a secessionist convention called by radical abolitionists, Parker was increasingly convinced that only war could eliminate slavery, and war was more acceptable to him than slavery. Although saddened by the violence of John Brown's antislavery victories in Kansas, he supported Brown and was a member of the secret Boston Committee of Six that provided moral and financial support for further efforts. He was out of the country at the time of the catastrophic raid on Harpers Ferry but wished he were home to defend the right.

As the 1850's passed, Parker's once-robust health declined, while his activities increased. In addition to his duties as minister of a congregation formally numbering some seven thousand, he continued writing and antislavery activism. He was delivering approximately one hundred lectures each year all over the East and North. In 1856-1857, he was slowed by pleurisy and other respiratory problems to a mere seventy lectures, but after a vacation in the spring of 1858 and an operation for fistula, he seemed on the road to recovery. He was back to work too soon, and although he managed to preach for New Year's Day of 1859, the next Sunday the congregation gathered only to receive a note that because of a serious lung hemorrhage Parker would not be able to come. Parker was suffering from the greatest killer of the nineteenth century: tuberculosis. His congregation sent him overseas in the hope that better climates would help, but as was so often the case before antibiotics, the disease could not be stopped. He died May 10, 1860, in Florence, Italy.

SIGNIFICANCE

Theodore Parker's life reflected much of the American spirit of reform and practicality. As a Transcendentalist, he was part of the first truly American school of philosophy, and his essays have been favorably compared with the work of Emerson. Parker never reached the poetic heights of Emerson, but he was better at clearly and systematically laying out the framework of his thought. He also injected a theme of empirical testing into the intuitive scheme of Transcendentalism. Parker was too good a scholar to accept the miraculous blithely. The less likely an event, the more proof he wanted before he would accept it.

Parker was also an important force in the development of liberal religion. His thought was critical and concrete rather than abstract and metaphysical. He rejected creeds and regarded atheism as impossible, except as the denial of the existence of higher law. Divorcing the essentials of Christianity from all authority but the individual's reason and conscience was clearly a step toward modernity and today's Unitarian-Universalist position that a sincere desire to find spiritual truth is the only requisite for membership.

Parker's reform efforts were also part of the reform tradition that has reappeared periodically throughout American history. His belief that the church should be a driving force in political reform might seem to defy the Jeffersonian tradition of separation of church and state, but Parker did not favor imposition of morality by legislation. The church was to lead by its example and show the society how much better it might be. Parker's reform spirit also had American democratic and egalitarian qualities. Even Abraham Lincoln seems to have learned from him, for Parker used a number of variations of the famous phrase about government of, by, and for the people. At least one example of this was communicated to Lincoln by his law partner, William Herndon, a friend of Parker. As he worked himself to death in the cause of abolitionism, Parker showed many of the finest characteristics of American reformers.

—Fred R. van Hartesveldt

FURTHER READING

Albrecht, Robert C. *Theodore Parker*. Boston: Twayne, 1971. A short but reasonably handled biography.

Chadwick, John W. *Theodore Parker: Preacher and Reformer*. Boston: Houghton Mifflin, 1900. Written by a Unitarian minister who knew and was inspired by Parker, this biography is rather uncritical but is important for its discussion of Parker's role in the development of Unitarianism.

Chesebrough, David B. *Theodore Parker: Orator of Superior Ideas*. Westport, Conn.: Greenwood Press, 1999. Examines Parker's rhetoric and rhetorical techniques and how his oratory affected mid-nineteenth century theology. Includes three of Parker's speeches, with introductions placing them in the proper context.

Collins, Robert E. *Theodore Parker: American Transcendentalist: A Critical Essay and a Collection of His Writings*. Metuchen, N.J.: Scarecrow Press, 1973. After a long interpretive essay by Collins, selections from Parker's writings are included for comparison with works by Emerson on similar subjects. Collins's conclusion that Parker was a more important Transcendentalist than Emerson is an overstatement.

Commager, Henry Steele. *Theodore Parker*. Boston: Little, Brown, 1936. Commager sometimes lets interpretive passages obscure the basic chronological structure of his book. He does a superb job, however, of setting Parker's life and work in context.

Grodzins, Dean. *American Heretic: Theodore Parker and Transcendentalism*. Chapel Hill: University of North Carolina Press, 2002. Focuses on the first phase of Parker's career, when he rose from poverty to become a major Transcendentalist prophet. Explores the religious roots of Transcendentalism and the ideas of Parker and Transcendentalist colleagues Emerson, Margaret Fuller, and Bronson Alcott.

Parker, Theodore. *The Slave Power*. Edited by James K. Hosmer. Boston: American Unitarian Association, 1916. Reprint. New York: Arno Press, 1969. This is a collection of Parker's abolitionist writings and is the most convenient source in which to find the text of his most powerful antislavery orations.

Wilber, Earl M. *A History of Unitarianism*. Boston: Beacon Press, 1977. A standard work on the subject; the section on American Unitarianism is very useful.

SEE ALSO: Henry Brougham; John Brown; Ralph Waldo Emerson; William Lloyd Garrison; Georg Wilhelm Friedrich Hegel; Julia Ward Howe; Samuel Gridley Howe; Abraham Lincoln; Horace Mann; Charles Sumner; Henry David Thoreau.

RELATED ARTICLES in *Great Events from History: The Nineteenth Century, 1801-1900:* 1836: Transcendental Movement Arises in New England; October 16-18, 1859: Brown's Raid on Harpers Ferry.

SIR HENRY PARKES
Australian politician

As premier of the colony of New South Wales through five terms, Parkes successfully promoted immigration to Australia, established public education, and sponsored the movement for federation that would lead to Australia's unification in the early twentieth century.

BORN: May 27, 1815; Stoneleigh, Warwickshire, England
DIED: April 27, 1896; Annandale, Sydney, New South Wales (now in Australia)
AREA OF ACHIEVEMENT: Government and politics

EARLY LIFE

Henry Parkes was the youngest of seven children of Thomas Parks (the spelling of the family name at the time) and his wife Martha. Thomas Parks was a tenant farmer on a property the Parks family had worked for generations, but in 1823 he was forced by accumulated debts to leave, and the entire family went to Birmingham. In the city, all the children had to work, and Henry Parkes, at the age of eight, found employment first as a rope maker and then as a laborer in the brickyards and on the highways, where conditions were harsh and treatment often cruel. He later was able to apprentice himself to a bone and ivory turner.

Although his parents were both uneducated, Henry himself learned to read and write and, at an early age, came to love literature, especially the works of William Shakespeare. Part of his education during this period no doubt included exposure to the extensive political agitation for reform taking place in Birmingham, where impassioned orators addressed mass meetings. Parkes was soon contributing prose and poems to the *Chartist*, and apparently also attended classes at the Mechanic's Institute in Birmingham. Having completed his apprenticeship in 1836, he set up a trade of his own in bone and ivory turning, and was married to Clarinda Varney, the daughter of a well-established businessperson who immediately disinherited her for the inappropriate marriage. Parkes, in his long career, was never successful in business, and his first venture failed within two years. The young couple then left Birmingham and moved to London, perhaps with some intention of emigrating, for after a few dire weeks of poverty, in which Parkes was again unable to establish himself, they announced in December of 1838 their decision to leave for Australia.

Parkes, his wife, and their two children sailed in March, 1839, as assisted immigrants on the *Strathfield-saye*, arriving in Sydney in July of that year, along with a third child born during the voyage. The pastoral boom of the 1830's was in progress and employment was hard to find in the city, so Parkes went up to the Penrith area to work as a laborer on the estate of Sir John Jamison. The difficult and poorly paid work dissatisfied him, and six months later he was in Sydney working first as a salesperson for an ironmonger, then as a hand in a brass foundry, and finally as a tide waiter for the Customs Department.

The latter position lasted three years and enabled Parkes to set his affairs upon a good enough foundation to try his hand again at his own trade. Subsequently, in 1845, he opened a business in ivory and toy manufacturing, and later he even tried branch shops in Maitland and Geelong, though they soon failed. It was during this period that Parkes put together his first volume of verse, entitled *Stolen Moments*, and found a hundred subscribers willing to finance it. The poems are conventional and didactic, but they do reveal the sincere and heartfelt thinking of a sensitive young man.

From the first, however, it was clearly politics that absorbed Parkes's energies; upon his arrival in Australia, he quickly became conversant with the political issues and questions of the day. Gradually, as he became known in Sydney, he became acquainted with leading citizens, and in 1848 he acted as organizing secretary for Robert Lowe's campaign against William Charles Wentworth for the Sydney seat on the Legislative Council. In 1849, Parkes was active in the protest against England's renewal of convict transportation to Australia, becoming a prominent public organizer and speaker. Finally, in 1849, Parkes entered fully into his political career with the founding of a daily newspaper, the *Empire*, a venture backed by a few wealthy friends and encouraged by many others; Parkes was now in a position to command attention and respect.

LIFE'S WORK

Parkes worked diligently and with delight at his journalistic labors on the *Empire* from 1853 to 1858. During that period the Legislative Council drafted and adopted a conservative constitution, under the direction of Wentworth, which heavily favored squatters and landowners at the expense of the middle class and small settlers. The liberals opposed it vigorously and formed a constitution committee of their own, of which Parkes was an important member.

Although the constitution came into operation in 1856, the liberals had organized themselves into an effective political force and were later able to mitigate some of the more regressive features of the new constitution through the passage of the Electoral Act of 1858 and the Land Acts of 1861. Parkes himself was elected to the new parliament's Legislative Assembly in 1856, having previously been a member of the old Legislative Council in 1854. He was thus able to use the *Empire* as an effective vehicle of liberal political opinion.

By 1857, however, Parkes owed more than fifty thousand pounds to the paper's creditors and in 1858 was forced to cease publication of the *Empire*. This latest business failure was a bitter blow to Parkes, for he had invested his time, money, and hopes into the paper, and it led him to consider entering the legal profession at the age of forty-three as a way to secure his economic well-being. Nevertheless, Parkes could not resist politics for long, and between 1858 and 1861 he was alternately in and out of Parliament. Between 1861 and 1863, he was in Great Britain as one of two commissioners sent there by the Legislative Assembly to encourage immigration, his wife, Clarinda, and the children having been left behind in Sydney. During this lecture tour of Great Britain, Parkes met several prominent and influential people, in particular Thomas Carlyle and Richard Cobden, the great advocate of free trade who, Parkes claimed, won him over.

Upon his return to Australia in 1863, Parkes was once again active in politics, and in 1864 he was again elected to Parliament. By this time, Parkes had many supporters and admirers, both for his political views and for his personal qualities of leadership, pious idealism, and sheer energy. He was clearly a politician of promise and had quickly and astutely mastered the skills of the dubious art of manipulative politics. Parkes could be guileful and ruthless, but he was considered effective by all.

In 1866, Parkes obtained his first cabinet position as colonial secretary in the government of James Martin, and during that period Parkes was responsible for the passing of the Public Schools Act of 1866, which enlarged and unified the system of national schools and was generally recognized as a progressive piece of legislation. This act was a major accomplishment for Parkes, and his close identification with the bill (and his subsequent position as president of the Council of Education) accorded him considerable public attention.

Parkes also persuaded Florence Nightingale to send a contingent of trained nurses to Sydney to improve the hospitals in the colony, an achievement of which he was proud. Although Parkes resigned from the government in 1870, having once again gone into bankruptcy, he returned the following year, and finally, in 1872, became premier at the age of fifty-seven. Thus began the ten-year period in which Parkes was premier three times, alternating with his chief rival, John Robertson (with whom he eventually forged a coalition lasting from 1878 to 1883). This was the summit of his political success, and his knighthood in 1877 seemed to confirm it.

Most of Parkes's accomplishments during this time were legislative and social: He helped reorganize the hospitals; he took an interest in the needs of delinquents and orphans and set up institutions for poor children; he continued to extend education reform; he sought to control the liquor trade more closely; he undertook numerous public works programs for roads, water systems, and railways; and he continued to encourage immigration to Australia from Great Britain. Parkes was well liked by the populace: His manner was dignified and his speech suitably platitudinous, his long white beard and white shock of hair gave him a masterful appearance, and his ministerial efforts appeared to be grounded in democratic principles. Parkes's views on matters were not always sharply distinct from those of his opposition—the 1880's and 1890's were a time of broad liberalism and reform, of widespread belief in "progress"—so his success was more often the result of his political skill and temperament than of his articulation of policy choices.

In 1881, Parkes became ill and was advised by his doctors to go abroad, which he did, while remaining premier, and spent eight months traveling in America and Great Britain. The trip turned into a triumphal procession in which he was hailed by politicians and entertained by eminent people on two continents, including several memorable days with Alfred, Lord Tennyson, who appears to have treated him as a fellow poet. Upon his return in late 1882, though, Parkes found that his political situation had eroded and his government was soon defeated.

After a short period serving in the parliament, Parkes once again departed for Great Britain in 1883, in part to find a way to improve his finances, and then returned to Australia in August of 1884. Back in Parliament briefly, he resigned over dissatisfaction with the state of politics, but stood for election again in 1885, when the government's action in sending troops to aid the British in the Sudan conflict angered Parkes. Then, in 1886, at the age of seventy-one, Parkes was once more premier. During the next two years, Parkes made some notable improvements, including the placing of the civil service and the railways under government commissions to avoid the abuses of political patronage. He also virtually banned the immigration of the Chinese, whose great numbers were considered a threat to the wage structure and economy of the country. In doing so, he may have averted serious racial conflicts that could have caused international repercussions.

These successes came at a difficult period for Parkes: Clarinda died in 1888, and his marriage in 1889 to Eleanor Dixon was not acceptable to polite society, or indeed to his own daughters. His financial problems continued: He once again declared bankruptcy in 1887 and assigned his estate to creditors. However, as the grand old man of Australian politics, Parkes was undeterred, and he continued to act with vigor and acumen; after a defeat in 1888 put him out of office, he came back within a few months and, as premier in 1889, formed his fifth and last ministry.

Despite these successes, Parkes's powers of leadership were waning, for the younger generation of politicians was increasingly impatient with his views and his style, and Parkes had some difficulty in maintaining unity among his cabinet ministers. The boldest move Parkes made during this last period in power, and the one for which he is most often remembered, came as a complete surprise to his cabinet and seemed to reassert his capacity to lead. Returning from a trip to Queensland in 1889, he stopped at the town of Tenterfield and delivered a resounding speech advocating, in urgent and eloquent terms, the federation of the then separate Australian colonies. This was by no means a new idea, but Parkes had now thrown his weight behind it and moved rapidly and forcefully to gain his goal.

In 1891, Parkes convened a federal convention in Sydney to draft a constitution. This was achieved, despite considerable difficulties and disagreements, in part because of the resolute efforts of Parkes and the persuasiveness of his impassioned oratory. Attempts were then made to have the new federal constitution ratified by all the colonies. However, Parkes was unable to convince the people of New South Wales that this should be their primary concern, and without what he considered sufficient public support, he delayed in putting the measure before Parliament. In 1891, tired and suffering from the consequences of a serious accident, Parkes resigned from office, and the federation bill was not acted upon until after his death.

For the next three years, Parkes continued to serve in Parliament, but his effectiveness was finished. He retired in 1894, but in 1895 made an ill-advised attempt to unseat his old rival within his own party, George Houston Reid, and after an unusually bitter campaign, in which Parkes attacked his previous allies, the free traders and the federalists, he was defeated. During the campaign, Parkes's second wife died, and, left in penniless circumstances with many children, he married a third time, to a young woman named Julia Lynch. Parkes was soon seriously ill with pneumonia, and on April 27, 1896, he died of a heart attack.

SIGNIFICANCE

Sir Henry Parkes spent almost half a century in public service, from the antitransportation movement during the 1840's to his last years in Parliament during the 1890's. His rise to prominence and power from humble beginnings is a testimony to the possibilities inherent in a democracy such as Australia's. His accomplishments were of a sort that may seem unglamorous and pedestrian, but they were instrumental in providing New South Wales (and later the whole of Australia) with the firm foundations of a responsive and responsible government. Matters of public education and welfare, of public amenities and works, are of the fabric of social cohesiveness, and Parkes labored to that end.

Not only was Parkes a politician in the sense of a man concerned with policy, but also he was one who understood the nature of party politics; as a leader he knew how to manipulate the machinery of government to his own advantage, and in a number of instances he revealed a certain pettiness and vindictiveness of character that suggests more the ruthless politician than the dignified statesman. Parkes saw himself as a man of the people, and often as the man of the hour, and this belief made him self-confident, though it also blinded him to his own worst defects and motives. The people may have laughed at his posturing and self-importance, at his chronic economic incompetence, but they were seldom scornful of Parkes. They accepted his foibles because they saw him as someone who had their interests at heart, and Parkes did much to repay that confidence.

Parkes is perhaps best remembered for his earliest accomplishment, the Education Act of 1866, and for his last accomplishment, the National Australian Convention for federation in 1891. The twenty-five years spanning these contributions were important years for the young colony, and Parkes did much to assist its growth and maturation. Although he did not live to see the advent of a federated Australia in 1901, he was surely a founder of the new nation.

—Paul Kane

FURTHER READING

Bavin, Sir Thomas. *Sir Henry Parkes: His Life and Work.* Sydney: Angus and Robertson, 1941. This volume contains the John Murtagh Macrossan lectures given by Sir Thomas Bavin in 1940. It is a useful work, providing a generous and judicious overview of Parkes's career and his significant contributions to Australia. Bavin makes good use of contemporary accounts and draws upon Parkes's own autobiography (see below).

Lyne, Charles E. *Life of Sir Henry Parkes.* Sydney: Angus and Robertson, 1896. This is a very early biography of Parkes and contains some interesting anecdotal information.

Martin, A. W. *Henry Parkes.* Melbourne, Vic.: Oxford University Press, 1964. This small booklet is a fine introduction to Parkes. Martin gives a balanced account and, in a short space, is able to draw a sympathetic and incisive portrait of the man. Some well-chosen illustrations accompany the text.

Palmer, Vance. *National Portraits.* Melbourne, Vic.: Melbourne University Press, 1960. This is a well-known collection of twenty-five brief lives of representative Australians. The chapter on Parkes, subtitled "The Politician," places his achievement within the context of the emerging nation. Stylishly written.

Parkes, Henry. *Fifty Years in the Making of Australian History.* London: Longmans, Green, 1892. Written near the end of his life, this autobiography begins with Parkes's arrival in Australia in 1839 and ends with the federation controversy of 1892. It is very much an apologia but, despite its tendentiousness, gives an excellent picture of the period.

Tennyson, Charles, and Hope Dyson. *Tennyson, Lincolnshire, and Australia.* Lincoln, England: The Lincolnshire Association and the Tennyson Society, 1974. This is a curious work, drawing upon the association of Parkes with the poet Tennyson. Contains some of their private correspondence.

Travers, Robert. *The Grand Old Man of Australian Politics: The Life and Times of Sir Henry Parkes.* Kenthurst, N.S.W.: Kangaroo Press, 1992. Comprehensive biography, describing Parkes's crucial role in the creation of an Australian federation.

SEE ALSO: Sir Edmund Barton; Thomas Carlyle; Richard Cobden; Alfred Deakin; Florence Nightingale.

RELATED ARTICLE in *Great Events from History: The Nineteenth Century, 1801-1900:* 1868: Last Convicts Land in Western Australia.

FRANCIS PARKMAN
American historian

The greatest of the nineteenth century American patrician historians, Parkman combined extensive research with an unparalleled literary artistry that continues to excite the imagination of modern readers. For many years, his seven-part series France and England in North America *was regarded as the definitive history of the three-sided struggle among the Indians, French, and English for dominion over the continent.*

BORN: September 16, 1823; Boston, Massachusetts
DIED: November 8, 1893; Jamaica Plain, Massachusetts
AREA OF ACHIEVEMENT: Historiography

EARLY LIFE

Francis Parkman was the son of Francis and Caroline (Hall) Parkman. His paternal grandfather had been one of Boston's wealthiest merchants. His father was pastor of the Old North Church and a pillar of Boston's Federalist-Unitarian establishment. On his mother's side, he traced his ancestry to the Puritan John Cotton. Because of his fragile health, Parkman was sent at the age of eight to live on his maternal grandfather's farm and attended school in nearby Medford.

Parkman returned to Boston at the age of thirteen, finished his preparatory work at the Chauncey Place School, and entered Harvard in 1840. He had acquired from his roamings on a stretch of untamed woodland at the edge of his grandfather's farm a romantic attachment to nature in the wild. His reading of the novels of James Fenimore Cooper sparked his interest in Indians, "the American forest," and the "Old French War." He was temperamentally a compulsively intense personality, driven by "passion" and "tenacious eagerness." During his sophomore year at Harvard, he appears to have decided upon what became his life's work: to write the dual story of the conquest of the Indians by the French and English and their struggle in turn for mastery. "The theme," he later recalled, "fascinated me, and I was haunted by wilderness images day and night."

At Harvard, Parkman was active in student extracurricular affairs, serving as president of the Hasty Pudding Club. He received sufficiently respectable grades in his course work for selection to Phi Beta Kappa. He spent his summer vacations tramping and canoeing in the forests of northern New England and the adjacent parts of Canada. Parkman hoped—in vain, as events turned out—that a strenuous regimen of outdoor living would strengthen his sickness-prone physique. He simultaneously took the opportunity to begin collecting material for his planned history project, filling his notebook with measurements of forts, descriptions of battle sites, reminiscences of survivors, and names and addresses of people in possession of old letters.

In the autumn of 1843, Parkman suffered a nervous illness and temporarily left Harvard for a tour of Europe to recuperate. He returned in time to be graduated with his class in August, 1844. At his father's behest, he went on to law school at Harvard. Although profiting from his exposure to the rules for the testing and use of evidence, he could not muster much enthusiasm for the law as such. His interests were primarily literary. His first appearance in print came in 1845, when he published in the *Knickerbocker Magazine* five sketches based upon his vacation trips. Although he was awarded his LL.B. in January, 1846, he never applied for admission to the bar.

After receiving his law degree, Parkman set out on what proved to be the formative experience of his life—a trip to the Western plains, partly in the hope of improving his health, partly to observe at firsthand Indian life. Camping for several weeks with a band of Lakota (Sioux), he immersed himself in their habits, customs, and ways of thinking. During those weeks he contracted a mysterious ailment that left him a broken man physically on his return to Boston in October, 1846.

Parkman's eyesight was so impaired that he could barely read, and he suffered from a nervous condition that made him unable to concentrate for longer than brief spurts. He still managed to dictate to a cousin who had accompanied him an account of their adventures that was serialized as "The Oregon Trail" in the *Knickerbocker Magazine* over a two-year span beginning in February, 1847. The account came out in book form in 1849 under the title *The California and Oregon Trail* (the shorter title was resumed with the 1872 edition). Parkman's experience with the Lakota shattered any illusions he may

Francis Parkman. (Library of Congress)

have gained from reading novels about the noble savage. "For the most part," he underlined,

> a civilized white man can discover very few points of sympathy between his own nature and that of an Indian. With every disposition to do justice to their good qualities, he must be conscious that an impassable gulf lies between him and his red brethren. Nay, so alien to himself do they appear, that, after breathing the air of the prairie for a few months or weeks, he begins to look upon them as a troublesome and dangerous species of wild beast.

LIFE'S WORK

In 1848, Parkman began work on what became *History of the Conspiracy of Pontiac and the Indian War After the Conquest of Canada* (1851). He had a frame built of parallel wires to guide his hand while writing with his eyes closed in a dark room. For the most part, however, he relied upon others reading the source materials to him and transcribing his words. At first, his progress was painfully slow—the readings limited to a half-hour per sitting and his output averaging six lines a day. Gradually, however, he pushed himself to work for longer periods and successfully completed the two volumes within two and a half years.

Parkman's new work dealt with the Indian uprising in 1763-1765 against English occupation of the Western territories after the French surrender. His purpose, he explained, was "to portray the American forest and the American Indian at the period when both received their final doom." He divided his story into two distinct phases. During the first, the Indians triumphantly pushed the English back; in the second, the English turned the tide in a successful counterattack. Parkman's portrayal of Pontiac as the central figure on the Indian side was effective drama but inaccurate history. Later scholars have found that Pontiac was simply one Indian chief among many. The work's larger importance lies in how Parkman, in his introductory background chapters, sketched in outline the theme that he would develop more fully in his seven-part *France and England in North America* (1865-1892): the collision of rival cultures culminating in the English triumph on the Plains of Abraham in September, 1759.

History of the Conspiracy of Pontiac and the Indian War After the Conquest of Canada appeared in 1851. The first installment of *France and England in North America*, titled *Pioneers of France in the New World*, did not come out until 1865. The delay was partly a result of the amount of research involved. The major difficulty, however, was health problems and family tragedies that would have broken the spirit of a weaker personality.

On May 13, 1850, Parkman married Catherine Scollay Bigelow, the daughter of a Boston doctor. The couple had one son and two daughters. In 1853, however, he suffered a relapse in his nervous condition that forced him to give up his historical work temporarily. A man who always needed an interest, Parkman, during his enforced withdrawal from scholarship, wrote his only novel, *Vassall Morton* (1856). Its hero, reflecting Parkman's own image of himself, is a high-spirited, outdoors-loving young man of high social position who succeeds in overcoming melodramatic trials and tribulations.

Parkman himself was unable to cope with his own personal crises at that time. The death of his son in 1857, followed by that of his wife within a year, precipitated a severe breakdown in 1858. Although these health problems kept him out of the

fighting, the Civil War had a major influence on his approach to the rivalry between the French and the English in the seventeenth and eighteenth centuries as a struggle, akin to the one under way in his own time, between "Liberty and Absolutism."

Pioneers of France in the New World focuses on the founding of Quebec during the early seventeenth century under the leadership of Samuel de Champlain. The next volume in the series, *The Jesuits in North America in the Seventeenth Century* (1867), had as its major protagonists the Jesuit missionaries, such as Jean de Brébeuf, Charles Garnier, and Isaac Jogues, who tried to convert the Canadian Indians to Roman Catholicism. The third volume, which appeared in 1869 as *The Discovery of the Great West*, traces the explorations of Robert La Salle in the area of the Great Lakes and then down the Mississippi River and across what is now Texas and Arkansas during the 1670's and 1680's.

Parkman's next two titles, *The Old Régime in Canada* (1874) and *Count Frontenac and New France Under Louis XIV* (1877), chronicle the political, social, and military history of New France during the last half of the seventeenth century. Their major theme is the corruption that came to pervade, and undermine, French colonial society despite the valiant, but unsuccessful, bid by Louis de Buade Frontenac to reverse the decay. Fearful lest he die before reaching the climax of his story, Parkman jumped ahead in the two volumes of *Montcalm and Wolfe* (1884) to deal with the final phase of the French-English struggle starting during the early 1750's and culminating in the surrender of Canada in 1763. In 1892, he filled in the gap with the two-volume *A Half-Century of Conflict*, in which he dealt with the fifty years of intermittent conflict from Frontenac's death in 1698 to the beginning of the French and Indian War during the 1750's.

PARKMAN'S NONFICTION WORKS	
1849	*The California and Oregon Trail*
1851	*History of the Conspiracy of Pontiac and the Indian War After the Conquest of Canada*
1865	*Pioneers of France in the New World*
1867	*The Jesuits in North America in the Seventeenth Century*
1869	*The Discovery of the Great West* (revised as *La Salle and the Discovery of the Great West*, 1879)
1874	*The Old Regime in Canada*
1877	*Count Frontenac and New France Under Louis XIV*
1884	*Montcalm and Wolfe*
1892	*A Half-Century of Conflict*

The work rested upon painstaking research in primary sources. Parkman even boasted that the "statements of secondary writers have been accepted only when found to conform to the evidence of contemporaries, whose writings have been sifted and collated with the greatest care." He relied primarily upon the massive compilations of documents that had been published during the "documania" that had swept the United States in the aftermath of the War of 1812. At the same time, Parkman spent freely from the money he inherited from his father to purchase documents and have copies made of archival materials in this country and abroad. When formerly inaccessible La Salle documents became available, he rewrote *The Discovery of the Great West* to incorporate the new information. The revised version appeared in 1879 with the new title *La Salle and the Discovery of the Great West*.

Parkman never succumbed to the illusion of late nineteenth century scientific history that the facts spoke for themselves. "Faithfulness to the truth of history," he emphasized,

> involves far more than a research, however patient and scrupulous, into special facts. Such facts may be detailed with the most minute exactness, and yet the narrative, taken as a whole, may be unmeaning or untrue. The narrator must seek to imbue himself with the life and spirit of the time. He must study events in their bearings near and remote; in the character, habits, and manners of those who took part in them. He must himself be, as it were, a sharer or a spectator of the action he describes.

In pursuit of that goal, Parkman personally visited the sites about which he wrote. One of his major strengths was his feeling for the physical setting in which his story unfolded. His early writings occasionally suffered from labored prose and excessive detail. As time went on, however, his descriptions became terser, his imagery sharper. Parkman saw heroic leaders as the primary shapers of history. His own special forte was the delineation of personality. His technique was to build up a composite portrait by drawing upon his protagonist's own words and the accounts by contemporaries before assaying the individual himself. His appraisal of Frontenac strikingly illustrates his mastery of character portrayal.

> What perhaps may be least forgiven him is the barbarity of the warfare that he waged, and the cruelties that he permitted. He had seen too many towns sacked to be much subject to the scruples of modern humanitarianism; yet he was no whit more ruthless than his times and

his surroundings, and some of his contemporaries find fault with him for not allowing more Indian captives to be tortured. Many surpassed him in cruelty, none equalled him in capacity and vigor. When civilized enemies were once within his power, he treated them, according to their degree, with a chivalrous courtesy, or a gentle kindness. If he was a hot and pertinacious foe, he was also a fast friend; and he excited love and hatred in about equal measure. His attitude toward public enemies was always proud and peremptory, yet his courage was guided by so clear a sagacity that he never was forced to recede from the position he had taken.

Notwithstanding such attempts at evenhandedness when dealing with individuals, Parkman shared the prejudices of his time and class. He was a vocal opponent of woman suffrage; his comments on what he called "the mazes of feminine psychology" were almost uniformly unflattering. No democrat, he made no secret of his contempt for society's lower orders. He dismissed the hardworking German farmers of Pennsylvania as "a swarm of . . . peasants . . . who for the most part were dull and ignorant boors." He was no more enamored of the poorer whites of colonial Virginia, considering them "of low origin," "vicious," and "as untaught as the warmest friend of popular ignorance could wish."

Parkman saw universal manhood suffrage as "the source of all the dangers which threaten the United States"; he pictured the immigrants of his own time as "barbarians . . . masses of imported ignorance and hereditary ineptitude." He was a social Darwinist before the publication of *On the Origin of Species by Means of Natural Selection* (1859). When describing in *The Oregon Trail* the "cannibal warfare" he witnessed among fishes in a pond, he ridiculed the dreams by softhearted philanthropists of a peaceful millennium. From minnows to men, he philosophized, life was incessant conflict, and he had no doubt that the outcome of the struggle for North America among the Indians, French, and English accorded with the "law of the survival of the fittest."

A thoroughgoing ethnocentrism marred Parkman's historical outlook. He pictured the Indians as barbarous savages: treacherous, deceitful, "a murder-loving race" filled with "insensate fury" and animated by "homicidal frenzy." "The Indians," he wrote in a typical descriptive passage, "howled like wolves, yelled like enraged cougars." Their white opponents "were much like the hunters of wolves, catamounts, and other dangerous beasts, except that the chase of this fierce and wily human game demanded far more hardihood and skill." As he put the matter bluntly in an 1886 public letter that dealt with contemporary white-Indian relations, "a few hordes of savages cannot be permitted to hold in perpetual barbarism the land which might sustain a hundred millions of civilized men."

Despite Parkman's admiration for some individual Frenchmen, they were an inferior breed compared to Anglo-Saxons. "The Germanic race, and especially the Anglo-Saxon branch of it," he wrote in his conclusion to *The Old Régime in Canada*,

> is peculiarly masculine, and, therefore, peculiarly fitted for self-government. It submits its action habitually to the guidance of reason. . . . The French Celt is cast in a different mould . . . he is impatient of delay, is impelled always to extremes, and does not readily sacrifice a present inclination to an ultimate good.

The fact that the English won and the French lost was no accident.

> The cause lies chiefly in the vast advantage drawn by England from the historical training of her people in habits of reflection, forecast, industry, and self-reliance,—a training which enabled them to adopt and maintain an invigorating system of self-rule, totally inapplicable to their rivals.

Despite the almost constant pain he suffered, Parkman did not surrender to invalidism. He had a wide circle of friends and carried on an extensive correspondence. He had an excellent sense of humor, and his writings are dotted with sharp quips. He never lost his love for the outdoors and continued his camping trips as much as his health permitted. He took up flower-growing as a hobby during the 1850's, when incapacitated from pursuing his scholarly work, and grew so fascinated that the study of horticulture became a passion second only to history. His major achievement in this line was his development of a hybrid crimson lily named *Lilium Parkmanni* in his honor. His specialty, however, was roses, and his *The Book of Roses* (1866) was regarded for many years as the best guide to their cultivation.

Parkman served as a member of the Harvard Overseers (1868-1871 and 1874-1876) and as a fellow of the corporation (1875-1888), he was one of the founders of the Archeological Institute of America in 1879, and he played a leading role in the establishment of the American School of Classical Studies in Athens, Greece. Shortly after finishing *A Half-Century of Conflict*, he suffered an attack of pleurisy that proved almost fatal.

He died November 8, 1893, of peritonitis at his home in Jamaica Plain (now part of Boston).

SIGNIFICANCE

Commentators have differed about Parkman's place in American historiography. There are those who put him with the literary historians of the romantic school such as John L. Motley, William Hickling Prescott, and George Bancroft. Others see him as a forerunner of the late nineteenth century scientific historians. In a sense, both views are correct: Parkman had a foot in both camps. He attracted an immense readership during his lifetime. His friend Henry Adams summed up the predominant contemporary appraisal when he rated Parkman "in the front rank of living English historians."

At the same time, Parkman enjoyed a higher reputation among professional academic historians than any other of his fellow amateurs except possibly Adams himself. Those who dealt with the same period did not simply follow Parkman's chronological framework but also relied heavily upon his work for information. One scholar went so far as to state that "Parkman never makes a mistake, certainly never a glaring one." Even Vernon Louis Parrington in his *Main Currents in American Thought* (1927-1930) acknowledged that the "Brahmin mind has contributed to American letters no more brilliant work." As late as 1953, the account in the standard *Literary History of the United States* (1948) concluded that "Parkman's whole method may be accurately summarized as an attempt to bring back the past just as it was."

During the late twentieth century, Parkman's reputation suffered an eclipse. Judged by modern standards, he had major shortcomings as a historian. The French-English rivalry in the New World was only a minor aspect of the worldwide struggle under way between those powers, but Parkman largely failed to explore the dynamics of that broader conflict. Even as regards its North American phase, Parkman's episodic, narrative approach focusing upon heroic personalities runs counter to the prevailing tendency to emphasize the role of larger social, economic, and cultural forces.

The heaviest attack on Parkman has come from ethnographers over his treatment of the Indians; he has even been accused of deliberately distorting evidence to put the Indians in the worst possible light. Such criticisms miss the point. As Frederick Jackson Turner rightly observed, Parkman was "the greatest painter of historical pictures that this country—perhaps it is not too much to say, that any country—has produced." The chorus of praise greeting the 1983 republication of *France and England in North America* in the Library of America series attests Parkman's "extraordinary power" as a literary artist. Notwithstanding its limitations, Parkman's history constitutes what a reviewer of the new edition aptly called "our great national epic."

—*John Braeman*

FURTHER READING

Doughty, Howard. *Francis Parkman*. New York: Macmillan, 1962. Although biographical in format, this work is primarily an appraisal of Parkman's writings, focusing upon their literary and artistic qualities from the point of view of a layman rather than a professional historian.

Gale, Robert L. *Francis Parkman*. New York: Twayne, 1973. A rather pedestrian biographical survey followed by volume-by-volume summaries of the major works.

Jacobs, Wilbur R. *Francis Parkman, Historian as Hero: The Formative Years*. Austin: University of Texas Press, 1991. An analysis of Parkman's historiography, questioning if his work was truth or fiction, objective or colored by Parkman's conservative Brahmin values.

Jennings, Francis. "Francis Parkman: A Brahmin Among Untouchables." *William and Mary Quarterly* 42 (July, 1985): 305-328. An important attempt to debunk Parkman's reputation for accuracy and impartiality by exposing his racism and his distortion of the evidence in order to place the Indians in the worst possible light.

Pease, Otis A. *Parkman's History: The Historian as Literary Artist*. New Haven, Conn.: Yale University Press, 1953. A brief but perceptive analysis of "the preconceptions and interests" shaping Parkman's historical approach.

Van Tassel, David D. *Recording America's Past: An Interpretation of the Development of Historical Studies in America, 1607-1884*. Chicago: University of Chicago Press, 1960. Places Parkman in the context of the development of historical scholarship in the United States.

Vitzthum, Richard C. *The American Compromise: Theme and Method in the Histories of Bancroft, Parkman, and Adams*. Norman: University of Oklahoma Press, 1974. Primarily an exercise in "literary criticism" based upon detailed textual explication.

Wade, Mason. *Francis Parkman: Heroic Historian*. New York: Viking Press, 1942. The fullest and most detailed biography, based upon thorough research of Parkman's correspondence, journals, and notes. The work is marred only by the author's tendency toward hagiography.

SEE ALSO: Henry Adams; George Bancroft; James Fenimore Cooper; William Hickling Prescott.

RELATED ARTICLE in *Great Events from History: The Nineteenth Century, 1801-1900:* 1824: Ranke Develops Systematic History.

CHARLES STEWART PARNELL
Irish politician

One of the leading figures in Irish nationalist history, Parnell fused disparate peoples and organizations into a cohesive Irish Nationalist party for the purpose of achieving home rule for Ireland.

BORN: June 27, 1846; Avondale, County Wicklow, Ireland
DIED: October 6, 1891; Brighton, Sussex, England
AREA OF ACHIEVEMENT: Government and politics

EARLY LIFE

Charles Stewart Parnell was born on the Parnell family estate, the eighth child of John Henry and Delia Stewart Parnell. His father's family was Anglo-Irish, while his mother was of American ancestry, although not much should be made of this fact. His heritage was Protestant, but he was to become more of an unbeliever than a believer. Parnell was hardly serious about his education, even during his three and a half years at Cambridge. When he left Cambridge, he returned to Avondale, which he had inherited on his father's death in 1859.

Parnell was a tall, athletic-looking man. He wore a beard and a mustache, but contemporaries regarded his eyes, which were a reddish-brown, as his most distinctive feature. He possessed an iron will, but was mild and gentle in personal intercourse. A brother described him as having a "courteous but frigid exterior," and claimed that he became even more reserved as he matured. Parnell also had a nervous temperament.

LIFE'S WORK

Parnell was first returned to the House of Commons in April, 1875, as a member for Meath. He entered Parliament as a proponent of home rule for Ireland, and it was as a member of Parliament that he was to make his name, although his maiden speech was uneventful except for the assertion that Ireland was a nation, not a geographical fragment of England. He was early recognized as one of the more advanced "home rulers" and became a supporter of Joseph Biggar's policy of obstructing English legislation as a way to pressure England into making concessions to Ireland. The most blatant use of this procedure occurred on July 31 and August 1, 1877, when the House was kept in session continuously for forty-five hours as seven Irishmen, including Parnell, thwarted the wishes of three hundred Englishmen.

By 1879, Parnell was becoming the leader of the nationalist movement. He was president of the Home Rule Confederation of Great Britain and of the recently

Charles Stewart Parnell. (Library of Congress)

formed Irish National Land League but had not been chosen as Isaac Butt's successor as leader of the Irish parliamentary party after Butt's death. That honor had gone to an avowed moderate, William Shaw, although his tenure was short-lived. After the general election of 1880, which saw Parnell begin to assert his authority over the party and to emerge from the election with twenty-four supporters out of sixty-three home rulers, Parnell was elected as chairman of the parliamentary party. One of his supporters for the leadership was William Henry O'Shea, and it was not long before Parnell was addressing O'Shea's wife, Katherine, as "My dearest love." This was an association that was to have momentous consequences.

Bringing together Irishmen of different persuasions was Parnell's great accomplishment. From 1879 to 1885, he devoted his energies in and out of Parliament to promoting the national cause. In Parliament, he could be cooperative, as he was in enacting the Third Reform Bill, or he could be intransigent, as he and his supporters were in using the tactic of obstruction.

Out of Parliament, Parnell was occupied with the development of tactics that would demonstrate to the Irish people that he was the leader who could deliver concessions that were desired by both the extremists and the constitutionalists. He thus flirted with the Land League for a time and partially initiated and then supported the practice of making social lepers out of those Irishmen who dared to lease a property from which an Irish tenant had been evicted, a practice that became known as boycotting. His association with the extremists resulted in his being imprisoned in Kilmainham jail from October 13, 1881, to May 2, 1882. This period of imprisonment only solidified Parnell's hold on Ireland. By August, 1885, John O'Leary, the Fenian leader and editor of the *Irish People*, was remarking that

> Mr. Parnell is the undoubted choice of the Irish people just now, and as long as that is so, and clearly so, I think it is the duty of all Irishmen, even Irishmen of my way of thinking, to take heed that they throw no obstacle in the way of his carrying out the mandate with which he has been intrusted.

Parnell's career was fast approaching its climax. He saw that climax as the grant of self-government to Ireland. To that end, he proceeded to prepare for the general election of 1885 under the newly enlarged franchise of the reforms of 1884-1885. What he wanted to emerge from the election was a highly disciplined party of eighty or more members in the House of Commons that would hold the balance of power between the two English parties and would thereby be in a position to play one off against the other to see which would make the most concessions for Irish support. The elections produced the desired results.

Parnell secured the election of eighty-six home rulers, a clear demonstration that he was the acknowledged leader of Ireland, and even of Ulster, for his party had secured a majority of one in that province. All home rulers had taken the pledge that they would vote as instructed by the leaders of the party. Furthermore, neither English party had emerged with a majority over its opponent and the Irish combined. Parnell could, therefore, keep either party in or out of power as he chose. He was, even more so than when Timothy M. Healy applied the term to him in 1880, "the uncrowned king of Ireland," a title that was to cling to his name to his death and beyond.

Although circumstances looked promising for Parnell and the Irish, reality was to prove otherwise. The Conservatives concluded that there was no future for them in making concessions to Ireland, and the Liberals were not united in support of concessions. William Ewart Gladstone led those Liberals who were willing to concede home rule, but Joseph Chamberlain, leader of the Radical section, and Lord Hartington (Spencer Compton Cavendish, later eighth duke of Devonshire), leader of the Whig section, were to split from the Liberal Party. Gladstone's Home Rule Bill was, therefore, defeated; ninety-three Liberals voted with the Conservatives against it. When a dissolution revealed that the country was even more anti-home rule than Parliament had been, the Conservatives were to come into office and remain in office, except for three years, for a twenty-year period. By the time the Liberals returned to office in 1892, Parnell was dead.

In the intervening years, Parnell's fortunes were to decline, rise to unprecedented heights, and then fall precipitously. Parnell and his party remained associated with the Liberals with the hope that once the Liberals were returned to office a new Home Rule Bill would be introduced and this time it would pass. Even before the First Home Rule Bill was introduced, however, Parnell's enemies were plotting his downfall. Their plan was to link him with criminal activities in Ireland, and they found a willing and naïve accomplice in the *Times*. A series of forged letters were sold to that paper and were printed in 1887 under the heading of "Parnellism and Crime," linking Parnell to the so-called Phoenix

Park murders, the murder of the newly appointed chief secretary and the undersecretary in Phoenix Park in 1882.

The publication of the series coincided with the debate in Parliament on a new coercion bill. The timing of publication, along with the fact that the letters had been previously submitted to a distinguished lawyer, who was skeptical of their authenticity and who advised the *Times* against publication, has led some to speculate that the *Times* and the government were working together to discredit Parnell and Irish nationalism, thereby enabling the government to enact stringent coercive measures against Irish nationalists. Whatever the truth may be, Parnell's response to the accusations was one of outward indifference. In Parliament, he denied that he had written the letters, but he took no further immediate action. Parnell's inaction was partly a result of ill health. For some time he had been suffering from illness, about which the details are unknown, but which may have been Bright's disease.

When Parnell did take action, he asked for the appointment of a select committee to investigate the charges against him. The government refused a select committee but did enact legislation for the appointment of a special commission to investigate not only the charge that Parnell was implicated in the Phoenix Park murders but also the activities of the Land League, with which Parnell was no longer on the best of terms. In other words, the question of whether Parnell had written the letters that implicated him in the Phoenix Park murders was to be only a minor part of the investigation.

The government had apparently become aware that the letters were suspect, and they did not want Parnell and Ireland to be regarded as injured parties when it was proven that Parnell had not written the letters attributed to him. Rather, the English government wanted to continue to rule Ireland with a strong hand under the new coercion law that had been enacted. The special commission legislation was passed, and the three judges conducted their investigation. The letters were proven to be forgeries, and the forger was revealed. The special commission also investigated the Land League, however, and when their report was debated in the Commons, government spokespersons and supporters dwelt upon the activities of the Land League rather than upon the fact that Parnell had been vindicated.

Parnell's vindication came in 1889, but almost immediately he had a new problem. Captain O'Shea sued his wife for divorce and named Parnell as corespondent. The divorce case ruined Parnell's political career and was partially responsible for his death. O'Shea secured his divorce and Parnell then married Katherine, but his party removed him as leader and the Roman Catholic Church would no longer support him. With a segment of the party remaining loyal to him, he believed that he could recoup his position by demonstrating that he retained the support of the Irish people. Consequently he ran in by-elections, but this effort was too much of a strain for his already weakened constitution. He died in his wife's arms on October 6, 1891.

SIGNIFICANCE

Charles Stewart Parnell was a remarkable man. A landowner and a Protestant, he became the leader of tenant farmers and Catholics in a nationalist movement that came close to achieving self-government for Ireland. He was also remarkable in that he was able to moderate between the constitutionalists and the extremists and to persuade them to cooperate in a common objective. The fact that he almost succeeded is a testimony to his ability, vision, and firmness of will. No other Irish leader, except perhaps Eamon de Valera, has since held such influence over the Irish people.

—*Albert A. Hayden*

FURTHER READING

Abels, Jules. *The Parnell Tragedy*. New York: Macmillan, 1966. A popular account of the life of Parnell. The reader must use caution in separating fact from speculation.

Callanan, Frank. *The Parnell Split, 1890-1891*. Syracuse, N.Y.: Syracuse University Press, 1992. Chronicles the events that occurred after Parnell was named as corespondent in Kitty O'Shea's divorce suit. Callanan describes how the reactionary views of Timothy H. Healy, a critic of Parnell, played an important role in Parnell's downfall.

Foster, R. F. *Charles Stewart Parnell: The Man and His Family*. Atlantic Highlands, N.J.: Humanities Press,

1976. This is a supplement to the Lyons's biography that deals more with the personal side of Parnell's life.

Kee, Robert. *The Laurel and the Ivy: The Story of Charles Robert Parnell and Irish Nationalism*. New York: Penguin Books, 1993. Exhaustive biography, tracing Parnell's political career and analyzing his impact on Irish nationalism and British politics.

Larkin, Emmett. *The Roman Catholic Church in Ireland and the Fall of Parnell, 1888-1891*. Chapel Hill: University of North Carolina Press, 1979. This is a volume in Larkin's history of the Roman Catholic Church in Ireland and is especially useful for understanding Parnell's relations with the Church.

Lyons, F. S. L. *Charles Stewart Parnell*. London: William Collins, 1977. The best biography of Parnell by one of the best of Irish historians. A thoroughly scholarly work.

_____. *The Fall of Parnell*. Toronto: University of Toronto Press, 1960. The best discussion of the divorce case and all its implications.

_____. *Ireland Since the Famine*. New York: Charles Scribner's Sons, 1971. A good general history of Ireland for the period of Parnell's life.

O'Brien, R. Barry. *Life of Charles Stewart Parnell*. 2 vols. New York: Harper and Bros., 1898. Reprint. New York: Greenwood Press, 1969. A chronological biography of Parnell by one of his contemporaries. Originally published in 1898.

SEE ALSO: Joseph Chamberlain; Fourteenth Earl of Derby; William Edward Forster; William Ewart Gladstone.

RELATED ARTICLES in *Great Events from History: The Nineteenth Century, 1801-1900:* September-November, 1880: Irish Tenant Farmers Stage First "Boycott"; December 6, 1884: British Parliament Passes the Franchise Act of 1884; June, 1886-September 9, 1893: Irish Home Rule Debate Dominates British Politics.

LOUIS PASTEUR
French bacteriologist

Through his pioneering work in crystallography, Pasteur established the discipline of stereochemistry (left-handedness and right-handedness in organic structures). He spent the bulk of his career founding modern microbiology and making exciting discoveries in immunology and bacteriology—a field that he virtually created.

BORN: December 27, 1822; Dôle, Jura, France
DIED: September 28, 1895; Villenueve-l'Étang, near Saint Cloud, France
AREAS OF ACHIEVEMENT: Chemistry, science and technology

EARLY LIFE

Louis Pasteur (PAHS-tewr) grew up in Arbois, a small town near the town of his birth. There, his father, Jean-Joseph, a veteran of Napoleon I's army, operated a tannery. His mother, Jeanne-Étiennette Roqui, was a gardener's daughter. The best portraits of his parents were done in pastels by young Louis himself, who was an excellent artist. He, like them, was of medium height and dark-haired with a high forehead. His nearsightedness was said to have enhanced his ability to see small details close up. In his maturity, he wore the beard and mustache of most males of his time.

Louis was a late bloomer, and his grades in school were only slightly above average. He attended the Collège d'Arbois, and late in his career there, he became inspired and desired to enter the prestigious École Normale Supérieure in Paris. He left Arbois in 1838 and entered Barbet's preparatory school in Paris but became so homesick that his father had to bring him home. In 1839, Louis enrolled in the Collège Royal at Besançon, in his home province of Franche Comté. Away from home but not far from it, the young scholar partially supported himself with a student assistantship and received his bachelor of science degree in 1842. Although accepted to the École Normale Supérieure, Pasteur believed that he was not yet ready to enter, and thus he spent a year at Barbet's preparatory school before finally matriculating in the fall of 1843.

Pasteur did well at the École Normale Supérieure, passing high on the teachers' examination in 1845 and quite high in his comprehensive exams the following year. In 1847, he received his doctorate in chemistry and soon found employment as a professor, first at the University of Dijon, where he taught physics for a semester, and then at the University of Strasbourg, where in 1849 he obtained a position in the chemistry department. It was also in Strasbourg that Pasteur met Marie Laurent, the twenty-two-year-old woman whom he soon made his wife. Their marriage lasted a lifetime and produced five children, although three of the daughters died early from typhoid. Throughout his life, Pasteur was politically conservative except for a youthful involvement in the revolutions of 1848, and he was a thoroughgoing supporter of the Second Empire under Napoleon III. Indeed, he received considerable grants and recognition from the emperor and empress personally.

LIFE'S WORK

As early as 1848, Pasteur was publishing his work on crystals, which he had begun for his doctoral research. Working with tartaric acid, he searched for the solution as to why one form of the acid twisted to the right the light rays passing through it, while another form (paratartaric or racemic acid) did not rotate the plane of the light rays.

The two forms of the acid were chemically identical, but Pasteur discovered that racemic acid had crystals that were either left-handed or right-handed—each the mirror image of the other. Using tweezers, he laboriously hand-separated the dried crystals into left and right piles. Then he dissolved each pile and found to his satisfaction that the left-handed crystal solution rotated light rays to the left and the right-handed to the right. When the two solutions were then mixed in equal amounts, no rotation occurred—the mixture was optically inactive. This breakthrough established Pasteur's reputation as a scientist, because it opened the door to stereochemistry, a new way of studying the molecular composition of substances. Pasteur had begun to understand dissymmetry, which characterizes not only organic forms but most inorganic forms as well.

As he continued his research on crystallography, Pasteur moved to the University of Lille, where he served as a dean as well as a professor from 1854 to 1857. While at Lille, Pasteur was approached by a man seeking expert help in explaining why some of his vats of sugar-beet juice, which he was fermenting prior to distilling alcohol from the mash, had been going bad. Pasteur had been urged by his superiors to serve practical ends as well as pure science, and, as it happened, Pasteur's own research into the composition of organic molecules had caused him to want to know how fermentation modified those molecules. Pasteur was eager to use the sugar-beet industry as a laboratory.

The scientist examined the vats and took samples. Under his vertically mounted microscope, Pasteur detected small, round globules of yeast from the "good" samples but found that the "bad" ones contained rodlike microorganisms, bacilli. He assumed that the yeasts, which he observed multiplying by budding, were the cause of fermenting beet sugar into the desired alcohol, but the rods were a mystery.

After considerable effort, he succeeded in formulating a soup in which he was able to culture the bacilli. After introducing only a few of the rods into the sterile solution, he saw them multiply into millions of vibrating germs. They were alive, and they were what crowded out the yeast and transformed the sugar into lactic acid—the acid of sour milk. Pasteur wrote a paper on his discovery entitled "Mémoire sur la fermentation appellée lactique" (memoir on the fermentation called lactic), which was published by the French Academy of Sciences in 1857. This paper was hailed as the initial proof that germs cause fermentation.

Pasteur's article of 1857 was the second great stride of his career, and as a result he was called to Paris and made director of scientific studies at the École Normale Supérieure. His elevated post, however, did not provide him with his own laboratory, so he created one for himself in two rooms in the attic. There he proceeded to demonstrate the extreme complexity of the processes involved in alcoholic fermentation. Chemists had previously expressed the conversion of sugar into ethyl alcohol and carbonic acid by means of a simple, inorganic formula, but Pasteur detailed the complex role of brewer's yeast in digesting the sugar into a number of compounds, of which alcohol was only the most important.

Continuing his work on microbes, Pasteur found that some bacteria required the absence of oxygen in order to survive, whereas others needed oxygen to live. The former he termed "anaerobic," and he named the latter "aerobic"—nomenclature used by science to the present day, as Pasteur was the first to bring to scientific and public attention the two different kinds of bacteria. Antoni van Leeuwenhoek and Lazzaro Spallanzani had earlier observed anaerobic bacteria but had failed to attract much notice to the discovery.

Pasteur then conducted a lengthy experiment on the canning of food, a process discovered by his fellow countryman François Appert in the time of Napoleon I. Pasteur showed conclusively that the heating of sealed containers killed the microbes that caused fermentation

Louis Pasteur. (Library of Congress)

and putrefaction. That was the secret of food preservation. He explained that microbes are necessary for decomposition of organic matter into its inorganic components and that without such microbes all the plants and animals that had ever lived would have their dead remains choking the surface of the planet.

Pasteur also proved that microbes came only from other microbes, that life came from life, and that there was no spontaneous generation. Leeuwenhoek two hundred years earlier had disproved spontaneous generation, but few had been willing to listen. Pasteur was so insistent that he forced people to pay attention. To illustrate that microbes can be carried through the air, Pasteur and his assistants exposed many sterile cultures briefly to the air of a deep basement in Paris, the surface-level air in Paris, the air of a vineyard on a hill of the Jura Mountains, and finally the air high on the slopes of Mont Blanc. Pasteur found that the higher and more rural the area the lower the percentage of cultures that were contaminated. The only low-lying location that had pure air was the nearly draft-free deep cellar in Paris.

Next Pasteur and his chief assistant, Émile Duclaux, set up a makeshift field laboratory in Pasteur's hometown of Arbois. Wine producers in the area had been having difficulty, as their output was sometimes ropy, acid, oily, or bitter. Looking through his microscope, Pasteur startled the vintners by correctly pronouncing what was wrong with each sample without tasting it. To prevent the spoilage, Pasteur recommended a treatment that came to be known as "pasteurization"—heating the wine, once fermentation was complete, to a certain temperature below boiling and holding it there for a specified period of time. The temperature could be lower if the time were lengthened and vice versa. When farmers objected to cooking their wine, Pasteur explained that the natural acidity of their product made it less hospitable to germs and that the required temperature was really quite low. Milk, beer, cider, and other liquids could be similarly preserved, and Pasteur designed special equipment for commercial pasteurization.

One of Pasteur's former professors, J. B. Dumas, begged Pasteur to investigate a disease of silkworms, pébrine, a blight that was devastating a main industry in south central France. Between 1865 and 1870, Pasteur spent several months of each year in and around Alais (modern Alès), the center of the nation's silk culture. Pasteur's confusion about what ailed the silkworms was compounded, as he eventually discovered, by the fact that the worms were suffering not from a single disease but from two different microbial infections.

Before he attained a breakthrough in the silkworm diseases, however, Pasteur suffered a cerebral hemorrhage in October, 1868, at the age of forty-five. Many thought that he would surely die; his left side was completely paralyzed. However, he regained partial use of his left side, and he walked, though with a severe limp. He depended on his assistants to do much of the manipulation required by his experiments, but his mind remained keen, and he never relinquished control over his laboratories. He had finished the rescue of the silk industry by 1870.

Pasteur, whose name was a household word in France and who had greatly assisted the French sugar-beet, wine, vinegar, silk, and beer industries, moved comparatively late in his career into the field of immunology. He confirmed the work of Robert Koch in Germany, who had discovered the complete life cycle of the anthrax bacillus, the cause of the animal (and sometimes human) disease anthrax, but he greatly desired to outdo the German. After considerable experimentation with animals, Pasteur announced that he had invented a vaccine, composed of weakened bacilli, which if injected into an animal would confer immunity against anthrax.

It was something Koch had never done. Skeptical French veterinarians in 1881 challenged Pasteur to a dramatic public experiment to test the immunization. Pasteur's assistants cautioned against accepting, as the vaccine had not been field-tested and a public failure could be devastating. Pasteur was adamant, however, and they caught the train for Pouilly-le-Fort, a village near Melun, southeast of Paris. Twenty-four sheep, one goat, and six cows were immunized, it was hoped, by Pasteur's assistant, the physician Émile Roux, with two injections of serum twelve days apart. Two weeks later, those animals and an equal-sized control group of animals were injected with a powerful culture of anthrax bacilli. All the immunized animals survived; all the others died; France went wild with the news.

Pasteur next turned to conquer rabies, probably motivated by childhood memories of an attack on his town by a rabid wolf. Sucking foam from the mouths of caged mad dogs, Pasteur and his men never found a responsible microbe, as hydrophobia is caused by a virus—something too small to be seen with a light microscope—but the scientists made a vaccine and used it successfully on animals. Then a mother brought in her son, bitten by a mad dog and sure to die. Pasteur ordered the child inoculated, and the child lived. Soon others came, even from distant Russia and the United States, and, except where too much time had elapsed, the cure was effective.

It was fitting climax to a brilliant career. On his seventieth birthday, a great celebration was held to honor Pasteur. Pasteur's son had to deliver his father's speech, in which Pasteur said that it gave him immense happiness to "have contributed in some way to the progress and good of humanity."

SIGNIFICANCE

Louis Pasteur is best known for his work in bacteriology, a field that he virtually founded. His discoveries contributed greatly to the control and treatment of cholera, diphtheria, tetanus, tuberculosis, and other diseases. His studies of the transmission of infection also contributed to the development of antiseptic procedures in surgery. His discovery of vaccines to prevent anthrax and other diseases of animals had an enormous impact not only in France but also worldwide. Although less widely known than his contributions to immunology, Pasteur's pioneering researches in crystallography were of fundamental importance. Among the many great scientists of the nineteenth century, Pasteur stands in the first rank.

—Allan D. Charles

FURTHER READING

Compton, Piers. *The Genius of Louis Pasteur*. New York: Macmillan, 1932. A readable and thorough account of Pasteur's life and contributions, this book has several interesting photographs of people, places, and events in his life.

Cuny, Hilaire. *Louis Pasteur: The Man and His Theories*. Translated by Patrick Evans. London: Souvenir Press, 1965. This book provides detail without being overwhelming. Cuny's explanations of the technical aspects of Pasteur's work are readily comprehensible to the layperson.

Debré, Patrice. *Louis Pasteur*. Translated by Elborg Forster. Baltimore: Johns Hopkins University Press, 1998. Comprehensive study of Pasteur's life and work written by a French immunologist who describes his subject as "a living symbol, embodying both science and France." Debrée describes the scientific details of Pasteur's experiments in simple, understandable language.

De Kruif, Paul. *Microbe Hunters*. New York: Pocket Books, 1950. Although more superficial than the full-length biographies, this book has two exquisitely entertaining chapters on Pasteur that convey the excitement inherent in making scientific breakthroughs that result in saving lives and industries.

Dubos, René. *Louis Pasteur: Free Lance of Science*. Translated by Elizabeth Dussauze. New York: Charles Scribner's Sons, 1976. This book is thorough and gives a good perspective on Pasteur. Includes a large photographic section.

Duclaux, Émile. *Pasteur: The History of a Mind*. Translated by Erwin Smith and Florence Hedges. Philadelphia: W. B. Saunders, 1920. Reprint. Metuchen, N.J.: Scarecrow Press, 1973. Written by a man who studied and worked under Pasteur, this book provides many insights into Pasteur's thinking. Duclaux deals exclusively with Pasteur's professional life and not with his personal life, and gives a balanced treatment with proper credit to Pasteur's rival researchers.

Geison, Gerald L. *The Private Science of Louis Pasteur*. Princeton, N.J.: Princeton University Press, 1995. Revisionist and controversial biography based upon Geison's extensive study of Pasteur's unpublished correspondence, lecture notes, and workbooks, Geison found significant differences between Pasteur's public positions and private records, concluding that some of Pasteur's experiments were tainted by lies and scientific, if not moral, misconduct.

Vallery-Radot, René. *The Life of Pasteur*. Translated by R. L. Devonshire. Mineola, N.Y.: Dover, 1960. This is the standard biography of Pasteur and was written by Pasteur's son-in-law. The book provides many quotations from documentary sources and gives an inside look at Pasteur, his life and his work.

SEE ALSO: Emil von Behring; Ferdinand Julius Cohn; Robert Koch; Sir Edwin Ray Lankester; Joseph Lister; Napoleon I; Napoleon III; Ignaz Philipp Semmelweis.

RELATED ARTICLES in *Great Events from History: The Nineteenth Century, 1801-1900:* May, 1847: Semmelweis Develops Antiseptic Procedures; 1857: Pasteur Begins Developing Germ Theory and Microbiology; 1867: Lister Publishes His Theory on Antiseptic Surgery; March 24, 1882: Koch Announces His Discovery of the Tuberculosis Bacillus; December 11, 1890: Behring Discovers the Diphtheria Antitoxin; August 20, 1897: Ross Establishes Malaria's Transmission Vector.

WALTER PATER
English writer

Pater's emphasis upon the importance of sensibility and feeling made him a central figure in the "art for art's sake" movement that marked the transition from Victorian realism to twentieth century modernism.

BORN: August 4, 1839; London, England
DIED: July 30, 1894; Oxford, England
ALSO KNOWN AS: Walter Horatio Pater (full name)
AREAS OF ACHIEVEMENT: Literature, art

EARLY LIFE
Walter Horatio Pater (PAY-ter) was the son of Richard Pater, a former Roman Catholic surgeon who died in 1842. His mother, née Maria Hill, came from a northern family and was a member of the Church of England. According to family tradition, their most distinguished ancestor was the French painter Jean-Baptiste Pater (1695-1736), although the English branch of the Paters had become prominent merchants in the lace trade on the Norfolk-Suffolk coast. After his father's death, Pater's family moved to Enfield, from which he entered King's School, Canterbury, in 1853 and then matriculated at Oxford's Queen's College in 1858.

At Oxford, Pater studied Plato with the legendary professor of Greek Benjamin Jowett, became interested in German philosophy as the result of two visits to Germany, and was graduated with a degree in classics in 1862. He remained at Oxford and tutored private pupils until elected a Fellow of Brasenose College in 1865, the year in which he also made an extensive tour of Italy. His discovery of the achievements of the Italian Renaissance resulted in a series of essays on Leonardo da Vinci, Sandro Botticelli, Michelangelo, and other major figures, which were collected in his first book, *Studies in the History of the Renaissance* (1873).

Pater settled upon his major intellectual interests during a period of great aesthetic controversy. The "art for art's sake" philosophy espoused by the poets Dante Gabriel Rossetti and Algernon Charles Swinburne was in full bloom, as many of the era's creative talents rebelled against what they viewed as the crass materialism of Victorian society. Pater's dislike of any sort of unpleasantness kept him from engaging in the more partisan aspects of this conflict, but his stress upon the cultivation of aesthetic sensibilities made him an influential—if often reluctant—ally of those advocating greater freedom for the artistic temperament.

Although Pater's love of the fine arts was characterized by an almost religious fervor, his personal appearance often surprised those who knew him only from his writings. His clean-shaven cheeks and short, neat mustache were unusual in an age when extensive facial hair was the male norm, and in combination with his six-foot height and solid build often led to his being described as a dead ringer for a military officer. This impression was supported by his simple, precisely tailored clothes and the distinctive manner in which he walked—quickly and with a noticeable swing of his shoulders. A high, receding forehead and sparkling eyes set close together rounded out a public image that struck most contemporary commentators as quite at variance with the nature of his literary accomplishments.

LIFE'S WORK
The essays collected in *Studies in the History of the Renaissance* were adopted as a kind of manifesto by what became known as the aesthetic movement, which included Rossetti, Swinburne, and such Pre-Raphaelite artists as John Everett Millais and W. Holman Hunt among its members. Pater's writing was lauded for having turned criticism into one of the fine arts, although those opposed to aestheticism attacked it as sterile, subjective, and dangerously hedonistic. Particularly controversial was the conclusion to *Studies in the History of the Renaissance*, in which Pater argued that those who would succeed in life must "burn always with this hard, gemlike flame." To many Victorian sensibilities this seemed a positively immoral basis for a philosophy of life: Thus, the conclusion was omitted from the book's second edition (*The Renaissance: Studies in Art and Poetry*, 1877) and only restored to its third edition (1888) in a revised and much less inflammatory version.

Pater's life at Oxford revolved around the home that he maintained with his two unmarried sisters, where a few friends and disciples served as a sounding board for his ideas on literature and art. He had little to do with the administrative affairs of his college, and on a typical day might well not leave the house except for a short evening walk. Despite his avoidance of publicity, Pater was held in high regard by his colleagues: The Brasenose College chapel contains a memorial showing him in the center of a group consisting of Leonardo da Vinci, Michelangelo, Dante, and Plato.

Much of Pater's work was first published in periodicals such as *Fortnightly Review*, *Westminster Review*, *Pall Mall Gazette*, and *The Athenaeum*, and it was then collected in volumes such as *Imaginary Portraits* (1887), *Appreciations* (1889), and *Plato and Platonism: A Series of Lectures* (1893). As the title of the second of these suggests, Pater's critical faculties were directed toward the discovery of excellence rather than the detection of failure. He largely disregarded matters of technique, and instead sought to elucidate the qualities of temperament and the relevant aesthetic contexts that lay behind the actual work of art. For Pater, the artist has a valuable message for the informed, aware, and sympathetic audience, and it is the responsibility of the critic to respond to art in a manner that conveys its significant spiritual aspects.

As attacks upon his position mounted, among them an unflattering fictional caricature in William Hurrell Mallock's satire *The New Republic* (1877), Pater decided to write a major work that would demonstrate how his ideas enhanced the encounter with life's aesthetic elements. *Marius the Epicurean* (1885) is a loosely structured novel organized around the experiences of its protagonist, whose coming of age in second century Rome brings him into contact with a wide range of religious and philosophic ideals. At the end of the book, Marius is inclined toward but not yet fully convinced of the validity of Christianity, a conclusion that many critics found unsatisfactory in its tacit approval of heretical views. It nevertheless accurately reflected Pater's belief that it was openness to experience rather than the insistence upon dogmatic certainties that characterized the truly sensitive soul, and the book became one of the key texts for adherents of the aesthetic movement.

Pater's later years found him venturing a bit further into the social whirl. He rented a house in London, began to be seen in literary society, and even gave a few public lectures—in which his extreme nervousness was evident—on Renaissance art and literature. The year 1894 found him at the pinnacle of his success, an object of veneration by such young talents as Oscar Wilde and William Butler Yeats and the recipient of an honorary doctorate from the University of Glasgow. In June of that year, however, he was suddenly taken ill with rheumatic fever and then pleurisy, and on July 30, he died of heart failure occasioned by his long illness. Although he was deeply mourned by his many friends and disciples, it was in a sense appropriate that a life dedicated to the appreciation of beauty should cease at the apex rather than the nadir of its accomplishments.

SIGNIFICANCE

Walter Pater's role in the sudden decline of the Victorian ethos and the equally rapid ascendancy of literary modernism was a crucial one. The fact that he was an extraordinarily shy, almost reclusive figure for much of his life meant that his influence rested upon his writings rather than a charismatic personality, and as a result he was taken seriously by the many intellectuals who viewed more flamboyant aesthetes—Wilde, most notoriously—as objects of ridicule rather than respect. Pater's solid academic background and early training in philosophy also helped to make his ideas palatable to many members of the educational establishment.

Pater's work also found many enthusiasts outside the ivory towers of England's great universities. His championing of the subjective approach to critical appreciation was immensely liberating to those reared in an atmosphere of Victorian deference to tradition and order, because it in effect substituted fresh individual responses for stale received opinions. Taking Pater as their guide, many people found the courage to express their own opinions without worrying about whether these were in line with the conventional wisdom.

In hindsight, Pater necessarily assumes the role of an early prophet in a revolution that has now been largely won. In addition to his historical importance as an advocate of the primacy of the developed aesthetic sense, however, Pater's elegant literary style can still be enjoyed by connoisseurs of fine writing, not least because it succeeds in exemplifying in prose what his heroes had achieved in the fine arts. Although the figures of such spiritual descendants as Wilde and Yeats now far overshadow that of Pater, it is important to remember that he was one of the first to oppose a dead and oppressive past with a vision of the capacity for enjoyment latent in everyone's endowments of feeling and sensibility.

—*Paul Stuewe*

FURTHER READING

Benson, Arthur Christopher. *Walter Pater*. London: Macmillan, 1906. A typical example of Macmillan's English Men of Letters series, in which a light tone and the absence of scholarly apparatus conceal a thorough acquaintance with the subject. Although Benson got many of his facts wrong, his deft sketches of Pater's Oxford background and dominant personality traits still make the book worth consulting.

Daley, Kenneth. *The Rescue of Romanticism: Walter Pater and John Ruskin*. Athens: Ohio University Press,

2001. Examines the close intellectual relationship of Pater and Ruskin, two of the Victorian era's most important art critics, who, in Daley's opinion, were theorists of Romanticism.

De Laura, David J. *Hebrew and Hellene in Victorian England: Newman, Arnold, and Pater*. Austin: University of Texas Press, 1970. A detailed investigation of the intellectual and personal relations maintained by three significant Victorian figures. The book is closely reasoned and not always easy to follow, but it is nevertheless a rewarding study that is particularly good on the history of the aesthetic movement.

Donoghue, Denis. *Walter Pater: Lover of Strange Souls*. New York: Knopf, 1995. A scholarly study of Pater's literary influence. Donoghue argues that Pater's tone of voice is heard in the works of James Joyce, T. S. Eliot, Virginia Woolf, and other modern writers.

Levey, Michael. *The Case of Walter Pater*. London: Thames and Hudson, 1978. Levey describes his work as a biography and includes an adequate account of Pater's early years, but his real focus is on his life as an Oxford don and the autobiographical nature of his writings. Levey often illuminates the connections between Pater's life and work, although he sometimes comes up with speculations that seem insufficiently grounded in historical fact.

Monsman, Gerald. *Walter Pater's Art of Autobiography*. New Haven, Conn.: Yale University Press, 1980. This attempt to abstract an autobiography from Pater's fiction theorizes that whatever the ostensible subject, he was in fact always meditating on the death of his parents. A Freudian interpretation expressed in the latest modes of textual analysis; an interesting and provocative, if not always convincing, effort.

Pater, Walter. *Letters of Walter Pater*. Edited by Lawrence Evans. Oxford, England: Oxford University Press, 1970. Contains 272 of Pater's generally brief and uninformative letters. This material has been well researched and annotated, and the reader gains a good idea of what Pater's daily routine was like, but little idea of what really engaged his more subtle thought processes.

Stein, Richard L. *The Ritual of Interpretation: The Fine Arts as Literature in Ruskin, Rossetti, and Pater*. Cambridge, Mass.: Harvard University Press, 1975. Stein argues that writing about art was a distinctive genre for the Victorians, and he discusses his three subjects in terms of their literary treatment of painting, sculpture, and architecture. The best elucidation of Pater's art criticism and its cultural antecedents.

Wright, Thomas. *The Life of Walter Pater*. 2 vols. London: Everett, 1907. Wright is constantly pointing out mistakes in Benson's *Walter Pater*, and it must be admitted that Wright's documentation is much superior. Wright seems to have little feel, however, for Pater's elusive personality and is often an irritatingly clumsy writer. An essential but by no means polished resource.

SEE ALSO: Daniel and Alexander Macmillan; John Ruskin; Hippolyte Taine; Oscar Wilde.

RELATED ARTICLE in *Great Events from History: The Nineteenth Century, 1801-1900:* Late 1870's: Post-Impressionist Movement Begins.

A. B. PATERSON
Australian writer

Paterson's popular poetry celebrating the Australian Outback helped to establish a national identity that led the country out of its colonial state into nationhood.

BORN: February 17, 1864; Narrambla, New South Wales, Australia

DIED: February 2, 1941; Sydney, Australia

ALSO KNOWN AS: Andrew Barton Paterson (full name); Banjo (pseudonym)

AREAS OF ACHIEVEMENT: Literature, communications

EARLY LIFE

Andrew Barton Paterson was born on a sprawling ranch in New South Wales, Australia's original colony, on the southeastern edge of the continent. His parents, Andrew Bogle and Rose Isabella Paterson, were early settlers in the remote region called the Yass district. Known as Barty to his family, Andrew received his earliest education at home and then attended a school in the nearby town of Binalong. As a boy, he witnessed at firsthand the strength and courage of the country folk as they carved out their livelihoods in an inhospitable land. His early experiences served him well in adulthood, when he used his writing to celebrate the Australian landscape and the hardy breed of men and women who inhabited it.

At the age of ten, Andrew went to Sydney, the major city in New South Wales, to attend Sydney Grammar School. After finishing school when he was sixteen, he entered a Sydney law firm, Spain and Salway, as a clerk. In 1886, he became a full-fledged lawyer and with a partner established the legal firm of Street and Paterson.

While practicing law, Paterson started publishing verses in the *Sydney Mail* and the *Bulletin*. The latter, an influential national newspaper established in 1880, had a literary section with a strong nationalistic tone that specialized in fiction and verse that extolled life in rural areas—that is, the vast regions in the country's center known as the "bush." At the suggestion of the *Bulletin* editor, Paterson submitted a manuscript to Angus & Robertson, a pioneering Australian publisher. *The Man from Snowy River, and Other Verses* appeared in 1895 and established Paterson as the major literary figure in Australia and a best-selling writer in Australia second only to Rudyard Kipling, another poet from the British Empire. Within six months, five editions of Paterson's book had sold out, and it remained in print more than a century later.

LIFE'S WORK

As a lawyer and part-time poet, Paterson wrote under the pseudonym "Banjo"—a name that he borrowed from the family's racehorse. In 1902, after returning from South Africa, where he served as a special correspondent for the *Sydney Morning Herald* during the South African (Boer) War, he left the legal profession to pursue a writing and journalistic career. He retained his pen name and became known as A. B. "Banjo" Paterson.

In 1903 Paterson married Alice Walker and settled in Sydney. He and his wife had two children together. As a married man with a family, Paterson took up full-time journalistic work, first editing the *Evening News*, then the *Australian Town and Country Journal*. When World War I broke out in 1914, he went to Europe as a correspondent. Disappointed with his assignment, he returned home and enlisted in the Remount Service, an organization that furnished horses to members of the Australian cavalry serving in the Middle East. After the war ended in 1918, he returned to Sydney and took up the editorship of the *Sydney Sportsman*.

Paterson published two more poetry collections that were similar in subject matter to his first book and equally successful: *Rio Grande's Last Race, and Other Verses* (1902) and *Saltbush Bill J. P., and Other Verses* (1917). He also tried his hand at fiction by publishing two novels, *An Outback Marriage* (1906) and *The Shearer's Colt* (1936), and a book of short stories, *Three Elephant Power, and Other Stories* (1917). In 1934, he published *Happy Dispatches*, a memoir that recounted his travels, adventures, and experiences as a correspondent. He made an important contribution to Australian folk art by compiling the anthology *Old Bush Songs* (1905), a collection of fifty songs and ballads from Australian oral traditions that might have been lost otherwise.

In spite of Paterson's literary glorification of life in the bush, he spent the rest of his years in Sydney, except for brief periods on a country property, which he gave up in 1919, when he settled permanently in the city. As a young man he had developed a strong interest in sports, including cricket, tennis, polo, and rowing, which he continued to follow. He devoted much of his time to his greatest passion, horses and the racetrack. Admiring horses for their endurance, courage, and skill, Paterson immortalized their feats in several of his ballads. Paterson's rich and productive life ended on his death on February 2, 1941—a few days before his seventy-seventh birthday.

SIGNIFICANCE

Even if A. B. Paterson had written nothing after *The Man from Snowy River, and Other Verses*, he would have gained a permanent place in Australian literature. During the same year that he published that book, 1895, he also composed the ballad "Waltzing Matilda" during a trip to Queensland, then a separate British colony north of New South Wales. That ballad's nimble words and catchy tune, which was adapted from a Scottish song, soon spread around Queensland. It gained a wider audience in 1903, when the version known today was issued on sheet music. Often considered Australia's unofficial national anthem, "Waltzing Matilda" represents Paterson at his best, as he captures the bush spirit by relying on the colorful slang that had evolved in the Australian Outback.

Paterson's celebration of bush life in *The Man From Snowy River, and Other Verses* appeared at an opportune time. The 1890's saw the rise of a movement toward the federation of Australia's six colonies—New South Wales, Victoria, Queensland, South Australia, Tasmania, and Western Australia. In 1901, the Commonwealth of Australia was officially inaugurated, and Australia became a nation rather than a hodgepodge of colonies.

Paterson made one of the most significant contributions to federation through his unadorned and straightforward writing that helped to give the colonists a single national identity. Like the characters in Paterson's ballads, they could see themselves as stalwart, courageous, and humble folk creating a distinctive culture,

turning a harsh land into a prosperous one, and retaining their independence. The well-traveled, city-dwelling, and sophisticated Paterson transformed the bush into an Arcadia—one that never truly existed except in his imag-

---

"WALTZING MATILDA"

Although this song has spread around the world, its lyrics require a glossary for those unfamiliar with its Australian slang. For example, "waltzing" actually means carrying and "matilda" means a swag or a bundle of personal belongings wrapped inside a blanket. The song opens with a "swagman" (a drifter) camped beside a "billabong" (stagnant pool). He sees a "jumbuck" (sheep) at the waterhole, kills the animal, and stuffs it in his "tucker-bag" (receptacle for food). The "squatter" (a rancher occupying government land) arrives with three policemen. Rather than give into authority and forfeit his freedom, the swagman jumps into the billabong. As he drowns he repeats the haunting line, "You'll come a-waltzing Matilda with me." The defiance and courage that the swagman displays in the face of authority epitomizes the ways of the bush that Paterson eulogized in his work. The poem's italicized refrain is repeated after each verse. In each case, however, its third line is the same as the third line of the verse that precedes it. The verse's last two lines are performed in a hushed tone, before resuming the energetic refrain.

> Once a jolly swagman camped by a billabong
> Under the shade of a coolibah tree
> And he sang as he watched and waited 'til his billy boiled
> You'll come a-waltzing matilda with me
>
> *Waltzing matilda, waltzing matilda*
> *You'll come a waltzing matilda with me*
> *And he sang as he watched and waited 'til his billy boiled*
> *You'll come a-waltzing matilda with me*
>
> Down came a jumbuck to dri-ink at that billabong
> Up jumped the swagman and grabbed him with glee
> And he sang as he stuffed that jumbuck in his tucker-bag
> You'll come a-waltzing matilda with me
>
> Up rode the squatter, mounted on his thoroughbred
> Up rode the troopers, one, two, three
> "Where's that jolly jumbuck you've got in your tucker-bag?"
> You'll come a-waltzing matilda with me
>
> Up jumped the swagman and sprang into that billabong
> "You'll never take me alive!" said he
> And his ghost may be heard as you pa-ass by that billabong
> You'll come a-waltzing matilda with me

Source: A. B. Paterson, "Waltzing Matilda." Electronic text from Australian National University community service pages, www.anu.edu.au/people. Accessed on September 24, 2005.

ination. In contrast to the realistic writing of his contemporary Henry Lawson (1867-1922), drought, fire, flood, dust and flies, economic hardships, isolation, and shattered lives never play a part in Paterson's romanticized version of the Outback.

Paterson's bush myth continues to define Australians, both at home and abroad, even though approximately 80 percent of Australia's early twenty-first century population lived in five major coastal cities. Paul Hogan's "Crocodile Dundee," who first captured the imagination of international moviegoers in 1986, is a direct descendant of the expert horseman Clancy in "The Man from Snowy River" and the intrepid swagman in "Waltzing Matilda."

—Robert Ross

FURTHER READING

Hall, Timothy. *"Banjo" Paterson's High Country.* Sydney: Angus & Robertson, 1989. Photographs and text record the Snowy River region that was the setting for several of Paterson's ballads.

Oliff, Lorna. *Andrew Barton Paterson.* New York: Twayne, 1971. Analyzes Paterson's writing within a biographical framework. Excellent introductory study.

Roderick, Colin Arthur. *Banjo Paterson: Poet by Accident.* Sydney: Allen & Unwin, 1993. Takes a contemporary look at Paterson and focuses on his continuing influence. Provides extensive biographical materials and discussions of Paterson's work.

Semmler, Clement. *The Banjo of the Bush: The Life and Times of A. B. Banjo Paterson.* Brisbane: University of Queensland Press, 1984. A thorough biographical study that sets Paterson's life and writing within the Australian context.

Smith, Roff. "Australia's Bard of the Bush: The Real Man from Snowy River." *National Geographic* (August, 2004): 2-29. Lavishly illustrated article that stresses Paterson's continuing influence on Australian attitudes toward the bush through firsthand observations, contemporary interviews, and biographical details. Excellent introduction to the man and his work.

Webby, Elizabeth, ed. *The Cambridge Companion to Australian Literature.* Cambridge, England: Cambridge University Press, 2000. Surveys the development of Australian writing in all genres and places Paterson in the larger picture.

Wilde, William H., Joy Hooton, and Barry Andrews, eds. *The Oxford Companion to Australian Literature.* Melbourne, Vic.: Oxford University Press, 1985. Includes an extended discussion of Paterson's life and work, as well as a history of "Waltzing Matilda."

SEE ALSO: Sir Edmund Barton; Alfred Deakin; Nathaniel Hawthorne; Rudyard Kipling; John MacArthur.

RELATED ARTICLES in *Great Events from History: The Nineteenth Century, 1801-1900:* 1851: Gold Is Discovered in New South Wales; 1868: Last Convicts Land in Western Australia.

ELIZABETH PALMER PEABODY
American educator

Peabody founded the first English-language kindergarten in the United States, published the Kindergarten Messenger, *promoted Friedrich Froebel's educational theories after studying his methods for a year in Germany, and ran a book shop in Boston that became a gathering place for New England intellectuals.*

BORN: May 16, 1804; Billerica, Massachusetts
DIED: January 3, 1894; Boston, Massachusetts
AREA OF ACHIEVEMENT: Education

EARLY LIFE

Elizabeth Palmer Peabody was the daughter of Nathaniel Peabody, a teacher who became a dentist, and Elizabeth Palmer Peabody, who ran an experimental school in Salem, Massachusetts. Elizabeth was the oldest of the seven Peabody children, four of whom were girls. Her parents both concerned themselves directly with their children's education. When Elizabeth was quite young, her father taught her Latin and encouraged her to study other languages. By the age of sixteen, Elizabeth had a reasonable mastery of ten different languages.

Elizabeth's mother believed that all her students, including Elizabeth, should be encouraged to strive toward achieving the highest educational goals possible. She individualized her instruction in ways that would enhance her students' self-confidence. In an era when children were often expected to be seen and not heard, the emphasis of Elizabeth's mother on self-expression in her teaching was revolutionary.

Clearly a prodigy, Elizabeth developed strong backgrounds in philosophy, history, literature, and theology at an age when many young women were still playing with their dolls. Before long, she was teaching at her mother's school. At the age of sixteen, she opened her own school in Lancaster, Massachusetts. After that school failed in 1723, she spent two years in Maine as a governess and tutor to the children of two wealthy families. This period essentially marked the end of Elizabeth's informal teaching apprenticeship. Her next venture, embarked upon with her sister Mary, was to open a school in Brookline, Massachusetts.

LIFE'S WORK

Peabody's path toward Transcendentalism, the philosophy she came to espouse and that most influenced her thinking, grew out of her coming to know William Ellery Channing, a liberal-minded Unitarian preacher. Channing had first impressed Elizabeth during her childhood when she had heard him preach in Salem. She began corresponding with Channing during her residence in Maine, but her close association with him began only in 1826, when he enrolled his only daughter in Elizabeth's Brookline school.

Intrigued by Channing's engaging intellect, Elizabeth encouraged him to confer frequently with her about his daughter's academic progress. In these conferences the two shared their educational philosophies and Channing introduced her to the philosophical tenets of Emanuel Swedenborg, the noted eighteenth century Swedish Transcendentalist. During the late 1820's and throughout the 1830's, Channing and Peabody explored the philosophical currents of their day, often joined by other intellectuals.

In 1832, Elizabeth was forced to close her school when she could no longer meet its expenses. She then struggled along, living on tutorial fees and on the meager royalties from her book *First Steps to the Study of History* (1832). She and her sisters lived in a Boston boarding house in which the educational pioneer Horace Mann also resided. Elizabeth formed a close friendship with him and the two seemed destined to marry; however, Mann instead married Elizabeth's sister Mary.

Bronson Alcott often participated in the Peabody-Channing discussions. In 1834, Elizabeth became Alcott's assistant at his Temple School in Boston. Elizabeth continued the work she had begun earlier as Channing's copyist, preparing many of his papers for publication. Between 1826 and 1844, she prepared more than fifty of his sermons for press. At the same time, she was being exposed to the educational philosophies of both Alcott and Mann.

During the 1830's, Transcendentalism became the strongest philosophical force in New England. In 1837, when the Transcendentalist Club was formed, Elizabeth Peabody and Margaret Fuller became charter members and were the only women to gain membership. Transcendentalism touted the primacy of the spiritual over the material, of mind over matter.

In 1835, Elizabeth published *Record of a School*, which was essentially the journal she kept during her work with Alcott. This publication brought Bronson Alcott, who soon published his own book, *Conversations with Children on the Gospels*, to public attention. Alcott included some excerpts from Elizabeth's journal. Both books were considered revolutionary in their day. Alcott's book, in particular, evoked harsh criticism from many quarters. Although Elizabeth was embarrassed by portions of Alcott's book, she came to his defense in a long article.

Elizabeth's defense of Alcott brought her into the public eye in ways that affected her professional life negatively. In 1836, after resigning from Temple School, she was unable to find gainful employment. The national economy was weakening during the months leading up to the so-called Panic of 1837. Elizabeth's only recourse was to return to her family's home in Salem. Over the next four years, she lived a marginal existence there without a job and with little income.

During this otherwise bleak period in her life, Elizabeth's association with Ralph Waldo Emerson, whom she had known since the 1820's when he taught her Greek, was a saving grace for her. On her visits to Emerson in Concord, she introduced him to the mystical and little-known poet Jones Very, whose excellence Emerson quickly appreciated. In 1839, Emerson edited and published Very's *Poems and Essay*, through which Very was introduced to the literary world. Also during this period, Elizabeth used her connections to secure for

Elizabeth Palmer Peabody. (Library of Congress)

Nathaniel Hawthorne a post in the Boston Custom House. In 1842, Hawthorne married Elizabeth's sister Sophia.

Finally, in 1839, Elizabeth moved to Boston with her sisters. The following year, she converted the parlor of their house into one of the most interesting book stores in New England. It quickly became a gathering place for New England intellectuals, mostly those espousing the Transcendentalism to which Elizabeth subscribed. This movement began to fade during the mid-1840's, and by 1850, Elizabeth closed her book store, but not before she had established herself as the first female publisher in the United States, printing and distributing important works of many writers, including Henry David Thoreau's landmark essay, "On Civil Disobedience."

Elizabeth now directed her energies into promoting Christian-Transcendental education for young people. She taught in various venues during the 1850's and 1860's. Between 1850 and 1884 she produced ten books and more than fifty articles on education. In 1859, she first heard of the kindergarten movement founded in Germany by Friedrich Froebel. The next year, she opened the first English-speaking kindergarten in the United States. This school was well received, as was Elizabeth's book *Moral Culture of Infancy and Kindergarten Guide* (1863).

Unsure that she had truly grasped Froebel's concepts, Elizabeth visited kindergartens in Germany that were run according to Froebel's ideal during 1867-1868. On her return, she continued to teach and, in 1873, began publishing her *Kindergarten Messenger*, which, in the two years it existed, introduced the kindergarten concept across the United States.

In her later years, Peabody taught in Bronson Alcott's Concord School of Philosophy and continued to publish. She never tired of engaging in conversations about philosophy and education. She died in Boston on January 3, 1894, during her ninetieth year.

SIGNIFICANCE

Elizabeth Peabody was not a militant crusader for women's rights. She had little need to be. She lived in an environment of liberal intellectuals who accepted her for who she was and her work for what it was. She was intellectually equal to the most renowned New England intellectuals of her age. She is remembered both for founding the first English-speaking kindergarten and for promoting Friedrich Froebel's educational ideals in the United States. She was also a formidable Transcendental philosopher, having been exposed for years to the Transcendentalism of such luminaries as Alcott Bronson and William Ellery Channing, both of whom introduced her to Transcendental thought as it existed in Europe.

A major portion of Peabody's legacy consists of the books she published during her lifetime, both her own and those of such notable authors as Raph Waldo Emerson and Henry David Thoreau. Peabody was a successful organizer, able quite deftly to persuade people to work toward her most cherished goals.

—*R. Baird Shuman*

FURTHER READING

Baylor, Ruth M. *Elizabeth Palmer Peabody: Kindergarten Pioneer*. Philadelphia: University of Pennsylvania Press, 1965. Thoughtful, well-documented study that captures the essence of what Peabody achieved as the founder, along with Margarethe Shurz, of the kindergarten movement in the United States.

Marshall, Megan. *The Peabody Sisters: Three Women Who Ignited American Romanticism*. Boston: Houghton Mifflin, 2005. Combined biography of Elizabeth and her two younger sisters, Mary and Sophia. Meticulously detailed, the book illuminates the sisters' lives and times.

Ronda, Bruce A., ed. *Letters of Elizabeth Palmer Peabody: American Renaissance Woman*. Middlebury, Conn.: Wesleyan University Press, 1984. Reading Peabody's correspondence reveals the growth of her thinking from its earliest stages through her studies of Froebel in Germany.

Tharpe, Louise Hall. *The Peabody Sisters of Salem*. Boston: Little, Brown, 1950. This book remains the most thorough and reliable source on the Peabody sisters, detailing well their lives and contributions.

Warren, James Perrin. *Culture of Eloquence: Oratory and Reform in Antebellum America*. University Park: Pennsylvania State University Press, 1999. In chapter 4, "Fuller, Peabody, and the Mother Tongue," Warren explores the dynamics of how Elizabeth Peabody disseminated her educational and transcendental ideas.

SEE ALSO: Felix Adler; Bronson Alcott; Dorothea Beale; William Ellery Channing; Ralph Waldo Emerson; Friedrich Froebel; Margaret Fuller; Horace Mann; Henry David Thoreau.

RELATED ARTICLE in *Great Events from History: The Nineteenth Century, 1801-1900:* 1820's-1830's: Free Public School Movement.

PEDRO I
Portuguese-born emperor of Brazil (r. 1822-1831)

Pedro I was the heir to the Portuguese throne—which he briefly held—but through a historical accident he grew up in colonial Brazil and became a leader of that colony's independence movement, which made him the first emperor of independent Brazil. However, military defeats and personal scandals during his comparatively brief reign forced him to abdicate, and he returned to Portugal, where his last significant act was to secure the throne of his native land for his daughter.

BORN: October 12, 1798; Lisbon, Portugal
DIED: September 24, 1834; Lisbon, Portugal
ALSO KNOWN AS: Antonio Pedro de Alcântara Bourbon (birth name); Dom Pedro I; Pedro IV; Peter I
AREA OF ACHIEVEMENT: Government and politics

EARLY LIFE

Dom Pedro I (PAY-throh) was born in a royal palace near Lisbon, the son of Portugal's future king Dom João (John) VI. His mother was the Infanta Carlota Joaquina de Bourbon, a daughter of the king of Spain. Pedro was educated privately, mainly by members of clergy. His interests, however, lay not in scholarship but in physical and athletic activities. His upbringing was somewhat chaotic. His parents were quarrelsome. His father was a genial but unkempt figure; his mother was a demanding and authoritative one. The boon companion of his youthful carousing, "Chalaça" (meaning the "joker" or "prankster"), was among Dom Pedro's closest friends and most trusted Brazilian advisers.

In 1808, Dom Pedro and the entire royal family fled from Portugal to Rio de Janeiro in colonial Brazil to escape the forces of Napoleon Bonaparte, which were invading the Iberian peninsula. While still exiled in Brazil, his father became king of Portugal and raised the colony of Brazil to the status of a kingdom. As the next in line to the Portuguese throne, nineteen-year-old Dom Pedro married the Archduchess Leopoldina of Austria, a daughter of the last Holy Roman Emperor, in 1817. Of the seven children that Pedro would have with his wife, the eldest would eventually become queen of Portugal, Maria II (da Glória); and the youngest would become the second emperor of Brazil, Pedro II. Pedro also had numerous other offspring with various mistresses in Brazil, Uruguay, France, and Portugal.

LIFE'S WORK

In 1821, six years after the collapse of the French Empire, the Portuguese parliament required that Dom João VI return to Portugal. The following year, it demanded that Crown Prince Dom Pedro also return. However, the young prince refused, defiantly announcing that he would stay in Brazil with the the response famously associated with him: "*Fico!*" (I will remain!). On September 7, 1822, along the banks of the Ipiranga River in the province of São Paulo, he declared Brazil separated from Portugal with the battle cry "*Independência ou Morte!*" (independence or death!). By the end of the year he was crowned, in the cathedral of Rio de Janeiro, as emperor of Brazil. The new sovereign realm was designated an "empire" both for its continental size—which was nearly one hundred times greater than that of Portugal—and its recent role as having been the center of the Portuguese Empire.

A dashing figure who played historical roles on two continents, Dom Pedro led a brief, ill-fated life. After Brazil achieved its independence, a constituent assembly began to write a constitution for the new country. In the wake of the overthrow of absolutist regimes in Europe by Napoleon and under the influence of British liberal politics, the young sovereign was committed to constitutional monarchy, to ruling under a written charter of rights and responsibilities among shared powers. However, concerned that the document did not give adequate authority to the monarchy to moderate among competing factions, Pedro dissolved the constituent body and issued his own constitution. This action considerably alienated liberal political forces that earlier had welcomed his declaration of independence.

In 1826, Pedro's father, Dom João VI, died. As the king's designated heir, Dom Pedro briefly assumed the title as Dom Pedro IV of Portugal. However, according to his own Brazilian constitution, he was not authorized to assume such a role. He therefore abdicated and placed his eldest daughter, then seven years old, on the throne as Maria II (also Maria da Glória) and tried to arrange for his brother Miguel to act as her regent. However, Miguel, who was the leader of the antiliberal forces in Portugal, considered himself the rightful heir. Pedro then tried to arrange for Miguel to marry Maria da Glória and serve as her regent, but instead of marrying his niece, Miguel assumed the throne for himself in 1828.

Meanwhile, Dom Pedro's attentions were consumed by a series of crises in Brazil. From the beginning of his reign, Brazil had been at war with neighboring Argentina over Brazil's occupation of the province of Uruguay. During 1826, the young monarch personally directed Brazilian forces there. However, Brazil lost the war, and Uruguay became independent in 1828, thereby serving the British interest in a buffer state between Brazil and Argentina. Thus, during a brief period, Dom Pedro suffered the losses of the Portuguese throne for his daughter and the territory of Uruguay for Brazil. He was left politically bankrupt in international adventures.

Pedro's personal affairs brought him further damage. At the time of independence, he had acquired a mistress in São Paulo named Domitila de Castro Canto e Melo, who was married to a low-ranking army officer. Pedro installed her and her entourage in a prominent residence near the royal palace in Rio de Janeiro and made her marchioness of Santos. He had five children with her. Pedro's wife felt so humiliated by Pedro's brazen affair that she died during childbirth in 1826. A popular outcry then arose against Pedro, for both the public scandal of openly keeping a mistress and the tragic death of the empress, who was a beloved figure noted for her charity and benevolence. In response to public criticisms, Dom Pedro separated from his mistress, so that he could attract a second wife among the European nobility. In 1829, he married Archduchess Amelia of Bavaria, the granddaughter of the French empress Joséphine, the first wife of Napoleon I. Dom Pedro had one daughter with his second wife.

In 1831, a political crisis proved the final blow to Pedro's reign in Brazil. His Portuguese birth had come to isolate him from the preponderance of Brazilian-born advisers who were increasingly surrounding him, and he was challenged over his ability to determine ministerial appointments. With his constitutional authority compromised, he abdicated the Brazilian throne on April 7, 1831. Now designated the duke of Bragança—after a city in northeastern Brazil—he resolved to return to Portugal to reestablish his daughter as queen of that country.

After residing briefly in Great Britain, Dom Pedro proceeded to the Azores, a group of Portuguese islands in the Atlantic that opposed the reactionary rule of his brother Miguel. There, Dom Pedro organized a force to invade Portugal and to establish a liberal constitutional monarchy under Maria da Glória. Supported by the British, but with many fewer troops than Miguel, Dom Pedro invaded Portugal in 1832. He occupied the northern city of Porto, a key commercial center, which favored a liberal regime. Besieged in Porto by the enemy, Pedro had his naval forces move south. He victoriously entered Lisbon by the middle of the following year.

The final battles of the war occurred during spring of 1834, with Miguel defeated and entering into exile. After Maria II was restored to the throne, she reigned until 1853. Dom Pedro, however, succumbed to tuberculosis, which had been wasting him for some months. He died on September 24, 1834, expiring in the royal palace where he had been born nearly thirty-six years earlier.

SIGNIFICANCE

Dom Pedro had a personality that was both engaging and mercurial. He left as a legacy within both Brazilian and Portuguese political history a nucleus for the principle of constitutional government. Nonetheless, he also reflected the elitist and unstable nature of Brazil's government through his authoritarian decree of the nation's first constitution and an abdication that was a consequence of both his personal whims and the political rivalries in which he was pitted. Most tellingly, he recognized the debilitating socioeconomic trap of slavery in which Brazilian history was caught. However, his insight tragically did not give him the personal or political weight to unmake it.

Despite his flaws and failures, Pedro I was nonetheless the founder of Brazilian independence. Within that role and over the forgiving course of time, he has risen to become an iconic figure of Brazilian history, the symbol of the country's nationhood. His mortal remains were returned to Brazil in 1972 during commemorations of the sesquicentennial of Brazilian independence.

—Edward A. Riedinger

FURTHER READING

Barman, Roderick J. *Brazil: The Forging of a Nation, 1798-1852.* Stanford, Calif.: Stanford University Press, 1999. Reviews events and key figures of Brazilian independence and nation building from late colonial to imperial period.

Bethel, Leslie, ed. *Brazil: Empire and Republic, 1822-1930.* Cambridge, England: Cambridge University Press, 1989. Comprehensive overview of political, economic, and social history of imperial and early republican Brazil by six leading specialists.

Costa, Sergio Corrêa da. *Every Inch a King: A Biography of Dom Pedro I, First Emperor of Brazil.* London: Hale, 1972. Detailed biography, translated from Portuguese to English, of Dom Pedro I by a leading Brazilian scholar.

Kaiser, Gloria. *Dona Leopoldina: The Habsburg Empress of Brazil.* Riverside, Calif.: Ariadne Press, 1998. Novel by an Austrian author, translated from German, that re-creates the life of Dom Pedro's first wife, with its trials and frustrations, based on correspondence with her family.

Macaulay, Neill. *Dom Pedro: The Struggle for Liberty in Brazil and Portugal, 1798-1834.* Durham, N.C.: Duke University Press, 1986. Scholarly study of Dom Pedro I tracing his life, particularly political and military actions, in relation to his commitment to liberal constitutional monarchy.

SEE ALSO: Simón Bolívar; Napoleon I; Pedro II; José de San Martín.

RELATED ARTICLES in *Great Events from History: The Nineteenth Century, 1801-1900:* September 7, 1822: Brazil Becomes Independent; 1828-1834: Portugal's Miguelite Wars.

PEDRO II
Emperor of Brazil (r. 1840-1889)

During the early years of his nearly fifty-year reign as emperor of Brazil, Pedro II stabilized the country politically and presided over fundamental economic developments. However, a draining war against Paraguay and the nation's divisive campaign against slavery undermined his rule until he was forced to abdicate.

BORN: December 2, 1825; Rio de Janeiro, Brazil
DIED: December 5, 1891; Paris, France
ALSO KNOWN AS: Pedro de Alcântara (birth name); Dom Pedro II
AREA OF ACHIEVEMENT: Government and politics

EARLY LIFE

Dom Pedro II (PAY-throh) was the Brazilian-born son of the first emperor of Brazil, Dom Pedro I, and the latter's Austrian wife, the Archduchess Leopoldina, daughter of the last Holy Roman Emperor. The youngest of seven children, Pedro lost his mother a year after he was born when she died from complications during childbirth. In 1831, when he was five years old, his father was forced to abdicate and leave the country, leaving him behind as the heir to the Brazilian throne.

Because Dom Pedro was too young to rule, a regency governed the country until he was declared of age in 1840, with leading figures of the period carefully guiding his education. Meanwhile, the death of his father in Portugal in 1834 left young Pedro orphaned. His oldest sister, Maria da Glória, became queen of Portugal, and Dom Pedro's reign as the second emperor of Brazil began officially with the declaration of his majority in 1840. His coronation occurred one year later.

LIFE'S WORK

The declaration of the majority of Dom Pedro II when he was only fourteen years old occurred as a consequence of the eroding authority of Brazil's central government under the regency. Addressing this rising anarchy was the immediate priority of the young monarch and his advisers. Supported by an exceptionally skilled and dedicated military officer, later ennobled as the duke of Caxias, the young monarch was able to suppress revolts in several provinces.

By the end of the first decade of Pedro's reign, the interior of the country was pacified. In addition the economy prospered due to the growing importance of coffee exports. During the previous three centuries, Brazil's prosperity had been based first on sugar and later on gold. The climate and soil in the highlands of southeastern Brazil were ideal for coffee growing, and its cultivation came to make the province of São Paulo one of the wealthiest and most economically dynamic in the empire.

Dom Pedro earnestly encouraged technical and cultural advances, supporting numerous projects for capital investment, banking, railroads, shipping, public health, and education. On the occasion of the centennial of the independence of the United States, in 1876, he visited that country. During a meeting with Alexander Graham Bell, he witnessed the operation of a telephone and afterward had the first telephone system installed in Brazil. The emperor also had temporarily as his chaplain the Brazilian inventor of wireless communication, Father Roberto Landell de Moura.

Dom Pedro acquired a reputation as a benign and progressive ruler, a magnanimous sovereign. However, he presided over an essentially archaic social regime, in which virtually all labor was performed by slaves, and most property and income were dominated by a small elite. Pedro favored constitutional monarchy and parliamentary democracy. However, the electoral franchise was quite limited in a realm such as his, a vast patriarchal plantation slavocracy. Conservative and liberal political parties existed, but had little of any electoral competitiveness, and political offices were allotted among members of the landed elites. Dom Pedro presided over a realm to which he gave conscientious attention, but was, at the same, the keystone of a regime with which he was fundamentally unsympathetic.

War and abolition eventually proved the downfall of the Brazilian empire and its last emperor. From 1864 to 1870, Brazil, Argentina, and Uruguay were in a war with Paraguay. This triple alliance of countries was ultimately victorious, and Brazil and the duke of Caxias made the greatest contributions to that victory. However, at the end of the war, the Brazilian army observed the sad condition of its impoverished soldiers, products of the archaic society from which they originated.

During the 1870's, the military increasingly became the focus of dissatisfaction with the imperial regime, viewing it as a feudal relic that hindered the economic and social progress of the country. To the military, the aging Dom Pedro increasingly came to appear as the representative of a society that compromised the security of Brazil, weakening it against modern and industrializing countries. Brazil needed a republican form of government, equal to any other country in the Americas.

Furthermore, the end of the U.S. Civil War in 1865 meant that Brazil remained the last major bastion of slavery in the Western Hemisphere. Dom Pedro favored the end of slavery. However, slave labor was the backbone not only of the national economy and society but also of the regime over which he presided. His opposition to slavery alienated from him some of the most conservative landed gentry, a key segment that traditionally had supported the monarchy. In addition, Pedro alienated the Roman Catholic hierarchy by favoring a separation of church and state, and he adhered to freemasonry.

Pedro had hoped progressively to replace slavery with free labor built on new European immigration. However, most European emigrants preferred to go to the United States or Argentina, where free labor markets were already established. Brazil abolished slavery in stages. First, in 1850, the importation of slaves was legally abolished. Next, all children born of slaves after 1871 were to become free when they reached their majority, and aged slaves were freed in 1885. The final stage, total abolition, occurred in 1888.

This last act of abolition, however, was not undertaken by Dom Pedro. Ill and overburdened, he was traveling abroad at that time, leaving his daughter Princess Isabel as regent in his place, and she signed the act of abolition. When Pedro returned to Brazil, he found himself in a country that no longer had any economic, political, or intellectual rationale to justify his regime. The empire was further jeopardized by the fact that Dom Pedro's successor would be his daughter Isabel, and a woman would not be welcome as a ruler in an overwhelmingly patriarchal society. Moreover, Isabel was not married to a Brazilian but to a French aristocrat.

On November 15, 1889, while Emperor Pedro was resting at his palace in the mountains near Rio de Janeiro, the armed forces declared that the empire was abolished, replaced by a republic. On receiving this news, the emperor offered no resistance. By that time, he was considered unreliable by political conservatives and irrelevant by liberals. He departed with his immediate family, setting sail for exile in Europe. The following year he died while staying at a hotel in Paris. Pedro and his empress are buried in the cathedral of Petropolis, the mountain retreat that was the summer seat of the imperial court. The palace there is now a museum commemorat-

ing his life and work and housing the former crown jewels.

In 1843, Pedro married Princess Teresa Cristina, the daughter of Francis I, king of the Two Sicilies. With her he had four children. Two sons, Afonso and Pedro, died in infancy; and one of his daughters, Leopoldina, predeceased her parents. His second child, and older daughter, was Princess Isabel. Over the following century, some descendants of Pedro II remained pretenders to the Brazilian throne, and a small monarchical party maintained a tenuous existence within Brazil.

SIGNIFICANCE

For no other figure in nineteenth century Brazil are there more images than those of Emperor Pedro II. However, it is the pictures of the closing years of his reign and life, of an aged figure, sad and meditative, that have come most to represent the tragic nature of his rule. He was a respected figure, recognized for his intelligence and humanity, and his authority during his time was rarely questioned. Nonetheless, he was powerless to undo what he himself recognized as the most debilitating aspect of Brazilian society and development: slavery. His tragedy was to be powerless against the socioeconomic condition that was the basis of his political position. Nonetheless, beyond the lasting images of the end of his reign should be balanced the vigor and hope of its beginning. Its accomplishments included foundations for Brazilian parliamentary, cultural, and intellectual development. He also supported innovations in Brazilian economic, commercial, and technical endeavors.

Pedro's limitations were those that lay across all Brazilian society. As a slavocracy, Brazil was made up not of owners of property or participants in society but by those owned as property and marginal to its social dynamic. No foundations or innovations could penetrate any deeper than the superficial layer of elites that composed the active whole of the country.

—*Edward A. Riedinger*

FURTHER READING

Barman, Roderick J. *Citizen Emperor: Pedro II and the Making of Brazil, 1825-91*. Stanford, Calif.: Stanford University Press, 1999. Details life of second emperor of Brazil within context of constitutional monarchy with recognized political responsibilities and limits; clarifies personal, political, and socioeconomic factors that contributed to successes and failures of his reign.

Bernstein, Harry. *Dom Pedro II*. New York: Twayne, 1973. Biography of Dom Pedro in a series on major historical figures in Europe and the Americas that offers concise biographies for general readership.

Bethel, Leslie. *Brazil: Empire and Republic, 1822-1930.* Cambridge, England: Cambridge University Press, 1989. Places reign of Pedro II within context of Brazil's first century of independence.

Schwarcz, Lilia Moritz. *The Emperor's Beard: Dom Pedro II and the Tropical Monarchy of Brazil.* New York: Hill & Wang, 2004. Translation of work by leading Brazilian historian, emphasizing evolving imagery of Dom Pedro II during his reign. Amply illustrated.

Simmons, Charles Willis. *Marshal Deodoro and the Fall of Dom Pedro II.* Durham, N.C.: Duke University Press, 1966. Details final stages of Brazilan empire and monarchy in confrontation between Pedro II and the head of military forces, Marshal Deodora da Fonseca, who established the republic in 1889.

Williams, Mary Wilhelmine. *Dom Pedro, the Magnanimous, Second Emperor of Brazil.* Chapel Hill: University of North Carolina Press, 1937. Earliest scholarly work in English on life of Pedro II, emphasizing his conscientiousness and sagacity.

SEE ALSO: Alexander Graham Bell; Joaquim Maria Machado de Assis; Pedro I; André Rebouças; Domingo Faustino Sarmiento.
RELATED ARTICLES in *Great Events from History: The Nineteenth Century, 1801-1900:* September 7, 1822: Brazil Becomes Independent; May 1, 1865-June 20, 1870: Paraguayan War.

SIR ROBERT PEEL
Prime minister of Great Britain (1834-1835, 1841-1846)

A Tory politician, Peel broke with party doctrine to reform the criminal code, create an effective police force, legalize labor unions, and repeal the Corn Laws, thereby ensuring the success of free trade and leaving a legacy of fundamental reforms in Great Britain.

BORN: February 5, 1788; near Bury, Lancashire, England
DIED: July 2, 1850; London, England
ALSO KNOWN AS: Second Baronet Peel
AREA OF ACHIEVEMENT: Government and politics

EARLY LIFE

Robert Peel was born in a cottage near Chamber Hall, his family's manor house in Lancashire. His father, Sir Robert Peel, and his mother, née Ellen Yates, were the children of partners who owned a successful cotton mill. The senior Peel's father had been a skilled craftsperson who had founded the family fortune by manufacturing cotton textiles. The Peels thus were part of the new commercial aristocracy, only two generations removed from Yorkshire yeomen. The senior Peel, independently wealthy, had won a seat in Parliament, served in William Pitt's cabinet, and been rewarded with a baronetcy.

Young Robert Peel was educated at Marrow and at Christ Church, Oxford University, where he distinguished himself as a first-rate scholar in classics, history, and mathematics. He was a deeply religious High Church Anglican but was never interested in theological debate.

In 1809, at the age of twenty-two, Peel joined his father in the ranks of the Tory Party in Parliament. After brief periods in lesser offices, he accepted the post of secretary for Ireland. For five years, between 1812 and 1817, he stirred extreme reactions of hatred and admiration for his administration of Ireland. He pursued a repressive policy depending heavily on armed force to keep order. He earned a reputation as a thorough bigot for his opposition to Roman Catholic emancipation, which meant principally the right of Roman Catholics to hold public office. At the same time, Peel created the Irish Constabulary, an efficient police force that was to be a valuable model for his later work with the London police.

In 1817, Peel resigned the uncongenial Irish secretaryship and was rewarded by his party with a parliamentary seat representing Oxford University, his alma mater. His policies in Ireland had made him the natural spokesperson for Oxford, which was known for its unyielding Anglican conservatism.

In 1820, Peel married. His wife, Julia, daughter of General Sir John Floyd, bore him five sons and two daughters. His devoted family formed a solid pillar of strength during the stormy years of his controversial political career.

LIFE'S WORK

From 1822 to 1827, Peel held the cabinet post of home secretary. With regard to Ireland and Catholic emancipation, he held to his old views. In other areas, however, his unyielding antireform Toryism showed signs of softening.

Peel took a leading role in convening a special parliamentary committee to investigate the condition of the working class. Francis Place, the former tailor who was to become the founder of British labor unionism, selected representative workers, coached them carefully, and brought them to the committee to offer testimony, through the collusion of Joseph Hume, a brilliant parliamentary radical. Thus, Peel, whose own fortune rested on the factory system, became a willing aid to those seeking to legalize the formation of labor unions and strikes. In 1824, the Combination Acts and the Statutes of Apprentices, which had previously prevented strikes, were repealed.

Inspired by the earlier work of Sir Samuel Romilly and Sir James Mackintosh, Peel took the initiative in 1825-1826 in passing the Five Acts, a series of ordinances that reformed criminal law. By the end of the first quarter of the nineteenth century, it was no longer possible to get juries to bring in guilty verdicts that carried mandatory death sentences for such crimes as stealing a shilling's worth of merchandise or appearing on a highway masked or in blackface. The great object of the Five Acts was to fit punishment to crime. Peel accepted the dictate that the certainty of punishment is more important than the severity of penalty.

During a second term as home secretary, in 1829, Peel created the London Metropolitan Police, the source of the ultimately fabled Scotland Yard. The fact that the police came to be called "Peelers" in Ireland and "Bobbies" in London constitutes a memorial to the same home secretary.

During his second term as home secretary, Peel entered the next phase in what his opponents termed a betrayal of old principles. In 1828, he joined in support of the repeal of the Test and Corporation Acts, which had previously ensured that only Anglicans and Presbyterians could hold office in the British Isles. In 1828, these rights were extended to nonconformist or dissenting Protestant denominations that had enjoyed freedom of religion since 1689 but whose members had been denied the right to hold office or to send their sons to Oxford or Cambridge Universities.

The full emancipation of Roman Catholics was another matter. In the popular mind, Roman Catholicism

Sir Robert Peel. (Courtesy, The University of Texas at Austin)

was still associated with the legends of "Bloody Mary Tudor," John Foxe's *The Book of Martyrs* (1559), and the alleged sinister intentions of King James II. The fact that most British Roman Catholics were Irish compounded theological and ethnic hatreds.

Nevertheless, a practical politician such as Peel found it easier to overcome old prejudices when he observed that the Irish had learned the fine art of political organization under the inspired leadership of the Protestant Irish nationalist Daniel O'Connell, who had founded the Catholic Association in 1823. O'Connell had proved that the Irish had the capacity to support and vote for Protestant parliamentary representatives pledged to Catholic emancipation and to do so in a disciplined and nonviolent fashion. Peel, who had a healthy respect for Irish violence, was perhaps more impressed with O'Connell's use of the electoral apparatus to attain his goals within the British system. Thus, it was Peel and the arch-Tory Arthur Wellesley, the duke of Wellington, who persuaded King George IV to approve Catholic emancipation in 1829.

Peel's support of Catholic emancipation briefly cost him his seat in Parliament. He was too valuable for the

Tories to lose, however, and he was back almost immediately. The firmness with which Peel opposed Charles Grey's parliamentary reform bill of 1832 regained for him many of the Tory allies he had lost over the issue of Catholic emancipation. It was Peel who rebuilt the Tory Party, which had fallen to a mere 150 members in Commons after Grey's Whig triumph.

In 1834, Peel became prime minister for the first time. His parliamentary majority was too precarious, however, and his cabinet fell. Interestingly, the issue that forced his resignation was a proposal to devote the surplus income of the Anglican Church in Ireland to Irish nonsectarian education. He was thirty-four years premature with an idea later passed into law by his great disciple, William Ewart Gladstone.

Peel's second and final tenure of the prime ministership occurred between 1841 and 1846. In foreign affairs, the ministry enjoyed two notable successes. An Afghan war was ended under honorable terms, and war was avoided with the United States by a settlement of the borders of Maine and Oregon. These years are chiefly remembered, however, for Peel's adoption of free trade. For twenty years, he had moved closer to the ideas of economists such as David Ricardo and pragmatic capitalists such as William Huskisson—after all, his own roots were not in the old aristocracy, which owed its wealth to agriculture, but in the new aristocracy, which had grown rich in the Industrial Revolution. In that sense, he had never been one with the country squires who made up the backbone of Toryism.

Thus, in 1842, Peel imposed an income tax to absorb a budget deficit. By the time that he left office, the Treasury boasted a surplus. Until the crucial year 1845, he managed to cut tariff rates on about 450 items, most of them raw materials not produced in Great Britain. Here again, Peel actually increased tariff income, as he approached free trade. His conversion to free trade raised criticism but did not precipitate party rebellion, because he did not speak of opening Great Britain to the free importation of foreign wheat.

The Corn Laws protecting aristocratic landowners from the competition of foreign wheat were regarded as sacred. The aristocracy asserted that a financially secure gentry was the only class in society prepared by heredity, education, and tradition to serve their country in the armed forces and in government without regard to personal financial reward. Since 1836, however, under the leadership of Richard Cobden and John Bright, the Anti-Corn Law League had argued that eliminating the Corn Laws would reduce the price of bread, lower the cost of

living, and permit foreign grain producers to sell agricultural produce in Great Britain, thereby increasing their purchases of British goods.

Peel might have been content to refrain from touching the Corn Laws since they were so essential to maintaining Tory strength, rebuilt with such difficulty since 1832. Nature, however, intervened. An Irish potato famine plunged that island into starvation and despair in 1845. The price of food staples flew so high that only a repeal of the Corn Laws could solve the crisis of millions of people faced with penury, starvation, or emigration. Peel could no longer defend the Corn Laws and abandoned them. In 1846, he finally formed a cabinet that was committed to repeal of the Corn Laws. The parliamentary debate was bitter; the Tory Party split in two.

Benjamin Disraeli turned against his mentor, Sir Robert Peel, and led that large faction of the Tories who regarded the repeal of the Corn Laws as equivalent to social revolution and the destruction of the old aristocracy. Gladstone, by contrast, stood by his prime minister. The Tory ministry leading the fight for repeal knew that they were ending their own tenure of office because they could obtain repeal only with the help of Lord John Russell and the Whigs. In a magnificent gesture of self-sacrifice, Peel lost his own chance ever to be prime minister again and sent his party into twenty-eight years of eclipse. Nevertheless, by his adoption of a low revenue tariff system of free trade, he gave Great Britain forty years of unparalleled prosperity and that special brand of national optimism that historians refer to as mid-Victorian self-confidence.

Out of office, though still in Parliament, Peel lent his generous support to the Whig-Liberal cabinet in repealing the Navigation Acts in 1849. He also made a vain effort, in his last days, to obtain full civil rights for the Jews. On June 29, 1850, he suffered fatal injuries while horseback riding in a park near his London home. He died on July 2.

SIGNIFICANCE

Sir Robert Peel must be remembered as the quintessential political pragmatist. An Anglican whose birth and education had infused him with a deep mistrust of Irish Catholics, he ended by doing more for them than any English leader had done before. He developed the Royal Irish Constabulary to carry out repressive measures, but ended by creating a London Metropolitan Police Force that became a model for maintaining order in a free society. By birth and education he belonged to the Tory gentry, but practical experience made him sympathetic to labor unions, legal strikes, and ultimately to laissez-faire capitalist free trade.

In a word, Peel held to no fixed position if experience proved him wrong. In the end, he enjoyed the respect and even the affection of those who at various times in his career had called him a renegade turncoat.

—Arnold Blumberg

FURTHER READING

Cecil, Algernon. *Queen Victoria and Her Prime Ministers*. London: Eyre and Spottiswoode, 1953. A serious examination of Victoria's long reign and her view of the ministers who served her. In the examination of sixty-three years, Peel's role is retrospectively modest.

Conacher, J. B. *The Peelites and the Party System, 1846-1852*. Newton Abbot, England: David and Charles, 1972. Explores the fate of the Tories who followed Peel when he broke with Disraeli and the party loyalists in 1846. Some, like Gladstone, went on to become leaders in the Whig Party as it became the Liberal Party.

Evans, Eric J. *Sir Robert Peel: Statesmanship, Power, and Party*. London: Routledge, 1991. Brief (82-page) discussion of Peel's political career. Evans argues that Peel was more successful as an administrator than as a politician.

Gash, Norman. *Sir Robert Peel: The Life of Sir Robert Peel After 1830*. Totowa, N.J.: Rowman & Littlefield, 1972. A solid, well-written, meticulously documented biography that should be the first work consulted by anyone interested in Peel.

Jenkins, T. A. *Sir Robert Peel*. New York: St. Martin's Press, 1999. An examination of Peel's political career, analyzing the achievements of his ministry. Jenkins views Peel as a link between Toryism and progressivism.

Jones, Wilbur Devereux. *The Peelites, 1846-1857*. Columbus: Ohio State University Press, 1972. Like the Conacher volume (see above), this serious and well-documented work traces the impact of the disaffected Tories on the Whig-Liberal Party.

Parker, Charles Stuart, ed. *Sir Robert Peel, from His Private Papers*. 3 vols. London: John Murray, 1891-1899. Reprint. New York: Kraus, 1970. As the collection was published by the trustees of Peel's estate, and

as Sir Robert's grandson George Peel wrote a eulogistic chapter, it may be assumed that this valuable source is accurate but selective and incomplete.

Peel, Sir Robert. *Memoirs by the Right Honourable Sir Robert Peel*. 2 vols. London: John Murray, 1856-1859. Reprint. New York: Kraus, 1969. The memoirs were published by Earl Stanhope and Edward Cardwell on behalf of the trustees of the Peel estate, six years after Sir Robert's death. This valuable source reflects what the deceased hoped would be posterity's judgment of his work.

_____. *The Speeches of the Late Right Honourable Sir Robert Peel, Bart., Delivered in the House of Commons, with a General Explanatory Index, and a Brief Chronological Summary of the Various Subjects on which the Speeches Were Delivered*. 4 vols. London: G. Routledge, 1853. Reprint. New York: Kraus, 1972. A valuable primary source.

Ramsay, Anna Augusta Whittal. *Sir Robert Peel*. Salem, N.H.: Ayer, 1928. Reprint. Freeport, N.Y.: Books for Libraries Press, 1969. A solid, scholarly, and well-written study of Peel's life. It is particularly good for analyses of the political alignments that affected Peel's choices of policy.

Victoria, Queen of Great Britain. *The Letters of Queen Victoria: A Selection from Her Majesty's Correspondence Between the Years 1837 and 1861*. Edited by Arthur Christopher Benson and Viscount Esher. 3 vols. New York: Longmans, Green, 1907. Offers revealing comment by the queen on her benign relationship to Peel.

SEE ALSO: John Bright; Richard Cobden; Benjamin Disraeli; George IV; William Ewart Gladstone; Daniel O'Connell; Francis Place; David Ricardo; Baron John Russell; Duke of Wellington.

RELATED ARTICLES in *Great Events from History: The Nineteenth Century, 1801-1900:* May 9, 1828-April 13, 1829: Roman Catholic Emancipation; June 4, 1832: British Parliament Passes the Reform Act of 1832; September 9, 1835: British Parliament Passes Municipal Corporations Act; 1845-1854: Great Irish Famine; June 15, 1846: British Parliament Repeals the Corn Laws; June 15, 1846: United States Acquires Oregon Territory.

CHARLES SANDERS PEIRCE
American philosopher

Although he was largely unrecognized by his contemporaries—apart from his contribution to pragmatism—Peirce developed a system of philosophy that attempted to reconcile the nineteenth century's faith in empirical science with its love of the metaphysical absolute. His difficult and often confusing ideas anticipated problems central to twentieth century philosophy.

BORN: September 10, 1839; Cambridge, Massachusetts
DIED: April 19, 1914; near Milford, Pennsylvania
AREA OF ACHIEVEMENT: Philosophy

EARLY LIFE

Charles Sanders Peirce was the son of Benjamin Peirce, one of the foremost American mathematicians. During his childhood, his mother, Sarah Hunt (Mills) Peirce, took second place to his dynamic father, who personally supervised the boy's education and provided a role model that inspired but also proved impossible to emulate. Convinced of his son's genius, Benjamin Peirce encouraged his precocious development. Charles began the study of chemistry at the age of eight, started an intense scrutiny of logic at twelve, and faced rigorous training in mathematics throughout his childhood. In the latter case, he was seldom given general principles or theorems. Instead, he was expected to work them out on his own.

At sixteen, Peirce entered Harvard, where his father was professor of mathematics. Contrary to expectations, Peirce proved a less than brilliant student, and he was graduated, in 1859, seventy-first out of a class of ninety-one. Probably too young and certainly too much the nonconformist to fit into the rigid educational system of nineteenth century Harvard, Peirce's inauspicious beginning in institutional academics was prophetic. Though he would continue his education, receiving a master's degree from Harvard in 1862 and a bachelor's degree in chemistry the following year, his future did not lead to a distinguished career in academics or, indeed, in any conventional pursuit. His lot in life, in spite of so much promise, was frustration and apparent failure.

Peirce's difficulty in adjusting to the world of ordinary men was related to his unusual and often trying personality. Always his father's favorite, Peirce became convinced of his own genius and impatient with those who failed to recognize the obvious. Shielded and overindulged as a child, Peirce never developed the social skills required for practical affairs nor the self-discipline necessary to make his own grandiose vision a reality. Such problems were exaggerated by his passion for perfection and his abstract turn of mind. Peirce found real happiness only in the rarefied world of his own philosophical speculation.

As a youth, Peirce both attracted and repelled. Always prone to the dramatic gesture and, when he was inclined, a brilliant conversationalist, he could be an entertaining companion, but he could also use his rapier wit as a weapon. Of medium height, dark, swarthy, and fastidious in matters of dress, the handsome young Peirce reveled in his reputation as a lady's man and spent much energy in seeking the "good life." He actually paid an expert to train his palate so that he could become a connoisseur of fine wines. In 1862, Peirce married Harriet Melusina Fay, three years his senior and infinitely more mature and self-possessed. A feminist and intellectual in her own right, "Zina" worshipped her captive "genius" and labored for years to keep him out of serious trouble while restraining his extravagance. However, she could also be jealous and possessive, and, though Peirce would experience some stability under Zina's influence, the marriage was doomed.

LIFE'S WORK

Upon his graduation from Harvard, Peirce went to work for the United States Coast and Geodetic Survey, a position acquired through his father's influence. Benjamin Peirce served as a consulting geometer for the organization and became its superintendent in 1867. Charles Peirce remained with the survey in various capacities until 1891, when he was asked to resign. This bureaucratic career, while terminated in less-than-desirable circumstances, was not without accomplishments. His deep commitment to the experimental method helped put the survey on a firm scientific basis, and Peirce himself became internationally known for his work on gravity research.

Peirce also continued an association with Harvard, once again through his father's influence, holding temporary lectureships in logic in 1865-1866 and 1869-1870 and from 1872 to 1875 serving as assistant at the Harvard Observatory. His observatory work on the measurement of light provided data for the only book he published during his lifetime, *Photometric Researches* (1878). Peirce hoped for a permanent appointment at Harvard, but his lack of a doctoral degree, his erratic lifestyle, and a typically personal quarrel with Harvard president Charles W. Eliot made the dream impossible.

More important than Peirce's actual work, the atmosphere and personal contacts at Harvard helped mold his philosophical outlook. Never idle, Peirce spent his spare time studying the work of Immanuel Kant, the ideas of the medieval scholastics, and various theories in logic and mathematics. The most useful forum for his developing ideas was the so-called Metaphysical Club.

In the meetings of this unusual group, which included William James, Oliver Wendell Holmes, Jr., Francis E. Abbot, and Chauncey Wright, among others, Peirce had the opportunity to test his theories before a critical audience. It was there that he used the term "pragmatism" to describe the relationship between a conception and its effects that allows one to understand the actual meaning of the original conception by knowing its effects. Although Peirce intended his idea as a theory of meaning, William James, more than twenty years later, would popularize the term and expand it far beyond the original intention. In fact, objecting to his friend's interpretation, Peirce, in 1905, coined the term "pragmaticism" to distinguish his thought from James's version.

In his Harvard years, Peirce began to write articles for *The Journal of Speculative Philosophy* and other scholarly publications, as well as more popular magazines such as *Popular Science Monthly*. Such articles, along with numerous book reviews, provided his major public outlet for the remainder of his life. Ignored by much of the philosophical community, these writings contained important contributions to logic, mathematics, and metaphysics.

Peirce finally got his chance to teach when he was hired as a part-time lecturer at Johns Hopkins University in 1879. Apparently an effective teacher, he produced some of his best work in logic and scientific methodology at Johns Hopkins. However, his erratic behavior, coupled with his divorce from his first wife and remarriage to a twenty-six-year-old French woman, the mysterious Mme Juliette Pourtalai, made it difficult for the authorities to accept him, no matter how brilliant, as part of the faculty. In 1884, Peirce was dismissed from his position because of unsuitable activities of a moral nature, probably connected with his divorce and remarriage.

Peirce's second marriage began a phase of his life that would be philosophically productive but personally frustrating, ending in self-imposed exile. In 1887, his academic career hopelessly in shambles and his labors for the survey drawing to a conclusion, Peirce moved to Milford, Pennsylvania, a resort area on the Delaware river. With a small inheritance, he was able to purchase land and begin construction of an elaborately planned home he called "Arisbe." Though Peirce was able to live in his retreat for the remainder of his life, the mansion was never really completed.

Typically, Peirce had overextended himself. When he lost his government salary in 1891 and suffered severe losses in the depression of 1893, he began a long slide into poverty. His closest and always tolerant friend, William James, tried to help as much as possible, arranging for a series of lectures in Boston in 1898 and finally persuading Harvard to allow the notorious philosopher to give a series of lectures at the university in 1903. No effort, however, even by the most famous American philosopher, would make Peirce acceptable to established society in the nineteenth century. Finally, James began collecting donations for a Peirce fund from interested and unnamed friends. From 1907 until his death in 1914, Peirce was largely supported by this fund, which amounted to about thirteen hundred dollars a year. Peirce, who had often been jealous of James and attacked his version of pragmatism with undisguised contempt, paid his friend a typical compliment by adopting Santiago (St. James) as part of his name in 1909.

Even in his last years, which were marred by illness, Peirce was productive. He continued to work in isolation, leaving behind a massive collection of papers. Ironically, Harvard, the institution that had so often rejected him, recognized his worth and purchased the manuscripts from his widow. Between 1931 and 1935, the six volumes of the *Collected Papers of Charles Sanders Peirce*, edited by Charles Hartshorne and Paul Weiss, were published by Harvard. This collection began what amounted to a revolution in American academic philosophy, making the ideas of Peirce a touchstone for twentieth century philosophical inquiry.

The exact nature of Peirce's contribution to understanding is by no means clear. Numerous scholars have spent careers examining his writings, never reaching a consensus. The confusion is rooted in the nature of Peirce's work itself. Not satisfied with a contribution in a single area of inquiry, Peirce envisioned a vast architectonic system ending in a complete explanation of all human knowledge. In short, Peirce strove to be a modern Aristotle. Although admirable, this goal ran up against a central dilemma in human thought, providing a source of tension within Peirce's system as well as within the world in which he lived.

Science, in the last years of the nineteenth century, revealed a limited vision of reality, of what could be known. The world, according to this view, consisted of matter and could be fully explained through the scientific method. Many thinkers, unable to accept this so-called positivistic version of reality, countered with an explanation based on the mind itself as the source of everything. Best represented in the Idealism of Georg Wilhelm Friedrich Hegel, this view had spawned many variations. Peirce could not fully accept either position. Positivism seemed to deny the possibility of metaphysics or, perhaps better, a universe with meaning that could be understood by human beings. Idealism seemed hopelessly subjective, denying the possibility of actually knowing the physical universe.

Peirce set out to reconcile the irreconcilable by carefully examining immediate experience. Characteristically, this examination would be grounded on clear and precise thinking such as his famous "pragmatic maxim." He also rejected nominalism and accepted the position of the medieval scholastic Duns Scotus on the reality of Universals. Peirce insisted that cognition itself is reality, and everything that is real is knowable. The structure of experience is revealed in what he called "phaneroscopy." This term is typical of Peirce's obsession with the invention of new words to explain concepts, which is one of the reasons his ideas are so difficult.

Phaneroscopy is roughly analogous to the modern concept of phenomenology. From his phenomenological basis, Peirce deduced three categories or qualities of experience that he termed Firstness, Secondness, and Thirdness. This division of experience allowed him to move from an essentially psychological analysis to logic itself through what he called the "semiotic," or the doctrine of signs. By signs, Peirce essentially meant those things in the mind that stand for the real things of the world. A word, for example, would be a sign but only one kind of sign. Peirce's analysis of signs and their relationships was a vast and complicated explanation of how human beings think and provides the logical basis for his whole system.

A complete discussion of this difficult and obscure argument is not possible in this context, but most modern philosophers would agree that it constitutes Peirce's most important contribution to philosophy, particularly logic. Its obscurity, however, has led to many different interpretations. Phenomenologists, for example, find considerable comfort in his explanation of experience, while the logical positivists, who seldom agree with phenomenologists, also see their ideas reflected in

Peirce's theory of signs. In fact, most philosophical systems in the twentieth century found some part of Peirce's ideas important in either a positive or a negative way.

Peirce's logic, however, was only the foundation of a broad system that included a complete theory of knowledge as well as cosmological speculations. This system, while not as widely accepted as his semiotic, includes a number of important concepts. For example, Peirce develops what he calls "tychism," or the doctrine of chance, which explains irregularities within nature. This idea should be balanced with "synechism," which is the doctrine that continuity is a basic feature of the world. Here again, Peirce reconciles the irreconcilable, and the result provides a reasonable picture of the actual condition of scientific inquiry.

Synechism represents scientific law, which Peirce calls habit, without which one could not understand the operation of the natural world. Tychism, however, explains how change is possible and prevents a deterministic version of reality, which is the logical result of scientific law. Science then, while based on research that, if pursued to infinity, will result in "truth," must in the practical world be based on probability. Even in logic itself, one cannot be sure that all statements are correct. Although not denying absolute truth, this concept, which Peirce called "fallibilism," provides a healthy corrective to those who are convinced that they have found the ultimate answer to reality.

SIGNIFICANCE

Few can profess to understand all of Peirce's philosophy, and his work will probably never appeal to the average person unschooled in the mysteries of philosophical discourse. Nevertheless, his attack on the central dilemma of modern thought, created by scientific advance and its almost inevitable clash with human values, is the necessary starting point for many twentieth century philosophers and, through their work, has a profound influence on the way the world is viewed.

It may be true that Peirce ultimately failed in his attempt to reconcile the "hard" world of science with cherished human values represented by the "soft" world of Idealism, but, unlike his tragic personal life, his philosophy was certainly a glorious failure. Moreover, Peirce remained a true optimist who believed in the inevitability of human progress through reason. His system of thought, while far from perfect, did provide a view of reality that would make such progress possible. His first rule of reason demanded that the road to new knowledge always be left open. The greatest sin against reasoning, he believed, consisted in adopting a set of beliefs that would erect a barrier in the path of the search for truth.

—*David Warren Bowen*

FURTHER READING

Almeder, Robert F. *The Philosophy of Charles S. Peirce: A Critical Introduction.* Totowa, N.J.: Rowman & Littlefield, 1980. An analysis of Peirce's philosophy, stressing his epistemological realism, which contains a perceptive and detailed discussion of his theory of knowledge.

Conkin, Paul K. *Puritans and Pragmatists: Eight Eminent American Thinkers.* Bloomington: Indiana University Press, 1968. One of the finest overviews of American intellectual history. Places Peirce within the context of the development of American thought between Jonathan Edwards and George Santayana.

De Waal, Cornelis. *On Peirce.* Belmont, Calif.: Wadsworth/Thomson Learning, 2001. Brief (91-page) overview of Peirce's philosophy, designed to introduce his ideas to students.

_____. *On Pragmatism.* Belmont, Calif.: Wadsworth/Thomson Learning, 2005. Describes the main figures and the central issues of pragmatism, with individual chapters devoted to Peirce, Dewey, James, and other philosophers.

Goudge, Thomas A. *The Thought of C. S. Peirce.* Toronto: University of Toronto Press, 1950. One of the most perceptive studies of Peirce's thought. Sees Peirce's philosophy as resting on a conflict within his personality that produced tendencies toward both naturalism and Transcendentalism.

Misak, Cheryl, ed. *The Cambridge Companion to Peirce.* New York: Cambridge University Press, 2004. Collection of essays discussing Peirce's philosophy and his place within the pragmatist tradition. The essays include examinations of Peirce and medieval thought, his account of perception, and his theory of signs.

Moore, Edward C. *American Pragmatism: Peirce, James, and Dewey.* New York: Columbia University Press, 1961. An analysis of American pragmatism based on its three primary figures. Provides an excellent comparison of their different positions.

Potter, Vincent G. *Charles S. Peirce: On Norms and Ideals.* Amherst: University of Massachusetts Press, 1967. An analysis of Peirce's attempt to establish aesthetics, ethics, and logic as the three normative sciences. The author places particular emphasis on the role of "habit" in the universe.

Reilly, Francis E. *Charles Peirce's Theory of Scientific Method.* New York: Fordham University Press, 1970. A discussion of Peirce's ideas concerning the method and the philosophy of science.

Skagestad, Peter. *The Road of Inquiry: Charles Peirce's Realism.* New York: Columbia University Press, 1981. Focuses on Peirce's theory of scientific method but also contains an introduction with considerable biographical information.

SEE ALSO: F. H. Bradley; Georg Wilhelm Friedrich Hegel; Oliver Wendell Holmes; William James.

RELATED ARTICLES in *Great Events from History: The Nineteenth Century, 1801-1900:* April, 1807: Hegel Publishes *The Phenomenology of Spirit*; 1819: Schopenhauer Publishes *The World as Will and Idea.*

MATTHEW C. PERRY
American naval officer

One of the towering figures in nineteenth century American naval history, Perry had a U.S. Navy career that spanned almost half a century. He commanded ships and fleets with distinction in peace and in war; he also proposed and accomplished reforms in naval architecture, ordnance, and organization, and through skillful negotiation introduced Japan into the modern community of nations.

BORN: April 10, 1794; Newport, Rhode Island
DIED: March 4, 1858; New York, New York
ALSO KNOWN AS: Matthew Calbraith Perry (full name)
AREAS OF ACHIEVEMENT: Military, diplomacy

EARLY LIFE

Matthew Calbraith Perry was the son of Christopher Raymond Perry, a descendant of original Quaker settlers of Rhode Island who served in privateers and Continental warships during the American Revolution. The senior Perry met his Irish wife, Sarah Wallace Alexander, when he was a paroled prisoner in Ireland in 1781. Matthew's eldest brother, Oliver Hazard Perry, was the hero of the Battle of Lake Erie in 1813 and Matthew Perry's greatest hero.

In 1809, Matthew Perry was assigned as a midshipman to the schooner *Revenge*. A year later he transferred to the frigate *President*, in which he served in 1811 in the engagement with HMS *Little Belt* and in the War of 1812, when he was wounded slightly in the inconclusive fight with HMS *Belvidera*.

On December 24, 1814, he married Jane Slidell (1797-1879), daughter of a New York merchant, who bore him ten children. Their three sons and one of their sons-in-law were all navy or marine officers.

In 1815, Perry was assigned to the brig *Chippewa*, which was part of the Mediterranean Squadron, and at the end of this cruise he applied for furlough and commanded one, and perhaps more, of his father-in-law's merchant ships.

LIFE'S WORK

In 1819, Perry returned to naval service as first lieutenant in the corvette *Cyane*, which escorted the first settlers sent to Liberia by the American Colonization Society and patrolled the coast of West Africa to suppress the slave trade. Two years later, he was commanding the schooner *Shark* in African waters and the West Indies, where the navy was attempting to suppress piracy. Perry was of great assistance to the Liberian settlers in their efforts to establish their republic and was primarily responsible for the selection of the site of Monrovia.

From 1824 to 1827, Perry served as first lieutenant and later as acting commander in the battleship *North Carolina* in the Mediterranean Squadron. At this time the two responsibilities of the squadron, commanded by Commodore John Rodgers, were the protection of American shipping during the Greek war of independence and the implementation of a naval treaty with Turkey. Rodgers achieved both goals.

After service in the Charlestown naval yard, Perry was given command of the sloop-of-war *Concord* and in 1830 was responsible for conveying Minister John Randolph to St. Petersburg. This voyage was followed by two more years in the Mediterranean.

By this time Perry had developed all the skills that distinguished the rest of his naval career: total mastery of seamanship, a commanding presence, a great sense of duty and personal rectitude, negotiating skills of a high order, and a capacity for sympathy with people of diverse cultures. Much of this no doubt derived from his devout Episcopalianism, but it also was a product of high intelligence, which was reflected in a broad range of scholarly interests, particularly in history, ethnology, languages, and science.

When Perry was serving in the Mediterranean in this cruise, President Andrew Jackson was seeking agreements by which the European powers would agree to pay for spoliation of American commerce during the Napoleonic wars. In 1832, Perry commanded a squadron sent to Naples to support the efforts of American negotiators to collect payments from the Kingdom of the Two Sicilies. This show of strength apparently tipped the scales to produce the agreement of October, 1832.

The three greatest achievements of Perry's career were his efforts to modernize the navy, his service in the Mexican War, and his command of the expedition that first established formal relations with Japan.

From 1833, when he accepted command of the New York recruiting station, until 1843, when he ended his tenure as commander of the Brooklyn naval yard, Perry campaigned for naval reform. In an 1837 article, he outlined in detail the inadequacies of the United States Navy, which was eighth in the world, trailing even Turkey and Egypt and far behind Great Britain and France in naval architecture and ordnance. Perry is correctly considered the founder of the steam navy.

Perry campaigned for construction of steam warships, and he initiated the action that led to the creation of the navy's Engineering Corps. He argued for the adoption of shell guns, invented the collapsible smokestack, advocated iron hulls for river gunboats, and recommended the creation of an independent Lighthouse Board. In addition, he was deeply involved in efforts to cure the old navy's problem of manpower procurement. During the early nineteenth century, crews were usually made up by robbing the merchant service and by recruiting foreigners and social misfits. Perry agitated for the creation of an apprentice system and for a school ship for their training. The attempted mutiny on the *Somers* in 1842 discredited this system, but that failure led to implementation of another of Perry's proposals: the creation of the Naval Academy.

In 1843, Perry was assigned to the command of the African Squadron, and in this capacity he negotiated a treaty with the local chiefs on the Ivory Coast, in which the chiefs agreed not to molest missionaries or plunder trading ships. He also was influential in settling differences between the immigrants and the native population of Liberia.

In the Mexican War, Perry first served as vice commodore of naval forces on the Mexican coast, subordinate to Commodore David Conner. He captured Frontera in October, 1846, and sailed fifty miles up the Rio Grijalva to attack Villahermosa and to capture nine enemy warships there. In November, he participated in the capture of Tampico, and the following month occupied Ciudad de Carmen. In March, 1847, he succeeded Conner as commodore and landed naval guns and guncrews to support the troops Conner had landed to besiege Veracruz.

By the time Veracruz surrendered on March 29, 1847, Perry was commanding the largest American fleet up to that time—twenty-three vessels. In April, he attacked Tuxpan, destroying the forts and carrying off the guns captured by the Mexicans when an American brig ran aground. His second attack on Villahermosa in June, 1847, was his greatest achievement in the war. He again advanced up the Grijalva to the underwater obstacles laid down by the enemy, then landed eleven hundred men and led them personally on their three-mile march through Mexican defenses to capture Villahermosa.

The Japan expedition originated in Perry's memorandum to the secretary of the navy in the winter of 1851, in which he suggested that friendly relations could be achieved with Japan by a show of naval strength. He did not want command of the expedition, but he accepted it in January, 1852. His selection of ships and officers was careful, and his logistical planning was so effective that the colliers for refueling his steamers were in their assigned positions throughout the voyage. Before he could depart, however, he was ordered to investigate charges of British interference with American fishermen on the Canadian coast. His report on his findings led to the reciprocity treaty of 1854.

Perry's squadron arrived at Okinawa, then an independent kingdom, in May, 1853, and he established relations that enabled him to negotiate a treaty in the following year. After a side trip to the Bonin Islands, where, on Chichi Jima, he bought fifty acres as a possible coaling station, the squadron reached Tokyo Bay on July 8, 1853.

Perry's behavior with the Japanese was remarkable for its combination of austere reserve, firmness, and cordiality. The Japanese sent minor officials to order the American ships away, but Perry dealt with them only through his subordinates, insisting on dealing with officials who could speak for the emperor. When Japanese guard boats attempted to ring his ships, he ordered them

Matthew C. Perry. (Courtesy, Naval Historical Center)

off under threat of opening fire. Finally, when it did not appear that the Japanese would accept President Fillmore's letter under any conditions, Perry informed them that if they would not accept it within a sufficient time he would land at Edo (Tokyo) in force and deliver it himself.

On July 14, Perry was invited to land with an armed retinue at Kurihama, near the mouth of Tokyo Bay, and, amid great formality on both sides, two Japanese officials accepted Fillmore's letter.

After wintering in Hong Kong, Perry returned to Japan in February, 1854, for further negotiations and landed in March. By the treaty of March 31, the Japanese granted two fueling ports, at Hakodate on Tsugaru Strait on southern Hokkaido and at Shimoda on the Izu Peninsula on Honshū. Although the treaty did not make arrangements for trade, it did give Americans free access to the areas around the ports and arranged for shipwrecked American sailors to be sent to those ports for repatriation. Perry examined the port of Shimoda and, after sailing to Hakodate to ensure that it was acceptable, he returned to Shimoda in June and reached further agreements with the Japanese on currency exchange, pilotage, and port dues. After sailing to Okinawa to negotiate the Treaty of Naha in July, 1854, he led his forces back to Hong Kong and with the treaty returned to the United States by commercial steamers.

In his last years, Perry enjoyed enormous public respect for his achievements in Japan. He devoted his time to service on the Naval Efficiency Board, which was engaged in weeding out overage naval officers, and concentrated much of his attention on the preparation of the official narrative of the Japan expedition and on writing several articles that revealed a great sense of the importance of the Pacific in future American naval and political strategy. He was convinced that Russia would be the future Pacific rival of the United States and that it was crucially important to acquire coaling stations and naval bases in the western Pacific. Meanwhile, as a result of his achievements, the European powers were able to obtain treaties with Japan, and a trade agreement between the United States and Japan was achieved in 1858. Perry died in New York City on March 4, 1858.

SIGNIFICANCE

Perry distinguished himself in his long naval career both as a commander and as a diplomat. Possessing not only the great skills in combat leadership that made him the most distinguished American naval officer of the Mexican War but also a remarkable combination of tact, firm-

ness, patience, and empathy that enabled him to achieve great results as a negotiator, he succeeded both in founding the modern United States Navy and in using naval power to establish mutually productive relations with Japan.

Perry's success in the latter case led him to the conclusion that the Pacific was to become his country's future arena of power and influence, and he made proposals for establishing naval bases in the Pacific that, if they had not disappeared in the domestic crisis in which the United States found itself during the 1850's, might well have prevented the rupture of Japanese-American relations during the 1930's. Perry recognized international political realities in the Pacific at a time when virtually every other American was concerned with the task of conquering and developing the continent and securing domestic harmony. When the United States finally accepted international responsibility, it was obliged to fight a terrible war with the country with which Perry had established amicable relations and to maintain the presence in the Pacific that he had favored in the first place.

—*Robert L. Berner*

FURTHER READING

Barrows, Edward M. *The Great Commodore*. Indianapolis, Ind.: Bobbs-Merrill, 1935. The best biography until it was superseded by that of Morison. Somewhat dated on the subject of the Japan expedition.

Hawks, Francis L. *Narrative of the Expedition of an American Squadron to the China Seas and Japan*. Edited by Sidney Wallach. New York: Coward-McCann, 1952. A convenient modern abridgement of the journals and reports of the Japan expedition. (The original was published in three volumes in 1856.)

Kuhn, Ferdinand. "Yankee Sailor Who Opened Japan." *National Geographic Magazine* 104 (July, 1953): 85-102. A general account of Perry's achievements in Japan, well illustrated with contemporary prints, many of them by Japanese artists.

Morison, Samuel Eliot. *"Old Bruin": Commodore Matthew Calbraith Perry, 1794-1858*. Boston: Little, Brown, 1967. The definitive biography, by the most distinguished American naval historian. Full account of Perry's personal and professional life, with thorough treatment of social and political background, including the *Somers* affair and the achievements of Perry's father and brother.

Paullin, Charles Oscar. "The First American Treaty with Japan: 1851-1854." In *Diplomatic Negotiations of American Naval Officers, 1778-1883*. Baltimore:

Johns Hopkins University Press, 1912. Paullin was the outstanding student of this subject, and this chapter is a sound, basic account of Perry's accomplishments in Japan.

Pineau, Roger, ed. *The Japan Expedition, 1852-1854: The Personal Journal of Commodore Matthew C. Perry*. Washington, D.C.: Smithsonian Institution Press, 1968. A fine edition of Perry's journal, hitherto unpublished, with splendid color plates of watercolors and prints made during the voyage.

Schroeder, John H. *Matthew Calbraith Perry: Antebellum Sailor and Diplomat*. Annapolis, Md.: Naval Institute Press, 2001. An assessment of Perry's long military career, including his efforts to modernize the U.S. Navy.

Walworth, Arthur. *Black Ships Off Japan*. New York: Alfred A. Knopf, 1946. A popular account of the Japan expedition, essentially accurate though its interpretation of Perry's character and behavior should be checked against that of Morison.

Wiley, Peter Booth, and Korogi Ichiro. *Yankees in the Land of the Gods: Commodore Perry and the Opening of Japan*. New York: Viking Press, 1990. Popular and detailed account of Perry's expedition to Japan, describing his journey's impact on Japanese government and foreign relations and on U.S. relations with Japan.

SEE ALSO: Stephen Decatur; David G. Farragut; Hiroshige; Ii Naosuke; Itō Hirobumi; Andrew Jackson; Oliver Hazard Perry; Saigō Takamori.

RELATED ARTICLE in *Great Events from History: The Nineteenth Century, 1801-1900:* March 31, 1854: Perry Opens Japan to Western Trade.

OLIVER HAZARD PERRY
American naval officer

The brother of Matthew C. Perry, Oliver Hazard Perry was one of the first naval heroes in American history. His skillful seamanship and tactical tenacity in the War of 1812 provided an example of leadership and courage to the officers and crews of the young republic's fledgling navy.

BORN: August 20, 1785; Rocky Brook, South Kingston, Rhode Island
DIED: August 23, 1819; near Port of Spain, Trinidad
AREA OF ACHIEVEMENT: Military

EARLY LIFE

Oliver Hazard Perry was born into a family of Rhode Island seamen. His father, Christopher Raymond Perry, broke with the clan's tradition of Quaker pacifism to fight in the American Revolution. Four of Christopher's sons served in the United States Navy, one of whom was Matthew C. Perry, the famed naval commander and diplomat who opened Japan to Western commerce and thought.

Oliver Perry was reared in Newport, Rhode Island, and educated by his mother, Sarah Wallace Perry. At the age of fourteen, he signed on as a midshipman on his father's vessel, USS *General Greene*. Four years later, he was a lieutenant on the twenty-eight-gun frigate USS *Adams*. Between 1803 and 1806, during the Tripolitan War, he served aboard the *Constellation*, captained the twelve-gun frigate *Nautilus*, and eventually transferred to the forty-four-gun frigate *Constitution* in Commodore John Rodgers's squadron. During the next six years, he directed the construction of various gunboats and commanded a schooner in American waters.

In 1811, Perry married Elizabeth Champlin Mason of Newport. They eventually had five children, two of whom became military officers.

LIFE'S WORK

The outbreak of war found Perry commanding a gunboat flotilla at Newport, but in early 1813 he reported to Presque Isle (modern Erie), Pennsylvania, where he immediately began constructing vessels and organizing a crew in the midst of a wilderness. Captain Perry found himself engaged in a naval arms race with Captain Robert H. Barclay of the Royal Navy, who was patrolling Lake Erie and building his own vessels at a rapid pace. Perry's flotilla was under the overall command of Commodore Isaac Chauncey, stationed at Sackett's Harbor, New York, on the southeastern shore of Lake Ontario.

While the ship construction proceeded at Presque Isle, Perry joined Chauncey and General Henry Dearborn and superintended the naval gunfire and amphibious landing support of the attack on Fort George at the mouth of the Niagara River, May 27, 1813. Perry's conduct in this operation was a model of interservice cooperation. The success of the Fort George attack allowed Perry to move to Lake Erie five small vessels and fifty sailors.

At Presque Isle, Perry spent the spring and summer building, equipping, officering, and manning his small fleet of ten vessels, the largest of which were the USS *Lawrence* and the USS *Niagara*, each of 480 tons burden. To take his flotilla onto the lake, Perry had to cross the bar outside the harbor, a feat he could not accomplish in the presence of an enemy force since the shallow waters required that the guns and equipment of the vessels be removed before the ships could pass over. For inexplicable reasons, Captain Barclay relaxed his vigilance and allowed his foe the opportunity in early August to enter the lake unmolested. The battle for Lake Erie may well have been won at the Presque Isle bar, because crossing it allowed the Americans to achieve superior naval power on the lake.

Hoisting his flag on the *Lawrence* and with Lieutenant Jesse Duncan Elliott commanding the *Niagara*, Commodore Perry set out to fight Barclay's force and to cooperate with General William Henry Harrison's army, then encamped at Fort Meigs (west of modern Toledo, Ohio). Harrison could not advance toward Detroit unless Perry

Oliver Hazard Perry. (Library of Congress)

secured his lines of supply along the western shore of Lake Erie. After conferring with General Harrison, Perry located Barclay's fleet at Fort Malden, near the mouth of the Detroit River, but confrontation was delayed because of contrary winds and illness among Perry's crew. The Americans retired to Put-in-Bay in the Bass Islands, near modern Sandusky, where Perry received crew reinforcements from Harrison and awaited Barclay's decision to leave the protection of Fort Malden. Though outgunned, Barclay had to risk an engagement because Perry's dominance of the lake denied the British supplies for their troops in the Detroit vicinity.

The encounter, on September 10, 1813, should have been easily won by the Americans because Perry's two twenty-gun vessels gave a decided weight of metal advantage over the single twenty-gun HMS *Detroit* commanded by Barclay. Moreover, the initial wind advantage enjoyed by the British was lost because of a change in direction that allowed the Americans the power of initiative. Perry intended the *Lawrence* to engage the *Detroit* and the *Niagara* to attack HMS *Queen Charlotte*, the second largest of the British vessels. Not only did Elliott not engage the *Queen Charlotte*, but he also allowed that vessel to support the *Detroit* against the *Lawrence*.

The result was that despite the heavy damage his flagship inflicted upon the *Detroit*, Perry found his vessel a wreck, its guns disabled, and most of its crew casualties. He transferred his flag to the undamaged *Niagara*, which he then took into action and quickly destroyed and captured the British vessels. His succinct message to General Harrison—"We have met the enemy and they are ours; two ships, two brigs, one schooner, and one sloop"—constitutes a model laconic after-action report. Elliott's conduct in this battle remains controversial and left a legacy of dispute with Perry that lasted long after the latter's death.

Perry's victory dramatically changed the military situation in the Middle West. Harrison quickly retook Detroit and pursued the British-Canadian-Indian forces eastward. Perry's vessels supported him, and when the two armies met at the Battle of the Thames on October 5, the naval captain acted as an aide to the general and assisted in the forming of the battle line.

Perry relinquished his command and made a triumphant tour to Newport. President James Madison promoted him to the permanent rank of captain, and Congress added five thousand dollars to the seventy-five hundred dollars in prize money that was his due and requested that the president give him a gold medal. In July, 1814, Perry took command of the newly commissioned

USS *Java* at Baltimore but was unable to take the vessel to sea because of the British blockade and the ship's still uncompleted state. While in this capacity, he commanded a battery of seamen who harassed the British fleet as it withdrew down the Potomac after the raid on Washington.

On the return of peace with Britain in 1815, Perry took a squadron into the Mediterranean to assist Commodore Stephen Decatur in redressing American grievances against Algiers and Tripoli, whose cruisers had captured numerous American vessels and seamen since 1812. During this cruise, he engaged in a number of diplomatic efforts. He also became involved in a dispute with Marine Captain John Heath, which grew so embittered that, in a fit of passion, Perry struck the *Java*'s marine detachment commander. The incident resulted in a court-martial and a mild reprimand. Still unsatisfied, Heath would eventually engage Perry in a duel that ended with both unhurt and Perry not firing his weapon.

In 1819, Perry undertook a diplomatic mission to Venezuela. He conducted the delicate venture successfully but died of yellow fever contracted during the trip. Perry was buried on Trinidad. In a token of respect for his military prowess and post-battle humanitarianism, his funeral procession received full British honors. Seven years later, his body was returned to Newport for reburial and was marked with a granite obelisk erected by the state of Rhode Island.

SIGNIFICANCE

The key to Oliver Hazard Perry's reputation is victory on Lake Erie. There, he demonstrated the elements of professionalism, presence, and determination that elicited the admiration of his officers and men. As he had done earlier at Fort George, in his support of General Harrison's ground force, Perry exhibited a degree of interservice cooperation uncharacteristic of many subsequent army-navy efforts. One of the few heroes in a war that was divisive, his achievement of capturing a Royal Navy fleet was unprecedented in American history. However, Perry was more than a distinguished warrior and seaman. His diplomatic efforts in North Africa and South America were typical naval endeavors of his day, and they set the tone for his younger brother's famous expedition to Japan. In the final analysis, his career, like that of John Paul Jones, Stephen Decatur, Thomas Macdonough, and James Lawrence, provided an example of valor, dedication, leadership, and patriotism that influenced American sailors for years to follow.

—David Curtis Skaggs

FURTHER READING

Dutton, Charles J. *Oliver Hazard Perry*. New York: Longmans, Green, 1935. The standard but undistinguished biographical study.

Forester, Cecil S. *The Age of Fighting Sail: The Story of the Naval War of 1812*. Garden City, N.Y.: Doubleday, 1956. A popular history by the author of the Horatio Hornblower stories, this is a good introduction to the problems confronted by Perry and his contemporaries.

Hitsman, J. Mackay. *The Incredible War of 1812: A Military History*. Toronto: University of Toronto Press, 1965. Written from a Canadian perspective, this is a solid history with a strong focus on the war on the Great Lakes.

MacKenzie, Alexander Slidell. *The Life of Commodore Oliver Hazard Perry*. 2 vols. New York: Harper and Brothers, 1840. A highly laudatory account by a naval officer who served under Perry, this study is notable for the numerous personal recollections that MacKenzie collected and for its defensive tone in the Perry-Elliott and Perry-Heath controversies.

Mahan, Alfred Thayer. *Sea Power in Its Relations to the War of 1812*. 2 vols. Boston: Little, Brown, 1905. Volume 2 contains this distinguished naval historian's account of the Battle of Lake Erie; Mahan stoutly defends Perry's conduct.

Morison, Samuel Eliot. *"Old Bruin": Commodore Matthew Calbraith Perry, 1794-1858: The American Naval Officer Who Helped Found Liberia*. Boston: Little, Brown, 1967. This account by a famous naval historian of the career of Perry's younger brother provides both family background and an analysis of the United States Navy during the early nineteenth century.

Skaggs, David Curtis, and Gerald T. Altoff. *A Signal Victory: The Lake Erie Campaign, 1812-1813*. Annapolis, Md.: Naval Institute Press, 1997. This history of the campaign describes how the United States and Great Britain sought to control the strategic Lake Erie frontier, with their struggle culminating in the decisive battle in 1813. Recounts the battle, analyzing the leadership of Perry and his British opponent, Commodore Robert H. Barclay.

SEE ALSO: Stephen Decatur; David G. Farragut; William Henry Harrison; Matthew C. Perry.

RELATED ARTICLE in *Great Events from History: The Nineteenth Century, 1801-1900:* June 18, 1812-December 24, 1814: War of 1812.

JOHANN HEINRICH PESTALOZZI
Swiss educator

Pestalozzi spent his life seeking ways to help students improve their learning skills so that they could develop into effective adults. His method was based upon imparting an awareness of, and encouraging direct interaction with, objects, progressing from simple steps to more complex ones in an orderly pattern, thereby achieving harmonious organic development.

BORN: January 12, 1746; Zurich, Switzerland
DIED: February 17, 1827; Brugg, Switzerland
AREA OF ACHIEVEMENT: Education

EARLY LIFE

Italians who immigrated to Switzerland from Locarno during the sixteenth century, the Pestalozzis settled in Zurich. By 1746, when Johann Heinrich Pestalozzi (PEHS-tah-lot-see) was born, the family had been in Zurich for two hundred years and had been accorded the full rights of citizens—a privilege in a city of 145,000, only 5,000 of whom were citizens. Heinrich was the youngest of Johann Baptist and Suzanne Hotz Pestalozzi's three children. Johann, a surgeon, died in 1751 at the age of thirty-three, leaving the family in straitened circumstances. Because Pestalozzi was a sickly child, his mother sheltered him, seldom allowing him to play with other children or to do chores. He was exposed to the poor when he visited his paternal grandfather, a clergyman near Zurich. The young Pestalozzi developed an interest in and sympathy for the poor.

At Zurich's Collegium Carolinum, Pestalozzi, an indifferent student, developed a consuming love for his country that led him to join the Helvetic Society and to write articles about the poor and suffering for its publication. Upon graduating from Collegium Carolinum, Pestalozzi entered the University of Zurich but abandoned his university studies soon after starting them. Having read Jean-Jacques Rousseau, Pestalozzi was particularly affected by *Émile: Ou, De l'éducation* (1762; *Emilius and Sophia: Or, A New System of Education*, 1762-1763). Rousseau's glorification of the natural life led Pestalozzi to spend the year 1767 studying agriculture. In 1768, he bought acreage near Birr and devoted himself to cultivating it. The failure of this venture in 1774 caused him to lose everything he owned except the house, Neuhof, which dominated his property, and a plot on which he raised food for his wife, Anna, whom he had married in 1769, and their son, Jean-Jacques, named for Rousseau.

By 1773, Pestalozzi had turned Neuhof into a school where he taught poor and unfit children to become cotton spinners. He taught them mathematics and catechism as they worked, and after work the boys gardened while the girls learned sewing and cooking. Pestalozzi also taught them the skills of basic literacy. The school attracted more than fifty unkempt students, ages six to eighteen. Pestalozzi, a slim, gentle man with a kind, understanding smile, reformed many of them, serving simultaneously as teacher and surrogate father. Nevertheless, in 1779 the school closed for lack of funds.

LIFE'S WORK

Pestalozzi was a dreamer, a true idealist, motivated primarily by his concern for those less fortunate than he and by his intense loyalty to Switzerland. He felt a deep personal commitment to make life better for his fellow humans, and he went through life seeking ways to bring about such an outcome as a way of improving society.

Pestalozzi's exposure to teaching during the five years at Neuhof suggested to him ways to create a better society and convinced him that social amelioration, his highest goal, proceeded from the bottom up by enabling the children of the poor to find a means of sustaining themselves, of gaining self-respect through productive work such as the cotton spinning that he taught them. He was not satisfied, however, for these students to be merely cotton spinners. He expected them to work with their minds, to elevate their thinking, and to imbue their lives with a dimension that typical workers lack. His ultimate aim was to make them functioning, effective members of the ideal democratic society that he envisioned for Switzerland. He thought education was society's obligation to all of its young. His ideas were precursors of the universal free education that was later widely accepted in developed nations.

Ruined financially by the failure of his school, Pestalozzi sought to make money by entering literary contests and thus began his career in writing. He first published *Abendstunde eines Einsiedlers* (1780; *Evening Hours of a Hermit*, 1912), which articulated his notion that human beings must work at developing their inner powers and that such development can be accomplished best within a wholesome family environment supplemented by a well-designed educational program free to everyone.

Johann Heinrich Pestalozzi. (Library of Congress)

The publication of *Lienhard und Gertrud: Ein Buch für das Volk* (1781; *Leonard and Gertrude: A Popular Story*, 1800), in which Gertrude reforms her heavy-drinking spouse and, aided by the local schoolmaster, saves her community from corruption, brought Pestalozzi great attention. With this book, Pestalozzi invented the biographical novel. Before 1787, the initial novel was followed by three sequels, the most important of which is *Christoph und Else lesen in den abendstunden das Buch "Lienhard und Gertrud"* (1782; Christopher and Elsa read the book *Leonard and Gertrude* in the evening), in which Pestalozzi attempts a less sentimental, more socially critical appeal than that in the earlier book, which a sentimental reading public had misinterpreted.

It was not until two decades later, however, that *Wie Gertrud ihre Kinder lehrt* (1801; *How Gertrude Teaches Her Children*, 1894), consisting of fourteen letters about education, appeared, making its mark as the most coherent expression of Pestalozzi's educational tenets. If his books had brought him recognition, they brought him neither job offers nor money. He struggled to survive. He even made a desperate attempt to publish a newspaper,

Ein Schweizer-Blatt, but this weekly soon failed. Nevertheless, the venture was important to Pestalozzi's development because, as editor, he wrote about how the state should deal with criminals, proposing the same sort of humane treatment for prisoners that he had accorded his students at Neuhof.

It was not until Pestalozzi was past fifty that he had another opportunity to work with children. The French invasion of Stans was a wholesale slaughter. When the French retreated, orphans had to be cared for. The Swiss government established a residential school for them, with Pestalozzi as head. Starting with fifty children, the school soon had eighty in residence. Pestalozzi worked with these students, assisted only by a housekeeper. The operation went reasonably well, even though the canton's dominant Catholic population viewed Pestalozzi, a Protestant, with suspicion.

After six months, the orphanage was taken over by the French, who again invaded the city, as a hospital. Pestalozzi, who was emotionally and physically spent, did not return to the orphanage when the facility was returned to that purpose. Instead, at the age of fifty-two, he became an assistant teacher in the poorest school in Burgdorf, where again he instituted his radical methods of discouraging rote learning, emphasizing understanding, and having students learn from observing and working with objects.

Not long after his initial assignment in Burgdorf, Pestalozzi was appointed sole teacher in a school of about sixty students from poor families. He could now implement the methods in which he most believed. Soon, the government helped him establish in Burgdorf Castle a school that attracted children from affluent families, not the kinds of students that most interested Pestalozzi. It was during this period that Pestalozzi published *How Gertrude Teaches Her Children*, the book that more than any other established his reputation.

When the government requisitioned Burgdorf, Pestalozzi was finally in a position to establish his own experimental school. After a brief, abortive attempt to work with Philipp Emanuel von Fellenberg at Hofwyl, Pestalozzi established his school at Yverdon in 1805. The school became important not only as an institution where children learned by novel methods that emphasized discovery, the understanding of concepts, and proceeding from the simple to the complex but also as a school that provided teacher training for hundreds of prospective teachers. Soon, governments from surrounding nations subsidized study at Yverdon for their most promising teachers.

Pestalozzi's methods were controversial throughout his lifetime. He was convinced that education is a growing and changing process, not a fixed one. At its best, education, thought Pestalozzi, could address and cure most social ills. He believed that education must be secular rather than religious. He valued the senses over the intellect, perhaps moving further in that direction than was prudent.

Not all Pestalozzi's methods worked to the best advantage of students. For example, employing his idea that one should proceed from the simple to the complex, Pestalozzi had beginning readers learn small syllabic constituents of words before they read whole words. He had them memorize an imposingly large "syllabary" consisting of hundreds of items such as *am, em, im, om*, and *um* before they tackled words. Methods of this sort, although hypothetically interesting, proved counterproductive.

In addition, the methods were applied to fields such as drawing, in which Pestalozzi had students draw constituent shapes—curves, lines, and circles—in isolation rather than drawing entities. His obsession with formal analysis limited his students and frustrated some teacher trainees at Yverdon, a number of whom, including Friedrich Froebel, became critical of Pestalozzi's method. When Yverdon closed in 1825, however, two years before its founder's death, it had made a significant impact upon education in the Western world. Objection to some of the specifics of Pestalozzi's pedagogy in no way diminishes the effect it had upon education, particularly at the elementary level.

SIGNIFICANCE

Johann Heinrich Pestalozzi succeeded at little during his first fifty years. Had he not founded Yverdon, his books would document his social and educational philosophy. His influence, however, would be less far-ranging than it was after he gathered around him a coterie of disciples who would help propagate his work after Yverdon's closing and his death.

Had Pestalozzi died at fifty, he would not have had the opportunity to practice in any sustained way the pedagogy that he developed. Yverdon became his laboratory. If Pestalozzi had a salient shortcoming, it was that he refused to admit the ineffectiveness of some of the methods in which he believed. This shortcoming, however, was more than counterbalanced by his devotion to children and by the sincerity of his effort.

The Pestalozzi legacy points in several directions. His school at Yverdon became a model for laboratory schools and for teacher-training institutions throughout the world. The normal school in the United States is an outgrowth of Yverdon. Pestalozzi's emphasis on having children learn by doing rather than by reading or hearing about things leads directly to John Dewey and other progressive educators who came indirectly under Pestalozzi's influence.

Maria Montessori's object-centered education, which led to the establishment of Montessori schools throughout the world, employs the Pestalozzi method of learning through observing objects and arriving at generalizations from those observations. The notion of engaging the senses in learning activities can be traced to Pestalozzi and such contemporaries of his as Johann Bernhard Basedow, Froebel, and Rousseau.

Pestalozzi's idea that education is the right of all children, not widespread in his time, is a prevailing tenet in most countries today, as is the separation of schools from religious authority, a radical view during the early nineteenth century. Few educational theorists have had the diverse effect upon modern educational practices that Pestalozzi had, though much of his significant work came after he had experienced a lifetime of failure.

—R. Baird Shuman

FURTHER READING

Downs, Robert B. *Heinrich Pestalozzi: Father of Modern Pedagogy*. Boston: Twayne, 1975. This brief biography is well researched and well written, although its bibliography of primary sources is slightly disappointing. The chronology at the beginning of the book is a helpful, ready resource.

Green, J. A. *The Educational Ideas of Pestalozzi*. New York: W. B. Clive, 1914. Reprint. New York: Greenwood Press, 1969. A small book that reproduces well-selected samples of Pestalozzi's most significant writing. Provides an excellent overview of the intellectual development of the man and his ideas.

Gutek, Gerald Lee. *Pestalozzi and Education*. New York: Random House, 1968. This fascinating book is the most comprehensive account of the development of Pestalozzi's educational philosophy. An indispensable source.

Mueller, Gustav E. "Heinrich Pestalozzi: His Life and Work." *Harvard Educational Review* 16 (1946): 141-159. A brilliant article that places Pestalozzi in a broad cultural context and demonstrates how his influence has pervaded most aspects of modern educational thought. Carefully researched and well reasoned.

Pestalozzianum and the Zentralbibliothek, Zürich, ed. *Pestalozzi and His Times: A Pictorial Record*. New York: G. E. Stechert, 1928. This handsome book contains a fine introduction that goes deeply into Pestalozzi's background before presenting nearly one hundred pictures of the man, his family, places he lived and worked, and manuscript pages. An extraordinary book.

Schultz, Lucille M. *The Young Composers: Composition's Beginnings in Nineteenth-Century Schools*. Carbondale: Southern Illinois University Press, 1999. Traces the development of school-based writing instruction, crediting Pestalozzi's ideas with altering composition training to make it more child-centered and less an imitation of college-level course work.

Silber, Käte, *Pestalozzi: The Man and His Work*. London: Routledge & Kegan Paul, 1965. A good treatment of Pestalozzi and the range of his ideas. This book supplants the earlier works and brings to light some of Pestalozzi's writing about topics other than education.

SEE ALSO: Friedrich Froebell; Jakob Steiner.

RELATED ARTICLE in *Great Events from History: The Nineteenth Century, 1801-1900:* September 12, 1848: Swiss Confederation Is Formed.

WENDELL PHILLIPS
American social reformer

Phillips was one of the foremost orators and writers in the American abolitionist and other social movements through the mid-nineteenth century.

BORN: November 29, 1811; Boston, Massachusetts
DIED: February 2, 1884; Boston, Massachusetts
AREA OF ACHIEVEMENT: Social reform

EARLY LIFE
Wendell Phillips traced his American ancestry to the Reverend Mr. George Phillips, who came to Massachusetts with John Winthrop in 1630 on the *Arbella*. His father, John Phillips, was a prominent Boston politician, who served as a judge, as the presiding officer of the state senate, and as the first mayor of Boston under that city's corporate charter, as well as on the Harvard Board of Overseers. One of his relatives was the founder of Phillips Andover Academy, while another founded Phillips Exeter Academy. Wendell's mother, Sarah Walley, was the devoutly Calvinist daughter of a middle-class Boston merchant. Although Sarah came from a less distinguished family than her husband, she could trace her American ancestry to the early seventeenth century.

As a child, Phillips received the typical education of a Boston patrician. He attended Boston Latin School, where he won distinctions for his oratory, was graduated from Harvard College in 1831, and then studied at Harvard's new law school under Justice Joseph Story until 1834.

As a young lawyer, Phillips could look forward to what appeared to be a certain and successful future. Phillips was already financially secure from his inheritance.

Politically, Phillips was fully in the tradition of conservative New England Federalists. He wrote in his Harvard class book of 1831, "I love the Puritans, honor Cromwell, idolize Chatham and Hurrah for Webster." He was connected by social class, and often by blood, to the most powerful and important families in Massachusetts. He was already noted as an unusually talented speaker and writer. In addition, he was healthy, physically fit, tall, handsome, and aristocratic in his bearing. Later in life, when proper Bostonians shunned him for his abolitionist activities, Phillips condescendingly retorted that his detractors were "men of no family."

By 1835, Phillips was on his way to building a successful and profitable law practice. Phillips was not particularly enthusiastic about law practice, but he probably would not have needed to continue in the field for long. Like his father, Phillips could have looked forward to a successful career in politics, which would have been enhanced by his remarkable speaking ability, brilliant mind, and superb debating skills. In October, 1837, Phillips solidified his position in Boston society when he married Ann Terry Greene, the orphaned daughter of a wealthy and prominent Boston merchant. In that year, however, Phillips abandoned his law practice and society life for a fulltime career as an abolitionist agitator, social reformer, and professional orator.

LIFE'S WORK
In 1837, Phillips's life changed dramatically. In March, he gave a short speech supporting abolition at the Massachusetts Anti-Slavery Society. By the end of 1837, Phil-

lips was a professional abolitionist speaker. This shift—from a socially prominent lawyer to a leading speaker for a despised group of radical reformers—was the result of his heritage, his marriage, and the events of the mid-1830's.

As an educated patrician, Phillips firmly believed in noblesse oblige. It was not inconsistent for him to champion the rights of an oppressed minority. Indeed, moderate opposition to slavery was part of his Federalist political background and his Puritan social and cultural heritage. Phillips was, in fact, a profoundly religious man whose Puritan background no doubt led him to a movement such as abolition, which sought to root out the most sinful American institution—slavery.

Phillips's relationship with Ann Terry Greene was critical to his development as an abolitionist. When he met Greene, she was already a committed abolitionist, active in the Boston Female Anti-Slavery Society. While courting Ann in 1836, Wendell met William Lloyd Garrison and the other abolitionists whom he soon would join. Although an invalid most of her life, Ann was actively involved in Wendell's career, giving him both intellectual and emotional support. Phillips claimed not only that Ann made him into an abolitionist but also that she was always ahead of him in analyzing the social issues of the movement.

Throughout their marriage, Ann encouraged Phillips to remain uncompromising in his opposition to slavery, in his support of the freemen, and in support of the rights of women. Their only major political disagreement was over the rights of the Irish. Ann retained the anti-Irish bias of most Bostonians of her class; Wendell saw the Irish as an exploited class, much like blacks, and thus in need of an eloquent champion to further their search for social justice. When he met Ann in 1836, Phillips was not yet an abolitionist. Two events, one in 1835 and the other in 1837, coalesced with his relationship with Ann and his background to bring Phillips into the antislavery movement.

In 1835, a mob dragged the abolitionist editor William Lloyd Garrison through the streets of Boston with a rope around his body. Phillips witnessed the event with shock and outrage. At the time, Phillips was not sympathetic to abolition. However, he considered himself to be fully a son of the American Revolution. As such, he believed in free speech for all, even radicals such as Garrison. The threatened lynching of Garrison violated Phillips's sense of order and constitutional rights. The young patrician lawyer now had a new view of the abolitionists—as protectors of civil liberties, because they were the victims of intolerance.

Wendell Phillips. (Library of Congress)

Phillips was even more profoundly affected by the death of Elijah Lovejoy, an abolitionist printer in Alton, Illinois. In 1837, Lovejoy was thrice attacked by mobs that threw his press into the Mississippi River. When a fourth press arrived in Alton, Lovejoy vowed to defend it. In the process, he was killed. At a meeting called to denounce this event, James T. Austin, Massachusetts's antiabolitionist attorney general, took the floor and gave an eloquent speech attacking Lovejoy. Austin compared Lovejoy's killers to the revolutionaries who organized the Boston Tea Party and declared that Lovejoy was "presumptuous and imprudent" for challenging the sentiments of the day. Phillips, still relatively unknown in Boston and not yet a committed abolitionist, immediately took the floor to answer Austin. His response electrified the crowd in Boston's Faneuil Hall; the printed version had a similar effect on those who read it. Pointing to the portraits of revolutionary leaders on the wall of Faneuil Hall, Phillips declared

> Sir, when I heard the gentleman [Austin] lay down principles which place the murderers of Alton side by side with Otis and Hancock, with Quincy and Adams, I

thought those pictured lips would have broken into voice to rebuke the recreant American, the slanderer of the dead. . . . Sir, for the sentiment he has uttered, on soil consecrated by the prayers of Puritans and the blood of patriots, the earth should have yawned and swallowed him up.

Phillips then went on to defend the rights of free speech and of the press and to attack those who would deny it to abolitionists.

This speech was the beginning of Phillips's career as the greatest abolitionist speaker of the day. Indeed, in an age of great orators, Phillips may have been the best. Besides speaking on abolition, Phillips often gave lectures on artistic and cultural topics and on other political issues. He was in constant demand and made a good living from his speaking tours. Phillips gave one nonpolitical lecture, entitled "The Lost Arts," more than two thousand times in his career and earned more than $150,000 from it.

As an antislavery agitator, Phillips was noted for his "eloquence of abuse." Northern politicians who supported slavery risked the wrath of his wit. Edward Everett was "a whining spaniel," Senator Robert Winthrop "a bastard who has stolen the name Winthrop," and Daniel Webster "a great mass of dough." Abraham Lincoln, who had once represented a slaveowner in a fugitive slave case, was "the slave hound from Illinois." When lecturing, Phillips could be abusively eloquent without even using words. During one speech, he mentioned the name of a United States attorney who was notorious for his support of the Fugitive Slave Law. Phillips then stopped his speech, asked for a glass of water, rinsed his mouth, spat the water out, and continued.

Besides his marvelous rhetoric, Phillips made important intellectual contributions to the antislavery movement. Phillips accepted Garrison's analysis that the Constitution was "a covenant with death and an agreement in Hell" that favored slavery. Because Phillips could not conscientiously support the Constitution, he ceased to practice law shortly after joining the abolitionist movement. However, he applied his legal training and knowledge to his speeches, articles, and pamphlets. His analysis of the Constitutional Convention, *The Constitution a Pro-Slavery Compact: Or, Selections from the Madison Papers* (1844), was particularly important to the Garrisonian analysis of the American government.

More important than his antislavery theory was the role he developed as a professional agitator. Phillips was harsh, extreme, and unfair in his speeches and his pam-

phlets. His rhetoric, however, was purposeful. He sought to enrage the people of the North by dwelling on the horrors of slavery. In a speech on slavery, he would assert that "The South is one great brothel, where half a million women are flogged into prostitution." His goal was to force his audiences to contemplate the evil of slavery. Phillips succeeded far better than any of his contemporaries.

In 1860, Phillips opposed Lincoln, as he had almost all other politicians, because the latter was not sufficiently antislavery. During the Civil War, however, Phillips's agitation was sympathetic to Lincoln and the cause of the Union. He intuitively understood that the war would destroy slavery, and he supported the Emancipation Proclamation, even though it did not extend to all slaves in the nation.

Unlike many abolitionists, Phillips did not discontinue his work with the end of the war and the adoption of the Thirteenth Amendment. In 1865, he severed his relationship with his longtime associate Garrison because the latter wanted to dissolve his American Anti-Slavery Society. Phillips thought that the job of the abolitionists remained unfulfilled. Emancipation alone was insufficient; Phillips was farsighted enough to realize that freedom required granting full political and social equality to former slaves. Thus, Phillips remained a tireless supporter of equal rights for the freedmen throughout the 1870's.

With the Constitution no longer proslavery, Phillips felt free to participate in politics. In 1870, he ran for governor of Massachusetts on the Labor Reform ticket and received twenty thousand votes. By this time, Phillips divided his energies between caring for his invalid wife, agitating for the rights of the freedmen, and opposing the exploitation of workers in the emerging industrial economy. He agitated for an eight-hour day and a reorganization of the nation's economy to protect the poor and the working classes from the robber barons of the Gilded Age. By the time of his death in 1884, Phillips was a full-fledged labor radical, as indicated by his last major publication, *The Labor Question* (1884).

SIGNIFICANCE

In 1881, Phillips was invited back to his alma mater to give the Phi Beta Kappa address. In his speech, titled "The Scholar in a Republic," Phillips argued that the role of an educated man in a free society is "to help those less favored in life." This had been the life of Phillips. In an age of great orators, he was among the best. Born to lead the elite, he led instead a movement that sought freedom for those at the bottom of society. He provided hard logic, brilliant rhetoric, and a measure of upper-class cachet for the antislavery movement. Phillips flourished on the fringes of American politics, consciously creating an "office" for himself as an agitator. Phillips never made policy. Nevertheless, by helping to create an antislavery constituency, Phillips was able to influence politics and politicians throughout his career. In the process of opposing slavery, Phillips helped legitimize the professional agitator in American politics and society.

— *Paul Finkelman*

FURTHER READING

Bartlett, Irving H. *Wendell and Ann Phillips: The Community of Reform, 1840-1880.* New York: W. W. Norton, 1979. A brief biography of Phillips and his wife, based on a large collection of Phillips family letters discovered during the 1970's. Includes many letters written to and from Ann and Wendell Phillips. Focuses on the private life, as well as the public life, of the Phillipses.

_____. *Wendell Phillips: Boston Brahmin.* Boston: Little, Brown, 1961. A sympathetic modern biography of Phillips. Covers his entire career, focusing almost entirely on his public life.

Filler, Louis, ed. *Wendell Phillips on Civil Rights and Freedom.* New York: Hill and Wang, 1965. A short collection of some of Phillips's greatest speeches. This volume begins with his brilliant defense of Elijah Lovejoy's right to publish an antislavery newspaper.

Hofstadter, Richard. "Wendell Phillips: The Patrician as Agitator." In *The American Political Tradition.* New York: Alfred A. Knopf, 1949. A superb essay on Phillips and his role as an agitator. One of the first modern reappraisals of Phillips.

Korngold, Ralph. *Two Friends of Man: The Story of William Lloyd Garrison and Wendell Phillips.* Boston: Little, Brown, 1950. Study of the two leaders of the radical or Garrisonian wing of the abolitionist movement.

Stewart, James Brewer. *Holy Warriors.* New York: Hill and Wang, 1976. A superb short history of the antislavery movement that places Phillips in the context of other abolitionists. An excellent introduction to history of abolition.

_____. *Wendell Phillips, Liberty's Hero.* Baton Rouge: Louisiana State University Press, 1986. Comprehensive biography, tracing Phillips's life, involvement in the abolitionist movement, and influence of his wife, Ann. Stewart demonstrates how Phillips played a greater role in the abolitionist movement than was previously understood.

Wiecek, William M. *The Sources of Antislavery Constitutionalism in America: 1760-1848.* Ithaca, N.Y.: Cornell University Press, 1977. Study of abolitionist thought, which places the ideas and theories of Phillips in context with other antislavery thinkers.

SEE ALSO: Lydia Maria Child; Frederick Douglass; Charlotte Forten; William Lloyd Garrison; Abraham Lincoln; Joseph Story; Harriet Tubman; Daniel Webster.

RELATED ARTICLES in *Great Events from History: The Nineteenth Century, 1801-1900:* January 1, 1831: Garrison Begins Publishing *The Liberator*; December, 1833: American Anti-Slavery Society Is Founded; December 6, 1865: Thirteenth Amendment Is Ratified; May 10, 1866: Suffragists Protest the Fourteenth Amendment; February 17-18, 1890: Women's Rights Associations Unite.

FRANKLIN PIERCE
President of the United States (1853-1857)

After service in his state's legislature and in both houses of Congress, Pierce became the nation's fourteenth president, serving during the turbulent mid-1850's. Though well liked by both northerners and southerners, he was irresolute on critical issues and did nothing to slow the movement toward civil war.

BORN: November 23, 1804; Hillsborough, New Hampshire
DIED: October 8, 1869; Concord, New Hampshire
ALSO KNOWN AS: Young Hickory
AREA OF ACHIEVEMENT: Government and politics

EARLY LIFE

Franklin Pierce was the son of Benjamin Pierce, an American Revolutionary War veteran and two-term governor of New Hampshire (1827-1828, 1829-1830). His mother, Anna Kendrick, was his father's second wife. Frank, as family and friends called him, was the sixth of their eight children.

Frank attended local schools before enrolling in Bowdoin College. Overcoming homesickness and early academic nonchalance, he was graduated fifth in the class of 1824. Classmates there included John P. Hale, the 1852 Free-Soil Party's presidential candidate; Calvin Stowe, the husband of Harriet Beecher Stowe; and writers Henry Wadsworth Longfellow and Nathaniel Hawthorne. Pierce became close friends with Hawthorne, and the novelist later penned his campaign biography. Pierce taught school during semester breaks, but his major interest during his college years seemed to be the college battalion, in which he served as an officer.

After graduation, Pierce studied in several law offices, including that of later U.S. senator and Supreme Court justice Levi Woodbury of Portsmouth. He was admitted to the bar in 1827 and immediately assisted in his father's successful bid for the governorship. When his father was reelected in 1829, he simultaneously gained a seat in the state legislature.

LIFE'S WORK

His political rise was steady. When first elected to the legislature, Pierce was named chairman of the Committee on Education. Later he served as chairman of the Committee on Towns and Parishes. In 1831, Governor Samuel Dinsmoor named him his military aide with the rank of colonel, and that same year and the next he served as Speaker of the House. In March, 1833, though he was not yet thirty years old, he was elected to the U.S. House of Representatives. By this time, his political course was already set. He had enjoyed rapid success because of his support for his father and the Democratic Party. From then on, he gave total loyalty to the party and to its experienced politicians.

Pierce served in the House from 1833 to 1837 before advancing to the Senate for one term (1837-1842). His service was undistinguished. He deferred to his elders (when he entered the Senate, it was its youngest member). He made no memorable speech and sponsored no key legislation. He served on several committees, eventually gaining the chairmanship of the Senate Pension Committee. He consistently accepted the southern view on slavery, and was strongly antiabolitionist, a staunch defender of the Democratic Party, and a strong opponent of the Whig program. For example, he supported the southern position on the Gag Rule and defended Andrew Jackson's opposition to internal improvements.

It was during these years that Pierce made the political contacts and created the impression that would result in his later nomination and election to the presidency. He came to be known as an accommodating person, fun loving, and always anxious to please. He seemed perfectly content to follow party policy, and he gave proper respect to his elders. He was a New Englander whom southerners trusted. He formed a close friendship with Jefferson Davis during these years.

In 1834, Pierce married Jane Means Appleton, the daughter of a former Bowdoin College president and Congregational minister. Throughout their married life, she suffered from a variety of physical illnesses, anxiety, and depression; in addition, she held strict Calvinistic views on life. In contrast to her sociable husband, she felt uncomfortable in social settings and consequently stayed away from Washington, D.C., as much as she could. Like many congressmen of that age, Pierce lived in a boardinghouse with several colleagues, and he joined them in drinking to try to compensate for the boredom of his existence. Pierce was no alcoholic, but he was incapable of holding any liquor. The smallest amount inebriated him. This problem, combined with his wife's unhappiness, which was exacerbated by the death of a newborn child, convinced Pierce in 1842 that he should go back to New Hampshire. There he promised his wife that he would never drink again or return to Washington.

In New Hampshire, Pierce became a successful law-

Franklin Pierce. (Library of Congress)

yer. He did not spend much time analyzing legal principles because he was easily able to ingratiate himself with
juries and win his cases that way. He was of medium
height and military bearing, dark, handsome, and an excellent dresser. People who met him at social and political gatherings liked him immediately.

During these years, Pierce also played an active role
in New Hampshire's Democratic politics. He was a driving force in most of the party's campaigns, achieving
good success, though he lost out to college classmate
Hale in a party dispute over Texas annexation. President
James K. Polk offered him the attorney generalship, and
his party wanted to return him to the Senate. He declined
both offers.

When the Mexican War broke out, Pierce's long-held
interest in military matters and his desire for more excitement than his Concord law practice provided caused him
to volunteer as a private. Before he donned his uniform,
he had gained the rank of brigadier general. He made
many friends among the enlisted men, and General Winfield Scott named him one of the three commissioners
who attempted to negotiate an unsuccessful truce. His
combat record was much less sparkling. During his first

combat in the Mexico City campaign, his horse stumbled, banging Pierce against the saddle horn and then
falling on his leg. He fainted. Though still in pain when
he was revived, he continued, only to twist his knee and
faint again when he encountered the enemy. Later, he became bedridden with a severe case of diarrhea. He was
happy when the conclusion of the war enabled him to return home.

Pierce resumed his legal and political pursuits. He
supported the Compromise of 1850 and became president of the state constitutional convention. He helped rid
the state party of an antislavery gubernatorial candidate
and thereby improved his reputation in the South. When
his former law tutor, Levi Woodbury, the state's choice
for the 1852 Democratic presidential nomination, died in
September, 1851, Pierce became New Hampshire's new
favorite son. Remembering his promise to his wife, however, he said he would consider the nomination only in
case the convention deadlocked. That was precisely what
happened. None of the Democratic front-runners, James
Buchanan, Lewis Cass, Stephen A. Douglas, and William L. Marcy, was able to obtain the necessary two-
thirds of the convention ballots. On the thirty-fifth stale-
mated ballot, Pierce's name was introduced. He was a
northerner with southern principles and a person everyone seemed to like. These characteristics carried the day.
On the forty-ninth ballot, he gained the nomination.
When his wife learned the news, she fainted from shock.

The 1852 presidential campaign between Pierce,
Whig candidate Winfield Scott, and Free-Soiler Hale
was issueless. Pierce made no formal speeches; according to the custom of the time, he allowed his supporters to
campaign for him. Hawthorne quickly wrote a laudatory
biography, and others worked to overcome the accusation that Pierce was a drunkard, a coward, and an anti-
Catholic. (The latter accusation came from an anti-Catholic provision remaining in the revised New Hampshire
constitution.) In a Boston speech the previous year, he
had called for the enforcement of the Fugitive Slave Law
yet voiced his belief that it was inhuman, so he had to
work hard to repair damage in the South from that remark. He never denied the statement but insisted he had
been misrepresented, and this seemed to satisfy his critics. He won the general election 254 to 42 in electoral
votes, although he had a popular margin of only forty-
four thousand.

At first, Pierce made good progress in organizing his
administration. Then tragedy struck. He, his wife, and
their eleven-year-old son, Benjamin, were riding the
train from Boston to Concord when, without warning,

their car toppled off the embankment. Benjamin was killed. Neither Pierce nor his wife was ever able to recover from the shock. They vainly sought to find meaning in the freak accident. Pierce wondered if his son's death was God's punishment for his sins. Jane Pierce concluded that God had taken the boy so her husband could give his undivided attention to the presidency.

Pierce thus entered office in a state of turmoil. The feeling of insecurity that caused him to want to please others and follow his party's line now received further reinforcement from the guilt and self-doubts resulting from his son's death. The reaction of Pierce's wife only added to his burdens. Quite by accident, she learned from a friend that her husband, far from not wanting to return to Washington as he had insisted, had actually worked hard to get the nomination. She had lost her son; now she learned that her husband had deceived her. She locked the bedroom door, seldom even appearing for public functions. Eventually she spent most of her time writing little notes to her dead son, apologizing for her lack of affection during his life.

Pierce became president determined to adhere to old-line Democratic policy, with a strong dose of expansionist ideas. However, everything he tried seemed to fail. He attempted to broaden the base of support for his administration by giving patronage to all segments of the party, but loyal supporters, especially southerners, became angry. He made decisions on what he considered to be principle but lost political support in the process. Most significantly, he did not seem to understand that slavery, especially its expansion into the territories, was a powder keg. He had always considered public opinion to be the stuff of demagogues, so he believed he could ignore the strong negative feelings about slavery that were gaining ground in the North.

Pierce seemed incapable of providing effective direction to his administration. His cabinet, the only one in history to remain intact for an entire term, was weak, but its members had to exert their authority since he did not. Jefferson Davis, the secretary of war, emerged as the most powerful of the group.

The tragedy of Franklin Pierce was that he was president during a time of major crisis and conflict. Pierce's presidency was dominated by controversy and even violence: the Kansas-Nebraska Act, Bleeding Kansas, Bloody Sumner, the Ostend Manifesto, the Gadsden Purchase, the destruction of the Whig Party and the birth of the Republican Party. The nation cried out for leadership, for some kind of direction, but Pierce was unable to provide it. Events seemed to provide their own impetus, and he seemed incapable of di-

THE MEXICAN BORDER SETTLEMENT

A notable achievement of Franklin Pierce's presidency was the federal government's acquisition of a strip of Mexican territory, known as the Gadsden Purchase, and the settlement of a long-standing border dispute with Mexico. Pierce commented on this settlement in his second state of the union address.

The treaty lately concluded between the United States and Mexico settled some of our most embarrassing difficulties with that country, but numerous claims upon it for wrongs and injuries to our citizens remained unadjusted, and many new cases have been recently added to the former list of grievances. Our legation has been earnest in its endeavors to obtain from the Mexican Government a favorable consideration of these claims, but hitherto without success. This failure is probably in some measure to be ascribed to the disturbed condition of that country. It has been my anxious desire to maintain friendly relations with the Mexican Republic and to cause its rights and territories to be respected, not only by our citizens, but by foreigners who have resorted to the United States for the purpose of organizing hostile expeditions against some of the States of that Republic. The defenseless condition in which its frontiers have been left has stimulated lawless adventurers to embark in these enterprises and greatly increased the difficulty of enforcing our obligations of neutrality. Regarding it as my solemn duty to fulfill efficiently these obligations not only toward Mexico, but other foreign nations, I have exerted all the powers with which I am invested to defeat such proceedings and bring to punishment those who by taking a part therein violated our laws. The energy and activity of our civil and military authorities have frustrated the designs of those who meditated expeditions of this character except in two instances. One of these, composed of foreigners, was at first countenanced and aided by the Mexican Government itself, it having been deceived as to their real object. The other, small in number, eluded the vigilance of the magistrates at San Francisco and succeeded in reaching the Mexican territories; but the effective measures taken by this Government compelled the abandonment of the undertaking.

The commission to establish the new line between the United States and Mexico, according to the provisions of the treaty of the 30th of December last, has been organized, and the work is already commenced.

Source: Franklin Pierce, "State of the Union Address," December 4, 1854.

recting them. His prosouthern and antiabolitionist attitudes, his desire to please, and his uncertainty about his own capabilities did not allow him to act effectively.

The Kansas-Nebraska Act demonstrated the problem quite clearly. Pierce believed that this law providing for popular sovereignty would effectively solve the controversy over slavery in the territories. He never understood why it resulted in violence instead. Increasingly, slavery was becoming a moral issue, but he continued to treat it as merely another solvable disagreement. He and the nation paid the price.

Despite the ever more obvious failure of his presidency, Pierce hoped for renomination, authoring his 1855 annual address as a campaign document. He excoriated the new Republican Party. He reminded Americans about the need for compromise and recognition of the concept of states' rights. He claimed that despite the South's longtime willingness to compromise, as, for example, in the Missouri Compromise, the North now refused to respond in kind. The Kansas-Nebraska Act was good legislation, Pierce argued, and it could solve the problem of slavery in the territories if it were allowed to; Republicans and other antislavery fanatics had to recognize that the South had rights, too. No one could arbitrarily limit slavery. Pierce believed that such fanaticism would result only in national disruption, and did anyone really want to destroy the interests of twenty-five million Americans for the benefit of a few Africans?

Pierce's battle cry brought down a torrent of criticism. When the Democratic National Convention met in 1856, it chose James Buchanan as its candidate, snubbing Pierce and making him the only sitting president who wanted to run for reelection not to receive his party's renomination for a second term. He was bitterly disappointed and went on a three-year tour of Europe. When the Civil War erupted, Pierce first supported the Union effort, but he quickly reverted to his prosouthern position. In a July 4, 1863, Concord speech, he blasted Lincoln's policy on civil rights and emancipation and proclaimed the attempt to preserve the Union by force to be futile. While he spoke, word filtered through the crowd of the Union victory at Gettysburg. Once again events had passed Pierce by. He lived another six years, but he played no further public role. He died on October 8, 1869, in Concord, New Hampshire.

SIGNIFICANCE

Franklin Pierce's life was filled with contradiction. He was an outgoing man who married a recluse. He was a northerner, but he held southern attitudes on the major is-

sue of the day, slavery. He gained the presidency because he seemed to be what the nation wanted: an amiable man whom neither northerners nor southerners found offensive. However, it was this appealing inoffensiveness, actually a lack of firm purposefulness, which doomed his presidency from the start. The nation's problems needed determination and skill of the highest order; in Franklin Pierce, the nation gained an irresolute man, overcome with personal problems, who did not understand the crisis swirling around him and was carried along by events instead of directing them.

—*John F. Marszalek*

FURTHER READING

Freehling, William W. "Franklin Pierce." In *The Presidents: A Reference History*, edited by Henry F. Graff. New York: Charles Scribner's Sons, 1984. A highly critical evaluation of Pierce. The New Hampshire politician is portrayed as a weak, vacillating individual whose mediocrity was the major reason why he was electable in 1852, and why he failed during his term.

Gara, Larry. *The Presidency of Franklin Pierce*. Lawrence: University Press of Kansas, 1991. Gara defines Pierce as a man of "limited ability" who was "overwhelmed" by the presidency, unable to provide the vision and leadership needed to halt the spread of slavery.

Kane, Joseph N. *Facts About the Presidents: A Compilation of Biographical and Historical Data*. 3d ed. New York: H. W. Wilson, 1974. A compilation of basic factual information on all the American presidents. Unusual or unique aspects about each president's administration are included.

Nevins, Allen. *Ordeal of the Union: A House Dividing, 1852-1857*. Vol. 2. New York: Charles Scribner's Sons, 1947. An excellent discussion of the Pierce years with insightful commentary on how his personality affected his policy. Nevins believes that Pierce's basic weaknesses doomed his presidency because they prevented him from taking the strong positions on national issues that the times required.

Nichols, Roy F. "The Causes of the Civil War." In *Interpreting American History: Conversations with Historians*, edited by John A. Garraty. Vol. 1. New York: Macmillan, 1970. A brief discussion of the White House relationship of Mr. and Mrs. Pierce. Nichols points out that Jane Pierce never recovered from the death of her son and became a virtual recluse in the White House.

_____. *Franklin Pierce: Young Hickory of the Granite Hills*. Philadelphia: University of Pennsylvania Press, 1931. This is the standard biography of the fourteenth president, detailed yet appealingly written. It emphasizes that, rather than outstanding ability, Pierce's physical attractiveness, his Mexican War military reputation, his ability to convince people with his oratory, his party regularity, and his pro-South policy gained him the 1852 Democratic nomination and eventually the presidency.

Taylor, Lloyd C., Jr. "Jane Means Appleton Pierce." In *Notable American Women, 1607-1950*, edited by Edward T. James. Vol. 3. Cambridge, Mass.: Belknap Press of Harvard University Press, 1971. A brief sketch of Pierce's wife that discusses how religious rigidity fostered a repressed personality that gave way under the strain of public life and the death of a young child.

Wallner, Peter A. *Franklin Pierce: New Hampshire's Favorite Son*. Concord, N.H.: Plaidswede, 2004. Volume 1 of this projected two-volume biography concludes on the night of Pierce's presidential inauguration. Wallner traces Pierce's career as a trial lawyer and New Hampshire politician and describes his presidential campaign.

SEE ALSO: James Buchanan; Caleb Cushing; Jefferson Davis; Stephen A. Douglas; Millard Fillmore; Nathaniel Hawthorne; Andrew Jackson; Henry Wadsworth Longfellow; James K. Polk; Winfield Scott; Harriet Beecher Stowe.

RELATED ARTICLES in *Great Events from History: The Nineteenth Century, 1801-1900:* December 31, 1853: Gadsden Purchase Completes the U.S.-Mexican Border; May 30, 1854: Congress Passes Kansas-Nebraska Act; June 16, 1855-May 1, 1857: Walker Invades Nicaragua; May, 1856-August, 1858: Bleeding Kansas.

ZEBULON PIKE
American explorer

One of the most important American explorers of his time, Pike helped to open the American Southwest to U.S. interests, and he gave his name to Colorado's Pikes Peak, which became famous as a symbol of the goals of Western pioneers.

BORN: January 5, 1779; Lamberton (now Trenton), New Jersey

DIED: April 27, 1813; York (now Toronto), Ontario, Canada

ALSO KNOWN AS: Zebulon Montgomery Pike (full name)

AREAS OF ACHIEVEMENT: Exploration, military

EARLY LIFE

The son of a U.S. Army major and the former Isabella Brown, Zebulon Pike was primarily raised on army posts in western Pennsylvania and Fort Washington, Ohio (now Cincinnati), while his father served under General James Wilkinson. Wilkinson, known to be wily, unscrupulous, and ambitious, would prove to be the predominant figure in the younger Pike's military and exploratory career.

A crack shot and expert outdoorsman, Pike entered his father's company as a cadet when he turned twenty years of age but found himself relegated to the job of quartermastering supplies. He served on posts in Indiana and Illinois in essentially a peacetime army with no prospects for distinction until Wilkinson decided to use Pike in two expeditions exploring the opening American West. It is possible that Pike found favor with his father's former commander when he eloped with Clarissa Brown, a cousin on Pike's mother's side and the daughter of a Wilkinson family friend.

In 1805, after President Thomas Jefferson's Louisiana Purchase and the commission of the Meriwether Lewis and William Clark expedition, the newly appointed Governor Wilkinson set up his headquarters in St. Louis, Missouri. There he prepared several expeditions to explore the upper Louisiana Territory, to establish the authority of the U.S. government over Indian tribes, and to discover the source of the Mississippi River. It is also possible that Wilkinson used Pike as leader of one of these expeditions to test British reactions to American incursions into the fur-trapping country and further used the expedition to test Pike's capabilities for future commands.

On July 30, 1805, Lieutenant Pike received his orders; he left St. Louis on August 5 with a twenty-man party. Pike's team trekked two thousand miles by keelboat and on foot north to upper Minnesota. On September 23, Pike made a treaty with the Lakota (Sioux) Indians, purchasing one thousand acres of land that later became Minneapolis/St.Paul. On February 21 Pike reached Leech Lake, which he wrongly claimed was the source of the Mississippi. After wintering in the area, he returned on April 30, 1806. His tour was deemed successful, although Pike was disappointed that President Jefferson did not give him the accolades showered on Lewis and Clark's ongoing reports. Nevertheless, Wilkinson determined that Pike was dependable. Three days after Pike's return, Wilkinson told him he would command an especially important expedition into the Southwest.

LIFE'S WORK

Although his motives and purposes remain uncertain, Wilkinson gave Pike command of a second expedition ostensibly to discover the headwaters of the Arkansas and Red Rivers and to explore them as far as the Spanish settlements of New Mexico in "New Spain." In addition, Pike was to accompany a party of Osage prisoners of war back to their country and effect a peace treaty between them and neighboring tribes, notably the strategically important Comanche. Wilkinson, a double agent for the Spanish court, cautioned Pike not to give the Spanish military cause for offense and not to reveal American interest in the economic, strategic, and settlement possibilities of the region.

Oddly, Wilkinson did not provide Pike with enough provisions for the trip, did not assign enough men to repel a serious Indian attack, and did not obtain governmental authority for the expedition. Some historians believe Wilkinson planned to betray Pike to the Spanish in order to spark an international incident, although his own son was part of the company. It is possible Pike had an unspoken agreement with Wilkinson, went beyond his orders, or was an inept geographer; in any event, subsequent actions would cast this expedition under a cloud of mystery.

With a party of twenty-two men, including eighteen from his previous trip, Pike left on July 15, 1806, and marched west to the Arkansas River. Slowed by inclement weather, he moved through Pawnee villages on the Republic River in what is now Kansas. There he learned that six hundred Spanish troops were looking for him. Pike ignored Pawnee warnings to turn back and sent five men, including the younger Wilkinson, to follow the Arkansas River south and return to St. Louis to report. Although not successful in his attempts to meet with Comanche chiefs, Pike was able to persuade the Pawnees

that they should change their allegiance from Spanish to American interests.

After following Spanish trails en route to Santa Fe, on November 15, 1806, Pike saw Pikes Peak for the first time. Pike originally named the mountain "Grand Peak," but his cartographers labeled it "Pikes Peak" on their maps, even though the mountain was well known to the Spanish, Indians, and trappers who had previously crossed the region. On November 26, Pike made one attempt to climb the mountain but was unsuccessful given the cold winter storms; he most likely climbed a nearby peak rather than the one that came to bear his name. Pike later predicted that no one would ever reach the summit of Pikes Peak. Pike then turned southwest, following Indian trails, and suffered from snow and ice in the Rocky Mountains of Colorado and upper New Mexico. Pike then found himself traveling in circles, moving north instead of south and unable to determine which way to proceed. After leaving behind three men incapacitated by frostbite, Pike finally came to a halt when he believed he had again found the Red River.

After building a log fort to defend his party against Indians near what turned out to be the upper Rio Grande, on February 26 he was discovered by one hundred Spanish cavalry troops. They invited Pike to come to Santa Fe, where he and his men were held under arrest for illegal entry. Despite Spanish fears that Pike's and other excursions into their territory were evidence of future American invasions, Pike easily made friends with local authorities. Pike was treated well, but the Spanish confiscated most of his papers (some were hidden in his men's rifle barrels). Pike's party was then escorted to Chihuahua, Mexico, and then Pike and his surviving men returned through Texas and were released in Natchitoches, Louisiana, on July 1, 1807.

Pike then went to Washington, D.C., but was busy with military business and did not present his report until January, 1808. By the time of his return, Wilkinson had been disgraced, and Pike found that his own efforts were treated with indifference or contempt, particularly because he maintained Wilkinson's innocence in conspiring with former vice president Aaron Burr to create a new republic in the Southwest by seizing Spanish lands. Tainted by the Wilkinson furor, Pike and his men were not given the usual land grants awarded by Congress to other explorers.

Pike's narrative of the trip was published in 1810. It presented the Great Plains to the American public for the first time as a Great American Desert. Pike claimed the region did not have sufficient timber to support settle-

Zebulon Pike. (Library of Congress)

pose of spying for Wilkinson and Aaron Burr, and only secondarily to gather topographical data. Later historians have refuted the charge, noting that extensive publicity preceded Pike's trip and that Pike did not know Spanish. They also suggest that if Pike were part of the Burr conspiracy, he would logically have gone directly to the Southwest instead of following the Arkansas River.

SIGNIFICANCE

Pike's western expedition pointed the way for new commercial interests, helped temporarily promote peace with the Indians, and helped establish U.S. domain over the territory. Pike's *An Account of Expeditions to the Sources of the Mississippi* (1810), although hastily compiled, inaccurate, and misleading, aroused American curiosity about the West. His account of the weakness of Spanish authority in Santa Fe and the profitability of trading with Mexico stirred entrepreneurs and politicians to expand into Texas, setting the stage for the Mexican War.

Some historians give Pike credit for helping to establish the myth of the Great American Desert, which retarded growth into the Great Plains. Pike's report also foreshadowed the later moves by the American government to push Indian tribes onto less desirable lands. Subsequent editions of Pike's journals were more dependable and more carefully organized, although not as honest or important as those of the Lewis and Clark dispatches, from which Pike heavily cribbed his own data.

In 1820, Dr. Edwin James became the first man on record to climb Pikes Peak. Julia Archibald Holmes became the first woman to reach the summit in 1858. During that same year, "Pikes Peak or Bust!" became a familiar slogan painted on the wagons of gold miners attracted to the region. Although few gold fortunes were made, the slogan made the mountain a national landmark. In 1893, Katherine Lee Bates, a Massachusetts author and teacher, composed the lyrics to "America the Beautiful," inspired by the view from the summit. The peak later became an important tourist attraction; visitors are able to reach the top by cog railway, car, or by foot. The Pikes Peak Cog Railroad was built in 1891 and is still in operation. Built in 1916, the Pikes Peak Toll Road is the second highest highway in the world. Pike County, Georgia, and its county seat, Zebulon, were named after Pike in 1856.

—Wesley Britton

ments, but he believed the desert would prove a useful buffer between the United States and Mexico. Furthermore, he claimed the plains would serve as an area to confine Indian tribes. Promoted to lieutenant colonel, in 1811 Pike was briefly under arrest for insubordination during the investigation of Wilkinson's possible involvement with the Burr conspiracy. Pike was completely exonerated on all charges. Wilkinson's role remains controversial and is still the subject of scholarly debate.

Becoming a general at the outset of the War of 1812, Pike was determined to find fame in combat or die. In April of 1813, Pike led sixteen hundred troops invading York (now Toronto), Canada, and was mortally wounded when the British deliberately set off a powder magazine. After a stone broke his spine, Pike lived long enough to hear the cries of his victorious men. As a gesture of respect, a captured British flag was placed under his head.

In 1908, Dr. H. E. Bolton discovered in Mexican archives some original papers confiscated during Pike's southwestern expedition of 1806. From these documents, Bolton and other historians concluded that Pike's second expedition was mounted primarily for the pur-

FURTHER READING

Carter, Carrol J. *Pike in Colorado*. Fort Collins, Colo.: Old Army Press, 1978. Carter's short, eighty-two-page volume focuses on Pike's discovery of Pikes Peak and his Colorado journey.

Hart, Stephen H., and Archer B. Hulbert, eds. *Zebulon Pike's Arkansas Journal.* Westport, Conn.: Greenwood Press, 1972. This edition focuses on Pike's lower Mississippi travels, augmenting Pike's accounts with interpretations based on recently discovered maps.

Hollon, W. Eugene. *The Lost Pathfinder: Zebulon Montgomery Pike.* Norman: University of Oklahoma Press, 1949. A longtime standard biography, Hollon's work is frequently cited as the most authoritative study of Pike's career.

Hyslop, Stephen G. "An Explorer or a Spy?" *American History* 37, no. 3 (August, 2002): 58. Describes Pike's Western explorations, including his alleged espionage activities for Aaron Burr.

Jackson, Donald, ed. *The Journals of Zebulon Pike, with Letters and Related Documents.* Norman: University of Oklahoma Press, 1966. Jackson's edition of Pike's journal is supplemented with both related documents and scholarly interpretations of Pike's accounts based on information discovered after Pike's death.

Montgomery, M. R. *Jefferson and the Gun-men: How the West Was Almost Lost.* New York: Crown, 2000. A chronicle of the Burr conspiracy, including Pike and Wilkinson's involvement in the scheme.

Pike, Zebulon Montgomery. *The Expeditions of Zebulon Montgomery Pike.* Edited by Elliott Coues. 2 vols. New York: Dover, 1987. Originally published in three volumes in 1895, these firsthand accounts of Pike's travels are accompanied by maps.

Sanford, William R., and Carl R. Green. *Zebulon Pike: Explorer of the Southwest.* Springfield, N.J.: Enslow, 1996. As part of the Legendary Heroes of the Wild West series, this biography is intended for the general reader.

Stallones, Jared. *Zebulon Pike and the Explorers of the American Southwest.* New York: Chelsea House, 1992. With an introductory essay by former Apollo astronaut Michael Collins, this short, critical overview of Pike emphasizes Pike's ineptitude and reliance on Wilkinson, portraying Pike as an unlucky man later mythologized as an American hero.

Terrell, John U. *Zebulon Pike: The Life and Times of an Adventurer.* New York: Weybright and Talley, 1968. Terrell is especially helpful discussing Pike's connections with his times, and color maps help illustrate Pike's journeys.

SEE ALSO: Aaron Burr; Meriwether Lewis and William Clark; Jedediah Smith.

RELATED ARTICLES in *Great Events from History: The Nineteenth Century, 1801-1900:* May 14, 1804-September 23, 1806: Lewis and Clark Expedition; July 15, 1806-July 1, 1807: Pike Explores the American Southwest; May, 1842-1854: Frémont Explores the American West; March 2, 1853-1857: Pacific Railroad Surveys.

LYDIA E. PINKHAM
American business leader

Through extensive advertising of a patent medicine bearing her name and image, Pinkham became one of the most widely known American women of the nineteenth century. Although the claims her company made for the medical benefits that her product offered were dubious, she and her family made a substantial contribution to changing the nature of marketing retail products.

BORN: February 9, 1819; Lynn, Massachusetts
DIED: May 17, 1883; Lynn, Massachusetts
ALSO KNOWN AS: Lydia Estes Pinkham (full name); Lydia Estes (birth name)
AREAS OF ACHIEVEMENT: Business, medicine

EARLY LIFE

Lydia Estes Pinkham was born Lydia Estes into a New England Quaker family, the tenth of twelve children. Her father, William Estes, was a shoemaker who took up farming. Her mother, Rebecca Estes, became a follower of Emanuel Swedenborg, an eighteenth century Swedish scientist and theologian who claimed special knowledge of the afterlife. Followers of Swedenborg were typically abolitionists, and Lydia seems to have taken that cause to heart, as at the age of sixteen she joined the Lynn Female Anti-Slavery Society.

Lydia attended Lynn Academy and after graduation became a teacher. In 1843, she met Isaac Pinkham, a young widower whom she married that same year.

In addition to a daughter from his previous marriage, the Pinkhams had several more children over the years, and Lydia spent the next thirty years as a homemaker. Her husband found it hard to settle down to one job and frequently spent more money than he earned. In 1857, they moved to Bedford, Massachusetts, where Isaac tried farming. After three years he gave up farming, and they returned to Lynn, where they remained through the rest of their marriage.

LIFE'S WORK

Lydia's entry into the business world was the culmination of several forces. As a result of land investments Isaac made over the years, the family gradually reached a moderate level of financial security. However, due to several bank failures in 1873, their finances deteriorated to the point that Isaac was sued and almost jailed for debts he was unable to pay. The family managed somehow to remain solvent, but their situation was precarious.

Several years earlier, Isaac had been given the formula for an herbal concoction that Lydia used as an herbal medicine for female complaints. Lydia had experimented with adding new herbs to the mixture and had tested it on members of the family and friends, many of whom believed it helped them. Lydia herself had never considered advertising and selling her medicine, but with the financial difficulties the family was facing, her son Daniel suggested that she try selling it.

In 1875, Lydia began selling her herbal medicine, which she called Lydia E. Pinkham's Vegetable Compound. It was made up of several different ground herbs and had an ethyl alcohol content of roughly 20 percent, which made it the equivalent of forty-proof liquor. The alcohol was justified, according to the product's label, because it was "used solely as a solvent and preservative." Each bottle contained 14.5 ounces of liquid and was sold for one dollar. Lydia also prepared a four-page pamphlet, titled *Guide for Women*, that gave health tips,

---

PINKHAM'S VEGETABLE COMPOUND

LYDIA E. PINKHAM'S
VEGETABLE COMPOUND
IS A POSITIVE CURE

*For all those painful Complaints and Weaknesses
so common to our best female population.*

It will cure entirely the worst forms of Female Complaints, all Ovarian troubles, Inflammation, Ulceration, Falling and Displacements of the Womb, and the consequent Spinal Weakness, and is particularly adapted to the Change of Life.

It will dissolve and expel Tumors from the Uterus in an early stage of development. The tendency to cancerous humors there is checked very speedily by its use. It removes faintness, flatulency, destroys all craving for stimulants, and relieves weakness of the stomach. It cures Bloating, Headaches, Nervous Prostration, General Debility, Sleepless, Depression and Indigestion.

That feeling of bearing down, causing pain, weight and backache, is always permanently cured by its use.

It will at all times and under all circumstances act in harmony with the laws that govern the female system. For the cure of Kidney Complaints of either sex this Compound is unsurpassed.

Lydia E. Pinkham's Vegetable Compound is prepared at Lynn, Mass. Price, $1.00; six bottles for $5.00. Sent by mail in the form of Pills, also in the form of Lozenges, on receipt of price. $1.00 per box, for either. Send for pamphlet. All letters of inquiry promptly answered. Address as above.

No family should be without LYDIA E. PINKHAM'S LIVER PILLS. They cure Constipation, Biliousness, and Torpidity of the Liver. 25 cents per box.

Source: Biomed Library, University of California, Los Angeles.

---

including the recommendation to take Lydia E. Pinkham's Vegetable Compound.

In 1876, the family incorporated the Lydia E. Pinkham Medicine Company. One of Lydia's sons, Will Pinkham, was listed as the company's proprietor, rather than Lydia's husband, because Will had no outstanding debts. Daniel and Will proceeded to market their product on the road, persuading druggists in a variety of cities and towns to stock the compound. Sales were initially small, so the family experimented with different types of advertising and distributing pamphlets. In an effort to attract a broader clientele, Daniel suggested that Lydia claim that her product benefited other organs of the body, in addition to the female uterus.

The first glimmers of success came when Daniel placed his mother's entire pamphlet as an advertisement in the *Boston Herald*. At first, the rest of the family considered it a foolish expense; however, the ad increased sales enough to encourage the family to put more effort and funds into advertising. They soon hired T. C. Evans to create newspaper ads.

The real turning point in sales came when Daniel suggested that the label for their medicine needed improvement. He decided that putting the picture of a young, healthy woman on the label would help increase sales. Although Lydia herself was sixty years old by that time, she did have a healthy appearance, so she posed for the photograph that began to appear on compound labels. Her image then became the trademark for Lydia E. Pinkham's Vegetable Compound. Who would not trust the advice of the grandmotherly figure on her products' labels?

Lydia's picture also appeared in newspaper and magazine ads. The ads became so widespread that Lydia E. Pinkham's name soon was known by almost all American women and by many men. Sales increased so quickly that the family was offered a large sum for their company and the trademark that went with it, but the family expected sales to continue to grow and refused the offer.

In 1879, Lydia's company began inviting people who read their ads to write to Lydia with their medical questions, promising that Lydia herself would answer the letters. For example, a woman with a prolapsed uterus wrote,

> Dr. tells me I can have the trouble removed but thought I would write and ask you if the compound would do it before I submitted to an operation with Doctor's tools, a thing I have not much faith in.

Lydia's reply:

> By all means avoid instrumental treatment for your trouble. Use the compound as you have been using it—faithfully and patiently—and it will eventually work a cure.

As this response suggests, the Pinkhams claimed that their compound could cure a broad range of ailments. They originally advertised the compound primarily as a cure for "female weakness," a euphemism for any number of "female problems." However, as time passed, the family broadened their claims for the product to encompass cures for a long list of medical ailments. Moreover, their advertising became increasingly elaborate, describing medical symptoms in subtle ways that encouraged readers to diagnose their own problems—always with the cure being the compound. Many "sufferers" were likely healthy, but because of Lydia E. Pinkham's ads

they considered themselves sick and in need of her product.

By 1881, the Pinkhams' business was strong, but personal tragedy struck Lydia. After fighting tuberculosis for two years, Daniel Pinkham died at the age of thirty-two. Later during the same year, twenty-eight-year-old Will died from lung disease. Late in the following year, Lydia herself suffered a stroke from which she never recovered. On May 17, 1883, she died in Lynn at the age of sixty-four.

Sales of Lydia's compound at the time of her death totaled $300,000 per year. Her company continued on without her for many years, but so far as the public knew, she was still alive, as the company continued to use her image as its trademark, while inviting readers to write letters to her. In 1905, this minor fraud was finally revealed when Mark Sullivan, who was hired to investigate patent medicine claims, published a photograph of Lydia's gravestone.

SIGNIFICANCE

Lydia Pinkham is best known for the picture on the labels of her products and in the many ads placed in newspapers and magazines. However, her greater significance lies in her innovations in marketing. Advertising was in its infancy when she began selling her compound. The success her company had through extensive, almost ubiquitous, advertising showed the power of this new medium. Moreover, her company's use of her picture as a trademark was a bold, successful move that has continued to be improved upon ever since.

Although Pinkham did not make a significant mark in the woman suffrage movement, she was concerned with women's issues. She also had strong convictions about other social problems such as slavery. Her contribution to woman suffrage was her success in the business world. Business was a man's world in her day, and she led the way to change that. The fact that her legacy long lived on in the company bearing her name also shows her business sense.

The Lydia E. Pinkham Medicine Company continued to sell products until the 1950's. Lydia's picture remained their trademark, but other things changed. In response to government concerns about alcohol content in patent medicines, the company finally removed alcohol from its compound in 1914. Over the ensuing years, sales of the compound gradually diminished as more laws were enacted to restrict claims made on patent medicine labels.

—Bryan D. Ness

FURTHER READING

Applegate, Edd. *Personalities and Products: A Historical Perspective on Advertising in America*. Westport, Conn.: Greenwood Press, 1998. Contains a chapter on Lydia Pinkham focusing on her role in improving nineteenth century advertising methods.

Fite, Gilbert C. *The Southern Country Editor*. Columbia: University of South Carolina Press, 1991. Contains a chapter concerning Lydia Pinkham and the company she founded.

Fox, Stephen. *The Mirror Makers: A History of American Advertising and Its Creators*. Urbana: University of Illinois Press, 1997. Contains a chapter about Lydia Pinkham and pinpoints her role in innovations in advertising.

Stage, Sarah. *Female Complaints: Lydia Pinkham and the Business of Women's Medicine*. New York: W. W. Norton, 1979. A thorough historical analysis of Lydia Pinkham and her times.

Wasburn, Robert C. *Life and Times of Lydia E. Pinkham*. Manchester, N.H.: Ayer, 1976. A biographical account of Lydia Pinkham's life and the times in which she lived.

SEE ALSO: Eleuthère Irénée du Pont; Marshall Field; Montgomery Ward.

RELATED ARTICLES in *Great Events from History: The Nineteenth Century, 1801-1900:* 1869: First Modern Department Store Opens in Paris; May 8, 1886: Pemberton Introduces Coca-Cola.

CAMILLE PISSARRO
French artist

Pissarro contributed to the formation of Impressionist techniques and thus to the Impressionist movement in France in the last half of the nineteenth century. In addition, he played an instrumental role in establishing a series of exhibitions to promote the work of the Impressionist artists.

BORN: July 10, 1830; Charlotte Amalie, St. Thomas, Danish West Indies (now in U.S. Virgin Islands)
DIED: November 13, 1903; Paris, France
ALSO KNOWN AS: Jacob-Abraham-Camille Pissarro (full name)
AREA OF ACHIEVEMENT: Art

EARLY LIFE

Born in the capital of the West Indian island of St. Thomas, Jacob Camille Pissarro (PEE-sah-roh) was the third of four sons of Jewish parents, Frédéric Pissarro and Rachel Manzano-Ponie Petit. His father's family had left Bordeaux, France, in search of a better life and settled on St. Thomas, where they established a family-operated trading store. To his father's displeasure, Camille spent his youthful years roaming the luxurious paths of the island, preferring to sketch and paint rather than work in the family business. At the age of twelve, Camille was sent to school in Passy, a suburb of Paris.

In Passy, the young Pissarro was encouraged by his schoolmaster to nurture his obvious talent, despite ex-

plicit instructions from his father that he was to be educated in business. After five years in Passy, his father called him home. The time in France, however, had left its mark on Pissarro. For the next five years, Pissarro preferred to sit by the docks, drawing and sketching the ships, or to hike across the island in search of suitable motifs for his sketchbook. During one of these excursions, he encountered Fritz Melbye, a Danish marine and landscape artist who encouraged Pissarro in developing a method of working outside, "in the fresh air" (*en plein air*), which he continued throughout most of his career. In 1852, the two artists moved to Caracas, Venezuela, where Pissarro remained for two years, painting continuously and interacting with the energetic artistic community in the capital. The years in Venezuela awakened Pissarro to his own ignorance of technique and of new directions then being taken in art. He left for France in 1855, never to see his homeland again.

Pissarro was twenty-five when he arrived in Paris, enthusiastic but naïve and already sporting the full, Old Testament prophet beard for which he became famous among his friends. While attending the Universal Exhibition, he discovered the work of Camille Corot, whose reputation, as both a painter and a teacher, was then at its height. Despite his youth and inexperience, Pissarro managed to show his work to the great master. Corot was favorably impressed, encouraging Pissarro to focus on developing what he termed values, or the harmony between two tones, in his work.

LIFE'S WORK

The meeting with Corot in 1855 set Pissarro on a path that he was to follow, with only occasional digressions, for the remainder of his artistic career. Heeding Corot's advice, he began to pay particular attention to the importance of tonal values in creating a truly harmonious work. He practiced a lifelong attention to the importance of drawing, to self-discipline manifested in daily exercising of his craft, to *pleinairisme* ("plain-airism"), to painting what he felt, and to painting not bit by bit but rather working on the whole canvas at once. In all of this he followed the tenets established by Corot. This focus on sensation ultimately became the basis of Pissarro's work.

In 1858, Pissarro moved to Montmorency in order to paint the landscape *en plein air*. This first move to the country announced Pissarro's lifelong struggle to reject the bourgeois oppressiveness of the city in favor of simpler, rural settings. Although later in life he was often to return to Paris, staying in various hotels and painting views of the city from his window, in his early years, he preferred the bucolic setting of the countryside to the bustle of urban life. During his frequent trips to the city, he developed friendships with most of the young avant-garde artists of the time, such as Paul Cézanne and Pierre-Auguste Renoir. Because of his natural ability to offer criticism and guidance without offending the delicate egos of his colleagues, Pissarro quickly became a trustworthy and articulate spokesperson for the diverse group of artists soon to be known collectively as the Impressionists.

In 1871, Pissarro married Julie Vellay. Their first of seven children, Lucien, became an accomplished artist in his own right. Although much in love during the early years of their marriage, the couple's constant financial struggles turned Julie into a sharp-tongued, unsupportive partner in later years. From all accounts, except those of Julie, Pissarro was a loving father. Nevertheless, his financial responsibility to his children never deterred him from resolutely continuing his painting even in the worst of times.

Firmly established among the Impressionists in Paris by 1863, Pissarro exhibited three paintings at the Salon des Refusés, an exhibit organized for those artists whose work had been refused by the judges for the official Salon exhibit of that year. The system of exhibitions was tightly regulated at the time by official judges (under the auspices of the emperor himself), who sought to establish national, and thus conservative, tastes in art. The Salon des Refusés was approved by the emperor in response to the artistic outcry against the conservatism of the official Salon art. Here were presented the most revolutionary works of the day. The exhibition drew desultory remarks from critics, derision, and the laughter of incomprehension from the general public. Pissarro's works went virtually unnoticed as all attention was focused on Édouard Manet's scandalous masterpiece, *Luncheon on the Grass* (1863), which depicted a naked female model accompanied on a picnic by two clothed gentlemen.

Infuriated by the public's total disinterest in his work, Pissarro was nevertheless convinced of the rightness of the new direction he was taking with his compatriots. Unlike the realistic artists whose works were being shown in the grand Salons, Pissarro and the other Impressionists sought first to capture the fugitive effects of light on a subject at a particular moment in time. Through the use of bold colors, slashing brushstrokes, and motifs chosen from everyday life, these young iconoclasts attempted to transform on canvas an effect of an impression of reality into a visually more personal, thus in their view more realistic, representation of the world.

By 1874, Pissarro was one of the acknowledged leaders of the Impressionist movement and assisted in organizing an Exhibition of the Society of Painters, Sculptors, Engravers, etc., the first of eight Impressionist exhibitions. The show included the works of Edgar Degas, Claude Monet, Berthe Morisot, Renoir, Alfred Sisley, and Cézanne. Although his work elicited only negative reactions, during the late 1870's and early 1880's he continued to paint in the Impressionist mode, experimenting with colors and different brushstrokes. Gradually he developed a highly personal and easily identifiable style, known as "Pissarro's *tricotage*" (knitting), consisting of parallel cross-hatchings of varying dimensions, which give his work of this period a distinctive sense of movement and textural unity.

Pissarro's art took a dramatic turn in October, 1885, after a meeting with the painter Georges Seurat. Influenced by then-current scientific theories of color and its perception by the human eye, Seurat departed from the Impressionists to develop a pointillist, or divisionist, style of painting using small dots of color rather than brushstrokes. Seurat's neo-Impressionist work announced a dramatically new intent to make visible the subjective rather than, as the Impressionists had sought to do, to make the objective world subjective. Pissarro exhibited his divisionist work alongside that of Seurat in May, 1887, but without success.

Pissarro's neo-Impressionist phase lasted about five years, although strictly pointillist technique distinguishes only part of his work of this period. Although his works sold poorly, he made many new friends, particularly among the Symbolist poets and writers who regarded neo-Impressionism as a visual translation of their quest toward verbal fluidity and musicality. He was also developing a strong sense of the social function of art as a supportive statement of the need for societal change, as professed by the active group of anarchists in Paris with whom he was acquainted. Melding politics and aesthetics, his work contains numerous scenes of peasants working cooperatively and serenely in the fields, content in their distance from the harsh realities of industrialization. By the late 1880's, Pissarro had found the divisionist methods tedious and abandoned the technique.

A retrospective exhibit of Pissarro's work in January, 1892, proved popular with critics and public, particularly a series of landscapes and landmarks painted during a trip to London. All seventy-one works exhibited were sold, finally establishing the artist's commercial success at the age of sixty-two. His continued association with various revolutionary groups resulted in his having to flee to Belgium in 1894.

In his final years, Pissarro enjoyed the rewards of a lifetime of hard work. Financial security came with an exhibition in 1896 of a series of paintings of the Seine executed in Rouen. Two final series of works, one of the Parisian Grands Boulevards, the other of the Avenue de l'Opéra, capped his career with critical and public acclaim. Having rented in 1900 a small apartment in Paris, he spent his last years focusing his vision on urban motifs: views of the Louvre, the Pont-Neuf, and the Tuileries Gardens. At the age of seventy-three, he developed an abcess of the prostate gland. Having always believed in the country wisdom of homeopathic medicine, he refused the necessary operation and succumbed to septicemia in 1903.

SIGNIFICANCE

Camille Pissarro never produced a signature painting that critics regard as his masterpiece. One may speak of a series of masterful works, yet no single work stands clearly above the rest. Perhaps this is true, as one critic has suggested, because Pissarro saw art as "a continual search after the eternally changing." His love of fall and winter scenes—for example, his fascination with light playing on snow-covered hills and streets—led him to paint dozens of canvases of Pontoise and its environs, each distinctive yet most effectively viewed as one part of a corporate vision of the village.

The internal coherence of each painting was supremely important for Pissarro. His son Lucien identified the dominant characteristic as a concern for *les valeurs rapprochées* (closely related values of color). Viewing Pissarro's work over a forty-year period from 1863 to 1903, one notes that while the artist often adjusted his style to his subject, he was always ruled by the immediacy of sensations brought into direct experience with his motif, sensations that he then struggled to order into an "idea of unity." Although his work was generally not appreciated in his own lifetime, critical consensus has established his rightful place among the giants of the Impressionist movement.

—William C. Griffin

FURTHER READING

Adler, Kathleen. *Camille Pissarro: A Biography*. London: B. T. Batsford, 1978. A short, 190-page biography, which was the first to reconstruct Pissarro's life for the English reader. The work contains numerous illustrations and photographs of the artist and his family. The useful combination of endnotes and bibliography into one document provides the reader with easy access to secondary sources, arranged chronologically.

Lloyd, Christopher, ed. *Studies on Camille Pissarro*. New York: Routledge and Kegan Paul, 1986. A series of essays covering diverse aspects of Pissarro's life and work, authored by some of the most eminent of modern Pissarro critics. Several previously unexplored aspects of Pissarro's work are examined, such as the link between his political philosophy and his art, and the possible influence of Rembrandt on Pissarro's etchings.

Pissarro, Joachim. *Camille Pissarro*. New York: H. N. Abrams, 1993. An objective reassessment of Pissarro's art by his great-grandson, an art historian and curator. Initial chapters provide a chronological overview of Pissarro's work, while later chapters focus on specific genres, including market scenes, landscapes, and interiors. Includes 354 illustrations (205 of them in color).

Rewald, John, ed. *Camille Pissarro*. New York: Harry N. Abrams, 1963. Perhaps the best of the relatively few collections of Pissarro's work in print, included in the Library of Great Painters series. A short introduction highlights the principal events in the artist's life and identifies major influences. Historical and aesthetic commentaries accompany each color plate.

Shikes, Ralph E., and Paula Harper. *Pissarro: His Life and Work*. New York: Horizon Press, 1980. A thorough and sensitive rendering of Pissarro's life in the context of his artistic evolution. The work contains twenty-one color plates and black-and-white reproductions. Drawing from material previously unpublished, the authors seek to reveal the complex and contradictory character of the artist. A current bibliography and detailed index assist both the casual and serious reader.

Stone, Irving. *Depths of Glory: A Biographical Novel of Camille Pissarro*. Garden City, N.Y.: Doubleday, 1985. Although a biographical novel, Stone's work scrupulously follows the documented details and spirit of Pissarro's life. A splendid evocation of the times by the author of similar works on the lives of Vincent van Gogh and Michelangelo. The serious reader will not be deterred by the novel's six hundred compellingly written pages.

Ward, Martha. *Pissarro, Neo-Impressionism, and the Spaces of the Avant-Garde*. Chicago: University of Chicago Press, 1996. Tracks the development and reception of the neo-Impressionists, a group of French artists and critics who, during the 1880's and 1890's, created a modern vanguard movement. Discusses the work of Pissarro and the other artists in the group.

SEE ALSO: Paul Cézanne; Edgar Degas; Paul Gauguin; Vincent van Gogh; Édouard Manet; Pierre-Auguste Renoir; Henri Rousseau; Georges Seurat.

RELATED ARTICLE in *Great Events from History: The Nineteenth Century, 1801-1900:* April 15, 1874: First Impressionist Exhibition.

PIUS IX
Roman Catholic pope (1846-1878)

Pius was elected pope shortly before Europe's revolutions of 1848. His was to be the longest papal reign in history. He led the Church through a difficult period into the era of Italian unity; in spite of the bitter conflict between church and state, he left the Church stronger at his death.

BORN: May 13, 1792; Senigallia, Papal States (now in Italy)
DIED: February 7, 1878; Rome, Italy
ALSO KNOWN AS: Giovanni Maria Mastai-Ferretti (birth name); Blessed Pius IX
AREAS OF ACHIEVEMENT: Church government, religion and theology

EARLY LIFE

Giovanni Maria Mastai-Ferretti was born into a family of lesser Italian nobility in the Marches only a few years before Napoleon I marched into Italy. He studied at Viterbo and at a seminary in Rome, where he developed a vocation for the priesthood. He suffered from epilepsy in his youth and consequently his application for service in the Swiss Guard was refused. He later recovered and was ordained as a priest in 1819. He was sent on a papal mission to Chile (1823-1825), his only experience of foreign travel. He was director of a Roman orphanage, Tata Giovanni, from 1825 to 1827, thereafter serving in the Papal States as archbishop of Spoleto (1827-1832) and bishop of Imola (1832-1840).

Gregory XVI elevated Mastai-Ferretti to cardinal in 1840. In these early years, Archbishop Mastai-Ferretti gained a deserved reputation as a devoted leader of his flock, and he was remembered with gratitude by his congregations as a man of sincere spiritual humility who set aside time to visit the poor and showed a special devotion to children. He also observed directly the consequences of the reactionary rule of Pope Gregory, and his recognition of the need for reform in the Papal States earned for him the reputation of a liberal.

At Imola, he formed a friendship with the liberal Count Giuseppe Pasolini, who introduced him to Vincenzo Gioberti's *Del primato morale e civile degli Italiani* (1843; of the civic and moral primacy of Italians). Gioberti was a Turinese priest whose earlier enthusiasm for Giuseppe Mazzini's ideas about Italian unity had raised suspicions about his orthodoxy. His thesis was that only the pope had the authority to bring unity to Italy, and the solution to the burning question of the Risorgimento was a federation of states under the presidency of the pope. At this period of Mastai-Ferretti's life, the reformist ideas of Gioberti were appealing, and he took a copy of the book with him when he was summoned to Rome for the conclave upon the death of Gregory XVI in 1846.

LIFE'S WORK

Mastai-Ferretti was elected pope on the fourth ballot, on June 16, 1846. He was the compromise candidate, between a liberal cardinal, to his left, and the former secretary of state to Gregory XVI, the reactionary Luigi Cardinal Lambruschini, to his right. He adopted the name of Pius for his revered Pius VII, once Napoleon's prisoner, who had helped the young Mastai-Ferretti enter the priesthood. Roman and European opinion was ecstatic. A liberal pope had been chosen, and it was widely believed that the days of absolute papal control of the Romagna were numbered.

One of Pius's first acts as pope was to grant amnesty to political prisoners and exiles. He granted freedom of the press, introduced street lighting to Rome, and established a new Roman Council (composed of an overwhelming majority of laymen, many of whom held openly republican views). He finally bent to the temper of the times and conceded a constitution in March, 1848. These reforms, however, were more the result of popular pressure than spontaneous concessions granted freely from above. The new pope was worried that he had unleashed forces beyond his control. When Venice and Milan, followed by Charles Albert of Piedmont, rose against the Austrian occupation, the pope refused to assume the symbolic leadership of the national struggle. In his allocution of April 29, 1848, he stated that, as the vicar of Christ on earth, he would not wage war on another Catholic power. That was the moment when the Papacy and the secular leaders of the Risorgimento parted company.

When the pope's prime minister, Count Pellegrino Rossi, was murdered on November 15, 1848, Pius was forced to flee Rome in disguise and seek asylum in Gaeta under the protection of King Ferdinand of Naples. A republic was declared in Rome, and Mazzini was summoned to lead it, with Giuseppe Garibaldi in charge of the defenses. From Gaeta, the pope appealed to the Catholic powers to overthrow the insurgents, and the French government (under the republican president Louis Napoleon) found itself in the embarrassing position of sending a small force to challenge a sister republic. The Roman republic collapsed in July, 1849, but the pope did not return until the following April.

Henceforth all pretense at accommodation with secular reformers was abandoned. Under the stewardship of the astute secretary of state, Giacomo Cardinal Antonelli, the Papal States prepared for a return to paternalism. The groundwork was laid for a growing conflict between church and state as Charles Albert of Piedmont,

under King Victor Emmanuel II of Savoy and his chief minister Count Cavour, assumed the initiative in the final struggle for Italian unity. In Piedmont, the pope had to endure the spectacle of the sequestration of church property, the abolition of religious orders, and the assumption of all educational responsibilities by the state. In Cavour he found a far more formidable adversary than Mazzini and Garibaldi, for Cavour was a brilliant and occasionally unscrupulous politician prepared to impose his will.

As the power of the secular state expanded, so papal territory shrank. As the Piedmontese drove the Austrians out of Lombardy in 1859, Cavour sent forces into the Romagna to wrest it from the rule of the Papacy. The loss of the Papal States was a heavy blow, for Pius considered this territory an essential part of the Church's patrimony, granted by God in perpetuity. For Cavour and most western European leaders, however, the Papal States were a thorn in the side of modern progress, a medieval impediment in the path of the secular future.

In the two decades after 1850, the pope presided over a great international expansion and revival of the Roman Catholic Church and the spread of its teachings. In 1864, he published the encyclical *Quanta Cura* along with the

Pius IX. (Library of Congress)

Syllabus of Errors, denouncing virtually every social and moral belief that had achieved general acceptance since the French Revolution. The gesture was intended to be an assertion of papal authority in spite of the loss of the Romagna and adjoining territories. Between 1860 and 1870, Rome was defended by French troops provided by Napoleon III, who was acting under pressure from French Catholics; he found himself now in opposition to Charles Albert of Piedmont, whose ambitions he had earlier, as president of a republic rather than emperor, supported. The outbreak of the Franco-Prussian War in July, 1870, however, led to the withdrawal of the French occupational force and the collapse of papal resistance to the government of King Victor Emmanuel. The last obstacle to Italian unity was removed and the pope retreated to the Vatican Palace.

It was Pius who cast himself in the role of "the prisoner of the Vatican," but only after he rejected a generous offer of settlement from the government (the Law of Guarantees). He thus set the pattern for his successors by refusing to come to terms with the secular institutions of power and attempting to persuade Catholics not to participate in the political life of the state.

It was not a coincidence that the Vatican Council summoned by Pius in 1869 proclaimed the pope infallible in all declarations on faith and morals in order to regain a hegemony in the spiritual sphere that had been lost in the temporal. Outbreaks of anticlericalism in Europe culminated in the abrogation of the concordat with Austria in 1874, followed by the aggressive anti-Catholic campaign (*Kulturkampf*) launched by Otto von Bismarck in Germany in 1875, which included the expulsion of Jesuits and a dissolution of Catholic schools. In spite of his isolation and doctrinally intransigent stance toward the modern world, Pius retained until the end not only the affection of the faithful but also that of the Roman populace in general, as well as the esteem of his opponents. Pius died peacefully on February 7, 1878.

SIGNIFICANCE

Although Pius's reign may be viewed as a disaster politically, ecclesiastically it recorded some major successes. Because he was not a skillful diplomat or an experienced politician, these occurred in the area of doctrine. Three events above all stand out. In 1853, Pius set about defining the dogma of the virginity of Mary. Demands for such a definition were initially received from the lower ranks of the religious orders and the Catholic laity. The pope then requested advice from his bishops, after which the doctrine was defined by a panel of experts. It was the

pope himself (who had played an active role in all the proceedings) who read the proclamation at a ceremony in St. Peter's on December 8, 1854.

The Syllabus of Errors—published ten years to the day after the proclamation on Mary—is a trenchant expression of orthodoxy, setting the Church consciously at odds with a heterodox world that it deplores. Eighty propositions are listed and condemned in the syllabus, including pantheism, rationalism, liberalism, socialism, and communism. All the "principles of '89"—the heredity of the French Revolution—that had infiltrated themselves into the myriad struggles for reform in the nineteenth century and had contributed to the secularization of civic life are denounced by the syllabus. The document is above all remembered for its final condemnation of the hope that the Papacy can be reconciled to progress, liberalism, and modern civilization.

A similar theological conservatism is evident in the question of papal infallibility endorsed by the Vatican Council of 1869-1870. The pope was not well served by an unauthorized and imprudent article in a Jesuit publication suggesting that the doctrine would be presented in council and accepted without debate. This was by no means the intention, but it offered an opportunity to anti-Catholic forces to claim that the pope was in the hands of the Jesuits. The result was that the question was debated at inordinate length, but its ultimate ratification by a vast majority of the assembled bishops was a personal triumph for Pius.

Taken together, these three questions of dogma illustrate the major concerns of Pius IX at a time when the Church, under fire from progressive and secular forces, sought to assert doctrinal unity behind the authority of God's appointed vicar on earth in order to keep a hold on the faith of its followers and to lead them into the modern era. Pius himself was not implacably opposed to every aspect of modern life; as pope, however, he saw his first duty as consolidating the power of the Church around the issue of faith and his second as securing a permanent place for the Church among the nation states of the new age.

—Harry Lawton

FURTHER READING

Corrigan, Raymond. *The Church and the Nineteenth Century*. Milwaukee: Bruce, 1938. A pro-papal view by a Jesuit historian of Pius's career and his struggle with the major historical events of his reign, the challenge of republican and monarchical government. There are separate chapters on the unification of Italy, the doctrine of the Immaculate Conception, and the Syllabus of Errors.

Flint, James B. *Great Britain and the Holy See: The Diplomatic Relations Question, 1846-1852*. Washington, D.C.: Catholic University of America Press, 2003. Examines the failure of British Prime Minister Earl Russell to establish diplomatic relations with Pope Pius IX. Flint maintains the papal government refused to establish relations because it feared that British diplomats might recommend unwelcome reforms in the Roman Catholic Church, or might use the church to make Catholic Ireland more amenable to British rule.

Hales, E. E. Y. *The Catholic Church in the Modern World*. New York: Hanover House, 1958. Hales returns to the central episodes referred to in his biography (see below), here treated with more specific historical detail and discussion. Chapters 7 through 11 deal with the major themes and struggles of Pius's reign, while his career as a whole is set in the broader history of the Church from the French Revolution to Italian fascism and the postwar democracy.

_____. *Pio Nono*. London: Eyre & Spotiswoode, 1954. The fullest study of the pope's career in English and essential reading for the student or scholar. This is a political biography written as a defense of Pius's position vis-à-vis contemporary liberalism, the Roman republic, and Catholic progressives. Informative on his relations with Cavour, Victor Emmanuel, and Napoleon III.

John, Eric, ed. *The Popes, a Concise Biographical History*. New York: Hawthorn Books, 1964. An encyclopedia of the lives of all the popes, each one written in all essential detail. The tone is pro-Catholic but not unctuous. The section on Pius IX is full, complete, and objective, while presenting an essentially sympathetic portrait of a troubled pontiff.

Kelly, John N. D. *The Oxford Dictionary of Popes*. New York: Oxford University Press, 1986. The pages on Pius are concise and detailed, clear on the major doctrinal contributions made by Pius to Catholic thinking. A useful introduction that will send students on to the complete biographies.

Kretzer, David I. *Prisoner of the Vatican: The Popes' Secret Plot to Capture Rome from the New Italian State*. Boston: Houghton Mifflin, 2004. Using previously unopened Vatican archives, Kretzer recounts how Popes Pius IX, Leo XIII, and other members of the clergy sought to dismantle the new Italian state and regain control of Rome.

Rendina, Claudio. *I papi, storia e segreti*. Rome: Newton Compton, 1983. Another encyclopedia of papal biographies, this one written from a more skeptical point of view, underlining occasional scandals within the Papacy and those reactionary positions undertaken by all popes that aroused indignation in the opinion of non-Catholic Europe. Rendina's commentary on Pius IX, as in other cases, is enlivened by quotations from contemporary satirists in verse or prose.

SEE ALSO: Otto von Bismarck; Count Cavour; Giuseppe Garibaldi; Vincenzo Gioberti; Leo XIII; Giuseppe Mazzini; Napoleon I; Napoleon III.

RELATED ARTICLES in *Great Events from History: The Nineteenth Century, 1801-1900:* January 12, 1848-August 28, 1849: Italian Revolution of 1848; December 2, 1852: Louis Napoleon Bonaparte Becomes Emperor of France; December 8, 1854: Pius IX Decrees the Immaculate Conception Dogma; December 8, 1869-October 20, 1870: Vatican I Decrees Papal Infallibility Dogma; 1871-1877: *Kulturkampf* Against the Catholic Church in Germany.

FRANCIS PLACE
English politician

Although Place never held an official position in the British government, he worked effectively for the advancement of organizations and legislation for the betterment of working persons and was an important figure during an era of fundamental political reforms.

BORN: November 3, 1771; London, England
DIED: January 1, 1854; London, England
AREAS OF ACHIEVEMENT: Government and politics, social reform

EARLY LIFE

Francis Place was born in a private debtors' prison near London's Drury Lane Theatre Royal. His father, Simon Place, had in his early years been a baker; at the time of Francis's birth, he was bailiff to the Marshalsea Court and operator of a debtors' lockup house. The elder Place's propensity for gambling lost for him and his family their home and livelihood on at least three occasions. Nevertheless, although he was strict with his four children and often cuffed the boys rather than answer their questions, he saw to their education in the manner of the times.

At four, young Francis was instructed by an old woman in Bell Street. After that, he and his brother attended boys' schools, where they were taught the rudiments of reading, writing, mathematics, and biblical studies. Place attributed his attainment of "right notions" and "power of reasoning" to the efforts of his last headmaster, who encouraged analytical thinking through regular discussion and rewards. Self-confidence, perseverance, industry, and a strong desire for learning were the result. From this time onward, Place read omnivorously, borrowing books and reading at bookstalls until he could afford a library of his own.

At fourteen, Place was apprenticed to a leather-breeches maker; he had chosen to learn a trade rather than read for the law. In the shop he enjoyed a fair amount of liberty, as long as he did his work, and by the age of eighteen he became a journeyman. Like most young men of his age, he ran with a street gang and frequented taverns. At the same time, though he was a conscientious worker and was steadily employed in various shops, he was never able to make a "respectable appearance," a goal dear to his heart.

With little in the way of worldly goods but with high hopes of one day owning his own business, Place married Elizabeth Chadd, the daughter of servants, on March 17, 1791. He was nineteen years of age; she was seventeen. At that time, Place described himself as muscular and short (five feet, six inches), with black curly hair and beard.

The leather-breeches trade was in decline, but by taking assignments from several masters, in two years Place reached what seemed a secure position. It was during this year, 1793, that a strike by the Breeches Makers Benefit Society deprived him of his employment, even though he was not actually involved with the society. For eight months, he and his family nearly starved, but Place learned valuable lessons. He set up a system for making the strikers' money last and helped organize other trades. He also gained an intense appreciation of the plight of those who labored in abject poverty.

In June, 1794, Place joined the London Corresponding Society, a group of artisans and small shopkeepers who were concerned with "the unequal Representation of the People in Parliament." He became a member of the general committee and the executive committee, where he met aware, intelligent men who attended weekly readings and discussions. He also helped write their new constitution. Later that same year, Place was chosen to prepare the successful defense of several members accused of treason, Thomas Hardy, the founder, among them.

The tensions of the war years, resultant government restraints, the suspension of habeas corpus, and the Treasonable Practices Act and Seditious Meetings Act of 1795 caused a decline. Nevertheless, Place and his friend John Ashley worked to keep the group together and financially solvent. When many of their colleagues insisted on holding a public meeting (prohibited by the new law), Ashley and Place withdrew (June, 1797). A year later the whole committee was seized by Middlesex magistrates, and not long after, the organization dissolved. The society had served Place well, and he reciprocated by raising money for the families of the imprisoned.

During these years, Place had been working independently and, despite periods of hardship, refused to go back to journeyman status. Never again would he be dependent upon an employer. On April 8, 1799, he realized his dream. He and Richard Wild, his boarder and colleague, opened a tailor shop at 29 Charing Cross. Frugal habits and hard work earned for them the necessary creditors and customers, and their business flourished. A year and a half later, his scheming partner left Place with his wife and four children virtually penniless. Fortunately for him, his reputation had been made, lenders came to his aid, and he was able to set up a new business, first on Brydges Street, and by spring, at 16 Charing Cross. By 1816, his net profits exceeded three thousand pounds, and in 1817, he was able to turn his business over to his son and engage in public pursuits. By this time, there were ten living children of the fifteen born to him.

LIFE'S WORK

Place had become an elector for Westminster by virtue of his residence at Charing Cross in 1800. By the time of the 1805 and 1807 elections, his business well established, he became interested in the machinations of the election process whereby Whigs and Tories simply divided the two seats. The duke of Northumberland's "beef, beer, and bread" purchase of votes sickened Place, and he worked to elect the Radical candidate, Sir Francis Burdett. The Westminster Committee was successful and became the key political unit in the district, with Place its chief organizer. His library became a meeting place for political discussion, and in time, leading political figures and their representatives gathered there to discuss and learn.

Place met and became friendly with many scholars, among them William Godwin, whose book *An Enquiry Concerning Political Justice, and Its Influence on General Virtue and Happiness* (1793) had provided the impetus for Place's venture into employer status. However, his well-meant attempt to rescue Godwin from financial chaos was foiled by Godwin himself, and Place severed their relationship. His experiences with James Mill, whom he met in 1808, and Jeremy Bentham, whom he met in 1812, were happier. When Place joined them in their studies at Ford Abbey in Devon for several weeks in the summer of 1817, he became a devoted disciple of utilitarianism.

Place later assisted Mill in copying, proofreading, and indexing his *History of British India* (1817). Place also aided Bentham in evaluating his *Rationale of Judicial Evidence* (1827) and in managing his business affairs. Along with other disciples, Place helped write Bentham's later books from his notes. Place believed in Bentham's practical approach to problems and shared his dedication to the principle that social policy should be determined according to "the greatest happiness of the greatest number."

When the Royal Lancastrian Association, a group dedicated to bringing education to the London poor through a system of student monitors, fell on hard times,

Place and Mill both extended aid. Place served on the committee of its successor, the British and Foreign School Society, with the goal of organizing primary and secondary schools throughout London. Though the project failed, it became the prototype for later efforts. Place made a more lasting contribution in helping to found the London Mechanics Institute in 1823. He and Dr. George Birkbeck, who lectured to workingmen, saw to it that there was middle-class participation, that subject matter was mainly technical and scientific, and that orthodox political ideas were followed. As Birkbeck College, the school later became part of the University of London.

Place's interest in Thomas Robert Malthus's *An Essay on the Principle of Population as It Affects the Future Improvement of Society, with Remarks on the Speculations of M. Godwin, M. Condorcet, and Other Writers* (1798) led him to ponder the multiplying population and shrinking resources. Although he could agree with Malthus's theory of population, that people multiply geometrically while food can only expand arithmetically, his own experiences militated against the abstinence and late marriage that Malthus advocated. In 1822, he published his only book, *Illustrations and Proofs of the Principle of Population*. In it, Place argued for conscientious contraception, although he is seldom credited with being the first to do so publicly.

Place's greatest triumph, according to his biographer, Graham Wallas, was his single-handed repeal of the Combination Laws. A law enacted in 1721 regulated the number of journeyman tailors; a second, enacted in 1799, prevented laborers from combining to change hours or wages. Place collected eight volumes of evidence illustrating the injustices suffered by workmen under these laws. Workers could be whipped or jailed for not accepting their masters' terms and even have their wages withheld if they banded together to demand money owed to them.

At the same time, masters were demanding stiffer laws. Place began working to repeal these laws in 1814. Through writing articles and petitions and carefully instructing his protégé, the parliamentarian Joseph Hume, he finally won a parliamentary committee in 1824. Hume chaired the committee, and Place prepared endless instructions. Workers came to his home to give their stories, and he coached them to give their testimony. He set up questions for Hume to ask and rebuttals for objections. He reviewed each day's proceedings and set up outlines and indexes for Hume. He then drew up resolutions that were directly incorporated into the bill. Many setbacks followed, but the law passed both houses of

Parliament in 1824, and a somewhat more restrictive law followed in 1825.

Place's wife, Elizabeth Chadd, died in 1824, and Place married a Mrs. Chatterly in 1830, from whom he was separated in 1851. In 1853, financial problems prompted his move to Brompton Square.

The reform spirit of England coincided with Place's period of peak performance. The July Revolution of 1830 in France, together with the death of King George IV and the accession of William IV, motivated the Radicals to pressure the Whigs for parliamentary reform. People everywhere held meetings in cities, towns, and parishes; artisans and workers met in their associations; farmworkers carried on rick burning. Hard times made the situation tense, and even Place, a normally peaceful reformer, thought that violence might be necessary to bring about change. At the same time, he chaired meetings and helped organize the Parliamentary Candidates' Society and the National Political Union.

After the first bill was rejected by the Lords on October 8, 1831, Place sponsored a peaceful procession, and urged members of Parliament to propose a second bill. Tempers were running high when the Lords refused the second bill and the king refused to create new peers. Lord Grey resigned, and the duke of Wellington set out to form a government of repression. The Birmingham Political Union threatened insurrection and contacted Place and the Parliament. At Place's connivance, it was decided that a run on the banks would thwart the duke. The scheme worked, Grey came back to power, and the third bill passed the Lords on June 4. Place had successfully steered a course between insurrection and stand-pat conservatism. He had advised workers and government leaders. The Reform Bill was only the beginning of the democratization of the English system, but Place was pleased that the people had asserted themselves and yet was satisfied that the bill did not grant the common people full power.

From 1834 to 1836, Place worked for the reorganization of local government through the Poor Law and the Municipal Corporation Act. He was enthusiastic about both and had unrequited hopes of becoming a Poor Law Commissioner. Place waged a campaign against the Newspaper Stamp Tax (enacted in 1819, it stipulated a four-penny duty on all periodicals under six pence) as a "Tax on Knowledge." In 1836, the tax was dropped to a penny; it was not abolished until 1855, the year after his death.

Disappointment with the Reform Bill and hard times led to a new drive for working-class solidarity during the mid-1830's. The Grand National Trades Union grew, and the home secretary, Lord Melbourne, talked of new combination laws. Place worked with laborers to apprise them of their rights and keep them within the law. In 1837, he helped William Lovett organize the Working Men's Association and in 1838 drafted the People's Charter. Chartism failed as a revolutionary movement, but five of its six goals (universal manhood suffrage, an abolition of property qualifications for members of Parliament, salaries for members, equal electoral districts, and a secret ballot) later became part of the English system.

Place's involvement with the Anti-Corn Law League took him to Manchester in November of 1841 in cold and rainy weather. He never recovered from the resulting illness, and in 1844, he suffered a cerebral attack. Unable to read very much but still dedicated to the workers, Place spent his last years organizing clippings and pamphlets related to their history and assembling them into 181 volumes. He died in his sleep at the home of his two unmarried daughters on January 1, 1854.

SIGNIFICANCE

It is difficult to assess the long-term influence of a man such as Francis Place. He has been criticized for lack of creativity, yet the time period in which he lived demanded just such characteristics as he possessed: a keen and receptive mind, analytical abilities, unflagging industry, and dogged persistence. His early experiences provided him with great understanding of and sympathy for workingmen. Though he never held an official position, he worked endlessly in their interest; that he sometimes pursued programs later rejected (for example, the Poor Law) is not surprising.

It is a commentary on both Place's intellect and his character that he made friends and worked with many luminaries of the day and was consulted by men of all classes. Place foresaw the rise of the democratic system and the concomitant decline in both the aristocracy as a class and the House of Lords as an institution. The fact that he worked diligently that workers might be prepared for the change through education and a gradual expansion of rights makes Place a key figure in the glorious history of England's peaceful change.

—*Marjorie Kratz*

FURTHER READING

Cole, G. D. H., and Raymond Postgate. *The Common People, 1746-1946.* London: Methuen, 1963. Indispensable background reading for a broad understanding of the working-class movement and the conditions that fostered it. Place and his activities are well covered.

Johnson, Dorothy Catherine. *Pioneers of Reform: Cobbett, Owen, Place, Shaftsbury, Cobden, Bright.* London: Methuen, 1929. Reprint. New York: B. Franklin, 1968. A brief and closely reasoned account of Place's life and career. Johnson sees her subject as without sympathy or emotion, a practical man of action. She traces the development of his philosophy through his contacts, especially with the utilitarians, and describes his political activities. Good brief rundown.

Miles, Dudley. *Francis Place, 1771-1854: The Life of a Remarkable Radical.* New York: St. Martin's Press, 1988. Comprehensive biography covering the full range of Place's political and social activism.

Place, Francis. *The Autobiography of Francis Place, 1771-1854.* Edited by Mary Thale. Cambridge, England: Cambridge University Press, 1972. Place traces his intellectual and political development together with his early economic fortunes. However, his work with the Combination Laws is mentioned only briefly, and his later political activity, not at all. Letters to friends and relatives are included.

_____. *Illustrations and Proofs of the Principle of Population.* London: Longmans, Green, 1822. Reprint. New York: Augustus M. Kelley, 1967. Well-read and politically and socially aware, Place came to believe that Malthus's ideas of moral restraint for population control were completely impractical. They did not conform to experience or utility and were contrary to human nature. In this book, he reviews Malthus's ideas step by step and comes out unequivocally for early marriage as a prevention for promiscuity, and contraception as a remedy for its consequences.

_____. *London Radicalism, 1830-1843: A Selection from the Papers of Francis Place.* Edited by D. J. Rowe. London: London Record Society, 1970. A unique collection, selected from Place's vast number of papers. Concentrates on the Reform Bill and the major organizations: The National Union of the Working Classes and the National Political Union. Limited coverage is given to the London Working Men's Association. Valuable for providing examples of Place's vast industry as well as of his lesser known ideas and activities.

Wallas, Graham. *The Life of Francis Place, 1771-1854.* New York: Longmans, Green, 1898. 4th ed. London: Allen and Unwin, 1951. The only full-length biography of the subject. Wallas utilized all of Place's papers, except for the many volumes that he collected in his final years. Well written, this work incorporates the then unpublished autobiography, often in Place's own words, and provides a good picture of the subject and his development in the context of the times.

Ward, John Towers. *Chartism.* New York: Harper and Row, 1973. Beginning with a brief chapter, "The Antecedents," Ward traces the reform impulse through the Chartist years. He puts Place in historical context and relates his activities to those of his reformist contemporaries.

SEE ALSO: George IV; Thomas Hardy; Thomas Robert Malthus; James Mill; Duke of Wellington; William IV.

RELATED ARTICLES in *Great Events from History: The Nineteenth Century, 1801-1900:* 1824: British Parliament Repeals the Combination Acts; June 4, 1832: British Parliament Passes the Reform Act of 1832; May 8, 1838-April 10, 1848: Chartist Movement.

KONSTANTIN PETROVICH POBEDONOSTSEV
Russian religious leader

As director general of the Holy Synod and tutor to Czars Alexander III and Nicholas II, Pobedonostsev was a major contributor to the preservation of the autocratic governmental system in Russia against the forces of modernization.

BORN: May 21, 1827; Moscow, Russia
DIED: March 23, 1907; St. Petersburg, Russia
AREA OF ACHIEVEMENT: Government and politics

EARLY LIFE

Konstantin Petrovich Pobedonostsev (pah-bye-dah-NAH-tsef) was one of eleven children. His father was the son of a Russian Orthodox priest and trained for the priesthood but instead became a professor of rhetoric and Russian literature at the University of Moscow. Little is known about Konstantin's mother, except that she was a descendant of an old-service noble family from near Kostroma. Konstantin, educated at home by his father, entered the School of Jurisprudence in St. Petersburg at thirteen; the school prepared him and others from gentry families for service in law courts and the judicial and legal branches of the imperial bureaucracy. Pobedonostsev spoke, read, and wrote in seven foreign languages and read widely throughout his life in the classics and in Russian and Western history and literature. Although he believed that an educated Russia must give special attention to western Europe and its achievements, there remained a basic tension in him throughout his life between a fascination with European ideas and a growing admiration for Russian traditions and institutions.

Upon his graduation in 1846, Pobedonostsev returned to Moscow as a law clerk in the eighth department of the senate. Established by Peter the Great as the highest state institution to supervise all judicial, financial, and administrative affairs, by the nineteenth century the senate had evolved into the supreme court for judicial affairs and appeals against administrative acts of the government. Pobedonostsev's rise in senate employment was rapid and steady. By 1853, he was secretary of the seventh department; in 1857 he became secretary to both the seventh and eighth departments; and by 1863 he was named executive secretary of the eighth department.

Pobedonostsev's education and training in the senate, along with his numerous publications, singled him out as an unusually promising young scholar, teacher (he was appointed lecturer in Russian civil law at the University

of Moscow in 1859), and administrator. As the government of Alexander II struggled with reforms following Russia's defeat in the Crimean War of 1853-1856, Pobedonostsev's work singled him out as one who could make an important contribution. The reforming decade of the 1860's was a turning point in both Pobedonostsev's career and his thinking.

LIFE'S WORK

In 1861, Pobedonostsev was appointed tutor in Russian history and law for the heir to the throne, Nicholas Alexandrovich. Upon the death of Nicholas from tuberculosis in 1865, Pobedonostsev continued as tutor for the new heir, the future Alexander III. This appointment was a key one in Pobedonostsev's life, removing him from the study and classroom and placing him in a position from which he would eventually exercise a profound influence on the course of late nineteenth century Russian history.

From 1866 to 1880, Pobedonostsev's rise through the bureaucracy continued to be steady and rapid. In 1868, he was named a senator, and in 1872 he was appointed a member of the Council of State, the major advisory body to the czar on projected laws and administration of the non-Russian areas of the empire. In April, 1880, he was appointed director general of the Holy Synod. The synod, also established by Peter the Great, replaced the patriarch as head of the Russian Orthodox Church and was one of the most important branches of the central government. As director general, a position he would hold for the next twenty-five years, Pobedonostsev was the czar's representative to this ruling body of the state church. Through this position, Pobedonostsev came to wield considerable influence over such aspects of government policy as education, access to information, social legislation, and civil rights.

The decade of the 1860's, associated with the Great Reforms of Alexander II, was an exhilarating time, but it proved to be the last time the autocratic system attempted to reform itself. Although the reconstruction of society was concerned mainly with the emancipation of the serfs, most state institutions were subjected to intense scrutiny that resulted in various degrees of reorganization. Pobedonostsev's numerous studies advocating reform of the judicial system resulted in his appointment to work on the draft of the judicial reform of 1864.

Although these early years might be termed his "liberal" period, the Polish uprising of 1863 and the resulting revolutionary unrest in Russia's major cities and towns came as a deep shock. Pobedonostsev began to turn against the introduction of new ideas and institutions, arguing instead that what Russia needed was more, not less, government control and supervision. His scholarly interests soon reflected this overall change in his outlook. Whereas up to 1864 his research reflected a certain criticism of some of Russia's central institutions, Pobedonostsev now devoted more time to the study of Russian civil law. His research resulted in the publication of his most important work, the three-volume *Kurs grazhdanskago prava* (1868-1880; course on civil law), which won for him high repute as a legal scholar. At the same time, Pobedonostsev became increasingly vocal in his belief that Russia must rely on its traditional values and institutions and reject the importation of alien ideas.

The rise of the revolutionary movement, culminating in the assassination of Alexander II in 1881, turned many in government and society against his policies of reform. Pobedonostsev was among those who saw liberalism as a fundamental threat to the principle of autocratic government and advised Alexander III that the czar's duty was to protect his people from the projects of constitutional reform associated with the last years of his father's reign. It was Pobedonostsev who drafted the famous manifesto of April 19, 1881, that ended all serious consideration of political reform in Russia for the next generation. From then on, the tall, thin, balding Pobedonostsev, peering out at the world from behind small, wire-rimmed glasses, was associated with the reactionary policies linked to the reign of Alexander III. His appointment as tutor to the future Nicholas II ensured that the autocratic system would not adjust itself to the new social and political movements of the day.

Pobedonostsev's political philosophy was spelled out coherently and succinctly in his most famous book, the collection of essays entitled *Moskovskii sbornik* (1896; *Reflections of a Russian Statesman*, 1898). Like many reactionary philosophers before and after him, Pobedonostsev vilified human nature as evil, worthless, and rebellious. Therefore, he believed that those who advocated reason instead of faith as the proper guide for human actions were fundamentally wrong. The enormous size of Russia, plus its complex national composition and the ignorance and economic backwardness of its peasantry, all pointed to the folly of introducing any concept of responsible government, freedom of the press, secular education, or laissez-faire economics. Instead, Pobe-

donostsev believed, society should be based on those traditional values and institutions that had shaped its character over the centuries. Thus Pobedonostsev, although widely read in European and American social and political literature, opposed any and all arguments for their application in the case of Russia.

There was a basic inconsistency in Pobedonostsev's thinking that can best be seen in his attitude toward Russia's minority peoples and religions. Although he always insisted that human beings were products of a historical tradition, Pobedonostsev refused to concede to Russia's minorities the right to defend their cultural and historical form of life against the encroachments and bureaucratic enactments of the Russian state. In this case, he was more interested in the stability and extension of the autocratic system and argued continuously in support of those Russification policies that so alienated the minorities in the empire.

The revolution of 1905 overthrew autocratic government in Russia and established a constitutional monarchy with civil liberties and an extended franchise for a new legislative assembly. Pobedonostsev played no role in this crisis. The results of the revolution, by introducing institutions and values he had consistently resisted, merely confirmed his pessimism about human nature and the future of Russia. In October, 1905, he retired quietly from his position as director general of the Holy Synod. Although he remained on the Council of State, he no longer played a role in government. His last days, filled with illness, were passed quietly in his residence, working on his ongoing project of translating the Bible into Russian. It was there that he died in 1907. He was buried with little fanfare in the garden of Saint Vladimir's, a finishing school for young women planning to marry priests and work in parish schools.

SIGNIFICANCE

Konstantin Petrovich Pobedonostsev is an excellent example of the conservative bureaucratic statesman associated with the reigns of the last two czars of Russia. Convinced as he was of the evil and weak nature of human beings, Pobedonostsev believed that the only institutions that might save the Russian people were the state, the Orthodox Church, and the family. Of these he believed the state was central. These beliefs were used to justify his support for arbitrary and authoritarian government. Thus, in facing the momentous changes engulfing Western civilization during the late nineteenth century, Pobedonostsev set himself squarely against them all in the name of Russia's traditional values and institutions.

Because Pobedonostsev believed that a people's educational system reflected their society, it is not surprising that he had a deep interest in the educational policies of the empire. He believed that the educational system must remain firmly under the control of the autocratic system and the state church. The system he envisioned had as its first priority the instillation of a firm religious foundation in its students, along with an emphasis on patriotism and love of autocracy. Pobedonostsev bears considerable responsibility for the ruling that kept Russian higher education in shackles until the 1905 revolution restored some semblance of autonomy.

Although he was suspicious of higher education as destabilizing for society, Pobedonostsev emphasized the role of the parish school as best suited to serve the interests of order. During his years as director general of the Holy Synod, he was instrumental in allocating resources to develop the parish school system throughout the country. By 1900, half of all elementary schools were under the control of the synod, while slightly more than a third of all children receiving primary education were enrolled in parish schools, wherein they were taught the proper values of an autocratic society.

As tutor to the last two czars and as director general of the Holy Synod for twenty-five years, Pobedonostsev was in a position to wield considerable influence on late imperial Russia. His opposition to all elements of liberalism and his support for the Russification of the national minorities made him, in the popular eye, the "grey eminence" behind the reign of Alexander III. Thus Pobedonostsev contributed to those policies that eventually caused a revolution that destroyed the entire imperial order.

—Jack M. Lauber

FURTHER READING

Adams, Arthur E. "Pobedonostsev's Religious Politics." *Church History* 22 (1953): 314-326. Pobedonostsev subordinated the Orthodox Church to the state in the name of political stability and state security. His efforts to strengthen and to extend Orthodoxy into the non-Russian provinces and among heretics and dissenters was motivated not by a desire to save souls but by a desire to preserve the Russian Empire.

_____. "Pobedonostsev's Thought Control." *The Russian Review* 11 (1953): 241-246. In his effort to control Russia's thought, Pobedonostsev used his official position in the state and church to persecute those whom he found dangerous to the stability of the system and to promote the careers of those whose views were in harmony with his own.

Basil, John D. "Konstantin Petrovich Pobedonostsev: An Argument for a Russian State Church." *Church History* 64, no. 1 (March, 1995): 44. Analyzes the importance of Pobedonostsev's thought and activities in the changing relationship of the church and state in late imperial Russia.

Byrnes, Robert F. "Dostoevsky and Pobedonostsev." In *Essays in Russian and Soviet History*, edited by John Shelton Curtiss. New York: Columbia University Press, 1962. Explores the close relationship between Pobedonostsev and Fyodor Dostoevski during the decade of the 1870's. While Soviet historians have argued that Dostoevski was influenced greatly by Pobedonostsev, especially in the writing of his later novels, evidence indicates this was not so.

_____. *Pobedonostsev: His Life and Thought.* Bloomington: Indiana University Press, 1968. A standard biography, presenting an account of Pobedonostsev's life along with a discussion and analysis of his major writings and sociopolitical philosophy. Emphasizes his conservatism and his influence both at court and through the Holy Synod to maintain order and stability within the empire.

_____. "Pobedonostsev on the Instruments of Russian Government." In *Continuity and Change in Russian and Soviet Thought*, edited by Ernest J. Simmons. Cambridge, Mass.: Harvard University Press, 1955. Analyzes Pobedonostsev's political philosophy, emphasizing his view that the duty of absolute government was to distinguish between right and wrong, good and evil, and to ensure social stability. The character of the state was formed by its national religious faith and its traditional political and social institutions.

Pobedonostsev, Konstantin P. *Reflections of a Russian Statesman.* Translated by Robert Crozier Long. London: G. Richards, 1898. Reprint. Ann Arbor: University of Michigan Press, 1965. An eloquent and readable plea in support of the values and institutions of traditional Russia. Expounds Pobedonostsev's belief in the evil and perverse nature of the human being and his social philosophy of stability and order through autocratic government and the Orthodox Church.

Polunov, A. Iu. "Konstantin Petrovich Pobedonostsev: Man and Politician." *Russian Studies in History* 39, no. 4 (Spring, 2001): 8. Profile of Pobedonostsev, examining his reputation, career, achievements, views on major issues, and role in imperial Russian politics and government.

Thaden, Edward C. *Conservative Nationalism in Nineteenth Century Russia*. Seattle: University of Washington Press, 1964. Chapter 13, entitled "Bureaucratic Nationalism," discusses Pobedonostsev's thought and contribution to Russification policies toward the national and religious minorities in the empire. In support of these policies, Pobedonostsev was not averse to the use of the power of the state to educate and coerce or to the use of the parish schools to indoctrinate youth in the values of traditional Russia.

SEE ALSO: Alexander II; Grigori Yefimovich Rasputin.

RELATED ARTICLE in *Great Events from History: The Nineteenth Century, 1801-1900:* January 4, 1894: Franco-Russian Alliance.

EDGAR ALLAN POE
American poet and short story writer

In addition to his achievements as one of the towering figures in American literature, Poe was influential in making magazine publishing an important force in the literary world of the nineteenth century.

BORN: January 19, 1809; Boston, Massachusetts
DIED: October 7, 1849; Baltimore, Maryland
AREA OF ACHIEVEMENT: Literature

EARLY LIFE

Edgar Allan Poe was the son of Elizabeth Arnold Poe, a talented actor from an English theatrical family. Because Poe's father, David Poe, Jr., a traveling actor of Irish descent, was neither talented nor responsible, the family suffered financially. After apparently separating from David Poe, Elizabeth died in Richmond, Virginia, in 1811. The young Edgar, though not legally adopted, was taken in by a wealthy Scottish tobacco exporter, John Allan, from whom Poe took his middle name.

For most of his early life, Poe lived in Richmond with the Allans, with the exception of a five-year period between 1815 and 1820 that he spent in England, where he attended Manor House School, near London. Back in America, he attended an academy until 1826, when he entered the University of Virginia. He withdrew less than a year later, however, because of various debts, many of them from gambling; Poe did not have the money to pay, and his foster father refused to help. After quarreling with Allan about these debts, Poe left for Boston in the spring of 1827; shortly thereafter, perhaps because he was short of money, he enrolled in the United States Army under the name "Edgar A. Perry."

In the summer of 1827, Poe's first book, *Tamerlane, and Other Poems*, published under the anonym "A Bostonian," appeared, but it was little noticed by the reading public or by the critics. In January, 1829, he was promoted to the rank of sergeant major and was honorably discharged at his own request three months later. In December, 1829, Poe's second book, *Al Aaraaf, Tamerlane, and Minor Poems*, was published, and it was well received by the critics. Shortly thereafter, Poe entered West Point Military Academy, possibly as a way to get into his foster father's good graces.

After less than a year in school, Poe was discharged from West Point by court-martial for neglecting his military duties. Most biographers agree that Poe deliberately provoked his discharge because he had tired of West Point. Others suggest that he could not stay because John Allan refused to pay Poe's bills any longer, although he would not permit Poe to resign. After West Point, Poe went to New York, where, with the help of some money raised by his West Point friends, he published *Poems by Edgar A. Poe, Second Edition*. After moving to Baltimore, where he lived at the home of his aunt, Mrs. Clemm, Poe entered five short stories in a contest sponsored by the *Philadelphia Saturday Courier*. Although he did not win the prize, the newspaper published all five of his pieces. In June, 1833, he entered another contest sponsored by the *Baltimore Saturday Visiter* and this time won the prize of fifty dollars for his story "Ms. Found in a Bottle." From this point until his death in 1849, Poe was very much involved in the world of American magazine publishing.

LIFE'S WORK

During the next two years, Poe continued writing stories and trying to get them published. Even with the help of a new and influential friend, John Pendleton Kennedy, a lawyer and writer, he was mostly unsuccessful. Poe's financial situation became even more desperate when, in

1834, John Allan died and left Poe out of his will. Kennedy finally persuaded the *Southern Literary Messenger* to publish several of Poe's stories and to offer Poe the job of editor, a position that he kept from 1835 to 1837. During this time, Poe published stories and poems in the *Messenger*, but it was with his extensive publication of criticism that he began to make his mark in American letters.

Although much of Poe's early criticism is routine review work, he began in his reviews to consider the basic nature of poetry and short fiction and to develop theoretical analyses of these two genres, drawing upon the criticism of A. W. Schlegel, in Germany, and Samuel Taylor Coleridge, in England. Poe's most important contribution to criticism is his discussion of the distinctive generic characteristics of short fiction, in a famous review of Nathaniel Hawthorne's *Twice-Told Tales* (1837). Poe makes such a convincing case for the organic unity of short fiction, argues so strongly for its dependence on a unified effect, and so clearly shows how the form is more closely allied to the poem than to the novel that his ideas have influenced literary critics ever since.

In 1836, Poe married his thirteen-year-old cousin, Virginia Clemm, a decision that, because of her age and rela-

Edgar Allan Poe. (Library of Congress)

tionship to Poe, has made him the subject of much adverse criticism and psychological speculation. In 1837, after disagreements with the owner of the *Messenger*, Poe moved to New York to look for editorial work. There he completed the writing of *The Narrative of Arthur Gordon Pym* (1838), his only long fiction, a novella-length metaphysical adventure. Unable to find work in New York, Poe moved to Philadelphia and published his first important short story, a Platonic romance titled "Ligeia." In 1839, he joined the editorial staff of *Burton's Gentlemen's Magazine*, where he published two of his greatest stories, "The Fall of the House of Usher" and "William Wilson."

In 1840, Poe left *Burton's* and tried, unsuccessfully, to establish his own literary magazine. He did, however, publish a collection of his stories, *Tales of the Grotesque and Arabesque* (1840), as well as become an editor of *Graham's Magazine*, where he published his first tale of ratiocination, "The Murders in the Rue Morgue." In this landmark story, he created the famous detective Auguste Dupin, the forerunner of Sherlock Holmes and thus of countless other private detectives in literature and film. A biographical sketch published at that time described Poe as short, slender, and well-proportioned, with a fair complexion, gray eyes, black hair, and an extremely broad forehead.

In 1842, Poe left *Graham's* to try once again to establish his own literary magazine, but not before publishing two important pieces of criticism: a long review of the poet Henry Wadsworth Longfellow, in which he established his definition of poetry as being the "Rhythmical Creation of Beauty," and his review of Hawthorne, in which he defined the short tale as the creation of a unified effect. Between 1842 and 1844, after Poe moved to New York to join the editorial staff of the *New York Mirror*, he published many of his most important stories, including "The Masque of the Red Death," "The Pit and the Pendulum," "The Black Cat," and two more ratiocinative stories, "The Mystery of Marie Roget" and "The Gold Bug." It was with the publication of his most famous poem, "The Raven," in 1845, however, that he finally achieved popular success.

Poe left the *New York Mirror* to join a new weekly periodical, the *Broadway Journal*, in February of 1845, where he continued the literary war against Longfellow begun in a review written for the *Mirror*. The series of accusations, attacks, and counterattacks that ensued damaged Poe's reputation as a critic at the very point in his career when he had established his critical genius. Poe's collection of stories, *Tales*, was published in July, 1845, to good reviews. Soon after, Poe became the sole editor and

POE'S MAJOR WORKS

SHORT FICTION
1840   *Tales of the Grotesque and Arabesque*
1843   *The Prose Romances of Edgar Allan Poe*
1845   *Tales*

LONG FICTION
1838   *The Narrative of Arthur Gordon Pym*

DRAMA
1868   *Politian*

POETRY
1827   *Tamerlane, and Other Poems*
1829   *Al Aaraaf, Tamerlane, and Minor Poems*
1831   *Poems*
1845   *The Raven, and Other Poems*
1848   *Eureka: A Prose Poem*

then proprietor of the *Broadway Journal*. In November, he published his collection *The Raven, and Other Poems*.

The year 1846 marked the beginning of Poe's decline. In January, the *Broadway Journal* ceased publication, and soon after, Poe was involved in both a personal scandal with two female literary admirers and a bitter battle with the literary establishment. Moreover, Poe's wife was quite ill, a fact that necessitated Poe's moving his family some thirteen miles outside the city to a rural cottage at Fordham. When Virginia died on January 30, 1847, Poe collapsed. Although he never fully recovered from this series of assaults on his already nervous condition, in the following year he published what he considered to be the capstone of his career, *Eureka: A Prose Poem*, which he presented as an examination of the origin of all things.

In the summer of 1849, Poe left for Richmond, Virginia, in the hope, once more, of starting a literary magazine. On September 24, he delivered a lecture, "The Poetic Principle," at Richmond, in what was to be his last public appearance. From that time until he was found semiconscious on the streets of Baltimore, Maryland, little is known of his activities. He never recovered, and he died on Sunday morning, October 7, in Washington College Hospital.

SIGNIFICANCE

Edgar Allan Poe is important in the history of American literature and American culture in two significant ways. First, he developed short fiction as a genre that was to

have a major impact on American literature and publishing throughout the nineteenth century. His stories and criticism have been models and guides for writers in this characteristically American genre up to the present time. No one interested in the short-story form can afford to ignore his ideas or his fiction. Poe was influential in making American literature more philosophical and metaphysical than it had been before.

Second, and perhaps most important, Poe helped to make periodical publishing more important in American literary culture. American writers during the mid-nineteenth century were often discouraged by the easy accessibility of British novels. Lack of copyright laws made the works of the great English writers readily available at low cost. Thus, American writers could not compete in this genre. Periodical publishing, and the short story as the favored genre of this medium, was the American way of fighting back. Poe was an important figure in this battle to make the United States a literary force in world culture.

The problem with Poe, however, is that he is too often thought of as the author of some vivid yet insignificant horror stories. Moreover, Poe's personality is often erroneously maligned: He has been called a drunk, a drug addict, a hack, a sex pervert, and an exploiter. As a result of these errors, myths, and oversimplifications, it is often difficult for readers to take his works seriously. The truth is, however, that Edgar Allan Poe, both in his criticism and in his dark, metaphysically mysterious stories, helped create a literature that made America a cultural force not to be ignored.

—*Charles E. May*

FURTHER READING

Allen, Hervey. *Israfel: The Life and Times of Edgar Allan Poe.* 2 vols. New York: George H. Doran, 1926. Reprint. New York: Farrar and Rinehart, 1956. A romantic narrative of Poe's life, valuable for the information drawn from letters between Poe and John Allan.

Buranelli, Vincent. *Edgar Allan Poe.* 2d ed. Boston: Twayne, 1977. A somewhat sketchy study of Poe's fiction, poetry, and criticism, but still a good introduction to his work.

Carlson, Eric W., ed. *A Companion to Poe Studies.* Westport, Conn.: Greenwood Press, 1996. Collection of essays examining various aspects of Poe's life and literature.

_____. *The Recognition of Edgar Allan Poe: Selected Criticism Since 1829.* Ann Arbor: University of Michigan Press, 1966. A valuable collection of some of the most influential critical remarks about Poe by artists, writers, and critics.

Hayes, Kevin J., ed. *The Cambridge Companion to Edgar Allan Poe*. New York: Cambridge University Press, 2002. Compilation of essays examining Poe's life, work, and influence, including discussions of his aesthetic theory, humor, science fiction, and place within American popular culture.

Hoffman, Daniel. *PoePoePoePoePoePoePoe*. Garden City, N.Y.: Doubleday, 1972. An idiosyncratic and highly personal account of one critic's fascination with Poe that echoes the fascination of countless readers. Often Freudian and sometimes far-fetched, the book provides stimulating reading and suggestive criticism.

Hutchisson, James M. *Poe*. Jackson: University Press of Mississippi, 2005. Biography focusing on Poe's southern identity and literary influence. Recounts the events of Poe's life and career and provides a critical overview of his major works.

Jacobs, Robert D. *Poe: Journalist and Critic*. Baton Rouge: Louisiana State University Press, 1969. An extensive study of Poe's career as editor, reviewer, and critic. Shows how Poe's critical ideas derived from and influenced periodical publishing during the mid-nineteenth century.

Moss, Sidney P. *Poe's Literary Battles: The Critic in the Context of His Literary Milieu*. Durham, N.C.: Duke University Press, 1963. A well-researched study of Poe's controversial battles with Longfellow and the many literary cliques of nineteenth century American publishing.

Quinn, Arthur Hobson. *Edgar Allan Poe: A Critical Biography*. New York: D. Appleton-Century, 1941. Reprint. Baltimore: Johns Hopkins University Press, 1998. Although this book is somewhat outdated in its critical analysis of Poe's works, it is the best and most complete biography, informed by Quinn's knowledge of Poe's literary milieu and his extensive research into Poe's correspondence.

Quinn, Patrick F. *The French Face of Edgar Poe*. Carbondale: Southern Illinois University Press, 1957. Ironically, Poe's fiction, poetry, and criticism had more influence on French literature in the nineteenth century than on American literature. Quinn's book explains why.

SEE ALSO: Charles Baudelaire; Samuel Taylor Coleridge; Nathaniel Hawthorne; Washington Irving; Henry Wadsworth Longfellow; Guy de Maupassant; Odilon Redon; Jules Verne.

RELATED ARTICLES in *Great Events from History: The Nineteenth Century, 1801-1900:* c. 1884-1924: Decadent Movement Flourishes; December, 1887: Conan Doyle Introduces Sherlock Holmes.

HENRI POINCARÉ
French mathematician

One of the most important mathematicians of the late nineteenth century, Poincaré developed the theory of automorphic functions, did extensive work in celestial mechanics and mathematical physics, and was a codiscoverer of the special theory of relativity. His writing style was so clear that his books about the philosophy of science were read widely by the general public and translated into many languages.

BORN: April 29, 1854; Nancy, France
DIED: July 17, 1912; Paris, France
ALSO KNOWN AS: Jules Henri Poincaré (full name)
AREAS OF ACHIEVEMENT: Mathematics, physics

EARLY LIFE

Henri Poincaré (pwahn-kah-ray) was born into one of the most distinguished families of France's Lorraine region.

His father, Leon, was a physician, and one of his cousins, Raymond, became president of the French Republic during World War I. Henri and his sister were adored by their mother, and she devoted herself to their education and rearing. When he was five, Henri contracted diphtheria, and the resulting weakness may have influenced his entire life. Because he was unable to join the other boys in their rough play, Henri was forced to entertain himself with intellectual pursuits. He developed a remarkable memory so that he could even cite page numbers for information in books that he had read many years earlier. In addition, because his eyesight was poor, he learned most of his classwork by listening, because he could not see the blackboard. Thus, he was forced to develop the ability to see spatial relationships in his mind at an early age.

Although he was a good student in his early years, there was no indication of his impending greatness until he was a teenager. He won first prize in a French national competition and in 1873 entered the École Polytechnique, where he exhibited his brilliance in mathematics. Upon his graduation, Poincaré entered the École des Mines in 1875 to study engineering. Although he was a careful student who did his work adequately, Poincaré spent much of his time pursuing mathematics as a recreation. He continued his practice of mathematics during his apprenticeship as a mining engineer.

Poincaré was not an extremely attractive man; he had thinning blond hair, wore glasses, and was short in stature; he was known for being absentminded and clumsy. Nevertheless, he maintained a happy personal life. He married at the age of twenty-seven, fathered four children, whom he adored, and never wanted for friends, because he was by nature humble and interested in other people.

LIFE'S WORK

In 1879, Poincaré submitted the doctoral thesis in mathematics that he had written during his work as an engineer, and he received his degree that same year. The subject was the first of his great achievements: the theory of differential equations. His first appointment was as a lecturer of mathematical analysis at the University of Caen in 1879, and in 1881 he was invited to join the faculty at the University of Paris. He continued this appointment until his death in 1912, although by then his responsibilities had expanded to include mechanics and physics.

During his tenure, he was elected to the Académie des Sciences in 1887 and the Académie Française in 1908. this second appointment is most unusual for a mathematician, for it is given to honor literary achievements and is thus a sure indication of his lucid writing style. He was named president of the Académie des Sciences in 1906. Other awards included a Fellowship in the Royal Society in 1894, the Prix Poncelet, Prix Reynaud, and Prix Bolyai, and gold medals from the Lobachevsky Fund.

Much of Poincaré's early work was in differential equations, a branch of calculus that is linked directly to the physical world. It was natural, then, for him to turn his attention from pure mathematics to physics and celestial mechanics. However, in his pursuit of solutions of physical and mechanical problems, he often created new tools of pure mathematics.

Poincaré was first drawn to celestial mechanics and astronomical physics by the classical three-body problem, which concerns the gravitational influence and distortions that three independent bodies in space would ex-

Henri Poincaré. (Library of Congress)

ert on one another; it held his interest throughout his life. Poincaré published partial results in his early years at the Sorbonne and later published work broadening the number of objects from three to any number. His results won for him a prize that had been offered by King Oscar II of Sweden.

In celestial mechanics, Poincaré was the first person to demand rigor in computations: He found the approximations used commonly at the time to be unacceptable, because they introduced obvious errors into the work. Consequently, more powerful mathematics had to be developed. This work was not centered on any one branch of mathematics but instead included calculus, algebra, number theory, non-Euclidean geometry, and topology. In fact, the field of topology was begun in large part with Poincaré's study of orbits. He published much of this work in *Les Méthodes nouvelles de la mécanique céleste* (new methods in celestial mechanics), in three volumes between 1892 and 1899.

Poincaré's other early achievement was in the theory of automorphic functions—a method for expressing functions in terms of parameters in mathematical analysis. These are functions that remain relatively unchanged though they are acted on by a series of transformations. He found that one class of these, which he called Fuchsian (for German mathematician Immanuel Fuchs), was related to non-Euclidean geometry, and this became an important insight. Indeed, there was some argument over priority in this development between Poincaré and German mathematician Christian Felix Klein; however, scientific historians agree that Poincaré was the developer of these theories.

It seems that all branches of mathematics held Poincaré's interest. Poincaré was essential to the development of algebraic geometry. Of particular importance is his development of a parametric representation of functions. For example, the general equation of a circle $x^2 + y^2 = r^2$ can be rewritten as two equations that describe the variables x and y in terms of some angle A. The equations $x = r$ sine A and $y = r$ cosine A are the equivalent of the original equation since $x^2 + y^2 = r^2$ sine$^2 A + r^2$ cosine$^2 A = r^2$ (sine$^2 A$ + cosine$^2 A$), which in turn equals r^2 since sine^2 + cosine$^2 = 1$. Many problems can be solved using parameters that do not yield to any other methods.

Poincaré is equally important in physics. Although Albert Einstein is generally known for his theory of relativity, the special theory of relativity was discovered independently by Poincaré. He and Einstein arrived at the theory from completely different viewpoints, Einstein from light and Poincaré from electromagnetism, at about the same time (Einstein's first work was published in 1905, and Poincaré's was published in 1906). There can be no doubt that both men deserve a share of the credit. When Poincaré became aware of Einstein's work, he was quite enthusiastic and supportive of the Swiss physicist even though most scientists were skeptical. Max Planck, who developed quantum theory, was another physicist who was recognized by Poincaré while he was being scorned by others. In addition, Poincaré developed the mathematics required for countless physical discoveries during the early twentieth century. An example is the wireless telegraph. He also developed the theory of the equilibrium of fluid bodies rotating in space.

Poincaré had a rare gift for a mathematician: He was able to write clearly and to make mathematics and science exciting to people whose educations were directed toward other fields. One of his most widely known works in the philosophy of science, *Science et méthode* (1908; *Science and Method*, 1914), is devoted to a study of how scientists and mathematicians create. Poincaré believed that some things in mathematics are known intuitively rather than from observation or from classic logic. His articles and books in the philosophy of science were av-

idly read and translated into most of the European languages and even into Japanese.

Poincaré continued in relatively good health until 1908, and in 1912 he died of an embolism following minor surgery. The church Saint-Jacques-de-Haut-Pas, the site of his funeral several days later, was filled with eminent persons from all fields who had come to pay a last tribute to his greatness.

SIGNIFICANCE

Henri Poincaré was clearly one of the great mathematicians of his time. In fact, some believe that he had no peer. He won virtually every mathematical prize available, and he also won several scientific awards. His work entered every field of mathematics at the time, and he created at least one new branch called algebraic topology. His discoveries inspired other mathematicians for years after his death. In addition, Poincaré did first-rate work in celestial mechanics and was a codiscoverer of the theory of relativity.

The more than thirty books and five hundred papers that Poincaré published are a testament to his prolific career, especially since he died during his productive years. In addition, his writings on the philosophy of science sparked public interest in mathematics and the physical sciences and foreshadowed the intuitionist school of philosophy. These works have helped define the way human beings think about mathematical and scientific creation and will continue to do so for years to come. The practical applications of Poincaré's work are numerous. Differential functions are the primary mathematics used in engineering and some of the physical sciences; his work in celestial mechanics was completely different from past works and altered the field's course. In addition, he offered many new ideas in pure mathematics.

Perhaps the most articulate tribute to Poincaré was given in the official report of the 1905 Bolyai Prize written by Gustave Rados: "Henri Poincaré is incontestably the first and most powerful investigator of the present time in the domain of mathematics and mathematical physics."

—*Celeste Williams Brockington*

FURTHER READING

Barrow-Greene, June. *Poincaré and the Three-Body Problem.* Providence, R.I.: American Mathematics Society, 1996. Describes how Poincaré accidentally discovered chaos theory. Aimed at readers with an advanced level of mathematical knowledge.

Bell, E. T. "The Last Universalist." In *Men of Mathematics.* New York: Simon & Schuster, 1937. This book is a series of twenty-nine chapters, each introducing a different mathematician from the early Greeks to the early twentieth century. Its account of Poincaré focuses on three areas: the theory of automorphic functions, celestial mechanics and mathematical physics, and the philosophy of science. Biographical information is also included.

Galison, Peter. *Einstein's Clocks, Poincaré's Maps: Empires of Time*. New York: W. W. Norton, 2003. Examines how Poincaré and Einstein created the modern conception of time through their ideas about relativity.

Nordmann, Charles. "Henri Poincaré: His Scientific Work, His Philosophy." In *Annual Report of the Board of Regents of the Smithsonian Institution*. Washington, D.C.: Government Printing Office, 1913. Nordmann includes not only a summary of Poincaré's work and philosophy as the title indicates but also a considerable amount of biographical information.

Poincaré, Henri. *The Foundations of Science*. Translated by George Bruce Halsted. New York: Science Press, 1913. Contains a preface by Poincaré and an introduction by Josiah Royce. Argues Poincaré's philosophy of science.

_____. "The Future of Mathematics." In *Annual Report of the Board of Regents of the Smithsonian Institution*. Washington, D.C.: Government Printing Office, 1910. This article represents Poincaré at his best. After a brief introduction, he guides the reader through most of the prominent fields of mathematics and predicts what he believed was to come. His explanations are excellent.

_____. *Mathematics and Science: Last Essays*. Translated by John W. Balduc. Reprint. Mineola, N.Y.: Dover, 1963. Another work in the philosophy of science.

Slosson, Edwin E. "Henri Poincaré." In *Major Prophets of Today*. Freeport, N.Y.: Books for Libraries Press, 1968. Slosson chose several representatives from the modern era whom he viewed as having lasting prominence. His article on Poincaré includes biographical information as well as a discussion of Poincaré's work in mathematics and philosophy.

Zahar, Eli. *Poincaré's Philosophy: From Conventionalism to Phenomenology*. Chicago: Open Court, 2001. Traces the development of Poincaré's philosophy, discussing his thoughts about general science, geometry, mathematics, relativity, and other subjects.

SEE ALSO: Niels Henrik Abel; Joseph Fourier.

RELATED ARTICLES in *Great Events from History: The Nineteenth Century, 1801-1900:* 1899: Hilbert Publishes *The Foundations of Geometry*; 1900: Lebesgue Develops New Integration Theory.

JAMES K. POLK
President of the United States (1845-1849)

Polk served only one term as president of the United States but used his authority to expand the nation nearly to its continental limits, while adding power and prestige to the presidency.

BORN: November 2, 1795; Mecklenburg County, North Carolina
DIED: June 15, 1849; Nashville, Tennessee
ALSO KNOWN AS: James Knox Polk (full name)
AREA OF ACHIEVEMENT: Government and politics

EARLY LIFE

James Knox Polk was the son of Samuel and Jane Knox Polk, members of large Scotch-Irish families whose forebears had begun migrating to North America late in the previous century. When James was eleven, Samuel moved the family westward to the Duck River Valley in middle Tennessee, where he became both a prosperous farmer and a prominent resident. The family was staunchly Jeffersonian in its politics, while Jane Polk was a rigid Presbyterian.

Young James was small in stature—of average height or less according to various accounts—and was never robust. At seventeen, he had a gallstone removed (without anesthesia), and thereafter his health improved somewhat. It became obvious early, however, that he would never be strong enough to farm, and contrary to his father's wish that he become a merchant, Polk decided on a law career with politics as his goal. For this goal, some education was necessary. He had been a studious youth but until the age of eighteen had had little formal schooling. Thereafter, he applied himself totally and entered the sophomore class at the University of North Carolina at the age of twenty. Two and a half years later, he was graduated with honors. Characteristically, he had worked diligently, but the drain on his physical reserves was so great that he was too ill to travel home for several months.

Upon his return to Columbia, Tennessee, Polk read law in the offices of one of the state's most prominent public figures, Felix Grundy. Through Grundy's sponsorship, Polk began his political career as clerk of the state senate in 1819 and was admitted to the bar the following year. Prospering as a lawyer, he was elected to the Tennessee legislature in 1823 and aligned himself with the supporters of the state's most famous citizen, Andrew Jackson. Soon he became friendly with Jackson, a presidential candidate in 1824, aided Old Hickory's election to the U.S. Senate, and thereafter was always associated with his fellow Tennessean.

On New Year's Day, 1824, Polk married Sarah Childress, a member of a prominent middle Tennessee family. Described as not particularly pretty, she was vivacious, friendly, and devoted, and the marriage, although childless, was apparently happy. By this time Polk's health had improved, but he remained slender, with an upright posture and a grim face below a broad forehead. According to contemporaries, he was always impeccably dressed, as befitted a promising young lawyer and sometime militia colonel on the governor's staff. Now nearly thirty, he was considered one of the state's rising Jacksonians.

LIFE'S WORK

Impressed with his legislative record and legal as well as martial success, in 1825 the Jackson faction supported Polk's bid for a seat in the House of Representatives against four opponents. His victory by a decisive plurality after a spirited campaign solidified his position among the followers of General Jackson. For the next four years, during the administration of President John Quincy Adams, Polk was in the forefront of the Jacksonians, who were determined to overturn the alleged "corrupt bargain" that had denied Jackson the presidency in 1824 and elect their man in 1828.

During the debates on the Adams program, considered too nationalistic by most congressmen, Polk seized numerous opportunities to express his opposition and to stand with the embryonic Democratic Party. He aided in reviving the "corrupt bargain" charge and spoke for economy, majority rule, and limited government. He embraced the party position against the protective tariff, internal improvements, and banks. Only on the question of slavery did he equivocate, as he would always do. Slavery was an evil, he believed, yet doing away with it

was fraught with peril. It was best that all concerned recognize its existence and live with it as peacefully as possible.

The issues before Congress during the Adams term commanded less attention than the Jacksonians' primary goal—the election of Jackson. In this effort, Polk played an increasingly important part as his abilities and devotion to the cause became more evident. In the bitter campaign of 1828, he constantly defended Jackson and carried on an extensive correspondence with him at his home in the Hermitage. Victory for Jackson followed and, despite interparty infighting for the position of successor to the new president, the future of the Jacksonian party looked promising.

In the next decade, Polk's rise in the party hierarchy was steady. He served as chairman of the House Ways and Means Committee in Jackson's first term and played a leading role in the president's victory in the Bank War. He enjoyed a growing reputation for speeches and reports showing much preparation, logic, and clarity. In 1835, he was elected Speaker of the House, and was reelected two years later. His four years in the chair, where he was the first to function as a party leader and to attempt

James K. Polk. (Library of Congress)

to guide through a program, proved to be trying. The Whig Party was gaining strength while the slavery issue was intruding in the House, resulting in the passage of the infamous "gag rule." In the middle of his second term as Speaker, Polk decided to become a candidate for governor of Tennessee rather than risk probable defeat for reelection. By now the recognized leader of the party forces in his home state, he won by a narrow margin in 1839.

Once again, Polk was the first incumbent to use an office for political purposes as a party leader. However, since the governor had little real power and Whig opposition continued strong, Governor Polk was able to accomplish little in his single two-year term. When the victorious Whig presidential candidate, William Henry Harrison, easily carried Tennessee in 1840, Polk's chances for another gubernatorial term appeared to be slim. He was defeated for reelection in 1841 and failed again two years later. For the only time in his career, he was out of office.

On the national level, Polk's position in the party remained secure. In 1840, he was a leading candidate for the vice presidential nomination on the ticket with President Martin Van Buren but withdrew when the convention decided against making a nomination. Polk then began to work toward the nomination four years later, when it was expected that the former president would again contend for the top place. In the meantime, he repaired political fences and kept in touch with Van Buren and other party leaders.

Polk's comeback, which led to his nomination as the Democratic standard-bearer in 1844, is one of the best-known episodes in American political history. Expansionism, justified as "Manifest Destiny," was in the air as Texas clamored for admission to the Union while American eyes were on California and Oregon. It was expected that the presidential race would be between former presi-

---

WAR WITH MEXICO

In his second state of the union address, delivered in December, 1845, President James K. Polk spoke at length on the rupture of diplomatic relations with Mexico that was to lead to the Mexican War the following year.

I regret to inform you that our relations with Mexico since your last session have not been of the amicable character which it is our desire to cultivate with all foreign nations. On the 6th day of March last the Mexican envoy extraordinary and minister plenipotentiary to the United States made a formal protest in the name of his Government against the joint resolution passed by Congress "for the annexation of Texas to the United States," which he chose to regard as a violation of the rights of Mexico, and in consequence of it he demanded his passports. He was informed that the Government of the United States did not consider this joint resolution as a violation of any of the rights of Mexico, or that it afforded any just cause of offense to his Government; that the Republic of Texas was an independent power, owing no allegiance to Mexico and constituting no part of her territory or rightful sovereignty and jurisdiction. He was also assured that it was the sincere desire of this Government to maintain with that of Mexico relations of peace and good understanding. That functionary, however, notwithstanding these representations and assurances, abruptly terminated his mission and shortly afterwards left the country. Our envoy extraordinary and minister plenipotentiary to Mexico was refused all official intercourse with that Government, and, after remaining several months, by the permission of his own Government he returned to the United States. Thus, by the acts of Mexico, all diplomatic intercourse between the two countries was suspended.

Since that time Mexico has until recently occupied an attitude of hostility toward the United States—has been marshaling and organizing armies, issuing proclamations, and avowing the intention to make war on the United States, either by an open declaration or by invading Texas. Both the Congress and convention of the people of Texas invited this Government to send an army into that territory to protect and defend them against the menaced attack. The moment the terms of annexation offered by the United States were accepted by Texas the latter became so far a part of our own country as to make it our duty to afford such protection and defense. I therefore deemed it proper, as a precautionary measure, to order a strong squadron to the coasts of Mexico and to concentrate an efficient military force on the western frontier of Texas. . . .

Source: James K. Polk, "State of the Union Address," December 2, 1845.

---

dent Van Buren and Whig Henry Clay. When both announced their opposition to the annexation of Texas, however, Van Buren's chances for the nomination faded. In the party convention in May, he withdrew when his cause looked hopeless, and on the ninth ballot delegates turned to Polk, who had declared for annexation weeks earlier. Although his nomination, recalled as the first "dark horse" selection, was a surprise to most voters, it was the result of much hard work and a correct recognition of the mood of the electorate.

In the ensuing campaign, Whig candidate Clay and his supporters obscured the issues by asking, "Who is James K. Polk?" Democrats responded by linking "Young Hickory" to the aged former president, vacillating on controversial matters such as the tariff and stressing annexation as a national, not sectional, question. After an exciting campaign, Polk won a narrow victory brought about in part because a number of potential Clay voters cast ballots for an antislavery candidate. In his inaugural address, President Polk announced a brief but positive program. He called for settling the Oregon question (Congress had voted to annex Texas by joint resolution a few days earlier) by its "reoccupation" and for the acquisition of California. The tariff was to be reduced to a revenue level, and the Independent Treasury, killed by the Whigs, would be reestablished. Unique among American chief executives, Polk carried out his entire program.

The new president assumed his duties, determined to be in control. He appointed able cabinet members, many of whom were friends, and he consulted them and Congress frequently, although he made his own decisions. Seldom away from his desk, he was constantly besieged by office seekers who placed an added drain on his limited strength and energy. Not surprisingly, his appointments were largely "deserving" Democrats.

Foreign affairs immediately commanded Polk's attention. Oregon, occupied jointly with England since 1818, was rapidly filling up with Americans who anticipated eventual absorption by the United States. It was "clear and unquestionable," the president declared in his inaugural, that Oregon belonged to the United States. However, he revealed to the British minister his willingness to compromise at the forty-ninth parallel. A negative response evoked from Polk a hint of war and a request in his first annual message for congressional sanction for termination of joint occupation. For the first time, there was a presidential reference to the Monroe Doctrine as justification for action, and war talk, including demands for "Fifty-four Forty or Fight," was heard. Neither nation wanted war, so the British countered with Polk's original suggestion, it was accepted, and a treaty was completed, setting the boundary at the forty-ninth parallel, where it has remained.

In the meantime, the Mexicans had not accepted the loss of Texas, and they now maintained that the southern boundary was the Nueces River, not the Rio Grande, as the Texans claimed. Polk agreed with the Texans and also feared that the British might interfere there, as well as in California and New Mexico. As tensions increased, he sent to Mexico City an offer of some thirty million dollars for the entire area. When the offer was refused, he ordered General Zachary Taylor to move his troops into the disputed section. A predictable clash took place, but before word reached Washington, Polk had decided to ask for war. Congress responded with a declaration on May 13, 1846. Although American forces were victorious from the beginning, the Mexican War, called "Mr. Polk's War," was among the most unpopular in the nation's history. Opposition to it was voiced in Congress, in the press, and among the people. Even though the two leading generals professed to be members of the party, Whigs led the protests, which tended to increase Polk's strongly partisan attitudes.

To a greater extent than any previous chief executive, Polk took his role as commander in chief seriously. His military experience was meager, yet he planned grand strategy, was personally involved in military appointments and promotions, and took the lead in peacemaking. His emissary (although technically recalled) completed with a defeated Mexico a satisfactory treaty that ceded California and New Mexico to the United States and recognized the annexation of Texas in return for some fifteen million dollars. Polk decided to accept the offer. The Senate narrowly approved the treaty on February 2, 1848, and the continental limits of the nation had almost been reached. Near the end of his term, Polk looked longingly at other areas, such as Cuba, but nothing further was done.

In Congress, the remainder of Polk's limited program was approved. The Independent Treasury was reestablished and remained in existence into the next century. In addition, the tariff was reduced considerably. Although these successes seemed to indicate party harmony, the Democrats actually were engaged in much interparty wrangling, adding to the president's many problems.

Of more lasting effect was the revival of antislavery agitation as a result of the possible addition of territory. In the midst of the war, as an appropriations measure was debated in Congress, Representative David Wilmot of Pennsylvania proposed an amendment banning slavery in any territory acquired from Mexico. This so-called Wilmot Proviso was never approved, yet it rekindled sectional animosities that finally led to secession some fifteen years later. Polk, a slaveholder who seldom thought of slavery in moral terms—he believed that the solution was the extension of the Missouri Compromise Line to the Pacific—was not directly involved in the ensuing agitation during the remainder of his term, yet the legacy of sectional bitterness continued to be linked to his administration.

In his acceptance letter in 1844, Polk declared that he would not be a candidate for a second time, the first nominee ever to do so. As his term drew to a close, he refused to reconsider. His health remained poor, and the split within his party was unsettling. His outlook did not improve with the election of one of the Mexican War generals, Zachary Taylor, as his successor.

Following Taylor's inauguration, the Polks slowly made their way home, often delayed by the poor health of the former president and well-meaning attempts by supporters to entertain them. Polk never fully recovered (his main complaint was chronic diarrhea) and he died June 15, 1849, slightly more than fourteen weeks after leaving office. His considerable estate, including a Mississippi plantation, was left to his widow, who lived until 1891, witnessing the tragic sectional split and devastating war brought about in part by the events associated with her husband's presidency.

SIGNIFICANCE

The youngest presidential candidate elected up to that time and often called the strongest chief executive between Andrew Jackson and Abraham Lincoln, James K. Polk raised the presidency in public esteem. Although humorless, partisan, and totally without charisma, he was devoted to the office and impressed all those around him with his dedication and diligence. Nothing was allowed to interfere with the carrying out of his duties—except that no business was conducted on Sundays unless in an emergency. Unlike most occupants of the office—into the twenty-first century—he seldom was away from the capital and was absent a total of only six weeks in four years.

Under his leadership, a relatively brief, successful war was fought with Mexico, the annexation of Texas was completed, the most troublesome dispute with England was resolved, and the nation expanded almost to its continental limits. These accomplishments came about despite Polk's frail constitution and sharp political differences with the Whig Party and among his fellow Democrats. However, his successes only added to the increasing sectional tensions that would soon tear the nation apart and cause a long, costly conflict.

—C. L. Grant

FURTHER READING

Bergeron, Paul H. *The Presidency of James K. Polk.* Lawrence: University Press of Kansas, 1987. Bergeron rates Polk as one of the strongest and most active presidents.

Cutler, Wayne, et al., eds. *Correspondence of James K. Polk.* 10 vols. Nashville, Tenn.: Vanderbilt University Press, 1969-2004. A well-edited, complete publication of all extant Polk papers. An indispensable source for the history of the period.

Dusinberre, William. *Slavemaster President: The Double Career of James Polk.* New York: Oxford University Press, 2003. Re-creates life at Polk's cotton plantation, describing the brutal and often short life of its slaves. Dusinberre speculates that Polk's support for slavery may have precipitated the Civil War.

Haynes, Sam W. *James K. Polk and the Expansionist Impulse.* Edited by Oscar Handlin. 2d ed. New York: Longman, 2002. Biography of Polk focusing on his support for expanding American territory. Haynes places Polk's expansionism in political and social context.

McCormac, Eugene Irving. *James K. Polk: A Political Biography.* Berkeley: University of California Press, 1922. Reprint. New York: Russell and Russell, 1965. First published in 1922 and somewhat dated, it was for many years the standard political biography of Polk. Still useful for an account of the political maneuvering in the Jackson years.

Mahin, Dean B. *Olive Branch and Sword: The United States and Mexico, 1845-1848.* Jefferson, N.C.: McFarland, 1997. A diplomatic history of the Mexican War, focusing on the policies of the Polk administration and the negotiations of American diplomat Nicholas Trist.

Quaife, Milo Milton, ed. *The Diary of James K. Polk.* 4 vols. Chicago: A. C. McClurg, 1910. Reprint. *Polk: The Diary of a President, 1845-1849.* Edited by Allan Nevins. New York: Longmans, Green, 1929. Only five hundred copies of the original diary were printed. Written between August 26, 1845, and June 2, 1849, it is highly personal and apparently was not written with an eye on future historians. As a result of the 1929 publication, in which selections of the earlier publication appeared, Polk's presidency was reassessed and his reputation considerably enhanced.

Schroeder, John H. *Mr. Polk's War: American Opposition and Dissent, 1846-1848.* Madison: University of Wisconsin Press, 1973. A provocative study of public opinion during the Mexican War. Conclusion is that Polk not only decided on the war before learning of the firing on American troops but also welcomed the conflict as a way to fulfill his expansionist plans.

Seigenthaler, John. *James K. Polk.* New York: Times Books, 2003. Seigenthaler concludes that Polk was a successful president who attained the four goals of his administration: lowering tariffs, establishing an independent federal treasury, acquiring the Oregon Territory from Great Britain, and making California an American territory.

Sellers, Charles Grier, Jr. *James K. Polk: Jacksonian, 1795-1843*. Princeton, N.J.: Princeton University Press, 1957.

_____. *James K. Polk: Continentalist, 1843-1846*. Princeton, N.J.: Princeton University Press, 1966. These volumes constitute the best treatment of Polk and his times up to the introduction of the Wilmot Proviso, a portent of things to come. Well-balanced and thoroughly researched, the study established Polk's claim to be considered one of the "near great" presidents.

Weems, John Edward. *To Conquer a Peace: The War Between the United States and Mexico*. Garden City, N.Y.: Doubleday, 1974. A popular treatment of the war. Largely undocumented but interesting and basi-cally sound. Weems believes that Polk hoped to avoid war by making a show of force.

SEE ALSO: John Quincy Adams; George Bancroft; Thomas Hart Benton; James Buchanan; Henry Clay; William Henry Harrison; Andrew Jackson; Abraham Lincoln; Zachary Taylor; Martin Van Buren.

RELATED ARTICLES in *Great Events from History: The Nineteenth Century, 1801-1900:* September 16, 1810-September 28, 1821: Mexican War of Independence; May 8, 1846: Battle of Palo Alto; June 15, 1846: United States Acquires Oregon Territory; June 30, 1846-January 13, 1847: United States Occupies California and the Southwest; August 1, 1846: Establishment of Independent U.S. Treasury; August 10, 1846: Smithsonian Institution Is Founded; January 19-February 3, 1847: Taos Rebellion; January 24, 1848: California Gold Rush Begins; February 2, 1848: Treaty of Guadalupe Hidalgo Ends Mexican War.

ALEKSANDR STEPANOVICH POPOV
Russian engineer and inventor

A member of the first wave of important twentieth century Russian engineers, Popov was a pioneer in the invention of radio and its applications. He also contributed to the development of X-ray photography. Outside Russia, he contributed to the development of radio in France.

BORN: March 16, 1859; Turinskiye Rudniki (now Krasnoturinsk), Perm, Russia
DIED: January 13, 1906; St. Petersburg, Russia
AREA OF ACHIEVEMENT: Science and technology

EARLY LIFE

Aleksandr Stepanovich Popov (pah-pahf) was born in a village in Perm, a marshy area of northeastern Russia, just west of the Ural Mountains. Despite its relative isolation, Perm was an area of ancient Russian settlement, first made famous by Saint Stephen of Perm. Saint Stephen converted the pagan Permians after he proved incombustible when they attempted to burn him at the stake. For many generations, the clergy provided Perm's only intelligentsia. Popov was the fourth child in a priest's family of seven children. Though Popov left his village, he loved Perm and in later life took numerous photographs of his native landscape, which form an important collection.

By Popov's time, copper and iron mines, as well as a few factories, were in operation near his village. As a child, he is supposed to have built models of factory and mining equipment. He was educated in seminaries and seemed destined to enter the priesthood, but at the age of eighteen he decided instead to pursue his growing interest in mathematics and physics. He moved to St. Petersburg to attend the university, which was then nearing the apogee of its reputation in science. Among Popov's distinguished teachers were the chemist Dmitry Mendeleyev and the physicists Fyodor Petrushevsky and Orest Khvolson. The University of St. Petersburg was one of the first to offer courses on the physics of electricity and magnetism and had a fine physics laboratory run by Popov's mentor Vladimir Lermantov.

While a student from 1878 to 1882, Popov always worked, not only to support himself and to contribute to the support of his siblings but also to support his wife, Raisa Gorbunov, whom he married before graduating. Gorbunov pursued medical studies and eventually became a physician. Popov found most congenial employment with a newly founded St. Petersburg company, Elektrotekhnik, which built and maintained small electric stations around the city.

As a student, Popov took part in the world's first electrical exhibition, in 1880, organized by a branch of the Russian Technical Society, which had just founded a new journal, *Elektrichestvo*. The exhibition was intended to raise money to fund the new publication and was a great success; it ran for a full month, attracting thousands of visitors. Popov worked as a guide throughout the exhibition, explaining the new marvels of technology to the public—a role that he was later to continue in public lectures and demonstrations, overcoming his initial shyness. A photograph of him from his student years shows a handsome, rather delicate-looking youth; later, he suffered from heart problems.

Popov was graduated from the faculty of mathematics and physics of the University of St. Petersburg with the degree of candidate (equivalent to a doctorate without a dissertation). His earliest research papers, published in *Elektrichestvo*, focused on the generation of electricity and the conversion of thermal energy into mechanical energy. He was trained in the spirit of concrete application of science, not for personal gain but for the good of others.

Upon his graduation, Popov accepted a position at the Russian navy's most prestigious training institute, the Mine Officers' (or Torpedo) School in Kronstadt, on the Gulf of Finland, where he worked from 1883 to 1901. The Kronstadt facility had Russia's most advanced physics laboratory, and Popov was soon in charge of it. He also gave free public lectures, in which he shared his advanced knowledge, delighting in finding ways to make technology accessible to the average person. He had only the most limited funds at his disposal and learned cabinetmaking and glassblowing in order to construct innovative apparatuses himself. Every summer, he supplemented his income by running the electrical power plant for the annual fair at Nizhni-Novgorod (modern Gorky).

LIFE'S WORK
At the Mine Officers' School in 1889, Popov reproduced Heinrich Hertz's experiments with electromagnetic waves. In the same year, in order to popularize both the Hertz oscillator and the field of electrical engineering in general, Popov gave a series of public lectures on the recent research done on the relationship between light and electric phenomena. These lectures made him see the need for an apparatus to demonstrate, before a large audience, the presence of the waves generated by the Hertz oscillator.

Popov constructed a better detector of electromagnetic waves, which led to his invention of a lightningstorm detector and a radio in 1895. He began with the electromagnetic-wave detector (later called a coherer) invented by the French physicist Édouard Branly and improved it so that it could be used reliably outside laboratory conditions. By the beginning of 1895, Popov had evolved the primitive coherer into a complete radio receiver. By the spring of 1895, Popov had a radio transmitter ready to complement his receiver; it was based on a modified Hertz oscillator excited by an induction coil. Using the two devices, he conducted radio communication experiments in the physics laboratory and in the garden of the Mine Officers' School. In the course of these experiments, he added a new element of his own, the radio antenna.

Popov successfully demonstrated his system of wireless communication and presented a formal paper to an audience of scientists from the Russian Physics and Chemistry Society on May 7, 1895. A report on his demonstration appeared in the Russian press on May 12, 1895, followed by other reports in late 1895 and early 1896. It is on the basis of this work that Russia claims primacy for the invention of wireless radio communication, although the young Italian physicist Guglielmo Marconi secured a patent on his own radio in the summer of 1896, won the Nobel Prize in 1909, and superseded Popov's achievements.

Initially, the components of Marconi's radio, being tested by the British Telegraph Agency in 1896, were kept secret. When the structure of Marconi's radio was finally revealed in 1897, however, it was identical to Popov's: an enhanced coherer with antenna and Hertz oscillator excited by an induction coil. The detailed description of Marconi's invention was published in the British professional engineering journal, *The Electrician*, in 1897. Popov and other Russian engineers read it and were shocked by the coincidence. Popov declined to accuse Marconi of theft, saying in an address to the First All-Russian Electrotechnical Congress in 1900:

> Was my instrument known to Marconi or not? The latter is very likely more probable. At any rate my combination of the relay, tube, and electromagnetic tapper served as the basis of Marconi's first patent as a new combination of already known instruments.

Popov had no interest in a vainglorious contest for primacy but did wish his achievements to be acknowledged. In an 1897 article published in *The Electrician*, he took exception to a lengthy article just published by the British journal on the subject of the coherer and the radio, in which Popov's contribution was not even mentioned.

From May of 1895 onward, Popov continued to work with his wireless system, to lecture, and to give demonstrations. Noting that the device was sensitive to lightning discharges, he set it to record oscillations on paper, clearly indicating the approach of storms. From the summer of 1895, Popov's lightning-storm detector was put to effective, long-term use by the Russian Forestry Institute.

On March 24, 1896, Popov sent the world's first wireless message in Morse code across a distance of 250 meters, between two buildings. The message consisted of two words: "Heinrich Hertz." The witnesses were scientists of the St. Petersburg Physics Society, holding a meeting at the University of St. Petersburg. Unfortunately for his future fame outside Russia, Popov was distracted from his radio work by his curiosity about the latest scientific phenomenon, X rays, discovered by Wilhelm Conrad Röntgen late in 1895. Popov was drawn to investigate these in 1896 and was the first in Russia to take X-ray photographs of objects and human limbs.

Newspaper reports of Marconi's patent broke in the fall of 1896, spurring Popov to fresh efforts. Popov increased the distance of radio communication. He achieved ship-to-shore communication across six hundred meters in 1897; by 1901, he had expanded that to 150 kilometers. His work was simultaneously experimental and practical, being applied in rescue missions at sea almost immediately. He experimented with wavelengths lying on the boundary between the decimeter and meter ranges. He predicted the development of broadcasting and the possibility of detecting the directionality of radio waves.

Popov was energetic about making foreign contacts and broadening his expertise. In 1893, he attended the Chicago World's Fair, where he delivered a lecture; he witnessed the Third International Electrical Congress being held in Chicago at the same time. In a letter sent from the United States, he expressed a strong intention to visit Thomas Edison's laboratory, but it is not known whether he actually did so. He visited New York and Philadelphia. During the late 1890's, he made several trips to France and Germany to examine radio stations there. In Russia, he was much in demand as a consultant on the establishment of electrical power plants and civilian wireless telegraph stations.

In 1899, Popov built a headphone message receiver and then went to Paris to work with the French engineer Eugène Ducretet. As a result, Popov's headset (patented in 1901) was manufactured in Russia and France from 1901 to 1904 and was widely used. In 1900, he returned to Paris to collaborate with Lieutenant Tissot, one of the pioneers of French radio, on numerous improvements in radio design.

While civilian use of wireless radio was expanding, the Russian navy was slow to apply it. Because of Popov's on-site work, Russia's Baltic Fleet, harbored at Kronstadt, was supplied with both radios and trained personnel. Under the prodding of Vice Admiral Stepan Makarov, a commander based in Kronstadt who took an interest in Popov's work, Popov began to receive modest funding. Unfortunately for Russia, there was no radio equipment aboard its Pacific fleet at the outbreak of the Russo-Japanese War of 1904-1905.

At this point, Popov was at last given a position worthy of his standing and achievement. Having been a professor at the St. Petersburg Electrotechnical Institute since 1901, he was unanimously elected rector in late 1905. Two weeks after his election, his entire faculty passed a resolution condemning "any forcible interference by the authorities in the life of the institute," referring chiefly to police searches of student dormitories and to student arrests.

Popov, who suffered from a weak heart and high blood pressure, was summoned to the office of the St. Petersburg governor for a stormy interview. He refused to back down and returned home in a shaken state. He died of cerebral hemorrhage a few days later, at the age of forty-six.

SIGNIFICANCE

Aleksandr Stepanovich Popov belongs to the long line of Russian scientists not much appreciated by their government in their lifetimes. There is a consistent succession, from Paul von Schilling-Cannstadt, who in 1832 installed one of the world's first telegraph connections (which ran between the Communications Ministry and the czar's Winter Palace but was never used), to Dmitry Mendeleyev (who was dismissed from his university post under government pressure), to Andrei Sakharov (who wasted years in the closed city of Gorky for political reasons).

While the rest of the world raced to master the wireless radio and its applications, funding teams of researchers, the Russian government—of which Popov was an employee—let Popov work alone, in his limited spare time. On two occasions, in 1925 and again in 1945, the Soviet government remembered Popov and effusively honored him. The regime had so little credibility on other fronts, however, that such honors added nothing to, and may have actually harmed, Popov's international repute.

Popov—who did invent a wireless radio, the components and operating principles of which were in essence the same as those of the Marconi radio patented a year later—disparaged suggestions that he had been copied, modestly noting that he had simply put together components that individually were already known. In a time of intense scientific interest in electromagnetic waves, the hour was ripe for such an invention, whose appearance was perhaps inevitable. Popov was content to be part of the world of scientific discovery and to share his knowledge even with the nonscientific public.

Popov belonged to the first wave of what became the substantial, proud, and little-understood caste of Russia's early twentieth century engineers. Like the highly educated characters in the plays of his scientifically trained contemporary Anton Chekhov, Popov and other members of the technical intelligentsia looked forward to a humane, enlightened future that they did not expect personally to see.

—*D. Gosselin Nakeeb*

FURTHER READING

Popov, Alexander. "An Application of the Coherer." *The Electrician*, 1897. Popov's article translated into English, reflecting his precise mind and talent for educating.

Radovsky, M. *Alexander Popov: Inventor of Radio.* Translated by G. Yankovsky. Moscow: Foreign Languages, 1957. The most comprehensive study of the life and work of Popov. This work is intended for the general reader as part of the Men of Russian Science series. Contains abundant footnotes to sources but no bibliography. Photographs of persons, equipment, and sites are included.

Smith-Rose, R. L. "Marconi, Popov, and the Dawn of Radiocommunication." *Electronics and Power* 10 (1964): 76-79. This article presents the British view that Marconi should be given primacy.

Süsskind, Charles. "Popov and the Beginnings of Radiotelegraphy." *Proceedings of the Institute of Radio Engineers* 50 (1962): 2036-2047. Reprinted as a separate pamphlet by the San Francisco Press in 1962 and 1973, this article utilizes Soviet sources and is favorable to the Russian view of Popov's primacy.

Weightman, Gavin. *Signor Marconi's Magic Box: The Remarkable Invention of the Nineteenth Century and the Amateur Inventor Whose Genius Sparked a Revolution.* Cambridge, Mass.: Da Capo Press, 2003. Although there is only one mention of the Popov-Ducretet wireless system, and two references to Popov in the text, this book provides an overall context in which to understand the invention of radio.

SEE ALSO: Anton Chekhov; Thomas Alva Edison; Hermann von Helmholtz; Nikola Tesla.

RELATED ARTICLES in *Great Events from History: The Nineteenth Century, 1801-1900:* June, 1896: Marconi Patents the Wireless Telegraph; December 15, 1900: General Electric Opens Research Laboratory.

JOHN WESLEY POWELL
American explorer

Powell led the first party of exploration to descend the gorges of the Green and Colorado Rivers by boat, stimulating interest in the geology and scenic wonders of the Grand Canyon. He also helped to establish the concepts of large-scale damming and irrigation projects as the keys to settlement and agricultural survival in the arid lands of the American West beyond the one hundredth meridian.

BORN: March 24, 1834; Mount Morris, New York
DIED: September 23, 1902; Haven, Maine
AREA OF ACHIEVEMENT: Exploration

EARLY LIFE

John Wesley Powell was the son of a circuit-riding Methodist minister who supplemented his income by farming and tailoring. In 1841, when Powell was about seven years old, the family moved from New York to Ohio. The abolitionist views of the Powell family were not well received in Ohio, and John Wesley had such a difficult time at school that he was eventually placed under the direction of a private schoolmaster. This proved a significant experience, for the young Powell accompanied his tutor on biological field trips and developed a strong interest in both biological and physical science. The family eventually moved on to Illinois, where John Wesley grew to maturity. He spent several years combining a career as a teacher in Wisconsin and Illinois with sporadic attendance at several colleges, including Wheaton, Oberlin, and Illinois College. During this period he undertook extensive natural history excursions and ambitious journeys by boat down the Illinois, Des Moines, Ohio, and

Mississippi Rivers from St. Paul all the way to New Orleans.

When the Civil War came, Powell immediately enlisted as a private in an Illinois volunteer infantry company. He rose quickly through the ranks and became a student of military engineering and fortifications. He met and became a friend of General Ulysses S. Grant and eventually commander of his own battery in an Illinois artillery unit. He led his battery into the fierce struggle at the Hornet's Nest in the Battle of Shiloh, where he was hit by a Minié ball, requiring the amputation of his right arm. Despite his injury he continued in service, seeing action and carrying out important duties in a number of major campaigns and rising to the rank of brevet lieutenant colonel.

After the war, Powell returned to Illinois and became professor of natural history at Illinois Wesleyan College, later moving to Illinois Normal University at Bloomington. By this time he had become accustomed to taking his students into the field as part of their training, but he was increasingly obsessed with the desire to reach further afield. He was particularly drawn by the glamour and mystery of the trans-Mississippi West and began to assemble the ingredients that would allow him to make his first major expedition into that area.

Powell was instrumental in the establishment of a state natural history museum in Bloomington, and as its first curator he secured funding from several governmental and private sources to undertake a collecting expedition into the West. His friendship with General Grant enabled him to arrange for low-cost rations from army posts and for military protection for part of his trip. In 1867, the expedition, including students, amateur naturalists, teachers, and family members, set out from Council Bluffs on the first of Powell's major expeditions. The summer was spent examining the country and collecting specimens in the Colorado Rockies, and Powell remained after most of his party returned east and journeyed along the Grand River in Colorado.

During the following summer, Powell returned to the Rockies with an expedition of twenty-five people, sponsorship from various Illinois state institutions, and encouragement from officials of the Smithsonian Institution, who were intrigued by his plans to explore among the rivers and high peaks of Colorado. After time collecting specimens in the Middle Park region, in late August Powell and six of his party made the first ascent of Long's Peak. They then moved into the White River basin, intending to follow it down to the Green River and on to a winter reconnaissance of the Colorado River.

John Wesley Powell. (Library of Congress)

By then Powell had become thoroughly captivated by Western adventuring and scientific exploration and was obsessed by the unknown mysteries and legends of the Colorado. He had actively promoted his ideas and successfully publicized his activities and plans and had something of a reputation as an explorer and scientist, as well as good connections in the political and scientific communities. Although this five-foot-six, bearded veteran with only one arm hardly looked the part of the great explorer, Major John Wesley Powell was on the threshold of one of the great Western adventures.

LIFE'S WORK

The gorges of the Green and Colorado Rivers were among the few remaining unexplored areas on the North American continent. The legends that had been constructed out of the tales of Indians, mountain men, and other sources told of a region of enormous waterfalls, vicious whirlpools and rapids, and enormous rock cliffs that offered no escape or refuge from the punishment of the river. Essentially Powell and his men would plunge into a river descent of nearly nine hundred miles with no real idea of what terrors and adventures lay before them.

Back east, Powell made the best preparations he could. A Chicagoan built four small wooden boats, one sixteen feet long of pine, the other three twenty-one feet, of oak, with watertight compartments. Powell secured some financial support from a variety of public and private sources, although most of the meager financing came out of his own pocket. He assembled a varied group of nine companions, and on May 24, 1869, after several weeks of training, they set off down the Green River toward the Colorado.

The explorers were on the river for ninety-two days. Their small vessels plunged through turbulent rapids, foaming cataracts, and towering canyon walls that at least matched most of the myths and legends. Two boats were lost, one expeditioner deserted early, and three others were killed by Indians as they gave up on the river journey and attempted to climb out of the Grand Canyon. A confidence man surfaced who claimed that he was the only survivor of a wreck beneath a falls that had claimed the lives of the other members of the expedition, and newspapers across the country reported that Powell's party had been defeated by the river. By the time they in fact surfaced at a Mormon settlement below the canyon, Powell and his men had explored the Colorado River and the Grand Canyon and had discovered the last unknown river and mountain range in the American West. Powell's prodigious expedition marked him immediately as an American hero and one of the great explorers in the nation's history. It also meant that he could attract support and financing for further activities.

Powell returned to the Colorado two years later and retraced his original steps, now with the sponsorship of the Smithsonian Institution and the Department of the Interior. This expedition was a more determinedly scientific endeavor, operating as a survey group, the United States Geological and Geographical Survey of the Rocky Mountains, and they undertook a careful study, survey, and mapping of the canyon country.

Powell became fascinated with the question not only of how the region—its canyons, plateaus, and mountains—looked but also of how they

had been formed. He undertook additional Western expeditions and employed men who explored the high plateaus of Utah, the Colorado Plateau, Zion and Bryce canyons, and the Henry and Uinta mountains. The work of Powell and his associates introduced the idea of vast processes of uplift and erosion as responsible for the topography of the canyon and plateau country. They helped to popularize the geological concept of "base level of erosion." Powell's findings and ideas were published as *Explorations of the Colorado River of the West and Its Tributaries* (1875; revised and enlarged in 1895 under the title *Canyons of the Colorado*).

Powell's interest in the topography and geology of the Western regions led him naturally to a concern about the management of its lands. In 1878 he published *A Report on the Lands of the Arid Region of the United States*, which has been described as among the most important works ever produced by an American. Powell rejected both the concept of the inexhaustibility of natural resources and the idea that the West was the "Great American Desert" and not capable of supporting substantial settlement. Powell's familiarity with the West had convinced him that its lands and climate west of the one

---

THE ANCIENT CLIFF DWELLERS

John Wesley Powell published the findings of his explorations of the Southwest in Canyons of Colorado, *in which he had much to say about the ruins of earlier Indian societies.*

Perhaps the most interesting ruins of America are found in this region. The ancient pueblos found here are of superior structure, but they were all built by a people whom the Navajos displaced when they migrated from the far North. Wherever there is water, near by an ancient ruin may be found; and these ruins are gathered about centers, the centers being larger pueblos and the scattered ruins representing single houses. The ancient people lived in villages, or pueblos, but during the growing season they scattered about by the springs and streams to cultivate the soil by irrigation, and wherever there was a little farm or garden patch, there was built a summer house of stone. When times of war came, especially when they were invaded by the Navajos, these ancient people left their homes in the pueblos and by the streams and constructed temporary homes in the cliffs and canyon walls. Such cliff ruins are abundant throughout the region, intimately the ancient pueblo peoples succumbed to the prowess of the Navajos and were driven out. A part joined related tribes in the valley of the Rio Grande; others joined the Zuni and the people of Tusayan; and still others pushed on beyond the Little Colorado to the San Francisco Plateau and far down into the valley of the Gila.

Source: John Wesley Powell, *Canyons of the Colorado* (Meadville, Pa.: Flood & Vincent, 1895), chapter 2.

hundredth meridian were simply not suitable for development under policies that had been shaped by the conditions in the eastern regions. The arid lands of the West required a different strategy, and the key was water management.

Powell argued that the arid regions would not support the traditional family farm on the eastern model and that the lands of the West should be categorized and utilized according to their most efficient uses for grazing, lumbering, mining, farming, and other purposes. Water should be considered a precious resource to be allocated by the community for the benefit of society in general rather than a privileged few. Government should undertake large-scale damming and irrigation projects so that the arid regions could be "reclaimed" and become productive. Powell's ideas represented a significant departure from the conventional wisdom regarding land use and the West, and his prestige as an explorer and scientist, coupled with his office as director of the United States Geological Survey from 1881 to 1894, put him in a position to be enormously influential in shaping the establishment in 1902 of the United States Bureau of Reclamation, which helped to make water management one of the major components of the early conservation movement.

During his Western expeditions, Powell had become fascinated by the cultures of the Indian tribes of the region, and it is characteristic of the man that he became a student of anthropology and headed the Bureau of Ethnology of the Smithsonian Institution during the same period that he led the Geological Survey. In 1880 he published his *Introduction to the Study of Indian Languages.*

Major Powell's retirement in 1894 was brought about partially because of physical ailments and partially because of his frustration in trying to get his ideas implemented. Ironically, his death in 1902 coincided with the passage of the Reclamation Act, which institutionalized many of his theories concerning land and water management.

SIGNIFICANCE

Powell's career was significant on several fronts. As an explorer, his journey down the Colorado River through the Grand Canyon in 1869 ranks as one of the epic American adventures. His scientific background and interests prepared him for important accomplishments in mapping, surveying, and studying the geology of the plateau and canyon country, and for long service as director of the United States Geological Survey. During the same period, he headed the Bureau of Ethnology of the Smithsonian Institution. Powell became most interested in the

problems of proper management and utilization of the lands in the arid West and was convinced that intelligent water management was the key to its development. He is one of the fathers of the concept of "reclamation" of arid lands through the construction of dams and irrigation projects.

—*James E. Fickle*

FURTHER READING

Bartlett, Richard A. *Great Surveys of the American West.* Norman: University of Oklahoma Press, 1962. A comprehensive treatment that includes the work of Powell.

Darrah, William C. *Powell of the Colorado.* Princeton, N.J.: Princeton University Press, 1951. A useful scholarly biography. Well researched, drawing on some unpublished sources, but rather colorless. Includes illustrations.

Exploring the American West, 1803-1879 (National Park Handbook no. 116). Washington, D.C.: Government Printing Office, 1982. This 128-page booklet is profusely illustrated and contains several photographs of Powell and his survey. The text is by William H. Goetzmann.

Fradkin, Philip L. *A River, No More: The Colorado River and the West.* New York: Alfred A. Knopf, 1981. Focusing upon the Colorado River and its tributaries, Fradkin discusses the federal land and water policies that shaped much of the West. Powell's role in the evolution of these developments is considered.

Goetzmann, William H. *Exploration and Empire: The Explorer and the Scientist in the Winning of the American West.* New York: Alfred A. Knopf, 1966. This Pulitzer Prize-winning book is the standard general treatment of the role of exploration in the American West. Contains a chapter dealing with Powell's life and career.

Powell, John Wesley. *Seeing Things Whole: The Essential John Wesley Powell.* Edited by William de Buys. Washington, D.C.: Island Press/Shearwater Books, 2001. A collection of Powell's writings, including selections from *A Report on the Lands of the Arid Region*, and writings expressing his ideas about civilization, western settlement, and allocation of natural resources. The selections are annotated and have introductions placing them within the proper context.

Savage, Henry, Jr. *Discovering America, 1700-1875.* New York: Harper and Row, 1979. A very readable survey that is particularly good on the nineteenth century explorations.

Schwartz, Seymour I., and Ralph E. Ehrenberg. *The Mapping of America*. New York: Harry N. Abrams, 1980. An enormously detailed and lavishly illustrated history.

Stegner, Wallace. *Beyond the Hundredth Meridian: John Wesley Powell and the Second Opening of the West*. Boston: Houghton Mifflin, 1954. The standard biography. Stegner brings a novelist's gifts to his compelling narrative. Illustrations juxtapose early artists' renderings of the Grand Canyon with some of the first photographs of the region.

Wild, Peter. *Pioneer Conservationists of Western America*. Missoula, Mont.: Mountain, 1979. A brief, breezy, superficial account that contains a chapter on Powell's explorations and theories.

Worster, Donald. *A River Running West: The Life of John Wesley Powell*. New York: Oxford University Press,

2001. Thorough, detailed account of Powell's life from his childhood through his years directing the Bureau of American Ethnology.

SEE ALSO: Kit Carson; Ulysses S. Grant; Zebulon Pike; Jedediah Smith.
RELATED ARTICLES in *Great Events from History: The Nineteenth Century, 1801-1900:* May 14, 1804-September 23, 1806: Lewis and Clark Expedition; July 15, 1806-July 1, 1807: Pike Explores the American Southwest; September 8, 1810-May, 1812: Astorian Expeditions Explore the Pacific Northwest Coast; 1822-1831: Jedediah Smith Explores the Far West; May, 1842-1854: Frémont Explores the American West; March 2, 1853-1857: Pacific Railroad Surveys.

WILLIAM HICKLING PRESCOTT
American historian

One of the first great American historians, Prescott proved that historical writing could achieve the permanence of literature. He introduced to American historiography all the methods of modern scholarship and remains the most distinguished historian in the English language of sixteenth century Spain and Spanish America.

BORN: May 4, 1796; Salem, Massachusetts
DIED: January 28, 1859; Boston, Massachusetts
AREA OF ACHIEVEMENT: Historiography

EARLY LIFE

William Hickling Prescott was the son of William Prescott, a lawyer and judge who prospered in investments in industry, real estate, and the India trade. His paternal grandfather was Colonel William Prescott, the hero of the Battle of Bunker Hill. Prescott's mother, Catherine Greene Hickling, was the daughter of another wealthy New England family. Prescott attended private schools in Salem and another in Boston when the family moved there in 1808. At Harvard, he suffered an injury to his left eye during a boyish fracas in the dining hall, which led to a lifetime of trouble with his eyesight. This event is the basis of the myth that he achieved literary fame in spite of blindness. Actually, he was never totally blind, but his eyesight and his general health were poor throughout his life.

When he was graduated from Harvard in 1814, Prescott's study of the law in preparation for joining his father's firm was cut short by impaired vision and rheumatic pains, and his parents sent him abroad for his health, first to the Azores, where his maternal grandfather was the American consul. He returned to Boston in 1817, after two years in England, France, and Italy, convinced that he would never be able to practice law. During the winter of 1817-1818, he was confined to a darkened room, where his sister read to him while he wrestled with the question of what career to pursue.

Prescott's first published work, an article on Lord Byron, appeared in the *North American Review* in 1821. By this time, he was determined to be a man of letters, a career made possible by the readers and secretaries whom he could afford to employ. In 1820, he married Susan Amory, the daughter of a wealthy Boston merchant, and he embarked on the systematic study of European literature. During the next nine years, he continued to publish essays on a variety of literary subjects while studying Italian and Spanish literature.

LIFE'S WORK

Prescott's study of the literature of Spain led to his determination to write a history of the reign of the fifteenth century monarchs Ferdinand and Isabella. Doubly isolated from documentary sources by his poor eyesight and his distance from Spanish libraries but blessed with sufficient wealth, Prescott employed full-time secretaries to read to him and to take dictation, and his many contacts in European libraries made possible a form of research that was remarkably complete, considering his difficulties.

Prescott's friends in Europe found and made copies of often obscure documentary sources, and his remarkable memory gave him the ability to keep a large amount of historical information in mind as he organized his subject. *History of the Reign of Ferdinand and Isabella the Catholic* (1838), the result of eight years of writing, was, for a historical work, a remarkable success, both in the United States and in England. Though later historians have charged that Prescott ignored the ordinary people of Spain in concentrating on the life of the Spanish court, it must be remembered that it was politics, diplomacy, and war, not "common life," that furnished subjects for historians in Prescott's time. This first work reveals high standards of objectivity, it is thoroughly documented, and Spanish historians have always considered it a basic contribution to fifteenth century historiography. All this is even more remarkable for being the achievement of a self-trained historian.

Prescott's success with his first book encouraged him to embark on the writing of the two works for which he is most famous, his accounts of the destruction of the Aztec and Inca empires by the conquistadors of Hernán Cortés and Francisco Pizarro. *History of the Conquest of Mexico* (1843) produced for Prescott a remarkable number of honors, including memberships in various historical societies in the United States and in Europe, honorary degrees, and, most significant, a membership in the Royal Academy of History in Madrid.

The book on Mexico, which has been issued in two hundred editions and has been his most translated book, is considered by most students of Prescott to be his masterpiece, admired particularly for its graceful style and overall design. It is a supreme example of the work of the first great generation of American historians—Prescott, Francis Parkman, and John Lothrop Motley—who, being unburdened by any philosophy of history, subordinated deep analyses of social background and lengthy explanations of the causes of events to simple narrative history written for both the edification and entertainment of the reader.

History of the Conquest of Peru (1847) was written in two years. The speed of its composition is an indication of the success of Prescott's mastery of the subject of sixteenth century Spain, his methods of research, and particularly the remarkable network of friends he had established in Spanish libraries. This work has not enjoyed the scholarly respect that *History of the Conquest of Mexico* has achieved, but this is less because of failing powers in its author than of the subject itself: Prescott found much less to admire in Pizarro than he had found in Cortés.

William Hickling Prescott. (Library of Congress)

ularly the remarkable network of friends he had established in Spanish libraries. This work has not enjoyed the scholarly respect that *History of the Conquest of Mexico* has achieved, but this is less because of failing powers in its author than of the subject itself: Prescott found much less to admire in Pizarro than he had found in Cortés.

In 1850, he traveled in Europe, where he was a great social success and where, among other honors, he received a doctorate from Oxford University. The first two volumes of his fourth work, *History of the Reign of Philip the Second, King of Spain*, were published in 1855, and the final, third volume appeared in December, 1858, only a month before his death on January 28, 1859. This is the least of his four major works, probably because of the bad health that plagued him while he was writing it but also because he found so little to admire in his subject.

Prescott's four historical works are his primary claim to fame as a historian and man of letters. He also published "The Life of Charles V After His Abdication" (1856) as a supplement to William Robertson's *The History of the Reign of the Emperor Charles the Fifth* (1769), and what he called "some of my periodical trumpery" appeared as *Biographical and Critical Miscellanies* in 1845.

In spite of his physical ailments, Prescott's private life was serene. He was the father of four children, he enjoyed a wide circle of personal and professional friends, and he maintained a comfortable rhythm of the seasons as he worked in his library in Boston in the winter and spent his summers at Nahant or at the ancestral Prescott farm.

Prescott was in many ways a typical Boston Brahmin, a Unitarian in religion, a Federalist in politics and later a Whig, and a man with strong social concerns for his community and a belief that wealth confers obligations on the wealthy. Early in life, he was influential in the establishment in Massachusetts of an institution for the care of the blind, and he supported the Boston Atheneum all of his life. He earned the respect of many Mexican and Spanish friends by opposing the Mexican War and the Pierce administration's designs on Cuba, and like most New England intellectuals, he opposed the Fugitive Slave Law and voted for John C. Frémont in 1856. He was a complex man who, in spite of his physical impairment, enjoyed social activity and gracious living, and he was a frequent help to other writers and researchers, but his ambition as a historian and man of letters triumphed over the double burden of ill health and social position while his wealth made possible research that no other American of his time could have achieved.

SIGNIFICANCE

William Hickling Prescott combined thorough research and literary gifts to produce historical works that must be considered contributions both to historical knowledge and to American literature. Though he concentrated on the colorful aspects of his subjects and ignored the more prosaic and mundane life of common people, he produced remarkable examples of narrative and helped to raise historical writing in the United States from the often parochial concerns of his predecessors while avoiding the dullness that characterizes much of the admittedly fuller social and economic histories of later generations of historians.

The fact that Prescott's work is eminently readable has obscured his importance as the first American historian to employ modern methods of historical research, an achievement that is even more remarkable when one takes account of the fact that he was completely self-trained and that he was burdened with ill health all of his life. Furthermore, at a time when American literary and

historical interests, in the aftermath of revolution and nation-building, were almost inevitably turned inward, he made American readers conscious of cultures beyond their borders while helping to give American literature an international reputation.

—*Robert L. Berner*

FURTHER READING

Charvat, William, and Michael Kraus, eds. *William Hickling Prescott: Representative Selections*. New York: American Book, 1943. This selection of passages from Prescott's writing is supplemented by a brief account of his life and discussions of his literary style and the philosophical and political premises of his work.

Darnell, Donald G. *William Hickling Prescott*. Boston: Twayne, 1975. Primarily concerned with Prescott as a man of letters, Darnell provides a brief account of his life, a balanced assessment of his achievement as a historian, and lengthy examinations of each of his four major works.

Gardiner, C. Harvey. *William Hickling Prescott: A Biography*. Austin: University of Texas Press, 1969. The definitive biography by the most distinguished Prescott scholar, based on a thorough knowledge of primary sources and not likely to be superseded. A balanced assessment of Prescott's achievement as a historian and man of letters and a full treatment of his complex personality and private life.

Levin, David. *History as Romantic Art: Bancroft, Prescott, Motley, and Parkman*. Stanford, Calif.: Stanford University Press, 1959. A study of the first generation of American historians, their romanticism, and its effects on their writing, which Levin often considers unfortunate. His assessments of Prescott should be checked against Gardiner's.

Ogden, Rollo. *William Hickling Prescott*. Boston: Houghton Mifflin, 1904. Apparently intended to supplement George Ticknor's biography, it devotes more attention to Prescott as a person and takes greater account of his private papers. The best biography before Gardiner's.

Peck, Harry Thurston. *William Hickling Prescott*. New York: Macmillan, 1905. A brief biography that makes no use of primary sources but includes a useful discussion of Prescott's literary style.

Prescott, William Hickling. *The Literary Memoranda of William Hickling Prescott*. Edited by C. Harvey Gardiner. 2 vols. Norman: University of Oklahoma Press, 1961. A collection of Prescott's private papers, which provide essential insight into his methods as a writer and researcher.

Ticknor, George. *Life of William Hickling Prescott*. Philadelphia: J. B. Lippincott, 1863. Ticknor, himself the author of a major history of Spanish literature, knew Prescott intimately, but his biography provides no insight into his subject's personality and little of his social and intellectual background. Includes useful appendixes on the history of the Prescott family.

Wertheimer, Eric. *Imagined Empires: Incas, Aztecs, and the New World of American Literature, 1771-1876*. New York: Cambridge University Press, 1999. Examines the writings of Prescott and other historians and authors who wrote about Latin America. Wertheimer maintains that early Americans took a great interest in South American civilizations, and this interest reflected the emerging role of the United States as an empire in the New World.

Williams, Stanley T. *The Spanish Background of American Literature*. 2 vols. New Haven, Conn.: Yale University Press, 1955. Includes a chapter on Prescott and provides insights into the sources of nineteenth century American interest in Spain and Spanish America.

SEE ALSO: Lord Byron; Fanny Calderón de la Barca; John C. Frémont; Francis Parkman.

RELATED ARTICLES in *Great Events from History: The Nineteenth Century, 1801-1900:* 1824: Ranke Develops Systematic History; November, 1839: Stephens Begins Uncovering Mayan Antiquities.

PIERRE-JOSEPH PROUDHON
French journalist and social reformer

Proudhon's greatest activity was as a journalist and pamphleteer. Hailed by his followers as the uncompromising champion of human liberty, Proudhon voiced the discontentment of the revolutionary period of nineteenth century France. His influence on French politics extended well into the twentieth century.

BORN: January 15, 1809; Besançon, France
DIED: January 19, 1865; Paris, France
AREAS OF ACHIEVEMENT: Philosophy, journalism

EARLY LIFE

Pierre-Joseph Proudhon (prew-dahn) was born in a rural French town. Although the political and social climates were important influences on Proudhon's life, the experiences he had as a child growing up in a working-class family shaped his philosophical views in even more important ways. Proudhon's father, who was a brewer and, later, a cooper, went bankrupt because, unlike most brewers, he sold his measure of drink for a just price. Penniless after the loss of his business, Proudhon's father was forced to move his family to a small farm near Burgille. Between the ages of eight and twelve, Proudhon worked as a cowherd, an experience that forged in him a lifelong identity with the peasant class.

Proudhon's formal education began in 1820, when his mother arranged with the parish priest for him to attend the local college, which was the nineteenth century equivalent of high school. The stigma of poverty suddenly became very real to him when he contrasted his clothes with those of his wealthier comrades. Smarting from the insults of the other children, Proudhon protected himself from further pain by adopting a surly, sullen personality. During his fourth year at school, Proudhon read François Fénelon's *Démonstration de l'existence de Dieu* (1713; *A Demonstration of the Existence of God*, 1713), which introduced him to the tenets of atheism. Proudhon then ceased to practice religion at the age of sixteen and began his lifelong war against the Church.

Proudhon's life changed drastically on the eve of his graduation. Sensing that something was wrong when neither of his parents was present, Proudhon rushed home to find that his father, who had become a landless laborer, had lost everything in a last desperate lawsuit. Years later, Proudhon used his father's inability to own farmland as the basis for his belief that society excluded the poor from the ownership of property.

At the age of eighteen, Proudhon was forced to abandon his formal education and take up a trade. He was apprenticed to the Besançon firm of the Gauthier brothers, which specialized in general theological publications. Proudhon became proud of his trade as a proofreader because it made him independent. At home among the printers, who were men of his own class, he found that he had traded the isolation of the middle-class school for the comradely atmosphere of the workshop.

The printshop also enabled Proudhon to continue his studies, in an informal way, for it was there that he developed his first intellectual passions. His budding interest in language was cultivated by a young editor named Fallot, who was the first great personal influence on Proudhon's life. It was there too that Proudhon was introduced to the works of the utopian thinker Charles Fourier. Fourier's position that a more efficient economy can revolutionize society from within is reflected in the anarchical doctrines of Proudhon's greatest works.

Another lesson Proudhon learned at the printshop was that mastering a trade does not guarantee a living, as it would in a just society. His apprenticeship came to an end as a result of the revolution of 1830, which overthrew the restored Bourbons. Although Proudhon hated to be out of work, he was infected with the spirit of revolution, which stayed with him throughout his life.

Proudhon's friend Fallot persuaded him to move to Paris and apply for the Suard scholarship. During their visit to Paris, Fallot provided Proudhon with moral and financial support, because he was convinced that Proudhon had a great future ahead of him as a philosopher and a writer. When Fallot was stricken with cholera, however, Proudhon declined to accept his friend's generosity any longer and began seeking employment in the printing houses of Paris, but to no avail. Discouraged, Proudhon left Fallot to convalesce by himself in Paris.

LIFE'S WORK

A turning point for Proudhon came with the publication of his book *Qu'est-ce que la propriété?* (1840; *What Is Property?*, 1876). The book was actually a showcase for his answer to this question—"Property is theft"—and it gained for Proudhon an immediate audience among those working-class citizens who had become disillusioned with Louis-Philippe, a king who clearly favored the privileged classes. Ironically, though, Proudhon was a defender of public property; he objected to the practice of drawing unearned income from rental property. This book represented a dramatic departure from the popular utopian theories embraced by most socialists of the day in that it employed economic, political, and social science as a means of viewing social problems.

Among the people who were attracted to Proudhon's theories was Karl Marx. In 1842, Marx praised *What Is Property?* and met Proudhon in Paris. Because Proudhon had studied economic science in more depth than Marx had, Marx probably learned more from their meeting than did Proudhon. Two years later, though, Marx became disenchanted with Proudhon after the publication

Pierre-Joseph Proudhon. (Library of Congress)

in 1846 of Proudhon's first major work, *Système des contradictions économiques: Ou, Philosophie de la misère* (1846; *System of Economic Contradictions*, 1888).

Proudhon hoped that the revolutions of 1848 would bring his theories to fruition by deposing Louis-Philippe. He became the editor of a radical journal *Le Représentant du peuple* (the representative of the people), in which he recorded one of the best eyewitness accounts of the revolution. During that same year, he was elected to the office of radical deputy. Surprisingly, Proudhon did not ally himself with the socialist Left. During his brief term in office, he voted against the resolution proclaiming the "right to work" and against the adoption of the constitution establishing the democratic Second Republic. His chief activity during his term in office was the founding of a "People's Bank," which would be a center of various workingmen's associations and would overcome the scarcity of money and credit by universalizing the rate of exchange.

The feasibility of such a bank will never be known, because it was closed after only two months of operation when Proudhon's career as a deputy came to an abrupt end. In 1849, Proudhon was arrested for writing violent articles attacking Napoleon III and was sentenced to three years in the Saint-Pelagie prison. Proudhon fled to

Belgium but was promptly arrested when he returned to Paris under an assumed name to liquidate his bank, which had foundered in his absence.

Proudhon's imprisonment actually proved to be a fortunate experience because it afforded him ample time to study and write. He also founded a newspaper, *Le Voix du peuple* (the voice of the people). In *Les Confessions d'un révolutionnaire* (1849; the confessions of a revolutionary), written while he was in prison, Proudhon traced the history of the revolutionary movement in France from 1789 to 1849.

In *Idée générale de la révolution au XIXe siècle* (1851; *The General Idea of the Revolution in the Nineteenth Century*, 1923), Proudhon appealed to the bourgeois to make their peace with the workers. *La Révolution sociale démontrée par le coup d'état du 2 décembre* (1852; the revolution demonstrated by the coup d'état), which was published a month after the release of Proudhon from prison, hailed the overthrow of the Second Republic as a giant step toward progress. Proudhon also proposed that anarchy was the true end of the social evolution of the nineteenth century. Because Proudhon suggested that Napoleon III should avoid making the same mistakes as Napoleon I, the book was banned by the minister of police. Nevertheless, the book created a sensation in France.

The most important event that occurred while Proudhon was in prison was his marriage to Euphrasie Piegard, an uneducated seamstress, whose management skills and resilience made her a suitable mate for a revolutionary. By marrying outside the Church, he indicated his contempt for the clergy. Marriage was good for Proudhon, and his happiness convinced him that marriage was an essential part of a just society.

The three years following Proudhon's release from prison were marked by uncertainty and fear. By the end of 1852, Napoleon III's reign was in crisis, and any writer who opposed him or the Crimean War was immediately ostracized. Proudhon's attempts to start a journal through which he could persuade the regime of Napoleon III to move to the left against the Church was thwarted by the Jesuits. With his journalistic career at an end, Proudhon began a series of literary projects.

The year 1855 saw a significant shift in Proudhon's philosophical outlook. He arrived at the conclusion that what was needed was not a political system under which everyone benefited but a transformation of humankind's consciousness. Proudhon's new concern with ethics resulted in his *De la justice dans la révolution et dans l'église* (about the justice of the revolution and the Church) in 1858. This three-volume work, which ranks as one of the greatest socialist studies of the nineteenth century, attacks the defenders of the status quo, including the Roman Catholic Church.

Although the book enjoyed great success, the anger that Proudhon had exhibited in this manifesto of defiance outraged the government and the Church. Once again, Proudhon was given a fine and a prison sentence. Proudhon submitted a petition to the senate, but to no avail; he was sentenced to three years' imprisonment and ordered to pay a fine of four thousand francs. His publisher received a fine as well. Proudhon again fled to Belgium, where he settled as a mathematics professor under the assumed name of Durfort.

Though Proudhon's publisher refused to accept any more of his political works, Proudhon continued to write. The last of Proudhon's great treatises, *La Guerre et la paix* (war and peace), appeared in 1861. This two-volume work explored Proudhon's view that only through war could man obtain justice and settle conflicts between nations. Proudhon also held that women must serve the state only as housewives and mothers in order to ensure a strong, virile nation. In response, Proudhon was branded a reactionary, a renegade, and a warmonger by both citizens and journalists.

Proudhon was forced to flee Belgium when his opposition to the nationalist movement, which he had expressed in various newspaper articles, created a furor. A large segment of readers objected to a statement in one of these articles that seemed to favor the annexation of Belgium by France.

After returning to France, Proudhon threw himself into his work, producing four books in only two years. This final burst of creativity was his last attempt to persuade the workers to abstain from political activity while the imperial administration continued to distort the workings of universal suffrage. *La Fédération de l'unité en Italie* (1863; the federal principle and the unity of Italy) contains what is considered by many to be the best explanation of the federal principle that has ever been written. *De la capacité politique des classes ouvrières* (1863; of the political capacity of the working classes), inspired by the workers' refusal to support the candidates of the Second Empire in the legislative election of 1863, reflects Proudhon's new confidence in the proletariat. He now believed that the workers could be a force for achieving mutualism.

Although Proudhon's mental faculties remained sharp, his health deteriorated rapidly in the last two years of his life. He died of an undetermined illness on January 19, 1865.

SIGNIFICANCE

Pierre-Joseph Proudhon was a radical thinker who was incapable of identifying completely with any single political ideology. Early in his career, Proudhon was a revolutionary who denounced the established political and economic institutions. As he grew older, he began to absorb some of those bourgeois values that he had scorned in his youth, such as the importance of the family and the inheritance of property. Thus, he is best described as a man of contradictions, a radical, a realist, and a moralist. In fact, he was viewed as a dissenter by other dissenters of the day: liberals, democrats, and republicans, as well as his fellow socialists.

Proudhon's influence on French politics extended well into the twentieth century. In the Paris Commune of 1871, Proudhon's political views carried more weight than did those of Marx. By the end of the nineteenth century, however, Proudhon's teachings seem to have been overshadowed by the Marxists. Through anarchism, Proudhon's influence was transferred to revolutionary syndicalism, which dominated French trade unionism into the twentieth century. The syndicalists favored a violent approach to the class struggle and employed the general strike as a weapon. Just before World War II, though, French trade unionism turned away from Proudhon as it began to cater to various political factions.

—*Alan Brown*

FURTHER READING

Brogan, D. W. *Proudhon*. London: H. Hamilton, 1934. A short but complete biography that includes summaries and critiques of Proudhon's work. The first half of the book does an excellent job of outlining those influences that shaped him as a writer and a thinker.

Ehrenberg, John. *Proudhon and His Age*. Atlantic Highlands, N.J.: Humanities Press, 1996. Social biography, placing Proudhon's life and thought within the context of a changing French society.

Ferrarotti, Franco. *An Invitation to Classical Sociology: Meditations on Some Great Social Thinkers*. Lanham, Md.: Lexington Books, 2003. Examines the development of sociology by analyzing the social thought of Proudhon and others who have made contributions to the field.

Hall, Constance Margaret. *The Sociology of Pierre Joseph Proudhon, 1809-1865*. New York: Philosophical Library, 1971. A penetrating analysis of Proudhon's political philosophy and the effects it had on nineteenth century France. The brief biographical sketch in the beginning of the volume is an excellent introduction to Proudhon's life and times.

Knowles, Rob. *Political Economy from Below: Economic Thought in Communitarian Anarchism, 1840-1914*. New York: Routledge, 2004. Examines the philosophy of communitarian anarchy, a form of socialism that denies the need for the state or other authority over an individual and requires the individual to live within a community of others. Knowles begins his study with the ideas of Proudhon in around 1840.

Morland, David. *Demanding the Impossible? Human Nature and Politics in Nineteenth-Century Anarchism*. London: Cassell, 1997. Examines the philosophies of Proudhon, Mikhail Bakunin, and Pyotr Alekseyevich Kropotkin to explore the relationship between anarchism's notion of human nature and its vision of a stateless society.

Ritter, Alan. *The Political Thought of Pierre-Joseph Proudhon*. Princeton, N.J.: Princeton University Press, 1969. A detailed study of Proudhon's political views that explains the historical events that spawned his ideas and describes how Proudhon's theories have been interpreted in various times. Also demonstrates how Proudhon attempted to integrate revolutionary, realistic, and moral concepts into a cohesive political theory.

Woodcock, George. *Pierre-Joseph Proudhon*. New York: Macmillan, 1956. A standard biography of Proudhon's life, combining voluminous details of his personal life with a discussion and critique of his writings and philosophical views. Provides invaluable insights into the turbulent historical period of which Proudhon was a product and shows the role that he played as a catalyst in these events. Emphasizes Proudhon's willingness to suffer as a result of his devotion to his principles.

SEE ALSO: Mikhail Bakunin; Gustave Courbet; Charles Fourier; Aleksandr Herzen; Jean Jaurès; Karl Marx; Napoleon I; Napoleon III.

RELATED ARTICLES in *Great Events from History: The Nineteenth Century, 1801-1900:* September 28, 1864: First International Is Founded; March 18-May 28, 1871: Paris Commune.

AUGUSTUS WELBY NORTHMORE PUGIN
English architect

Best remembered for designing Great Britain's Houses of Parliament, Pugin designed and built more than one hundred distinctive buildings during his short career and wrote treatises promoting the Gothic revival in church architecture.

BORN: March 1, 1812; London, England
DIED: September 14, 1852; London, England
AREA OF ACHIEVEMENT: Architecture

EARLY LIFE

Augustus Welby Northmore Pugin (pew-jihn) was the only son of Augustus Charles Pugin, a French immigrant architectural illustrator, who was fifty when his son was born, and a Calvinist mother, Catherine Welby. His parents were educators who ran a school for training architects and illustrators. In England, young Pugin attended class field trips and learned early to measure and draw buildings. He traveled with classes to France, absorbing the quiet grandeur of the medieval cathedrals. His memories of the crypts of the Continental cathedrals would later fire his interest in the Catholic faith.

When Pugin was twenty-three, his father died, leaving an unfinished manuscript, *Examples of Gothic Architecture* (1835). Pugin undertook to fulfill his father's contract for the book, demonstrating his skill and interest in architecture. His education in the field continued, without an apprenticeship. Pugin worked diligently to complete the manuscript, while traveling to study medieval art history and find clients.

Meanwhile, his domestic life inspired his building a home for his second wife, Louisa (his first wife, Anne, having died in childbirth). Saint Marie's Grange had a pleasing view and its own chapel, but it was soon too small for a growing family. When Pugin tried to sell the house, he found that his tastes were not average. The house did not imitate the fantastic castles and cottages of the day, and it took some time for his growing reputation to make the house salable.

Though reared as a Nonconformist, Pugin converted to Catholicism at the age of twenty-six, several years after the Catholic Emancipation Act. He found Roman Catholic churches in England in poor condition after the Reformation years, their beauty and solemnity sadly diminished. His estimation of the state of the faith was further diminished by the performance of ceremonies without proper attention to details. Trompe l'oeil, artificial flowers, pagan symbols, and shabby upkeep he found in-

compatible with the aims of the faith. This grave dismay at the condition of his chosen church, and his sense of the Roman Catholic Church, specifically the English branch, manifested itself in a lifelong study of the Church in the medieval world, a time when church power was at its greatest. This scholarship would be the foundation of his building, decorating, and writing endeavors.

A look of serious contemplation is apparent in a portrait of Pugin by J. R. Herbert. Framed in an ecclesiastically styled piece decorated with quatrefoils and intertwined carved ribbons bearing the legend "En Avant," Pugin's face and hands seem to float above the dark background. Thin brows and a churlish mouth on a fleshy face seem loath to let the compass and pencil in hand remain still for posing. Pugin was always eager to attack his work—at a hare's pace.

LIFE'S WORK

As far as Pugin was concerned, the baroque London church St. Mary Woolnoth could keep the hours. Pugin designed churches with bell towers, rather than clock towers, to call the faithful. He believed that the proper concern of church architecture was not the temporal function of classical architectural forms. The influence of Greek and Roman forms Pugin could only regard with contempt as pagan creations, designed for the worship of idols. Not only was the spiritual inspiration defective, but also the current vogue for Roman designs, with the low slope to the roofs, according to Pugin was unsuitable to the severities of the English climate.

In the Gothic Pugin found the "only correct expression of the faith, wants and needs of our country." Pugin applied these principles by use of local materials, scrupulous attention to church liturgy, and study of medieval Gothic churches.

August, 1839, marked the opening of Pugin's first completed church, St. Mary's, Uttoxeter. Commissioned by John Talbot, the earl of Shrewsbury, who would present Pugin with several additional commissions, the church was a monumental accomplishment for Pugin. He called it "the first Catholic structure erected in this country in strict accordance with the rules of ancient ecclesiastical architecture since the days of the pretended reformation."

Though this church earned his praise, it was not Pugin's ideal. Its success showed Pugin's ability to work gracefully within the constraints of a particular job. A simple church in comparison to his later works, it was mostly brick, though Pugin preferred stone, and it had no side aisles.

The inside was illuminated by Pugin's window of preference, a large round one over the door (usually he had to make do with the tall, pointed ones). The nave's high ceiling created a grand space separated from the chancel by a rood, or cross, which foreshadowed Pugin's use of rood screens. In the chancel, Pugin's reredos, or altar screen, featured eight angels in niches. Curtains to either side of the altar protected the clergy from breezes. To the right, Pugin included the three seats of the sedilia and sacrarium; to the left, a place for holding the consecrated hosts on Maundy Thursday.

This church, like his others, was not a mere copy of medieval designs. Pugin combined the Gothic design vocabulary, sometimes even adapting local medieval patterns, with available materials and the restraints of budget and location to create original solutions to the challenge of church building—with his particular ecclesiastical standards in mind.

For best achieving these standards in his own work, Pugin preferred St. Giles', Cheadle, another of his early churches commissioned by the earl of Shrewsbury. Metalwork, vestments, and other accessories designed by Pugin and executed at the Hardman works in Birmingham furnished the interior. Begun in 1840 and completed six years later, the church was built from local stone, with local alabaster for the altar. Massive in scale with a two-hundred-foot spire, elaborate in decorations rich with symbolism, and sumptuous in colors all the way up the walls and over the ceiling, St. Giles' was immediately impressive and distinctively Pugin's.

Whereas St. Giles' had the tower in the center of the west side with the main entrance, Pugin's last churches advocated asymmetry, with the towers standing at the end of aisles or to the side of the nave.

While experimenting with tower location, Pugin was also developing his interior aesthetics. His Irish churches, which showed a remarkable respect for indigenous architecture and materials, contrasted with the ornamentation of St. Giles'. St. Mary's Cathedral, Killarney, begun in 1842 but completed after Pugin's death with altar and reredos by his son Edward, was designed as a huge cruciform structure of stone crowned by a spire above the crossing. Irregular stones suggested a solid and immovable landmark, yet still drew the eye upward. Inside, the plain stone walls directed one to the detail in the pointed arches marching up the side aisles to the chancel.

It was not in the innovative achievements of design that Pugin found the most satisfaction. Late in his brief life, he commented that it was his writings that contributed the most to the advancement of Gothic principles. *Contrasts* (1836), his first book, subtitled "Or, A Parallel Between the Noble Edifices of the Fourteenth and Fifteenth Centuries, and Similar Buildings of the Present Day, Shewing the Present Decay of Taste," sarcastically examines the "advances" of the Reformation and finds them wanting. *The True Principles of Pointed or Christian Architecture: Set Forth in Two Lectures Delivered at St. Marie's, Oscott*, which followed in 1841, called for a rational examination of the Gothic to find it the form exclusively appropriate for ecclesiastical building. All upward design elements he found emblematic of the Resurrection, a further reason to complete spires on towers (the other being to shed precipitation). He also used the opportunity to strike another blow at classical design, "Greek temples are utterly inapplicable to the purpose of Christian churches . . . the architecture and arrangement of which have originated in their wants and purpose."

The Ecclesiological Society, later called the Cambridge Camden Society, a self-appointed hierarchy of judges on church design in England and abroad, found Pugin too broad-minded in his definition of good architecture. They contended that his principles were not exclusive to Gothic intention. In fact, a reader might be inclined to attribute Pugin's philosophy to the Bauhaus, nearly a century away: For Pugin, ". . . there should be no features about a building which are not necessary for convenience, construction, or propriety." Further,

> In pure architecture the smallest detail should *have a meaning or serve a purpose*; and even the construction itself *should vary with the material employed*, and the designs should be adapted to the material in which they are executed.

Despite the subservience of form to function and the concern for truth to materials, Pugin would not build by the glass-box standard of the twentieth century. As a Victorian, he added the caveat that there should be ornament suitable to the purpose of the building. He backed the rhetoric with dictionaries of forms suitable for decorating: *Designs for Gold and Silversmiths* (1836), *Floriated Ornament: A Series of Thirty-one Designs* (1849), and *Glossary of Ecclesiastical Ornament and Costume* (1844, 1846, 1868).

For architects merely imitating a style, a group most offensive to Pugin, a little dictionary was a dangerous thing. Decoration, he believed, should be an integral part of the structure. His warning to the imitators was little short of a moral imperative:

> The severity of Christian architecture requires a *reasonable purpose for the introduction of the smallest detail*, and daily experience proves that those who attempt this glorious style without any fixed idea of its unalterable rules, are certain to end in miserable failures.

Pugin's most famous commission, however, was not ecclesiastical. Sir Charles Barry had been impressed with Pugin's work, completing projects assigned to his father around the time of his death. When the competition for replacing the Houses of Parliament opened in 1835, Barry hired Pugin to draw his plans. After being awarded the commission, Barry hired Pugin to draw revisions, and later to design the innumerable details of decorating the interiors of the Houses. Under Barry's exacting standards, Pugin created a full range of secular furnishings with a distinctly Gothic flavor. Not only would Pugin create the design for a particular piece, but he would also detail the manufacturing specifications for John Hardman, in the case of metalwork, or other artisans for tile, wallpaper, furniture, or glass.

SIGNIFICANCE

Though the Houses of Parliament remain intact, time has undone much of the Pugin gallery. Fashion, as well as official decree, has had its way with some of his designs. Decay and demolition have obliterated others. Larger congregations called for additions to his small parish churchs, often obscuring the original lines and intention of Pugin's work. Before the beginning of the twentieth century, many of Pugin's principles were declared obsolete. Within a century of the publishing of *The True Principles of Pointed or Christian Architecture*, Pope Pius XII officially sanctioned removal of Pugin's beloved rood screens.

The Houses of Parliament and the churches that remain show Pugin's success in executing his intentions. His deep understanding of the Gothic style allowed him to transcend design by imitation. He analyzed the essence of design, participating in the canon ranging from Durandus to Charles-Édouard Le Corbusier.

The relentless pace of Pugin's life, a pace commensurate with the century after his own, combined with his pursuit of the ideals belonging to a time five centuries prior to his own, left him mad in the end, and he died insane. He had, however, the final satisfaction of being buried in his own properly designed church, St. Augustine, Ramsgate.

—Ellen Clark

FURTHER READING

Anson, Peter F. *Fashions in Church Furnishings, 1840-1940*. London: Faith Press, 1960. Begins with chapters on the early Victorian era and on Pugin. Very good source on the decoration of churches and altars in the context of the social and ecclesiastical ferment that these details sometimes stirred.

Atterbury, Paul, ed. *A. W. N. Pugin: Master of Gothic Revival*. New Haven, Conn.: Published for the Bard Graduate Center for Studies in the Decorative Arts, New York, by Yale University Press, 1995. A catalog published to accompany an exhibit at the Bard Graduate Center. Contains ten essays about Pugin, including a biographical sketch, and discussions of the Gothic sensibility, Pugin's interior design, Pugin's Catholic churches in England and Ireland, and Pugin and the Gothic Revival movement in France and North America.

Atterbury, Paul, and Clive Wainwright, eds. *Pugin: A Gothic Passion*. New Haven, Conn.: Yale University Press, 1994. A catalog published to accompany an exhibit at the Victoria and Albert Museum in London. Contains twelve essays offering a complete appraisal of Pugin's life and achievements, including discussions of his architectural style; his theater, domestic, and church architecture; and his wallpaper, furniture, and book design.

Foster, Richard. *Discovering English Churches*. New York: Oxford University Press, 1982. Covering the architectural development of parish churches from the fourth century through the Gothic revival, this book presents the church-building heritage that Pugin researched for inspiration for his designs. Valuable for its glossary of architectural and ecclesiastical terms.

Pugin, A. Welby. *An Apology for the Revival of Christian Architecture in England*. London: John Weale, 1843. Reprint. Oxford, England: St. Barnabas Press, 1969. This book is Pugin's argument for the revival of old forms and an explanation for the correct approach to employing the Gothic mode. Truly a delight as it castigates Christopher Wren and dismisses the sightseeing architects who brought back nonindigenous design from their travels.

_____. *The True Principles of Pointed or Christian Architecture: Set Forth in Two Lectures Delivered at*

St. Marie's, Oscott. London: John Weale, 1841. Reprint. New York: St. Martin's Press, 1973. Includes Pugin's engravings and his opinions on the proper manner of construction and ornamentation of buildings, especially churches.

Stanton, Phoebe. *The Gothic Revival and American Church Architecture*. Baltimore: Johns Hopkins University Press, 1968. Though the perspective is from "the Colonies," the Pugin influence in England and abroad permeates this account of nineteenth century church building. The history of the contentions between various ecclesiastical societies points out the superior achievement of a single individual who could rise above the ferment—not only in his architectural criticism but in the actual building as well.

_____. *Pugin*. New York: Viking Press, 1972. A well-organized, well-researched biography that benefits from an occasional look at Foster's glossary (see above). Nice balance between Pugin, the man, and Pugin, the author and architect. Stanton's bibliographies also recommend Sir Kenneth Clark's *The Gothic Revival* (1928), and Benjamin Ferrey's *Recollections of A. N. Welby Pugin and His Father Augustus Pugin* (1861).

Watkin, David. *Morality and Architecture*. Oxford, England: Clarendon Press, 1977. Examines the tradition of critics and designers who have aspired to the Platonic ideal in their architectural undertakings. An especially good book to consider in the light of Pugin's severe criticism of his own designs.

SEE ALSO: Sir Charles Barry; William Morris; John Nash; Sir George Gilbert Scott; George Edmund Street.

RELATED ARTICLES in *Great Events from History: The Nineteenth Century, 1801-1900:* July 14, 1833: Oxford Movement Begins; Fall, 1848: Pre-Raphaelite Brotherhood Begins.

JOSEPH PULITZER
American journalist

An icon in American journalism because of the prizes that bear his name, Pulitzer capitalized on sensationalism but at the same time combined a strong social conscience with a superb grasp of journalistic techniques. He made his New York World *the prototype of the modern American newspaper.*

BORN: April 10, 1847; Mako, Hungary
DIED: October 29, 1911; Charleston, South Carolina
AREA OF ACHIEVEMENT: Journalism

EARLY LIFE
Born in Hungary, Joseph Pulitzer (PEWL-iht-ser) was the son of Philip Pulitzer, a Magyar-Jewish grain dealer who was affluent enough to retire by 1853, when the family moved to Budapest. His mother, who had been born Louise Berger, was Austro-German and Catholic. Pulitzer and his younger brother and sister (another brother died early) were educated by private tutors; he became fluent in German and French as well as his native Hungarian.

By the age of seventeen, Pulitzer was ready to make his own way. Brilliant, independent, and intensely ambitious, he first sought fame in the military. Having been rejected for enlistment by several European armies—his eyesight was poor—he was approached by Union army recruiting agents, who were considerably less selective. Thus it was that Pulitzer came to the United States and, in September, 1864, enlisted in the Lincoln Cavalry. His military career was short, undistinguished, and unhappy; discharged in July, 1865, with little money and no immediate prospects, he settled in St. Louis, Missouri, where there was a large German community.

Photographs of the beardless, bespectacled young Pulitzer show a profile seemingly tailor-made for the caricaturist: a prominent, beaky nose and an up-pointed, witchlike chin. At six feet two and a half inches, he was a tall man for his time, slender and ungainly. When he arrived in St. Louis, he spoke only the most rudimentary English. Nevertheless, his exceptional abilities and his capacity for hard work were soon noticed, and, after a series of subsistence jobs, he was hired as a reporter for the *Westliche Post*, an influential German-language paper with a strong reform bent. This association provided Pulitzer's entrée into politics, and he was elected to the Missouri state legislature in 1869. His financial acumen soon became evident as well, and by his mid-twenties he was able to enjoy a long vacation in Europe.

By the time of his marriage, in June, 1878 (his bride, the beautiful Kate Davis, was a distant cousin of the former president of the Confederacy), Pulitzer had achieved the kind of success that most immigrants could only dream of, but the direction that his life would take was not yet clear. Maintaining a desultory law practice, he continued to take an active interest in politics, but, impatient, imperious, he was ill suited to the demands of office. Later in 1878, however, he made what proved to be a decisive choice of vocation.

LIFE'S WORK

It was in December of 1878 that Pulitzer, acting through an intermediary, purchased at auction in St. Louis the bankrupt *Evening Dispatch*. The paper's sixteen-year history had been marked by failure, but it did possess a Western Associated Press franchise—a consideration that prompted the publisher of a recently established rival paper, the *Post*, to propose a merger exactly as Pulitzer had planned. For the first issue of the *Post and Dispatch* (soon to become simply the *Post-Dispatch*), Pulitzer wrote an editorial that ringingly asserted the paper's independence from special interests and its dedication to reform:

> The POST and DISPATCH will serve no party but the people; will be no organ of "Republicanism," but the organ of truth; will follow no caucuses [*sic*] but its own convictions; will not support the "Administration," but criticise it; will oppose all frauds and shams wherever and whatever they are; will advocate principles and ideas rather than prejudices and partisanship.

Although Pulitzer's great achievements are associated with New York, he laid the foundation for those achievements in St. Louis in the years from 1878 to 1883 with the *Post-Dispatch*. As publisher and editor, he was involved in every phase of the paper's operation. He was an editor of genius, as his memos to his staff attest: Even in the twenty-first century, his notes could serve as a course in newspaper journalism. Always a shrewd judge of talent, he hired the gifted editor of the *Baltimore Gazette*, John A. Cockerill, to serve as managing editor of the *Post-Dispatch*; Cockerill later followed him to New York.

Pulitzer's ability to find good employees and treat them well played an integral part in his success: The average salary of the reporters for the *Post-Dispatch* was the highest of any paper in the country, and at a time when vacations were a luxury, every employee of the *Post-Dispatch* enjoyed a paid two-week vacation each summer. Pulitzer was, then, an inspiring leader and a relatively enlightened employer, but working for him was

Joseph Pulitzer. (Library of Congress)

difficult: He had a pronounced dictatorial streak, which became much stronger as he grew older, and he could be ruthless in his judgments.

Having developed in St. Louis the brand of journalism that was to make him the most influential newspaperman of his time, Pulitzer was ready to move to New York—where, ironically, his brother Albert was prospering with the *Morning Journal*, which he had founded in 1882. (The arrival of another Pulitzer was not welcomed by Albert; never close, the brothers were permanently estranged thereafter.) The opportunity came in 1883, when Pulitzer bought the failing *New York World* from financier Jay Gould for $346,000; the deal was closed not long after Pulitzer's thirty-sixth birthday.

Although a young man, Pulitzer was in poor health: His eyesight was failing, and he suffered from a nervous disorder. (In a later age, he would probably have been diagnosed as manic depressive.) Moreover, the continuing profitability of the *Post-Dispatch* notwithstanding, in purchasing the *New York World* he had incurred an enormous debt. Such were the unpromising circumstances in which Pulitzer entered the arena of New York journalism, yet within a short time his *New York World* reigned supreme: The paper that sold fifteen thousand copies daily in 1883 sold almost fifteen million daily in 1898.

Great as his success was, Pulitzer was never fully able to savor it. In 1890, still in his early forties, he was compelled by blindness and the worsening condition of his nerves to give up firsthand supervision of the *New York World* although he kept in close touch with his editors, firing off innumerable memos.

Pulitzer's mood swings and other manifestations of his illness made him a difficult companion for his wife and their children (four daughters, one of whom died in infancy and another of whom, her father's favorite, died at seventeen, and three sons, one of whom, Joseph Pulitzer, Jr., became a noted newspaperman in his own right, despite a conspicuous lack of paternal confidence in his abilities). Pulitzer spent much of the time in later years traveling; near the end of his life, his preferred residence was his magnificently appointed yacht *Liberty*, where, as was his custom, newspapers, magazines, and books were read to him in great abundance and where distractions and annoyances were minimized. It was on the *Liberty* that he died, on October 29, 1911. Among the provisions in his will was the establishment of the Pulitzer Prizes, annual awards in journalism and arts and letters; also included was a one-million-dollar bequest to the soon-to-be-opened Columbia School of Journalism, which he had endowed in 1903.

SIGNIFICANCE

In countless ways, Pulitzer caught the democratic, egalitarian spirit of America, an achievement reflected in the enormous influence of his journalistic style. The *New York World* was a pioneer in increased sports coverage, especially of boxing and baseball. People from every walk of life—tradesmen and judges, firemen and Brooklyn belles—were featured in line-drawn portraits (photojournalism did not begin until the Spanish-American War), often accompanied by brief biographical sketches. That American institution, the Sunday funnies, can also be traced to the *New York World*, where, in 1894, the first colored comic strip appeared.

Pulitzer was able to accomplish so much because, to an extraordinary degree, his own character mirrored all the contradictions that distinguished late nineteenth century America. Genuinely idealistic, Pulitzer crusaded against widespread corruption and injustice, bringing to public attention, for example, the inhuman conditions in which many immigrants were forced to live and work. Certainly this sense of conscience was one key to the *New York World*'s success.

At the same time, however, Pulitzer was a master of sensationalism. Others before him had used lurid stories of crime, sex, and disaster to attract readers, but Pulitzer took this material and, with bold headlines, illustrations (diagrams of murder scenes were particularly popular), and first-rate reporting, made it both appealing and acceptable to a wide range of readers. Indeed, Pulitzer rarely challenged the essentially conservative values of his readers (values that he largely shared), whether the subject was women's rights or the plight of the unemployed.

Pulitzer's legacy is most visible in the prizes that bear his name, synonymous with excellence in journalism. Less obvious but more pervasive is his impact on the way in which Americans get the news, not only in the morning paper but also on television, where sensationalism with a social conscience has enjoyed great success.

—*John Wilson*

FURTHER READING

Barrett, James Wyman. *Joseph Pulitzer and His "World."* New York: Vanguard Press, 1941. An anecdotal biography by the last city editor of the *New York World*. Although the focus is on Pulitzer, the last three chapters follow the fate of the *New York World* after his death to the paper's last issue in 1931. Valuable for its insider's view but rambling and undocumented.

Brian, Denis. *Pulitzer: A Life*. New York: John Wiley & Sons, 2001. The only comprehensive biography since Swanberg (see below). Relies heavily upon information contained in earlier works.

Juergens, George. *Joseph Pulitzer and the "New York World."* Princeton, N.J.: Princeton University Press, 1966. The best single book on Pulitzer's "new journalism." Concentrates on the crucial years from 1883 to 1885, though later developments are also noted. Juergens's approach is thematic rather than chronological; he provides a clear, objective, well-documented analysis of Pulitzer's journalistic techniques and their revolutionary impact.

King, Homer W. *Pulitzer's Prize Editor: A Biography of John A. Cockerill, 1845-1896*. Durham, N.C.: Duke University Press, 1965. A colorful account of Cockerill's career before, during, and after his tenure with Pulitzer. Perhaps exaggerates Cockerill's contributions to Pulitzer's success but offers a needed corrective to other accounts.

Rammelkamp, Julian S. *Pulitzer's "Post-Dispatch,"* *1878-1883*. Princeton, N.J.: Princeton University

Press, 1967. Stresses the significance of Pulitzer's St. Louis years, scanted in most studies. A valuable, well-documented study, as much social history (particularly concerned with the growth of the middle-class reform movement) as journalistic history.

Seitz, Don C. *Joseph Pulitzer: His Life and Letters.* New York: Simon & Schuster, 1924. Badly dated, this intimate portrait by Pulitzer's longtime business manager nevertheless remains indispensable; all subsequent biographers have drawn on it.

Swanberg, W. A. *Pulitzer.* New York: Charles Scribner's Sons, 1967. Popular biography, marred by some irritating mannerisms, but the only full-scale life of Pulitzer since Barrett's book of 1941. Generally balanced and well researched, drawing extensively on the Pulitzer papers at Columbia University and the Library of Congress.

Turner, Hy B. *When Giants Ruled: The Story of Park Row, New York's Great Newspaper Street.* New York: Fordham University Press, 1999. This history of the New York City newspaper business during the mid-nineteenth and early twentieth centuries includes information about Pulitzer and the other publishers of the era. Chronicles the newspaper circulation wars and the contributions of reporters, illustrators, and cartoonists.

Wittke, Carl. *The German-Language Press in America.* Lexington: University Press of Kentucky, 1957. Mentions Pulitzer only in passing but provides a detailed account of the milieu in which he made his beginning as a journalist and in which his political views were formed.

SEE ALSO: James Gordon Bennett; Mary Baker Eddy; Horace Greeley; Edward Wyllis Scripps; John Walter II.

RELATED ARTICLES in *Great Events from History: The Nineteenth Century, 1801-1900:* October 28, 1886: Statue of Liberty Is Dedicated; 1895: Rise of Yellow Journalism; 1895-1898: Hearst-Pulitzer Circulation War.

E. B. PUSEY
English religious leader

Pusey was a leader of the Oxford Movement to revive Anglo-Catholic doctrines and practices in the life of the Church of England, a defender of the Bible against attacks from higher criticism, and a distinguished scholar in Semitic languages.

BORN: August 22, 1800; Pusey, Berkshire, England
DIED: September 16, 1882; Ascot Priory, Berkshire, England
ALSO KNOWN AS: Edward Bouverie Pusey (full name)
AREA OF ACHIEVEMENT: Religion and theology

EARLY LIFE

Edward Bouverie Pusey (PEW-zih) was born into an English family with French Huguenot roots. His father, Philip Bouverie, assumed the name Pusey when he succeeded to the Pusey manor in 1789. Edward's paternal grandfather was the first Viscount Folkestone. Pusey received his early education at a school in Mitchum, Surrey, operated by Anglican clergyman Richard Roberts. From there he went to Eton in 1812, where he studied under the tutorial guidance of Edward Maltby, who later became bishop of Durham. In 1819, he enrolled at Christ Church College, Oxford, where he earned high distinction in classical studies. In 1824, Pusey obtained a fellowship at Oriel College, Oxford, evidently in recognition of his outstanding scholarship. His Latin-language essay on the colonial expansion of ancient Greece and Rome won for him a university award that enhanced his reputation for erudition.

Pusey received a bachelor's degree in 1822 and a master's degree in 1825, and he spent the periods of June to September, 1825, and June, 1826, to July, 1827, in Germany at the universities of Göttingen, Berlin, and Bonn. While in that country he studied under some of Europe's most illustrious theologians, all but one of whom espoused the higher critical approach to the Bible and a rationalist interpretation of historic Christian doctrine. Pusey's exposure to this teaching came as a result of contacts with Friedrich Schleiermacher, Johann August Wilhelm Neander, Johann Gottfried Eichorn, and other noteworthy academicians.

Although Pusey established a cordial relationship with some of his German professors, and though he proved to be a brilliant student in their classes, he rejected higher criticism and became an outspoken defender of traditional Christian doctrines. The teaching of Ernst Wilhelm Hengstenberg, a professor at Berlin, seems to have encouraged Pusey to maintain his belief in the historical accuracy and divine authority of the Scriptures. Hengstenberg, once a rationalist himself, had begun moving toward pietism when Pusey met him, and both eventually became famous champions of orthodoxy, Hengstenberg in Lutheranism, his pupil in Anglicanism.

While in Germany Pusey mastered the Hebrew, Syriac, and Arabic languages, which equipped him well for work as an exegetical commentator on various books of the Old Testament.

Soon after returning to England, Pusey was married and was ordained a member of the clergy; he published *An Historical Enquiry into the Probable Causes of the Rationalist Character Lately Predominant in the Theology of Germany* in 1828. In this book the author sounded an alarm to fellow Anglicans to guard their church against German teachings that, he feared, might infect England and impair the religious health of its national church. Perhaps because of his awkward style, some readers misunderstood the book and contended mistakenly that Pusey was actually a rationalist himself. Pusey was never satisfied with this book, and later in life he took steps to prevent anyone from reprinting it.

LIFE'S WORK

The year 1828 was a turning point in Pusey's career, when the duke of Wellington nominated him Regius Professor of Hebrew at Oxford, a position he retained until he died. By 1828, he had established his reputation through his studies in Germany and by his learned publications. As Regius Professor he continued the work of his celebrated predecessor, Alexander Nicoll, in collecting and editing Arabic manuscripts, and he taught Hebrew language classes with the devotion of a theologian dedicated to the exposition of the Old Testament. Pusey's students were numerous, and many were preparing for the ministry. He had a particular concern to convey to them his own confidence in the inspiration and reliability of the Bible.

In addition to his expert teaching, Pusey wrote extensively and published two profound commentaries on selected Old Testament books. *Daniel the Prophet* appeared in 1864, and *The Minor Prophets with a Commentary Explanatory and Practical* was published between 1860 and 1877. Both of these works reflect the author's staunch conservatism in doctrine and his aggressive defense of the Scriptures against higher criticism.

Pusey defended the authenticity of Daniel against scholars who assigned the authorship of the book to the Maccabean era. He contended that it is the work of the sixth century B.C.E. prophet whose name it bears, and he related that he had selected this Old Testament book as a battleground on which he wanted to fight those who contended for the later date. In the course of stating his case, Pusey argued that the critical method of Bible study arose from the disbelief of its exponents. He wrote that he hoped to "shake the confidence of the young in their would-be misleaders. . . . Disbelief ha[s] been the parent, not the offspring of their criticism." In *The Minor Prophets*, he interpreted the bizarre experience of Jonah in the belly of a fish as literal history, and he accepted at face value Christ's claim that the entombment of Jonah in the sea monster prophesied his own burial and bodily resurrection.

The Hebrew Psalter was one of Pusey's favorite portions of the Bible. He studied the Psalms devotedly and entered numerous marginal notes, many of which are cross-references to other texts in the Bible. He intended to revise the King James Version, and for that purpose he used one special copy of the Scriptures in which he inserted corrections and emendations to the text. He completed the revisions in Job and Psalms and did extensive work on the Minor Prophets and the Pentateuch. Pusey did not, however, complete this project or publish what he had finished. In his will he expressed doubts about his textual revisions and directed that his work not be published. He began his effort to revise the King James Version in 1827, but after 1833 he directed his energies to other projects, principally to the Oxford Movement.

The Oxford Movement arose in response to the spread of skepticism that had originated in the eighteenth century and that had prompted considerable interest, especially among Liberal politicians, to reduce the wealth and privileges of the Church of England. Its adherents opposed liberalism—by which they meant materialism, rationalism, indifference to religious doctrines, and state control of the Anglican Church. Oxford Movement leaders decried Evangelicalism, Methodism, and those vigorous Protestants who vociferously denounced the Papacy.

The movement began formally in 1833, when John Keble, a renowned religious poet associated with Oriel College, preached a sermon subsequently published as *National Apostasy, Considered in a Sermon Preached in St. Mary's* (1833). Keble called fellow Anglicans to rise to the defense of their church and its rights that the Liberal government threatened to violate by reducing the number of bishops and exerting increasing control over ecclesiastical affairs. Soon able preachers and scholars from Oxford University began publishing *Tracts for the Times*, pamphlets designed to effect wide dissemination of their concerns. John Henry Newman became the most famous of these Tractarians, and Pusey adhered to the movement late in 1834 or early in 1835, probably at the urging of his friend Newman.

Pusey feared that the political victory that the Liberals had secured in 1832 would not only threaten the structure of the Anglican Church but also encourage the spread of indifference toward Christianity in general. His first written contribution to the Oxford Movement was a treatise on baptism, which appeared in three portions as tracts sixty-seven, sixty-eight, and sixty-nine. After the issuing of these compositions, the tracts became essays of great substance rather than simple pamphlets. Newman rejoiced at Pusey's contributions and hailed his adherence to the movement as greatly enhancing its credibility.

As a Tractarian, Pusey wrote extensively on theological themes. In *Scriptural Views of Holy Baptism* (1836), he argued that this sacrament unites one with Christ through regeneration, an interpretation widely held by High Church Anglicans but rejected by most members of the Evangelical wing of the Church of England. Although there was much criticism of his position, Pusey's teaching on baptism eventually gained broad acceptance within his church.

Ever since the Church of England had broken with the Papacy in the sixteenth century, its scholars had been divided in their understanding of the sacrament of the Eucharist. Pusey set forth an Anglo-Catholic view of this matter in a sermon preached at Oxford in May, 1843. He affirmed the Real Presence of Christ and portrayed the Eucharist as a means of comfort to penitents.

Although he seems to have remained within the borders of Anglican doctrine, Dr. G. Fausett, professor of divinity, charged that the sermon contained heresy. The vice chancellor of the university then initiated proceedings against Pusey. A committee of six theologians examined the case, and Fausett was one of the six. The university statute governing such matters did not guarantee the accused a hearing, and Pusey did not receive one. The committee concluded that he had violated the doctrines of the Anglican Church, and the vice chancellor suspended him from preaching at the university for two years. Pusey received no formal notice about the identity of his accuser but learned it at second hand. University officials did not reveal exactly what were the offensive

portions of the sermon, and even William Ewart Gladstone and Justice John Taylor Coleridge could not obtain an explanation on his behalf.

Pusey tried to show that his understanding of the Eucharist concurred with that of early church fathers, but his opponents dismissed that as advocacy of transubstantiation, which he really did not espouse. Pusey believed the presence of Christ in the sacrament to be a mystery beyond explanation.

Because High Church Anglicans in general and Oxford Movement leaders in particular believed that the Bible should be interpreted with reference to the fathers, ancient creeds, and liturgical traditions, Pusey initiated work on *Library of Fathers of the Holy Catholic Church Anterior to the Division of East and West* (1838-1885), a project that extended eventually to forty-eight volumes. Keble and Newman were joint editors. Although Pusey had full confidence in the truth of Scripture, he maintained that the Church must preserve ancient doctrines against modern private interpretations that, he believed, were the besetting sins of the Evangelicals both within and without the Church of England. He appreciated the Evangelicals' reverence for the Bible, but he disliked their rejection of Catholic sacramental teachings. Pusey, for example, accused them of rationalism in their denial of baptismal regeneration.

Because the Oxford Movement stressed the Catholicity of Anglican beliefs so vigorously, its leaders were often accused of being Roman Catholics at heart, as attacks on Pusey's view of the Eucharist attest. Suspicions about Romanist leanings were not entirely unfounded, for in 1845 John Henry Newman left the Oxford Movement to join the papal church. Pusey, however, despite his friend's efforts to woo him, remained a convinced Anglican.

Pusey disliked the great veneration for the Virgin Mary in Catholicism, and he regarded it as a major barrier to reunion between the Roman and Anglican churches. He tried to dissuade people from following Newman's example, claiming that the Church of England preserved the true doctrine of the sacraments and apostolic succession of bishops and genuine Catholic teachings. He published *The Doctrine of the Real Presence* (1855) and *The Real Presence* (1857) to support his contention.

Despite his defense of the Anglican Church against the claims of Rome, Pusey recognized that the two churches had much in common, and he wished that they could be reunited. He expressed this desire in *An Eirenicon* (1865-1876). There he cited Roman Catholic teachings about purgatory and indulgences, together with the position of the Virgin Mary, as chief obstacles to re-union. After Vatican Council I promulgated the dogma of papal infallibility in 1870, Pusey lost all hope for official reconciliation with Rome.

Although the Evangelicals often accused Pusey of Romanism, he maintained a remarkably generous attitude toward them. Whereas Newman and other spokespeople for the Oxford Movement strongly disdained the Protestant Reformers of the sixteenth century, Pusey was restrained in his criticisms of their teachings. When the Evangelicals proposed erecting a martyrs' memorial in Oxford to honor the reformers, he supported the effort, even though his colleagues in the movement regarded it as a device to embarrass them. Pusey's rather kindly disposition toward the Protestants is especially noteworthy when one realizes that he founded an order of Anglican nuns and composed the first manual to guide Anglican clergymen when hearing confessions.

The leaders of the Oxford Movement did not extol learning for its own sake but were scholar-zealots committed to a cause. They defended a definite body of doctrine that, they believed, constituted the heart of Christianity, as the career of Pusey illustrates. Pusey was the most erudite advocate of this view. He seems never to have doubted what he believed, and he had little patience with Christians who lacked religious fervor. He did, however, sympathize with people who, because of intellectual problems, did not believe. He had great concern for the spiritual well-being of the wealthy, whom he often reminded of their obligation to aid the poor, and his order of nuns became famous for its ministry to the poverty-stricken residents of urban areas.

SIGNIFICANCE

E. B. Pusey strove valiantly to combat secularism in an increasingly materialist society. Among Oxford Movement leaders he was probably the most independent thinker. In contrast to Newman, who wanted the Anglican Church to elect its own bishops, Pusey appealed to the Crown to prevent unworthy men from becoming prelates. At first, he did not have episcopal approval for his plan to establish a religious order of nuns, but that did not deter him. Unlike others in the Oxford Movement who, because of subscription to apostolic succession, stressed obedience to bishops, he sometimes acted on his own without much regard for episcopal authority.

Although Pusey's resistance to higher criticism and his doctrinal conservatism did not prevail in the Church of England, his view of the sacraments, his order of nuns,

and his espousal of Catholic traditions have remained potent influences in the worldwide Anglican communion.

—James E. McGoldrick

FURTHER READING

Brilioth, Yngve. *The Anglican Revival: Studies in the Oxford Movement*. London: Longmans, Green, 1925. Reprint. 1975. This is still one of the most reliable surveys of the movement, one that no student of religion in the Victorian era can afford to ignore.

Brose, Olive. *Church and Parliament*. Stanford, Calif.: Stanford University Press, 1959. This basically political account helps one to place the Oxford Movement within the context of English Liberal reformist thinking and legislation.

Chadwick, Owen. *The Mind of the Oxford Movement*. London: A. and C. Black, 1960.

_____. *The Victorian Church*. 2 vols. New York: Oxford University Press, 1966. Chadwick's two works are masterpieces of thorough scholarship and readable prose. They are invaluable for this subject.

Church, Richard William. *The Oxford Movement, Twelve Years, 1833-1845*. New York: Macmillan, 1891. Reprint. Edited by Geoffrey Best. Chicago: University of Chicago Press, 1970. This reprint brings to modern readers the insights of one who participated in the movement and wrote the first account of its founding and early history. Although the author wrote as an enthusiast, he was duly critical of his colleagues.

Elder, Gregory P. *Chronic Vigour: Darwin, Anglicans, Catholics, and the Development of a Doctrine of Providential Evolution*. Lanham, Md.: University Press of America, 1996. Examines the Anglican clergymen who knew and endorsed Darwin's theory of evolution, and altered their theology in response to it. The first chapter of the book discusses Pusey's connection to Darwin.

Fairweather, Eugene. *The Oxford Movement*. New York: Oxford University Press, 1964. A profound analysis by a skilled church historian.

Liddon, H. P. *Life of Edward Bouverie Pusey*. Edited by John O. Johnston and Robert J. Wilson. 4 vols. London: Longmans, Green, 1893-1897. Despite its age and the author's great devotion to Pusey, this remains the standard biography.

Newman, John Henry. *Apologia Pro Vita Sua*. London: Longman, Green, 1864. Rev. ed. Edited by Daniel M. O'Connell. Chicago: Loyola University Press, 1930. An indispensable primary source for the careers of both Newman and Pusey.

Pusey, Edward Bouverie. *Daniel the Prophet*. London: John Henry and James Parker, 1864. Reprint. New York: Funk and Wagnalls, 1885.

_____. *Occasional Sermons Selected from Published Sermons of E. B. Pusey*. London: Walter Smith, 1884. Specimens of Pusey's pulpit work that show that he was a rather awkward preacher but one who proclaimed his message with great fervor.

_____, ed. *The Minor Prophets with Commentary Explanatory and Practical*. 6 vols. Oxford, England: Parker, 1860-1877. Reprint. 2 vols. New York: Funk and Wagnalls, 1885. This effort offers the best evidence of the amazing erudition of Pusey and shows his method as an apologist for traditional beliefs, theological and biblical.

SEE ALSO: Thomas Arnold; William Ewart Gladstone; Frederic Harrison; John Henry Newman; Friedrich Schleiermacher; Duke of Wellington.

RELATED ARTICLES in *Great Events from History: The Nineteenth Century, 1801-1900:* July 14, 1833: Oxford Movement Begins; October 9, 1845: Newman Becomes a Roman Catholic.

ALEXANDER PUSHKIN
Russian poet

Revered by generations of Russian writers, Pushkin left his greatest legacy in his poetry. His literary memory is compounded by the fact that his works inspired internationally celebrated operas, ballets, and films.

BORN: June 6, 1799; Moscow, Russia
DIED: February 10, 1837; St. Petersburg, Russia
ALSO KNOWN AS: Alexander Sergeyevich Pushkin (full name)
AREA OF ACHIEVEMENT: Literature

EARLY LIFE

Alexander Pushkin (PEWSH-kyihn) was the son of a tenant of a ministerial steward and a mother who was descended from an Abyssinian who had become the adopted godson and personal secretary of Peter the Great. Sergey Lvovich, Alexander's father, was more interested in drawing rooms and theaters than in his estate, which he left to the mismanagement of his wife, Nadezhda Osipovna Hannibal.

With curly, chestnut-colored hair, Alexander was a sallow, thick-lipped, and dreamy-eyed child. Neglected by his parents, who preferred his younger brother Leo and his elder sister Olga, he turned to his nanny, Arina Rodionovna, who regaled him with legends and songs about wizards, princesses, knights-errant, and elves. He also enjoyed the company of his maternal grandmother, Marya Hannibal, and it was at her country estate that Pushkin learned to love his native language.

As soon as he was old enough to read, he had a number of tutors, but he was a poor student. In 1811, he entered the lyceum in Tsarskoye Selo, a school instituted and sponsored by imperial decree, where he studied everything from religion and philosophy to swimming and horsemanship. At the age of fourteen, Pushkin published his first poem, "To a Poet-Friend," in the well-respected *European Herald*. His official entry into the literary world occurred on January 8, 1815, when, as part of his qualifying examination for the upper school, he recited his own poem "Recollections of Tsarskoye Selo" before distinguished guests. His remarkable use of language, rhythm, onomatopoeia, and references to myth established him as a prodigy.

During 1817, Pushkin's last year at school, he befriended hussars stationed at Tsarskoye Selo and joined them in bouts of drinking and gambling. After his graduation, he was appointed to the Ministry of Foreign Affairs, but in 1818 he joined the Society of the Green Lamp, a literary club with liberal political leanings. The next year, he was suspected of collaborating with revolutionaries. Further complications arose with the publication in 1820 of his long poem *Ruslan i Lyudmila* (English translation, 1936). This poem created enormous controversy, winning praise for its epic quality but drawing condemnation for, among other things, its atheism. Pushkin was forced into exile on Ascension Day, May 6, 1820. He spent the next few years in the south of Russia, especially in Yekaterinenshtadt, the Caucasus, and Kishinev.

LIFE'S WORK

Befriended by Nicholas Raevsky, the younger son of a general celebrated for his exploits in the Napoleonic Wars, Pushkin was invited to holiday with the Raevsky family in the Caucasus, which fueled his imagination for his poem *Kavkazskiy plennik* (1822; *The Prisoner of the Caucasus*, 1895). Raevsky's elder brother Alexander was the model for the poet's sneering Mephistophelean hero in "The Demon" of the same year.

As his literary fame increased, so did his social notoriety. He continued to be extravagant in misconduct, surviving a duel against an officer whom he had accused of cheating at baccarat and using the incident in his short story "Vystrel" (1831; "The Shot"). Pushkin finally resigned from the government in 1824, but the emperor transferred him to the Pushkin estate in the deserted province of Mikhailovka, near Pskov. There he lived in sparse, unheated quarters, without books or his customary amusements. He wrote to friends requesting copies of works by William Shakespeare, Friedrich Schiller, Johann Wolfgang von Goethe, George Gordon, Lord Byron, Miguel de Cervantes, Dante, Petrarch, John Milton, and Tacitus.

Engrossed in his own idiosyncratic activities, Pushkin neglected the family farm. During this period, he completed *Tsygany* (1827; *The Gypsies*, 1957), a verse tale based on his experiences in Bessarabia, a story of defeated egotism. Strong on description, it had affected, bombastic dialogue. *Graf Nulin* (1827; *Count Nulin*,

Alexander Pushkin. (Library of Congress)

1972), a thin, rather banal response to Shakespeare's *The Rape of Lucrece* (1594), shocked readers with its sexual frankness. Pushkin wrote many lyric poems in the same year, including "André Chenier," about the poet-martyr of the French Revolution. Its theme of heroic independence was regarded suspiciously by government censors, who deleted all references to the revolution. Pushkin's political consciousness was further exercised in his drama *Boris Godunov* (1831; English translation, 1918), a powerful story of ambition, murder, and retribution. Never produced in Pushkin's own time, the play was savaged by critics, who thought it massively disorganized because it shifted focus from Czar Boris to the Impostor Dmitry.

This professional setback was coupled with trouble ensuing from Pushkin's friendship with several conspirators in the Decembrist Revolt on December 4, 1825, against Czar Nicholas I, who had ascended the throne after Alexander I had died suddenly in November. Sick with fury and shame for having had to plead for compassion over his friendship with a key conspirator, Pushkin was escorted to the emperor, who appointed himself the writer's censor and commanded the court to take note of the new, repentant Pushkin.

In Moscow, Pushkin lived with a friend and was invited to salons and parties of the famous, but the secret police watched him diligently. The czar wanted the poet supervised continually and tested Pushkin's loyalty and liberalism by both subtle and unsubtle means. Pushkin grew tired of Moscow and left for St. Petersburg, where he saw little of his parents. He was investigated rather belatedly for his authorship of *Gavriiliada* (1822; *Gabriel: A Poem*, 1926) and later was reprimanded for traveling without authorization.

Pushkin's writing remained calm and controlled, though his life was not. In October, 1828, he began *Poltava* (1829; English translation, 1936), a poem on Peter the Great. Also that year, his beloved nanny Rodionovna died in St. Petersburg, and he met sixteen-year-old Natalya Goncharov in Moscow in the winter, falling victim to her youthful beauty. Natalya was to be his victimizing "madonna," for she was a vain, shallow creature. He became engaged to Natalya on May 6, 1830, but a cholera epidemic forced him to Boldino, where he composed *Povesti Belkina* (1831; *The Tales of Belkin*, 1947), his first sustained fictional work, and almost completed his masterpiece *Evgeny Onegin* (1825-1833; *Eugene Onegin*, 1881), which he had started in 1823.

Written as a novel in sonnet sequences, *Eugene Onegin* was modern in its devastating sociological criticism

PUSHKIN'S MAJOR WORKS

POETRY

1820	*Ruslan i Lyudmila* (*Ruslan and Liudmila*, 1936)
1822	*Gavriiliada* (*Gabriel: A Poem*, 1926)
1822	*Kavkazskiy plennik* (*The Prisoner of the Caucasus*, 1895)
1827	*Bakhchisaraiskiy fontan* (*The Fountain of Bakhchisarai*, 1849)
1827	*Graf Nulin* (*Count Nulin*, 1972)
1827	*Tsygany* (*The Gypsies*, 1957)
1829	*Poltava* (English translation, 1936)
1833	*Domik v Kolomne* (*The Little House at Kolomna*, 1977)
1833	*Skazka o mertvoy tsarevne* (*The Tale of the Dead Princess*, 1924)
1833	*Skazka o rybake ir rybke* (*The Tale of the Fisherman and the Fish*, 1926)
1833	*Skazka o tsare Saltane* (*The Tale of Tsar Saltan*, 1950)
1834	*Skazka o zolotom petushke* (*The Tale of the Golden Cockerel*, 1918)
1837	*Medniy vsadnik* (*The Bronze Horseman*, 1899)

FICTION

Years in left column are earliest dates of production or publication.

1825-1832, 1833	*Evgeny Onegin* (*Eugene Onegin*, 1881)
1828-1841	*Arap Petra velikogo* (*Peter the Great's Negro*, 1896)
1834	*Kirdzhali* (English translation, 1896)
1834	*Pikovaya dama* (*The Queen of Spades*, 1858)
1836	*Kapitanskaya dochka* (*The Captain's Daughter*, 1846)
1841	*Dubrovsky* (English translation, 1892)
1841	*Yegipetskiye nochi* (*Egyptian Nights*, 1896)
1857	*Istoriya sela Goryukhina* (*History of the Village of Goryukhino*, 1966)

DRAMA

1831	*Boris Godunov* (English translation, 1918)
1852	*Skupoy rytsar* (*The Covetous Knight*, 1925)
1839	*Kamyenny gost* (*The Stone Guest*, 1936)
1832	*Motsart i Salyeri* (*Mozart and Salieri*, 1920)
1833	*Pir vo vryemya chumy* (*The Feast in Time of the Plague*, 1925)
1838	*Rusalka* (*The Water Nymph*, 1924)

finities with such figures as Goethe's Werner and Byron's Childe Harold, and he stands as the first hero of Russian realism.

Pushkin's marriage to Natalya in September, 1831, was followed by a move to St. Petersburg, where he served as historiographer and where his mounting debts compounded his anxieties. The next five years were solid successes as far as his literary achievements were concerned. In 1837, he was elected to the Russian Academy.

The final four years of Pushkin's life marked a transition from poetry to prose. In 1834, he produced *Skazka o zolotom petushke* (*The Tale of the Golden Cockerel*, 1918) in verse, but he found more renown with the novella *Pikovaya dama* (1834; *The Queen of Spades*, 1896), which bore comparison with *Eugene Onegin*. Its themes of destruction, death, and madness were underlined by subtle symbolism in a manner reminiscent of his great French contemporary Stendhal.

Pushkin's final masterpiece was *Kapitanskaya dochka* (1836; *The Captain's Daughter*, 1846), a historical novella set during the period of the Pugachev Rebellion. The hero is a young officer loyal to the queen who runs the gamut of happiness, pain, and vindication both in love and in honor. In this work, Pushkin conjoins story and history, fashioning a thoroughly credible romance while also creating an interesting portrait of the rebel leader Emelyan Ivanovich Pugachev by presenting him through the sensitivities of less important characters. The alternation of scenes of love and domestic calm with scenes of battle and camp precedes Leo Tolstoy's orchestration of similar scenes in *Voyna i mir* (1865-1869; *War and Peace*, 1886), although Pushkin's scale is smaller.

Despite his literary prowess, Pushkin found himself caught up in a spiral of destructive passions. His wife, though by now the mother of his four children, was still a

amid the doomed Romanticism of the central characters. Technically, the story was in eight cantos, each stanza in four-foot iambics, alternating between masculine and feminine rhymes. It was the first occasion that Pushkin had used a regular stanzaic arrangement for a long poem, and the "Onegin" stanza with its final rhymed couplet was probably derived from Byron's *ottava rima*. It was the figure of Onegin, however, that sealed the importance of the work, for the melancholy Romantic had af-

flirt. Besides being the emperor's special interest, she became the object of admiration of Baron Georges-Charles D'Anthès, the adopted godson of Baron Heckeren. On November 4, 1836, Pushkin received an anonymous "diploma," designating him a member of the "Order of Cuckolds." In response, Pushkin challenged D'Anthès to a duel, which was avoided by skillful manipulation on the part of Heckeren. On his friend's advice, D'Anthès married someone else and tried unsuccessfully to make peace with Pushkin. Matters came to a head with a duel on February 8, 1837, in which D'Anthès suffered a superficial rib injury while Pushkin was mortally wounded. Howling in agony, Pushkin turned to his wife to absolve her of any guilt for his death. He died on February 10.

SIGNIFICANCE

There is no critical disagreement over Alexander Pushkin's legacy to succeeding generations of Russian writers in prose and poetry. His mature work drew on a variety of genres and influences, and he can no more be limited by the term "Romantic" than the term "realist." He was not a rebel by nature, so his Romanticism remained a force of circumstance. His most outstanding successes, *Eugene Onegin, The Queen of Spades*, and *The Captain's Daughter*, show a tension between a Romantic emotionalism and a cool intellect that moderates his tendency toward excess.

Although the tone of his writing varies almost as much as his inconstant temperament in life, the total body of his writing is charged with satirical humor and implicit sociological criticism. The most explicit evidence of this lies in works such as *Ruslan and Liudmila, Gabriel, Count Nulin*, and *Eugene Onegin*. Versatile in everything from verse epistles to lyrics and narratives, from historical studies to Romantic tragedies, Pushkin was preeminently a poet and novella writer.

The paradox of Pushkin was that he was intensely Russian even when he was derivatively French. His landscape was thoroughly indigenous, as were his most memorable characters. His plays (of which only *Boris Godunov* has the scope and intensity of a major work) follow history's course even as they move into humankind's inner world of mind, spirit, and will. Although at first there is little that is Slavic about Pushkin, his work evokes some of the most cherished memories of Russia's past and his own times.

—*Keith Garebian*

FURTHER READING

Binyon, T. J. *Pushkin: A Biography*. London: Harper-Collins, 2002. Well-reviewed biography, focusing on Pushkin's turbulent life. Binyon quotes passages of Pushkin's poetry to provide a better understanding of the poet's personal experiences.

Bloom, Harold, ed. *Alexander Pushkin*. New York: Chelsea House, 1987. Edited with an introduction by Harold Bloom, one of the major postmodernist critics, this is a representative selection of some of the best academic criticism on Pushkin. Opens with an introductory critical essay by Bloom and a note that comments on the eleven individual essays that follow. Includes discussions of Pushkin's poetry, prose, language, imagination, and image as a Russian national poet. Contains a chronology and a bibliography.

Feinstein, Elaine. *Pushkin: A Biography*. Hopewell, N.J.: Ecco Press, 1998. Details Pushkin's volatile life and personality. Features selections from his poetry (some of which were translated by the author) to demonstrate how Pushkin's work displayed "the facility of Byron, the sensuous richness of Keats and a bawdy wit reminiscent of Chaucer."

Mirsky, D. S. *Pushkin*. New York: E. P. Dutton, 1926. A critical biography that is sometimes unsatisfyingly brief in its treatment of many works, but reveals much about Pushkin's psychology.

Simmons, Ernest J. *Pushkin*. Cambridge, Mass.: Harvard University Press, 1937. A well-documented account of Pushkin's life, although it contains no rigorous discussion of his work.

Troyat, Henri. *Pushkin*. Translated by Nancy Amphoux. Garden City, N.Y.: Doubleday, 1970. A massive but compelling biography that is richly evocative of Pushkin's life and times, while giving detailed analyses of all of his significant writing. Although highly laudatory of the artist, it never forgets to present the man in all of his emotional mutations.

Vickery, Walter N. *Alexander Pushkin*. New York: Twayne, 1970. A useful guide for nonspecialist readers that conforms to a house style favoring much plot description and generalized comment. Its main focus is on Pushkin's themes and poetic personality.

SEE ALSO: Alexander I; Lord Byron; Fyodor Dostoevski; Nikolai Gogol; Mikhail Lermontov; Nikolay Ivanovich Lobachevsky; Modest Mussorgsky; Nicholas I; Nikolay Rimsky-Korsakov; Stendhal; Peter Ilich Tchaikovsky; Leo Tolstoy.

RELATED ARTICLES in *Great Events from History: The Nineteenth Century, 1801-1900:* June 23-December 14, 1812: Napoleon Invades Russia; December, 1849: Dostoevski Is Exiled to Siberia.

SIR HENRY RAEBURN
Scottish painter

For nearly forty years, Raeburn reigned as the leading portrait painter in his native Scotland, and he left a valuable pictorial record of many prominent and affluent personages of late eighteenth and early nineteenth century Scottish society.

BORN: March 4, 1756; Stockbridge (now in Edinburgh), Scotland
DIED: July 8, 1823; Edinburgh, Scotland
AREA OF ACHIEVEMENT: Art

EARLY LIFE

Henry Raeburn was the younger son of Robert and Ann Elder Raeburn. His family had long been associated with agriculture in the Scottish Lowlands, but his father had abandoned that life for a career in textile manufacturing, eventually becoming a successful mill owner. Both of his parents died when young Henry was only six, leaving him in the care of his elder brother, William.

In 1765, Raeburn enrolled at Heriot's Hospital, a prestigious private school in Edinburgh that provided its students with the classical education customary for a gentleman. Raeburn, who displayed a fondness for caricature while in school, received only a few years of formal education before being apprenticed at the age of fifteen to James Gilliland, a jeweler and goldsmith. Early in his apprenticeship, Raeburn began painting miniature portraits of his friends during his spare time. Gilliland, recognizing his potential, introduced his apprentice to the engraver David Deuchar. Raeburn received occasional drawing lessons from Deuchar and through him met David Martin, then considered Edinburgh's preeminent painter. Martin did not give Raeburn any formal instruction but permitted him to use his studio and allowed him to copy some of his works. Their budding friendship ended when Martin accused Raeburn of selling one of the copies he had made.

The aspiring young artist thus received remarkably little formal instruction. During the 1770's, Edinburgh was a city with neither a public art gallery nor frequent artistic exhibitions where he could study the works of acknowledged masters. However, many middle- and upper-class homes contained portraits, which Raeburn undoubtedly examined; and reproductions of works by such established painters as George Romney and Sir Joshua Reynolds were also readily available. Raeburn was fortunate in that Edinburgh was an expanding and increasingly prosperous community during the late eigh-

teenth century, creating a ready-made market for a determined and talented painter who could supply a steady stream of portraits to its citizens.

Raeburn's success in selling some of his miniatures, few of which survive, enabled him to negotiate a release from his apprenticeship and devote his energy to a full-time career as a portraitist. His earliest known full-size work in oil, *George Chalmers of Pittencrieff*, dates from 1776, but it is impossible to date accurately any of the other portraits from his early period, from 1776 to 1784.

Raeburn never endured the severe financial difficulties that plagued so many aspiring artists. His good friend John Clerk, a noted lawyer, introduced him to many prospective clients, and from his early twenties the artist had sufficient commissions to live comfortably. His financial future was secured by his 1778 marriage to Ann Edgar Leslie, a wealthy widow twelve years his senior and already the mother of three. Pleasant and supportive, Ann Raeburn proved to be an excellent wife. The couple had two sons, Peter and Henry, the elder of whom died as an adolescent.

LIFE'S WORK

During the late eighteenth century, it was still commonplace for aspiring artists to study abroad in order to observe the works of the great masters. In his late twenties and now comfortable financially, Raeburn decided to follow this tradition. He first traveled to London, where he met Reynolds, then president of the Royal Academy and the preeminent figure in the British art world. Reynolds permitted him to work in his studio for several weeks and was impressed by the young Scot's abilities. He strongly advised Raeburn to go to Rome and, not knowing of his financial situation, even offered him financial assistance. Raeburn declined the money but gratefully accepted the letters of introduction that Reynolds provided.

During his two years in Rome, Raeburn probably did not produce any full-scale portraits but instead devoted himself to the study of the great works of art that abounded in the city. He became friends with Pompeo Batoni, then a leading artist, who had painted many outdoor portraits of visiting Scots; Raeburn was also influenced by the antiquary and art dealer James Byrnes. Although his Italian sojourn did not radically transform Raeburn's style or subject matter, it undoubtedly had an effect on his use of poses, color, and tonality. After his return to Edinburgh in 1787, Raeburn rapidly replaced Martin as the city's leading portraitist, a status he maintained until his death. By 1795, Raeburn was able to move from his studio on George Street to more spacious accommodations at York Place, which he personally designed. In addition to his own studio, York Place also contained a large gallery where the public could view his works. He actively promoted artistic exhibitions in the city and freely lent his gallery for such purposes.

Described by contemporaries as a tall, robust man with a rather florid complexion, Raeburn enjoyed a prominent position in Edinburgh society, free from major rivals or controversies. An interesting conversationalist who was fond of anecdotes, the amiable portraitist became friends with many of the city's prominent citizens and achieved a social status denied to all but the most successful artists of the period.

Nothing was bohemian or unconventional about Raeburn's lifestyle. He enjoyed golf, fishing, and archery, as well as long walks in the country. He also retained a lifelong interest in architecture and had a passion for building miniature ships and models. As a painter, Raeburn was a diligent and dependable worker. Rising at seven,

Sir Henry Raeburn. (The Granger Collection, New York)

he was at work in his studio by nine and usually saw three or four sitters a day, keeping each of them between one and a half and two hours. He usually finished work by five and dined at six, thus freeing his evenings for time with family, friends, and hobbies.

When painting, Raeburn worked with much greater spontaneity than did most of his contemporaries. He never made preliminary sketches or drawings, but instead preferred to paint directly onto the canvas, starting with the forehead, chin, nose, and mouth. His free, bold brushwork resembled that of the Spanish master Diego Velázquez, examples of whose work Raeburn probably had studied in Rome. Raeburn believed that nothing should divert attention from the face, and his heads are more finely done than other parts of the body. His aim was always to capture the personality of the sitter, and many of his portraits have a delightful informality, with the subject relaxed in a chair.

Knowing that his portraits would be placed high on the walls of many homes, Raeburn preferred to paint his subjects from an angle similar to that from which they would eventually be viewed. He therefore placed them on a platform in his studio and, after studying them for some time, would magically begin to capture their likeness, sometimes employing a brush up to a yard long.

Although he bowed to the tradition, popularized by such artists as Thomas Gainsborough and Reynolds, of including scenic settings as backgrounds for some of his portraits, Raeburn believed that such landscapes should not detract from the individuality of his sitter. In many of his portraits, he completely eliminated the background or reduced it to simple drapery. Raeburn's blunt, bold brushwork produced figures with squarish, solid countenances. His style changed remarkably little over the decades, although his tonality became lighter and his lighting less artificial in his later years. Contemporaries occasionally criticized his technique for being overly simplified and lacking in richness of color and refinement.

Despite Raeburn's prominence in Edinburgh, he long remained isolated from the center of the British artistic world and achieved a reputation in London only late in life; his visits to the capital were infrequent. In 1792, he sent his first three works to the city for the annual Royal Academy exhibition. The largest of these, a magnificent portrait of Sir John Clerk and his wife, arrived too late to be hung, but one of the aldermen, John Boydell, arranged for the portrait to be shown at the Shakespeare Gallery, where it attracted some favorable attention in the press.

Raeburn did not start regularly sending works to London until 1810, the year he seriously contemplated moving to the capital. John Hoppner, a fashionable London artist, had just died, and Raeburn considered taking over Hoppner's house and practice. It is possible that he considered the move because of recent difficulties caused by his son's financial failures. To recoup his losses, Raeburn had been forced to sell York Place and had even accepted commissions to copy portraits done by other artists—a rather unusual step for someone of his reputation. Ultimately, however, Raeburn abandoned the idea of relocating in London and decided to stay in his native city, where he had no serious competitors and his reputation was impregnable.

Gradually, the London establishment officially recognized the Scottish painter's abilities. He was elected an associate member of the Royal Academy in 1812 and, after failing to be elected to one of the two vacancies in 1814, was ultimately elevated to full membership in 1815. Further recognition came during the final years of his life. During George IV's visit to Edinburgh in 1822, Raeburn was knighted, thus earning the same social status achieved by Reynolds in the previous century. In May, 1823, Raeburn was appointed the king's painter in Scotland, but he did not live long enough to paint a planned portrait of the monarch in Highland dress. His last work was a portrait of Sir Walter Scott. Shortly after accompanying Scott and several others on an expedition to Ravensheugh Castle in Fife, Raeburn succumbed to a mysterious ailment and died, on July 8, 1823.

SIGNIFICANCE

Often referred to as the "Scottish Reynolds," Sir Henry Raeburn left a valuable legacy of portraits of the Scottish society whose values and ideas he shared. Portraiture was the only type of painting he attempted, in part because it brought the most dependable and lucrative commissions. The exact number of Raeburn portraits remains unknown; he kept no record of his sitters, so neither an accurate chronology nor the exact quantity of his work is known. He produced at least seven hundred portraits during his long and productive career. Almost all of his famous Scottish contemporaries—such as Adam Smith, James Boswell, and David Hume—sat for Raeburn portraits, the main exception being Robert Burns. Raeburn's series of Highland chiefs in native garb, the most famous being *The MacNab*, gained particular popularity. However, the majority of his portraits were of various lawyers, academics, military officers, and others of the professional class who wished to have their likenesses preserved for posterity.

Raeburn's work remained relatively unknown outside Scotland until the twentieth century, in part because so much of it remained in private collections. By 1900, however, major galleries eagerly sought to acquire his portraits. Many critics now rank him as one of the most important figures in British art during the late eighteenth and early nineteenth centuries.

With his quiet, undramatic lifestyle hundreds of miles away from the turmoil of the London art world, Raeburn was long a rather obscure figure, and much less is known about the details of his life and work than is known about such contemporaries as Gainsborough, Reynolds, or Joseph Turner. Nevertheless, Raeburn's reputation as a superb portraitist seems secure. His diligent promotion of art in Scotland and his engrossing portraits undoubtedly provided a significant contribution to Great Britain's expanding role in the visual arts.

—Tom L. Auffenberg

FURTHER READING

Armstrong, Sir Walter. *Sir Henry Raeburn*. London: W. Heinemann, 1901. The standard biography, by a prominent art historian who also wrote works on Reynolds, Gainsborough, and Turner. Includes a catalog of Raeburn's paintings, prepared with the assistance of James L. Caw.

Arts Council of Great Britain, Scottish Committee. *Raeburn Bicentenary Exhibition*. Edinburgh: National Gallery of Scotland, 1956. Prepared as a catalog for the special Edinburgh exhibition celebrating the bicentennial of Raeburn's birth, this work includes an introductory biographical essay by David Baxandall and detailed explanatory notes about fifty-three of Raeburn's portraits.

Brotchie, Theodore C. F. *Henry Raeburn, 1756-1823*. London: Cassell, 1924. Includes a brief bibliography, as well as a chart showing the prices paid for some of Raeburn's paintings between 1907 and 1922.

Caw, James L. *Raeburn*. London: T. C. and E. C. Jack, 1909. A brief study by the former director of the National Gallery of Scotland and leading authority on Scottish art history. Includes some original letters as well as eight color illustrations of Raeburn's portraits.

Greig, James. *Sir Henry Raeburn, R.A.* London: Connoisseur, 1911. Includes a fairly extensive catalog of Raeburn's paintings, selected correspondence, and numerous black-and-white reproductions.

Irwin, David, and Francina Irwin. *Scottish Painters at Home and Abroad, 1700-1900*. London: Faber and Faber, 1975. Takes advantage of the latest scholarly discoveries and contains a lively and well-written section on Raeburn and his influence, as well as making specific comments on many of his paintings. Contains a useful bibliography of books and articles.

Smith, Bill, and Selina Skiipwith. *A History of Scottish Art*. London: Merrell in association with The Fleming-Wyfold Art Foundation, 2003. This overview of Scottish art includes information about Raeburn.

Thomson, Duncan, and Lynne Gladstone-Millar. *The Skating Minister: The Story Behind the Painting*. Edinburgh: National Galleries of Scotland/National Museums of Scotland, 2004. Originally published in 1997 as *The Reverend Robert Walker Skating on Duddingston Loch by Sir Henry Raeburn*. Examines Raeburn's painting of his friend, the Reverend Robert Walker, ice skating. Explores the relationship between the artist and his subject, why Raeburn painted Walker in this unusual way, and why the painting has become so well known.

Whitley, William T. *Art in England*. 2 vols. New York: Macmillan, 1928, 1930. Reprint. New York: Hacker Art Books, 1973. A detailed account of the English art world of 1800-1837; proves useful for discussing Raeburn's relations with the Royal Academy. Corrects certain errors found in earlier studies. Includes numerous contemporary press reactions to Raeburn paintings exhibited in London during this period.

SEE ALSO: John Constable; George IV; William Holman Hunt; John Singer Sargent; Sir Walter Scott; J. M. W. Turner; James McNeill Whistler.

RELATED ARTICLE in *Great Events from History: The Nineteenth Century, 1801-1900:* 1814: Scott Publishes *Waverley*.

MAHADEV GOVIND RANADE
Indian social reformer

Ranade was a social reformer and political leader who attempted to bring about change in colonial India through peaceful means, while believing that Indians should use British overrule as an opportunity to reform their country, and was one of the founders of India's most powerful political party, the Indian National Congress.

BORN: January 18, 1842; Niphad, India
DIED: January 16, 1901; Pune, India
ALSO KNOWN AS: Mahadeo Govind Ranade
AREAS OF ACHIEVEMENT: Social reform, law, government and politics

EARLY LIFE

Mahadev Govind Ranade (MAH-hah-dayv goh-VIHND RAH-nah-day) was born in the Indian state of Maharashtra to a Hindu Chitpavan Brahman family. His father was a government official. His given name was Mahadev, but people called him Mahadeo, and he is known by both names. Until the age of fifteen he was raised at Kolhapur. From 1851 to 1856, he attended Kolhapur English School, where he was so quiet and calm a pupil that his behavior masked his academic brilliance. In 1856, two years after he married Sakhubai Dandekhar, he went to Elphinstone College in Bombay, where he became a voracious reader. He matricu-

lated there in 1859 and received his bachelor's degree in 1862.

From 1863 to 1866, Ranade was a teaching fellow at Bombay University, and he received his law degree in 1866. In 1868, he was appointed assistant professor of English and history at Elphinstone College. In 1871, he passed his advocate examination and was appointed a judge of a Bombay court equivalent to an American small claims court. There he began the legal career for which he became professionally renowned. In 1873, his first wife died and he married Ramabai (1862-1924).

LIFE'S WORK

When British-educated Indians in Maharashtra founded the Prarthana Samaj, or Prayer Society, in 1867, Ranade immediately became a member. It was the first of many reform and political movements in which he would become involved. All the societies and schools in which he became involved were in one way or another connected with his deeply held belief in the value of education or in social reform and in religious service.

Ranade also pursued an active political career and a distinguished legal career. Between 1885 and 1894, he served three one-year terms as an appointed member of the Bombay Legislative Council. In 1886, he was appointed to the government of India Finance Committee. His legal appointments included "small causes courts" in

ORGANIZATIONS THAT RANADE FOUNDED OR COFOUNDED	
1873	Elocution Society
1878	Sahitya Parishad
1878	Society for Promoting Marathi Books
1880	New English School
1881	elementary school for girls in Poona
1884	Deccan Association
1885	Indian National Congress
1887	Indian National Social Conference
1891	Industrial Conference of Western India
1894	Deccan Vernacular Translation Society
1896	Deccan Sabha

Poona (1867), Nasik (1878), and Dhulia (1879). In 1881, he was appointed a presidency magistrate for Bombay and joint judge of the Deccan Agriculturists' Relief Act. From then until 1893, he made annual tours of the district. In 1893, he was appointed to the Bombay High Court; during that the same year, he was also elected to the Bombay University Senate—one of his many appointments to educational boards.

Most members of the Prarthana Society were Chitpavan and Saraswat Brahmans, but the organization was also supported by Gujerati merchants and Parsis. The organization set up a managing committee to organize the Sunday services at which *bhakti* hymns were chanted, and lectures and readings from Hindu, Christian, and Buddhist scriptures were delivered. Members pledged to worship one God and to find truth in all religions.

In 1874, Ranade wrote *A Theist's Confession of Faith*, a tract that created an ideological basis for the Prayer Society that was reflected in its creed when a new meeting hall was opened. The creed stated that members would not use carved or painted images or symbols employed by other religious sects, while at the same time they would not condemn other religious groups that used them. Moreover, members pledged not to acknowledge any one book as the infallible word of God, while not condemning any books used by others.

Members of the society had an intellectual, rather than an emotional, approach to both religious and social issues and attempted to reform others along these lines. In 1873, the society started a night school for working people and started a journal, the *Subodh Patrika*. Members advocated a variety of Hindu reform: ending the ban on remarriage of widows, abolishing caste restrictions, abolishing child marriage, and educating women. How-

ever, the organization took a cautious approach and left it to individual members to advance these issues.

The society opened more than twenty branches in Maharashtra, Madras, and the south. In addition to its Sunday services, it created a free reading room, a library, night schools for working people, an orphanage, and, in 1906, a mission dedicated to the disadvantaged classes. Between 1878 and 1896, Ranade himself edited a daily newspaper, *Induprakash*, to further his ideas on reforming social and religious traditions, but he also believed in economic reforms. One of his modernist ideas was that agricultural banks should be set up to lend money directly to poor farmers in order to bypass extortionist moneylenders. Another was the creation of joint stock companies to start new industries. In 1885, he was one of the founding members of the Indian National Congress.

SIGNIFICANCE

Ranade saw himself as a teacher and was hailed as a guru by many of the moderate leaders of the day. He was also admired by his great "radical" political rival, Bal Gangadhar Tilak (1856-1920). Indeed, there were few areas of Maharashtrian life that remained untouched by Ranade and his reforming spirit. Through his various educational and social organizations and his fervent belief in social, economic, and political progress, he served as an inspiration to an entire generation, and his following continued into the twentieth century under the leadership of his disciple Gopal Krishna Gokhale (1866-1915). Ranade's nonsectarian and noncommunal beliefs were also shared by many others, including Mohandas K. Gandhi (1869-1948). By the end of his life, Ranade's stature was so great that he was truly a legend in his own time.

—*Roger D. Long*

FURTHER READING

Brown, D. Mackenzie. *Indian Nationalist Thought from Ranade to Bhave*. Berkeley: University of California Press, 1961. This short classic study places Ranade's political thought in historical and comparative perspective by comparing one of his writings with writings of other political leaders, including Gandhi.

Grover, Verinder, ed. *Political Thinkers of Modern India*. Vol. 3. New Delhi: Deep and Deep, 1990. This useful volume contains short biographical pieces on Ranade and offers a selection of his essays and speeches that includes "The Rise of Maratha Power," "The Key to Progress," "Indian Political Economy," "The Reorganisation of Rural Credit in India," and nine others, mostly on economic themes.

Jones, Kenneth W. *Socio-Religious Movements in British India*. Cambridge, England: Cambridge University Press, 1989. A contribution to *The New Cambridge History of India*, this volume places Ranade's thought in perspective with the numerous other reform movements from the eighteenth to the twentieth century.

Parvate, T. V. *Mahadev Govind Ranade: A Biography*. New York: Asia Publishing House, 1964. This erudite and rich biography not only presents the life of Ranade in chronological order but also offers useful essays on a numebr of topics such as his second wife and Gandhi.

Ranade, Ramabai. *Ranade: His Wife's Reminiscences*. Translated by Kusumavati Deshpande. New Delhi: Ministry of Information and Broadcasting, Government of India, 1963. Ranade educated his second wife Ramabai personally, and she became an activist on behalf of women and continued on his work after his death. Her *Reminiscences*, originally written in Marathi, provide an important record of Ranade's life, ideas, and activities.

Tucker, Richard P. *Ranade and the Roots of Indian Nationalism*. 1972. Chicago: University of Chicago Press, 1976. This well-written and well-researched book shows how Ranade's liberal political beliefs were increasingly becoming questioned by the end of his life as Indians (and Ranade himself) became impatient at the pace of political reforms.

SEE ALSO: Dadabhai Naoroji; Rammohan Ray; Iswar Chandra Vidyasagar; Vivekananda.

RELATED ARTICLE in *Great Events from History: The Nineteenth Century, 1801-1900:* 1885: Indian National Congress Is Founded.

RANJIT SINGH
Sikh ruler of the Punjab (r. 1792-1839)

Ranjit Singh was the first person to unify the vast and ethnically diverse Punjab region and became the first—and only—sovereign ruler over all Sikhs, as well as Hindus and Muslims living within his domain.

BORN: November 13, 1780; Gujranwala, India (now in Pakistan)

DIED: June 27, 1839; Lahore, Punjab (now in Pakistan)

ALSO KNOWN AS: Budh Singh (birth name); Runjut Singh; Lion of the Punjab

AREAS OF ACHIEVEMENT: Government and politics, warfare and conquest

EARLY LIFE

Ranjit Singh was born Budh Singh, the son of the Sukerchakia Sikh ruler (*misldar*) Sardar Mahan Singh of Gujranwala and his wife, Raj Kaur, who was also known as Mai Malwain of Jind. He was renamed Ranjit, for "victor in battle," by his warrior father following the latter's victory over the Chattahs, a local Muslim tribe.

Ranjit had no formal education but could understand spoken Punjabi and Persian. During his early youth, he lost one eye to an attack of smallpox but nevertheless became proficient in physical exercises, martial arts, and especially in horseback riding. At the age of ten he experienced his first military action during his father's campaign against the Bhangi chiefs (Sardars) of Lahore, who had rushed to liberate the nearby fort of Sodhran that Ranjit's father had besieged.

After his father died in 1792, Ranjit stepped into the leadership role, but he spent much of his time hunting and in similar indulgences while the affairs of the confederacy (*misl*) were managed by his mother, assisted by Diwan Lakhpat. During one of Ranjit's hunting expeditions, when he was thirteen, he faced a murderous assault on his life by a rival Sikh ruler and succeeded in killing his would-be assassin.

At the age of fifteen, Ranjit married Mehtab Kaur, a girl from the Kanhaya confederacy of Batala. Although the marriage never worked out satisfactorily for either partner, Ranjit compensated for his loveless life by pursuing power and glory with the help of his wife's community, the Kanhaya Sikhs. In 1798, he took a second wife, Raj Kaur (who was renamed Datar Kaur), a sister of the ruler of the Nakkai Sikhs. Around that same time, he dismissed his diwan and assumed responsibility for state affairs himself. He was then eighteen years old.

LIFE'S WORK

At the time Ranjit assumed full powers, the political situation in the Punjab region was complicated and tense.

The region had twelve Sikh confederacies that were mutually suspicious of one another. It also had one district that was controlled by Pathans and another that was controlled by an English adventurer named George Thomas. Meanwhile, the entire region faced possible invasions from Afghans in the northeast, Rajputs in the north, Gurkhas in the northwest, the British in the east, and Marathas in the southeast. However, the biggest menace to a united and free Punjab came from the Afghans. Since the conquest of their strongman Ahmad Shah Abdali in 1752, they had looked upon most of northern India, including the Punjab, as part of their empire. During 1795-1797, Abdali's grandson Shah Zaman twice tried to invade the Punjab. On November 27, 1798, he occupied Lahore, the chief city of the Punjab, but had to return home to deal with a crisis there.

After Zaman's departure, the people of Lahore—Hindus, Sikhs, and Muslims—decided to break the stranglehold of three inept Bhangi chiefs and invited Ranjit to take over the city. Ranjit occupied Lahore on July 7, 1799. On April 12, 1801, he assumed the title of maharaja. Possession of the ancient city of Lahore made the young Ranjit the most powerful chieftain in northern India.

During the following year, another Bhangi stronghold, the great city of Amritsar, surrendered to Ranjit's army and his allies. Over the next several years, Ranjit conquered all the Cis-Sutlej states. The internal political turmoil in Afghanistan encouraged him to expand his sway westward; in 1804 he set out to conquer the dependencies of the Afghan Empire east of the Indus River. He easily cowed the local Muslim chiefs of the region between the Ravi and Indus Rivers into submission and conquered the mid-Indus region during 1820-1821. Afterward that region served as a secure buffer against Afghan inroads into the Punjab.

The secure establishment of Ranjit Singh's authority in the Punjab forced the East India Company, which governed most of India in the name of Great Britain, to enter into amicable relations with his government. As early as 1808, a British mission led by Sir Charles Metcalfe visited Ranjit. That mission resulted in the Treaty of Amritsar (April 25, 1809), by which Britain recognized Maharaja Ranjit Singh's sovereignty over territories north of the Sutlej River and promised perpetual friendship between him and the British.

The Treaty of Amritsar barred Ranjit's eastward expansion, thereby preventing the union of all Sikh territories under a single state. Ranjit instead turned his attention to the north—to Kangra and the hill states occupied by the Gurkhas. Both regions soon came under his sway. He then took Multan in 1818, Kashmir in 1819, Peshawar in 1823, and Leh in Ladhak in 1836. His domain eventually covered more than one-quarter million square miles of prosperous and strategically sensitive territory of South Asia.

Maharaja Ranjit Singh's power and status reached their peak during the 1830's, the last decade of his life, when he was reckoned as a powerful and resourceful Indian prince by both the English and the French. On October 26, 1831, a meeting was arranged between him and Lord William Bentinck, the British governor-general of India.

Though practically illiterate, Ranjit was a patron of arts and letters. He patronized such renowned poets as Fakir Aziz-ud-Din, Syed Muhammad Hashim, Ahmad, and Qadir Yar.

Ranjit Singh. (The Granger Collection, New York)

These were writers whose creative talent led to the flourishing of heroic verse and a variety of Punjabi, Urdu, and Hindi poetic forms. During Ranjit Singh's reign, the renowned Sikh theologian Bhai Santokh Singh published two celebrated works, *Nanak Parkash* and *Gur Partap Surya*. Although a true man of the world and bon vivant, Ranjit was also a deeply religious man of eclectic faith. He respected both Sikh scriptures and Islam's holy Qurʾān.

Although an active man throughout his life, Ranjit Singh suffered from several bouts of paralysis. He survived the first two attacks in 1826 and 1834 but was severely weakened by a third attack in December, 1838. On June 27, 1839, he succumbed to a fourth attack and died in Lahore.

SIGNIFICANCE

Ranjit Singh created the new state of Punjab not by merely by military means but also through a calculated policy of accommodation and conciliation with the Sikh, Rajput, and Pathan peoples of the region. He presided over the new ruling classes in his kingdom, which encompassed Sikhs, Jats, Khatris, Brahmans, Sayyids, Pathans, and Europeans, and allowed them to share in the distribution of the resources of the state as ministers, courtiers, provincial governors, and commanders. Surrounded by hostile neighbors, the ruling classes as well as the people at large developed a heightened Punjab identity that transcended the communal differences making for a multicultural and yet a cohesive regional state.

—*Narasingha P. Sil*

FURTHER READING

Bakshi, S. R. *History of the Punjab: Maharaja Ranjit Singh*. New Delhi: Anmol, 1991. A detailed scholarly account of the rise of Ranjit Singh and Anglo-Sikh relations during his reign. A valuable work of reference.

Banerjee, Anil C. *The New History of Modern India, 1707-1947*. 1983. Kolkata, India: K. P. Bagchi, 1992. The seventh chapter is a critical analysis of Ranjit Singh's reign by a noted expert on the history of the Punjab. Succinct and solid scholarship.

Banga, Indu. "The Punjab Under Sikh Rule: Formation of a Regional State." In *History and Ideology: The Khalsa over Three Hundred Years*, edited by J. S. Grewal and Indu Banga. New Delhi: Tulika Books, 1999. An insightful assessment by a distinguished historian of Ranjit Singh's achievement as the architect of the state of Punjab.

Duggal, K. S. *Ranjit Singh: A Secular Sikh Sovereign*. New Delhi: Abhinav, 1989. An illustrated biography by a leading Punjabi novelist and scholar. Useful for both specialists and lay readers.

Grewal, J. S., and Indu Banga, eds. *Maharaja Ranjit Singh and His Times*. Amritsar: Guru Nanak Dev University, 1980. A collection of research papers by the historians of the Punjab's leading university, including several distinguished specialists.

Khullar, K. K. *Maharaja Ranjit Singh*. New Delhi: Hem, 1980. A work of solid scholarship with an informative appendix containing a note on indigenous historiography, and texts of the treaties entered into by Ranjit Singh.

Lafont, Jean-Marie. *Maharaja Ranjit Singh: Lord of the Five Rivers*. New York: Oxford University Press, 2002. Examines Singh's achievements, focusing on how he and the Punjabi people established a state in the Land of the Five Rivers.

Osborne, W. G. *Ranjit Singh: The Lion of the Punjab*. 1840. 2d ed. Calcutta, India: Susil Gupta, 1952. A contemporary British estimate of Ranjit Singh as a ruler and an eyewitness account of his court in Lahore.

Singh, Khushwant. *Ranjit Singh: Maharajah of the Punjab*. London: Allen & Unwin, 1962. A popular biography by a well-known critic and historian.

SEE ALSO: First Marquis of Dalhousie; John Laird Mair Lawrence.

RELATED ARTICLES in *Great Events from History: The Nineteenth Century, 1801-1900:* November 5, 1817-June 3, 1818: Third Maratha War; April, 1848-March, 1849: Second Anglo-Sikh War; May 10, 1857-July 8, 1858: Sepoy Mutiny Against British Rule.

LEOPOLD VON RANKE
German historian

Ranke is considered the founder of modern historical scholarship and a founder of the German idea of history. His historical works rank as classics of modern historiography.

BORN: December 21, 1795; Wiehe, Thuringia, Saxony (now in Germany)
DIED: May 23, 1886; Berlin, Germany
AREA OF ACHIEVEMENT: Historiography

EARLY LIFE

The father of Leopold von Ranke (RAHNG-kee), Gottlob Israel Ranke, was a lawyer, but the Lutheran ministry was the traditional profession of the family. Ranke's parents expected him, as the eldest of nine children, to follow a career in the Church. After an early education in local schools, he was sent to Schulpforta, a famous German public school known for the quality of its humanistic, classical curriculum. Ranke studied philology and theology at the University of Leipzig and received a doctoral degree in 1817 for a dissertation on the political ideas of Thucydides.

As a student, Ranke adopted the critical philological method of Barthold Niebuhr, a statesman and scholar whose *Römische Geschichte* (1811-1832; *History of Rome*, 1828-1842) reconstructed the historical origins of the Roman state. Ranke admired Niebuhr's history but not his clumsy prose. A master stylist himself, he was early influenced by the German of Martin Luther and Johann Wolfgang von Goethe. Although he remained a devout Lutheran, Ranke declined to enter the ministry. The classics and philology interested him more than dogma. In 1818, he became a master of classical languages in the gymnasium in Frankfurt an der Oder. Entrusted with the teaching of history, Ranke was led to write his first book, *Geschichte der romanischen und germanischen Völker von 1494 bis 1514* (1824; *History of the Latin and Teutonic Nations from 1494 to 1514*, 1887), in which he applied his philological training to the field of modern history. Ranke was called in 1824 to the University of Berlin, where he taught until 1871.

Ranke's students left a vivid vignette of their master. He is described as a slight figure with dark, curly hair, a low voice, a lively speaking manner, penetrating blue eyes, and a serene temperament. He, in turn, took a paternalistic interest in his students, who eventually filled almost every chair of history in Germany. Surrounded by his children and grandchildren (he married Clara Graves,

daughter of an Irish barrister, in 1843, and the couple had two sons and a daughter), he would say that he had another and older family, his pupils and their pupils.

LIFE'S WORK

In the programmatic preface to *History of the Latin and Teutonic Nations from 1494 to 1514*, Ranke gave a new direction to historical studies by declaring that it was not the duty of the historian to judge the past for the benefit of the present or the future. It was only "to show what actually occurred." This matter-of-fact statement was directed against the historiography of the Enlightenment, which had given history an abstractly defined end and viewed it as an ascending process in which a later age was superior to an earlier one. According to Ranke each age was unique, "each period is equally close to God."

In the appendix of his first book, Ranke added that he had found traditional histories untrustworthy; they did not correspond with the evidence he found in contemporary documents. For his history, he wrote, he had relied only on original sources, critically sifted and cross-examined. Ranke's ambition to use only "the purest, most immediate documents" led him to the Italian archives in 1827. In Italy, where he gratified his "archival obsession" for three years, Ranke became the first scholar to examine the famous *relazioni*, secret reports Venetian ambassadors had submitted to their government after diplomatic missions to the courts of Europe. In such materials, Ranke believed, the historian could divine the core and secret of human events. Upon his return to the University of Berlin, where he became a full professor in 1836, Ranke created the historical seminar and instructed advanced students in *Quellenkritik*, the critical study of the sources.

Ranke spurned the schematic history of the philosophers but he was, nevertheless, a generalist. Through the perception of the particular, the historian was to grasp the inner connection and complete whole of history. As a devout Christian, Ranke believed that the unity and tendency of the historical experience were an expression of divine purpose—the "hand of God" was evident in the particular and the universal.

Divine action in the historical world was largely realized through nations or states, Ranke contended, a theory he developed in "Political Dialogue" (1836) and "The Great Powers" (1833), famous essays written while he was editor of the political journal *Historisch-politische Zeitschrift* (historical-political review) from 1832 to 1836. Ranke argued that there was no ideal political constitution. States developed their own genius and institutional forms: That was the task set them by God. Accordingly, power embodied in the nation-state was ethically good: It was an expression of God's will. This conception or idea of history, reflected in all of Ranke's historical studies, affirmed the importance of the great powers and identified the state as an ethical institution whose interests were in harmony with the general good.

While on his tour of the Italian archives, Ranke outlined the course of his future studies: first Italian, then French, English, and German studies. He turned to German history before the French and English, but otherwise the early outline of his life's work was followed faithfully. The national histories were capped by nine volumes of world history, *Weltgeschichte* (1881-1888; partial translation as *Universal History*, 1884), begun in his eighty-sixth year.

Ranke's Italian project, published from 1834 to 1836 in three volumes, was *Die römischen Päpste in den letzten 4 Jahrhunderten* (*The History of the Popes During the Last Four Centuries*, 1907), considered by many his finest work in form and matter. Ranke approached the popes as a historian fascinated by their role in world history, but they were also a subject in which he found the "thought of God." The history of the popes was followed by *Deutsche Geschichte im Zeitalter der Reformation* (1839-1847; *History of the Reformation in Germany*, 1845-1847), a six-volume history received in Germany as a national classic, although Ranke himself thought it inferior to his study of the popes. As the first of the Reformation volumes appeared, Frederick William IV recognized Ranke's eminence as a scholar and appointed him, in 1841, historiographer of the Prussian state. Ranke was ennobled, thereby adding "von" to his name, in 1865.

In the two decades after his study of the Reformation, Ranke wrote his massive histories of the great powers, all focusing on developments from the fifteenth to the eighteenth century. *Neun Bücher preussischer Geschichte* (nine books of Prussian history), a study later expanded to twelve books, appeared in 1847-1848, and *Englische Geschichte, vornehmlich im 16 und 17 Jahrhundert* (*A History of England Principally in the Seventeenth Century*, 1966) was issued in six volumes between 1859 and 1868.

In Ranke's opinion, the most important features of history between 1492 and 1789 were the creation of the

modern state, the rise of the great powers, and the establishment of the state system. He appreciated the role of ideas in history and suggested that historians should pay attention to population, churches, agriculture, industry, and transportation. In practice, however, he was a political and diplomatic historian, and he focused almost exclusively on courts and chanceries. Later historians, with a greater interest in the evolution of society, assigned ideas and social and economic forces far more important roles in historiography. On the other hand, while he was the motive force behind the creation of an encyclopedia of German national biography, Ranke himself wrote little biography; exceptions were short biographical studies of Frederick the Great and Frederick William IV. For Ranke, the individual was important only when he played an active or leading role in general history.

It is not surprising that Ranke elected to spend his final years, although infirm and unable to read or write, preparing a world history. He was able to produce eight volumes, taking his story to the end of the fifteenth century, before his death in May, 1886, at the age of ninety. The universal history, although incomplete, was a fitting

Leopold von Ranke. (Library of Congress)

conclusion to Ranke's career: To comprehend the whole while obeying the dictates of exact research, he had written during the 1860's, was the ideal goal of the historian.

SIGNIFICANCE

Leopold von Ranke is commonly identified as an empirical, nonphilosophical historian, the founder of the "scientific school" of history. This image is one-sided but not invalid. Ranke sought to write history as it actually happened, free of philosophical presuppositions, and he contributed a critical method that emphasized the use of documentary sources. He suggested that national cultures and periods of history should be examined on their own terms. German historians, however, also appreciated Ranke as a contemplative thinker, and most of his successors accepted his emphasis on the central role of the state and of foreign affairs in the European experience. Many, too, adopted his concept of the spiritual character of power, a theme that runs through Ranke's writings. It was only after World War II that leading German historians concluded that Ranke had been insufficiently pessimistic regarding power and the state.

Ranke's own works, and he published a large number of historical classics, are still valuable. They are largely free of bias and show an insight and style that make them profitable reading for modern students of history.

—*J. A. Thompson*

FURTHER READING

Gay, Peter. "Ranke: The Respectful Critic." In *Style in History*. New York: McGraw-Hill, 1974. Reprint. New York: W. W. Norton, 1988. A perceptive and gracefully written essay on Ranke as dramatist, scientist, and believer.

Geyl, Pieter. "Ranke in the Light of the Catastrophe." In *Debates with Historians*. Groningen, the Netherlands: J. B. Wolters, 1955. A strong indictment of Ranke's idea that power was an expression of divine activity in the historical world.

Gilbert, Felix. *History: Politics or Culture: Reflections on Ranke and Burckhardt*. Princeton, N.J.: Princeton University Press, 1990. In five essays, Gilbert points out the similarities between Ranke and Jacob Burckhardt, two major historians of the early nineteenth century. Emphasizes the novelty and originality of Ranke's ideas about history.

Gooch, G. P. "Ranke." In *History and Historians in the Nineteenth Century*. London: Longmans, Green, 1913.

_____. "Ranke's Critics and Pupils." In *History and Historians in the Nineteenth Century*. London: Longmans, Green, 1913. Two of the best brief studies in English on Ranke.

Higham, John, Leonard Krieger, and Felix Gilbert. *History*. Englewood Cliffs, N.J.: Prentice-Hall, 1965. A useful discussion of Ranke's influence in the professionalization of history in Europe and the United States.

Iggers, Georg G. *The German Conception of History: The National Tradition of Historical Thought from Herder to the Present*. Middletown, Conn.: Wesleyan University Press, 1968. A valuable interpretative survey of the theoretical presuppositions and political values of German historians. Ranke is identified as a founder of a school that not only adopted the critical method but also viewed the state as an ethical good.

_____. "The Image of Ranke in American and German Historical Thought." *History and Theory* 2 (1962): 17-40. A survey of divergent images of Ranke held by German and American historians.

Iggers, Georg G., and James M. Powell, eds. *Leopold von Ranke and the Shaping of the Historical Discipline*. Syracuse, N.Y.: Syracuse University Press, 1990. Collection of papers delivered at a 1986 conference to mark the centennial of Ranke's death. The papers place him in the context of the developing historical discipline and discuss various issues in European historiography.

Van Laue, Theodore H. *Leopold Ranke: The Formative Years*. Princeton, N.J.: Princeton University Press, 1950. Traces the development of Ranke's historical ideas in the context of contemporary Germany from 1795 to 1836. It includes Ranke's essays "Political Dialogue" and "The Great Powers" in translation as well as a useful bibliographical essay.

SEE ALSO: George Bancroft; Jules Michelet; Theodor Mommsen; Barthold Georg Niebuhr; William Hickling Prescott; William IV.

RELATED ARTICLE in *Great Events from History: The Nineteenth Century, 1801-1900:* 1824: Ranke Develops Systematic History.

GRIGORI YEFIMOVICH RASPUTIN
Russian mystic

Because of his apparently mystic ability to amelioriate the hemophilia of the heir to the Russian throne, Rasputin ingratiated himself to Czar Nicholas II and Empress Alexandra. Rasputin's profligate ways and the refusal of the rulers to believe the scandal he consistently generated increased the estrangement between the rulers and their people, thus contributing to the Russian Revolution.

BORN: c. 1870; Pokrovskoye, Siberia, Russia
DIED: December 30, 1916; Petrograd (now St. Petersburg), Russia
ALSO KNOWN AS: Grigori Yefimovich Novykh (birth name); Grigori Efimovich Rasputin; Grigory Yefymovich Rasputin
AREAS OF ACHIEVEMENT: Government and politics, religion and theology

EARLY LIFE

The exact date of the birth of Grigori Yefimovich Rasputin (rahs-PEW-tyihn) is unknown, as was true for most Russian peasants at the time he was born. As a young boy, Rasputin exhibited a remarkable ability to commune with and heal animals. Although illiterate, he liked to memorize Scripture, and at the age of eighteen, he had a vision of the Virgin Mary. Legend claims that he also possessed gifts of precognition and clairvoyance, but villagers later remembered him primarily for his excessive drinking and proclivity toward sexual depravity. These apparently irreconcilable impressions were indicative of his whole life: Times of prayer and generosity coexisted with epic debauchery. He was variously viewed as a pious holy man and an insatiable satyr.

In 1889 Rasputin married Praskovya Fedorovna Dubrovina, who bore him three children. Rasputin became a farmer, but he was apparently unwilling to abandon his disorderly life; his drinking increased, and he was accused of petty thievery. He soon moved to a nearby monastery where he lived as a monk for three months. Some sources claim that the trouble he had stirred up in Pokrovskoye made temporarily vanishing a prudent idea. His time at the monastery proved to be a watershed. He permanently gave up tobacco and meat, and he temporarily gave up alcohol. He appeared nervous and restless, with moods swinging between severe depression and religious ecstasy. He prayed frequently, learned to read the Orthodox liturgy, and memorized

huge segments of Scripture. He also began to attract followers.

Within one month of his return from the monastery, Rasputin embarked on a series of long pilgrimages, traveling to holy shrines as a religious mendicant begging for food and lodging. Between pilgrimages, he awed his growing circle of admirers with descriptions of the holy places he had visited. Rasputin's physical endurance and self-confidence enabled him to spend the better part of a decade meandering throughout Siberia. He was welcomed into homes as a true holy man, perhaps because of his uncanny ability to recognize people with troubled minds and provide a calming peace.

Rasputin's wanderings eventually brought him into contact with Russian aristocrats, many of whom were awed by his magnetic personality. In 1903 he visited Kazan, a religiously important city, where his piousness so impressed officials of the Russian Orthodox Church that he was welcomed as a true holy man. By ingratiating himself with progressively more important holy officers, he managed to gain valuable friends and allies. Rasputin's triumphant acceptance in Kazan paved the way for his welcome reception by the upper-class society of St. Petersburg, the Russian Empire's capital city.

LIFE'S WORK

Rasputin, fortified by introductions to important religious and political personages, took up residence in St. Petersburg in 1905. The aristocratic citizens were fascinated by this unruly and unkempt peasant from the Siberian wasteland. His status as a religious teacher soon attracted a coterie of fawning disciples, mostly women. Rasputin expounded perverted twists to Christian doctrine, including the idea that salvation could be achieved only through repentance; therefore, one had to sin in order to have the opportunity to repent. His doctrine resolved the fundamental, seemingly irreconcilable conflict between religion and carnal appetites. He was always willing to help provide salvation through sexual sin for the many attractive, willing women who flocked to his apartment.

Alexandra Fedorovna, the wife of Czar Nicholas II and empress of Russia, had given birth to four daughters before producing an heir to the Russian throne, Alexei, on July 30, 1904. Shortly after Alexei's birth, his parents learned that he was a hemophiliac; any bruise caused painful internal hemorrhaging, and the slightest injury

Grigori Yefimovich Rasputin. (The Granger Collection, New York)

could be fatal. Because hemophilia was incurable and because simple childhood accidents could lead to days of unrelenting agony, the czar and empress lived in a state of relentless distress. They sought solace through holy men, clairvoyants, and other dabblers in the occult arts whom they hoped could help relieve the sufferings of the heir apparent.

Rasputin's reputation for marvelous healing powers soon brought him to the attention of the royal couple. When he was introduced to them in October, 1905, they were convinced that this simple yet devout man was the very holy man for whom they were searching. Their faith was not entirely misplaced. When young Alexei next suffered from serious internal bleeding, Rasputin's bedside prayers caused an immediate improvement. The doctors had thought that Alexei would not survive, but he soon recovered. Over the next decade, Rasputin consistently alleviated the young heir's suffering. Whatever the explanation, there can be no doubt that his soothing presence or his prayers were effective. To the empress, Rasputin was a saint whom God used to effect miraculous cures.

Although Rasputin's debauchery continued to escalate, he always maintained a pious facade before the royal family. They trusted him implicitly and soon began to seek his council for appointments in the church hierarchy. Rasputin cleverly placed his cronies in important posts and had his enemies transferred to distant provinces. He soon began to meddle in civil appointments as well. His double life required supporters in key government posts and the dispatching of enemies. As his power grew, his spiritual demeanor eroded, and his ambition for political control was progressively magnified.

By accepting bribes to help people gain political offices or achieve their goals, Rasputin also accumulated considerable wealth, although his inherent generosity caused him to give much of it to needy people. Influential merchants flocked to Rasputin's sitting room, where the miracle-worker simplified business transactions by short-circuiting typical bureaucratic delays. He scribbled a few words to people whose help he needed, and his access to the czar assured that the simple sentence worked wonders.

As his political power grew, so did his number of enemies, including many former allies who had lost confidence in him. When drunk, he often boasted about his control over the czar and empress, causing ordinary citizens to lose faith in a monarch who would allow an ignorant lout of a peasant to be virtually omnipotent. Any incompetent fool who struck the fancy of this arrogant peasant could easily be assigned to an important ministerial post, while those best qualified were ignored. Nicholas and Alexandra lived in blissful ignorance of the escalating problems caused by Rasputin's political meddling. Harassed by perpetual fear for the heir and reassured by Rasputin's miraculous cures, they turned a deaf ear to all warnings.

As the number of Rasputin's enemies increased, so did the number of murder plots being hatched against him. In November of 1916, four noblemen formed a conspiracy to eliminate Rasputin. The conspirators, headed by Prince Felix Yusupov, lured Rasputin to Yusupov's palace during the late night of December 29 to poison him with potassium cyanide. Although Prince Yusupov later claimed that they murdered Rasputin for the idealistic and patriotic reasons of saving the Russian autocracy, the lofty aims were not justified by the hypocritical means and their cowardly denials when later accused of murder.

Rasputin had been told that he was being taken to meet Yusupov's beautiful wife, although she was not even in St. Petersburg at the time. Yusupov brought

Rasputin into a basement room and served him poisoned cakes and poisoned wine while the others waited upstairs. Although enough poison had been used to kill a battalion, the lethal cakes and wine seemed to have no noticeable effect. A disconcerted Yusupov raced upstairs, retrieved a small revolver, and returned to shoot Rasputin. He appeared to die instantly, and Yusupov left.

Returning later to examine the corpse, the prince noticed Rasputin's left eyelid trembling. Suddenly Rasputin's eyes popped open, and he jumped up and seized Yusupov by the neck. The prince ran up the stairs in horror; the others bounded down the stairs just in time to see Rasputin sprinting across the courtyard toward an open gate. After taking two shots in the back, Rasputin collapsed in the snow. The conspirators kicked him in the head to convince themselves that he was finally dead. They then bound the body with ropes and dumped it off a bridge over the Neva River through a hole in the ice.

The body was not found for several days, but when it was recovered it became apparent that Rasputin had still been alive when he was thrown into the water. One arm was half out of the rope, and his lungs were full of water, indicating that the actual cause of death was drowning. Rasputin was buried on the grounds of the czar's palace, but during the night of March 22-23, 1917, a crowd of rebel soldiers exhumed the grave and carried the coffin to a nearby forest, where the decomposing body was burned on an improvised pyre.

SIGNIFICANCE

Because of Empress Alexandra's concern for young Alexei, she would believe no ill rumors about Rasputin. He had incredible power over her, and he misused it for his own nefarious purposes. Czar Nicholas II was a timid and vacillating man who consistently acquiesced to his wife's demands. If Rasputin wanted someone put into or out of office, he had only to mention it to the empress, who would request it of the czar.

The heavy casualties suffered by the Russian army during the first years of World War I caused the czar to take command of the troops at the front lines in 1915, effectively leaving Alexandra and Rasputin in charge of the country. Competent ministers were dismissed and replaced by Rasputin's unpopular and incompetent nominees. In just one year there were five interior ministers, three war ministers, four agriculture ministers, and three justice ministers. Economic conditions deteriorated, transportation was chaotic, and supplies for the military were chronically short.

Rasputin's constant meddling in political affairs had weakened an already weak government beyond the point of no return. By 1917 the czar had no credibility with his people or with government officials. Scarcely two months after Rasputin's murder, the czar was forced to abdicate, and a moderate provisional government took control. In October, 1917, the Bolsheviks seized power, and the country degenerated into a civil war that ultimately transformed the communist regime into a dictatorship of terror. Although one cannot claim that Rasputin was responsible for the Russian Revolution, by fueling the rising tide of discontent against the monarchy, he was certainly a major contributing factor.

—*George R. Plitnik*

FURTHER READING

Fulop-Miller, René. *Rasputin: The Holy Devil*. New York: Garden City, 1928. One of the earliest accounts of Rasputin's life. The author succeeds in presenting the divergent facets of Rasputin's personality in a well-researched and unbiased manner.

Furhmann, Joseph. *Rasputin: A Life*. New York: Praeger, 1990. A well-researched history written from the perspective that there were always two Rasputins, the "real" one and the one who was said to exist. Furhmann consistently strives to disentangle these two.

Moynahan, Brian. *Rasputin: The Saint Who Sinned*. New York: Random House, 1997. This volume's meticulous attention to detail and historical accuracy does not render it any less readable.

Myles, Douglas. *Rasputin: Satyr, Saint, or Satan*. New York: McGraw-Hill, 1990. Myles provides a well-written and highly entertaining account of the Rasputin story. This work includes a glossary of foreign words with a guide to their pronunciation.

Radzinsky, Edvard. *The Rasputin File*. Translated from the Russian by Judson Rosengrant. New York: Nan Talese/Doubleday, 2000. In 1917, a revolutionary commission compiled an evidentiary file to determine the cause of Rasputin's death. Radzinsky obtained the file and uses it and other sources to present a detailed account of Rasputin's actions from 1903 until his death in 1916. Recommended for readers with a specialized knowledge of Russian history.

Rasputin, Maria, and Patte Barham. *Rasputin: The Man Behind the Myth—A Personal Memoir*. Englewood Cliffs, N.J.: Prentice-Hall, 1977. These personal and favorably biased recollections were written by Rasputin's daughter six decades after his murder. Several of the accounts clash with other, less biased, evidence.

Youssoupov (Yusupov), Felix. *Rasputin: His Malignant Influence and His Assassination.* 1927. Reprint. Salisbury, N.C.: Documentary Publications, 1976. This is an obviously biased apologia written by Rasputin's primary murderer ten years after the event. He maintains that Rasputin was the devil incarnate and that his murder was justified and necessary to save the Russian monarchy.

SEE ALSO: Alexander II; Konstantin Petrovich Pobedonostsev.

RELATED ARTICLE in *Great Events from History: The Nineteenth Century, 1801-1900:* January 4, 1894: Franco-Russian Alliance.

RAMMOHAN RAY
Indian religious leader and social reformer

Remembered as the founder of modern India, Ray left writings that have become the putative source for almost all India's social and religious reformist ideals. He saw the Hinduism of his day as a debased form of a purer monotheism practiced in India during a prehistoric Golden Age. He also found many social customs of his own day—the forced suicide of widows and child marriage, for example—as decadent, medieval accretions on the noble patterns of the Vedic age.

BORN: May 22, 1772; Rādhānagar, Bengal (now in India)

DIED: September 27, 1833; Bristol, England

ALSO KNOWN AS: Rammohun Ray; Rammohun Roy; Raja Rammohun Ray

AREAS OF ACHIEVEMENT: Religion and theology, social reform

EARLY LIFE

Rammohan Ray was born into a Kulin family and married twice while still in his early teens. Among Bengalis of the eighteenth and early nineteenth centuries, priests (Brahmans) of the Kulin class ranked only slightly lower than the gods. Their inferiors customarily addressed them as "Lord" (*Thakur*). They also emulated the Kulin's dialect of Bengali and almost everything about their style. Kulin boys were much in demand as husbands and often had more than one wife.

Ray's father's ancestors had long before assimilated themselves into the culture of India's Muslim rulers and had served in many governmental posts. His father was a landowner (*zamindar*) who fell on hard times in later life. In 1800, his father was jailed for debt, and he died in poverty in 1803. Ray's mother's family had not moved so close to Indo-Islamic culture and supported themselves as ritual specialists.

As a boy, Ray studied Arabic and Persian and was sent to Patna in Bihar, which, as a center for Muslim learning, offered better instruction than his hometown school. That was a common practice among Hindus who adopted the cosmopolitan culture of Muslims. Ray acquired a knowledge of Islamic doctrine as well as an interest in the mystical teachings of the Sufis. These two philosophies may have been responsible for his lifelong iconoclasm. According to his own autobiographical notes, while still a teenager he criticized his father's devotion to images of the gods and was thrown out of the house. Ray seems to have romanticized his recollections of the next decade of his life, claiming a journey to Tibet to study Buddhism and a lengthy stay in Benares to learn Sanskrit. Because in later life he wanted to be considered an authority on ancient Hindu religious texts, he may have exaggerated his knowledge of the classical language.

Between 1797 and 1802, Ray seems to have spent much of his time in Calcutta, the burgeoning capital of Bengal and British India, where he acted as a moneylender. Many of his clients were young Englishmen employed by the East India Company. In this way his name became known in government circles, and he received an appointment in the Revenue Department. He eventually became a deputy district collector, the highest civil post an Indian could hold. During his active career, he invested in real estate, and by his early forties he had an ample fortune that allowed him to retire to Calcutta in 1815.

LIFE'S WORK

Beginning during the 1770's, a number of Englishmen began to expand their knowledge of India's non-Muslim traditions. Sir William Jones and Henry Colebrooke, among others, acquired a better-than-rudimentary knowledge of Sanskrit. As they discovered that an enormous body of literature existed in that tongue, they conceded to ancient Indian civilization a classical status analogous to that of Greece and Rome in Western tradition. Their efforts in the reconstruction of the history of India earned for them the sobriquet "Orientalist."

The work of the Orientalists had two institutional foci. The first was the Asiatic Society of Bengal, founded in 1784, and the second the College of Fort William, established in 1800. Although the former was a typical learned society of the period that met regularly to hear papers by members on a variety of subjects published in the society's journal, the second was an unprecedented attempt to train the East India Company's servants in the languages of the peoples they expected to govern. Few of those young men proved to be able scholars, but the professors of the College of Fort William, with the help of numerous Indian assistants, kept extending their knowledge of Sanskrit and the texts written in it.

During his earlier stays in Calcutta, Ray had contacts with Englishmen active in the college. He began to learn English and became fluent in the language. He was not, however, alone in his interests and contacts with the British. A number of other Bengali intellectuals had similar connections and concerns. They imbibed a number of ideas that had originated with British scholars such as Jones and Colebrooke. One of the most important of these was the notion that Hindu civilization had enjoyed a Golden Age during which India produced a lofty and subtle religiophilosophical system every bit as valuable as that of the Greeks and Romans. They also believed that, in that halcyon time, India's society was well organized and featured a balance between the various classes.

For the Orientalists, as well as for such Indians as Ray who subscribed to their ideas, a major problem was explaining how the Golden Age had disappeared to be replaced by the polytheism, idolatry, and caste inequalities of their own day. Following the British lead, Ray and others saw Muslims as the cause of that decline. Despite a Muslim presence in the subcontinent of more than nine hundred years' duration, as well as the prominence of Hindus in Muslim governments from the beginning of their rule, they began describing Muslims as foreign tyrants whose oppression brought on Hindu decadence. Because Ray maintained close personal ties to Muslims—in 1831, he became the Mughal emperor's first ambassador to the Court of Saint James—perhaps he espoused this opinion only as a way of inspiring his coreligionists, never thinking that the notion would have so long a life or such ultimately fatal consequences.

In 1815, Ray published *Translation of an Abridgment of the "Vedant": Or, Resolution of All the Veds, the Most Celebrated and Revised Work of Brahminical Theology*. In this book, he emphasized monotheist religious views, claiming that a pure monotheism was the true doctrine taught by Indian religious texts, especially the *Upanishads*, also known as the "End of the Vedas" (*Vedanta*). To reinforce these assertions, Ray translated several of the more than three hundred *Upanishads*. In his emphasis on monotheism—belief in a personal God—rather than monism—the assertion that all reality is an impersonal, featureless "One"—Ray seems to be reflecting his dependence not on the original Sanskrit texts but on Persian translations of them ordered by the Mughal prince Dara Shikoh.

The *Upanishads* tended to stress monism, but as a Muslim Dara slanted his translations toward monotheism in order to make it seem that the texts were closer to Islam. Some of Ray's more perceptive critics pointed out that his interpretations proved that he did not have the Sanskrit learning required to give authoritative explanations of sacred literature. Ray's other concerns also provoked opposition.

As did most other religious critics in India's history, Ray soon became embroiled in controversies over social practices. He made the fate of Bengali women his special cause. At the time, women were uneducated, treated as weak creatures subject to the whims of their brutish husbands, and never allowed to leave their homes. Ray supported many measures to protect them. He championed attempts to outlaw the burning of widows on their husbands' funeral pyres. Though followed by only a few high-status families, the custom dictated that a woman volunteer for this fate, thus proving herself a "virtuous female" (*satī*). In practice, relatives used the occasion to avoid, through murder, having to support an unwanted female. He also opposed the practice of child marriage, which sometimes created widows who were eight or nine years old. Even though they were not consigned to the mortuary fires, these girls were forced to lead dreary lives either as the celibate servants of their in-laws or as unmarriageable burdens on their own parents and brothers.

Though many of his views derived ultimately from the Orientalists, Ray did not invariably support all of their schemes. For example, when some proposed the establishment of a Sanskrit college, he opposed the move, believing that it was better to teach English to Indians than to immerse them in an archaic language. In this instance, he seems to have anticipated the anti-Orientalist reaction that arose in the government of India during the 1840's and that dominated educational policy throughout the British period.

Ray's interest in religion blossomed in Calcutta. He became a defender of his purified version of Hinduism against attacks by missionaries. He found himself drawn closer to the teaching of the Unitarians, who were emerging during the 1820's as a distinct and, to the minds of most Christians, heretical sect. Their monotheism, iconoclasm, and refusal to assert the absolute superiority of Christian revelation attracted Ray. He began corresponding with leading Unitarians in England and the United States; at one point, he contemplated finishing his life in the United States in order to be close to William Ellery Channing. *The Precepts of Jesus, the Guide to Peace and Happiness*, published in 1820, displayed the Unitarian influence. In it, he selected only those passages of the New Testament that contained some moral injunction and ignored those mentioning miracles or that contained assertions of Jesus' divinity. Although Ray often said that his heart was with the Unitarians, he never formally joined their church, preferring always to be known as a Hindu.

In 1828, Ray and a few associates founded the Brahmo Sabha (later called the Brahmo Samaj), or "Society of God." In general, this church was supposed to promulgate reformed religious and social principles. The Brahmo Sabha had little time to evolve as an organization before Ray in 1831 accepted the post of Mughal ambassador to England and left Calcutta forever. After his departure, the organization became moribund until it was revived some nine years later. By the time he left the city, Ray's staunchest friends were either Muslims or British Unitarians. Most of his fellow Hindus either condemned or ignored him. In England, his health ebbed and his fortune dwindled. He became a much-revered figure among English Unitarians and died in one of their homes. A Unitarian minister preached his funeral sermon.

SIGNIFICANCE

Though today universally acknowledged as the founder of modern India, Rammohan Ray was not fully recognized while he lived. The work of providing him with this identity began in the years following his death. Debendranath Tagore revived the Brahmo Sabha (calling it the Brahmo Samaj) in the years 1840 through 1842 and realized that the society required a spiritual leader to give it cohesion. Tagore, whose family produced several of Bengal's leading intellectual and literary lights, began to edit Ray's Persian, English, and Bengali writings. Af-

ter K. C. Mitra published a biography of Ray in the *Calcutta Review* of 1845, the practice of crediting Ray for the invention of everything modern and progressive became common. Ray's importance, however, may well have been in his being typical of an era when Indians of many faiths and Englishmen cooperated in securing European recognition of India's civilization as one of the world's most influential and important traditions.

—*Gregory C. Kozlowski*

FURTHER READING

Basham, A. L., ed. *A Cultural History of India*. Oxford, England: Clarendon Press, 1975. Contains thirty-five essays discussing almost every aspect of India's history from ancient times to the present. By judicious reading, a beginner will be able to discover the broader intellectual and social context in which Ray and other reformist thinkers worked.

Bhattacharya, Haridas, ed. *Religions*. Vol. 4 in *Cultural Heritage of India*. Calcutta, India: Ramakrishna Mission, 1969. The last volume in a series of books cataloging many aspects of the religious and social traditions of Indian life. Shows that Hinduism is a term loosely connecting a number of very different religious tendencies. The essay on the Brahmo Samaj describes Ray's influence on this group and its place in nineteenth and twentieth century India.

Farquhar, J. N. *Modern Religious Movements in India*. Reprint. Delhi, India: Munshiram Manoharlal, 1967. Originally written by a sympathetic Christian missionary. The many reprintings of this book demonstrate its value as an introductory text. It has a clear style easily accessible to students. Although a number of its views should be modified by reference to the work of modern scholars, notably David Kopf's books listed below, it remains a readable introduction to Ray and his era.

Hay, Stephen N., ed. *Modern Indian and Pakistan*. Vol. 2 in *Sources of Indian Tradition*. 2d ed. New York: Columbia University Press, 1988. A valuable anthology of translations from primary sources, introductory essays, and comments on the sources. Places brief selections from Ray's writings in the context of his own time as well as relating them to the work of later generations of reformers.

Heimsath, Charles H. *Indian Nationalism and Hindu Social Reform*. Princeton, N.J.: Princeton University Press, 1964. Makes the vital connection between religious/social reform, its critics, and India's nationalist movement. The programs of both reformers and their critics must be understood as part of India's long drive for independence. Also has the merit of covering reformist movements in all the major cultural regions of the subcontinent.

Kopf, David. *The Brahmo Samaj and the Shaping of the Modern Indian Mind*. Princeton, N.J.: Princeton University Press, 1979. Together with the book cited below, this work provides a comprehensive and insightful history of Bengali intellectual life from the late eighteenth century to the early twentieth century. The first chapters give a succinct and penetrating appraisal of Ray's influence on modernizing Bengalis. Also describes Tagore's role in establishing Ray as the founder of modern India.

_____. *British Orientalism and the Bengal Renaissance: The Dynamics of Indian Modernization, 1773-1835*. Berkeley: University of California Press, 1969. This valuable work demonstrates the complex interchanges between Englishmen and Indians that added a new dimension to Bengali intellectual life. Provides a history of the College of Fort William and places Ray's career in the context of Orientalist labors. Also

charts the anti-Orientalist reaction of the 1830's and 1840's.

Robertson, Bruce Carlisle. *Raja Rammahan Ray: The Father of Modern India*. Delhi, India: Oxford University Press, 1995. Robertson describes how Ray's ideas set the agenda for modern India, creating a vision of an independent, pluralistic society based upon the principles of the *Upanishads*.

Salmond, Noel A. *Hindu Iconclasts: Rammohun Roy, Dayananda Sarasvati, and Nineteenth-Century Polemics Against Idoltary*. Waterloo, Ont.: Published for the Canadian Corporation for Studies in Religion by Wilfrid Laurier University Press, 2004. Scholarly study analyzing the ideas of Ray and others who challenged Hindu practices of idolatry. Examines other aspects of Ray's religious thinking.

SEE ALSO: William Ellery Channing; Dadabhai Naoroji.
RELATED ARTICLE in *Great Events from History: The Nineteenth Century, 1801-1900:* 1885: Indian National Congress Is Founded.

ANDRÉ REBOUÇAS
Brazilian engineer and abolitionist

The grandson of a freed slave, Rebouças demonstrated that upward social mobility was possible for some people of color in nineteenth century Brazil. Trained as an engineer, he directed large construction projects designed to modernize Brazil; he also became involved in the abolitionist struggle and helped bring about the end of slavery in Brazil.

BORN: January 13, 1838; Cachoeira, Bahia, Brazil
DIED: May 9, 1898; Funchal, Madeira
ALSO KNOWN AS: André Pinto Rebouças (full name)
AREAS OF ACHIEVEMENT: Government and politics, engineering

EARLY LIFE

André Rebouças (reh-BOH-suhs) was born in Brazil's sugar-producing province of Bahia. His grandfather had immigrated to Brazil from Portugal and married a freed black woman. Their mixed-race children were encouraged to pursue studies that focused on the high culture of Europe. Their oldest son, the uncle of André Rebouças, followed a career in music. Proficient on violin and pi-

ano, he completed his training in France and Italy. Upon returning to Brazil he became an orchestra conductor who was much admired for the violin solos he played on a Stradivarius that he brought from Europe. Another son, André's father, became a well-known lawyer. Self-taught in classical languages and literature, he was both a talented lawyer and an astute politician. During the early 1820's he took the side of those who supported an independent Brazil ruled by Pedro I. For his efforts in bringing his province of Bahia into the nativist fold, he was rewarded with a special commendation from the new emperor as well as with appointments to public office. In 1828, he was elected to the National Assembly.

When André was eight years old, his family moved to the capital city of Rio de Janeiro. While living in Bahia, his father had taken charge of his education. In Rio, however, André was enrolled in local schools, in which he prepared successfully for the difficult entrance examination for the prestigious national military academy. A brilliant student at the academy, he completed his training in mathematics and engineering at the top of his class. It was customary for the best graduates of the military academy to be granted scholarships to complete their educations in Europe. However, because André was considered a "mulatto," he was denied that honor, so his father paid for him to go to Europe himself.

Rebouças returned from Europe in 1861. Three years later, Brazil went to war with Paraguay in 1864. Rebouças immediately joined the Volunteers of the Fatherland and was sent to the front, where he advised military commanders on strategy. Dismayed at the lack of preparation evident in Brazil's army, he became committed to modernizing the military. However, he became one of the thousands of soldiers who contracted smallpox in Paraguay and had to return to Rio de Janeiro in 1866 to convalesce.

LIFE'S WORK

With his exceptionally fine mind and solid training, Rebouças rose to professional and political prominence during the 1870's. Imbued with the spirit of his age, he was determined to help launch Brazil into the modern era. Although he had friends and admirers in the highest circles of government, racial prejudice at times hindered his professional opportunities. For example, when he was hired to oversee the building of a modern customs house and docks in Rio de Janeiro, he was paid only one-third the salary that his British predecessor had earned.

Frustrated by the roadblocks he faced while in government service, Rebouças became convinced that politicians were hindering Brazil's move forward into the industrial era. He also came to believe that the Brazilian economy, built on African slavery, did not provide the necessary incentives to foster modernization. Only a radical transformation of the social base, aided by large-scale European immigration, would bring progress to his nation. Like many prosperous Brazilians, Rebouças and his family owned slaves, but they freed them in 1870.

During the 1870's, after being rejected several times because of his skin color, Rebouças was given a professorship at Brazil's prestigious Polytechnical School. When he became involved in the abolitionist campaigns of the 1880's, he encouraged his students to support the cause of freedom for slaves. He befriended the most influential abolitionists, wrote newspaper articles and pamphlets in favor of abolition, and contributed a large portion of his private funds to promote abolition. In his view, a modern Brazil would be possible only after eliminating the concentration of land in the hands of a few families. He therefore urged that significant land reform accompany abolition so that freed slaves and European immigrants might have access to land of their own.

As a young man, Rebouças had believed Brazil should follow the North American model of industrialization and supported republicanism. During the 1880's, however, he became convinced that a Brazilian republic would be at the mercy of an agricultural oligarchy that would block land reform, so he changed his position to support a constitutional monarchy in which the monarch would promote the reforms that must be undertaken for the good of the nation.

Rebouças was a prolific writer. Not only did he keep a detailed diary, but he also wrote frequent letters to influential friends and to editors of major newspapers in Rio de Janeiro, and contributed articles to newspapers in Brazil and abroad—including *The Times* of London. His writings enabled him to share with a broad audience his vision of the future of Brazil and the need to end slavery.

In time, Rebouças became a good friend of Brazil's Emperor Pedro II. After slavery was abolished in 1888, Rebouças deepened his support for Brazil's royal family. When a military coup deposed the emperor and installed a republic in 1889, Rebouças's hopes for a modern Brazil guided by a benevolent king were dashed. He decided to leave Brazil and accompanied the emperor into exile in Europe. After Pedro's death in 1891, Rebouças traveled to Africa but became disenchanted with life there. In 1893, he settled on the Portuguese island of Madeira.

Although Rebouças yearned for Brazil, and his friends there urged him to return home, he felt he could not. As his health and financial situation deteriorated, he became increasingly despondent. On May 9, 1898, exactly ten years after the Brazilian parliament had passed the law freeing the slaves, he was found dead on a beach at Funchal. At the time, many people suspected that he had committed suicide. In any case, it was generally agreed that his death was a sad end to the life of a person who had contributed much to his country.

SIGNIFICANCE

André Rebouças illustrates the opportunities—and the limitations—open to Brazilians of all races in the nineteenth century. Although he lived in a nation marked by African slavery and intense racial prejudice, his own family transcended the barriers of race and rose to positions of high influence. They did this primarily by accepting the cultural values of the white elite. Rebouças is remembered in Brazil for participating in the abolitionist campaign and for his vision of a modern Brazil built on agrarian reform. He also became a poignant symbol of those who saw in Brazil's enlightened monarchy the best hope for a brighter future and were devastated by its demise. In honor of his contributions as an engineer, the longest tunnel in Rio de Janeiro, linking the suburbs to the city, was named for him.

—*Joan E. Meznar*

FURTHER READING
Andrews, George Reid. *Afro-Latin America, 1800-2000.* New York: Oxford University Press, 2004. The author provides an excellent background to abolition in Brazil, setting Rebouças in the context of his friendship with Brazil's abolitionist emperor.
Azevedo, Celia Maria Marinho de. *Abolitionism in the United States and Brazil: A Comparative Perspective.* New York: Garland, 1995. In this comparative study, the author highlights Rebouças's view that slavery in Brazil hindered development and his hope that European immigration would promote progress.
Conrad, Robert Edgar. *Children of God's Fire: A Documentary History of Black Slavery in Brazil.* University Park: Pennsylvania State University Press, 1994. An excellent collection of primary source materials on Brazilian slavery, including an excerpt from Rebouças's diary in which he described the racism he experienced during a visit to New York City in 1873.
_____. *The Destruction of Brazilian Slavery, 1850-1888.* Berkeley: University of California Press, 1972. Includes a thorough account of the abolitionist activities of Rebouças, who was one of several mulattoes who struggled in different ways to eradicate slavery in Brazil.

Nabuco, Carolina. *The Life of Joaquim Nabuco.* Translated by Ronald Hilton. Stanford: Stanford University Press, 1950. In this biography of one of Brazil's leading abolitionists, his daughter describes some of the people who collaborated with him in the struggle to end slavery in Brazil. André Rebouças became a good friend of Joaquim Nabuco as they worked together to promote abolition.
Skidmore, Thomas E. "Racial Ideas and Social Policy in Brazil, 1870-1940." In *The Idea of Race in Latin America, 1870-1940*, edited by Richard Graham. Austin: University of Texas Press, 1990. Useful for a description of the black middle class to which Rebouças belonged, and its contribution to the struggle against slavery.
Spitzer, Leo. *Lives in Between: Assimilation and Marginality in Austria, Brazil, West Africa, 1780-1945.* Cambridge, England: Cambridge University Press, 1989. The best account available in English of three generations of the Rebouças family. Important for its biographical information, it also discusses the implications of upward mobility in Brazil through "whitening" and assimilating into the dominant culture.

SEE ALSO: Joaquim Maria Machado de Assis; Pedro I; Pedro II.
RELATED ARTICLES in *Great Events from History: The Nineteenth Century, 1801-1900:* September 7, 1822: Brazil Becomes Independent; May 1, 1865-June 20, 1870: Paraguayan War.

RED CLOUD
Native American leader

Red Cloud led the Lakota (Sioux) Indians through a difficult period, effectively resisting the onrush of American westward advance and later helping the Lakota make the transition to reservation life under American rule.

BORN: 1822; Blue Creek, near North Platte (now in Nebraska)
DIED: December 10, 1909; Pine Ridge, South Dakota
ALSO KNOWN AS: Makhpíya-Lúta (birth name)
AREA OF ACHIEVEMENT: Government and politics

EARLY LIFE
Red Cloud was born into the Oglala subtribe of the Teton branch of Lakota, or Dakota people (more popularly

known as Sioux) on the high plains of what is now Nebraska. His father, a headman in the Brulé subtribe, was named Lone Man, and his mother was Walks-as-She-Thinks, a member of the Saone subtribe. There is disagreement over the origins of the name Red Cloud. Some sources contend that it was a family name used by his father and grandfather, while others claim that it was coined as a description of the way his scarlet-blanketed warriors covered the hills like a red cloud.

Little is known about Red Cloud's early life. His father died when he was young, and he was reared in the camp of Chief Old Smoke, a maternal uncle. He undoubtedly spent his boyhood learning skills that were important to Lakota men at the time, including hunting, riding, and shooting. Plains Culture Indians sometimes conducted raids against enemies, and Red Cloud joined his first war party and took his first scalp at the age of sixteen. Thereafter, he was always quick to participate in expeditions against Pawnee, Crows, or Ute. Other Oglala frequently retold Red Cloud's colorful exploits in battle. During a raid against the Crows, he killed the warrior guarding the ponies and then ran off with fifty horses. This was a highly respected deed among Plains Indians, whose horses were central to their way of life. On an expedition against the Pawnee, Red Cloud killed four of the enemy—an unusually high number in a type of warfare in which casualties were normally low.

During the early 1840's, most Oglala bands camped around Fort Laramie on the North Platte River, where they could obtain a variety of goods from white traders. Red Cloud was part of a band known as the Bad Faces, or Smoke People, under the leadership of his uncle, Old Smoke. Another band in the area, the Koya, was led by Bull Bear, the most dominant headman among the Oglala and commonly recognized as their chief. The two groups frequently quarreled. One day in the fall of 1841, after young men of both sides had been drinking, a member of the Bad Faces stole a Koya woman. Bull Bear led a force to the Bad Face camp and shot the father of the young man who had taken the woman. The Bad Faces retaliated, and when a shot to the leg downed Bull Bear, Red Cloud rushed in and killed him. This event led to a split among the Oglala that lasted for many years. It also elevated Red Cloud's standing among the Bad Faces, and shortly after the incident he organized and led a war party of his own against the Pawnee.

Soon after recovering from wounds suffered in that raid, Red Cloud married a young Lakota woman named Pretty Owl. Sources disagree as to whether he thereafter remained monogamous or took multiple wives, a common practice among prominent Lakota. There is no agreement on how many children he fathered, although five is the number most accepted by scholars. Over the next two decades, Red Cloud's reputation and status continued to grow. By the mid-1860's, he was a ruggedly handsome man of medium stature with penetrating eyes and a confident and commanding presence. He was also a band headman and a leading warrior with an increasing following among the Bad Faces. Lakota social and political structure was decentralized; no one person had authority over the whole group. Instead, certain leaders were recognized as chiefs on the basis of ability and achievement. An important member of his band, at this time Red Cloud was not yet a chief.

Red Cloud. (National Archives)

LIFE'S WORK

In the several decades before the Civil War, traders began operating in Lakota territory, followed by wagon trains, telegraph construction, and more. The Lakota welcomed most of the traders and at least tolerated most of the wagon trains, even though whites disrupted hunting by killing indiscriminately and chasing many animals away from traditional hunting grounds. By the closing years of the Civil War, American traffic across the northern plains increased even further. The discovery of gold in the mountains of Montana in late 1862 enticed more whites to cross Lakota land, leading to friction and occasional clashes. The final straw came when the government sent soldiers in to build forts and protect passage along a popular route known as the Bozeman Trail that linked Montana with the Oregon Trail.

In 1865, many Lakota, including Red Cloud, took up arms in resistance. Several Lakota leaders signed a treaty in the spring of 1866 that would open the Bozeman Trail, but Red Cloud and his many followers held out, insisting on a removal of soldiers. The government tried to ignore Red Cloud for a time, but the Lakota almost completely closed down travel and obstructed efforts to construct the forts. This was the high point in Red Cloud's career as a military strategist. He led his men to a number of victories, most notably the annihilation of Captain William J. Fetterman and eighty-two soldiers in an incident known to whites as the Fetterman Massacre and to Indians as the Battle of a Hundred Slain. In November of 1868, when, after negotiations, the army withdrew the troops and abandoned the forts, Red Cloud finally ended the war.

This victory increased Red Cloud's standing among his people, although he still was not the Lakota's exclusive leader. The U.S. government, however, assumed that he was the head chief and dealt with him as such. During the late 1860's, there was talk of creating a reservation for the Lakota, and Red Cloud surprised everyone by announcing that he would go to Washington, D.C., and talk about the idea.

Some have argued that Red Cloud was motivated by a desire to gain the status among the Lakota that he already enjoyed in the view of federal officials. On the other hand, he may have realized that since many white Westerners opposed a reservation and preferred the extermination of Indians, a reservation, combined with the withdrawal of troops from all Lakota lands, an important objective to Red Cloud, might be the best compromise he could achieve. He and twenty other Lakota leaders were escorted to the nation's capital in 1870 with great ceremony. Red Cloud did not win everything he wanted, but he clearly emerged as the most famous Native American of his time. He was applauded by many easterners who sympathized with Indians and saw Red Cloud as a symbol of justifiable response to white advance.

In 1871, Red Cloud settled on the newly created reservation, at the agency named after him. Then, only a few years later, gold was discovered in the Black Hills portion of the reserve, and the government pressured the Lakota to sell the area. When negotiations broke down, events quickly escalated into the Sioux War of 1876-1877. With one eye on the government, Red Cloud publicly opposed the armed action undertaken by some Lakota to stop the flood of prospectors onto their lands, but privately he seemed to sanction such moves.

Red Cloud frequently became embroiled in political battles with federal agents on the reservation. He tried to win whatever provisions and concessions he could to ease his people's suffering, and he resisted government efforts to break down traditional cultural and political life. When many Lakota became involved in the controversial Ghost Dance in 1889-1890, Red Cloud avoided early commitment to or open encouragement of partici-

pation. Many dancers, however, believed that they indeed had his support. Red Cloud's frequent compromise position and his seeming cooperation with government agents sometimes made him suspect among some of his people, and, as a consequence, his influence steadily eroded. He died on the reservation on December 10, 1909.

SIGNIFICANCE

Red Cloud emerged as a military and political leader at a dramatic and tragic time in the history of the Lakota people. Onetime powerful nomadic buffalo hunters, they were going through far-reaching changes. American westward advance constricted their land base, destroyed the buffalo upon which their economy depended, and ultimately brought about their impoverishment. Moreover, government attempts to destroy traditional Lakota ways of life on the reservation, while never completely successful, resulted in cultural shock.

For a time, Red Cloud resisted militarily as effectively as any Native American leader ever had. Then, when American domination became clear, he attempted delicately to balance the two worlds of Indian and white, hoping to win the best results possible for his people under the circumstances. This was a difficult task, and he did not satisfy everyone. He was attacked from both sides—by whites for not doing more to encourage his followers to assimilate into the white world, and by some Lakota for being too willing to give in to government authorities.

Red Cloud stood as a symbol to many Indians (and some whites) of strong defense of homelands and culture, while to other whites he epitomized the worst in Indian treachery and savagery. For both sides, the name Red Cloud conveyed immense power and meaning. During the 1960's and 1970's, with the rise of the Red Power movement and a rejuvenation of Indian culture, he again became a symbol—this time to a generation of young Indian (and sometimes white) political activists who found inspiration in what they saw as his defiance in the face of unjust authority.

—Larry W. Burt

FURTHER READING

Allen, Charles Wesley. *Autobiography of Red Cloud: War Leader of the Oglalas.* Edited by R. Eli Paul. Helena: Montana Historical Society Press, 1997. Red Cloud gave an oral account of his life to a historian in 1893, and Allen later prepared a manuscript with Red Cloud's recollections. The manuscript languished in the offices of the Nebraska State Historical Society for decades until it was published by the Montana Historical Society in 1997.

Cook, James H. *Fifty Years on the Old Frontier*. New Haven, Conn.: Yale University Press, 1923. Neither scholarly nor complete in its coverage of Red Cloud, it does contain some interesting, colorful, and first-hand descriptions of the Lakota leader and some of his exploits by a prominent frontiersman and close friend.

DeMallie, Raymond J., ed. *The Sixth Grandfather: Black Elk's Teachings Given to John G. Neihardt*. Lincoln: University of Nebraska Press, 1984. Does not focus on Red Cloud's life specifically, but provides direct accounts of various events in his life, especially surrounding the 1875-1876 Black Hills controversy, as told by Black Elk and other Lakota participants to poet John Neihardt.

Goodyear, Frank H., III. *Red Cloud: Photographs of a Lakota Chief*. Lincoln: University of Nebraska Press, 2003. Red Cloud was photographed many times because he believed these photographs helped him serve as a mediator between the Oglala Lakota and the federal government. This book contains more than eighty photographs by Mathew Brady, Edward Curtis, and other photographers. It also features a biographical and historical analysis written by Goodyear.

Hyde, George E. *Red Cloud's Folk: A History of the Oglala Sioux Indians*. Norman: University of Oklahoma Press, 1937. Less complete and authoritative than the more recent book by James C. Olson, but generally well written and reliable. Focuses on the earliest period of which historians have any knowledge of Lakota history to about the end of the Sioux War of 1876-1877.

_____. *A Sioux Chronicle*. Norman: University of Oklahoma Press, 1956. A continuation of *Red Cloud's Folk* that carries the story of the Oglala to the tragedy at Wounded Knee in 1890. Contains less information about Red Cloud, because his role was diminishing by the end of the nineteenth century. However, it does offer useful material on Red Cloud's part in Lakota history after the creation of the reservation during the 1870's.

Olson, James C. *Red Cloud and the Sioux Problem*. Lincoln: University of Nebraska Press, 1965. The best and most complete account of Red Cloud. Except for some background information on the Lakota and Red Cloud's early life, it begins with the period immediately after the Civil War and ends with the death of Red Cloud in 1909.

Robinson, Doane. *A History of the Dakota or Sioux Indians*. Aberdeen, S.D.: News Printing, 1904. Reprint. Minneapolis, Minn.: Ross and Haines, 1958. First printed by the South Dakota State Historical Society in 1904, this book bears the mark of scholarship in an earlier era in its attitude toward Indians. It is so factually solid and complete that it still stands as an important source for information on Red Cloud.

Utley, Robert M. *The Last Days of the Sioux Nation*. New Haven, Conn.: Yale University Press, 1963. An excellent history of the events surrounding the famous Massacre of Wounded Knee, including material about Red Cloud's participation in that event that reveals something about his role in Lakota society in 1890.

SEE ALSO: Crazy Horse; Sitting Bull; Tecumseh.

RELATED ARTICLES in *Great Events from History: The Nineteenth Century, 1801-1900:* August 17, 1862-December 28, 1863: Great Sioux War; June 13, 1866-November 6, 1868: Red Cloud's War; December 21, 1866: Fetterman Massacre; December 29, 1890: Wounded Knee Massacre.

ODILON REDON
French painter

Through long years of artistic experimentation, Redon developed a mysterious, nostalgic, melancholy, and sometimes humorous fantasy world in his paintings, prints, and drawings. This world became his distinctive contribution to the allusive art movement of the end of the nineteenth century called Symbolism that anticipated twentieth century Surrealism.

BORN: April 20, 1840; Bordeaux, France
DIED: July 6, 1916; Paris, France
ALSO KNOWN AS: Bertrand-Jean Redon (birth name)
AREA OF ACHIEVEMENT: Art

EARLY LIFE

Originally christened Bertrand-Jean, Odilon Redon (ree-dahn) was always known by his nickname, the masculine version of his mother's name, Marie-Odile. She was an American from New Orleans, Louisiana, where Redon's French father had established a lucrative business. Shortly before Redon's birth, his father brought the family permanently back to France. Redon was a sickly child; as a young boy, he was sent to live with an aged uncle at a rural family estate near Bordeaux. The boy lived a reclusive life close to nature, drawing the natural beauty around him and creating his own fantasy world. As an adult, he frequently returned to this home, which served as an unending source of inspiration. A nostalgia for this boyhood home never left him. From the age of eleven, he received professional art training. Originally, his goal was to become an architect, but it became clear that he did not possess the mathematical skills required for such a profession. At that point, his father allowed him to pursue training as an artist.

Redon was keenly interested in playing the violin and reading contemporary literature. His reading included works by Edgar Allan Poe, Charles Baudelaire, Gustave Flaubert, and, later, Stéphane Mallarmé. Both of these interests provided excellent background for his eventual artistic direction. The Symbolist style, with which Redon was allied, included musicians, writers, and visual artists. It favored an approach that suggested an emotional tone that was often pessimistic or melancholy, as well as mystical and fantastic, and certainly disturbing, which the viewer was encouraged to imaginatively embellish. Redon created prints, paintings, and drawings that developed these themes and often drew on the works of his favorite writers. Compared with the best-known works of the Symbolists, Redon's art had a benign cast to it that was more melancholy than disturbing.

LIFE'S WORK

At the age of twenty-five, Redon began studying painting in Paris under the Romantic-style artist Jean-Léon Gérôme. This was not a happy period for Redon. His teacher's philosophical attitude toward art was not agreeable to Redon, and he could not fit into the rigid studio regimen. He needed instruction that included a great deal of artistic freedom of expression. Gérôme's regimen emphasized the realistic reproduction of a subject, but realism was never a productive approach for Redon. Nature only provided a launchpad for his imagination.

In 1863, Redon returned to Bordeaux and continued a more productive period of work and study with his friend, the printmaker Rodolphe Bresdin, who taught him etching and engraving techniques. However, it was Bresdin's highly imaginative subject matter that really sparked Redon's interest. It was at this time that Redon immersed himself in the exploration of the graphic possibilities of black and white in both printmaking and drawing. The experimentation directed his work for the rest of his life. He readily understood the mysterious possibilities of shadowy, subtly graded darks that created an atmosphere of fantasy and otherworldliness. Redon studied the graphic works of German artist Albrecht Dürer and the dark-light contrasts of Rembrandt's etchings to learn technique. Francisco de Goya's etchings and engravings were also a strong influence on Redon, who was interested not only in Goya's graphic techniques but also in the psychological fantasy of such works as his *Caprichos* series (1799). Redon enjoyed creating other worlds that were less specific than those painted by Goya. In 1885, Redon created a lithographic series called *Hommage à Goya* to celebrate his enthusiasm for the Spanish artist.

Redon transferred the skill he had developed in rich dark-light effects to his charcoal drawings, which he called *noirs*, and then to lithography. Between 1879 and 1899, he produced twelve series in various graphic techniques, many of which had strong literary associations. The series were based on contemporary poems and novels but were not illustrations for them. Instead, literature provided the stimulus for his own independent interpretations, such as *À Edgar Poe* (1882). During the 1890's,

Redon drew charcoals and lithographs as separate works based on Baudelaire's poetry collection, *Les Fleurs du mal* (1857; *Flowers of Evil*, 1931).

Two important nonartistic events shaped Redon's life. The first were the horrors that he experienced as a soldier in the Franco-Prussian War of 1870. The tragedies he witnessed affected what was already a pessimistic and imaginative mind. The other event was a happy one. In 1880, at the age of forty, Redon married. His wife, Camille, was an understanding spouse who competently handled the business side of their lives and raised their son.

Redon's many series of graphic works, along with charcoal drawings, dominated his output for many years. Around 1890, his numerous oil paintings and pastel drawings became more colorful, and the subject matter became more optimistic and less melancholy. This direction grew stronger when, in 1897, the rural family home in which he grew up was sold. It was as if a dark cloud had passed, and it allowed his work to develop in a more positive direction. Rich colors grew more dominant for the remainder of his career. This, too, was consonant with Symbolist theory, which promoted color for its emotional associations.

Redon created a range of imagery that he repeatedly used. A typical example of an image that he used in many different guises in which the context revealed its meaning was an independent eye. The eye first appeared in an 1878 charcoal drawing, *The Eye Balloon*. The floating eye looks up as it carries its basket above a featureless landscape. A silly element is injected into the scene by the addition of a fringe of eyelashes along the top of the balloon. The image invokes a freedom of consciousness sailing above the trials of daily cares, while the humor of the lashes leavens the seriousness. The combination of the deeply serious and a touch of humor was a frequent characteristic Redon's work. The eye balloon in a different guise can also mean a retreat into isolation. The eye sometimes appeared alone or as part of another object, such as at the center of an unfurling leaf or flower to anthropomorphize or humanize the consciousness of the plant.

A related but more complicated recurrent image was a severed head with (usually) closed eyes. This image had its acknowledged origin in the severed heads of murder victims, but Redon's usage, while it did suggest death, had less sinister connections. The closed eyes suggested a dream world, reserve, separation from life, and a higher purpose in the transcendent. Multiple meanings were typical of Symbolist mystical suggestion.

Flower imagery was another related symbol. A flower could be a human head with the previously mentioned multiple meanings attached to it. Flower or plant growth also suggested primordial themes that explored the concept of life-forms before the human race existed and related that to transcendent consciousness. The complexity of interrelated ideas had a basic appeal for Symbolist artists.

In 1903, Redon received official recognition from the French government when he was made a Chevalier of the Legion of Honor. Another honor followed in 1904, when the French government purchased one of his paintings. He was well enough known by then that an entire room was devoted to his works at the autumn art exhibition in Paris. By this time, his work displayed less tension and anxiety: He often painted portraits and flowers, explored mythological subjects, and used brilliant colors. In 1913, Redon's international fame grew when he was included in the controversial Armory Show in New York City. This exhibition introduced modern art in its various forms to the United States and was much discussed, praised, or damned depending on the critic.

SIGNIFICANCE

Odilon Redon did not find his mature voice until he was forty years old. After that time, his works were exhibited widely in France and the United States. As a Symbolist artist, he developed the image of the eye balloon floating freely above the world as a personal and universal metaphor for the questing soul. This allusive image, which developed from Redon's identity as an outsider in society and the art world, eventually influenced the Surrealist art movement of the 1920's and 1930's, which delved into the dream and fantasy worlds explored by Freudian psychology. The Surrealists, in their turn, became an ever-present influence on the art of the twentieth century.

—*Ann Stewart Balakier*

FURTHER READING

Bacou, Roseline. *Odilon Redon: Pastels*. Translated by Beatrice Rehl. New York: George Braziller, 1987. This monograph on Redon's pastels includes seventy color reproductions with a short discussion of each. Bacou's introduction discusses the pastels by referring to quotations from figures in the Paris art world. Included are two short but important documents about Redon's life: The first is made up of photographs of Redon, and the second is a twelve-page autobiography.

Delevoy, Robert L. *Symbolists and Symbolism*. New York: Rizzoli, 1982. Delevoy defines Symbolism by discussing the various topics that constitute approaches to subject. This short work is profusely illustrated with examples by a large number of artists, including Redon.

Druick, Douglas W., ed. *Odilon Redon: Prince of Dreams, 1840-1916*. Chicago: Art Institute of Chicago, 1994. This is a sizable exhibition catalog (464 pages) celebrating the centennial of Redon's first retrospective exhibition. It contains the fullest treatment available in English of the artist's biography, extensive reproduction of his works, examples of artistic influences, and an analysis of his working techniques. The extensive bibliography contains all of Redon's published art criticism and personal journals.

Eisenman, Stephen F. *The Temptation of Saint Redon: Biography, Ideology, and Style in the "Noirs" of Odilon Redon*. Chicago: University of Chicago Press, 1992. This study investigates Redon's utopian subject matter, which the author sees as reconciling the artist's feelings of powerlessness that stemmed from a lonely childhood.

Keay, Carolyn, ed. *Odilon Redon*. New York: Rizzoli, 1977. This short introduction to Redon's work contains sixty-six color and black-and-white reproductions.

Mathieu, Pierre-Louis. *The Symbolist Generation: 1870-1910*. New York: Rizzoli, 1990. Mathieu discusses the Symbolist style by defining the subgroups within the movement and identifying the differences created by geographical location.

Théberge, Pierre. *Lost Paradise: Symbolist Europe*. Montreal, Que.: Montreal Museum of Fine Arts, 1995. This 555-page exhibition catalog gives a comprehensive presentation of the Symbolist art movement. The discussion centers on the various topics that the style used as subjects.

Werner, Alfred. *The Graphic Works of Odilon Redon*. New York: Dover, 1969. This is the most complete overview of Redon's graphic works published with an English introduction. Two hundred nine lithographs, etchings, and engravings are included. The ten-page introduction is short but pithy.

Wilson, Michael. *Nature and Imagination: The Work of Odilon Redon*. London: Phaidon Press, 1978. Wilson provides a short but thorough discussion of the life and artistic career of Redon. The book contains seventy illustrations, many in color, with a few examples of works by artists who influenced Redon.

SEE ALSO: Charles Baudelaire; Gustave Flaubert; Paul Gauguin; Théodore Géricault; Edgar Allan Poe; Pierre-Auguste Renoir; Noah Webster.

RELATED ARTICLES in *Great Events from History: The Nineteenth Century, 1801-1900:* May 15, 1863: Paris's Salon des Refusés Opens; 1892-1895: Toulouse-Lautrec Paints *At the Moulin Rouge*.

WALTER REED
American physician

Reed served as the head of the commission that designed and conducted the experiments that proved that yellow fever was transmitted by mosquito bites, thus making control of this terrible disease possible and enabling the construction of projects such as the Panama Canal.

BORN: September 13, 1851; Belroi, Virginia
DIED: November 22, 1902; Washington, D.C.
AREA OF ACHIEVEMENT: Medicine

EARLY LIFE
Walter Reed was the youngest of five children. His mother, Pharaba White, was the first wife of his father, Lemuel Sutton Reed, a Methodist minister. From the first, it seemed as if Reed were destined to live a gypsy-like existence. As an adult, he would reside in a nearly endless series of army camps; as a child, his family moved frequently as his father was sent to parish after parish in the regions of southeastern Virginia and eastern North Carolina. In 1865, however, the Reeds achieved some stability with a move to Charlottesville, Virginia, and Walter was able to attend school with some regularity. In 1866, he entered the University of Virginia, receiving a medical degree in 1869.

Feeling the need for more clinical experience, Reed next enrolled in the medical school of Bellevue Hospital in New York City, where, at the age of nineteen, he completed study for his second medical degree. A year's internship followed in New York's Infant's Hospital, after which he became a physician in two other hospitals in the New York area while also serving as a sanitary inspector for the Brooklyn Board of Health.

LIFE'S WORK

Unhappy with the insecurity of life as a public physician, yet having no good prospects for private practice, Reed decided upon a career in the military and, in 1875, passed the examinations that earned for him a commission as first lieutenant in the Army Medical Corps. He married Emilie Lawrence in 1876, and shortly afterward was transferred to Fort Lowell in Arizona. His wife soon joined him, and their son Lawrence was born in 1877. A daughter, Blossom, followed in 1883. The Reed children lived much the same restless life as their father had as a youngster as they followed him in almost annual moves from army post to army post in Arizona, Nebraska, Minnesota, and Alabama.

These wanderings in the West were interrupted briefly in 1889, when Reed was appointed surgeon for army recruits in Baltimore. While stationed there, he sought and was given permission to work in Johns Hopkins Hospital, where he took courses in bacteriology and pathology. It was not, however, until 1893, when Reed returned to the East to stay, that his career finally began to flourish. In that year, he was promoted to the rank of major, assigned the position of professor of bacteriology and clinical microscopy at the recently established Army Medical School in Washington, D.C., and given the position of curator of the Army Medical Museum as well.

In 1896, Reed received his first real opportunity to demonstrate his ability as a medical investigator when he tracked down the cause of near-epidemic malaria among troops in the Washington barracks and in nearby Fort Myer, Virginia. In addition, in 1898, he chaired a committee that investigated the spread of typhoid fever in army camps. All this was excellent preparation for the task that Reed was about to undertake, and the task for which he is famous—that of resolving the riddle of yellow fever's transmission.

Yellow fever had been the scourge of the Caribbean Islands and the regions bordering on the Gulf of Mexico, as well as other port cities in North America and Brazil, for more than two centuries and had claimed hundreds of thousands of lives. Its abrupt but mysterious appearances and disappearances had long been the subject of controversy among physicians. Many believed the disease to be contagious, while many others were convinced that it was caused by local climatic conditions that created poisoned air (miasmata). By the end of the nineteenth century, much of the medical world had accepted the contagionists' view, believing that the disease was spread by fomites (items such as clothing or bedding used by a yellow fever victim).

For at least a century, a few physicians had been skeptical of both explanations. Dr. John Crawford of Baltimore is sometimes credited with advancing a mosquito theory toward the end of the eighteenth century, as are Josiah Nott of Mobile, Alabama, and the French naturalist Louis Daniel Beauperthuy at about the midpoint in the nineteenth century. The real credit for a mosquito theory, however, belongs to the Cuban physician Carlos Juan Finlay, who, in 1881, not only suggested that mosquitoes were responsible for the transmission of yellow fever but also narrowed the focus to the *Aëdes aegypti* (then called *Stegomyia fasciata*) mosquito. Finlay's difficulty was that he could not prove his theory.

In 1896, an Italian physician, Giuseppe Sanarelli, claimed to have isolated the causative agent of yellow fever, and Reed, along with army physician James Carroll, was assigned the task of investigating that claim. They soon demonstrated it to be groundless, but this was only the beginning of Reed's work on yellow fever. He volun-

Walter Reed. (Library of Congress)

teered for duty during the war with Spain over the question of Cuban independence, but only got to Cuba after the war was over, arriving in Havana in 1899, to investigate a typhoid outbreak, and again in 1900, as the head of a commission sent to investigate the reasons for an outbreak of yellow fever among American troops still stationed on the island. Carroll, Aristides Agramonte, and Jesse Lazear made up the remainder of the commission.

At first, they made little progress with yellow fever, for their efforts were directed toward showing that the bacillus that Sanarelli believed to cause yellow fever was actually part of the group of hog cholera bacillus. It was only after Reed had investigated an outbreak of a disease originally thought to be malaria among soldiers in Pinar del Rio that the commission settled down to its task. The disease in question turned out to be yellow fever, and the circumstances surrounding the death of one of the soldiers who had been a prisoner and locked in a cell particularly intrigued Reed because none of his cellmates had gotten yellow fever, not even the one who had taken his bunk and bedding. This fact seemed to discredit the fomite theory, and Reed wrote later that at this point he began to suspect that some insect was capable of transmitting the disease.

It was also at this point that several important findings began to converge. In 1894, Sir Patrick Manson had suggested that mosquitoes might be responsible for the transmission of malaria, and in 1897, Sir Ronald Ross had proved it. On the other hand, malaria was a very different disease from yellow fever. One of the reasons why Finlay had been unable to prove that the *Aëdes aegypti* mosquito was responsible for spreading yellow fever was that he (and everyone else) was unaware of the long period (generally nine to sixteen days) of incubation the yellow fever virus requires in the stomach of a mosquito before that mosquito is capable of passing the disease along to a human host. In May of 1900, Henry Rose Carter of the United States Marine Hospital Service published his observations on outbreaks of the disease in Mississippi that for the first time revealed the lengthy incubation period.

Then, in the summer of 1900, the members of the commission met with Finlay, who placed the records of his experiments at their disposal. They had decided to test Finlay's theory using human subjects for the experiments.

Reed returned to Washington but was back in Cuba in September, upon learning that Lazear, who had permitted himself to be bitten by an infected mosquito, was dead from yellow fever and that Carroll was seriously ill with the disease. It seemed that Finlay had indeed been correct, and Reed at this juncture designed and conducted the experiments that produced twenty-two more cases in soldier volunteers, proving once and for all that the female *Aëdes aegypti* mosquito was responsible for epidemic yellow fever. Armed with this knowledge, Major W. C. Gorgas was able to free Havana of the disease quickly and then eradicate it in Panama (making construction of the canal possible), while others wiped out yellow fever in urban centers elsewhere in the hemisphere. More than three decades would elapse before another form of the disease called jungle yellow fever would be discovered in some of the monkey populations of that area and in those of Africa. With this discovery came the realization that the disease could not be completely eradicated, but only controlled.

Reed did not live long enough to see the whole of this triumph of humankind over yellow fever. After completing his experiments in Cuba, he returned, in 1901, to Washington, a hero and the recipient of many honors. He resumed his teaching duties but died in late 1902 of complications that developed following surgery on his ruptured appendix.

SIGNIFICANCE

In no small part because of a sensationalist American press, Reed (as Cuban physicians and historians in particular have pointed out) has probably received too much credit for the solution of the age-old mystery of yellow fever's transmission. However, Reed himself was always modest about his role in the matter and quick to pass along that credit to Finlay, and to his associates Carroll, Lazear, and Agramonte.

In truth, however, Reed was entitled to a lion's share of the credit. Finlay had not been able to prove the truth of his mosquito hypothesis, and Reed's colleagues were narrow specialists; Carroll was a bacteriologist, Lazear, a mosquito specialist, and Agramonte, a pathologist. Thus, it was Reed who successfully drew the work of these and others together and organized the experiments that made the final definitive breakthrough.

Although his early career gives no hint of this kind of ability, his activities in investigating malaria and typhoid outbreaks during the years immediately prior to his yellow fever work surely prepared him well for that work. In all these undertakings, Reed revealed a fine scientific mind, and his success in the tropical medicine field, heretofore dominated by Europeans, brought much prestige to American science and American scientific education. Thus it is fitting that the small monument over his resting place in Arlington National Cemetery bears the inscription, "He gave to man control over that dreadful scourge Yellow Fever."

—Kenneth F. Kiple

FURTHER READING

Bean, William B. *Walter Reed: A Biography*. Charlottesville: University Press of Virginia, 1982. Despite its lack of documentation, it is clear that this study, by the leading authority on Reed, has been extensively researched, and as a full-length biography it has the virtue of providing a balanced account of Reed's life rather than concentrating excessively on his yellow fever work alone. Thus, it provides an excellent description of medicine and the military between the Civil War and the war with Spain.

Carter, Henry Rose. *Yellow Fever: An Epidemiological and Historical Study of Its Place of Origin*. Edited by Laura Armistead Carter and Wade Hampton Frost. Baltimore: Williams and Wilkins, 1931. The author, himself one of the major actors in the drama of the conquest of yellow fever, provides a thorough examination of the history of the disease as well as an account of its ultimate surrender to science.

Chappell, Gordon S. "Surgeon at Fort Sidney: Captain Walter Reed's Experiences, 1883-1884." *Nebraska History* 54 (1973): 419-443. Focuses on Reed's year of service as the chief medical officer at Fort Sidney, a Nebraska military post. An interesting glimpse of a slice of Reed's early career.

Dormandy, Thomas. *Moments of Truth: Four Creators of Modern Medicine*. Hoboken, N.J.: Wiley, 2003. Part 4 of this book contains six chapters examining Reed's life, career, and contributions to modern medicine.

Gilmore, Hugh R. "Malaria at Washington Barracks and Fort Myer." *Bulletin of the History of Medicine* 29 (1955): 346-351. This is a brief description of the careful epidemiological investigation of a malaria outbreak among soldiers in the Washington, D.C., area carried out by Reed in 1896.

Kelly, Howard A. *Walter Reed and Yellow Fever*. 3d rev. ed. Baltimore: Norman, Remington, 1923. The first scholarly and satisfactory biography of Reed despite its uncritical nature. It traces his life from birth to death, but, as the title indicates, it places most of the emphasis on the work done by Reed and his associates on yellow fever.

Pierce, John R., and Jim Writer. *Yellow Jack: How Yellow Fever Ravaged America and Walter Reed Discovered Its Deadly Secrets*. Hoboken, N.J.: Wiley, 2005. Chronicles the rise and fall of yellow fever, focusing on the impact of the disease in America. Describes Reed's successful efforts to eradicate the disease.

Truby, Albert E. *Memoir of Walter Reed: The Yellow Fever Episode*. New York: Paul B. Hoeber, 1943. This work, as the title indicates, is not biographical in nature but rather concentrates on the methods and techniques employed by Reed and his colleagues to demonstrate that the mosquito was indeed the carrier of yellow fever. In the process, the study also provides a fine background sketch of the Army Medical Corps and the conditions in Cuba with which Reed met upon his arrival.

SEE ALSO: Emil von Behring; Marie Anne Victorine Boivin; Sir William Osler; Ignaz Philipp Semmelweis; Rudolf Virchow.

RELATED ARTICLES in *Great Events from History: The Nineteenth Century, 1801-1900:* May 4, 1805-1830: Exploration of West Africa; May, 1847: Semmelweis Develops Antiseptic Procedures; August 20, 1897: Ross Establishes Malaria's Transmission Vector; June, 1900-1904: Suppression of Yellow Fever.

FREDERIC REMINGTON
American artist

One of the best-remembered American artists of the nineteenth century, Remington created drawings and bronzes that recorded the Old West before it vanished, thus preserving it for later generations.

BORN: October 4, 1861; Canton, New York
DIED: December 26, 1909; Ridgefield, Connecticut
ALSO KNOWN AS: Frederic Sackrider Remington (full name)
AREA OF ACHIEVEMENT: Art

EARLY LIFE

Frederic Sackrider Remington was the only child of Clara Bascomb Sackrider and Seth Pierrepont Remington, a newspaper editor and publisher. His early childhood was marked by the four-year absence of his father, who was a lieutenant colonel in the Civil War. Upon his father's return, Remington eagerly listened to his tales of the cavalry and the West; perhaps Remington's lifelong fascination with the horse can be traced to this period. At any rate, Remington grew up sketching horses, cowboys, Indians, and soldiers. His artistic ability pleased his father, whom he idolized, but did not satisfy his practical mother, who envisioned for him a career in business. School never received much of his attention; instead, his childhood revolved around fishing, swimming, and other outdoor activities.

In 1878, after two years at a military academy in Massachusetts, Remington entered Yale and its newly established School of Art and Architecture. In the college weekly, *Courant*, he published his first drawing, *College Riff-Raff* (1879), a cartoon of a bruised football player. Despite his interest in art, he was soon bored by the study of classical painting and sculpture, but he discovered a new diversion, football. Tall, robust, and burly, he was a natural football player and became a forward on the varsity team.

In 1880, Remington's father died, leaving him a modest inheritance. Finding himself financially independent, at least momentarily, he left Yale against his mother's wishes, after having completed less than two years. In Canton, he tried several jobs, but none was to his liking. In the summer of 1880, upon meeting Eva Adele Caten of Gloversville, New York, he fell deeply in love and asked her father for her hand, but he was refused on the grounds that his future was not promising. Remington, dejected, left to find his fortune in the West. Working as a cowboy and a scout did not make him rich, but as a result of the

trip he sold a sketch, *Cow-boys of Arizona: Roused by a Scout* (1882), to *Harper's Weekly*, his first appearance in a major magazine, a milestone even if the sketch was redrawn by a staff artist.

In 1883, Remington bought a sheep ranch in Kansas. However, the difficult and lonely work induced him to sell it in 1884. With the last of his inheritance, he invested in a saloon. Although the business was successful, his unscrupulous partners tricked him out of his share. After selling a few drawings to a Kansas City art dealer, he began seriously to consider an art career. In retrospect, he said of his interest in drawing, "I knew the wild riders and the vacant land were about to vanish forever. . . . Without knowing exactly how to do it, I began to record some facts around me and the more I looked the more the panorama unfolded." Thus, he began the task of chronicling the West before it disappeared.

Returning to New York, Remington again approached Eva's father, who relented, perhaps because Eva would have no other. After being married on October 1, 1884, he and his bride set out for Kansas City to establish their home. A steady income was not to be found, however, so after less than a year Eva returned to New York, and Remington resumed his travels through the West. At one time, he prospected for gold; at another, he rode with an army unit in search of Apaches, but always he sketched.

Realizing that New York City, with its many publishers, was the place for an aspiring illustrator, he returned in 1885 and, with Eva, set up a household in Brooklyn. The early days were difficult as he doggedly tried to sell his drawings, but the turning point came in 1886, when *Harper's Weekly* published on its cover his drawing *The Apache War: Indian Scouts on Geronimo's Trail* (1886). Soon Remington's work began to appear regularly in major magazines.

LIFE'S WORK

In the years following 1886, Remington became recognized as the foremost illustrator of his day. Over his lifetime, his drawings, numbering more than twenty-seven hundred, were published in forty-one different periodicals. His illustrations, with their Western themes, struck a responsive chord in the American public, whose curiosity had been aroused by the tales of gold and Indians, circulating out of the Wild West.

After 1886, Remington went West every summer to sketch and to collect Indian artifacts and cowboy para-

Frederic Remington. (Library of Congress)

phernalia. At other times, he traveled on assignment for magazines. In 1888, he covered the army campaign against the Apache. In 1890, he was in the Badlands of South Dakota, documenting the Plains Indian Wars. Traveling with the army, he experienced at first hand several brief skirmishes with the Lakota. The Wounded Knee Massacre, the last battle of the Indian Wars, took place a few miles from where he was situated.

When the Spanish-American War erupted, Remington, representing *Harper's Weekly* and William Randolph Hearst's New York *Journal*, went to Cuba. Arriving with the cavalry, he witnessed the assault of San Juan Hill. One of his paintings, *Charge of the Rough Riders of San Juan Hill* (1899), depicted Theodore Roosevelt, his friend of ten years, leading his men. Roosevelt's charge probably occurred more in Remington's imagination than in fact. Roosevelt, however, used the drawing to his advantage in creating his image as a soldier and hero that would later prove useful to his political future.

Remington illustrated not only articles but also books, the first being *Mexico Today* (1886) by Solomon Buck-

ley Griffin. In 1890, nearly thirty, he illustrated Henry Wadsworth Longfellow's *The Song of Hiawatha* (1855), the popularity of which can be attributed partly to Remington's drawings. He illustrated books by Owen Wister, the noted writer of Western tales, and, in 1892, he did the drawings for Francis Parkman's *The Oregon Trail* (1892). In all, he illustrated more than 140 books.

Remington also wrote about the West he loved. His first signed articles, published in 1888, concerned the Lakota uprising. In 1895, he published the first of his eight books, *Pony Tracks*, a collection of his articles concerning army life. In 1902, he wrote a novel, *John Ermine of the Yellowstone*, a romantic Western, which, in 1903, he adapted for the stage. The drawings for the novel posed a problem: How was he to illustrate a love story when he rarely sketched women? He solved his dilemma when he hired the well-known illustrator Charles Dana Gibson to draw the female figures.

In addition to being known as a pen-and-ink illustrator, Remington was also a popular oil painter. Beginning in 1887, his work was accepted in major exhibitions, often receiving prizes. He was an associate member of the prestigious National Academy of Design and a member of the National Institute of Arts and Letters. Remington's favorite subject for his paintings as well as for his illustrations was the Old West, a world full of cowboys, Indians, and horses. His paintings typically emphasize action; the scene might be of riders and horses wildly racing for safety, as in *A Dash for Timber* (1889), or of men besieged, as in *The Fight for the Water Hole* (probably painted 1895-1902). His paintings tell the story of the taming of the West. The fur traders, scouts, and soldiers populating his canvases conquer the West through their determination and strength while the Indians, noble but also cruel, are shown in their losing struggle.

In 1895, after watching the sculptor Frederic W. Ruckstull at work, Remington tried the new medium; the result was *The Bronco Buster*, a casting of which was later presented to Theodore Roosevelt by the Rough Riders on their return from the Spanish-American War. Over the next fourteen years, he produced twenty-five sculptures, all except one focusing on a Western theme. His bronzes have the same focus on action and the same attentiveness to details that distinguish his drawings.

Remington was a disciplined artist: He would rise at six and draw until the early afternoon; later in the evening, he would return to his studio to plan his work for the next day. He was also a highly successful artist. First known as an illustrator, he also made his mark as a writer, painter, and sculptor. On December 26, 1909, at the age of forty-eight, he died of complications from an appendectomy. His art can be found at the Remington Art Museum in Ogdensburg, New York, and at the Amon Carter Museum of Western Art, in Fort Worth, Texas. The Thomas Gilcrease Institute of History and Art houses a large collection of Remington bronzes.

SIGNIFICANCE

Through his illustrations, paintings, and bronzes, Remington created the image of the West held by most Americans. The lonely cowboy, the savage Indian, the limitless land, the noble horse, the brave soldiers who battle against overwhelming odds, and the pioneers who never question their right to settle the land are all in his paintings.

Remington's illustrations and drawings have been valued as a documentary of the West. His rendering of the costumes of the Indian tribes, the different breeds of the horses, and the details of the soldiers' dress have been praised for their authenticity. Some critics argue that Remington also romanticized the West, indicating the many buffalo skulls that litter his paintings, and others suggest that his work owes as much to his imagination as to fact, citing the historically inaccurate costumes of the Indians in *The Song of Hiawatha*. Both evaluations are correct.

Remington was highly accurate in his early drawings, which were usually based on sketches done in the West, but the later paintings were often imagined reconstructions of fact and fantasy, portraying the spirit of the West rather than a particular moment. However, whatever faults might be found in his paintings, they do not obscure the fact that Remington had a tremendous impact on how Americans view the West. Many would agree with Owen Wister, "Remington is not merely an artist; he is a national treasure."

—*Barbara Wiedemann*

FURTHER READING

Anderson, Nancy K., et al. *Frederic Remington: The Color of Night*. Princeton, N.J.: Princeton University Press, 2003. In the final decade of his life Remington created seventy-two paintings depicting the color of night. This book accompanied an exhibit of these nocturnes and features three essays placing the works within a literary, aesthetic, and technological context. Includes reproductions of the paintings.

Baigell, Matthew. *The Western Art of Frederic Remington*. New York: Random House, 1976. Contains a short introduction to Remington's life and work followed by color plates of Remington's paintings from 1887 to 1909. Baigell is critical of Remington's portrayal of the West, suggesting that it is a romanticized version.

Dippie, Brian W. *The Frederic Remington Art Museum Collection*. New York: Harry N. Abrams, 2001. A catalog of Remington's work held by the Frederic Remington Art Museum in Ogdensburg, New York. Features a detailed analysis of the holdings, with excerpts from Remington's letters, diaries, and sketchbooks. There are 333 illustrations.

Ewers, John C. *Artists of the Old West*. Garden City, N.Y.: Doubleday, 1973. Contains chapters devoted to the artists who popularized the West, including George Catlin, Albert Bierstadt, Frederic Remington, and Charles M. Russell. Discusses Remington's experiences during the Plains Indian War.

Jackson, Marta, ed. *The Illustrations of Frederic Remington*. New York: Crown, 1970. A brief account of Remington's life, followed by drawings that are arranged by subject. Many of the drawings are not found in other books. Includes a brief commentary by Owen Wister on Remington's artistic contribution.

McCracken, Harold. *Frederic Remington: Artist of the Old West*. Philadelphia: J. B. Lippincott, 1947. A widely recognized biography. Contains colorful anecdotes gathered from Remington's friends and relatives. A glowing appraisal of Remington's artistic contribution. McCracken supplies a useful list of all of Remington's drawings, books, and bronzes. Includes forty-eight plates of paintings, pastels, and bronzes.

Nemerov, Alexander. *Frederic Remington and Turn-of-the-Century America*. New Haven, Conn.: Yale University Press, 1995. Nemerov argues that Remington was not merely an illustrator of Western frontier scenes, but also the creator of complex, imaginative art.

Richardson, E. P. *Painting in America: The Story of 450 Years*. New York: Thomas Y. Crowell, 1956. An authoritative study of American painting. Praises Remington as an illustrator who realistically recorded the West but criticizes the "crude and raw" color of his paintings.

Samuels, Peggy, and Harold Samuels. *Frederic Remington*. Garden City, N.Y.: Doubleday, 1982. This massive but readable biography is the most thorough, most balanced study of Remington to date. Although the authors hold their subject in high regard, they do not fail to acknowledge his flaws. Their account emphasizes the influence of Impressionism on his later work.

Vorpahl, Ben Merchant. *Frederic Remington and the West: With the Eye of the Mind*. Austin: University of Texas Press, 1978. Traces how Remington was influenced by the West and how he, in turn, shaped the public's image of the frontier. An academic study, ranging widely in literature and social history.

Wear, Bruce. *The Bronze World of Frederic Remington*. Tulsa, Okla.: Gaylord, 1966. Discusses the bronzes, how they were cast, Remington's involvement with the production, and the problem of forgeries. The text is followed by plates of the bronzes and pertinent information about each work.

SEE ALSO: George Caleb Bingham; Geronimo; Henry Wadsworth Longfellow; Francis Parkman.

RELATED ARTICLES in *Great Events from History: The Nineteenth Century, 1801-1900:* 1895: Rise of Yellow Journalism; 1895-1898: Hearst-Pulitzer Circulation War.

ERNEST RENAN
French writer

Renan's writings encompass the areas of religion, history, science, and morality. His controversial biography of Jesus Christ illustrates his ongoing theme of resolution of contradictions by emphasizing the problem of reconciling the historical and the spiritually divine Jesus.

BORN: February 28, 1823; Tréguier, Côtes-du-Nord, France
DIED: October 2, 1892; Paris, France
ALSO KNOWN AS: Joseph-Ernest Renan (full name)
AREAS OF ACHIEVEMENT: Historiography, religion and theology

EARLY LIFE

Joseph-Ernest Renan (ree-nahn) was born in a town in Brittany that was in many respects a religious center. His youth was shaded by a veil of devout Roman Catholicism, to which he, in accordance with his mother's most intense wishes and his own strong inclinations, was committed. His father, Philibert, was a grocer and seaman. His mother, Magdelaine Féger, was widowed when Ernest was five years old, her husband having drowned—it has not been determined whether accidentally or otherwise—at sea. Ernest Renan had a brother, Alain, born in 1809, and a sister, Henriette, born in 1811. His sister was profoundly influential in his life, and his attachment to her is lyrically expressed in *Ma Sœur Henriette* (1895; *My Sister Henrietta*, 1895), which was initially published in a limited edition of one hundred copies in 1862 as *Henriette Renan: Souvenir pour ceux qui l'ont connue* (Henriette Renan: a remembrance for those who knew her) and reprinted posthumously.

From 1832 to 1838, Renan was a student at the Ecclesiastical School in Tréguier, while his sister, having failed to establish a private school for girls, accepted a teaching position in Paris. In 1838, Renan moved to Paris and studied rhetoric at the seminary of Saint-Nicolas du Chardonnet. After three years, he moved to the seminary of Issy-les-Moulineux outside Paris, where his study of philosophy began to bring about his wavering in religious faith. His sister, with whom he was to maintain an ongoing correspondence, had moved, during this time, to Poland, where she found employment as a governess. From Issy-les-Moulineux, he moved in 1849 to the parent seminary of Saint-Sulpice and entered upon his study of theology.

In his academic progression from rhetoric to philosophy to theology, the normal pattern of seminary education in France, Renan developed a devotion to literature, a skeptical turn of mind, and a sense of alienation in his separation, first, from Brittany and, later, from his mother. He remained firmly within his faith, however, and in 1844 became a tonsured cleric in evidence of his call to the priesthood. After a year, he came to realize that he lacked belief sufficient to this vocation, and his rationalism and scientific propensity led him to abandon the ecclesiastical for the secular life. His sister Henriette supported him in his decision and commended his firmness of purpose and strength of will.

Renan then set his life's course toward reconciling the two worlds that, as he assured his mother in her disappointment, were not, to his mind, separate. The world of Jesus (the world of religion) and the world of science contradicted each other but were not mutually exclusive. To his own way of thinking, he had departed from Jesus so as to be better able to follow Jesus.

LIFE'S WORK

In 1845, at the age of twenty-two, Renan, believing that his own emotions and his own thoughts were his God, became a tutor, an ultimately successful candidate for the *baccalauréat* and *licence* (roughly equivalent to the bachelor's and master's degrees in the United States), a friend of the chemist Marcellin Berthelot, and a student of the Semitic languages (of which he was soon to become a professor).

Two years later, Renan won the Volney Prize for his essay on the history of the Semitic languages. His friendship with the scientist, which proved to be lifelong, and his own predilection for science, along with his Semitic studies, adumbrated his major contributions to intellectual history and to the history of ideas; these are his *Histoire des origines du christianisme* (1863-1882; *The History of the Origins of Christianity*, 1890) and *L'Avenir de la science* (1890; *The Future of Science*, 1890). Renan completed his work on *The Future of Science* in 1849, three years before the publication of his doctoral dissertation, *Averroès et l'Averroïsme* (1852). Segments of the text of *The Future of Science* appeared in journals, periodicals, and other of his books, but its full publication, with only minor revisions of the original, materialized only two years before his death.

One of the primary focuses of *The Future of Science* is criticism, a subject that Renan had initially expounded in his *Cahiers de jeunesse* (1845-1846; youthful notebooks). Renan's views on criticism as an intellectual activity anticipated much of the direction that was to be taken by post-World War II critical theorists. For him, true criticism was universal in character and was decidedly not to be limited to literary criticism and even more decidedly not to be identified with judgment and measurements against standards of form and composition.

Renan believed that beauty was open-ended and not subject to the closure that is implied by the concept of an absolute. He saw criticism as a creative use of the powers of interpretation and a conceptual conjunction of history, topography, philosophy, and morality. Like the deconstructionists of the twentieth century, he disregarded the demarcations of disciplines and sought to reconcile the disciplines through comparativism, eclecticism, and synthesis; comparison served him in science, literature, and religion as the great tool of criticism. *The Future of Science* begins with the simple statement, "Only one thing is necessary." The one thing proves to be, after all syntheses have been unified, science as that religion that comprises human feeling and human thought.

Ernest Renan. (Library of Congress)

H. W. Wardman recognizes in *The Future of Science* the idea that "philosophy is a human science born of the union of philology and historical sympathy," and this prompts him effectively to conclude that Renan's philosopher is "a kind of seer fitted by his insight into human nature to take over from the Church the spiritual leadership of mankind." Philology, according to Renan, is "the science of the products of the human mind."

Renan's notion of history is an extension of Victor Cousin's concept of the three ages: a primary age informed by religion without science, a secondary age informed by science without religion, and a final age informed by both religion and science. The historical process is the development of the divine. In the final age, the development will have been concluded and God will be manifestly whole. The future of science, then, is the fulfillment of religion, that is to say, God.

Renan's masterwork was a seven-volume study, *The History of the Origins of Christianity*. The first of these volumes, *Vie de Jésus* (1863; *The Life of Jesus*, 1864), is the most famous and is the work for which Renan is best known. At the time of its publication, Renan had been married to Cornélie Scheffer for seven years, had become the father of two girls, the first having died eight months after birth, and had, in 1861, lost in death his sister Henriette, to whose soul he dedicated this work.

The life of Jesus, according to Renan, is the focal event of world history; it brought about the spiritual revolution that was the culmination of seven centuries of Jewish history and that in the subsequent three centuries would be established as a religion. This entire period of one thousand years is presented by Renan as embracing the origins of Christianity.

Renan depicts Jesus as a superior, indeed a sublime, person but not as a god. His Jesus let his followers believe that he was God as he taught them the ways to fulfill their subjectivity. He holds that Jesus' immediate followers and their successors invented, in belief and desire, the Resurrection:

> The life of Jesus ends, as far as the historian is concerned, with his last sigh. But so great was the mark he had made in the hearts of his disciples and several devoted women that for a few more weeks he was alive to them and he consoled them.

This passage from chapter 26 is representative of the secular Jesus whom hosts of Renan's critics rejected and protested against. The whole of chapters 26 and 27 was, for example, among the exclusions from the French Book Club's ornately bound and illustrated 1970 abridg-

ment of *The History of the Origins of Christianity*. The Christian clergy and laity assailed the book for its profanation and its author's apostasy. Literary critics frowned upon the idyllic and romantic Galilee that it painted and upon its overly genteel characterization of Jesus. The book became an international best seller, however, going through eight printings in the first three months of its publication.

The second volume of *The History of the Origins of Christianity* appeared in 1866; it is a historiography of the Apostles, from 33 to 45 C.E., and an investigation into the continuing apotheosis of Jesus by way of visionary presumption, amplification of legend, and adaptation of mythical traditions. His third volume, *La Vie de saint Paul* (1869; *Saint Paul*, 1869), dedicated to his wife, who had accompanied him in his retracing of the travels of his subject, is replete with the topography and accoutrements of epic. Saint Paul is here reminiscent of the Homeric Odysseus: a man of action and purpose.

The fourth volume (1873), following the New Testament's book of Revelation as Renan's second and third volumes follow, respectively, the book of Acts and the Pauline Epistles, studies Emperor Nero as the Antichrist. The fifth volume (1877) expatiates upon the second Christian generation and the production of the first four books of the New Testament, the basis of his life of Jesus. He applauds Matthew and Mark as the genuinely divine increment of Christianity, berates Luke as special pleading, and sees John as fraudulent save for its recounting of various of Jesus' teachings. (Only nine of this volume's twenty-seven chapters are included in the above-mentioned French Book Club edition.) The sixth volume (1879) details the defeat of Gnosticism and Montanism and the establishment of the Orthodox Christian church. The concluding volume (1881) centers on Emperor Marcus Aurelius (161-180) and the end of the ancient world.

From 1888 to the year of his death, Renan published three of the five volumes of his last historical opus, *Histoire du peuple d'Israël* (*History of the People of Israel*, 1888-1895), the last two volumes of which were published posthumously in 1893. He looked upon this work as his completion of the history of Christianity's origins and as his ex-

---

RECOLLECTIONS OF YOUTH

One should never write except upon that which one loves. Oblivion and silence are the proper punishments to be inflicted upon all that we meet with in the way of what is ungainly or vulgar in the course of our journey through life. Referring to a past which is dear to me, I have spoken of it with kindly sympathy; but I should be sorry to create any misapprehension, and to be taken for an uncompromising reactionist. I love the past, but I envy the future. It would have been very pleasant to have lived upon this planet at as late a period as possible. [René] Descartes would be delighted if he could read some trivial work on natural philosophy and cosmography written in the present day. The fourth form school boy of our age is acquainted with truths to know which Archimedes would have laid down his life. What would we not give to be able to get a glimpse of some book which will be used as a school-primer a hundred years hence?

Source: Ernest Renan, "Preface," in *Recollections of My Youth*, translated by C. B. Pitman (London: Chapman and Hall, 1897).

position of the Jewish "subsoil" of Jesus' roots. The ten books of this work trace the development of Jewish monotheism, messianism, and religious mission—a development that entailed the sacrifice of nationalistic power to spiritual identity.

Renan died on October 2, 1892, from pneumonia and cardiac complications. Although his death was painful, it came after he had gained personal satisfaction from completing his life's work.

SIGNIFICANCE

Ernest Renan's monuments are *The Future of Science, The History of the Origins of Christianity*, and *History of the People of Israel*. His other works are many, and they warrant careful study by anyone seriously interested in his contributions to modern thought. These include, apart from other works already mentioned, his correspondence, his *Souvenirs d'enfance et de jeunesse* (1876-1882; *Recollections of My Youth*, 1883), his *Discours et conférences* (1887; speeches and lectures), his philosophical dialogues, and his four philosophical dramas: *Caliban, suite de "La Tempête": Drame philosophique* (1878; *Caliban: A Philosophical Drama Continuing "The Tempest" of William Shakespeare*, 1896), *L'Eau de jouvence* (1881; the fountain of youth), *Le Prêtre de Némi* (1886; the priest of Nemi), and *L'Abbesse de Jouarre* (1886; the abbess of Jouarre).

Renan is an outstanding example of the thinker whose crisis of spirit is resolved by his work. Like the English poet William Cowper (1731-1800), who adjusted to his unshakable belief that he was damned by engaging in constant literary effort, Renan overcame his loss of faith with a creative scholarship that brought him spiritual contentment.

In his spiritual secularism and his universal criticism, Renan was ahead of his time. His attitudes and ideas anticipated those of certain significant twentieth century theologians (for example, Hans Küng), literary artists (Miguel de Unamuno y Jugo), and critical theorists (Michel Foucault and René Girard), but his twentieth century successors not only found broader and more consistent readerships but also outdistanced him in depth and caliber of expression, though not in exquisiteness of prose.

Renan saw himself as a man of two worlds: religion and science. He belongs as well to two different temporal worlds: the nineteenth century, in which his ideas were uncommon and thereby largely unheeded, and the twentieth century, in which his ideas were largely unheeded because they had become commonplace.

—Roy Arthur Swanson

FURTHER READING

Chadbourne, Richard M. *Ernest Renan.* New York: Twayne, 1968. An admirable and admiring account of the life and works of Renan, touching upon all the qualities that make Renan a "great historian, critic, and artist." This is one of the finest volumes in Twayne's World Authors series, and an excellent secondary work on Renan.

_____. *Ernest Renan as an Essayist.* Ithaca, N.Y.: Cornell University Press, 1957. Examines Renan's contribution to the tradition of French essay-writing. Chadbourne stresses the seriousness of purpose that is to be found in the essays as against the author's propensity for irony, humor, and open-ended play. Considering that he may have made Renan appear overly serious, Chadbourne corrects the impression in his *Ernest Renan*.

Gore, Charles. Introduction to *The Life of Jesus*, by Ernest Renan. New York: E. P. Dutton, 1927. Gore offers an excellent summary of the reception of Renan's *The Life of Jesus* by critics, liberals, and orthodox Christians. He also offers a vindication of Renan as a historian whose estimation of the historical value of the New Testament documents had come to be recognized as essentially correct. Gore's translation, the second into English and the first in international importance, should also be of interest to any reader seeking familiarity with Renan's most famous work.

Gore, Keith. "Ernest Renan: A Positive Ethics?" *French Studies* 41 (April, 1987): 141-154. A concise account of Renan's philosophical adjustment to his break with the Church and to the political situation in France (Second Empire, Franco-Prussian War, Third Republic). In a long footnote, Gore insists, contrary to assertions by H. W. Wardman (in a book written in 1979 in French), that in the ethical sphere, Renan was pragmatic, not metaphysical.

Lee, David C. J. *Ernest Renan: In the Shadow of Faith.* London: Duckworth, 1996. Focuses on Renan's decision to abandon the Church for a secular career, examining the conflict inherent in this decision. Lee argues that Renan's Jesus biography was successful because Renan's writing featured a religious nostalgia that was common to the literature of his age.

Neff, Emery. *The Poetry of History: The Contribution of Literature and Literary Scholarship to the Writing of History Since Voltaire.* New York: Columbia University Press, 1947. An appraisal of Renan's historiography as the work of a man of letters. Informative comparison of Renan's work to that of Jacob Burckhardt and John Richard Green. Neff makes a case for the long-term worth of Renan's distinctive and effective style of historical inquiry.

Schweitzer, Albert. *The Quest of the Historical Jesus: A Critical Study of Its Progress from Reimarus to Wrede*. Translated by W. Montgomery. London: Adam & Charles Black, 1954. Chapter 13 is devoted to Renan's *The Life of Jesus*. Schweitzer calls Renan's essay on the sources for the life of Jesus "a literary masterpiece" but finds the work inconsistent in its estimate and use of the Fourth Gospel and in its thoroughgoing "insincerity." Passing attention is accorded to Renan in other chapters.

Wardman, H. W. *Ernest Renan: A Critical Biography*. London: Athlone Press, 1964. The emphasis in this biography is upon Renan's life and work in the context of his times. Wardman offers a consistent characterization of Renan, noting, for example, Renan's fear of his work becoming outdated or being proved wrong by posterity, as well as Renan's metaphysical anxieties.

Wilson, Edmund. *To the Finland Station: A Study in the Writing and Acting of History*. New York: Harcourt Brace, 1940. Reprint. New York: Farrar, Straus & Giroux, 1972. Places Renan within the revolutionary tradition in Europe. Part 6 of chapter 1 discusses Renan in the context of the decline of the revolutionary tradition and praises *The History of the Origins of Christianity* as "a masterpiece—perhaps the greatest of all histories of ideas." Elsewhere in his text, Wilson suggests that Renan's moral force diminishes in proportion to his urbane tolerance of error and his diplomatic dissimulation.

SEE ALSO: Auguste Comte; Jamāl al-Dīn al-Afghānī; Albrecht Ritschl.

RELATED ARTICLE in *Great Events from History: The Nineteenth Century, 1801-1900:* 1835: Finney Lectures on "Revivals of Religion."

PIERRE-AUGUSTE RENOIR
French painter

One of the greatest of the French Impressionists, Renoir painted in the open air, handling the paint loosely, dissolving masses, and abandoning local colors. He differed, however, from most other Impressionists in his concentration on the human figure and in his strong interest in portraiture.

BORN: February 25, 1841; Limoges, France
DIED: December 3, 1919; Cagnes-sur-Mer, France
AREA OF ACHIEVEMENT: Art

EARLY LIFE

Pierre-Auguste Renoir (reh-nwahr) was the son of Léonard Renoir, a poor painter who moved his family from Limoges to Paris in 1845, when Pierre-Auguste was four years old. There the young Renoir, who displayed talent for music as well as for drawing, was enrolled in the choir school of the parish church of Saint-Roch. His elder sister Lisa first exposed him to painting at the age of nine by taking him to the Louvre. He would doodle in his exercise books in school, and he was later encouraged in art by Lisa's fiancé, the illustrator Charles Leray.

At the age of thirteen, Renoir was apprenticed to the Lévy Frères firm of porcelain painters, for whom he painted decorative bouquets on dishware in an eighteenth century style. During his lunch periods, he hurried to the Louvre, where he practiced his drawing; later, in 1860, he was given official permission to copy there. After losing his job in the porcelain atelier in 1858, when the firm went bankrupt, he painted fans for a living, copying on them pictures of the rococo artists François Boucher, Jean-Honoré Fragonard, Nicolas Lancret, and Antoine Watteau. The sense of joy and gracefulness encapsulated in that phase of French painting would later be found in Renoir's own work.

Renoir enrolled in 1862 in the academically oriented studio of Charles Gleyre, a mediocre Swiss painter, where he met Jean Frédéric Bazille, Claude Monet, and Alfred Sisley. At gatherings at the home of a relative of Bazille, he met the painter Édouard Manet, the poet Charles Baudelaire, and the novelist Théophile Gautier. Leaving Gleyre's studio the next year, Renoir painted with his friends in the Fontainebleau Forest in order to sketch the landscape and move toward greater naturalism. They stayed at Chailly, near the encampment of the Barbizon painters, and Renoir met there the Barbizonist Narcisse Virgile Diaz de La Peña. The major influence on Renoir's work from 1867 to 1870 was exerted by

Gustave Courbet, whose heavy modeling, massive figures, and use of the palette knife can be seen reflected in Renoir's rendering of the nude in *Diane Chassereuse* (1867). In that picture there can be discerned, too, the influence of Manet in the use of an obviously contemporary figure to pose for a mythological scene.

LIFE'S WORK

In the spring of 1868, Renoir and Bazille moved to a studio in the rue de la Paix, where Monet would occasionally join them. In the evenings, they often went to the Café Guerbois, where there would be much talk of painting, with Manet as the presiding figure, the painter Paul Cézanne, the printmaker Félix Bracquemond, Henri Fantin-Latour, Constantin Guys, and Sisley, and the novelists Émile Zola and Gautier.

Renoir's leap into full-blown Impressionism occurred in 1869 with his paintings of *La Grenouillière*, the bathing place and floating restaurant at Bougival on the Seine. His intention was to combine the sense of poetry of the rococo with a motif from contemporary life. His strokes are broken. About half of the painted surface is given to the shimmering water, and light and atmosphere have become the unifying elements. Renoir and Monet painted side by side at that spot, and their compositions and placement of boats and figures on water-surrounded platforms are almost identical, except that Renoir gives somewhat more prominence to the figures.

During that time, as the supporter of his mistress Camille and her son Claude, Renoir struggled to make ends meet and often borrowed from Bazille. In 1870, he was drafted for the Franco-Prussian War. He believed that it was his duty to serve and was sent first to Bordeaux and later to Tarbes. Back in Paris by March 18, 1871, Renoir continued in the Impressionist manner through the 1870's.

In his work Renoir gave no indication of the political unrest of the times; his most ambitious paintings of the next years were of streets filled with leisurely strollers and of beautiful young people enjoying their carefree existence in the open air. *Dancing at the Moulin de la Galette, Montmartre* (1876) shows couples dancing at a popular open-air spot while other people converse and drink at the outdoor tables, a custom on Sunday afternoons. The crowd swirls about, with Renoir focusing on no single person or couple, giving

a sense of randomness. Some figures are cut by the edge of the canvas. All seem to be enjoying themselves to the utmost, with no hint of anything troubling. Renoir once said, "The earth as the paradise of the gods, that is what I want to paint."

In 1874, Renoir took an active part in the organization of the Impressionist group and participated in some of the group's exhibitions. In spite of his adherence to what was then stylistically avant-garde, he also exhibited more conservative paintings at the salon and was commissioned to do portraits of prominent people. His portrait *Madame Charpentier and Her Children* (1878) was dignified and can be considered to be related to Impressionism mainly in the casual postures of the sitters. In the Charpentier circle he met Zola once again, as well as the author Alphonse Daudet, the critic Edmond de Goncourt, and the diplomat-banker Paul Bérard, who was to be a steadfast patron. From the mid-1870's, as Renoir began to obtain portrait commissions and as his pictures began to be collected, his circumstances improved.

In the spring of 1881, Renoir traveled to Algiers and then in the fall to Venice, Rome, and Naples, where he was impressed by the works of Raphael and by Pompeian frescoes. He became disaffected with his Impressionist

Pierre-Auguste Renoir. (Library of Congress)

involvement, convinced that he had lost much of his ability to draw. He said to the dealer Ambrose Vollard, "There is a greater variety of light outdoors than in the studio . . . because of this, light plays far too important a part, you have no time to work out the composition."

Throughout the 1880's, Renoir gave figures a much firmer outline instead of partially dissolving them in light. He made preparatory drawings and grouped figures according to deliberate schemas, sometimes based on a specific monument of the past. The three sculpturesque nudes in *Les Grandes Baigneuses* (c. 1887) are based on a seventeenth century relief by François Girardon at Versailles. From 1888 on, his nudes became heavier, with broader hips, longer torsos, more-rounded legs, and smaller breasts, as he tried to capture something of the monumentality of the antique. In 1895, becoming interested in the plays of the ancient Greeks, he painted a series dealing with the Oedipus story.

Renoir, who so admired health, robustness, and joie de vivre, in later life had to cope with serious illness. In 1888, he visited Cézanne at Aix; Cézanne cared for him while he was ill. Arthritis combined with rheumatism became his chief affliction. In 1894, he began to walk with two canes. He traveled to various spas in the hope of finding a cure and wintered in the south. In 1913, he was confined to a wheelchair.

After 1892, Renoir had no financial worries, as a large one-man show that year at Durand-Ruel's proved a turning point. (Monet had introduced him to the dealer in the summer of 1872, and Durand-Ruel had done much during the 1880's to further the prices of Renoir's paintings.) Renoir also married rather late in life. His marriage with Aline Charigot in 1882 produced three sons: Pierre was born in 1885, Jean in 1893, and Claude in 1901.

In his children, Renoir found a new subject matter, yet he also continued to paint his radiant nudes, which during the 1890's were painted outside any environmental context and seemed to glow from within. Toward the end of Renoir's life, for example, as in the painting *Judgment of Paris* (1914), the nudes became bulbous and awkwardly heavy, perhaps reflecting the artist's own hampered mobility. Renoir also became engaged in sculpture from 1907. He was encouraged in this direction when he was visited that year by the sculptor Aristide Maillol, who did a bust of him.

Renoir's sculptures are improvisations on his late paintings, with massive figures in slow movements. These include the *Judgment of Paris* (1916) and *Blacksmith (Fire)* (1916). As he had a disability that left him with little dexterity in his hands, Renoir made drawings for the design, and an assistant, adding and subtracting according to his directions, built up the model in clay. In 1918, Renoir because completely immobilized and had to be carried. Nevertheless, before his death the next year, he made a last visit to the Louvre to see the old masters.

SIGNIFICANCE

Although usually considered as one of the inner group of the French Impressionists, Renoir was in important ways atypical. Like the other painters, he portrayed (at first glance) the life of the times, but actually what he presented were young men and women in modern clothes acting as though they were in an arcadia devoid of the stresses of the day. In his evocation of a never-never land, he is as close, in spirit, to the rococo painters of the eighteenth century as he is to the Impressionists.

Unlike other Impressionists, Renoir makes little use of open spaces, sometimes expanding or contracting to convey the tensions of modern life. He did not much explore flattenings, unusual perspectives, or cutting of figures (a device sometimes found in Renoir's paintings but seldom made much of). Renoir is perhaps best known for his paintings of figures rather than landscapes, unlike the other Impressionists. His paintings of nudes, especially, gained for him recognition, and his later nudes, with the unusual use of pigments providing a glowing, curiously weightless look, have provoked much interest.

—Abraham A. Davidson

FURTHER READING

Bailey, Colin B. *Renoir's Portraits: Impressions of an Age*. New Haven, Conn.: Yale University Press in Association with National Gallery of Canada, Ottawa, 1997. This book, published to accompany an exhibition, contains an essay examining Renoir's work as a portraitist, with detailed descriptions of his subjects. Includes reproductions of his portraits.

Barnes, Albert C., and Violette De Mazia. *The Art of Renoir*. New York: Minton, Balch, 1935. Barnes was a noted and eccentric collector who amassed some two hundred of Renoir's paintings. Barnes sees Renoir as an artist of the first rank. The text, however, is full of flowery phraseology and vague terminology. Barnes makes comparisons with Cézanne and others in his attempt to fit Renoir into a quasi-abstract mold.

Benjamin, Roger. *Renoir and Algeria*. New Haven, Conn.: Yale University Press, 2003. Renoir visited Algeria in 1881 and 1882, creating two dozen paintings of Algerian scenes and people. This book, which accompanied an exhibition of Renoir's Algeria paintings, analyzes the paintings and the influence of Orientalism on other works by the artist. Also includes an essay providing historical and cultural background about Algeria and the French presence there in the nineteenth century.

Renoir, Auguste. *Pierre Auguste Renoir*. Introduction by Walter Pach. New York: Harry N. Abrams, 1950. Includes large, excellent color plates. Discusses Renoir's handling of his subjects, his use of color, and his composition.

Renoir, Jean. *Renoir, My Father*. Translated by Randolph Weaver and Dorothy Weaver. Boston: Little, Brown, 1962. The artist's son, a film director, recounts his father's life, touching on the artist's friends, travels, tastes, and beliefs. The reproductions are few and in black and white, but the volume includes photographs of the artist and his family, and pictures of Manet, Camille Pissarro, and Cézanne.

Sagner-Düchting, Karin. *Renoir, Paris and the Belle Epoque*. New York: Prestel, 1996. Examines how Paris was a primary influence on Renoir's paintings, with analysis of the nudes, portraits, and plein air paintings created there.

"Special Section: A Renoir Symposium." *Art in America* 74 (March, 1986): 102-125. Includes the responses of various scholars to the 1986 Renoir retrospective held at the Grand Palais in Paris, the National Gallery in London, and the Museum of Fine Arts in Boston. Suggests that Renoir's reputation seems either to be on the wane or undergoing a major reassessment (with greater importance, for example, accorded the late glowing nudes).

Wadley, Nicholas, ed. *Renoir: A Retrospective*. New York: H. L. Levin, 1987. This authoritative work has contemporary accounts and evaluations.

Wheldon, Keith. *Renoir and His Art*. New York: Hamlyn, 1975. A brief but readable account of the life and development of Renoir's art. Includes comments from such scholars as John Rewald and Fritz Novotny. About half of the 102 plates are in color, and some are full-page reproductions.

White, Barbara E. *Renoir: His Life, Art, and Letters*. New York: Harry N. Abrams, 1984. White's work is useful because of its color illustrations, but its chief value lies in its use of Renoir's correspondence. White sees much of Renoir's work as derived from Monet and others.

SEE ALSO: Charles Baudelaire; Paul Cézanne; Gustave Courbet; Edgar Degas; Eugène Delacroix; Paul Gauguin; Édouard Manet; Camille Pissarro; Georges Seurat; Émile Zola.

RELATED ARTICLE in *Great Events from History: The Nineteenth Century, 1801-1900:* April 15, 1874: First Impressionist Exhibition.

CECIL RHODES
English-born South African politician and industrialist

An unabashed exponent of British imperialism, Rhodes was a business tycoon who used the wealth he amassed from South Africa's diamond and goldfields to extend British influence into Central Africa, and he bequeathed his fortune to a scholarship fund bearing his name to bring the best young minds of the English-speaking world together at his beloved Oxford University.

BORN: July 5, 1853; Bishop Stortford, Hertfordshire, England
DIED: March 26, 1902; Muizenberg, Cape Colony, South Africa
ALSO KNOWN AS: Cecil John Rhodes (full name)
AREAS OF ACHIEVEMENT: Business, government and politics

EARLY LIFE

Cecil John Rhodes was the fifth son of an English parish vicar, Francis William Rhodes, and his second wife, Louisa Peacock. The family consisted of nine sons, four of whom entered the army, and two daughters; none of the children ever married. Cecil attended the local grammar school from 1861 to 1869 but was not an outstanding student. At sixteen, his health failed, and, rather than entering university, he was sent to South Africa.

Rhodes landed at Durban on South Africa's east coast, on October 1, 1870, and proceeded to join his eldest brother, Herbert, who had migrated to Natal and was seeking to grow cotton there. Herbert was frequently absent from the farm, and thus while still in his teens, Cecil was made responsible for the management of the operation.

Even at this early age, Rhodes indicated those managerial skills that would make him a success in the diamond and goldfields of Southern Africa. In his spare time he continued a private reading program, for Rhodes had made a decision: He would one day return to England and pay his own way through Oxford University. These dreams, however, were momentarily circumvented. Diamonds had been discovered in the Orange Free State, in what ultimately became known as the Kimberley Division. Herbert left cotton farming for diamond prospecting in January, 1871, and Cecil followed him in October. In the fresh air of the high African veldt, the younger Rhodes recovered his health. The fear of tuberculosis that had originally taken him to Africa was never to plague him again, as long as he remained there, although he soon was to manifest a heart condition that would ultimately cost him his life. The next decade in Rhodes's life was to be extraordinarily complex, alternating between managing the brothers' interests in diamonds and, after 1873, matriculating at Oxford.

In October, 1873, after modest success in the Kimberley fields, Rhodes returned to Great Britain to fulfill his ambition of attending Oxford. Although frustrated in his desire to attend University College, he was recommended to and was able to gain entry into Oriel. During this first term at Oxford, Rhodes caught a chill and was diagnosed as having only six months to live; he therefore interrupted his education to return to Africa, where his lungs were no longer a problem. Over the next several years, increasing involvement in business matters in Africa prevented his returning to Oxford full time, but he kept terms whenever possible and as a result of his determination was able to pass the bachelor of arts examination in 1881. As in his grammar schooling, Rhodes was not a scholar, but these years were significant in the formation of his outlook on life.

Rhodes devoured and absorbed books or ideas that appealed to him. Three authors and their ideas made a deep impression on the Oxford undergraduate: Aristotle's *Ethics* emphasized man developing his facilities to their fullest, Edward Gibbon's *The History of the Decline and Fall of the Roman Empire* (1776-1788) provided Rhodes with a creed that the Roman imperium had fallen on nineteenth century Great Britain's shoulders, and John Ruskin's lectures outlined a gospel of public service. These ideas were absorbed at Oxford, and no later experiences seem to have altered these impressions; in fact, experience seems to have strengthened them in his faith, and their influence is to be seen in the first of his wills, in 1877.

The young Rhodes is described by his contemporaries as a slender youth, retiring in nature and with absolutely no interest in women. Maturity was to increase his stature; he became a six-footer with a broad chest and a massive head with wavy brown hair that became white in his later years. Rhodes was not what would normally be considered a good speaker, seeming to dream aloud, but he was an effective one, as indicated by his ability to persuade men to his way of thinking.

LIFE'S WORK

While Rhodes was pursuing his education, his African career made rapid progress, and he soon was to identify completely with the subcontinent. From 1874 on, he was in partnership with Charles Dunell Rudd, and gradually these two increased their Kimberley holdings, concentrating their efforts on one of the two major mines, the De Beers mine. Rhodes quickly proved to be one of the shrewdest and ablest speculators in the district, with one major rival in Barney Barnato.

Cecil Rhodes. (Library of Congress)

The year 1874 was a difficult one in Kimberley; illness attacked the miners and problems in the mines forced many to give up, but Rhodes persevered and took advantage of others' problems to acquire their concessions. Both Rhodes and Barnato recognized the basic problem within the diamond industry: As long as individual miners produced diamonds and sold them on an unregulated market, no real progress was possible. Both saw in an amalgamation of the mines and regulation of supply (and thus of price) the solution to the industry's problems. To this end, on April 1, 1880, Rhodes and his associates formed the De Beers Mining Company, with £200,000 in capital.

This was not Rhodes's only dream. In 1875, he spent eight months traveling through Bechuanaland and the Transvaal on a trip that opened his eyes to the potential of central Southern Africa and was to shape his vision of the African future. His dream was to secure this land for English occupation, to cooperate with the Afrikaners (Boers) inhabiting the Orange Free State and Transvaal (officially known as the South African Republic), and ultimately, to create a federation of self-governing South African colonies under British rule—but not without the full assent and cooperation of the Afrikaner population. Meanwhile, Rhodes had suffered his first serious heart attack and made his first will, dated September 19, 1877. Although several later wills would be drafted, Rhodes always adhered to the basic ideas expressed in this first one: his estate's assets were to be used to fund a society to promote

the extension of British rule throughout the world, the perfecting of a system of emigration from the United Kingdom and colonization by British subjects of all lands wherein the means of livelihood are attainable by energy, labour and enterprise . . . the ultimate recovery of the United States of America as an integral part of the British Empire, the consolidation of the whole Empire, the inauguration of a system of Colonial Representation of the Imperial Parliament which may tend to weld together the disjointed members of the Empire, and finally the foundation of so great a power as to hereafter render wars impossible and promote the best interests of humanity.

These ideas were to dominate his life. Within this confession of faith may be seen his dream of a British-dominated South Africa, the nucleus of the Rhodes scholarships, and, fifty years before its realization, thinking that would produce the British Commonwealth of Nations.

Meanwhile, Rhodes had taken on another obligation. In 1880, Griqualand West was absorbed into the Cape Colony, thus gaining representation in the Cape parliament. Cecil Rhodes was elected one of the two representatives for Barkly West in 1880. He took his seat in the Cape legislature the following year, and was to represent that constituency for the remainder of his life. As a member of the Cape parliament, Rhodes sought to further his African dream, maintaining the widest degree of local self-government and simultaneously organizing and promoting British colonization as a means of extending British influence and domination over the land south of the Central African lakes.

Rhodes concentrated his initial efforts on obtaining British (or Cape) control over Bechuanaland, a vast inhospitable territory north of the Orange River through which ran the only practical route to the coveted northern lands—lands that were the object of German, Portuguese, and Transvaal Afrikaner ambitions. An imperial protectorate was proclaimed over this region early in 1884, and a year later the southern portion of this territory became part of Cape Colony, with the northern portion remaining an imperial protectorate.

Within a year, new developments were to broaden Rhodes's horizons. In 1886, gold was discovered on the Rand in the Transvaal, starting a gold rush that Rhodes was ultimately to join. Also, Rhodes was attracted to the vast expanse of territory north of the Limpopo River. This land, that of the Ndebele (or Matabele) under their king, Lobengula, became as Bechuanaland had been, the focus of attention for several powers, and on October 30, 1888, Lobengula signed a convention with the British granting them mineral rights to his land and promising to make no additional concessions.

It became clear that the London government was not interested in additional costly colonial involvement, so Rhodes inquired if a chartered company would be acceptable. On this basis, the British South Africa Company was chartered July 13, 1889, with the right to develop land between the Limpopo and Zambesi Rivers, land that was soon named Rhodesia (later, Southern Rhodesia, and now, Zimbabwe). Subsequently, this same company extended its interests beyond the Zambesi to the southern shore of Lake Tanganyika, in a further effort to bring all Africa from the Cape to Cairo under the British flag. These new acquisitions subsequently became Northern Rhodesia.

While these colonizing activities were being promoted, Rhodes was consolidating his position in the diamond mines. Gradually the De Beers Mining Company had been absorbing claims, as had Barnato at Kimberley, and it became obvious that sooner or later one of these entrepreneurs would have to absorb the other. In July, 1887, Rhodes bought out the assets of a French interest, and on March 13, 1888, Rhodes's and Barnato's interests were consolidated as the De Beers Consolidated Mines, with Rhodes as chairman. This company was not limited to producing and marketing diamonds; at Rhodes's insistence, it was authorized to acquire, settle, and exploit lands in Africa and to raise and maintain such military force as necessary in the pursuit of its objectives. It was Rhodes's companies, not the imperial or the Cape governments, that undertook the construction of a rail line into the interior as an initial step in Rhodes's dream of a Cape to Cairo railroad.

After less than a decade in the Cape parliament, Rhodes became prime minister of the Cape in July, 1890, gaining and keeping power by the votes of both the British and Afrikaners. As prime minister, Rhodes sought to diminish as much as possible the interference of the British government in local affairs, but simultaneously he promoted the dream of an imperial federation. To this end he subscribed ten thousand pounds in 1888 to the Irish Home Rule movement; he believed Irish self-government was a necessary step on the road to imperial federation. The Cape prospered under Rhodes's leadership, but at the end of 1895 a decision was made and a course of action adopted that was to bring his downfall. Perhaps Rhodes believed that his heart condition doomed him to an early death and that to realize his dreams more impulsive steps had to be taken.

Rhodes had vainly sought the cooperation of the Transvaal's president, Paul Kruger, to complete the South African federation. Relations were exacerbated by the Afrikaner treatment of the foreign gold mine workers (the Uitlanders) of the Witwatersrand (at Johannesburg). Although these workers produced the wealth of the Transvaal, they were discriminated against and their needed mining supplies were heavily taxed. In December, 1895, the Uitlanders despaired of a peaceful resolution to their grievances and determined to seek reform by violence; Rhodes was asked to support this endeavor and he agreed. A plan was worked out by which Uitlanders would rebel in Johannesburg and would ask for Cape assistance to make good their claims. Meanwhile, Rhodes had sent money and arms to the Uitlanders and simultaneously authorized Dr. Leander Starr Jameson to organize the force to respond to the Johannesburg appeal.

In the confusion, Jameson launched his invasion precipitously, on December 27, 1895, and his forces were

defeated and captured by Transvaal Afrikaners within ten days. Although Rhodes had no direct responsibility for the raid, he resigned his premiership on January 6, 1896. A Cape investigation in the matter condemned Rhodes's actions, while absolving him of responsibility for the Jameson Raid; a British inquiry in 1897 found him guilty of grave breaches of duty as prime minister.

For the remainder of his life, Rhodes devoted himself to the development of Rhodesia and consolidating his loyal party in the Cape parliament. In 1896, he was personally involved in the pacification of the Ndebele and Shona revolts against company rule. With the outbreak of the South African War in October, 1899, Rhodes made his way to Kimberley and participated in the four-month siege of that city but emerged with his health broken. Business took him to Great Britain in 1901 and 1902, yet he returned to Africa to die in his adopted land at the age of forty-eight on March 26, 1902.

SIGNIFICANCE

Cecil Rhodes's influence did not end with his death. His major legacy was the scholarships to Oxford that bear his name. Except for small personal bequests, the overwhelming bulk of his fortune of approximately six million pounds was left to public service. Part represents the Rhodes scholarships: two students from each state or territory in the United States, three from each of eighteen British colonies, and an additional fifteen from Germany were granted Oxford scholarships. This plan was the final result of that boyish dream outlined in the first will of 1877 to create a society to promote Great Britain's worldwide position. Additional sums were left to Oriel College, and land was bequeathed to provide for a university in Rhodesia.

Although Rhodes's hasty actions in 1895 doomed the immediate federation of the two English colonies and two Afrikaner republics, this scheme remained in the forefront of his mind. The restoration of responsible government and the federation of the four states into the Union of South Africa in 1909 represented a posthumous and partial fulfillment of Rhodes's dreams. Developments in South Africa since 1960 have deviated from his dreams.

Rather than becoming part of a British-dominated Africa, Bechuanaland and the two Rhodesias became independent: Northern Rhodesia as Zambia (1964), Bechuanaland as Botswana (1966), and Southern Rhodesia as Zimbabwe (1980). Even Rhodes's beloved Cape (as a component of the Union of South Africa) declared its status as an independent republic in 1961, thus severing ties with Great Britain.

The most important piece of legislation enacted during Rhodes's premiership has influenced attitudes toward Africans ever since. This act, the Glen Grey Act of 1894, provided the blueprint for the modern apartheid system adopted by the South African government in 1948. Rhodes believed that the African must be disciplined by work and must be relegated to his own districts where he would be allowed to own property. No matter how much they might prosper, Africans would never gain the Cape franchise and would be allowed to vote only for their local councils. Thus the native homeland (Bantustan) policy of the South African government also stems from a decision reached by Rhodes.

—Ronald O. Moore

FURTHER READING

Flint, John. *Cecil Rhodes*. Boston: Little, Brown, 1974. A volume in the Library of World Biography. Flint approaches his protagonist as a fascinating case study of a self-made man who bartered wealth for political power and who manipulated British imperialism for his own ends. Critical, with a low regard for Rhodes's abilities.

Galbraith, John S. *Crown and Charter: Early Years of the British South African Company*. Berkeley: University of California Press, 1974. Example of the newer specialized studies regarding Rhodes and his activities; focuses on the internal policies and motives of the British South Africa Company and suggests deceitful dealings by the company and its agents with African societies.

Gross, Felix. *Rhodes of Africa*. New York: Praeger, 1957. Written by a South African journalist, this book lacks the documentation needed to support its generally critical approach to Rhodes; views him as an unscrupulous adventurer and hints at shady financial dealings and homosexual tendencies.

Leasor, James. *Rhodes and Barnato: Architects of Empire*. London: Leo Cooper, 1997. Compares and contrasts the careers and personalities of two Englishmen who made their fortunes in the South African diamond industry—Rhodes and Barney Barnato, a part-time boxer and music hall comedian who became one of England's wealthiest tycoons.

Millin, Sarah Gertrude. *Cecil Rhodes*. New York: Harper and Brothers, 1933. A fair and impressionistic biography appropriate for the chaotic life of the subject; written by one who loved Africa as much as Rhodes did. More concerned with Rhodes's personal side than Williams is.

Porter, Bernard. *The Lion's Share: A Short History of British Imperialism, 1850-1983*. 2d ed. New York: Longman, 1984. Brief, judicious general history of the British Empire during the age of the New Imperialism, allowing comparison of Rhodes's activities in Africa with events in other areas.

Thomas, Anthony. *Rhodes*. New York: St. Martin's Press, 1996. Balanced biography written by a South African documentary film producer. Thomas criticizes Rhodes's racist and politically corrupt methods of building white-dominated states, but appreciates his subject's forceful personality.

Williams, Basil. *Cecil Rhodes*. London: Constable, 1921. The first academic study of Rhodes, written by an author who was acquainted with Rhodes and most of the personalities figuring in the biography. The work is not uncritical, especially of the Jameson Raid, but is still largely an apologia for Rhodes and his work.

Wilson, Monica, and Leonard Thompson, eds. *The Oxford History of South Africa*. 2 vols. New York: Oxford University Press, 1969, 1971. The second volume, dealing with the period after 1870, is useful in providing a detailed background for Rhodes's career and impact on South Africa.

SEE ALSO: Joseph Chamberlain; Sir George Goldie; H. Rider Haggard; Rudyard Kipling; Paul Kruger; Lobengula; John Ruskin; Olive Schreiner.

RELATED ARTICLES in *Great Events from History: The Nineteenth Century, 1801-1900:* June 21, 1884: Gold Is Discovered in the Transvaal; November 15, 1884-February 16, 1885: Berlin Conference Lays Groundwork for the Partition of Africa; March 13, 1888: Rhodes Amalgamates Kimberley Diamondfields; October 11, 1899-May 31, 1902: South African War.

DAVID RICARDO
English economist

Acknowledged as the founder of political economy, Ricardo was the most influential of the early nineteenth century thinkers who formalized the growing science of economics. His impact on economics has continued into the twenty-first century.

BORN: April 18, 1772; London, England
DIED: September 11, 1823; Gatcombe Park, Gloucestershire, England
AREA OF ACHIEVEMENT: Philosophy

EARLY LIFE

Born in England, David Ricardo was descended from Jewish-Spanish ancestors who had migrated to Italy and then to Holland before 1700. His father, Abraham Israel Ricardo, left Holland while in his early twenties to visit England, where he remained. He became a citizen, married Abigail Delvalle, from a well-to-do Jewish merchant family, and established himself as a successful merchant-banker with a broker's license. The family was important in the London Jewish community. David was the third child, and third son, of fifteen children.

Groomed to enter the family business, David received practical schooling in England and then was sent to Holland to continue his education in a commercial school under the care of an uncle. After two years in Holland he returned to England for a final year of schooling, after which he entered his father's business, at the age of fourteen.

Ricardo soon became involved in high-level financing of bills of exchange and public securities, quickly becoming a respected participant in the world of finance. His ability, however, led to conflict with his father over the latter's role as chief of the family. When Ricardo reached the age of twenty-one, he married a Quaker woman, Priscilla Ann Wilkinson, and was instantly ostracized by his family. Priscilla, too, was ostracized, but with less severity. David never again had any dealings with his mother; he was removed from his godfather's will as of the date of the wedding. By 1810, he was, however, fully reconciled with his father.

Ricardo was a small man and well proportioned. His skin appears to have been darker than the typical Englishman's; his eyes were reported to evince intelligence and thoughtfulness. His voice was high and squeaky, perhaps an advantage in Parliament, because that made it distinct. Although he was not robust or athletic, he enjoyed good health.

LIFE'S WORK

Ricardo, in 1793, was on his own. He and Priscilla leased a house in the Kennington Place area of London, followed by two more nearby in the next three years—each larger than the last. Having begun speculating in the stock market prior to his marriage, he was respected by private bankers, who provided him with a line of credit.

In 1796, Ricardo expanded his interests, becoming an avid amateur mineralogist. (In 1807, he would be one of the first members of the Geological Society.) In 1799, while he and Priscilla were in Bath for her health, David read Adam Smith's *The Wealth of Nations* (1776), the first work on capitalist economics. He immediately took an interest in political economy, the subject that would become his area of achievement.

During the years of the wars with revolutionary and Napoleonic France, Ricardo was active in war finance through purchase of government bonds and the creation of the professionalized stock exchange. He also served as an officer in volunteer military units. As one of a thousand originators of the London Institution, an organization to promote science, literature, and the arts, he made friends with the publisher of the *Morning Chronicle*, James Perry.

In 1797, the British government had suspended gold payments and issued paper bank notes. The effects of bank failures and inflation had created a long-standing controversy identified as "paper against gold." Perry asked Ricardo to write about the issue, which he did in 1809, publishing an essay titled "The Price of Gold." The next year, he published *The High Price of Bullion: A Proof of the Depreciation of Banknotes* and became a public figure. His next publication was *A Reply to Mr. Bosanquet's Practical Observation on the Report of the Bullion Committee* (1811), considered the best controversial work on an economic topic to that date. His argument in both pieces was that government should control the supply of paper currency to reflect accurately the value of gold bullion. Ricardo, the successful man of finance, had become the public theorist.

By 1809, Ricardo was active in the Unitarian Church. Priscilla and the children eventually became Anglicans, but David would not do so. He was attracted to Unitarianism for its respect for reasoned toleration.

With escalating costs as the war with France neared its end in 1815, Ricardo and others loyally continued to buy and deal in bonds. When Napoleon was finally defeated at Waterloo, the market soared, and Ricardo made a fortune. He purchased a grand London home—on land used for the American Embassy in the twentieth century—and the estate of Gatcombe in Gloucestershire, where as chief landholder he was expected to perform extensive community services. He also indulged in support of the arts, book collecting, educational reform, and intellectual discussions with such thinkers as Jeremy Bentham, James Mill (father of John Stuart Mill), and Thomas Malthus.

In 1815, Ricardo published his critique of the Corn Laws, *An Essay on the Influence of a Low Price of Corn on the Profits of Stock*. The Corn Laws were a means of guaranteeing English grain producers a high price for their products. Ricardo contended that they were an artificial interference with the workings of the market and thus benefited the landowner at the expense of everyone else.

By 1817, Ricardo had taken much of the profit from his war bonds and invested in other areas: in land, French bonds, and mortgages, which allowed him to retire from day-to-day business and devote time to other activities, including the writing of his *On the Principles of Political Economy and Taxation* (1817) and participation in Parliament.

On the Principles of Political Economy and Taxation was Ricardo's account of the growing discipline of economics. Ricardo propounded seven principles upon which an economy is based. First, the cost of production determines price. Second, the amount of labor required determines the value of an item. (This idea was based on Smith's "labor theory of value"; in the 1821 edition Ricardo conceded that the cost of production might also influence value.) The third principle described a rent theory based on Malthus's idea of population growth outstripping food production and wherein rent was the difference in price between the most and least productive acres. (Ricardo contended that this created permanent conflict between landowners and capitalists.) Further, for Ricardo there is a fixed supply of money for wages—the amount of capital in circulation—and as capital increases, population grows, more land is rented, capital profits shrink, and wages are lowered.

Ricardo's fifth principle is that when wages fall below a minimum for survival, population drops as a result of war, pestilence, and disease (Malthus's contention). According to Ricardo's sixth principle, "diminishing returns" set in when capitalists must spend more on subsistence wages and therefore have less to invest and expand production. Ricardo's seventh and last principle

is based on a quantity theory of money that projects rising prices resulting from an increased supply of gold, through domestic or foreign trade. These principles became the basis for economics as a scientific study, and some are at the heart of late twentieth century schools of thought.

In exchange for a four-thousand-pound fee and a large mortgage loan, Ricardo was given the House of Commons seat of Portarlington by the earl of Portarlington. He took his seat in Parliament on February 26, 1819. His first speech, a month later, was on a bill to reform the Poor Laws. Not a great orator, Ricardo reluctantly joined in debate, but his wisdom on matters relating to economics was always in demand.

In 1820, Ricardo was reelected. He would retain his seat in the House of Commons until his death in 1823. His politics were decidedly those in support of tolerance, individual rights, and limits on the size of government. He attacked the Corn Laws, usury laws, bounties, economic restrictions, and Robert Owen's pastoral socialist schemes. He supported an annuity plan for the poor, the reduction of taxes, and the idea of paying off the national debt with a onetime tax on all land.

On July 12, 1822, Ricardo and family boarded a steamboat at the Tower of London steps and headed for the Continent for a five-month Grand Tour. The tour started in Amsterdam and extended to Leghorn, near Florence, Italy, where Spanish Jews had first migrated around 1600. In 1823, Ricardo was joined in Parliament by Joseph Hume, an advocate of the ideas of James Mill and Bentham. The two joined forces, voicing concern over the need for parliamentary reform. Ricardo began work on a plan to create a national bank (published after his death, in 1824). He also drew up plans for refurbishing Gatcombe. An earache, first noted in Italy, recurred early in September. Ricardo died of a mastoid infection near noon on September 11, 1823. He was buried in the churchyard at Hardenhuish.

SIGNIFICANCE

David Ricardo managed in his lifetime to meld the world of finance with the life of the mind and the good of the body politic. Personally successful in business, he systematized the general principles of what would become the science of economics. Gifted in the practical, he contributed an original view on the theoretical. During the later years of his life, Ricardo expanded his interest to politics, tempering what he saw as the laws by which political economies worked with a concern for toleration, justice, and the public good.

Although his ideas have been superseded or modified by new theoretical approaches to economics, Ricardo managed to influence all positions on the economic spectrum, from the proponents of laissez-faire capitalism to those of socialism.

—Lance Williams

FURTHER READING

Churchman, Nancy. *David Ricardo on Public Debt.* New York: Palgrave, 2001. An analysis of Ricardo's ideas about public debt, describing how those ideas connect with his other economic theories.

Grampp, William D. "Scots, Jews, and Subversives Among the Dismal Scientists." *Journal of Economic History* 36 (September, 1976): 543-571. An account of the abuse hurled at Ricardo and other political economists because they were Scots, Jews, or political radicals. Ricardo is shown to have been damned also for being a stockbroker.

Heilbroner, Robert L. *The Worldly Philosophers.* 6th ed. New York: Simon & Schuster, 1986. Chapter 4 is titled "The Gloomy Presentiments of Parson Malthus and David Ricardo." The gloom from Malthus concerns his theories on population. Ricardo is presented as a theorist dealing with abstractions—abstract workers, abstract capitalists. A good comparison of their ideas.

Henderson, John P. *The Life and Economics of David Ricardo.* With supplemental chapters by John B. Davis; edited by Warren J. Samuels and Gilbert B. Davis. Boston: Kluwer Academic, 1997. Comprehensive, intellectual biography, recounting Ricardo's early years, career, economic theories, and relationships with Thomas Malthus and other classical economists.

Hollander, Jacob H. *David Ricardo: A Centenary Estimate.* New York: August M. Kelley, 1968. A reprint of the 1910 edition, from three lectures at Harvard University in 1910, Hollander's book is helpful in understanding the connection between later writings and his parliamentary activities.

Kuhn, W. E. *The Evolution of Economic Thought.* Cincinnati, Ohio: South-Western, 1963. Includes a short sketch of Ricardo's life and contribution to economic ideas and public life. Also includes an analysis of Ricardo's monetary and banking theory in chapter 9.

Marshall, Alfred. *Principles of Economics.* 8th ed. London: Macmillan, 1920. A discussion of the fundamental economic law of value. The human side of Ricardo is seen as a barrier to a clear exposition of his ideas. Marshall contends that Ricardo's unwillingness to repeat his ideas, to explain them in greater detail, led to errors of omission.

Peach, Terry. *Interpreting Ricardo.* New York: Cambridge University Press, 1993. Explains the full range of Ricardo's economic theories, including his ideas about profits, the law of markets, and the labor theory of value.

Ricardo, David. *Biographical Miscellany.* Vol. 10 in *The Works and Correspondence of David Ricardo.* Edited by Piero Sraffa. Cambridge, England: Cambridge University Press, 1955. A collection of sketches and other personal data. The one source with some information about his physical appearance. A helpful volume of memorabilia. The most revealing personality glimpses, however, are in *Maria Edgeworth, Letters from England, 1813-1844,* edited by Christina Colvin (Oxford, England: Oxford University Press, 1971).

Weatherall, David. *David Ricardo: A Biography.* The Hague: Martinus Nijhoff, 1976. The most readable, human account. Particularly useful insights into the events that affected Ricardo and his times.

SEE ALSO: Thomas Robert Malthus; Karl Marx; James Mill; John Stuart Mill; Robert Owen.

RELATED ARTICLES in *Great Events from History: The Nineteenth Century, 1801-1900:* 1817: Ricardo Identifies Seven Key Economic Principles; 1833: British Parliament Passes the Factory Act; June 15, 1846: British Parliament Repeals the Corn Laws.

ELLEN SWALLOW RICHARDS
American chemist and social reformer

The first American woman to become a professional chemist, Richards was a writer, reformer, teacher, and scientist who believed that science should be applied to practical issues. As an advocate for commercial food safety and public sanitation, she helped found the discipline of home economics and played an important role in the passage of public health measures and in the advancement of women's education.

BORN: December 3, 1842; Dunstable, Massachusetts
DIED: March 30, 1911; Boston, Massachusetts
ALSO KNOWN AS: Ellen Henrietta Swallow (birth name); Ellen H. Richards
AREAS OF ACHIEVEMENT: Chemistry, education, social reform

EARLY LIFE

Ellen Swallow Richards was born Ellen Swallow, the daughter of Peter Swallow and Fanny Gould Taylor, who were both New England teachers. As a child, she received home schooling that combined book and practical learning until she was sixteen. Her father then bought a general store in Westford in which Ellen worked, while studying Latin, French, German, classical literature, science, and mathematics at the local academy. At home, she learned the skills of housekeeping. At the store she developed a business sense by keeping the accounts and doing the purchasing, which often required her to travel to Boston. Her observations of housewives debating the relative merits of salertus and baking soda—which she knew were exactly the same substances—helped her to understand of the power of marketing.

In 1868, Ellen entered Vassar College, where she took as many science courses as she could and graduated with a degree in chemistry in 1870. At Vassar, her organic chemistry professor insisted that science should solve practical problems and trained his students to analyze common substances, such as bread. Upon graduation, Ellen could not find employment. One firm encouraged her to further her studies in chemistry. Because no women's college offered more science than Vassar, from which she had already graduated, she applied to the Massachusetts Institute of Technology (MIT), which had been founded in 1865. After some deliberation, the professors decided to admit her as a special student and waived her tuition.

Ellen entered MIT in January, 1871. To support herself, she tutored, translated scientific articles written in German into English, and ran the boardinghouse in which she lived. Soon, her skills in chemical analysis attracted the attention of William R. Nichols, whom the state board of health had chosen to study sewerage and the water supply. Nichols made Ellen his assistant and thus enabled her to come into contact with the most advanced work in sanitation. In 1873, she received a bachelor's degree in chemistry from MIT and, concurrently, a master's degree from Vassar. For two years she remained at MIT, which allowed her to pursue graduate studies but refused to grant her a doctorate. In 1875, she married Robert H. Richards, a mining engineering professor at MIT.

LIFE'S WORK

Ellen Richards's life's work reflected her interests in public health, education, nutrition, the environment, and home economics. She was the first woman to earn a degree at MIT, the first to be appointed an instructor in sani-

Ellen Swallow Richards. (Courtesy, MIT Museum)

tary chemistry there, in 1884, and the first to join the American Association for the Advancement of Science. Her experiences as Nichols's assistant helped to establish her reputation as an analytical chemist and contributed to her lifelong interest in sanitation and public health. After the Manufacturers' Mutual Fire Insurance Company hired her as a consulting chemist to study the problem of fires and explosions in textile mills in 1884, she analyzed the combustion points and volatility of the often cheap and low-grade oils and dyes used by the mills. Her findings provided information that the insurers used to force mill owners to purchase better materials and to devise safety standards for their workers.

In 1887, Richards supervised another water study for the Massachusetts Board of Health. Her study produced the first water-purity tables and enabled Massachusetts to pass the nation's first water-quality standards. It also led to the construction of the world's first modern sewage treatment facilities. At the annual meeting of the American Public Health Association in Boston in 1896, Richards argued that unhealthy and unsanitary school environments were killing two hundred schoolchildren per year and causing five thousand cases of illness. When local officials refused to act on her recommendations, she and her supporters took the issue to the Massachusetts legislature, which eventually enacted sanitary reforms for all aspects of state schools, from the administration to the students.

Education for both professional women and homemakers occupied Richards's attention as well. She met with the Women's Education Association to garner financial support for a woman's laboratory at MIT, which had offered a space. The laboratory opened in late 1876 under the direction of Professor John Ordway, with Richards as the unpaid assistant. The new lab attracted women who went on to become science teachers at colleges and high schools. In 1883, the lab was torn down, five years after MIT began to admit women into its regular programs.

In 1878-1879, Richards and her MIT lab students tested staple foods that were on the market and discovered significant and widespread adulterations. Massachusetts passed its first food and drug acts in 1882 and 1884, using the chemical analyses detailed in Richards's report published by the Board of Health. The Women's Laboratory also analyzed other household substances, including papers, woods, cloth, and furniture and discovered, for example, arsenic in wallpaper and mercury in fabrics. Their findings also elucidated the chemical properties of cleaning agents and the processes of cooking.

Richards studied the chemical breakdown of macronutrients, such as carbohydrates, and had a special interest in bread—of which the average American ate one pound every day. Richards developed specific recommendations for wives and mothers on how to bake the better and healthier bread. Richards published her findings in two small books, *The Chemistry of Cooking and Cleaning* (1882) and *Food Materials and Their Adulterations* (1886).

One of Richards's goals was to educate the working poor on how to achieve the most nutrition for the least money—an expression of her commitment to economy and efficiency. In 1890, she opened the New England Kitchen with a threefold purpose: to collect information on the food supplies and tastes of the working class, to use materials that were usually wasted, and to cook the most economical and nutritious foods to sell for home consumption. This effort led Richards to plan the Rumsford Kitchen for the 1893 Chicago World's Fair, where visitors were offered pamphlets on nutrition and could purchase balanced meals, whose food values were computed. Another outgrowth of Richards's New England Kitchen was the school lunch program. In 1884, the New England Kitchen took over this task from school janitors and ultimately provided five thousand high school pupils with lunches. Many institutions, such as schools and hospitals, consequently consulted Richards for nutritional advice.

In 1892, Richards coined the word "ecology" (borrowed from the German morphologist Ernst Haeckel) for the study of domestic science, and late in her life wrote a book on euthenics, which addressed her concern that environmental degradation injured human health. Richards was involved in many organizations and helped found the American Association of University Women. She also served as the first president of the American Home Economics Association, which was organized in late 1908, and published fourteen books and a number of articles. After leading a busy and productive life, she died of heart failure in Boston on March 30, 1911, during her sixty-ninth year.

SIGNIFICANCE

Ellen Swallow Richards's faith in science and the necessity of reform reflected the spirit of the Progressive movement. Some of her efforts also caused controversies, and her challenges to industry to consider human health and safety met with some resistance. Although her virtual isolation from collegial support and her lack of credentials hampered her efforts, she achieved remarkable success in social reform, public health education, and the popularization of science. She also challenged, less successfully, the prevailing social Darwinist view that so-called inferior genes caused human problems, and argued that poor nutrition and lack of sanitation threatened children's intelligence. Moreover, she challenged the authorities to understand public health issues and to implement safety measures.

Late twentieth century scholarship reinterpreted Richards's work in terms of feminism and environmentalism. Challenging prevailing social theory, Richards argued that traditional woman's work had calculable economic value in the capitalist system. She recognized the changes in gender roles that were brought about by industrialization, and while she seemingly tended to relegate women to the home, she also advocated the sharing of domestic duties by men and desired to empower women by giving them the scientific knowledge to control their immediate environments.

—Kristen L. Zacharias

FURTHER READING

Breton, Mary Joy. *Women Pioneers for the Environment.* Boston: Northeastern University Press, 1998. Chapter 2 presents an overview of Richards's work in public sanitation, education, and domestic science.

Clarke, Robert. *Ellen Swallow: The Woman Who Founded Ecology.* Chicago: Follett, 1973. Focuses on Richards's role in founding the modern environmental movement in the United States.

Edwards, June. *Women in American Education, 1820-1955: The Female Force and Educational Reform.* Westport, Conn.: Greenwood Press, 2002. Chapter 4 examines Richards's philosophy of teaching, which focused on hands-on experience, as well as her promotion of science education for the public and for women in particular.

Hunt, Caroline L. *The Life of Ellen H. Richards, 1842-1911.* Washington, D.C.: American Home Economics Association, 1958. First published in 1912, this book is outdated in its writing style but offers a useful perspective on Richards's role in the development of home economics.

Lippincott, Gail. "Rhetorical Chemistry." *Journal of Business and Technical Communication* 17, no. 1 (January, 2003): 10-49. Examines how two of Richards's papers, one addressed to male scientists and the other to clubwomen, employed different rhetorical techniques and concludes that she displayed rhetorical sophistication. Places the analysis in the context of technology, gender, and communication.

Richardson, Barbara. "Ellen Swallow Richards: 'Humanistic Oekologist,' 'Applied Sociologist,' and the Founding of Sociology." *American Sociologist* 33, no. 3 (Fall, 2002): 21-57. Interpretation of Richards's work as a scientist and social reformer within a feminist framework. Argues that she challenged academic models of social change. Valuable also for its placement of her work in its historical context.

SEE ALSO: Ernst Haeckel; Maria Mitchell.

RELATED ARTICLES in *Great Events from History: The Nineteenth Century, 1801-1900:* May 12, 1857: New York Infirmary for Indigent Women and Children Opens; 1869-1871: Mendeleyev Develops the Periodic Table of Elements; May 1-October 30, 1893: Chicago World's Fair.

ABBY SAGE RICHARDSON
American writer

Richardson was a successful but far from an important author and playwright. Her fame derives primarily from her central role in the celebrated trial of her former husband for murdering her second husband. The case helped to call attention to laws that unjustly made it difficult for women to win divorces from abusive husbands.

BORN: October 14, 1837; Lowell, Massachusetts
DIED: December 5, 1900; Rome, Italy
ALSO KNOWN AS: Abby Sage (birth name); Abby Sage McFarland
AREAS OF ACHIEVEMENT: Theater, women's rights

EARLY LIFE

Abby Sage Richardson was born Abby Sage, the daughter of William and Abigail Sage. Her father was a member of an established New England family descended from the mid-seventeenth century Welsh immigrant David Sage and his wife Mary Willcox. When Abby was five, the family moved from Massachusetts to Manchester, New Hampshire.

The eldest of three surviving children, Abby had a precocious interest in books and read whatever she could, including a miniature edition of William Shakespeare's plays. As she grew older, she trained to become a teacher at the Normal School in New Hampshire. After graduating in 1855, she taught elementary school in New Haven, Connecticut.

In the spring of 1857, Abby met Daniel McFarland (1818-1880), an alcoholic land speculator who had had a brief career as a college instructor of elocution and who was a nonpracticing member of the Massachusetts bar. To the articulate but inexperienced Abby, the twenty-years-older McFarland was a sophisticated and learned man who moved in the wealthy, progressive circles that she aspired to enter. Marriage to him seemed to Abby an ideal match of two cultivated minds, and on December 14, 1857, they wed in Boston.

Over the next ten years, during which time Abby had two children, she found that preserving her marriage to McFarland was becoming an ordeal. She traveled constantly with her husband to further his land ventures until 1863, when she drew on her wealthy social connections to get her husband work as a provost marshal for the military draft under the Enrollment Act. During that period, their marriage was strained by McFarland's heavy drinking, his resentment of the fact that Abby was supporting the family through her paid readings, and by her having to shuttle between her parents' homes and their own rooming houses in New York and New Jersey as their money ran out.

LIFE'S WORK

Like many other mid-nineteenth century American women who were denied careers and whose economic status was desperate, Abby turned to lecturing and writing to earn money. Private readings that she had begun in homes in the West had been so well received that her husband—whose business schemes almost invariably failed—trained her as an actor. However, no immediate work resulted. Meanwhile, although her husband expressed his resentment of her role as primary provider for the family in invective and abuse, he accepted her money readily.

Abby's readings from the poetry of Henry Wadsworth Longfellow, John Greenleaf Whittier, and others and from Shakespeare's plays attracted the attention of some of society's powerful figures. These included Mrs. John F. Cleveland, a sister of Horace Greeley, the editor of the *New York Tribune*, and Charlotte and Samuel Sinclair, the publisher of the *New York Tribune*. In addition to doing readings, Abby wrote a collection of poems, *Percy's Year of Rhymes*, that was published in Boston in 1866.

During that same year, 1866, Abby was befriended by the noted *Tribune* journalist Lucia Gilbert Calhoun, who introduced her to the manager of the Winter Garden Theater. In that theater, Abby embarked on a short-lived stage career under the stage name "Miss Cushing." On one occasion, she appeared played Nerissa opposite the distinguished actor Edwin Booth in Shakespeare's *The Merchant of Venice* (pr. c. 1596-1597). Also during that year, she met Albert Deane Richardson, a widowed *Tribune* journalist and travel correspondent. Richardson boarded in the same house as the McFarlands and unavoidably observed their fractured marriage.

In 1867, Abby continued to write and act and received both moral and material support from the Sinclairs and the Calhouns and professional advice from Albert Deane Richardson. She wrote essays for the *Riverside Magazine for Young People* and a children's column for the *Independent*. The American Publishing company, of Hartford, Connecticut, published her next book of poems, *Pebbles and Sunshine*.

In February, 1867, Abby finally recognized that her long effort to preserve her marriage to a violent alcoholic had failed and told McFarland that she was leaving him. In March, a drunken McFarland shot and wounded Richardson, as he was escorting Abby home from the theater. Mortified by the publicity that the shooting attracted, Abby resigned from the theater and moved with her two children to Boston. During that same month, McFarland began a custody proceeding that won him custody of Abby's older son, Percy, in November. Eager to claim his wife again, he sued her for "alienation of affections."

Meanwhile, Abby continued to support herself and her younger son, Daniel, whom she renamed William Sage. She wrote book reviews and articles for the *New York Tribune*, the *Atlantic Monthly*, and the *Independent*. She chose not to divorce McFarland in New York State, whose laws required a claim of adultery, even though McFarland was guilty of that offense. Instead, she moved to Indianapolis, Indiana, where divorce laws were broader. There, in October, 1869, she won a divorce from McFarland on grounds of cruelty.

After returning to Massachusetts, Abby visited Richardson and made plans to move to New York with him. On November 25, 1869, McFarland shot Richardson again, in the *Tribune* building lobby, gravely injuring him. Five days later, on November 30, the well-known Protestant cleric Reverend Henry Ward Beecher conducted a marriage between Abby and Richardson on what proved to be the latter's deathbed, as Richardson died two days later.

McFarland's ensuing murder trial was a national sensation, setting women's rights advocates such as

THE ACQUITTAL OF RICHARDSON'S FORMER HUSBAND

After Abby Sage Richardson's former husband, Daniel McFarland, was acquitted of the murder of her second husband, Albert Deane Richardson, Abby swore out this affidavit and had it published in the New York Tribune *the day after McFarland's trial ended.*

You have heard my true story. I said when I began that I would tell the whole and I have. I think the same thing might have happened to any man or woman who lives, without bringing to them either remorse or shame.

I believe now, as I have believed for years, that Mr. McFarland was a man born to do a murder. The fact that he was always uttering threats of bloodshed does not so much convince me of this as the fact of his temperament, which had become one of uncontrollable violence. I believe he feared this himself. Often during our early married life, when I told him in his reasonable moments that he would kill me in some of his fits of passion, he asserted with vehemence that he "should never harm a hair of my head." Towards the last of my life with him, however, he said in answer to my expressed fears, "I shall never harm you, if I *know* you," which convinced me that he not feel sure of himself. I believe that if I had stayed with him, sooner or later I should have been the victim of his blind fury.

I write this without malice or hard feeling against him. Mr. McFarland married me a girl in years, a child in experience. In every way he abused his claim in me, he turned my love to bitterness, he took all the bloom and sweetness from my life. When I went away, and he found I had begun, perhaps, to feel a hope of happiness, his wounded vanity and desire for revenge turned his naturally made temper into blackest madness. He swore to my friends, by all the fiends that he "would rob me of my reputation, my children, all I held dear." He has done so, and I pity him from my soul.

There are those who say that my marriage to Albert Richardson was the act that led to Mr. McFarland's acquittal by setting the public against Mr. Richardson. If so, it does not matter. As I have said, I wished Mr. McFarland no ill, and I believe that he was, and is, insane. I believe he would have been acquitted in any event, justice being so lax in New York, malignity so strong and the sympathy for crime so increased for a criminal who commits a capital offense. Indeed it seems as if we need only commit murder to have all the public sympathy. Perhaps it is a protest against capital punishment and may end in its abolition. If so it will leave its good fruits.

There is but one word more today, and I will say it briefly. It is well known that I was on trial before a New Y4ork Court as much as Daniel McFarland, and for a crime more heinous and more bitterly punished in a woman than murder committed by a man. And it is clearly seen by all who see dispassionately that wherever a loop-hole was opened for any truth about my conduct or Mr. Richardson's it was immediately stopped. I have tasted to its dregs the cup of justice which, in the nineteenth century men born of women mete out to one whose worst crime was the mistake of marrying a man who was half madman from natural inheritance, half brute from natural proclivity. Of the justice I have received let those who have read my story be witness.

Source: George Cooper, *Lost Love* (New York: Pantheon Books, 1994), pp. 230, 232.

Elizabeth Cady Stanton against lawyers and the press, who attacked Abby as an adulterer and used the McFarland case to defend the conservative position on reforms of laws respecting marriage and women's property rights. McFarland was acquitted, ostensibly because of his insanity plea, but more likely because of the defense's argument that he had acted on the unwritten biblical law that a man was not a murderer if he killed his wife's lover in a passionate defense of his patriarchal rights and property, which included his wife. McFarland did not trouble Abby again.

Widowed and left with Richardson's three children and her own son to support, Abby moved to Chicago, where she continued writing for magazines and newspapers and resumed her public readings. Now using the name Abby Sage Richardson, she edited a collection of her husband's essays, *Garnered Sheaves from the Writings of A. D. Richardson* (1871), and wrote a book that she and her late husband had hoped to write together, *The History of Our Country from Its Discovery by Columbus to the Celebration of the Centennial Anniversary of Its Declaration of Independence* (1875). She also edited and published *Stories from Old English Poetry* (1872), *Songs from the Old Dramatists* (1873), and *Familiar Talks on English Literature* (1881).

During her last decade life, when she was recognized as one of the grand old women of New York's literary and theater world, she wrote plays. These included *Donna Quixote* (1890), a bitterly contested adaptation of Mark Twain's *The Prince and the Pauper* (1890), and, in collaboration with Grace Livingston Furniss, *A Colonial Girl* and the highly successful *Pride of Jennico* (1900). During a tour of Italy with her son William, she died in Rome on December 5, 1900, at the age of sixty-three.

SIGNIFICANCE

Abby Sage Richardson retains a minor reputation as one of many "scribbling women" of the nineteenth century, whose earnings were directly determined by audience demand for the sentimental and the domestic, as evidenced by one of her late works, *Old Love-Letters: Or, Letters of Sentiment Written by Persons Eminent in English Literature and History* (1882). The scandalous crisis of her divorce from Daniel McFarland has earned her far greater renown, particularly in the history of American family law and in the women's rights movement of her time, when the United States was divided over issues such as the right of women to independence through divorce and was alarmed by the threat that di-

vorce posed to the traditional patriarchal rules of marriage.

—Marion Sheila McAvey

FURTHER READING

Basch, Norma. *Framing American Divorce: From the Revolutionary Generation to the Victorians*. Berkeley: University of California Press, 1999. Analyzes the social and cultural anxiety over legal changes in divorce over two centuries. The McFarland-Richardson case highlighted the inflammatory association of divorce and women's rights with cultural and moral decline in the United States.

Cooper, George. *Lost Love: A True Story of Passion, Murder, and Justice in Old New York*. New York: Pantheon, 1994. A well-documented narrative of the lives of Abby Sage Richardson, Daniel McFarland, and Albert Deane Richardson, ending with the sensational murder trial. Includes a detailed bibliography, excerpts from contemporary newspaper accounts, trial transcripts, letters, and illustrations.

Demarest, Phyllis Gordon. *The Naked Risk*. Garden City, N.Y.: Doubleday, 1954. A fictional account of the relationships between Abby Sage Richardson and her husbands.

Fatout, Paul. "Mark Twain: Litigant." *American Literature* 31, no. 1 (1959): 30-45. Details the successful lawsuit brought against Abby Sage Richardson, Mark Twain, and producer Daniel Frohman, brought by Edward H. House, who had an agreement with Twain to dramatize the latter's novel *The Prince and the Pauper* before contracted with Richardson to dramatize his novel.

Hartog, Hendrik. "Lawyering, Husbands' Rights, and the 'Unwritten Law' in Nineteenth-Century America." *Journal of American History* 84, no. 1 (1997): 67-96. Places the McFarland-Richardson murder trial within the context of legal-cultural battles over the reform of American divorce laws, especially the threat to patriarchal code of the "unwritten law" that permitted enraged husbands, brothers, and female victims to murder seducers.

Ireland, Robert. "Insanity and the Unwritten Law." *American Journal of Legal History* 32, no. 2 (1998): 157-172. Studies the ways in which medical definitions of insanity expanded during the nineteenth century to facilitate acquittals in murder trials involving the unwritten law permitting husbands to kill libertines who seduced their wives.

SEE ALSO: Henry Ward Beecher; Edwin Booth; Horace Greeley; Henry Wadsworth Longfellow; Adah Isaacs Menken; Elizabeth Cady Stanton; Mark Twain; John Greenleaf Whittier.

RELATED ARTICLE in *Great Events from History: The Nineteenth Century, 1801-1900:* c. 1801-1850: Professional Theaters Spread Throughout America.

HENRY HOBSON RICHARDSON
American architect

By absorbing early medieval stylistic ideas, suffusing them with his own vision, and adapting them to the needs of his own time, Richardson earned his reputation as one of the greatest American architects.

BORN: September 29, 1838; Priestley plantation, St. James Parish, Louisiana
DIED: April 27, 1886; Brookline, Massachusetts
AREA OF ACHIEVEMENT: Architecture

EARLY LIFE

Henry Hobson Richardson had a distinguished ancestor in Joseph Priestley, one of the founders of modern chemistry, whose granddaughter Caroline married Henry Dickenson Richardson, a partner in a Louisiana cotton business, and gave birth to the future architect in 1838. The boy attended school in New Orleans and was destined for West Point, but the academy rejected him for stuttering. Having shown early promise in drawing and in mathematics, young Richardson entered Harvard College, with the goal of becoming a civil engineer. His academic work was unspectacular; his friendships, however, were constructive ones. He numbered among his friends Henry Adams, the future historian, and several young men who later helped him obtain commissions.

Richardson's Class of 1859 photograph shows wide-set eyes in a rather long, thin face with dark, wavy hair. Although he looked serious, his classmates found him buoyant and personable. Another photograph taken in Paris, where he decided to study architecture at the École des Beaux Arts upon his graduation, confirms contemporary accounts of him as tall, slim, and clean-shaven.

Returning to the United States at around the end of the Civil War, Richardson chose New York over his native Louisiana as the best location for a beginning architect. His first commission, in 1866, for a new Unitarian Church in Springfield, Massachusetts, most likely arose from his college friendship with the son of an influential supporter of the project. In January of 1867, his career well launched, he married Julia Gorham Hayden, to whom he had been engaged since before his Parisian sojourn. The couple would have six children. Several factors—among them, early commissions in New England and the fact that his wife was a native of Cambridge, Massachusetts—suggested a move to the Boston area, and by 1874 the Richardsons had settled in Brookline, where he would continue to live and work.

LIFE'S WORK

The Romanesque qualities for which Richardson would become famous began to appear in the third church he designed, the Brattle Square Church in Boston's Back Bay, for which he won a competition in 1870. Taking advantage of local materials, he chose Roxbury pudding stone for this building, whose most original feature is its 176-foot corner tower, which has arches forming a carriageway at the bottom and smaller belfry arches above a frieze of sacramental figures, with a pyramidal roof. The tower is somewhat detached from the church, in the manner of the Italian campanile.

One indication of Richardson's spreading fame was a commission for the Buffalo State Hospital buildings, also in 1870. Another was his selection, two years later, as designer of Trinity Church in Boston's Copley Square, while the Brattle Square Church was still under construction nearby. Because this part of Boston is built on fill and is watery below the surface, the weight of the planned church required four thousand wooden piles beneath its foundation, and construction took more than three years.

This elaborate project included a sanctuary and a parish house that Richardson connected to the church by an open cloister. Built of granite with brownstone trim from local quarries and topped with a red tile upper roof, the church forms a Greek cross with a central tower based on one in Salamanca, Spain, as adapted by Stanford White, then Richardson's assistant and later a noted architect. John La Farge, one of the premier artists of his time, designed the windows and interior decoration. It is an elaborate and colorful church, both inside and out, with elements of Gothic and high, round Romanesque arches, all of which exemplify Richardson's genius for combining and modifying different styles to produce a unique, self-expressive result. Although additions, many of them unfortunate, have altered the church since Richardson's time, it remains one of his most famous and admired structures.

Richardson enjoyed the opportunity to work at a time when small towns and cities in New England were seeking larger and more gracious public library buildings. Beginning in 1877, Richardson designed libraries for Woburn, North Easton, Quincy, and Malden, Massachusetts, as well as one for the University of Vermont. Although his fondness for massive structures ran counter to the American Library Association's standards for flexibility in library design, all of his library buildings remained in use more than a century later. The Thomas Crane Public Library in Quincy, of Quincy granite, again with brownstone trim, is the simplest and is generally considered his finest. It is a rectangular structure of three main parts: stack wing with tiered alcoves, central hall, and reading room. Its asymmetrical front entrance is a low, broad Syrian arch surmounted by a gable. To the left of the arch is a circular stair tower with a low, conical roof. Asymmetrical end gables mark both ends of the building, for which Richardson also designed the original furniture.

Richardson also designed two additions to his alma mater: Sever Hall (1878) and Austin Hall (1881). The former uses red brick to harmonize with the older architecture of Harvard Yard, while the latter, for Harvard Law School, is sandstone with an elaborately carved entry arch and interior fireplace. More than a century after its construction, Austin Hall continued to be used mainly for its original purpose. Most architectural historians date Richardson's maturity from the period in which these two educational buildings were designed, as well as the Crane Memorial Library (1880).

Richardson worked as a collaborator on the sprawling Albany, New York, capital over a period of many years beginning in 1875, but his most personal monument in Albany is its city hall, with a beautiful 202-foot corner tower, another design of 1880. In that year, construction began on a more unusual project, the Ames Monument in Wyoming, which commemorated two brothers' contributions to the completion and administration of the Union Pacific Railroad. It is a granite pyramid, sixty feet square at its base and sixty feet high, erected near the railroad's highest point above sea level. Medallions bearing busts of Oakes and Oliver Ames decorate the east and west faces, respectively. Twenty years after it was built,

the railroad relocated to the south, and the nearby town of Sherman lost its economic base and disappeared. For most of the twentieth century, the monument has stood isolated and reachable only by secondary roads.

Other Richardsonian structures have fared worse. A number of his Massachusetts railroad stations have been demolished, others violently altered or allowed to fall into ruin; few continued as stations during the 1980's. His most celebrated commercial building, the Marshall Field Wholesale Store in Chicago, designed in 1885, was made of rock-faced red Missouri granite and red sandstone. Groups of windows were topped by arches at the fourth floor level of this seven-story building; narrower arches capped single rows of fifth- and sixth-story windows. The simplicity and harmonious proportions of this store can be admired today only in photographs, for, in 1930, the owner demolished it in favor of a parking lot.

Among his many other structures, Richardson designed a stone and a metal bridge in Boston's Fenway during the early 1880's, the Allegheny County courthouse and jail in Pittsburgh (1883-1884), and a considerable number of private residences, both of wood and stone, large and small, from the East Coast to St. Louis. Two of the latter, the William Watts Sherman House in Newport, Rhode Island (1874), and the J. J. Glessner House in Chicago (1885), have, along with Trinity Church, Sever Hall, the Allegheny County buildings, and the New York State capitol, been designated National Historic Landmarks.

Like all prominent architects, Richardson had to face the problems of popularity. As his work expanded, so did his workforce, and he found it necessary to delegate more authority and exercise less personal supervision over his projects. During the 1880's, he took on too much work, but he chose his assistants and construction firms carefully and would not tolerate shoddy work. Charles McKim and Stanford White of his office went on to renown in a firm of their own.

Richardson was a convivial man who enjoyed good company, good food, and good wine. Photographs of him in his maturity show the formerly slender architect to be a massive man with a full mustache and a bushy beard. One anecdote has three of his assistants standing together able to wrap themselves in one of his coats. Although his creative energy continued to flow, Bright's disease took its toll in his final years, increasingly limiting the mobility of a man whose work was frequently in progress in several scattered locations. In 1886, only a year after an *American Architect and Building News* poll rated five of his buildings among the ten finest in the United States, with Trinity Church first, and while his fame was finally reaching Europe, where American building had never been taken seriously, Henry Hobson Richardson died at the age of forty-seven.

SIGNIFICANCE

When Richardson began his work during the 1860's, civic buildings in the United States were likely to follow classical or Renaissance styles, churches often followed the Victorian Gothic, while commercial structures were most often mere utilitarian boxes. Thus, Richardson's boast that he would design anything from a chicken coop to a cathedral reflects no mere indiscriminate appetite for building but a rejection of outworn conventions and an affirmation that a developed architectural sensibility might apply itself to any sort of building. The more one studies the range of Richardson's work—public, commercial, religious, and private buildings—the more clearly they can be seen as the expression of his artistic vision. A suburban or village railroad station was to be taken as seriously as a church and was as worthy of beauty.

At the same time, Richardson did not neglect the requirements of the task at hand. He preserved his independence and would not yield to clients' notions that were inconsistent with his own ideas, but neither was he indifferent to their requirements. His buildings became more functional and less ornate as his career proceeded. His placement of windows, for example, was dictated not by formal requirements of the exterior facade only but by interior needs. Richardson was the first American architect to combine creativity of the highest order with receptiveness to the needs of contemporaries. In a period of divorce between aesthetic and utilitarian concerns, Richardson united them in his mature work.

Richardson's influence, powerful for several decades after his death, was not always beneficial. Certain features of his design—the arches, towers, and rough stone exteriors—were easy to imitate, but the Richardsonian integrity that fused these and other less obvious elements into an artistic whole was not. In the years following his death, some of the most notable architectural talents occupied themselves with the requirements of the skyscraper, which implied not great masses of masonry but skeletons of steel and lower floor windows on a scale incompatible with typical Richardsonian materials and designs.

Although it is difficult to determine what contribution Richardson might have made had he lived longer, the work he left did not point toward the twentieth century.

In large American cities, even Boston, which resisted it into the 1960's, the skyscraper became an economic inevitability. The glassy John Hancock Building now dwarfs nearby Trinity Church. Richardson's greatest commercial building, the Field Store, was wiped out as an anachronism as early as 1930 in downtown Chicago. Vast bland airports have supplanted Richardson's railroad stations as symbols of America on the move.

In recent decades, however, the value of Richardson buildings has been recognized more widely. The National Historic Landmark Program, which began in 1960, and the National Register of Historic Places Program, dating from 1966, offer substantial protection, the National Register including thirty-two of Richardson's works. The harmony and solid beauty of his best churches, libraries, and private homes continue to answer human needs left unsatisfied by the buildings that have come to dominate urban skylines.

—*Robert P. Ellis*

FURTHER READING

Breisch, Kenneth A. *Henry Hobson Richardson and the Small Public Library in America: A Study in Typology*. Cambridge, Mass.: MIT Press, 1997. Examines Richardson's designs for five public libraries, describing his architectural style and the historical background of these buildings.

Hitchcock, Henry-Russell. *The Architecture of H. H. Richardson and His Times*. Hamden, Conn.: Archon Books, 1961. The most thorough of the twentieth century studies of Richardson's work, this book contains some biographical facts and a learned, if often dogmatic, evaluation of his subject's significance.

_____. *Richardson as a Victorian Architect*. Northampton, Mass.: Smith College Pamphlets, 1966. A lecture based on a seminar given at Harvard University in 1965. Hitchcock adroitly relates Richardson's work to the diverse strands that make up the complicated conception that is "Victorian architecture."

Mumford, Lewis. *The Brown Decades: A Study of the Arts in America, 1865-1895*. New York: Harcourt Brace, 1931. Reprint. New York: Dover, 1955. Mumford argues that Richardson, in using metal skeletons in two of his late commercial buildings, laid the basis for bridging the gap between stone construction and the ensuing steel-and-glass age. An eloquent appreciation of Richardson's contribution to his profession.

Ochsner, Jeffrey Karl. *H. H. Richardson: Complete Architectural Works*. Cambridge, Mass.: MIT Press,

1982. This handsome book includes not only photographs and plans of proposed and completed Richardson projects but also views of the author and his studios that provide valuable insights into his working habits. Biographical information is restricted chiefly to the details of his business life. Extensive bibliographies and appendixes showing the locations of his buildings and indicating their preservation status mark this meticulously researched volume.

O'Gorman, James F. *H. H. Richardson and His Office: Selected Drawings.* Cambridge, Mass.: Department of Printing and Graphic Arts, Harvard College Library, 1974. O'Gorman's thirty-page introductory essay is particularly useful for its attention to the architect's working methods.

_____. *Living Architecture: A Biography of H. H. Richardson.* Photographs by Cervin Robinson. New York: Simon & Schuster, 1997. O'Gorman, the most productive Richardsonian scholar since Hitchcock, evaluates the architect's life and work. The book is particularly valuable for its more than 150 photographs of Richardson's buildings.

_____, ed. *The Makers of Trinity Church in the City of Boston.* Amherst: University of Massachusetts Press, 2004. A collection of ten essays, each one describing the contributions of a person or persons responsible for the construction, decoration, and use of the church. Includes essays about Richardson's roles as architect and creator of the church furnishings.

Roger, Laura Wood. *F. L. O.: A Biography of Frederick Law Olmsted.* Baltimore: Johns Hopkins University Press, 1974. Scattered references to Richardson and also a detailed account of the happy collaboration of Richardson with the greatest landscape architect of his time.

Russell, John. "Henry Hobson Richardson." *American Heritage* 32 (October/November, 1981): 48-59. A lively and beautifully illustrated essay by an art critic who sees Richardson as the transformer—even the creator—of the architectural profession in the United States.

Van Rensselaer, Marianna Griswold. *Henry Hobson Richardson and His Works.* Boston: Houghton Mifflin, 1888. Reprint. New York: Dover, 1969. All students of Richardson are heavily indebted to Van Rensselaer, who wrote the only true biography of a man whom she knew personally and whose work she understood thoroughly. Commissioned as a tribute to Richardson shortly after his death, the book remains a readable and valuable account of his works. Virtually all of the limited personal information to be had about its subject is to be found here.

SEE ALSO: Henry Adams; Marshall Field.

RELATED ARTICLES in *Great Events from History: The Nineteenth Century, 1801-1900:* May, 1819: Unitarian Church Is Founded; May 24, 1883: Brooklyn Bridge Opens.

LOUIS RIEL
Canadian political leader

One of the most controversial figures in Canadian history, Riel led two popular revolt movements in the west and played a crucial role in the creation of the provinces of Manitoba and Saskatchewan.

BORN: October 22, 1844; St. Boniface, Assiniboia (now Winnipeg, Manitoba, Canada)
DIED: November 16, 1885; Regina, Northwest Territories (now in Saskatchewan), Canada
ALSO KNOWN AS: Louis David Riel, Jr.
AREA OF ACHIEVEMENT: Government and politics

EARLY LIFE
Louis Riel (LEW-ee ree-EHL) was born and raised in the Red River Valley of Manitoba. Because his paternal

grandmother had Dene Indian ancestry, his family were regarded as Metis—people of mixed European and Indian heritage. Like his father, Louis went east to Montreal to study as a young man. In the tradition of his family, he was a devout Roman Catholic and was doing well at the Seminary of St. Sulpice, but the death of his father in 1864 seems to have interrupted his studies for the priesthood. He then went through a difficult period, studying law for a time in the office of Rodolfe Laflamme, and coming under the influence of the conservative backlash, which had resulted from the thwarted Quebec Rebellion of 1837-1839.

After the end of a disappointing love affair, Riel left Montreal and lived in Chicago and St. Paul, Minnesota, for several months before returning to Manitoba in 1869.

On his return to Canada, Riel landed in the middle of a political storm over the change in status of the territory. The Hudson's Bay Company was in the process of ceding its sovereignty over Rupert's Land, which included Manitoba, to the newly created Dominion of Canada, and the Metis people believed that they were being overlooked in the negotiations regarding this transfer of authority. Riel's father had been a leader in the struggle to break the fur-trading monopoly of the Hudson's Bay Company in the area in 1849. As an intelligent, educated, and traveled young man, Louis Riel was well situated and equipped to assume a role of leadership among his people despite being only twenty-five years old.

LIFE'S WORK

The Canadian Dominion Lands homesteading program, which was introduced after confederation in 1867, had trouble accommodating the Metis population of the northwest. First, members of communities wishing to use the system to homestead needed some familiarity with the English language, and most Metis spoke only French or Indian languages. Second, the Dominion Lands program was intended for farmers, not for people such as the Metis, whose subsistence was based on fishing and trapping. Third, the program was intended for new arrivals, not for people already established in the area. Finally, the Dominion Lands method of surveying in rectangular lots went against the system of dividing land that had been used traditionally in Quebec, where settlers got small amounts of river frontage and long, narrow strips of land extending back from the river.

The law recognized the Metis and their settlements. Surveyors sent to the western frontier by the Canadian government were supposed to accept established claims and to be sensitive to local situations. However, they were not trained diplomats, and friction often resulted. On October 10, 1869, Louis Riel led a party of eighteen Metis who blocked the progress of a surveyor named A. C. Webb in the first confrontation of what became known as the Red River Resistance. On November 2, 120 armed men led by Riel moved into Fort Garry (where Winnipeg is now located), which had formerly been occupied by the Hudson's Bay Company. They proclaimed themselves the provisional government of Manitoba on December 27. When William McDougall, who had been appointed by Canada as the first governor of the province, arrived, the rebels refused him entry and sent him packing back to Ottawa. The provisional government then sent a delegation to Ottawa to negotiate the terms under which Manitoba would join the new Canadian Confederation.

At that moment, there was a good deal of sympathy for Riel and his cohorts among the Canadian population. However, the execution of an English prisoner named Thomas Scott cut deeply into that goodwill. Scott had tried to escape twice and was apparently a difficult and disagreeable prisoner. Riel and the Council of War that he assembled believed that maintaining good order and discipline required the strictest measures and had Scott put in front of a firing squad on March 4, 1870. Most English-speaking Canadians considered Scott's execution an unjustified act of cold-blooded political expediency.

On May 12, 1870, the Manitoba Act became law and Manitoba joined the dominion as a province. The act met the legitimate demands of Manitoba's provisional government, but the amnesty that had been discussed for participants in the resistance never materialized. Those who participated in the execution of Thomas Scott were murdered by vigilantes or chased off. A warrant was issued for Riel's arrest, and a member of the Canadian parliament from Ontario took it upon himself to offer a five-thousand-dollar reward for Riel's capture. Riel became a fugitive, and although he was elected by citizens of Manitoba three times to represent them in the Canadian parliament, he was never able to take his seat in Ottawa.

For almost fifteen years, Riel suffered in silence and labored in obscurity. He believed deeply that he had a mission from God to lead his Metis people to some historic destiny, but all political avenues of expression were blocked. His frustration finally became too much for him, and he spent several years institutionalized under psychiatric treatment in Quebec. In 1875, he was finally granted amnesty—with the condition that he stay out of Manitoba for five more years. His vagabond existence seemed to end during the early 1880's, when he married Marguerite Belhumeur, started a family, and took a job teaching in Montana. He even became a U.S. citizen in 1883, but the call of his Canadian destiny came once again.

A delegation from the Batoche area of Saskatchewan led by Gabriel Dumont sought out Riel in Montana and asked for his help in dealing with several problems involving the Canadian government. Riel packed up his wife and two young children, went to Saskatchewan, and became the leader of a movement that became known as the Northwest, or Second Riel, Rebellion. The main issues involved land distribution and were similar to those that had arisen in Manitoba fifteen years earlier. Newly

RIEL'S LAST TESTAMENT

On November 6, 1885, while Louis Riel waited in Regina Prison for his execution four days later, he wrote this last testament.

I make my will, following the advice of Reverend Father Alexis Andre, my charitable confessor and most devoted director of conscience. In the name of the Father, of the Son and of the Holy Ghost. I declare that this is my last will, and that I write it freely in full possession of my mental faculties. The date of my death having been fixed for next November 10, and since it is possible that the sentence be carried out, I declare in advance that my submission to the dictates of Providence is sincere, that, with entire freedom of action under the influence of the Divine grace of Our Lord Jesus Christ, my will conforms with the doctrine of the Roman Catholic, Apostolic Church. In it I was born, and through it, also, I have been redeemed. I have retracted what I said and professed contrary to its doctrine, and I retract this again.

I ask pardon for the scandal I caused. I do not wish any difference as big as a pin head to exist between me and the priests of Jesus Christ. If I must die on the 10th of this month, that is, in four days, I want to do all in my power with the help of my Divine Saviour to die in perfect harmony with my Creator, my Redeemer, my Sanctifier, and with the Holy Catholic Church. If God wishes to grant me the inestimable gift of life, I, for my part want to mount the scaffold and resign myself to the will of Providence, remaining detached, as I am today, from all earthly things, for I understand that the surest way to act well is to carry out one's plans—in a completely disinterested manner, without passion, without agitation, under God's eyes, loving one's neighbour, friends and enemies as oneself for the love of God.

I thank my good and gentle mother for having loved me with so Christian a love. I ask her pardon for the faults I am guilty of against her love, and the respect and obedience which I owe her. I also ask her pardon for the sins I have committed against my duties towards my beloved and regretted father and against his revered memory. I thank my brothers and sisters for the great love and kindness they have had for me. I also ask them pardon for all the errors I may be guilty of in their eyes. I thank my relatives and those of my wife for the affection and goodwill they have always shown me especially my affectionate and well-loved father-in-law; my mother-in-law, brothers-in-law, and sisters-in-law. From them, also, I beg forgiveness for anything in my conduct which was not good or might have been bad.

I give a warm and friendly handclasp to my friends of all ages, class and condition. I thank them for the services they rendered me. I express my gratitude to my friends on both sides of the frontier who were so kind as to take care of my public affairs, to the Oblates of Mary Immaculate, to the Society of St. Sulpice, and to the Grey Nuns for all the benefits I have received from them since my childhood. I offer them my thanks. I have benefactors on the other side of the frontier, friends whose goodness for me has been beyond measure. I ask them to accept my thanks and to charitably excuse my faults. If my conduct has offended in anyway, in small or great matters, I ask pardon, asking them to take into account any excuse that might be in my favour; and as to the sum of my true faults, my culpabilities, I trust that they will have the goodness to forgive my before God and man. With all my heart and mind, with all my strength and with all my soul, I pardon those who have caused me sorrow and harm, who have persecuted me, who without reason have fought me for fifteen year, who gave me only the pretence of a trial, who condemned me to death; and I forgive them totally as I ask God to pardon me totally for all my sins in the name of Jesus Christ.

I thank my wife for her goodness and charity towards me, for her patient share in my painful work and difficult undertakings. I beg her to pardon me the suffering I caused her voluntarily. I enjoin her to care for our little children, to raise them in a Christian manner, with special attention to all relating to good companions. It is my desire that my children be raised with great attention to all that concerns obedience to the Church. I exhort them to show the greatest respect, the greatest docility, and the most complete affection for their good mother, I leave neither gold nor silver to my children, but I beseech God in His infinite mercy, I beseech the womb of God's mercy to fill my mind and heart with the true father's benediction that I wish to give to them: Jean, my son, Angelique, my daughter; I bless you in the name of the Father, the Son and the Holy Ghost. May you seek to know God's will and be faithful in accomplishing it in all piety and sincerity; may you practise virtue, firmly and simply, without show or pretence; may you do the most good possible without failing others within the limits of an upright obedience to the ordained clergy, priests and bishops, especially your Bishop and your Confessor. I bless you so that your death may be gentle, edifying, good and holy in the eyes of the Church and of Jesus Christ Our Lord, Amen. I bless you, finally, that you may seek and find the Kingdom of God and that you may moreover rest in Jesus, Mary and Joseph. Pray for me. I leave my testament with Rev. Father Alexis Andre, my Confessor. I beg my friends from everywhere to keep Father Andre's name side by side with mine. I love Father Andre. Louis David Riel, son of Louis Riel and of Julie de Lagimodiere.

Source: Auguste Henri de Trémaudan, *Hold High Your Heads: History of the Métis Nation in Western Canada.* 1936. Translated by Elizabeth Maguet (Winnipeg, Man.: Pemmican, 1982).

arrived English settlers were swamping the territory and putting pressure on the Metis population. By then, the buffalo herds on which the Metis depended were gone, and living off the land by fishing and trapping was no longer possible. Inexperienced in modern commerce and agriculture, the Metis had trouble adjusting to changing times, and the Canadian government failed to respond to their needs.

The Northwest Rebellion was a much larger uprising than the Manitoba Resistance had been. Some eight thousand Canadian soldiers under the command of Major General Frederick D. Middleton were sent to crush a few hundred Metis and their handful of Cree and Assiniboine allies. Bloody confrontations at Duck Lake, Battleford, and Fish Creek were preliminary to the last stand of Louis Riel at the Battle of Batoche in May of 1885. Finally, on May 15, he was captured and taken to Regina to stand trial for high treason.

Modern standards of due process cast a suspicious light on the treatment of Riel after he was taken prisoner. The selection of his jury and the jurisdiction of the stipendiary magistrates who heard his case now appear questionable. Most observers agree that the official inquiry into Riel's sanity that was arranged by Prime Minister John A. Macdonald was a political charade. However, Riel himself did not complain in the diaries that he kept during the last days of his life. By all accounts he forgave his enemies and accepted his fate with good grace. He is said to have ascended the scaffold to his own hanging in a state of inner peace when he was executed in Regina on November 16, 1885.

SIGNIFICANCE

Sympathy for Louis Riel has grown in Canada with the passage of time since his death. Although he clearly made mistakes, the demands he made of the government in both his major confrontations are generally considered to have been justified, and most of his demands were eventually met. In 1997, a private members bill was introduced to the Canadian parliament to revoke his conviction for high treason, but it was still being revised and debated during the first years of the twenty-first century.

The modern nation of Canada was founded on the marriage of two European peoples in the New World, the French and the English. Many Canadians, including Pierre Trudeau, who was Canada's prime minister during the 1970's and early 1980's, have enjoyed this kind of mixed heritage. Trudeau's policy of coast-to-coast bilingualism is a cultural extension of the same unifying impulse. The Metis leader Louis Riel has come to symbolize the bringing together of disparate elements into a whole. To a growing number of modern Canadians, Riel symbolizes a united Canada.

—*Steven Lehman*

FURTHER READING

Charlebois, Peter. *The Life of Louis Riel*. Toronto: NC Press, 1975. An illustrated, very sympathetic, and readable biography.

Dumont, Gabriel. *Gabriel Dumont Speaks*. Vancouver: Talon Books, 1993. The personal account of the Second Riel Rebellion by the Metis military commander.

Flanagan, Thomas. *Riel and the Rebellion*. Toronto: University of Toronto Press, 2000. The issues involved in the Second Riel Rebellion presented from the point of view of the Canadian government.

Friesen, John W. *The Riel/Real Story*. Ottawa: Borealis Press, 1996. Focuses on the importance of Riel in creating and shaping Metis culture.

Riel, Louis. *The Diaries of Louis Riel*. Edited by Thomas Flanagan. Edmonton: T. H. Best, 1975. Letters, notes, visions, prophecies, and prayers written by Riel in jail during the last few months of his life.

SEE ALSO: James Jerome Hill; Sir John Alexander Macdonald; David Thompson.

RELATED ARTICLES in *Great Events from History: The Nineteenth Century, 1801-1900:* October 23-December 16, 1837: Rebellions Rock British Canada; October 11, 1869-July 15, 1870: First Riel Rebellion; September, 1878: Macdonald Returns as Canada's Prime Minister; March 19, 1885: Second Riel Rebellion Begins.

ARTHUR RIMBAUD
French poet

Rimbaud became one of the most influential of the French Symbolist poets through his vigorous writings and his dramatic personal history.

BORN: October 20, 1854; Charleville, France
DIED: November 10, 1891; Marseilles, France
ALSO KNOWN AS: Jean-Nicolas-Arthur Rimbaud (full name)
AREA OF ACHIEVEMENT: Literature

EARLY LIFE

Jean-Nicholas-Arthur Rimbaud (rahn-boh) was the second son of Frédéric Rimbaud, a career army officer, and Vitalie Cuif, an austerely devout and conscientious woman of peasant stock. Seldom at the family's Charleville home, Captain Rimbaud left the family forever in September, 1860, after several violent clashes with his wife. Madame Rimbaud reared her children to be examples of propriety and devoted herself to the complete control of their thoughts and actions. The eldest child, Frédéric, was slow, but Arthur showed early promise. The boys entered school together in 1861. In 1865, they were transferred to the Collège de Charleville. Arthur soon outstripped his brother academically, met outstanding success in all studies but mathematics, and won an overwhelming list of year's end prizes.

The young Rimbaud is described as angelic, with blue eyes and round cheeks—an ideal schoolboy. Madame Rimbaud separated her sons from the other boys at school, but eventually they found a long-term friend in Ernest Delahaye, later to be Rimbaud's biographer. Rimbaud's skill in French prose composition and Latin verse won for him the respect of his classmates. The principal of the *collège* indulged him, lent books to his prodigy, and enjoyed Rimbaud's success in academic competitions.

By early 1870, Rimbaud was leading a double life. Outwardly obedient, he read voraciously in all periods and points of view and formed a global view based on revolution against middle-class norms. He hoped to become a journalist and escape his mother, with whom he identified all civil and religious restrictions. He shared long walks with Delahaye, with whom he read and discussed poetry. Several of his Latin poems had already been published when his first long piece of French verse appeared in January, 1870. In the same month, Georges Izambard joined the faculty of the *collège* as a teacher of rhetoric. Izambard was very young, a political liberal,

and a poet in his own right. He encouraged Rimbaud, lent him books, and discussed poetry with him. Through him, Rimbaud met Paul Bretagne, a friend of the famous poet Paul Verlaine. The boy was intoxicated by this link with Paris and found an outlet in poems celebrating nature and poetic aspirations as well as satires on the good bourgeois of Charleville.

On July 18, Napoleon III declared war on Prussia. When classes ended, Izambard left Charleville. Rimbaud's older brother ran away to follow the army. Delahaye was his only resource. Isolated, disgusted by bourgeois patriotism, and determined to rebel, Rimbaud ran away. On August 29, he made his first attempt, which ended with imprisonment in Paris for traveling without a ticket. Izambard posted bail and returned him to his mother.

Between October, 1870, and April, 1871, Rimbaud ran away three more times. Many poems written during this period are violent, revolutionary attacks on bourgeois society and the national government. The sixteen-year-old Rimbaud was probably in Paris in late April, 1871, during the last days of the Paris Commune, but left before the Thiers government retook the capital in the "bloody week" of May 7-14. During this stay, the runaway schoolboy witnessed wild scenes and possibly suffered homosexual rape. He also knew hunger and exposure and returned home ill and filthy. His personality and behavior had undergone a dramatic change. He was now determined to break his own ties to normal life.

LIFE'S WORK

On May 13 and 15, 1871, Rimbaud wrote his "Lettre du voyant" ("Seer Letter"), tumbling verses and exhortations as he described his ideal visionary poet. The Seer must reach new visions by a reasoned dismantling of all senses and create a new language, in which the senses join to shape material and poetic futures. No suffering or self-sacrifice is too great to reach this end, and other horrible workers will carry on after the individual's death. In a catalog of French poets of the past, Rimbaud heaps scorn on most but names Verlaine a Seer and true poet. Although Rimbaud had not yet met Verlaine, in September, 1871, he twice sent him poems and confided in him as an admired master. Verlaine, who was twenty-seven years old, married, and soon to be a father, was living with his in-laws. He took up a collection, sent for Rimbaud, and offered him temporary lodging with his wife's family. Rimbaud's single most famous poem, "Le Ba-teau ivre" ("The Drunken Boat"), was written as an intro-duction to Parisian poets before he left Charleville.

The inflexible young Rimbaud was immediately rec-ognized by Verlaine's circle as a sort of evil angel and ge-nius. He bent all of his energies to fulfilling his ideal of the Seer in his own life and Verlaine's. He provoked a se-ries of violent confrontations with Verlaine's friends and family, moved from lodging to lodging, occasionally on the streets, returned to Charleville, but always urged the older man to free himself from his settled life.

On July 7, 1872, the two poets left Paris for Belgium and continued to London, where they installed them-selves and began to learn English. Their relationship was marked by frequent violent quarrels, separations, and Verlaine's illness. In the course of the year ending July, 1873, the older poet saw himself hopelessly alienated from his wife and the French literary world. In her suit for legal separation, Mathilde Verlaine accused him of ho-mosexuality, a charge he always denied. Leaving Rim-baud penniless in London on July 3, 1873, Verlaine went to Brussels, with the plan either to reconcile with his wife or kill himself. He was joined in Belgium by his mother and Rimbaud. On July 10, Verlaine shot Rimbaud in the left arm. He was arrested on Rimbaud's complaint and spent eighteen months in Belgian prisons. He was re-leased in January, 1875.

Most of Rimbaud's major verse works were written during the two years spent in close contact with Verlaine. Those years were spent in the hardest kind of living, sup-ported by money from Verlaine's mother, with alcohol and hashish used as tools in a deliberate dismantling of his mind for poetry's sake. He had begun work on prose poems, which Verlaine would later publish as *Les Illumi-nations* (1886; *Illuminations*, 1932). He had written a major piece, "La Chasse Spirituelle" (the spiritual chase), now lost. During a period in Charleville, he had begun *Une Saison en enfer* (1873; *A Season in Hell*, 1932). Verlaine's arrest shook him, and he tried unsuccessfully to withdraw charges; he then retired to his mother's farm in Roche, where he finished *A Season in Hell*. This work, published in October, 1873, is the only book Rimbaud ever saw into print. He obtained at the printer's only a dozen copies; the rest of the printing was discovered in storage there in 1901. He left one copy at Verlaine's prison and embarked for Paris with the intention of dis-tributing the rest in the hope of favorable reviews.

Although Verlaine was older and known as a violent drunk, Rimbaud was blamed for his imprisonment and was ostracized by Parisian literary circles. Their hostility

Arthur Rimbaud. (Library of Congress)

led him to burn his copies of *A Season in Hell* when he re-turned to Roche. Many believe this to be the end of his lit-erary life. Evidence suggests, however, that he continued working on prose poems after the publication of *A Sea-son in Hell*, during a stay in London with the Provençal poet Germain Nouveau in the spring of 1874. This part-nership ended abruptly when Nouveau realized the de-gree of ostracism awaiting Rimbaud's friends. Verlaine and Nouveau both were involved in copying Rimbaud's works, and it is almost entirely through Verlaine's efforts that Rimbaud's verse and *Illuminations* were published.

Sometime during the months following the departure of Nouveau, Rimbaud stopped writing literature. From 1875 to 1880, the former poet traveled. He studied Ger-man in Stuttgart, crossed the winter Alps on foot, visited Austria and Italy, and wandered with a Scandinavian circus.

Rimbaud went as far as Java in the Dutch colonial army, then deserted and worked his way to Europe on ship. Illness sent him home more than once. He studied piano and foreign languages, and even taught. He worked as an overseer for an engineering firm on Cyprus in 1878. In the end, he became a merchant working out of

Aden and Harar in Africa, first as an agent for a French firm (beginning in 1880) and eventually on his own, trading in gold, coffee, skins, guns, and small goods for local consumption. He was one of the first white men to travel into the Shoa region of Ethiopia. The facts of his African years have less impact than the aura of adventure they lend his life. When he died of generalized carcinoma in Marseilles, the phenomenal spread of his literary reputation had just begun, and his absence from the scene enhanced public appreciation of his work.

SIGNIFICANCE

Arthur Rimbaud's role as a literary meteor, a sort of fallen angel, was enough to guarantee for him a place as an icon of modern poetry. A large school of admirers, among them the great Christian poet Paul Claudel, saw him as a supreme example of spiritual adventure, a poet who pushed the quest for faith to its ultimate limits. An equally ardent school of thought sees the young poet as an unrepentant, Luciferian rebel. The study of Rimbaud's writings, with their shattering power of imagination, involves the reader in an absorbing enigma—the contemplation of language pursued into silence. Even though his work spanned barely five years, it can hardly be matched. Few walk away from Rimbaud in indifference.

—*Anne W. Sienkewicz*

FURTHER READING

Fowlie, Wallace. *Rimbaud*. Chicago: University of Chicago Press, 1965. This elegantly written work is especially focused on *Illuminations*. It gives an outline of Rimbaud's life, coupled with detailed literary and psychological analysis of key Rimbaud texts. Includes a selected bibliography.

Petitfils, Pierre. *Rimbaud*. Translated by Alan Sheridan. Charlottesville: University Press of Virginia, 1987. One of the most complete of the Rimbaud biographies available in English. A thoroughly scholarly, yet accessible work that argues for an essential unity in Rimbaud's years as a poet and his mature life. The author does not analyze Rimbaud's writings as litera-ture, but as evidence in the study of his life. An extensive bibliography is included.

Rimbaud, Arthur. *Complete Works, Selected Letters*. Translated with an introduction by Wallace Fowlie. Chicago: University of Chicago Press, 1966. This is the translation of Rimbaud's poems used by Pierre Petitfils in his *Rimbaud*, reposing on the solid basis of Fowlie's long studies of the poet and his period.

Robb, Graham. *Rimbaud*. New York: W. W. Norton, 2000. An unsentimental, scholarly biography. Rimbaud emerges as a man with a restless intellect who allowed no compromise with convention nor tenderness for other people's weakness.

St.-Aubyn, F. C. *Arthur Rimbaud*. Boston: Twayne, 1975. Part of Twayne's World Authors series, intended for undergraduate student research. Includes a chronology, a short biography, and an annotated bibliography.

Starkie, Enid. *Arthur Rimbaud*. Winchester, Mass.: Faber & Faber, 1938. Rev. ed. New York: W. W. Norton, 1961. The standard English Rimbaud biographer for many years, Starkie writes from an intimate psychological viewpoint about the works and life of the poet. A short bibliography is included.

Steinmetz, Jean-Luc. *Arthur Rimbaud: Presence of an Engima*. Translated by Jon Graham. New York: Welcome Rain, 2001. English translation of a French biography recounting the events of Rimbaud's life.

Wilson, Edmund. *Axel's Castle: A Study in the Imaginative Literature of 1870-1930*. New York: Charles Scribner's Sons, 1936. The prominent American literary critic relates the life and work of Rimbaud to the literary movements of his day. The French poet is thus juxtaposed to William Butler Yeats, T. S. Eliot, and Gertrude Stein. Somewhat dated but still valuable.

SEE ALSO: Napoleon III; Odilon Redon; Georges Seurat.
RELATED ARTICLES in *Great Events from History: The Nineteenth Century, 1801-1900:* c. 1884-1924: Decadent Movement Flourishes; December 22, 1894: Debussy's *Prelude to the Afternoon of a Faun* Premieres.

NIKOLAY RIMSKY-KORSAKOV
Russian composer

One of the greatest and most prolific of Russian composers, Rimsky-Korsakov embodied in his music the nationalist spirit that was so important an element in late nineteenth century Russian culture. He composed fifteen operas, in addition to symphonies, concerti, chamber music, and solo pieces for piano and voice.

BORN: March 18, 1844; Tikhvin, Russia
DIED: June 21, 1908; Lyubensk, St. Petersburg District, Russia
ALSO KNOWN AS: Nikolay Andreyevich Rimsky-Korsakov (full name)
AREA OF ACHIEVEMENT: Music

EARLY LIFE

Nikolay Rimsky-Korsakov (REEM-skee kahrs-ah-KAHF) was born into a family of the Russian gentry. Although he demonstrated an early aptitude for music, family tradition required that he pursue a service career, and in 1856 he entered the Imperial Russian Navy, remaining on active duty until 1865. Somehow, however, he managed to compose. He had early made the acquaintance of Mily Alekseyevich Balakirev and, in time, sent him the manuscript of a first symphony, for which the latter arranged a public performance in December, 1865.

After 1865, Rimsky-Korsakov lived almost continuously in St. Petersburg, displaying an enviable ability to compose with an ease and rapidity that would characterize his entire career, for there was little of the artist's angst in him. He soon became one of the group known as "the Five" or "the Mighty Handful"—the others were Balakirev, Aleksandr Borodin, César Antonovich Cui, and Modest Mussorgsky—all of whom were dedicated to the creation of a distinctly Russian musical idiom.

With the premiere of his first opera, *Pskovityanka* (1873; *The Maid of Pskov*), Rimsky-Korsakov's place among contemporary Russian composers was assured. Two years earlier, in 1871, he had been appointed the professor of composition and instrumentation at the St. Petersburg Conservatory, a position that he would occupy, except for a few months in 1905, for the remainder of his life. In 1874, he took over from Balakirev as director and conductor of the Free School Concerts, an arrangement that continued until 1881, and between 1886 and 1900 he was conductor of the newly established Russian Symphony concerts. By then, however, Rimsky-

Korsakov had emerged as indubitably the most prolific of the Mighty Handful. He was blessed with a creative energy, a fluency of invention, and a melodic prodigality that, together with his devotion to traditional Russian folk song and folk melody, made him the embodiment of that phase of late nineteenth century Russian culture in which so many writers, artists, and musicians sought a return to a pre-Petrine Slavic heritage.

Rimsky-Korsakov experimented with most forms of musical composition, and although the bulk of his output was operatic, he wrote three symphonies, several symphonic suites, concerti for various instruments, a respectable corpus of chamber music (including three string quartets), solo pieces for the piano, choral works, and many songs. *Antar* (his second symphony, composed in 1868), *Skazka: A Fairy Tale* (1879-1880), *Capriccio espagnol* (1887), *Scheherazade* (1888), and the *Russian Easter Festival Overture* (1888) have remained perennial favorites. All exemplify Rimsky-Korsakov's qualities as a composer—melodic inventiveness, strong rhythms, and brilliant orchestration.

LIFE'S WORK

It is primarily as a composer of operas that Rimsky-Korsakov occupies his prominent place in Russian music. He completed fifteen operas, and, of these, only three have non-Russian subject matter: *Mozart and Salieri*, based upon Alexander Pushkin's poem (first performed in Moscow in 1898); *Servilia*, based upon a Roman play by the popular contemporary dramatist Lev Mey (first performed in St. Petersburg in 1902); and *Pan Voyevoda*, with a Polish setting (first performed in St. Petersburg in 1904). His first opera, *The Maid of Pskov*, was also based upon a play by Mey. *The Maid of Pskov* is based upon a true episode, Ivan the Terrible's visitation upon the city in 1569, and the czar himself is one of Rimsky-Korsakov's most successful character roles. It was a favorite role with the famous bass Fyodor Chaliapin, and Rimsky-Korsakov thought him inimitable in it.

Rimsky-Korsakov's second complete opera, *Maskaya noch* (*May Night*), based upon a story by Nikolai Gogol, was well received at its premiere at the Maryinsky in 1880. Two years later, in 1882, the Maryinsky witnessed the opening of what is perhaps his best-loved opera, *Snegurochka* (*The Snow Maiden*). Rimsky-Korsakov himself was extremely pleased with this work, in which he believed he had achieved for the first time a smooth-

Nikolay Rimsky-Korsakov. (Library of Congress)

flowing recitative and in which the vocal writing as a whole constituted an advance upon his earlier work. *The Snow Maiden* was followed by *Mlada* (1892); *Christmas Eve* (1895), based upon a story by Gogol; and the magnificent, sprawling *Sadko* (1898), constructed from material taken from the *bylini*, the epic songs of medieval Russia, all three exemplifying his love of fantasy, folklore, and the fairy tale. In 1898, he returned to the subject matter of his first opera, *The Maid of Pskov*, and set to music Mey's original prologue, *Boyarinya Vera Sheloga*. It received its premiere in Moscow later that same year.

Rimsky-Korsakov now felt himself ready to fulfill a long-standing ambition, the composition of an opera based upon the subject matter of Mey's play *Tsarskaya nevesta* (*The Tsar's Bride*). For this, he seems to have intended something rather different from his earlier operas. "The style of this opera," he declared:

> was to be cantilena par excellence; the arias and soliloquies were planned for development within the limits of the dramatic situation; I had in mind vocal ensembles, genuine, finished and not at all in the form of any casual and fleeting linking of voices with others. . . .

The Tsar's Bride was given its premiere in Moscow in 1899. Moscow was also the location for the opening nights of *Skazka o tsare Saltane* (1900; *The Tale of Tsar Saltan*), based upon a poem by Pushkin, and the rarely performed *Kashchey bessmertny* (1902; *Kashchey the Immortal*).

By then, however, Rimsky-Korsakov was absorbed in the composition of what is widely regarded as his greatest work, *Skazaniye o nevidimom grade kitezhe i deve Fevroniy* (1907; *The Legend of the Invisible City of Kitezh and the Maid Fevronia*), a story linking the thirteenth century Mongol invasion of Russia, the legend of Saint Fevronia of Murom, and the pagan animism of pre-Christian Russia on which he had previously drawn for *The Snow Maiden*. The result was a work of profound spirituality, which has been called, not inappropriately, the Russian *Parsifal*. It had its premiere at the Maryinsky in 1907, while the composer was at work upon his last opera, *Zolotoy petushok* (1909; *The Golden Cockerel*).

Among Soviet audiences, Rimsky-Korsakov's operas (of which *The Snow Maiden*, *Sadko*, *The Legend of the Invisible City of Kitezh and the Maid Fevronia*, and *The Golden Cockerel* may be regarded as the most original) enjoy enormous popularity. Outside the Soviet Union, they have not traveled well and are best known in the West through a series of brilliant orchestral suites (those of *Mlada*, *Christmas Eve*, *The Tale of Tsar Saltan*, and *The Golden Cockerel*).

SIGNIFICANCE

Nikolay Rimsky-Korsakov's role in the development of Russian music was seminal, for in addition to his numerous compositions that now occupy a secure niche in the concert halls and opera houses of the Soviet Union and the world, he left his mark upon Russian music in two other ways. Because he possessed a temperament that did not feel threatened by creativity in others and because of his genuine interest in the work of fellow composers, he willingly undertook the completion of a number of important works by others left unfinished at the time of their deaths. No less significant for the future, his many years as a teacher at the St. Petersburg Conservatory meant that, for the last three decades of the nineteenth century and for the opening years of the twentieth, few young Russian instrumentalists or composers did not have firsthand exposure to him both as an instructor and as a generous, nurturing mentor.

A man of great personal integrity, a liberal, and a staunch opponent of the virulent anti-Semitism that flourished during the reigns of the last two czars, Rimsky-

Korsakov found himself increasingly alienated from a regime in which reaction had replaced reform. In March, 1905, he sent a letter to the periodical *Rus* urging the case for the autonomy of the conservatory from the control of the Imperial Russian Musical Academy. He also sent an open letter to the director of the conservatory protesting police surveillance of the students. As a result of these actions, he was summarily dismissed from the professorship that he had held for thirty-four years. That was not the end of the matter, however, for his dismissal prompted the resignation from the faculty of, among others, Aleksandr Glazunov and Anatoly Lyadov. Before the end of the year, the conservatory attained sufficient independence to elect Glazunov its new director and, shortly thereafter, Rimsky-Korsakov was reinstated.

This episode does not seem to have interfered with Rimsky-Korsakov's habitually busy schedule. During the summer of 1905, he revised and supervised the printing of *The Legend of the Invisible City of Kitezh and the Maid Fevronia*, which had its premiere in 1907, and during 1906-1907 he worked on *The Golden Cockerel*. Then the censor intervened, ordering the omission of the entire introduction, the epilogue, and forty-five lines of the text. It has been suggested that the ban was motivated by the opera's subject matter, that the misadventures of the foolish King Dodon could be interpreted as a satire on the czar's court or his disastrous mismanagement of the Russo-Japanese War of 1905, but it is more likely that it was retribution for his publicly expressed liberal sentiments. Rimsky-Korsakov never saw *The Golden Cockerel* staged, for he died on June 21, 1908. Its first performance was given in Moscow in October, 1909.

—*Gavin R. G. Hambly*

FURTHER READING

Abraham, Gerald. *Essays in Russian and East European Music*. Oxford, England: Clarendon Press, 1985. The relevant essays in this collection are "*Pskovityanya*: The Original Version of Rimsky-Korsakov's First Opera," "Satire and Symbolism in *The Golden Cockerel*," and "Arab Melodies in Rimsky-Korsakov and Borodin."

_____. *Studies in Russian Music*. London: William Reeves, 1935. This earlier collection of Abraham's essays includes "Rimsky-Korsakov's First Opera," "Rimsky-Korsakov's Gogol Operas," "Snegurochka (Snow Maiden)," "Sadko," "The Tsar's Bride," "Kitezh," and "The Golden Cockerel."

Borovsky, Victor. *Chaliapin: A Critical Biography*. New York: Alfred A. Knopf, 1988. This definitive biography of the great Russian bass describes how Chaliapin interpreted the roles of Ivan the Terrible in *The Maid of Pskov* and Antonio Salieri in *Mozart and Salieri*.

Calvocoressi, Michel D., and Gerald Abraham. *Masters of Russian Music*. New York: Alfred A. Knopf, 1936. The best general account of Rimsky-Korsakov's life and work. Both scholarly and readable.

Ridenour, Robert C. *Nationalism, Modernism, and Personal Rivalry in Nineteenth-Century Russian Music*. Ann Arbor, Mich.: UMI Research Press, 1981. A scholarly investigation of Rimsky-Korsakov's circle and their critics to 1873.

Rimsky-Korsakov, Nikolay Andreyevich. *My Musical Life*. Translated by Judah A. Joffe. New York: Alfred A. Knopf, 1942. Essential reading for understanding the outlook and personality of the composer.

Seroff, Victor I. *The Mighty Five: The Cradle of Russian National Music*. New York: Allen, Towne, & Heath, 1948. A popular account of Rimsky-Korsakov's circle of colleagues and friends.

Taruskin, Richard. *Opera and Drama in Russia as Preached and Practiced in the 1860's*. Ann Arbor, Mich.: UMI Research Press, 1981. An important study of the theatrical background to the theory and practice of opera as developed among the Mighty Handful.

SEE ALSO: Aleksandr Borodin; Nikolai Gogol; Modest Mussorgsky; Alexander Pushkin; Peter Ilich Tchaikovsky.

RELATED ARTICLE in *Great Events from History: The Nineteenth Century, 1801-1900:* December 22, 1894: Debussy's *Prelude to the Afternoon of a Faun* Premieres.

ALBRECHT RITSCHL
German religious leader

Ritschl contributed to the liberalizing of nineteenth century Protestant theology by moving its concerns away from the speculative, neo-Scholastic abstractions that the faithful could not understand toward a renewal of a practical examination of the life of Jesus Christ as revealed in the New Testament. Because Christ was the perfect manifestation of the love of God, believers could have a model upon which to make proper value judgments.

BORN: March 25, 1822; Berlin, Prussia (now in Germany)

DIED: March 20, 1889; Göttingen, Germany

ALSO KNOWN AS: Albrecht Benjamin Ritschl (full name)

AREA OF ACHIEVEMENT: Religion and theology

EARLY LIFE

Albrecht Ritschl (RIHCH-ehl) came from a solid religious background. His father, Carl Ritschl, was a bishop and general superintendent of the Lutheran Church in Pomerania, and the boy grew up in the town of Stettin. He was an excellent student throughout his preuniversity career, excelling in languages and science. His mind welcomed complex information, because it gave him an opportunity to see how complexity grew and came together to formulate antithetical arguments that endlessly repeated the process. It was no doubt his penchant for synthesis that drew him early to the revolutionary work of Georg Wilhelm Friedrich Hegel, the leading professor at the University of Berlin during the first part of the nineteenth century.

Ritschl pursued his education at a number of prestigious universities during the years from 1839 to 1846. He studied at the University of Bonn and Halle, where he received his doctoral degree in 1843, and then pursued postdoctoral work at Heidelburg and Tübingen, where he studied church history with one of its leading scholars, Ferdinand Christian Baur. Baur became, for the next ten years or so, Ritschl's major mentor and influence. Ritschl's earliest scholarly works came out of the deep influence of Baur and his Tübingen school, which was an amalgamation of theologians and biblical scholars and historians that had been highly influenced by Hegel and his so-called conflict model of human history. This model proposed that history, like all other components of naturalistic process, works itself out in terms of the convergence of conflicting elements that then fall into necessary opposition and then form a new synthesis of meaning. History, like everything else in nature, operates within the laws of process, and Hegel had delineated the terms of those laws in his famous model of thesis, antithesis, and synthesis.

It was this Hegelian method of Baur and the Tübingen school that had informed Ritschl's first major scholarly work, *Das Evangelium Marcions und das Kanonische Evangelium des Lucas* (1846; the Gospel of Marcion and the canonical Gospel of Luke), and the success of this work established his career at the University of Bonn, where he became a full professor in 1859 at the age of thirty-seven. Although this early work on the Gospel of Luke broke no new scholarly ground, it was an intelligently reasoned and lucidly written examination done within the mode of the Tübingen school of radical New Testament criticism.

It was Ritschl's next book, however, that broke all ties to Baur and his followers. During the years following the publication of his highly abstract book on the Gospel of Luke, Ritschl became increasingly disillusioned and disturbed at the intensified metaphysical approaches that theological and biblical studies were following. With each new theoretical-speculative volume emerging, the laity, the community of Christian believers, was being left behind, buried in the impossibly complex language and heady intellectualism of German scholarship.

Ritschl had found, however, an anchor and antidote to the cause of the increasing abstraction, Hegelian historical process, and he discovered it during the writing of his next book, which concerned the intellectual and spiritual ethos of the early Christianity of the first and second centuries. He performed a simple process of laying the emphasis on the first word, the adjective "historical," and removing it from the word "process." He found that the solid ground of history could save him from involvement in the endless speculative abstractions of the Hegelian dialectic.

Ritschl's next study was of the early Church Fathers and led him, historically, to the earliest forms of Christianity. He found that the closer Christianity came to the temporal and physical proximity of Jesus Christ—and to the earliest apostles and Church Fathers, the roots of the faith—the simpler and more pristine the message of Christianity became. History, then, stopped the Hegelian cyclic process and led him back linearly to the essential simplicity of the message of the Gospels. After Ritschl disengaged himself from this cyclic model of history and attached himself to a linear model, he found relief in the bedrock of history.

In the second edition (1857) of his *Die Entstehung der altkatholischen Kirche* (1850; the rise of the old Roman Catholic Church), Ritschl announced the dramatic break, both personal and intellectual, with his mentor Ferdinand Baur. The move was a shattering blow to his former teacher. Two years later, Ritschl was appointed a full professor at the University of Bonn, rejecting similar offers from such prestigious schools as Strasbourg and Berlin. He became, then, the principal founder and exponent of what would be known as the liberal Protestant theological school that took root and flourished until just after World War I.

LIFE'S WORK

Ritschl's work after his major break with Baur proceeded with a serious redirection and reevaluation of the whole Christian enterprise. After he found the anchor of hope in reinstating the historical Jesus Christ as the principal model for a Christian lifestyle and direction, a linearly sanctioned one at that, he was able to develop the major tenets of his revolutionary project. His basic working premise was the adaptation of a view regarding the moral nature of human beings that was new within the basic beliefs of Christianity:

> In every religion what is sought, with the help of the superhuman spiritual power reverenced by man, is a solution of the contradiction in which man finds himself as both a part of nature and a spiritual personality claiming to dominate nature.

Although this was his definitive statement of his views on humankind's moral nature made in his next work, the monumental three-volume study *Die christliche Lehre von der Rechtfertigung und Versöhnuns* (1870-1874; *The Christian Doctrine of Justification and Reconciliation*, 1872-1900), his lectures and publications from 1857 through the 1860's thoroughly embodied this view.

What Ritschl had done, in effect, was to move Christianity away from its persistent and losing battles with two of its primary demons: the overly intellectualized speculations of natural philosophy on one hand, and the emotionalism of Pietism, on the other. Indeed, Ritschl's second major three-volume work was his definitive attack on such emotional subjectivism. Ritschl had to concede Immanuel Kant's proposition that humankind was unable to show evidence of or prove through any rational arguments the existence of God and, therefore, what a Christian's duty is to God. Therefore, he was forced to discard the overly neat proofs of God's existence simply because they started from outside personal Christianity and built on general ideas unconnected either with biblical revelation or with a living Christian faith.

What was left for the sincere Christian was the other end of the philosophical spectrum: subjectivism and its expression, mysticism. Without rational proof of God's existence and influence in the world, the seeker after God is left with his own subjective responses and feelings about his experiences and, therefore, runs the risk of mistaking the knowledge of his own religious consciousness for some kind of valid knowledge of God. Ritschl, having found a way back to the authentic roots of Christianity via history, leaps over the mystical and rationalistic barriers and exhorts the Christian to return to the original message of the New Testament as it was presented by Martin Luther himself. The original message is available, he argued, in the life and revelation of Jesus Christ directly observed through a rigorously historical examination of the texts themselves.

In short, what Ritschl offered was an enfreshened vision of the very purpose of Christianity. Religion should stop engaging in fruitless searches for direct knowledge of God. Kant proved such efforts hopeless. Humans must also admit that they are part of nature and, therefore, are divided beings who must constantly war with their natural impulses. However, human beings are also gifted with two qualities that lift them above mere beast consciousness: self-consciousness and the ability to assign value to their actions. Humans are capable of making moral and ethical choices that the lower animals are not. Those gifts qualify them, then, to assume moral domination in the world that, as Christians, they are obliged to do.

In positing these enlightened views on the moral nature of human beings, Ritschl does away with several key Christian beliefs. He reveals unmistakably Romantic views when he dismisses the Calvinist view of humankind's innate depravity. Human beings, he believes, are basically good but must continually war with their animal impulses. With one dramatic gesture, Ritschl does away with Satan, Original Sin, and innate depravity. Humans are, however, divided beings who need the example of Jesus Christ, who bridged the gulf between his animal and spiritual impulses. Out of humankind's recognition of its plight, humans derive their sense of obligation to rule over the natural world, to take dominion and stewardship over it, and to attempt to shape it into what Ritschl called the "Kingdom of God on earth."

Ritschl, in his magnum opus, *The Christian Doctrine of Justification and Reconciliation*, changed the older, guilt-laden term "justification," which had earlier meant the "forgiveness of sins," to mean the lifting of "guilt-consciousness" and a consequent bridging of the gulf between God and humankind. The second stage of the transforming operation he called "reconciliation," God's free act of mending the split between God and humankind through the life example and death of Jesus Christ. It was the original intention of the great Protestant Reformers, he claims, to restore "justification and reconciliation" to their previous central positions within early Christianity and to tap its infinitely vital energies and use them to renew the original force and meaning of Christianity.

The first volume of the work delineated the various propositions he used to make his points. The third volume lays out what the results and effects of the reorganization of the entire Christian enterprise will be. If Christianity returns to the early pragmatic interpretation of "justification and reconciliation" based upon replacing the knowledge about God with the practical revelations made in the life of Jesus Christ and recoverable through a historical study of the New Testament, the possibility of an ethical human community comes into being.

By 1864, Ritschl had moved to the University of Göttingen as a full professor, where he finished his two major works and taught not only biblical subjects but also dogmatics and ethics. His last twenty-five years at Göttingen brought forth his full powers as both a thinker and a writer. He died quietly there on March 20, 1889.

SIGNIFICANCE

The achievement of Albrecht Ritschl was so significant during the late nineteenth and early twentieth centuries that theologians have invented the term "Ritschlianism." Unquestionably, Ritschl became the most famous proponent of the new liberal Protestant theology during those years. His major works, *The Christian Doctrine of Justification and Reconciliation* and *Geschichte des Pietismus* (1880-1886; the history of Pietism), brought Protestant theology into the modern era by denying the validity of its endless oscillations between highly abstract, speculative debate over whether God can be known and how He can be known and the overly subjective, emotional, and mystical avenues into the divine mystery.

Before Ritschl could approach these seemingly insurmountable projects, he first had to admit that Kant had been correct and that Christianity was forced to discard any remaining vestiges of natural philosophy. History must replace metaphysical speculation as an avenue to certainty, but a certainty only verified through action, not ideas. Jesus Christ's life and death immediately, simultaneously, and permanently effected justification and reconciliation and created the possibility of an ethical human community.

—*Patrick Meanor*

FURTHER READING

Barth, Karl. *Protestant Thought: From Rousseau to Ritschl*. Translated by Brian Cozens. New York: Harper & Brothers, 1959. Although renowned for a brutal attack on Ritschl and other liberal Protestant theologians, Barth nevertheless delivers a brilliant summary of all the various theological schools leading up to Ritschl and places him at the conclusion of a tradition that was summarily destroyed by World War I.

Heron, Alasdair I. C. *A Century of Protestant Theology*. Philadelphia: Westminster Press, 1980. In a chapter devoted to Friedrich Schleiermacher and Ritschl, the author clearly distinguishes their unique contributions but shows that Ritschl was forced to reject the older theologian's overemphasis on what came to be called "the theology of feeling." Succinct and highly informative.

Jodock, Darrell, ed. *Ritschl in Retrospect: History, Community, and Science*. Minneapolis, Minn.: Augsburg Fortress Press, 1995. Essays by historians and theologians who reassess Ritschl's ideas on reviving the Reformation tradition, the communal dimensions of the church, community, the relationship of science and the church, and other topics.

Lotz, David W. *Ritschl and Luther: A Fresh Perspective on Albrecht Ritschl's Theology in the Light of His Luther Study*. Nashville: Abingdon Press, 1974. Lotz devoted much time and energy to revealing exactly what Ritschl derived from his own deep study of Martin Luther's major contributions to theology, particularly Luther's interpretations and explanations of the terms "justification and reconciliation."

Mackintosh, H. R. *Types of Modern Theology: Schleiermacher to Barth*. London: Collins, 1964. The first and, perhaps, still the most comprehensive treatment of Ritschl that is not an entire book. Mackintosh clearly places Ritschl in a nineteenth century tradition and shows how he emerges from Schleiermacher, corrects him, and creates the way for other important theologians. There are many points in Ritschl's approach that clearly disturb Mackintosh, but he explicates him with fairness and equanimity. Highly recommended.

Marsh, Clive. *Albrecht Ritschl and the Problem of the Historical Jesus.* Lewiston, N.Y.: E. Mellen Press, 1992. An analysis of Ritschl's ideas about the life and work of Jesus Christ.

Richmond, James. *Ritschl, a Reappraisal: A Study in Systematic Theology.* London: Collins, 1978. Richmond shows how theologians are reviving Ritschl since he seems to have so closely foreshadowed the more existential modern theologians. This is one of several correctives to certain Barthian neoorthodox criticisms.

Tillich, Paul. *Perspectives on Nineteenth and Twentieth Century Protestant Theology.* Edited with an introduction by Carl E. Braaten. New York: Harper & Row, 1967. Although he does not offer a comprehensive treatment of Ritschl, Tillich discusses Ritschl's influence on American theology long after it seemed dead in Germany. He credits the Ritschlians with introducing Kantianism into theology and labeling Kant the philosopher of Protestantism. Highly informative and intelligent.

SEE ALSO: Georg Wilhelm Friedrich Hegel; Friedrich Nietzsche.

RELATED ARTICLE in *Great Events from History: The Nineteenth Century, 1801-1900:* October 9, 1845: Newman Becomes a Roman Catholic.

JOHN D. ROCKEFELLER
American industrialist and philanthropist

One of the major industrialists and philanthropists in American history, Rockefeller pioneered in raising the scale of business organization through his phenomenally successful Standard Oil Company; he also raised the scale of philanthropic giving.

BORN: July 8, 1839; Richford, New York
DIED: May 23, 1937; Ormond Beach, Florida
ALSO KNOWN AS: John Davison Rockefeller (full name)
AREAS OF ACHIEVEMENT: Business, patronage of the arts

EARLY LIFE

John Davison Rockefeller was the son of Eliza Davison and William Avery Rockefeller. His father owned a farm and traded such commodities as salt and lumber. The family, which included John's older sister, two younger sisters, and two younger brothers, moved frequently: first to Moravia, New York; then to Owego, New York; and finally, to Cleveland, Ohio. John's education was irregular, but he studied hard and did have two years at Cleveland High School. His father, who by that time had become a wandering vendor of patent medicine, encouraged him to go into business. John especially liked mathematics, and he took a three-month course in bookkeeping at Folsom's Commercial College.

In selecting a job, Rockefeller was not as much interested in the salary as he was in the possibilities a position offered for learning about the business world. He selected a large and diversified merchant firm and started as a bookkeeper at a salary of $3.50 per week. After three and a half years, he left to form his own wholesale grain and grocery business with Maurice B. Clark. Together, the two had only four thousand dollars; during their first year, however, they grossed $450,000 and netted a fourteen-hundred-dollar profit. The following year, the Civil War began. The war gave Rockefeller, along with a number of other leading postwar industrialists, the opportunity to make his initial pile of money. Business at Cleveland-based Clark and Rockefeller boomed with major orders coming in from the army, other cities, and Europe. Rather than miss these business opportunities fighting in the Civil War, Rockefeller avoided the draft by paying for a substitute to fight in his place.

During these early business years, Rockefeller displayed the character traits and personal lifestyle that would be with him throughout his life. A devout Baptist, Rockefeller remained active in that church, even after becoming fabulously successful in business. For years, he taught Sunday school and served on church boards with streetcar conductors and other working-class people. He also took seriously the biblical injunction to give away one-tenth of what he earned, even when starting out at a low salary. He lived simply, had few pleasures, and was devoted to his family.

In 1864, Rockefeller married Laura Celestia Spelman, whose father was a prosperous businessperson.

Eventually, they had four children who lived to adulthood: three daughters, Bessie, Alta, and Edith, and a son, John D. Rockefeller II, of whom his father was quite proud. The family lived in a large, comfortable, but not ostentatious house in Cleveland until moving to New York during the 1880's. Rockefeller instilled a sense of industry and public responsibility in his offspring that extended down to the third and fourth generations, producing one vice president (Nelson) and three state governors (Nelson of New York, Winthrop of Arkansas, and John D. IV of West Virginia). Of all the leading American industrial families, the Rockefeller dynasty became the most remarkable.

LIFE'S WORK

It was possible for John D. Rockefeller to gain a monopolistic fortune in the oil business because of certain conditions that existed at that time. Oil was first used for medicinal purposes. Oil strikes in Pennsylvania during the 1850's greatly increased the supply. To find other uses for the product, the Pennsylvania Rock Oil Company hired Yale chemist Benjamin Silliman, Jr. Silliman discovered that oil could be distilled into kerosene for burning in lamps, and he also noted its lubricating qualities. At the time, oil was obtained by skimming off what floated on the surface of water-filled ditches and springs.

With other uses, however, drilling quickly became economically productive. Independent oil wells and small-scale refineries sprang up in great profusion in northwestern Pennsylvania, and refineries also proliferated in Cleveland. The oil business was chaotic, with numerous small operators, overproduction, cutthroat competition, and alternating periods of boom and bust. Rockefeller perceived that whoever could bring order to this industry could make a fabulous fortune.

In 1863, Rockefeller began his involvement with the oil business. He and his wholesale grocery partners, along with refining expert Samuel Andrews, built a refinery in Cleveland. His wholesale grocery partners proved too cautious for Rockefeller's taste. In 1865, he decided to buy out the three Clark brothers, get entirely out of the wholesale grocery business, and devote himself to oil. By the end of the year, the firm of Rockefeller and Andrews had an oil refinery that was producing at least twice as much as any other single refinery of Cleveland's nearly thirty refineries.

Rockefeller prospered more than his competitors because of his foresight, attention to detail, emphasis on efficiency, lack of toleration for waste, and growing reputation as a successful businessperson. These qualities allowed him to borrow heavily from bankers and to attract partners who brought additional capital to his firm. Henry M. Flagler joined Rockefeller in 1867, bringing with him a substantial amount of money and the ability to negotiate ever lower railroad shipping rates. Railroad rates were unregulated then, with railroads commonly giving favored shippers rebates on their publicly stated rates. The larger the shipper, the more favorable the rate. Rockefeller was able to play two railroads off against

John D. Rockefeller. (Library of Congress)

each other and water transportation off against the railroads. In turn, his lower shipping rates allowed him to undersell his competitors, steadily driving them out of business.

Meanwhile, Rockefeller implemented a policy of vertical integration. To cut his firm's dependence on related businesses, he began making his own barrels and then bought his own timber tracts to supply his cooperage plant. He owned his warehouses, bought his own tank cars, and, to the extent possible, owned or produced the raw materials and transportation he needed to operate. Finally, he fought waste by using kerosene by-products to become the oil industry's leading producer of paraffin and machine lubricants.

In 1870, to accommodate additional growth, Rockefeller converted his partnership into a joint-stock corporation, the Standard Oil Company of Ohio. Meanwhile, Thomas A. Scott of the Pennsylvania Railroad began organizing certain railroads, oil refiners, and well owners into the infamous South Improvement Company. The purpose was to form a monopoly and get rebates on their competitors' shipments. The public reaction was hostile, and the South Improvement Company quickly lost its charter. Rockefeller had been part of this scheme, which badly tarnished his reputation. However, through the South Improvement Company, he acquired another wealthy partner, Cleveland refiner Oliver H. Payne.

Furthermore, Standard Oil decided to proceed on its own to create a monopoly in the oil business. Early in 1872, Rockefeller offered to buy out nearly all remaining Cleveland oil refineries. Owners could either accept a cash offer, take the offer in Standard Oil stock, or be driven out of business. With the South Improvement Company still a live entity and given the size of Standard Oil itself, most refiners sold out. Some claimed that they had been pressured into taking less than their businesses were worth, but those who acquired Standard stock did make small fortunes. Rockefeller accomplished this takeover of his Cleveland competitors in three months. From Cleveland, Standard then proceeded to acquire refineries in Pittsburgh, in Philadelphia, and on Long Island. By 1875, the firm was refining half of the oil products in the United States. Rockefeller's next step was to gain control of pipelines, oil terminals, kerosene distributors, and additional plants. He also attracted rival oilman John D. Archbold to his firm. By 1878, Rockefeller had secured his monopolistic position.

During the 1880's, Standard Oil continued to grow. The firm acquired new oil fields, built new refineries,

and developed new refining methods. Under the direction of John's brother, William Rockefeller, the firm also expanded into the international market. Standard Oil products were a familiar sight in Asia, Africa, South America, and even Central Europe, where Standard encountered stiff competition from cheap Russian oil. Also, Standard Oil pioneered in corporate organization. Rockefeller employed the best legal talent to devise the concept of the trust. That meant that the stock of Standard's subsidiaries and related companies was combined with Standard's stock, new certificates were issued, and an executive committee with Rockefeller at the head assumed control. During 1883-1884, he transferred the corporate headquarters to New York City. However, Standard Oil never took total control of the oil industry. While accounting for 80-90 percent of oil produced in the United States and making substantial profits, Standard did lower the price of its products. Rockefeller had stabilized a chaotic industry.

In the process, Rockefeller became powerful and was feared and vilified. The lack of railroad rate regulation did much to make his monopoly possible. Unfair railroad rates upset many more people than Rockefeller's business competitors. The public began agitating for railroad rate regulation, first at the state level and then for the Interstate Commerce Act, passed in 1887. Because that law was largely ineffective, agitation continued until railroad rates were finally effectively regulated in the twentieth century. Throughout this agitation, the outstanding example of how unregulated railroad rates could lead to powerful monopolies was Standard Oil.

The New York legislature investigated Standard Oil in 1879 and again in 1888. Henry Demarest Lloyd published an exposé in the *Atlantic Monthly* in March, 1881. Congress sought to dampen the public's concern with the Sherman Antitrust Act of 1890. When that law went initially unenforced, muckrakers again attacked. The best-known exposé was Ida M. Tarbell's *History of the Standard Oil Company* (1904). Rockefeller always refused to respond directly to these attacks. His attitude was that his products spoke for themselves. Not until 1905 did Standard Oil hire its first public relations expert. Nevertheless, the federal government proceeded to prosecute Standard Oil for violating the Sherman Antitrust Act. Under court order, the company broke into smaller, separate companies in 1911.

Rockefeller's wealth at one point approached $900 million. What to do with all this money posed a dilemma. He invested in the stock market and, during the 1890's, gained control of the Mesabi Range, the richest iron ore field in the United States. Within a few years, however, he sold his Range holdings to Andrew Carnegie. Increasingly, his interests were turning to philanthropy, where his impact was tremendous.

At first, Rockefeller's gifts to hospitals, colleges, and other institutions were haphazard, and his gifts were sometimes misused. Soon, however, he began to apply some of his principles for making money—of attention to detail and organization—to giving money away. He virtually made the University of Chicago with a founding gift in 1889 of $600,000 and later gifts (some from his son) totaling $80 million. He created the Rockefeller Institute for Medical Research in 1901 and the General Education Board in 1902. The latter helped to revolutionize medical education, fought the spread of hookworm, and worked to improve southern agriculture. His philanthropy was further systematized with the creation of the Rockefeller Foundation in 1913. He gave away more than a half billion dollars, and the influence of his philanthropic institutions has continued to grow after his death. Rockefeller had turned over active leadership of the Standard Oil Company in 1897 but lived until 1937, dying at the age of ninety-seven.

SIGNIFICANCE

John D. Rockefeller succeeded as a businessperson and a philanthropist in part because of his personal qualities and in part because of his times. He had an uncanny ability to identify and secure leading executive talent. The extreme care with which he made decisions was accompanied by a boldness of action and accuracy of vision unmatched in his field. Furthermore, he had the steadiness to compete in a rough, competitive, "survival of the fittest" environment where there were few laws and regulations. Indeed, he turned this freewheeling environment to his advantage.

Rockefeller was able to build Standard Oil because of such conditions as the general absence of effective railroad rate regulation and lack of an income tax. He went into the oil business at a time when it was taking off, and good luck was with him when the gasoline-powered automobile came along to increase demand. He regarded himself as a trustee of his wealth and became, perhaps, the outstanding philanthropist in the United States. Finally, he instilled an obligation for public service in his descendants. Of all the "robber barons" of his generation, his long-range impact may have been the greatest.

—*Judith Ann Trolander*

FURTHER READING

Abels, Jules. *The Rockefeller Billions: The Story of the World's Most Stupendous Fortune*. New York: Macmillan, 1965. Scholarly, readable, with a good selection of photographs of Rockefeller, his family, business associates, and houses. Generally, Abels is favorably disposed toward Rockefeller.

Carr, Albert A. *John D. Rockefeller's Secret Weapon*. New York: McGraw-Hill, 1962. Focuses on the role that the Union Tank Car Company, established by Rockefeller and the key to his transportation system, played in the success of Standard Oil. In 1891, the company became a separate corporation from Standard Oil in response to the Sherman Antitrust Act. Carr covers the history of Union Tank Car up to 1961.

Chernow, Ron D. *Titan: The Life of John D. Rockefeller, Sr.* New York: Random House, 1998. Well-written, meticulously researched biography based on newly acquired archival materials. Chernow recounts the details of Rockefeller's life and career, describing his human side as well as his misdeeds.

Collier, Peter, and David Horowitz. *The Rockefellers: An American Dynasty*. New York: Holt, Rinehart and Winston, 1976. The bulk of this book is on John D. Rockefeller's descendants, down through his great-grandchildren, the impact his fortune has had on them, and their sense of public responsibility.

Hawke, David F. *John D.: The Founding Father of the Rockefellers*. New York: Harper and Row, 1980. A chatty, popular account, this slim volume is not too extensively footnoted but is based on archival sources along with more detailed secondary sources, especially Nevins's 1940 biography.

Josephson, Matthew. *The Robber Barons: The Great American Capitalists, 1861-1901*. New York: Harcourt, Brace, 1934. Reprint. Harcourt, Brace, and World, 1962. In this critical account, Rockefeller is only one among many late nineteenth century industrialists, but the book is excellent for setting him in the context of his time. Josephson is critical of the business practices and extensive power of Rockefeller and his associates.

Nevins, Allan. *John D. Rockefeller: The Heroic Age of American Enterprise*. New York: Charles Scribner's Sons, 1940. Nevins is the scholarly authority on Rockefeller. This two-volume work was the most comprehensive, carefully researched, and balanced source on Rockefeller until Nevins's 1953 book appeared.

_____. *Study in Power: John D. Rockefeller, Industrialist and Philanthropist.* New York: Charles Scribner's Sons, 1953. More of a second biography of his subject than a revision, this book incorporates material based on a large amount of documents not available to Nevins in his earlier biography; it also reflects a maturing of Nevins's analysis. Both Nevins biographies can be profitably consulted.

SEE ALSO: Andrew Carnegie; William Rainey Harper; Cornelius Vanderbilt.
RELATED ARTICLES in *Great Events from History: The Nineteenth Century, 1801-1900:* January 10, 1870: Standard Oil Company Is Incorporated; January 2, 1882: Standard Oil Trust Is Organized; July 20, 1890: Harrison Signs the Sherman Antitrust Act.

AUGUSTE RODIN
French sculptor

One of the greatest sculptors of all time, Rodin has been hailed for both the monumentality and the psychological penetration of his sculpture. Much of his work has a kinetic quality, a dynamism that takes over the solid material of his sculpture, transforming it into the expression of a towering personality.

BORN: November 12, 1840; Paris, France
DIED: November 17, 1917; Meudon, France
ALSO KNOWN AS: François-Auguste-René Rodin (full name)
AREA OF ACHIEVEMENT: Art

EARLY LIFE

The youngest of two children in a French working-class home, Auguste Rodin (roh-dahn) was educated with great care under the supervision of his uncle in a friar's school until he was fourteen. By the age of ten, he had already shown an interest in drawing, and it was thought that he would become an artisan. His teachers were impressed with his dedication and talent and encouraged him to believe that he would one day become a fine artist. However, his early years were not full of success. Indeed, he failed three times to gain acceptance at the École des Beaux-Arts, where he had hoped to study sculpture.

Working as a craftsperson, Rodin studied on his own the work of Antoine-Louis Bayre (1795-1875), who was famous for his lifelike depictions of animals. He also assisted Albert-Ernest Carrier-Belleuse (1824-1887) in his studio, beginning in 1864, and closely followed developments in the world of contemporary sculpture. His early sculptures, one of his father (c. 1860) and one of Father Pierre-Julien Eymard (1863), already exhibit his dexterous and precise sense for the human face. Father Eymard, the superior of the Societas Sanctissimi Sacramenti, profoundly impressed and touched Rodin, who had stayed briefly in a cloister before deciding that the religious life did not suit him.

Still largely unacknowledged, Rodin traveled to Italy in 1875 to study the sculpture of Donatello and Michelangelo. Not being able to afford a long trip, he soon returned to France with great enthusiasm for the Italian masters, which resulted in his sculpture, *The Age of Bronze*, a work that was so lifelike he was accused of having taken a mold of a live model. Other artists came to his defense in what was to be the first of many controversies concerning Rodin's techniques and choices of subject matter.

By the late 1870's, the state was acquiring sculptures such as *Saint John the Baptist Preaching*, which were every bit as realistic as *The Age of Bronze*, for by now the temper of the age was beginning to swing Rodin's way, valuing precisely his uncanny ability to render the human figure in bronze as if it were alive. Rather than accepting traditional sculpture with stereotypical gestures, Rodin had accustomed his contemporaries to a startling, almost photographic depiction of the individual, of a peasant-faced Saint John, for example, crooking one finger of his extended right arm while dropping his left arm, slightly flexed, to his side. This portrait of man in action, in mid-stride, with a body that reflected an inner psychological life and purposiveness, was a stunning achievement.

LIFE'S WORK

Now a figure of considerable influence, Rodin was courted and given many commissions, including one that involved the decoration of a door for the future Museum of Decorative Arts. Inspired by Dante's *Inferno*, Rodin chose to create *The Gates of Hell*, a work of enormous ambition that he never finished and perhaps never could, for as William Hale notes, the sculptor took as his subject

Auguste Rodin. (Library of Congress)

the creation of chaos itself. Kept in his studio until his death, the work reflects the artist's constant experimentations with style and his engagement with all the inchoate human desires that are never quite fulfilled.

Seated atop this magnificent work is the world-famous statue *The Thinker*. He is at once a perfectly realized and enigmatic figure. With his chin resting on his bent right hand, and his upper body leaning forward in somber meditation, he is evocative of a powerful human intellect but also of a brooding, perhaps dissatisfied nature for whom thought itself does not suffice. Various commentators have noted that this powerfully muscled figure is out of proportion—a deliberate ploy to increase the tension of the pose, to use physical power to suggest mental strength. Behind the thinker, in the tympanum, are the vacant-faced figures of the damned, engaged in their ghastly dance of death while other falling figures suggest horror and the frustration of failed lives. On the twenty-one-foot-tall door (thirteen feet wide and three feet deep), the artist uses the size of human figures (ranging from six inches to four feet) to portray the differentiated scale of a world of human sufferers.

Rodin repeatedly flouted his society's notion of what was dignified and presentable. His commissioned sculpture of Victor Hugo was rejected because he produced a seated rather than a standing figure. Even more bitterness was occasioned by his monument to Honoré de Balzac, which many of his contemporaries considered to be grotesque, a violent and swollen piece that was called "an obscenity," "a toad in a sack," "this lump of plaster kicked together by a lunatic," and the like. Rodin was aiming, however, not for a faithful likeness of his subject but for a visceral rendering of his extraordinary imagination and body of work.

Rodin pursued his sculpting subjects as if he were a biographer, and in the case of Balzac went so far as to visit the places where the novelist's fiction was set. Balzac had died at the age of fifty-one, his body exhausted from having produced his novels so intensely and rapidly. Rodin contacted Balzac's tailor to get a measure of his clothes, he checked accounts of the writer's physical appearance, and he exercised his conception of the writer by sculpting more than twenty studies of his head and body. Many of these preliminary efforts were realistic portraits, as though Rodin preferred to work with the outward facts and burrow more deeply into his subject's interior life. The result was a huge figure with a bull neck, a distorted face, and an immense torso—the point being that here was an artist whose very physical presence was magnificently marked by the lives he had imagined. The statue was like a thing of nature, with the figure's features erupting from the surface like volcanic life itself.

Rodin's work in marble—*The Kiss* (1886), for example—has been more accessible and a great favorite with the public. A highly erotic man and artist, Rodin has accentuated the effect of the embrace by the angle he has chosen, which has the woman's right leg thrusting forward while the man's fingers touch her thigh. There is an equality in the embrace, a mutuality (emphasized by the touching of their feet and the entwinement of their legs) that seems perfect.

By 1900, Rodin was recognized as the foremost sculptor of his period. Soon he would travel to do a bust of George Bernard Shaw (1906) and sculptures of English and American notables. In 1905, forty-two of his works were exhibited in the Luxembourg Museum. He continued to innovate, creating human figures that emphasize his interest in the motion and position of bodies. By fragmenting these sculptures, taking away certain physical features, expressions, and bodily parts, he accentuated his art. His *Walking Man* is headless, because nothing must distract from his study of the shift in weight, the rhythm of musculature, and the placement of the feet—all of which contribute to an appreciation of how a man walks. Rodin believed in the principle of leaving out something, of an understatement that allows other features or themes to be seen more clearly.

SIGNIFICANCE

Auguste Rodin was both a great scholar and a creator of art. No artist of his stature has exceeded his ability to learn from his predecessors. He was also very much a man of the nineteenth century, taking a profound interest in individual lives, treating his preparations for portrait sculpture the way a modern psychological biographer does his or her research and writing, amassing evidence but also probing for the heart of the subject. He welcomed new tools—the camera, for example—not only to record his work, to help him in modeling and studying his subjects, but also to assist him in capturing reality from new points of view.

There are many accounts of Rodin working in his studio. The biography by Frederic V. Grunfeld contains many passages that show how carefully Rodin studied the nude human body—not simply to attain accuracy of presentation but also to use physical details, the tone and the play of different muscle groups, to suggest mental and spiritual life. Rodin knew that he had to imbue outward forms with a sense of inner life. His statues are not static. They have the dynamism of Renaissance forms, of the works by Donatello that Rodin admired so profusely, but Rodin's work has something more: the pulsing of muscles that reflect interior energies. It is as if the sculptor makes what is invisible visible.

Notoriously slow in executing his commissions, Rodin was known to keep works many years past their deadlines, half-finished, awaiting his inspiration and his maturing conception of what the work could yield to him. In some cases, as in his work on Victor Hugo, he never did find the right form, the appropriate means of expression for his subject. In others, as with his work on Balzac, he was determined to shape a figure that revealed all he had to say about this titanic figure of literature.

Perhaps more than any other sculptor, Rodin concerned himself with sculpture and its relationship to nature. His pieces are renowned for the way they take the light, for the artist's realization that the meaning of form depends upon how it reacts with its environment. A work that has no context, or does not create a context for itself, is a work that is only half-realized. Few great artists have matched Rodin's exquisite sense of the wholeness of art, of the perfect work that creates its own standards, its own way of measuring itself and the world around it.

—*Carl Rollyson*

FURTHER READING

Butler, Ruth. *Rodin: The Shape of Genius*. New Haven, Conn.: Yale University Press, 1993. Insightful, comprehensive biography, using previously unpublished letters as source material. Particularly good at describing Rodin's relationships with women and the politics of the artistic community.

Champigneulle, Bernard. *Rodin*. New York: Harry N. Abrams, 1967. A sound biographical and critical study, with superb black-and-white and color plates, notes, and a list of illustrations. No bibliography and only an inadequate index.

Elsen, Albert E. *In Rodin's Studio: A Photographic Record of Sculpture in the Making*. Ithaca, N.Y.: Cornell University Press, 1980. A fascinating study of the way Rodin used and was influenced by photography in the creation of his work. Photographs of Rodin and his studio, as well as of his work in various stages of composition, make this an extraordinarily valuable study.

Grunfeld, Frederic V. *Rodin: A Biography*. New York: Henry Holt, 1987. The first full-scale biography of Rodin to appear since 1936. Grunfeld has found and taken advantage of many new sources. His huge book is well written, copiously illustrated, and enhanced by a full bibliography, extensive notes, and a comprehensive index. Written for both scholars and a larger, general audience, this biography is essential reading.

Hale, William Harlan. *The World of Rodin, 1840-1917*. New York: Time-Life Books, 1969. A copiously illustrated, life-and-times approach to the artist's life that includes a chronology of artists, a bibliography, a comprehensive index, and "A Guide to the Gates of Hell," detailing the architectural features and figures of this complex masterpiece.

Rodin, Auguste. *Rodin Sculptures*. Selected by Ludwig Goldscheider. London: Phaidon Press, 1970. Large, handsome black-and-white reproductions of Rodin's most important works. This work is enhanced by detailed notes on plates and succinct introductions to the artist's life and work.

Vilain, Jacques, et al. *Rodin at the Musée Rodin*. Translated from French by Judith Hayward. London: Scala

Books, 1997. Catalog of Rodin's works held by the museum. Museum curators have compiled a chronological study of Rodin's career, a biographical sketch of the artist, and photographs and written descriptions of Rodin's major works.

SEE ALSO: Honoré de Balzac; Antonio Canova; Victor Hugo; Augustus Saint-Gaudens.
RELATED ARTICLE in *Great Events from History: The Nineteenth Century, 1801-1900:* 1888: Rodin Exhibits *The Thinker.*

JOHN AUGUSTUS ROEBLING
German-born American engineer

An academically trained civil engineer who worked in the middle decades of the nineteenth century when such talents were rare in the United States, Roebling fully exploited the potentialities of the suspension bridge, placing the United States in the forefront in construction of long-span, stable, heavy-load-bearing bridges for generations.

BORN: June 12, 1806; Mühlhausen, Prussia (now in Germany)
DIED: July 22, 1869; Brooklyn Heights, New York
AREA OF ACHIEVEMENT: Engineering

EARLY LIFE

John Augustus Roebling (ROHB-lihng) was born in one of the German states of the Confederation of the Rhine that was incorporated into Prussia in 1815. The second largest of the German states, Prussia was in most respects the most advanced. Roebling's parents were respected citizens of their ancient walled town, which was rich in Gothic architecture that later became one of the motifs in Roebling's own work. Mühlhausen similarly enjoyed a rich cultural heritage, Johann Sebastian Bach, among other noted figures, having worked there. Because rapidly growing Berlin was Prussia's political and cultural center, Roebling was sent to Berlin's Royal Polytechnic School in 1822. When he was graduated in 1826, he had studied civil engineering, architecture, mathematics, and philosophy (under Georg Wilhelm Friedrich Hegel) and completed a senior thesis on suspension bridges.

LIFE'S WORK

After graduation, Roebling was employed for the next three years as a civil engineer on both public and military works for the Prussian government. Prussia, however, was an autocratic state in which the liberal, republican views that were to take root in the German state until 1848, views Roebling shared, withered. Because of such opinions, Roebling was officially listed as a subversive,

and his career accordingly ended. Seeking a freer reign for his career and for his political convictions, he emigrated to Saxonburg in eastern Pennsylvania.

Over the next six years, Roebling unsuccessfully attempted farming. With the craze for internal improvements, particularly for canals and railroads, in full swing and trained engineers rare, Roebling returned to engineering in 1837, initially as a surveyor for the Beaver River Canal, then shortly afterward for the Pennsylvania Railroad. The enormous anthracite deposits of northeastern Pennsylvania, the frenzy to find economical means of getting the coal to market as it increasingly became the nation's principal domestic and industrial fuel, ensured a demand for bridges.

In 1844, at the age of thirty-eight, Roebling earned his first commission, partly on the strength of his invention, in 1840, of a method of manufacturing wire-rope cable, essential for stable, heavy-duty suspension work. His first project, built to carry the Pennsylvania State Canal across the Allegheny River at Pittsburgh, was a suspension aqueduct for canal boats. Its masonry towers foreshadowed an Egyptian motif later to reappear in the Brooklyn Bridge. Roebling's next four commissions, also aqueducts, were for the Delaware and Hudson Canal, a company then redesigning its anthracite-carrying canals from the coalfields of northeastern Pennsylvania to tidewater ports better able to compete with railroads. All were multispan suspension structures. Convenient for navigation, they were built without falsework—one of the advantages of suspension construction. Each consisted of troughlike flumes capable of carrying boats of sixty or more tons. The flumes were solidly embanked with fitted timbers and into transverse floor beams, all buttressed with sidewall trusses.

As on the famed Delaware Aqueduct, which remained in use until the 1970's, the shore piers and masonry spans were company built. All the suspension work and its loads were designed and built by Roebling. Indeed, the Delaware Aqueduct was a handsome, thousand-foot span hung on eight-and-one-half-inch wrought-iron cables. Aware of the cable's coming importance, Roebling, in fact, founded his own wire-cable factory in Trenton, New Jersey, in 1849, just prior to completion of his Delaware and Hudson commissions.

In the meantime, a fire in Pittsburgh and the destruction of the Monongahela River's Smithfield Bridge in 1846 brought him a commission for his first vehicular suspension bridge. With two shore abutments and six river spans, it stretched fifteen hundred feet. The deck was carried by wrought-iron rods hung from wire cables, which Roebling spun onshore. Until traffic weights became too great, the bridge was in all regards a success, resulting, late during the 1850's, in construction of an identical bridge over the Allegheny River at Pittsburgh's Sixth Street. In this case, however, there were two differences: First, Roebling spun his wire cable on the bridge; second, his son, Washington, joined him, thus inaugurating his own career.

In 1851, John Roebling undertook his greatest challenge yet: construction of a railway suspension bridge across the Niagara River at Niagara Falls, New York. After a brilliant career, Charles Ellet, Roebling's predecessor, resigned his commission for the job, effectively end-

ing his career. Moreover, leading engineers in both the United States and Europe considered the task impossible. Roebling designed a double-decked structure: the upper one carrying the mainline of the Grand Trunk Railway and the Great Western Railway of Canada, and the lower one serving normal vehicular traffic. The Niagara gorge was deep; the river was deep and swift; the span to be covered on an absolute level was 821 feet from shore to shore. Roebling's design consisted of four ten-inch cables, each of 3,640 wires, hung from masonry towers. Characteristically, the load was carried by the cables and reticulations of radiating stays. Roebling completed this, the first of the world's railway suspension bridges, in 1855.

Meanwhile, Roebling rebuilt an Ellet bridge at Wheeling, West Virginia, and by 1856, he had embarked on ten years of frustrations—finances, ice, floods, and war—constructing a twelve-hundred-foot span across the Ohio River between Cincinnati and Covington, Kentucky. Since its opening in January, 1867, nevertheless, with its design unaltered, it continues in use, an even greater tribute to his engineering genius, tenacity, and industry than his remarkable Niagara Bridge.

Roebling's last and monumental work was begun in 1867, with his appointment as chief engineer for the New York Bridge Company, whose objective was bridging the East River between lower Manhattan and Brooklyn, then two separate cities. The growth of each dictated a need for the most efficient connections. River traffic was enormous; rail and shipping connections were awkward and inefficient; and, though a tidal river, the East River severed both cities and halted traffic by freezing over or being covered with ice floes periodically. Proposals for a bridge began at least by 1811, and, in 1857, Roebling made his own bid. The Civil War and objections from the United States Army Engineers shelved work until 1869. Roebling designed an unprecedented structure with a main span of 1,595 feet.

Though built to Roebling's specifications, the great bridge, which came to symbolize not only New York's greatness but also the aesthetic and structural abilities of American engineering, was completed by Washington Roebling fourteen years after his father's death. On his initial survey in July, 1869, John Roebling's toes were crushed against pilings by a ferry, and he died of a tetanus infection July 22, 1869, in Brooklyn Heights, New York.

John Augustus Roebling. (Library of Congress)

SIGNIFICANCE

Although Roebling has been popularly identified with the design of the magnificent Brooklyn Bridge, an American symbol as well as an example of artistic engineering, one of his major contributions lies elsewhere: He, along with a handful of others, demonstrated the necessity for, and the superiority of, professionally trained engineers and the passing of those who, however ingeniously, even brilliantly, worked by "guess and by God." This was especially true of bridge builders, who were increasingly confronted by the broad, swift rivers of America and by the vastly heavier burdens that had to be borne by their structures during rapid industrialization.

Roebling did not invent the suspension bridge: As a simple form it was thousands of years old. On a modest scale and in modest circumstances, suspensions were being improved even as his career began. The precision of his designs, his mastery of wire-cable manufacture and use, and his mathematical assessment of loads and stresses that lend special character to all of his constructions, whether his aqueducts, his Wheeling, Pittsburgh, Cincinnati, or Niagara structures, however, made him the acknowledged master of suspension forms. By his boldness in adapting his designs to the peculiar needs of the American environment, he revolutionized bridge construction throughout the world. This was a legacy passed on not only by his son's completion of the Brooklyn Bridge but also by professional engineers everywhere.

—Clifton K. Yearley and Kerrie L. MacPherson

FURTHER READING

Cadbury, Deborah. *Dreams of Iron and Steel: Seven Wonders of the Nineteenth Century, from the Building of the London Sewers to the Panama Canal.* New York: Fourth Estate, 2004. A popular history of major nineteenth century construction projects, including the Brooklyn Bridge. Provides information about Roebling's involvement in the project as well as details of the bridge's design and construction.

Condit, Carl W. *American Building: Materials and Techniques from the Beginning of Colonial Settlements to the Present.* Chicago: University of Chicago Press, 1982. A standard study; chapters 8 and 12 are on Roebling. Excellent technical discussion of bridge construction, including the suspension work of Roebling, among others. Also strong on historical contexts of these developments. Readable and widely available.

_____. *American Building Art: The Nineteenth Century.* New York: Oxford University Press, 1960. As excellent as all of Condit's studies. Concentration not only on building techniques but also on the aesthetics of structural architecture. Chapter 5 is particularly relevant to Roebling and suspension bridges.

Kirby, Richard S., and Philip G. Laurson. *The Early Years of Civil Engineering.* New Haven, Conn.: Yale University Press, 1932. Standard and excellent. Includes portraits and brief biographical sketches of Roebling and many other major civil engineers of national and international note. Chapter 5 is especially relevant.

Latimer, Margaret, Brooks Hindle, and Melvin Kranzberg. *Bridge to the Future: A Centennial Celebration of the Brooklyn Bridge.* New York: New York Academy of Sciences, 1984. A literary as well as a technical survey. Sound and accurate.

McCullogh, David G. *The Great Bridge: The Epic Story of the Brooklyn Bridge.* New York: Simon & Schuster, 1972. Reprint 2001. A detailed, well-written, and meticulously researched popular history of the Brooklyn Bridge. The 2001 reprint includes a new introduction by the author.

Steinman, David B., and Sara Ruth Watson. *Bridges and Their Builders.* New York: G. P. Putnam's Sons, 1941. Expertly done by engineering scholars. A fine survey.

Vogel, Robert M. *Roebling's Delaware and Hudson Canal Aqueducts.* Washington, D.C.: Smithsonian Institution Press, 1971. Fine monograph on Roebling's early work. Technically detailed with reproductions of Roebling's designs. Useful for understanding Roebling's later works.

SEE ALSO: Isambard Kingdom Brunel; Marc Isambard Brunel; James Buchanan Eads; Gustave Eiffel; Georg Wilhelm Friedrich Hegel; Thomas Telford.

RELATED ARTICLE in *Great Events from History: The Nineteenth Century, 1801-1900:* May 24, 1883: Brooklyn Bridge Opens.

WILHELM CONRAD RÖNTGEN
German physicist

Röntgen made important contributions to several areas of physics but is best known for his revolutionary discovery of X rays and his investigations of their properties.

BORN: March 27, 1845; Lennep, Prussia (now Remscheid, Germany)
DIED: February 10, 1923; Munich, Germany
ALSO KNOWN AS: Wilhelm Konrad Röntgen; Wilhelm Conrad Roentgen
AREAS OF ACHIEVEMENT: Science and technology, physics

EARLY LIFE

Wilhelm Conrad Röntgen (RAHNT-gehn) was the only child of Friedrich Conrad Röntgen, a German textile manufacturer and merchant, and Charlotte Constanza Frowein, who came from a Dutch family of merchants. When "Willi," as he was called as a child, was three, his family moved to Apeldoorn, his mother's hometown in Holland. There Willi attended primary public school and later became a student at Kostschool, a private boarding school. In 1862, he went to Utrecht, where he entered a secondary technical school, from which he was later expelled for refusing to inform on a fellow student who had drawn an unflattering caricature of a teacher. Although he attended some classes at the University of Utrecht, he was unable to become a formal student because he lacked a secondary-school diploma. He resolved his academic problems by passing the difficult entrance examination of the recently established Federal Institute of Technology (or Polytechnic) in Zurich, Switzerland.

In November of 1865, Röntgen began his education as a mechanical engineer. Over the next three years, he studied various technical courses but found his greatest fulfillment in a physics course taught by Rudolf Clausius, a distinguished scientist who helped found modern thermodynamics. Röntgen eventually passed his final examinations with excellent grades and received his diploma on August 6, 1869.

Röntgen remained in Zurich after graduation to work in the laboratory of August Kundt, a Polytechnic physics professor who had befriended him. Röntgen studied different gases to see if they all expanded uniformly with increases in temperature, as predicted by Gay-Lussac's law, and discovered that some had expanded to greater volumes than the law predicted. Less than a year later, he submitted his dissertation, "Studies on Gases," to the University of Zurich, which granted him a doctorate on June 22, 1869. While working in Zurich, Röntgen met his future wife, Anna Bertha Ludwig, who shared his interests in natural history and hiking. In 1871, when Kundt accepted a position at the University of Würzburg, Röntgen accompanied him as his assistant, and the following year he married Bertha.

LIFE'S WORK

Röntgen's lack of a secondary-school diploma again hindered his academic advancement at Würzburg, so he and his wife subsequently moved, with Kundt, to the Kaiser Wilhelm University in Strasbourg. On the basis of the success of his scientific investigations with Kundt, he received an offer of a full professorship from the Agricultural Academy in Hohenheim, Württemberg, in 1875. However, he was unhappy with that institution's experimental facilities and returned to Strasbourg one and one-half years later as an assistant professor in theoretical physics.

Röntgen wrote a series of papers on the properties of gases that exhibited his growing skills as an experimental physicist, and in 1879 he was offered the chair of physics at the University of Giessen. During his ensuing nine years at Giessen, he did important work on crystals, their generation of electricity when subjected to heat (pyro-electricity), and their generation of electricity when subjected to mechanical stress (piezoelectricity). His greatest discovery, however, was his confirmation of a prediction made by the Scottish physicist James Clerk Maxwell that a magnetic field would be generated within dielectrics such as glass plates when they are moved back and forth between two electrically charged plates. The Dutch physicist Hendrik Antoon Lorentz named this effect, which Röntgen detected with a sensitive device, the "roentgen current." Röntgen later considered this discovery as an important step in his work on X rays.

Recognition of Röntgen's accomplishments in physics brought him offers from other universities. In 1888, he turned down the chair of physics at the University of Utrecht but accepted the University of Würzburg's proposal to occupy Kundt's former position. During his first six years at Würzburg, he published seventeen papers on such topics as the properties of solids and liquids. His fame as a physicist and respect for his political sagacity led to his election in 1894 to the rectorship of the univer-

Wilhelm Conrad Röntgen. (Courtesy, Yale University)

sity. One year later, he left his position as rector and took up a new field of scientific research.

Philipp Lenard, a Hungarian-German physicist, had been studying cathode rays by means of an apparatus he constructed that allowed what some called "Lenard rays" to enter the air beyond the apparatus. Röntgen became interested in exploring these rays, and on November 8, 1895, he wrapped a cathode-ray tube with a "close-fitted shield of black paper" to observe the narrow beam of rays from the tube. By chance, he noticed that a paper coated on one side with barium platinocyanide and located some distance from the tube glowed with a brilliant fluorescence. This puzzled him because cathode rays had an effective range of only a few centimeters. He therefore suspected that he might have come upon a previously unknown kind of radiation.

Over the next several weeks, Röntgen investigated these new rays by directing the invisible beam through paper, wood, and thin sheets of aluminum, copper, silver, gold, and platinum. He was amazed to discover that these materials were transparent to the rays, which were impeded only by sheets of lead. He also discovered that these "X rays"—as he called them, "for the sake of brev-

ity"—traveled in straight lines, were unaffected by magnets or electrically charged plates, and could ionize gases. Unlike light rays, X rays could neither be reflected from a mirror nor refracted in a prism. On the other hand, they could, like light rays, blacken photographic plates; when Röntgen directed an X-ray beam through his wife's hand and onto a photographic plate, an image of the bones wondrously appeared.

On December 28, 1895, when Röntgen announced his discoveries to the world, both scientists and the public were fascinated by these mysterious rays that could reveal the skeletons inside living humans. Physicians in Europe and America quickly put them to medical use in diagnosing broken bones and foreign objects in human bodies. Röntgen knew that his rays had commercial potential, but, out of altruism, he refused to patent his discovery.

Kaiser William II was the first dignitary to honor Röntgen with an award, on January 14, 1896. The kaiser's award was following by many others, culminating in Röntgen's reception of the first Nobel Prize in Physics in 1901. By that time he had accepted a distinguished position as professor of experimental physics and head of the physical institute at the University of Munich, where he would remain for the next twenty years. During that period, he witnessed X rays being used by physicians to treat skin diseases and cancer and by physicists to study atomic arrangements in crystals. His own work centered on crystals, their electrical conductivity, and the influence of radiation on them.

During his professorship at Munich, Röntgen dedicated himself to what he saw as his sacred duty to advance scientific knowledge. However, he also had to take time to defend himself against the claims that other scientists had observed the effects of X rays before him. However, although Lenard may have observed fluorescence near a Crookes tube, he never investigated this observation in the way that Röntgen later did.

Although Röntgen received many honors on the occasion of his seventieth birthday in 1915, the privations brought by World War I had a negative influence on his scientific work. After the war he was deeply affected by the sufferings of his wife, who died in 1919 after a long illness. Furthermore, he, like most Germans, was troubled by postwar political turmoil, ruinous inflation, and food shortages. His own health began to fail, and other physicists took over his work. Röntgen diagnosed his condition as carcinoma of the intestine. He died in Munich during the morning of February 10, 1923, and his ashes were later deposited at the family grave in Giessen.

SIGNIFICANCE

The medical applications of X rays were quickly recognized, but the impact of X rays on physics and chemistry proved to be even more momentous. For example, Henry Becquerel's investigation of X rays led directly to his discovery of radioactivity. In 1912, Max von Laue suggested that X rays might be diffracted by crystals, and scientists soon discovered that diffracted rays allowed them to determine the three-dimensional structures of many crystals. The English physicist Henry Moseley discovered characteristic X rays emitted by each of the chemical elements, leading to a deeper understanding of the periodic table. So significant were these and other discoveries that some scholars called Röntgen's discovery of X rays the event that initiated the "Second Scientific Revolution" because it ushered in the modern physics of the twentieth century, just as the discoveries of Galileo Galilei, Johannes Kepler, and Isaac Newton had forged the New Science of the seventeenth century.

With the passage of time, practical uses of X rays multiplied. So many medical applications were developed that an entirely new medical specialty, radiology, was created. Engineers used X rays to study stresses in various materials and the strengths of welds. Dentists used them to detect cavities in teeth. Archaeologists used them to study mummies and other artifacts without harming the objects. Computer technicians used them to etch integrated circuits. Workers and airports and seaports used them to inspect luggage and cargo. Astronomers studied X rays emanating from different parts of the universe to help them understand stars, pulsars, and black holes. In computerized axial tomography scientists used high-resolution X-ray pictures to study healthy and diseased human brains. These examples do not exhaust the significant applications that continue to be discovered over a century after Röntgen first found and characterized these powerful rays.

—*Robert J. Paradowski*

FURTHER READING

Baigrie, Brian S. *Scientific Revolutions: Primary Texts in the History of Science.* Upper Saddle River, N.J.: Pearson Prentice Hall, 2004. This anthology, based on the conviction that scientific discoveries are best understood through classic texts, contains a chapter, "Shadow Pictures," with an English translation of Röntgen's "On a New Type of Rays" preceded by a helpful historical introduction.

Bleich, Alan Ralph. *The Story of X-Rays from Röntgen to Isotopes.* New York: Dover, 1960. Bleich, a professor of radiology, devotes the first two chapters of his book to Röntgen's discovery of X rays and the remaining chapters to their applications in medicine, industry, scientific research, and art.

Glasser, Otto. *Wilhelm Conrad Röntgen and the Early History of Roentgen Rays.* Springfield, Ill.: Charles C Thomas, 1995. This reprint, with a new introduction, derives from what was once the standard Röntgen biography first published in 1931, expanded in a second edition in 1945 to commemorate the centennial of Röntgen's birth, and revised again in 1959.

Kevles, Bettyann H. *Naked to the Bone: Medical Imaging in the Twentieth Century.* New Brunswick, N.J.: Rutgers University Press, 1997. This narrative history for the nonscientist analyzes how X rays fostered such new technologies as computerized tomography and magnetic resonance imaging. The author also discusses how X rays transformed medicine, criminology, and certain visual, literary, and fine arts.

Nitski, W. Robert. *The Life of Wilhelm Conrad Röntgen, Discoverer of the X Ray.* Tucson: University of Arizona Press, 1971. This popular biography, which incorporates primary source material into the narrative, concentrates on Röntgen's researches before, during, and after the discovery of X rays. Chronology, bibliography, and index, with English translations of Röntgen's three most famous papers.

SEE ALSO: The Becquerel Family; Joseph-Louis Gay-Lussac; Samuel Pierpont Langley; James Clerk Maxwell; Aleksandr Stepanovich Popov.

RELATED ARTICLES in *Great Events from History: The Nineteenth Century, 1801-1900:* November 9, 1895: Röntgen Discovers X Rays; December 14, 1900: Articulation of Quantum Theory; December 15, 1900: General Electric Opens Research Laboratory.

SIR JAMES CLARK ROSS
English explorer

Ross was one of the greatest of polar explorers. Through determined and efficient leadership, he discovered the North Magnetic Pole, mapped hundreds of miles of coastline, and discovered scores of geographical features at both ends of the globe.

BORN: April 15, 1800; London, England
DIED: April 3, 1862; Aylesbury, Buckinghamshire, England
AREA OF ACHIEVEMENT: Exploration

EARLY LIFE

James Clark Ross was born in London, England, of Scottish parents, but little is known of his boyhood until he joined the Royal Navy at the age of twelve under the guidance of his uncle, Sir John Ross, a commander in the Royal Navy. Probably fulfilling a family tradition, young Ross was taken onboard his uncle's ship as a first-class volunteer and was promoted rather quickly to midshipman and then to master's mate on the same vessel. He served with his uncle in the Baltic Sea, White Sea, and English Channel and on the west coast of Scotland. In 1818, when Ross was eighteen, he served as midshipman on the *Isabella* with his uncle, who commanded an Arctic expedition in a futile search for a northwest passage through the Canadian Arctic from the Atlantic to the Pacific Ocean.

The following year, Ross volunteered for service with William Edward Parry, who had been given command of the next Arctic voyage. Parry returned in 1820, having explored half the Northwest Passage and having accomplished far more than any previous explorer in that region. In the ensuing wave of public enthusiasm to finish the task of discovery, Parry was commissioned to command his second voyage to the Arctic. Ross was again assigned as midshipman on an expedition that consumed two years searching for an "Open Polar Sea." Ross functioned as naturalist, collecting birds, mammals, marine life, and plants.

Ross frequently accompanied Parry onshore to make observations. Despite its scientific data and extensive natural history collection, however, the voyage, from the standpoint of its purpose, was a failure. Ross sailed with Parry on a third voyage to the Arctic (1824-1825), which was disastrous. During a storm, one of Parry's ships, the *Fury*, was driven hard into the ice, and Parry was forced to abandon it. This was Parry's last expedition in search of the Northwest Passage, but he and Ross made an over-land assault on the North Pole. Traveling by sledge and dragging boats, they came within five hundred miles of the North Pole, a record unsurpassed for over fifty years.

LIFE'S WORK

In 1829, Ross, having been promoted to commander, sailed with his uncle, Commander John Ross, as his second-in-command on an Arctic exploration. James, seaman and scientist, and the active officer with the most Arctic experience in the Royal Navy, was the logical choice for a new try for the Northwest Passage. The expedition had fired the public imagination in that John had replaced the traditional sailing ship with a steam vessel, the *Victory*, thought to be superior for driving through ice. However, the machinery malfunctioned and progress was painfully slow; John, upon reaching Greenland, junked the engine and returned the *Victory* to a sailing vessel to the approval of all officers and crew.

James's wintering experiences with Parry proved invaluable. When the ship was snugged down for winter in Felix Harbor off Melville Island, he arranged exercise, activities, school instruction, and work for everyone. He instituted a new system of diet, patterned after the Eskimos, that ensured that the crew remain healthy. In the spring, James went on several hunting and fishing expeditions with Eskimo sledge parties and, with their help, mapped the coastlines.

During the second winter that they were trapped in the ice in Felix Harbor, James launched an expedition to the west coast of Boothia Peninsula (named for John's friend and benefactor, Felix Booth), where he discovered the North Magnetic Pole in 1831. After a third winter trapped in the ice, John determined to abandon the *Victory* and travel by sledge for Fury Beach. There, a canvas-covered house was constructed for living quarters, and supplies from Parry's abandoned ship, *Fury*, got them through the fourth Arctic winter. The following August, they were rescued by a whaler, and, after four and one-half years in the Arctic, they arrived in London in late September, 1833.

Beyond their miraculous return, the Rosses' expedition compiled results unequaled for many years. In addition to the discovery of the North Magnetic Pole, hundreds of miles of previously unknown coast were surveyed, and hundreds of miles of new shoreline were discovered. The Gulf of Boothia was discovered, and James had crossed the strait now named for him (Ross Strait).

In 1834, James Ross was promoted to post captain and, as a leading authority on terrestrial magnetism, was ordered to conduct the first systematic survey of the British Isles. This work was interrupted in 1836, when he was given command of the *Cove* and sent to the relief of eleven whalers containing about six hundred men who were frozen in the ice in Davis Strait, which separates Greenland from Baffin Island. Three hundred miles from Greenland, the *Cove* was struck by a tremendous storm, and only through the calm orders of Ross was the ship, although damaged, saved. Ross faced down a near mutiny of his crew to learn in Greenland that all vessels but one, which was never found, were safe.

Ross was the most experienced officer in Arctic navigation, having spent eight winters and fifteen navigable seasons in the Arctic region, and was also an expert in terrestrial magnetism. As the British Admiralty's choice to lead a proposed naval expedition to the Antarctic, Ross and his eminently qualified and carefully chosen crew departed on the afternoon of September 25, 1839. The two small but heavy ships, the *Erebus* and the *Terror*, which had been reinforced to withstand ice pressure, crossed the equator on December 3 and, after stopping at various points to set up observatories, reached Tasmania in August, 1840.

Cheered by the prospect of geographical discovery, Ross steered the *Erebus* and the *Terror* across the Antarctic Circle, breaking through the pack ice with ease. Heading for the South Magnetic Pole, Ross was disheartened to discover that the blink on the horizon was snow-covered mountain peaks. He sailed westerly in the sea that now bears his name and surveyed the magnificent mountain ranges, naming one of them the Admiralty Range, for the Lords Commissioners of the Admiralty, and the other for eminent members of the Royal Society and British Association.

An active volcano, 12,400 feet high and belching flame and smoke, was named Mount Erebus, while a smaller, inactive volcano was named Mount Terror. Hopes of reaching the South Magnetic Pole were dashed when Ross encountered a perpendicular wall of ice between 150 and 200 feet high directly in front of him that stretched as far as the eye could see. Ross followed this barrier (his name for what was later named the Ross Ice Shelf) to the east for over two hundred miles but, unable to move any farther south, reluctantly turned back to Tasmania for the winter.

Ross's second voyage into the Antarctic was disappointing, but the dangers were much greater. A terrific storm drove both ships into an ice pack that inflicted considerable damage and would have destroyed the vessels had they not been reinforced against ice. Ross managed to attain only a slightly higher latitude than the previous year before returning northward. On the way, a fierce gale caused a violent collision between the two ships, entangling the rigging and dashing the ships against each other. Gradually, the *Terror* forged past the *Erebus*, leaving the *Erebus* completely disabled. Rough weather continued as Ross called it a season and limped into the Falkland Islands. On his third cruise into the Antarctic, he was stopped again by the ice pack in March, 1843. As the season was too far advanced to attempt more, Ross signaled the *Terror* to turn back. He arrived in England in September of 1843 following an absence of four years and five months.

Ross's journey to Antarctica was one of the greatest voyages of discovery and exploration ever made. His geographical discoveries overshadowed the principal purpose of magnetic observation. Despite his disappointment at not reaching the South Magnetic Pole, his discoveries of Victoria Land, McMurdo Sound, Ross Sea, and the spectacular Ross Ice Shelf, among other geographical features, marked important advances in the knowledge of Antarctica.

Sir James Clark Ross. (Library of Congress)

On his return from Antarctica, Ross married Ann Coulman, but only after he contracted with her father never to go on any more long polar voyages. Long known as the "navy's handsomest man," he was eager to settle down on an estate he bought at Aylesbury. The terrible strain of long expeditions had taken its toll on his iron constitution, and he needed rest. He was given a knighthood and received an honorary degree from Oxford. He also wrote an account of his voyages and served as a consultant on Arctic matters.

In November, 1847, Lady Ross consented to allow her husband to command a rescue expedition in search of Commander John Franklin. The two-year voyage was a failure, for it was learned that Franklin and his crew had perished before Ross had left England. Ross returned exhausted and broken in health. Lady Ross died unexpectedly in 1857, and Ross died in 1862.

SIGNIFICANCE

Sir James Clark Ross was a sailor's sailor, an officer whose skill in ice navigation and nerves of steel saved ships and men on various occasions. Patient and fearless, he endured the privation and suffering of the long sledge journeys by virtue of his own strength, stamina, and judgment.

Ross's enormous contributions to knowledge through magnetic observation, specimen collection, mapping, and discovery were largely possible because of his foresight and planning. By surrounding himself with men of scientific as well as Arctic experience, his expeditions were better equipped and therefore more successful than many of those of his contemporaries.

An introvert, Ross developed techniques that made other explorers' tasks easier. One of his most significant contributions was his hard-won knowledge that successful exploration depends upon providing for the health, comfort, and safety of the men. Succeeding explorers benefited from his wintering techniques in which the ship's deck, under the housing, was covered with two and one-half feet of snow, trod down to a solid mass of ice, and covered with sand. Men were supplied with the best-quality warm clothing.

Ross's insistence upon regular activity, work, and exercises for the men relieved boredom and supported morale. Unusually large stores of preserved meat and vegetables were laid in, reducing the chance of scurvy to a minimum. Frequent hunting and fishing expeditions also provided dietary supplements. Ross was one of the first Europeans to understand that increasing the quantity of food per man, especially the large use of oil and fat

meats, was essential to successful Arctic living. Healthy men who returned from Ross's expeditions and the many others that followed owed their lives to his acumen.

—Mary Hurd

FURTHER READING

Dodge, Ernest S. *The Polar Rosses: John and James Clark Ross and Their Explorations.* New York: Barnes and Noble, 1973. Covers the explorations and related activities of both men. Gives detailed accounts of experiences that follow James Ross's log as well as insight into his working relationship with the British Admiralty.

King, H. G. R. *The Antarctic.* New York: Arco, 1969. Provides an introduction to Antarctic science along with basic facts concerning Antarctic geography, natural history, and exploration. Contains a short but informative section on Ross.

Langley, Michael. *When the Pole Star Shone: A History of Exploration.* London: George G. Harrap, 1972. Contains a history of exploration from ancient times to Neil Armstrong's landing on the moon. Includes chapters on polar navigators and the siege of the poles, with maps, sketches, and illustrations.

Mountfield, David. *A History of Polar Exploration.* London: Hamlyn, 1974. Interesting focus on the experiences of men who explored polar regions and major obstacles they had to overcome. Contains an excellent section on Ross. Includes maps, illustrations, and sketches.

Ross, M. J. *Polar Pioneers: John Ross and James Clark Ross.* Montreal: McGill-Queen's University Press, 1994. A chronicle of the two men's expeditions to the polar regions, written by the great-grandson of James Clark Ross. Describes John Ross's two Arctic voyages and James Clark Ross's scientific expedition to Antarctica. Includes black-and-white illustrations.

Sykes, Percy. *A History of Exploration: From the Earliest Times to the Present Day.* Westport, Conn.: Greenwood Press, 1949. An extensive history of exploration from earliest to modern times with emphasis on more remote areas of the world. Includes a brief but informative section on Ross.

SEE ALSO: Sir John Franklin.

JOHN ROSS
Native American leader

As a leader of the Cherokee nation during its ordeal of forced removal and civil war, Ross is the supreme example of nineteenth century Native American statesmanship.

BORN: October 3, 1790; Turkey Town, Cherokee
   Nation (near present-day Center, Alabama)
DIED: August 1, 1866; Washington, D.C.
ALSO KNOWN AS: Coowescoowe (birth name)
AREA OF ACHIEVEMENT: Government and politics

EARLY LIFE

Born in a Cherokee settlement in Alabama, John Ross was by blood only one-eighth Cherokee. His mother, Mollie McDonald, was the granddaughter of a Cherokee woman, but his father, the trader Daniel Ross, and all of his mother's other ancestors were Scottish. His father, while securing a tutor for his children and sending Ross to an academy near Kingston, Tennessee, did not want to stamp out his children's Cherokee identity, and his mother gave him a deep sense of loyalty to the tribe, to their ancient lands and traditions, and to the ideal of Cherokee unity. As a son of three generations of Scottish traders, Ross early showed an interest in business. In 1813, he formed a partnership with Timothy Meigs at Rossville, near modern Chattanooga, and two years later another with his brother Lewis Ross; during the Creek War of 1813-1814, when Cherokee warriors fought in Andrew Jackson's army, he did a lucrative business filling government contracts. During the Creek War, he served as adjutant in a company of Cherokee cavalry.

By the mid-1820's, his increasing involvement in the political affairs of the Cherokee nation caused him to abandon business. In 1827, he settled at Coosa, Georgia, thirty miles from the new Cherokee capital at New Echota, and established himself as a planter, with a substantial house, orchards and herds, quarters for his twenty slaves, and a lucrative ferry.

Ross served as a member of four Cherokee delegations to Washington between 1816 and 1825 and was president of the tribe's National Committee in 1818, when it resisted the attempt of Tennessee to persuade the tribe to surrender their lands in that state. In 1822, he was a cosigner of a resolution of the National Committee that the Cherokee would not recognize any treaty that surrendered Cherokee land. In 1823, Ross earned for himself the undying loyalty of the majority of the tribe when he

rejected a bribe offered by federal commissioners and publicly denounced them in a meeting of the National Committee.

LIFE'S WORK

Ross was president of the convention that in 1827 produced the Cherokee constitution. This document, in its assignment of powers to three branches of government, its bicameral legislature, and its four-year term for the principal chief, was modeled on the Constitution of the United States. In 1828, he was elected principal chief, an office that he held until his death, and in 1829 he went to Washington on the first of many embassies that he undertook in that capacity.

The Cherokee established their republic within the context of an ongoing struggle to maintain their traditional claims against state governments, particularly that of Georgia. In 1802, Georgia had ceded to the United States its western territory (what later became Alabama and Mississippi) in exchange for a promise that all Native Americans would be removed from Georgia. A substantial number of Cherokee, accepting removal, surrendered their land rights and moved west. (One of them was the great Cherokee genius Sequoya, who gave his people a syllabary for their language.)

With the inauguration of Andrew Jackson, who was determined to send the Cherokee west, and the discovery of gold on Cherokee land, it was clear that removal was almost inevitable. Ross was determined to exhaust every legal and political recourse, however, before submitting to the superior physical might of the U.S. government. Though Jackson was willing to assert the power of the federal government—even if it meant war—to put down any movement in South Carolina for "nullification" of the Constitution, he declared that in the Cherokee case he would not interfere with state sovereignty. As a result, his Indian Removal Bill of 1830 included the provision that any Native American who chose not to remove was subject to state law. Georgia therefore refused to recognize the legitimacy of the Cherokee republic and made no effort to prevent white squatters from moving into the Cherokee country. These official attitudes and the chaos caused by the gold rush produced a state of anarchy in which, on one occasion, Ross himself barely escaped assassination.

By 1833, pressure by the government of Georgia and by the Jackson administration was producing dissension among the Cherokee themselves. John Ridge, son of an influential Cherokee family, and Elias Boudinot, editor of the *Cherokee Phoenix*, were both working for acceptance of removal and were thus undermining the efforts of Ross, who wanted the tribe to resist removal, and if it were inevitable, to accept it only on the best possible terms.

In 1835, returning from a trip to Washington, Ross found his land and house occupied by a white man, who was able to present a legal title granted by Georgia. In the same year, the Ridge faction signed the Treaty of New Echota, accepting removal. In spite of the fact that it was signed by only a handful of Cherokee, in spite of opposition by the Cherokee who had already settled in the West, in spite of a protest signed by fourteen thousand Cherokee, and in spite of Henry Clay's opposition in the Senate, it was approved by the Senate in May, 1836, and signed by Jackson.

Under the conditions of the treaty, the Cherokee were given two years to prepare for removal, and Ross spent that time in further hopeless efforts to persuade the government to give the entire Cherokee people opportunity to accept or reject the treaty. The removal itself was flawed by looting, arson, and even grave-robbing by white squatters; disease was inevitable in the stockades that served as holding pens; of the thirteen thousand people who were removed, probably four thousand, including Ross's wife, died on the "Trail of Tears."

In his first years in Oklahoma, Ross devoted all of his energies to his efforts to unite three Cherokee factions: his own Nationalist followers, the Ridge-Boudinot faction that had accepted removal, and the Old Settlers, who had formed their own government and did not want to merge with the easterners. In July, 1839, a convention wrote a new constitution, virtually the same as that of 1827, and passed the Act of Union, which was ratified by all parties.

In spite of Ross's efforts for Cherokee unity, extremists in his own party exacted the traditional Cherokee penalty for selling tribal lands when they murdered Ridge and Boudinot. Ross was not involved in these crimes and did not condone them, but they were a source of disharmony in the tribe as long as he lived, and they were the primary reason that he had difficulty negotiating a new treaty with the government in an attempt to guarantee Cherokee claims to their Oklahoma lands. Ross had opposed removal because he knew that if the government were allowed to confiscate the Georgia lands they could confiscate lands in Oklahoma later. The government refused to agree to guarantees, however, be-

cause the followers of Ridge and Boudinot claimed that Ross was responsible for the murders; finally, in 1846, the Polk administration signed a treaty acceptable to all parties.

On September 2, 1844, Ross married Mary Bryan Stapler, daughter of a Delaware merchant, who bore him two children. The period from the 1846 treaty until the Civil War was a relatively happy time for Ross and for his people. He prospered as a merchant, raised livestock, and contributed much of his wealth to charities on behalf of poor Cherokee; under his guidance, seminaries and a Cherokee newspaper were established.

Though, by 1860, Ross owned fifty slaves, he opposed slavery on principle, and this issue during the 1850's was another source of tribal dissension, his full-blood followers opposing it and the mixed-bloods favoring it. When the war began and agents were working among the Oklahoma tribes on behalf of the Confederacy, Ross favored neutrality and adherence to the 1846 treaty. Only when the neighboring tribes accepted a Confederate alliance and the Cherokee nation was virtually surrounded was Ross willing to accept an alliance. However, in June, 1862, when Union forces finally arrived from Kansas, he welcomed them, though he and his family were forced to leave the Cherokee country as refugees when the Union forces withdrew. His four sons by his first wife served in the Union Army, and one of them died in a Confederate prison.

For the next three years, Ross was in the East working to persuade the Lincoln administration to send federal troops to the Cherokee country and to feed the six thousand pro-Union Cherokee who had taken refuge in Kansas. The last year of the war was a particularly unhappy time for him because of the illness of his wife, who died in July, 1865.

When Ross died on August 1, 1866, he was in Washington negotiating a peace treaty with the U.S. government and fighting the efforts of the Cherokee faction that had been pro-South in the war to get federal approval of a permanently divided tribe. The treaty that was proclaimed ten days after his death was his last contribution to the cause of Cherokee unity.

SIGNIFICANCE

John Ross was passionately devoted to the ancestral homeland of the Cherokee and to their cultural traditions, but when he recognized that removal might be inevitable he submitted to it in order to reestablish a unified Cherokee nation on the frontier; his people's achievement of a remarkable blend of tribal traditions and white man's political and economic methods was his greatest monument. Though he was "by blood" only one-eighth Cherokee, he grew up as a Cherokee, identified with the Cherokee people, and devoted his life to the great cause of tribal unity. The Cherokee tragedy, which remains permanently fixed as one of the most disgraceful acts of the American people, stands in contrast to the life of the man who was probably the most distinguished Native American political leader of the nineteenth century and who resembles Lincoln both in his political skills and in his vision of union as the only basis for peace and justice.

—*Robert L. Berner*

FURTHER READING

Eaton, Rachel Caroline. *John Ross and the Cherokee Indians*. Chicago: University of Chicago Press, 1921. A doctoral dissertation that concentrates on the Cherokees' political ordeal during Ross's lifetime. Essentially accurate, though apparently written without access to all the early documents.

Jahoda, Gloria. *The Trail of Tears*. New York: Wings Books, 1995. Recounts the Cherokees' forced removal and resettlement west of the Mississippi River.

McLoughlin, William G. *After the Trail of Tears: The Cherokees' Struggle for Sovereignty, 1839-1880*. Chapel Hill: University of North Carolina Press, 1993. Examines the social, cultural, and political history of the Cherokee Nation in the forty years after the tribe was forced to resettle in Oklahoma. Describes Ross's leadership during this period.

Meserve, John Bartlett. "Chief John Ross." *Chronicles of Oklahoma* 13 (December, 1935): 421-437. A brief but balanced account of Ross's life, though flawed by several errors in detail.

Moulton, Gary. *John Ross: Cherokee Chief*. Athens: University of Georgia Press, 1978. The best and most nearly definitive account of Ross's life and political struggles. Most useful because of its copious notes, which provide all the apparatus necessary for further study.

Starkey, Marion L. *The Cherokee Nation*. New York: Alfred A. Knopf, 1946. A semipopular account of Cherokee history from the beginnings to removal, with a final chapter devoted to later events. Written from the point of view of the missionaries to the Cherokee and perhaps overly sympathetic to the Treaty Party.

Wardell, Morris L. *A Political History of the Cherokee Nation, 1838-1907*. Norman: University of Oklahoma Press, 1938. A scholarly account of the Cherokee from removal to Oklahoma statehood. Refers to Ross in passing.

Woodward, Grace Steele. *The Cherokees*. Norman: University of Oklahoma Press, 1963. The best general account of the full range of Cherokee history, from first white contact to the late twentieth century. A fuller and much more balanced history than Starkey's book.

SEE ALSO: Henry Clay; Andrew Jackson; Sequoyah.

RELATED ARTICLES in *Great Events from History: The Nineteenth Century, 1801-1900:* February 21, 1828: *Cherokee Phoenix* Begins Publication; 1830-1842: Trail of Tears; May 28, 1830: Congress Passes Indian Removal Act; March 18, 1831, and March 3, 1832: Cherokee Cases; June 23, 1865: Watie Is Last Confederate General to Surrender.

CHRISTINA ROSSETTI
English poet

Rossetti's verse, characterized by a richly sensuous expression of spiritual longings, and her technical skill in writing musical yet vigorous lines gave her a unique voice among Victorian poets.

BORN: December 5, 1830; London, England
DIED: December 29, 1894; London, England
ALSO KNOWN AS: Christina Georgina Rossetti (full name); Ellen Alleyne (pseudonym)
AREA OF ACHIEVEMENT: Literature

EARLY LIFE

A lifelong Londoner, Christina Rossetti (roh-ZEHT-ee) was born in 1830 into an Anglo-Italian family. Her father, Gabriele Rossetti, an expatriate Italian poet, had become a professor of Italian at King's College, London. Her mother, Frances (née Polidori) Rossetti, a former governess, was the daughter of another Italian emigrant, Gaetano, and the sister of the John Polidori who had been Lord Byron's physician.

By maintaining stronger ties with frequent Italian guests—patriots, writers, and musicians—than with proper English middle-class families, Christina's parents gave her and her three older siblings an unconventional bilingual upbringing that encouraged artistic and intellectual pursuits. Christina's father, an apostate Roman Catholic, left the children's education and discipline to her mother, a fervent Anglican and a model Victorian wife. All four Rossetti children were precocious, producing illustrated stories and poems in their early years, with Christina and her older brother, Dante Gabriel, frequently competing in sonnet-writing contests. Christina and Gabriel are also said to have shared the most passionate or "Italian" temperament among the children.

A family crisis marked Christina's entry into adolescence. Her father's deteriorating eyesight and chronic bronchitis invalided him, seriously reducing the family income. Often delegated to stay at home as her father's caretaker, Christina herself fell ill in the summer of 1845. She became weak, suffering chest pains, palpitations, and a feeling of suffocation. Because of the indefiniteness of diagnosis from her several reputable physicians, biographers have tended to interpret this malady as a nervous breakdown brought on by entering puberty. A few trips to the seashore partly restored Christina's health, however. By 1847, she had written more than forty poems, which her grandfather Gaetano printed on his own press as *Verses*. Soon after this family publication, Christina followed her brother William into print in the *Athenaeum*, an important literary weekly, with two poems that Gabriel had urged her to submit. Thus at the age of seventeen, Christina publicly announced her calling as a poet.

LIFE'S WORK

From a spirited, even unruly child Christina grew into a self-contained young woman aspiring to her sister Maria's piety and sacrificing such worldly pleasures as chess, opera, and theater to Anglican High Church principles. Moreover, renunciation in the face of strong desire or attraction became an early theme in her poetry, as in her life. However, her letters reveal that her devoutness left intact both her sense of humor and her ambitions for her writing, which she worked on steadily all her life, except during times of serious illness.

Christina never chose to deny herself creative or intellectual sustenance—which in 1848 came to her through associating with members of the Pre-Raphaelite Brotherhood, formed by Dante Gabriel, William Holman Hunt, and John Everett Millais to challenge the old-fashioned academic art traditions of the day. The group's other members included three less-well-known artists and William Rossetti. In addition to participating in the lively aesthetic discussions of the group when it met at the Rossetti home, Christina occasionally served as a model for the painters and offered suggestions for the group's short-lived journal, *The Germ*. She also published seven lyrics in the journal. Her contributions to the first issue were unsigned; her contributions to the second and third issues were signed under the pseudonym Ellen Alleyne.

The year 1848 also brough Christina a marriage proposal from James Collinson, a Brotherhood painter known to her previously from church. She initially refused his proposal because of his Roman Catholic tendencies but later gave him an ambivalent acceptance, contingent upon his return to the Anglican fold. The engagement lasted until 1850, when Christina gave up on Collinson after his formal conversion to Roman Catholicism. More than a decade later, she would reject another marriage proposal because of her religious qualms; on the latter occasion it would be Charles Bagot Cayley's agnosticism.

As disciplined in familial as in religious matters, Christina joined her mother in teaching school in Somerset from 1851 to 1854 to improve the family's financial situation. Even during a period of depression following her broken engagement, the failure of the Somerset school venture, and the deaths of two grandparents and her father, Christina continued to write and to have individual poems accepted by various magazines and anthologies. Although she was relieved that her poor health spared her from having to work as a governess, she sought a wider horizon in 1854 by volunteering to assist the nursing work of Florence Nightingale in the Crimean War.

Christina was not quite twenty-four years at that time and she was rejected by Nightingale because of her youth. She then remained at home with her mother, her unmarried sister Maria, the family breadwinner William, and, eventually, two elderly aunts. Helping her mother run the household for two decades and then taking care of the older generation made Christina's life emphatically domestic, but she was neither sheltered from reality nor reclusive. Although more constrained than Gabriel and William, she nevertheless visited relatives and friends in England, traveled to France and Italy, undertook parish duties, continued to frequent her brothers' bohemian circles, took part in campaigns against child prostitution and vivisection, and did volunteer work at the St. Mary Magdalene Home for Fallen Women in Highgate. She socialized with—and won admiration from—such literary luminaries as Lewis Carroll, Robert Browning, Barbara Leigh Smith Bodichon, and Algernon Swinburne.

In 1862, Christina joined the ranks of recognized writers with her first published book, *Goblin Market, and Other Poems*, which Gabriel illustrated for her. Both critics and readers greeted the book enthusiastically. This was a happy period for Christina, as the volume's success coincided with her new engagement to Cayley. Four years later, *The Prince's Progress, and Other Poems* (1866), also illustrated by Gabriel, appeared to similar acclaim and established her as one of the period's foremost literati.

Middle age brought personal challenges in the midst of Christina's professional success. Even as her elderly companions were beginning to need more of her care, she herself was diagnosed in 1871 with Graves' disease, a deforming and enervating thyroid malfunction. When she and her mother felt compelled to find a new residence because of William's marriage to Lucy Madox Brown, an atheist, in 1874, Maria also left, to join an Anglican sisterhood. During that same year, Christina published her first volume of devotional prose,

Christina Rossetti. (Courtesy, The University of Texas at Austin)

Annus Domini, whose contents indicated her ever-increasing reliance on her religious faith for solace in adversity.

Before her death in 1894 from cancer, Christina saw into print a half-dozen other religious works and three collected editions of earlier poems, including the best-selling *Verses* of 1893. After being confined to her sickbed, she alternated between expressions of brave serenity and gloom about her fate. Toward the end, her nightly screams—perhaps from pain, perhaps from spiritual anguish—disturbed her closest neighbor. She finally died on December 29, 1894, at the age of sixty-four. After a funeral service that included the singing of one of her own poems, she was buried in Highgate Cemetery. Her only surviving sibling, William, supervised two posthumous anthologies of her verses.

SIGNIFICANCE

A year before Christina Rossetti's death, the *Athenaeum* extolled her as "one of the greatest of living poets," while

---

"GOBLIN MARKET"

The first and last stanzas of Christina Rossetti's Gothic masterpiece convey much of the flavor of the three-thousand-word poem.

Morning and evening
Maids heard the goblins cry:
"Come buy our orchard fruits,
Come buy, come buy:
Apples and quinces,
Lemons and oranges,
Plump unpecked cherries,
Melons and raspberries,
Bloom-down-cheeked peaches,
Swart-headed mulberries,
Wild free-born cranberries,
Crab-apples, dewberries,
Pine-apples, blackberries,
Apricots, strawberries;—
All ripe together
In summer weather,—
Morns that pass by,
Fair eves that fly;
Come buy, come buy:
Our grapes fresh from the vine,
Pomegranates full and fine,
Dates and sharp bullaces,
Rare pears and greengages,
Damsons and bilberries,
Taste them and try:
Currants and gooseberries,
Bright-fire-like barberries,
Figs to fill your mouth,
Citrons from the South,
Sweet to tongue and sound to eye;
Come buy, come buy."

. . . .

Life out of death.
That night long Lizzie watched by her,
Counted her pulse's flagging stir,
Felt for her breath,
Held water to her lips, and cooled her face
With tears and fanning leaves:

But when the first birds chirped about their eaves,
And early reapers plodded to the place
Of golden sheaves,
And dew-wet grass
Bowed in the morning winds so brisk to pass,
And new buds with new day
Opened of cup-like lilies on the stream,
Laura awoke as from a dream,
Laughed in the innocent old way,
Hugged Lizzie but not twice or thrice;
Her gleaming locks showed not one thread of grey,
Her breath was sweet as May
And light danced in her eyes.

Days, weeks, months, years
Afterwards, when both were wives
With children of their own;
Their mother-hearts beset with fears,
Their lives bound up in tender lives;
Laura would call the little ones
And tell them other early prime,
Those pleasant days long gone
Of not-returning time:
Would talk about the haunted glen,
The wicked, quaint fruit-merchant men,
Their fruits like honey to the throat
But poison in the blood;
(Men sell not such in any town:)
Would tell them how her sister stood
In deadly peril to do her good,
And win the fiery antidote:
Then joining hands to little hands
Would bid them cling together,
"For there is no friend like a sister
In calm or stormy weather;
To cheer one on the tedious way,
To fetch one if one goes astray,
To lift one if one totters down,
To strengthen whilst one stands."

Source: Christina Rossetti, *Goblin Market* (London: Macmillan, 1893).

the *Saturday Review* similarly numbered her among "the foremost poets of the age." As the writer of more than one thousand poems and eight books of prose, Rossetti was emphatically prolific. She also worked in an impressive range of genres: lyrical and narrative poems, children's verse, nonsense rhymes, religious poetry, short stories for both adults and children, prayers and religious commentary, and even several poems composed in Italian. Equally impressive was her technical expertise, which led her contemporaries to rank her along Alfred, Lord Tennyson, and Robert Browning. Two innovative hallmarks of Rossetti's style that pleased critics were her simple yet resonant diction and her reliance on short, irregularly rhymed lines.

Rossetti became the most popular devotional writer of her day. Meanwhile, in poems combining spiritual themes with sensuously textured imagery in the tradition of Tennyson and John Keats, she announced her Pre-Raphaelite affinities—which in her Gothic masterpiece *Goblin Market* and *The Prince's Progress* found far more critical approbation than had previously greeted Pre-Raphaelite works by William Morris, Swinburne, and her brother Gabriel.

Finally, as one of only four major nineteenth century Anglo-American women poets, Christina contributed to a growing tradition of professional female authorship. Along with Emily Brontë, Emily Dickinson, and Elizabeth Barrett Browning, she confirmed the possibility of women's genius in poetry. Like Barrett Browning before her, Christina Rossetti lived to see herself lauded for excellent craftsmanship in a jealously guarded masculine field and emulated by younger women.

—*Margaret Bozenna Goscilo*

FURTHER READING

Bellas, Ralph A. *Christina Rossetti*. Boston: Twayne, 1977. Overview of Rossetti's career that devotes separate chapters to her juvenilia, two sonnet sequences, devotional poems, short stories, children's verse, and religious prose.

Gilbert, Sandra M., and Susan Gubar. *The Madwoman in the Attic: The Woman Writer and the Nineteenth-Century Literary Imagination*. New Haven, Conn.: Yale University Press, 1979. A chapter titled "The Aesthetics of Renunciation" is a feminist exploration of the prose narrative *Maude* and *Goblin Market* that links Rossetti, Elizabeth Barrett Browning, and Emily Dickinson as voices of passionate renunciation.

Jones, Kathleen. *Learning Not to Be First: The Life of Christina Rossetti*. Gloucestershire: Windrush Press, 1991. A feminist reading of Rossetti's career, with emphasis on her friendships with other women and her affinities with such women writers as Elizabeth Barrett Browning, Laetitia Elizabeth Landon, and Dora Greenwell. Includes photographs.

Marsh, Jan. *Christina Rossetti: A Literary Biography*. London: Jonathan Cape, 1994. Detailed biography by a leading Pre-Raphaelite scholar that includes close readings of Rossetti's poems. Includes photographs.

Packer, Lona Mosk. *Christina Rossetti*. Berkeley: University of California Press, 1963. Focuses on its subject's emotional life and claims to solve many biographical conundrums by interpreting Rossetti's relationship with William Bell Scott as a romantic one. Includes photographs and reproductions of portraits.

Thomas, Frances. *Christina Rossetti*. Hanley Swan, England: Self-Publishing Association, 1992. Relies heavily on Rossetti's letters to her friends and information about her daily occupations to get to the complex person behind the saintly myth. Includes photographs of people and residences.

SEE ALSO: Barbara Leigh Smith Bodichon; The Brontë Sisters; Elizabeth Barrett Browning; Lord Byron; Lewis Carroll; Emily Dickinson; William Holman Hunt; John Keats; Daniel and Alexander Macmillan; William Morris; Florence Nightingale.

RELATED ARTICLE in *Great Events from History: The Nineteenth Century, 1801-1900:* Fall, 1848: Pre-Raphaelite Brotherhood Begins.

GIOACCHINO ROSSINI
Italian composer

Rossini was one of the greatest composers of Italian opera in the nineteenth century. In almost forty works for the operatic stage, he created some of the last and finest specimens of the opera buffa *and also numerous serious operas that laid the foundation for the ensuing generation of Italian Romantic composers. His brilliant overtures have enjoyed a separate life as concert pieces.*

BORN: February 29, 1792; Pesaro, Papal States (now in Italy)
DIED: November 13, 1868; Passy, France
ALSO KNOWN AS: Gioacchino Antonio Rossini (full name)
AREA OF ACHIEVEMENT: Music

EARLY LIFE

Gioacchino Rossini (rohs-see-nee) was the son of musicians: His father, Giuseppe, was a horn player, and his mother, Anna (née Guidarini), was a soprano who, though musically untutored, sang minor roles in provincial theaters. Rossini's childhood coincided with Napoleon I's Italian campaigns, and his hometown of Pesaro on the Adriatic changed hands numerous times; the elder Rossini, an enthusiastic republican, was briefly imprisoned by papal authorities in 1800. Despite vicissitudes, Rossini's early life was not unhappy. Tradition has it that the young Rossini was unusually high-spirited and prankish, early manifestations no doubt of a drollery that was to remain with him in maturity.

The Rossini family settled in Bologna in 1804. For Rossini, this was a stroke of good fortune: He was able in 1806 to enter the Liceo Musicale, one of the finest music schools in Italy. The fact that he had already acquired considerable prowess as a musician is attested by his election in the same year to the Accademia Filarmonica of Bologna, a remarkable honor for a fourteen-year-old. At the conservatory, Rossini's studies in counterpoint were directed by Padre Stanislao Mattei, a strict traditionalist whose rigorous method helped Rossini attain a well-regulated and fluent compositional technique.

Rossini's studies at the Liceo continued until 1810. By this time he had already completed his first opera, a serious work entitled *Demetrio e Polibio*, which would receive its first performance in 1812. Rossini's actual public debut as an opera composer was with a comic work, a one-act farce entitled *La cambiale di matrimonio* presented at the Teatro San Moisè in Venice in Novem-

ber, 1810. The opera was a triumph. Already the eighteen-year-old composer displayed evidence of the élan and wit that were to be the hallmarks of his later works. The success of *La cambiale di matrimonio* propelled Rossini into a mad whirl of opera composition: In the next twenty-six months, he composed six more comic works and established himself in the front rank of young composers. By age twenty-one, Rossini was a veteran of the operatic wars and a national celebrity; he was poised on the brink of international acclaim.

The larger-than-life Rossini personality had also begun to emerge. Witty and gregarious, Rossini cut a wide swath in society. Precocious in his interest in the opposite sex, he paid a price for his indulgences: Several venereal infections led to chronic urological problems in his middle years. Rossini was slender and attractive as a young man but soon fell prey to baldness and corpulence; all extant photographs show him well fleshed and bewigged.

LIFE'S WORK

Rossini emerged as a composer at a time when Italian opera was in transition. The *opera seria* (serious opera) as it had been cultivated in the eighteenth century was moribund; its rigidly conventionalized formality and its reliance on artificial mythological or classical plots caused it to wilt in the hotter artistic climate of the nineteenth century. *Opera buffa*, as it had been cultivated by Wolfgang Amadeus Mozart, was still a vital genre, but it had entered its final phase; it, too, was ultimately an expression of eighteenth century sensibilities.

Although Rossini remains most closely identified with *opera buffa* through the continuing appeal of works such as *The Barber of Seville* (1816), the clear majority of his operas after his apprentice phase were tragic or heroic works that may be viewed as attempts to recast the *opera seria* in nineteenth century terms. Ironically, Rossini himself remained ambivalent about the emerging Romantic style. Though he helped to shape the Romantic taste in librettos, and though he virtually invented the formal structure of the Romantic melodrama, he was reluctant to succumb fully to the wholesale emotional intensity of the Romantic style.

Nevertheless, the work that first brought Rossini international fame was the proto-Romantic *Tancredi*, a serious opera that was first performed at the Teatro La Fenice in Venice in February of 1813. The libretto, drawn from Voltaire and Torquato Tasso, presents a costume drama of no particular distinction, but it afforded Rossini the opportunity to experiment with new methods of formal organization. Most of the formal conventions that sustained Rossini in later works are here present at least in embryonic state. These forms include the opening choral introduction interrupted by a solo, the multipart ensemble finale, and the extended *scena* for principal characters. A large measure of *Tancredi*'s success had to do, however, with its sheer tunefulness. *Tancredi*'s act 1 cavatina "Di tanti palpiti," for example, became an international hit by nineteenth century standards.

The decade following the premiere of *Tancredi* in 1813 marked the peak of Rossini's productivity as a composer of Italian opera. Rossini completed twenty-five operas in this span, including comic gems such as *L'italiani in Algeri* (1813), *The Barber of Seville, La cenerentola* (1817), and dramatic or tragic works such as *Otello* (1816), *Mosè in Egitto* (1818), *La donna del lago* (1819), and *Semiramide* (1823). As Rossini moved from triumph to triumph, he attained a celebrity that was virtually without precedent in the music world. Stendhal was

Gioacchino Rossini. (Library of Congress)

guilty of only modest exaggeration when he wrote of Rossini in 1824:

> Napoleon is dead; but a new conqueror has already shown himself to the world; and from Moscow to Naples, from London to Vienna, from Paris to Calcutta, his name is constantly on every tongue.

The Barber of Seville was undoubtedly Rossini's comic masterpiece. Although the work was first given under the title *Almaviva* in order to discourage comparison with a popular opera on the same subject by Giovanni Paisiello, Rossini's work soon eclipsed the older opera in popularity and has remained his most frequently given stage work. The opera stands in the older *opera buffa* tradition, but it has a quality of manic humor that is uniquely Rossinian.

From late 1815 until 1823, Rossini made Naples the base of his operations; ten of nineteen operas produced during this span were written for Neapolitan stages. At Naples, he became romantically involved with one of his prima donnas, the soprano Isabella Colbran. Rossini and Colbran were married in 1822, but the union was not enduring, and separation followed quickly.

The enormous and unbroken popularity of *The Barber of Seville* has obscured the fact that most of Rossini's operas in the Neapolitan period were serious. Of particular note were *Otello* and *La donna del lago*. The former was Rossini's only Shakespearean opera, and though the libretto lamentably perverts William Shakespeare's drama, the score is one of Rossini's most ambitious efforts to synthesize music and text. The entire last act presents itself as a musicodramatic unit rather than as a string of pieces; Rossini himself considered it to be one of his finest achievements. *La donna del lago*, based on Sir Walter Scott's *The Lady of the Lake*, demonstrates Rossini's interest in the literature of his day and was evidently the first of the many nineteenth century operas inspired by the writings of Scott.

In the final phase of his career, Rossini was drawn to Paris. Although three of his four operas with French texts were in fact revisions of earlier Italian works, Rossini's last opera, *Guillaume Tell* (1829), was newly composed and is his largest, and arguably his greatest, work. The tale of the Swiss patriot William Tell loosely follows Friedrich Schiller's play of that name and provided Rossini with a grand canvas on which to work. He responded with some of his finest music. The overture, whose electrifying gallop at the close has become a cliché, is nevertheless a superb inspiration.

After *Guillaume Tell* came the so-called great renunciation: Rossini simply ceased to compose operas. Numerous explanations have been adduced to account for his abrupt retirement: that he had said all that he had to say, that he was uncomfortable with the advent of unbridled Romanticism, that he deplored the decline of vocal standards, that he was suffering from ill health. In all probability, each of these factors contributed to Rossini's decision.

The early years of Rossini's retirement were plagued by ill health. During this period, he was nursed solicitously by his new mistress, the former courtesan Olympe Pélissier, whom he married in 1846. During the mid-1850's, Rossini settled permanently in Paris. For the remainder of his life, Rossini was treated like a *grand seigneur*; his salon was a magnet for young composers, and his pungent observations and jests were widely circulated.

Only a few compositions date from the long retirement. The two most impressive are sacred works: the highly dramatic *Stabat mater* (1832) and the *Petite messe solennelle* (1853). Rossini also composed numerous epigrammatic and parodistic works for piano that he called *Péchés de vieillesse* (1835; sins of my old age).

SIGNIFICANCE

Of the great nineteenth century Italian opera composers, only the mature Giuseppe Verdi surpassed Gioacchino Rossini in sheer compositional inspiration. In style, wit, originality, brio, and technical fluency, Rossini was abundantly endowed. Where Rossini was able to concentrate these gifts—in the comic operas and the overtures—he was able to achieve both critical and popular success. Ironically, Rossini did his most original work in a genre—the romantic *melodrama*—for which he was not fully suited by taste and temperament. In works such as *Otello, La donna del lago*, and *Guillaume Tell*, Rossini charted the course for the next generation of opera composers. However, Rossini himself was reluctant to cross the threshold into the new age. His legacy is nevertheless substantial: His thirty-nine operas form a trove that has not yet been fully brought to light.

—*Steven W. Shrader*

FURTHER READING

Gossett, Philip. "Gioacchino Rossini." In *The New Grove Masters of Italian Opera*. New York, W. W. Norton, 1983. Gossett's seventy-page essay, together with a full list of works, constitutes a reworking of his earlier entry for *The New Grove Dictionary* and is perhaps the most reliable and up-to-date account of Rossini generally available.

Senici, Emanuele, ed. *The Cambridge Companion to Rossini*. New York: Cambridge University Press, 2004. Collection of essays about Rossini's life and music. The book is divided into four parts, with essays about Rossini's biography and reception, words and music (including essays on the librettos of his operas and his compositional methods), representative operas, and performance.

Servadio, Gaia. *Rossini*. New York. Carroll & Graf, 2003. Biography based on newly discovered material. Servadio focuses on Rossini's life, rather than his music, describing how he sought to overcome a poor and unhappy childhood by becoming a successful and prolific composer.

Stendhal. *Life of Rossini*. Translated and annotated by Richard N. Coe. New York: Orion Press, 1970. Stendhal's famous biography has the merits of contemporaneity and literary brilliance. It was, however, a work of polemical journalism, not of scholarship, and it is marred by many inaccuracies.

Till, Nicolas. *Rossini: His Life and Times*. New York: Hippocrene Books, 1983. This lavishly illustrated work is perhaps the best short introduction to Rossini's life and work for the general reader. Till provides excellent descriptions of Rossini's social and professional milieu and offers intelligent critical judgments couched in highly readable prose.

Toye, Francis. *Rossini: A Study in Tragi-comedy*. New York: Alfred A. Knopf, 1947. First published in 1934, Toye's work engagingly championed Rossini and his works at a time when the composer's stock among music critics was low. Though perhaps overly reliant on the three-volume study by Giuseppe Radiciotti in Italian, this genial work remains valuable.

Weinstock, Herbert. *Rossini: A Biography*. New York: Alfred A. Knopf, 1968. The most exhaustive account of Rossini's life in English, Weinstock's work is the product of impressive research and contains extensive notes, appendixes, and a lengthy bibliography.

SEE ALSO: Hector Berlioz; Gaetano Donizetti; Napoleon I; Jacques Offenbach; Niccolò Paganini; Sir Walter Scott; Stendhal; Giuseppe Verdi.

RELATED ARTICLE in *Great Events from History: The Nineteenth Century, 1801-1900:* February 20, 1816: Rossini's *The Barber of Seville* Debuts.

THE ROTHSCHILD FAMILY
German financiers

The Rothschild family developed one of the most successful banking and investment companies of all time. By locating branches in a number of major cities while keeping the business a family matter, they coordinated international operations and provided services to clients and governments that were unavailable elsewhere.

MAYER AMSCHEL ROTHSCHILD

BORN: February 23, 1744; Frankfurt am Main (now in Germany)
DIED: September 19, 1812; Frankfurt am Main
ALSO KNOWN AS: Mayer Amschel Bauer (birth name)

AMSCHEL MAYER ROTHSCHILD

BORN: June 12, 1773; Frankfurt am Main (now in Germany)
DIED: December 6, 1855; Frankfurt am Main

SALOMON MAYER ROTHSCHILD

BORN: September 9, 1774; Frankfurt am Main (now in Germany)
DIED: July 27, 1855; Paris, France

NATHAN MAYER ROTHSCHILD

BORN: September 16, 1777; Frankfurt am Main (now in Germany)
DIED: July 28, 1836; Frankfurt am Main

CARL MAYER ROTHSCHILD

BORN: April 24, 1788; Frankfurt am Main (now in Germany)
DIED: March 10, 1855; Naples, Kingdom of the Two Sicilies (now in Italy)
ALSO KNOWN AS: Karl Mayer Rothschild

JAMES MAYER ROTHSCHILD

BORN: May 15, 1792; Frankfurt am Main (now in Germany)
DIED: November 15, 1868; Paris, France
ALSO KNOWN AS: Jacob Mayer Rothschild
AREA OF ACHIEVEMENT: Business

EARLY LIVES

Mayer Amschel Rothschild was born in the Frankfurt ghetto in 1744. His parents died only eleven years later of smallpox, but traveling with his peddler father had already had an impact on the boy. In the patchwork of principalities making up the eighteenth century Holy Roman Empire, even a minor trader might visit several countries in a day or two. Mayer Amschel was thus introduced at an early age to the mysteries of money exchanging. Although his parents had enrolled him in a Jewish religious school that prepared students to be scholars, after their deaths he was able to convince relatives that he would be better off in a business career. In 1757, an apprenticeship at the Oppenheimer Bank in Hannover was arranged. He returned to Frankfurt in 1763.

Mayer Amschel had become a dealer in rare coins, and in 1765 a connection made in Hannover arranged for him to display his wares for Prince William of Hesse, whose avarice was legendary. For four years, Mayer Amschel sold coins at bargain prices to the prince, getting little for his trouble. Later, however, he was able to buy the house the family had been renting, which became his home and office. He had an illustrated catalog printed. Most important, he married Gutle Schnapper in 1770. The union was fruitful: Five sons and five daughters grew to adulthood. The sons—Amschel, Salomon, Nathan, Carl, and James—would build the family business into a worldwide concern.

Mayer Amschel continued to court William, who was combining enterprises such as renting mercenaries to England for use in America and an inheritance to become enormously wealthy. His break came because of a friendship with Carl Buderus, William's chief financial adviser. Mayer Amschel had given Buderus a valuable coin, and upon making a second visit to William in his new establishment in Kassel, Mayer Amschel got his first commission. This was the beginning of a relationship that proved extremely profitable to all concerned. By the 1790's, the family was comfortably well off and about to embark on the enterprise that would make it an international financial force.

LIVES' WORK

Annoyed by the haughtiness of an English cotton salesperson, the twenty-one-year-old Nathan resolved to go to England and conduct business for the family; he would become the most successful of the entire clan. The stocky, powerful Nathan was roundheaded with coarse features; his speech was crude, and he never lost his German accent. Interested in little but business, he was soon established as a major financier and trader in a variety of commodities, taking good advantage of the demands created by the French Revolutionary Wars. On the Continent, the Rothschilds were of enormous service in concealing valuables from the emperor's rapacious agents, but in England Nathan, at least at times, used the funds transferred for investment in bonds in more speculative investments. When he had to account for sums, he bought the requested bonds, making up the interest so that William of Hesse earned as much as if the bonds had been bought when ordered. This was all arranged in partnership with Carl Buderus, who helped hide the operation from William and became rich in the process.

The Rothschild firm was now extremely successful, thanks to its financial manipulations. Another factor was the increased business provoked in London and Frankfurt by the French blockade, which forced the opening of new markets as well as shifting old ones to Rothschild advantage. In 1810, the firm was renamed M. A. Rothschild and Sons, with Mayer Amschel and the four sons still in Frankfurt having shares—Nathan, in enemy territory, could get nothing legally but was promised his share when the political situation made it possible.

Mayer Amschel Rothschild. (Library of Congress)

Nathan had, the year before, established his own bank in England and was beginning to be brought into government financial arrangements. In 1814, he had a hand in the very profitable process of collecting loans and transferring the funds to the duke of Wellington in the Peninsula. In addition, he created an excellent system of couriers, carrier pigeons, and other means of communication, which usually meant that he had information about European events before his competitors and often was able to buy or sell government bonds to advantage. While Nathan was expanding the holdings of the English branch, his brothers were spreading family institutions around Europe. James had settled in Paris, where he had had some opportunity to help with Nathan's efforts to supply money to Wellington in Spain.

In 1819, a wave of liberal-nationalist feeling broke over the German Confederation, threatening the Rothschilds both as bankers who supported the conservative policies of Metternich and as Jews. The family was urged to abandon Frankfurt for Paris. Upon hearing of this, Metternich sent word that the Rothschilds would be welcome in Vienna, and subsequently he arranged for the Rothschild bank to raise an enormous loan for the Austrian government. Despite some troubling moments and charges of corruption, the bonds involved proved profitable for the bank and a good investment for purchasers. As the loan required much attention, Salomon opened a branch of the bank in Vienna. In 1821, Carl, the least forceful of the brothers, became the agent for the bank to raise a loan in Naples to help the Austrian government with the cost of maintaining an occupation to prevent revolution. His success not only improved the standing of the family in Vienna but also resulted in his remaining to open a new branch. In 1822, Metternich requested that the emperor bestow baronies on the five brothers.

Amschel, the only brother to be orthodox or slim, remained in Frankfurt, eventually becoming treasurer to the German Confederation and extremely influential in the financial policy-making of the Prussian government. The Rothschilds had become part of the economic and social elite.

Trouble arose when the Revolution of 1830 toppled the Bourbon government, for James Rothschild, deeply involved with government finance, did not believe the government was in trouble. Initial losses were serious, but the excellent communications system maintained by the family allowed Nathan and Salomon to sell French securities early and to rebuy at great profits. James's dependable, fiscally conservative management soon caught the attention of the July Monarch, Louis-Philippe, and James was brought back into a major role in French government finance.

The death of Nathan, while in Frankfurt to attend the 1836 wedding of his son Lionel, left James in Paris as the head of the family. Increasingly involved in the finances of both the government and Louis-Philippe personally, James's fortune approached fifty million pounds. His circle of friends included both aristocrats and intellectuals such as George Sand and Honoré de Balzac. Always pressed to support one cause or another, James gave generously only to be criticized for meanness by the rejected and unsatisfied.

In the middle of the century, the Rothschild business interest turned to railroads, resulting in much profit in Austria, Italy, and France. Efforts were also made to support international peace, as in 1840 when in Paris and Vienna the governments were soothed so that war would not destroy prosperity. In 1848, Carl persuaded the government of Naples to make liberal concessions to the revolutionaries and defuse the threat that in so many places led to violence.

In Paris, revolution again proved expensive. Not only was money invested in government securities at risk but also James's villa in the Bois de Boulogne was burned by the mob. In Vienna, Salomon had to abandon his house to the mob; Salomon went to Frankfurt, never returning to Vienna. James clung to his base in Paris and, by attaching himself to Eugène Cavaignac, minister of war in the new revolutionary government, was soon back in the thick of politics and finance. Having been the bitter foes of Napoleon I, the Rothschilds were hardly eager for the advent of another. Their hopes were frustrated, however, when Louis-Napoleon Bonaparte was elected president of the Second Republic and then in 1852 declared himself Emperor Napoleon III.

In England, Lionel (1808-1879), already prominent in the business when his father died, became senior partner aided by his brothers, Mayer, Anthony, and Nathaniel. The second English generation began to move the family into traditional English upper-class patterns. Estates were purchased; Rothschilds were also becoming known for charity, art collecting, and hunting. Although the patriarch might not have approved of his sons' charitable impulses or artistic and sporting avocations, he would have been warmly in favor of their efforts to further the removal of civil and social disabilities from Jews. Although few Rothschilds felt much affinity for the outward forms of religion, they remained sensitive to their heritage.

Lionel, who devoted himself to the business, was urged by his friend, the great conservative politician Benjamin Disraeli, to seek a seat in the House of Commons. As members had to take an oath "on my true faith as a Christian," Jews were barred. In 1847, Lionel was elected to Parliament as a Liberal candidate for the City of London (the business district of the metropolis); although Commons passed a bill to allow him to take his seat, the bill was rejected by the House of Lords. Six times over the next eleven years, Lionel was reelected only to be turned away, despite the support of Disraeli. Finally in 1858, after a seventh electoral triumph, the Lords yielded, and Lionel became the first practicing Jew to be a member of Parliament.

Membership in Parliament was only one element of becoming prominent in English society. The upper classes were tied together by relationships forged in public schools (the equivalent of private preparatory schools in the United States) and the two universities. As the University of Oxford had a religious test for graduation, the University of Cambridge was the institution for those of nonorthodox religious opinions; Cambridge did, however, require attendance at Anglican chapel.

Although exceptions had been made for Lionel's brother Mayer and at least one other Jew, the requirement was not dropped by the university until 1856, and even then individual colleges could retain it. The change facilitated the matriculation of Lionel's son Nathan Mayer (called Natty) in 1859. Having distinguished himself socially at Cambridge and certainly having no lack of wealth, Natty made himself a force in Liberal politics and in 1885 became the first Jewish peer. His cousin Hannah married the earl of Rosebery, a future prime minister, in 1878. Thus by the end of the nineteenth century, the Rothschilds were not only among the most wealthy of the English but also were firmly ensconced among the social and political elite.

On the Continent, Rothschild fortunes were more mixed during the middle years of the nineteenth century. In 1855, three of the original five brothers died: Carl of Naples, Salomon of Vienna, and Amschel of Frankfurt. The family was not quickly welcomed into the confidences of Napoleon III's government, although James's personal tie to the Empress Eugénie prevented complete ostracism. Although the French Rothschilds were frozen out of the organization of the Crédit Mobilier, a new French financial institution that, with government support, was enormously successful, Anselm, the son of Salomon of Vienna, took the lead in developing the Kreditanstalt, a similar business in Vienna.

By the late 1850's, a third generation—Alphonse of Paris (James lived until 1868), Anselm of Vienna, Lionel of London, and Mayer Carl of Frankfurt—were cooperating as well as the original brothers had. The Italian War of 1859-1860 strained the Crédit Mobilier, resulting in a cosmetic reconciliation between the emperor and the Rothschilds. The same war began Italian unification, and, with the collapse of Naples as an independent state, the Rothschild Bank there was closed. It would not be reopened.

A growing public role was common for the family during the late nineteenth century. The Franco-Prussian War (1870-1871) did the Rothschild business no real harm and, because the bank managed the payment of the French indemnity, in the long run resulted in a profit. In England, Alfred Rothschild was appointed a director of the Bank of England in 1868, and, when Natty became a peer, his cousin Ferdinand replaced him in Parliament.

The end of the century found Rothschilds still running the family business but pursuing widely divergent non-business interests. For example, Edmond devoted his time and money to supporting the establishment of colonies of poor Jews in Palestine, Lionel Walter (1868-1937) became well known as a naturalist, and Henri (1872-1947) was a successful physician and playwright.

SIGNIFICANCE

The Rothschild family holds an extraordinary place in the world of international finance. In less than fifty years, the family went from poverty in the Frankfurt ghetto to control of one of the richest and most powerful banks in the world. Further, the family held its place throughout the turbulent nineteenth century. The Rothschild Bank was an early example of an international company with the twist that its branches were all controlled directly by family members and operated with an eye to the benefit of the entire clan. It is not surprising that, with their wealth and excellent communications system, the family was involved in the public financial operations in all the countries in which they had banks. More unusual is that, despite some use of bribery, the Rothschilds do not seem to have enriched themselves via corruption. The members of the family have generally been committed to serious public service as well as to profit-making.

Rothschilds have also done much to eliminate discrimination against Jews. Never stinting in the use of money and renown in the cause of coreligionists, they accomplished much. Elimination of restrictions on Jewish property holding in Habsburg territories; access to the

Parliament, university, and peerage in England; and membership in the social elite of France are only some of their achievements. If noblesse oblige can be applied to the status of wealth, then it seems appropriate for the four generations of Rothschilds between 1758 and 1900.

—*Fred R. van Hartesveldt*

FURTHER READING

Corti, Count Egon Caesar. *The Rise of the House of Rothschild.* Translated by Brian Lunn and Beatrix Lunn. London: Victor Gollancz, 1928. An account of the early years of the Rothschild rise to prominence and wealth. Its focus on the first generations makes it particularly useful, because the early years are generally less well known.

Cowles, Virginia. *The Rothschilds: A Family of Fortune.* New York: Alfred A. Knopf, 1973. A popular family history recounting the story of the Rothschilds from their origins in eighteenth century Frankfurt to multinational prominence during the mid-twentieth century. The book is well written and corrects some of the most common myths about the Rothschilds, but it does leave other legends untouched.

Davis, Richard. *The English Rothschilds.* Chapel Hill: University of North Carolina Press, 1983. The author, an excellent scholar, based this book on the Rothschild family papers and a detailed knowledge of the period; the style makes it a volume for both the general reader and the serious student. There is no better source of information or bibliography for the English branch of the family.

Ferguson, Niall. *The House of Rothschild: Money's Prophets, 1798-1848.* New York: Penguin Books, 1999.

_____. *The House of Rothschild: The World's Banker, 1849-1998.* Rev. ed. New York: Penguin Books, 2000. Meticulously detailed, balanced, and readable account of the Rothschild family's rise and decline. Focuses on the family's public career, not on the personal and psychological aspects of individual family members.

Lottman, Herbert R. *The French Rothschilds: The Great Banking Dynasty Through Two Turbulent Centuries.* New York: Crown, 1995. Focuses on the French branch of the family, providing a detailed and accessible chronicle of its history from the reign of Napoleon Bonaparte through the government of François Mitterrand.

Morton, Frederic. *Rothschilds: A Family Portrait.* New York: Atheneum, 1962. Useful account of the family's history. The general focus makes it particularly desirable for the study of the family rather than of individual members.

Roth, Cecil. *The Magnificent Rothschilds*. London: Robert Hale, 1939. Long the standard general history of the family, this book, while still valuable, is dated. It is a complete, well-researched, and well-written account.

SEE ALSO: Honoré de Balzac; Benjamin Disraeli; Theodor Herzl; Metternich; Napoleon I; Napoleon III; George Sand; Duke of Wellington.

RELATED ARTICLES in *Great Events from History: The Nineteenth Century, 1801-1900:* July 26, 1858: Rothschild Is First Jewish Member of British Parliament; February, 1896-August, 1897: Herzl Founds the Zionist Movement.

HENRI ROUSSEAU
French painter

Rousseau was the best known of the "naïve" artists of the late nineteenth century. His deceptively primitive paintings possessed a mysterious poetry that transcended their often banal subject matter and childlike technique to inspire such later artistic movements as Surrealism.

BORN: May 21, 1844; Laval, France
DIED: September 2, 1910; Paris, France
ALSO KNOWN AS: Henri-Julien-Félix Rousseau (full name); Le Douanier (The Customs Officer)
AREA OF ACHIEVEMENT: Art

EARLY LIFE

When Henri-Julien-Félix Rousseau was born, his father, Julien, worked as a tinsmith and lived in Beuchheresse Gate, a remnant of the old fortified wall that had once surrounded the French town of Laval. Never financially well off, Julien had debts that grew to be so overwhelming that his creditors seized his house when Henri was only seven years old. The Rousseau family then left Laval, leaving young Henri as a boarder at the local school. He proved to be a below-average student but did win several medals for art and singing.

Rousseau left school when he was fifteen and obtained a job in a lawyer's office in Angers, where he worked for three years before signing up for a seven-year tour in the army in 1863. He later claimed that he had served with French forces in Mexico, but this seems to have been the product of his desire to promote himself rather than a historical fact. Rousseau married a young woman named Clémence from Saint-Germain-en-Laye in 1869 while still in the army, and the young couple settled in Paris after his discharge from the service in 1871. Although he initially resumed his premilitary occupation as a law clerk, Rousseau soon managed to obtain a position manning one of the toll booths that marked the entry

into Paris. His nickname, *le douanier* (the customs collector), derived from this job with the Paris Municipal Toll Service.

Although Rousseau settled comfortably into his role as a minor functionary, his personal life contained a great deal of tragedy. Clémence bore nine children in rapid succession, but only one, a daughter named Julia, survived to adulthood. Seven of their other children died in infancy, and one son lived to be eighteen. Clémence died giving birth to the last of these ill-fated children. Rousseau would never marry again, although he would pursue a number of women throughout the rest of his life and unsuccessfully propose to many of them.

Rousseau later claimed that it was his lack of financial security that forced him to take the position as a toll booth collector and temporarily forsake his love of art. However, his undemanding job did provide him with ample time to pursue his hobby, and he frequently took time off work to paint. As he practiced, he grew increasingly confident in his talent and began thinking of making painting his full-time vocation. The death of Clémence appears to have pushed him to make his decision. Shortly after her death, he retired from the customs service in 1885, sent his two surviving children to live with relatives in Angers, and devoted himself exclusively to his art.

LIFE'S WORK

Rousseau marked his entry as a professional artist by exhibiting a number of his paintings at the official Salon des Artistes Français in 1885. He considered himself an "academic" painter at the time and had received advice and encouragement from two fairly prominent painters of this school, Gérôme and Félix Clément. However, his work received a hostile reception at the salon. Spectators slashed two of his paintings with knives,

Henri Rousseau. (Library of Congress)

and the judges had all of his works removed from the exhibition and declared that they were not up to the standards of the salon.

Most artists would have given up in the face of such universal condemnation of their work. However, if this hostile reception bothered Rousseau, he gave no indication in public. He did abandon his goal to exhibit at the official salon and instead began to show his work at the newly created Salon des Indépendants, an annual art exhibit that showcased the work of new artists. The new salon did not have a jury, so nearly all who wanted to exhibit their work were free to do so without fear of rejection. Rousseau took advantage of this "open door" policy and exhibited four of his paintings at the 1886 session of the Salon des Indépendants. Even though the public and critics still ignored his work, he sincerely believed that

he was part of the artistic community since he had now shown his paintings in a public exhibit.

Rousseau's difficulty in gaining recognition for his work stemmed from the fact that it was difficult to ascertain what he was trying to do. Although he claimed to be a painter in the classic academic style, his work did not adhere at all to the standards of this school. His paintings often demonstrated a childlike technique that included glaring disproportions in perspective and exaggerated characterizations. His subject matter was often banal, drawn frequently from book and catalog illustrations that attracted his eye. He often portrayed human characters in stiff, unnatural poses and simplified their facial expressions in an almost cartoonish manner. Even more disturbing for many of his contemporaries was the fact that it was never clear whether Rousseau's technique represented an intentional distortion of reality or merely reflected a severely limited talent.

Rousseau did not appear to have been upset by the criticism leveled at his work. Even though critics accused him of "painting with his feet" and viciously attacked every new painting that he presented at the annual shows of the Salon des Indépendants, he continued to remain completely oblivious to their barbs. Many scholars agree that his immunity to criticism was the product of his naïve personality and have claimed that he frequently mistook sarcastic comments as praise.

The founders of the avant-garde movement in France, notably the playwright Alfred Jarry and the journalist Guillaume Apollinaire, took Rousseau under their wing and promoted his work. It was through their efforts that Rousseau met such innovative contemporary artists as Pablo Picasso, Paul Gauguin, and Camille Pissarro—all of whom admired aspects of his work. This acceptance by a segment of the avant-garde community buttressed Rousseau's own estimation of his work, but it brought him little financial success. His entry into this bohemian community also proved to be a mixed blessing. Many of his new "friends" exploited his childlike naïveté to pull a series of pranks on him. For example, Gauguin once told Rousseau that he had been awarded a government commission for a painting.

Rousseau believed that story without question and promptly went to the Ministry of Fine Arts to receive his money and instructions. On another occasion, one of his friends sent him a phony letter from the president of France inviting him to dinner. Rousseau blithely went to the president's mansion at the appointed day and time, only to be turned away at the door. Rousseau would later claim that the invitation had been real but that he had forgotten to wear formal attire and had been asked to come back another day.

These pranks never caused Rousseau to reject his new friends. In fact, beginning in 1907, he began to hold "soirées familiales et artistiques"—parties to which he invited everyone whom he knew. These parties became celebrated events on the Left Bank in Paris and regularly attracted a large number of artists and intellectuals, including Georges Braque and Picasso. At the same time, Rousseau's reputation as a painter began to improve, thanks primarily to the efforts of Apollinaire, who tirelessly championed his work.

Certain critics began to identify Rousseau with the fauvist movement (which also included Henri Matisse and Braque), and the young painters of this school also accepted Rousseau as one of their own. In fact, when a collection of fauvist paintings was organized for the 1905 Salon d'Automne, Rousseau's *The Hungry Lion* (1905) was accorded a place of honor next to the work of Matisse, Braque, Georges Roualt, and Raoul Dufy. This acceptance was highlighted by a huge banquet given by Picasso in Rousseau's honor in 1908. Although this event was partially put on in jest, it nonetheless reflected the warm feelings that the Parisian artistic community held for the eccentric and guileless *le douanier*.

Despite a growing appreciation of his work in certain sophisticated quarters, Rousseau still faced a great deal of scorn from mainstream critics and the general public during the last years of his life and found it difficult to support himself through his art. When he died in 1910 from blood poisoning, he was buried in a pauper's grave in Paris. One year later, painter Robert Delaunay and Rousseau's former landlord collected enough money from Rousseau's former acquaintances to buy him a regular cemetery plot and a small tombstone. In 1924, his remains and tombstone were moved to the Parc de la Perrin in Laval.

SIGNIFICANCE

After Rousseau's death, critics and the public alike finally realized the value of his work. His use of color, his attention to detail, and his unusual renderings of often banal subjects revealed a fresh artistic vision that is often stunning in its impact on the viewer. One is struck by the innocence and enthusiasm in his work, characteristics that would later gain the admiration of the Surrealists and expressionists.

In Rousseau's most famous paintings, such as *The Dream* (1910), *The Sleeping Gypsy* (1897), *The Football*

Players (1908), and *Carnival Evening* (1886), an aura of mystery and wonder pervades the canvas, challenging the viewers' sense of reality and forcing them to acknowledge Rousseau's alternative interpretation of the world. Henri Rousseau viewed the world around him in a very original way, and his art, which embodied his unique view, still impresses viewers with its combination of simplicity, drama, and insight. His artistic legacy has outlasted the criticisms of his numerous contemporary detractors and continues to inspire generation after generation of painters. Rousseau always knew that he was a talented painter; it has just taken the rest of the world a little time to catch up with him.

—*Christopher E. Guthrie*

FURTHER READING

Adriani, Götz. *Henri Rousseau.* Translated by Scott Kleager and Jenny Marsh. New Haven, Conn.: Yale University Press, 2001. This book accompanied an exhibit of Rousseau's work at the Kuntshalle Tübingen in Tübingen, Germany. Götz, director of the Kuntshalle Tübingen, provides an introductory essay discussing Rousseau's life in Paris, his method of painting, and the critical reception of his work. Götz also analyzes the fifty-nine paintings featured in the exhibit and other paintings by Rousseau. Contains full-color reproductions of the fifty-nine paintings and photographs of Rousseau, his friends, and acquaintances.

Alley, Ronald. *Portrait of a Primitive: The Art of Henri Rousseau.* New York: Dutton, 1978. Alley provides a straightforward narrative of the life and work of Rousseau that emphasizes his contribution to the primitive art movement of the twentieth century.

Ehrlich, Doreen. *Henri Rousseau.* New York: Smithmark, 1995. This work stresses that Rousseau's work had an important influence on future generations of artists despite his nonacceptance by the art establishment during his lifetime.

Keay, Carolyn. *Henri Rousseau, le douanier.* New York: Rizzoli, 1976. This book is short on biographical details, concentrating instead on a thorough examination of Rousseau's paintings and future influence.

Rich, Daniel. *Henri Rousseau.* New York: Museum of Modern Art, 1946. This is the first book in English to recognize the importance of Rousseau's work in shaping subsequent artistic movements in the twentieth century.

Schmalenbach, Werner. *Henri Rousseau: Dreams of the Jungle.* New York: International Book Import Service, 1998. Schmalenbach examines the jungle paintings that Rousseau produced late in his career and investigates the issue of their inspiration and influence.

Shattuck, Roger. *The Banquet Years: The Origins of the Avant-Garde in France, 1885 to World War I.* New York: Vintage Books, 1968. Shattuck argues that Rousseau, along with Guillaume Apollinaire, Erik Satie, and Alfred Jarry, personified the modernist movement in France during the late nineteenth century.

Vallier, Dora. *Henri Rousseau.* New York: Crown, 1979. This book offers a comprehensive analysis of Rousseau's painting. The text draws heavily on the artist's own writings about his work.

SEE ALSO: Paul Gauguin; Camille Pissarro.

RELATED ARTICLES in *Great Events from History: The Nineteenth Century, 1801-1900:* May 15, 1863: Paris's Salon des Refusés Opens; 1892-1895: Toulouse-Lautrec Paints *At the Moulin Rouge.*

JOHN RUSKIN
English writer

Ruskin was the most influential critic of art and architecture in the nineteenth century, promoting the notion that art had a moral purpose; as a social critic, he worked to undercut notions of laissez-faire economics and utilitarianism, championing the dignity of individual workers and the need for national programs of education and welfare.

BORN: February 8, 1819; London, England
DIED: January 20, 1900; Coniston, Lancashire, England
AREAS OF ACHIEVEMENT: Art, social reform

EARLY LIFE

John Ruskin's parents, wine merchant John James Ruskin and his wife Margaret, were convinced that their child was destined for greatness. With this future in mind, they reared him in sheltered comfort, keeping him from activities that might lead to injury, affording him few opportunities to play with children his own age. Young John read the Bible with his devout mother, who believed he would one day be a great divine, and listened to the works of Sir Walter Scott and other literary luminaries read by his father, who thought John destined for fame as a poet. In the isolation of his home, Herne Hill, outside London, Ruskin wrote poetry and sketched for amusement. There, too, he was privately tutored in preparation for entry into Oxford.

Business activities meant frequent trips for his father, and as a child Ruskin had ample opportunity to see both Great Britain and later the Continent in his parents' company. On a trip through France in 1835, he met Adèle Domecq, eldest daughter of his father's business partner; unaccustomed to the company of young females, Ruskin fell helplessly and confusedly in love. For several years

he harbored deep feelings for Adèle, but he was eventually disappointed when she married a French nobleman in 1840.

Meanwhile, Ruskin was already writing on subjects that would occupy him for much of his adult life: art and architecture. He had published scientific papers when he was only fifteen, and had already published poetry before he enrolled at Oxford in 1837. While a student there, he began a series for *Architectural Magazine* titled "The Poetry of Architecture"; these essays stress the importance of landscape art as an expression of the artist's view of nature, not mere slavish imitation—a theme he would elaborate in his multivolume *Modern Painters* (1843-1860).

Ruskin's life at Oxford was by most standards unusual. Friends at Christ Church College knew him as a friendly sort, slender, with reddish hair, and pale blue eyes accentuated by the blue cravat he wore. Though he resided at the college, his mother had taken rooms nearby to oversee his education. For three years, Ruskin strove for the Newdigate Prize for poetry, largely at his father's insistence, winning the prize in 1839. However, he found his preparation for Oxford insufficient in some areas and eventually had to take a leave of absence to recover from a stress-related illness. Not until 1842 did he receive a bachelor's degree, taking a double fourth in classics and mathematics.

LIFE'S WORK

Ruskin's emergence into the public forum came as a result of his passion for art. Long an admirer of the iconoclastic painter J. M. W. Turner, in 1842 Ruskin found himself compelled to undertake a systematic defense of the artist to rebut a savage review of Turner's work. At the same time, his family moved to Denmark Hill, which was to be Ruskin's home for three decades. There he wrote diligently what eventually became the first of a multivolume work explaining the principles that characterize great art: power, imitation, truth, beauty, and relation. The first volume of *Modern Painters* was published in 1843; Ruskin identified himself on the title page simply as "A Graduate of Oxford," ostensibly to mask the fact that he was so young to write so authoritatively.

Modern Painters was favorably received, and Ruskin set about immediately to continue his study. In 1845, he was allowed to travel to the Continent without his parents for the first time. In Italy he studied the works of antiquity and the Renaissance, a period for which Ruskin had great antipathy. He also spent considerable time studying the architecture of the cities through which he traveled. As a consequence, the second volume of *Modern Painters* did not follow slavishly the plan set out in the first volume and implied in its title; instead, Ruskin digressed to discuss the art he had observed during his more recent trips.

The success of his work made Ruskin popular socially, and his parents hoped he would eventually marry Charlotte Lockhart, granddaughter of Sir Walter Scott. Ruskin, however, had other ideas; he fell in love with Euphemia ("Effie") Gray, daughter of a Perth businessperson. After some months of awkward courtship, they were married, on April 10, 1848.

Marriage did not change Ruskin's lifestyle greatly; he continued his travels and writings, preparing studies of architecture that appeared in 1849 as *The Seven Lamps of Architecture*. Further investigations, and deeper thought about the relationship between great buildings and those who built them, resulted in the three volumes published in 1851-1853 as *The Stones of Venice*. In the work, Ruskin argues that one can read a city's history in its architecture, and make judgments about a society based on the kind of buildings it erects. During this same period, Ruskin began what was to be a lifelong defense of the Pre-Raphaelite painters and poets.

Meanwhile, relations between Ruskin and his wife deteriorated, as John's parents found their daughter-in-law an interloper in their close-knit family, a view their son came to share. By 1854, Effie could no longer stand the constant upbraiding and mental harassment; she fled back to her family, initiating a suit for annulment on the grounds that the marriage had never been consummated. Ruskin did not contest the suit. Two years later, Effie married the painter John Everett Millais, with whom she had a large family.

John Ruskin.

Freed from the constraints of married life, Ruskin returned to his parents' home and resumed work on *Modern Painters*. The third volume appeared in January, 1856; the fourth followed in April. In these books, Ruskin stated clearly his belief that great art can be produced only by men who feel acutely and nobly. At the same time, he began developing what was to become an important thesis in his later works: the inextricable relationship between art and the economy.

In 1857, Ruskin spent considerable time cataloging the nineteen thousand drawings that Turner had bequeathed to the nation upon his death in 1851. During that same year, Ruskin delivered a series of lectures in Manchester. In them, he argued for public patronage of the arts, straying from strict commentary about art to remark on the status of Great Britain's economy and the ways in which the masses were being exploited and impoverished.

By 1860, Ruskin had finally finished *Modern Painters*. In the seventeen years during which he worked on this magnum opus, he had grown significantly in the appreciation of various artists, developed a moralistic theory of art and architecture, and suffered several personal setbacks. Never one to deal well with women, Ruskin found himself associating often with young ladies, even girls; his affiliation with Margaret Bell's girls' school at Winnington was one way in which he satisfied his psychological needs to share such company. A chance meeting in 1858 led to his infatuation with ten-year-old Rose La Touche. For more than a decade he pursued her affection, eventually proposing marriage when she turned eighteen (he was forty-seven at the time). Her continual rejection brought anguish to Ruskin, an anguish that found its way into his public writings through a series of private symbols and obscure autobiographical references.

Though he had spoken publicly and written often about the state of the economy for some time before 1860, in that year Ruskin emerged as a major critic of current economic and social programs. In the fifth volume of *Modern Painters*, he launched what would amount to a crusade, with himself cast in the role of Saint George against the dragon of a country obsessed with money and unwilling to recognize the dignity of its laborers. Meanwhile, Ruskin composed a series of essays on political economy for the new *Cornhill Magazine*. However, these were too controversial, and the editor, William Makepeace Thackeray, was forced to cancel them after several had appeared. Undaunted, Ruskin published the complete set in 1862 in a volume titled *Unto This Last*.

Ruskin's father objected to his son's new field of inquiry, and the early 1860's were difficult years. The senior Ruskin's death in 1864 freed Ruskin from constant criticisms but left him to care for his mother until she died in 1871. To help at Denmark Hill, Ruskin's cousin Joan Agnew came for a brief visit—and stayed almost constantly for the rest of the century, first assisting with Mrs. Ruskin, then serving as a younger companion and later nurse for Ruskin himself. Their relationship, which became quite intimate in its own way, survived Joan's marriage to Arthur Severn.

Throughout the 1860's Ruskin devoted himself to writing about economic issues, trying to relate the disparate branches of his studies into a coherent vision of human society. In 1867, he began writing "open letters" on a variety of social and economic issues. The first series he collected in 1872 as *Munera Pulveris*. A year earlier, he had initiated a monthly series of letters (which slowed in frequency after several years) addressed to the workingmen of Great Britain. Titling his series *Fors Clavigera* (1871-1884), a name he said implied "force" or "fortune" in the first word and "strength" or "patience" in the second, Ruskin wrote on a wide variety of topics, mingling autobiography and private symbology in tracts about art, politics, and economics. Many were considered incomprehensible by even the most astute Ruskin devotees; the intended audience was undoubtedly confused, even bewildered, by this strange mixture of personal narrative and public pronouncement.

Ruskin's commitment to social issues did not keep him from pursuing his work in art. In 1870, he as-

---

ON PERFECTION IN ART AND ARCHITECTURE

I should be led far from the matter in hand, if I were to pursue this interesting subject. Enough, I trust, has been said to show the reader that the rudeness or imperfection which at first rendered the term "Gothic" one of reproach is indeed, when rightly understood, one of the most noble characters of Christian architecture, and not only a noble but an *essential* one. It seems a fantastic paradox, but it is nevertheless a most important truth, that no architecture can be truly noble which is not imperfect. And this is easily demonstrable. For since the architect, whom we will suppose capable of doing all in perfection, cannot execute the whole with his own hands, he must either make slaves of his workmen in the old Greek, and present English fashion, and level his work to a slave's capacities, which is to degrade it; or else he must take his workmen as he finds them, and let them show their weaknesses together with their strength, which will involve the Gothic imperfection, but render the whole work as noble as the intellect of the age can make it.

But the principle may be stated more broadly still. I have confined the illustration of it to architecture, but I must not leave it as if true of architecture only. Hitherto I have used the words imperfect and perfect merely to distinguish between work grossly unskilful, and work executed with average precision and science; and I have been pleading that any degree of unskilfulness should be admitted, so only that the labourer's mind had room for expression. But, accurately speaking, no good work whatever can be perfect, and *the demand for perfection is always a sign of a misunderstanding of the ends of art*.

Source: John Ruskin, "Characteristics of Gothic Architecture," in *Selections from the Works of John Ruskin*, edited by Chauncey B. Tinker (Cambridge, Mass.: Houghton Mifflin, 1908).

sumed the Slade Professorship of Art at Oxford, the first professor of art appointed in Great Britain. For several years, he used that forum to further his ideas concerning the relationship between art and religion, and art and morality. He also assembled a fine collection of works to illustrate his lectures, eventually bequeathing them to the university. In 1871, he funded a new school of art at Oxford, the Ruskin School of Drawing, still among the most prestigious of such institutions.

Meanwhile, Ruskin tried to implement some of the social theories about which he had written. In 1871, he officially founded the Guild of St. George, a utopian society to promote humanistic living. Though the project eventually failed, Ruskin worked diligently to obtain land to establish ideal communities where men could share the products of their labors, and where they could enjoy the beauties of art (much of which Ruskin himself obtained for these planned communities).

The death of Rose La Touche in 1875 may have been responsible for the frenzy of work in which Ruskin engaged for the next several years. He continued to visit the Continent, to write new works or revise those that he thought required a change of focus, and to promote social causes. During the late 1870's, he began to suffer from intermittent fits of mental instability. Fighting the effects of this illness, Ruskin worked on a host of projects, including his autobiography, *Praeterita*, left unfinished in 1889 when his condition worsened to the point that he lost all capacity for work. In effect, he spent the last eleven years of his life totally incapacitated, simply existing at his home under the care of Joan Agnew Severn. He died in 1900 and was buried in the churchyard at Coniston.

SIGNIFICANCE

Author of more than a hundred books and pamphlets on subjects ranging from art to politics, John Ruskin was one of the most influential writers of his age. To him is owed the recognition of the greatness of the painter Turner and the group of painters and poets known as the Pre-Raphaelite Brotherhood. More significant, Ruskin established principles for evaluating art that became touchstones for later critics and art historians. Although his notion that all great art is inherently moral may have subsequently been discredited, his method of close reading of paintings and especially of architecture has had marked influence on the study of these art forms. Ironically, his imperative judgment that art has value for society, and is not simply ornament, led to the development of the art for art's sake movement, which also claimed an inherent value for art—but divorced from any utilitarian or moral value.

Like many other social commentators, Ruskin attracted a contemporary following, but subsequent generations have not sought his work as a model for their society. He was influential in bringing his countrymen to see the dangers of Benthamism and similar systems that treated people as ciphers.

Even though his direct influence on theories of art and economics has waned, Ruskin remains a significant figure in the living tradition of English literature. His best writings, laden with echoes of the Bible and literary classics, are often cited as models of the richness that can be achieved by one whose prose approaches poetry in style, allusion, and use of metaphor.

—*Laurence W. Mazzeno*

FURTHER READING

Abse, Joan. *John Ruskin: Passionate Moralist.* New York: Alfred A. Knopf, 1981. Carefully researched biography focusing on Ruskin's efforts to promote various causes, and noting the importance that events in his personal life had in shaping his writings and public lectures. Includes a valuable bibliography of primary and secondary sources for those wishing to read more by or about Ruskin.

Batchelor, John. *John Ruskin: A Life.* New York: Carroll & Graf, 2000. Perceptive biography, describing how Ruskin turned his self-destructive unhappiness into his crusading ideas about the value of art and the dignity of work. Analyzes and summarizes Ruskin's writings.

Burd, Van Akin, ed. *The Ruskin Family Letters: The Correspondence of John James Ruskin, His Wife, and Their Son, John, 1801-1843.* 2 vols. Ithaca, N.Y.: Cornell University Press, 1973. These important letters between Ruskin and his parents, covering the first forty years of Ruskin's life, provide valuable insight into the role his parents played in Ruskin's development as a critic. The letters also expand, or in some instances correct, information provided in Ruskin's autobiography, *Praeterita*.

Cook, E. T. *The Life of John Ruskin.* 2 vols. London: George Allen, 1911. The first detailed biography of Ruskin, written by one of the editors of the standard edition of Ruskin's works. Contains significant excerpts from letters and diaries but omits details of Ruskin's decade-long relationship with Rose La Touche and his battle with mental instability.

Hilton, Tim. *John Ruskin.* 2 vols. New Haven, Conn.: Yale University Press, 1985-2000. A scholarly biography based on a comprehensive study of available documents at the major Ruskin collections. Stresses the significance of Ruskin's later work, highlighting the writings on society and the economy, especially *Fors Clavigera*. Attempts to correct errors, lapses, and omissions in earlier biographies, especially those of Cook and other Victorian and Edwardian chroniclers.

Hunt, John Dixon. *The Wider Sea: A Life of John Ruskin.* New York: Viking Press, 1982. Detailed, comprehensive biography that highlights the importance of travel in shaping Ruskin's ideas. Concentrates on Ruskin's personal life, providing brief analyses of individual works.

Ruskin, John. *The Diaries of John Ruskin.* Edited by Joan Evan and J. H. Whitehouse. 3 vols. Oxford, England: Clarendon Press, 1956-1959. Though not a complete collation of such materials, these diaries are a key to understanding Ruskin's method of composition and reveal much about the way his mind worked as an artist, a traveler, and an observer of life.

_____. *John Ruskin: Selected Writings.* Edited with an introduction and notes by Dinah Birch. New ed. New York: Oxford University Press, 2004. The selections include excerpts from *Modern Painters*, *The Stones of Venice*, and Ruskin's writings about science and math. Birch's introduction provides an overview of Ruskin's life and ideas. Includes some of Ruskin's own illustrations.

_____. *Praeterita.* New York: Oxford University Press, 1978. Ruskin's celebrated autobiography, highly selective in its presentation of details from the author's earlier life. Written between Ruskin's bouts with mental illness, it was intended to present those things that had given him enjoyment. Hence, stress is placed on travel and relationships with his parents and mentors; there is no discussion, however, of his six-year marriage.

SEE ALSO: Octavia Hill; William Holman Hunt; Sir Walter Scott; William Makepeace Thackeray; J. M. W. Turner; James McNeill Whistler.

RELATED ARTICLES in *Great Events from History: The Nineteenth Century, 1801-1900:* Fall, 1848: Pre-Raphaelite Brotherhood Begins; 1884: New Guilds Promote the Arts and Crafts Movement.

JOHN RUSSELL
Prime minister of Great Britain (1846-1852; 1865-1866)

One of the leading Whig politicians of nineteenth century Great Britain, Russell held cabinet offices for all but seven of the years between 1830 and 1866, and was twice prime minister. He was not always the most effective British political leader of his era, but he played important roles in some of the most sweeping political reforms of the nineteenth century.

BORN: August 18, 1792; London, England
DIED: May 28, 1878; Pembroke Lodge, Richmond Park, England
ALSO KNOWN AS: Lord John Russell; First Earl Russell; Viscount Amberley and of Ardsalla; Russell of Kingston Russell
AREA OF ACHIEVEMENT: Government and politics

EARLY LIFE
A younger son of the fifth duke of Bedford, John Russell came from a family that had historical ties with the English Reformation, the parliamentary cause in the Civil War, the opposition to the Catholic king, James II, the Glorious Revolution, and the Whig opposition to William Pitt the Younger's anti-French measures. Russell lived and breathed his family's history, and the events of the seventeenth and eighteenth centuries were as real to him as those of the nineteenth. His ancestor Lord William Russell was executed in 1683 for his part in the plot to exclude James II from the throne. Parliament over king, Whigs over Tories, Protestant truth over Roman Catholic obscurantism: These were the principles for which Russell believed his family stood.

Born two months prematurely, Russell, when fully grown, stood only about five feet, five inches tall and was frail of health. His size was a handicap in politics and a caricaturist's dream: His friends called him "Jack the Giantkiller"; his enemies drew him as a child. He married a widow, and the nickname "the widow's mite" followed. After study with tutors, Russell attended the University of Edinburgh; he also traveled in Portugal, Spain, and Italy, and he visited Napoleon at Elba. He enjoyed the title "Lord John" Russell as the younger son of a duke, and it is by this name that history knows him best.

Lord John entered the House of Commons in 1813 for the family pocket borough of Tavistock. He represented this area and several other constituencies until 1841, when he was returned for the City of London; he held that prestigious seat until 1861, when he was elevated to the peerage. His early political career, from 1813 to 1830, proved him to be an advanced Whig, supporting parliamentary reform, Dissenters' rights, and Roman Catholic Emancipation. Although not a great debater, he was able to hold the attention of the Commons through the force of his argument. This ability united with his family background to bring him to a position of leadership among the Whigs.

LIFE'S WORK

Russell was not immediately given a cabinet post when the Charles Grey ministry came to power in 1830. He served on the committee that drafted the Great Reform Bill, and he piloted it through the House of Commons. His great national popularity as a reformer dates from this period. He served as home secretary (1835-1839) and colonial secretary (1839-1841) under Lord Melbourne. During these years, Russell continued to express his advanced Whig views, supporting Dissenters' rights, reform of Irish grievances, the rationalization of the revenues of the Church of England, the Municipal Corporations Act, and other reforms in the areas of prisons, the Poor Law, and education. Although distasteful to the more conservative Whigs (Lord Stanley, the earl of Ripon, and Sir James Graham resigned over Russell's proposal to confiscate revenues of the Irish church), Russell's proposals did not go far enough to suit the Philosophical Radicals, the Irish, and the militant Nonconformists. They had little choice but to support him, however, for the Conservatives were worse.

Lord John emerged as the leader of the Whig opposition during Robert Peel's ministry (1841-1846). When the Conservatives split over the questions of endowing the Irish Roman Catholic seminary at Maynooth and repealing the Corn Laws, Russell formed a government. He was prime minister from 1846 to 1852.

Russell's ministry continued the pattern of moderate Whig reforms set during the 1830's. The state's role in education, factories, and public health expanded. The Whigs supported representative and responsible government for the colonies. They persevered in their policies of free trade and laissez-faire economics, eliminating the last vestiges of protective tariffs. In the three areas of Ireland, foreign policy, and religious policy, however, the Russell ministry was unfortunate.

Russell's ministry coincided with the Irish Potato Famine. The government did not respond well to this disaster. Although it attempted to alleviate the famine with a large public works program, it believed that free market economics would solve the problem of famine. Although free market economics did not work, given the special circumstances of the Irish situation, the government, determined not to deviate from economic orthodoxy, refused to permit the direct relief necessary to prevent starvation. This policy promoted Irish discontent and terrorism, and it created the myth, still held in the twenty-first century, that the British had tried to starve the Irish.

In foreign policy, Russell came into conflict with Foreign Secretary Lord Palmerston. Russell imagined that the unification of Italy would both promote liberal political institutions and damage the Roman Catholic Church. Palmerston, although himself a liberal, was an experienced diplomat concerned to promote international stability and British national interests. Moreover, Palmerston ran his foreign policy independently of his cabinet colleagues. This created conflicts that made it rather difficult for the government to respond effectively to the revolutions of 1848 and to the rise of Louis-Napoleon Bonaparte (Napoleon III) in France.

It was Russell's religious policy, however, that caused the loudest quarrels, that helped bring down his government in 1852, and that ultimately destroyed his career. As has been noted, his support of Dissenters' rights and of church reform alienated Anglicans and Conservatives, yet he did not go far enough to satisfy the more extreme Dissenters. When it came to Roman Catholics, his policies were so contradictory that they managed to alienate everyone. Russell supported the Maynooth endowment, and he proposed the concurrent endowment of Anglicans and Roman Catholics in Ireland. However, he denounced Roman Catholicism as "superstitious" during the Papal Aggression crisis of 1850-1851 (when a papal hierarchy was created for Great Britain) and passed penal legislation against its bishops. His measures, offensive to Roman Catholics, were too weak to satisfy the anti-Catholics.

Russell was not blessed with a docile cabinet, and some of his ministers, especially Chancellor of the Exchequer Charles Wood and Lord Privy Seal the earl of Minto, were inept. Russell was more liberal than most of his colleagues, who prevented him from introducing measures for further parliamentary reform.

All these factors combined to bring the Russell ministry to such a state of weakness by February, 1852, that Lord Palmerston (who had been fired from the cabinet the previous December) was able to bring it down.

SIGNIFICANCE

It is the judgment of Lord John Russell's biographer, John Prest, that Russell ought to have retired from public life in 1852. Despite all the problems of his ministry, he stood in high public esteem as a reformer and as a man of honest and dedicated character. Russell, however, had not known when enough was enough. He continued in public office: foreign secretary, minister without portfolio, and Lord President of the Privy Council in the ill-fated Whig-Peelite Aberdeen Coalition (1852-1855); foreign secretary in the Palmerston ministry (1859-1865); and prime minister again (1865-1866) after Palmerston's death.

Russell's record in those offices was dismal, as he could not escape Palmerston's domination. During his tenure as foreign secretary, Russell directed most of his energies to domestic matters, especially abortive reform bills, and relied upon Palmerston and the rest of the cabinet to set foreign policy.

Russell was not the most successful of Queen Victoria's prime ministers. He issued public statements and committed his cabinet to policies without consulting his colleagues and without considering the consequences. Oftentimes, he announced a policy without having any idea of how to translate sentiment into practical legislation. He did not have a firm grasp of foreign policy and seemed to believe that foreign rulers were prepared to adopt without debate schemes that Lord Palmerston thought nonsensical. Russell was especially troubled when it came to religion, for he seemed unable or unwilling to devise programs that were politically feasible; he constructed schemes that were impracticable, unsystematic, and superficial.

The roots of Russell's muddle are to be found in his religious peculiarities. He was a Protestant insofar as he was hostile to Roman Catholicism, but he was no orthodox Christian. He believed that a religious establishment should be maintained to propagate rational religion and honest behavior, but he denied that Anglican clergymen were more than a species of civil servant. With respect to his personal faith, Russell had inherited eighteenth century skepticism, anticlericalism, rationalism, and latitudinarianism. His second wife, née Frances Elliot, daughter of the earl of Minto, influenced his views. A Scots Calvinist of unusual scrupulosity, Lady John was an extreme anticlericalist who eventually gravitated to the Plymouth Brethren sect. She encouraged Russell to extremism in his views.

Russell's character and career reflect both the contributions of the Whig Party to Victorian politics and that party's limitations. He consistently supported measures that he thought would improve British institutions, but all too often he was unable to translate his ideas into programs that would work. He died on May 28, 1878, at Pembroke Lodge, a royal house in Richmond Park, placed by the queen at Russell's disposal.

—*D. G. Paz*

FURTHER READING

Arnstein, Walter L. *Britain Yesterday and Today: 1830 to the Present*. Vol. 4 in *A History of England*. 4th ed. Lexington, Mass.: D. C. Heath, 1983. A very readable survey of English history, useful for background.

Brown, Lucy M., and Ian R. Christie. *Bibliography of British History, 1789-1851*. Oxford, England: Clarendon Press, 1977. This bibliography of writings on British history for this period is organized by subject and is well indexed.

Ellens, J. P. "Lord John Russell and the Church Rate Conflict: The Struggle for a Broad Church, 1834-1868." *Journal of British Studies* 26 (1987): 232-257. A thoughtful and well-researched study of Russell's views and actions on an important issue connected with church-state relations.

Kerr, Donal A. *A Nation of Beggars? Priests, People, and Politics in Famine Ireland, 1846-1852*. New York: Oxford University Press, 1994. Examines Russell's efforts to improve the life of Irish Catholics by changing the landlord-tenant system and upgrading the status of the Catholic Church.

Paz, D. G. "Another Look at Lord John Russell and the Papal Aggression, 1850." *Historian* 45 (1982): 47-64. Analyzes Russell's actions in an important religious controversy and argues that his anti-Catholicism stemmed from his unique religious views and his impetuous personality.

Prest, John. *Lord John Russell*. New York: Macmillan, 1972. The definitive biography; integrates Russell's public career and quirks of personality.

Russell, First Earl. *The Early Correspondence of Lord John Russell, 1805-1840*. Edited by Rollo Russell. 2 vols. London: T. Fisher Unwin, 1913. More poorly edited than Gooch's work (see below), with errors of transcription, but it does make the documents available.

_____. *The Later Correspondence of Lord John Russell, 1840-1878*. Edited by G. P. Gooch. 2 vols. London: Longmans, 1925. Not well edited, but useful.

_____. *Recollections and Suggestions, 1813-1873*. Boston: Roberts Brothers, 1875. Russell's autobiography. Although Russell himself was not especially self-perceptive, this memoir reveals much about his character.

Scherer, Paul. *Lord John Russell: A Biography*. Selinsgrove, Pa.: Susquehanna University Press, 1999. The first scholarly biography since Prest's book (see above). Scherer bases his biography on new documentation, focusing on Russell's career after 1852, his work as foreign secretary under Prime Minister Palmerston, and his private life.

Walpole, Spencer. *The Life of Lord John Russell*. 2 vols. London: Longmans, Green, 1889. Reprint. New York: Greenwood Press, 1968. A typical Victorian "double-decker" biography. Although replaced by Prest, its virtue lies in the documents that it prints, for Walpole was a good historian and careful transcriber.

SEE ALSO: Fourteenth Earl of Derby; Benjamin Disraeli; Napoleon III; Lord Palmerston; Sir Robert Peel; Queen Victoria.

RELATED ARTICLES in *Great Events from History: The Nineteenth Century, 1801-1900:* May 9, 1828-April 13, 1829: Roman Catholic Emancipation; September 9, 1835: British Parliament Passes Municipal Corporations Act; October 23-December 16, 1837: Rebellions Rock British Canada; February 10, 1841: Upper and Lower Canada Unite; June 15, 1846: British Parliament Repeals the Corn Laws; July 26, 1858: Rothschild Is First Jewish Member of British Parliament; August, 1867: British Parliament Passes the Reform Act of 1867.

SACAGAWEA
Native American explorer

Sacagawea was the only woman who accompanied the Lewis and Clark Expedition in its exploration of the territory acquired through the Louisiana Purchase, but as the expedition's primary guide and interpreter, she played a major role in its success.

BORN: c. 1788; central Idaho
DIED: December 20, 1812; Fort Manuel, Dakota
  Territory (now in South Dakota)
ALSO KNOWN AS: Sagagawea; Sakakawea; Sacajawea;
  Bird Woman
AREA OF ACHIEVEMENT: Exploration

EARLY LIFE

Sacagawea (sahk-ah-jah-WEE-ah) was born into a band of northern Shoshone Indians, whose base was the Lemhi Valley of central Idaho. Her name translates as "Bird Woman" (Hidatsa) or "Boat Pusher" (Shoshonean). The northern Shoshone, sometimes referred to as Snake Indians (a name given them by the French because of the use of painted snakes on sticks to frighten their enemies), were a wandering people, living by hunting, gathering, and fishing. As a child, Sacagawea traveled through the mountains and valleys of Idaho, northwest Wyoming, and western Montana. In 1800, at about age twelve, Sacagawea and her kin were encamped during a hunting foray at the Three Forks of the Missouri (between modern Butte and Bozeman, Montana) when they were attacked by a war party of Hidatsas (also called Minnetarees), a Siouan tribe; about ten Shoshone were killed, and Sacagawea and several other children were made captives. Sacagawea was taken to reside with the Hidatsas at the village of Metaharta near the junction of the Knife and Missouri Rivers (in modern North Dakota).

Shortly after her capture, Sacagawea was sold as a wife to fur trader Toussaint Charbonneau. A French-Canadian who had developed skills as an interpreter, Charbonneau had been living with the Hidatsas for five years. At the time that Sacagawea became his squaw, Charbonneau had one or two other Indian wives.

All that is known of Sacagawea for certain is found in the journals and letters of Meriwether Lewis, William Clark, and several other participants in the expedition of the Corps of Discovery, 1804-1806, along with meager references in other sources. The Lewis and Clark party, commissioned by President Thomas Jefferson to find a route to the Pacific and to make scientific observations along the way, traveled on the first leg of their journey up the Missouri River to the mouth of the Knife River, near which they established Fort Mandan (near modern Bismarck, North Dakota) as their winter headquarters. The site was in the vicinity of Mandan and Hidasta villages. Here the expedition's leaders made preparations for the next leg of their journey and collected information on the Indians and topography of the far West.

LIFE'S WORK

Sacagawea's association with the Lewis and Clark expedition began on November 4, 1804, when she accompanied her husband to Fort Mandan. She presented the officers with four buffalo robes. Charbonneau was willing to serve as interpreter, but only on condition that Sacagawea be permitted to go along on the journey. After agreeing to those terms, Lewis and Clark hired Charbonneau. At Fort Mandan on February 11, 1805, Sacagawea gave birth to Jean-Baptiste Charbonneau. Thus, along with the some thirty men, the "squaw woman" and baby became members of the exploring group.

The expedition set out from Fort Mandan on April 7, 1805. Charbonneau and Sacagawea at different times were referred to in the journals as "interpreter and interpretess." Sacagawea's knowledge of Hidatsa and Shoshonean proved of great aid in communicating with the two tribes with which the expedition primarily had contact. Later, when the expedition made contact with Pacific coast Indians, Sacagawea managed to assist in communicating with those peoples even though she did not speak their language. Her services as a guide were helpful only when the expedition sought out Shoshone Indians in the region of the Continental Divide in order to find direction and assistance in leaving the mountains westward. Carrying her baby on her back in cord netting, Sacagawea stayed with one or several of the main groups of explorers, never venturing out scouting on her own. Little Baptiste enlivened the camp circles, and Clark, unlike Lewis, became fond of both baby and mother.

Several times on the westward journey Sacagawea was seriously ill, and once she and Charbonneau were nearly swept away in a flash flood. In May of 1805, Sacagawea demonstrated her resourcefulness by retrieving many valuable articles that had washed out of a canoe during a rainstorm. Lewis and Clark named a stream "Sâh-câ-ger we-âh" (*Sah ca gah we a*), or "bird woman's River," which at a later time was renamed Crooked Creek. Not the least of Sacagawea's contributions was finding sustenance in the forests, identifying flora that Indians considered edible. She helped to gather berries, wild onions, beans, artichokes, and roots. She cooked and mended clothes.

On reaching the Three Forks of the Missouri, Sacagawea recognized landmarks and rightly conjectured where the Shoshone might be during the hunting season. A band of these Indians was found along the Lemhi River. Sacagawea began "to dance and show every mark of the most extravagant joy . . . sucking her fingers at the same time to indicate that they were of her native tribe." The tribe's leader, Cameahwait, turned out to be Sacagawea's brother (or possibly cousin). Lewis and Clark established a cordial relationship with Sacagawea's kinsmen and were able to obtain twenty-nine horses and an Indian guide through the rest of the mountains.

As it came down from the mountains, the exploring party made dugout canoes at the forks of the Clearwater River, and then followed an all-water route along that stream, the Snake River, and the Columbia River to the Pacific coast. At the mouth of the Columbia River, just below present Astoria, Oregon, the adventurers built Fort Clatsop, where they spent the winter. Sacagawea was an important asset as the expedition covered the final phase of the journey. "The wife of Shabono our interpreter," wrote William Clark on October 13, 1805, "reconsiles all the Indians, as to our friendly intentions a woman with a party of men is a token of peace."

Besides her recognition of topography that aided in finding the Shoshones, Sacagawea's other contribution as guide occurred on the return trip. During the crossing of the eastern Rockies by Clark's party (Lewis took a more northerly route), Sacagawea showed the way from Three Forks through the mountains by way of the Bozeman Pass to the Yellowstone River. Lewis and Clark reunited near the junction of the Missouri and the Yellowstone. Sacagawea, Charbonneau, and infant Baptiste accompanied the expedition down the Missouri River only as far as the Hidatsa villages at the mouth of the Knife River. On April 17, 1806, they "took leave" of the exploring group. Clark offered to take Sacagawea's baby, whom Clark called "Pomp," with him to St. Louis to be reared and educated as his adopted son. Sacagawea, who consented to the proposal, insisted that the infant, then nineteen months old, be weaned first.

With the conclusion of the Lewis and Clark expedition, details about Sacagawea's life become sketchy. In the fall of 1809, the Charbonneau family visited St. Louis. Charbonneau purchased a small farm on the Missouri River just north of St. Louis from Clark, who had been named Indian superintendent for the Louisiana Territory. In 1811, Charbonneau sold back the tract to Clark. Sacagawea yearned to return to her homeland. Charbonneau enlisted in a fur trading expedition conducted by Manuel Lisa. In April of 1811, Sacagawea and Charbonneau headed up river in one of Lisa's boats. One observer on board at the time commented that Sacagawea appeared sickly.

Sacagawea left Jean-Baptiste Charbonneau with Clark in St. Louis. On August 11, 1813, an orphan's court appointed Clark as the child's guardian. Sacagawea's son went on to have a far-ranging career. At the age of eighteen, he joined a western tour of the

Sacagawea. (Courtesy, Smithsonian, National Postal Museum)

young Prince Paul Wilhelm of Württemberg, and afterward went to Europe, where he resided with the prince for six years. The two men returned to America in 1829, and again explored the western country. Jean-Baptiste thereafter was employed as a fur trapper for fifteen years by the American Fur Company. He later served as an army guide during the Mexican War. Joining the gold rush of 1849, Jean-Baptiste set up residence in Placer County, California. Traveling through Montana in May of 1866, he died of pneumonia.

There once was a lively controversy over the correct determination of the date and place of Sacagawea's death. Grace Raymond Hebard, a professor at the University of Wyoming, published the biography *Sacajawea* in 1933, in which she went to great lengths to prove that Sacagawea died on April 9, 1884. Hebard traced the alleged wanderings of the "Bird Woman" to the time that she settled down on the Wind River Reservation in Wyoming. Hebard made a substantial case, based on oral testimony of persons who had known the "Bird Woman"; the hearsay related to known details of the Lewis and Clark expedition. Hebard also relied upon ethnological authorities.

At the heart of the controversy is a journal entry of John Luttig, resident fur company clerk at Fort Manuel. On December 20, 1812, he recorded: "this Evening the Wife of Charbonneau, a Snake Squaw died of a putrid fever she was a good and the best Women in the fort, aged abt 25 years she left an infant girl." It is known that Sacagawea had given birth to a daughter, Lizette. The Luttig journal was not published until 1920. Hebard claimed that the death notice referred to Charbonneau's other Shoshone wife, Otter Woman. The issue, however, seems put to rest by the discovery in 1955 of a document in William Clark's journal dated to the years 1825 to 1828. Clark's list of the status of members of his expedition states: "Se car ja we au Dead." Nevertheless, the notion that Sacagawea lived until the 1880's continues to have support.

SIGNIFICANCE

Sacagawea had a fourfold impact on the Lewis and Clark expedition. Though she viewed much of the country the group traversed for the first time, her geographical knowledge was most important in locating the Shoshones in the Rocky Mountains and directing Clark's party through the Bozeman Pass. At crucial instances her services as a translator were essential, and she served as a contact agent. Perhaps, most of all, as an Indian mother with a young baby, she dispelled many of the fears of the Indians encountered on the journey, particularly the fear that the expedition might harm them.

Sacagawea may be credited as a primary factor in ensuring the success of the Lewis and Clark expedition. Sacagawea also contributed to the uplifting of morale. Throughout the venture she exhibited courage, resourcefulness, coolness, and congeniality. The presence of mother and baby encouraged a certain civilized restraint among the members of the party. Henry Brackenridge, who met Sacagawea in April of 1811, said that she was "a good creature, of a mild and gentle disposition." Clark expressed regrets at the end of the expedition that no special reward could be given to Sacagawea. In many ways she was more valuable to the expedition than her husband, who ultimately received compensation for their efforts.

Sacagawea's place in history was long neglected. Interest in her life, however, gained momentum with the centenary celebrations of the Lewis and Clark expedition during the early twentieth century and especially with the rise of the suffrage movement, which saw in Sacagawea a person of womanly virtues and independence. Eva Emery Dye's novel, *The Conquest: The True Story of Lewis and Clark* (1902), did much during the course of its ten editions to popularize an exaggerated role of Sacagawea on the famous journey of discovery.

Sacagawea attracted new attention in 2000, when the U.S. Mint began issuing a new dollar coin with her image on the front. Images of American Indians had been used on many earlier coins—such as the "Indian head" penny and the "buffalo" nickel—but new Sacagawea dollar was the first coin to feature the image of a specific Indian person.

—*Harry M. Ward*

FURTHER READING

Anderson, Irving. "A Charbonneau Family Portrait." *American West* 17 (Spring, 1980): 4-13, 58-64. Written for a popular audience, this article provides a thorough and reliable account of the lives of Sacagawea, her husband Toussaint, and her son Jean-Baptiste.

Chuinard, E. G. "The Actual Role of the Bird Woman." *Montana: The Magazine of Western History* 26 (Summer, 1976): 18-29. Emphasizes the role of Sacagawea as a guide and contact agent and challenges the exaggeration of her actual accomplishments.

Clark, Ella E., and Margot Edmonds. *Sacagawea of the Lewis and Clark Expedition.* Berkeley: University of California Press, 1979. Includes discussion of Sacagawea's life and the efforts made to popularize her legend. Although they provide a relatively accurate account, the authors choose to accept the discredited theory that Sacagawea lived until 1884.

Howard, Harold P. *Sacajawea*. Norman: University of Oklahoma Press, 1971. A balanced biography aimed at a general audience, this work attempts to sort out fact from legend in the life of Sacagawea.

Hunsaker, Joyce Badgley. *Sacagawea Speaks: Beyond the Shining Mountains with Lewis and Clark*. Guilford, Conn.: Two Dot Books, 2001. Sacagawea recounts her experiences with the Corps of Discovery. Hunsaker uses oral tradition, scholarly research, anecdotes, and other materials to compile Sacagawea's first-person narrative.

Jackson, Donald, ed. *Letters of the Lewis and Clark Expedition, with Related Documents, 1783-1854*. 2d ed. 2 vols. Urbana: University of Illinois Press, 1978. Contains a variety of letters, journal entries, and other papers relevant to the activities of the expedition. Sheds some light on the contribution of the Charbonneau family.

Nelson, W. Dale. *Interpreters with Lewis and Clark: The Story of Sacagawea and Toussaint Charbonneau*. Denton: University of North Texas Press, 2003. Examines the contributions of Toussaint and Sacagawea to the Lewis and Clark expedition. Nelson seeks to rehabilitate Toussaint's character and reputation.

Perdue, Theda, ed. *Sifters: Native American Women's Lives*. New York: Oxford University Press, 2001. Chapter 4 in this collection of biographies focuses on the myth and reality of Sacagawea's life.

Ronda, James P. *Lewis and Clark Among the Indians*. Lincoln: University of Nebraska Press, 1984. This scholarly study examines the contact made between the Lewis and Clark expedition and the Indians. Provides insights into Sacagawea's contributions to the success of the expedition. Includes an appendix that evaluates various books and articles about Sacagawea.

SEE ALSO: Meriwether Lewis and William Clark; Zebulon Pike; Jedediah Smith.

RELATED ARTICLES in *Great Events from History: The Nineteenth Century, 1801-1900:* May 14, 1804-September 23, 1806: Lewis and Clark Expedition; July 15, 1806-July 1, 1807: Pike Explores the American Southwest; June 15, 1846: United States Acquires Oregon Territory.

SAʿĪD IBN SULṬĀN
Sultan of Oman, Muscat, and Zanzibar (r. 1804, 1806-1856)

Saʿīd was the dominating force in the western Indian Ocean through the first half of the nineteenth century. After moving his capital from Oman to Zanzibar, he controlled East African trade, opened diplomatic relations with the United States and European powers, and made Zanzibar the world center of clove production.

BORN: 1791; Oman
DIED: October 19, 1856; aboard ship on the Indian Ocean
ALSO KNOWN AS: Saʿīd ibn Sulṭān ibn Aḥmad ibn Saʿīd al-Būsaʿīdī (full name); Saʿīd Imām; Saʿīd Sayyid; Sayyid Saʿīd; Seyyid Saʿīd
AREA OF ACHIEVEMENT: Government and politics

EARLY LIFE
Sayyid Saʿīd (SAH-yihd SAH-ihd) was born in the Oman sultanate at the southeastern end of the Arabian Peninsula. He would eventually become the third member of the al-Busaʿīdi dynasty to rule Oman. After a Persian invasion of Oman and a civil war, his grandfather Aḥmad ibn Saʿīd took control of Oman in 1749.

Oman had long been involved in trade from the major seaports of Suhar and Muscat, reaching as far east as China. During the early sixteenth century the Portuguese conquered Muscat and used that port as their trading base to India until 1650. Under Aḥmad ibn Saʿīd, a large Omani navy was established that drove pirates from the Persian Gulf and restored trade, especially with the east coast of Africa. Hamad ibn Saʿīd (r. 1783-1792) conquered the town of Kilwa on the coast of what is now southern Tanzania, installed a governor, and began exacting tribute.

The latter half of the eighteenth century was also marked by the ambitions of both Great Britain and France in controlling the northwestern part of the Indian Ocean. In 1798, Sultan ibn Aḥmad (1792-1804) concluded a treaty with Britain, the first between a Persian Gulf state and a European nation. However, the sultan also continued to nurture a favorable relationship with the French ruler, Napoleon I. At that time, Oman was also weakened by internal threats. The ultraconservative Wahhabi of central Arabia had moved eastward around the turn of the nineteenth century and had established a stronghold at Buraymi, two hundred miles from Muscat, from which they attacked Sultan ibn Aḥmad and exacted tribute from him. When he was killed in 1804, Oman appeared near dissolution.

For more than a year, the nine grandsons of Aḥmad ibn Saʿīd competed with one another for power. Among them was Saʿīd ibn Sulṭān. Saʿīd's cousin Badr ibn Sayf initially prevailed by gaining control of Muscat with the backing of the Wahhabi. However, most Omanis did oppose the newly enforced puritanical practices of the Wahhabi. In early 1806, Saʿīd ibn Sulṭān, although only fifteen years old, assumed leadership by assassinating Bedr, personally stabbing him with a dagger. At first Saʿīd shared the throne with his older brother Salim, but Saʿīd eventually emerged a popular folk hero and leader. He chose for himself the title *Sayyid*, rather than the religious title *Imam* used by his predecessors, and signaled a style of leadership that would prevail for a half a century.

Saʿīd ibn Sulṭān. (The Granger Collection, New York)

LIFE'S WORK

In spite of his youth, Sayyid ibn Saʿīd proved an astute leader. He assumed a neutral position in the Napoleonic Wars that were raging in Europe and was able to acquire assistance from both Great Britain and France in expelling the Wahhabi from Oman and suppressing pirating. The latter achievement won him favor with Americans, whose ship *Essex* had recently been attacked by pirates who massacred the crew. Saʿīd took advantage of the situation to expand the role of Oman in trade along the African coast.

It was not long until Saʿīd was invited to intervene in political matters in Africa. In 1811, a war broke out along the coast of what is now Kenya, when the Mazrui rulers of the port of Mombasa began expanding northward to take control of Pate Island. This action was followed a year later by the Battle of Shela, a failed attempt by the Mazrui to take the island town of Lamu. Lamu sought Saʿīd's support and accepted an Omani governorship on the island. By 1822, Saʿīd had established garrisons on both Pate and Pemba. He continued his involvement against the Mazuri until he eventually gained control of Mombasa. In 1828, he paid his first visit to the East African coast in order to sign a peace treaty with the Mazrui. He completed the visit with a three-month stay on the large island of Zanzibar.

In 1799, Saʿīd's father had established an Omani cogovernorship over Zanzibar. Saʿīd was soon able to achieve a monopoly for the trade of slaves and ivory. The importance of Zanzibari trade became so great that he paid several more visits during the 1830's. Finally, in 1840, he moved the seat of his government from Muscat to Zanzibar. One of his first decisions during his visits was to introduce the cultivation of cloves and other spices to Zanzibar, which had fertile soil and favorable growing conditions. At that time, cloves were in demand in Europe and North America for use as preservatives for meat. The international clove trade soon dominated Omani commerce. In addition, Saʿīd financed trading caravans that reached deep into the interior of East Africa, extending as far as Lake Tanganyika in 1837.

Meanwhile, in 1833, Saʿīd signed a trade agreement with the United States. Over the next two years no fewer than thirty-two American ships docked at Zanzibar. In 1845, John Bertram and Company of Salem, Massachusetts, opened offices on Zanzibar and was beginning to purchase local gum, cloves, and other products in exchange for American cotton and hardware. Zanzibar's extensive trade with Salem is documented by the Peabody Museum in Salem, where the only known au-

SAʿĪD IBN SULṬĀN REMEMBERED BY HIS DAUGHTER

Saʿīd's daughter Sayyida Salma, who was born in 1844, married a German and took the name Emily Ruete, under which she published Memoirs of an Arabian Princess from Zanzibar *in 1888. This passage from her book's first chapter offers an intimate glimpse of her father.*

My father, Seyyid Saïd, bore the double appellation of Sultan of Zanzibar and Imam of Muscat, that of Imam being a religious title and one originally borne by my great-grandfather Ahmed, a hereditary title, moreover, which every member of our family has a right to append to his signature.

As one of Seyyid Saïd's youngest children, I never knew him without his venerable white beard. Taller in stature than the average, his face expressed remarkable kindness and amiability though at the same time his appearance could not but command immediate respect. Despite his pleasure in war and conquest, he was a model for us all, whether as parent or ruler. His highest ideal was justice, and in a case of delinquency he would make no distinction between one of his own sons and an ordinary slave. Above all, he was humility itself before God the Almighty; unlike so many of great estate, arrogant pride was foreign to his nature, and more than once, when a common slave of long and faithful service took a wife, my father would have a horse saddled, and ride off alone to offer the newly wedded couple his good wishes in person. . . .

Source: Emily Ruete, *Memoirs of an Arabian Princess from Zanzibar*, translated by Lionel Strachey (New York: Doubleday, Page, 1907), chapter 1.

thentic portrait of Sayyid Saʿīd is housed. British and French interest in Zanzibar also continued. The British followed the United States by signing a trade agreement with Saʿīd in 1839, and the French signed an agreement in 1844. Soon western consulates were established on Zanzibar.

Because of strong British opposition to the slave trade, diplomatic negotiations with Saʿīd focused on the most affective way to end slavery. In 1822, the British signed the Moresby Treaty with Saʿīd to curtail the spread of slavery. In 1845, the sultan signed a further treaty with Colonel Atkins Hamerton, the first British consul in Zanzibar, to limit the trade to territories within the sultan's possessions. This agreement left a number of loopholes that allowed the external slave trade to continue. Meanwhile, the great increase in spice production on Zanzibar fostered the growth of large plantations that depended on slave labor. Although Zanzibar continued to export slaves, with some restrictions, the greatest need was for slaves to work in clove and coconut production on Zanzibar and neighboring Pemba Island. Essentially a merchant prince, the sultan prolonged the slave trade to serve his commercial needs. Slavery would not be abolished on Zanzibar until 1897.

Sayyid Saʿīd had a large family. His principal wife was Azze bint Sef, of the royal house of Oman. It is estimated that he also had as many as seventy-five secondary wives and concubines and many children. At the time of his death, thirty-six of his children were known still to be living.

After Saʿīd died in October, 1856, conflict among his sons centered on his succession. Two years earlier, he had returned to Muscat to deal with local matters, leaving his son Khalid as acting governor on Zanzibar. When Khalid died a few months after Saʿīd left, another son, Majid, took his place. Saʿīd had entrusted to the British consul Hamerton the guidance of his sons in his absence, so the transition went smoothly. When Saʿīd finally sailed back to Zanzibar in October, 1856, he died aboard his ship midway through voyage. His nineteen-year-old son Barghash attempted a plot to take over the throne that involved secretly carrying Saʿīd's body ashore and burying it near the palace. However, Hamerton put down the rebellion and installed the twenty-one-year-old Majid as the new sultan. Afterward, the sultanate split when another of Saʿīd's sons, Thuwain, took over the rule of Muscat. The governments of Zanzibar and Muscat were never reunited. Zanzibar's al-Busaʿīdi dynasty was overthrown in 1964, but Saʿīd's descendants were still ruling Oman in the early twenty-first century.

SIGNIFICANCE

Sayyid Saʿīd is known for transforming Zanzibar from a minor island fishing community to a major trade center with connections throughout the Indian Ocean and the rest of the world. His decision to move the capital of Oman to the island opened the door for the transformation of East Africa through contacts with non-African nations. In addition to the Arab influx that influenced East Africa's Swahili language and helped foster the spread of Islam, he encouraged merchants from India to manage trade, and he signed important trade agreements, not only with European powers such as Great Britain and France, but also with the United States of America. His interest in farming led to the introduction of cloves, making Zanzibar the spice capital of the world.

Saʿīd has also been credited with beginning the negotiations with the British that eventually abolished the slave trade in East Africa. However, his trade policies actually increased the numbers of slaves moving through Zanzibar, and that fact actually prolonged the institution of slavery through his introduction of large plantations on the island.

—*Fred Strickert*

FURTHER READING

Bennett, Norman Robert. *The Arab State of Zanzibar: A Bibliography*. Boston: G. K. Hall, 1984. Comprehensive bibliography of Zanzibar, with many references to works discussing Saʿīd.

Coupland, Reginald. *East Africa and Its Invaders: From the Earliest Times to the Death of Seyyid Said in 1856*. New York: Russell & Russell, 1965. Originally published in 1938, this study has been criticized as not always accurate, but it remains a useful resource.

Nicolini, Beatrice, and Penelope-Jane Watson. *Makran, Oman, and Zanzibar: Three-Terminal Cultural Corridor in the Western Indian Ocean, 1799-1856*. Leiden: Brill, 2004. Historical study that focuses on relationship between the sultan of Zanzibar and European powers.

Oliver, Roland, and Gervase Matthew, eds. *History of East Africa*. Vol. 1. Oxford, England: Clarendon Press, 1963. A scholarly and detailed treatment that includes the sultan's life.

Ruete, Emily. *Memoirs of an Arabian Princess from Zanzibar*. New York: M. Wiener Publishers, 1989. Generally accepted as an authentic memoir of life in the sultan's Zanzibar palace by one of Saʿīd's daughters. Born in 1844 as Sayyida Salma, Emily Ruete married a German merchant and left the island in 1866. Her memoirs were first published in German in 1888 and in English in 1907.

SEE ALSO: Sir Richard Francis Burton; Napoleon I; Tippu Tib.

RELATED ARTICLES in *Great Events from History: The Nineteenth Century, 1801-1900:* 1814-1879: Exploration of Arabia; 1873-1897: Zanzibar Outlaws Slavery.

SAIGŌ TAKAMORI
Japanese politician

Saigō's military leadership and political support were instrumental in the events leading to the demise of Japan's last feudal government in 1868, while his championing of samurai ideals, culminating in the failed 1877 Satsuma Revolt, during the early Meiji reform era, earned for him the reputation as one of the last supporters of an honorable but outdated value system he ironically helped destroy.

BORN: 1827/1828; Kagoshima, Kyūshū, Japan
DIED: September 24, 1877; Kagoshima, Kyūshū, Japan
ALSO KNOWN AS: Saigō Kichibē or Saigō Kichinosukē (birth name); Nanshū (pseudonym)
AREA OF ACHIEVEMENT: Government and politics

EARLY LIFE

The eldest of seven children of a low-ranking samurai serving as head of the Satsuma accounts department, Saigō Takamori (si-go tah-kah-moh-ree) was born in the castle town of Satsuma, on the southern island of Kyūshū, a *tozama* domain ruled by the Shimazu clan.

The Tokugawa Bakufu military government was a feudal polity controlling from its capital at Edo (modern Tokyo) about 260 hereditary *han* (domains) ruled by local daimyo lords. Former enemies of the Tokugawa clan were included in this arrangement as *tozama* (outside lords), and their lands were latent repositories of anti-Bakufu sentiments.

Once proud fighting men, many samurai, as a result of the Pax Tokugawa, had become bureaucrats, assisting their lords in various administrative capacities. Saigō's father was such a retainer. Proud of his warrior heritage, yet reduced to the role of a fiscal manager, he struggled to supplement his low salary by farming.

Saigō, a heavyset boy with a thick neck, bushy eyebrows, and penetrating eyes, was reared among memories of his family's samurai heritage and his domain's proud history. During his youth, Saigō was trained in the fighting arts and had inculcated in him the principles of *Bushidō*, the code of samurai ethics. His formal learning occurred at the *Zōshikan*, the Satsuma clan school. There he received a traditional education grounded in neo-Confucian ethics, the activist moral philosophy of the Ming Chinese philosopher Wang Yangming, complemented by swordsmanship, Zen meditation, the nativist Shinto beliefs, and regular school subjects. He had a reputation for being a mischievous, headstrong, inarticulate, yet brave and charismatic young man. His burly stature and weight stood him well in sumo wrestling matches, but it also made him the butt of classmates' jokes. Upon finishing school at sixteen, he became an assistant clerk in the county magistrate's office.

Saigō became politically active when he became involved in a succession dispute within the domain's ruling family by siding with Shimazu Nariakira, who became daimyo in 1851, two years before Commodore Matthew C. Perry steamed into Uraga Bay near Edo with a squadron of "black ships" to demand an end to the self-imposed seclusion policy begun during the 1630's.

In recognition of his crucial support for his lord's rise to power, Saigō was taken into Nariakira's service. His presence at Nariakira's Kagoshima headquarters gave him entrée into the inner circle of Satsuma political discussions and policy-making. Saigō, from 1855 to 1858, traveled to Edo and Kyoto as Nariakira's private emissary in the complex political maneuvering among shogunate, imperial court, and daimyo over a commercial treaty that had been proposed by American consul general Townsend Harris and the naming of an heir to the childless shogun Takugawa Iesada.

Nariakira's political star eclipsed in 1858, when his preferred Hitotsubashi line candidate for shogun was rejected in favor of the Kii line. The victory of the Kii proponents brought to power Ii Naosuke, who became great elder in the summer of 1858. Ii signed the Harris treaty without court approval in July and launched the Ansei purge (1858-1860) to oust those opposing him and the shogunal policy of *kaikoku* (open the country).

Nariakira died in August, 1858. In despair at the loss of his patron and now on the political outside, Saigō resolved to commit suicide; he was dissuaded from doing so by Gesshō, a proimperialist Buddhist monk, who was also on Ii's purge list. Together they fled from Kyoto to Satsuma, where the authorities would not give them protection. They decided in a joint suicide pact to drown themselves in Kagoshima Bay. Gessho succeeded; Saigō, however, was retrieved from the water and, after recovering, banished to Amami Oshima in the Ryukyu Islands.

Nariakira's half brother Hisamitsu had become regent for his son Tadayoshi, the new lord of Satsuma. Hisamitsu, persuaded by Saigō's boyhood friend Ōkubo Toshimichi, decided to send troops to Kyoto to support

the emperor and then march on Edo to force reforms on the Bakufu. Ōkubo interceded with Hisamitsu for Saigō's return. On March 12, 1862, Saigō was recalled to Satsuma and soon consented to head an advance party of Satsuma troops to Kyoto. He irked Hisamitsu by holding discussions in Kyoto with radical *rōnin* (masterless samurai) wanting to overthrow the Bakufu. Consequently, he was ordered into a second exile (only six months after his pardon) to the islands south of Satsuma. Saigō spent his second banishment (1862-1864) brooding over his failure to avenge his honor through suicide, practicing his calligraphy, wrestling, writing poetry, and starting a family with a commoner, by whom he had two sons (he would take an official wife, Itoko, in 1865).

LIFE'S WORK

Again at the urging of Ōkubo, Saigō's second exile ended on April 4, 1864. After Ii Naosuke was assassinated by samurai extremists in March, 1860, the weakened shogunate tried to reach an accommodation with the pro-emperor, antiforeign forces in Kyoto. Given the title of war minister, Saigō was sent to Kyoto to serve as a Satsuma watchdog. There he faced plotters from the *tozama han* Chōshū (a Satsuma rival), maneuvering to overthrow the Bakufu elements at court. Saigō and his men helped pro-Bakufu Aizu samurai expel the Chōshū troops from Kyoto. Chōshū was declared rebellious, and a punitive expedition was authorized by the Bakufu to chastise this southwestern domain. Saigō was a leader of the December, 1864, Chōshū expedition that forced the domain to apologize, surrender some land, disband its militia, and have some leaders commit suicide. Saigō was instrumental in preventing a harsher treatment of Chōshū.

By 1865, however, Chōshū was rebuilding itself after an internal revolt by midrank samurai. Satsuma was now concerned that the Bakufu was becoming more powerful. Saigō and others began aiding loyalists such as Sakamoto Ryōma, a young Tosa (another outside domain) samurai, and certain Kyoto nobles allied with Iwakura Tomomi, an important court official. Saigō also met Great Britain's first envoy to Japan, Sir Harry Parkes, to try to persuade the English from wholeheartedly supporting the Bakufu. These efforts impressed Chōshū: the two *han*, burying differences in favor of a united front against the Bakufu, their common enemy, entered an alliance in March, 1866. A powerful *tozama* coalition, soon augmented by Tosa, was in place to challenge the Tokugawa. When a second punitive Bakufu-led army (without Satsuma participation, at Saigō's insistence) was launched against Chōshū in the summer of 1866, the strengthened Chōshū domain had no trouble repelling them.

The ascendancy of Tokugawa Yoshinobu to the shogunate late in 1866 revived the central government; reforms were initiated and Western military matériel was secured. In the face of Satsuma opposition, however, the shogun had to agree in the fall of 1867 to a Tosa compromise requiring him to step down and join the daimyo ranks as the head of a power-sharing council. There was fear that the Tokugawa, still the strongest of the daimyo, might reassert its right to national rule; to counter this threat, Satsuma troops entered Kyoto, where Saigō and others, with the support of Iwakura, formulated a proclamation to be issued in the name of the fifteen-year-old emperor Mutsuhito, declaring the restoration of imperial rule.

On January 3, 1868, this proclamation was made in the context of a coup d'état in Kyoto led by Saigō. The office of shogun was officially ended; the Tokugawa were ordered to surrender all lands and titles, a demand that Yoshinobu refused. Saigō, a junior councillor in the new provisional government, led loyalist troops against holdout Bakufu forces, winning the Battle of Toba-Fushimi. His troops continued mop-up campaigns, which lasted until Edo castle was surrendered and the last Bakufu naval forces were defeated. Victorious in battle, Saigō spared most of his enemies, including the ousted shogun. The emperor, his reign title changed to Meiji (enlightened rule), was nominally restored in 1868, but the political future of the new government, transferred to the former Tokugawa seat of power, renamed Tokyo (eastern capital), was in the hands of a small coterie of young middle- and low-rank samurai from the domains of Satsuma, Chōshū, Tosa, and Hizen.

As the fighting diminished in 1868, Saigō returned to Kagoshima along with many of his soldiers. Whereas his colleague Ōkubo stayed in Tokyo to launch the Meiji regime, Saigō entered semiretirement, working as a clan councillor. He was a national military hero. The court offered him the third rank junior grade to recognize his contributions to the restoration, but he declined in self-deprecating tones, because such an honor would have put him at a rank higher than his daimyo. Realizing that Saigō's nonparticipation in the government and his influence at home could be troublesome, Iwakura, serving as an imperial messenger and accompanied by Ōkubo and Yamagata Aritomo, called on Saigō in January, 1871, with a direct order from the emperor, requiring his participation in the Tokyo government. Ever loyal, he acqui-

esced to the imperial command, becoming a chief counselor of state. He thus joined Ōkubo, Kido Kōin (Chōshū), Itagaki Taisuke (Tosa), and Ōkuma Shigenobu (Hizen) in a coalition government representing the leading pre-Meiji restoration *han*.

In 1871, confident that their reforms had firmly established them in power, Iwakura led more than half of the government's leaders on a year-and-a-half-long trip to observe at first hand the United States and Europe and to persuade the Western powers to revise the unequal treaties. Saigō, Itagaki, and Ōkuma were left in charge of a caretaker government bound by written promises not to initiate any new policies while the Iwakura Mission was abroad. In the area of foreign policy, however, independent action was contemplated. When Korea, under Chinese suzerainty, rejected Japanese overtures to recognize the Meiji government, Saigō wanted to go to Korea alone and provoke the Koreans to kill him, thus forcing Japan into war. Earlier, when fifty-four Ryukyuans were attacked by Taiwanese aborigines in 1871, he had called for a punitive expedition against Formosa. Saigō favored a foreign war to create a role for the many samurai who had been replaced by the new conscript army of commoners and who looked to him for leadership.

Before Saigō could have his permission to go to Korea confirmed by the emperor, Iwakura returned and persuaded Ōkubo to head the opposition to Saigō's plans. Ōkubo, the pragmatic realist, and Saigō, the romantic idealist, clashed over the *seikan* (conquer Korea) issue, ending their decades-long friendship. Iwakura followed Ōkubo's efforts by forcing Saigō and his prowar partisans out of the government. To save face, it was announced that Saigō and many Satsuma supporters were leaving the government because of poor health. This was his irreversible break with the Meiji government, now dominated by the Ōkubo faction.

Takamori's retirement was outwardly peacefully spent romping in the Kagoshima woods with his dogs and composing poetry; there was, however, a political dimension to his retirement as well. He founded several private schools to train Satsuma youth in the fighting arts and traditional ethics. Elsewhere, as samurai were being stripped of their class privileges and becoming impoverished by the financially strapped government's reduction of their stipends, resentment turned into rebellion. In 1874, two thousand Saga samurai revolted unsuccessfully under Etō Shimpei, who had left the government when Saigō had. There were similar failed samurai uprisings in Kumamoto and Hagi two years later.

Wary of what Saigō might do, police informants watched for signs of disquiet in Kagoshima. The government decided to remove by ship a cache of arms from Kagoshima to prevent Saigō's followers from arming themselves. Hotheaded young samurai attacked the imperial arsenals to forestall the arms' removal, precipitating the 1877 Satsuma Revolt. Saigō, probably aware of the futility of the rebellion, backed his followers, reaffirming his allegiance to the emperor while berating the evil politicians who surrounded him. Saigō's twenty-five thousand men faced at least three times as many government forces. A disastrous battle over Kumamoto castle depleted the rebel army, and its remnants were pursued throughout Kyūshū. In a cave at Shiroyama, Saigō rejected a request from Yamagata to surrender. As he was attempting to escape, he was wounded by a bullet. A samurai to the end, Saigō, to avoid capture and shame, committed ritual disembowelment on September 24, 1877.

SIGNIFICANCE

Ending his life a traitor to the state he had helped to found, Saigō Takamori became a hero in death. In 1890, the emperor Meiji pardoned him posthumously and restored his titles. This apotheosis, coming at a time when the Meiji oligarchy was secure in its power, reflected the popular verdict that Saigō had been a sincere, patriotic hero representative of samurai values nostalgically celebrated in a modernizing Japan that was struggling for an accommodation with its feudal past. The Satsuma Revolt and Saigō's suicide for the cause were not only his but also the country's last backward glances at a consciously discarded tradition, the lofty virtues of which still resonated in the hearts—if not the minds—of many Japanese.

Saigō's life bracketed the sweeping changes that in a short period ended a feudal regime and established a centralized nation-state in its place. Although the majority of the Meiji Restoration leaders looked forward, Saigō clutched at a past symbolic of the pure samurai motives his political activism espoused. For later eras, Saigō's life and deeds would be a manipulatable legacy, often with altered facts, that would provide a model for jingoistic foreign adventurists, right-wing nationalists, and out-of-power political dissidents, who would claim him as their source of inspiration. Saigō's life was so complex that liberals, Westernizers, and other more progressive elements could similarly adopt the Satsuma warrior as their own.

—*William M. Zanella*

FURTHER READING

Beasley, W. G. *The Meiji Restoration*. Stanford, Calif.: Stanford University Press, 1972. The most comprehensive treatment of the late Tokugawa to early Meiji period, with useful glossaries and a bibliography. Saigō's role in the important events of the time are woven into this factual and analytical narrative.

Buck, James H. "The Satsuma Rebellion of 1877." *Monumenta Nipponica* 28 (Winter, 1973): 427-446. A thorough account of the samurai uprising and Saigō's participation, emphasizing the military and political maneuvers of the rebel and imperial forces.

Hillsborough, Romulus. *Samurai Sketches: From the Bloody Final Years of the Shogun*. San Francisco: Ridgeback Press, 2001. This collection of sketches about the overthrow of the Tokugawa shogunate includes information about Saigō, listed under the name Saigō Kichinosuke in the book's index.

Iwata, Masakazu. *Ōkubo Toshimichi: The Bismarck of Japan*. Berkeley: University of California Press, 1964. A biography of Saigō's Satsuma compatriot, with numerous references to Saigō's life where it intertwined with Ōkubo's. Provides an overall view of Satsuma politics and the domain's role in the restoration movement and early Meiji government.

Jansen, Marius B. *Sakamoto Ryōma and the Meiji Restoration*. Stanford, Calif.: Stanford University Press, 1961. Though focusing on this Tosa loyalist samurai, numerous references to Saigō are interlaced in this biographical narrative, describing the downfall of the Tokugawa shogunate.

Mayo, Marlene. "The Korean Crisis of 1873 and Early Meiji Foreign Policy." *Journal of Asian Studies* 31 (August, 1972): 793-819. An analysis of the background of and the reasons for the aborted Korean plan of Saigō and the political maneuvering that defeated it, placed in an overview of emerging Meiji diplomatic concerns.

Morris, Ivan. *The Nobility of Failure: Tragic Heroes in the History of Japan*. New York: Holt, Rinehart and Winston, 1975. Chapter 9, "The Apotheosis of Saigō the Great," is an excellent English account of Saigō's life, analyzed as part of the Japanese fascination for failed heroes. Very useful notes contain additional biographical details.

Ravina, Mark. *The Last Samurai: The Life and Battles of Saigō Takamori*. Hoboken, N.J.: John Wiley & Sons,

2004. Popular biography, recounting Saigō's life and participation in the Satsuma Revolt.

Yates, Charles L. *Saigō Takamori: The Man Behind the Myth.* New York: Kegan Paul, 1995. The first English-language biography of Saigō examines his life and near-mythic status in Japanese history.

SEE ALSO: Ii Naosuke; Itō Hirobumi; Mutsuhito; Matthew C. Perry.

RELATED ARTICLES in *Great Events from History: The Nineteenth Century, 1801-1900:* January 3, 1868: Japan's Meiji Restoration; January-September 24, 1877: Former Samurai Rise in Satsuma Rebellion.

AUGUSTUS SAINT-GAUDENS
Irish-born American sculptor

Saint-Gaudens's memorial statues of the greatest American men and women are generally regarded as among the most beautiful and inspired examples of late nineteenth century artistic realism, which reached its zenith partly because of the popularity of his work.

BORN: March 1, 1848; Dublin, Ireland
DIED: August 3, 1907; Cornish, New Hampshire
AREA OF ACHIEVEMENT: Art

EARLY LIFE

Augustus Saint-Gaudens (sahnt goh-denz) was the son of Bernard Paul Ernest Saint-Gaudens, formerly of the village of Aspet in southern France, a shoemaker who emigrated to London and then Dublin. It was in the latter city that he met and married Mary McGuiness, a handcrafter of slippers formerly from Bally Mahon, County Longford. Their first children, George and Louis, died in childhood; then Augustus was born in Dublin; finally, Andrew and another Louis were born in the United States.

The family emigrated from Ireland to the United States in 1848, during Augustus's infancy and the ruinous potato famine. The small family arrived at Boston but soon moved to New York City. Here the children were brought up in the Catholic faith and attended public schools. A patron of the arts, Dr. Cornelius Rea Agnew, saw some pen-and-ink drawings by the child Augustus in his father's shop and recommended that he be apprenticed to an artist. Accordingly, in 1861, when he was thirteen, the boy began his apprenticeship under a stern taskmaster named Avet, a stone-cameo cutter.

The Civil War years and the personalities of that era impressed themselves upon the sensitive mind of the budding artist. Later, he would portray several of them in examples of his greatest works. He came to detest Avet, however, and almost turned his back on portraiture until he found employment with the shell-cameo artist Jules LeBrethon and was accepted as a student at the distin-

guished drawing school of the Cooper Institute. Before the war drew to a close in 1865, he was admitted to the still more prestigious National Academy of Design. His skills greatly heightened and his family's finances much improved by his earnings, Saint-Gaudens sailed for Europe at the age of nineteen.

LIFE'S WORK

In Paris, Saint-Gaudens obtained employment with an Italian cameo cutter and enrolled in a small art school and then in the world famous school of fine arts, L'École des Beaux-Arts. Here, Saint-Gaudens learned much of low relief and the special art of sculpture. In 1868, the American produced his first such work, a bronze bust of his father.

Several lifelong friendships were formed in the five years before Saint-Gaudens returned to the United States in 1872, one with Alfred Garnier, one with Paul Bion, and another with the Portuguese Soares dos Reis. These accomplished young artists reinforced one another's desire to persevere in the face of brutal criticism and dwindling funds. Saint-Gaudens, with some of his friends from L'École des Beaux-Arts, lived for a while in Rome; there he completed several classic busts and his statues *Hiawatha* and *Silence*, later placed in Saratoga and New York City, respectively.

Saint-Gaudens's brief return home, to New York, led to several commissioned works. During this time, his patrons included Senator William Evarts of New York, Edward Stoughton, Edward Pierrepont, Elihu Root, and L. H. Willard. Now a productive artist, he chose to live in Rome for the next three years, returning to the United States to stay in 1875. Before his return, he met and became engaged to an American girl in Rome, Augusta F. Homer.

The wedding took place at Roxbury, Massachusetts, on June 4, 1877. Both Augustus and Augusta were dark, average in height, and slim. Augusta was considered by far the better-looking of the two, as Augustus's chin and nose were long and angular. Augustus also maintained a mustache and, generally, a beard of some kind. Their one child, Homer, was born in 1880. Back in New York, artist John La Farge helped Saint-Gaudens obtain such important assignments as the statue of Admiral David Farragut for placement in Madison Square, New York City, the St. Thomas (Episcopal) Church reliefs, also in New York, and those of the Edward King tomb in Newport, Rhode Island.

Early during the 1880's, Saint-Gaudens began a friendship that was to have a great impact on both his life and his work. A Swedish-born model, Alberta Hulgren or Hultgren, became his mistress; rechristened Davida (she later used the name Davida Johnson Clarke), she became his muse as well. The details of this relationship, long suppressed, remain sketchy. For many years, Saint-Gaudens maintained a separate household for Davida, by whom he had a son; her likeness is evident in a number of Saint-Gaudens's idealized female figures.

It was during this decade, too, that Saint-Gaudens fully established himself as an artist. By 1880, he had already completed the Morgan Tomb's *Angels*, the statue

Augustus Saint-Gaudens. (Library of Congress)

of Robert Richard Randall for Sailors' Snug Harbor, Staten Island, and several medallion and plaque low reliefs such as those of fellow artist Bastien-Lepage and friend Dr. Henry Shiff. A friend of whom he did caricatures was Charles Follen McKim. Another friend and patron, Stanford White, made valuable contacts on his behalf. In the years that followed, Saint-Gaudens added to his fame with statues or reliefs of Robert Louis Stevenson, William Dean Howells, the children of Jacob H. Schiff, Kenyon Cox, Peter Cooper, Princeton president James McCosh, Mrs. Grover Cleveland, General John A. Logan, General William T. Sherman, and Abraham Lincoln. The Lincoln statue was highly regarded, and it came to rest, appropriately enough, in Lincoln Park in Chicago.

Saint-Gaudens's other works included *The Puritan*, in Springfield, Massachusetts, a winged *Victory* on the Sherman Monument, *Amor Caritas*, caryatids, other glorified women, eagles for gold coins, horses, and angels. He taught courses at the Art Students' League in New York, accepted pupils readily at his studio on Thirty-sixth Street (most notably Frederick W. MacMonnies), and helped found the Society of American Artists and other groups to promote and advance the fine arts. His advice to aspiring artists was to "conceive an idea and then stick to it." Those who "hang on" will be "the only ones who amount to anything."

In 1891, Saint-Gaudens's most celebrated creation was unveiled: The slim nudity of his *Diana*, high on the tower of Stanford White's Madison Square Garden, provoked comment throughout the city of New York. (A second *Diana*, slightly altered and improved, later took the place of the first.) Many artists today, however, regard Saint-Gaudens's 1891 monument to Mrs. Henry Adams in Rock Creek Cemetery, Washington, D.C., and especially the relief he did there, commonly entitled *Grief*, as his greatest work.

Late in life, Saint-Gaudens suffered two great shocks: He lost his studio in a fire, and then he lost his fast friend and patron White to a pistol bullet. The fire, in October, 1904, destroyed many small pieces of his life's work. The murder of White, a noted architect with a flamboyant lifestyle, was carried out by crazed playboy Harry K. Thaw in June, 1906, and was a scandalous affair. Saint-Gaudens died August 3, 1907, following a bout of poor health, in his beloved vacation site of Cornish, New Hampshire.

SIGNIFICANCE

Realistic sculpture reached its zenith of popularity during the lifetime of Augustus Saint-Gaudens, and his own contributions helped to keep it popular. Although many of his works, busts, reliefs, and complete statues are simply of wealthy patrons and their friends, his most memorable creations are largely associated with the great men and women of his lifetime, including Lincoln, Farragut, and Sherman. His work is both inspired and inspirational, ideal for the dramatic memorial and the noble sentiment. It expresses feelings of passion, confidence, and courage; it is timely yet timeless.

—Joseph E. Suppiger

FURTHER READING

Cortissoz, Royal. *Augustus Saint-Gaudens*. Boston: Houghton Mifflin, 1907. The author, a specialist in the field of American art and artists in the nineteenth century, has produced an effective though somewhat rambling biography.

Cox, Kenyon. *Old Masters and New*. New York: Fox, Duffield, 1905. Cox was a close friend of Saint-Gaudens, and his insight into the subject's work is especially valuable. While dealing with such different artists as Michelangelo and James Whistler, he does set aside a chapter entitled "The Early Work of Saint-Gaudens," wherein the sculptor's Sherman is given particularly close inspection.

Duffy, Henry J., and John H. Dryfhout. *Augustus Saint-Gaudens: American Sculptor of the Gilded Age*. Washington, D.C.: Trust for Museum Exhibitions in cooperation with the Saint-Gaudens National Historic Site, Cornish, N.H., 2003. Catalog accompanying a Saint-Gaudens exhibition, featuring photographs of his work and essays about the sculptor written by Duffy and Dryfhout, the curator and superintendent, respectively, of the Saint-Gaudens National Historic Site.

Greenthal, Kathryn. *Augustus Saint-Gaudens: Master Sculptor*. New York: Metropolitan Museum of Art, 1985. An excellent, thoroughly researched study. Among the 181 illustrations are twelve superb color plates. Includes an extensive bibliography.

Hind, Charles Lewis. *Augustus Saint-Gaudens*. New York: International Studio, John Lane, 1908. The author, a prolific biographer at the turn of the century, produced in this volume a well-illustrated, if rather shallow, biography.

Saint-Gaudens, Augustus. *Augustus Saint-Gaudens, 1848-1907: A Master of American Sculpture*. Toulouse, France: Musée des Augustins, 1999. Catalog accompanying a French exhibition of Saint-Gaudens's work. Includes essays about the collections at the Saint-Gaudens National Historic Site, Saint-Gaudens's reception in France, his influence upon American sculpture, his Civil War monuments, and other topics.

_____. *The Reminiscences of Augustus Saint-Gaudens*. 2 vols. Edited by Homer Saint-Gaudens. New York: Century, 1913. The son of the subject and himself a knowledgeable artist, Homer Saint-Gaudens speaks with authority. Inasmuch as he quotes his father extensively, Homer Saint-Gaudens is regarded as the editor, but he is generous with his own observations.

Taft, Lorado. *History of American Sculpture*. New York: Macmillan, 1903. This book is the best illustrated work available on the masterpieces of Saint-Gaudens and his contemporaries. Taft's lucid commentaries and beautiful full-page photogravures were so well received that this book went through several revisions and reprints.

Wilkinson, Burke. *Uncommon Clay: The Life and Work of Augustus Saint Gaudens*. San Diego, Calif.: Harcourt Brace Jovanovich, 1985. The work of a novelist and popular biographer, this spirited account portrays Saint-Gaudens as part passionate romantic, part "Renaissance soldier of fortune." Provides information unavailable elsewhere, particularly concerning Davida Clarke, whose role in Saint-Gaudens's life is perhaps exaggerated by Wilkinson. Well documented; includes a useful section of illustrations.

SEE ALSO: Henry Adams; Grover Cleveland; David G. Farragut; Abraham Lincoln; Auguste Rodin; Robert Louis Stevenson.

RELATED ARTICLE in *Great Events from History: The Nineteenth Century, 1801-1900:* May 1-October 30, 1893: Chicago World's Fair.

HENRI DE SAINT-SIMON
French sociologist

Regarded as the founder of French socialism and a major early progenitor of the discipline of sociology, the influential Saint-Simon called attention to the value of society's productive classes in the nineteenth century and the need for social reorganization with those natural leaders at the helm. Through his preachments and writings, he inspired practical developments in banking, engineering, feminism, and concern with the plight of the lower classes.

BORN: October 17, 1760; Paris, France
DIED: May 19, 1825; Paris, France
ALSO KNOWN AS: Claude-Henri de Rouvroy (birth name)
AREAS OF ACHIEVEMENT: Sociology, social reform, scholarship

EARLY LIFE

Henri de Saint-Simon (sahn-see-mohn), the future comte de Saint-Simon, considered himself destined for glory because he was the grandnephew of the French king Louis XIV's courtier, the duc de Saint-Simon. Henri's parents, Balthazar-Henri and Blanche-Elizabeth, were cousins descended from different branches of the aristocratic Saint-Simon family.

After an early education provided by tutors, Henri followed his father in seeking a military career. By late 1779, when he was only nineteen years old, he had attained the rank of captain in an infantry regiment and was part of the French contingent supporting the North American colonists in their War of Independence against Great Britain. As a marine officer, he served admirably with the Marquis de Lafayette and General George Washington at the siege of Yorktown.

After the American Revolution ended, Saint-Simon spent several years participating in military campaigns in the Caribbean. At that time, he conceived one of his earliest schemes: a canal connecting the Atlantic and Pacific Oceans across the Isthmus of Panama. After returning to Europe in 1784, Saint-Simon continued his military career, adding to it minor diplomatic roles and another proposal for a fanciful engineering scheme: a canal connecting Madrid, Spain, with the Atlantic Ocean.

Saint-Simon's role in the French Revolution, which began in 1789, was largely insignificant, but he seems to have supported the republican goals against the monarchy. Renouncing his aristocratic connections, he took advantage of the fluid political and social situation in France to speculate in national land purchases, finally achieving the affluence he had long sought. After briefly being imprisoned during the Revolution's Reign of Terror, Saint-Simon resumed his business ventures during the ensuring Directory period and immersed himself in a society of indulgence and learning. While hosting a salon, he cultivated associations with scientists, bankers, and industrialists—all people who were essential to his plans to reorganize society.

LIFE'S WORK

After the turn of the nineteenth century, Saint-Simon's recently acquired fortune was diminishing, and he spent the remainder of his life in financial uncertainty. The years between 1807 and 1813 were beset with financial struggles with a former business partner. He continually sought recognition for his ideas and projects, but his entreaties to Emperor Napoleon I were ignored. His complex and mercurial life was punctuated by a nervous breakdown in 1813, and he attempted suicide in 1823.

Throughout his personal hardships, Saint-Simon remained committed to the dual goals of personal glory and society's advancement, and he managed an outpouring of creative work. In 1803, he presented his first major work, *Lettres d'un habitant de Genève à ses contemporains* (letters of an inhabitant of Geneva to his contemporaries), in which he glorified the role of the new sciences that would be harnessed for social peace and progress. Influenced by physiology and its view of society as an organism, Saint-Simon believed that the methods of science would lead to the understanding of the structure and laws of society. He had imbibed the Enlightenment's focus on unlimited progress, especially as outlined by the Marquis de Condorcet. He regarded the eighteenth century, with its Enlightenment and upheavals, as "critical and revolutionary" and expected the nineteenth century to focus on the "inventive and organizational." He solicited patrons to support the scientific leaders who would join together to form a "Council of Newton," to which he also welcomed women scientists.

The ten-year period that began in 1814 was especially productive for Saint-Simon. With the assistance of several astute collaborators, most importantly the historian Augustin Thierry and the philosopher Auguste Comte, he publicized his most seminal ideas. His prophetic *De la réorganisation de la société européenne* (1814; on the reorganization of European society) envisioned a European federation with a national parliament that would decide the common interests of Europe. Inspired by the Abbe de Saint-Pierre's *Project for Perpetual Peace* (1713) and based on the "natural" alliance of England and France, this association would facilitate commercial intercourse and internal travel, provide European-wide public education, and have the power to adjudicate disputes among its members. In 1815, reacting to the increasing roles of bankers and industrial entrepreneurs in France's Restoration period, Saint-Simon proposed the creation of a special national credit bank with headquarters in Paris and branches throughout the country.

By 1817 Saint-Simon's earlier focus on the centrality of science had shifted to a preoccupation with the benefits of the new industrial age. In line with France's accelerating industrialization, his writings ennobled industry as the source of all wealth and power. In *The Organizer* (1819), Saint-Simon condemned the parasitic roles of the aristocrats who then held power and advocated their replacement by the "industrials," members of what he considered productive groups, such as bankers, artisans, engineers, scientists, industrialists, civil servants, and agriculturists, who contributed to the actual richness of society. With this reorganization of society, the exploitation of humans by other humans would be superseded by humankind's exploitation of nature: "The administration of things will replace the government of man."

Saint-Simon conceded that nobles and priests had provided material and moral guidance in earlier stages of historical development, particularly in the theological and feudal era. However, he regarded them as having become anachronistic in a positive age when the productivity and superior intelligence of industrialists gave the latter the human and divine mandate to lead.

In *Industrial System* (1821-1822) and *Catechism of the Industrialists* (1823), Saint-Simon added to the advantages of industrial leadership. Naturally inclined to commanding people in daily tasks, they would maintain order and prevent violence and ensure the greatest good for the greatest number. This model was indeed a hierarchical structure without pretensions to egalitarianism or democracy, which would be unnecessary with proper reorganization and administration. Manual workers would not be placed in leadership roles, but their interests would be secured. Interestingly, Saint-Simon predicted that his theories would eventually spread through France and Europe, then to other parts of the world.

Although Saint-Simon had earlier sought to abandon metaphysical speculation in favor of positive knowl-

edge, in *Nouveau Christianisme* (1825; new Christianity), his goal was to harmonize a this-worldly, non-dogmatic religion with a society based on science and industry. Continuing a theme established earlier in *Lettres*, and revisited in *Industrial System*, Saint-Simon attacked the papacy and clergy for their betrayal of the moral interests of the people, calling for a renewed morality based on brotherhood, social salvation, and attention to society's neediest groups, "the amelioration of the moral and physical existence of the poorest class." In numerous works Saint-Simon emphasized the role of public education in establishing these ideas in society but believed that the schools must be oriented toward positive science.

After his death in 1825, Saint-Simon's followers distilled his views in the *Exposition of the Doctrine of Saint-Simon* (1828-1830) and in many other writings and preachments. The so-called Saint-Simonians further popularized their master's theories by denouncing the eighteenth century's critical approaches and "egotism" in favor of cooperation, love and brotherhood, and order and progress. They promoted at once society's material and spiritual interests, seeing Saint-Simon's ideas as the fulfillment of Jesus' teachings in an industrial world. With their assault on private property and rights of inheritance, and their call for the emancipation of woman and the equality of the sexes, Saint-Simon's followers had a profound impact on European socialist and feminist movements during the 1830's and 1840's. As bankers and engineers they were to have influential careers, even designing such projects as the Suez Canal.

SIGNIFICANCE

Saint-Simon was the first major European theorist to grasp not only the potential but also the contradictions of industrial society in the nineteenth century, even to the point of analyzing disparate class interests. He tirelessly championed a reorganization of French and European society that would at once maximize the talents of its naturally productive individuals while also addressing the needs of the less fortunate, and in this he influenced Marxism and other later socialist movements. His proto-socialist, technocratic vision of society emphasized the role of proper administration rather than governance in polities of the future.

A pioneering figure in the positivistic movement that extolled science and laws applicable to human society, Saint-Simon inspired many bankers, engineers, and social thinkers who helped to transform Europe and the world in the late modern era. His social theories have earned him a unique position in the development of French socialism and the discipline of sociology, and he was an early exponent of European federation and public education. As a Romantic personality he was perhaps equally inspirational, and he and his followers captured the imagination of belles-lettrists, musicians, and artists.

—*William H. Alexander*

FURTHER READING

Dondo, Mathurin. *The French Faust: Henri de Saint-Simon*. New York: Philosophical Library, 1955. This is a solid summary of the life and ideas of Saint-Simon with numerous enlightening passages from the master's works.

Manuel, Frank. *The New World of Henri Saint-Simon*. Cambridge, Mass.: Harvard University Press, 1956. Although somewhat dated, this is still the best and most comprehensive study of Saint-Simon, by an intellectual historian who situates him culturally and politically.

_____. *The Prophets of Paris*. Cambridge, Mass.: Harvard University Press, 1962. This minor classic has separate chapters juxtaposing Saint-Simon and his followers with other major French social thinkers of the eighteenth and nineteenth centuries, such as the Marquis de Condorcet, who influenced Saint-Simon, and Auguste Comte, Saint-Simon's collaborator who developed positivism into a system.

Musso, Pierre, ed. *L'actualité du Saint-Simonisme*. Paris: Press Universitaires de France, 2004. Based on a 2003 colloquium, this collection of French-language essays offers twenty-first century interpretations and also traces the international influence of Saint-Simon and the Saint-Simonians.

SEE ALSO: Auguste Comte; Wilhelm Liebknecht; Lester Frank Ward.

RELATED ARTICLES in *Great Events from History: The Nineteenth Century, 1801-1900:* 1839: Blanc Publishes *The Organization of Labour*; 1851-1854: Comte Advances His Theory of Positivism.

THIRD MARQUIS OF SALISBURY
Prime minister of Great Britain (1885-1886; 1886-1892; 1895-1902)

Salisbury served as prime minister of Great Britain three times and as foreign secretary four times. In guiding British domestic and foreign policies during the last quarter of the nineteenth century with a steady and firm hand, he overshadowed the influence of all his political rivals through the last years of the nineteenth century.

BORN: February 3, 1830; Hatfield, Hertfordshire, England
DIED: August 22, 1903; Hatfield, Hertfordshire, England
ALSO KNOWN AS: Robert Cecil (birth name); Robert Arthur Talbot Gascoyne-Cecil (full name); earl of Salisbury; Viscount Cranborne; Baron Cecil of Essendon
AREA OF ACHIEVEMENT: Government and politics

EARLY LIFE

The third Marquis of Salisbury was born Robert Arthur Talbot Gascoyne-Cecil on the Cecil family's English estate in Hertfordshire. His father was James Brownlow Gascoyne-Cecil, second Marquis of Salisbury, and his mother was Frances Mary Gascoyne, an heir to estates in Lancashire and Essex. Cecil, who was, according to his daughter Lady Gwendolen, "a nervous sensitive child in mind and body," suffered an irreparable loss when his mother died before he was ten.

After being taught by a local clergyman, Cecil spent a miserable period at a preparatory boarding school. When Cecil was ten, he was sent to Eton, where he did quite well in his academic subjects, but he despised his fellow Etonians for their constant bullying; his time there did nothing to improve his shy and withdrawn personality. When Cecil was fifteen, his father rescued him from his misery at Eton by removing him from the school. For the next two years, Cecil spent what he later called the happiest time of his childhood being tutored at his home at Hatfield. During this period, Cecil discovered an interest in botany, which he retained for the rest of his life; he also spent hours reading in the family library.

Just before he was eighteen, in 1848, Cecil went up to Christ Church, Oxford, to study mathematics. While at Oxford, he manifested his first interest in politics and became treasurer and secretary of the Oxford Union. His tenure at Oxford lasted only two years before he suffered a physical and mental breakdown; he was granted an honorary fourth-class degree.

After leaving Oxford, Cecil suffered a further breakdown of his health; on his doctor's orders, he was sent, in 1851, on a two-year journey to Australia and New Zealand. During his travels, he regained his health although he was quite pessimistic about his future career; he did not want to practice law, and he saw little hope for securing a seat in the House of Commons. Cecil's pessimism soon faded when his father obtained for him the vacant seat of Stamford, Lincolnshire, the borough of Stamford being under the control of one of Cecil's cousins. In August, 1853, Cecil was elected, unopposed, as a Conservative member of Parliament for Stamford; he remained unopposed for the next fifteen years. Cecil also competed for and was elected to a fellowship in All Souls College, Oxford, in 1853.

Salisbury's first years in Parliament were of little inspiration, and he continued to have serious problems with his physical and mental health. At six feet, four inches, and with a thin, stooping figure, the poorly dressed Cecil was not impressive physically, but his spirits took a dramatic turn for the better with his introduction to Georgina Alderson, the daughter of a Norfolk judge. Despite his father's objection to the marriage (on the grounds that she lacked the necessary social and eco-

Third Marquis of Salisbury. (Library of Congress)

nomic status), Cecil married Georgina in July, 1857. The outgoing and optimistic Georgina provided a solid counterbalance to her shy and pessimistic husband.

Because he needed to support his wife and a growing family, Cecil turned during the 1850's and 1860's to journalism as a way to supplement his precarious finances. He contributed a number of articles to the *Quarterly Review* and to the *Saturday Review*, which was owned by his brother-in-law. Cecil, who had entered Parliament in 1853 at the age of twenty-three, did not feel comfortable with the Tory leadership of the fourteenth earl of Derby and Benjamin Disraeli, and he became gloomy about the character of the current political system. He acquired, during this period, a reputation as an independent thinker who was, both in his articles and in his speeches before the Commons, prepared to criticize his own party's policies and leaders.

Cecil's opposition to his party's leadership climaxed during the 1850's and 1860's with his determination to prevent any parliamentary reform of the British electoral system. He opposed any significant increase in the size of the British electorate, believing that any radical change in the electoral system, such as the enfranchisement of the working classes, would irreparably harm the British system of checks and balances. When the Conservatives led by the earl of Derby and Disraeli introduced, in early 1867, a reform bill that gave the franchise to all urban taxpayers, Cecil resigned his recently acquired seat in the cabinet.

During this period of debate over parliamentary reform, Cecil had assumed the courtesy title of Lord Cranborne and had become heir to the Salisbury title upon the death of his older brother. At his father's death in April, 1868, Cecil inherited the Hatfield estates and became the third Marquis of Salisbury. His achievements, which make him one of Great Britain's greatest statesmen, were to be attained while leading his party from the House of Lords.

LIFE'S WORK

The new Lord Salisbury's move to the House of Lords did not prevent him from criticizing the programs and policies of William Ewart Gladstone's Liberal government of 1868-1874. Although politics occupied much of his time during this period, Salisbury also found time to chair the Great Eastern Railway and was elected in 1869 as chancellor of Oxford University. He also spent much of his time at Hatfield with his growing family.

After the stunning victory of the Conservatives in the general election in 1874, Disraeli persuaded Salisbury to return to his former post as secretary of state for India in the new Conservative cabinet. It was during the Disraeli administration of 1874-1880 that Salisbury was propelled into prominence in foreign affairs and was established in his reputation as one of Great Britain's greatest diplomatic statesmen. After Russia invaded Turkey's possessions in 1877, both countries signed a peace treaty that forced the Turks to place their Balkan territories under Russian control. Disagreeing with the British cabinet's decision not to recognize the treaty, the fifteenth earl of Derby resigned as foreign secretary, and Salisbury took his place in March, 1878. Salisbury successfully negotiated the terms of treaties with both Russia and Turkey, which paved the way for the famous Congress of Berlin, held in the summer of 1878. Although Disraeli commanded most of the attention at the congress, it was Salisbury's masterful diplomacy that succeeded in preserving the balance of power in the Balkans.

The Conservatives fell from power in the general election of spring, 1880, and Gladstone formed his second ministry (1880-1885); Salisbury was chosen to lead the Conservatives in the House of Lords when Lord Beaconsfield (Disraeli) died in April, 1881. Upon Gladstone's defeat in May, 1885, over a budget issue, Salisbury reluctantly became prime minister for the first time; during his administration, the question of Irish home rule dominated much of the debate. Salisbury, who served as his own foreign secretary, devoted much of his time during his brief ministry to Ireland and international problems, including the renewed tensions in the Balkans. After suffering defeat in the November, 1885, general election, Salisbury resigned as prime minister in January, 1886.

With the defeat of Gladstone's Irish Home Rule Bill in June, 1886, ninety-three Liberals (also known as Liberal Unionists) deserted the Liberal Party. Because of Salisbury's ability to persuade local Conservatives to give the Liberal Unionists free races in their constituencies, Salisbury and the Unionists triumphed in July, 1886, in the general election. He formed his second ministry, which would last until 1892.

The first months of Salisbury's second administration were dominated by the mercurial personality of Lord Randolph Churchill, who served as Leader of the Commons and Chancellor of the Exchequer. Churchill, who was constantly at odds with his fellow cabinet members, was allowed to resign over a budget issue in December, 1886; Salisbury, not Churchill, would run the 1886-1892 Conservative administration. The major domestic achievement of this administration was the passage of the Local Government Act of 1888, which created elected county councils in England and Wales. Other important pieces of domestic legislation included acts for mine regulation, working-class housing, and free education. Salisbury, who had taken over the Foreign Office in January, 1887, devoted much of his time and energy to international and colonial affairs. He made good use of his diplomatic skills in fending off the encroachments of France, Germany, and Portugal during the European partition of Africa. Although by no means a crusading imperialist, Salisbury was determined to safeguard British interests in Africa.

With the Liberal victory at the polls in 1892, Salisbury lost control of the government for three years. Nevertheless, although Gladstone managed to pass an Irish Home Rule Bill through the Commons in 1893, Salisbury and others decisively defeated the bill in the upper chamber. Salisbury and the Conservatives returned to power with a convincing victory in the general election of summer, 1895; Salisbury would now serve as prime minister uninterrupted until his retirement in 1902.

Although heavily involved with foreign policy during his last administration, Salisbury did not ignore domestic and social issues. He pushed through acts concerned with workmen's compensation, vaccination, food and drugs, working-class housing, and Irish land purchase. In his foreign policy, all Salisbury's skillful diplomacy was needed to avert a war between Great Britain and France over the French intrusion into the Upper Nile. Salisbury was also involved in the successful negotiation between the United States and Great Britain over a boundary dispute between Venezuela and British Guiana. His diplomatic skills did not, however, prevent the outbreak of the South African (Boer) War from 1899 through 1902 between Great Britain and the Afrikaner republics of Transvaal and the Orange Free State. Salisbury had supported the policy of achieving British control of the Transvaal, but he only reluctantly supported Great Britain's entry into the South African War.

Soon after the Conservative government was returned to power in the fall, 1900, election, the tired, seventy-year-old Salisbury gave up the Foreign Office. Now in declining health, he waited until the South African War had been settled and a peace treaty signed before he handed his resignation to Edward VII on July 11, 1902. A little more than a year later, on August 22, 1903, Salisbury died at Hatfield.

SIGNIFICANCE

Robert Cecil, Lord Salisbury, prime minister for nearly fourteen years, was one of Great Britain's most influential statesmen of the late Victorian period. Although Disraeli and Gladstone dominated mid-Victorian politics, Salisbury overshadowed all of his rivals in foreign and domestic affairs. He was the last British statesman to head the government from the House of Lords and not from the House of Commons.

Salisbury is best known as one of Great Britain's great foreign policy statesmen. Although he was no jingoistic imperialist, the British Empire grew during his tenure as foreign secretary and prime minister. He did not actively promote the expansion of the British Empire but instead ensured that Great Britain's interests were protected abroad. Salisbury, who despised secret diplomacy, believed that foreign affairs should be conducted in the open and opposed interference in the internal affairs of other nations. He conducted his foreign policy in a deliberate and methodical manner.

Although no diehard resister of change, Salisbury attempted in his domestic policies to reconcile individual liberties and freedoms with social and political stability. A firm believer in self-help in certain domestic areas, such as working-class housing reform, he was nevertheless willing to use the power of the state to address pressing problems that he believed threatened the entire fabric of British society.

Salisbury was in many ways the architect of the modern Conservative British Party; he made effective use of Gladstone's Irish home rule program to provide a secure base in the Conservative Party for moderate Liberals who had fled their own party over the home rule issue. Unlike many of his political contemporaries, he devoted considerable time and energy to managing party affairs. With his numerous speeches to Conservative associations, he was one of the first British politicians to make effective use of the stump speech to articulate his political opinions, and he also made effective use of Victorian periodicals to publicize his conservative views.

Salisbury was not the charismatic type of politician who needed society's adulation; he preferred to spend his time with his family at Hatfield or with his scientific experiments in his basement laboratory. Ironically, the shy and reserved Salisbury, who wanted to avoid publicity, served in the limelight for much of the last quarter of the nineteenth century as one of Great Britain's most famous and influential statesmen.

—Neil Kunze

FURTHER READING

Bentley, Michael. *Lord Salisbury's World: Conservative Environments in Late-Victorian Britain.* New York: Cambridge University Press, 2001. An examination of the political thought and worldview of Salisbury and other late-Victorian conservatives, providing a context in which to better understand Salisbury's political career.

Cecil, Lady Gwendolen. *Life of Robert, Marquis of Salisbury.* 4 vols. London: Hodder and Stoughton, 1921-1932. Any study of Salisbury must begin with this definitive biography by his daughter; however, Lady Gwendolen's massive work follows her father only to the end of his second ministry in 1892.

Grenville, J. A. S. *Lord Salisbury and Foreign Policy: The Close of the Nineteenth Century.* London: Athlone Press, 1964. Salisbury's foreign policy has received much attention from scholars, and this study is a perceptive analysis of Salisbury's foreign policy between 1895 and 1902.

Kennedy, A. L. *Salisbury, 1830-1903: Portrait of a Statesman.* London: John Murray, 1953. Kennedy offers a very readable portrait of Salisbury. Except for his coverage of the 1892-1903 period, however, he adds little that cannot be found in the more complete study of Salisbury by his daughter.

Marsh, Peter. *The Discipline of Popular Government: Lord Salisbury's Domestic Statecraft, 1881-1902.* Hassocks, England: Harvester Press, 1978. Although the majority of works on Salisbury have focused on Salisbury and his foreign policy, this well-researched and well-written book is a welcome addition to the growing body of literature concerned with the domestic and party leader.

Pinto-Duschinsky, Michael. *The Political Thought of Lord Salisbury, 1854-1868.* London: Constable, 1967. Through a detailed analysis of Salisbury's articles for the *Quarterly Review* and the *Saturday Review*, the author effectively examines the fundamental assumptions of Salisbury's political philosophy.

Roberts, Andrew. *Salisbury: Victorian Titan.* London: Weidenfeld & Nicolson, 1999. Comprehensive, exhaustively researched biography, exploring Salisbury's private life, careers as a journalist and politician, and character and intellect.

Salisbury, Third Marquess of. *Lord Salisbury on Politics: A Selection from His Articles in the Quarterly Review, 1860-1883.* Edited by Paul Smith. Cambridge, England: Cambridge University Press, 1972. Salisbury wrote thirty-three articles for the Tory

Quarterly Review between 1860 and 1883; Smith presents a valuable analysis of Salisbury's ideas on politics in his introduction and skillful editing of seven of these articles.

Steele, David. *Lord Salisbury: A Political Biography*. London: LCL Press, 1999. A reappraisal of Salisbury's political career, focusing on his both his domestic and foreign policies.

Taylor, Robert. *Lord Salisbury*. New York: St. Martin's Press, 1975. Taylor has written the best single-volume work on Salisbury; while others have concentrated on Salisbury's foreign policy, Taylor devotes most of his study to his subject's domestic record. The

book also contains an excellent bibliography of the major primary and secondary sources.

SEE ALSO: Joseph Chamberlain; Fourteenth Earl of Derby; Benjamin Disraeli; William Ewart Gladstone.

RELATED ARTICLES in *Great Events from History: The Nineteenth Century, 1801-1900:* December 6, 1884: British Parliament Passes the Franchise Act of 1884; June, 1886-September 9, 1893: Irish Home Rule Debate Dominates British Politics; 1889: Great Britain Strengthens Its Royal Navy; July 10-November 3, 1898: Fashoda Incident Pits France vs. Britain.

SAMORY TOURÉ
West African resistance leader

Samory Touré established a Muslim empire in western Africa, stretching from Sierra Leone to the Ivory Coast region. He conquered and enslaved African enemies to finance his military resistance to French colonial expansion and defend the territory he acquired. As a champion of African protonationalism, he helped inspire later African independence movements.

BORN: c. 1830; Manyambaladugu, Sise Kingdom, West Africa (now in Guinea)
DIED: June 2, 1900; Ndjole, Gabon
ALSO KNOWN AS: Samory; Black Napoleon of the Sudan
AREAS OF ACHIEVEMENT: Warfare and conquest, government and politics

EARLY LIFE
Samory Touré (sahm-oh-REE too-RAY) was born in the Sise Kingdom in a region of West Africa that is now part of the modern nation of Guinea. Little is now known about his parents, who were apparently traders (*Dyula*), beyond the fact that they were Mandingo, or Mandinka, and his father's lineage was part of the Touré clan. According to a Mande epic, his father was Kemo Lanfia, and his mother was Sona Kamara. Oral histories indicate that many members of the Touré clan were Muslim merchants. Little is also known about Samory's childhood; however, Mande epics depict him as a naughty child who was a natural leader who liked to persuade friends to play pranks on neighbors.

When Samory was seventeen, he pursued trading such goods as cloth and cows to please his family and allow him to describe himself as a *Dyula*. As a young man, Samory became aware of growing European efforts to exploit African resources and seize lands to form colonies. The growing foreign intrusions in West Africa altered relationships among African communities, which competed to acquire wealth and privilege from European trade. The acquisition of European weapons enabled some communities to defeat others and seize property and power.

Samory found that he disliked trading and took to developing soldierly skills, aspiring to become a military leader. In 1848, when he was about eighteen years old, he rescued his mother after she was captured during a Sise clan raid. Realizing he could benefit from Sise weapons and knowledge, he worked for them for about seven years, according to epics, while mastering their weapons. After Samory and his mother left the Sises, he applied his new skills, fighting with the Berete army against the Sises. After two years, Samory returned home.

LIFE'S WORK
In 1861, Mande leaders designated Samory a war chief (*keletigi*). Swearing that he would defend his people from their Sise and Berete enemies, he built up an army and appointed his sons, brothers, and selected friends as representatives and commanders, while gathering his forces near Sanankoro. Access to area rivers provided Samory and his army convenient transportation to the nearby areas he sought to control.

When the ruler of the powerful Tukolor (Toucouleur) Empire, al-Hājj 'Umar Tal, died in 1864, his territory around the upper Niger River became vulnerable to enemy acquisition. Like other military leaders and chiefs, Samory realized he could seize land because of the unstable conditions and persuaded allies to support his ambitions. He wanted to establish a kingdom defended by devoted, capable soldiers armed with weapons equivalent or superior to those used by his European and African foes. Samory secured breech-loading rifles from Sierra Leone sources and took control of gold mines at Buré to finance his military campaigns. He also sold ivory to pay for guns and employed blacksmiths to repair and make new weapons.

In 1878, Samory declared he was the military ruler of the Wassulu (Wassoulou) Empire that he created. Establishing a capital at Bissandugu, in which is now Côte d'Ivoire (Ivory Coast), Samory initiated trade with Tokolor and emphasized his political rights to represent his empire in transactions with other states. During the following year, he seized Kankan, a trading community located near significant roads Samory needed to control. He continued to subdue tribes and their states and secured vast holdings. He demanded that tribes pay him large tributes, which he used to strengthen his military forces. He rewarded his troops on merit and loyalty and expected them to perform both agricultural and military duties.

In addition to military action, Samory pursued diplomacy with selected African rulers and Europeans in West Africa, especially British colonists in Sierra Leone. He traded with Futa Jallon representatives, exchanging slaves for weapons and livestock. Assuming the Islamic title *almani*, designating a prayer leader, Samory demanded that all people living within his empire become Muslims. He arranged his territory into ten sections with a centralized Islamic administration and ordered the construction of mosques and religious educational facilities.

Samory vowed to remove French colonists from West Africa. After attempting diplomatic methods of persuading the French to leave, he resorted to military actions when the French refused. He challenged French forces that entered his empire to reach French territory in the Ivory Coast. In February, 1882, French soldiers fought Samory's troops at Kenyeran, which Samory's followers were attempting to capture. Distracted from their target, Samory's army focused on countering the French assault. This first major confrontation with a French force taught Samory that the French were formidable opponents, so he began planning new defensive strategies.

Samory next acquired territory closer to Liberia for future weapons support and purchased additional British rifles. The French colonel A. V. A. Combes targeted Samory's goldfields in 1885 but retreated when Samory's men effectively cut off French communications. The next year, Samory agreed to terms of the Treaty of Bissandougou. He accepted a western border at the Niger River and briefly submitted to French supervision in a protectorate to secure temporary peace while he regrouped his forces.

Almost forty thousand men, representing infantry and cavalry, served in Samory Touré's army in 1887. Desiring to rebuild his empire, Samory resumed offensive operations to acquire new territory by ordering his troops to occupy Sikasso (Mali). However, the French encouraged Samory's new subjects to rebel and supplied them with material support, thereby cutting into Samory's military strength. During the late 1880's, Samory agreed to treaty conditions, conceding to the French some disputed land. In 1890, the signing of the Brussels Convention by European powers ended Samory's access to his most effective weapons when British sources no longer supplied him with rifles.

Meanwhile, both the French and Samory's forces continued to fight for territory in West Africa. The French colonel Louis Archinard assaulted Kankan in March, 1891. Outgunned by French artillery, Samory guided troops away from Kankan to battle the French elsewhere and defeated French forces at Dabadugu in September. Colonel Humbert and his troops secured Bissandugu in June, 1892. Despite his ambitions, Samory was unable to defeat the French. As French troops pursued him, Samory moved east into the Ivory Coast region, burning crops and villages as he passed through to prevent the French from using them and slowing their progress. He secured Dabakala in 1893 and directed guerrilla raiders against nearby French targets, harassing them for three years.

After defeating most of Samory's allies, the French concentrated on finding Samory. French commandant Louis Goudraud finally captured Samory at Guelemou while he trying to make his way to Liberia, on September 29, 1898. Charging him with treason, the French imprisoned him on the Ogooeé River island of Ndjole, in the French Equatorial Africa colony of Gabon, far from his homeland. There, Samory contracted pneumonia and died in exile on June 2, 1900.

SIGNIFICANCE

Samory Touré influenced West African history long after his death. His followers continued seeking independence from French rulers, praising how Samory had hindered colonial expansion and served as an inspiring example of resistance tactics. Samory's critics, however, emphasized the brutality of his tactics and his trading in slaves.

Although the empire that Samory created soon ceased to exist, Samory shaped the formation of modern Guinea by serving as a national hero who had resisted colonialism. Declaring he was Samory's great-grandson—a claim some scholars have questioned—Sekou Touré (1922-1984) became the first person elected modern Guinea's president after that country gained independence from France in 1958. He stressed his anticolonial heritage to retain political prestige.

During Sekou Touré's presidency, he approved issuing a Guinea postage stamp featuring Samory. Benin also issued a Samory postage stamp, celebrating his legacy of resistance to foreign control that ultimately helped achieve independence in West Africa. Modern African storytellers still perform epics that chronicle Samory's life and military achievements. In 1988, playwright Massa Makan Diabate published *A Hyena with an Empty Stomach*, depicting Samory. In 2000, North Korean leaders dedicated a statue of Samory at Conakry, Guinea, to recognize the centennial of his death.

—*Elizabeth D. Schafer*

FURTHER READING

Ajayi, J. F. Ade, ed. *Africa in the Nineteenth Century Until the 1880s*. Berkeley: University of California Press, 1989. This sixth volume in the UNESCO General History of Africa incorporates information concerning Samory's family, community, motivations for his decisions, and rise to power.

Boahen, A. Adu, ed. *Africa Under Colonial Domination, 1880-1935*. Berkeley: University of California Press, 1985. This seventh volume in the UNESCO General History of Africa stresses how Samory preferred fighting to diplomacy and explains the strategies he employed to acquire and maintain effective weapons.

Gann, Lewis H., and Peter Duigan, eds. *The History and Politics of Colonialism 1870-1914*. Vol. 1 in *Colonialism in Africa, 1870-1960*. Cambridge, England: Cambridge University Press, 1969. Chapters by Henri Brunschwig and John D. Hargreaves discuss West African leaders' reactions to European intrusions in African territory and their strategies to resist colonialism.

Johnson, John William, Thomas A. Hale, and Stephen Belcher, eds. *Oral Epics from Africa: Vibrant Voices from a Vast Continent*. Bloomington: Indiana University Press, 1997. Includes a partial epic depicting Samory collected by scholar David Conrad in Kissidougou, Guinea, in 1994. Discusses the role of oral storytelling to transmit African history.

Niane, Djibril Tamsir. "The Origins of Samori's State." *Mande Studies* 3 (2001): 7-14. Part of a special journal volume commemorating the centenary of Samory's death. This issue contains six articles about Samory that discuss such topics as Samory's allies, his weapons technology, and imperialism in West Africa.

Oliver, Roland, and G. N. Sanderson, eds. *From 1870 to 1905*. Vol. 6 in *The Cambridge History of Africa*. Cambridge, England: Cambridge University Press, 1985. Two chapters focusing on West Africa provide details about how local Africans reacted to Samory's demands for Islamic conformity, the harsh treatment that Samory inflicted on them, and their decisions to assist the French during military campaigns.

SEE ALSO: Cetshwayo; Louis Faidherbe; Menelik II; 'Uthman dan Fodio.

RELATED ARTICLE in *Great Events from History: The Nineteenth Century, 1801-1900:* May 4, 1805-1830: Exploration of West Africa.

JOSÉ DE SAN MARTÍN
South American military and nationalist leader

San Martín ranks among the great liberation leaders of the Western Hemisphere. He altered the course of history with his bold movements in Argentina, Chile, and Peru, accomplishing feats that lesser leaders could never have accomplished, while changing the map of South America.

BORN: February 25, 1778; Yapeyú, viceroyalty of Río de la Plata (now in Argentina)
DIED: August 17, 1850; Boulogne-sur-Mer, France
ALSO KNOWN AS: José Francisco de San Martín (full name)
AREA OF ACHIEVEMENT: Military

EARLY LIFE

José Francisco de San Martín (sahn mahr-TEEN) was born in a village on the Uruguay River in what is now northeastern Argentina, where his father, Juan, a career army officer, was administrator. The youngest of four sons, he was educated in Madrid following his father's transfer there in 1785. Two years later, following in the footsteps of his father and older brothers, he requested a cadetship in the Spanish army.

San Martín's first military experience began at the age of fifteen in Morocco, in a Spanish engagement against local Muslim warlords. He also fought in the French Revolution and in the Napoleonic Wars. In 1808, Napoleon I sent French troops into Spain to reach Portugal, which had traded with France's archenemy Great Britain in defiance of Napoleon's wishes. This invasion, along with Napoleon's removal of the Spanish king, caused a furor among the Spanish, who mounted a guerrilla war against the French invaders. San Martín joined the fight against the French by enlisting in the service of the Spanish provisional government (junta), which had been established at Seville. San Martín distinguished himself in battle, receiving a medal and promotions.

For more than twenty years, San Martín served his king with faith and dedication. He had gained valuable experience and had received recognition for his distinguished service. It has been speculated that he did not believe that he had been adequately recognized and, for that reason, he decided to return to his native land and participate in revolutionary events there. San Martín was a Creole, a Spaniard born in the New World, and there was discrimination against Creoles in favor of Spanish-born Peninsulars. Also, in Spain, he had formed friendships with English officers who had imbued him with the revolutionary ideas of the Enlightenment. In 1812, he refused a promotion and returned to Buenos Aires to embark on an enterprise that would gain for him everlasting fame—the independence of South America.

LIFE'S WORK

The thirty-four-year-old San Martín returned to Buenos Aires, which in 1812 was in the middle of revolutionary activities. Creoles in Argentina had created a provisional government in the name of the deposed Spanish king Ferdinand VII. Realizing that San Martín would be a valuable member of their military forces because of his experience in Spain, the government gave him command of the army of Upper Peru, which had been defeated by Royalists and was recuperating in Tucumán. San Martín's military genius shone as he improved the soldiers, who lacked discipline and training.

Although not all biographers agree, many have asserted that San Martín founded a secret pseudo-Masonic society, the Lautaro Lodge, whose members dedicated themselves to the independence of South America from Spain. At any rate, San Martín was strongly dedicated to his native country's independence, and he believed that the provisional government should declare independence and abandon any pretense of loyalty to Ferdinand.

In 1814, San Martín asked to be relieved of his command, declaring that he was in poor health. He was then appointed governor-intendant of the province of Cuyo, which enjoyed a better climate than his previous residence in Tucumán. The real reason for this change, however, was San Martín's secret plan to defeat the Spanish in South America by attacking their stronghold in Peru, not through Upper Peru as the provisional government proposed but by creating a small, well-disciplined army in Mendoza, the capital of Cuyo, to cross the Andes Mountains and defeat the Royalists in Chile and then proceed to Lima, the capital of Peru, by sea. Mendoza was located at the eastern end of a strategic pass leading across the Andes to Chile. San Martín believed that independence would not be accomplished until the Spanish stronghold of Lima was captured.

For three years, San Martín devoted all of his considerable energy to his bold and daring plan—recruiting, training, and equipping his army of the Andes. The years in Cuyo were in many ways the happiest years of his life. Shortly after his arrival in Buenos Aires, he had married fifteen-year-old María de los Remedios Escalada, the daughter of a wealthy Creole merchant. Their only child, Mercedes, was born in 1816, during his governorship in Cuyo. San Martín was an efficient administrator, accomplishing much for the people of Mendoza. He was popular there, proving to be charming and persuasive with the people even though he never pretended to be a politician. He was a tall, broad-shouldered, handsome man with a large aquiline nose, thick black hair, and large, bushy whiskers. His complexion was dark, and he had dark, piercing eyes. He looked every inch the soldier, with a commanding presence.

In 1816, San Martín persuaded the Buenos Aires government to assist him in his bold scheme. Juan Martín Pueyrredón, head of the government, appointed him commander in chief of the army of the Andes. By January, 1817, San Martín's army of more than three thousand soldiers was ready to march across the snow-covered Andes and fulfill its mission. His soldiers successfully traversed the rugged mountains and, twenty-one days later, appeared before the astonished Spaniards on the Chilean side of the Andes. This amazing feat has been compared to Napoleon's march across the Alps in 1800 and Hannibal's similar march in the Punic Wars. San Martín's feat, however, had a greater effect on history, because it prepared the way for the independence of Chile and Peru from Spain.

San Martín's forces inflicted a decisive blow against the Royalist army on February 12 at Chacabuco, which opened the way to Santiago, the Chilean capital. Two days later, his army jubilantly entered Santiago unopposed. Declining offices and promotions from the grateful Chileans, he continued with his plan to attack Lima by sea from some fifteen hundred miles away. To accomplish that, a navy was needed. There were still substantial Royalist forces in Chile, and another battle had to be fought to secure Chile's independence. This battle, fought in April, 1818, at Maipú, near Santiago, ended any further Royalist threat.

A year later, in preparation for his expedition against Peru, San Martín was appointed brigadier general of the Chilean army, projected to be some six thousand strong. In the meantime, a navy was being created in Chile for the upcoming invasion. The Chileans had enlisted the valuable assistance of Thomas, Lord Cochrane, a former English naval officer, who was made the commander of Chile's navy. San Martín's plans, however, were almost thwarted by events in Argentina, where political leaders were arguing over what form the government should take. Many favored a monarchy, as San Martín did, but agreement could not be reached. Amid this discord, the

José de San Martín. (Library of Congress)

Argentine government ordered San Martín and his army to recross the Andes and return to Argentina. He refused but left his resignation up to his men, who insisted that he remain their commander. The Chilean government reinforced this revolutionary act by appointing San Martín commander in chief of liberation.

In August, 1820, the invasion of Peru, the last stronghold of Spanish power in South America, began. San Martín made it clear to his soldiers that their objective was to free, not to conquer, their Peruvian brothers. Upon his arrival in Peru, Spanish officials in Lima attempted to negotiate a compromise with San Martín, who insisted that Spain recognize the independence of Peru. San Martín proposed that a junta govern Peru for the time being; ultimately, he envisioned a constitutional monarchy for South America, with a king or emperor from the Spanish royal family. Soon, however, the negotiations broke down.

Peruvians in the north had been influenced by San Martín's writings and speeches calling for independence, and it was undoubtedly their demand for independence that caused the viceroy to evacuate the loyalist troops from Lima and the coast, leaving the way clear for

San Martín to occupy the capital, which he quietly did on June 12, 1821. The independence of Peru was proclaimed officially on July 28, 1821, amid jubilation. Events, however, would soon turn against San Martín.

In August, 1821, San Martín announced that he would assume the title of protector of Peru, with full military and civil power, in order to deal with counterrevolutionary plots and the opposition of the powerful elite in Lima to San Martín's social reforms. Although he declared that he had no ambitious motives, many of his followers voiced criticism. There were also rumors that he wanted to be king. Matters were exacerbated when Lord Cochrane quarreled with San Martín and left Peru with his squadron of ships. San Martín was struck with a sudden illness that confined him to bed. Meanwhile, a large Royalist army gathered near Lima, challenging San Martín to a battle that he refused to join because of his smaller force.

Amid this unhappy state of affairs, San Martín announced that he would meet with Simón Bolívar, the liberator of Colombia, at Guayaquil to discuss plans for the complete liberation of Peru. The famous meeting of the two giants of South American independence took place on July 26 and 27, 1822. It has never been clear exactly what transpired at the meeting, but after it San Martín abruptly withdrew from public life. It is possible that San Martín withdrew because he saw that Bolívar possessed the greater resources necessary to win the final victory over the powerful Royalist army in Peru.

San Martín returned to Argentina, where he received the news of his wife's death. He left an indifferent and hostile Argentina with his young daughter and spent the remainder of his life in exile in Europe, where he suffered from poor health, poverty, and bitterness. He died in Boulogne-sur-Mer, France, on August 17, 1850, unaware that history would elevate him to legendary stature.

SIGNIFICANCE

José de San Martín's claim to fame emanated from his bold and daring plan to cross the Andes, liberate Chile, and establish a base from which to attack Peru by sea and thus complete the liberation of southern South America. He was a great leader of men, inspiring them to great feats of endurance. He was a man of action rather than of reflection; he won battles and left other matters to statesmen. At the same time, it should be noted that he was a man who reflected the spirit of his age, because he was a believer in the ideals of the eighteenth century Enlightenment as evidenced in his ideas of independence and his strong support of education and social reforms. He was a rational man who correctly reasoned that South America was not ready for the republican type of government found in the United States. He supported monarchy as the solution to the chaos he saw emerging around him.

San Martín altered the course of history with his bold movements in Argentina, Chile, and Peru. A lesser man would never have accomplished what he did. He truly deserves to be remembered alongside other liberators in the New World, such as George Washington and Simón Bolívar.

—James E. Southerland

FURTHER READING

Harvey, Robert. *Liberators: Latin America's Struggle for Independence, 1810-1830*. Woodstock, N.Y.: Overlook Press, 2000. A history of Latin America's struggle to overthrow Spanish rule, focusing on San Martín and six other liberation leaders.

Metford, J. C. J. *San Martín: The Liberator*. New York: Philosophical Library, 1950. A very readable, well-balanced, and scholarly account of San Martín's life. The author attempts to separate the man from the legend.

Mitre, Bartolomé. *The Emancipation of South America*. Translated by William Pilling. London: Chapman & Hall, 1893. A translation and condensation of Mitre's exhaustive multivolume *Historia de San Martín y de la emancipación sud-americana* (1887-1888), which is considered a classic. Poetically written. Combines a helpful index and a map.

Robertson, William Spence. *Rise of the Spanish-American Republics as Told in the Lives of Their Liberators*. New York: D. Appleton, 1918. Contains an excellent chapter on San Martín. Offers a well-written and well-researched summary of San Martín's role in the independence of Argentina, Chile, and Peru.

Rodríguez O., Jaime E. *The Independence of Spanish America*. New York: Cambridge University Press, 1998. Covers the wars for independence in Mexico and South America between 1808 and 1826, including information about San Martín's role in the independence movement.

Rojas, Ricardo. *San Martín: Knight of the Andes*. Translated by Herschel Brickell and Carlos Videla. New York: Doubleday, Doran, 1945. A sympathetic, very readable biography. The author believes that San Martín belongs to the "race of armed Saints" that includes Lohengrin and Parsifal. Helpful backnotes and an index.

Schoellkopf, Anna. *Don José de San Martín, 1778-1850: A Study of His Career.* New York: Boni and Liveright, 1924. A small volume, taken almost entirely from Mitre's works, including several verbatim quotations. Contains several illustrations and a helpful map of South America.

SEE ALSO: Simón Bolívar; Napoleon I; Bernardo O'Higgins; Antonio José de Sucre.
RELATED ARTICLES in *Great Events from History: The Nineteenth Century, 1801-1900:* January 18, 1817-July 28, 1821: San Martín's Military Campaigns; September 7, 1822: Brazil Becomes Independent.

GEORGE SAND
French writer

An idealistic, sometimes even mystical, novelist, Sand contributed to nineteenth century French literature a prodigious number of important romantic novels, travel writings, and political essays.

BORN: July 1, 1804; Paris, France
DIED: June 8, 1876; Nohant, France
ALSO KNOWN AS: Amandine-Aurore-Lucile Dupin (birth name); Amandine-Aurore-Lucile Dupin Dudevant; Baronne Dudevant
AREA OF ACHIEVEMENT: Literature

EARLY LIFE

In many ways, George Sand's early life reads like one of her more improbable romantic novels, with her socially mismatched parents, her eccentric aristocratic grandmother, her unorthodox tutors, her flirtation with Roman Catholicism, her unfortunate marriage, her idealistic quest for love, and her close proximity to the political upheavals of her age. She was born Amandine-Aurore-Lucile Dupin during the year of Napoleon I's coronation. When she was only four years old, her father, Maurice Dupin, a dashing officer in Napoleon's army, and a grandson of the illustrious Marshal of Saxe, was thrown from a Spanish stallion and died instantly. Aurore was left alternately in the care of her mother, Sophie, the low-born daughter of a tavern keeper, and her fraternal grandmother, Mme Dupin de Francueil, a woman of aristocratic background and tastes.

Aurore endured the constant emotional and social friction between her two guardians until 1817, when she was sent to the Couvent des Anglaises in Paris to finish her education. At the convent, she was much appreciated by the nuns, despite her somewhat headstrong ways, and even felt the mystical attractions of a religious vocation. In 1820, to circumvent her taking the veil, Mme Dupin de Francueil brought Aurore home to the family estate at Nohant in Berry. There she learned to ride cross-saddle with her brother Hippolyte Chatiron, began to wear men's clothing for riding, and was taught to shoot by Stephane Ajasson de Grandsagne.

In the summer of 1821, Aurore's grandmother had a severe stroke, and Aurore nursed Mme Dupin de Francueil, an unusually difficult patient, until her death in December of the same year. Shortly afterward, in September of 1822, Aurore married Second Lieutenant Casimir Dudevant, bringing him a large estate of 400,000 francs. Her first child, Maurice Dudevant, was born in June of 1823. Her second child, Solange, probably fathered by Stephane Ajasson de Grandsagne, was born in September of 1828, and signaled the continued deterioration of her hasty marriage to the then-financially dependent and increasingly unpleasant Casimir.

In 1831, Aurore left her husband, and Nohant, for Paris, where she lived with her literary mentor, Jules Sandeau. Together, they coauthored articles for the French publication *Le Figaro* and, under the pen name Jules Sand, published an apprentice novel, *Rose et Blanche* (1831). During the early 1830's, Paris was in turmoil, in the aftermath of the July Revolution, and Aurore Dudevant was writing her first independent novel, to be published under the pseudonym George Sand.

LIFE'S WORK

In May of 1832, *Indiana* (English translation, 1833) was published. It was an immediate popular and critical success, launching a distinguished literary career that was to flourish unabated for forty-four prolific years. Sand followed up her first triumph rapidly, in only six short months, with an equally relished novel, *Valentine* (1832; English translation, 1902). This short period of time between novels was a good indication of the famous, almost notorious, fluency with which Sand was to write throughout her life.

In 1833, Sand published *Lélia* (English translation, 1978), and these three early works, along with the ones

	SAND'S NOVELS
1832	*Indiana* (English translation, 1833)
1832	*Valentine* (English translation, 1902)
1833, 1839	*Lélia* (English translation, 1978)
1837	*Mauprat* (English translation, 1870)
1839	*Spiridion* (English translation, 1842)
1840	*Le Compagnon du tour de France* (*The Companion of the Tour of France*, 1976; also as *The Journeyman Joiner*, 1847)
1842-1843	*Consuelo* (English translation, 1846)
1843-1844	*La Comtesse de Rudolstadt* (*The Countess of Rudolstadt*, 1847)
1844	*Jeanne*
1845	*Le Meunier d'Angibault* (*The Miller of Angibault*, 1847)
1846	*Lucrezia Floriani*
1846	*La Mare au diable* (*The Devil's Pool*, 1929; also as *The Enchanted Lake*, 1850)
1847	*Le Péché de M. Antoine* (*The Sin of Monsieur Antoine*, 1900)
1848-1849	*La Petite Fadette* (*Fanchon the Cricket*, 1864; also as *Little Fadette*, 1850)
1850	*François le champi* (*Francis the Waif*, 1889)
1853	*Les Maîtres sonneurs* (*The Bagpipers*, 1890)
1859	*Elle et lui* (*She and He*, 1902)
1861	*Le Marquis de Villemer* (*The Marquis of Villemer*, 1871)
1861	*La Ville noire*
1863	*Mademoiselle la Quintinie*
1868	*Mademoiselle Merquem* (English translation, 1868)
1876	*Marianne* (novella; English translation, 1883)

a Traveller, 1847), as well as the later novel *Elle et lui* (1859; *She and He*, 1902). *Consuelo* (1842-1843; English translation, 1846), the story of a charming prima donna, which evokes so beautifully the musical world of the eighteenth century, was written during her long liaison with Frédéric Chopin. With George Sand, life and art seem always to imitate each other.

The works of Sand's second period, probably influenced by the socialist prophet Pierre Leroux, take a religious tone and concern for the common people, which were already present in Sand's earlier works. *Spiridion* (1839; English translation, 1842), which is a mystical story set in a monastery, and *Le Meunier d'Angibault* (1845; *The Miller of Angibault*, 1847), which has a man of the people for its hero, are typical of the novels of this political period, in which she was also establishing the socialist *Revue indépendante* (1841) with Pierre Leroux and gaining the reputation that would make her the unofficial minister of propaganda after the abdication of Louis-Philippe in 1848.

As much as Sand's heart was in the revolution, and as hard as she worked for government reforms in her own province of Berry, she was sorely disillusioned by the reckless and often-irrational behavior of both the proletariat and the bourgeois participants. After the coup of 1851, Sand focused her political work on interceding with Napoleon III on behalf of numerous imprisoned or exiled republicans. His fortunate admiration for her work made her an unusually successful advocate.

La Mare au diable (1846; *The Enchanted Lake*, 1850), *François le champi* (1850; *Francis the Waif*, 1889), and *La Petite Fadette* (1848-1849; *Little Fadette*, 1850) are Rousseauesque paeans to the beauties of nature and the essential goodness of plain, simple peasants, no matter how hard their lives might be, or what difficulties circumstance might put in their way. These novels are a direct and startling contrast to her intense involvement in French politics, and are often considered her most beautiful and authentic works. The characters in these novels are clearly modeled on the Berrichon peasants whom she had known from childhood.

that followed, *Jacques* (1834; English translation, 1847) and *Mauprat* (1837; English translation, 1870), were typical of Sand's characteristic concerns: the relationship between men and women, class differences in French society, marriage laws and conventions, and the romantic quest for passionate love. There is no question that Sand, when writing these early novels, was drawing on the experience of her own socially mixed parentage, her unhappy union with Casimir Dudevant, and her passionate but troublesome affair with the poet Alfred de Musset.

Critical interest in Sand's life and loves has always competed with interest in her works, and this is not surprising when one considers how much they are intertwined. It was, in fact, her ill-fated trip to Venice with Musset in 1833 that provided the material for her highly acclaimed *Lettres d'un voyageur* (1837; *Letters of*

During the 1850's, Sand's son Maurice had become fascinated with puppet theater, an interest that soon captivated Sand and eventually resulted in her writing a number of plays for the Paris theater. Her fluent, almost poetic, style was not suited to the theater of the day, however, and her plays did not bring her the popularity or the financial rewards of her earlier writings.

Through the last twenty-five years of her life, Sand continued to publish novels with remarkable felicity, at least partly to support her estate at Nohant. The jewel of her later years is undoubtedly her autobiography, *Histoire de ma vie* (1854-1855; *History of My Life*, 1901), written to finance her daughter's dowry and to settle a number of pressing debts. This enormous work, of close to half a million words, first ran in 138 installments in the Parisian newspaper *La Presse*.

History of My Life is not exactly an autobiography in the modern, or conventional, sense of the word, since more than one-third of the book is really about her editing of her father's correspondence with her grandmother; since it is quite restrained about the private details of her relationships with such interesting and renowned artists as Prosper Mérimée, Jules Sandeau, Alfred de Musset, Frédéric Chopin, and Alexandre Manceau; since it was written fully twenty-one years before her death; and since it is full of seemingly unrelated digressions and didactic passages. Nevertheless, this amorphous tome is an unparalleled source of information about Sand's early life and fundamental ideas.

In her final two decades, Sand's literary output was primarily miscellaneous, with one of the outstanding features being a copious correspondence with other important writers, such as Gustave Flaubert. Sand was a diligent letter writer; more than twenty thousand of her letters are still extant.

George Sand died on June 8, 1876, of an intestinal occlusion, but not before she had seen the dawn of the republic in France, and not before she had spent her early morning hours writing as usual. She was buried at her beloved Nohant, and her funeral was attended by such notables as Prince Jérôme Bonaparte, Alexandre Dumas, *fils*, and Gustave Flaubert, as well as by the grief-stricken peasants of the district of Berry.

SIGNIFICANCE

Ivan Turgenev said of George Sand, "What a brave man she was, and what a good woman!" Sand's androgyny, which expressed itself sometimes in her smoking and masculine clothing, and sometimes in the motherly solicitude with which she cared for her friends and lovers, is only one of the many dichotomies that are so characteristic of her life and work. It is important to remember that Sand was a woman with aristocratic blood and a family estate, who wrote socialist novels and worked for the republic.

Despite her idealism, Sand was always the practical and financial center of her family. She was a famous Parisian and an avid traveler, who loved the quiet countryside of Berry with an almost spiritual devotion. She was a woman who had high respect for marriage but who also wrote some of the most damning criticism of the institution ever written. She was in all ways a woman, and a writer, who captured, in both her life and her works, the conflicted spirit of her age.

—*Cynthia Lee Katona*

FURTHER READING

Barry, Joseph. *Infamous Woman: The Life of George Sand*. New York: Doubleday, 1977. An enthusiastic biography of George Sand by an author who sees her as "our existential contemporary." Especially useful for its long quotations from her correspondence, and for its well-chosen illustrations, including a manuscript page in Sand's own hand from her diary dated August 21, 1865.

Cate, Curtis. *George Sand: A Biography*. New York: Avon Books, 1975. This is the definitive biography of Sand for English-speaking readers. Cate follows the personal, literary, social, family, and economic life of Sand from her birth and the crowning of Napoleon in 1804, to her death and the rise of the republic in 1876.

Crecelius, Kathryn J. *Family Romances: George Sand's Early Novels*. Bloomington: Indiana University Press, 1987. A study of George Sand's early novels, with an emphasis on Sigmund Freud's concept of the Oedipal struggle.

Dickenson, Donna. *George Sand*. New York: Berg, 1988. In this largely feminist analysis of Sand's life and work, Dickenson attempts to reinterpret some of the staples of the George Sand myth. She argues, for example, that Sand was a more professional and careful writer than critics, who look only at her prolific output, are usually willing to admit. She also combats the image of Sand as an omnivorous, devouring lover.

Glasgow, Janis, ed. *George Sand: Collected Essays*. Troy, N.Y.: Whitson, 1985. This collection of essays, in both French and English, is an unusual example of Franco-American scholarly cooperation.

Harlan, Elizabeth. *George Sand*. New Haven, Conn.: Yale University Press, 2004. Harlan argues that the question of identity is at the root of Sand's writing, and examines her personal and literary obsession with this question.

Jack, Belinda. *George Sand: A Woman's Life Writ Large*. New York: Knopf, 2000. Biography exploring the connections between Sand's life and literature. Jack maintains that Sand used her literature to probe her psyche and to prepare her for life.

Sand, George. *My Life*. Translated by Dan Hofstadter. New York: Harper & Row, 1979. Because Sand's original French autobiography was exceedingly large and rambling, overly focused on her family before her birth, written long before her career was completed, and was not especially frank about her liaisons with other famous artists, Hofstadter has wisely abridged his translation of Sand's autobiography for English readers.

_____. *She and He*. Translated by George B. Ives. Chicago: Cassandra Editions, 1978. This clearly autobiographical novel is a fictionalized account of Sand's stormy affair with the artist Alfred de Musset. Thérèse's and Laurent's sojourn in Italy and Laurent's near-fatal illness closely resemble the events of Sand's life with Musset from 1833 to 1835.

Thomson, Patricia. *George Sand and the Victorians: Her Influence and Reputation in Nineteenth Century England*. New York: Columbia University Press, 1976. Thomson explores the connections between George Sand and Jane Carlyle, Elizabeth Barrett Browning, Charlotte and Emily Brontë, Matthew Arnold, George Eliot, Thomas Hardy, and Henry James. There is an especially good chapter entitled "George Sand and English Reviewers."

SEE ALSO: Frédéric Chopin; Gustave Flaubert; Napoleon I; Napoleon III; Ivan Turgenev.

RELATED ARTICLE in *Great Events from History: The Nineteenth Century, 1801-1900:* October 1-December 15, 1856: Flaubert Publishes *Madame Bovary*.

ANTONIO LÓPEZ DE SANTA ANNA
Mexican military leader and politician

Santa Anna dominated Mexico during the first forty years of its independence. Although his many presidencies and other power struggles were endemic to his time, he bears the greatest responsibility for the loss of territory to the United States and for retarding the development of political maturity in Mexico.

BORN: February 21, 1794; Jalapa, Veracruz, Mexico
DIED: June 21, 1876; Mexico City, Mexico
AREAS OF ACHIEVEMENT: Government and politics, military

EARLY LIFE

Antonio López de Santa Anna (SAHN-tah AH-nah) was born on the family estate in eastern Mexico during the last decades of the Spanish Empire in the Americas. His family, of Spanish origin, had only arrived in Mexico a few years before his birth. The facts of his birth made him a *criollo*—a person born in America of recent Spanish origin—and that status would later influence his decisions in future political alliances.

Santa Anna had little formal education and did not get along well with his classmates when he was obliged to go to school. His only real interests from an early age were things military. In 1810, after a brief, failed attempt at a career in commerce in the city of Veracruz, he joined a local regiment of the Spanish army as a cadet. He soon transferred to a cavalry regiment and spent the next four years helping to subdue rebellions against Spain in what is now northeastern Mexico. He was promoted twice in 1812 for his service.

In 1813 Santa Anna saw action in Texas against both Mexican and American rebels. This first encounter with American rebels and the "war to the death" tactics that he witnessed Spain use against them would be important in his later dealings with Texas and the United States. After his return to Veracruz in 1814, he confined his military activities to putting down rebellions within the local region. He served as an aide to one of the last viceroys of Mexico in 1817, an assignment that took him briefly, and for the first time, to Mexico City. His spare time was spent furthering his education, particularly on military matters. It is important to note that Santa Anna did not like the pomp of Mexico City and preferred to spend his time in Veracruz. This would be a lifelong pattern in which his home province would provide the requisite base of operations for his many rebellions.

In 1820 a revolt of Spanish troops in Spain forced the king to restore the earlier, radical constitution of 1812. When this news reached Mexico, it set in motion a number of rebellions by *criollo* military officers within the ranks of local Spanish forces. Led by Agustín de Iturbide, these forces proclaimed an independent Mexico in 1821. Shortly after this proclamation, Santa Anna switched sides and declared his support for Iturbide and independence. This act was the first of a number of rebellions and changes of loyalty that characterized Santa Anna's future life; it also signaled his new role as a major public figure. The pattern of pronouncing against an existing government and the promulgation of a "plan" that set forth the rebel leader's concerns was the standard means of operation in Mexico during the first half of the nineteenth century. Therefore, Santa Anna's use of it was nothing unusual.

LIFE'S WORK

Santa Anna aided in securing the 1821 Treaty of Córdoba, in which Spain recognized Mexico's independence. For this and other revolutionary activity, Iturbide promoted him to brigadier general. Within one year, he broke with Iturbide and proclaimed a federal republic in 1822. He served briefly in the Yucatan, married in 1825, and generally remained out of the public eye until 1829, when he defeated Spanish forces at Tampico, bringing considerable glory to himself nationwide. In the light of this glory, he rebelled against the government in 1832 and was elected president in March, 1833. He immediately retired to his estates, leaving the daily government to his vice president and leaving the way open for a takeover of the government in 1834, when he proclaimed a centrist republic to replace the previous federal one.

Given dictatorial powers, Santa Anna turned his attention to crushing anticentrist revolts in Texas and Zacatecas. He defeated Texan forces at the Alamo and Goliad in March, 1836. These two campaigns showed a brutal side of Santa Anna, one contradicted by his good treatment and even adoption of Texan prisoners during the 1840's. Within one month of these victories, he was captured at the San Jacinto River by Sam Houston, forced to sign treaties recognizing Texan independence, and sent to Washington, D.C., before returning to Mexico.

After spending the next year in relative disgrace and seclusion, Santa Anna returned to national attention with the loss of a leg during the Pastry Wars of 1838-1839. Riding this wave of glory, he now hurried to defend

Anastasio Bustamante, the same president he had ousted in 1832. Santa Anna served as a dictator from March to July, 1839, while Bustamante was away. Economic and political collapse led Santa Anna to revolt and gain power in 1841. In December, 1842, he again assumed dictatorial powers by abolishing a short-lived republic. He was elected president by a hand-picked assembly in 1843.

Between 1842 and 1844, Santa Anna increased the size of the army, undertook works of urban renewal, and furthered his cult of personalism through statues, medals, and the military honors accorded the reburial of his lost leg. At this time he also revised Mexican public education and revitalized the Academia de San Carlos, the nation's premiere art institute. Decline began in 1844: Taxes for his elaborate lifestyle were too high, and rebellions broke out in the north and in the Yucatan. By 1845, crowds were defacing his monuments. Amid all this, his first wife died, but he soon remarried. In May of 1845, rebels captured Santa Anna, put him in prison, and then exiled him to Cuba "for life."

Santa Anna returned triumphantly to Mexico on September 16, 1846, from his Cuban exile, having convinced U.S. diplomats that he alone could deliver more Mexican territory to the United States without a war. He then denounced negotiations and called for war with the United States. He was elected president on December 6, 1846. Santa Anna showed indecisiveness in the war with the United States. The Battle of Buena Vista was a standoff, but Santa Anna retreated to Mexico City to quell political infighting. Within one year of his own return to Mexico, Santa Anna witnessed the American occupation of Mexico City. He fled to Jamaica.

From Jamaica, Santa Anna went to Colombia. From there, he was recalled to Mexico to save a nation in chaos that saw no solution to its problems. He was elected president in March of 1853 with dictatorial power and by December had assumed the title of "His Most Serene Highness." Faced with many of the same problems that existed in his previous tenure of office, Santa Anna sold the territory of the American southwest known as the Gadsden Purchase to the United States in an effort to refill the public coffers. Facing failure on all fronts, he sailed into exile again in 1855, first to Colombia and then to Saint Thomas in the modern U.S. Virgin Islands. This would be his last flight from power.

Despite his exile, Santa Anna could not avoid Mexican politics. He returned to his country in 1864 to support the French-backed emperor Maximilian. Within one month of his return, the French expelled him. In true fashion, Santa Anna turned his efforts to toppling Maximilian, spending considerable time in the United States propounding his ideas. While trying to enter Mexico in 1867, Santa Anna was imprisoned for nearly six months. Having lost most of his land and wealth and feeling the end at hand, he wrote his will. In November, 1867, he began his final exile, first in Cuba, then in the Bahamas. A broken Santa Anna returned to Mexico under an amnesty in 1874. Having returned home, he completed his memoirs and died on June 21, 1876. He was buried the next day near Guadalupe Hidalgo.

SIGNIFICANCE

The period from the 1820's to the mid-1850's is often referred to as the Age of Santa Anna, for no other single force had such a constant and powerful effect on Mexico at this time. In many respects, Santa Anna's life was similar to that of many of his contemporaries, for these same years saw constant short-term governments that ranged the political spectrum from federal republic and central republic to dictatorship and monarchy. Few presidents served out their full terms of office, and military rebellions were the norm.

Santa Anna served five times as elected head of state and took power on several other occasions. When he ruled, he ruled absolutely, usually with a careful eye to clients' interests. When he was not in power, he made it difficult for strong opposition to develop. He represented the typical military leader of both his time in Mexico and in other areas of Spanish America by his cultivation of personalism, which substituted loyalty to and patronage from the person of the military leader rather than political institutions.

This cult of personalism and the use of armed forces to propound and defend it effectively retarded the growth of strong political institutions in Mexico. Santa Anna's alternate protection of and attacks on the Roman Catholic Church reflected the divided opinions of his day and presaged the Reform of 1857 and even the strong anticlericalism of the 1930's. Driven by personal ambition and lack of education, Santa Anna is best seen as an opportunist who could raise an army from nothing and turn disastrous defeats into resounding personal achievements through a timely preempting of rising popular or elite demands. He is best remembered as the one person who is most responsible for the alienation to the United States of roughly half of Mexico's territory.

—*St. John Robinson*

FURTHER READING

Calcott, Wilfred H. *Santa Anna: The Story of an Enigma Who Once Was Mexico*. Reprint. Hamden, Conn.: Archon, 1967. Reprinted from an earlier 1936 edition, this is the first major modern treatment of Santa Anna. It presents the contradictions present in Santa Anna's personality and the problems they posed for effective rule in Mexico.

Costeloe, Michael P. *The Central Republic in Mexico, 1835-1846: "Hombres de Bien" in the Age of Santa Anna*. Cambridge, England: Cambridge University Press, 1993. Costeloe studies the men of position and wealth in Mexico as they interacted with Santa Anna as clients and opponents. The author presents Santa Anna as one of this group, explaining to some degree his move to a more autocratic government.

Hardin, Stephen L. *The Alamo, 1836: Santa Anna's Texas Campaign*. Westport, Conn.: Praeger, 2004. Recounts Santa Anna's slaughter of about two hundred people at the Alamo on March 6, 1836, and how this action set off the war for Texas independence.

Jones, Oakah L. *Santa Anna*. New York: Twayne, 1968. Part of Twayne's Rulers and Statesmen of the World series, this is a detailed account and remains one of the standard biographies of Santa Anna. Includes a handy chronology.

Lynch, John. *Caudillos in Spanish America, 1800-1850*. Oxford, England: Oxford University Press, 1992. Lynch treats the origins, characteristics, and development of the *caudillo* (military-political leader) through the formative years of the Spanish American republics. He then analyzes the careers of four *caudillos*, one of whom is Santa Anna, and finds him the least constructive of the figures studied.

O'Brien, Steven. *Antonio Lopez de Santa Anna*. New York: Chelsea House, 1992. Part of the Hispanics of Achievement series, this book, written for a younger audience, presents Santa Anna in a generally favorable light. Some illustrations included.

Olivera, Ruth R., and Liliane Crété. *Life in Mexico Under Santa Anna, 1822-1855*. Norman: University of Oklahoma Press, 1991. Largely based on the observations and comments of visitors to Mexico and important residents there, this work presents an overview of daily life during the "Age of Santa Anna." Olivera covers the arts, industry, festivals, and social classes. This is one of the few studies to present Santa Anna in other than purely military or political context.

Santa Anna, Antonio Lopez de. *The Eagle: The Autobiography of Santa Anna*. Austin, Tex.: State House

Press, 1988. A translation of Santa Anna's account of his life and achievements. Although it is quite readable, Santa Anna generally presents himself as the victim of the conspiracies or incompetence of others, which is very much in the style of Santa Anna's other publications.

Scheina, Robert L. *Santa Anna: A Curse Upon Mexico.* Washington, D.C.: Brassey's, 2002. A military and political history of Santa Anna, depicting him as a political opportunist but a brave and resourceful military leader.

SEE ALSO: Fanny Calderón de la Barca; David Crockett; Porfirio Díaz; Sam Houston; Benito Juárez.

RELATED ARTICLES in *Great Events from History: The Nineteenth Century, 1801-1900:* September 16, 1810-September 28, 1821: Mexican War of Independence; October 2, 1835-April 21, 1836: Texas Revolution; June 30, 1846-January 13, 1847: United States Occupies California and the Southwest; February 2, 1848: Treaty of Guadalupe Hidalgo Ends Mexican War; December 31, 1853: Gadsden Purchase Completes the U.S.-Mexican Border.

LA SARAGOSSA
Spanish military leader

Because of an act of extraordinary courage during the French siege of Saragossa, the woman who became legendary as "La Saragossa" symbolized Spanish resistance to Napoleon's forces during a crucial period of invasion in the Peninsular War.

BORN: 1786; Tortosa, Catalonia, Spain
DIED: 1857; Saragossa, Spain
ALSO KNOWN AS: Maria Agustina Saragossa y Domenech (birth name); Maria Agustina; Maid of Saragossa
AREA OF ACHIEVEMENT: Military

EARLY LIFE

Little is known about the childhood of Maria Agustina Saragossa y Domenech. She grew up in a period during which Franco-Spanish relations were frequently tense and, at times, openly hostile and belligerent. After the French Revolution of 1789 and the establishment of the revolutionary regime in France, Spain occupied a precarious international position. The revolutionary regime, having tried and executed the Bourbon monarchs in France, had no qualms about dissolving the Family Compact of 1761, which had allied the Bourbon monarchs throughout Europe, and attacking the Spanish monarchy.

In 1793 France officially declared war on Spain, causing a vicious anti-French fervor throughout the Iberian Peninsula as religious leaders and village volunteers rallied around military leaders to fight the French. Although peace was declared between the countries three years later, intense hatred continued to strain their relations, which soured irrevocably in 1808 when Napoleon Bonaparte and his officials refused to recognize Ferdinand VII, the newly crowned Bourbon monarch. Instead, Napoleon installed his elder brother, Joseph Bonaparte, upon the Spanish throne to make Spain obedient to France. A nationwide revolt ensued as Spain struggled against French domination. Before being assisted by the British in 1809, the Spanish fought alone for one year under circumstances that profoundly affected most Spaniards, including Maria Agustina.

LIFE'S WORK

Agustina gained her fame and legend by the heroic action she took when the French decided to besiege Saragossa, her native city. Napoleon's Iberian forces, after successfully conquering the Spanish cities of Tudela, Mallen, Alagon, and Epila, turned their attention toward Saragossa, the former Caesar Augusta of Roman Hispania and the capital of Aragon. The city occupied a fairly breachable position, being flanked only by the Ebro River on the north, an open plain to the south, and the Hueva stream to the east and southeast.

Saragossa itself was in the wilderness of Aragon and had no access to the sea or communication with nearby cities. However, a twelve-foot wall surrounded the city, and many of the massive interior buildings, including several monasteries and the old Moorish stronghold, the Aljafería, had proved virtually impervious throughout centuries of warfare. The Spanish forces at Saragossa were not very sizable, numbering only one thousand regulars to be supplemented by five or six thousand civilians with little military training and few weapons. Nevertheless, pockets of resistance formed, particularly around different military leaders. José de Palafox, the leader of the Aragonese revolt and a native of Saragossa, helped form a junta made up of his friends and relatives.

When the French troops arrived on June 15, 1808, brigadier general Charles Lefebre-Desnoüettes pressed for Saragossa's surrender, anticipating a swift capitulation and a triumphant march into Aragon's capital. He did not want to lay traditional siege because he had few men and resources at his disposal after his other campaigns. The French general determined the weakest part of the city's defenses and successfully attacked the fortifications at one of the farthest external points, at Monte Torrero. Upon his order, some French soldiers managed to break through the Spanish defenses before the guns were in place, but most were slain while the remaining French forces retreated, which helped encourage the city's resistance.

Incensed by the breach in security, Spanish leaders later ordered the officer in command to be tried and hanged publicly to instill fear and patriotic fervor into the town's inhabitants so they would work fervently to repel the French onslaught. The French general had completely underestimated the rebellious spirit of the Saragossans, who managed to repel the first French assault. At the end of the first day, the French army retired to an area one mile from the city's wall between the two rivers to await supplies and reinforcements. The French had lost almost seven hundred men in the fray, and Lefebre-Desnoüettes wanted to wait.

This reprieve from battle allowed Saragossa to form a more organized and deadly defense. Over the next several weeks, every inhabitant in the city worked in some capacity to fortify Saragossa's defense. Women and children made uniforms, while men fortified buildings, made ammunition, burned outlying houses, cut down trees, and readied weapons. Private homes became fortresses and bastions of defense. Everyone, including Agustina, prepared for a fierce and bloody battle.

On the morning of July 2, 1808, the French launched a full assault in six strategic areas: the cavalry barracks, the Aljafería Castle, and the gates of Portillo, Carmen, Sancho, and Santa Engracia. The Spanish, under the leadership of Palafox, sought to direct their defense from the centrally located monastery of San Francisco. The men worked the cannons feverishly as their comrades died about them. Agustina gained her fame from a critical moment in the siege during which the French offense began to surmount the weakening defense at the strategically vital Portillo gate. The defensive position of the gate suddenly became vulnerable as artillery personnel serving the battery lay dying and defenders began to scat-

ter. Rather than allow the French infantry to pour through an irreparably weakened stronghold, Agustina took a lit fuse from the hands of her dead fiancé or husband, an artilleryman, and touched it to a cannon loaded with gunshot. Heedless of the carnage all about her, she shot the guns one after another, all the while, according to some accounts, deriding the cowardice of men fighting on both sides of the battle.

Agustina's actions instantly revived the Spanish defense and checked the French advance, which had moved to within one hundred meters of the guns. Although wounded in the battle, she fervently compelled her compatriots to arms. Men and women alike seemed to have admired and followed her example. She inspired at least one woman to take over the cannon from a dead soldier posted at the Santa Engracia battery and fire it at French infantry. Matching the patriotism of Agustina, Palafox refused to surrender, choosing instead to lead the city's inhabitants in a fight to the death. This proved unnecessary as the French soldiers broke ranks, many leaving their weapons behind in their flight. Until November, the Spanish successfully withstood the long-lasting siege.

After the first siege, the Saragossans were widely admired and honored throughout Spain. Every Spanish town produced plays such as *Los Patriotas de Aragon* (the patriots of Aragon) that depicted the Saragossans' defiance in the face of Napoleon's troops. Agustina earned the name "La Saragossa" and became famous in her own right throughout Spain and much of Europe. For her valiant and heroic actions, Agustina received a commendation from Palafox, the rank and salary of a gunner, and a shield of honor that was sewn to her sleeve.

Over the next several months, Saragossa's inhabitants worked to regain and fortify their defensive position, expecting that they would be able to again withstand a ferocious assault. The second siege began at the end of December, 1808, and seemed at first to follow the pattern of the first. Acting as an official gunner, Agustina was wounded in the defense of the city. Despite the best efforts of Agustina and the Saragossans, the siege lasted only until the middle of February, 1809. Although La Saragossa and the other city inhabitants fought gamely, even offensively at times, the French finally occupied the city. In those three months, Saragossa lost 54,000 people, with only 12,000 to 15,000 inhabitants remaining alive. Agustina miraculously survived the second siege and, along with all the inhabitants of Saragossa, was rounded up by the French before being dispersed throughout Aragon.

Little else is known of the woman heroically named La Saragossa. Occasional accounts of her actions surfaced in later years as French and Spanish soldiers alike bragged about having seen her in action at Saragossa or having met her in other skirmishes with the French. In each tale, her beauty, intelligence, and, most of all, her bravery in the face of adversity garnered her great honor, although few of these rumors can be substantiated or documented.

Agustina's legend and heroic reputation persist in poetry and art as well. The nineteenth century English Romantic poet Lord Byron saw La Saragossa in Seville wearing many medals and orders at the command of the junta and was inspired to write a verse about her that was read throughout Europe. In *Childe Harold's Pilgrimage* (1812-1818, 1819), he wrote

> Her lover sinks—she sheds no ill-tim'd tear
> Her chief is slain—she fills his fatal post
> Her fellows flee—she checks their base career
> The foe retires—she heads the sallying host:
> Who can appease like her a lover's ghost?
> Who can avenge so well a leader's fall?
> What maid retrieve when man's flush'd hope is lost?
> Who hang so fiercely on the flying Gaul,
> Foil'd by a woman's hand, before a batter'd wall?

These verses illustrate how Lord Byron commemorated La Saragossa and helped vivify her legend in the imagination of his readers.

Francisco de Goya, a nineteenth century Spanish painter from Saragossa, further immortalized her legend in his series entitled *Los desastres de la guerra* (1810-1814; the disasters of war), an expression of his disgust at the barbarity and bloodshed of the Peninsular War and his admiration of La Saragossa. One of his works, titled *Qué Valor*, depicts Agustina standing at the cannon amid the bodies of her fallen comrades ready to light the fuse and spur the Spanish defense to action. This painting was destroyed by the French in 1809. Two other painters, Juan Gálvez and Ferdinand Brambila, were commissioned by the restored Ferdinand VII to sketch scenes of Saragossa's heroics and devastation and produced an etching of Agustina and the cannon in a series titled *Las Ruinos de Zaragoza* (the ruins of Saragossa).

When Agustina died in 1857, her body was returned to Saragossa and buried in the Portilla Church alongside the other heroes of Saragossa. A statue and cannon stand outside the church in honor of her memory.

SIGNIFICANCE

Maria Agustina, as La Saragossa, clearly personified Spain's fierce resistance to Napoleon's incursions, not only at the sieges of Saragossa but also throughout the larger Peninsular War. Arguably, the prolonged defiance of the Saragossans wreaked havoc on Napoleon's campaigns in Spain and lowered the morale and fighting ability of his soldiers. Although the individual efforts of Agustina may not have had a permanent effect after the first siege and France was ultimately victorious, La Saragossa symbolized resistance, patriotism, and perseverance among the Spanish.

—Susanna Calkins

FURTHER READING

Esdaile, Charles J. *Fighting Napoleon: Guerillas, Bandits, and Adventurers in Spain, 1808-1814.* New Haven, Conn.: Yale University Press, 2004. Focuses on the Spanish peasants, bandits and other guerilla fighters (like La Saragossa) who attacked the French army, assessing the contributions they made to the Peninsular War.

_____. *The Peninsular War: A New History.* New York: Palgrave MacMillan, 2002. A comprehensive history of the war, providing details of the battles as well as the political and social dimensions of the conflict.

_____. *The Spanish Army in the Peninsular War.* Manchester, England: Manchester University Press, 1988. Esdaile traces the history of the Spanish army from 1788 to 1814, and the impact of the French Revolution and the Napoleonic wars on Spain.

Gates, David. *The Spanish Ulcer: A History of the Peninsular War.* New York: W. W. Norton, 1986. This book contains detailed sections on the first and second sieges of Saragossa within the context of the larger Peninsular War.

Lovett, Gabriel H. *Napoleon and the Birth of Modern Spain.* 2 vols. New York: New York University Press, 1965. This two-volume set offers a comprehensive survey of Napoleon's wars in the Iberian Peninsula. A chapter on "Heroic Zaragoza" explains how Saragossa attempted to withstand the French forces and describes La Saragossa's patriotism.

Lynch, John. *Bourbon Spain 1700-1808.* Oxford, England: Basil Blackwell, 1989. Lynch provides an insightful and comprehensive overview of the crises facing the Bourbon monarchy in Spain. The book contains a bibliographic essay on different aspects of the Spanish Bourbon regime.

Rudorff, Raymond. *War to the Death: The Sieges of Saragossa, 1808-1809*. New York: Macmillan, 1974. Rudorff offers one of the most comprehensive accounts of the two invasions of Saragossa. The book also contains several illustrations, including Goya's *Qué Valor* and other paintings concerning the sieges.

Tranie, J., and Juan Carlos Carmigniani. *Napoleon's War in Spain: French Peninsular Campaigns, 1807-1814*. Harrisburg, Pa.: Arms and Armour Press, 1982. This highly illustrated account of Napoleon's wars in Spain contains more description than analysis and includes a useful chronology of his military campaigns throughout Spain and Portugal.

SEE ALSO: Lord Byron; Napoleon I.
RELATED ARTICLES in *Great Events from History: The Nineteenth Century, 1801-1900:* May 2, 1808-November, 1813: Peninsular War in Spain; July 22, 1812: Battle of Salamanca; March, 1814: Goya Paints *Third of May 1808: Execution of the Citizens of Madrid*.

JOHN SINGER SARGENT
American painter

Sargent was one of the greatest American painters of his time, but most of his influences and training were European. He was particularly renowned for his magnificent portraiture, which earned for him a reputation as a modern Anthony Van Dyck.

BORN: January 12, 1856; Florence, Italy
DIED: April 15, 1925; London, England
AREA OF ACHIEVEMENT: Art

EARLY LIFE

John Singer Sargent was the son of Mary Newbold Singer Sargent, an incurable romantic. In 1854, she induced her husband, Dr. FitzWilliam Sargent, to abandon his medical practice and their comfortable, predictable bourgeois existence and move to Europe. Mary had recently come into a decent inheritance from her father, a wealthy fur merchant, and now saw no reason to live out her life among the dull, middle-class surroundings of Philadelphia. The transplanted Sargents usually spent their summers in northern France, Germany, or England, and headed to southern France or Italy during the winter, living in rented apartments. Florence, Italy, could be characterized as the family's "home base." There, the Sargents' eldest child, John, was born and attended school.

John Singer Sargent displayed a high degree of intellectual maturity, but his formal education was frequently interrupted by the family's travels. In addition to English, he spoke Italian, German, and French fluently; he became an accomplished pianist; he knew European literature, history, and art. His mother constantly hauled him around to museums and cathedrals; she was an enthusiastic watercolorist and encouraged him to make art his career, much to the dismay of her husband, who wanted his son to become a sailor. It was Mary Sargent who had her way, and John was allowed to attend the Academy of Fine Arts in Florence. The young student enthusiastically filled sketchbooks with drawings of classical monuments, copies of old master paintings, and still lifes; he drew people and scenes that he observed on his various travels. His parents showed his work to professional artists, and, when these experts confirmed John's talent, it was decided that he should be sent to Paris to further his studies.

Sargent arrived in the French capital in late spring of 1874 and was accepted by Charles Jurand Carolus-Duran, a famous academic portraitist, to join his atelier for advanced students; Sargent also passed the examinations for admission to the École des Beaux-Arts. He thus received one of the best formal art educations of his day. The Beaux Arts gave him a solid grounding in academism; Carolus-Duran taught him to paint in half-tones and trained him to eliminate all that was not essential from his composition.

Sargent was also influenced by such artists as Édouard Manet and Eugène Boudin and some of the Impressionists; like them, he spent his summers in the French provinces painting outdoors. His progress was rapid. One of his paintings, *En route pour la pêche* (also known as *The Oyster Gatherers of Cancale*), which resulted from a summer in Brittany, won a second-class medal at the Salon of 1878, a great personal achievement for a young unknown artist. Carolus-Duran thought so highly of his pupil that he invited him to help paint the *Triumph of Marie de' Medici*, a large mural commissioned for the ceiling of the Luxembourg Palace.

Sargent helped color the design of the mural but was also allowed to paint the two allegorical figures on either side of the principal portrait of Marie de' Medici; he also painted a bystander with the features of Carolus-Duran, who was so pleased that he allowed his pupil to paint a more formal portrait of him. The work, a remarkably perceptive representation done in half-tones and selective highlights, was artistically the culmination of the lessons Sargent had been taught. The portrait, both chronologically and artistically, marked the beginning of his professional career.

LIFE'S WORK

Sargent established his own studio (first on the rue Notre-Dame des Champs, later on the rue Berthier) and began to enjoy life as a rising young society artist. It was extremely difficult for a foreigner to break into the French market, however, and most of his commissions at that time came from wealthy foreigners living or visiting abroad. He did do an uncommissioned full-length portrait, *Madame Gautreau* (1884), which he hoped would open some doors, but the work was badly received at the Salon of 1884. Nevertheless, Sargent hardly suffered from lack of praise. According to Henry James, he was so talented that even on the threshold of his career he had nothing more to learn.

During this period, Sargent also did some subject paintings, such as the exotic *El Jaleo* (1882), a picture of a Gypsy dancer he saw while on a visit to Spain. For the most part, however, he did not stray far from his main source of income, although he became increasingly disenchanted with working in the French capital. His commissions had begun to decline, and he had not received the proper respect he thought he deserved. From time to time, his work had taken him to England as the wealthy British had less hesitation about having their portraits painted by foreigners than did the French.

Sargent passed the summer of 1885 at Broadway in the Cotswolds, where he did a number of landscapes. At that time, he apparently decided to make his residence in the British Isles more permanent; the following year, he closed down his Paris studio and moved to London, renting a studio previously occupied by James McNeill Whistler. The British capital would be his home for the rest of his life.

Commissions for portraits came slowly at first—some potential patrons, accustomed to the formalism of the Royal Academy, found his technique a bit too avant-garde—but gradually, he was commissioned for more and more work, until he had almost more than he could handle. Although the English art scene was not as exciting as the one he had left in Paris, Sargent's personal associations in the British capital were more congenial and fulfilling. Many of his clients were wealthy Americans, and one of these, Henry Marquand, invited him, in 1887, to come to the United States (to Newport, Rhode Island) to paint a portrait of his wife with the prospect of other commissions from Marquand's well-heeled friends.

Sargent's trip to the United States lasted eight months. He completed twelve formal portraits and had a one-man show in Boston in January, 1888, which received rave reviews. Everywhere he went, he was treated as a great artist and was appreciated in a way it seemed he had never

John Singer Sargent. (Library of Congress)

been in Europe. However, he returned to England; during the summer of 1888, he painted a series of pictures in the Impressionist style of Claude Monet, for whom he had an intense admiration. After this interlude, he returned to full-time portraiture.

One of Sargent's most famous portraits, *Ellen Terry as Lady Macbeth* (1889), he solicited himself. He returned to the United States in December, 1889, for another series of portraits, but he was also commissioned to decorate the upper landing of the Boston Public Library, a project that would occupy him intermittently for the next quarter of a century. As his theme, Sargent chose the development of religious thought from its pagan origin, through Old Testament times, to Christianity. The actual painting was done in England on canvas and transported to Boston. Although Sargent considered the work to be one of his major contributions to contemporary art, the murals did not display his talent at its best.

Throughout the last years of the Victorian period and the following Edwardian period, Sargent was widely regarded as the greatest portrait painter in England, his status confirmed by the number of commissions he was now receiving from the British aristocracy and by his election to full membership in the Royal Academy in 1897. However, the more famous he became and the greater the requests for his services, the more his interest in portraiture declined. He undoubtedly recognized that his work was suffering from repetition and a tendency toward formalism and artificiality. Consequently, from 1910 onward, he devoted the major part of his time to landscapes, journeying to Spain, the Holy Land, Egypt, Majorca, Corfu, and, especially, the Alpine region and Italy for subject matter. He chose the subjects that pleased him, beginning his work early in the day, having plopped his easel down wherever the spirit moved him. Sargent continued to work in oils, but most of his production was now in watercolors.

Sargent was in the Austrian Tirol when World War I broke out. The local military authorities refused him permission to leave the country, and he remained in the village of Colfushg and continued to paint. He apparently took little interest in the course of hostilities, which he regarded as collective madness; he naïvely believed that fighting was suspended on Sundays. Finally, he managed to leave Austria and make it to Italy, through France, and back to England, where he resumed work on the mural for the Boston library.

Sargent came again to the United States in 1916, and, on this trip, accepted another commission for a mural: for the rotunda of the Boston Museum of Fine Arts. When he returned to England in April, 1918, he was asked by the Ministry of Information's War Artists Committee to do a painting emphasizing wartime Anglo-American cooperation. He went to France to do research, staying there six months until October, one month before the armistice. The result was *Gassed*, painted in his London studio, which shows a line of Allied soldiers, eyes bandaged, being led one after the other toward a dressing station. The picture was displayed at the Royal Academy in 1919 and became an instant sensation, being judged one of the best paintings to come out that year.

Sargent now came more frequently to the United States, his work on his wall decorations monopolizing much of his time and energy. He was there from 1919 to 1920; he returned again in 1921 and in 1923, and he was planning to make a return trip to oversee the installation of his museum paintings. Just before he was scheduled to leave, on April 15, 1925, Sargent died of a heart attack, following a farewell party given by his sister. He was found with an open copy of Voltaire's *Philosophical Dictionary* (1764) beside him. His death drew national attention, marked by a memorial service in London's St. Paul's cathedral.

SIGNIFICANCE

Like a great actor who devotes too much of his talent to soap operas instead of to the classics, Sargent for most of his productive life painted works lacking in spiritual depth and imaginative force, works that he was later to regret having done. "I *hate* to paint portraits! I hope I never paint another portrait in my life. . . . I want now to experiment in more imaginary fields," he said.

However, portraits were what Sargent did best. When he was good, he was excellent; when he was bad, he was still extraordinary. For example, his portrait *Woodrow Wilson* (1917), not generally considered to be one of his best, is remarkable in the way it captures the humorless, messianic Wilsonian stare. Sargent's misfortune was to live at a time when painting the famous and haut-monde was increasingly looked on with derision.

Although Sargent refused to accept any commissions in which he did not have complete artistic freedom, he remained acutely sensitive to the social and professional stature of his subjects, whom he frequently placed in his paintings in theatrical or symbolic surroundings. Sargent was a businessperson who gave his sitters what they paid for. He posed them on Louis XV settees, in front of marble pillars, standing beside huge cloisonné vases, some wearing top hats and highly polished riding boots, as in *Lord Ribblesdale* (1902), or plumed bonnets, as in *Lady*

Sassoon (1907), or adorned, as in *The Wyndham Sisters* (1899), in dresses worth small fortunes. Sargent was clearly an artist of fin de siècle conspicuous consumers, and he served them well.

Americans claimed Sargent as one of their own, but in training and performance he was completely European. Sargent based his style on Europe's traditional artistic values as expressed by the artists he admired. He never tired of going to museums to learn from the great artists of the past, such as Diego Velázquez, Titian, Tintoretto, Peter Paul Rubens, and, above all, Frans Hals, whose loose brushwork became Sargent's own trademark.

Sargent's painterly style was enlivened with splashes of clear color that attested the lessons he had learned from the Impressionists. He was never able to adapt his palette completely to theirs, however, and sometimes he became too garish or somber. "One day the American painter Sargent came here to paint with me," Monet recalled. "I gave him my colors and he wanted black, and I told him: 'But I haven't any.' 'Then I can't paint,' he cried and added, 'How do you do it!'"

Sargent came the closest to Impressionism in his watercolors, especially those he did in Venice, which also reveal him at his spontaneous and individualistic best. However, if Sargent had failings as a painter, they were failings of theme, not of expertise, for his was overpowering and could rival that of the finest painters of any age.

—*Wm. Laird Kleine-Ahlbrandt*

FURTHER READING

Charteris, Evan Edward. *John Sargent*. New York: Charles Scribner's Sons, 1927. This official biography is built largely from quotations, letters, and anecdotes. The author, who was a personal friend of Sargent, was too close to his subject to be truly objective, and the painter's personality remains elusive. Sargent is revealed as tremendously dedicated, hardworking, and self-critical, but such traits alone are hardly the stuff of drama.

Davis, Deborah. *Strapless: John Singer Sargent and the Fall of Madame X*. New York: Jeremy Tarcher/Penguin Group, 2003. The story of *Madame X*, Sargent's painting of a woman in a black evening gown. Describes how Sargent won the commission for the painting, the work's reception, and how the painting changed the life of Sargent and its subject, Virginie Gautreau.

Lubin, David M. *Act of Portrayal: Eakins, Sargent, James*. New Haven, Conn.: Yale University Press, 1985. Contains extensive sexual-sociological analysis of Sargent's famous portrait of the Boit children, *The Daughters of Edward Boit* (1882). Essentially an exercise in speculation and provocation, showing that what is not known about a painting need not stand in the way of intellectualizing about its meaning.

McSpadden, J. Walker. *Famous Painters of America*. New York: Dodd, Mead, 1916. A brief description of Sargent's life and work, written during his lifetime in obvious recognition and appreciation of his genius. Argues that despite his thoroughly European training and formation, "Americans may rightfully claim Sargent."

Memorial Exhibition of the Works of the Late John Singer Sargent. Boston: Museum of Fine Arts, 1925. A catalog of some of Sargent's most famous works, commemorating the unveiling of his mural decorations in the Boston Public Library. The works on display came almost exclusively from American collections, helping to reinforce the artist's image as a native son.

Mount, Charles Merril. *John Singer Sargent*. New York: W. W. Norton, 1955. A complete, well-researched, and lavishly documented account in which even the most insignificant aspects of Sargent's life seem worthy of inclusion. Mount, who is also a portraitist, offers intelligent and perceptive commentary about his subject's style and techniques.

Olson, Stanley. *John Singer Sargent: His Portrait*. New York: St. Martin's Press, 1986. A literate, sympathetic, but objective biography, particularly strong in its portrayal of the varied figures who played a part in Sargent's life. Includes a small selection of illustrations.

Ormond, Richard, and Elaine Kilmurray. *John Singer Sargent: Complete Paintings*. 3 vols. New Haven, Conn.: Published for the Paul Mellon Centre for Studies in British Art by Yale University Press, 1998-2003. A definitive *catalogue raisonné* of Singer's works in oil, watercolor, and pastel, with many of the paintings reproduced in color. The paintings are arranged chronologically, with documentation about each painting's subject, the circumstances of its creation, its artistic techniques, and its place within Singer's total body of work. The first volume, *John Singer Sargent: The Early Portraits*, covers the artist's years in France and England through his first professional trip to the United States in 1887; volume two, *John Singer Sargent: Portraits of the 1890's*, focuses on his work between 1889 and 1900; the final volume, *John Singer Sargent: The Later Portraits*, presents his work from 1900 through 1925.

SEE ALSO: Henry James; Édouard Manet; Ellen Terry; James McNeill Whistler.

RELATED ARTICLES in *Great Events from History: The Nineteenth Century, 1801-1900:* Fall, 1848: Pre-Raphaelite Brotherhood Begins; 1892-1895: Toulouse-Lautrec Paints *At the Moulin Rouge.*

DOMINGO FAUSTINO SARMIENTO
President of Argentina (1868-1874)

While he was president of Argentina, Sarmiento emphasized the importance of public education for national development and integration. He was an acute observer of his own society and wrote a penetrating study of the political and cultural roots of Argentina that revealed the forces underlying the national tendency toward authoritarian government.

BORN: February 14, 1811; San Juan, Viceroyalty of the Rio de la Plata (now in Argentina)
DIED: September 11, 1888; Asunción, Paraguay
AREAS OF ACHIEVEMENT: Government and politics, education

EARLY LIFE

Domingo Faustino Sarmiento (Doh-MEEN-goh Fows-TEEN-oh Sahr-mee-YEHN-to) was born when Argentina was still a dominion of Spain known as the Viceroyalty of La Plata. He was raised in a home of sparse means in the province of San Juan, a mountainous northwestern territory of Argentina that during colonial times had been part of Chile. Through self-instruction and the support of a clerical relative, he was able to obtain an elementary education and by mid-adolescence was already helping to teach classes.

Meanwhile, in 1816, when Sarmiento was only five years old, Argentina became the first South American country to achieve independence. However, a fragmenting period of civil strife soon followed. Out of the chaos emerged regional political strongmen, known as *caudillos*. The chief among these men were Juan Facundo Quiroga and Juan Manuel de Rosas. The former consolidated control over the country's northern interior provinces from the late 1820's until his assassination in 1835. The latter, and the most powerful of the *caudillos*, ruled over the country's richest province, Buenos Aires, from 1835 to 1852. The *caudillos* advocated a federal government in which Argentina would comprise an association of sovereign provinces. They were opposed by unitarists, who hoped to modernize the country by incorporating its vast and disparate provinces into a nation consolidated under a strong central government.

As Sarmiento grew up, he joined the political debate opposed to *caudillos* and rose to captain in the local militia trying to fend off Quiroga's advance into San Juan. Quiroga's victory forced Sarmiento to flee into exile in Chile in 1831, and he did not return to Argentina until 1836, after Quiroga died, by which time he was twenty-five years old.

LIFE'S WORK

Throughout Argentina the Generation of 1837 arose, the first group of Argentine leaders to come of age since the nation's independence. They were moved by Romantic literary appeals to revolutionary social change as they confronted the abyss of anarchy and the morass of *caudillo* repression into which the young Argentine nation had sunk. Sarmiento became part of this movement in San Juan. Advocating the importance of education of all in forming a new Argentina, he founded a school for girls in 1839. During that same year, he also founded a literary periodical, *El Zonda* (hot wind), whose acerbic political criticism brought down government reprisals that again forced him into Chilean exile in 1840. He did not return until 1852.

During his years of exile, Sarmiento developed as both a writer and educator. He worked for several Chilean newspapers, including the noted *El Mercurio*, and continued his interest in politics. He also published his most noted books. In 1845, the most famous book appeared, *Civilización y barbarie: vida de Juan Facundo Quiroga, y aspecto físico, costumbres, y hábitos de la República Argentina* (1845; *Life in the Argentine Republic in the Days of the Tyrants: Or, Civilization and Barbarism*). Ostensibly a biography of Quiroga, the book was essentially a denunciation of the Rosas dictatorship at the height of its power and also presented a critique of the elite socioeconomic system that created arbitrary and ultimately unstable governments.

In 1849, Sarmiento published *De la educacion popular*, a book emphasizing the value of mass public education as a means of modernizing and stabilizing a country. The following year appeared *Arjirópolis*, a plan for reorganizing Argentina in a Confederated States of the Rio de la Plata.

Supported and admired by the Chilean government, Sarmiento was made head of that country's first teacher-training school. He traveled widely in Europe and the Americas, making contacts in the United States with the American educational pioneers Horace and Mary Peabody Mann. Horace Mann greatly influenced how Sarmiento would formulate public education in Chile and Argentina, and Mann's wife late translated *Facundo* into English and maintained an extensive correspondence with Sarmiento.

Events in Argentina during the 1850's brought Sarmiento back to his home country, where he then played his most decisive political role. He joined military forces that were being organized in Uruguay to overthrow Rosas. Rosas was ousted in 1852, and a new constitution was written the following year. The constitution was progressively amended so that by 1862 a relatively stable government under the presidency of Bartolomé Mitre emerged. As an ally of Mitre, Sarmiento became governor of San Juan in 1862 and instituted educational, administrative, and electoral reforms. In 1864, he was appointed ambassador to the United States. While he was abroad in 1868, Argentina elected him to succeed Mitre. He returned home and assumed the presidency in October.

As president, Sarmiento put into effect on a national scale the ideas and projects that had long distinguished him. Building on the policies of Mitre, he continued to encourage immigration, welcoming waves of new European settlers. When he conducted the first national census in 1869, he was disturbed to find that nearly three of every four Argentines were illiterate. He then quadrupled the number of children in elementary schools, to well over 100,000, and established many specialized schools, following American and European models.

Pursuing the ideal of a modernized, integrated Argentina, Sarmiento increased the number of railway and telegraph lines, roads, and bridges and welcomed British investment capital. The expanding infrastructure reached ever farther into the fertile interior of the country, which would eventually produce a cornucopia of cereals and meat for export to industrializing Europe. In 1870, he ended a war with Paraguay that had begun in 1865 and in which his son Dominguito had died. (Sarmiento had been estranged from his wife, Benita Martínez, since 1860.)

In 1874, Sarmiento was succeeded in the presidency by his duly elected successor, Nicolas Avellaneda, who continued his and Mitre's national development policies. After Sarmiento left the presidency, he became a senator from San Juan and served as a minister in the Avellaneda government, as director of schools in Buenos Aires, and as director of national education. He was eventually promoted to the rank of general and had his collected writings published in a set of fifty-two volumes. For reasons of health he moved to Asunción, Paraguay, in 1887. He died there on September 11, 1888, at the age of seventy-seven.

SIGNIFICANCE

Sarmiento is a monumental figure in Argentine history. In one person, he constituted a composite of historic figures. Like the American president Abraham Lincoln—of whom he wrote a biography—and the Mexican president Benito Juárez, Sarmiento rose from humble origins to play a decisive role in his country's formation. Like the American educator Horace Mann, he was a key figure in forging the rationale and structure of public education in Argentina and Chile. Like the French essayist Alexis de Tocqueville, who famously wrote on the nature of the American character, Sarmiento described with keen insight the nature of the Argentine character. Together with Mitre and Avellaneda, he formed the precedent of stable presidential succession.

Constitutional and electoral stability in Argentina endured into the early twentieth century. However, the extraordinary expansion of the Argentine economy and development of its society during the late nineteenth century occurred within a framework of vastly unequal land ownership and distribution of wealth. Such socioeconomic chasms eventually destabilized Argentina, resulting in the rise of a modern *caudillo*, Juan Perón, during the late 1940's. Perón was followed by alternating military and civilian regimes that aggravated political instability, and the educational policies and accomplishments of Sarmiento and his colleagues were not sufficient to overcome this imbalance. His legacy is to have helped create a population that is articulate in expressing its sociopolitical stresses but economically hampered in reversing them.

—Edward A. Riedinger

FURTHER READING

Bravo, Héctor Félix. "Domingo Faustino Sarmiento, 1811-88." *Prospects: Quarterly Review of Comparative Education* 24, no. 3/4 (1994): 487-500. Synopsis of the origin, development, and nature of Sarmiento's ideas on education together with a bibliography of his principal works on the subject.

Bunkley, Allison Williams. *Life of Sarmiento*. Princeton, N.J.: Princeton University Press, 1952. Most detailed, scholarly biography of Sarmiento in English, with illustrations and an extensive bibliography.

Criscenti, Joseph, ed. *Sarmiento and His Argentina*. Boulder, Colo.: L. Rienner, 1993. Collection of articles by scholars covering Sarmiento's policies on topics ranging from immigration and Indians to women, education, and modernization.

Halperín Donghi, Tulio, ed. *Sarmiento, Author of a Nation*. Berkeley: University of California Press, 1994. Edited by a noted specialist in Argentine history, this collection of articles by various scholars examines literary and political aspects of Sarmiento's life.

Katra, William H. *The Argentine Generation of 1837: Echeverría, Alberdi, Sarmiento, Mitre*. Madison, N.J.: Farleigh Dickinson University Press, 1996. Detailed study of debate that occurred in shadow and the aftermath of the Rosas dictatorship among four of the leading intellectual and political leaders forging the Argentine nation.

Patton, Elva Clayton. *Sarmiento in the United States*. Evansville, Ind.: University of Evansville Press, 1976. Study of the periods when Sarmiento lived and traveled in the United States, reviewing his reactions to American culture and examining the influence on him of nineteenth century American public education movement.

Shumway, Nicholas. *The Invention of Argentina*. Berkeley: University of California Press, 1991. Insightful study of Argentine intellectual life in the nineteenth century, examining the ideas of Sarmiento and others in forging his country's identity.

Sorensen, Diana. *"Facundo" and the Construction of Argentine Culture*. Austin: University of Texas Press, 1996. Examines Sarmiento's book *Civilización y barbarie: vida de Juan Facundo Quiroga* for its contributions to Argentine intellectual life, seeing its often contradictory readings as themselves constituting a composite cultural construct.

SEE ALSO: Benito Juárez; Abraham Lincoln; Horace Mann; Clorinda Matto de Turner; Bernardo O'Higgins; Pedro II; José de San Martín; Alexis de Tocqueville.

RELATED ARTICLE in *Great Events from History: The Nineteenth Century, 1801-1900:* May 1, 1865-June 20, 1870: Paraguayan War.